# AFL '98

## THE OFFICIAL STATISTICAL HISTORY OF THE AFL

Edited by Michael Lovett

Produced by the Australian Football League
Designed by SlatteryΔDavis Pty Ltd
Paginated by Myriad Communications Pty Ltd
Printed and bound by Australia by Griffin Press Pty Ltd
Photographs courtesy of Sporting Pix

ISBN 1 86330 629 3

# AFL '98

## THE OFFICIAL STATISTICAL HISTORY OF THE AFL

**Edited by Michael Lovett**

**A publication of the Australian Football League**

Communications Manager: Tony Peek
Managing Editor: Geoff Slattery
Copy Editor: Janelle Ward
AFL statistics by Col Hutchinson
Key player statistics by APB Sports
Player profiles by Michael Lovett, Greg Hobbs, Peter Ryan
Grand Final reviews by Michael Roberts
Additional research by Andrew Lake

# CONTENTS

## DEFINITIONS

There have been several changes to the AFL competition since the end of the 1996 season. This explanation will clarify the AFL's position regarding names and records.

**WESTERN BULLDOGS:** As part of a new marketing direction, Footscray changed its name to the Western Bulldogs last year. To eliminate any confusion, all records before the start of 1997 refer to the name Footscray, or an abbreviation thereof. From 1997 on, all records refer to the club as the Western Bulldogs (or abbreviation).

**BRISBANE/FITZROY:** The merger between Fitzroy and the Brisbane Bears resulted in the formation of a new club, the Brisbane Lions, However, to preserve the history and tradition of both clubs, particularly Fitzroy, which was a founding member of the AFL, a line has been drawn on the records from 1996 dating back to 1897 (in Fitzroy's case) and 1987 (in the Bears' case). Records of the new team, the Brisbane Lions, started in 1997 and continue henceforth

**Michael Lovett, Editor**

# FAST PHONE
# NUMBERS

AFL .................(03) 9643 1999
AFL Media fax ..(03) 9650 3189
Adelaide ..........(08) 8347 2322
Brisbane...........(07) 3335 1777
Carlton .............(03) 9387 1400
Collingwood......(03) 9419 9222
Essendon .........(03) 9230 0300
Fremantle.........(09) 9430 8975
Geelong............(03) 5221 3355
Hawthorn .........(03) 9816 2222
Melbourne ........(03) 9650 9052
North Melb .......(03) 9326 8666
Port Adelaide ...(08) 8447 4044
Richmond .........(03) 9429 5333
St Kilda ............(03) 9555 6688
Sydney .............(02) 9332 9123
West Coast ......(09) 9381 1111
West. Bulldogs .(03) 9689 3100

# Statistics tell the story

### By Michael Lovett,
### Publications Editor

Some football followers are consumed by statistics. Others could not care less and maintain that the most important statistic will be recorded on Saturday, September 26, this year, by the team that drinks from the premiership cup.

However, our feedback tends to suggest those in the latter category are in the minority and that fans are searching endlessly for statistics that go way beyond who took the most marks or had the most handballs and kicks.

Statistics tell us about trends and patterns emerging in the game. It could be anything from which club has fared best at the National Draft to why certain players continually poll well in the Brownlow Medal.

Certainly coaches and football clubs are consumed by statistics and it is a fair bet that every one of the AFL's 16 clubs will have several copies of *AFL '98* on file for reference and research. Some, we are told, buy in bulk and issue them to players.

It is important that everyone, including supporters, has access to the sort of information clubs have at their fingertips. This is the third year the AFL's official statistical guide has been on sale to the public and the response and feedback has been extremely positive.

We have received suggestions on improvements to the guide and some have been acted upon. For instance, the section covering finals and Grand Finals (1931-97) is now a complete year-by-year account, including ladders, finals results and Grand Final details (teams, scores, best players, goalkickers, Norm Smith Medallists and a brief description of each Grand Final).

Since it was introduced in 1986, various forms of the draft have put a new slant on recruiting players. At first, it was all a bit of a mystery to the average fan, but it would be fair to say that the draft is now accepted as an important part of football culture.

It can be a complicated process as clubs trade, deal and select the best talent they can. In this year's guide, we have researched the history of every player taken in the draft and have provided a ready reference as to how and when a particular player was drafted and/or traded.

As football moves into the new millenium, it is important that we record the history of the draft from day one and maintain a year-by-year account of player movement. For some, the recruiting and trading of players is just as fascinating as whether they can kick both feet or take a mark running with the flight of the ball.

Other changes this year include the listing of premier teams in major state competitions such as the VFL, SANFL and WAFL. The records of the Brisbane Bears and Fitzroy have been recorded to reflect the history of the merged clubs.

Every player on a senior list has been profiled and there is instant and valuable information about every team — from the club's phone number to its win-loss record. Supporting all this detail are reports on the award winners and achievers of the 1997 season. That means if you follow the Adelaide Crows or you admire the way Robert Harvey plays football, you have some enjoyable reading ahead.

The greatest achiever for 1997 was, of course, Adelaide, whose effort in jumping from 12th in 1996 to first in '97 is the biggest single improvement in the history of the VFL/AFL.

Its performance was even better when you consider it also became the first side to win four finals to take out the premiership.

It should not be forgotten that St Kilda also made one giant step for football-kind when it moved from 10th in 1996 to second in '97. Had St Kilda triumphed, it would have put its name in the records as the biggest improver in a season.

Once again, we are delighted to present this guide to the general public and not just to the clubs and media as was the case until a few years ago. Keep it handy; it will be a constant reference point.

As you will see, it has been a case of fine tuning rather than a complete overhaul. After all, it defies logic to change something that is quite definitive.

# Dramatic Brownlow win

**R**ecent history tells us to expect the unexpected on Brownlow Medal night. Few would have been surprised by the events that unfolded at the Crown Entertainment Complex on September 22, 1997.

In 1993, Gavin Wanganeen won the Brownlow with 18 votes, just one ahead of Carlton's Greg Williams, who went unrecognised for a 40-plus possession game earlier that season.

A year later, Williams was all smiles after he polled 30 votes to win his second Brownlow — yet West Coast's Peter Matera polled a staggering 28 votes to finish second. In any other year in the history of the award, that would have won the Eagles' speedster a medal.

On to 1996, and two of the best young players in the competition, the Brisbane Bears' Michael Voss and Essendon's James Hird, could not be separated in votes or spirit. They polled 21 votes each and became soul mates.

But spare a thought for another young champion, North Melbourne's Corey McKernan. He, too, finished on 21 votes, but was ruled ineligible after incurring a one-week suspension during the season. McKernan became the first ineligible player in Brownlow Medal history to have been denied a win because of suspension.

And so to 1997 and it was another night of high drama as St Kilda's Robert Harvey did what most pundits and punters had predicted: he added a Brownlow Medal to his imposing collection of individual honors, a medal to put alongside three club best and fairest awards, three EJ Whitten Medals and selection (five times) in the All-Australian team.

But while Harvey's win was thoroughly deserved and was another triumph in a memorable season for the Saints, it was achieved against a backdrop of controversy.

Western Bulldogs star Chris Grant went one better than McKernan the previous season by polling more votes than the winner. But Grant, who finished on 27 votes, one ahead of Harvey, had also incurred the wrath of the

**MEDAL MAN:** Robert Harvey claimed football's highest individual honor, the Brownlow Medal, in 1997.

Tribunal during the season — a one-match penalty for an indiscretion in a round-seven match against Hawthorn.

Fortunately, the two players involved — Grant and Harvey — displayed champion qualities other than those we have seen on the field. In his victory speech, Harvey immediately acknowledged Grant's misfortune and the St Kilda ruck-rover won many points for that, not the least with some disappointed Bulldogs fans.

Grant, like McKernan the year before, had known his fate for much of the season and while inwardly he was hurting, he kept his feelings to himself and showed great character during what must have been a difficult time.

For Harvey, only a premiership medallion would have made it a better season. By the end of the year, he led the AFL in possessions — 756 after he pulled up stumps in the Grand Final, almost 100 ahead of teammate Nathan Burke on 669.

Some of them were absolute gems, such as his goal from the boundary line in wet conditions against West Coast in round 11.

It is not only Harvey's ability to get the ball on a regular basis that sets him apart. The amount of ground he covers week in, week out, has most would-be taggers shaking in their boots at the thought of shadowing him.

He dodges and side-steps like a ballroom champion and slips out of tackles as though he is flicking a moth off his jumper. At 26, Harvey is in the prime of his career and should not only chalk up 300-plus games, but could go down as one of the game's greatest runners/on-ballers.

Harvey finished five votes ahead of Matera who, like Geelong's Garry Hocking, is developing a reputation as the eternal bridesmaid on Brownlow night. Sydney captain Paul Kelly, a winner in 1995, also polled 21 votes to finish tied with Matera. **— Michael Lovett**

# McLeod's ripping finale

**P**lay six inspirational quarters of football in succession in mid-June and people might talk about it for a day or even two. Do what Adelaide midfielder Andrew McLeod did and play six ripping quarters in the last six quarters of the football year and people will be talking about you for the rest of their lives. It earned McLeod both a Norm Smith and a premiership medal.

For Adelaide supporters to say his performance came at the right time is like saying a parachute opened at the right time — before you hit the ground. At half-time of the first preliminary final against the Western Bulldogs, the Crows, outsiders at the start of the game, were 31 points behind. Someone needed to produce something special.

McLeod's move at half-time into the midfield proved a match-winner as the Crows overcame their deficit to win by two points. His urgency and readiness to take risks around the middle of the ground was the spring that created a torrent of opportunities and enabled Adelaide to fall into its first Grand Final.

On Grand Final day, McLeod looked as comfortable on the MCG, as other men from Darwin — Michael Long (Norm Smith Medal 1993) and Maurice Rioli (Norm Smith Medal 1982) — had looked before him. It was in stark contrast to the day he first arrived down south to, relatively speaking, the big smoke of Adelaide.

Through watery eyes he surveyed his new home as his dad, Jock, left him in town to pursue his dream of playing AFL football. He began by playing with Port Adelaide under-9s in the SANFL in 1994.

**ON THE RUN:** He ran all day and always stayed at least a step ahead of his opponents. In the end, Adelaide's Andrew McLeod had the Saints on the run and earned the Norm Smith Medal for his trouble.

His Grand Final began at half-back on St Kilda's Matthew Lappin. In the first quarter, he was out of the starting blocks quicker than Carl Lewis. He had nine touches before the corporate lunch-goers had settled in their seats. St Kilda pumped the footy forward, McLeod gathered it in and pushed it back the other way.

In the second quarter, Blight moved him into the centre of the ground looking to get more value from him. His play when the Crows were under pressure from a Barry Hall-led St Kilda surge kept victory within view.

He would bounce on the balls of his feet, break tackles and stand up when St Kilda's tackling was at its fiercest. McLeod kept shelling out handballs or getting away kicks, persisting like a parent carrying on a conversation even when the kids are crawling all over him or her.

In the last half, he ran and ran and ran. Hunched forward ready to pounce at every pack situation, he took hard ball after hard ball. Then, as the Crows began to look like winners half-way through the last quarter, he planted himself forward of the centre circle and kept pounding the ball into a forward line full of Darren Jarmans, Shane Ellens and Troy Bonds. He finished the game with 18 kicks, 11 marks and 13 handballs.

At 21, he wasn't the youngest player to win the Norm Smith Medal — Wayne Harmes, the first winner in 1979, was 19 — but he was one of the most deserved. Tough, resolute and courageous, McLeod had a game and a year that won't be forgotten — by him or anyone else. — **Peter Ryan**

# Modra's mixed fortunes

At one stage of his pop star-like fame, Tony Modra was being mentioned in the same breath as Sir Donald Bradman as South Australia's greatest sporting hero. With comparisons such as that, little wonder Modra tries to keep a low profile.

But in what was, until the arrival of Port Adelaide, a one-team town, Modra was perceived as an occasionally spectacular player who suffered an inferiority complex because of the attention placed on him from the other side of the fence.

When the Crows won and Modra played well, the fans adored him. When the Crows lost and Modra didn't get a touch, there were more sightings of him than Elvis having a night on the town.

Yet those close to Modra say he is a quiet bloke who likes to surf and, yes, he has been caught doing a few things he regrets. But at the end of the day, he should be judged on his football talents and there is no doubt he has plenty of those.

Last year, he won the Coleman Medal, booting 81 goals during the home and away season (the award is based on home and away season goals only).

It was Modra's first Coleman Medal, even though he had kicked 129 by the end of the 1993 season, finals included. The Coleman Medal of that year went to Geelong's Gary Ablett, who had kicked 124 to the end of the home and away season.

Mere mention here of Ablett's name makes an interesting comparison. Like Ablett, Modra prefers to keep a low profile but, while not as robust and strong as the former Geelong champion, Modra could be

**MODRA MANIA:** He has the looks of a box office star, but Tony Modra likes to keep a low profile and let his goalkicking do the talking.

equally as spectacular, particularly in the air.

And like Ablett, and perhaps Peter Daicos beforehand, Modra possesses an amazing ability to conjure up goals from all sorts of angles and positions when the ball hits the ground.

Ablett and Modra share another bond. When Malcolm Blight arrived to coach Geelong in 1989, he turned Ablett's career around. Under Blight, Ablett booted exactly half his career goals (515) in just six seasons at an average of 4.5 goals per game. That included one season (1991) when he went into temporary retirement and kicked only 28 goals in 12 games.

Certainly Modra was starting to regain form in 1996 under Robert Shaw after a lean year in 1995 (40 goals), but surely his eyes must have lit up with the arrival of Blight who immediately structured a quicker midfield which suited Modra's lead and leap style.

The best part about Modra's 1997 season was that, from the outside, he really appeared to be enjoying his football. The saddest part was that, after struggling with a knee problem towards the end of the season, he seriously damaged his other knee during the preliminary final against the Western Bulldogs and is unlikely to see any game time in 1998.

But even after that memorable win over the Bulldogs and seven days later when the Crows hoisted the cup sans Modra, he lapped up the celebrations as though he had booted seven goals himself. A team man and a team player to the end.

**— Michael Lovett**

**9**

# The best, say the players

Robert Harvey was the deserved winner of the AFL Players' Association's most valuable player award in 1997. It was one of many awards he won during the year, including the Brownlow Medal, but is one he rates highly as it is awarded by the players. Peer recognition has no peer.

Such is Harvey's skill and daring on a football field that you almost hope he will get himself into trouble so you can watch him get out of it — rather like watching a rodeo clown.

Harvey runs all day, picking up possession after possession with such regularity that the word monotonous might apply.

**PERFECTION:** For the Saints, Robert Harvey (left) is a dream player. For the Swans, Paul Kelly is courage personified.

This year, he was instrumental in lifting the Saints into the Grand Final.

His performance in the preliminary final was as close to perfection as a midfielder can achieve on a footy field. It had 77,000 people watching in awe.

In the Grand Final, he was battered from pillar to post, but still knocked up getting the ball more than 35 times. It is only upon reflection that one can truly appreciate his awesome contribution to the Saints' effort on that day. His modesty off the field combined with his brilliance on it make him one of the AFL's most popular players.

The Sydney Swans' Paul Kelly was voted the AFL Players' Association's most courageous player for the fourth year in succession.

Describing Paul Kelly as courageous is hardly riveting conversation. It's like saying Don Bradman could bat or Kieren Perkins can swim. But recognition of his fearless attack on the football and his will to win is warranted.

It is hard to imagine a Sydney side without the almost spindly, but square-shouldered, No. 14 underneath the packs.

Kelly's rise to the exalted status he enjoys has not come about merely through courage. He is a player of enormous skill and has a capacity to keep working against the odds.

Once again this year, he didn't miss a game. He led the Swans into the finals for the second year in succession. He won his club's best and fairest for the fourth time and he finished on the third line of Brownlow voting, tying with West Coast's Peter Matera on 21 votes, with only Robert Harvey and Chris Grant ahead of him.

Kelly was subjected to some fierce tagging this year — his clashes with the Western Bulldogs' Tony Liberatore received much publicity — but through it all, he never once committed an undisciplined act. They were the type of efforts that coaches and commentators like to call "real courage". It means keeping your eye on the ball, when all around you seem intent on ending your day.

Robert Harvey, most valuable; Paul Kelly, most courageous. Tell us something we didn't know.

— **Peter Ryan**

# Port's young star on the rise

As the Adelaide Crows completed their celebratory lap on Grand Final day last year, Michael Wilson stood at the front row of the middle deck of the Great Southern Stand and took it all in.

Below him were delirious Crows' supporters. Hugging the boundary line, and each other, were 21 jubilant Adelaide players all trying to share the famous cup.

The Port Adelaide youngster was clearly impressed with what he was watching — not so much that it was his rivals from Adelaide lapping up the glory, but you got the feeling that special moment was being stored away and that one day he wants to be running a lap of honor.

If the debut season of Port Power and their rising young star is any indication, it won't be too far away. After all, Wilson has tasted success with Port in the SANFL as a teenager playing in the 1995 and '96 premiership teams, but an AFL premiership ... well, perhaps the seeds have been planted.

The tough left-footer who plays more like a 31-year-old than a 21-year-old was one of a host of Port Adelaide players to make a big impact in their first season. In the end, Wilson's impact was bigger than any young player in the competition because he finished as the winner of the Norwich Rising Star award.

Wilson was a revelation, tagging opposition stars yet winning the ball at will. He has been likened to Tony Shaw, Barry Rowlings and Mark Thompson — three very tough and uncompromising left-footers.

It was another outstanding year for young players and those eligible for the Norwich Rising Star award (those aged under 21 and who have not played more than 10 games at the start of the year).

The Sydney Swans had outstanding youngsters in Stefan Carey and Troy Cook, Richmond's Joel Bowden was going great guns until he was injured in round eight and Essendon appears to have unearthed a fine young talent in Blake Caracella. **— Michael Lovett**

**YOUNG STAR:** Michael Wilson celebrates his victory in the 1997 Norwich Rising Star award.

## 1997 NORWICH RISING STAR NOMINATIONS

Rd
1 — Lance Whitnall (Carlton)
2 — Joel Bowden (Richmond)
3 — Bowen Lockwood (Port Adelaide)
4 — Michael Wilson (Port Adelaide)
5 — Heath Black (Fremantle)
6 — Adam Houlihan (Geelong)
7 — Brendon Lade (Port Adelaide)
8 — Daniel Bradshaw (Brisbane Lions)
9 — Stefan Carey (Sydney)
10 — Shane Woewodin (Melbourne)
11 — Troy Cook (Sydney)
12 — Kane Johnson (Adelaide)
13 — Blake Caracella (Essendon)
14 — Michael Braun (West Coast)
15 — Peter Vardy (Adelaide)
16 — Carl Steinfort (Geelong)
17 — Brad Scott (Hawthorn)
18 — Mal Michael (Collingwood)
19 — Michael Gardiner (West Coast)
20 — Robert Powell (Richmond)
21 — Nathan Eagleton (Port Adelaide)
22 — Angelo Lekkas (Hawthorn)

# Playing the numbers game

Figuratively speaking, there were some big numbers hitting the headlines last season … and we're not just referring to player contracts.

• 1200 was the number of AFL goals kicked by Hawthorn champion Jason Dunstall in round seven, 1997. He became only the second player in history — behind Collingwood's Gordon Coventry (1299 goals) — to kick that many goals. Unfortunately, Dunstall injured a knee the very next week against Carlton to miss the rest of the season and remain on 1200 goals.

• 240 was the number of consecutive AFL games played by Melbourne's Irish ruckman, Jim Stynes, in the Demons' final match of the season.

• 5,842,139 was the record number of people who attended AFL home and away games.

• 2721 was the combined total of games played by 12 of the game's retiring greats — Geelong's Gary Ablett, Paul Couch and Billy Brownless, Hawthorn's Chris Langford and Darrin Pritchard, Carlton's Greg Williams, Justin Madden and Stephen Kernahan, Brisbane Lions' Michael McLean, Melbourne's Craig Turley and Andrew Obst and Essendon's Mark Harvey.

• Seven was the number of seasons it took the Adelaide Crows to bag its first premiership.

• 13.4 was the percentage difference which kept Port Adelaide out of the final eight in its debut year after it tied with the Brisbane Lions on 42 points.

• 81 was the number of goals kicked by Adelaide's Tony Modra to win the Coleman Medal at the end of the home and away season. It was the lowest winning total in the award's history.

• 26 was the number of Brownlow votes polled by St Kilda's Robert Harvey who became the first Brownlow medallist to poll the second highest number of votes. The

**EVER-READY:**
Melbourne's Jim Stynes just keeps on keeping on.

Western Bulldogs' Chris Grant had polled 27 votes, but was ineligible due to a one-week suspension for striking Hawthorn's Nick Holland in round seven.

• 225 was the number of games in which Stephen Kernahan had captained Carlton in round 18 to make him the longest-serving captain in AFL history. Essendon legend Dick Reynolds' record of 224 had stood since 1950.

• 416 games as coach is the total required by the Bombers' Kevin Sheedy as he closes on Reynolds' record as longest-serving coach of Essendon. Sheedy coached his 400th Essendon game in round 22.

• 400 was the number of games notched by field umpire Rowan Sawers in the round 14 clash between Geelong and Collingwood. That's earning your free kicks.

• 29.11 (185) was the highest score for the year, recorded by the Adelaide Crows when they defeated Richmond by 137 points in round 17. Richmond coach Robert Walls was sacked the next week.

• 3.9 (27) was the lowest score of the year, recorded by Melbourne in round nine. And guess what? Melbourne coach Neil Balme was sacked the next week.

• Three was the number of St Kilda players to top League charts. Nathan Burke led the kicks list with 469; Stewart Loewe, marks, with 192, and Robert Harvey, handballs, with 303.

• Four was the record number of finals matches the Adelaide Crows had to win to take home the premiership. Collingwood, in 1980, and Melbourne, in 1988, won three finals in a row only to be wiped out by record margins in the Grand Final, while North Melbourne, in 1977, played in five finals winning three, drawing one and losing one to win the flag. Adelaide Crows' coach Malcolm Blight was in that Kangaroos' team.

**— Peter Ryan**

# Crows rule in year of records

Season 1997 was a historic, record-breaking year. Adelaide was premier for the first time, there were record attendances, record television ratings and record club memberships.

Adelaide became the first club since Hawthorn in 1961 to win the premiership in its first Grand Final. It was truly a grand occasion which capped a slashing finals series by the Crows.

Adelaide became the second non-Victorian club to win the title, following West Coast, which was premier in 1992 and '94. And two finals were played at Football Park for the first time.

The Grand Final crowd of 98,828 was the biggest since 101,861 fans saw Hawthorn beat Carlton in 1986. It was a record since the completion of the Great Southern Stand in 1992 which provided more seats and less standing room, reducing capacity to just on 100,000.

Pre-game entertainment at the Grand Final was provided by Marina Prior, James Morrison, Tommy Emmanuel, Nathan Cavaleri, Tommy Tycho, Cafe of the Gates of Salvation, Kelley Abbey, Colleen Hewett, a cast and crew of 2000 and more than 1000 props.

A record attendance of 297,410 watched the 15 games in the pre-season Ansett Australia Cup series, won by Carlton. The grand final, watched by 74,786, was played at the MCG for the first time.

Much interest in 1997 centred on Port Adelaide, the new club in the competition. Many believed Port would struggle, but its first victory came in round three against Geelong and in the finish, it missed playing in the finals on percentage only. Its ninth placing in year one with 10 wins and a draw was hailed as highly successful.

In the home and away series, two coaches lost their jobs — Neil Balme at Melbourne and Robert Walls at Richmond.

Hawthorn's Chris Langford was the only player to reach the 300-game milestone in '97 and was one of several notable players to retire. Others to depart included teammates Darrin Pritchard, Ray Jencke and John Platten; Gary Ablett, Bill Brownless and Paul Couch (Geelong); Stephen Kernahan, Greg Williams, Justin Madden and Earl Spalding (Carlton); Ben Allan (Fremantle); Michael McLean and Scott McIvor (Brisbane Lions) and Mark Harvey (Essendon).

In the year's two State of Origin games, Victoria beat South Australia at Football Park and the Allies won against Western Australia at Subiaco.

At the season's end, the Coca-Cola All-Australian side was announced with Paul Kelly (Sydney) captain and Stan Alves (St Kilda) coach.

Major award winners were: Brownlow Medal — Robert Harvey (St Kilda); Norm Smith Medal — Andrew McLeod (Adelaide); Coleman Medal — Tony Modra (Adelaide); EJ Whitten Medal — Gavin Brown (Victoria); Fos Williams Medal — Brayden Lyle (South Australia); Graham Moss Medal — Scott Cummings (Western Australia), Alex Jesaulenko Medal — Nathan Buckley (The Allies); Norwich Rising Star — Michael Wilson (Port Adelaide).

Richmond won the AFL reserves' title, Sandringham the VFL grand final and North Ballarat Rebels the TAC Cup under-18s grand final.

The AFL's major sponsor was again Coca-Cola and the Channel Seven Network again had the TV rights.

Attendances and receipts for the season: home and away rounds (22) — attendance 5,842,591, receipts $26,077,935; finals (9) — attendance 560,406, receipts $15,466,562.

There was again a final eight and the finals break-up was: MCG (6 games) 420,221, Football Park (2) 90,150, Waverley Park (1) 50,035.

Ansett Australia Cup pre-season competition (15 games): attendance 297,410, receipts $1,909,071. Both were records.

Club membership of 382,345 was also a record.

Home and away admission: adults $12.50, visiting adult member $10.50, concession $6.50, children under 15 $1.70, children under six free, family $25.

Grand Final: adult $70, concession $37 (including Bass booking fee of $1.50 and a training levy of $1 on all tickets).

— **Greg Hobbs**

# Young and the old combine

Once again it was a special combination of talent that made up the 1997 All-Australian team. That mix covered 10 of the AFL's 16 clubs and ranged from 21-year-old Austinn Jones to 34-year-old Paul Roos.

St Kilda covered itself in glory in 1997 and it was no surprise to see the Saints represented by four players — Robert Harvey, Nathan Burke, Peter Everitt and the youthful Jones.

Harvey and Burke have been regular members of the All-Australian team. Burke was selected in 1993 and '96 and in '97 was named vice-captain to Sydney's Paul Kelly.

Harvey, the 1997 Brownlow Medallist, was first selected in 1992 and, apart from 1993, has been selected every year since. Obviously the selectors did not have to spend too many hours mulling over his inclusion.

Everitt and Jones were both selected for the first time and the long and the short of the Saints, as it were, had terrific seasons. Everitt's selection covered, in some way, for the disappointment of missing the Grand Final due to injury, while the jockey-sized Jones scorched the grass at grounds all over the country. To complete a big season for the Saints, Stan Alves was named coach of the year.

Other first time selections were David King, Adam Heuskes, Rohan Smith, Daryn Cresswell, Michael O'Loughlin and Fraser Gehrig, while Paul Salmon was selected under a different concept back in 1987 and '88 when the team was named after interstate games.

There were 13 changes to the 1996 All-Australian side with the following players missing selection: Chris Mainwaring, Shane Crawford, James Hird, Wayne Carey, Mit-

**DEBUT:** Port Adelaide's Adam Heuskes was selected in the All-Australian team for the first time.

chell White, Michael Voss, Tony Lockett, Darren Jarman, Corey McKernan, Craig Lambert, Glen Archer, Matthew Richardson and Garry Hocking.

St Kilda and Sydney each had four players selected, while at the other end of the scale, Geelong, Brisbane Lions, Richmond, Essendon, Fremantle and Melbourne were not represented. In the case of the Cats and the Lions, both finalists in 1997, it reflected the evenness of the two sides.

Hayden Kennedy, who was in charge of his second Grand Final, was named All-Australian umpire.

The selection panel comprised Gerard Healy, Ross Glendinning, Kevin Bartlett, Leigh Matthews and Neil Kerley, AFL general manager — football operations Ian Collins and AFL football administration manager Rod Austin. AFL chief executive officer Wayne Jackson was the non-voting chairman.
— **Michael Lovett**

---

## 1997 ALL-AUSTRALIAN TEAM

**B:** David King (NM), Stephen Silvagni (Carl), Paul Roos (Syd)
**HB:** Peter Matera (WC), Michael Sexton (Carl), Adam Heuskes (PA)
**C:** Austinn Jones (St K), Craig Bradley (Carl), Nathan Buckley (Coll)
**HF:** Rohan Smith (WB), Chris Grant (WB), Michael O'Loughlin (Syd)
**F:** Fraser Gehrig (WC), Tony Modra (Adel), Paul Kelly (Syd) (c)
**R:** Paul Salmon (Haw), Robert Harvey (St K), Nathan Burke (St K) (v-c)
**IC:** Peter Everitt (St K), Daryn Cresswell (Syd), Mark Ricciuto (Adel)
**Coach:** Stan Alves
**Umpire:** Hayden Kennedy

# Alves' dream turnaround

**R**emarkably, Stan Alves' most memorable and successful season as an AFL coach came in the same year that could very well have seen the end of him.

No, Stan Alves won't forget season 1997. He went to the brink, survived the early hardship and in the final analysis wasn't chasing a wooden spoon but a premiership.

The turnaround was of such magnitude that Alves, who looked one game away from the sack in April, was named the coach of the AFL's 1997 All-Australian side in September. It was a very, very sweet pill to swallow.

The big disappointment for Alves was the loss in the Grand Final against Adelaide. But, when the dust had settled and when he had time to contemplate, there must have been much personal satisfaction attached to a year that was going so wrong, then dramatically righted itself.

Losing that big game on the last Saturday in September hurt, but it could have been much worse back in April.

St Kilda went to Brisbane in round two and lost by 97 points. The pressure on Alves intensified. He called a meeting of the players and was ready to resign, but the players pledged their support. After the first two games St Kilda was on the bottom without a win and Alves was on a tightrope.

At one point during this early-season drama, club president Andrew Plymton spoke to Alves about the team's direction. He said Alves did not plead for sympathy but stressed he had a plan and said "let's stick to the plan, it's going to pay off".

After round six, St Kilda was still second bottom. Yet from these grim times the Saints rallied with four straight wins. After round eight they were in the top eight and the great transformation continued to reshape the club. When the home and away season finished, St Kilda was top of the pack, in No.1 berth with 15 wins and seven losses.

Those who had sought Alves' blood were now patting his back. There wouldn't be an execution at Moorabbin in 1997; maybe, thought the St Kilda throngs, a premiership celebration instead.

Alves, always a firm believer in his own doctrine, had his coaching confidence

**PLAN:** Stan Alves told the Saints to stick to his plan and they would be rewarded. They nearly were.

topped up like never before. In his 89th game as coach of the club, he had his men in the finals for the first time. It had been a long time coming.

Many believed it would happen in 1996 after St Kilda had beaten Carlton to win the pre-season Ansett Australia Cup and looked good in doing it. But, the balloon was soon pricked when the premiership season came along.

St Kilda and Alves, despite all the early hurdles, gave their supporters the works in 1997. First up in the finals were the Brisbane Lions at Waverley Park. This was the club that almost brought St Kilda and Alves to their knees five months earlier. But, in Melbourne and hurt by injuries, the Brisbane Lions were no match. North Melbourne, in the preliminary final, was the next club to fall to the Alves onslaught and this opened the door to the Grand Final.

This was almost all too hard to believe.

Finally, St Kilda went under to Adelaide. While Alves was disappointed and drained, he had lived to fight another day in 1998 and his crowning as coach of the year was richly deserved.

As a player, Alves gave his all in 226 games with Melbourne, but never once took part in a final. He crossed to North Melbourne and played in the 1997 premiership side and now he is chasing more gold at St Kilda.

In the 1990s, the side finishing second has gone on to win the premiership the following year only once — West Coast in 1992. That is something for Stan Alves to chew on. I think he can chew contentedly.

**15**

# Fight or die, said Blight, and so the Crows learnt to fly

It was a premiership that people knew was up for grabs. Anyone could win it — St Kilda, the Western Bulldogs, North Melbourne, Geelong, West Coast, the Brisbane Lions, Sydney and … Adelaide? Nah, not Adelaide. Anyone else though. In six seasons in the AFL, the Crows were the worst thing you can become in sport — a running joke.

September 1997 would change that perception — forever.

New coach Malcolm Blight came out firing. His stinging public comments after a round two loss in Melbourne against Richmond on both the developing culture of the club and a couple of individual performances — most notably that of ruckman David Pittman's first quarter — were a call to arms. Blight's clear message was that he was not about to accept mediocrity and the club would not survive if the players were prepared to.

**TRAILBLAZERS:** The first Adelaide side to win an AFL premiership and were they happy!

Still, it appeared the message had not sunk in as two rounds later the Crows were humiliated by newcomer Port Adelaide.

Then, the players got it. The next week they beat ladder leader the Western Bulldogs, in Victoria, by 10 goals. The same day, Shaun Rehn, the All-Australian ruckman from 1994, came back from his second knee reconstruction. He'd played only six games in the previous two years.

The Crows won five of the next six, losing only to Collingwood at Victoria Park by one point. These six wins weren't soft wins either as three were in Melbourne and one in Perth on a Monday night. Everyone had lifted. Mark Bickley, Mark Ricciuto, Nigel Smart — the new leadership group — were superb. Tony Modra had begun his assault on the Coleman Medal. From being spineless, the club had one of the most effective spines in the game — Andrew McLeod across half-back, Peter Caven at centre half-back, Matthew Robran at centre half-forward. And they had the wildcard — Darren Jarman.

But when September came, the Crows were in fourth spot. They had a home final, but it was not a great place from which to win a flag. They would have to win four consecutive finals and that had never been done. They beat the West Coast Eagles in week one. They were behind at three-quarter time against Geelong and won. At half-time in the preliminary final in Melbourne against the Western Bulldogs, they were 31 points down and Modra was out for the season with a knee injury. They won by two points with Jarman kicking the winning goal.

In the Grand Final, they were behind again, by 13 points at half-time. They were missing their two 1997 All-Australians —Modra and Ricciuto — and on their interchange was one fit player. They responded with six goals in the third quarter and eight in the last.

Jarman kicked six. Half-back flanker Shane Ellen kicked five after kicking only three goals in his 38-game career. And Troy Bond, the man dropped from Carlton's 1995 premiership side, kicked four. McLeod blitzed, while three ruckmen, Rehn, Pittman and Aaron Keating, kept the Saints guessing.

They had won the premiership by 33 points. It was the first team ever to win all four finals to win the flag; the sixth side to win the flag from fourth and the first Adelaide premiership side. — **Peter Ryan**

# Anatomy of a premier team

## Grand Final Line-up

B: Hart, Jameson, Goodwin
HB: McLeod, Pittman, Caven
C: Koster, Bickley, Connell
HF: Sampson, Robra, Rintoul
F: Bond, Ellen, Smart
R: Rehn, Johnson, Jarman
Int: Keating, James, Edwards

## Grand Final Score

**Adelaide**
3.8  5.10  11.11  19.11 (125)
**St Kilda**
3.6  7.11  9.13  13.16 (94)

Best: Adelaide — McLeod, Jarman, Rehn, Ellen, Johnson, Goodwin.
Goals: Adelaide — Jarman 6, Ellen 5, Bond 4, Smart, Goodwin, Rintoul, Caven.

Two Adelaide Crows players — Mark Ricciuto and Tony Modra — were selected in the 1997 All-Australian team. Both missed playing in the premiership side because of injury.

## 1997 Stats Record

Home and away: Played 22. Won 13, lost 9
Finals: Played 4. Won 4, lost 0

## Individuals

Most kicks: Darren Jarman 381
Most marks: Peter Caven 116 (16th in AFL)
Most handballs: Mark Bickley 197 (15th in AFL)
Most frees for: David Pittman 40 (5th in AFL)
Most frees against: Darren Jarman 51 (1st in AFL)
Most goals: Tony Modra 84 goals (1st in AFL)
Most hitouts: David Pittman 317 (4th in AFL)

Most tackles: Mark Bickley 80 (2nd in AFL)
Most shepherds: Kym Koster 19

## The Team

Average kicks per game: 195
Average marks per game: 72
Average handballs per game: 91
Average tackles per game: 33

## Premiership Team Averages

Height: 186cm
Weight: 86kg
Age: 24
Played every game: Mark Bickley, Ben Hart, Andrew McLeod
Oldest player: 30 years 8 months — Darren Jarman, born 28/1/67
Youngest player: 19 years 6 months — Kane Johnson, born 15/3/78
Most games: Darren Jarman, 152 games
Least games: Aaron Keating, 3 games
Tallest player: Shaun Rehn, 203cm
Shortest player(s): Clay Sampson, Mark Bickley, Brett James, 178cm

## Wealth of Experience

More than 200 games: 0
150-200 games: 1 player
100-150 games: 4 players
50-100 games: 9 players
25-50 games: 2 players
0-25 games: 5 players

## Tall Timber

200-210cm: 3
190-200cm: 4
180-190cm: 10
178-180cm: 4

## The Scores

Highest score: R17 29.11 (185) v Richmond 7.6 (48)
Lowest score: R21 6.12 (48) v Collingwood 5.9 (39)
Average score for (home and away): 14.12 (96)
Average score against (home and away): 11.13 (79)
Average winning margin (home and away): 47 points
Average losing margin (home and away): 24 points
Greatest winning margin: 137 points v Richmond R17
Greatest losing margin: 56 points v Geelong R13

## Average Scores Per Quarter

**HOME AND AWAY**

|  | Adelaide | Opposition |  |
| --- | --- | --- | --- |
| 1st quarter: | 24 points | 21 points | won qtr 11 |
| 2nd quarter: | 24 points | 17 points | won qtr 16 |
| 3rd quarter: | 22 points | 21 points | won qtr 11 |
| 4th quarter: | 27 points | 20 points | won qtr 15 |

**FINALS**

|  | Adelaide | Opposition |  |
| --- | --- | --- | --- |
| 1st quarter: | 17 points | 21 points | won qtr 2 |
| 2nd quarter: | 25 points | 26 points | won qtr 3 |
| 3rd quarter: | 22 points | 17 points | won qtr 3 |
| 4th quarter: | 33 points | 14 points | won qtr 4 |

Only team to win all four finals to win the premiership.

## Crows at a glance

**ADDRESS:** Turner Drive, West Lakes, SA 5021
**POSTAL ADDRESS:** PO Box 10, West Lakes, SA 5021
**TELEPHONE:** (08) 8347 2322
**FACSIMILE:** (08) 8347 2118
**WEB SITE:** www.afc.com.au
**MELBOURNE ADDRESS:** Suite 5, 2 Claremont St, South Yarra, Vic 3141
**MELBOURNE TELEPHONE:** (03) 9827 9111
**MELBOURNE FACSIMILE:** (03) 9827 9112
**CHAIRMAN:** Bob Hammond
**CHIEF EXECUTIVE OFFICER:** Bill Sanders
**GENERAL MANAGER, FOOTBALL OPERATIONS:** John Reid
**FOOTBALL ADMINISTRATION OFFICER:** John Condon
**MARKETING MANAGER:** Shane Fuller: Facsimile (08) 8347 3237
**COMMUNICATIONS MANAGER:** Steven Trigg (email: strigg@afc.com.au)
**RECRUITING MANAGER:** James Fantasia
**COACHING STAFF:** Malcolm Blight (senior), Darel Hart (assistant)
**SELECTION COMMITTEE:** Malcolm Blight, Terry Moore, Darel Hart, John Reid, Neil Craig, Peter Maynard
**TRAINING SERVICES MANAGER:** Trevor Jaques
**CLUB DOCTOR:** Brian Sando
**CLUB PHYSIOTHERAPIST:** Kevin Whitford
**JOINED AFL:** 1991
**HOME GROUND:** Football Park, West Lakes, South Australia
**GROUND DIMENSIONS:** 170m by 135m
**OFFICIAL COLORS:** Guernsey: Navy blue, red and gold hoops. Shorts: Navy blue. Socks: Navy blue, red and gold hoops
**PREMIERSHIPS:** 1997
**RECORD HOME ATTENDANCE:** 48,522 — August 29, 1993 v Collingwood

# ADELAIDE
# Now to keep the fire in the belly

In the 1990s, the good clubs are just like good businesses — professional, accountable and innovative. Adelaide has always had the money. It needed direction.

Last year, with new coach Malcolm Blight, the Crows gained innovation, respect, integrity and self-belief. With new captain Mark Bickley, they displayed professionalism and accountability.

After hitting rock bottom early with a devastating loss to new chum Port Adelaide, they picked themselves off the canvas. In the finals, Adelaide registered four gutsy victories — two at home, two at the MCG.

In the 1997 preliminary final against the Western Bulldogs, Adelaide became the first team to win a final outside its home state since West Coast won the premiership in 1994. Sixteen teams had tried and failed in that three-year period.

And the Crows won the flag without their injured 1997 All-Australians Mark Ricciuto (their highest vote-getter in the Brownlow) and Tony Modra (winner of the Coleman Medal for leading goalkicker in the AFL).

So what's in store? In the 1990s, no side has followed up a premiership with a placing higher than North Melbourne's fourth last year.

Adelaide will be without Tony Modra for most of 1998 as he recovers from the knee reconstruction forced by an injury in the preliminary final. However, Shaun Rehn, returning from a second knee reconstruction, was back to his best by the end of last year.

Riccuito will be back and the confidence given to all the younger players by a premiership should be enough to spur them again. Matthew Robran must continue to improve at centre half-forward and Ian Downsborough has been recruited as an insurance policy.

Mark Stevens, from North Melbourne, will have opportunities as a middle-sized running player, something Adelaide lacks. The most difficult thing will be for the players who made their names in the finals series to accept that success can only be repeated by hard work. Blight, a man who has achieved just about everything there is to achieve as a player and a coach in AFL football, has the challenge in front of him.

Adelaide still has great talent, with Andrew McLeod, Darren Jarman, Mark Bickley, Peter Caven, Ben Hart and Nigel Smart at the forefront. It also has good young players Peter Vardy, Simon Goodwin, Kane Johnson, Andrew Eccles, Tyson Edwards and Tom Gilligan with much to prove.

— **Peter Ryan**

## THE YEAR AHEAD

| Rd | Date | Opponent | Venue | Home/ Away | Time (local) |
|----|------|----------|-------|------------|--------------|
| 1 | March 28 | Carlton | OO | A | 2.10pm |
| 2 | April 5 | Fremantle | FP | H | 1.40pm |
| 3 | April 12 | St Kilda | P | A | 2.10pm |
| 4 | April 19 | Port Adelaide | FP | A | 1.40pm |
| 5 | April 26 | Geelong | FP | H | 2.50pm |
| 6 | May 3 | North Melbourne | MCG | A | 2.10pm |
| 7 | May 10 | West Coast | FP | H | 1.40pm |
| 8 | May 17 | Richmond | FP | H | 12.10pm |
| 9 | May 23 (N) | Brisbane Lions | G | A | 7.40pm |
| 10 | May 31 | Melbourne | FP | H | 1.40pm |
| 11 | June 7 | Western Bulldogs | OO | A | 2.10pm |
| 12 | June 13 (N) | Essendon | FP | H | 8.10pm |
| 13 | June 20 | Collingwood | MCG | A | 2.10pm |
| 14 | June 28 | Sydney | SCG | A | 12.40pm |
| 15 | July 5 | Hawthorn | FP | H | 12.10pm |
| 16 | July 17 (N) | Carlton | FP | H | 8.10pm |
| 17 | July 24 (N) | Fremantle | S | A | 6.40pm |
| 18 | August 1 (N) | St Kilda | FP | H | 8.10pm |
| 19 | August 9 | Port Adelaide | FP | H | 2.50pm |
| 20 | August 15 | Geelong | KP | A | 2.10pm |
| 21 | August 22 (N) | North Melbourne | FP | H | 8.10pm |
| 22 | August 29 (N) | West Coast | S | A | 6.40pm |

## 1997 AT A GLANCE

**W:** R1: Adelaide 20.12 (132) v Brisbane Lions 14.12 (96) (FP)
**L:** R2: Richmond 19.14 (128) v Adelaide 15.10 (100) (MCG)
**L:** R3: Carlton 15.18 (108) v Adelaide 12.8 (80) (OO)
**L:** R4: Adelaide 11.6 (72) v Port Adelaide 11.17 (83) (FP)
**W:** R5: Western Bulldogs 9.17 (71) v Adelaide 19.7 (121) (OO)
**L:** R6: Collingwood 13.6 (84) v Adelaide 11.17 (83) (VP)

### SNAPSHOT

**Games:** 26
**Won:** 17 **Lost:** 9
**Ladder finish:** 4
**Players used:** 35

**W:** R7: Adelaide 18.18 (126) v Essendon 11.7 (73) (FP)
**W:** R8: Adelaide 22.12 (144) v Sydney 8.7 (55) (FP)
**W:** R9: Hawthorn 13.10 (88) v Adelaide 14.18 (102) (P)
**W:** R10: Fremantle 10.12 (72) v Adelaide 16.9 (105) (S)
**W:** R11: Melbourne 5.15 (45) v Adelaide 14.13 (97) (MCG)
**L:** R12: Adelaide 12.11 (83) v North Melbourne 16.9 (105) (FP)
**L:** R13: Geelong 17.8 (110) v Adelaide 7.12 (54) (KP)
**W:** R14: Adelaide 16.10 (106) v West Coast 4.7 (31) (FP)
**W:** R15: Adelaide 10.16 (76) v St Kilda 9.12 (66) (FP)
**L:** R16: Brisbane Lions 17.16 (118) v Adelaide 13.9 (87) (G)
**W:** R17: Adelaide 29.11 (185) v Richmond 7.6 (48) (FP)
**W:** R18: Adelaide 18.19 (127) v Carlton 13.8 (86) (FP)
**W:** R19: Port Adelaide 9.4 (58) v Adelaide 9.11 (65) (FP)
**L:** R20: Adelaide 7.18 (60) v Western Bulldogs 16.7 (103) (FP)
**W:** R21: Adelaide 6.12 (48) v Collingwood 5.9 (39) (FP)
**L:** R22: Essendon 16.6 (102) v Adelaide 14.14 (98) (OO)

# The Coach

## Malcolm Blight

**Born:** 16/2/50

In his first year as coach of Adelaide, Malcolm Blight steered the Crows from 12th in '96 through the uncharted territory of four consecutive finals wins to the flag and the greatest improvement ever.

Blight took risks — as he always has — and they paid off. He publicly criticised his players in an attempt to change the culture of his new club, then underplayed their morale-sapping loss to Port Adelaide early last season. Blight set realistic goals about winning out of Adelaide, gave opportunities to youngsters, established a new leadership group and set about restoring respectability to the club.

In the Grand Final against St Kilda, Blight made moves — Ellen to full-forward, Pittman to centre half-back, McLeod to the midfield, Jarman contesting in the centre then running forward and Goodwin running off the back of the centre square — that changed the dynamics of the contest. Blight was in his fourth Grand Final as coach — something no current coach has come close to achieving — but had experienced only losses with Geelong.

## AT A GLANCE

### COACHING RECORD
**North Melbourne**

| Season | P | W | L | D | Pos |
|--------|----|----|----|----|-----|
| 1981 | 16 | 6 | 10 | — | 8 |

**Geelong**

| Season | P | W | L | D | Pos |
|--------|----|----|----|----|-----|
| 1989 | 26 | 18 | 8 | — | 2 |
| 1990 | 22 | 8 | 14 | — | 10 |
| 1991 | 25 | 17 | 8 | — | 3 |
| 1992 | 26 | 18 | 8 | — | 2 |
| 1993 | 20 | 12 | 8 | — | 7 |
| 1994 | 26 | 16 | 10 | — | 2 |
| | 145 | 89 | 56 | | |

**Adelaide**

| Season | P | W | L | D | Pos |
|--------|----|----|----|----|-----|
| 1997 | 26 | 17 | 9 | — | 4 |
| **Total** | **187** | **112** | **75** | | |

## WIN/LOSS RECORD

| Against | P | W (N) | L (N) | D (N) |
|---|---|---|---|---|
| Brisbane Bears | 9 | 7 (2) | 2 (1) | 0 |
| Brisbane Lions | 2 | 1 | 1 (1) | 0 |
| Carlton | 11 | 3 (1) | 8 | 0 |
| Collingwood | 11 | 2 (1) | 9 (3) | 0 |
| Essendon | 12 | 4 (3) | 8 (1) | 0 |
| Fitzroy | 9 | 6 (4) | 3 (1) | 0 |
| Fremantle | 3 | 3 (3) | 0 | 0 |
| Geelong | 11 | 5 (4) | 6 | 0 |
| Hawthorn | 11 | 5 (2) | 6 (1) | 0 |
| Melbourne | 10 | 7 (5) | 3 | 0 |
| North Melb | 10 | 4 (2) | 6 (3) | 0 |
| Port Adel | 2 | 1 | 1 | 0 |
| Richmond | 11 | 6 (2) | 5 (4) | 0 |
| St Kilda | 12 | 7 (3) | 4 (1) | 1 |
| Sydney | 11 | 6 (4) | 5 (2) | 0 |
| West Coast | 12 | 5 (4) | 7 (2) | 0 |
| W Bulldogs | 12 | 5 (3) | 7 | 0 |
| **TOTALS** | **159** | **77 (43)** | **81 (20)** | **1 (0)** |

*(N) Premiership matches played at night*

## WINNING RUNS

6 v Brisbane Bears (1991– 1994)
5 v Richmond (1991–1993)
4 v Melbourne (1993–1997)
3 v North Melb (1991–1993)
3 v Geelong (1992–1994)
3 v Sydney (1992–1994)
3 v St Kilda (1992–1993); (1995–1996)
3 v Fremantle (1995–1997)
2 v Fitzroy (1992–1993); (1996)
2 v West Coast (1993); (1994–1995); (1997–)
1 v Collingwood (1993); (1997–)
1 v W Bulldogs (1991); (1993); (1995); (1997–)
1 v Carlton (1991); (1994); (1997–)
1 v Hawthorn (1991); (1992); (1993); (1997–)
1 v Port Adelaide (1997)
1 v Brisbane Lions (1997)

## 1997 BEST AND FAIREST

Five members of the match committee award scores out of 10 to their five best players.

**1** Andrew McLeod (409)
**2** Darren Jarman (389)
**3** Mark Ricciuto (296)
**4** Ben Hart (272)
**5** Peter Craven (270)
**6** Mark Bickley (228)
**7** Nigel Smart (227)
**8** Kym Koster (195)
**9** Tony Modra (167)
**10** David Pittman (157)

## GAMES RECORDS

**144** Mark Bickley (1991– )
**142** Nigel Smart (1991– )
**133** Ben Hart (1992– )
**132** Rod Jameson (1991– )
**117** Chris McDermott (1991–96)
**113** Tony McGuinness (1991–96)
**110** Andrew Jarman (1991–96)
**110** Tony Modra (1992– )
**110** Matthew Liptak (1991– )
**104** Mark Ricciuto (1993– )

## GOALS RECORDS

**421** Tony Modra (1992– )
**124** Matthew Liptak (1991– )
**100** Scott Hodges (1991–93; 1996)
**95** Rod Jameson (1991– )
**92** Andrew Jarman (1991–96)

## HIGHS AND LOWS

| Against | Highest | Lowest | G. W. Margin | G. L. Margin |
|---|---|---|---|---|
| Brisbane Bears | 23.18.156 (1991) | 6.10.46 (1995) | 66 (1991) | 30 (1995) |
| Brisbane Lions | 20.12.132 (1997) | 13.9.87 (1997) | 36 (1997) | 31 (1997) |
| Carlton | 22.18.150 (1994) | 7.13.55 (1991) | 66 (1994) | 79 (1993) |
| Collingwood | 19.21.135 (1993) | 5.7.37 (1991) | 24 (1993) | 123 (1991) |
| Essendon | 23.23.161 (1996) | 6.11.47 (1991) | 96 (1996) | 122 (1995) |
| Fitzroy | 26.10.166 (1996) | 7.8.50 (1991) | 99 (1996) | 33 (1995) |
| Fremantle | 20.12.132 (1996) | 16.9.105 (1997) | 96 (1996) | — |
| Geelong | 24.25.169 (1992) | 5.8.38 (1994) | 91 (1992) | 123 (1992) |
| Hawthorn | 24.11.155 (1991) | 6.11.47 (1994) | 86 (1991) | 97 (1994) |
| Melbourne | 23.8.146 (1995) | 9.13.67 (1992) | 59 (1993) | 51 (1996) |
| North Melb | 28.12.180 (1991) | 9.11.65 (1995) | 73 (1991) | 80 (1994) |
| Port Adel | 11.6.72 (1997) | 9.11.65 (1997) | 7 (1997) | 11 (1997) |
| Richmond | 29.11.185 (1997) | 9.4.58 (1995) | 139 (1993) | 46 (1996) |
| St Kilda | 23.18.156 (1993) | 4.7.31 (1991) | 93 (1993) | 131 (1991) |
| Sydney | 24.10.154 (1994) | 10.15.75 (1994) | 90 (1996) | 57 (1995) |
| West Coast | 16.10.106 (1997) | 5.12.42 (1995) | 75 (1997) | 135 (1995) |
| W Bulldogs | 19.14.128 (1991) | 4.10.34 (1994) | 50 (1997) | 87 (1992) |

## THE LEADERSHIP AT ADELAIDE

| Year | Pos | Coach | Captain | Best & Fairest | Leading Goalkicker | |
|---|---|---|---|---|---|---|
| 1991 | 9 | G. Cornes | C. McDermott | M. Mickan | R. Jameson | 49 |
| 1992 | 9 | G. Cornes | C. McDermott | C. McDermott | S. Hodges | 48 |
| 1993 | 3 | G. Cornes | C. McDermott | T. McGuinness | T. Modra | 129 |
| 1994 | 11 | G. Cornes | C. McDermott | S. Rehn | T. Modra | 70 |
| 1995 | 11 | R. Shaw | T. McGuinness | M. Connell | T. Modra | 42 |
| 1996 | 12 | R. Shaw | T. McGuinness | M. Liptak | T. Modra | 75 |
| 1997 | 1 | M. Blight | M. Bickley | A. McLeod | T. Modra | 84 |

# PLAYER PROFILES

## NATHAN BASSETT
Had a frustrating year in 1997, moving from Norwood to Melbourne to be on its rookie list, then breaking his sternum when on the verge of playing senior football. A middle-sized utility whom Adelaide is happy to have back. Expect a contribution this year.

## MARK BICKLEY
Made captain in 1997, as much for his qualities off the field as his ability on it. Produced his best last year when Adelaide needed him. Best on ground in Adelaide's first final at home against the West Coast Eagles. A persistent midfielder who is great at working the ball out of the centre and a ferocious tackler who was in the top-10 possession winners in the AFL last season. Has not missed a game for three years and has been with the Crows since day one in 1991. In the past, has been a very underrated player, but captains of premiership teams don't remain that way for long, and Bickley is now part of what is recognised as one of the strongest midfields in the competition.
**Player honors:** 2nd best and fairest 1993, 3rd best and fairest 1992; premiership side 1997. Captain since 1997.

## TROY BOND
A premiership player with Adelaide after missing out on Carlton's 1995 triumph when dropped from its Grand Final side to make way for the returning Scott Camporeale. At the time, he left the Blues a very disappointed young man but has now realised his premiership dream. A handy, crumbing forward who is devastating late last year, kicking nine out of his 20 goals for the year in the finals, including one in each quarter of the Grand Final. Developed confidence as the season wore on and is a great finisher. Difficult to match up on as he plays taller than he is and manages to kick goals when the pressure is on.
**Player honors:** AFL Norwich Rising Star nominee 1994; premiership side 1997.
**Previous AFL club:** Carlton (1994-95: 36 games, 26 goals).

## PETER CAVEN
Last year became one of the most attacking defenders and improved players in the game at centre half-back. In the Grand Final, he became a luxury at half-back, a position more suitable for a player of his size. Took the most marks of any Adelaide player, has great run out of defence and great consistency. The left-footer spent time at Fitzroy and Sydney — playing more than half his games in the seconds — before joining the Crows and playing 42 of a possible 48 games in two years. Still remembered in Sydney after being cleaned up by Tony Lockett (then with St Kilda) and the extent of his injuries after the clash. However, it has not affected his ability to run hard and straight at the ball. His toughness and resilience indicates last year was not just one out of the box, but realisation of a player with plenty of talent. Finished fifth in Adelaide's best and fairest in 1997. Plays his 100th game first up in 1998.
**Player honors:** premiership side 1997.

**Previous AFL clubs:** Fitzroy (1991-93: 39 games, 17 goals), Sydney (1994-95: 18 games, 4 goals).

## MATT CONNELL
Overcame injury problems to play well on the wing in Adelaide's premiership side. A reliable player who picks up plenty of kicks and is well suited to Adelaide's long-kicking, tight-checking style. Not overly quick, but rarely beaten and links in well particularly on the big Football Park arena. Is yet to return to his best and fairest form of 1995, but is a luxury on a wing or running through the midfield and adds handy depth to the Crows' on-ball set-up.
**Player honors:** Adelaide best and fairest 1995; premiership side 1997.
**Previous AFL club:** West Coast Eagles (1993: 3 games, 0 goals).

## TIM COOK
Played four games early last season without consolidating a position, but certainly didn't disgrace himself. Has filled a forward pocket role in his senior appearances, but is struggling to move into Adelaide's strong midfield. Toned up a bit and with extra fitness is looking for a big year.

## GREG DEMPSEY
Missed two-thirds of last season because of problems with a quad muscle, so was unable to show his wares in his first season with the club. The West Adelaide on-baller will be looking for a bit more luck this year.

## IAN DOWNSBOROUGH
Joins his third club in three years. The West Coast Eagles traded him to Port Adelaide at the end of 1996 to net No. 1 draft choice Michael Gardiner and he was swapped for Brett Chalmers at the close of the 1997 season. Malcolm Blight has made noises that the Crows might be able to use him as a tall mobile centre half-forward/forward pocket. Downsborough is definitely mobile and can play at either end of the ground. Has the talent to get back on track following a frustrating 14 months interrupted by illness and movement between clubs. Early practice match form encouraging.
**Previous AFL clubs:** West Coast Eagles (1995-96: 20 games, 5 goals); Port Adelaide (1997: 7 games, 2 goals).

## ANDREW ECCLES
Came from Victoria's Preston Knights in 1996 as a 17-year-old after winning their best and fairest and being named in the All-Australian side. Looked good early in '97 when he played two Ansett Australia Cup games, but was unable to break into the senior side in the AFL premiership season. Performed well for Norwood reserves in the finals last season, but by the start of the 1998 season the opinion was that he may need more time. A versatile player who is team-orientated. He has an excellent spring, is a strong mark and runs straight at the football.

## TYSON EDWARDS
Showed his ability in the Grand Final when coming off the bench to provide drive from the half-back line where he played on the ever dangerous Nicky Winmar. At only 21, he plays in a similar mould to Andrew

McLeod. Edwards has an exciting leap, good hands and, despite his inexperience, plays in a very confident manner. Would be expected to improve further over the next couple of seasons.
**Player honors:** premiership side 1997.

## SHANE ELLEN
From obscurity to a household name was the story of last season for Ellen, when he kicked five goals in the Grand Final after starting at full-forward. The surprise move reaped two goals in the first quarter, making Ellen so confident that when he moved to the more familiar half-back in the second half, he drifted forward to kick three more goals for the game. A versatile and serviceable player who had not previously had a big impact, largely because of a succession of injuries. At 25, and with a huge confidence booster under his belt, Ellen could make his mark — if injury-free — in 1998. He is a good kick for goal and marks well in front of his face. He will, however, get more attention this year from opposition sides. The loss of Tony Modra for most of 1998 will create further opportunities in attack.
**Player honors:** premiership side 1997.
**Previous AFL club:** Western Bulldogs (1993-1995: 11 games, 1 goal).

## ASHLEY FERNEE
The young ruckman/defender is taking time to develop as he enters his third season with the Crows. Played two games for Adelaide in 1996 after being drafted from the Calder Cannons in 1995, but copped a couple of injuries and has struggled since for South Adelaide. Could show results for the experience he has gained.

## TOM GILLIGAN
Made his debut in round three last year in a side depleted of talls because of injury. Acquitted himself well in three games, then played for Port Adelaide in the SANFL for the rest of the season. Tired towards the finish — as is often the case with young players entering AFL football — but the youngster showed good early form and should build on that this season. Is at a club stacked with similar sized players so just making senior football will be a fair achievement at this stage. Possesses an outstanding leap and shapes as a good long-term prospect.

## SIMON GOODWIN
Made his debut in round one last year, but managed only six home and away games because of injury before returning for a great finals series. Kicked a pressure goal late in the preliminary final against the Western Bulldogs. Helped turn the tide after half-time in the Grand Final when asked to run off the back of the centre square at all centre bounces giving the Crows first use of the footy on many occasions out of the middle. A tough, straight-at-the-football left-footer who rarely loses a contest or makes an unforced error.
**Player honors:** premiership side 1997.

## BEN HART
Given more of a leadership role, Hart responded to recognition that he was a player Adelaide wanted to build the club around. Revelling in the 'back yourself'

philosophy of coach Malcolm Blight, he returned to the attacking style of defence that won him much respect early in his career. Seemed to lose his way for a couple of seasons but was a model of consistency throughout 1997. Only 23, but very cool in a crisis. A desperate, high-leaping, exciting defender, Hart helped turn the preliminary final last year with his hard running and shut down St Kilda's Jason Heatley in the Grand Final. A player who benefited from being able to settle in one position in defence.
**Player honors:** All-Australian 1992, 1993; premiership side 1997.

## BRETT JAMES
Lucky in the finish to make the Grand Final team, when included at the expense of Trent Ormond-Allen. Proved very capable, filling a hole in defence, and was a deserved part of the victory. Used in specific roles last year after crossing from Collingwood at the end of 1996 and both player and club reaped the rewards. James is also capable as a high quality 'run-with' player showing great early season form in that role last year.
**Player honors:** premiership side 1997.
**Previous AFL club:** Collingwood (1994-96: 42 games, 26 goals).

## ROD JAMESON
An experienced campaigner used either to match up on key opposition forwards or to go forward himself. (He kicked six in the last round last year). A strong, versatile, hard-running player who lined up at full-back in last year's Grand Final before a hamstring tear kept him off the ground from quarter time. Has been with the club since the start and although he has had his share of injuries, he thoroughly deserved a premiership medallion.
**Player honors:** Adelaide leading goalkicker 1991; premiership side 1997.

## DARREN JARMAN
Answered all doubters with a huge second half in the Grand Final when he kicked six goals (five in the last quarter). This followed a match-winning last quarter in the preliminary final when he kicked the winning goal. Kicked 39 goals in 24 games — an awesome contribution from a running player — and finished second in Adelaide's best and fairest. A great tackler when he hasn't got the footy, Jarman, now in his 30s, will probably never produce consistency to match his brilliance, yet is still one of the most important players in the game. Seeing Jarman with the ball on the string is one of the more enjoyable sights in AFL football. His disposal is the best in the competition and he has incredible evasive skills. Showed his versatility in both the preliminary and Grand Finals, being the match-winner when moved to full-forward late in both games. Now has the distinction of playing in premiership sides at two clubs. Was overcoming a groin injury during the pre-season, but was expected to be fully fit by the start of the season.
**Player honors:** 2nd Brownlow Medal 1995; Hawthorn best and fairest 1995, 2nd Hawthorn best and fairest 1992; Adelaide 2nd best and fairest 1997, Adelaide equal 3rd best and fairest 1996; All-Australian 1992, 1995, 1996; Hawthorn night series premiership side

1991, 1992; Hawthorn premiership side 1991; Adelaide premiership side 1997.
**Previous club:** Hawthorn (1991-1995: 109 games, 122 goals).

### KANE JOHNSON
Arrived at the Crows from the Eastern Ranges after being selected at No. 27 in the 1995 National Draft. Consolidated on flashes he had shown in two games in 1996, by being a valuable premiership player and playing in 23 games. Is now looking as if he was a bargain pick-up. Tagged Brownlow Medallist Robert Harvey on Grand Final day and did well. A tall, running player who is becoming more attacking with experience. Has a great temperament, is disciplined and appears capable of becoming one of the keys in an Adelaide Crows' midfield. Will continue to improve.
**Player honors:** premiership side 1997; AFL Norwich Rising Star nominee 1997.

### AARON KEATING
Surprise selection in preliminary final for only his second game, replacing suspended ruckman David Pittman. His preliminary final performance was good, but he struggled in the Grand Final when used sparingly. Broke a pelvic bone in his round one debut last year. A huge man who will develop into a ruckman of some quality. As the third ruckman, behind Shaun Rehn and David Pittman, the youngster must force his way into the line-up as he did for the Grand Final.
**Player honors:** premiership side 1997.

### KYM KOSTER
The bow-legged wingman came back from a knee reconstruction — after an injury in 1996 — in round three of last year to be one of the quickest, most creative wingmen in the game. Played the next 24 games straight and was rarely out of the best players. Won the Crows' best team player award for 1997. Injects toughness and pace, carrying with him a belief that Adelaide can win anywhere. Koster also has good vision and a determination which ensures he does all the hard things that can quickly change a team's performance. Another player who can also be used in a 'run-with' role. Koster finished eighth in Adelaide's best and fairest.
**Player honors:** premiership side 1997.
**Previous AFL club:** Western Bulldogs (1994-95: 38 games, 13 goals).

### NICK LAIDLAW
Knuckled down in 1997 after being initially shocked by the requirements of AFL football. The Crows say he was their most improved youngster, playing senior football for Sturt and performing well by year's end. Is a former captain of South Australia in the AFL Under-18 National Championships.

### MATTHEW LIPTAK
Combining his career as a doctor and footballer has always been an incredible balancing act for this talented half-forward flanker, but constant hamstring problems kept the 1996 club best and fairest away for most of 1997 and, sadly, the chance to play in a premiership side. It threatens to hamper his 1998 season as he wasn't fully recovered by the time the Ansett Australia Cup began. Liptak is a very reliable

midfielder/forward capable on both sides of his body and very handy around goals.
**Player honors:** best and fairest 1996.

### ANDREW McLEOD
A golden year for this talented player from the Northern Territory. He won the Norm Smith Medal for a slashing performance in the Grand Final and was club best and fairest in a premiership year. He found his niche across half-back (where he played most of his footy in Darwin) being both attacking and, at times, impassable. It was his match-winning efforts in the midfield during the finals series that put his name in lights. Not surprisingly, he attracted the attention of other clubs and was seriously considering a big offer to move north and join the Brisbane Lions. To the collective sighs of relief in Adelaide, he was persuaded to stay with the Crows. At only 21, he could become not only one of the most damaging, but also one of the most recognised footballers in the game in 1998.
**Player honors:** best and fairest 1997; Norm Smith Medal 1997; AFL Norwich Rising Star nominee 1995; premiership side 1997.

### TONY MODRA
Missed out on playing in the Grand Final last year, because of injury, but his performances were instrumental in the team's improvement. Despite a form slump that saw him kick only six goals in his last seven games, he won his first Coleman Medal with 81 goals in the home and away rounds (84 for the year) and All-Australian selection. Unfortunately, he missed his ultimate goal — to play in a premiership side — but despite what must have been mixed feelings, he heartily joined in the premiership celebrations. His reaction indicated an increasing maturity from a player who has suffered, at times, from the adulation a pop star might receive. Has had a knee reconstruction after being injured in the first quarter of last year's preliminary final and is making good progress. However, Adelaide says there will be no return before July and maybe not at all in 1998.
**Player honors:** 3rd best and fairest 1993; Fos Williams Medallist 1996; All-Australian team 1993, 1997; Coleman Medal 1997; leading goalkicker 1993, 1994, 1995, 1996, 1997.

### TRENT ORMOND-ALLEN
Played in two finals last year after a courageous comeback from a broken jaw suffered in round 18. However, glandular fever kept him out of the Grand Final. A newcomer at Adelaide last year after two years with Melbourne, Ormond-Allen was aggressive and able to tag key playmakers, surprising many with his hard-at-the-footy approach. His resolve was important in changing perception about Adelaide. He was able to join in full training before Christmas and Adelaide doesn't believe the illness has hampered his preparation for this season.
**Previous AFL club:** Melbourne (1995-96: 8 games, 1 goal).

### IAN PERRIE
A potential key position player at AFL level, who had a fantastic game with East Perth in the reserves grand final last year. Named in the All-Australian under-18 side and showed good form over summer in trial games.

## LANCE PICIOANE

Dashing ruck rover with an outstanding junior record. His father played with Marconi, represented Victoria and was in the Australian soccer squad. An explosive player with an ability to move freely in heavy traffic and pinpoint a teammate. Captain of Victoria Metro at under-16 level, where he was best player at the 1995 National Schoolboys Championship. Was an All-Australian at under-18 level last year. Adelaide has been impressed with his early season form and he would be expected to play senior football at some stage this season.

## DAVID PITTMAN

Became one of the best known names in football in April 1997 when new coach Malcolm Blight publicly described him, after his first quarter against Richmond, as "the most pathetic ruckman I've ever seen in my entire life in footy". Blight later said his quote had been taken out of context but his reaction was certainly one of the more furious outbursts a coach has made on his own player in recent times. Came back from the lambaste to play a crucial role in the premiership side, playing well in the unusual role of centre half-back on Stewart Loewe in the Grand Final. A talented ruckman, Pittman is a luxury to have as second string to Shaun Rehn. His improvement was highlighted when he finished 10th in Adelaide's best and fairest.
**Player honors:** premiership side 1997.

## SHAUN REHN

One of the most important players in the AFL, Rehn returned in round five from his second knee reconstruction after playing only three games in each of 1995 and '96. Of the 22 games he played in 1997, the Crows won 16. Apart from Darren Jarman he was probably Adelaide's most important player during the finals and his performance in a closely fought semifinal final against Geelong was pivotal. Can consistently mark around the ground and win ruck contest after ruck contest. His courage in successfully returning to football after a two-year lay-off was fantastic. A genuine star.
**Player honors:** best and fairest 1994; All-Australian 1994; premiership side 1997.

## MARK RICCIUTO

Missed last year's finals series because of a persistent groin/hernia injury, but put in a brilliant year. Provided run through the midfield, gained plenty of the ball and disposed of it creatively. Finished in the top-six in Brownlow voting, was third in the club best and fairest and won All-Australian selection for the second time. At only 22, and with 104 games under his belt, the joint vice-captain is a key part of one of the best midfields in the game. Ricciuto's capacity to use his body strength is well known, but last year he showed the complete package, relying on his skill to inspire the Crows. Had several operations at the end of the season to overcome leg problems and had returned to running by mid-November. Was still not quite right by Ansett Australia Cup time and Adelaide was taking no risks with him early in the season.
**Player honors:** 3rd best and fairest 1994, 1997; All-Australian 1994, 1997; AFL Norwich Rising Star nominee 1993.

## CHAD RINTOUL

In and out of the side in his debut year, but the forward pocket was there at the finish to help win the flag. Needs to improve in certain areas, but should build on the form he showed last year. Nuggety and often bobs up with a goal when Adelaide is struggling for an avenue home. Works hard to keep the ball in attack.
**Player honors:** premiership side 1997.

## MATTHEW ROBRAN

Played a major role at centre half-forward in the Crows' ascent up the ladder. Made the position his own and was on fire mid-season after coming back in round seven from injury. Form dropped slightly by season's end, when he kicked only three goals in the last eight matches. Marks well and is a booming kick capable of kicking a goal from 60 metres out. Slight problems with a knee over summer didn't hamper his preparation greatly, although he missed the start of the Ansett Australia Cup. Looms as a key player this season, particularly in the absence of Tony Modra, as he could play at full-forward as well as centre half-forward. A player who the opposition can never be sure it has beaten, as he is capable of turning his form around quickly and can make damaging use of a few possessions.
**Player honors:** premiership side 1997.
**Previous AFL club:** Hawthorn (1991: 7 games, 5 goals).

## CLAY SAMPSON

Returned to South Australia in 1997 after two years at Melbourne. Broke into the Crows' line-up in round 17 and didn't miss a game for the rest of the year. Suffered a cork thigh early in the Grand Final and had to leave the ground. Not a big possession-winner, but has good evasive skills and is damaging when he has the ball. Capable of kicking goals at crucial stages as evidenced by his match-winning effort against Richmond in the Ansett Australia Cup earlier this year.
**Player honors:** premiership side 1997.
**Previous AFL club:** Melbourne (1995-96: 13 games, 1 goal).

## NIGEL SMART

Capable of playing in every key position on the ground. Not only a fantastic mark and a booming kick, but loves running with the ball to quickly rebound out of defence. Has the capacity to change a game when moved from defence into attack or vice-versa. A class player who adds value through his superb leadership skills and his talent to change the flow of a game. Another player who seems to have blossomed under Malcolm Blight and still has plenty of good football ahead of him.
**Player honors:** 2nd best and fairest 1996, 3rd best and fairest 1991; All-Australian team 1991, 1993; premiership side 1997.

## BARRY STANDFIELD

Was playing the best football of his career early last year up forward. Kicked 20 goals in the first eight games as a tall second fiddle to Tony Modra. An injury and then a loss of form saw him lose his spot and never regain it — even when Pittman missed the preliminary final because of suspension. Will not want to miss any more opportunities when they come his way this season. Could be an early option to cover for Modra, although his mobility, and therefore ability to apply defensive pressure, must be of concern.

**Previous AFL club:** Western Bulldogs (1989-96: 98 games, 38 goals).

## LINDEN STEVENS

Grew up in Singapore playing soccer and participating in cross-country running. Last year, demonstrated his versatility by playing 13 games for Sturt. Adelaide will be looking at him as a half-forward option, but is expecting him to take time.

## MARK STEVENS

Joined North Melbourne in 1995, but struggled to cement a place, playing eight games in each of his first two seasons and five in 1997. A fresh start with the reigning premier gives him another crack after he was picked up in exchange for Jason McCartney. A versatile player who has shown ability up forward at times, he would be a difficult player to match up on.

**Previous AFL club:** North Melbourne (1995-97: 21 games, 20 goals).

## JAMES THIESSEN

Had three seasons in the SANFL with Norwood, after playing seven AFL games with Richmond in 1993 before being delisted. Has good pace and could develop into a handy wingman/on-baller. At 23, the Crows will be hoping he can step straight into senior football.

**Previous AFL club:** Richmond (1993: 7 games, 1 goal).

## SIMON TREGENZA

Sought by Port Adelaide during trade negotiations, but the Crows weren't about to relinquish him. The speedy wingman showed good form after returning from a knee reconstruction, but then suffered minor problems with the grafts and copped a calf injury that ended his season. Has always been a part of the Crows' best team with his ball-carrying ability and mental toughness, but needs a solid year to re-establish himself.

**Player honors:** 3rd best and fairest 1995; Fos Williams Medallist 1995.

## PETER VARDY

Missed out on playing in the Grand Final because of a broken collarbone. His last act for 1997 was to kick a team-lifting goal in the tight semi-final against Geelong. One of the toughest young half-forwards in the game, he's capable of kicking goals on the run and is a hard tackler. High up in AFL Norwich Rising Star award voting and when he develops further, could become a vital goalkicking midfielder for Adelaide. Had an interrupted pre-season, but Adelaide will be hoping for another solid year from this high quality youngster.

**Player honors:** AFL Norwich Rising Star nominee 1997.

# ROOKIE LIST

## SUDJAI COOK

Born in Vietnam, Cook was rover in Norwood's premiership side last year. Played very well in that game and was a winner of the McCullin Medal awarded at under-17 level to South Australia's best player. Roves well, has a bit of pace and would be capable of immediately stepping up if needed.

## TIM DAVIS

A well-built centre half-back, Davis is young in footy terms according to Adelaide. This summer was his first training with the Crows and they have been impressed with his work ethic and ability. Only 20, but Adelaide believes, given time, he will be a good player.

## STEVEN HALL

Originally from Queensland, Hall has played the last three seasons at Woodville/West Torrens and last season was its best and fairest. A full-back capable of playing in both key defensive posts. At 23, this is the last year he can be on a rookie list.

## BEN MARSH

A tall ruckman who was on Adelaide's supplementary list last season. The club has seen improvement and believes he is worth persevering with. Performed well in early season practice games.

# ADELAIDE

| Name (# = rookie) | No. | Born | Height | Weight | Recruited from |
|---|---|---|---|---|---|
| Nathan Bassett | 8 | 7/12/76 | 192 | 90 | NORWOOD (SA)/MELB RESERVES |
| Mark Bickley | 26 | 4/8/69 | 178 | 82 | SOUTH ADELAIDE (SA) |
| Troy Bond | 18 | 14/7/73 | 179 | 76 | PORT ADELAIDE (SA)/CARLTON |
| Peter Caven | 44 | 16/5/70 | 190 | 85 | MONTMORENCY/FITZROY/SYDNEY |
| Matthew Connell | 14 | 3/8/72 | 181 | 76 | SUBIACO (WA)/WEST COAST |
| Tim Cook | 2 | 20/2/74 | 176 | 75 | CENTRAL DISTRICT (SA) |
| Greg Dempsey | 38 | 19/2/74 | 176 | 75 | WEST ADELAIDE (SA) |
| Ian Downsborough | 17 | 19/1/72 | 192 | 94 | WEST PERTH (WA)/WEST COAST/PORT ADEL |
| Andrew Eccles | 33 | 1/6/79 | 188 | 96 | ELTHAM /NORTHERN U18 |
| Tyson Edwards | 9 | 6/8/76 | 180 | 76 | WEST ADELAIDE (SA) |
| Shane Ellen | 13 | 1/1/73 | 191 | 90 | MELTON/FOOTSCRAY |
| Ashley Fernee | 1 | 24/6/77 | 196 | 84 | EAST KEILOR/CALDER U18 |
| Tom Gilligan | 31 | 3/11/78 | 198 | 96 | FRANKSTON BOMBERS/DANDEN-STHN U18 |
| Simon Goodwin | 36 | 26/12/76 | 186 | 80 | SOUTH ADELAIDE (SA) |
| Ben Hart | 34 | 9/7/74 | 191 | 84 | NORTH ADELAIDE (SA) |
| Brett James | 11 | 15/12/72 | 178 | 78 | NORWOOD (SA)/COLLINGWOOD |
| Rod Jameson | 35 | 30/6/70 | 185 | 87 | GLENELG (SA) |
| Darren Jarman | 3 | 28/1/67 | 183 | 86 | NORTH ADELAIDE (SA)/HAWTHORN |
| Kane Johnson | 28 | 15/3/78 | 185 | 80 | RINGWOOD/EASTERN U18 |
| Aaron Keating | 20 | 24/5/74 | 200 | 102 | NORWOOD (SA) |
| Kym Koster | 5 | 1/2/73 | 182 | 79 | SOUTH ADELAIDE (SA)/FOOTSCRAY |
| Nick Laidlaw | 25 | 27/2/78 | 186 | 80 | STURT (SA) |
| Matthew Liptak | 27 | 30/4/70 | 178 | 79 | GLENELG (SA) |
| Andrew McLeod | 23 | 4/8/76 | 179 | 88 | DARWIN (NT)/PORT ADELAIDE (SA) |
| Tony Modra | 6 | 1/3/69 | 188 | 91 | WEST ADELAIDE (SA) |
| Trent Ormond-Allen | 21 | 11/6/76 | 179 | 80 | PORT ADELAIDE (SA)/MELBOURNE |
| Ian Perrie | 22 | 9/4/79 | 191 | 96 | EAST PERTH (WA) |
| Lance Picioane | 4 | 7/6/80 | 183 | 82 | ESSENDON GRAMMAR/WESTERN U18 |
| David Pittman | 15 | 23/2/69 | 201 | 103 | NORWOOD (SA) |
| Shaun Rehn | 52 | 17/8/71 | 203 | 106 | WEST ADELAIDE (SA) |
| Mark Ricciuto | 32 | 8/6/75 | 182 | 92 | WEST ADELAIDE (SA) |
| Chad Rintoul | 42 | 31/7/74 | 180 | 82 | EAST FREMANTLE (WA) |
| Matthew Robran | 10 | 19/3/71 | 193 | 99 | NORWOOD (SA)/HAWTHORN |
| Clay Sampson | 24 | 24/2/76 | 178 | 79 | SOUTH ADELAIDE (SA)/MELBOURNE |
| Nigel Smart | 7 | 21/5/69 | 188 | 92 | SOUTH ADELAIDE (SA) |
| Barry Standfield | 16 | 13/2/70 | 193 | 90 | FISH CREEK/FOOTSCRAY |
| Linden Stevens | 39 | 13/6/78 | 186 | 80 | STURT (SA) |
| Mark Stevens | 19 | 25/10/75 | 190 | 84 | HEYFIELD/GIPPSLAND U18/NORTH MELB |
| James Thiessen | 29 | 10/2/74 | 180 | 80 | BRENTWOOD/RICHMOND/NORWOOD (SA) |
| Simon Tregenza | 12 | 9/3/71 | 182 | 86 | PORT ADELAIDE (SA) |
| Peter Vardy | 30 | 26/1/76 | 181 | 83 | CENTRAL DISTRICT (SA) |
| Sudjai Cook # | N/A | 27/6/76 | 176 | 79 | NORWOOD (SA) |
| Tim Davis # | N/A | 31/8/77 | 193 | 90 | NORTH ADELAIDE (SA) |
| Steven Hall # | N/A | 3/7/75 | 193 | 89 | WOODVILLE-WEST TORRENS (SA) |
| Ben Marsh # | N/A | 9/7/76 | 202 | 98 | WEST ADELAIDE (SA) |
| Total/(Average) *On 26/2/98 | | (24.0 yrs)* | (186) | (86) | |

# PLAYERS 1998

| Debut | HOME & AWAY | | 1997 | | FINALS | | GRAND FINALS | | | NIGHT SERIES | | STATE OF ORIGIN | |
|---|---|---|---|---|---|---|---|---|---|---|---|---|---|
| | Gms | Gls | Gms | Gls | Gms | Gls | Gms | Gls | Won | Gms | Gls | Gms | Gls |
| | 0 | 0 | 0 | 0 | | | | | | 0 | 0 | | |
| 1991 | 144 | 43 | 26 | 12 | 7 | 1 | 1 | 0 | 1 | 15 | 3 | 6 | 0 |
| 1994 | 74 | 60 | 18 | 20 | 8 | 11 | 1 | 4 | 1 | 3 | 2 | 1 | 0 |
| 1991 | 99 | 44 | 22 | 6 | 4 | 1 | 1 | 1 | 1 | 12 | 6 | 0 | 0 |
| 1993 | 55 | 16 | 17 | 6 | 4 | 1 | 1 | 0 | 1 | 11 | 7 | 2 | 1 |
| 1997 | 4 | 3 | 4 | 3 | | | | | | 0 | 0 | 0 | 0 |
| | 0 | 0 | 0 | 0 | | | | | | 2 | 1 | 0 | 0 |
| 1995 | 27 | 7 | 7 | 2 | 1 | 0 | | | | 5 | 0 | 0 | 0 |
| | 0 | 0 | 0 | 0 | | | | | | 2 | 0 | 0 | 0 |
| 1995 | 46 | 14 | 17 | 5 | 3 | 0 | 1 | 0 | 1 | 4 | 0 | 0 | 0 |
| 1993 | 38 | 5 | 10 | 5 | 5 | 5 | 1 | 5 | 1 | 0 | 0 | 0 | 0 |
| 1996 | 2 | 0 | 0 | 0 | | | | | | 0 | 0 | 0 | 0 |
| 1997 | 3 | 1 | 3 | 1 | | | | | | 0 | 0 | 0 | 0 |
| 1997 | 10 | 4 | 10 | 4 | 4 | 2 | 1 | 1 | 1 | 0 | 0 | 0 | 0 |
| 1992 | 133 | 26 | 26 | 2 | 5 | 1 | 1 | 0 | 1 | 13 | 1 | 6 | 0 |
| 1994 | 59 | 29 | 17 | 3 | 1 | 0 | 1 | 0 | 1 | 4 | 2 | 0 | 0 |
| 1991 | 132 | 95 | 22 | 9 | 5 | 2 | 1 | 0 | 1 | 15 | 8 | 1 | 0 |
| 1991 | 152 | 207 | 24 | 39 | 10 | 15 | 2 | 6 | 2 | 16 | 13 | 8 | 16 |
| 1996 | 25 | 7 | 23 | 7 | 4 | 1 | 1 | 0 | 1 | 4 | 0 | 0 | 0 |
| 1997 | 3 | 0 | 3 | 0 | 2 | 0 | 1 | 0 | 1 | 2 | 0 | 0 | 0 |
| 1994 | 71 | 29 | 24 | 12 | 7 | 4 | 1 | 0 | 1 | 3 | 3 | 0 | 0 |
| | 0 | 0 | 0 | 0 | | | | | | 0 | 0 | 0 | 0 |
| 1991 | 110 | 124 | 7 | 9 | 3 | 5 | | | | 10 | 9 | 1 | 1 |
| 1995 | 60 | 47 | 26 | 10 | 4 | 2 | 1 | 0 | 1 | 3 | 0 | 1 | 0 |
| 1992 | 110 | 421 | 25 | 84 | 6 | 13 | | | | 14 | 54 | 6 | 24 |
| 1995 | 26 | 1 | 18 | 0 | 2 | 0 | | | | 2 | 0 | 0 | 0 |
| | 0 | 0 | 0 | 0 | | | | | | 0 | 0 | 0 | 0 |
| | 0 | 0 | 0 | 0 | | | | | | 0 | 0 | 0 | 0 |
| 1992 | 98 | 23 | 23 | 4 | 6 | 0 | 1 | 0 | 1 | 15 | 2 | 5 | 1 |
| 1991 | 92 | 36 | 22 | 11 | 7 | 3 | 1 | 0 | 1 | 10 | 13 | 1 | 0 |
| 1993 | 104 | 61 | 21 | 6 | 3 | 0 | | | | 13 | 4 | 4 | 2 |
| 1997 | 11 | 8 | 11 | 8 | 4 | 4 | 1 | 1 | 1 | 2 | 1 | 0 | 0 |
| 1991 | 67 | 61 | 19 | 24 | 5 | 4 | 1 | 0 | 1 | 11 | 1 | 3 | 4 |
| 1995 | 23 | 6 | 10 | 5 | 4 | 2 | 1 | 0 | 1 | 3 | 0 | 0 | 0 |
| 1991 | 142 | 72 | 22 | 13 | 7 | 10 | 1 | 0 | 1 | 17 | 4 | 6 | 0 |
| 1989 | 111 | 61 | 13 | 23 | 6 | 2 | | | | 10 | 6 | 0 | 0 |
| | 0 | 0 | 0 | 0 | | | | | | 0 | 0 | 0 | 0 |
| 1995 | 21 | 20 | 5 | 1 | | | | | | 5 | 4 | 0 | 0 |
| 1993 | 0 | 0 | 0 | 0 | | | | | | 0 | 0 | 0 | 0 |
| 1991 | 97 | 16 | 10 | 1 | 3 | 0 | | | | 17 | 8 | 3 | 0 |
| 1996 | 31 | 33 | 24 | 28 | 2 | 2 | | | | 2 | 3 | 0 | 0 |
| | 0 | 0 | 0 | 0 | | | | | | 0 | 0 | | |
| | 0 | 0 | 0 | 0 | | | | | | 0 | 0 | | |
| | 0 | 0 | 0 | 0 | | | | | | 0 | 0 | | |
| | 0 | 0 | 0 | 0 | | | | | | 0 | 0 | | |
| | (53) | (39) | 529 | 363 | 132 | 91 | 22 | 18 | 22 | 245 | 155 | 54 | 49 |

## Lions at a glance

**ADDRESS:** Brisbane Office: "The Gabba", 840 Stanley St, Woolloongabba, Qld 4102
Melbourne Office: 460 High St, Northcote, Vic 3070

**POSTAL ADDRESS:** Brisbane: PO Box 1535, Coorparoo D.C., Queensland 4151.
Melbourne: PO Box 82, Northcote, Vic 3070

**TELEPHONE:** Brisbane (07) 3335 1777, Melbourne (03) 9482 7000

**FACSIMILE:** Brisbane (07) 3891 1222 (Admin/Marketing), (07) 3891 2955 (Football/Media); (07) 3891 5929 (CEO); Melbourne (03) 9482 7155

**WEB SITE:** www.lions.com.au

**EMAIL:** email@lions.com.au

**CHAIRMAN:** Noel Gordon

**CHIEF EXECUTIVE:** Andrew Ireland

**DIRECTOR OF FOOTBALL:** Scott Clayton

**FOOTBALL MANAGER:** Shane Johnson

**VICTORIAN MANAGER:** Kinnear Beatson

**MEDIA/PR MANAGER:** Peter Blucher

**MARKETING MANAGER:** Judy Kilby

**COACHING STAFF:** John Northey (senior); Roger Merrett (assistant); Rod O'Riley (development)

**SELECTION COMMITTEE:** Scott Clayton (Chairman), John Northey, Roger Merrett, Rod O'Riley, Dr Alan Mackenzie

**CLUB DOCTOR:** Alan Mackenzie

**CLUB PHYSIOTHERAPIST:** Jim Eustace

**FOUNDED:** November 1, 1996

**HOME GROUND:** "The Gabba"

**GROUND DIMENSIONS:** 165m by 145m

**OFFICIAL COLORS:** Jumper: maroon, gold lion, blue yoke and gold and white trim. Shorts: maroon. Socks: maroon, with blue and gold stripes.

**PREMIERSHIPS:** Brisbane Bears: Nil; Fitzroy: 1898, 1899, 1904, 1905, 1913, 1916, 1922, 1944

**BROWNLOW MEDALLISTS:** Brisbane Bears: Michael Voss (1996 tied); Fitzroy: Haydn Bunton (1931, 1932, 1935); "Chicken" Smallhorn (1933); "Dinny" Ryan (1936); Allan Ruthven (1950); Kevin Murray (1969); Bernie Quinlan (1981 tied)

**RECORD HOME ATTENDANCE:** (Gabba) — 21,644, May 17, 1996 v Collingwood

# BRISBANE LIONS
# Best ahead for fit and settled Lions

On face value, it would appear the best is yet to come for the Brisbane Lions. Touted by the media and no less an authority than Essendon coach Kevin Sheedy as certainties for the flag in '97, the Lions could not drum up any consistency.

A combination of injuries, poor form and the struggle to get the best out of its eight Fitzroy imports saw the Brisbane Lions limp into the eight.

The side won its last game for 1997 in round 18 (it drew with Port Adelaide at the Gabba in round 20) and after losing in rounds 21 and 22, fell into the eight when other teams blew their chances.

To no one's surprise, it made a hasty exit, losing the qualifying final against St Kilda. The Lions' fortunes fluctuated wildly at times — they lost four in succession from rounds five to eight and won five in a row between rounds 12 and 16. That roller-coaster ride took its toll in the end.

So, too, did injuries, notably to Jarrod Molloy, who was shaping as the best of the eight players taken by the Brisbane Lions as part of the merger.

After breaking a wrist early in the season, Molloy damaged a knee on his return. However, in the 10 games he played, he gave the Lions a strong physical presence in attack.

He also allowed Alastair Lynch to play most of his football at full-back and the Lions co-captain was able to settle both body and mind after an 18-month battle with Chronic Fatigue Syndrome.

Perhaps the biggest blow for the Lions came when 1996 Brownlow Medallist Michael Voss hurt a knee and was forced to miss the final five games. His absence, together with long-term injuries to Andrew Bews, Chris Scott and Brad Boyd, robbed the Lions of some badly needed leadership and experience — a problem compounded by the retirement of Roger Merrett at the end of '96.

Despite all those setbacks, the Lions have much to look forward to in 1998. There is no doubt they will be a more settled unit after the honeymoon period of the merger and those who were sidelined in 1997 are all expected to be back bigger and better this season.

An injection of youth has been provided via the 1997 National Draft and some selective trading and, combined with a draw that includes 11 games at the Gabba, the Brisbane Lions should be in a position to push themselves back into top-four contention.

— **Michael Lovett**

## THE YEAR AHEAD

| Rd | Date | Opponent | Venue | Home/<br>Away | Time<br>(local) |
|----|------|----------|-------|------|------|
| 1 | March 28 (N) | Western Bulldogs | G | A | 7.40pm |
| 2 | April 4 (N) | Sydney | SCG | A | 7.40pm |
| 3 | April 13 | Melbourne | G | H | 2.10pm |
| 4 | April 19 | North Melbourne | MCG | A | 2.10pm |
| 5 | April 25 | Hawthorn | P | A | 2.10pm |
| 6 | May 1 (N) | Richmond | G | H | 7.40pm |
| 7 | May 9 | St Kilda | P | A | 2.10pm |
| 8 | May 15 (N) | Essendon | MCG | A | 7.40pm |
| 9 | May 23 (N) | Adelaide | G | H | 7.40pm |
| 10 | May 30 | Carlton | OO | A | 2.10pm |
| 11 | June 7 | Fremantle | S | A | 12.10pm |
| 12 | June 14 (N) | Port Adelaide | G | H | 8.10pm |
| 13 | June 20 | Geelong | KP | A | 2.10pm |
| 14 | June 28 | Collingwood | G | H | 12.40pm |
| 15 | July 4 (N) | West Coast | G | H | 7.40pm |
| 16 | July 18 | Western Bulldogs | OO | A | 2.10pm |
| 17 | July 26 | Sydney | G | H | 2.10pm |
| 18 | August 1 | Melbourne | P | A | 2.10pm |
| 19 | August 7 (N) | North Melbourne | G | H | 7.40pm |
| 20 | August 15 (N) | Hawthorn | G | H | 7.40pm |
| 21 | August 22 | Richmond | MCG | A | 2.10pm |
| 22 | August 29 (N) | St Kilda | G | H | 7.40pm |

## 1997 AT A GLANCE

**L:** R1: Adelaide 20.12 (132) v Brisbane Lions 14.12 (96) (FP)
**W:** R2: Brisbane Lions 23.16 (154) v St.Kilda 7.15 (57) (G)
**L:** R3: Hawthorn 12.15 (87) v Brisbane Lions 11.9 (75) (WP)
**W:** R4: Brisbane Lions 15.19 (109) v North Melb 12.11 (83) (G)
**L:** R5: Port Adelaide 10.13 (73) v Brisbane Lions 10.11 (71) (FP)
**L:** R6: Essendon 15.12 (102) v Brisbane Lions 9.17 (71) (KP)
**L:** R7: Brisbane Lions 8.12 (60) v West Coast 21.13 (139) (G)

### SNAPSHOT

**Games:** 23
**Wins:** 10 **Losses:** 12
**Drawn:** 1
**Ladder Finish:** 8th
**Players Used:** 37

**L:** R8: Fremantle 14.14 (98) v Brisbane Lions 15.3 (93) (S)
**W:** R9: Brisbane Lions 19.12 (126) v Geelong 15.8 (98) (G)
**W:** R10: Brisbane Lions 13.14 (92) v Sydney 13.11 (89) (G)
**L:** R11: Carlton 12.12 (84) v Brisbane Lions 9.9 (63) (OO)
**W:** R12: Melbourne 7.8 (50) v Brisbane Lions 21.9 (135) (MCG)
**W:** R13: Brisbane Lions 11.22 (88) v Collingwood 11.7 (73) (G)
**W:** R14: Brisbane Lions 7.26 (68) v Richmond 7.8 (50) (G)
**W:** R15: Western Bulldogs 11.7 (73) v Bris Lions 21.11 (137) (OO)
**W:** R16: Brisbane Lions 17.16 (118) v Adelaide 13.9 (87) (G)
**L:** R17: St.Kilda 12.20 (92) v Brisbane Lions 5.14 (44) (WP)
**W:** R18: Brisbane Lions 21.15 (141) v Hawthorn 11.5 (71) (G)
**L:** R19: North Melb 17.14 (116) v Brisbane Lions 9.5 (59) (MCG)
**D:** R20: Brisbane Lions 13.15 (93) v Port Adelaide 13.15 (93) (G)
**L:** R21: Brisbane Lions 15.12 (102) v Essendon 16.10 (106) (G)
**L:** R22: West Coast 18.12 (120) v Brisbane Lions 11.15 (81) (W)

# The Coach

**John Northey**

**Born:**
29/6/1943

John Northey did not exactly have to pick up the pieces in 1996 when he moved to Brisbane, but he has overseen a period of change. The merger between Fitzroy and the Brisbane Bears brought a change of culture for some players and Northey has had the task of putting the on-field pieces into place.

It was a difficult assignment in 1997, but the Brisbane Lions made the finals. One of the AFL's most experienced coaches, Northey will be keen to go a couple better in 1998.

## AT A GLANCE

**COACHING RECORD**

| | | | | | |
|---|---|---|---|---|---|
| **Sydney** | | | | | |
| **Season** | **P** | **W** | **L** | **D** | **Pos** |
| 1985 | 22 | 6 | 16 | — | 10 |
| **Melbourne** | | | | | |
| **Season** | **P** | **W** | **L** | **D** | **Pos** |
| 1986 | 22 | 7 | 15 | — | 11 |
| 1987 | 25 | 14 | 11 | — | 3 |
| 1988 | 26 | 16 | 10 | — | 2 |
| 1989 | 24 | 15 | 9 | — | 4 |
| 1990 | 24 | 17 | 7 | — | 4 |
| 1991 | 24 | 14 | 10 | — | 4 |
| 1992 | 22 | 7 | 14 | 1 | 11 |
| | 167 | 90 | 76 | 1 | |
| **Richmond** | | | | | |
| **Season** | **P** | **W** | **L** | **D** | **Pos** |
| 1993 | 20 | 4 | 16 | — | 14 |
| 1994 | 22 | 12 | 10 | — | 9 |
| 1995 | 25 | 16 | 8 | 1 | 4 |
| | 67 | 32 | 34 | 1 | |
| **Brisbane Bears** | | | | | |
| **Season** | **P** | **W** | **L** | **D** | **Pos** |
| 1996 | 25 | 17 | 7 | 1 | 3 |
| **Brisbane Lions** | | | | | |
| **Season** | **P** | **W** | **L** | **D** | **Pos** |
| 1997 | 23 | 10 | 12 | 1 | 8 |
| **Total** | **304** | **155** | **145** | **4** | |

## WIN/LOSS RECORD

| Against | P | W (N) | L (N) | D (N) |
|---|---|---|---|---|
| Adelaide | 2 | 1 (1) | 1 (0) | 0 |
| Carlton | 1 | 0 (0) | 1 (0) | 0 |
| Collingwood | 1 | 1 (1) | 0 | 0 |
| Essendon | 2 | 0 | 2 (1) | 0 |
| Fremantle | 1 | 0 | 1 (0) | 0 |
| Geelong | 1 | 1 (0) | 0 | 0 |
| Hawthorn | 2 | 1 (1) | 1 (0) | 0 |
| Melbourne | 1 | 1 (0) | 0 | 0 |
| North Melb | 2 | 1 (0) | 1 (1) | 0 |
| Port Adel | 2 | 0 | 1 (0) | 1 (1) |
| Richmond | 1 | 1 (0) | 0 | 0 |
| St Kilda | 3 | 1 (0) | 2 (0) | 0 |
| Sydney | 1 | 1 (0) | 0 | 0 |
| West Coast | 2 | 0 | 2 (1) | 0 |
| W Bulldogs | 1 | 1 (0) | 0 | 0 |
| **TOTALS** | **23** | **10 (3)** | **12 (3)** | **1 (1)** |

*(N) Premiership matches played at night*

## WINNING RUNS

1 v Adelaide (1997– )
1 v Collingwood (1997– )
1 v Geelong (1997– )
1 v Hawthorn (1997– )
1 v Melbourne (1997– )
1 v Richmond (1997– )
1 v Sydney (1997– )
1 v Western Bulldogs (1997– )

## 1997 BEST AND FAIREST

Four members of the match committee can award 1-15 votes each week. A maximum of five votes is awarded to any one player and there is no obligation to use the 15 votes available.

1 Matthew Clarke (90)
2 Nigel Lappin (80)
3 Marcus Ashcroft (79)
4 Justin Leppitsch (74)
5 Danny Dickfos (71)
6 Craig Lambert (70)
7 Darryl White (69)
8 Shaun Hart (48)
9 Tristan Lynch (41)
10 Alastair Lynch (38)

## GAMES RECORDS

23 Marcus Ashcroft (1997– )
22 Danny Dickfos (1997– )
22 Justin Leppitsch (1997– )
21 Richard Champion (1997– )
21 Matthew Clarke (1997– )
21 Adrian Fletcher (1997– )
21 Nigel Lappin (1997– )
21 Tristan Lynch (1997– )

## GOALS RECORDS

50 Justin Leppitsch (1997– )
35 Daniel Bradshaw (1997– )
21 Jarrod Molloy (1997– )
20 Jason Akermanis (1997– )

## THE LEADERSHIP AT THE BRISBANE LIONS

| Year | Pos | Coach | Captain | Best & Fairest | Leading Goalkicker | |
|---|---|---|---|---|---|---|
| 1997 | 8 | J. Northey | A. Lynch<br>M. Voss | M. Clarke | J. Leppitsch | 50 |

## HIGHS AND LOWS

| Against | Highest | Lowest | G. W. Margin | G. L. Margin |
|---|---|---|---|---|
| Adelaide | 17.16.118 (1997) | 14.12.96 (1997) | 31 (1997) | 36 (1997) |
| Carlton | 9.9.63 (1997) | 9.9.63 (1997) | — | 21 (1997) |
| Collingwood | 11.22.88 (1997) | 11.22.88 (1997) | 15 (1997) | — |
| Essendon | 15.12.102 (1997) | 9.17.71 (1997) | — | 31 (1997) |
| Fremantle | 15.3.93 (1997) | 15.3.93 (1997) | — | 5 (1997) |
| Geelong | 19.12.126 (1997) | 19.12.126 (1997) | 28 (1997) | — |
| Hawthorn | 21.15.141 (1997) | 11.9.75 (1997) | 70 (1997) | 12 (1997) |
| Melbourne | 21.9.135 (1997) | 21.9.135 (1997) | 85 (1997) | — |
| North Melb | 15.19.109 (1997) | 9.5.59 (1997) | 26 (1997) | 57 (1997) |
| Port Adel | 13.15.93 (1997) | 10.11.71 (1997) | — | 2 (1997) |
| Richmond | 7.26.68 (1997) | 7.26.68 (1997) | 18 (1997) | — |
| St Kilda | 23.16.154 (1997) | 5.14.44 (1997) | 97 (1997) | 48 (1997) |
| Sydney | 13.14.92 (1997) | 13.14.92 (1997) | 3 (1997) | — |
| West Coast | 11.15.81 (1997) | 8.12.60 (1997) | — | 79 (1997) |
| W Bulldogs | 21.11.137 (1997) | 21.11.137 (1997) | 64 (1997) | — |

## PLAYER PROFILES

### JASON AKERMANIS

Electrifying wingman/forward with great skill and goal sense in his fourth year. Product of QSFL club Mayne, he kicked 32 goals in 1996 to be fourth on the Brisbane Bears' list and in 1997, after a slow start caused by hamstring injuries and indifferent form, he was fourth on the Brisbane Lions' list with 20 goals. A confidence player, he has matured as a footballer and, at only 21, has a big future. A former under-18 All-Australian player, he represented The Allies in 1996 and '97 and is one of the League's quickest players.

**Brisbane Bears record:** 1995-96 (38 games, 44 goals).

### MARCUS ASHCROFT

At 26, a veteran of nine years in the AFL and last year was the club's most professional player and third in best and fairest voting. A Gold Coast product, he is a quick, skilful and versatile midfielder/tagger. Very disciplined in his approach to any on-field role he is given and his refusal to be beaten by bigger names than himself has seen him rise to highly respected status in AFL football. The only Lion to play every game last year, he finished the season on an unbroken run of 115 games, having not missed a game since round 20, 1992. A 1995, '96 and '97 Allies representative and a vice-captain since 1994.

**Player honors:** 3rd Brisbane Bears best and fairest 1991, 1993, 1994; third Brisbane Lions best and fairest 1997.

**Brisbane Bears record:** 1989-96 (52 games, 84 goals).

### SCOTT BAMFORD

Slightly built wingman with blistering pace and immaculate skills. A product of North Adelaide and the No. 4 selection in the 1995 National Draft. Made a real impact in his first AFL season with Fitzroy in 1996, when one of only four Lions to play every game. Took time to settle into the Brisbane Lions after the merger and spent time mid-year in the QSFL. Outstanding form in the last six weeks of the '97 season. Looks too young and wiry to play AFL football, but such is his energy and persistence that he causes havoc when he has the football.

**Player honors:** 3rd Fitzroy best and fairest 1996.

**Previous AFL club:** Fitzroy (1996: 22 games, 6 goals).

### TRENT BARTLETT

Powerful Tasmanian key defender who didn't play an AFL game in 1997 when crucified by three ankle operations. Former Tasmanian captain in the AFL National Under-18 Championships and an All-Australian pick. Third-round choice in the 1993 National Draft and shaped as a long-term prospect after playing eight AFL games in 1995 and 14 in 1996 as a teenager. Now 21 and in his fifth year. A fearless type who shapes as a likely centre half-back.

**Brisbane Bears record:** 1995-96 (22 games, 1 goal).

### ANDREW BEWS

Veteran defender and superb clubman in his 17th AFL season, his fifth in Brisbane and possibly his last. A valuable performer in 1997 in between frustrating minor injuries and shelved any retirement plans when he missed the finals for the second consecutive year due to injury. A long-serving Victorian representative, a former Geelong captain and Grand Final player, he is the fourth-oldest player in the League. Commands great respect as a desperate ball-winner, is a good mark for his size and wily as an old Cat should be. The Lions' oldest and most experienced player by 88 games and almost four years and shapes as a key leadership figure in a young side. Qualified for AFL life membership in 1997 and at the start of season '98 needed 24 games for his triple century.

**Player honors:** Geelong 3rd best and fairest 1985, 2nd best and fairest 1987; All-Australian 1987, 1989; Geelong captain 1990, 1991.

**Previous AFL club:** Geelong (1982-93: 207 games, 132 goals).

**Brisbane Bears record:** 1994-96 (56 games, 2 goals).

### SIMON BLACK

Left-footed wingman/midfielder from East Fremantle who won under-18 All-Australian selection in 1997 and was regarded as WA's best player at this level. A schoolboy distance running champion, he was a bargain pick-up at No. 31 in the 1997 National Draft. No surprise if he plays some AFL football this year.

### BRAD BOYD

Former Fitzroy ruck-rover who will look to re-ignite his career after back and hamstring injuries restricted him to 20 minutes of AFL football against Geelong in round nine in 1997. Had major surgery in September '97 to stabilise his back and was encouraged by progress made over summer. A former Collingwood under-19 captain, he was traded to Fitzroy for Tony Woods before playing League football and made his debut in 1992. Was Fitzroy skipper at 23 and carried a heavy load through the club's demise, yet played for Victoria in 1994 and '95. Will be a prize 1998 'recruit' if his body holds up. When fit, he is a very good midfielder who plays tall and adds a tough dimension to the centre.

**Player honors:** 2nd Fitzroy best and fairest 1994, best and fairest 1995; Fitzroy captain 1995, 1996.

**Previous AFL club:** Fitzroy (1992-96: 70 games, 49 goals).

### DANIEL BRADSHAW

Third-year full-forward who at 18 shapes as a future champion. Won the Lions' best first-year player award in 1997 and finished fifth in the AFL Norwich Rising Star. A bargain fourth-round pick at the 1995 National Draft. From Wodonga, has exceptional jumping ability, strong hands, an unflappable temperament and is a reliable kick for goal. Booted 35 goals in 16 games last year — including six against Geelong and seven against Hawthorn, both at the Gabba — to be second on the club list behind Leppitsch. One of the more exciting marks to emerge in the competition, he looks, with maturity, capable of holding down centre half-forward.

**Player honors:** AFL Norwich Rising Star nominee 1997.

**Brisbane Bears record:** 1996 (3 games, 0 goals).

### NICK CARTER

Third-year player from Golden Square and the Bendigo Pioneers under-18s, he is a quick, aggressive wingman who was a second-round selection in the 1995 National Draft. Played 17 of 22 games with Fitzroy in 1996 and in his third game was best afield with 31 possessions in the Lions' only win of the year against Fremantle. Managed just two senior games in a difficult post-merger transition period, but is regarded as a promising talent.
**Player honors:** AFL Norwich Rising Star nominee 1996.
**Previous AFL club:** Fitzroy (1996: 17 games, 4 goals).

### RICHARD CHAMPION

Veteran defender and standout clubman now in his eighth AFL season. Originally from Kadina in South Australia, was a second-round draft pick in 1988 but played a further three years at Woodville before joining the Brisbane Bears in 1991. Served a three-year 'apprenticeship', mixing spasmodic brilliance with frustrating inconsistency, before finishing fifth, sixth and sixth in the 1994, '95 and '96 best and fairest awards. In 1996, he was recognised as one of the best full-backs in the competition, but last year his attacking game came under pressure as his form dropped away slightly and he was forced, on occasion, to move out from the full-back position. Was disappointed when failed to secure the SA State of Origin jumper he had worn in 1992, '94, '95 and '96 and will be desperate to regain his best in '98.
**Brisbane Bears record:** 1991-96 (119 games, 37 goals).

### MATTHEW CLARKE

Inaugural winner of the Merrett/Murray Medal as 1997 club champion and a superbly athletic ruckman who ranks among the AFL's best. Has established a reputation as a tap ruckman of the highest order. A veterinary science student who calls Mt Gambier (South Australia) home, Clarke is a Richmond cast-off who played under-19s with the Tigers in 1991. Claimed by the Brisbane Bears at the 1992 Pre-Season Draft and played at South Adelaide in 1992 before moving north. Spent most of his first season in Brisbane sidelined with recurring foot stress fractures. A 1995, '96 and '97 SA State of Origin representative.
**Player honors:** Brisbane Lions best and fairest 1997; 2nd Brisbane Bears best and fairest 1994, 1996; AFL Norwich Rising Star nominee 1994.
**Brisbane Bears record:** 1993-96 (69 games, 6 goals).

### SHANE CLAYTON

Skilful half-back flanker, originally from Bundoora, who enters his third year of League football aged 19. A 1994 and '95 premiership player with the Northern Knights under-18s and a 1995 Victorian under-18 selection. Played 13 games with Fitzroy as a schoolboy in 1996. Managed just three games with the Brisbane Lions in 1997, but impressed enormously after initially being reluctant to move north. Son of former AFL umpire Ian Clayton.
**Previous AFL club:** Fitzroy (1996: 13 games, 1 goal).

### DANNY DICKFOS

Iron-willed defender who has made a big impact in the past two years following a long overdue introduction to AFL football. Had an illustrious QSFL career with Windsor-Zillmere/North Brisbane and rejected countless approaches from the Brisbane Bears and rival clubs dating back to his teens. Slotted superbly into the Brisbane Bears' defence in 1996, when he shared best first-year player honors with Clark Keating. Was even better in 1997, playing with new-found confidence, finishing fifth in the best and fairest, winning the Bill Cavanagh "1%er of the Year" award and making his Allies State of Origin debut. A favorite with his teammates and a cult figure with Lions fans, Dickfos announced in a late-season post-match interview that he had been married the day before to the surprise of half his teammates. A great acquisition.
**Brisbane Bears record:** 1996 (22 games, 0 goals).

### ANDREW GOWERS

Veteran wingman/utility set for his 11th AFL season and the only Lions player with an AFL premiership medallion won at Hawthorn in 1991. A product of Melbourne's Xavier College, he joined the Brisbane Bears in 1995 after a seven-year stint at Hawthorn. Missed 15 weeks' football with back-related hamstring problems in '97, but finished on a high note. An ever reliable wingman/defender.
**Player honors:** Hawthorn premiership side 1991; Hawthorn night series premiership side 1992.
**Previous AFL club:** Hawthorn (1988-94: 89 games, 54 goals).
**Brisbane Bears record:** 1995-96 (30 games, 7 goals).

### SHAUN HART

Workaholic midfielder/utility from Shepparton entering his ninth AFL season. An early third-round draft selection in 1989, the 26-year-old is among the League's fittest players and one of the strongest on a bodyweight basis. Has had five top-10 best and fairest finishes, including an eighth last year, and was in the reserves' premiership team in 1991. Was best first-year player in 1990 and most professional player in '92. A one-time tagger, this pocket-sized left-footer has established himself as a quality goal-kicking midfielder, but has been underrated by the football public for most of his career.
**Player honors:** 3rd Brisbane Bears best and fairest 1995.
**Brisbane Bears record:** 1990-96 (102 games, 81 goals).

### RORY HILTON

Exciting newcomer from the Murray Bushrangers under-18s who is raring to go after almost 21 months out of the game following a knee reconstruction in July '96. Brisbane Bears scouts claimed him at No. 3 in the 1996 National Draft, despite knowing he wouldn't play in '97. A hard and skilful utility player who will wear the No. 19 jumper made famous by Michael McLean, he played his first practice match in the Brisbane Lions colors in February 1998.

### CHRIS JOHNSON

Exciting running utility who enters his fifth AFL season

aged 21. Originally from Jacana, he was the No. 7 selection in the 1993 National Draft and a regular at Fitzroy, where he was fifth in the 1996 best and fairest. Struggled for fitness and consistency in Brisbane in 1997 and asked to be traded to a Melbourne-based club over the summer. However, was happy to honor the final two years of his Lions contract when a suitable deal could not be arranged. Will need to get super-fit if he is to maximise his huge potential as a small, aggressive footballer who loves to take a high mark.

**Player honors:** AFL Norwich Rising Star nominee 1994; Fitzroy leading goal-kicker 1995.

**Previous AFL club:** Fitzroy (1994-96: 59 games, 67 goals).

### CLARK KEATING

Key long-term prospect at centre half-forward who has been on the Brisbane list since 15 and now enters his third AFL season at 22. Originally from the Gold Coast, he played 14 games in 1996 to share best first-year player honors with Danny Dickfos, but missed the finals due to a serious foot injury suffered in round 20. Rejected a big offer from Port Adelaide to stay with the merger club in 1997, but after playing the first 20 games and making his Allies State of Origin debut, a knee injury meant he again missed the finals. Can spell Matthew Clarke in the ruck and use his bulk to bring smaller players into the game by forcing the ball to the ground.

**Brisbane Bears record:** 1996 (14 games, 9 goals).

### MATTHEW KENNEDY

Gold Coast utility product and 100-gamer who enters his ninth AFL season at the crossroads. A genuine utility, he made a name for himself at centre half-back in the 1996 finals after playing chiefly as a wingman in his early days. Struggled to hold his spot in '97, playing just 11 games before a shoulder injury in the QSFL ended a disappointing year. Son of former St Kilda player Des Kennedy.

**Brisbane Bears record:** 1990-96 (113 games, 25 goals).

### CRAIG LAMBERT

Quality midfielder who ranks as one of the game's premier hard ball winners and enters his 11th AFL season within striking distance of 200 games. A six-year player at Richmond who moved to Brisbane in 1994 via the Pre-Season Draft, he is among a select group with best and fairest honors at two clubs. In each of the past two years, he has been denied a possible best and fairest win due to late season injury. A prodigious and prolific handball exponent, he is a long-serving Victorian representative who each week faces an opposition tag. Missed five games before the 1997 finals due to calf problems and underwent major back surgery last October. The midfield will rely heavily on his bullocking work, particularly with the departure of another hard ball winner, Adrian Fletcher, to Fremantle.

**Player honors:** Richmond best and fairest 1991; 2nd Richmond best and fairest 1989; Brisbane Bears best and fairest 1994; 3rd Brisbane Bears best and fairest 1996; All-Australian 1996.

**Previous AFL club:** Richmond (1988-93: 123 games, 53 goals).

**Brisbane Bears record:** 1994-96 (49 games, 19 goals).

### NIGEL LAPPIN

Tall, classy midfielder/utility with immaculate skills who finished second to Matthew Clarke in the inaugural Merrett/Murray Medal in 1997. From Chiltern, in northern Victoria, he was the No. 2 selection in the 1993 National Draft and in 1996 become the first Brisbane Bears player to wear the Big V. Best and fairest Brisbane Bears finishes of 27th, 13th and fifth and second last year in the Brisbane Lions highlight his improvement. After a 1997 season in which he played primarily as a running half-back flanker, he is set to move into the midfield where his pace and good evasive skills will make him difficult to stop through the centre.

**Player honors:** 2nd Brisbane Lions best and fairest 1997.

**Brisbane Bears record:** 1994-96 (61 games, 40 goals).

### STEVEN LAWRENCE

Gold Coast product who made an inspirational comeback in 1997 after reconstructive knee surgery in 1995 and '96. Spent the first 14 weeks of the '97 season with QSFL club Southport, but returned to the seniors against the Western Bulldogs in round 15 and held his place through to the finals. The son of former St Kilda captain Barry Lawrence, he is a fearless defender/midfielder who overcame an off-season back stress fracture.

**Player honors:** AFL Norwich Rising Star nominee 1995.

**Brisbane Bears record:** 1995-96 (13 games, 1 goals).

### JUSTIN LEPPITSCH

Exciting key forward who became a household name over summer when rival clubs chased the out-of-contract redhead. Signed a long-term deal and at 22, begins his sixth season. Originally from Berwick, in Melbourne, he was the No. 4 selection in the 1992 National Draft after a standout junior career. Missed virtually two years due to a knee reconstruction early in 1993. Played 17 games in his 1995 comeback, but not until 1996, when he kicked 45 goals to be second on the Brisbane Bears list, did he really look the goods. Took over as the Lions' focal point in 1997, kicked his 50th goal in the qualifying final against St Kilda and finished fourth in the best and fairest count after winning Victorian State of Origin squad selection mid-year. Quick on the lead, spectacular overhead and a reliable kick for goal. Also boasts that dash of flare which makes him a crowd favorite.

**Player honors:** Brisbane Lions leading goalkicker 1997.

**Brisbane Bears record:** 1993-96 (44 games, 58 goals).

### ALASTAIR LYNCH

Champion key position utility who is set to recapture his brilliant best after two broken collarbones in 1994 and a career-threatening three-year battle with Chronic Fatigue Syndrome which forced him to miss the 1995 season. From Wynyard, in Tasmania, he was a six-year standout at Fitzroy, where he became one of the League's premier players. Has been a shadow of his former self in Brisbane, despite three top-10 best and fairest finishes. Settled in well at full-back in the second half of 1997 and was easily the Lions' best in their last two games. Shared the Lions captaincy with Michael Voss last year and received Lions life membership last October. Has done a full pre-season for the first time in five years. A great mark, fearless in his approach at the footy and an inspirational leader. The Brisbane Lions can only benefit from his presence.

**Player honors:** 2nd Fitzroy best and fairest 1991, 3rd Fitzroy best and fairest 1992, Fitzroy best and fairest 1993; All-Australian 1993; Fitzroy leading goalkicker 1993; Brisbane Bears leading goalkicker 1996; Brisbane Lions co-captain 1997.

**Previous AFL club:** Fitzroy (1988-93: 120 games, 173 goals).

**Brisbane Bears record:** 1994-96 (32 games, 89 goals).

## TRISTAN LYNCH
No-frills defender/tagger who made his AFL debut with Brisbane in 1996 after two years on the Richmond supplementary list. Born in Launceston and raised in Sale, he was drafted by Collingwood in 1992 before being delisted four months later without playing a game. Followed John Northey to Brisbane via the 1996 Pre-Season Draft and played 21 of a possible 24 games before adding 21 last year to finish ninth in the best and fairest. A wobbly determined running style disguises his excellent balance and his courage is sometimes scary to the casual observer.

**Brisbane Bears record:** 1996 (21 games, 1 goal).

## BEAU McDONALD
An athletic 200cm beanpole ruckman who is the nephew of Garry and Allan Sidebottom. Played with the Swan Districts colts in 1997 in only his second year of football and was a project selection at No. 74 in the National Draft.

## CRAIG McRAE
Lightning fast half-forward, dangerous around goal and has a prodigious left-foot kick. Opposition players try hard to put him off his game around half-forward with constant niggling tactics. A Glenelg product, he was a bonus pick-up in the 1994 Pre-Season Draft. After a further 12 months in the Adelaide competition, he headed north to play every game in 1995 and kicked 28 goals to earn best first-year player honors with the Brisbane Bears. Battled recurring groin problems in 1996-97, but when fit a dangerous proposition. Kicked 28 goals in 16 games in '96 and 18 goals in 19 games in '97.

**Brisbane Bears record:** 1995-96 (39 games, 56 goals).

## JARROD MOLLOY
Strong, robust former Fitzroy key position utility who had an injury nightmare in his first season in Brisbane after the merger, yet was a key player in 10 games when fit and clubman of the year. Before injury, Molloy was emerging as the toughest forward going around, raging in attack in a manner reminis-

cent of Tony Lockett. Missed eight weeks with a broken wrist after a round three mishap against Hawthorn and in his seventh comeback game, also against Hawthorn, he did a knee. A successful reconstruction had him on target for an early-season return, but he required further wrist surgery in November. The son of former Fitzroy player Shane Molloy hails from Box Hill and was a Victorian under-18 and Preston Knights under-18 premiership player in 1993. Won Fitzroy's best first-year player award in 1994 and was fourth in the 1996 best and fairest. The Brisbane Lions have picked up a player capable of swinging matches.

**Player honors:** AFL Norwich Rising Star nominee 1994.

**Previous AFL club:** Fitzroy (1994-96: 59 games, 54 goals).

## TIM NOTTING
Tall, athletic wingman/utility chosen at No. 26 in the 1996 National Draft. A product of Stawell, he played with the Ballarat Rebels and took part in a handful of reserves games with Richmond in 1996 before playing a full season with Mt Gravatt in the QSFL in 1997.

## SHANE O'BREE
Accomplished centreman who captained the North Ballarat Rebels' under-18 premiership side in 1997. Was 10th pick in the 1997 National Draft after being considered unlucky to miss selection as a 17-year-old 12 months earlier. Originally from Beaufort, outside Ballarat, he is the nephew of former Richmond, Collingwood and Footscray forward Allan 'Butch' Edwards and the grandson of former Footscray 100-gamer Frank 'Dolly' Aked senior. Appeals as a ready-made player.

## MARCUS PICKEN
Son of former Collingwood champion Billy Picken, he is a tall, running half-back flanker and a key figure in 1997 TAC Cup premier side North Ballarat. Hails from Monivae College in Hamilton, western Victoria, and played senior football with MacArthur from the age of 14. Chosen at No. 55 in the National Draft after the Pies declined to forgo a second-round pick to take him under the father/son rule. Has great potential and could be a smoky.

## LUKE POWER
Slightly built but lightning fast and skilful rover/wingman from the Oakleigh Chargers under-18s and Trinity Grammar and the No. 5 pick in the 1997 National Draft. Won under-18 All-Australian selection over the past three years and knowledgeable scouts say he has the capacity to play at AFL level in 1998. If given time to settle in to a new environment, should be a valuable choice for the Brisbane Lions, who have shown an ability to pick players with good all-round qualities.

## SCOTT RALPH
Tall running player with excellent athleticism from QSFL club Morningside, best suited at wing/half-back. A Queensland standout at the 1997 National Under-18 Championships and was picked up at No. 51 in the National Draft.

## BEN ROBBINS

Diminutive midfielder from Maffra, in eastern Victoria, who spent two years on the West Coast Eagles list, including the '96 season with Perth in the WAFL, before joining the Brisbane Bears in a pre-draft trade at the end of 1995. A fearless bore-in type, he did well to make five AFL appearances in 1996 and was a '97 regular, despite an eight-week lay-off mid-year with ankle problems. Son of former Richmond player Graham Robbins.
**Brisbane Bears record:** 1996 (5 games, 1 goal).

## BRAD SCOTT

Identical twin of Chris Scott who was traded from Hawthorn for Nathan Chapman and John Barker. A defender/tagger from the Eastern Ranges under-18s, he was drafted by Hawthorn in 1994, but delisted after one year. Won the 1996 Hawthorn reserves best and fairest as a supplementary list player, was re-drafted and in 1997 played every game to finish ninth in the best and fairest. Will fulfil a life-long dream to play in the same team as Chris and shapes as a disciplined and team-oriented addition. There are not many harder workers in the game.
**Player honors:** AFL Norwich Rising Star nominee 1997.
**Previous AFL club:** Hawthorn (1997: 22 games, 6 goals).

## CHRIS SCOTT

Committed running utility in his fifth year who played only five games in 1997 due to a broken collarbone and recurring hamstring problems. A product of the 1992 Eastern Ranges and Victorian under-18 side, he underlined his huge potential in winning the 1994 AFL Norwich Rising Star award and finished 10th and eighth in the Brisbane Bears' best and fairest in 1994 and '96. Very talented and will be buoyed by the arrival of twin brother Brad.
**Player honors:** AFL Norwich Rising Star 1994.
**Brisbane Bears record:** 1994-96 (55 games, 23 goals).

## DION SCOTT

Injury-prone key position utility who continues to fight to consolidate an AFL career which is now nine years old. Originally from Devonport and taken at No. 9 by Sydney in the 1988 National Draft, he has battled a broken neck and a knee reconstruction among countless other injuries. Played six games in four years in Sydney and 56 in five years in Brisbane, including seven in 1997. In a team with so many good tall marking players, Scott is often used as a call-up when needed, rather than first picked. It is a situation he would like to change this season.
**Previous AFL club:** Sydney (1990-92: 6 games, 0 goals).
**Brisbane Bears record:** 1993-96 (49 games, 39 goals).

## NICK TRASK

Left-footed midfielder/goalsneak from the Eastern Ranges under-18s who was a second-round pick at the 1995 National Draft. Had five games of AFL football in 1997, including the final against St Kilda. Showed glimpses of what it takes after an injury-dis-rupted first season in Brisbane in '96, but will need to work enormously hard.

## BRETT VOSS

Younger brother of the 1996 Brownlow Medallist and Lions captain Michael, he played his first three AFL games in the first half of 1997 without making a huge impact. A product of QSFL club Morningside, he is a midfielder/half-forward who joined the club on a Queensland priority at the 1995 National Draft.

## MICHAEL VOSS

A genuine superstar who missed the last five rounds of the 1997 season plus the final (a period when the Brisbane Lions won one, drew one and lost four) due to a knee injury, but will be fully fit to start '98. Born in Orbost in eastern Victoria, but a Queens-lander from the age of 11, he became the youngest Bear to play in the AFL when he made his debut in 1992 at 17 years and 11 days. A midfielder/utility with skills and maturity beyond his years, he won back-to-back best and fairest awards in 1995 and '96 and shared the 1996 Brownlow Medal with James Hird. Became the League's youngest captain last year, sharing the position with Alastair Lynch. Has had 12 months to settle into the job and get used to the endless tagging that follows superstars and is set for a huge '98.
**Player honors:** Brownlow Medal 1996; Brisbane Bears best and fairest 1995, 1996; All-Australian 1996; Brisbane Lions co-captain 1997, 1998.
**Brisbane Bears record:** 1992-96 (79 games, 72 goals).

## DARRYL WHITE

Exciting defender/utility originally from Alice Springs who boasts that freakish ability to do almost anything. In six years, he has got better and better at consistently applying his talents and is coming off a standout '97 in which he became a dynamic attacking force at half-back and finished seventh in the best and fairest. A 1995, '96 and '97 Allies State of Origin representative, he was one of only four players to kick 100 goals for the Bears and will long remember his first — the 1992 AFL goal of the year.
**Brisbane Bears record:** 1992-96 (90 games, 106 goals).

## DEREK WIRTH

Strong and athletic teenage key position prospect who is looking to make a mark in his third year on the Brisbane Lions list. Standout Queensland under-18 player who joined the club on a local priority at the 1995 National Draft and was a member of the Mt Gravatt sides beaten in the 1996 and '97 QSFL grand finals.

# ROOKIE LIST

### TATE DAY

Teenager who was plucked from virtual obscurity by the Lions after standing out in a practice match earlier this year. Selected as a local zone rookie, Day, who has represented Queensland at the AFL Under-18 National Championships, can play on the forward line or in the ruck.

# BRISBANE LIONS

| Name (# = rookie) | No. | Born | Height | Weight | Recruited from |
|---|---|---|---|---|---|
| Jason Akermanis | 12 | 24/2/77 | 177 | 78 | MAYNE (QLD) |
| Marcus Ashcroft | 10 | 25/9/71 | 184 | 85 | SOUTHPORT (QLD) |
| Scott Bamford | 34 | 23/6/74 | 183 | 68 | NORTH ADELAIDE (SA)/FITZROY |
| Trent Bartlett | 17 | 26/11/76 | 190 | 98 | DELORAINE (TAS) |
| Andrew Bews | 25 | 19/7/64 | 175 | 81 | NORTH GEELONG/GEELONG |
| Simon Black | 20 | 3/4/79 | 184 | 71 | EAST FREMANTLE (WA) |
| Brad Boyd | 9 | 10/8/71 | 189 | 86 | BUNDOORA/COLLINGWOOD RESERVES/FITZROY |
| Daniel Bradshaw | 36 | 21/11/78 | 186 | 88 | WODONGA |
| Nick Carter | 37 | 28/4/78 | 179 | 84 | GOLDEN SQUARE/BENDIGO U18/FITZROY |
| Richard Champion | 1 | 14/4/68 | 186 | 94 | WOODVILLE (SA) |
| Matthew Clarke | 16 | 18/9/73 | 198 | 100 | WEST GAMBIER (SA)/RICH U19/SOUTH ADELAIDE (SA) |
| Shane Clayton | 40 | 24/10/78 | 186 | 81 | BUNDOORA/NORTHERN U18/FITZROY |
| Danny Dickfos | 14 | 30/9/70 | 188 | 95 | NORTH BRISBANE (QLD) |
| Andrew Gowers | 8 | 11/4/69 | 191 | 85 | XAVIER COLLEGE/HAWTHORN |
| Shaun Hart | 32 | 17/5/71 | 175 | 74 | SHEPPARTON UNITED |
| Rory Hilton | 19 | 15/4/79 | 185 | 89 | WODONGA/MURRAY U18 |
| Chris Johnson | 2 | 30/5/76 | 177 | 86 | JACANA/NORTHERN U18/FITZROY |
| Clark Keating | 27 | 19/3/76 | 199 | 102 | SURFERS PARADISE (QLD) |
| Matthew Kennedy | 41 | 4/2/70 | 191 | 98 | SOUTHPORT (QLD) |
| Craig Lambert | 18 | 5/10/68 | 178 | 86 | DANDENONG/RICHMOND |
| Nigel Lappin | 44 | 21/6/76 | 187 | 86 | CHILTERN |
| Steven Lawrence | 15 | 19/5/76 | 177 | 82 | SOUTHPORT (QLD) |
| Justin Leppitsch | 23 | 1/10/75 | 188 | 95 | SPRINGVALE/SOUTHERN U18 |
| Tristan Lynch | 42 | 22/8/73 | 188 | 82 | SALE/RICHMOND RES |
| Alastair Lynch | 11 | 19/6/68 | 193 | 96 | HOBART (TAS)/FITZROY |
| Beau McDonald | 43 | 3/11/79 | 201 | 84 | SWAN DISTRICTS (WA) |
| Craig McRae | 4 | 22/9/73 | 176 | 72 | GLENELG (SA) |
| Jarrod Molloy | 7 | 12/5/76 | 189 | 100 | NORTHERN U18/BOX HILL/FITZROY |
| Tim Notting | 39 | 21/10/78 | 182 | 82 | NAVARRE/BALLARAT U18 |
| Shane O'Bree | 21 | 15/3/79 | 182 | 81 | BEAUFORT/NORTH BALLARAT U18 |
| Marcus Picken | 24 | 9/10/79 | 186 | 80 | McARTHUR/NORTH BALLARAT U18 |
| Luke Power | 6 | 8/1/80 | 176 | 70 | BALWYN/OAKLEIGH U18 |
| Scott Ralph | 31 | 22/3/79 | 190 | 84 | MORNINGSIDE (QLD) |
| Ben Robbins | 28 | 27/12/76 | 181 | 77 | MAFFRA/GIPPSLAND U18/WEST COAST LIST |
| Brad Scott | 5 | 3/5/76 | 182 | 84 | EAST DONCASTER/EASTERN U18/HAWTHORN |
| Chris Scott | 22 | 3/5/76 | 181 | 85 | EAST CAMBERWELL/EASTERN U18 |
| Dion Scott | 38 | 1/4/70 | 190 | 102 | DEVONPORT (TAS)/SYDNEY |
| Nick Trask | 35 | 6/2/78 | 175 | 76 | VERMONT/EASTERN U18 |
| Brett Voss | 13 | 22/2/78 | 181 | 77 | MORNINGSIDE (QLD) |
| Michael Voss | 3 | 7/7/75 | 181 | 87 | MORNINGSIDE (QLD) |
| Darryl White | 33 | 12/6/73 | 186 | 87 | PIONEERS (NT) |
| Derek Wirth | 30 | 29/11/78 | 193 | 94 | MT GRAVATT (QLD) |
| Tate Day # | N/A | 12/9/78 | 188 | 85 | GOLD COAST (QLD) |
| **Total/(Average)**  *On 26/2/98 | | **(22.9 yrs)*** | **(185)** | **(86)** | |

# PLAYERS 1998

| Debut | HOME & AWAY | | 1997 | | FINALS | | GRAND FINALS | | | NIGHT SERIES | | STATE OF ORIGIN | |
|---|---|---|---|---|---|---|---|---|---|---|---|---|---|
| | Gms | Gls | Gms | Gls | Gms | Gls | Gms | Gls | Won | Gms | Gls | Gms | Gls |
| 1995 | 55 | 64 | 17 | 20 | 4 | 6 | | | | 5 | 4 | 2 | 0 |
| 1989 | 175 | 102 | 23 | 18 | 5 | 1 | | | | 9 | 2 | 5 | 5 |
| 1996 | 33 | 13 | 11 | 7 | 1 | | | | | 1 | 0 | 0 | 0 |
| 1995 | 22 | 1 | 0 | 0 | 1 | 1 | | | | 3 | 2 | 0 | 0 |
| 1982 | 276 | 134 | 13 | 0 | 11 | 5 | 1 | 1 | 0 | 21 | 6 | 12 | 6 |
| | 0 | 0 | 0 | 0 | | | | | | 0 | 0 | 0 | 0 |
| 1992 | 71 | 49 | 1 | 0 | | | | | | 9 | 2 | 2 | 1 |
| 1996 | 19 | 35 | 16 | 35 | 1 | 3 | | | | 2 | 0 | 0 | 0 |
| 1996 | 19 | 5 | 2 | 1 | | | | | | 1 | 0 | 0 | 0 |
| 1991 | 140 | 46 | 21 | 9 | 4 | 3 | | | | 10 | 0 | 4 | 1 |
| 1993 | 90 | 15 | 21 | 9 | 5 | 0 | | | | 5 | 2 | 3 | 0 |
| 1996 | 16 | 1 | 3 | 0 | | | | | | 1 | 0 | 0 | 0 |
| 1996 | 44 | 0 | 22 | 0 | 4 | 0 | | | | 4 | 0 | 3 | 0 |
| 1988 | 137 | 63 | 8 | 2 | 11 | 3 | 1 | 0 | 1 | 12 | 3 | 0 | 0 |
| 1990 | 121 | 92 | 19 | 11 | 5 | 4 | | | | 8 | 3 | 0 | 0 |
| | 0 | 0 | 0 | 0 | | | | | | 0 | 0 | 0 | 0 |
| 1994 | 78 | 78 | 19 | 11 | 1 | | | | | 3 | 0 | 0 | 0 |
| 1996 | 34 | 24 | 20 | 15 | | | | | | 1 | 0 | 1 | 0 |
| 1990 | 125 | 26 | 12 | 1 | 3 | 0 | | | | 8 | 2 | 2 | 0 |
| 1988 | 188 | 77 | 16 | 5 | 5 | 2 | | | | 12 | 2 | 7 | 3 |
| 1994 | 82 | 50 | 21 | 10 | 5 | 3 | | | | 7 | 2 | 2 | 0 |
| 1995 | 22 | 13 | 9 | 12 | 1 | 3 | | | | 1 | 0 | 0 | 0 |
| 1993 | 66 | 108 | 22 | 50 | 5 | 8 | | | | 4 | 5 | 0 | 0 |
| 1996 | 42 | 6 | 21 | 5 | 4 | 1 | | | | 2 | 2 | 0 | 0 |
| 1988 | 172 | 274 | 20 | 12 | 4 | 13 | | | | 15 | 12 | 6 | 1 |
| | 0 | 0 | 0 | 0 | | | | | | 0 | 0 | 0 | 0 |
| 1995 | 57 | 75 | 18 | 19 | 4 | 7 | | | | 4 | 4 | 0 | 0 |
| 1994 | 69 | 75 | 10 | 21 | | | | | | 6 | 4 | 0 | 0 |
| | 0 | 0 | 0 | 0 | | | | | | 0 | 0 | 0 | 0 |
| | 0 | 0 | 0 | 0 | | | | | | 0 | 0 | 0 | 0 |
| | 0 | 0 | 0 | 0 | | | | | | 0 | 0 | 0 | 0 |
| | 0 | 0 | 0 | 0 | | | | | | 0 | 0 | 0 | 0 |
| | 0 | 0 | 0 | 0 | | | | | | 0 | 0 | 0 | 0 |
| 1996 | 17 | 4 | 12 | 3 | 1 | 1 | | | | 1 | 1 | 0 | 0 |
| 1997 | 22 | 6 | 22 | 6 | | | | | | 0 | 0 | 0 | 0 |
| 1994 | 60 | 26 | 5 | 3 | 4 | 0 | | | | 5 | 0 | 0 | 0 |
| 1990 | 62 | 46 | 7 | 7 | 4 | 4 | | | | 5 | 2 | 1 | 0 |
| 1997 | 5 | 2 | 5 | 2 | 1 | | | | | 0 | 0 | 0 | 0 |
| 1997 | 3 | 0 | 3 | 0 | | | | | | 0 | 0 | 0 | 0 |
| 1992 | 96 | 81 | 17 | 9 | 3 | 2 | | | | 6 | 4 | 3 | 0 |
| 1992 | 109 | 109 | 19 | 3 | 5 | 4 | | | | 8 | 4 | 4 | 3 |
| | 0 | 0 | 0 | 0 | | | | | | 0 | 0 | 0 | 0 |
| | 0 | 0 | 0 | 0 | | | | | | 0 | 0 | | |
| | (60) | (40) | 455 | 306 | 102 | 74 | 2 | 1 | 1 | 179 | 68 | 57 | 20 |

**Blues at a glance**

**ADDRESS:** Optus Oval, Royal Parade, North Carlton, Vic 3054
**POSTAL ADDRESS:** PO Box 83, North Carlton, Vic 3054
**TELEPHONE:** (03) 9387 1400
**FACSIMILE:** (03) 9387 7805, (03) 9389 6247 (Football Department), (03) 9388 0326 (Marketing)
**WEB SITE:** www.carltonfc.com.au
**EMAIL:** blues@carltonfc.com.au
**PRESIDENT:** John Elliott
**CHIEF EXECUTIVE:** Stephen Gough
**FOOTBALL MANAGER:** Colin Kinnear
**COMMUNICATIONS MANAGER:** Ian Coutts
**RECRUITING MANAGER:** Shane O'Sullivan
**MARKETING MANAGER:** Adrian Lloyd
**COACHING STAFF:** David Parkin (senior); Wayne Brittain (assistant/reserves); Stephen Kernahan and Greg Williams (both part-time)
**SELECTION COMMITTEE:** Barry Richardson (chairman), David Parkin, Wayne Brittain, Adrian Gallagher, Stephen Kernahan
**CLUB DOCTORS:** Phillip Perlstein, Peter Baquie
**CLUB PHYSIOTHERAPISTS:** Ivan Gutierrez, Simon Nelson
**JOINED AFL:** 1897
**HOME GROUND:** Optus Oval, Princes Park, North Carlton
**GROUND DIMENSIONS:** 160m by 137m.
**OFFICIAL COLORS:** Guernsey: Dark navy blue with a white monogram. Socks: Dark navy blue. Shorts: Dark navy blue
**PREMIERSHIPS:** 1906-7-8, 1914-15, 1938, 1945, 1947, 1968, 1970, 1972, 1979, 1981, 1982, 1987, 1995
**BROWNLOW MEDALLISTS:** B. Deacon (1947), J. James (1961), G. Collis (1964), G. Williams (1994)
**RECORD ATTENDANCE:** 62,986 — 1945 Grand Final, Carlton v South Melbourne.
**RECORD HOME ATTENDANCE** (Optus Oval): 47,514 — May 25, 1963 v Geelong

# CARLTON

# Old hands must guide Blues again

In what really has been a changing of the guard at Carlton, the '98 line-up sees no Kernahan, Williams, Hanna, Madden, O'Sullivan or Spalding.

Many younger Carlton supporters have never known a Carlton without Kernahan as the leader and for a time, it seemed coach David Parkin might also be joining the exodus. Thankfully, in my opinion, he remains.

While Carlton had an opportunity to play in the 1997 finals right up to the final round, the club generally struggled. Age caught up with its champions and changes had to be made.

Craig Bradley, the side's most visible player in 1997, is one of the veterans to remain. He didn't win the best and fairest award as many thought he should, finishing second behind Brett Ratten. At 34, he remains a star, a constant kick-getter, and Carlton will need all of that.

Peter Dean, 33, Stephen Silvagni, 31 in May and Dean Rice, 30, are the other over-30s still on the list. Silvagni is vital in key roles at either end, but I have doubts about the rest.

The show will revolve around Bradley, defenders Michael Sexton, Andrew McKay and maybe injury-troubled Ang Christou, all-rounders Silvagni and Anthony Koutoufides, mid-fielders Ratten and Scott Camporeale and big man Matthew Allan.

General improvement can also be expected from the very promising Lance Whitnall. Aaron Hamill is talented and the club will be hoping young ruckman Mark Porter can come on and put pressure on semi-established follower Allan.

Allan is possibly the key to the operation. With the aerial power of Kernahan and the guile of Williams missing, there must be a handful of players who take big steps. One of them must be Allan.

The Blues received Sean Charles from Melbourne in pre-draft trading last October. He has been a problem player; a player with a liberal serving of talent who can kick stunning goals, but who has had injuries and form and concentration lapses.

At the National Draft, Carlton gained promising recruits Kris Massie — one of the jewels of the draft — and Adam Chatfield.

For a club that was in the top eight only three times in 1997, it's hard to go overboard about its chances in 1998, given that the influx of new blood has been modest. But with Carlton, you never know.

Parkin and president John Elliott hate losing.

— **Greg Hobbs**

## THE YEAR AHEAD

| Rd | Date | Opponent | Venue | Home/ Away | Time (local) |
|----|------|----------|-------|------------|--------------|
| 1 | March 28 | Adelaide | OO | H | 2.10pm |
| 2 | April 5 | Western Bulldogs | OO | A | 2.10pm |
| 3 | April 13 | Essendon | MCG | H | 2.10pm |
| 4 | April 19 | Melbourne | OO | H | 2.10pm |
| 5 | April 26 | St Kilda | P | A | 2.10pm |
| 6 | May 2 | Collingwood | MCG | H | 3.30pm |
| 7 | May 9 | Port Adelaide | OO | H | 2.10pm |
| 8 | May 17 | West Coast | S | A | 1.20pm |
| 9 | May 23 | North Melbourne | OO | H | 2.10pm |
| 10 | May 30 | Brisbane Lions | OO | H | 2.10pm |
| 11 | June 6 | Geelong | MCG | A | 3.30pm |
| 12 | June 13 | Sydney | OO | H | 2.10pm |
| 13 | June 21 | Fremantle | S | A | 1.20pm |
| 14 | June 27 | Hawthorn | OO | H | 2.10pm |
| 15 | July 3 (N) | Richmond | MCG | A | 7.40pm |
| 16 | July 17 (N) | Adelaide | FP | A | 8.10pm |
| 17 | July 25 | Western Bulldogs | OO | H | 2.10pm |
| 18 | August 2 | Essendon | MCG | A | 2.10pm |
| 19 | August 8 | Melbourne | MCG | A | 2.10pm |
| 20 | August 16 | St Kilda | MCG | H | 2.10pm |
| 21 | August 23 | Collingwood | MCG | A | 2.10pm |
| 22 | August 30 | Port Adelaide | FP | A | 2.50pm |

## 1997 AT A GLANCE

**L:** R1: Essendon 16.10 (106) v Carlton 15.9 (99) (MCG)

**L:** R2: North Melbourne 12.14 (86) v Carlton 8.12 (60) (MCG)

**W:** R3: Carlton 15.18 (108) v Adelaide 12.8 (80) (OO)

**W:** R4: Collingwood 12.12 (84) v Carlton 15.11 (101) (MCG)

**L:** R5: Carlton 12.14 (86) v Geelong 13.16 (94) (OO)

**L:** R6: Sydney 21.16 (142) v Carlton 11.17 (83) (SC)

**W:** R7: Richmond 10.16 (76) v Carlton 14.14 (98) (MCG)

**W:** R8: Carlton 15.16 (106) v Hawthorn 12.9 (81) (OO)

**W:** R9: Carlton 16.9 (105) v Fremantle 14.4 (88) (OO)

**L:** R10: Port Adelaide 14.9 (93) v Carlton 7.13 (55) (FP)

**SNAPSHOT**

Games: 22
Wins: 10 Losses: 12
Ladder finish: 11th
Players Used: 38

**W:** R11: Carlton 12.12 (84) v Brisbane Lions 9.9 (63) (OO)

**L:** R12: St Kilda 16.20 (116) v Carlton 12.13 (85) (WP)

**W:** R13: West Coast 11.13 (79) v Carlton 12.14 (86) (S)

**L:** R14: Carlton 11.8 (74) v Western Bulldogs 16.14 (110) (OO)

**L:** R15: Melbourne 18.11 (119) v Carlton 15.10 (100) (MCG)

**W:** R16: Carlton 25.15 (165) v Essendon 13.9 (87) (MCG)

**L:** R17: Carlton 7.16 (58) v North Melbourne 14.12 (96) (OO)

**L:** R18: Adelaide 18.19 (127) v Carlton 13.8 (86) (FP)

**W:** R19: Carlton 14.23 (107) v Collingwood 13.13 (91) (MCG)

**L:** R20: Geelong 13.17 (95) v Carlton 9.13 (67) (KP)

**W:** R21: Carlton 11.10 (76) v Sydney 5.11 (41) (OO)

**L:** R22: Carlton 13.11 (89) v Richmond 13.13 (91) (OO)

## The Coach

**David Parkin**

**Born:** 12/9/42

There was some speculation about David Parkin and his future as coach of Carlton after the 1997 season, but a few days before the Grand Final, he was re-appointed.

The Blues were well removed from Grand Final activities, having finished 11th with 10 wins and 12 losses in a disappointing season.

Parkin starts his 19th season as a senior League coach. He has coached 445 premiership season games to be sixth on the League coaches' long service list.

Parkin played all his League football with Hawthorn from 1961 to '74. He captained the 1971 premiership side and won a best and fairest award in 1965.

### AT A GLANCE

**COACHING RECORD**

**Hawthorn**

| Season | P | W | L | D | Pos |
|--------|----|----|----|---|-----|
| 1977 | 25 | 18 | 7 | — | 3 |
| 1978 | 25 | 19 | 6 | — | 1 |
| 1979 | 22 | 10 | 12 | — | 7 |
| 1980 | 22 | 10 | 12 | — | 8 |
| | 94 | 57 | 37 | — | |

**Fitzroy**

| Season | P | W | L | D | Pos |
|--------|----|----|----|---|-----|
| 1986 | 25 | 15 | 10 | — | 3 |
| 1987 | 22 | 8 | 14 | — | 11 |
| 1988 | 22 | 7 | 15 | — | 12 |
| | 69 | 30 | 39 | — | |

**Carlton**

| Season | P | W | L | D | Pos |
|--------|----|----|----|---|-----|
| 1981 | 24 | 19 | 5 | — | 1 |
| 1982 | 26 | 19 | 6 | 1 | 1 |
| 1983 | 23 | 13 | 10 | — | 5 |
| 1984 | 24 | 13 | 11 | — | 4 |
| 1985 | 23 | 15 | 8 | — | 5 |
| 1991 | 22 | 8 | 14 | — | 11 |
| 1992 | 22 | 14 | 8 | — | 7 |
| 1993 | 23 | 15 | 7 | 1 | 2 |
| 1994 | 24 | 15 | 9 | — | 5 |
| 1995 | 25 | 23 | 2 | — | 1 |
| 1996 | 24 | 15 | 9 | — | 6 |
| 1997 | 22 | 10 | 12 | — | 11 |
| | 282 | 179 | 101 | 2 | |
| **Total** | **445** | **266** | **177** | **2** | |

## WIN/LOSS RECORD

| Against | P | W (N) | L (N) | D (N) |
|---|---|---|---|---|
| Adelaide | 11 | 8 | 3 (1) | 0 |
| Brisbane Bears | 17 | 13 (2) | 4 (1) | 0 |
| Brisbane Lions | 1 | 1 | 0 | 0 |
| Collingwood | 215 | 111 (1) | 100 | 4 |
| Essendon | 204 | 109 (1) | 92 | 3 |
| Fitzroy | 197 | 120 | 72 | 5 |
| Fremantle | 4 | 3 | 1 | 0 |
| Geelong | 193 | 110 | 81 (1) | 2 |
| Hawthorn | 139 | 96 | 43 (1) | 0 |
| Melbourne | 184 | 104 | 78 | 2 |
| North Melb | 128 | 89 (4) | 39 (3) | 0 |
| Port Adel | 1 | 0 | 1 (1) | 0 |
| Richmond | 184 | 106 (2) | 76 (1) | 2 |
| St Kilda | 186 | 151 | 33 | 2 |
| Sydney | 197 | 122 (1) | 69 (2) | 6 |
| West Coast | 19 | 10 (1) | 9 (2) | 0 |
| W Bulldogs | 120 | 76 | 40 | 4 |
| University | 14 | 13 | 1 | 0 |
| **TOTALS** | **2014** | **1242 (12)** | **742 (13)** | **30 (0)** |

*(N) Premiership matches played at night*

## WINNING RUNS

25 v Hawthorn (1925–1938)
24 v Richmond (1908–1917)
16 v Fitzroy (1962–1971)
16 v Melbourne (1905–1911)
15 v St Kilda (1929–1936)
15 v Melbourne (1976–1983)
13 v Hawthorn (1945–1952)
13 v St Kilda (1902–1906)
13 v Essendon (1968–1974)
12 v Essendon (1932–1939)
12 v North Melb (1928–1935)
11 v St Kilda (1979–1984)
10 v Fitzroy (1934–1940)
10 v St Kilda (1944–1949); (1966–1971)
9 v Collingwood (1905–1909)
9 v W Bulldogs (1978–1982)
8 v Geelong (1970–1973)
8 v SM/Sydney (1970–1974); (1978–1982)
8 v Brisbane Bears (1992–1996)
4 v West Coast (1988–1989); (1994–1996)
4 v Adelaide (1994–1997)
2 v Fremantle (1997– )
1 v Brisbane Lions (1997)

## 1997 BEST AND FAIREST

Votes are awarded on a 5-4-3-2-1 system by four people on the match committee.

1 Brett Ratten (191)
2 Craig Bradley (182)
3 Andrew McKay (161)
4 Stephen Silvagni (114)
5 Michael Sexton (112)
6 Greg Williams (79)
7 Anthony Koutoufides (70)
8 Adrian Hickmott (55)
9 Matthew Allan (51)
10 Glenn Manton (45)

## GAMES RECORDS

356 Bruce Doull (1969–86)
328 John Nicholls (1957–74)
287 Justin Madden (1983–96)
268 Geoff Southby (1971–84)
267 Craig Bradley (1986– )
263 David McKay (1969–81)
256 Alex Jesaulenko (1967–79)
251 Stephen Kernahan (1986–97)
249 Peter Jones (1966–79)
243 Mark Maclure (1974–86)

## GOALS RECORDS

738 Stephen Kernahan (1986–97)
722 Harry Vallence (1926–38)
424 Alex Jesaulenko (1967–79)
397 Horrie Clover (1920–24; 1926–31)
370 Rod Ashman (1973–86)
367 Robert Walls (1967–78)
365 Ken Baxter (1938–41; 1945–50)
342 Vin Gardiner (1907–17)
327 Mark Maclure (1974–86)
307 John Nicholls (1957–74)

## HIGHS AND LOWS

| Against | Highest | Lowest | G. W. Margin | G. L. Margin |
|---|---|---|---|---|
| Adelaide | 24.12.156 (1993) | 6.12.48 (1991) | 79 (1993) | 66 (1994) |
| Brisbane Bears | 27.22.184 (1987) | 9.8.62 (1996) | 103 (1987) | 97 (1996) |
| Brisbane Lions | 12.12.84 (1997) | 12.12.84 (1997) | 21 (1997) | — |
| Collingwood | 28.10.178 (1943) | 0.6.6 (1898) | 104 (1943) | 102 (1977) |
| Essendon | 27.13.175 (1975) | 1.2.8 (1898) | 102 (1936) | 109 (1985) |
| Fitzroy | 27.19.181 (1993) | 1.1.7 (1898) | 97 (1995) | 94 (1904) |
| Fremantle | 23.7.145 (1996) | 6.13.49 (1996) | 61 (1996) | 53 (1996) |
| Geelong | 23.28.166 (1944) | 1.5.11 (1899) | 106 (1944) | 73 (1933) |
| Hawthorn | 30.30.210 (1969) | 4.12.36 (1971) | 128 (1969) | 98 (1991) |
| Melbourne | 25.15.165 (1986) | 1.2.8 (1903) | 116 (1986) | 81 (1897) |
| North Melb | 31.13.199 (1984) | 5.2.32 (1965) | 137 (1984) | 111 (1983) |
| Port Adel | 7.13.55 (1997) | 7.13.55 (1997) | — | 38 (1997) |
| Richmond | 28.9.177 (1972) | 3.10.28 (1924) | 115 (1984) | 77 (1978) |
| St Kilda | 24.26.170 (1977) | 2.5.17 (1918) | 140 (1985) | 56 (1995) |
| Sydney | 27.23.185 (1982) | 0.8.8 (1902) | 102 (1982) | 77 (1970) |
| West Coast | 29.17.191 (1987) | 6.13.49 (1994) | 87 (1987) | 76 (1989) |
| W Bulldogs | 30.21.201 (1982) | 1.10.16 (1991) | 129 (1982) | 59 (1989) |

## THE LEADERSHIP AT CARLTON

| Year | Pos | Coach | Captain | Best & Fairest | Leading Goalkicker | |
|------|-----|-------|---------|----------------|--------------------|---|
| 1931 | 3 | D. Minogue | R. Brew | | H. Vallence | 86 |
| 1932 | 2 | D. Minogue | C. Martyn | | H. Vallence | 97 |
| 1933 | 4 | D. Minogue | F. Gill | | H. Vallence | 84 |
| 1934 | 5 | D. Minogue | M. Johnson | C. Crisp | C. Crisp | 44 |
| 1935 | 4 | F. Maher | C. Davey | J. Francis | H. Vallence | 66 |
| 1936 | 4 | F. Maher | J. Francis | A. Clarke | H. Vallence | 86 |
| 1937 | 5 | P. Rowe | A. Clarke | D. McIntyre | H. Vallence | 39 |
| 1938 | 1 | B. Diggins | B. Diggins | C. Crisp | H. Vallence | 81 |
| 1939 | 5 | B. Diggins | B. Diggins | F. Gill | K. Baxter | 65 |
| 1940 | 5 | B. Diggins | B. Diggins | J. Francis | P. Schmidt | 55 |
| 1941 | 3 | P. Bentley | J. Francis | B. Chitty | P. Schmidt | 77 |
| 1942 | 5 | P. Bentley | J. Francis | J. Mooring | P. Schmidt | 47 |
| 1943 | 4 | P. Bentley | J. Francis | G. Gniel | J. Wrout | 33 |
| 1944 | 5 | P. Bentley | B. Atkinson | B. Chitty | J. Mooring | 42 |
| 1945 | 1 | P. Bentley | B. Chitty | R. Savage | L. Collins | 49 |
| 1946 | 6 | P. Bentley | B. Chitty | J. Howell | K. Baxter | 46 |
| 1947 | 1 | P. Bentley | E. Henfry | B. Deacon/E. Henfry | K. Baxter | 42 |
| 1948 | 6 | P. Bentley | E. Henfry | J. Howell | K. Baxter/R. Garby | 39 |
| 1949 | 2 | P. Bentley | E. Henfry | E. Henfry | K. Baxter | 46 |
| 1950 | 8 | P. Bentley | E. Henfry | A. Hodgson | K. Baxter | 43 |
| 1951 | 7 | P. Bentley | E. Henfry | J. Clark | K. Warburton | 48 |
| 1952 | 4 | P. Bentley | E. Henfry/K. Hands | O. Grieve | J. Howell | 42 |
| 1953 | 5 | P. Bentley | K. Hands | K. Hands | J. Spencer | 32 |
| 1954 | 8 | P. Bentley | K. Hands | W. Milroy | N. O'Brien | 45 |
| 1955 | 7 | P. Bentley | K. Hands | J. James | N. O'Brien | 73 |
| 1956 | 5 | J. Francis | K. Hands | D. Beasy | K. Hamilton | 22 |
| 1957 | 4 | J. Francis | K. Hands | B. Comben | G. Burke | 34 |
| 1958 | 7 | J. Francis | B. Comben | B. Comben | J. Heathcote | 19 |
| 1959 | 3 | K. Hands | B. Comben | J. Nicholls | Sergio Silvagni | 40 |
| 1960 | 7 | K. Hands | B. Comben | J. James | L. Brereton | 44 |
| 1961 | 8 | K. Hands | G. Donaldson | J. James | T. Carroll | 54 |
| 1962 | 2 | K. Hands | G. Donaldson | Sergio Silvagni | T. Carroll | 62 |
| 1963 | 6 | K. Hands | J. Nicholls | J. Nicholls | T. Carroll | 27 |
| 1964 | 10 | K. Hands | Sergio Silvagni | G. Collis | I. Nankervis | 18 |
| 1965 | 6 | R. Barassi | R. Barassi | J. Nichols | B. Quirk | 29 |
| 1966 | 7 | R. Barassi | R. Barassi | J. Nicholls | A. Gallagher | 24 |
| 1967 | 3 | R. Barassi | R. Barassi | J. Nicholls | B. Kekovich | 38 |
| 1968 | 1 | R. Barassi | R. Barassi/J. Nicholls | Sergio Silvagni | B. Kekovich | 59 |
| 1969 | 2 | R. Barassi | J. Nicholls | G. Crane | A. Jesaulenko | 66 |
| 1970 | 1 | R. Barassi | J. Nicholls | A. Gallagher | A. Jesaulenko | 115 |
| 1971 | 5 | R. Barassi | J. Nicholls | G. Southby | A. Jesaulenko | 56 |
| 1972 | 1 | J. Nicholls | J. Nicholls | G. Southby | G. Kennedy | 76 |
| 1973 | 2 | J. Nicholls | J. Nicholls | P. Jones | B. Walsh | 60 |
| 1974 | 7 | J. Nicholls | J. Nicholls/R. Walls | B. Doull | C. Davis | 45 |
| 1975 | 4 | J. Nicholls | A. Jesaulenko | A. Jesaulenko | R. Walls | 59 |
| 1976 | 3 | I. Thorogood | A. Jesaulenko | T. Keogh | R. Walls | 55 |
| 1977 | 6 | I. Thorogood | R. Walls | B. Doull | M. Maclure | 39 |
| 1978 | 4 | I. Stewart A. Jesaulenko | A. Jesaulenko | T. Keogh | R. Galt | 49 |
| 1979 | 1 | A. Jesaulenko | A. Jesaulenko | M. Fitzpatrick | K. Sheldon | 53 |
| 1980 | 4 | P. Jones | M. Fitzpatrick | B. Doull | W. Johnston | 51 |
| 1981 | 1 | D. Parkin | M. Fitzpatrick | K. Hunter | P. Bosustow | 59 |
| 1982 | 1 | D. Parkin | M. Fitzpatrick | J. Buckley | R. Ditchburn | 61 |
| 1983 | 5 | D. Parkin | M. Fitzpatrick | W. Johnston | K. Hunter | 43 |
| 1984 | 4 | D. Parkin | W. Johnston | B. Doull | W. Ralph | 55 |
| 1985 | 5 | D. Parkin | W. Johnston | J. Madden | M. Maclure | 48 |
| 1986 | 2 | R. Walls | M. Maclure | C. Bradley/W. Johnston | S. Kernahan | 62 |
| 1987 | 1 | R. Walls | S. Kernahan | S. Kernahan | S. Kernahan | 73 |
| 1988 | 3 | R. Walls | S. Kernahan | C. Bradley | S. Kernahan | 54 |
| 1989 | 8 | R. Walls A. Jesaulenko | S. Kernahan | S. Kernahan | S. Kernahan | 59 |
| 1990 | 8 | A. Jesaulenko | S. Kernahan | Stephen Silvagni | S. Kernahan | 69 |
| 1991 | 11 | D. Parkin | S. Kernahan | J. Madden | S. Kernahan | 46 |
| 1992 | 7 | D. Parkin | S. Kernahan | S. Kernahan | S. Kernahan | 83 |
| 1993 | 2 | D. Parkin | S. Kernahan | C. Bradley | S. Kernahan | 68 |
| 1994 | 5 | D. Parkin | S. Kernahan | G. Williams | S. Kernahan | 82 |
| 1995 | 1 | D. Parkin | S. Kernahan | B. Ratten | S. Kernahan | 63 |
| 1996 | 6 | D. Parkin | S. Kernahan | Stephen Silvagni | S. Kernahan | 56 |
| 1997 | 11 | D. Parkin | S. Kernahan | B. Ratten | A. Koutoufides | 28 |

# PLAYER PROFILES

## MATTHEW ALLAN

Starts the season as the flagship of the club's ruck division for the first time. While he may have effectively had that title at the start of 1997, Justin Madden was about the place as a back-up if required. Madden has now gone and Allan is without a safety net. He carried the ruck for much of last season, was ninth in the club voting and if he can lift a notch this year, will help overcome the exit of experienced players since last year. Has had medical treatment for a shin injury since '97.

**Player honors:** night series premiership side 1997.

## JACOB ANSTEY

Slipped into the Blues' line-up for the first time in 1997 and played nine games, plus another dozen in the reserves, taking his total there to 35. The former Canberra player has skill as a rover/forward pocket and relies heavily on his slickness because, in terms of build, there is not a lot of him. He will be endeavoring to cement a regular senior place this year — his third at Optus Oval.

## ANDREW BALKWILL

Aged 26 and has played just one senior game with Carlton — early last year. Had 19 games in the reserves last year, but the Blues obviously believe he has something to offer. A half-forward who can run all day and must flatter this year. Was part of Central District's SA finals campaign in 1996 and arrived at Optus Oval (with Ben Nelson) in a deal that saw Brent Heaver go to Port Adelaide.

## SIMON BEAUMONT

Left-footer who was heavily restricted in 1997 with a groin injury which resulted in surgery last August. Still troubled with the injury leading in to 1998. Played seven senior games and one in the reserves in '97 and is a fine half-forward/wingman who will be hoping to get a clearer run this year. Has been well tried in the reserves since 1994, playing 54 games. His groin problem is his biggest concern.

## CRAIG BLACK

Rover with promise and a member of the Dandenong Stingrays' losing grand final side in 1997. Carlton's third choice (55th overall) at the 1997 National Draft. Earlier in the year he played some games with the Carlton reserves and was a member of the Victoria Metro under-18 side.

## TONY BOURKE

Had surgery to repair a ruptured spleen after being accidentally knocked in the stomach in a pre-season Ansett Australia Cup game in 1997. His season was restricted to just three Ansett Australia Cup games, which was a hefty blow for the promising young centre half-forward/centre half-back/ruckman. Mobile and had been making steady progress until his setback. Drafted from East Ballarat in 1994, but is yet to play senior football in the major season.

## CRAIG BRADLEY

Evergreen at 34 and, pre-season, hampered by a groin injury. Is still a penetrating midfielder/on-baller who knocks up winning the ball. While several of his experienced teammates called it a day after last season, Bradley steams on and last year again won selection in the All-Australian side. Appointed skipper in 1998 after a long apprenticeship as vice-captain and said he hoped to play this year and next. Bradley was second in 1997 club voting and picked up 15 Brownlow Medal votes.

**Player honors:** best and fairest 1986 (equal), 1988, 1993; 2nd best and fairest 1989, 1991, 1995, 1997; 3rd best and fairest 1990; All-Australian 1986, 1993, 1994, 1995, 1997; Fos Williams Medal 1986, 1991, 1993; premiership sides 1987, 1995; night series premiership side 1997; captain 1998.

## FRASER BROWN

Tough centre-line/on-baller who needs a special year to regain lost ground following a chronic back-related hamstring injury which had further medical attention last October. Played only seven senior games in 1997 and in 1996, similar injuries kept him to 15 games. While the Blues have missed his gritty play, they have learnt to live without his regular presence. Trained cautiously for 1998 and still not 100 per cent when practice matches in full swing.

**Player honors:** premiership side 1995.

## SCOTT CAMPOREALE

Swift wingman who was struck down with glandular fever in 1997, causing him to miss eight matches. A fine player at Optus Oval since 1995, as evidenced by his solitary game in the reserves against 59 senior appearances. Must now assume a team leader role as the Blues try to re-establish themselves.

**Player honors:** AFL Norwich Rising Star nominee 1995; premiership side 1995; night series premiership side 1997.

## SEAN CHARLES

Showed uncanny skills with Melbourne, but injuries and a lack of consistency held him back. The Demons persisted, but Charles did not respond often enough and was exchanged for a third round draft selection (Matthew Blake, Bendigo Pioneers). Now has the chance to play a valuable role in the Blues' scoring set-up. Made his debut in 1992, but has played only 47 senior games and 28 in the reserves.

**Previous AFL club:** Melbourne (1992-97: 47 games, 60 goals).

## ADAM CHATFIELD

Interesting selection at the 1997 National Draft as Carlton's second choice (23rd overall). Played with Pennant Hills in Sydney, which seems an unlikely breeding ground. More recently was based at Canberra, had grooming with the NSW/ACT Rams and shows potential as a half-forward. Was the quickest player at the AFL draft camp last October, has good recovery and kicks long distances with either foot.

## ANG CHRISTOU

From a cult figure with the Blues fans and a 1995 All-Australian back pocket to an almost 'forgotten' player in 1997. Missed the second half of last season with a serious back (disc) injury and only time will tell if he can regain his place. Will certainly be a late starter in

'98. The Blues need him back firing and part of the renowned defence of Silvagni, Sexton, McKay, Manton and Dean. Too good a player to be in the grandstand.

**Player honors:** AFL Norwich Rising Star nominee 1993; premiership side 1995; night series premiership side 1997; All-Australian 1995.

### MATT CLAPE

Had a great first season in the premiership year of 1995 when he finished eighth in the best and fairest voting, but his standing has slipped. Sidelined for several games last year with a right knee injury and underwent surgery in August. The former West Coast Eagles forward played only 11 games last year and needs to produce a top season. Has a touch of class, but will have to consistently dig deep.

**Player honors:** premiership side 1995; night series premiership side 1997.

**Previous AFL club:** West Coast Eagles (1992-94: 29 games, 14 goals).

### PETER DEAN

One of a handful of Carlton over-30s left after last season, but the defender (and part-time forward) has held his ground and will start his 15th season with 235 games behind him. At 33, he is the second oldest player on the list (behind Craig Bradley) and his experience and keenness should again see him through. Has been a top-line defender, a strong clubman and is the only player at the club to serve under David Parkin during his two coaching stints.

**Player honors:** premiership sides 1987, 1995; night series premiership side 1997; 3rd best and fairest 1994.

### RON DE IULIO

Interrupted 1997 season with knee and back injuries, a four-match Tribunal suspension and was dropped at one stage. Will be anxious to win his share of votes. Had his left knee 'cleaned up' after last season, so should have more freedom. Looked like being traded a few years back, but turned his career around and has been a steady defender.

**Player honors:** night series premiership side 1997.

### ANTHONY FRANCHINA

Put into the senior side late in 1997 for two games to give him a taste of the tempo — and of things to come this year. Pacy half-forward and at 20, has already had 43 games in the reserves — 41 with Carlton (1996-97) and two with Fitzroy (1995). On Carlton's supplementary list in 1996 and is an up-and-comer who will be seeking more exposure.

### AARON HAMILL

A potential star who came to light in the AFL under-17 championships. Played 23 senior games in 1996 and '97 and won the club's Past Players' Association encouragement award in 1996. Had a few flat spots in '97 and was dropped three times, but still played 19 matches. Can play in defence and attack and has the talent to become an established player.

**Player honors:** night series premiership side 1997.

### ADRIAN HICKMOTT

Played in Geelong's losing Grand Final side against Carlton in 1995 and fronted up for Carlton in his next game through a trade. Promptly won Carlton's best first-year player award and finished 10th in the best and fairest voting. Jumped two rungs last year to eighth. Is seen at his best at half-back and in the back pocket and at the end of season 1997 had arthroscope attention to a knee. Needs only 11 games for 100.

**Previous AFL club:** Geelong (1992-95: 50 games, 24 goals).

### MATTHEW HOGG

Persistent all-rounder who always gives 110 per cent. Might lack pure skill, but has desire and a thirst for tough competition. Joined Carlton from Footscray in 1992 and needs only seven more games to bring up his 100 with the Blues in an overall total of 152. Throw in 45 reserves games and it has been a long career that started in the reserves in 1986 and in the seniors in 1988.

**Player honors:** premiership side 1995; night series premiership side 1997.

**Previous AFL club:** Footscray (1988-91: 59 games, 4 goals).

### TRENT HOPPNER

An elusive centreline player and rover who captained Preston Knights in 1997 and was Carlton's fourth selection (70th overall) at the National Draft. In 1997, also played with Victoria Metro at the AFL National Under-18 Championships. With a big changing of the guard at Optus Oval since last season, may be one of the youngsters to step up.

### DARREN HULME

Selected at the 1997 Pre-Season Draft after a stay on Carlton's supplementary list. Played several excellent games in the reserves as a rover and broke into the senior side in round 10. Had a taste, was dropped and then returned for the last five matches. Had five games with Sydney's reserves in 1995 and 13 with the Blues (1996-97). Is a nuggety type with courage and a strong will to win, but must work on his skills.

### JOHN HYNES

Injuries interrupted his 1997 season, but did enough at full-back with the Prahran Dragons for Carlton to select him fifth (80th overall) at the 1997 National Draft. Well down in the order, but several players have emerged from this lowly position to become League stars. The key is the transition from junior to senior football. Has also played with Cheltenham.

### CHRIS JACKSON

From the NSW country town of Hay and last year had a solid grounding of 19 games in the reserves. In 1996, also had a reserves match with the Western Bulldogs. Drafted in 1996 as a tall, key position player following impressive performances with the NSW/ACT Rams. Played at centre half-back in the Rams' losing grand final (against Preston Knights) in 1996. Not 20 until October.

### ANTHONY KOUTOUFIDES

Athletic all-rounder capable of brilliant football, but did not live up to expectations in 1997 when he finished seventh in the club voting. Fourth in '96 and equal sixth in '95. While he has been a strong contributor, there is a feeling he sometimes turns it on and off. Needs a big season to confidently take his place among the elite. Had 426 disposals in the home and away series last year, which had him 33rd on the AFL list.

**Player honors:** premiership side 1995; night series premiership side 1997; leading goalkicker 1997; All-Australian 1995.

### DAMIEN LOCK
Waiting for the senior nod following 23 reserves games — four in 1996 and 19 last year — and the word is he will play a good slice of senior football in '98. A running half-forward who is quick and can win the ball. Came from Eaglehawk, in country Victoria, as a pacy midfielder after Carlton took him as its second selection (behind Sam Smart) at the 1996 National Draft.

### GLENN MANTON
His run of 47 consecutive games came to an end in round 17 last year when he injured a hamstring. Back after two games and this excellent defender finished 10th in best and fairest voting. Was delisted by Essendon after 21 games (1992-94) and Carlton swooped at the 1995 Pre-Season Draft. Took his place on the backline and played in the 1995 Grand Final side. At Essendon, also played 51 reserves games.

**Player honors:** premiership side 1995; night series premiership side 1997; Essendon night series premiership sides 1993, 1994.

**Previous AFL club:** Essendon (1992-94: 21 games, 4 goals).

### KRIS MASSIE
Outstanding junior who lasted until the seventh pick at the 1997 National Draft. Was expected to be picked up as early as third. Excellent defender — a product of the Edithdale-Aspendale and Dandenong Stingrays clubs and a strong Collingwood supporter until draft day — who was an All-Australian at under-16 and under-18 levels.

### ANDREW McKAY
One of the best defenders in the business across half-back. Finished third in club voting in 1997 after an interrupted 1996 in which he did not figure in the top 10. Studied in Brisbane in '96, which disrupted his football schedule, but he was back in Melbourne last season and returned to his best. Played in all games in 1997 and is a player who gives nothing away and leaves little to chance. If you run off McKay and kick a goal, you earn it. One of the club's on-field leaders.

**Player honors:** All-Australian 1993; premiership side 1995; night series premiership side 1997; 3rd best and fairest 1997.

### JUSTIN MURPHY
Looked like being a wise draft choice by Richmond when he kicked five goals in his first game in 1994 against Essendon, but this competent wing/half-forward seemed to run his race at Punt Road and after only 12 games was traded to Carlton. In two seasons at Optus Oval, has played 37 games, which is a good result, but didn't figure in the top 10 in best and fairest voting in either season. Has had only eight games in the Blues' reserves — a sharp improvement on his 31 with Richmond.

**Player honors:** night series premiership side 1997.

**Previous AFL club:** Richmond (12 games, 9 goals).

### BEN NELSON
A half-back with just one senior game against his name at the end of 1997 and 12 in the reserves. Was part of a deal before the 1996 National Draft (with Carlton teammate Andrew Balkwill) that saw Carlton's Brent Heaver go to Port Adelaide. Had more than 50 games with SA club Sturt as a defender/midfielder. Troubled by a stress fracture in a foot in 1997 and his season was ended prematurely due to a knee problem. 1998 preparation set back by glandular fever.

### BRAD PEARCE
Explosive in the premiership year of 1995, kicking 52 goals, including four in the Grand Final. Was elevated to star status with his play on the half-forward line. However, has not had the same impact in the past two seasons and has battled groin, back and knee injuries. Played 15 games in 1996 and 11 last year. Must produce a series of top performances to win back respect. Played with the Brisbane Bears in 1993.

**Player honors:** premiership side 1995.

**Previous AFL club:** Brisbane Bears (1993: 2 games, 1 goal).

### MARK PORTER
Started 1997 on Carlton's rookie list but became a fully fledged list member when veteran Justin Madden retired. A young ruckman with great promise who has bulked up since last year when he played four senior games in the latter part of season. Is expected to make regular appearances in 1998. Palms the ball with authority and will be an excellent back-up to Matthew Allan — as Allan was to Madden for a few years. Has had 12 reserves games with Blues.

### BRETT RATTEN
Beat Craig Bradley in 1997 to win the best and fairest award for the second time and has had a knee repaired in readiness for 1998. Extensive worker around the midfield, underlined by his 261 handballs (2nd in the AFL in the home and away series) and 255 kicks — placing him ninth on the disposals list (home and away) in 1997. Again one of the best tacklers in the competition and his all-round presence is immense. Club voting over the past three years tells the story — winner in 1995, second in '96 and the winner again in '97.

**Player honors:** premiership side 1995; night series premiership side 1997; best and fairest 1995, 1997; 2nd best and fairest 1996.

### DEAN RICE
Hard-at-the-ball campaigner who plays it vigorously, whether stationed in defence or attack. Never takes a short step and while he may be a bit rough around the edges, has been a tremendous team player. Wore the Big V in his days at St Kilda. Has had to overcome two major reconstructions and had hamstring prob-

lems in 1997. But with so much football spirit in him, there is no holding him back. Is 30 in March, so it will get harder from now on.

**Player honors:** premiership side 1995; night series premiership side 1997.

**Previous AFL club:** St Kilda (1987-93: 116 games, 43 goals).

### MICHAEL SEXTON

Leading centre half-back in the competition in 1997, winning the position in the All-Australian side. The year before, he was in the back pocket in the All-Australian team. As Carlton fought for a finals berth late in 1997, it unfortunately did not have Sexton, who was laid up with a shoulder injury. Plays without fanfare and his fifth placing in the club voting last year followed second and third placings in previous seasons. Started with the Blues' reserves' in 1989 and made his senior debut in 1990.

**Player honors:** premiership side 1995; night series premiership side 1997; 2nd best and fairest 1993; 3rd best and fairest 1996; All-Australian 1996, 1997.

### STEPHEN SILVAGNI

Acknowledged as the best full-back in the AFL — he was chosen at full-back in the AFL Team of the Century in 1996 — and when the scoring dries up, he is often sent to full-forward to rectify the position. It seemed all was not well between Silvagni and the club over contractual arrangements, but signed on again and appointed vice-captain. Silvagni, who is over shoulder surgery, has been a brilliant, athletic competitor and is on his way to 250 games this year. Father Sergio played 239 games (1958-71), so it has been a huge family contribution.

**Player honors:** premiership sides 1987, 1995; best and fairest 1990, 1996; 2nd best and fairest 1994; 3rd best and fairest 1995; 3rd Brownlow Medal 1990; All-Australian 1988, 1990, 1994, 1995, 1996, 1997; AFL Team of Century 1996.

### SAM SMART

South Australian with a Norwood background who played in Carlton's 1997 night series premiership side, but did not get his next and only senior appearance until round 21. Is a 200cm centre half-forward/full-forward/ruckman with a good junior background in Teal Cup football and in 1994 was on the Adelaide Crows list. Carlton's No. 1 selection in the 1994 National Draft, but medical studies kept him in Adelaide until last year. Turns 23 in May and must make his presence felt this year.

**Player honors:** night series premiership side 1997.

### BEN THOMPSON

Member of the Queensland team at the 1996 AFL National Under-18 Championships and a defender with enough quality to prompt his selection by Carlton at the 1997 National Draft. He was the last of Carlton's six selections and the 83rd selection overall.

### ADAM WHITE

Played his first 10 senior games in 1997 — most of them in the first half of the season. This one-time East Burwood player has shown ability at half-forward/half-back and on the wing and is strong overhead. At 22, will strive hard to cement a place.

**Player honors:** night series premiership side 1997.

### ADRIAN WHITEHEAD

Had more than his share of injuries — hamstring, foot and shoulder — and will be anxious to get a better run in 1998. One of the lower-profile Blues, but is a willing and able all-rounder whose skills have quietly taken him to 62 games, plus 32 in the reserves, the last of them in 1996.

**Player honors:** AFL Norwich Rising Star nominee 1995; premiership side 1995; night series premiership side 1997.

### LANCE WHITNALL

Was being billed as the likely recruit of the year when he started last season. Joined Carlton under the father/son rule — Graeme Whitnall played 66 games — and kicked four goals in his first game in round one. Played 18 games (and four in the reserves) in his first season and although his form wavered, he has what it takes to become a top player. Was a brilliant junior and only 17 when he made his senior debut last year.

**Player honors:** Norwich Rising Star nominee 1997; night series premiership side 1997.

## ROOKIE LIST

### CAMERON BLIGHT

From Devonport in Tasmania and was second in the Tassie Mariners 1997 best and fairest voting. Represented Tasmania at the 1997 AFL National Under-18 Championships. Tall athlete and could develop into a key position backman.

### CLINT EVANS

From the Dandenong Stingrays and can play centre/wing/half-back/ruck-rover. Has played with Collingwood's reserves and has an impressive athletic background as a schoolboy sprinter. Trained with the Blues over summer.

### SIMON FLETCHER

Spent two years at Geelong and was well-blooded in the reserves, but did not manage a senior game. Delisted by Geelong shortly before the 1997 National Draft. Was troubled by a knee injury last year and trained with Carlton in the 1998 pre-season.

### SHANE FLYNN

Was on Carlton's supplementary list in 1997. Former Eastern Ranges (VSFL) youngster who shows promise as a tagger/on-baller.

### SCOTT FREEBORN

Was on Port Adelaide's list in 1997, but did not manage a game. Is 20 in May and a brother of North Melbourne 1996 premiership player Glenn Freeborn. Had a serious knee injury last year.

### DAMIAN LANG

Picked up by Sydney as a priority selection at the 1993 National Draft and played with the Port Adelaide Magpies over the past couple of years. Smart player in defence at full-back, centre half-back or back pocket who can pick up the 'talls'. Turned 22 in March.

**Previous AFL club:** Sydney (1994: 5 games, 4 goals).

# CARLTON

| Name (# = rookie) | No. | Born | Height | Weight | Recruited from |
|---|---|---|---|---|---|
| Matthew Allan | 24 | 26/2/75 | 198 | 102 | NORTH RINGWOOD |
| Jacob Anstey | 12 | 27/1/78 | 176 | 71 | TUGGERANONG (ACT) |
| Andrew Balkwill | 28 | 24/3/72 | 192 | 89 | CENTRAL DISTRICT (SA) |
| Simon Beaumont | 29 | 13/12/75 | 188 | 82 | EAST CAMBERWELL/CENTRAL U18 |
| Craig Black | 37 | 9/2/79 | 180 | 70 | ROSEBUD/DANDENONG U18 |
| Tony Bourke | 40 | 13/6/76 | 201 | 89 | EAST BALLARAT/BALLARAT U18 |
| Craig Bradley | 21 | 23/10/63 | 180 | 83 | PORT ADELAIDE (SA) |
| Fraser Brown | 20 | 18/8/70 | 181 | 89 | LILYDALE |
| Scott Camporeale | 16 | 11/8/75 | 180 | 76 | WOODVILLE-WEST TORRENS (SA) |
| Sean Charles | 10 | 18/5/75 | 182 | 83 | POWELLTOWN/MELBOURNE |
| Adam Chatfield | 13 | 22/6/79 | 189 | 78 | PENNANT HILLS (NSW)/NSW-ACT U18 |
| Ang Christou | 39 | 16/1/72 | 190 | 93 | EAST BRUNSWICK |
| Matt Clape | 6 | 28/5/69 | 187 | 86 | EAST PERTH (WA)/WEST COAST |
| Ron De Iulio | 34 | 15/4/72 | 180 | 81 | BOX HILL |
| Peter Dean | 35 | 9/3/65 | 188 | 85 | SOUTH BENDIGO |
| Anthony Franchina | 45 | 11/10/77 | 176 | 78 | NEWLANDS-COBURG/CALDER U18 |
| Aaron Hamill | 36 | 20/8/77 | 184 | 87 | TUGGERANONG (ACT) |
| Adrian Hickmott | 9 | 30/3/72 | 182 | 86 | HORSHAM/GEELONG |
| Matthew Hogg | 33 | 21/12/68 | 175 | 79 | EAST KEILOR/FOOTSCRAY |
| Trent Hoppner | 42 | 19/2/79 | 175 | 70 | HEIDELBERG/PRESTON U18 |
| Darren Hulme | 27 | 19/7/77 | 175 | 80 | FRANKSTON BOMBERS/DAND-STHN U18 |
| John Hynes | 26 | 23/2/79 | 184 | 85 | CHELTENHAM/PRAHRAN U18 |
| Chris Jackson | 38 | 7/10/78 | 193 | 90 | HAY/NSW-ACT U18 |
| Anthony Koutoufides | 43 | 18/1/73 | 190 | 95 | LALOR |
| Damien Lock | 17 | 1/10/78 | 179 | 73 | EAGLEHAWK/BENDIGO U18 |
| Glenn Manton | 22 | 1/6/73 | 185 | 86 | EAST KEILOR/ESSENDON |
| Kris Massie | 3 | 30/5/80 | 188 | 78 | EDITHVALE-ASPENDALE/DAND U18 |
| Andrew McKay | 5 | 14/4/70 | 185 | 89 | GLENELG (SA) |
| Justin Murphy | 18 | 24/4/76 | 183 | 90 | DE LA SALLE O.C./CENTRAL U18/RICHMOND |
| Ben Nelson | 15 | 23/1/77 | 184 | 91 | STURT (SA) |
| Brad Pearce | 19 | 16/8/71 | 185 | 86 | SOUTH LAUNCESTON (TAS)/BRISBANE |
| Mark Porter | 11 | 11/10/76 | 199 | 100 | COBURG |
| Brett Ratten | 7 | 11/7/71 | 184 | 92 | YARRA GLEN |
| Dean Rice | 23 | 17/3/68 | 180 | 92 | LONGWOOD/GEELONG RESERVES/ST KILDA |
| Michael Sexton | 14 | 5/3/71 | 192 | 90 | SANDHURST |
| Stephen Silvagni | 1 | 31/5/67 | 194 | 99 | MARCELLIN |
| Sam Smart | 25 | 2/5/75 | 200 | 101 | NORWOOD (SA) |
| Ben Thompson | 41 | 4/10/78 | 186 | 80 | KEDRON GRANGE (QLD) |
| Adam White | 30 | 9/1/76 | 188 | 89 | EAST BURWOOD/EASTERN U18 |
| Adrian Whitehead | 32 | 25/8/75 | 178 | 82 | WODONGA |
| Lance Whitnall | 8 | 23/8/79 | 190 | 91 | LALOR/NORTHERN U18 |
| Cameron Blight # | 48 | 8/9/79 | 188 | 88 | DEVONPORT/TAS U18 |
| Clint Evans # | 47 | 24/7/79 | 177 | 74 | BERWICK/DANDENONG U18 |
| Simon Fletcher # | 31 | 17/8/78 | 188 | 73 | GROVEDALE/GEELONG U18/GEELONG RESERVES |
| Shane Flynn # | 50 | 28/5/77 | 179 | 83 | BASIN/EASTERN U18 |
| Scott Freeborn # | 46 | 20/5/78 | 183 | 85 | WOODVILLE-WEST TORRENS (SA)/PORT ADEL LIST |
| Damian Lang # | 44 | 3/3/76 | 191 | 78 | LEETON (NSW) |
| **Total/(Average)**  *On 26/2/98 | | **(23.6 yrs)*** | **(186)** | **(86)** | |

# PLAYERS 1998

| Debut | HOME & AWAY Gms | Gls | 1997 Gms | Gls | FINALS Gms | Gls | GRAND FINALS Gms | Gls | Won | NIGHT SERIES Gms | Gls | STATE OF ORIGIN Gms | Gls |
|---|---|---|---|---|---|---|---|---|---|---|---|---|---|
| 1994 | 55 | 18 | 21 | 8 | 3 | 0 | | | | 10 | 4 | 0 | 0 |
| 1997 | 9 | 4 | 9 | 4 | | | | | | 2 | 0 | 0 | 0 |
| 1997 | 1 | 0 | 1 | 0 | | | | | | 0 | 0 | 0 | 0 |
| 1995 | 16 | 9 | 7 | 4 | | | | | | 4 | 4 | 0 | 0 |
| | 0 | 0 | 0 | 0 | | | | | | 0 | 0 | 0 | 0 |
| | 0 | 0 | 0 | 0 | | | | | | 3 | 0 | 0 | 0 |
| 1986 | 267 | 195 | 22 | 12 | 16 | 15 | 4 | 6 | 2 | 19 | 6 | 14 | 7 |
| 1989 | 129 | 83 | 7 | 5 | 10 | 5 | 2 | 0 | 1 | 13 | 5 | 0 | 0 |
| 1995 | 59 | 38 | 12 | 7 | 4 | 2 | 1 | 1 | 1 | 10 | 13 | 1 | 0 |
| 1992 | 47 | 60 | 18 | 17 | 2 | 7 | | | | 1 | 3 | 0 | 0 |
| | 0 | 0 | 0 | 0 | | | | | | 0 | 0 | 0 | 0 |
| 1991 | 105 | 17 | 8 | 0 | 10 | 3 | 2 | 0 | 1 | 12 | 1 | 2 | 0 |
| 1992 | 80 | 60 | 11 | 5 | 4 | 1 | 1 | 0 | 1 | 12 | 11 | 1 | 0 |
| 1992 | 69 | 53 | 8 | 1 | 4 | 0 | | | | 5 | 4 | 0 | 0 |
| 1984 | 235 | 36 | 20 | 7 | 15 | 3 | 3 | 0 | 2 | 18 | 4 | 2 | 0 |
| 1997 | 2 | 0 | 2 | 0 | | | | | | 0 | 0 | 0 | 0 |
| 1996 | 23 | 13 | 19 | 12 | 1 | 1 | | | | 4 | 5 | 0 | 0 |
| 1992 | 89 | 42 | 17 | 5 | 11 | 5 | 2 | 0 | 0 | 7 | 1 | 0 | 0 |
| 1988 | 152 | 38 | 18 | 6 | 8 | 0 | 2 | 0 | 1 | 14 | 9 | 1 | 0 |
| | 0 | 0 | 0 | 0 | | | | | | 0 | 0 | 0 | 0 |
| 1997 | 8 | 0 | 8 | 0 | | | | | | 0 | 0 | 0 | 0 |
| | 0 | 0 | 0 | 0 | | | | | | 0 | 0 | 0 | 0 |
| | 0 | 0 | 0 | 0 | | | | | | 0 | 0 | 0 | 0 |
| 1991 | 107 | 83 | 22 | 28 | 7 | 7 | 1 | 0 | 1 | 13 | 7 | 0 | 0 |
| | 0 | 0 | 0 | 0 | | | | | | 0 | 0 | 0 | 0 |
| 1992 | 77 | 23 | 20 | 10 | 5 | 1 | 1 | 0 | 1 | 17 | 9 | 0 | 0 |
| | 0 | 0 | 0 | 0 | | | | | | 0 | 0 | 0 | 0 |
| 1993 | 108 | 18 | 22 | 2 | 10 | 3 | 2 | 0 | 1 | 8 | 0 | 5 | 0 |
| 1994 | 49 | 54 | 21 | 26 | 2 | 1 | | | | 9 | 11 | 0 | 0 |
| 1997 | 1 | 0 | 1 | 0 | | | | | | 0 | 0 | 0 | 0 |
| 1993 | 53 | 104 | 11 | 16 | 3 | 9 | 1 | 4 | 1 | 5 | 13 | 0 | 0 |
| 1997 | 4 | 2 | 4 | 2 | | | | | | | | | |
| 1990 | 142 | 36 | 21 | 6 | 10 | 1 | 2 | 0 | 1 | 14 | 7 | 2 | 0 |
| 1987 | 153 | 70 | 10 | 2 | 5 | 3 | 1 | 1 | 1 | 13 | 4 | 2 | 1 |
| 1990 | 148 | 15 | 18 | 4 | 9 | 0 | 2 | 0 | 1 | 15 | 1 | 2 | 0 |
| 1985 | 230 | 152 | 18 | 25 | 18 | 1 | 3 | 0 | 2 | 20 | 4 | 10 | 3 |
| 1997 | 1 | 0 | 1 | 0 | | | | | | 1 | 0 | 0 | 0 |
| | 0 | 0 | 0 | 0 | | | | | | 0 | 0 | 0 | 0 |
| 1997 | 10 | 5 | 10 | 5 | | | | | | 4 | 0 | 0 | 0 |
| 1994 | 62 | 22 | 13 | 12 | 6 | 2 | 1 | 1 | 1 | 10 | 1 | 0 | 0 |
| 1997 | 18 | 19 | 18 | 19 | | | | | | 4 | 5 | 0 | 0 |
| | 0 | 0 | 0 | 0 | | | | | | 0 | 0 | | |
| | 0 | 0 | 0 | 0 | | | | | | 0 | 0 | | |
| | 0 | 0 | 0 | 0 | | | | | | 0 | 0 | | |
| | 0 | 0 | 0 | 0 | | | | | | 0 | 0 | | |
| | 0 | 0 | 0 | 0 | | | | | | 0 | 0 | | |
| 1994 | 5 | 4 | 0 | 0 | | | | | | 2 | 1 | | |
| | (61) | (31) | 418 | 250 | 163 | 70 | 31 | 13 | 19 | 267 | 132 | 42 | 11 |

## Magpies at a glance

**ADDRESS:** Lulie St., Collingwood, Vic 3067
**POSTAL ADDRESS:** PO Box 165, Abbotsford, Vic 3067
**TELEPHONE:** (03) 9419 9222
**FACSIMILE:** (03) 9419 3302
**WEB SITE:** www.collingwoodfc.com.au
**PRESIDENT:** Kevin Rose
**CHIEF EXECUTIVE:** John May
**FOOTBALL MANAGER:** David Wheadon
**MEDIA/PR MANAGER:** Karen Gilbert
**MARKETING MANAGER:** Anthony Barham
**NATIONAL RECRUITING MANAGER:** Noel Judkins
**COACHING STAFF:** Tony Shaw (senior), David Wheadon (assistant), Danny Frawley (reserves), Dr Noel Duncan (head of conditioning)
**SELECTION COMMITTEE:** Tony Shaw, Danny Frawley, David Wheadon
**CLUB DOCTOR:** Paul Blackman
**CLUB PHYSIOTHERAPIST:** David Francis
**JOINED AFL:** 1897
**HOME GROUND:** Victoria Park, Lulie Street, Collingwood and MCG.
**GROUND DIMENSIONS:** Victoria Park — 164m by 133m. Goals run east to west; MCG — 161m by 140m. Goals run east to west
**OFFICIAL COLORS:** Guernsey: Black and white vertical stripes on body and horizontal stripes on sleeves. Socks: Black. Shorts: Black
**PREMIERSHIPS:** 1902-3, 1910, 1917, 1919, 1927-8-9, 1930, 1935-6, 1953, 1958, 1990.
**BROWNLOW MEDALLISTS:** S. Coventry (1927); A. Collier (1929); H. Collier (1930 tied), M. Whelan (1939), D. Fothergill (1940 tied), L. Thompson (1972), P. Moore (1979).
**RECORD HOME ATTENDANCE,** (Victoria Park): 47,224 — April 26, 1948 v Sth Melb. (MCG): 94,825 — April 25, 1995 v Essendon

# COLLINGWOOD
# Finals or bust for haphazard Pies

The glare of failure shone on Collingwood last year. The Magpies were good enough, couldn't have been luckier with injuries, were on top of the ladder after eight rounds, had a good draw with only four games interstate (none in Perth) and had Nathan Buckley, Paul Williams, Gavin Brown, Scott Russell and Gavin Crosisca firing. Yet they still failed to make the final eight, winning only four out of their last 14 games.

But during that dark, gloomy period following coach Tony Shaw re-signing for two years, the Pies just couldn't kick a winning score. Somehow, from averaging 18 goals a game in the first eight rounds, the Woods could average only 11 goals for the next six rounds.

Coach Tony Shaw, frustrated at seeing a season that had promised so much slip away so quickly, was as confounded as anyone. He said that if Collingwood could not make the eight in 1998, a new coach might be needed.

Noel Judkins and David Wheadon were lured from Essendon as recruiting manager and football manager as criticism of Collingwood's recruiting in the 1990s reached a crescendo.

Buckley, Brown, Williams, Russell and Crosisca couldn't do more in 1998 than they did last season, so improvement needs to come from elsewhere. However, there are some positive signs.

Mal Michael came off the rookie list to hold down fullback. Chad Liddell and Richard Osborne played well in the backline at the end of last season, adding marking power and solidity in defence. A fit Scott Burns will be an asset as he showed only a glimpse of his best form, because of injury, in 1997. Jamie Tape, coming from Richmond, may release Burns into the midfield.

Mark Richardson has shown he has the ability to take on a tall in defence and may be used as a mobile running ruckman who can push forward to kick goals. However, the Rocca brothers are the keys. Saverio needs to kick pressure goals to get the monkey off his back, while Anthony is still learning but is capable of making a consistent impact — with natural improvement.

Picking up Clinton King from Sydney could give the Pies a crumbing goalkicking option. Damian Monkhorst is another with a chance to answer the critics. If fit, he still has a big role to play.

The Pies showed early last year that at their best they are among the best. The supporters and the internal mechanisms of the club won't accept another year out of the finals.

— **Peter Ryan**

## THE YEAR AHEAD

| Rd | Date | Opponent | Venue | Home/ Away | Time (local) |
|----|------|----------|-------|------------|--------------|
| 1 | March 28 | Hawthorn | MCG | H | 3.30pm |
| 2 | April 3 (N) | West Coast | S | A | 6.40pm |
| 3 | April 11 | Western Bulldogs | OO | A | 2.10pm |
| 4 | April 17 (N) | Richmond | MCG | H | 7.40pm |
| 5 | April 25 | Essendon | MCG | H | 3.30pm |
| 6 | May 2 | Carlton | MCG | A | 3.30pm |
| 7 | May 10 | Sydney | P | H | 2.10pm |
| 8 | May 17 | Melbourne | MCG | A | 2.10pm |
| 9 | May 24 | Port Adelaide | FP | A | 2.50pm |
| 10 | May 31 | Fremantle | VP | H | 2.10pm |
| 11 | June 8 | North Melbourne | MCG | A | 2.10pm |
| 12 | June 14 | St. Kilda | P | H | 2.10pm |
| 13 | June 20 | Adelaide | MCG | H | 2.10pm |
| 14 | June 28 | Brisbane Lions | G | A | 12.40pm |
| 15 | July 5 | Geelong | MCG | H | 2.10pm |
| 16 | July 18 | Hawthorn | P | A | 7.40pm |
| 17 | July 25 | West Coast | P | H | 2.10pm |
| 18 | July 31 (N) | Western Bulldogs | MCG | H | 7.40pm |
| 19 | August 9 | Richmond | MCG | A | 2.10pm |
| 20 | August 15 | Essendon | MCG | A | 2.10pm |
| 21 | August 23 | Carlton | MCG | H | 2.10pm |
| 22 | August 30 | Sydney | SCG | A | 12.40pm |

## 1997 AT A GLANCE

**W:** R1: Collingwood 26.10 (166) v Port Adelaide 13.9 (87) (MCG)
**W:** R2: Melbourne 7.14 (56) v Collingwood 24.19 (163) (MCG)
**L:** R3: St Kilda 19.11 (125) v Collingwood 17.16 (118) (WP)
**L:** R4: Collingwood 12.12 (84) v Carlton 15.11 (101) (MCG)
**W:** R5: Essendon 10.10 (70) v Collingwood 14.15 (99) (MCG)
**W:** R6: Collingwood 13.6 (84) v Adelaide 11.17 (83) (VP)

## SNAPSHOT

**Games:** 22
**Wins:** 10 **Losses:** 12
**Ladder Finish:** 10th
**Players Used:** 35

**W:** R7: North Melbourne 9.14 (68) v Collingwood 17.9 (111) (MCG)
**W:** R8: Collingwood 19.15 (129) v Western Bulldogs 11.17 (83) (MCG)
**L:** R9: Sydney 16.15 (111) v Collingwood 11.8 (74) (SCG)
**L:** R10: Hawthorn 16.12 (108) v Collingwood 8.7 (55) (P)
**L:** R11: Collingwood 10.11 (71) v Richmond 11.11 (77) (MCG)
**L:** R12: Collingwood 7.13 (55) v West Coast 11.5 (71) (VP)
**L:** R13: Brisbane Lions 11.22 (88) v Collingwood 11.7 (73) (G)
**L:** R14: Geelong 9.26 (80) v Collingwood 10.12 (72) (MCG)
**W:** R15: Collingwood 25.10 (160) v Fremantle 9.6 (60) (VP)
**L:** R16: Port Adelaide 17.9 (111) v Collingwood 8.10 (58) (FP)
**W:** R17: Collingwood 20.14 (134) v Melbourne 12.10 (82) (MCG)
**L:** R18: Collingwood 12.17 (89) v St Kilda 15.21 (111) (MCG)
**L:** R19: Carlton 14.23 (107) v Collingwood 13.13 (91) (MCG)
**W:** R20: Collingwood 13.13 (91) v Essendon 12.9 (81) (MCG)
**L:** R21: Adelaide 6.12 (48) v Collingwood 5.9 (39) (FP)
**W:** R22: Collingwood 18.14 (122) v Nth Melbourne 15.21 (111) (MCG)

# The Coach

**Tony Shaw**

**Born:** 23/7/60

June is not a good time for Tony Shaw. In two years as coach of Collingwood, he is yet to win a game in that month.

An eight-game losing streak in the middle of 1996 was matched last year by a six-game losing streak which saw Collingwood fall from top spot after round eight to 11th after round 14. Shaw was at a loss to explain why the season had spiralled downwards after such an auspicious start.

Shaw has been a revelation as coach. His strategies on kick-outs and the creation of loose players inside the Magpies' 50 metres — when they were working early last year — made Collingwood one of the most exciting and interesting teams to watch. He also introduced a full day's training on Mondays.

As the season turned awry, Shaw was frank in his assessments of the team and himself, shouldering the blame and asking the players to ask themselves some hard questions.

Shaw signed for a further two years in May last year, but said that nothing short of a finals appearance in 1998 would justify his staying on.

Shaw and the club want wins on the board — quickly.

## AT A GLANCE

**COACHING RECORD**
**Collingwood**

| Season | P | W | L | D | Pos |
|--------|---|---|---|---|-----|
| 1996 | 22 | 9 | 13 | — | 11 |
| 1996 | 22 | 10 | 12 | — | 10 |
| **Total** | **44** | **19** | **25** | | |

## WIN/LOSS RECORD

| Against | P | W (N) | L (N) | D (N) |
|---|---|---|---|---|
| Adelaide | 11 | 9 (3) | 2 (1) | 0 |
| Brisbane Bears | 15 | 13 (3) | 2 (1) | 0 |
| Brisbane Lions | 1 | 0 | 1 | 0 |
| Carlton | 215 | 100 | 111 (1) | 4 |
| Essendon | 196 | 110 (2) | 82 (1) | 4 |
| Fitzroy | 209 | 131 | 75 | 3 |
| Fremantle | 4 | 3 | 1 (1) | 0 |
| Geelong | 201 | 118 | 82 (1) | 1 |
| Hawthorn | 129 | 84 (1) | 45 | 0 |
| Melbourne | 209 | 133 (1) | 72 | 4 |
| North Melb | 131 | 90 (2) | 39 (3) | 2 |
| Port Adel | 2 | 1 | 1 (1) | 0 |
| Richmond | 177 | 102 | 74 (2) | 1 |
| St Kilda | 189 | 140 (1) | 48 (1) | 1 |
| Sydney | 196 | 124 (1) | 71 (2) | 1 |
| West Coast | 19 | 7 | 11 (1) | 1 |
| W Bulldogs | 123 | 91 (2) | 31 | 1 |
| University | 14 | 13 | 0 | 1 |
| | 2041 | 1269 (16) | 748 (17) | 24 (0) |

*(N) Premiership matches played at night*

## WINNING RUNS

29 v Hawthorn (1925–1941)
19 v Hawthorn (1944–1954)
18 v St Kilda (1897–1903)
17 v North Melb (1964–1973)
16 v SM/Sydney (1924–1933)
14 v W Bulldogs (1977–1983)
14 v Geelong (1901–1907)
13 v Melbourne (1928–1935); (1968–1974)
12 v Melbourne (1912–1921)
12 v North Melb (1925–1932); (1943–1949)
12 v St Kilda (1950–1957)
11 v Essendon (1932–1938)
11 v Fitzroy (1968–1973)
11 v Richmond (1909–1914)
11 v St. Kilda (1977–1982)
11 v Brisbane Bears (1987–1993)
10 v Essendon (1913–1919)
10 v W Bulldogs (1925–1932)
10 v Geelong (1955–1960)
10 v Melbourne (1922–1926); (1977–1981)
10 v North Melb (1933–1939)
5 v Carlton (1897–1899)
5 v Adelaide (1994–1997)
2 v West Coast (1989)
2 v Fremantle (1995–1996)
1 v Port Adelaide (1997)

## 1997 BEST AND FAIREST

A system of assessing each player according to position and performance of the task required. One vote awarded for a good game, two for very good and three for great. There is no limit on how many players can receive votes. Theoretically, if 18 players had a good game they could all receive a vote.

1 Gavin Brown (25)
2 Nathan Buckley (22)
3 Paul Williams (20)
4 Gavin Crosisca (18)
5 Scott Russell (17)
6 Scott Burns (10)
7 Mark Richardson (9)
  Saverio Rocca (9)
9 Mal Michael (8)
  Damian Monkhorst (8)
  Graham Wright (8)

## GAMES RECORDS

**313** Tony Shaw (1978–94)
**306** Gordon Coventry (1920–37)
**277** Wayne Richardson (1966–78)
**268** Len Thompson (1965–78)
**261** 'Jock' McHale (1903–18; 1920)
**253** Harry Collier (1926–40)
**250** Lou Richards (1941–55)
**250** Peter Daicos (1979–93)
**245** Phonse Kyne (1934–44; 1946–50)
**230** Dick Lee (1906–22)

## GOALS RECORDS

**1299** Gordon Coventry (1920–37)
**838** Peter McKenna (1965–75)
**707** Dick Lee (1906–22)
**549** Peter Daicos (1979–93)
**453** Albie Pannam (1933–43; 1945)
**423** Lou Richards (1941–55)
**386** Saverio Rocca (1992– )
**371** Brian Taylor (1985–90)
**337** Des Fothergill (1937–40; 1945–47)
**327** Ron Todd (1935–39)

## HIGHS AND LOWS

| Against | Highest | Lowest | G. W. Margin | G. L. Margin |
|---|---|---|---|---|
| Adelaide | 23.22.160 (1991) | 5.9.39 (1997) | 123 (1991) | 24 (1993) |
| Brisbane Bears | 26.16.172 (1991) | 11.11.77 (1994) | 101 (1991) | 44 (1994) |
| Brisbane Lions | 11.7.73 (1997) | 11.7.73 (1997) | — | 15 (1997) |
| Carlton | 24.14.158 (1971) | 0.9.9 (1900) | 102 (1977) | 104 (1943) |
| Essendon | 30.20.200 (1971) | 2.4.16 (1900) | 147 (1971) | 133 (1984) |
| Fitzroy | 25.17.167 (1930) | 1.5.11 (1898) | 101 (1967) | 95 (1945) |
| Fremantle | 25.10.160 (1997) | 11.16.82 (1996) | 100 (1997) | 24 (1996) |
| Geelong | 28.16.184 (1972) | 1.4.10 (1897) | 97 (1945) | 88 (1982) |
| Hawthorn | 25.19.169 (1979) | 4.12.36 (1961) | 105 (1979) | 125 (1987) |
| Melbourne | 27.11.173 (1996) | 2.2.14 (1960) | 109 (1919) | 94 (1939) |
| North Melb | 26.20.176 (1990) | 2.6.18 (1987) | 113 (1937) | 91 (1974) |
| Port Adel | 26.10.166 (1997) | 8.10.58 (1997) | 79 (1997) | 53 (1997) |
| Richmond | 24.17.161 (1992) | 2.13.25 (1927) | 101 (1986) | 138 (1942) |
| St Kilda | 32.19.211 (1980) | 3.8.26 (1907) | 178 (1979) | 62 (1963) |
| Sydney | 29.11.185 (1985) | 0.8.8 (1897) | 99 (1991) | 91 (1987) |
| West Coast | 20.9.129 (1989) | 7.9.51 (1988) | 59 (1990) | 81 (1991) |
| W Bulldogs | 28.16.184 (1926) | 4.4.28 (1962) | 126 (1926) | 56 (1955) |

## THE LEADERSHIP AT COLLINGWOOD

| Year | Pos | Coach | Captain | Best & Fairest | Leading Goalkicker | |
|------|-----|-------|---------|----------------|--------------------|---|
| 1933 | 6 | J. McHale | S. Coventry | G. Coventry | G. Coventry | 108 |
| 1934 | 4 | J. McHale | S. Coventry | A. Collier | G. Coventry | 105 |
| 1935 | 1 | J. McHale | H. Collier | A. Collier | G. Coventry | 88 |
| 1936 | 1 | J. McHale | H. Collier | J. Regan | G. Coventry | 60 |
| 1937 | 2 | J. McHale | H. Collier | D. Fothergill | G. Coventry | 72 |
| 1938 | 2 | J. McHale | H. Collier | D. Fothergill | R. Todd | 120 |
| 1939 | 2 | J. McHale | H. Collier | M. Whelan | R. Todd | 121 |
| 1940 | 8 | J. McHale | J. Regan | D. Fothergill | D. Fothergill | 56 |
| 1941 | 5 | J. McHale | J. Regan | F. Murphy | A. Pannam | 42 |
| 1942 | 11 | J. McHale | A. Kyne | A. Pannam | A. Pannam | 37 |
| 1943 | 10 | J. McHale | J. Regan | No award | A. Pannam | 40 |
| 1944 | 10 | J. McHale | P. Fricker | No award | L. Richards | 26 |
| 1945 | 3 | J. McHale | A. Pannam | No award | D. Fothergill | 62 |
| 1946 | 3 | J. McHale | A. Kyne | A. Kyne | D. Fothergill | 63 |
| 1947 | 5 | J. McHale | A. Kyne | A. Kyne | N. Mann | 48 |
| 1948 | 3 | J. McHale | A. Kyne | A. Kyne | L. Richards | 44 |
| 1949 | 4 | J. McHale | A. Kyne | R. Rose | J. Pimm | 34 |
| 1950 | 7 | A. Kyne | G. Hocking | C. Utting | L. Richards | 35 |
| 1951 | 3 | A. Kyne | G. Hocking | R. Rose | M. Dunstan | 40 |
| 1952 | 2 | A. Kyne | L. Richards | R. Rose | M. Dunstan | 43 |
| 1953 | 1 | A. Kyne | L. Richards | R. Rose | R. Rose | 36 |
| 1954 | 7 | A. Kyne | L. Richards | N. Mann | K. Bromage | 22 |
| 1955 | 2 | A. Kyne | L. Richards | D. Healey | K. Smale | 47 |
| 1956 | 2 | A. Kyne | N. Mann | W. Twomey | K. Smale | 33 |
| 1957 | 5 | A. Kyne | W. Twomey | M. Weideman | I. Brewer | 26 |
| 1958 | 1 | A. Kyne | F. Tuck | T. Merrett | I. Brewer | 73 |
| 1959 | 4 | A. Kyne | F. Tuck | T. Merrett | M. Weideman | 36 |
| 1960 | 2 | A. Kyne | M. Weideman | R. Gabelich | M. Weideman | 30 |
| 1961 | 9 | A. Kyne | M. Weideman | M. Weideman | K. Pay | 31 |
| 1962 | 7 | A. Kyne | M. Weideman | M. Weideman | M. Weideman | 48 |
| 1963 | 8 | A. Kyne | M. Weideman | D. Tuddenham | T. Waters | 50 |
| 1964 | 2 | R. Rose | R. Gabelich | I. Graham | T. Waters | 43 |
| 1965 | 3 | R. Rose | R. Gabelich | T. Steer | D. Norman | 32 |
| | | | J. Henderson | | | |
| 1966 | 2 | R. Rose | D. Tuddenham | T. Waters | I. Graham | 58 |
| 1967 | 4 | R. Rose | D. Tuddenham | L. Thompson | P. McKenna | 47 |
| 1968 | 7 | R. Rose | D. Tuddenham | L. Thompson | P. McKenna | 64 |
| 1969 | 3 | R. Rose | D. Tuddenham | B. Price | P. McKenna | 98 |
| 1970 | 2 | R. Rose | T. Waters | P. McKenna | P. McKenna | 143 |
| 1971 | 4 | R. Rose | T. Waters | | | |
| | | | W. Richardson | W. Richardson | P. McKenna | 134 |
| 1972 | 4 | N. Mann | W. Richardson | L. Thompson | P. McKenna | 130 |
| 1973 | 3 | N. Mann | W. Richardson | L. Thompson | P. McKenna | 86 |
| 1974 | 4 | N. Mann | W. Richardson | W. Richardson | P. McKenna | 69 |
| 1975 | 5 | M. Weideman | W. Richardson | P. Carman | P. Carman | 41 |
| 1976 | 12 | M. Weideman | D. Tuddenham | R. Hyde | P. Carman | 38 |
| 1977 | 2 | T. Hafey | M. Richardson | L. Thompson | P. Moore | 76 |
| 1978 | 3 | T. Hafey | L. Thompson | R. Shaw | P. Moore | 57 |
| 1979 | 2 | T. Hafey | R. Shaw | P. Moore | C. Davis | 88 |
| 1980 | 2 | T. Hafey | R. Shaw | P. Moore | C. Davis | 52 |
| 1981 | 2 | T. Hafey | P. Moore | M. Williams | P. Daicos | 76 |
| 1982 | 10 | T. Hafey/M. Erwin | P. Moore | P. Daicos | P. Daicos | 58 |
| 1983 | 6 | J. Cahill | M. Williams | W. Picken | M. Richardson | 49 |
| 1984 | 3 | J. Cahill | M. Williams | A. Shaw | M. Williams | 53 |
| 1985 | 7 | R. Rose | M. Williams | M. Williams | B. Taylor | 80 |
| 1986 | 6 | R. Rose/L. Matthews | M. Williams | W. Fellowes | B. Taylor | 100 |
| 1987 | 12 | L. Matthews | A. Shaw | D. Millane | B. Taylor | 60 |
| 1988 | 4 | L. Matthews | A. Shaw | P. Daicos | B. Taylor | 73 |
| 1989 | 5 | L. Matthews | A. Shaw | G. Brown | B. Taylor | 49 |
| 1990 | 1 | L. Matthews | A. Shaw | A. Shaw | P. Daicos | 97 |
| 1991 | 7 | L. Matthews | A. Shaw | T. Francis | P. Daicos | 75 |
| 1992 | 5 | L. Matthews | A. Shaw | M. McGuane | P. Daicos | 52 |
| 1993 | 8 | L. Matthews | A. Shaw | M. McGuane | S. Rocca | 73 |
| 1994 | 8 | L. Matthews | G. Brown | G. Brown/N. Buckley | S. Rocca | 49 |
| 1995 | 10 | L. Matthews | G. Brown | S. Rocca | S. Rocca | 93 |
| 1996 | 11 | T. Shaw | G. Brown | N. Buckley | S. Rocca | 66 |
| 1997 | 10 | T. Shaw | G. Brown | G. Brown | S. Rocca | 76 |

# PLAYER PROFILES

### GAVIN BROWN

Playing across half-back, Brown, 30, produced a top year to answer any doubters who had written him off at the start of the season. He played every game, won the best and fairest for the third time, captained Victoria and won the EJ Whitten Medal for best on ground as the Vics beat South Australia. His courage has never been doubted, just whether his body could continue to stand up to the rigors of AFL football. Despite expressing a preference for playing on the wing at times, Brown's attacking play off half-back was a highlight. He is rarely, if ever, beaten in a one-on-one contest and his marking and ability to dispose of the ball skilfully in heavy traffic is one of the game's highlights.

**Player honors:** best and fairest 1989, 1994 (equal), 1997; 2nd best and fairest 1991; 3rd best and fairest 1988 (equal); All-Australian 1991, 1994; EJ Whitten Medal 1989, 1997; premiership side 1990; captain since 1994; Victorian captain 1997.

### NATHAN BUCKLEY

One of the game's bonafide superstars. Didn't put in a bad performance in 1997 and his skill level, particularly his kicking, rose to another level. After round 22, he was the highest kick-getter in the AFL with 453 kicks (averaging 20.59 kicks per game). It is difficult to see how the Magpies would cope if Buckley was out for an extended time such is his capacity, at times, to almost single-handedly keep them in the contest. One of the most professional athletes in the game, runs all day and, above all else, hates losing. Playing in the midfield, his kicking out from full-back after a behind has made this part of the game an exciting spectacle. The only current player in Collingwood's Team of the Century last year and won the Jesaulenko Medal for his performance captaining The Allies. The fact that Buckley has kept firing for so long, yet Collingwood still hasn't been able to build a consistent winning combination around him, must haunt the Collingwood faithful.

**Player honors:** best and fairest 1994 (equal), 1996; 2nd best and fairest 1993, 1997; All-Australian 1996, 1997; Margarey Medal 1992; AFL Norwich Rising Star 1993; Jesaulenko Medal 1997; Allies captain 1997.

**Previous AFL club:** Brisbane Bears (1993: 20 games, 21 goals).

### SCOTT BURNS

Hampered by a groin injury in 1997 (osteitis-pubis, inflammation of the pubic bone) and apart from a slashing game against North Melbourne (20 kicks, 13 marks, 8 handballs), was incapable of showing his best form. Showed courage to play in 14 games for the year, but his reliability, either in defence or the midfield, were sorely missed. Burns and Collingwood finally gave into the problem by August 14 and he had an operation on his groin and missed early pre-season training. Fully fit, he is a tough reliable half-back flanker who runs straight and reads the play well.

**Player honors:** 2nd best and fairest 1996.

### GAVIN CROSISCA

Responded magnificently to being dropped for the round 12 game against the West Coast Eagles last year, returning as a crucial part of the midfield that tried hard to turn the season around. Only 29, tough as ankle-high boots and is assuming leadership responsibilities that come with experience. Played his 200th game in 1997. His game is so simple, disciplined (apart from an indiscretion against Adelaide in round 21, which gave away a vital 50-metre penalty) and reliable that it is hard to see the left-footer producing anything else but another great season.

**Player honors:** 3rd best and fairest 1989, 1995; premiership side 1990.

### SCOTT CROW

A dislocated collarbone suffered against Melbourne in round 17 ended his 1997 season. Is in the middle rung of Collingwood players, but gives indications that he is capable of more. Playing in the midfield, he is good in close and marks exceptionally well for his size, though his disposal sometimes lacks penetration. Well respected at Collingwood and even at current form is easily in the Pies' best team. Had a contract dispute over summer but it was quickly resolved by player and club.

**Previous AFL club:** Hawthorn (1993-95: 13 games, 2 goals).

### CHRIS CURRAN

An underrated run-with player who looked set to finally put together a full season of senior football. Played the first 12 games of 1997 — his highest yearly tally to date — and then broke down. A broken jaw suffered in a round 17 reserves game, as he made his way back, ended his season. There was speculation last October that he was offered to St Kilda as part of a deal to entice the Saints into trading Jamie Shanahan. Curran has been unlucky with injuries, but is a great survivor having played his first reserves game with Richmond in 1992. He enters 1998 with the benefit of a surgery-free summer — an unusual occurrence.

### MATTHEW FRANCIS

A tall, mobile ruckman who needs to improve his output. Doesn't take enough marks for his size (28 in 15 games in 1997), nor are his hitout totals very high (28 in 1997). Forced to shoulder all of the ruckwork in the final two rounds in 1997 when Monkhorst was out through suspension, he performed manfully against Adelaide and North Melbourne, which have two of the best big men in the game. This year the ruck position is up for grabs and Francis has resigned from his job to commit himself to full-time football.

**Previous AFL club:** Richmond (1990-92, 1994: 19 games, 13 goals).

### TONY FRANCIS

A persistent groin injury suffered in a Traralgon practice match virtually ruined his '97 season. Starting in round four, he copped a one-week suspension, then was injured again in round six. Played eight games after round 13, but his only performance of note was against Melbourne when he kicked four goals, including a dribbling miracle six-pointer. May be of value as a goalsneak in the forward pocket as it appears his days as a genuine high quality rover are over. Still one of the cheekiest little men in the business.

**Player honors:** best and fairest 1991; 3rd best and fairest 1996 (equal); All-Australian 1991; premiership side 1990.

## BRAD FULLER

A reasonable debut year in which he earned senior selection against the Brisbane Lions, registered one kick (in a short on-field stint) and was dropped the next week. Kicked 28 goals in 20 reserves games, despite being tagged most weeks after a big opening game in which he kicked five goals. A small opportunist type who has good skills.

## MICHAEL GARDINER

Drafted in 1996, but arrived from WA in December 1997 after completing university. A basketball background in WA means he may need time, but Collingwood will be hoping the tall youngster might be able to fit into a key post.

## SHANNON GIBSON

Drafted by Hawthorn in 1993 after being best on ground for the Preston Knights in their premiership win that year. In four seasons he managed just 25 AFL games, the highlight being five goals in the first half against Geelong last season.

**Previous AFL club:** Hawthorn (1995-97: 25 games, 18 goals).

## LUKE GODDEN

A semi-trailer would reverse if it saw Godden running straight at it. Played three games near the end of the season across half-back, before a cartilage problem kept him out of the last two. Despite doubts aired publicly by former Collingwood champion Peter Daicos about his capacity at AFL level, Godden performed reasonably well. Has a fierce determination and showed poise last year when in possession, particularly when under pressure against Essendon.

## CLINTON KING

The lightly built youngster from Victoria spent two years at the Sydney Swans and despite impressing in his brief appearances, wasn't able to break into the line-up. Has very good skills, evasive ability and goal-kicking prowess, but needs to develop his strength. Finished equal runner-up in the 1997 Gardiner Medal.

**Previous AFL club:** Sydney (1996-97: 9 games, 4 goals).

## BEN KINNEAR

Stand-out player in pyschomotor testing at AFL draft camp, scoring perfect 10s for hand movement speed, peripheral vision and peripheral awareness — the only player to do so. Spent last year playing at centre half-back for Central Districts' reserves and under-19s, impressing with his strength overhead, good concentration and discipline in defence. Represented South Australia in the 1997 AFL Under-18 National Championships.

## TROY KIRWEN

Late starter who joined Preston Knights halfway through 1997 and excelled at centre half-back. Very athletic, represented Victoria in basketball at under-19 level last year and was third in state high jump in the past two years. Turned 18 in December.

## CHAD LIDDELL

Moved into defence for the second half against Melbourne in round 17 and finally something clicked. Played the last six games in the back half and slotted in well. A great mark for his size and a tough, hard tackler.

## JOSH MAHONEY

Impressed in eight games in '97 with his courageous attack on the football and willingness to put his relatively small frame on the line. Unfortunately made mistakes that had drastic consequences on the scoreboard when Collingwood played Adelaide at the end of last year, but will have learnt a great deal from the experience. Had a solid debut year and will bulk up a bit more to suit his style of play.

## STUART MANGIN

Former Preston Knights premiership player drafted to Sydney in 1994 (No. 20). Played 63 games for 37 goals in the Swans reserves over three years before being traded to Collingwood. Was on the verge of senior selection several times, but injured himself before he could grab his chance. A strongly built left-footer and an excellent kick.

## ALEX McDONALD

Has played 41 out of a possible 44 games since joining the Magpies in 1996. Can match up on a variety of opponents, but needs to be tougher in winning contests and not just playing a link man role. Dropped a couple of times last season as Collingwood served notice it wasn't about to accept mediocrity from him.

**Player honors:** Hawthorn night series premiership 1991, 1992.

**Previous AFL club:** Hawthorn (1990-95: 46 games, 24 goals).

## MALCOLM MICHAEL

A rapid footballing ascension in 1997. Placed on the rookie list, he was put on the Magpies' senior list and made his debut in round seven against North Melbourne. Became the first player in the AFL to come off a rookie list to play senior football. Played at full-back and grew from a defensive spoiler to show glimpses of attacking defensive football. Earned an AFL Norwich Rising Star nomination and Collingwood was rapt with his progress.

**Player honors:** AFL Norwich Rising Star nominee 1997.

## DAMIAN MONKHORST

Made a fantastic start last season, then everything began to go wrong. Started looking aggressive, fit and skilful, but by season's end, appeared slow, lacking in confidence and at the crossroads. Needs to be fully fit to have an impact and struggled to adapt to players such as Peter Everitt running forward. Players of his quality don't just drop out of the sky, so it is up to Monkhorst to be fit and Collingwood to find the best way to use the big ruckman.

**Player honors:** 3rd best and fairest 1992 (equal), 1993, 1994; premiership side 1990.

## RICHARD OSBORNE

Played well in the last eight weeks of 1997 as an attacking half-back flanker. With the trend to having players run through the lines from half-back, he might just fill a role. It's just a pity he is reaching the end of his career. His qualities are his marking, pace — even at 33 — and long kicking.

**Player honors:** Fitzroy 2nd best and fairest 1984; Fitzroy leading goalkicker 1986, 1987, 1988, 1989, 1992; Western Bulldogs leading goalkicker 1995; Fitzroy captain 1991.

**Previous AFL clubs:** Fitzroy (1982-92: 187 games, 411 goals); Sydney (1993: 16 games, 39 goals); Western Bulldogs (1994-96: 51 games, 98 goals).

## STEPHEN PATTERSON

Was burning early in the season, but seemed to get lost midway before returning to capture three Brownlow votes in the last game. Needs to kick more goals if playing up forward or improve his general disposal to be a quality midfielder. Has pace and endurance, but is sometimes rushed and uncertain in his delivery by hand or foot. Played football full time last year.

## SIMON PRESTIGIACOMO

Had a nightmare game against St Kilda in round three last year and was dropped a week later. Earmarked to play at full-back — a tough call for a 19-year-old entering his second year — he had some second-year blues. After being tried a couple of times up the field later in the year, he was diagnosed as having glandular fever and his season was over. A tall, tight-checking player with good skills.

## ANDREW PUGSLEY

Impressed on the rookie list last year. Collingwood admits it is taking a bit of a punt, but he has good endurance, is an accurate kick for goal and in the second half of last year was kicking regular goals in the reserves, including a couple of bags of four and five.

## FRANK RASO

Played in two Preston Knights premierships, was vice-captain in 1997 and played a blinder in the preliminary final attempting to get them to their fifth consecutive premiership. Very quick, aggressive rover/ruck-rover type who is strong at the ball. Needs to polish up on his skills, but there will soon be a place for a rover in the Collingwood structure.

## MARK RICHARDSON

His loss to a thigh injury after playing the first 17 rounds in 1997 was a huge blow. One of the Pies' most consistent performers until that point, Richardson was like a new recruit for the Pies minding the opposition talls across half-back. It was a Shaw move in round three against St Kilda that unearthed his capacity there. Richardson is mobile, has a good pair of hands and his ability to read the play makes him useful around the ground as a second ruckman. Becoming crucial to the Pies' on-field balance.

## ANTHONY ROCCA

Exciting early last year, showing aggression at the contest and confidence in his ability. Form dropped away to such an extent that he started at centre half-back in the last round. A confidence player, but is only young and people at Collingwood are still willing to give him time. Was a high profile recruit without much senior experience and from that perspective, did well to kick 34 goals in 21 games.

**Previous AFL club:** Sydney (1995-96: 22 games, 11 goals).

## SAVERIO ROCCA

Second in the AFL's goalkicking in 1997, kicking 76 goals including one bag of 10 and one of nine. So why was he one of the most disappointing players in the game last year? Because he missed important goals from set shots whenever the pressure was on. Against Carlton both times and then cruelly under the national spotlight against Adelaide in round 21, he was unable to convert gettable chances. It was a letdown for the Pies as Rocca seemed to drop the bundle when things went wrong. Saverio has kicked 386 goals and is just 24, so has plenty of time and ability to answer his critics. And Collingwood supporters were among his most strident last year.

**Player honors:** best and fairest 1995; AFL Norwich Rising Star nominee 1993; leading goalkicker 1993, 1994, 1995, 1996, 1997.

## SCOTT RUSSELL

Ever reliable and once again highly placed in best and fairest voting. Also polled well in the Brownlow Medal. Played every game, mainly as a running half-back, picking up plenty of the ball. Had the most handballs for Collingwood last year, but his game is centred around his capacity to run tirelessly all day and attack from defence. An important player in the midfield structure.

**Player honors:** 3rd best and fairest 1990 (equal), 1991, 1992, 1996 (equal); premiership side 1990.

## ANDREW SCHAUBLE

Down on his sensational 1996 form last season, but was impeded by a rib and back injury suffered during a clash with Essendon's Dean Wallis. Sure ball-handling was not affected, but he certainly got less of the football. A tall, lean athlete with a great pair of hands who was tried as a mobile marking forward towards the end of last year with fair results. Has made his name as a slightly undersized centre half-back of high quality.

**Player honors:** AFL Norwich Rising Star nominee 1996.

## BRAD SMITH

A former Claremont and then Richmond reserves player. Very tall, but has good balance and rucks well. The Pies think he might be a late developer.

## JAMIE TAPE

Career has mirrored that of Richmond — the side he joined in 1994 from South Australia. As the Tigers climbed the ladder, Tape was superb, marking beautifully across half-back and attacking the football courageously. Those attributes then seemed to desert him as he was often caught out of position, appearing slow and his poor disposal was exposed in the last two years. Played only eight games in 1997, but if he can return to anywhere near his 1995 form, the Pies have gained a genuinely good player.

**Player honors:** AFL Norwich Rising Star nominee 1994.

**Previous AFL club:** Richmond (1994-97: 75 games, 4 goals).

## CHRIS TARRANT

Collingwood's first choice in the 1997 National Draft at No. 8, Tarrant is an exciting left-footed key position player. From South Mildura, he was the winner of the AFL life membership scholarship and an All-Australian at under-16 level in 1996. Underwent a shoulder reconstruction at the end of 1996, but recovered well before another setback — he broke his wrist — soured his pre-season.

## BRENT TUCKEY

Youngest, at 17, to come through the 1996 National Draft, Tuckey moved from Stawell and was on the verge of senior selection by the final round. Was completing VCE last year and trying to put a bit of bulk on his slender frame. Still needs work in that area, but he's quick for his height, marks well and played his most impressive football up forward last year. The Pies are hoping he can make it as a mobile ruck, key position type but are prepared to be patient.

## JAMES WASLEY

Rated as a flying machine, Wasley played 10 senior games for Norwood (a frequent Collingwood talent source) in 1997, but was not in its premiership side. Probably best suited to a wing, but still needs to work on his skills.

## SHANE WATSON

Played all but one match last season — missed through suspension — and appeared to be returning to near his best form at half-back before being knocked out against Richmond in round 11. Played the next week, but it took a while for him to regain his confidence. Started at Collingwood at full-forward and represented Victoria as a half-back flanker in 1993 — the year he was runner-up in Collingwood's best and fairest. Since then, has not settled in one position and has showed only glimpses of his true ability. A courageous footballer who is a good mark for his size and has reasonable disposal.
**Player honors:** 2nd best and fairest 1993.

## SCOTT WHISTON

Born in England, but moved to Australia at about the age of one. A super-fit triathlete who competed at South Australian state level. Played mostly schoolboy football and was a late starter to the game. A running half-back flanker who will need time to develop.

## JASON WILD

Run-with player given more opportunities this year. Can frustrate at times with his inaccurate disposal, which he needs to work on, but the redhead is a goer and with natural improvement, can fill a tagging role.

## PAUL WILLIAMS

Probably the best running goalkicker in the game. Is explosively quick, carries the ball well and is also an important centre square player. Lifted a notch, becoming a more consistent ball-getter and showed an ability to break free of taggers. Has an ability to pull off individual efforts resulting in goals from nowhere through sheer pace. Fantastic to watch.

**Player honors:** 2nd best and fairest 1995, 3rd best and fairest 1996 (equal), 1997.

## GRAHAM WRIGHT

Returned in round three, 1997, from a knee reconstruction and played every game until he hurt an ankle in round 20. Played mainly across half-back with the customary Wright courage, but was lacking a bit of the usual dash. Turns 30 this year and in 1997, looked to be nearing the end of his career. A great player for Collingwood. Was one of the new breed that provided the improvement necessary for a premiership and needs only 18 games to play 200. Definitely good enough when fit, even on last year's form, to be in the Pies' best 21.
**Player honors:** 2nd Brownlow Medal 1990, 3rd best and fairest 1990 (equal); premiership side 1990.

# ROOKIE LIST

## GEORGE BAKOULAS

A well-built key position player who has trained with Collingwood since November. The club has been impressed with his rate of improvement, describing him as probably their best player off the list in the pre-season. Has good pace, marking and jumping ability. Played with the Calder Cannons and was a state junior sprint champion.

## MARCUS BARHAM

Chosen towards the end of the 1996 National Draft, but was delisted after last year. Stress fractures denied him a pre-season in 1997, but he showed great improvement in 17 reserves games before problems with stress fractures again emerged. Needs to work on his skill levels and general fitness, but has trained hard since the delisting.

## ADAM COLLINGS

Big wraps from the Eastern Ranges sparked the Pies' interest. Didn't play last year due to a knee reconstruction but has good pace.

## FRANK DIMMATINA

Son of Frank, the former Richmond premiership player, and brother of Paul at the Western Bulldogs. Small, tough player from the Oakleigh Chargers. Has good pace, fair skills and attacks the footy hard.

## TARKYN LOCKYER

Strongly built back pocket player from East Fremantle, who has fair pace and is an excellent kick on both sides. Performed well for Western Australia in last year's AFL National Under-18 Championships. Has excellent vision.

## MARK MATTHEWS

Left-footer with solid build and good pace, who trained with St Kilda and Melbourne reserves this summer. Virtually didn't play footy for seven years as he concentrated on a burgeoning tennis career which saw him rated in the top five under-18 players in Australia. When an opportunity at an American university fell through, he returned to play football with Croydon, then Box Hill.

# COLLINGWOOD

| Name (# = rookie) | No. | Born | Height | Weight | Recruited from |
|---|---|---|---|---|---|
| Gavin Brown | 26 | 25/9/67 | 183 | 84 | TEMPLESTOWE |
| Nathan Buckley | 5 | 26/7/72 | 186 | 89 | SOUTHERN DISTS(NT)/PORT ADEL (SA)//BRISBANE |
| Scott Burns | 17 | 23/12/74 | 178 | 75 | NORWOOD (SA) |
| Gavin Crosisca | 28 | 15/9/68 | 188 | 89 | WESTERN DISTRICTS (QLD) |
| Scott Crow | 39 | 18/12/73 | 179 | 80 | PORT FAIRY/HAWTHORN |
| Chris Curran | 24 | 3/8/74 | 178 | 76 | BORONIA/RICHMOND RESERVES/BOX HILL |
| Matthew Francis | 9 | 29/8/70 | 196 | 86 | BALLAN/RICHMOND |
| Tony Francis | 2 | 1/4/69 | 171 | 74 | NORWOOD (SA) |
| Brad Fuller | 11 | 8/8/78 | 176 | 75 | EASTLAKE (ACT)/NSW-ACT U18 |
| Michael R. Gardiner | 37 | 22/3/78 | 197 | 92 | SUBIACO (WA) |
| Shannon Gibson | 38 | 7/11/75 | 181 | 84 | PRESTON/NORTHERN U18/HAWTHORN |
| Luke Godden | 43 | 21/9/78 | 180 | 80 | YARRAMBAT/NORTHERN U18 |
| Clinton King | 40 | 24/3/78 | 179 | 67 | HEATHERDALE/EASTERN U18/SYDNEY |
| Ben Kinnear | 30 | 27/2/79 | 192 | 88 | CENTRAL DISTRICT (SA) |
| Troy Kirwen | 45 | 20/12/79 | 190 | 80 | BUNDOORA/PRESTON U18 |
| Chad Liddell | 33 | 21/1/77 | 185 | 80 | MORDI-BRAESIDE/SOUTHERN U18 |
| Josh Mahoney | 8 | 31/10/77 | 183 | 78 | ST KEVINS/WESTERN U18/WILLIAMSTOWN |
| Stuart Mangin | 25 | 8/2/77 | 190 | 95 | MACLEOD/NORTHERN U18/SYDNEY RESERVES |
| Alex McDonald | 27 | 13/2/70 | 186 | 82 | BALLARAT YCW/HAWTHORN |
| Malcolm Michael | 48 | 24/6/77 | 190 | 88 | MORNINGSIDE (QLD) |
| Damian Monkhorst | 1 | 21/8/69 | 203 | 104 | WOORI YALLOCK |
| Richard Osborne | 44 | 16/6/64 | 182 | 86 | BULLEEN-TEMPLESTOWE/FITZ/SYD/FOOTS |
| Stephen Patterson | 6 | 4/1/71 | 175 | 72 | NORWOOD (SA) |
| Simon Prestigiacomo | 35 | 31/1/78 | 189 | 81 | RESEARCH/NORTHERN U18 |
| Andrew Pugsley | 47 | 25/7/78 | 186 | 81 | SCORESBY/EASTERN U18 |
| Frank Raso | 46 | 12/9/79 | 176 | 73 | PRESTON RSL/PRESTON U18 |
| Mark Richardson | 3 | 31/10/72 | 193 | 92 | MACLEOD |
| Anthony Rocca | 23 | 15/8/77 | 193 | 103 | NTH RESERVOIR-LAKESIDE/NORTHERN U18/SYDN |
| Saverio Rocca | 36 | 20/11/73 | 194 | 107 | NORTH RESERVOIR-LAKESIDE |
| Scott Russell | 29 | 7/5/70 | 180 | 75 | STURT (SA) |
| Andrew Schauble | 12 | 17/11/76 | 192 | 85 | XAVIER COLLEGE |
| Bradley Smith | 15 | 7/7/77 | 201 | 98 | CLAREMONT (WA)/RICHMOND RESERVES |
| Jamie Tape | 13 | 5/4/74 | 188 | 89 | WOODVILLE-WEST TORRENS (SA)/RICHMOND |
| Chris Tarrant | 20 | 18/12/80 | 191 | 78 | SOUTH MILDURA/BENDIGO U18 |
| Brent Tuckey | 21 | 27/8/79 | 191 | 78 | STAWELL/BALLARAT U18 |
| James Wasley | 16 | 19/7/79 | 183 | 76 | NORWOOD (SA) |
| Shane Watson | 14 | 17/2/74 | 185 | 80 | MONTMORENCY |
| Scott Whiston | 31 | 17/5/70 | 183 | 74 | CENTRAL DISTRICT (SA) |
| Jason Wild | 22 | 10/2/76 | 182 | 78 | COLLINGULLIE-ASHMONT (NSW) |
| Paul Williams | 10 | 3/4/73 | 177 | 81 | NORTH HOBART (TAS) |
| Graham Wright | 19 | 6/6/68 | 178 | 84 | DEVONPORT (TAS) |
| George Bakoulas # | 50 | 20/1/79 | 194 | 92 | TULLAMARINE/CALDER U18 |
| Marcus Barham # | 32 | 19/10/78 | 186 | 85 | GISBORNE/CALDER U18 |
| Adam Collings # | 52 | 3/3/79 | 181 | 78 | CROYDON/EASTERN U18 |
| Frank Dimattina # | 51 | 4/1/79 | 175 | 75 | BULLEEN-TEMPLESTOWE/OAKLEIGH U18 |
| Tarkyn Lockyer # | 53 | 30/10/79 | 176 | 76 | EAST FREMANTLE (WA) |
| Mark Matthews # | 41 | 14/7/77 | 176 | 76 | BOX HILL |
| **Total/(Average)** *On 26/2/98 | | **(23.1 yrs)*** | **(186)** | **(83)** | |

# PLAYERS 1998

| Debut | HOME & AWAY | | 1997 | | FINALS | | GRAND FINALS | | | NIGHT SERIES | | STATE OF ORIGIN | |
|---|---|---|---|---|---|---|---|---|---|---|---|---|---|
| | Gms | Gls | Gms | Gls | Gms | Gls | Gms | Gls | Won | Gms | Gls | Gms | Gls |
| 1987 | 204 | 145 | 22 | 1 | 9 | 21 | 1 | 2 | 1 | 11 | 9 | 11 | 2 |
| 1993 | 107 | 105 | 22 | 20 | 1 | 1 | | | | 8 | 8 | 4 | 8 |
| 1995 | 56 | 16 | 14 | 6 | | | | | | 3 | 0 | 1 | 0 |
| 1987 | 202 | 55 | 21 | 6 | 8 | 6 | 1 | 2 | 1 | 14 | 1 | 7 | 2 |
| 1993 | 49 | 17 | 14 | 8 | | | | | | 5 | 1 | 0 | 0 |
| 1995 | 31 | 13 | 12 | 8 | | | | | | 1 | 0 | 0 | 0 |
| 1990 | 44 | 23 | 15 | 8 | | | | | | 6 | 2 | 0 | 0 |
| 1990 | 132 | 94 | 10 | 8 | 6 | 7 | 1 | 0 | 1 | 7 | 3 | 6 | 4 |
| 1997 | 1 | 0 | 1 | 0 | | | | | | 1 | 0 | 0 | 0 |
| | 0 | 0 | 0 | 0 | | | | | | 0 | 0 | 0 | 0 |
| 1995 | 25 | 18 | 11 | 14 | | | | | | 1 | 1 | 0 | 0 |
| 1997 | 3 | 0 | 3 | 0 | | | | | | 0 | 0 | 0 | 0 |
| 1996 | 9 | 4 | 4 | 1 | | | | | | 0 | 0 | 0 | 0 |
| | 0 | 0 | 0 | 0 | | | | | | 0 | 0 | 0 | 0 |
| | 0 | 0 | 0 | 0 | | | | | | 0 | 0 | 0 | 0 |
| 1995 | 20 | 12 | 8 | 6 | | | | | | 2 | 3 | 0 | 0 |
| 1997 | 8 | 4 | 8 | 4 | | | | | | 1 | 0 | 0 | 0 |
| | 0 | 0 | 0 | 0 | | | | | | 1 | 0 | 0 | 0 |
| 1990 | 87 | 36 | 19 | 3 | 2 | 0 | | | | 11 | 2 | 0 | 0 |
| 1997 | 13 | 0 | 13 | 0 | | | | | | | | 0 | 0 |
| 1988 | 174 | 37 | 20 | 6 | 7 | 1 | 1 | 1 | 1 | 9 | 3 | 2 | 2 |
| 1982 | 269 | 568 | 15 | 20 | 9 | 12 | | | | 19 | 43 | 7 | 6 |
| 1995 | 57 | 60 | 18 | 14 | | | | | | 4 | 3 | 0 | 0 |
| 1996 | 18 | 0 | 6 | 0 | | | | | | 1 | 0 | 0 | 0 |
| | 0 | 0 | 0 | 0 | | | | | | 0 | 0 | 0 | 0 |
| | 0 | 0 | 0 | 0 | | | | | | 0 | 0 | 0 | 0 |
| 1991 | 65 | 51 | 17 | 6 | | | | | | 7 | 6 | 0 | 0 |
| 1995 | 43 | 45 | 21 | 34 | | | | | | 2 | 4 | 0 | 0 |
| 1992 | 110 | 386 | 21 | 76 | 1 | 0 | | | | 7 | 14 | 0 | 0 |
| 1990 | 167 | 102 | 22 | 11 | 6 | 7 | 1 | 2 | 1 | 10 | 6 | 8 | 9 |
| 1995 | 45 | 6 | 20 | 1 | | | | | | 1 | 0 | 0 | 0 |
| | 0 | 0 | 0 | 0 | | | | | | 0 | 0 | 0 | 0 |
| 1994 | 75 | 4 | 8 | 0 | 3 | 0 | | | | 5 | 0 | 1 | 0 |
| | 0 | 0 | 0 | 0 | | | | | | 0 | 0 | 0 | 0 |
| | 0 | 0 | 0 | 0 | | | | | | 0 | 0 | 0 | 0 |
| | 0 | 0 | 0 | 0 | | | | | | 0 | 0 | 0 | 0 |
| 1991 | 109 | 64 | 21 | 6 | 1 | 0 | | | | 9 | 4 | 1 | 0 |
| | 0 | 0 | 0 | 0 | | | | | | | | 0 | 0 |
| 1995 | 47 | 14 | 19 | 6 | | | | | | 3 | 1 | 0 | 0 |
| 1991 | 135 | 173 | 22 | 28 | 1 | 0 | | | | 5 | 4 | 4 | 7 |
| 1988 | 182 | 106 | 18 | 6 | 8 | 1 | 1 | 0 | 1 | 5 | 1 | 2 | 1 |
| | 0 | 0 | 0 | 0 | | | | | | 0 | 0 | | |
| | 0 | 0 | 0 | 0 | | | | | | 0 | 0 | | |
| | 0 | 0 | 0 | 0 | | | | | | 0 | 0 | | |
| | 0 | 0 | 0 | 0 | | | | | | 0 | 0 | | |
| | 0 | 0 | 0 | 0 | | | | | | 0 | 0 | | |
| | 0 | 0 | 0 | 0 | | | | | | 0 | 0 | | |
| | (61) | (53) | 445 | 307 | 62 | 56 | 6 | 7 | 6 | 159 | 119 | 54 | 41 |

## Bombers at a glance

**ADDRESS:** Napier Street, Essendon, Vic 3040
**POSTAL ADDRESS:** PO Box 17, Essendon, Vic 3040
**TELEPHONE:** (03) 9230 0300
**FACSIMILE:** (03) 9370 6804
**WEB SITE:** essendonfc.com.au
**CHAIRMAN:** Graeme McMahon
**CHIEF EXECUTIVE OFFICER:** Peter Jackson
**PLAYER DEVELOPMENT MANAGER:** Matthew Drain
**FOOTBALL ADMINISTRATION MANAGER:** Michael Quinlan
**MEMBERSHIP MANAGER:** Bernadette Dargan
**RECRUITING AND WELFARE MANAGER:** Adrian Dodoro
**COMMUNICATIONS MANAGER:** Alan Murphy
**COACHING STAFF:** Kevin Sheedy (senior); Robert Kerr (assistant, AFL), Mark Thompson (assistant, reserves), Mark Harvey (assistant)
**SELECTION COMMITTEE:** Kevin Sheedy, Charlie Payne (chairman), Mark Thompson, Kevin Egan, David Collins, Robert Kerr (ex-officio)
**CLUB DOCTORS:** Bruce Reid, Ian Reynolds
**CLUB PHYSIOTHERAPIST:** Bruce Connor
**JOINED AFL:** 1897
**HOME GROUND:** MCG, Yarra Park, Jolimont
**GROUND DIMENSIONS:** 161m by 140m. Goals run east to west
**TRAINING VENUE:** Windy Hill, Napier Street, Essendon
**OFFICIAL COLORS:** Guernsey: Black with a red sash. Socks: Red with black hoops. Shorts: Black
**PREMIERSHIPS:** 1897, 1901, 1911-12, 1923-24, 1942, 1946, 1949-50, 1962, 1965, 1984-85, 1993
**BROWNLOW MEDALLISTS:** R. S. Reynolds (1934, 1937, 1938), W. H. Hutchison (1952 tied, 1953), G. Moss, (1976), G. Wanganeen (1993), J. Hird (1996 tied)
**RECORD HOME ATTENDANCE:** 87,638 — April 12, 1993 v Collingwood

# ESSENDON

# Revamped and fit; Bombers look hot

After a horrific year in 1997, ruined by injuries, football department revamping, resignations and dashed expectations, Essendon finished in fine style, showing enough to be installed near the top of early premiership betting.

A six-point win over eventual premier Adelaide in the last round was a nice way to recognise Kevin Sheedy's 400th game as coach of Essendon and three-time Bomber premiership player Mark Harvey's last game of AFL football.

It ended a month in which the Bombers beat Geelong, the Brisbane Lions and the Crows and only just failed to beat Collingwood and North Melbourne.

In 1997, Essendon was gutted by long-term injuries to 1996 Brownlow Medallist James Hird (seven games), wingman Michael Long (five games), midfielder Mark Mercuri (11 games), tall forward Steven Alessio (nine games), goalsneak Darren Bewick (five games), utility David Calthorpe (five games) and the aggressive Barry Young (six games).

Its paucity of options forced it to play 41 players off its list of 42. Add this to football manager Danny Corcoran's mid-season defection to Melbourne and it appeared the wings had fallen off.

If necessity is the mother of invention, then for Sheedy, injuries are the big daddy of re-invention. Out of the mire rose some talented youngsters.

Matthew Lloyd was brilliant up forward in the absence of Hird, kicking 63 goals from 20 games and stamping himself as a real talent.

Blake Caracella, after 52 games for the Essendon reserves, is one of the most recognisable young players in the AFL and finished a close second in the Norwich Rising Star Award. Dustin Fletcher took his game to a new level. Scott Lucas is a tall mobile player who improves every time he runs out, while more experienced midfielders Joe Misiti and Sean Denham were fantastic all year.

Essendon was the only club not to make a trade during October — a clear indication of the faith it has in its list.

Eight youngsters were introduced to AFL football in 1997 with Jason Johnson, Gary Moorcroft, Chris Heffernan and Daniel McAlister showing they have the potential for long AFL careers.

Essendon managed to hang on to Che Cockatoo-Collins, who will be keen to atone for a mediocre year. He was close to joining North Melbourne last October before re-signing for two years.

— **Peter Ryan**

## THE YEAR AHEAD

| Rd | Date | Opponent | Venue | Home/ Away | Time (local) |
|----|------|----------|-------|------------|--------------|
| 1 | March 29 | Richmond | MCG | A | 2.10pm |
| 2 | April 5 | St Kilda | MCG | H | 2.10pm |
| 3 | April 13 | Carlton | MCG | A | 2.10pm |
| 4 | April 19 | Fremantle | P | H | 2.10pm |
| 5 | April 25 | Collingwood | MCG | A | 3.30pm |
| 6 | May 2 | Western Bulldogs | OO | A | 2.10pm |
| 7 | May 9 (N) | Geelong | MCG | H | 7.40pm |
| 8 | May 15 (N) | Brisbane Lions | MCG | H | 7.40pm |
| 9 | May 23 | Melbourne | MCG | A | 2.10pm |
| 10 | May 30 | Hawthorn | P | A | 3.30pm |
| 11 | June 5 (N) | Sydney | MCG | H | 7.40pm |
| 12 | June 13 (N) | Adelaide | FP | A | 8.10pm |
| 13 | June 19 (N) | West Coast | MCG | H | 7.40pm |
| 14 | June 26 (N) | North Melbourne | MCG | A | 7.40pm |
| 15 | July 4 | Port Adelaide | MCG | H | 2.10pm |
| 16 | July 19 | Richmond | MCG | H | 2.10pm |
| 17 | July 26 | St Kilda | P | A | 2.10pm |
| 18 | August 2 | Carlton | MCG | H | 2.10pm |
| 19 | August 8 (N) | Fremantle | S | A | 6.40pm |
| 20 | August 15 | Collingwood | MCG | H | 2.10pm |
| 21 | August 21 (N) | Western Bulldogs | MCG | H | 7.40pm |
| 22 | August 29 | Geelong | MCG | A | 2.10pm |

## 1997 AT A GLANCE

**W:** R1: Essendon 16.10 (106) v Carlton 15.9 (99) (MCG)

**W:** R2: Port Adelaide 8.12 (60) v Essendon 14.9 (93) (FP)

**W:** R3: Essendon 18.14 (122) v North Melbourne 12.8 (80) (MCG)

**L:** R4: Geelong 11.19 (85) v Essendon 11.12 (78) (MCG)

**L:** R5: Essendon 10.10 (70) v Collingwood 14.15 (99) (MCG)

**W:** R6: Essendon 15.12 (102) v Brisbane Lions 9.17 (71) (MCG)

**L:** R7: Adelaide 18.18 (126) v Essendon 11.7 (73) (FP)

**L:** R8: Essendon 14.16 (100) v St Kilda 18.16 (124) (MCG)

**L:** R9: West Coast 16.14 (110) v Essendon 13.7 (85) (S)

**L:** R10: Essendon 17.12 (114) v Western Bulldogs 20.16 (136) (MCG)

### SNAPSHOT

Games: 22
Wins: 9
Losses: 13
Ladder Finish: 14th
Players Used: 41

**L:** R11: Essendon 13.13 (91) v Hawthorn 17.22 (124) (MCG)

**L:** R12: Fremantle 24.13 (157) v Essendon 9.6 (60) (S)

**W:** R13: Richmond 4.10 (34) v Essendon 19.13 (127) (MCG)

**W:** R14: Essendon 18.12 (120) v Melbourne 8.9 (57) (MCG)

**L:** R15: Sydney 11.13 (79) v Essendon 11.12 (78) (SCG)

**L:** R16: Carlton 25.15 (165) v Essendon 13.9 (87) (MCG)

**L:** R17: Essendon 10.12 (72) v Port Adelaide 18.14 (122) (MCG)

**L:** R18: North Melbourne 11.17 (83) v Essendon 8.16 (64) (MCG)

**W:** R19: Essendon 11.7 (73) v Geelong 9.14 (68) (MCG)

**L:** R20: Collingwood 13.13 (91) v Essendon 12.9 (81) (MCG)

**W:** R21: Brisbane Lions 15.12 (102) v Essendon 16.10 (106) (G)

**W:** R22: Essendon 16.6 (102) v Adelaide 14.14 (98) (OO)

## The Coach

**Kevin Sheedy**

**Born:** 22/12/47

The wonder of modern coaching — Kevin Sheedy is about to enter his 18th consecutive season as coach of Essendon. In 1998, he will have a remodelled football department structure that leaves him as the ultimate decision-maker on football issues.

Criticised at times last year for spending too much time on areas outside his direct coaching role and even for not attending a game in which the Bombers' opponents were playing the next week, Sheedy showed he is never one to do the ordinary.

He has such confidence in the list Essendon has developed in the past couple of years that the club was the only one not involved in last October's player trading. Sheedy, having coached the Bombers in 400 games, is closing on Essendon legend Dick Reynolds' record of 415 games as Bomber coach.

### AT A GLANCE

**COACHING RECORD**
**Essendon**

| Season | P | W | L | D | Pos |
|--------|----|-----|-----|---|-----|
| 1981 | 23 | 16 | 7 | – | 5 |
| 1982 | 23 | 16 | 7 | – | 5 |
| 1983 | 26 | 18 | 8 | – | 2 |
| 1984 | 25 | 20 | 5 | – | 1 |
| 1985 | 24 | 21 | 3 | – | 1 |
| 1986 | 23 | 12 | 11 | – | 5 |
| 1987 | 22 | 9 | 12 | 1 | 9 |
| 1988 | 22 | 12 | 10 | – | 6 |
| 1989 | 25 | 18 | 7 | – | 3 |
| 1990 | 25 | 18 | 7 | – | 2 |
| 1991 | 23 | 13 | 10 | – | 6 |
| 1992 | 22 | 12 | 10 | – | 8 |
| 1993 | 24 | 16 | 7 | 1 | 1 |
| 1994 | 22 | 11 | 11 | – | 10 |
| 1995 | 24 | 15 | 7 | 2 | 5 |
| 1996 | 25 | 15 | 9 | 1 | 4 |
| 1997 | 22 | 9 | 13 | – | 14 |
| **Total** | **400** | **251** | **144** | **5** | |

## WIN/LOSS RECORD

| Against | P | W (N) | L (N) | D (N) |
|---|---|---|---|---|
| Adelaide | 12 | 8 (1) | 4 (3) | 0 |
| Brisbane Bears | 15 | 11 (3) | 4 (2) | 0 |
| Brisbane Lions | 2 | 2 (1) | 0 | 0 |
| Carlton | 204 | 92 | 109 (1) | 3 |
| Collingwood | 196 | 82 (1) | 110 (2) | 4 |
| Fitzroy | 197 | 112 (1) | 80 | 5 |
| Fremantle | 4 | 3 (1) | 1 | 0 |
| Geelong | 190 | 106 (2) | 79 | 5 |
| Hawthorn | 132 | 82 (1) | 50 | 0 |
| Melbourne | 188 | 114 | 72 | 2 |
| North Melb | 128 | 86 | 41 (5) | 1 |
| Port Adel | 2 | 1 | 1 (1) | 0 |
| Richmond | 163 | 86 | 73 | 4 (1) |
| St Kilda | 186 | 126 (1) | 56 | 4 |
| Sydney | 190 | 117 (2) | 72 (3) | 1 (1) |
| West Coast | 22 | 14 (2) | 8 (1) | 0 |
| W Bulldogs | 130 | 79 (1) | 50 | 1 |
| University | 14 | 12 | 2 | 0 |
| **TOTALS** | **1975** | **1133 (17)** | **812 (18)** | **30 (2)** |

*(N) Premiership matches played at night*

## WINNING RUNS

23 v St Kilda (1944–1957)
20 v St Kilda (1981–1991)
15 v Fitzroy (1962–1970)
15 v Hawthorn (1946–1954)
14 v Carlton (1897–1902)
14 v Melbourne (1980–1986)
14 v St Kilda (1897–1902)
13 v Hawthorn (1938–1944)
11 v Western Bulldogs (1963–1969)
11 v Melbourne (1905–1910)
10 v Western Bulldogs (1925–1929)
10 v Geelong (1982–1986)
10 v Carlton (1981–1985)
10 v Brisbane Bears (1987–1993)
9 v North Melb (1927–1932)
9 v SM/Sydney (1959–1964), (1971–1975)
7 v Richmond (1987–1991)
6 v Collingwood (1984–1986)
5 v West Coast (1988–1990)
4 v Adelaide (1992–1994)
3 v Fremantle (1995–1996)
2 v Brisbane Lions (1997)
1 v Port Adelaide (1997)

## 1997 BEST AND FAIREST

Three members of the match committee can select a maximum of eight players to receive up to 10 votes, with no obligation to award votes.

1 Sean Denham (258)
2 Joe Misiti (204)
3 Mathew Lloyd (203)
4 Sean Wellman (185)
5 Blake Carcella (176)
6 Dustin Fletcher (126)
7 Mark Mercuri (122)
8 Michael Prior (111)
9 Damien Hardwick (109)
10 Scott Lucas (108)

## GAMES RECORDS

378 Simon Madden (1974–92)
320 Dick Reynolds (1933–51)
307 Tim Watson (1977–91; 1993–94)
300 Garry Foulds (1974–89)
294 Terry Daniher (1978–92)
290 Bill Hutchison (1942–57)
266 Don McKenzie (1960–74)
264 Ken Fletcher (1967–80)
263 Jack Clarke (1951–67)
226 Gary O'Donnell (1987– )

## GOALS RECORDS

575 Simon Madden (1974–92)
537 John Coleman (1949–54)
509 Paul Salmon (1983–95)
496 Bill Hutchison (1942–57)
447 Terry Daniher (1978–92)
442 Dick Reynolds (1933–51)
420 Alan Noonan (1966–76)
415 Keith Forbes (1928–37)
372 Ted Freyer (1929–37)
361 Tom Reynolds (1937–44)

## HIGHS AND LOWS

| Against | Highest | Lowest | G. W. Margin | G. L. Margin |
|---|---|---|---|---|
| Adelaide | 27.20.182 (1995) | 8.10.58 (1994) | 122 (1995) | 96 (1996) |
| Brisbane Bears | 29.20.194 (1988) | 9.10.64 (1987) | 140 (1988) | 35 (1996) |
| Brisbane Lions | 16.10.106 (1997) | 15.12.102 (1997) | 31 (1997) | — |
| Carlton | 27.14.176 (1985) | 2.2.14 (1903) | 109 (1985) | 102 (1936) |
| Collingwood | 28.6.174 (1984) | 3.2.20 (1898) | 133 (1984) | 147 (1971) |
| Fitzroy | 24.22.166 (1995) | 0.9.9 (1899) | 103 (1985) | 96 (1979) |
| Fremantle | 21.9.135 (1995) | 9.6.60 (1997) | 48 (1995) | 97 (1997) |
| Geelong | 26.9.165 (1983) | 2.3.15 (1902) | 97 (1986) | 116 (1934) |
| Hawthorn | 26.16.172 (1968) | 5.13.43 (1974) | 107 (1944) | 160 (1992) |
| Melbourne | 27.20.182 (1986) | 1.8.14 (1907) | 122 (1986) | 90 (1927) |
| North Melb | 29.16.190 (1934) | 6.13.49 (1961) | 104 (1985) | 59 (1985) |
| Port Adel | 14.9.93 (1997) | 10.12.72 (1997) | 33 (1997) | 50 (1997) |
| Richmond | 25.20.170 (1960) | 3.4.22 (1918) | 125 (1960) | 74 (1983) |
| St Kilda | 28.21.189 (1944) | 1.7.13 (1906) | 120 (1911) | 68 (1975) |
| Sydney | 28.16.184 (1964) | 1.4.10 (1900) | 165 (1964) | 163 (1987) |
| West Coast | 25.10.160 (1989) | 5.14.44 (1994) | 142 (1989) | 99 (1988) |
| W Bulldogs | 32.16.208 (1982) | 2.11.23 (1955) | 146 (1982) | 100 (1977) |

# THE LEADERSHIP AT ESSENDON

| Year | Pos | Coach | Captain | Best & Fairest | Leading Goalkicker | |
|---|---|---|---|---|---|---|
| 1931 | 6 | G. Campbell | G. Campbell | T. Clarke | E. Freyer | 50 |
| 1932 | 6 | G. Campbell | G. Campbell | S. Carman | E. Freyer | 52 |
| 1933 | 12 | G. Campbell | G. Campbell | P. Walsh | E. Freyer | 51 |
| 1934 | 10 | C. May | K. Forbes | R. Reynolds | E. Freyer | 61 |
| 1935 | 8 | C. May | K. Forbes | K. Forbes | K. Forbes | 52 |
| 1936 | 8 | J. Baggott | J. Baggott | R. Reynolds | E. Freyer | 50 |
| 1937 | 10 | J. Baggott | K. Forbes | R. Reynolds | K. Forbes | 44 |
| 1938 | 7 | J. Baggott | L. Webster | R. Reynolds | T. Reynolds | 68 |
| 1939 | 6 | J. Baggott<br>R. Reynolds | R. Reynolds | R. Reynolds | T. Reynolds | 71 |
| 1940 | 3 | R. Reynolds | R. Reynolds | H. Torney | E. Bryce | 48 |
| 1941 | 2 | R. Reynolds | R. Reynolds | W. Buttsworth | T. Reynolds | 65 |
| 1942 | 1 | R. Reynolds | R. Reynolds | R. Reynolds | T. Reynolds | 61 |
| 1943 | 2 | R. Reynolds | R. Reynolds | R. Reynolds | R. Reynolds | 31 |
| 1944 | 3 | R. Reynolds | R. Reynolds | P. Bushby | R. Powell | 42 |
| 1945 | 8 | R. Reynolds | R. Reynolds | W. Buttsworth | W. Brittingham | 48 |
| 1946 | 1 | R. Reynolds | R. Reynolds | W. Hutchison | W. Brittingham | 66 |
| 1947 | 2 | R. Reynolds | R. Reynolds | W. Buttsworth | E. Leehane | 50 |
| 1948 | 2 | R. Reynolds | R. Reynolds | W. Hutchison | W. Hutchison | 52 |
| 1949 | 1 | R. Reynolds | R. Reynolds | J. Coleman | J. Coleman | 100 |
| 1950 | 1 | R. Reynolds | R. Reynolds | W. Hutchison | J. Coleman | 120 |
| 1951 | 2 | R. Reynolds | W. Hutchison | N. McDonald | J. Coleman | 75 |
| 1952 | 8 | R. Reynolds | W. Hutchison | W. Hutchison | J. Coleman | 103 |
| 1953 | 4 | R. Reynolds | W. Hutchison | W. Hutchison | J. Coleman | 97 |
| 1954 | 6 | R. Reynolds | W. Hutchison | J. Gill | J. Coleman | 42 |
| 1955 | 4 | R. Reynolds | W. Hutchison | W. Hutchison | H. Mitchell | 51 |
| 1956 | 6 | R. Reynolds | W. Hutchison | W. Hutchison | G. Willey | 33 |
| 1957 | 2 | R. Reynolds | W. Hutchison | R. Burgess | F. Gallagher | 34 |
| 1958 | 5 | R. Reynolds | J. Clarke | J. Clarke | J. Birt | 31 |
| 1959 | 2 | R. Reynolds | J. Clarke | H. Mitchell | R. Evans | 78 |
| 1960 | 4 | R. Reynolds | J. Clarke | R. Burgess | R. Evans | 67 |
| 1961 | 7 | J. Coleman | J. Clarke | J. Birt | H. Mitchell | 33 |
| 1962 | 1 | J. Coleman | J. Clarke | J. Clarke | C. Payne | 39 |
| 1963 | 6 | J. Coleman | J. Clarke | K. Fraser | C. Payne | 36 |
| 1964 | 4 | J. Coleman | J. Clarke | K. Fraser | H. Mitchell | 32 |
| 1965 | 1 | J. Coleman | K. Fraser | J. Birt | E. Fordham | 54 |
| 1966 | 3 | J. Coleman | K. Fraser | D. McKenzie | E. Fordham | 76 |
| 1967 | 6 | J. Coleman | K. Fraser | J. Birt | A. Noonan | 40 |
| 1968 | 2 | J. Clarke | K. Fraser | B. Davis | A. Noonan | 51 |
| 1969 | 6 | J. Clarke | D. McKenzie | B. Davis | A. Noonan | 43 |
| 1970 | 11 | J. Clarke | B. Davis | D. Gerlach | G. Blethyn | 33 |
| 1971 | 11 | J. Birt | B. Davis | B. Davis | A. Noonan | 31 |
| 1972 | 5 | D. Tuddenham | D. Tuddenham | N. Fields | G. Blethyn | 107 |
| 1973 | 5 | D. Tuddenham | D. Tuddenham | A. Wilson | A. Noonan | 63 |
| 1974 | 8 | D. Tuddenham | D. Tuddenham | G. Moss | A. Noonan | 77 |
| 1975 | 8 | D. Tuddenham | D. Tuddenham | G. Moss | A. Noonan | 48 |
| 1976 | 10 | W. Stephen | G. Moss | G. Moss | G. Blethyn | 39 |
| 1977 | 9 | W. Stephen | K. Fletcher | S. Madden | M. Crow | 38 |
| 1978 | 10 | B. Davis | K. Fletcher | K. Fletcher | W. Primmer | 47 |
| 1979 | 5 | B. Davis | K. Fletcher | S. Madden | T. Daniher | 57 |
| 1980 | 7 | B. Davis | S. Madden | T. Watson | S. Madden | 45 |
| 1981 | 5 | K. Sheedy | S. Madden | N. Daniher | A. Buhagiar | 42 |
| 1982 | 5 | K. Sheedy | R. Andrews | T. Daniher | S. Madden | 49 |
| 1983 | 2 | K. Sheedy | T. Daniher | S. Madden | T. Daniher | 64 |
| 1984 | 1 | K. Sheedy | T. Daniher | S. Madden | P. Salmon | 63 |
| 1985 | 1 | K. Sheedy | T. Daniher | T. Watson | M. Harvey | 48 |
| 1986 | 5 | K. Sheedy | T. Daniher | G. Hawker | A. Ezard | 47 |
| 1987 | 9 | K. Sheedy | T. Daniher | M. Thompson | P. Salmon | 43 |
| 1988 | 6 | K. Sheedy | T. Daniher | T. Watson | P. Salmon | 37 |
| 1989 | 3 | K. Sheedy | T. Watson | T. Watson | P. Salmon | 39 |
| 1990 | 2 | K. Sheedy | T. Watson | M. Thompson | P. Salmon | 43 |
| 1991 | 6 | K. Sheedy | T. Watson | A. Ezard | S. Madden | 42 |
| 1992 | 8 | K. Sheedy | M. Thompson | M. Harvey | P. Salmon | 59 |
| 1993 | 1 | K. Sheedy | M. Thompson | G. O'Donnell | P. Salmon | 65 |
| 1994 | 10 | K. Sheedy | M. Thompson | J. Hird | S. Cummings | 32 |
| 1995 | 5 | K. Sheedy | M. Thompson | J. Hird | J. Hird | 47 |
| 1996 | 4 | K. Sheedy | G. O'Donnell | J. Hird | J. Hird | 39 |
| 1997 | 14 | K. Sheedy | G. O'Donnell | S. Denham | M. Lloyd | 63 |

# PLAYER PROFILES

## STEVEN ALESSIO

Potentially among the top big men in the game, but such has been his misfortune with injuries — and in 1997 you can add a three-week suspension — that the mobile goalkicking ruckman hasn't been on the park long enough for him to make the mark he deserves. Made his debut in 1992 and has played only 78 games, with last year's return of nine being caused by a foot injury. As a late convert to Australian Football, he was always going to be a late developer, but now he must consolidate. At 26, Alessio could lead Essendon's ruck for the next five years and develop into a key player.

**Player honors:** night series premiership side 1993.

## MATTHEW BANKS

Made his debut at full-back last season in front of a full house at the MCG against Collingwood before he was probably ready for it. A tall defender and among the quickest in the club over 10 metres. Obviously green last year, but Essendon believes he needs to be pushed along to bring out his best. Played two games before fracturing an arm in the reserves. Essendon plans to give him a big pre-season to get him fit and then give him the opportunity to develop his confidence in the seniors.

## PAUL BARNARD

Frustrating 1997, despite looking fitter and more confident then ever when the season opened. Season came to a crushing end after only five games because of a recurring foot problem. The bald-headed, fiery defender loves to run with the ball, showing that his skill matches his bluster. Exciting to watch.

**Previous AFL club:** Hawthorn (1994-95: 11 games, 4 goals).

## PETER BERBAKOV

Performed well in the forward line for the first half of last season, leading strongly and marking consistently. His form dropped away once the surprise element had gone (he played in defence in 1996) and he was back in the reserves by the end of the year. Needs to settle in a position at either end of the ground.

## DARREN BEWICK

Ruptured his left knee (medial ligament) in a 1997 pre-season practice match in Alice Springs after earlier undergoing shoulder surgery. First appearance in round 15 made it difficult to find form — kicked only two goals from five games — and another knee scare in round 19 saw him out for the year. A pacy goal-sneak who is becoming smarter as he grows older. Capable of causing enormous damage around the forward line and gets plenty of the ball in the midfield.

**Player honors:** 2nd best and fairest 1991; night series premiership side 1993, 1994; premiership side 1993.

## JUSTIN BLUMFIELD

Given Tim Watson's No. 32 for the 1997 season, such is the future he is thought to have. Judged as a very exciting prospect and in a more settled line-up this year could excel. A physically well-developed player who is an excellent mark and very versatile.

## MARK BOLTON

Excelled at centre half-back in the 1997 AFL National Under-18 Championships. A good runner with a cross-country background, Essendon will be developing him in 1998. From the Bombers' perspective, any senior football will be a bonus.

## ANDREW BOMFORD

Appeared to have been given the opportunity he had been denied for so long when he made his debut for Essendon. Played 79 reserves games with Sydney before being picked up by the Bombers at No. 25 in the 1996 National Draft. Didn't begin a pre-season last year until after Christmas and then suffered stress fractures in a foot early in the season. Rated very highly by Essendon and this year, with a better preparation, his versatility, pace and toughness at the football will be a great asset.

## DAVID CALTHORPE

Nuggety half-back/winger who had his 1997 season ruined by injury with constant back-related hamstring problems. Managed only one game after round seven and completely missed the second half. Adds depth to the midfield and is capable of taking a game by the scruff of the neck with his bullocking runs. However, not an automatic selection now that Essendon has some similar young players emerging.

**Player honors:** EJ Whitten Medal 1994; night series premiership side 1994; premiership side 1993.

## BLAKE CARACELLA

The find of the season for Essendon, which had nurtured him for more than 50 reserves games before letting him make his debut last season. Finished second in the AFL Norwich Rising Star award, won plaudits for his games against Geelong and the Brisbane Lions and took the most courageous mark of the year running into a pack against the Cats. A lightly built running player with great skills and heaps of courage. Enters 1998 as one of the Bombers' brightest hopes.

**Player honors:** AFL Norwich Rising Star nominee 1997.

## CHE COCKATOO-COLLINS

Re-signed for two years after much interest from other clubs in the trading period. Essendon was prepared to trade him if he wanted to go and tried to arrange a swap for Port Adelaide's Bowen Lockwood. Cockatoo-Collins considered an offer from North Melbourne, but was influenced by teammate Michael Long. A precocious player who kicks goals from nowhere. Aggressive in his attack on the ball and more than capable of handling leadership responsibilities. Had a disappointing year last year, kicking only 17 goals from 17 games and was dropped late in the year before returning. The interest shown in him in pre-draft trading shows he is still highly rated.

**Player honors:** AFL Norwich Rising Star nominee 1994; night series premiership side 1994.

## SEAN DENHAM

Won his first club best and fairest last year after placings in 1994 (Essendon) and 1988 (Geelong). A great effort by the nuggety rover who was indirectly involved in one of the most controversial incidents of last season when Carlton's Greg Williams was reported for

pushing an umpire during a verbal exchange with Denham. A great possession winner, fantastic at centre clearances and an attacking run-with player.
**Player honors:** Essendon best and fairest 1997, 2nd best and fairest 1994; Geelong 3rd best and fairest 1988; Essendon night series premiership side 1993, Essendon premiership side 1993.
**Previous AFL club:** Geelong (1987-91: 44 games, 21 goals).

**JORDAN DOERING**
The forward/on-baller is a left-foot kick capable of commanding a quality opposition defender. Kicked seven goals for the Eastern Ranges in a TAC Cup final last year and kicked five goals for Carlton reserves. A young player with height, strength and mobility.

**BEN DOOLAN**
Hampered by a foot operation in 1997 that restricted him to 11 games. Has worked through the pressure created by his big money move from Sydney and has become a reliable performer when fit (finished fourth in the 1996 best and fairest). Marks well, doesn't lose many one-on-one duels and is as tough as nails. Expect a big year.
**Player honors:** night series premiership side 1994.
**Previous AFL club:** Sydney (1991-92: 25 games, 4 goals).

**SIMON EASTAUGH**
Spent time on Richmond's list, then had an outstanding year with Norwood last season playing in its premiership side. Expected to be capable of stepping straight into senior football as a back-up ruckman to Peter Somerville, with the capacity to assume the number one role if required.

**DUSTIN FLETCHER**
Made the jump in 1997 to class player, after a few years of inconsistent performances. Burned in the first game of the season and did not look back. Was hampered by a virus and then struggled with a knee injury, but played 16 excellent games. Can play at centre half-back, full-back (where he played in the 1993 premiership) or centre half-forward. Became a real on-field leader, beating all-comers. Only needs to back himself more by running off his opponent in defence to become a complete player. Will play a major role in Essendon's fortunes in the next decade.
**Player honors:** night series premiership side 1994, premiership side 1993; AFL Norwich Rising Star nominee 1993.

**MARK FRASER**
Speedster who is yet to cement a place in the Bombers' line-up after crossing from Collingwood at the start of 1995. Son of Essendon champion Ken Fraser, Mark seems to have found himself as first player out when changes are swung and struggles with hamstring problems. Capable of holding down a wing position, but needs to improve his disposal. At 26, must find a permanent role with Essendon this year.
**Previous club:** Collingwood (1992-94: 45 games, 23 goals).

**DAMIEN HARDWICK**
Small aggressive defender who has often landed himself in trouble at the Tribunal, but made a real effort in 1997 to curb this tendency to 'ask questions later'. Well-balanced, courageous and scruffy enough to engender respect. An attacking half-back flanker, who, despite his small stature, can play tall. Would find life much easier with some good key position players around him.

**CHRIS HEFFERNAN**
The No. 2 pick from the Geelong Falcons in the 1996 National Draft managed three games in the last four rounds and will have learnt much from the experience. Showed good skills. A level-headed youngster and one of the fittest players at the club. Expected to make the step this season.

**JAMES HIRD**
First a calf injury, then a stress fracture of a foot ruined his season. Kicked 18 goals in only seven appearances and was among the best each week. A few supporters had heart failure during contract negotiations last July, but he re-signed for three years at a reported $300,000 a year. He's worth every cent both as a player and as a club representative. Was doing all the running and kicking by late October last year, but was resting every second day. Has the all-clear and will be 100 per cent by round one. Potentially one of the great centre half-forwards and his absence last year will have sharpened his keenness. If it improves his football even one per cent, opposition clubs had better look out. Should rise to the added challenge of being appointed captain.
**Player honors:** Brownlow Medal 1996; best and fairest 1994, 1995, 1996; All-Australian 1995, 1996; AFL Norwich Rising Star nominee 1993; leading goalkicker 1995, 1996; premiership side 1993; night premiership sides 1993, 1994; captain 1998-.

**JASON JOHNSON**
A well-balanced running player who made his debut in round 18 and played three games. Seems to have plenty of time and runs hard and straight. Needs to work on his disposal, but looks a good prospect.

**JUDD LALICH**
Superstar at AFL draft camp. Great cricketer who played under-17 state cricket. Had back and knee problems, but broke into East Perth seniors at end of 1997. Quick and fit and has the potential to play across half-forward in a similar style to James Hird.

**MATTHEW LLOYD**
One of the most exciting players in the competition and only turns 20 in April. His start was delayed last year because of a ruptured spleen suffered in the 1996 preliminary final, but his year didn't suffer. Kicked 63 goals from 20 games and at times carried Essendon's forward line. Made an impressive debut for Victoria and finished third in the club best and fairest. A courageous full-forward who marks well and kicks beautifully. A graceful footballer to watch and will form a scary combination up forward with Hird. Joined Essendon as a 16-year-old and looks set to fulfil the high expectations placed on him over the next decade.
**Player honors:** 3rd best and fairest 1997; leading goalkicker 1997; AFL Norwich Rising Star nominee 1996.

## MICHAEL LONG

Has struggled with a troublesome knee for three of the past four seasons and managed only five games in 1997, giving the year away after round eight to undergo his second knee reconstruction. An inspirational and explosive player and one of the most important figures in the game — both for his footballing ability, his courageous leadership and his educational role in racial vilification issues. Needs to be carefully managed for the rest of his career in order to recapture his exciting form. Could play as an attacking half-back flanker to relieve some of the twisting stress on his knees.

**Player honors:** 2nd best and fairest 1995; All-Australian 1995; Norm Smith Medal 1993; night series premiership sides 1990, 1993; premiership side 1993.

## SCOTT LUCAS

A tall, mobile left-footer who stood up when required last year playing every game. Still gangly and developing, but his skills and pace for his size make him difficult to match-up on. Capable of kicking goals and although he may be just too small to hold down ruck, he will be very handy in this age of mobile tall players.

## DANIEL McALISTER

Played in the last two victories of the year, making his debut under coach Kevin Sheedy's policy of exposing some youngsters to senior football. Of Kiwi descent, he is still learning but has great pace and strength and likes moving the ball by hand. Only small, but Essendon has a high opinion of him and he could quickly become an exciting player.

## MARK MERCURI

A groin problem, a torn thigh, influenza and an injured shoulder stopped him from stringing together games in 1997. Managed 11 games, but was sorely missed. One of Essendon's key players and among the best midfielders in the game. Combines courage and ball-getting ability with great disposal and evasive skills and is the best small man overhead in the game. A potential match-winner.

**Player honors:** 2nd best and fairest 1996; AFL Norwich Rising Star nominee 1993; night series premiership sides 1993, 1994; premiership side 1993.

## JOE MISITI

Playing his most consistent football since 1993, 'Smokin' Joe was runner-up in the club's best and fairest, following on his third in '96. Dynamic in the midfield, always keen to run hard into defence to help out and plays well whether working with or against the tide. Looks to have matured in the past couple of years and improved his fitness, knowing that is the key to good form. A groin injury kept him out of the last three games of last season.

**Player honors:** 2nd best and fairest 1997, 3rd best and fairest 1996; AFL Norwich Rising Star nominee 1993; night series premiership sides 1993, 1994; premiership side 1993.

## GARY MOORCROFT

Winner of the 1994 Morrish Medal who came off the rookie list in 1997, played 11 games and improved in every one. Looks too small to play AFL football, but is courageous, gets plenty of the ball and tackles hard. Also capable of taking a spectacular mark reminiscent of a leaping Alan Ezard (former Essendon premiership player). Needs to improve his disposal, but shapes as a valuable acquisition.

## RYAN O'CONNOR

A car accident interrupted his pre-season last year and the big Tasmanian really struggled. He looked unfit and lost much of his confidence before being dropped late in the year. Was mentioned by the football media as a possible trade for the Bombers late in the season, but nothing eventuated. Spending more time on the ball with Alessio injured and Somerville struggling for form exposed his lack of pace. Has had a couple of operations (knee and ankle) over summer and plans to get really fit to have a big year. Potentially a dominating player.

**Player honors:** Jesaulenko Medal 1995; AFL Norwich Rising Star nominee 1995.

## GARY O'DONNELL

The bouncy, unstoppable veteran is a great leader as he hits his 33rd year and his 14th with Essendon. Has always played under Kevin Sheedy and is understandably excited about the future of the club. Form was consistent again in 1997 as he controlled the ball across half-back and was able to give the team a lift in the midfield when it was needed. One of the most respected players in the game, his experience is invaluable. Should be able to concentrate more on how own game now he has handed the captaincy to James Hird.

**Player honors:** best and fairest 1993, 2nd best and fairest 1989, 1990, 3rd best and fairest 1991, 1992 (equal) 1995; Michael Tuck Medal 1994; night series premiership sides 1990, 1993, 1994; premiership side 1993; captain 1996, 1997.

## RICKY OLARENSHAW

The way his head bobs and hair jumps as he bounces off players and baulks opponents, Olarenshaw sometimes moves as if he is playing guitar for the Easybeats back in '69. Last year, a four-week suspension in the first round for striking Carlton's Scott Camporeale got his season off to a disastrous start. However, he recovered to play 15 games for the year. A risky, but exciting half-back/winger who is yet to make the jump into the midfield. Is a bit one-sided and can be caught out because of that.

**Player honors:** AFL Norwich Rising Star nominee 1993; night series premiership side 1994; premiership side 1993.

## MICHAEL PRIOR

Embroiled in a racial vilification controversy after the round five clash against the Magpies when words were exchanged with Collingwood's (now Sydney's) Robbie Ahmat. Despite the impact it had on Prior, who denied racially vilifying Ahmat (it was resolved by the AFL Tribunal which cleared Prior), he managed to continue with the job. Played all 22 games, improving to be a very reliable half-back flanker versatile enough to move into the midfield where he kicked 10 goals. A typical modern half-back who marks well, runs straight and hard and has excellent long-kicking skills. Essendon's highest kick-winner in 1997.

**DEAN SOLOMON**

Tall defender from Broken Hill. Played for Bendigo Pioneers last year and made the All-Australian team playing for NSW/ACT Rams in the AFL National Under-18 Championships. Very strong, hard at the footy and second and third efforts are very good. Could be effective playing in attack, but at this stage suited to a position where he can run straight ahead. Compared with Dean Wallis in his approach to the footy.

**PETER SOMERVILLE**

Struggled for form in 1997 after suffering a stress fracture in a foot and had his worst year for a while. Played 13 games but didn't get anywhere near enough of the ball. This led to difficulties when his contract came up for renewal last year and he threatened to leave the club. Needs to lift and re-establish himself as the club's number one ruckman. Turning 30 he should, if he can, stay fit and be able to use his experience and talent to exert real influence from the ruck.
**Player honors:** premiership side 1993; night series premiership sides 1993, 1994.

**MICHAEL SYMONS**

The leaping pilot of Essendon's defence and a great player to watch, though often makes costly mistakes. A broken jaw after clashing with Geelong's Barry Stoneham finished Symons' '97 season. The small defender has a huge leap, is a good mark and plays courageous, attacking football. Must improve his disposal.
**Player honors:** night series premiership side 1994.

**ANDREW UKOVIC**

Lightly built player who made his debut in round 12 last season and played five games before heading back to the reserves where the Bombers were rapt with his form. Worked hard on the upper body over summer and the Bombers are expecting reward on their investment this season. Was paid a big compliment when he was handed Mark Harvey's No.1 jumper for the 1998 season. He should do it justice.

**DEAN WALLIS**

The tough man of Australian Football is absolutely fearless and used by Kevin Sheedy on opposition danger players. Frustrated by injury and played only 11 games in 1997. In defence, has improved his skills with time. Still capable of the cheeky, as evidenced by his smothering of Geelong's John Barnes' shot for goal in their round 19 clash last season. Expect him to annoy and frustrate opponents — and supporters — for another season.
**Player honors:** night series premiership side 1993; premiership side 1993.

**MATTHEW WATSON**

Ruckman who, after a slow start last year, played good solid football in the reserves and was rewarded with a senior game. Looking for more improvement this year and could possibly play as a centre half-back.

**SEAN WELLMAN**

Had his best season in the AFL last year, played every game mainly at full-back and finished fourth in the club's best and fairest. Lacks a bit of pace, but is a good mark (took 100 in 1997) and works feverishly to defeat his opponent on the last line of defence. Crossed from the Adelaide Crows for the 1996 season.

**Previous AFL club:** Adelaide Crows (1994-95: 34 games, 9 goals).

**TIM WILLIAMS**

The only Essendon player on the senior list not to have played a senior game in 1997. A torn thigh suffered mid-season cost him any opportunity. Played 14 reserves games and has a good grounding for senior football in 1998, where he could find a spot either on half-forward or in the midfield. Drafted from East Perth in 1996.

**BARRY YOUNG**

Another victim of Essendon's shocking injury run. Struggled to overcome a thigh injury and played only six games, although he was back playing well in the last three rounds. Played his 100th game last year and is ready to take on a leadership role. Can play in a variety of roles and is very aggressive at the ball.
**Previous AFL club:** Richmond (1989-93: 53 games, 23 goals).

## ROOKIE LIST

**ROBERT DIROSA**

Drafted by Geelong in the 1994 National Draft at No. 18 after an excellent junior career and then spent last year on the Western Bulldogs' supplementary list. Admired for his hard-at-the-footy approach. Taking a while to develop, but Essendon believes he has handy qualities.

**WINIS IMBI**

Born and raised in Papua-New Guinea and grew up playing soccer before his family settled in Portland, Victoria, eight years ago. By the age of 17, he had won the North Ballarat Rebels best and fairest and last season was one of Victoria Country's best players in the AFL National Under-18 Championships and an important member of the Rebels premiership side. A clever rover who reads the play well and works hard on the track.

**MARK JOHNSON**

Originally from the Calder Cannons and on Essendon's rookie list last season. Won the reserves best and fairest and Essendon felt he deserved another chance. Works hard on his skills, is tough at the football and, as a local boy, is a player Essendon wanted to support.

**LACHLAN OAKLEY**

Nephew of former AFL chief executive Ross Oakley and son of Denis Oakley, a gun full-forward for Sandringham in the late '50s and early '60s. An aggressive forward, Oakley played on the half-forward flank for Sandringham in its 1997 VFL premiership — his second year in senior football — and was a key player last season.

**DEAN RIOLI**

The nephew of former Richmond champion Maurice Rioli, who won the Norm Smith Medal in 1982. Played for South Fremantle last year, kicking four goals in the Westar Grand Final. Originally from Darwin, a profitable recruiting ground for the Bombers

# ESSENDON

| Name (# = rookie) | No. | Born | Height | Weight | Recruited from |
|---|---|---|---|---|---|
| Steven Alessio | 27 | 8/11/71 | 203 | 105 | ST OLIVERS |
| Matthew Banks | 39 | 20/7/76 | 199 | 105 | RINGWOOD/EASTERN U18 |
| Paul Barnard | 16 | 13/2/73 | 189 | 92 | EAST PERTH (WA)/HAWTHORN |
| Peter Berbakov | 20 | 22/8/73 | 188 | 87 | SUNBURY/ESSENDON U19/GLENELG (SA) |
| Darren Bewick | 8 | 21/8/67 | 176 | 81 | WEST PERTH (WA) |
| Justin Blumfield | 32 | 24/11/77 | 187 | 86 | TUGGERANONG (ACT) |
| Mark Bolton | 23 | 3/4/79 | 192 | 83 | RINGWOOD/EASTERN U18 |
| Andrew Bomford | 28 | 19/7/74 | 183 | 83 | NORTH SHORE (NSW)/SYDNEY RESERVES |
| David Calthorpe | 14 | 17/8/73 | 179 | 92 | EAST KEILOR |
| Blake Caracella | 33 | 15/3/77 | 186 | 84 | ST MARYS(VMFL)/NORTHERN U18 |
| Che Cockatoo-Collins | 9 | 5/3/75 | 186 | 76 | CITY COBRAS,CAIRNS (QLD)/PORT ADELAIDE (SA) |
| Sean Denham | 38 | 29/4/69 | 177 | 75 | MELTON SOUTH/GEELONG |
| Jordon Doering | 34 | 14/9/79 | 187 | 83 | SANDHURST/BENDIGO U18 |
| Ben Doolan | 22 | 10/1/73 | 182 | 89 | ALBURY (NSW)/SYDNEY |
| Simon Eastaugh | 36 | 12/6/73 | 200 | 98 | SHEPPARTON/RICHMOND RES/NORWOOD (SA) |
| Dustin Fletcher | 31 | 7/5/75 | 198 | 96 | ESSENDON GRAMMAR/WESTERN U18 |
| Mark Fraser | 30 | 4/2/71 | 183 | 80 | MONTMORENCY/COLLINGWOOD |
| Damien Hardwick | 11 | 18/8/72 | 179 | 78 | UPWEY-TECOMA/NTH MLB RESERVES/SPRINGVALE |
| Chris Heffernan | 26 | 29/1/79 | 186 | 82 | TERANG/GEELONG U18 |
| James Hird | 5 | 4/2/73 | 185 | 93 | AINSLIE (ACT) |
| Jason Johnson | 42 | 25/1/78 | 181 | 88 | KILMORE/CALDER U18 |
| Judd Lalich | 17 | 26/12/75 | 193 | 86 | EAST PERTH (WA) |
| Matthew Lloyd | 18 | 16/4/78 | 191 | 86 | AVONDALE HEIGHTS/WESTERN U18 |
| Michael Long | 13 | 1/10/69 | 178 | 79 | ST MARYS (NT) |
| Scott Lucas | 25 | 30/12/77 | 191 | 90 | CAMPERDOWN/GEELONG U18 |
| Daniel McAlister | 4 | 22/8/78 | 185 | 86 | SMITHTON/TAS U18 |
| Mark Mercuri | 2 | 21/2/74 | 180 | 77 | KEILOR PARK |
| Joe Misiti | 24 | 9/11/74 | 186 | 90 | KEILOR PARK |
| Gary Moorcroft | 29 | 16/4/76 | 173 | 80 | PRESTON/NORTHERN U18 |
| Ryan O'Connor | 3 | 27/6/74 | 195 | 104 | ULVERSTONE (TAS) |
| Gary O'Donnell | 10 | 12/5/65 | 181 | 85 | NORTH RINGWOOD |
| Ricky Olarenshaw | 47 | 1/2/73 | 182 | 80 | KEILOR |
| Michael Prior | 15 | 6/9/73 | 184 | 79 | EAST PERTH (WA) |
| Dean Solomon | 7 | 9/1/80 | 188 | 92 | NTH BROKEN HILL (NSW)/BENDIGO U18 |
| Peter Somerville | 19 | 8/7/68 | 195 | 97 | MOE |
| Michael Symons | 12 | 16/9/71 | 182 | 80 | SUBIACO (WA) |
| Andrew Ukovic | 1 | 23/11/78 | 187 | 76 | WEST COBURG/NORTHERN U18 |
| Dean Wallis | 21 | 27/8/69 | 190 | 94 | NHILL |
| Matthew Watson | 44 | 2/12/76 | 199 | 98 | WARRAGUL/GIPPSLAND U18 |
| Sean Wellman | 6 | 20/9/74 | 194 | 92 | NORTH ADELAIDE (SA)/ADELAIDE |
| Tim Williams | 40 | 22/9/75 | 194 | 94 | EAST PERTH (WA) |
| Barry Young | 35 | 26/6/70 | 184 | 87 | ST ARNAUD/RICHMOND |
| Robert DiRosa # | 50 | 4/7/77 | 183 | 80 | WERRIBEE/WESTERN U18/GEELONG/FOOTS RES |
| Winis Imbi # | 49 | 26/4/79 | 172 | 78 | PORTLAND/BALLARAT U18 |
| Mark Johnson # | 45 | 23/5/78 | 180 | 86 | SUNBURY/CALDER U18 |
| Lachlan Oakley # | 46 | 25/5/75 | 180 | 90 | SANDRINGHAM |
| Dean Rioli # | 43 | 20/5/78 | 180 | 85 | SOUTH FREMANTLE (WA) |
| Total/(Average) *On 26/2/98 | | (23.7 yrs)* | (187) | (87) | |

# PLAYERS 1998

| Debut | HOME & AWAY | | 1997 | | FINALS | | GRAND FINALS | | | NIGHT SERIES | | STATE OF ORIGIN | |
|---|---|---|---|---|---|---|---|---|---|---|---|---|---|
| | Gms | Gls | Gms | Gls | Gms | Gls | Gms | Gls | Won | Gms | Gls | Gms | Gls |
| 1992 | 78 | 87 | 9 | 11 | 5 | 14 | | | | 7 | 8 | 0 | 0 |
| 1997 | 2 | 1 | 2 | 1 | | | | | | 0 | 0 | 0 | 0 |
| 1994 | 31 | 7 | 5 | 0 | 2 | 0 | | | | 4 | 1 | 0 | 0 |
| 1996 | 28 | 10 | 11 | 10 | | | | | | 2 | 0 | 0 | 0 |
| 1988 | 172 | 266 | 5 | 2 | 14 | 23 | 2 | 1 | 1 | 12 | 16 | 4 | 4 |
| 1996 | 25 | 8 | 15 | 5 | 2 | 1 | | | | 1 | 2 | 0 | 0 |
| | 0 | 0 | 0 | 0 | | | | | | 0 | 0 | 0 | 0 |
| 1997 | 3 | 2 | 3 | 2 | | | | | | 1 | 0 | 0 | 0 |
| 1992 | 71 | 45 | 8 | 4 | 7 | 5 | 1 | 1 | 1 | 5 | 2 | 1 | 0 |
| 1997 | 17 | 25 | 17 | 25 | | | | | | 1 | 1 | 0 | 0 |
| 1994 | 71 | 97 | 17 | 17 | 3 | 6 | | | | 6 | 4 | 3 | 0 |
| 1987 | 159 | 62 | 22 | 8 | 11 | 6 | 1 | 1 | 1 | 12 | 4 | 0 | 0 |
| | 0 | 0 | 0 | 0 | | | | | | 0 | 0 | 0 | 0 |
| 1991 | 83 | 11 | 11 | 1 | 5 | 0 | | | | 6 | 0 | 2 | 0 |
| | 0 | 0 | 0 | 0 | | | | | | 0 | 0 | 0 | 0 |
| 1993 | 91 | 31 | 16 | 9 | 8 | 5 | 1 | 0 | 1 | 5 | 0 | 0 | 0 |
| 1992 | 69 | 32 | 11 | 5 | 2 | 0 | | | | 9 | 5 | 0 | 0 |
| 1994 | 65 | 12 | 15 | 3 | 4 | 1 | | | | 3 | 0 | 0 | 0 |
| 1997 | 3 | 0 | 3 | 0 | | | | | | 1 | 0 | 0 | 0 |
| 1992 | 95 | 167 | 7 | 18 | 8 | 12 | 1 | 2 | 1 | 10 | 18 | 1 | 3 |
| 1997 | 3 | 0 | 3 | 0 | | | | | | 0 | 0 | 0 | 0 |
| | 0 | 0 | 0 | 0 | | | | | | 0 | 0 | 0 | 0 |
| 1995 | 36 | 88 | 20 | 63 | 5 | 4 | | | | 3 | 1 | 1 | 3 |
| 1989 | 131 | 103 | 5 | 4 | 12 | 11 | 2 | 2 | 1 | 10 | 4 | 4 | 7 |
| 1996 | 36 | 34 | 22 | 23 | 1 | 0 | | | | 3 | 0 | 0 | 0 |
| 1997 | 2 | 0 | 2 | 0 | | | | | | 1 | 0 | 0 | 0 |
| 1992 | 90 | 127 | 11 | 12 | 8 | 16 | 1 | 3 | 1 | 10 | 9 | 2 | 5 |
| 1992 | 103 | 40 | 18 | 4 | 6 | 2 | 1 | 1 | 1 | 10 | 1 | 0 | 0 |
| 1995 | 12 | 7 | 11 | 7 | | | | | | 0 | 0 | 0 | 0 |
| 1994 | 49 | 39 | 16 | 12 | 2 | 0 | | | | 3 | 0 | 2 | 0 |
| 1987 | 226 | 85 | 20 | 8 | 16 | 7 | 2 | 0 | 1 | 18 | 4 | 9 | 0 |
| 1993 | 60 | 12 | 15 | 2 | 9 | 0 | 1 | 0 | 1 | 6 | 1 | 0 | 0 |
| 1994 | 47 | 15 | 22 | 10 | 2 | 0 | | | | 4 | 0 | 2 | 0 |
| | 0 | 0 | 0 | 0 | | | | | | 0 | 0 | 0 | 0 |
| 1988 | 134 | 87 | 13 | 1 | 11 | 3 | 2 | 1 | 1 | 14 | 11 | 1 | 1 |
| 1992 | 92 | 77 | 15 | 2 | 4 | 3 | | | | 7 | 2 | 1 | 0 |
| 1997 | 5 | 2 | 5 | 2 | | | | | | 1 | 1 | 0 | 0 |
| 1987 | 86 | 29 | 11 | 0 | 7 | 2 | 1 | 1 | 1 | 5 | 1 | 0 | 0 |
| 1997 | 1 | 0 | 1 | 0 | | | | | | 0 | 0 | 0 | 0 |
| 1994 | 65 | 11 | 22 | 2 | 2 | 0 | | | | 5 | 5 | 2 | 0 |
| | 0 | 0 | 0 | 0 | | | | | | 1 | 0 | 0 | 0 |
| 1989 | 106 | 58 | 6 | 3 | 5 | 0 | | | | 9 | 7 | 1 | 0 |
| 1995 | 3 | 0 | 0 | 0 | | | | | | 0 | 0 | | |
| | 0 | 0 | 0 | 0 | | | | | | 0 | 0 | | |
| | 0 | 0 | 0 | 0 | | | | | | 0 | 0 | | |
| | 0 | 0 | 0 | 0 | | | | | | 0 | 0 | | |
| | 0 | 0 | 0 | 0 | | | | | | 0 | 0 | | |
| | (56) | (40) | 415 | 276 | 161 | 121 | 16 | 13 | 12 | 195 | 108 | 36 | 23 |

## Dockers at a glance

**ADDRESS:** Level One, Wesley Way, 16 Market St, Fremantle 6160

**WEB SITE:** www.dockers.com.au

**EMAIL:** dockers@dockers.com.au

**POSTAL ADDRESS:** PO Box 381, Fremantle 6959

**TELEPHONE:** (08) 9430 8975

**FACSIMILE:** (08) 9430 8976

**PRESIDENT:** Ross Kelly

**CHIEF EXECUTIVE:** David Hatt

**FOOTBALL MANAGER:** Gerard McNeill

**MARKETING MANAGER:** Vern Reid

**RECRUITING MANAGER:** Phil Smart

**COACHING STAFF:** Gerard Neesham (senior), Stan Magro, Mark Riley, Ben Allan

**SELECTION COMMITTEE:** Gerard Neesham, Mark Riley, Ron Alexander (chairman), Ben Allan, Stan Magro

**RESOURCES MANAGER:** Tony Solin

**CLUB DOCTORS:** Ken Withers, David Day

**CLUB PHYSIOTHERAPISTS:** Ian Lowther, Jeff Boyle

**VICTORIAN MANAGER:** Wayne Hughes, 105 Kingsclere Ave, Keysborough 3173

**TELEPHONE:** (03) 9798 6842

**FACSIMILE:** (03) 9798 7725

**JOINED AFL:** 1995

**HOME GROUND:** Subiaco Oval and the WACA

**GROUND DIMENSIONS:** Subiaco Oval — 173m by 129m. WACA 165m by 129m.

**OFFICIAL COLORS:** Guernsey: Purple with one red and one green chest panel separated by a white anchor. Socks: Purple with green, white and red hoops around top. Shorts: Purple.

**RECORD HOME ATTENDANCE:** Subiaco — 39,844 — September 3, 1995 v West Coast WACA: 26,618 — April 26, 1996 v Melbourne

# FREMANTLE

# Time to step up for Dockers

Of all the so-called 'newcomers' to the AFL in the past decade, the hardest team to rate has been Fremantle. Like Port Adelaide, the Dockers were the second team to represent their state/city and at first glance it appears their record is none too flattering.

Fremantle has finished 13th, 13th and 12th since its debut in 1995, but there have been signs all along that the Dockers are not far away from mixing it with the best.

Improving their position one place in 1997 does not appear anything out of the ordinary, but last year could be seen as a watershed season. Had the Dockers beaten wooden-spooner Melbourne in round 22, they would have secured a place in the eight.

But luck, particularly with injuries, deserted them when it counted and they lost their final three games to finish with a 10-12 win-loss record.

In the past two years, the Dockers have won only three games outside Perth. They will have to follow the example of their cross-town rival West Coast and, more recently, Adelaide, and improve their record on the road if they are to break into the eight.

Plenty has been written and said about their style of play, but it seems the Dockers are now aiming for less flair and more reliability around the midfield. They have recruited proven performers such as Adrian Fletcher (Brisbane Lions) and Stuart Anderson (North Melbourne), two players who can almost act like traffic policemen directing play.

On the debit side, they have lost Ben Allan (retired) and Jeff White (Melbourne), but some of the younger brigade are starting to show the benefit of two or three seasons of AFL football.

Greg Harding, Craig Callaghan, Daniel Bandy, James Clement, Shane Parker and Luke Toia fall into that category and there has been experience and back-up from Dale Kickett, Peter Mann, Stephen O'Reilly and Andrew Wills. Two exciting youngsters to keen an eye on are Heath Black and Jess Sinclair.

The defence appears fairly well established with O'Reilly and Kickett leading a unit that is prepared to run and back itself, but the Dockers have struggled to find a regular target up forward.

Kingsley Hunter has had modest returns of 33 goals (1996) and 32 goals (1997) to head Fremantle's goal-kicking in the past two seasons. Last season he played only 11 games and perhaps there is a future for him in front of goal.

— **Michael Lovett**

## THE YEAR AHEAD

| Rd | Date | Opponent | Venue | Home/ Away | Time (local) |
|----|------|----------|-------|------------|--------------|
| 1 | March 29 | Melbourne | S | H | 1.20pm |
| 2 | April 5 | Adelaide | FP | A | 1.40pm |
| 3 | April 12 | West Coast | S | H | 1.20pm |
| 4 | April 19 | Essendon | P | H | 2.10pm |
| 5 | April 25 (N) | North Melbourne | W | H | 6.40pm |
| 6 | May 2 (N) | Port Adelaide | FP | A | 8.10pm |
| 7 | May 8 (N) | Hawthorn | W | H | 6.40pm |
| 8 | May 16 | Geelong | KP | A | 2.10pm |
| 9 | May 22 (N) | St Kilda | W | H | 6.40pm |
| 10 | May 31 | Collingwood | VP | A | 2.10pm |
| 11 | June 7 | Brisbane Lions | S | H | 12.10pm |
| 12 | June 14 | Western Bulldogs | OO | A | 2.10pm |
| 13 | June 21 | Carlton | S | H | 1.20pm |
| 14 | June 27 | Richmond | MCG | A | 2.10pm |
| 15 | July 5 | Sydney | S | H | 1.20pm |
| 16 | July 18 | Melbourne | MCG | A | 2.10pm |
| 17 | July 24 (N) | Adelaide | S | H | 6.40pm |
| 18 | August 2 | West Coast | S | H | 12.10pm |
| 19 | August 8 (N) | Essendon | S | H | 6.40pm |
| 20 | August 14 (N) | North Melbourne | MCG | A | 7.40pm |
| 21 | August 23 | Port Adelaide | S | H | 12.10pm |
| 22 | August 29 | Hawthorn | P | H | 2.10pm |

## 1997 AT A GLANCE

**W:** R1: Western Bulldogs 11.10 (76) v Fremantle 10.20 (80) (OO)
**W:** R2: Fremantle 13.9 (87) v Hawthorn 10.13 (73) (S)
**L:** R3: West Coast 16.15 (111) v Fremantle 9.17 (71) (S)
**L:** R4: Richmond 10.11 (71) v Fremantle 10.7 (67) (OO)
**W:** R5: Fremantle 16.11 (107) v St Kilda 15.11 (101) (S)
**L:** R6: Geelong 14.13 (97) v Fremantle 6.7 (43) (KP)

### SNAPSHOT

**Games:** 22
**Wins:** 10 **Losses:** 12
**Ladder Finish:** 12th
**Players Used:** 38

**W:** R7: Fremantle 17.22 (124) v Melbourne 10.9 (69) (W)
**W:** R8: Fremantle 14.14 (98) v Brisbane Lions 15.3 (93) (S)
**L:** R9: Carlton 16.9 (105) v Fremantle 14.4 (88) (OO)
**L:** R10: Fremantle 10.12 (72) v Adelaide 16.9 (105) (S)

**L:** R11: North Melbourne 15.15 (105) v Fremantle 12.7 (79) (MCG)
**W:** R12: Fremantle 24.13 (157) v Essendon 9.6 (60) (S)
**L:** R13: Port Adelaide 10.9 (69) v Fremantle 7.12 (54) (FP)
**W:** R14: Fremantle 6.12 (48) v Sydney 3.15 (33) (W)
**L:** R15: Collingwood 25.10 (160) v Fremantle 9.6 (60) (VP)
**W:** R16: Fremantle 15.7 (97) v Western Bulldogs 13.13 (91) (S)
**W:** R17: Hawthorn 9.8 (62) v Fremantle 10.11 (71) (P)
**L:** R18: Fremantle 7.7 (49) v West Coast 13.4 (82) (S)
**W:** R19: Fremantle 12.13 (85) v Richmond 5.12 (42) (W)
**L:** R20: St Kilda 12.5 (77) v Fremantle 9.10 (64) (P)
**L:** R21: Fremantle 9.14 (68) v Geelong 14.16 (100) (S)
**L:** R22: Melbourne 18.11 (119) v Fremantle 11.13 (79) (MCG)

## The Coach

**Gerard Neesham**

**Born:** 11/12/54

Gerard Neesham is back for his fourth year as coach of the Fremantle Dockers and by far his biggest test awaits him. Most experts consider the Dockers have done their three-year apprenticeship and that now is the time to make their move.

Neesham's contract was extended at the end of the 1997 season and his agenda is to get the Dockers inside the eight if not this year then certainly the next. They were knocking on the door in '97, but came up short at the finish.

He does not enjoy the highest profile of League coaches — perhaps a legacy of the fact that he had only a short stint in the VFL, playing nine games with Sydney in 1982, the year the South Melbourne club relocated to the Harbour City.

He made his name as a player in WA, amassing 218 games with East Fremantle, Swan Districts and Claremont. He played in premiership sides with East Fremantle (1985) and Swan Districts (1983, '84).

He coached Claremont from 1987 to '94 for 122 wins, 44 losses and three draws. There were six grand finals and four premierships (two as playing coach of Claremont in 1987 and '89). He was also WA state coach in 1988 and '94.

### AT A GLANCE

**COACHING RECORD**
Fremantle

| Season | P | W | L | D | Pos |
|--------|----|----|----|---|-----|
| 1995 | 22 | 8 | 14 | — | 13 |
| 1996 | 22 | 7 | 15 | — | 13 |
| 1997 | 22 | 10 | 12 | — | 12 |
| **Total** | **66** | **25** | **41** | | |

## WIN/LOSS RECORD

| Against | P | W (N) | L (N) | D (N) |
|---|---|---|---|---|
| Adelaide | 3 | 0 | 3 (3) | 0 |
| Brisbane Bears | 3 | 1 | 2 (1) | 0 |
| Brisbane Lions | 1 | 1 | 0 | 0 |
| Carlton | 4 | 1 | 3 | 0 |
| Collingwood | 4 | 1 (1) | 3 | 0 |
| Essendon | 4 | 1 | 3 (1) | 0 |
| Fitzroy | 4 | 3 | 1 | 0 |
| Geelong | 5 | 1 (1) | 4 | 0 |
| Hawthorn | 4 | 2 | 2 | 0 |
| Melbourne | 5 | 2 (2) | 3 (1) | 0 |
| North Melb | 3 | 0 | 3 (1) | 0 |
| Port Adel | 1 | 0 | 1 (1) | 0 |
| Richmond | 5 | 2 (1) | 3 | 0 |
| St Kilda | 4 | 2 (1) | 2 | 0 |
| Sydney | 5 | 5 (1) | 0 | 0 |
| West Coast | 6 | 0 | 6 | 0 |
| W Bulldogs | 5 | 3 | 2 | 0 |
| **TOTALS** | **66** | **25 (7)** | **41 (8)** | **0 (0)** |

*(N) Premiership matches played at night*

## WINNING RUNS

5 v Sydney (1995– )
2 v Hawthorn (1997– )
2 v Fitzroy (1995)
1 v Brisbane Bears (1995)
1 v Brisbane Lions (1997– )
1 v Geelong (1995)
1 v St Kilda (1995)
1 v Western Bulldogs (1995–)
1 v Carlton (1996)
1 v Richmond (1996); (1997– )
1 v Brisbane (1996); (1997)
1 v Melbourne (1996)
1 v Collingwood (1996)
1 v Essendon (1997– )

## 1997 BEST AND FAIREST

Four members of the match committee are allocated 10 votes to distribute to players. One player can receive a maximum of four votes per game.

1. Dale Kickett (93)
2. Shane Parker (76)
3. Craig Callaghan (74)
4. Andrew Wills (72)
5. Greg Harding (63)
6. Luke Toia (55)
7. Stephen O'Reilly (33)
8. Quenton Leach (26)
9. Gary Dhurrkay (24)
10. Mark Gale (23)

## GAMES RECORDS

63 Dale Kickett (1995– )
62 Stephen O'Reilly (1995– )
58 Peter Mann (1995– )
53 Quenton Leach (1995– )
51 Andrew Wills (1995– )

## GOALS RECORDS

79 Peter Mann (1995– )
65 Kingsley Hunter (1995– )
58 Andrew Wills (1995– )
55 Winston Abraham (1995–97)

## HIGHS AND LOWS

| Against | Highest | Lowest | G. W. Margin | G. L. Margin |
|---|---|---|---|---|
| Adelaide | 12.12.84 (1995) | 5.6.36 (1996) | — | 96 (1996) |
| Brisbane Bears | 17.18.120 (1995) | 10.10.70 (1996) | 66 (1995) | 25 (1996) |
| Brisbane Lions | 14.14.98 (1997) | 14.14.98 (1997) | 5 (1997) | — |
| Carlton | 15.12.102 (1996) | 7.7.49 (1995) | 53 (1996) | 61 (1996) |
| Collingwood | 15.16.106 (1996) | 9.6.60 (1997) | 24 (1996) | 100 (1997) |
| Essendon | 24.13.157 (1997) | 11.16.82 (1995) | 97 (1997) | 48 (1995) |
| Fitzroy | 24.13.157 (1996) | 10.16.76 (1996) | 86 (1996) | 31 (1996) |
| Geelong | 12.22.94 (1995) | 6.7.43 (1997) | 19 (1995) | 54 (1997) |
| Hawthorn | 13.9.87 (1997) | 7.11.53 (1996) | 14 (1997) | 57 (1996) |
| Melbourne | 17.22.124 (1997) | 7.8.50 (1995) | 55 (1997) | 52 (1995) |
| North Melb | 12.7.79 (1997) | 8.10.58 (1996) | — | 71 (1995) |
| Port Adel | 7.12.54 (1997) | 7.12.54 (1997) | — | 15 (1997) |
| Richmond | 17.18.120 (1996) | 10.7.67 (1997) | 54 (1996) | 7 (1995) |
| St Kilda | 20.11.131 (1995) | 9.10.64 (1997) | 71 (1995) | 23 (1996) |
| Sydney | 25.13.163 (1995) | 6.12.48 (1997) | 58 (1995) | — |
| West Coast | 9.17.71 (1997) | 6.9.45 (1996) | — | 85 (1995) |
| W Bulldogs | 17.14.116 (1995) | 10.20.80 (1997) | 31 (1995) | 18 (1996) |

## THE LEADERSHIP AT FREMANTLE

| Year | Pos | Coach | Captain | Best & Fairest | Leading Goalkicker | |
|---|---|---|---|---|---|---|
| 1995 | 13 | G. Neesham | B. Allan | P. Mann | P. Mann | 33 |
| 1996 | 13 | G. Neesham | B. Allan | S. O'Reilly | K. Hunter | 33 |
| 1997 | 12 | G. Neesham | P. Mann | D. Kickett | K. Hunter | 32 |

# PLAYER PROFILES

### STUART ANDERSON
Young defender who played in North Melbourne's 1996 premiership side only to find himself traded to another club 12 months later. Involved in a direct swap for the Dockers' Winston Abraham and probably faces the most crucial time of his career. Appeared to have many more years left in him at North, but had a disappointing 1997, spending part of it in the reserves. Regained his spot in the finals, but was not an impact player in either of the Roos' two September appearances. Now faces a new challenge in a side desperately in need of ready-made players. His style will suit the Dockers and he should provide plenty of drive running off the half-back flank.
**Player honors:** North Melbourne premiership side 1996; AFL Norwich Rising Star nominee 1995.
**Previous AFL club:** North Melbourne (1994-97: 61 games, 20 goals).

### DANIEL BANDY
This tall, athletic young ruckman is on the verge of making his mark in the AFL after showing great promise over the past three seasons. Can be used as an option in attack, but is at the stage of his career where he could become his club's No. 1 ruckman. Has had some injury setbacks, particularly in 1996 when he missed the second half of the season with a shoulder problem. Gave up a promising basketball career to concentrate on football. If he can remain injury-free, he could be on the verge of something big.
**Player honors:** AFL Norwich Rising Star nominee 1996.

### HEATH BLACK
Had a promising debut season, playing 15 games for the Dockers and winning an AFL Norwich Rising Star nomination. A product of the TAC Cup competition in Victoria, Black played some eye-catching games on the wing and can roam as a half-forward. Blessed with excellent disposal on his left foot, he looks to have a bright career. Appears to have settled in well in his adopted state and Fremantle has high hopes that he will develop into a quality running player. The question now is the second-year blues syndrome, but Black appears to be a mature type for one so young and should be a long-term prospect. Unfortunately, a groin injury required surgery over the pre-season and was expected to miss most of the first half of 1998.
**Player honors:** AFL Norwich Rising Star nominee 1997.

### CHRIS BOND
Tenacious on-baller who finds himself at his third AFL club. Started with Carlton in 1990, but played his best football with Richmond, particularly in 1994 and '95. Did not enjoy a great year in 1997, even though he played every game and finished 10th in the Tigers' best and fairest. With the Dockers looking for established players, they were prepared to trade their first round draft pick in exchange for Bond. They certainly have gained a player who will give nothing less than 100 per cent and the change of club at this stage of his career could be a turning point. Was a popular player at Punt Road and should provide experience and leadership in his new environment. Would be no surprise to see him leading by example and setting the pace for his younger teammates, both at training and on game day.
**Player honors:** Richmond best and fairest 1994.
**Previous AFL clubs:** Carlton (1990-92: 22 games, 8 goals), Richmond (1993-97: 100 games, 32 goals).

### MICHAEL BROWN
Did not kick on in 1997 after a reasonable debut season in 1996 when he played 10 games. Feisty key position player who has been used mainly in attack, but probably needs to harness his aggression. Has the sort of raw strength and ability that appeals and would be keen to cement a regular place in 1998 and beyond. Probably needs to get a few good games and goals on the board with Swan Districts and will be a late starter because of a shoulder operation.

### MATTHEW BURTON
Despite his height has never claimed the No. 1 ruck spot for the Dockers, but has shown great agility and mobility for one so tall. At 210cm, he is the AFL's tallest player and one of Fremantle's most popular characters. Has some young and spirited opposition vying for the No. 1 spot but is keen to prove himself as a consistent ruckman at this level. Palms the ball well and has a big height advantage over his opponents.

### CRAIG CALLAGHAN
Tough, speedy rover who has improved each year since 1995. Played 21 games in 1997 and was the only Fremantle player to win more than 300 kicks for the season. Was a durable performer, playing 21 of a possible 22 games and gives the impression he is ready to make a name for himself. Capped off a great season by finishing third in his club's best and fairest and looks set to become one of the top on-ballers in the competition. On the verge of a 50-game milestone at the start of 1998 and will be around the AFL scene for many years to come.
**Player honors:** 3rd best and fairest 1997; AFL Norwich Star nominee 1995, 1996.

### TRENT CARROLL
Looks set to push for a permanent senior place after playing six games in 1997. Could develop into a key position player and is best suited in defence. A former captain of Western Australia's under-18 team, Carroll played most of his junior football at centre half-forward but is more likely to be used in defence by the Dockers.

### SCOTT CHISHOLM
Dashing half-back flanker who is well suited to Fremantle's style of play. However, had a frustrating season in 1997 because of groin and back-related problems and was restricted to 14 games. When fully fit, plays with plenty of flair and is a crowd favorite. Goes by the nickname 'Prince' after claims that he is a distant relative of the royal family. One of the real characters of Fremantle's line-up and, more importantly, plays an integral role in the Dockers' running game.

## MICHAEL CLARK

Yet to play a game of AFL football and might be wondering what he has done wrong in his short time on the Dockers' list. Did not play any football in 1997 after a shoulder injury required major surgery (he also had shoulder problems in 1996). Was making good progress from his shoulder reconstruction and the Dockers believe this tall utility would have played senior football in 1998. However, a summer training mishap — he ruptured an anterior cruciate ligament — means he will miss his second successive season. The Dockers have great faith in his ability and will retain a spot on their list for him. Clark is the son of former Australian Test fast bowler Wayne Clark.

## JAMES CLEMENT

Big improver in 1997, playing 21 games and winning selection in the WA State of Origin side. Has the height to play in a variety of positions, but looked comfortable as a tall half-back flanker. Was forced to play up forward last year when Peter Mann was injured and made a reasonable fist of his new role. Should develop further in '98 because of his willingness to go hard at the ball.

## MATTHEW CLUCAS

Played only one senior game in 1997 — he was brought to Victoria for the travelling experience but the Dockers found themselves with injury problems on a terrible day at Geelong. Even though he was thrown to the wolves that day and did not play any more senior games, the Dockers have high hopes for this young rover. Was able to learn more about the game by playing for East Fremantle in the local competition and has a big chance to impress this season. One of many young hopefuls who will be eager to impress.

## TONY DELANEY

Probably at the crossroads of his career as he shapes up for his sixth season at this level. Talented and speedy, Delaney had a serious thigh injury in 1997 and was restricted to eight games. Has never been able to get any consistency at this level, mainly because of injuries, and 40 games since 1993 is not a big output. Most of his injuries have been soft tissue-related which has been extremely frustrating for both player and club. Needs to put it together this year, but is still young enough to make the grade.
**Player honors:** Essendon night series premiership side 1994.
**Previous AFL club:** Essendon (1993-94: 15 games, 9 goals).

## GARY DHURRKAY

Finished ninth in Fremantle's best and fairest last year, but does not play with a great deal of consistency. Has all the skills, especially long kicking, and his free-running style is suited to the Dockers. Now in his fourth season at League level, Dhurrkay is another player facing a make-or-break year. With Winston Abraham's departure to North Melbourne, he can expect more playing time.

## BRENDON FEDDEMA

Mobile big man who was discovered by the Dockers two years in the United States when he was studying at Regis University in Colorado. On his return to Australia last year, he was on the verge of senior selection when he hurt a knee at training. Had a knee reconstruction and is not expected to return until midway through the season. Will turn 24 early in the season and is yet to play at AFL level. His form in the local competition had been encouraging and he was showing signs he could make the grade.

## ADRIAN FLETCHER

Like a one-pace stayer, Fletcher just keeps going and going and in a trade for the No. 5 draft pick with the Brisbane Lions, he finds himself at his fourth AFL club. It's a big move from Brisbane to Fremantle, but there is no doubt the Dockers were after a midfield general to direct traffic through the centre. It appeared Fletcher was reluctant at first to be part of the trade, but the Lions felt his form had slipped after an outstanding year in 1996. Knocks up winning possessions and should be a great pick-up for the Dockers, who need a player of Fletcher's experience to link in with their running game. Overcame a lack of opportunities at Geelong and St Kilda to finally establish himself in Brisbane and at 28 no doubt believes he has plenty of good football in him.
**Player honors:** 2nd Brisbane Bears best and fairest 1995.
**Previous clubs:** Geelong (1989-91: 23 games, 10 goals), St Kilda (1992: 22 games, 10 goals), Brisbane Bears (1993-96: 86 games, 49 goals), Brisbane Lions (1997: 21 games, 4 goals).

## MARK GALE

Has been on the Dockers list since their inception, but managed only four games in his first two seasons. Stepped up last year, proving himself a very handy player running out of defence. Finished 10th in best and fairest voting and was named the club's rookie of the year. Has the opportunity to claim a regular place and will have gained plenty of confidence by playing 16 games last year. The Dockers were extremely pleased and say he has the right attitude to continue his 1997 form. Is the son of experienced international golfer Terry Gale and is a more than adequate player himself, playing off a handicap of two.

## TONY GODDEN

Former West Coast Eagles utility who has had little luck trying to establish himself as a permanent senior player. Had groin surgery last year and did not play at AFL level. The Dockers are confident he can push himself into their line-up in 1998. Has finals experience with the Eagles (three games), but his return of 20 games since 1993 is a concern. One of the fittest players on the Dockers squad and will probably be used in a tagging role.
**Previous AFL club:** West Coast Eagles (1993-95: 13 games, 8 goals).

## GREG HARDING

Continued on from where he left off in 1996 with another fine season for the Dockers in 1997. Cool defender who plays well under pressure and will continue to improve as he gains more experience. Was sorely missed when he injured a shoulder in a bone-jarring collision with St Kilda's Stewart Loewe in round 20 and was forced out of the final two rounds of '97. Has played 18 games in each of his two seasons with Fremantle and has impressed with his sure and precise play. At 21, appears to have a long career ahead of him.

**Player honors:** AFL Norwich Rising Star nominee 1996.

## DANIEL HARGRAVES

Young key position forward who has the chance to return to the form he showed in 1995 and '96 in a new environment. Last year, Hargraves had a season he would prefer to forget, playing just four games for the Bulldogs. Suffered a serious shoulder injury which kept him out for most of the first half of the year and was not able to re-establish himself when he returned. A strong mark and reliable kick, he should be a good acquisition for the Dockers. He will at least provide a marking option, something the Dockers have struggled with in their short time in the AFL.

**Player honors:** AFL Norwich Rising Star nominee 1995.

**Previous AFL club:** Western Bulldogs (1994-97: 38 games, 62 goals).

## BRODIE HOLLAND

Highly promising youngster from Tasmania who made a good impression with the Tassie Mariners in the TAC Cup competition. Represented Tasmania in athletics and, not surprisingly, is a dashing type. Captained the Mariners last year and averaged 25 possessions a game. Although he is the youngest player on the Dockers' list, Holland has already played senior football for Glenorchy (when he was just 15). Glenorchy was also the former home of Adrian Fletcher and no doubt the experienced midfielder will be taking the youngster under his wings. Like Fletcher, he is best suited in the midfield. Was Fremantle's third selection — 25th overall — in the 1997 National Draft.

## KINGSLEY HUNTER

Missed the first half of the 1997 season through injury, but booted 32 goals in the final 11 games to give the Dockers a badly needed focal point. Fremantle has not been able to produce a consistent goalkicker, but Hunter shapes as the player most likely. He is strong, leads well and can take a big grab — now he just needs to get more games under his belt. His kicking can sometimes let him down, but he has the size and potential to establish himself. Needs to get a full season under his belt and if he can kick 60 to 70 goals, the Dockers believe they will be close to making their first finals appearance.

**Player honors:** AFL Norwich Rising Star nominee 1996.

## TROY JOHNSON

Fremantle's fourth and final choice in the 1998 National Draft, Johnson was highly regarded as a teenager and was drafted by the Brisbane Bears in 1995. Had some problems off the field and played only two games, but has settled down back in Perth and played in South Fremantle's 1997 premiership team. Clever half-forward who will be keen to grab another chance. The Dockers have provided him with that opportunity and certainly believe he has the ability to play at AFL level.

**Previous AFL club:** Brisbane Bears (1996: 2 games, 0 goals).

## ANTHONY JONES

Played the first three games of 1997, one mid-season and then the last three. Had a fine season in '96 when he missed only one game, but struggled with knee injuries last year and the Dockers missed his presence in defence. Still young enough to make his mark and will be looking for a big year in 1998. An honest, no-frills type player, Jones would be in the Dockers' best line-up.

## DALE KICKETT

In three seasons has proved himself to be Fremantle's best and most reliable player after doing the rounds with four other AFL clubs. Has been a great player in defence and his consistency has been reflected in his polling in the club's best and fairest award over the past three years. One of the real success stories of recent times and there is no reason why he can't maintain that form. Will appreciate the addition of several experienced players in defence and around midfield which might relieve some of the pressure on him and enhance his natural game. Only Kickett and Shane Parker played all 22 games for the Dockers last year.

**Player honors:** best and fairest 1997, 2nd best and fairest 1995, 1996; Simpson Medal 1991, '93.

**Previous AFL clubs:** Fitzroy (1990: 15 games, 13 goals), West Coast Eagles (1991: 2 games, 0 goals), St Kilda (1992: 21 games, 20 goals), Essendon (1994: 8 games, 7 goals).

## STEVEN KOOPS

Talented youngster who had a frustrating run with hamstring problems in 1997. Showed his class returning from a long break to kick four goals in the final match of the season. Lively forward who was still in his teens at the start of the 1998 season and is a player worth watching as he gains more experience. Had an outstanding career as a junior and could be ready to blossom. Of all the young players on the Dockers' list, Koops shapes as the most exciting.

## QUENTON LEACH

Returned from a broken jaw in 1996 and played 21 of a possible 22 games in 1997. After playing almost exclusively as a defender in '95 and '96, was used in attack on a regular basis last season and appreciated the freedom. It is worth noting he played most of his junior football in attack. Achieved every player's dream when he displayed plenty of maturity to kick a goal after the siren to sink the Brisbane Lions in round eight. He might be in the superstar bracket, but he's very tough mentally and, when playing in defence, gives his opponents little room to move.

## PETER MANN

Achieved a personal milestone when elevated to club captain at the start of 1997, replacing Ben Allan, but did not enjoy a great season because of a combination of form and injury. Will have to lead from the front at centre half-forward as the Dockers don't have many tall, marking options up forward. There is no doubt the Dockers' skipper relies heavily on his marking and he will have to get his confidence up early in the season to lead his side from the front. Was elected president of the AFL Players' Association last year, replacing Justin Madden.

**Player honors:** best and fairest 1995; leading goal-kicker 1995; captain since 1997.

**Previous AFL club:** North Melbourne (1991-94: 39 games, 12 goals).

### ANDREW McGOVERN

Nothing pretty about his play, but this solid defender gets the job done and has been a consistent performer for the Dockers. Can play close and tight, much to the annoyance of opponents who appreciate a bit of freedom, and is deceptively quick. Suffered a broken leg towards the end of the season, but to no one's surprise, has worked hard to regain his fitness and adds depth and experience to the Dockers' list. Normally takes Fremantle's kick-ins and has an important role in the Dockers' set plays.

**Previous AFL club:** Sydney (1992-93: 20 games, 7 goals).

### SHAUN McMANUS

Just when his career looked like taking off, McManus had a wretched season in 1997. Suffered a serious knee injury in round three and was sidelined for the rest of the year. Has gone through the long, exhausting rehabilitation process and the Dockers are confident he will return to his dashing best on the wing. Was in the top 10 Fremantle players the previous season and providing he makes a full recovery, should again be a regular. The Dockers say he should be ready to resume playing at the start of the season.

**Player honors:** AFL Norwich Rising Star nominee 1995.

### CLEM MICHAEL

Talented youngster who is the son of former South Fremantle champion ruckman Stephen Michael who, in his prime in the late 1970s and early '80s, was feted by just about every Victorian club. Clem played in South Fremantle's 1997 premiership side in his first season at senior level and was most impressive, particularly in the finals. A stylish forward who is very cool under pressure. Still learning the game after playing basketball almost exclusively for two years. Was Fremantle's second pick, 21st overall, in the 1997 National Draft.

### JASON NORRISH

Best suited in a tagging role, Norrish played only eight games in 1997 because of continual groin problems. Tough, low-to-the-ground left-footer who reads the play well and doesn't mind getting in and under. Played in three finals for Melbourne in 1994 and has given Fremantle's midfield some badly needed experience. Should be a regular player when fully fit.

**Previous AFL club:** Melbourne (1993-94: 20 games 2 goals).

### STEPHEN O'REILLY

Maintained his rating as one of the best full-backs in the competition and showed just how much the Dockers depend on him when his hamstring injury probably cost them a spot in the finals. Missed the round 20 game against St Kilda, perhaps should not have played against Geelong in round 21 and was ruled out

of the must-win game against Melbourne in round 22. Was high on Fremantle's list of priorities when the Dockers were first formed and has not let them down. Strong defender who loves to run with the ball and boasts finals experience with Geelong. One of Fremantle's best on-field leaders.

**Player honors:** best and fairest 1996.

**Previous AFL club:** Geelong (1993-94: 36 games, 5 goals).

### DANIEL PARKER

Was given a chance to play at full-forward in the first half of the season in the absence of Kingsley Hunter. Kicked 16 goals in the first 10 games, but was not able to produce on a consistent basis. Needs more strength, but has the height to be a sound key position player. Can play in the ruck at a pinch, but the Dockers are hoping he can establish himself as a goalkicker in the local competition. Will be more opposition for places up forward this year, but has worked hard over summer and could be a player to watch.

### SHANE PARKER

One of the most improved players in the competition, Parker went from strength to strength in 1997. One of only two players (with Dale Kickett) to appear in all 22 games and was rewarded for his consistency with a high placing in the club's best and fairest award. Held down centre half-back for most of the season, despite having to play on taller opponents. Indeed, he was almost an unsung hero last season, claiming some handy scalps including Chris Grant and Matthew Richardson. Is a good mark for his size, reads the play well and is very quick. Should have the confidence now to establish himself.

**Player honors:** 2nd best and fairest 1997.

### JESS SINCLAIR

The Dockers would have been delighted with the debut season of this youngster from Victoria. Attacks the ball strongly and has good finishing skills, suggesting he will have a long career ahead of him. Played nine games in 1997 and will be eligible for an AFL Norwich Rising Star nomination in 1998. Had an excellent pre-season and impressed officials with his willingness to work hard. Should be one of several young players to emerge for the Dockers this season.

### LUKE TOIA

Looks a likely type after two impressive seasons at senior level. Was knocked from pillar to post during the latter stages of 1997, but showed plenty of courage and tenacity at the fall of the ball. With opposition sides playing him plenty of respect, it's fair indication he is rated as a player capable of igniting the Dockers, particularly at the centre bounces. Unfortunately, will have a delayed start to the '98 season because of a groin operation. Signed a three-year deal at the end of '97 and should develop into a quality midfielder. Another shining young light for the Dockers.

**Player honors:** AFL Norwich Rising Star nominee 1996.

### JAMES WALKER

One of the outstanding players in last year's TAC Cup competition, Walker is expected to be ready to play senior football. Quick, skilful winger whose best on ground performance for Victoria Country against Victoria Metro caught the eye at last year's AFL National Under-18 Championships. Was later selected to the All-Australian team. The Dockers rate him highly having taken him as their first selection, sixth overall, in the 1997 National Draft. Has impressed the club with his maturity and has settled quickly into his new football environment.

### CLIVE WATERHOUSE
Started to establish himself more in 1997, playing 15 games and netting a couple of bags of four goals. Runs hard and straight at the ball and is at the stage where he will have to live up to his No. 1 draft pick tag. Played in Port Adelaide's 1995 SANFL premiership side. Comes from a soccer background and started playing serious football only at 17. The pressure of being No. 1 draft pick has taken its toll on other players and at this stage the jury is still out on Waterhouse. Struggled early to fit into the Gerard Neesham style of play, but there were indications last year he is starting to adapt. If he can continue to find space and kick inspiring goals, he will leave his mark on the game.

### MARTIN WHITELAW
The second tallest player on Fremantle's list, Whitelaw is a developing young player who was given a chance in round 21 last year when the club's playing stocks were stretched to the limit. Had to take on an in-form Steven King from Geelong and while he struggled, he at least knows the level he has to achieve. Will take more time to develop, but has progressed satisfactorily and the departure of Jeff White means he will have more chances.

### ANDREW WILLS
Built his reputation as an opportunist forward, but stepped up last year to play a prominent role in Fremantle's midfield after two modest seasons in 1995 and '96. His pace and ball skills were well suited to the Dockers' style and enjoyed his best season in the AFL. Polled 15 votes to finish seventh in the Brownlow Medal and was close to winning selection in the Victorian State of Origin side. Has had back problems over the summer months and could be a late starter for the 1998 season.
**Previous AFL club:** Geelong (1991-94: 59 games, 43 goals).

## ROOKIE LIST

### BRAD DODD
Elusive half-forward/winger capable of playing a tagging role. Has played 32 games for East Fremantle after making his senior debut in 1996.

### CAMERON JACKSON
The tallest and heaviest player taken in the 1998 Rookie Draft, Jackson represents a swing from basketball — once perceived as the great threat to Australian Football — back to the nation's most popular sport. Jackson played in the National Basketball League for the Perth Wildcats and later the North Melbourne Giants but returned to football after living in football-crazy Melbourne for two years. Gave football away as a 16-year-old but his height and new-found passion for the game could turn out to be a bonus for the Dockers.

### PAUL MAHER
High leaping ruckman/forward who can also play in defence. Made his senior debut with Perth last season and played 17 games. Did pre-season training with the West Coast Eagles.

### JOHN NEESHAM
Nephew of Fremantle coach Gerard Neesham and another youngster who hails from a different sporting background. Represented Australia at last year's world junior championships in Cuba and has followed the family tradition of mixing football and water polo. Goes hard at the ball but has only played junior football in WA and will be given the chance to develop.

# FREMANTLE

| Name (# = rookie) | No. | Born | Height | Weight | Recruited from |
|---|---|---|---|---|---|
| Stuart Anderson | 6 | 27/6/74 | 181 | 83 | SALE/NORTH MELB |
| Daniel Bandy | 44 | 18/11/75 | 200 | 93 | PERTH (WA) |
| Heath Black | 7 | 28/5/79 | 177 | 75 | MAZENOD/OAKLEIGH U18 |
| Chris Bond | 32 | 26/1/69 | 178 | 81 | NORTH HOBART (TAS)/CARLTON/RICHMOND |
| Michael Brown | 18 | 20/9/76 | 190 | 94 | SWAN DISTRICTS (WA) |
| Matthew Burton | 24 | 19/5/70 | 210 | 103 | SUBIACO (WA) |
| Craig Callaghan | 42 | 9/3/76 | 173 | 76 | SWAN DISTRICTS (WA) |
| Trent Carroll | 46 | 28/4/78 | 191 | 88 | CLAREMONT (WA) |
| Scott Chisholm | 13 | 28/5/73 | 182 | 75 | CLAREMONT (WA) |
| Michael Clark | 39 | 31/3/78 | 192 | 86 | SWAN DISTRICTS (WA) |
| James Clement | 31 | 4/9/76 | 190 | 91 | SOUTH FREMANTLE (WA) |
| Matthew Clucas | 41 | 18/3/78 | 175 | 79 | EAST FREMANTLE (WA) |
| Tony Delaney | 30 | 27/12/75 | 183 | 85 | CLAREMONT (WA)/ESSENDON |
| Gary Dhurrkay | 19 | 4/3/74 | 181 | 86 | EAST FREMANTLE (WA) |
| Brendon Feddema | 35 | 14/5/74 | 190 | 88 | EAST FREMANTLE (WA) |
| Adrian Fletcher | 2 | 10/10/69 | 178 | 84 | GLENORCHY (TAS)/GEELONG/ST KILDA/BRISBANE |
| Mark Gale | 37 | 7/5/76 | 190 | 88 | CLAREMONT (WA) |
| Tony Godden | 22 | 19/4/72 | 183 | 81 | SUBIACO (WA)/WEST COAST |
| Greg Harding | 3 | 17/9/76 | 187 | 84 | CLAREMONT (WA) |
| Daniel Hargraves | 21 | 6/12/75 | 191 | 94 | POWELLTOWN/EASTERN U18/WSTRN BLDGS |
| Brodie Holland | 17 | 3/1/80 | 178 | 79 | GLENORCHY (TAS)/TASSIE U18 |
| Kingsley Hunter | 14 | 27/5/75 | 191 | 98 | CLAREMONT (WA) |
| Troy Johnson | 27 | 26/7/77 | 178 | 76 | STH FREM (WA)/BRISBANE/STH FREMANTLE (WA) |
| Anthony Jones | 38 | 19/12/74 | 186 | 92 | CLAREMONT (WA) |
| Dale Kickett | 11 | 4/5/68 | 179 | 77 | CLAREMONT(WA)/FITZ/WEST C/ST K/ESS |
| Steven Koops | 28 | 24/7/78 | 187 | 75 | WEST PERTH (WA) |
| Quenton Leach | 36 | 20/8/72 | 181 | 81 | CLAREMONT(WA) |
| Peter Mann | 9 | 7/9/70 | 194 | 88 | CLAREMONT (WA)/NORTH MELB |
| Andrew McGovern | 43 | 7/4/68 | 177 | 83 | CLAREMONT(WA)/SYDNEY |
| Shaun McManus | 8 | 9/2/76 | 180 | 78 | EAST FREMANTLE (WA) |
| Clem Michael | 16 | 16/7/76 | 182 | 85 | SOUTH FREMANTLE (WA) |
| Jason Norrish | 25 | 26/1/72 | 180 | 81 | CLAREMONT (WA)/MELBOURNE |
| Stephen O'Reilly | 10 | 9/11/72 | 195 | 102 | SWAN DISTRICTS (WA)/GEELONG |
| Daniel Parker | 5 | 25/5/74 | 198 | 92 | SUBIACO (WA) |
| Shane Parker | 23 | 18/2/73 | 188 | 84 | SUBIACO (WA) |
| Jess Sinclair | 15 | 26/8/78 | 180 | 75 | EAST RINGWOOD/EASTERN U18 |
| Luke Toia | 1 | 23/11/77 | 178 | 77 | SUBIACO (WA) |
| James Walker | 40 | 15/1/79 | 179 | 74 | LAKE WENDOUREE/NTH BALLARAT U18 |
| Clive Waterhouse | 26 | 23/6/74 | 184 | 87 | PORT ADELAIDE (SA) |
| Martin Whitelaw | 20 | 22/5/76 | 201 | 95 | WEST PERTH (WA) |
| Andrew Wills | 4 | 3/1/72 | 185 | 85 | BARWON/GEELONG |
| Brad Dodd # | N/A | 23/3/77 | 184 | 78 | EAST FREMANTLE (WA) |
| Cameron Jackson # | N/A | 6/8/75 | 205 | 102 | NO CLUB: BASKETBALLER |
| Paul Maher # | N/A | 11/6/76 | 190 | 86 | PERTH (WA) |
| John Neesham # | N/A | 18/1/79 | 174 | 75 | EAST FREMANTLE (WA) |
| Total/(Average) *On 26/2/98 | | (23.2 yrs)* | (185) | (85) | |

# PLAYERS 1998

| Debut | HOME & AWAY | | 1997 | | FINALS | | GRAND FINALS | | | NIGHT SERIES | | STATE OF ORIGIN | |
|---|---|---|---|---|---|---|---|---|---|---|---|---|---|
| | Gms | Gls | Gms | Gls | Gms | Gls | Gms | Gls | Won | Gms | Gls | Gms | Gls |
| 1994 | 61 | 20 | 20 | 7 | 7 | 2 | 1 | 0 | 1 | 3 | 1 | 0 | 0 |
| 1995 | 34 | 31 | 18 | 18 | | | | | | 3 | 1 | 2 | 1 |
| 1997 | 15 | 8 | 15 | 8 | | | | | | 0 | 0 | 0 | 0 |
| 1990 | 122 | 40 | 22 | 3 | 3 | 0 | | | | 5 | 1 | 6 | 1 |
| 1996 | 14 | 9 | 4 | 3 | | | | | | 1 | 0 | 0 | 0 |
| 1995 | 43 | 16 | 11 | 1 | | | | | | 1 | 0 | 1 | 0 |
| 1995 | 48 | 28 | 21 | 14 | | | | | | 3 | 2 | 1 | 1 |
| 1997 | 6 | 0 | 6 | 0 | | | | | | 0 | 0 | 0 | 0 |
| 1995 | 47 | 20 | 14 | 3 | | | | | | 3 | | 1 | 1 |
| | 0 | 0 | 0 | 0 | | | | | | 0 | 0 | 0 | 0 |
| 1996 | 33 | 5 | 21 | 4 | | | | | | 3 | 0 | 1 | 1 |
| 1997 | 1 | 0 | 1 | 0 | | | | | | 0 | 0 | 0 | 0 |
| 1993 | 40 | 18 | 8 | 0 | | | | | | 7 | 2 | 1 | 0 |
| 1995 | 41 | 41 | 15 | 7 | | | | | | 2 | 0 | 2 | 0 |
| | 0 | 0 | 0 | 0 | | | | | | 0 | 0 | 0 | 0 |
| 1989 | 152 | 73 | 21 | 4 | 7 | 2 | | | | 11 | 2 | 4 | 2 |
| 1995 | 21 | 4 | 16 | 2 | | | | | | 2 | 0 | 0 | 0 |
| 1993 | 20 | 13 | 0 | 0 | 3 | 1 | | | | 6 | 1 | 0 | 0 |
| 1996 | 36 | 1 | 18 | 1 | | | | | | 0 | 0 | 0 | 0 |
| 1994 | 38 | 62 | 4 | 3 | 1 | 1 | | | | 4 | 2 | 0 | 0 |
| | 0 | 0 | 0 | 0 | | | | | | 0 | 0 | 0 | 0 |
| 1995 | 30 | 65 | 11 | 32 | | | | | | 1 | 2 | 0 | 0 |
| 1996 | 2 | 0 | 0 | 0 | | | | | | 2 | 2 | 0 | 0 |
| 1995 | 39 | 1 | 7 | 0 | | | | | | 3 | 0 | 1 | 0 |
| 1990 | 109 | 48 | 22 | 1 | 2 | 2 | | | | 11 | 8 | 2 | 1 |
| 1996 | 10 | 13 | 4 | 7 | | | | | | 2 | 1 | 0 | 0 |
| 1995 | 53 | 26 | 21 | 17 | | | | | | 3 | 3 | 0 | 0 |
| 1991 | 97 | 91 | 17 | 20 | 3 | 0 | | | | 10 | 5 | 2 | 2 |
| 1992 | 64 | 8 | 18 | 0 | | | | | | 4 | 1 | 0 | 0 |
| 1995 | 37 | 25 | 3 | 1 | | | | | | 0 | 0 | 1 | 0 |
| | 0 | 0 | 0 | 0 | | | | | | 0 | 0 | 0 | 0 |
| 1993 | 62 | 7 | 8 | 0 | 3 | 0 | | | | 7 | 2 | 0 | 0 |
| 1993 | 98 | 9 | 20 | 0 | 4 | 0 | 1 | 0 | 0 | 6 | 0 | 2 | 0 |
| 1996 | 12 | 17 | 11 | 16 | | | | | | 2 | 3 | 0 | 0 |
| 1995 | 45 | 3 | 22 | 0 | | | | | | 2 | 0 | 0 | 0 |
| 1997 | 9 | 3 | 9 | 3 | | | | | | 0 | 0 | 0 | 0 |
| 1996 | 31 | 22 | 18 | 11 | | | | | | 2 | 2 | 1 | 0 |
| | 0 | 0 | 0 | 0 | | | | | | 0 | 0 | 0 | 0 |
| 1996 | 26 | 29 | 15 | 20 | | | | | | 3 | 2 | 0 | 0 |
| 1997 | 1 | 0 | 1 | 0 | | | | | | 0 | 0 | 0 | 0 |
| 1991 | 110 | 101 | 21 | 19 | 11 | 2 | 2 | 1 | 0 | 4 | 3 | 0 | 0 |
| | 0 | 0 | 0 | 0 | | | | | | 0 | 0 | | |
| | 0 | 0 | 0 | 0 | | | | | | 0 | 0 | | |
| | 0 | 0 | 0 | 0 | | | | | | 0 | 0 | | |
| | 0 | 0 | 0 | 0 | | | | | | 0 | 0 | | |
| | (39) | (21) | 463 | 225 | 44 | 10 | 4 | 1 | 1 | 116 | 46 | 28 | 10 |

## Cats at a glance

**ADDRESS:** Kardinia Park, Moorabool St, Geelong, VIC 3220

**POSTAL ADDRESS:** PO Box 461, Geelong, Vic 3220

**TELEPHONE:** (03) 5221 3355

**FACSIMILE:** (03) 5221 8462

**WEB SITE:** www.catnet.com.au/gfc

**PRESIDENT:** Ron Hovey

**CHIEF EXECUTIVE:** Philip Nunn

**GENERAL MANAGER — FOOTBALL DEPARTMENT:** Stephen Wells

**FOOTBALL MANAGER:** Garry Davidson

**MARKETING MANAGER:** Graeme Johnstone

**RECRUITING MANAGER:** Stephen Wells

**COACHING STAFF:** Gary Ayres (senior); Alan McConnell (development); Terry Bright (reserves)

**SELECTION COMMITTEE:** Gary Ayres, Alan McConnell, Terry Bright, Phillip Walsh, Gary Davidson

**CLUB DOCTOR:** Dr Hugh Seward

**SENIOR CLUB PHYSIOTHERAPIST:** Jeff Oxley

**JOINED AFL:** 1897

**HOME GROUND:** Kardinia Park, Moorabool St, Geelong

**GROUND DIMENSIONS:** 171m by 117m. Goals run north to south

**OFFICIAL COLORS:** Guernsey: Navy blue and white hoops. Socks: Navy blue and white hoops. Shorts: Navy blue

**PREMIERSHIPS:** 1925, 1931, 1937, 1951-52, 1963

**BROWNLOW MEDALLISTS:** E. Greeves (1924), B. Smith (1951), A. Lord (1962), P. Couch (1989)

**RECORD HOME ATTENDANCE** (Kardinia Park): 49,109 — August 30, 1952 v Carlton

# GEELONG

# Cats' youngsters make giant strides

Once the dust and disappointment had settled on Geelong's unfortunate finish to the 1997 season, the Cats, almost to a man, were calling: "Bring on the 1998 season".

And it is a different type of optimism that Geelong takes in to 1998. For the first time since 1984, the Cats will start without Gary Ablett, the player regarded by some as the greatest in the club's history.

They will also be without one of their most decorated players, centreman Paul Couch, but it is fair to say the club has been in transition mode for the past 12 months.

After all, Geelong went through all of 1997 without Ablett, while Couch managed just five games before calling it quits. Without much contribution from another favorite son in Billy Brownless, whose career is also over, the Cats fared better than most had predicted.

The emphasis at Kardinia Park has well and truly focused on youth and for that, coach Gary Ayres has made no apologies. The club has unearthed some exciting talent and blended it with a mix of players ready to take the next step.

Leading the department of youth is teenage ruckman Steven King, who has been elevated to the club's No. 1 ruck position and has taken on, and beaten, most of the competition's best. His supporting young cast includes Adam Houlihan, Darren Milburn, Jason Snell and Carl Steinfort. All five are products of the TAC Cup competition.

The new-look, hardened backline has been Ayres' greatest success and knowing how Hawthorn built its premiership glory on a miserly defence, it comes as no surprise. Brad Sholl, Ben Graham, Tim McGrath, Michael Mansfield and Brenton Sanderson were the mainstays.

The midfield also had a different look to it. With Couch missing and Garry Hocking not enjoying his best season, players such as Glenn Kilpatrick and Liam Pickering stepped up and a no-Ablett attack relied on the pinch-hitting of Ronnie Burns, Derek Hall and Paul Lynch, who, if he could get himself through an injury-free season, could elevate himself to star status.

The Cats came up short at the end of 1997, losing both finals, but had their share of misfortune when Leigh Colbert and Barry Stoneham missed crucial periods in the final weeks of the home and away season. There is much to look forward to at Kardinia Park.

— **Michael Lovett**

## THE YEAR AHEAD

| Rd | Date | Opponent | Venue | Home/ Away | Time (local) |
|---|---|---|---|---|---|
| 1 | March 28 | St Kilda | P | A | 2.10pm |
| 2 | April 4 | Richmond | KP | H | 2.10pm |
| 3 | April 12 | Sydney | SCG | A | 12.40pm |
| 4 | April 18 | Western Bulldogs | KP | H | 2.10pm |
| 5 | April 26 | Adelaide | FP | A | 2.50pm |
| 6 | May 2 | Hawthorn | KP | H | 2.10pm |
| 7 | May 9 (N) | Essendon | MCG | A | 7.40pm |
| 8 | May 16 | Fremantle | KP | H | 2.10pm |
| 9 | May 23 | West Coast | KP | H | 2.10pm |
| 10 | May 31 | North Melbourne | MCG | A | 2.10pm |
| 11 | June 6 | Carlton | MCG | H | 3.30pm |
| 12 | June 13 | Melbourne | MCG | A | 2.10pm |
| 13 | June 20 | Brisbane Lions | KP | H | 2.10pm |
| 14 | June 27 (N) | Port Adelaide | FP | A | 8.10pm |
| 15 | July 5 | Collingwood | MCG | A | 2.10pm |
| 16 | July 18 | St Kilda | KP | H | 2.10pm |
| 17 | July 26 | Richmond | MCG | A | 2.10pm |
| 18 | August 1 | Sydney | KP | H | 2.10pm |
| 19 | August 8 | Western Bulldogs | OO | A | 2.10pm |
| 20 | August 15 | Adelaide | KP | H | 2.10pm |
| 21 | August 23 | Hawthorn | P | A | 2.10pm |
| 22 | August 29 | Essendon | MCG | H | 2.10pm |

## 1997 AT A GLANCE

**L:** R1: Richmond 15.14 (104) v Geelong 13.17 (95) (MCG)

**W:** R2: Geelong 11.12 (78) v West Coast 11.6 (72) (KP)

**L:** R3: Port Adelaide 18.21 (129) v Geelong 14.6 (90) (FP)

**W:** R4: Geelong 11.19 (85) v Essendon 11.12 (78) (MCG)

**W:** R5: Carlton 12.14 (86) v Geelong 13.16 (94) (OO)

**W:** R6: Geelong 14.13 (97) v Fremantle 6.7 (43) (KP)

**W:** R7: Geelong 11.10 (76) v Sydney 6.8 (44) (KP)

### SNAPSHOT

**Games:** 24
**Wins:** 15
**Losses:** 9
**Ladder Finish:** 2nd
**Players Used:** 32

**W:** R8: Melbourne 7.7 (49) v Geelong 19.14 (128) (MCG)

**L:** R9: Brisbane Lions 19.12 (126) v Geelong 15.8 (98) (G)

**W:** R10: Geelong 16.11 (107) v St Kilda 11.13 (79) (KP)

**L:** R11: Western Bulldogs 14.12 (96) v Geelong 11.9 (75) (OO)

**L:** R12: Geelong 12.10 (82) v Hawthorn 13.10 (88) (KP)

**W:** R13: Geelong 17.8 (110) v Adelaide 7.12 (54) (KP)

**W:** R14: Geelong 9.26 (80) v Collingwood 10.12 (72) (MCG)

**W:** R15: North Melbourne 14.8 (92) v Geelong 15.12 (102) (MCG)

**W:** R16: Geelong 16.14 (110) v Richmond 12.6 (78) (KP)

**L:** R17: West Coast 20.9 (129) v Geelong 12.10 (82) (S)

**W:** R18: Geelong 25.9 (159) v Port Adelaide 11.8 (74) (KP)

**L:** R19: Essendon 11.7 (73) v Geelong 9.14 (68) (MCG)

**W:** R20: Geelong 13.17 (95) v Carlton 9.13 (67) (KP)

**W:** R21: Fremantle 9.14 (68) v Geelong 14.16 (100) (S)

**W:** R22: Sydney 13.12 (90) v Geelong 15.10 (100) (SCG)

## The Coach

### Gary Ayres

**Born:**
28/9/60

Gary Ayres had the burning ambition to succeed as a player and judging by his short time in the demanding world of coaching, his philosophy has not changed.

In three years as senior coach of Geelong — he was Malcolm Blight's assistant in 1994 — Ayres has taken the Cats into three finals series. But while the Cats have presented themselves as September regulars, Ayres knows there is unfinished business and he won't be satisfied until that elusive premiership flag is flying above the Geelong Town Hall.

He has already made his mark, overseeing the retirements of several prominent players and changing the playing structure of the Cats.

Gone are the free-wheeling days of big scores and little accountability to opposition players. In its place is a commitment to hard-nosed defence and a firm belief that youth is the only way to go.

Since the Cats were brushed aside by Carlton in the 1995 Grand Final, Ayres has put his faith in a regular back six and youngsters with an appetite to succeed in the AFL. It looks a very promising recipe.

### AT A GLANCE

**COACHING RECORD**
**Geelong**

| Season | P | W | L | D | Pos |
|---|---|---|---|---|---|
| 1995 | 25 | 18 | 7 | — | 2 |
| 1996 | 23 | 13 | 9 | 1 | 7 |
| 1997 | 24 | 15 | 9 | 1 | 7 |
| **Total** | **72** | **46** | **25** | **2** | |

## WIN/LOSS RECORD

| Against | P | W (N) | L (N) | D (N) |
|---|---|---|---|---|
| Adelaide | 11 | 6 | 5 (4) | 0 |
| Brisbane Bears | 15 | 10 (1) | 4 (1) | 1 |
| Brisbane Lions | 1 | 0 | 1 | 0 |
| Carlton | 193 | 81 (1) | 110 | 2 |
| Collingwood | 201 | 82 (1) | 118 | 1 |
| Essendon | 190 | 79 | 106 (2) | 5 |
| Fitzroy | 183 | 103 | 79 | 1 |
| Fremantle | 5 | 4 | 1 (1) | 0 |
| Hawthorn | 123 | 66 | 56 | 1 |
| Melbourne | 185 | 107 (1) | 77 | 1 |
| North Melb | 128 | 79 (3) | 48 (3) | 1 |
| Port Adel | 2 | 1 | 1 (1) | 0 |
| Richmond | 166 | 82 | 81 | 3 |
| St Kilda | 181 | 110 | 71 | 0 |
| Sydney | 187 | 102 (4) | 85 (1) | 0 |
| West Coast | 23 | 8 (1) | 15 (2) | 0 |
| W Bulldogs | 127 | 80 (2) | 45 | 2 |
| University | 14 | 8 | 6 | 0 |
| **TOTALS** | **1935** | **1008 (14)** | **909 (15)** | **18 (0)** |

*(N) Premiership matches played at night*

## WINNING RUNS

23 v North Melb (1925–1939)
16 v St Kilda (1897–1903)
12 v Carlton (1897–1902)
12 v Nth. Melb. (1962–1968)
11 v Western Bulldogs (1988–1994)
10 v Fitzroy (1964–1969)
10 v W Bulldogs (1949–1954); (1962–1968)
10 v Melbourne (1965–1970)
10 v St Kilda (1951–1957)
10 v Richmond (1990–1996)
8 v Hawthorn (1949–1953); (1963–1967)
7 v SM/Sydney (1949–1953); (1961–1964);
    (1966–1969); (1991– 1995)
6 v Collingwood (1923–1925)
5 v Essendon (1954–1956)
5 v Brisbane Bears (1991–1993)
4 v West Coast (1995–1997)
4 v Fremantle (1995– )
2 v Adelaide (1991–1992); (1994–1995 )
1 v Port Adelaide (1997– )

## 1997 BEST AND FAIREST

The four members of the match committee gave 4-3-2-1 votes for each of the home and away and finals games.

1   Liam Pickering (145)
2   Glenn Kilpatrick (137)
3   Michael Mansfield (127)
4   Brad Sholl (120)
5   Leigh Colbert (116)
6   Ben Graham (108)
7   Garry Hocking (101)
8   Tim McGrath (91)
9   Derek Hall (78)

## GAMES RECORDS

325   Ian Nankervis (1967–83)
300   John Newman (1964–80)
259   Paul Couch (1985–97)
253   Bruce Nankervis (1970–83)
248   Bill Goggin (1958–71)
245   Reg Hickey (1926–40)
245   Michael Turner (1974–88)
242   Gary Ablett (1984–96)
232   'Jocka' Todd (1922–34)
223   Neville Bruns (1978–92)

## GOALS RECORDS

1021   Gary Ablett (1984–96)
834   Doug Wade (1961–72)
441   Billy Brownless (1986–97)
429   Lindsay White (1941; 1944–50)
400   Cliff Rankin (1915; 1919–28)
389   Lloyd Hagger (1917–27; 1929)
339   Larry Donohue (1973–80)
333   Percy Martini (1909–15; 1917–20)
331   Terry Bright (1976–87)
303   George Moloney (1931–35)

## HIGHS AND LOWS

| Against | Highest | Lowest | G. W. Margin | G. L. Margin |
|---|---|---|---|---|
| Adelaide | 32.18.210 (1992) | 9.14.68 (1997) | 123 (1992) | 91 (1992) |
| Brisbane Bears | 37.17.239 (1992) | 10.18.78 (1987) | 164 (1992) | 66 (1990) |
| Brisbane Lions | 15.8.98 (1997) | 15.8.98 (1997) | — | 28 (1997) |
| Carlton | 22.12.144 (1925) | 3.4.22 (1919) | 73 (1933) | 106 (1944) |
| Collingwood | 23.18.156 (1940) | 3.2.20 (1902) | 88 (1982) | 97 (1945) |
| Essendon | 28.13.181 (1992) | 2.9.21 (1910) | 116 (1934) | 97 (1986) |
| Fitzroy | 29.10.184 (1987) | 0.8.8 (1899) | 127 (1996) | 123 (1944) |
| Fremantle | 17.10.112 (1996) | 10.15.75 (1995) | 54 (1997) | 19 (1995) |
| Hawthorn | 25.13.163 (1989) | 5.10.40 (1975) | 109 (1933) | 135 (1986) |
| Melbourne | 27.21.183 (1996) | 1.9.15 (1897) | 127 (1996) | 79 (1909) |
| North Melb | 29.18.192 (1992) | 4.11.35 (1958) | 114 (1981) | 68 (1982) |
| Port Adel | 25.9.159 (1997) | 14.6.90 (1997) | 85 (1997) | 39 (1997) |
| Richmond | 32.19.211 (1989) | 4.10.34 (1915) | 134 (1989) | 118 (1969) |
| St Kilda | 35.18.228 (1989) | 0.18.18 (1919) | 161 (1899) | 94 (1971) |
| Sydney | 26.11.167 (1978) | 3.1.19 (1899) | 104 (1976) | 109 (1933) |
| West Coast | 26.19.175 (1989) | 8.15.63 (1994) | 95 (1989) | 80 (1994) |
| W Bulldogs | 26.16.172 (1992) | 3.7.25 (1939) | 88 (1995) | 83 (1968) |

# THE LEADERSHIP AT GEELONG

| Year | Pos | Coach | Captain | Best & Fairest | Leading Goalkicker | |
|------|-----|-------|---------|----------------|-------------------|---|
| 1931 | 1 | C. Clymo | E. Baker | G. Todd | G. Moloney | 74 |
| 1932 | 5 | R. Hickey | R. Hickey | G. Moloney | G. Moloney | 109 |
| 1933 | 3 | A. Coghlan | R. Hickey | L. Hardiman | G. Moloney | 68 |
| 1934 | 3 | A. Coghlan | R. Hickey | R. Hickey | J. Metherell | 45 |
| 1935 | 9 | P. Parratt | R. Hickey | F. Hawking | J. Evans | 32 |
| 1936 | 5 | C. Dibbs/R. Hickey | C. Dibbs/R. Hickey | T. Quinn | J. Metherell | 58 |
| 1937 | 1 | R. Hickey | R. Hickey | T. Quinn | J. Metherell | 71 |
| 1938 | 3 | R. Hickey | R. Hickey | T. Arklay | C. Helmer | 74 |
| 1939 | 7 | R. Hickey | R. Hickey | J. Grant/L. Dean | N. Glenister | 36 |
| 1940 | 4 | R. Hickey | R. Hickey | T. Arklay | J. Grant | 47 |
| | | L. Laver | A. Everett | | | |
| | | A. Everett | | | | |
| 1941 | 10 | L. Metherell | T. Arklay | J. Knight | L. White | 67 |
| 1942 | | Did not compete | | | | |
| 1943 | | Did not compete | | | | |
| 1944 | 12 | T. Arklay | J. Butcher | J. Munday | L. White | 60 |
| 1945 | 11 | J. Williams | J. Butcher/L. White | J. Fitzgerald | V. Nankervis | 42 |
| 1946 | 10 | T. Quinn | J. Grant | G. Mahon | R. Renfrey | 28 |
| 1947 | 7 | T. Quinn | G. Gniel | L. White | L. White | 76 |
| 1948 | 9 | T. Quinn | L. White | B. Morrison | L. White | 86 |
| 1949 | 8 | R. Hickey | J. Fitzgerald | F. Flanagan | L. White | 53 |
| 1950 | 3 | R. Hickey | L. White | J. Hyde | G. Goninon | 45 |
| 1951 | 1 | R. Hickey | F. Flanagan | B. Smith | G. Goninon | 86 |
| 1952 | 1 | R. Hickey | F. Flanagan | G. Williams | G. Goninon | 59 |
| 1953 | 2 | R. Hickey | F. Flanagan | P. Pianto | G. Goninon | 65 |
| 1954 | 3 | R. Hickey | B. Smith | N. Sharp | F. Flanagan | 55 |
| 1955 | 3 | R. Hickey | R. Davis | G. Williams | N. Rayson | 80 |
| 1956 | 4 | R. Hickey | R. Davis | B. Smith | N. Rayson | 41 |
| 1957 | 12 | R. Hickey | R. Davis | R. Davis | F. Wooller | 56 |
| 1958 | 12 | R. Hickey | R. Davis | J. O'Neill | N. Trezise | 27 |
| 1959 | 10 | R. Hickey | N. Trezise | C. Rice | F. Wooller | 27 |
| 1960 | 9 | R. Davis | R. Hovey/C. Rice | F. Wooller | F. Wooller | 29 |
| 1961 | 6 | R. Davis | J. Yeates | R. West | D. Wade | 51 |
| 1962 | 3 | R. Davis | J. Yeates | A. Lord | D. Wade | 68 |
| 1963 | 1 | R. Davis | F. Wooller | G. Farmer | D. Wade | 48 |
| 1964 | 3 | R. Davis | F. Wooller | G. Farmer | D. Wade | 41 |
| 1965 | 4 | R. Davis | G. Farmer | P. Walker | G. Andrews | 35 |
| 1966 | 4 | P. Pianto | G. Farmer | D. Marshall | D. Wade | 52 |
| 1967 | 2 | P. Pianto | G. Farmer | W. Goggin | D. Wade | 96 |
| 1968 | 3 | P. Pianto | W. Goggin | J. Newman | D. Wade | 64 |
| 1969 | 4 | P. Pianto | W. Goggin | D. Wade | D. Wade | 127 |
| 1970 | 5 | P. Pianto | W. Goggin | W. Goggin | D. Wade | 74 |
| 1971 | 10 | W. McMaster | W. Goggin | D. Clarke | D. Wade | 94 |
| 1972 | 10 | W. McMaster | D. Wade | I. Nankervis | D. Wade | 90 |
| 1973 | 11 | G. Farmer | G. Ainsworth | B. Nankervis | D. Clarke | 45 |
| 1974 | 6 | G. Farmer | J. Newman | B. Nankervis | P. Sarah | 32 |
| 1975 | 11 | G. Farmer | J. Newman | J. Newman | L.Donohue/I.Nankervis | 29 |
| 1976 | 4 | R. Olsson | B. Nankervis | I. Nankervis | L. Donohue | 105 |
| 1977 | 8 | R. Olsson | B. Nankervis | I. Nankervis | L. Donohue | 63 |
| 1978 | 5 | R. Olsson | I. Nankervis | D. Clarke | L. Donohue | 95 |
| 1979 | 6 | R. Olsson | I. Nankervis | D. Clarke | D. Clarke | 40 |
| 1980 | 3 | W. Goggin | I. Nankervis | R. Blake | T. Bright | 59 |
| 1981 | 3 | W. Goggin | I. Nankervis | P. Featherby | T. Bright | 48 |
| 1982 | 9 | W. Goggin | B. Peake | J. Mossop | M. Turner | 40 |
| 1983 | 9 | T. Hafey | I. Nankervis | R. Card | T. Bright | 26 |
| 1984 | 6 | T. Hafey | M. Turner | G. Ablett | M. Jackson | 74 |
| 1985 | 6 | T. Hafey | N. Bruns | G. Williams | G. Ablett | 82 |
| 1986 | 9 | J. Devine | M. Turner | P. Couch | G. Ablett | 65 |
| 1987 | 6 | J. Devine | D. Bourke | M. Bos | B. Lindner | 62 |
| 1988 | 9 | J. Devine | D. Bourke | M. Bos | G. Ablett | 82 |
| 1989 | 2 | M. Blight | D. Bourke | P. Couch | G. Ablett | 87 |
| 1990 | 10 | M. Blight | A. Bews | B. Stoneham | G. Ablett | 75 |
| 1991 | 3 | M. Blight | A. Bews | G. Hocking | B. Brownless | 81 |
| 1992 | 2 | M. Blight | M. Bairstow | K. Hinkley | B. Brownless | 79 |
| 1993 | 7 | M. Blight | M. Bairstow | G. Hocking | G. Ablett | 124 |
| 1994 | 2 | M. Blight | M. Bairstow | G. Hocking | G. Ablett | 129 |
| 1995 | 2 | G. Ayres | G. Hocking/ | P. Couch | G. Ablett | 122 |
| | | | G. Ablett/K. Hinkley | | | |
| 1996 | 7 | G. Ayres | G. Ablett/B. Stoneham | G. Hocking | G. Ablett | 69 |
| 1997 | 5 | G. Ayres | B. Stoneham | L. Pickering | R. Burns | 50 |

# PLAYER PROFILES

## JOHN BARNES

It appears the Cats are gradually finding a new role for Barnes, whose grip on the No. 1 ruck position at Kardinia Park is now not permanent. The development of teenager Steven King, combined with Barnes' horrific arm injury in 1997, means he will have to play a support role. However, he has the height and marking ability to play as a key forward as well as providing back-up and experience in the ruck.

**Previous AFL club:** Essendon (1987-90: 12 games, 12 goals).

## GERRARD BENNETT

Big-marking youngster from the Tassie Mariners who had a bad start to his AFL career when he suffered a serious knee injury in the reserves. Has youth on his side and is expected to make a full recovery and could be given a chance at senior level later in the season.

## CRAIG BIDDISCOMBE

Started well in 1997, playing the first eight games, but tapered off and managed just two more senior appearances. Had some leg problems, but did not get much of a look in after losing his spot. Probably facing a testing season in 1998, but certainly has the talent.

**Player honors:** AFL Norwich Rising Star nominee 1996.

## CLINTON BIZZELL

Played four games in 1996, but suffered an early setback last year when he fell ill and did not return until midway through the season. Did not see any senior action in 1997, but the Cats have maintained their faith in him and the former Queensland youngster will be given a chance to press for senior selection again in 1998.

## LEIGH BROCKMAN

Tall, lightly built youngster who will be a project player for the Cats over the next couple of seasons. Was a high draft pick in 1996 and had a setback early in '97 when he suffered stress fractures in his feet. Will be developed as a ruckman of the future.

## PAUL BROWN

Experienced utility with almost 200 games of senior and reserves football to his credit. The past couple of years have been frustrating — he played just one senior game in 1996 and none last year. Has had patella tendon problems, but was starting to show some encouraging signs in the reserves towards the end of '97. Popular clubman and has the ability to play at both ends of the ground.

## RONNIE BURNS

Elusive forward who stepped up to be Geelong's leading goalkicker in 1997, playing a major role in the absence of Gary Ablett. Ideally needs a tall player alongside him to feed off, but has exceptional pace and ball-getting ability. Opposition sides have tried to work him to his unnatural right side and his form tapered off towards the end of '97 and during the finals. Has been a bargain pick up at No. 49 in the 1995 National Draft and plays a very important role for the Cats.

**Player honors:** leading goalkicker 1997.

## LEIGH COLBERT

An outstanding all-round player, he appears destined to become Geelong's next captain and, at 22 and with a 100-game milestone looming, he has the football world at his feet. He is not unlike Collingwood's Gavin Brown — a great mark for his size, has no shortage of courage and has skill and talent to burn. Probably the classiest act going around at Kardinia Park and was sorely missed in the latter stages of the '97 home and away season after taking a solid bump against the West Coast Eagles. Became part of the game's folklore with his unpaid mark in last year's semi-final against Adelaide.

**Player honors:** 3rd best and fairest 1996; AFL Norwich Rising Star nominee 1993.

## PAUL CORRIGAN

Gave the Cats good service in his debut year at senior level after playing on Melbourne's supplementary list in 1996. Played 15 games and although he lost his place in the final stages, showed enough dash and creativity to suggest he will bolster Geelong's midfield.

## TIM FINOCCHIARO

One of the most decorated players to come out of the Victorian junior system, Finocchiaro has been a standout centreman for the Eastern Ranges in the TAC Cup competition. Has won the Larke Medal as best player at the past two AFL National Under-18 Championships and was an All-Australian at both championships. Knocks up winning the ball and should be able to adapt to senior football almost immediately.

## BEN GRAHAM

Enjoyed his best and most consistent season for the Cats, playing all 22 games plus two finals and finished sixth in the best and fairest. Must have gone close to winning All-Australian selection as he was among the best-performed full-backs in the competition. Had two excellent games against Tony Lockett and with his confidence up, he was rarely beaten. His long kicking remains a feature, but he also seemed more at ease, both in the air and when the ball hit the ground. Came out of contract at the end of 1997, but has committed himself for at least another two seasons.

## DEREK HALL

His absence in Geelong's finals campaign might have been the difference between the September hard luck story and a Grand Final appearance. Hall was sidelined in both games with a calf injury and the Cats sorely missed his sure hands and his ability to present himself as a target. Missed another five games during the home and away season, yet finished in the top 12 marks of the AFL for '97. One of the best marks for his size in the competition and could be extremely dangerous in the Cats' new-look attack.

**Previous AFL club:** West Coast Eagles (1993: 2 games, 3 goals).

## TIM HARGREAVES

Aggressive forward who was traded to the Cats in exchange for Aaron Lord last year. He struggled for consistency and although he made his way back to the senior line-up at the end of the season, he did not set the world on fire. Certainly has the ability and at

22, has the chance to claim a regular spot as the Cats try different options up forward.

**Previous AFL club:** Hawthorn (1994-96: 42 games, 57 goals).

## GARRY HOCKING

Champion on-baller rated by some as one of the best in Geelong's long and proud history. Despite a modified training program to accommodate the wear and tear on his knees, Hocking still has plenty of good football ahead of him. Plays it tough, but has outstanding skills on both sides of the body and has won his club's best and fairest a record four times. Might not have the explosive pace of a few years ago and will probably start to spend less time on the ball, but could be very dangerous lurking near goals. Has reached his 200-game milestone and following the retirements of Ablett, Brownless and Couch, is Geelong's most experienced player.

**Player honors:** 2nd (equal) Brownlow Medal 1993; 3rd Brownlow Medal 1991, 1994, 1995; best and fairest 1991, 1993, 1994, 1996; 2nd best and fairest 1990; All-Australian 1991, 1993, 1994, 1996; Geelong captain (part) 1995.

## ADAM HOULIHAN

Caught the eye with an impressive performance on debut against Essendon in round four last year and looks to be an exciting young talent. Had a two-year apprenticeship in the reserves and this former jockey has grown in stature and confidence. Was dropped later in the season just to remind him that nothing can be taken for granted, but should develop into a regular senior player. Received the award for the Cats' best first year player.

**Player honors:** AFL Norwich Rising Star nominee 1997.

## GLENN KILPATRICK

Had a terrific season for his second AFL club, playing every game and finishing second in the best and fairest. There was even a quiet tip for him on Brownlow Medal night and this hard-working midfielder was one of the reasons Geelong finished second on the ladder at the end of the home and away season. Was named the Cats' most improved player in '97. By no means a speedster, Kilpatrick collected 506 possessions for the season to be Geelong's leading disposals man. At 25, he has grabbed his second chance in similar fashion to teammate Liam Pickering.

**Player honors:** 2nd best and fairest 1997; Magarey Medal (equal) 1995; Essendon night series premiership side 1994.

**Previous AFL club:** Essendon (1992-94: 26 games, 4 goals).

## STEVEN KING

It would be no surprise to see King go on to play 250-plus games and become one of the dominant big men in the competition. Together with the West Coast Eagles' Michael Gardiner, he is rated as the best young ruck prospect in the AFL and at 19, has an enormous future. Strong and aggressive, King is learning his craft week in, week out and has tremendous skills for such a big man. Lowered his colors to Shaun Rehn in last year's semi-final, but has rarely been overwhelmed and will be Geelong's No. 1 ruck-

man for years to come. Had an interrupted pre-season when he broke an arm late in 1997.

**Player honors:** AFL Norwich Rising Star nominee 1996.

## DANIEL LOWTHER

The former Preston Knights premiership captain played three senior games in 1997. Skilled on-baller who is part of Geelong's push for youth and quickness in its midfield. Now entering his third season with the Cats, Lowther will be looking for more chances at senior level. Won the club's best and fairest in the reserves in 1997.

## PAUL LYNCH

Exciting forward who tantalised Geelong supporters with some classy performances in 1997, justifying the Cats' decision to keep him on their list. However, Lynch has a long history of hamstring and groin-related injuries and has played only 43 games since 1993. If he can get himself fully fit, would be in the leading bracket of AFL players. Has left no stone unturned in his quest to shake off these persistent injuries — even to the extent of doing stretching routines used by leading ballet dancers. With spots opening up on Geelong's forward line, a fit Lynch would certainly be a welcome addition.

## MICHAEL MANSFIELD

Another great year for this dashing half-back flanker who has been among Geelong's most consistent players over the past four seasons. Mansfield is fiercely competitive and played an integral role marshalling one of the best defensive units in the AFL last year. Never one to take a backward step, he was also used in some pinch-hitting roles in attack as the Cats tried to cover the loss of Gary Ablett. Has an even greater leadership role to play now, but loves the challenge and intensity of AFL football.

**Player honors:** All-Australian 1994, 1995; 3rd best and fairest 1994, 1997.

## TIM McGRATH

Experienced and reliable defender who played 23 of a possible 24 games in 1997. Started the season slowly when he was dropped for the ill-fated game against Port Adelaide in round three, but quickly regained his spot and did not look back. Finished eighth in the club's best and fairest and laid the tackle of the season when he brought down North Melbourne's Darren Crocker in round 15. Since joining the Cats in 1992, McGrath has been an outstanding player and one of the mainstays of their defence. A popular player, McGrath was voted the best club man in 1997.

**Player honors:** 2nd best and fairest 1992; 3rd best and fairest 1993.

**Previous AFL club:** North Melbourne (1989-91: 7 games, 0 goals).

## JOEL McKAY

After trading their first round draft pick (No. 13) to the West Coast Eagles for Brett Spinks, the Cats worked their way back into the 1997 National Draft by gaining three selections for Matthew Robbins. One of them was pick No. 15 and the Cats were delighted to have secured McKay, an impressive youngster from the Murray Bushrangers. The Cats have picked up Steven

King and Adam Houlihan from the Bushrangers and they are confident this young defender can also make the grade. He captained the Victoria Country side at last year's AFL National Under-18 Championships and has been rated highly because of his excellent temperament.

### MARTIN McKINNON
The Cats have recruited well from other clubs in recent seasons and McKinnon is a good example of a player relishing a change of scenery. He showed considerable promise with the Adelaide Crows, but with more opportunities at Geelong, his confidence has grown. Best suited as a running, goalkicking option, but can play in defence and had an excellent game against former teammate Tony Modra in round 13 last year.
**Player honors:** AFL Norwich Rising Star nominee 1995.
**Previous AFL club:** Adelaide (1994-95: 25 games, 7 goals).

### DAVID MENSCH
An often-maligned player, Mensch has let himself and the Cats down in finals and until he overcomes that reputation, it is difficult to see him taking his game to another level. Missed a crucial goal in last year's semi-final against Adelaide, but the Cats have stuck with him knowing he has the ability to become a permanent fixture. Had to contend with injuries last year and has a chance to present himself as a marking option in attack.

### DARREN MILBURN
One of the bright sparks of Geelong's 1997 season and looks to be a player of considerable promise. Started the season well, but contracted glandular fever before returning in the latter stages to play in both finals. Among Geelong's best in the qualifying final loss to North Melbourne. A versatile player with a big future.

### LIAM PICKERING
A slow start because of injury, then quickly established himself as one of the hardest working and most efficient on-ballers in the competition last year. Finished the season as a deserved and popular winner of his club's best and fairest award — a high point of a career that looked like stagnating when North Melbourne axed him at the end of 1992. He has turned his career around at Geelong, winning acclaim from Malcolm Blight and later Gary Ayres for his work ethic and leadership skills. Was Geelong's best player during the finals and was also voted best team player and most constructive player for 1997.
**Player honors:** best and fairest 1997; 3rd best and fairest 1995.
**Previous AFL club:** North Melbourne (1989-92: 22 games, 8 goals).

### JAMES RAHILLY
Athletic half-back flanker from South Warrnambool who had been a consistent performer for the Geelong Falcons in the TAC Cup competition. Quick, strong and aggressive, he will be a player to watch as the Cats continue their policy of developing youngsters.

### PETER RICCARDI
Did not enjoy his greatest season and for the first time since 1994, found himself playing reserves football. As he did the previous season, Riccardi started well and was even used in some forward roles, highlighted by his six goals against the West Coast Eagles in round two. After a two-week spell, he returned in round 18 and just as his game appeared to be getting back in order, he turned in two ordinary games in the finals. Has all the talent and skill, but has to produce on a consistent basis.

### CAMERON ROBERTS
Former South Australian who played three senior games in the middle of the 1997 season. The Cats are keen to develop him into a key position player, preferably in attack, and he appears to have the size and strength to make a fist of it. Will improve with more experience.

### BRENTON SANDERSON
Became an important cog in the Cats' defensive unit, which was among the most miserly in the competition last year. Another player to make the most of another chance, Sanderson has grabbed his opportunity and run with it — literally. Likes to dash out of defence, uses the ball well and has no shortage of courage, as evidenced by his collision with the West Coast Eagles' Ashley McIntosh in round two last year.
**Previous AFL clubs:** Adelaide (1992-93: 6 games, 4 goals); Collingwood (1994: 4 games, 1 goal).

### MATTHEW SCARLETT
The second of Geelong's two father-son selections, Scarlett is the son of former Cats full-back John Scarlett. Rated a potential key defender like his father, Scarlett was an outstanding player for Victoria Country at the 1997 AFL National Under-18 Championships. Strong in the air and a fine kick.

### BRAD SHOLL
Dashing defender and occasional on-baller who has taken his game to another level since joining the Cats from North Melbourne in 1995. Has missed only one game in that time and has been a fantastic rebounding player, backing his judgment and setting up teammates with his ability to read the play. A big possession winner, Sholl polled 16 votes in the 1997 Brownlow Medal to finish sixth, but did not poll in the top three in his club's best and fairest (he finished fourth). However, his outstanding attitude to playing and training was recognised when he received an award for the "most determined and most dedicated player" of 1997.
**Player honors:** 2nd best and fairest 1996.
**Previous AFL club:** North Melbourne (1992, 1994: 2 games, 0 goals).

### HAMISH SIMPSON
Key position player who can play at either end, Simpson was part of the exchange for Shayne Breuer. Originally from Kedron Grange, he played with Woodville-West Torrens in the SANFL and played 15 games in the Cats' reserves in 1997. Was being touted as a possible option in attack when Geelong had injuries on the eve of the finals.

### SEAN SIMPSON
Geelong's best tagging and 'run-with' player, Simpson has performed some big tasks for the Cats in recent

years. Has played 100 games for Geelong and been praised by Gary Ayres for his ability to apply himself and play within team rules. Injuries interrupted his career last year, but is considered a good team man. Turns 28 at the start of the '98 season and should have a couple more years in him.

**Previous AFL club:** St Kilda (1988-90: 7 games, 1 goal).

## JASON SNELL

One of many young players Geelong is grooming for the future, Snell has a wonderful opportunity to press ahead as a midfielder or small forward. In two seasons with the Cats, he has shown ability to not only win the ball but finish off in front of goal. Booted five goals against Port Adelaide in round 18 last year and three against Sydney in a crucial clash at the SCG in the final round. Was also a good performer during Geelong's finals campaign.

## BRETT SPINKS

After making bold bids to secure a key forward of some experience, the Cats settled for the forgotten man of the West Coast Eagles. With just six games in the past three years, Spinks has not been as prominent as he would have liked, but hasn't always had the right opportunity. He was a fine player for Perth last year (he kicked 58 goals) and the Cats believe his height, strength and unfulfilled potential was worth a punt in exchange for their No. 13 pick in the 1997 National Draft. Following the retirements of Gary Ablett and Billy Brownless, the former Eagle will certainly get his chance at Kardinia Park.

**Player honors:** AFL Norwich Rising Star nominee 1994.
**Previous AFL club:** West Coast Eagles (1994-97: 21 games, 14 goals).

## CARL STEINFORT

Patience has been the key with Steinfort, but the Cats look set to reap the benefit of giving him a solid apprenticeship in the reserves. Played 22 of a possible 24 games for the Cats in 1997 and won an AFL Norwich Rising Star nomination for his effort against Richmond in round 16. Not quite tall enough for a key position role, Steinfort is best suited as a ruck-rover and has been able to shadow key opposition players. Plays with plenty of discipline and determination and looks to have a good future.

**Player honors:** AFL Norwich Rising Star nominee 1997.

## BARRY STONEHAM

A leader in every sense of the word, Stoneham's comeback to football has been one of the big positives at Kardinia Park over the past couple of seasons. Unfortunately, the legacy of breaking a leg late in 1994 at the height of his career and the ensuing complications, have reduced his pace and agility. However, he remains as competitive as ever, acting as a general on the forward line where he played most of his football in 1997. Apart from a costly three-week suspension, which forced him out of the final three rounds, Stoneham was able to stand up each week and that in itself was a bonus. With the retirements of Ablett, Brownless and Couch, he has an even greater role to play and he should be able to see out another couple of seasons.

**Player honors:** best and fairest 1990; 2nd best and fairest 1989; 3rd best and fairest 1992; All-Australian 1989, 1992; Geelong co-captain 1996, captain since 1997.

## GRANT TANNER

A highly regarded performer, Tanner has virtually been a regular since he joined the Cats in 1994. However, he will see little action in 1998 after seriously injuring a knee against Essendon in round 19 last year. When fully fit, he is a good running midfielder who can play at either end and he would be a bonus if he can return later this year.

## DAVID UGRINIC

A total of eight reserves matches is not a great statistic for this talented winger from South Australia. He was the Cats' first choice (No. 13 overall) in the 1993 National Draft, but elected to spend 1994 to '96 with Woodville-West Torrens in the SANFL. Played three reserves games flying in from SA in 1996 and decided to settle in Geelong last year in a bid to start his AFL career. However, he suffered patella tendon and hip injuries and managed only five games in the reserves.

## JUSTIN WOOD

Youngster from Tasmania who will join former Tassie Mariners teammates Gerrard Bennett and Leigh Brockman at Kardinia Park. Hails from Glenorchy and is a smart, well balanced flanker who has great endurance and uses the ball well. Will be given time to develop.

## MARC WOOLNOUGH

One of two father-son selections at the 1997 National Draft, Woolnough is the son of former Geelong and Collingwood utility Michael Woolnough. Playing for Queensland at last year's AFL National Under-18 Championships, he was an All-Australian selection at centre half-back. He has followed Geelong all his life and was most keen to join the Cats.

# ROOKIE LIST

## SHAUN BAXTER

Made a courageous return to the football field after being diagnosed with throat cancer while playing in the reserves for the Western Bulldogs in 1996. His plight was captured on a special documentary/film of the Bulldogs' 1996 season. Unfortunately, he could not break through for senior selection in 1997 and was delisted by the Bulldogs at the end of the season. However, Baxter, who hails from Bannockburn and played for the Geelong Falcons, was given a chance to train over summer with the Cats and will be grateful for the chance to at least make the rookie list. Has played mainly in defence.

## CHRIS HEMLEY

Geelong is hoping Hemley will be a late developer after spending three seasons with St Kilda for just one senior game before being delisted at the end of 1997. A local product from the Geelong Falcons, Hemley is a tall, key position player and will appreciate being back in a familiar environment.

**Previous AFL club:** St Kilda (1995: 1 game, 0 goals)

## PAUL LINDSAY

Tall, skilful ruckman from East Fremantle. Did pre-season training with Fremantle and would be a development player for the Cats.

# GEELONG

| Name (# = rookie) | No. | Born | Height | Weight | Recruited from |
|---|---|---|---|---|---|
| John Barnes | 6 | 1/6/69 | 193 | 95 | COBRAM/ESSENDON |
| Gerrard Bennett | 36 | 9/4/79 | 189 | 87 | NORTH HOBART/TAS U18 |
| Craig Biddiscombe | 30 | 21/9/76 | 185 | 77 | TRARALGON/GIPPSLAND U18 |
| Clint Bizzell | 9 | 28/6/76 | 188 | 84 | KEDRON GRANGE (QLD) |
| Leigh Brockman | 25 | 23/7/78 | 196 | 83 | NORTH HOBART/TAS U18 |
| Paul Brown | 40 | 6/5/69 | 187 | 87 | ECHUCA |
| Ronnie Burns | 8 | 13/3/73 | 179 | 80 | ST MARYS (NT)/WEST PERTH (WA) |
| Leigh Colbert | 2 | 7/6/75 | 192 | 85 | SOUTH BENDIGO |
| Paul Corrigan | 33 | 30/7/77 | 184 | 80 | HAILEYBURY COLL/DAND-STHN U18/MELB RES |
| Tim Finocchiaro | 43 | 19/6/79 | 177 | 80 | WARRANDYTE/EASTERN U18 |
| Ben Graham | 7 | 2/11/73 | 195 | 94 | LEOPOLD |
| Derek Hall | 19 | 29/11/70 | 189 | 89 | WEST PERTH (WA)/WEST COAST |
| Tim Hargreaves | 22 | 30/5/75 | 184 | 86 | BERRIGAN (NSW)/HAWTHORN |
| Garry Hocking | 32 | 8/10/68 | 181 | 82 | COBRAM |
| Adam Houlihan | 3 | 6/4/78 | 185 | 81 | COROWA-RUTHERGLEN/MURRAY U18 |
| Glenn Kilpatrick | 13 | 29/8/72 | 184 | 86 | STUDFIELD/ESSENDON/WEST ADELAIDE (SA) |
| Steven King | 1 | 22/11/78 | 200 | 93 | SHEPPARTON H.S./MURRAY U18 |
| Daniel Lowther | 29 | 19/4/77 | 179 | 75 | DIAMOND CREEK/NORTHERN U18 |
| Paul Lynch | 18 | 18/10/73 | 184 | 82 | ALVIE |
| Michael Mansfield | 21 | 8/8/71 | 184 | 83 | ST JOSEPHS |
| Tim McGrath | 17 | 7/10/70 | 190 | 96 | NORTH DANDENONG/NORTH MELB |
| Joel McKay | 38 | 16/7/79 | 182 | 72 | WODONGA/MURRAY U18 |
| Martin McKinnon | 28 | 5/7/75 | 189 | 89 | CENTRAL DISTRICT (SA)/ADELAIDE |
| David Mensch | 31 | 14/8/72 | 192 | 93 | GROVEDALE |
| Darren Milburn | 39 | 15/4/77 | 187 | 76 | KILMORE/CALDER U18 |
| Liam Pickering | 23 | 9/9/68 | 184 | 85 | STAWELL/NORTH MELB |
| James Rahilly | 34 | 15/6/79 | 186 | 75 | SOUTH WARRNAMBOOL/GEELONG U18 |
| Peter Riccardi | 15 | 17/12/72 | 182 | 85 | WEST ST PETERS |
| Cameron Roberts | 11 | 7/9/78 | 194 | 85 | NORTH ADELAIDE (SA) |
| Brenton Sanderson | 27 | 27/2/74 | 185 | 83 | STURT (SA)/ADELAIDE/COLLINGWOOD |
| Matthew Scarlett | 41 | 5/6/79 | 189 | 80 | ST JOSEPHS/GEELONG U18 |
| Brad Sholl | 12 | 10/11/72 | 183 | 81 | HORSHAM/NORTH MELB |
| Hamish Simpson | 24 | 17/1/76 | 191 | 90 | KEDRON GRANGE (QLD)/WOODV-W. TORRENS (SA) |
| Sean Simpson | 37 | 16/4/70 | 188 | 85 | EAST BALLARAT /ST KILDA |
| Jason Snell | 4 | 27/7/77 | 180 | 80 | UPWEY-TECOMA/EASTERN U18 |
| Brett Spinks | 14 | 7/11/73 | 194 | 106 | SOUTH FREMANTLE (WA)/WEST COAST |
| Carl Steinfort | 20 | 1/4/77 | 190 | 93 | MAZENOD O.C./CENTRAL U18 |
| Barry Stoneham | 26 | 9/2/68 | 194 | 95 | ST JOSEPHS |
| Grant Tanner | 10 | 24/7/70 | 184 | 80 | NORWOOD (SA) |
| David Ugrinic | 35 | 11/2/75 | 183 | 78 | WOODVILLE-WEST TORRENS (SA) |
| Justin Wood | 42 | 18/12/79 | 184 | 70 | GLENORCHY (TAS)/TASSIE U18 |
| Marc Woolnough | 16 | 20/5/80 | 189 | 79 | SOUTHPORT (QLD) |
| Shaun Baxter # | 46 | 2/10/77 | 185 | 85 | BANNOCKBURN/GEELONG U18/FOOTS RES |
| Chris Hemley # | 45 | 8/9/77 | 192 | 93 | BELL POST HILL/GEELONG U18/ST KILDA |
| Paul Lindsay # | 44 | 28/2/76 | 198 | 100 | EAST FREMANTLE (WA) |
| Total/(Average)  *On 26/2/98 | | (23.2 yrs)* | (187) | (84) | |

# PLAYERS 1998

| Debut | HOME & AWAY | | 1997 | | FINALS | | GRAND FINALS | | | NIGHT SERIES | | STATE OF ORIGIN | |
|---|---|---|---|---|---|---|---|---|---|---|---|---|---|
| | Gms | Gls | Gms | Gls | Gms | Gls | Gms | Gls | Won | Gms | Gls | Gms | Gls |
| 1987 | 126 | 59 | 15 | 12 | 15 | 6 | 3 | 0 | 0 | 11 | 9 | 2 | 0 |
| | 0 | 0 | 0 | 0 | | | | | | 0 | 0 | 0 | 0 |
| 1995 | 22 | 3 | 10 | 2 | | | | | | 3 | 2 | 0 | 0 |
| 1996 | 4 | 0 | 0 | 0 | | | | | | 0 | 0 | 0 | 0 |
| | 0 | 0 | 0 | 0 | | | | | | 0 | 0 | 0 | 0 |
| 1990 | 83 | 66 | 0 | 0 | 9 | 0 | 2 | 0 | 0 | 5 | 6 | 0 | 0 |
| 1996 | 45 | 81 | 24 | 50 | 3 | 2 | | | | 3 | 3 | 2 | 3 |
| 1993 | 85 | 41 | 20 | 15 | 10 | 4 | 2 | 0 | 0 | 7 | 3 | 2 | 1 |
| 1997 | 15 | 2 | 15 | 2 | | | | | | 4 | 1 | 0 | 0 |
| | 0 | 0 | 0 | 0 | | | | | | 0 | 0 | 0 | 0 |
| 1993 | 73 | 6 | 24 | 1 | 5 | 0 | 1 | 0 | 0 | 6 | 1 | 0 | 0 |
| 1993 | 53 | 59 | 17 | 26 | 1 | 1 | | | | 8 | 5 | 1 | 0 |
| 1994 | 53 | 68 | 11 | 11 | 3 | 0 | | | | 7 | 5 | 0 | 0 |
| 1987 | 207 | 197 | 20 | 27 | 20 | 20 | 4 | 0 | 0 | 16 | 5 | 6 | 7 |
| 1997 | 14 | 15 | 14 | 15 | 1 | 0 | | | | 2 | 1 | 0 | 0 |
| 1992 | 61 | 8 | 24 | 4 | 2 | 0 | | | | 11 | 1 | 0 | 0 |
| 1996 | 35 | 11 | 22 | 8 | 3 | 1 | | | | 2 | 0 | 0 | 0 |
| 1997 | 3 | 0 | 3 | 0 | | | | | | 1 | 0 | 0 | 0 |
| 1993 | 43 | 30 | 13 | 20 | 2 | 2 | | | | 7 | 5 | 0 | 0 |
| 1990 | 141 | 81 | 23 | 14 | 15 | 9 | 3 | 0 | 0 | 9 | 0 | 3 | 0 |
| 1989 | 145 | 12 | 23 | 1 | 13 | 1 | 3 | 0 | 0 | 7 | 2 | 0 | 0 |
| | 0 | 0 | 0 | 0 | | | | | | 0 | 0 | 0 | 0 |
| 1994 | 68 | 38 | 24 | 23 | 3 | 1 | | | | 9 | 5 | 1 | 0 |
| 1992 | 76 | 80 | 8 | 2 | 9 | 11 | 2 | 1 | 0 | 1 | 1 | 0 | 0 |
| 1997 | 10 | 5 | 10 | 5 | 2 | 1 | | | | 4 | 1 | 0 | 0 |
| 1989 | 107 | 51 | 20 | 10 | 9 | 8 | 2 | 1 | 0 | 10 | 6 | 1 | 0 |
| | 0 | 0 | 0 | 0 | | | | | | 0 | 0 | 0 | 0 |
| 1992 | 125 | 124 | 21 | 19 | 14 | 10 | 3 | 3 | 0 | 10 | 8 | 1 | 1 |
| 1997 | 3 | 0 | 3 | 0 | | | | | | 2 | 2 | 0 | 0 |
| 1992 | 65 | 17 | 21 | 8 | 5 | 1 | | | | 12 | 4 | 0 | 0 |
| | 0 | 0 | 0 | 0 | | | | | | 0 | 0 | 0 | 0 |
| 1993 | 73 | 17 | 24 | 8 | 6 | 1 | 1 | 0 | 0 | 4 | 0 | 0 | 0 |
| | 0 | 0 | 0 | 0 | | | | | | 0 | 0 | 0 | 0 |
| 1988 | 107 | 17 | 9 | 0 | 10 | 0 | 1 | 0 | 0 | 6 | 3 | 1 | 0 |
| 1996 | 13 | 16 | 10 | 13 | 2 | 1 | | | | 0 | 0 | 0 | 0 |
| 1994 | 21 | 14 | 2 | 0 | 1 | 0 | | | | 2 | 2 | 0 | 0 |
| 1996 | 24 | 11 | 22 | 11 | 3 | 1 | | | | 4 | 2 | 0 | 0 |
| 1986 | 194 | 167 | 21 | 7 | 14 | 14 | 2 | 3 | 0 | 18 | 13 | 7 | 2 |
| 1994 | 69 | 28 | 14 | 1 | 5 | 2 | 1 | 0 | 0 | 5 | 1 | 0 | 0 |
| | 0 | 1 | 0 | 0 | | | | | | 0 | 0 | 0 | 0 |
| | 0 | 0 | 0 | 0 | | | | | | 0 | 0 | 0 | 0 |
| | 0 | 0 | 0 | 0 | | | | | | 0 | 0 | 0 | 0 |
| | 0 | 0 | 0 | 0 | | | | | | 0 | 0 | | |
| 1995 | 1 | 0 | 0 | 0 | | | | | | 0 | 0 | | |
| | 0 | 0 | 0 | 0 | | | | | | 0 | 0 | | |
| | (52) | (32) | 487 | 315 | 185 | 97 | 30 | 8 | 0 | 196 | 97 | 27 | 14 |

## Hawks at a glance

**ADDRESS:** Linda Cres., Hawthorn, Vic 3122

**POSTAL ADDRESS:** Hawthorn Football Club, PO Box 52, Hawthorn Vic 3122

**TELEPHONE:** (03) 9816 2222

**FACSIMILE:** (03) 9816 2220

**PRESIDENT:** Ian Dicker

**CHIEF EXECUTIVE:** Michael Brown

**FOOTBALL MANAGER:** John Hook

**DIRECTOR OF MARKETING:** James Henderson

**COACHING STAFF:** Ken Judge (senior); Chris Connolly (assistant); Peter German (reserves)

**SELECTION COMMITTEE:** Kelvin Moore (chairman); Ken Judge, Chris Connolly, Peter German, Scott Maginness

**CLUB DOCTORS:** Peter Wilson, Bernie Crimmins

**CLUB PHYSIOTHERAPIST:** Barry Gavin

**JOINED AFL:** 1925

**HOME GROUND:** Waverley Park, Wellington Rd., Mulgrave

**GROUND DIMENSIONS:** 200m by 160m (fence to fence). Playing area: 165m by 142m.

**TRAINING VENUE:** Glenferrie Oval, Linda Cres., Hawthorn

**OFFICIAL COLORS:** Guernsey: Brown and gold vertical stripes on front, plain gold back. Socks: Brown and gold hooped. Shorts: Brown

**PREMIERSHIPS:** 1961, 1971, 1976, 1978, 1983, 1986, 1988-89, 1991

**BROWNLOW MEDALLISTS:** C. Austen (1949 tied), R. DiPierdomenico (1986 tied), J. Platten (1987 tied)

**RECORD HOME ATTENDANCE** (Waverley Park): 53,982 — August 18, 1990 v Collingwood

# HAWTHORN

# Hawks must post results on the field

Finishing last season with eight straight losses nearly overshadowed Hawthorn's great off-field achievement in turning around the club's financial situation.

Averting a merger and then building the second highest membership of any Victorian-based club was quite an achievement.

But results are what supporters remember and after promising so much, the Hawks fell away sharply.

Hawthorn's game-plan of accountability relies on a few better-than-average individuals to be playing well. As coach Ken Judge was quoted as saying halfway through the slump: "When we drift away from what we do well, we're a pretty ordinary side."

The injury list might not have been long, but it was all quality. Jason Dunstall was missing after round eight when his courageous comeback from a knee reconstruction was aborted when the knee 'went' again.

Shane Crawford didn't appear until round 10 and then fought a stress fracture in a foot for the whole season. His performances were still outstanding.

Anthony Condon played only four games. Chris Langford was able to combine footy and business only by round 13 and Nick Holland was out for five weeks — a period when Hawthorn lost the first five of eight losing games on end to blow its season out of the water.

The tightly knit unit that was in fifth spot after 14 rounds started to lose shape. Through it all, Paul Salmon was a constant and notched his second club best and fairest.

Judge, who signed a three-year contract after round 14, will be demanding that his talented players lift and will probably try a few new things as some of the stalwarts have moved on.

Dunstall might return, but Hawthorn won't get caught in the trap of waiting for saviors. He has resigned the captaincy and given himself every chance.

Daniel Harford's form last year dropped off after the State-of-Origin game to such an extent that the acid will be on him early. Mark Graham performed well at full-back early and might find himself back there this season.

The middle rung of players — Daniel Chick, Brendan Krummel, Craig Trelevan, Aaron Lord and Angelo Lekkas — can be very good in supporting roles and Jonathon Robran made a leap forward last year.

Picking up Nathan Chapman and John Barker from the Brisbane Lions in exchange for Brad Scott is a bonus for Hawthorn. And securing Joel Smith from St Kilda was a bonus long-term investment. — **Peter Ryan**

## THE YEAR AHEAD

| Rd | Date | Opponent | Venue | Home/ Away | Time (local) |
|----|------|----------|-------|------------|--------------|
| 1 | March 28 | Collingwood | MCG | A | 3.30pm |
| 2 | April 4 | Port Adelaide | P | H | 2.10pm |
| 3 | April 11 | Richmond | MCG | A | 3.30pm |
| 4 | April 18 | St Kilda | P | H | 3.30pm |
| 5 | April 25 | Brisbane Lions | P | H | 2.10pm |
| 6 | May 2 | Geelong | KP | A | 2.10pm |
| 7 | May 8 (N) | Fremantle | W | A | 6.40pm |
| 8 | May 17 | Western Bulldogs | P | H | 2.10pm |
| 9 | May 24 | Sydney | SCG | A | 12.40pm |
| 10 | May 30 | Essendon | P | H | 3.30pm |
| 11 | June 6 | Melbourne | P | H | 2.10pm |
| 12 | June 12 (N) | West Coast | W | A | 6.40pm |
| 13 | June 20 | North Melbourne | P | H | 2.10pm |
| 14 | June 27 | Carlton | OO | A | 2.10pm |
| 15 | July 5 | Adelaide | FP | A | 12.10pm |
| 16 | July 18 | Collingwood | P | H | 7.40pm |
| 17 | July 25 (N) | Port Adelaide | FP | A | 8.10pm |
| 18 | August 2 | Richmond | P | H | 2.10pm |
| 19 | August 8 | St Kilda | P | A | 2.10pm |
| 20 | August 15 (N) | Brisbane Lions | G | A | 7.40pm |
| 21 | August 23 | Geelong | P | H | 2.10pm |
| 22 | August 29 | Fremantle | P | H | 2.10pm |

## 1997 AT A GLANCE

**W:** R1: St Kilda 10.11 (71) v Hawthorn 11.11 (77) (P)

**L:** R2: Fremantle 13.9 (87) v Hawthorn 10.13 (73) (S)

**W:** R3: Hawthorn 12.15 (87) v Brisbane Lions 11.9 (75) (P)

**L:** R4: West Coast 17.10 (112) v Hawthorn 13.10 (88) (S)

**W:** R5: Hawthorn 15.9 (99) v Sydney 11.8 (74) (P)

**L:** R6: Hawthorn 14.9 (93) v North Melbourne 16.7 (103) (P)

**L:** R7: Western Bulldogs 19.19 (133) v Hawthorn 13.10 (88) (OO)

### SNAPSHOT

**Games:** 22
**Wins:** 8
**Losses:** 14
**Ladder Finish:** 15
**Players Used:** 34

**L:** R8: Carlton 15.16 (106) v Hawthorn 12.9 (81) (OO)

**L:** R9: Hawthorn 13.10 (88) v Adelaide 14.18 (102) (P)

**W:** R10: Hawthorn 16.12 (108) v Collingwood 8.7 (55) (P)

**W:** R11: Essendon 13.13 (91) v Hawthorn 17.22 (124) (MCG)

**W:** R12: Geelong 12.10 (82) v Hawthorn 13.10 (88) (KP)

**W:** R13: Hawthorn 17.16 (118) v Melbourne 7.13 (55) (P)

**W:** R14: Hawthorn 18.16 (124) v Port Adelaide 13.14 (92) (P)

**L:** R15: Richmond 22.13 (145) v Hawthorn 10.9 (69) (MCG)

**L:** R16: Hawthorn 9.8 (62) v St Kilda 20.21 (141) (P)

**L:** R17: Hawthorn 9.8 (62) v Fremantle 10.11 (71) (P)

**L:** R18: Brisbane Lions 21.15 (141) v Hawthorn 11.5 (71) (G)

**L:** R19: Hawthorn 10.6 (66) v West Coast 13.9 (87) (P)

**L:** R20: Sydney 20.15 (135) v Hawthorn 11.11 (77) (SCG)

**L:** R21: North Melbourne 10.21 (81) v Hawthorn 6.7 (43) (MCG)

**L:** R22: Hawthorn 13.9 (87) v Western Bulldogs 15.15 (105) (P)

## The Coach

### Ken Judge

**Born:**
15/8/58

It was a torrid end to 1997 for Ken Judge as Hawthorn lost its last eight games, tumbling from fifth spot (equal on points with Adelaide and St Kilda) to finish 15th.

The losing streak followed the re-signing of Judge on a contract lasting until the end of 1999. The Hawks wanted to make sure West Coast or Carlton weren't able to gain his services, as it was reported they were keen on securing him.

Judge's style is based on accountability of each player for an opponent. But injuries to, and absence of, key players, such as Crawford, Condon, Dunstall, Langford and Holland, at various times made the team fairly light on for talent.

Judge was not making excuses though and would expect improvement from some of the talented youngsters.

He expects players to play within their limitations, fulfilling their objectives for the good of the team. That message should have sunk in by the end of last season and Judge will be able to begin afresh with a new direction, free of the uncertainty that surrounded the club at the start of the 1997 pre-season.

### AT A GLANCE

**COACHING RECORD**

| | **Hawthorn** | | | | |
|--------|-----|-----|-----|-----|-----|
| Season | P | W | L | D | Pos |
| 1996 | 23 | 11 | 11 | 1 | 8 |
| 1996 | 22 | 8 | 14 | 0 | 15 |
| **Total** | **45** | **19** | **25** | **1** | |

## WIN/LOSS RECORD

| Against | P | W (N) | L (N) | D (N) |
|---|---|---|---|---|
| Adelaide | 11 | 6 (1) | 5 (2) | 0 |
| Brisbane Bears | 16 | 13 (1) | 3 (1) | 0 |
| Brisbane Lions | 2 | 1 | 1 (1) | 0 |
| Carlton | 139 | 43 (1) | 96 | 0 |
| Collingwood | 129 | 45 | 84 (1) | 0 |
| Essendon | 132 | 50 | 82 (1) | 0 |
| Fitzroy | 116 | 63 | 52 | 1 |
| Fremantle | 4 | 2 | 2 | 0 |
| Geelong | 123 | 56 | 66 | 1 |
| Melbourne | 132 | 65 (1) | 67 | 0 |
| North Melb | 141 | 78 (4) | 61 (3) | 2 |
| Port Adel | 1 | 1 | 0 | 0 |
| Richmond | 129 | 55 | 74 (1) | 0 |
| St Kilda | 130 | 67 (1) | 62 (1) | 1 |
| Sydney | 127 | 72 (1) | 53 (2) | 2 |
| W Bulldogs | 132 | 65 (1) | 66 | 1 |
| West Coast | 19 | 7 | 12 (2) | 0 |
| **TOTALS** | **1483** | **689 (11)** | **786 (15)** | **8 (0)** |

*(N) Premiership matches played at night*

## WINNING RUNS

22 v Melbourne (1973–1984)
20 v St Kilda (1979–1989)
16 v Richmond (1985–1994)
15 v Fitzroy (1963–1971)
14 v North Melb (1985–1993)
13 v SM/Sydney (1971–1977)
11 v SM/Sydney (1981–1986)
11 v Geelong (1985–1990)
10 v Richmond (1959–1964)
9 v Brisbane Bears (1990–1995)
7 v Carlton (1984–1986)
6 v Collingwood (1982–1984); (1985–1988); (1989–1992)
6 v Essendon (1987–1989)
6 v Western Bulldogs (1976–1978)
3 v West Coast (1988–1989)
2 v Adelaide (1993); (1994)
2 v Fremantle (1995–1996)
1 v Port Adelaide (1997– )
1 v Brisbane Lions (1997)

## 1997 BEST AND FAIREST

Team is divided into areas — backline, centre/on-ball, forwards — to assess who has played well and a maximum of four votes can be given to any one player. More than one player in the same area can be given the same votes. Votes allocated in Ansett Australia Cup games, home and away games and finals.

**1** Paul Salmon (26)
**2** Daniel Harford (21)
Aaron Lord (21)
**4** Mark Graham (19)
Nick Holland (19)
Tony Woods (19)
**7** Richard Taylor (18)
**8** Craig Treleven (17)
**9** Brad Scott (15)
**10** Brendan Krummel (14)

## GAMES RECORDS

**426** Michael Tuck (1972–91)
**332** Leigh Matthews (1969–85)
**303** Chris Langford (1983–97)
**302** Don Scott (1967–81)
**300** Kelvin Moore (1970–84)
**269** Gary Ayres (1978–93)
**264** Peter Knights (1969–85)
**258** John Platten (1986–97)
**256** Jason Dunstall (1985– )
**241** John Kennedy Junior (1979–91)

## GOALS RECORDS

**1200** Jason Dunstall (1985– )
**915** Leigh Matthews (1969–85)
**727** Peter Hudson (1967–74; 1977)
**629** Michael Moncrieff (1971–83)
**475** John Peck (1954–66)
**427** Dermott Brereton (1982–92)
**383** Alex Albiston (1936–42; 1945–49)
**320** Michael Tuck (1972–91)
**293** Gary Buckenara (1982–90)
**269** Bert Hyde (1925–35)

## HIGHS AND LOWS

| Against | Highest | Lowest | G. W. Margin | G. L. Margin |
|---|---|---|---|---|
| Adelaide | 23.20.158 (1991) | 7.16.58 (1995) | 97 (1994) | 86 (1991) |
| Brisbane Bears | 25.16.166 (1994) | 5.11.41 (1996) | 99 (1994) | 63 (1996) |
| Brisbane Lions | 12.15.87 (1997) | 11.5.71 (1997) | 12 (1997) | 70 (1997) |
| Carlton | 24.13.157 (1978) | 4.12.36 (1954) | 98 (1991) | 128 (1969) |
| Collingwood | 25.22.172 (1976) | 2.8.20 (1952) | 125 (1987) | 105 (1979) |
| Essendon | 32.24.216 (1992) | 3.7.25 (1944) | 160 (1992) | 107 (1944) |
| Fitzroy | 36.15.231 (1991) | 3.16.34 (1930) | 157 (1991) | 84 (1925) |
| Fremantle | 18.10.118 (1995) | 9.8.62 (1997) | 57 (1996) | 14 (1997) |
| Geelong | 35.15.225 (1986) | 3.6.24 (1933) | 135 (1986) | 109 (1933) |
| Melbourne | 26.22.178 (1982) | 1.7.13 (1926) | 115 (1983) | 141 (1926) |
| North Melb | 32.14.206 (1982) | 2.13.25 (1950) | 95 (1988) | 127 (1994) |
| Port Adel | 18.16.124 (1997) | 18.16.124 (1997) | 32 (1997) | — |
| Richmond | 28.17.185 (1984) | 3.11.29 (1925) | 101 (1986) | 114 (1967) |
| St Kilda | 25.41.191 (1977) | 5.5.35 (1955) | 129 (1983) | 109 (1950) |
| Sydney | 29.15.189 (1979) | 4.10.34 (1932) | 99 (1987) | 123 (1932) |
| West Coast | 19.27.141 (1989) | 6.9.45 (1993) | 91 (1989) | 82 (1991) |
| W Bulldogs | 28.26.194 (1982) | 3.10.28 (1953) | 143 (1982) | 112 (1946) |

# THE LEADERSHIP AT HAWTHORN

| Year | Pos | Coach | Captain | Best & Fairest | Leading Goalkicker | |
|------|-----|-------|---------|----------------|--------------------|---|
| 1931 | 11 | J. Harris | J. Harris | | J. Ryan | 39 |
| 1932 | 12 | J. Jackson | B. Mills | S. Spinks | J. Ryan | 37 |
| 1933 | 11 | A. Rademacher | B. Mills | B. Mills | E. Pool | 27 |
| | | W. Twomey | W. Twomey | | | |
| 1934 | 11 | W. Twomey | B. Mills | E. Loveless | J. Green | 80 |
| | | | | W. Twomey | | |
| 1935 | 10 | I. McAlpine | I. McAlpine | B. Mills | J. Green | 63 |
| 1936 | 9 | I. McAlpine | I. McAlpine | L. Murphy | N. Hillard | 26 |
| 1937 | 8 | I. McAlpine | I. McAlpine | L. Murphy | N. Hillard | 31 |
| 1938 | 11 | I. McAlpine | B. Mills | S. Spinks | A. Naismith | 30 |
| 1939 | 10 | L. Thomas | L. Thomas | B. Mills | A. Albiston | 37 |
| 1940 | 9 | B. Mills | B. Mills | A. Angwin | A. Naismith | 25 |
| 1941 | 12 | B. Mills | B. Mills | A. Albiston | A. Albiston | 57 |
| 1942 | 12 | R. Cazaly | J. Carmody | J. Barker | A. Albiston | 32 |
| 1943 | 5 | R. Cazaly | R. Williams | J. Bohan | W. Culpitt | 43 |
| 1944 | 11 | T. Lahiff | J. Bohan | J. Blackman | W. Culpitt | 57 |
| 1945 | 10 | K. Shea | K. Shea | J. Bohan | A. Albiston | 66 |
| 1946 | 12 | K. Shea | J. Bohan | A. Albiston | A. Prior | 52 |
| 1947 | 11 | A. Albiston | A. Albiston | W. Culpitt | A. Prior | 67 |
| 1948 | 11 | A. Albiston | A. Albiston | K. Curran | A. Prior | 47 |
| 1949 | 12 | A. Albiston | A. Albiston | C. Austen | A. Prior | 48 |
| 1950 | 12 | R. McCaskill | P. O'Donohue/K. Curran | J. Kennedy | G. Anderson | 21 |
| 1951 | 11 | R. McCaskill | P. O'Donohue | J. Kennedy | P. Cash | 26 |
| 1952 | 11 | R. McCaskill/J. Hale | P. O'Donohue | J. Kennedy | J. MacDonald | 26 |
| 1953 | 12 | J. Hale | E. Fletcher | E. Fletcher | K. Coghlan | 19 |
| 1954 | 9 | J. Hale | E. Fletcher | J. Kennedy | K. Coghlan | 27 |
| 1955 | 8 | J. Hale | J. Kennedy | G. Arthur | K. Coghlan | 28 |
| 1956 | 7 | J. Hale | J. Kennedy | R. Simmonds | J. Peck | 31 |
| 1957 | 3 | J. Hale | J. Kennedy | A. Hughes | T. Ingersoll | 33 |
| 1958 | 6 | J. Hale | J. Kennedy | G. Arthur | J. Peck | 27 |
| 1959 | 7 | J. Hale | J. Kennedy | A. Woodley | G. Young | 35 |
| 1960 | 5 | J. Kennedy | G. Arthur | B. Edwards | G. Young | 36 |
| 1961 | 1 | J. Kennedy | G. Arthur | I. Law | J. Peck | 49 |
| 1962 | 9 | J. Kennedy | G. Arthur | G. Arthur | J. Peck | 38 |
| 1963 | 2 | J. Kennedy | G. Arthur | I. Law | J. Peck | 75 |
| 1964 | 5 | G. Arthur | G. Arthur | I. Law | J. Peck | 68 |
| 1965 | 12 | G. Arthur | G. Arthur/J. Peck | D. Parkin | J. Peck | 56 |
| 1966 | 9 | P. O'Donohue | G. Arthur | R. Wilson | J. Peck | 32 |
| 1967 | 10 | J. Kennedy | G. Arthur | R. Keddie | P. Hudson | 57 |
| 1968 | 6 | J. Kennedy | G. Arthur | P. Hudson | P. Hudson | 125 |
| 1969 | 5 | J. Kennedy | D. Parkin | R. Keddie | P. Hudson | 120 |
| 1970 | 8 | J. Kennedy | D. Parkin | P. Hudson | P. Hudson | 146 |
| 1971 | 1 | J. Kennedy | D. Parkin | L. Matthews | P. Hudson | 150 |
| 1972 | 6 | J. Kennedy | D. Parkin | L. Matthews | P. Knights | 46 |
| 1973 | 7 | J. Kennedy | D. Parkin | D. Scott | L. Matthews | 51 |
| 1974 | 3 | J. Kennedy | P. Crimmins | L. Matthews | M. Moncrieff | 67 |
| 1975 | 2 | J. Kennedy | P. Crimmins | P. Knights | L. Matthews | 68 |
| 1976 | 1 | J. Kennedy | D. Scott | L. Matthews | M. Moncrieff | 97 |
| 1977 | 3 | D. Parkin | D. Scott | L. Matthews | P. Hudson | 110 |
| 1978 | 1 | D. Parkin | D. Scott | L. Matthews | M. Moncrieff | 90 |
| 1979 | 7 | D. Parkin | D. Scott | K. Moore | M. Moncrieff | 45 |
| 1980 | 8 | D. Parkin | D. Scott | L. Matthews | M. Moncrieff | 86 |
| 1981 | 6 | A. Jeans | L. Matthews | T. Wallace | L. Matthews | 48 |
| 1982 | 3 | A. Jeans | L. Matthews | L. Matthews | L. Matthews | 74 |
| 1983 | 1 | A. Jeans | L. Matthews | T. Wallace | L. Matthews | 79 |
| 1984 | 2 | A. Jeans | L. Matthews | R. Greene | L. Matthews | 77 |
| 1985 | 2 | A. Jeans | L. Matthews | D. Brereton | D. Brereton | 58 |
| 1986 | 1 | A. Jeans | M. Tuck | G. Ayres | J. Dunstall | 77 |
| 1987 | 2 | A. Jeans | M. Tuck | J. Platten | J. Dunstall | 94 |
| 1988 | 1 | A. Joyce | M. Tuck | J. Dunstall | J. Dunstall | 132 |
| 1989 | 1 | A. Jeans | M. Tuck | J. Dunstall | J. Dunstall | 138 |
| 1990 | 5 | A. Jeans | M. Tuck | A. Collins | J. Dunstall | 83 |
| 1991 | 1 | A. Joyce | M. Tuck | B. Allan | J. Dunstall | 82 |
| 1992 | 6 | A. Joyce | G. Ayres | J. Dunstall | J. Dunstall | 145 |
| 1993 | 6 | A. Joyce | G. Ayres | J. Dunstall | J. Dunstall | 123 |
| 1994 | 7 | P. Knights | C. Langford | J. Platten | J. Dunstall | 101 |
| 1995 | 15 | P. Knights | J. Dunstall | D. Jarman | J. Dunstall | 66 |
| 1996 | 8 | K. Judge | J. Dunstall | P. Salmon | J. Dunstall | 102 |
| 1997 | 15 | K. Judge | J. Dunstall | P. Salmon | N. Holland | 29 |

# PLAYER PROFILES

## MARCUS BALDWIN

From Finley, birthplace of the Crawford brothers. Tall lightly built player who the Hawks think will take a while to develop strengthwise. Showed pace on a wing for the NSW/ACT Rams in the AFL National Under-18 Championships and made the All-Australian side. Brother Peter played for Geelong.

## JOHN BARKER

Very versatile and capable of holding down a key position if required, though more value on a flank. Plays the game hard running straight and tackling strongly, but was never able to overcome injury problems to string games together for the Lions. Has played more than 50 games and is only just 23, so is at the cusp of a settled AFL career at Hawthorn if he can perform well this season.
**Player honors:** AFL Norwich Rising Star nominee 1994.
**Previous AFL clubs:** Fitzroy (1994-96: 47 games, 12 goals), Brisbane Lions (1997: 8 games, 1 goal).

## RANDALL BONE

Hawthorn is persisting with Bone as a back-up ruckman for Paul Salmon, despite the fact he played only two games last season and 27 since making his debut in 1992. A lumbering type of ruckman in the Paul Dear mould — though yet to have anywhere near the same impact — but has toned up in preparation for this season. Impresses with his attitude and certainly, at only 24, is still young for a player of his type. Salmon has a mortgage on the number one ruck spot, but Bone needs to make more of any chances he gets.
**Previous AFL club:** Adelaide (1992-93: 12 games, 13 goals).

## HAYDEN BURGIEL

Smart left-footer capable of playing in defence and attack. Second in best and fairest voting at Gippsland Power, where he was used as a designated kicker from full-back while playing in the midfield. Still has a lot to learn and needs to work on his endurance.

## NATHAN CHAPMAN

The 1992 No. 2 draft pick from Kangaroo Flat returns to Victoria from the Brisbane Lions with a big chance to display the talent everyone knows he has. After a huge debut year in 1993, playing at full-back for the Brisbane Bears, Chapman suffered form and injury problems and wasn't able to consolidate a position. Has a great build, good skills and can hold down a key position in defence. Won the final of the Herald-Sunkick on Grand Final day in 1991.
**Player honors:** AFL Norwich Rising Star nominee 1993.
**Previous AFL club:** Brisbane Bears (1993-96: 49 games, 12 goals), Brisbane Lions (1997: 11 games, 1 goal).

## DANIEL CHICK

Last season, played 21 games and kicked 28 goals before being dropped for the last game. Was used at full-forward in the absence of Jason Dunstall, but is not built for a key position. Leads well, is courageous and recorded the most tackles for the Hawks last year. Needs to play on a flank in a supporting role to be able to show his flair.
**Player honors:** AFL Norwich Rising Star nominee 1996.

## JUSTIN CRAWFORD

An off-field indiscretion early last season didn't help the settling process at his new club, although having brother Shane there would have helped. Strung together some good football in the middle of the season, playing as a tall aggressive half-forward. Can be expected to show improvement in his second season with the club since crossing from the Sydney Swans.
**Player honors:** AFL Norwich Rising Star nominee 1995.
**Previous AFL club:** Sydney Swans (1995-97: 17 games, 11 goals).

## SHANE CRAWFORD

Fractured the navicular bone in a foot in an Ansett Australia Cup game last year and didn't reappear until round 10. Played off the half-back flank and was virtually a week-to-week proposition as he still suffered from problems relating to the stress fracture. However, he didn't miss a game and played well in most. A genuinely good footballer, with the potential to be one of the greats of the game. Plays with bouncy enthusiasm, is rarely beaten, has the capacity to gather the ball in from any area in his vicinity and runs hard to support teammates.
**Player honors:** 2nd best and fairest 1995 (equal), 1996; All-Australian 1996, AFL Norwich Rising Star nominee 1993.

## TRENT CROAD

The standout forward in the TAC Cup competition last year. Won the Dandenong Stingrays best and fairest — a great effort for a 17-year-old — averaged eight marks a game, finished second in the TAC Cup coaches' award and third in the Morrish Medal. Earmarked as a good player, but admits he's still learning how to play centre half-forward. Expected to get a chance at senior football later this year, either at full-forward or full-back. Born in New Zealand where his grandfather Eric Boggs was an All Black in the 1940s.

## JASON DANILTCHENKO

Made his debut in 1993 but has played only 28 games for the Kangaroos, with opportunities denied by both an embarrassment of riches on North's forward line and injuries at unfortunate times. Last year, a knee injury suffered in round two saw him out until a surprise selection in the preliminary final when North lost to St Kilda. Will have more opportunities at Hawthorn where his marking, and long left-foot kicking will relieve a bit of the pressure on Nick Holland and give the Hawks more than one avenue to attack.
**Player honors:** North Melbourne night series premiership side 1993.
**Previous AFL club:** North Melbourne (1993-97: 28 games, 18 goals).

## MATTHEW DENNIS

Played in a premiership for Old Brighton in B-grade amateurs last season. Can play at either end of the ground, is a good reader of the play, has good disposal and is a strong mark. A level-headed youngster rated a big chance to step straight into senior football this year.

## BEN DIXON

Made his debut last season, playing in 11 games and kicking eight goals after having a huge pre-season that saw him retained on the list. Showed ability to finish around goal with penetrating left-foot kicks. Is not overly quick and doesn't get a lot of the ball, but leads well and appears confident. Had made moves to establish himself by the end of the season, but 1998 shapes as crucial.

## JASON DUNSTALL

At the top of the most respected players' list and suffered the saddest injury of last season when the anterior cruciate ligament in his left knee went again in round eight against Carlton. It was one week after he became only the second player in the history of the AFL — behind Collingwood's 1930s champion Gordon Coventry (1299 goals) — to kick 1200 goals. Had played seven consecutive games in his comeback from the first knee reconstruction at the end of 1996. Has resigned the captaincy to concentrate solely on his comeback, while refusing to commit himself to definitely making it. Aged 33, but is such a champion that if he can make it back, the Hawks will definitely benefit. Could still kick 100 goals for the record.
**Player honors:** 2nd Brownlow Medal 1988 (equal), 1992; 3rd Brownlow Medal 1989; best and fairest 1988, 1989, 1992, 1993, 2nd best and fairest 1994, 3rd best and fairest 1996; All-Australian 1988, 1989, 1992, 1994; EJ Whitten Medal 1989; Simpson Medal 1989; Coleman Medal 1988, 1989, 1992; leading goalkicker 1986, 1987, 1988, 1989, 1990, 1991, 1992, 1993, 1994, 1995, 1996; premiership sides 1986, 1988, 1989, 1991; night series premiership sides 1985, 1986, 1988, 1991, 1992; captain 1995–1997.

## KANE FRASER

Playing in the last game of the 1997 season wasn't a good enough result for Fraser, who is in his third year at the club. But there are hopes he can make it. Needs to work hard on his skills because he is capable of getting the football, but turns it over too often. Has good aerobic fitness, pace and is hard at the football.

## MARK GRAHAM

A foot injury interrupted his fantastic form at full-back early last season; form that was perhaps assisted by advice he sought from Chris Langford via email. After Graham had given Collingwood's Saverio Rocca a football lesson in round 10, coach Ken Judge thought he deserved to be included in the Victorian squad. A hard-running, attacking player, Graham is lightly framed but a brilliant mark and capable of matching — and defeating — the best players in the game. Used up forward towards the end of the season, such is his versatility, but will probably be asked to play in a key defensive position.
**Player honors:** AFL Norwich Rising Star nominee 1994.

## DANIEL HARFORD

Was burning early last season, polling nine Brownlow votes in the first six rounds in the No. 5 made famous by the late Peter Crimmins. His brilliant form culminated with a slashing performance for Victoria in the State of Origin game against South Australia, before he faded towards the end of the season as the team struggled. A talented young rover with an impeccable junior record and will be a great player. Courageous, hard running and not afraid to take on the best opponents. His lapse at the end of last season should focus his mind on 1998, although he had a minor setback at the start of the season with a groin injury.
**Player honors:** 2nd best and fairest 1997 (equal).

## JON HASSALL

Recruited at the start of 1997 as an anticipated replacement for veteran Andy Collins. Lightly built but determined and was used last year mainly in stopping roles that he filled reasonably well. Doesn't get enough of the ball and his disposal by foot lets him down.
**Player honors:** AFL Norwich Rising Star nominee 1994.
**Previous AFL club:** Collingwood (1994-96: 50 games, 12 goals).

## JONATHON HAY

Definitely one of the players Hawthorn is pinning its rebuilding hopes on. Played four games in 1997 for a taste of senior football and became a key player at reserves level. Has good pace and agility, but is still in the developing process.

## NICK HOLLAND

A knee injury that caused Holland to miss five games after round 14 last year (the start of Hawthorn's losing streak) was cited as the reason the Hawks fell away. His marking power was sorely missed up forward and his kicking had definitely improved before his injury. Showed more of a capacity to take control of a game given added responsibility with Dunstall injured and Langford busy. Finished fourth in the best and fairest, despite his five-week absence, and assumed more of a leadership role. Will have a pre-season this year unencumbered by trade talks/contract negotiations that have distracted in the previous two.
**Player honors:** 2nd best and fairest 1995 (equal); leading goalkicker 1997; AFL Norwich Rising Star 1995.

## DARREN KAPPLER

Long-kicking left-foot wingman/half-forward who missed the first half of last season due to groin surgery. Played 11 games for the season and is an important part of the midfield, particularly in the wide open spaces of Waverley. Game centres on providing sweeping drive from the half-forward line through his ability to kick long. Has entered the veteran class at 33, is in his 12th year in the game and has signed a one-year contract. Reliable rather than brilliant.
**Player honors:** Fitzroy best and fairest 1988.
**Previous AFL clubs:** Fitzroy (1987-91: 87 games, 51 goals), Sydney (1992-95: 59 games, 74 goals).

**HAYDON KILMARTIN**
Drafted by Melbourne at No. 31 in the 1991 National Draft from North Hobart, where he played 26 reserves games in 1992. Now 24, Kilmartin was desperate for another crack at AFL football after being runner-up in the Sandover Medal in 1997. Hawthorn interviewed him in November, but couldn't guarantee him anything except the opportunity to train. Kilmartin paid his own way to Victoria, financed his stay here over summer and was rewarded by being drafted at number 12 in the pre-season draft. A midfielder, Kilmartin has reasonable pace, good skills and is a right-footer, but is excellent on both sides of his body.

**BRENDAN KRUMMEL**
Kicked five goals from full-forward the week after Dunstall was out injured and looked a possible solution. Leads hard and has good skills, but wasn't able to hold down the key position in the long term. Is mobile for his size, but struggled when forced to take the best opposition defender each week. Played State of Origin football for Western Australia last season.
**Previous AFL clubs:** West Coast Eagles (1992-94: 9 games, 3 goals), Fremantle (1995: 1 game, 0 goals).

**STEPHEN LAWRENCE**
Re-invented himself across half-back in the past couple of years, managing 19 games last season. A talented ruckman early in his career, but hasn't really lived up to the expectations and hopes held for him in the '90s. At 28 and about to reach 150 games, needs to assume an on-field leadership role. Is tall, athletic and capable of matching it around the ground with the best mobile ruckmen in the game. Ideally could play a more attacking role in order to pose some match-up problems for the opposition and put Hawthorn back on the front foot.
**Player honors:** premiership side 1991; night series premiership side 1991.

**ANGELO LEKKAS**
Played every game in only his second year of AFL football. His consistency earned him the final AFL Norwich Rising Star nomination for '97 and praise from coach Ken Judge. A dour player who fits the coach's creed of accountability and playing within one's limitations. A great tackler, remains unflustered regardless of the situation and gets a lot of the football.
**Player honors:** AFL Norwich Rising Star nominee 1997.

**BRAD LLOYD**
The older brother of Essendon's Matthew Lloyd was on Hawthorn's supplementary list last season and won the Gardiner Medal (AFL reserves best and fairest). Hawthorn was keen to put him on its list for 1998, but was able to wait until draft pick No. 67 to snap him up. A highly skilled wingman/centreman who will step straight in to bolster the midfield.

**AARON LORD**
A fantastic beginning and middle part of last year that was soured slightly when poor form saw him dropped for round 18 then added as a late inclusion. Early form was so good he was equal second in the best and fairest — a tremendous effort in his first year at the club. A strong running player who can kick goals, Lord was the highest kick-winner for the Hawks in 1997 and their third highest goalkicker. The move to Hawthorn has been a definite plus for Lord, who at 22, should be a valuable midfielder for the Hawks.
**Player honors:** Hawthorn 2nd best and fairest 1997 (equal); AFL Norwich Rising Star nominee 1995.
**Previous AFL club:** Geelong (1994-96: 32 games, 19 goals).

**LUKE McCABE**
The No. 15 pick at the 1993 National Draft and still just off what is required at AFL level. Managed 11 games last year, mostly on a wing, but by year's end was out of the side. Needs a big year to convince the football world he is up to AFL standard.

**CHRIS OBST**
A courageous running defender from Melton South, who didn't have a pre-season in 1997 yet still made the Victoria Metro side and performed well. Showed excellent poise for the Western Jets in 1997, is a good mark and doesn't deviate. Hawthorn can expect rapid improvement after a big pre-season, but won't be rushing him.

**JADE RAWLINGS**
A couple of big marks in the reserves Grand Final in 1997 and a place among Hawthorn's best players made fans sit up and take notice. After being a low pick (No. 97) in the 1994 National Draft, the young Tasmanian showed some form, kicking five goals in the first half against Fremantle in round 17. However, he struggled to put four quarters together. Needs to be more consistent, but is capable.

**JONATHON ROBRAN**
From the famous South Australian footballing family and a very honest player last year. Played every game, mainly in defence, and employed mostly negative tactics to achieve a result. A tall, square-shouldered man, Robran is a workhorse with the capacity to hold down a key defensive post. He's 25 and appears, because of his build, to be a late developer. Needs to improve his marking power.

**PAUL SALMON**
A completely revitalised footballer. Second season for the Hawks was the same as the first — brilliant. Easily won his second Hawks best and fairest and was ruckman of the 1997 All-Australian team. His ruckwork is without peer and several times last season, his tapwork won games. Made the most hitouts in the AFL last season and was in the top 10 for marking, but it is his leadership and direction that makes him such a successful recruit. He missed one game late last year with a back problem.
**Player honors:** Hawthorn best and fairest 1996, 1997; All-Australian 1987, 1988, 1997; Tassie Medal 1988; Essendon leading goalkicker 1984, 1987, 1988, 1989, 1990, 1992, 1993; Essendon night series premiership sides 1990, 1994; Essendon premiership sides 1985, 1993.
**Previous AFL club:** Essendon (1983-95: 209 games, 509 goals).

**PAUL SHARKEY**
After four less than fruitful seasons with Collingwood,

finally indicated he wanted out and was traded for Shannon Gibson. Became a maligned player at Collingwood, but is fit, has good height and can run with the ball. Needs to get the footy more often, whether he plays in a run-with role or across half-back. Plenty of football left in him and his career wasn't going anywhere with the Magpies.
**Previous AFL club:** Collingwood (1994-97: 26 games, 4 goals).

### JOEL SMITH

Arrives at Hawthorn as one of the bigger stories of the off-season after he left St Kilda in controversial circumstances. The young forward and the Saints could not agree to terms over a new contract and both player and club left each other feeling jilted. Hawthorn, having lost many out-of-contract players, saw the chance to grab one of the AFL's brightest prospects and view him as a long-term player, despite a serious knee injury. Smith hurt himself in round 18 last year against Collingwood and faces a long stint on the sidelines. Classy mover on the ball or in attack and providing he makes a full recovery, he should be a 200-game player for the Hawks.
**Player honors:** AFL Norwich Rising Star nominee 1995; St Kilda night series premiership side 1996.
**Previous AFL club:** St Kilda (1995-97: 58 games, 51 goals).

### PHILLIP SMITH

Continued to impress all with his work ethic and desire to make AFL football. Looked good early last year, but failed to crack it for a senior game. A left-footer with a capacity to get the football who needs to work on his disposal.

### RICHARD TAYLOR

Gutsy on-baller who runs straight at the football. Had an impressive year in 1997 as a second string on-baller and finished seventh in the club's best and fairest. A reliable footballer rarely beaten and capable at times of doing something quite brilliant, such as his fearlessness. The confidence of having an injury-free season (Taylor suffered two knee reconstructions as a youngster) will help him take another step by becoming a more attacking player.

### RAYDEN TALLIS

Has worked hard at Hawthorn to re-establish himself after finishing the season at the crossroads with his future at Hawthorn uncertain. He also received a one-week suspension from the last game of the season underlining a disappointing 1997. Hawthorn is persisting with Tallis who needs to knuckle down to become a regular senior AFL player this season. A good run-with player when given the opportunity and has managed 53 AFL games in five seasons without ever really settling.
**Player honors:** AFL Norwich Rising Star nominee 1994.

### NATHAN THOMPSON

Bendigo Pioneers and the TAC Cup's leading goal-kicker in 1996 as a bulky full-forward from Kyneton. Missed out on being drafted, lost a lot of weight over the summer getting his fitness levels right for AFL football, trained with Williamstown and was on Hawthorn's supplementary list. A very strong player and a good mark who has earned his opportunity at AFL level through hard work.

### CRAIG TRELEVEN

Was burning in the first half of the season picking up his usual quota of high possessions before his form mirrored that of his team and fell away in the last third. Was sent a clear message when dropped near the end. Hails from East Fremantle and has been a good pick-up. A big possession winner with excellent skills on both sides of his body.
**Player honors:** Sandover Medal 1995.

### NATHAN TURVEY

Was expected to play senior football last year and his failure to do so was a disappointment. The recruit from South Fremantle, nicknamed 'Topsy', has good pace, but last year didn't work hard enough to use it. AFL career is at the crossroads as he needs to improve his work ethic to make the grade.

### RICHARD VANDENBURG

From Wentworth in NSW so was unable to be named by either Carlton or Hawthorn on their supplementary lists for 1997 because of AFL rules relating to the naming of supplementary list players. Went back to play in the VAFA with University Blues in A grade, where he made the state squad, before his season was ruined by a broken wrist suffered in a trailbike accident on the family farm at Wentworth. Very hard at the football, plays in the midfield and is thought to be definitely capable of playing at this level.

### TONY WOODS

Consistently good in his role as a run-with player and now, after three years, is a solid part of the make-up at Hawthorn following stints at Fitzroy and Collingwood. A smart footballer who relies on concentration, mental toughness and a good ability to read the play to match more naturally talented opponents. Nearing 100 games.
**Previous AFL clubs:** Fitzroy (1989-90: 13 games, 4 goals), Collingwood (1992-94: 18 games, 6 goals).

## ROOKIE LIST

### STEPHEN JURICA

Burst on to the AFL scene in 1995 when he played a crucial role at full-forward as Richmond tied with Essendon in front of a near full house at the MCG. Hasn't really delivered since, playing just five games in two years for the Tigers. One of Richmond's best in last year's reserves' grand final when the Tigers defeated the Hawks. Has trained with Hawthorn all summer and could be a target up forward or a mobile, if slightly small, ruckman.
**Player honors:** AFL Norwich Rising Star nominee 1995.
**Previous AFL club:** Richmond (1995-97: 18 games, 25 goals).

### GLEN BOWYER

A promising junior golfer from Wodonga, Bowyer had a very good year across half-back with the Murray Bushrangers. Played well in the TAC Cup finals last season, kicking three goals when swung into attack in their losing preliminary final.

# HAWTHORN

| Name (# = rookie) | No. | Born | Height | Weight | Recruited from |
|---|---|---|---|---|---|
| Marcus Baldwin | 26 | 24/10/79 | 194 | 81 | ASSUMPTION COLLEGE/CALDER U18 |
| John Barker | 27 | 19/2/75 | 193 | 91 | PASCOE VALE/NORTHERN U18/FITZROY/BRISBANE |
| Randall Bone | 16 | 13/11/73 | 194 | 98 | SOUTH ADELAIDE (SA)/ADELAIDE |
| Hayden Burgiel | 41 | 23/3/79 | 182 | 74 | MAFFRA/GIPPSLAND U18 |
| Nathan Chapman | 1 | 7/5/75 | 192 | 80 | KANGAROO FLAT/BRISBANE |
| Daniel Chick | 17 | 10/2/76 | 184 | 85 | EAST FREMANTLE (WA) |
| Justin Crawford | 23 | 20/3/77 | 183 | 85 | TOCUMWAL(NSW)/ASSUMPTION COLLEGE/SYDNEY |
| Shane Crawford | 9 | 9/9/74 | 175 | 77 | FINLEY (NSW)/ASSUMPTION COLLEGE |
| Trent Croad | 24 | 9/3/80 | 190 | 92 | NARRE WARREN/DANDENONG U18 |
| Jason Daniltchenko | 25 | 2/9/75 | 189 | 93 | BAYSWATER/NORTH MELB |
| Matthew Dennis | 28 | 11/2/78 | 189 | 87 | OLD BRIGHTON |
| Ben Dixon | 32 | 14/6/77 | 186 | 86 | YARRAWONGA/ASSUMPTION COLLEGE |
| Jason Dunstall | 19 | 14/8/64 | 188 | 100 | COORPAROO (QLD) |
| Kane Fraser | 39 | 22/7/77 | 185 | 88 | EAST RINGWOOD/EASTERN U18 |
| Mark Graham | 34 | 13/3/73 | 190 | 85 | BERWICK |
| Daniel Harford | 5 | 19/3/77 | 177 | 80 | ST MARYS (VMFL)/NORTHERN U18 |
| Jon Hassall | 13 | 14/8/73 | 173 | 76 | WARRANDYTE/COLLINGWOOD |
| Jonathan Hay | 3 | 13/8/79 | 194 | 87 | EAST FREMANTLE (WA) |
| Nick Holland | 2 | 29/7/74 | 195 | 100 | NORTH ADELAIDE (SA) |
| Darren Kappler | 11 | 23/1/65 | 183 | 84 | SOUTH ADELAIDE (SA)/FITZROY/SYDNEY |
| Haydon Kilmartin | 38 | 22/7/73 | 178 | 80 | NORTH HOBART (TAS)/MELB RES/EAST FREM (WA) |
| Brendan Krummel | 14 | 24/6/72 | 185 | 85 | EAST FREMANTLE (WA)/WEST COAST/FREMANTLE |
| Stephen Lawrence | 12 | 22/4/69 | 200 | 100 | MORNINGSIDE (QLD) |
| Angelo Lekkas | 37 | 29/6/76 | 185 | 86 | ALPHINGTON/NORTHERN U18 |
| Brad Lloyd | 18 | 16/9/75 | 182 | 81 | WILLIAMSTOWN |
| Aaron Lord | 15 | 21/7/75 | 182 | 89 | DONCASTER HEIGHTS/CENTRAL U18/GEELONG |
| Luke McCabe | 7 | 10/8/76 | 183 | 76 | CENTRAL DISTRICT (SA) |
| Chris Obst | 31 | 9/10/79 | 184 | 76 | MELTON/WESTERN U18 |
| Jade Rawlings | 20 | 9/10/77 | 195 | 87 | DEVONPORT (TAS) |
| Jonathon Robran | 10 | 21/10/72 | 196 | 94 | NORWOOD (SA) |
| Paul Salmon | 4 | 20/1/65 | 205 | 112 | NORTH RINGWOOD/ESSENDON |
| Paul Sharkey | 36 | 8/6/74 | 190 | 92 | SANDHURST/COLLINGWOOD |
| Joel Smith | 21 | 3/5/77 | 186 | 84 | YARRAWONGA/MURRAY U18/ST. KILDA |
| Phillip Smith | 33 | 7/8/78 | 183 | 83 | WEST PERTH (WA) |
| Rayden Tallis | 29 | 9/6/75 | 183 | 83 | WANTIRNA/EASTERN U18 |
| Richard Taylor | 6 | 14/7/73 | 175 | 75 | CAMBERWELL GRAMMAR |
| Nathan Thompson | 49 | 14/2/78 | 195 | 91 | KYNETON/BENDIGO U18 |
| Craig Treleven | 8 | 14/6/70 | 188 | 86 | EAST FREMANTLE (WA) |
| Nathan Turvey | 22 | 17/10/77 | 182 | 83 | SOUTH FREMANTLE (WA) |
| Richard Vandenberg | 35 | 14/1/77 | 180 | 80 | UNIVERSITY BLUES |
| Tony Woods | 30 | 2/7/69 | 185 | 85 | OLD PARADIANS/FITZROY/COLLINGWOOD |
| Glen Bowyer # | 43 | 28/12/79 | 181 | 83 | WODONGA/MURRAY U18 |
| Stephen Jurica # | 40 | 26/6/76 | 194 | 104 | SOUTH FREMANTLE (WA) |
| Total/(Average) *On 26/2/98 | | (23.0 yrs)* | (187) | (86) | |

# PLAYERS 1998

| Debut | HOME & AWAY | | 1997 | | FINALS | | GRAND FINALS | | | NIGHT SERIES | | STATE OF ORIGIN | |
|---|---|---|---|---|---|---|---|---|---|---|---|---|---|
| | Gms | Gls | Gms | Gls | Gms | Gls | Gms | Gls | Won | Gms | Gls | Gms | Gls |
| | 0 | 0 | 0 | 0 | | | | | | 0 | 0 | 0 | 0 |
| 1994 | 55 | 13 | 8 | 1 | | | | | | 3 | 0 | 0 | 0 |
| 1992 | 27 | 17 | 2 | 0 | 2 | 2 | | | | 1 | 0 | 0 | 0 |
| | 0 | 0 | 0 | 0 | | | | | | 0 | 0 | 0 | 0 |
| 1993 | 60 | 13 | 11 | 1 | 3 | 0 | | | | 5 | 0 | 0 | 0 |
| 1996 | 43 | 42 | 21 | 28 | 1 | 2 | | | | 2 | 0 | 1 | 0 |
| 1995 | 32 | 28 | 15 | 17 | 1 | 0 | | | | 3 | 2 | 0 | 0 |
| 1993 | 93 | 74 | 13 | 5 | 2 | 2 | | | | 7 | 3 | 2 | 2 |
| | 0 | 0 | 0 | 0 | | | | | | 0 | 0 | 0 | 0 |
| 1993 | 29 | 18 | 3 | 1 | 1 | 0 | | | | 9 | 4 | 0 | 0 |
| | 0 | 0 | 0 | 0 | | | | | | 0 | 0 | 0 | 0 |
| 1997 | 11 | 8 | 11 | 8 | | | | | | 0 | 0 | 0 | 0 |
| 1985 | 256 | 1200 | 8 | 21 | 21 | 78 | 5 | 23 | 4 | 29 | 116 | 8 | 24 |
| 1996 | 3 | 0 | 1 | 0 | | | | | | 0 | 0 | 0 | 0 |
| 1993 | 84 | 28 | 19 | 14 | 2 | 3 | | | | 3 | 1 | 0 | 0 |
| 1995 | 55 | 23 | 22 | 11 | 1 | 0 | | | | 2 | 0 | 1 | 0 |
| 1994 | 65 | 13 | 15 | 1 | 1 | 0 | | | | 7 | 2 | 0 | 0 |
| 1997 | 4 | 2 | 4 | 2 | | | | | | 0 | 0 | 0 | 0 |
| 1994 | 55 | 59 | 17 | 29 | 1 | 0 | | | | 6 | 2 | 2 | 3 |
| 1987 | 176 | 147 | 11 | 8 | 1 | 1 | | | | 17 | 15 | 2 | 1 |
| | 0 | 0 | 0 | 0 | | | | | | 0 | 0 | 0 | 0 |
| 1992 | 42 | 20 | 21 | 15 | 1 | 1 | | | | 3 | 1 | 1 | 0 |
| 1988 | 142 | 30 | 19 | 4 | 7 | 1 | 1 | 0 | 1 | 7 | 1 | 2 | 0 |
| 1996 | 25 | 2 | 22 | 2 | | | | | | 1 | 0 | 0 | 0 |
| | 0 | 0 | 0 | 0 | | | | | | | | | |
| 1994 | 54 | 41 | 22 | 22 | 4 | 4 | 1 | 0 | 0 | 3 | 2 | 0 | 0 |
| 1995 | 28 | 3 | 11 | 0 | 1 | 0 | | | | 1 | 0 | 0 | 0 |
| | 0 | 0 | 0 | 0 | | | | | | 0 | 0 | 0 | 0 |
| 1996 | 8 | 11 | 6 | 10 | | | | | | 1 | 1 | 0 | 0 |
| 1995 | 39 | 3 | 22 | 3 | | | | | | 1 | 0 | 0 | 0 |
| 1983 | 248 | 256 | 21 | 13 | 14 | 35 | 3 | 13 | 2 | 22 | 28 | 14 | 45 |
| 1994 | 26 | 4 | 5 | 1 | 1 | 0 | | | | 3 | 1 | 0 | 0 |
| 1995 | 58 | 51 | 16 | 23 | | | | | | 9 | 7 | 0 | 0 |
| | 0 | 0 | 0 | 0 | | | | | | 1 | 0 | 0 | 0 |
| 1994 | 53 | 10 | 10 | 2 | 1 | 0 | | | | 1 | 0 | 0 | 0 |
| 1992 | 53 | 21 | 20 | 8 | 1 | 0 | | | | 3 | 0 | 0 | 0 |
| | 0 | 0 | 0 | 0 | | | | | | 0 | 0 | 0 | 0 |
| 1996 | 40 | 11 | 19 | 4 | 1 | 0 | | | | 1 | 0 | 1 | 2 |
| | 0 | 0 | 0 | 0 | | | | | | 0 | 0 | 0 | 0 |
| | 0 | 0 | 0 | 0 | | | | | | 0 | 0 | 0 | 0 |
| 1989 | 93 | 22 | 22 | 3 | 2 | 2 | | | | 1 | 1 | 0 | 0 |
| | 0 | 0 | 0 | 0 | | | | | | 0 | 0 | | |
| 1995 | 18 | 25 | 3 | 0 | 1 | 1 | | | | 2 | 0 | | |
| | (48) | (53) | 417 | 257 | 70 | 131 | 10 | 36 | 7 | 152 | 187 | 34 | 77 |

## Demons at a glance

**ADDRESS:** 26 Jolimont Terrace, Jolimont 3002
**POSTAL ADDRESS:** Melbourne Football Club, PO Box 254, East Melbourne 3002
**TELEPHONE:** (03) 9650 9052
**FACSIMILE:** (03) 9654 6039
**WEB SITE:** www.demons.com.au
**EMAIL:** melbfc@demons.com.au
**PRESIDENT:** Joseph Gutnick
**CHIEF EXECUTIVE:** Cameron Schwab
**GENERAL MANAGER, FOOTBALL OPERATIONS:** Danny Corcoran (Address: Junction Oval, Cnr Fitzroy St & Lakeside Drive, St Kilda 3182. Phone: (03) 9534 8477, Fax: (03) 9534 8655)
**MARKETING MANAGER:** Elizabeth Crosthwaite
**BUSINESS MANAGER:** John Anderson
**COMMUNICATIONS MANAGER:** Gerard Murphy
**COACHING STAFF:** Neale Daniher (senior); Greg Hutchison (assistant); Chris Fagan (development and reserves)
**SELECTION COMMITTEE:** Greg Healy (chairman); Greg Hutchison, Neale Daniher, Chris Fagan, Bernie Sheehy
**CLUB DOCTORS:** Andrew Daff, Kal Fried
**CLUB PHYSIOTHERAPISTS:** Price Warren, Andrew Ronchi
**JOINED AFL:** 1897
**HOME GROUND:** MCG, Yarra Park, Jolimont
**GROUND DIMENSIONS:** 161m by 140m. Goals run east to west
**TRAINING VENUE:** Junction Oval, St Kilda
**OFFICIAL COLORS:** Guernsey: Navy blue with red V neck. Socks: Red. Shorts: Navy blue
**GAMES RECORD HOLDER:** Robert Flower — 272
**AFL CONSECUTIVE GAMES RECORD HOLDER:** Jim Stynes — 240
**PREMIERSHIPS:** 1900, 1926, 1939-40-41, 1948, 1955-56-57, 1959-60, 1964
**BROWNLOW MEDALLISTS:** I. P. Warne-Smith (1926, 1928), Dr Don Cordner (1946), B. Wilson (1982), P. Moore (1984), J. Stynes (1991)
**RECORD HOME ATTENDANCE** (MCG): 99,346 — June 15, 1958 v Collingwood

# MELBOURNE

# New challenge awaits Demons

It would be fair to say the past two seasons at Melbourne have not been exactly uneventful off the field, even if they have been ordinary on it.

In no particular order, the club has seen off a merger, a coach, a chairman, a chief executive, a football manager, a chairman of selectors and wondered, at times, what it had done wrong to cop so many injuries to top-line players.

But the past 12 months have seen a change in direction, starting from the top under chairman Joseph Gutnick and continuing with the appointments of Neale Daniher (coach), Cameron Schwab (chief executive) and Danny Corcoran (football manager).

Now comes the hard part — getting its act together on the field. For a club that has won just 20 of 66 games in the past three years, it is going to be a monumental task.

The 1997 season started and finished on a high, but in between there was a lot of anguish, heartbreak and plain hard luck.

The regular faces missing included Garry Lyon (5 games in '97), Stephen Tingay (3), Shaun Smith (11), Matthew Febey (11) and Glenn Lovett (14), while Paul Prymke and Craig Turley never got to the line.

Melbourne has also lost experience in the form of Andrew Obst (retired), but on the positive side David Schwarz improved spirit and morale at the club by making a welcome return from three major knee operations. The big forward played 10 games and while his first steps were understandably a little tentative, he was getting better each week.

As reflected in the Demons' best and fairest voting, the mainstays were the indefatigable Jim Stynes and tough on-baller Todd Viney. Once again, Melbourne will be relying heavily on these experienced players as the club goes through a re-building period to beat all re-building periods.

The Demons would have been delighted with the debut season of Shane Woewodin, while clever forward Jeff Farmer can only be better as more talent and experience is gathered around him.

Some of that talent will come from Jeff White, who has been lured back to Victoria from Fremantle and will get ample opportunity to fulfil the promise he showed with the Dockers. The arrival of Jamie Shanahan from St Kilda adds badly needed experience to the backline. It would be fairly safe to assume there is only one direction in which the Demons can head.

**— Michael Lovett**

## THE YEAR AHEAD

| Rd | Date | Opponent | Venue | Home/ Away | Time (local) |
|----|------|----------|-------|------------|--------------|
| 1 | March 29 | Fremantle | S | A | 1.20pm |
| 2 | April 4 | North Melbourne | MCG | H | 3.30pm |
| 3 | April 13 | Brisbane Lions | G | A | 2.10pm |
| 4 | April 19 | Carlton | OO | A | 2.10pm |
| 5 | April 26 | Port Adelaide | MCG | H | 2.10pm |
| 6 | May 3 | Sydney | SCG | A | 12.40pm |
| 7 | May 10 | Richmond | MCG | A | 2.10pm |
| 8 | May 17 | Collingwood | MCG | H | 2.10pm |
| 9 | May 23 | Essendon | MCG | H | 2.10pm |
| 10 | May 31 | Adelaide | FP | A | 1.40pm |
| 11 | June 6 | Hawthorn | P | A | 2.10pm |
| 12 | June 13 | Geelong | MCG | H | 2.10pm |
| 13 | June 21 | St Kilda | MCG | H | 2.10pm |
| 14 | June 28 | West Coast | S | A | 1.20pm |
| 15 | July 4 | Western Bulldogs | OO | A | 2.10pm |
| 16 | July 18 | Fremantle | MCG | H | 2.10pm |
| 17 | July 25 | North Melbourne | MCG | A | 2.10pm |
| 18 | August 1 | Brisbane Lions | P | A | 2.10pm |
| 19 | August 8 | Carlton | MCG | H | 2.10pm |
| 20 | August 16 | Port Adelaide | FP | A | 12.10pm |
| 21 | August 24 (N) | Sydney | MCG | H | 7.40pm |
| 22 | August 30 | Richmond | MCG | H | 2.10pm |

## 1997 AT A GLANCE

**W:** R1: North Melbourne 7.13 (55) v Melbourne 10.10 (70) (MCG)

**L:** R2: Melbourne 7.14 (56) v Collingwood 24.19 (163) (MCG)

**L:** R3: Sydney 15.9 (99) v Melbourne 14.7 (91) (SCG)

**L:** R4: Melbourne 13.9 (87) v Western Bulldogs 13.11 (89) (MCG)

**L:** R5: Melbourne 12.6 (78) v West Coast 19.12 (126) (MCG)

**L:** R6: St Kilda 17.19 (121) v Melbourne 4.11 (35) (P)

**L:** R7: Fremantle 17.22 (124) v Melbourne 10.9 (69) (W)

**L:** R8: Melbourne 7.7 (49) v Geelong 19.14 (128) (MCG)

**L:** R9: Port Adelaide 10.18 (78) v Melbourne 3.9 (27) (FP)

**W:** R10: Richmond 9.13 (67) v Melbourne 14.8 (92) (MCG)

### SNAPSHOT

**Games:** 22
**Wins:** 4 **Losses:** 18
**Ladder Finish:** 16th
**Players Used:** 38

**L:** R11: Melbourne 5.15 (45) v Adelaide 14.13 (97) (MCG)

**L:** R12: Melbourne 7.8 (50) v Brisbane Lions 21.9 (135) (MCG)

**L:** R13: Hawthorn 17.16 (118) v Melbourne 7.13 (55) (P)

**L:** R14: Essendon 18.12 (120) v Melbourne 8.9 (57) (MCG)

**W:** R15: Melbourne 18.11 (119) v Carlton 15.10 (100) (MCG)

**L:** R16: Melbourne 7.16 (58) v North Melbourne 17.12 (114) (MCG)

**L:** R17: Collingwood 20.14 (134) v Melbourne 12.10 (82) (MCG)

**L:** R18: Melbourne 7.11 (53) v Sydney 25.19 (169) (MCG)

**L:** R19: Western Bulldogs 14.18 (102) v Melbourne 9.10 (64) (OO)

**L:** R20: West Coast 15.7 (97) v Melbourne 7.17 (59) (W)

**L:** R21: Melbourne 8.14 (62) v St Kilda 17.12 (114) (MCG)

**W:** R22: Melbourne 18.11 (119) v Fremantle 11.13 (79) (MCG)

## The Coach

### Neale Daniher

**Born:** 15/2/51

It was never going to be a matter of would Neale Daniher become an AFL coach, but rather a case of when.

The former Essendon defender and member of one of the game's most famous football families was destined to coach at the top level once the right opportunity presented itself.

Now, after a two-year stint as assistant to Gerard Neesham at Fremantle, Daniher has the chance to make his mark, albeit from the bottom of the tree.

The Demons appointed Daniher ahead of other well-credentialled candidates including Greg Hutchison, the man who was asked to stand in after Neil Balme was sacked nine rounds into the 1997 season.

Of course, Daniher is a rookie coach in name only. Even during his injury-interrupted career with Essendon, good judges at Windy Hill knew he had the makings of a future coach and he was a member of the Bombers' coaching panel for several years.

He played with Werribee in the VFA in 1991 after finishing his playing career at Windy Hill in 1990 and returned to the Bombers as a specialist coach in 1992.

Daniher played 82 games and kicked 32 goals for the Bombers in three stints — 1979-81, 1985 and 1989-90. He will be remembered as one of the unluckiest players in football, having endured three major knee operations and missing the glory years when the Bombers won back-to-back flags in 1984-85.

## WIN/LOSS RECORD

| Against | P | W (N) | L (N) | D (N) |
|---|---|---|---|---|
| Adelaide | 10 | 3 | 7 (5) | 0 |
| Brisbane Bears | 17 | 12 (4) | 5 (2) | 0 |
| Brisbane Lions | 1 | 0 | 1 | 0 |
| Carlton | 184 | 78 | 104 | 2 |
| Collingwood | 209 | 72 | 133 (1) | 4 |
| Essendon | 188 | 72 | 114 | 2 |
| Fitzroy | 179 | 83 | 88 | 3 |
| Fremantle | 5 | 3 (1) | 2 (2) | 0 |
| Geelong | 185 | 77 | 107 (1) | 1 |
| Hawthorn | 132 | 67 | 65 (1) | 0 |
| North Melb | 128 | 74 (4) | 53 (2) | 1 |
| Port Adel | 1 | 0 | 1 (1) | 0 |
| Richmond | 157 | 68 (2) | 87 | 2 |
| St Kilda | 181 | 108 | 72 (1) | 1 |
| Sydney | 177 | 83 | 93 (1) | 1 |
| West Coast | 22 | 7 (2) | 15 (3) | 0 |
| University | 14 | 11 | 3 | 0 |
| W Bulldogs | 132 | 73 | 58 (1) | 1 |
| **TOTALS** | **1922** | **896 (13)** | **1008 (21)** | **18 (0)** |

*(N) Premiership matches played at night*

## WINNING RUNS

20 v North Melb (1953–1965)
15 v North Melb (1934–1942)
10 v North Melb (1926–1931)
10 v St Kilda (1945–1950)
9 v Geelong (1941–1947); (1957–1962)
9 v Hawthorn (1925–1930); (1932–1937)
8 v Brisbane Bears (1987–1991)
8 v Carlton (1954–1958)
8 v SM/Sydney (1937–1941); (1958–1962)
7 v Collingwood (1939–1941); (1955–1957)
7 v Essendon (1924–1928)
7 v Fitzroy (1963–1967)
7 v Western Bulldogs (1925–1928); (1934–1937)
7 v Richmond (1961–1965)
4 v West Coast (1989–1990)
2 v Adelaide (1992–1993)
1 v Fremantle (1995); (1996) (1997– )

## 1997 BEST AND FAIREST

Members of the match committee award five
players with scores out of 10 after each game.
1  Jim Stynes (404)
2  Todd Viney (355)
3  Andrew Leoncelli (185)
4  Glenn Lovett (179)
5  Anthony Ingerson (163)
6  Robert Pyman (155)
7  Adem Yze (128)
8  Marcus Seecamp (123)
9  Paul Hopgood (103)
10  Steven Febey (102)
    Anthony McDonald (102)

## GAMES RECORDS

272  Robert Flower (1973–87)
252  Brian Dixon (1954–68)
244  Jim Stynes (1987– )
235  Brett Lovett (1986– )
226  Stan Alves (1965–76)
224  Greg Wells (1969–80)
219  Gary Hardeman (1967–77; 1981)
216  Jack Mueller (1934–50)
213  Percy Beames (1931–44)
210  Norm Smith (1935–48)

## GOALS RECORDS

546  Norm Smith (1935–48)
411  Fred Fanning (1940; 1942–47)
383  Garry Lyon (1986– )
378  Jack Mueller (1934–50)
323  Percy Beames (1931–44)
315  Robert Flower (1973–87)
308  Ron Baggott (1935–42; 1945)
302  Bob Johnson Senior (1926–33)
295  Ron Barassi Junior (1953–64)
267  Bob Johnson Junior (1954–61)
267  George Margitich (1930–34)

## HIGHS AND LOWS

| Against | Highest | Lowest | G. W. Margin | G. L. Margin |
|---|---|---|---|---|
| Adelaide | 19.9.123 (1996) | 5.15.45 (1997) | 51 (1996) | 59 (1993) |
| Brisbane Bears | 22.21.153 (1987) | 6.10.46 (1996) | 89 (1993) | 77 (1996) |
| Brisbane Lions | 7.8.50 (1997) | 7.8.50 (1997) | — | 85 (1997) |
| Carlton | 23.17.155 (1991) | 2.4.16 (1899) | 81 (1897) | 116 (1986) |
| Collingwood | 25.18.168 (1982) | 1.5.11 (1898) | 94 (1939) | 109 (1919) |
| Essendon | 25.20.170 (1937) | 0.8.8 (1897) | 90 (1927) | 122 (1986) |
| Fitzroy | 27.18.180 (1991) | 0.2.2 (1899) | 131 (1991) | 190 (1979) |
| Fremantle | 18.11.119 (1997) | 8.11.59 (1996) | 52 (1995) | 55 (1997) |
| Geelong | 26.18.174 (1994) | 0.10.10 (1897) | 79 (1909) | 127 (1996) |
| Hawthorn | 26.20.176 (1940) | 3.11.29 (1966) | 141 (1926) | 115 (1983) |
| North Melb | 28.14.182 (1991) | 3.9.27 (1946) | 122 (1937) | 129 (1981) |
| Port Adel | 3.9.27 (1997) | 3.9.27 (1997) | — | 51 (1997) |
| Richmond | 26.19.175 (1993) | 4.10.34 (1910) | 121 (1993) | 93 (1980) |
| St Kilda | 27.13.175 (1977) | 2.13.25 (1908) | 105 (1948) | 86 (1997) |
| Sydney | 26.21.177 (1991) | 0.8.8 (1912) | 107 (1939) | 124 (1986) |
| West Coast | 21.13.139 (1990) | 2.8.20 (1991) | 61 (1987) | 106 (1996) |
| W Bulldogs | 23.21.159 (1984) | 3.9.27 (1932) | 80 (1943) | 120 (1985) |

# THE LEADERSHIP AT MELBOURNE

| Year | Pos | Coach | Captain | Best & Fairest | Leading Goalkicker | |
|------|-----|-------|---------|----------------|--------------------|---|
| 1931 | 8 | I. Warne-Smith | I. Warne-Smith | | G. Margitich | 66 |
| 1932 | 9 | I. Warne-Smith | F. Vine | | G. Margitich | 60 |
| 1933 | 10 | F. Hughes | F. Vine | | R. Johnson | 62 |
| 1934 | 6 | F. Hughes | C. Niven | | J. Mueller | 52 |
| 1935 | 6 | F. Hughes | C. Niven | A. La Fontaine | M. Gibb | 59 |
| 1936 | 3 | F. Hughes | A. La Fontaine | A. La Fontaine | E. Glass | 56 |
| 1937 | 3 | F. Hughes | A. La Fontaine | J. Mueller | R. Baggott | 51 |
| 1938 | 5 | F. Hughes | A. La Fontaine | N. Smith | N. Smith | 80 |
| 1939 | 1 | F. Hughes | A. La Fontaine | J. Mueller | N. Smith | 54 |
| 1940 | 1 | F. Hughes | A. La Fontaine | R. Baggott | N. Smith | 89 |
| 1941 | 1 | F. Hughes | A. La Fontaine | A. La Fontaine | N. Smith | 88 |
| 1942 | 8 | P. Beames | P. Beames | A. La Fontaine | F. Fanning | 37 |
| 1943 | 7 | P. Beames | P. Beames | Don Cordner | F. Fanning | 62 |
| 1944 | 8 | P. Beames | P. Beames | N. Smith | F. Fanning | 87 |
| 1945 | 9 | F. Hughes | N. Smith | F. Fanning | F. Fanning | 67 |
| 1946 | 2 | F. Hughes | N. Smith | J. Mueller | J. Mueller | 58 |
| 1947 | 6 | F. Hughes | N. Smith | W. Lock | F. Fanning | 97 |
| 1948 | 1 | F. Hughes | Don Cordner | A. Rodda | L. Arnold | 41 |
| 1949 | 5 | A. La Fontaine | Don Cordner | L. Dockett | R. McKenzie | 40 |
| 1950 | 4 | A. La Fontaine | S. McGrath | Denis Cordner | Denis Cordner | 36 |
| 1951 | 12 | A. La Fontaine | Denis Cordner | N. McMahen | R. McKenzie | 40 |
| 1952 | 6 | N. Smith | Denis Cordner | G. McGivern | N. Clarke | 49 |
| 1953 | 11 | N. Smith | Denis Cordner | K. Melville | R. McKenzie | 38 |
| 1954 | 2 | N. Smith | G. Collins | Denis Cordner | N. Clarke | 51 |
| 1955 | 1 | N. Smith | N. McMahen | S. Spencer | S. Spencer | 34 |
| 1956 | 1 | N. Smith | N. McMahen | S. Spencer | R. Johnson | 43 |
| 1957 | 1 | N. Smith | J. Beckwith | J. Beckwith | A. Webb | 56 |
| 1958 | 2 | N. Smith | J. Beckwith | L. Mithen | R. Barassi, A. Webb | 44 |
| 1959 | 1 | N. Smith | J. Beckwith | L. Mithen | R. Barassi | 46 |
| 1960 | 1 | N. Smith | R. Barassi | B. Dixon | I. Ridley | 38 |
| 1961 | 3 | N. Smith | R. Barassi | R. Barassi | R. Johnson | 36 |
| 1962 | 4 | N. Smith | R. Barassi | H. Mann | L. Mithen | 37 |
| 1963 | 3 | N. Smith | R. Barassi | H. Mann | B. Bourke | 48 |
| 1964 | 1 | N. Smith | R. Barassi | R. Barassi | J. Townsend | 35 |
| 1965 | 7 | N. Smith | H. Mann | J. Townsend | B. Vagg | 30 |
| 1966 | 11 | N. Smith | H. Mann | T. Leahy | B. Vagg | 20 |
| 1967 | 7 | N. Smith | H. Mann | H. Mann | H. Mann | 38 |
| 1968 | 8 | J. Beckwith | H. Mann | R. Groom | H. Mann | 29 |
| 1969 | 12 | J. Beckwith | R. Johnson | J. Townsend | R. Dillon | 48 |
| 1970 | 10 | J. Beckwith | F. Davis | F. Davis | R. Dillon | 41 |
| 1971 | 7 | I. Ridley | F. Davis | G. Wells | P. Callery | 38 |
| 1972 | 8 | I. Ridley | F. Davis | S. Alves | G. Parke | 63 |
| 1973 | 10 | I. Ridley | S. Alves | C. Ditterich | R. Brewer | 32 |
| 1974 | 12 | R. Skilton | S. Alves | S. Alves | R. Brewer | 40 |
| 1975 | 10 | R. Skilton | S. Alves | L. Fowler | G. Wells | 32 |
| 1976 | 6 | R. Skilton | S. Alves | G. Wells | R. Biffin | 47 |
| 1977 | 11 | R. Skilton | G. Wells | R. Flower | R. Brewer | 26 |
| 1978 | 12 | D. Jones | G. Wells | G. Baker | H. Coles | 33 |
| 1979 | 11 | C. Ditterich | C. Ditterich | L. Fowler | R. Flower | 33 |
| 1980 | 9 | C. Ditterich | C. Ditterich | L. Fowler | B. Crosswell | 31 |
| 1981 | 12 | R. Barassi | R. Flower | S. Smith | M. Jackson | 76 |
| 1982 | 8 | R. Barassi | R. Flower | S. Icke | Gerard Healy | 77 |
| 1983 | 8 | R. Barassi | R. Flower | A. Johnson | R. Flower | 40 |
| 1984 | 9 | R. Barassi | R. Flower | Gerard Healy | K. Templeton | 51 |
| 1985 | 11 | R. Barassi | R. Flower | D. Hughes | B. Wilson | 40 |
| 1986 | 11 | J. Northey | R. Flower | Greg Healy | Greg Healy | 35 |
| 1987 | 3 | J. Northey | R. Flower | S. Stretch | R. Flower | 47 |
| 1988 | 2 | J. Northey | Greg Healy | S. O'Dwyer | R. Jackson | 43 |
| 1989 | 4 | J. Northey | Greg Healy | A. Johnson | D. Bennett | 34 |
| 1990 | 4 | J. Northey | Greg Healy | G. Lyon | D. Bennett | 87 |
| 1991 | 4 | J. Northey | G. Lyon | J. Stynes | A. Jakovich | 71 |
| 1992 | 11 | J. Northey | G. Lyon | G. Lovett | A. Jakovich | 40 |
| 1993 | 10 | N. Balme | G. Lyon | T. Viney | A. Jakovich | 39 |
| 1994 | 4 | N. Balme | G. Lyon | G. Lyon | G. Lyon | 79 |
| 1995 | 9 | N. Balme | G. Lyon | J. Stynes | G. Lyon | 77 |
| 1996 | 14 | N. Balme | G. Lyon | J. Stynes | D. Neitz | 56 |
| 1997 | 16 | N. Balme | G. Lyon | J. Stynes | J. Farmer | 30 |
| | | G. Hutchison | | | D. Neitz | 30 |

# PLAYER PROFILES

## MATTHEW BLAKE
Hard-working young midfielder who knocked up winning possessions for the Bendigo Pioneers in last year's TAC Cup competition. Covers plenty of ground and his endurance should see him make his mark at League level.

## MARK BRADLY
Young ruckman who has spent the past two seasons learning his craft in the reserves. Has played 30 games and kicked 42 goals in the reserves and should be just about ready to press for senior selection. Another youngster, Leigh Newton, probably jumped ahead of him last year, but the Demons are looking at various options to assist Jim Stynes.

## NATHAN BROWN
Was drafted by the Demons on the strength of his outstanding season with West Adelaide in the SANFL. A late developer, Brown has plenty of responsibility playing on the ball and could be a readymade senior player. Played every game for West Adelaide in 1997.

## DAVID COCKATOO-COLLINS
Talented youngster who, together with his twin brother, has been given a patient grounding, but would be looking to increase his time in the seniors. Has played just two senior games (one in 1996 and another last year) and even though Melbourne's list is a lot stronger, has the chance to impress. The twins, younger brothers of Essendon's Che Cockatoo-Collins, turn 20 at the start of the season.

## DONALD COCKATOO-COLLINS
Probably developed a bit quicker than David, playing four games in 1997 and showing great potential, perhaps as a half-back flanker. Despite some talk of a trade involving the brothers, the Demons are committed to keeping them together.

## MATTHEW COLLINS
Talented Victorian youngster who was drafted by the Adelaide Crows in the 1994 National Draft, but had a couple of tough years on and off the field. Broke a leg in the SANFL in 1995 and made his debut for the Crows in 1996, going on to play eight games. However, found his chances limited last year and after becoming homesick, made it known he wanted to return to Victoria. Was part of a trade and should play senior football, probably in attack.
**Previous AFL club:** Adelaide (1996-97: 14 games, 2 goals).

## JEFF FARMER
Brilliant young forward capable of kicking team-lifting goals, but has not reached his full potential. With three years' experience under his belt, Farmer is at a stage where he could make a real name for himself. Quick and elusive, but probably needs to improve his fitness and the defensive side of his game. Finished the season on a high last year booting six goals in the final game against Fremantle.
**Player honors:** leading goalkicker (equal) 1997.

## MATTHEW FEBEY
It's been a long hard battle for Febey to establish himself in the AFL after he and twin brother Steven were selected by Melbourne in the inaugural National Draft in 1986. Matthew was delisted by the Demons at one stage, played country football in Victoria, returned to the Demons and has overcome many injury setbacks. When Matthew played his 100th game last year, the Febeys became the first twins in VFL/AFL history to each play 100 or more games. Matthew had knee problems during the season, but his experience will be invaluable as Melbourne goes through its rebuilding period.

## STEVEN FEBEY
Recovered from an injury-plagued 1996 season to again be one of the Demons' most reliable and consistent performers. Provides plenty of drive, usually from half-back, and his experience and leadership will be a big plus at a crucial time in Melbourne's history. Starts the season 20 games short of 200 games.
**Player honors:** night series premiership side 1989.

## DAMIEN GASPAR
Played the first 12 games of 1997, but suffered a groin injury and was ruled out for the rest of the season. Had to hold down full-back in an undermanned and inexperienced side and was starting to feel more comfortable when injury forced him out. Still young enough to make his mark.

## BRENT GRGIC
At just 18, this youngster from the Geelong area looks to have a great future. He was Melbourne's first choice in the 1996 National Draft (No. 11 overall) and due to circumstances beyond his control, was probably thrown in at the deep end earlier than the Demons had hoped. With so many injuries, Melbourne decided to risk him as a 17-year-old in senior company last year and he made a decent fist of it, playing the last nine games. Has great skill and poise and could develop into a key position player. He is not related to West Coast Eagles ruckman Ilija Grgic.

## PAUL HOPGOOD
Solid performer over five seasons at senior level for the Demons. Nothing flashy about him, but gets the job done either in defence or when he has been used further up the field. Finished eighth in Melbourne's best and fairest and has virtually been a regular over the past couple of seasons.

## ANTHONY INGERSON
Former Adelaide key position player who has been a good pick-up for the Demons, playing 18 games in his first season (1996) and all 22 last year. An awkward looking kick for a left-footer, Ingerson has long arms and can make life tough for opponents, particularly when he has been used in defence. Finished fifth in the Demons' best and fairest count.
**Previous AFL club:** Adelaide (1992-95: 37 games, 25 goals).

## TRAVIS JOHNSTONE
Rated by many as the finest midfielder to come out of the draft in the 1990s. Was the strong tip to be the No. 1 draft choice in 1997 and it was no surprise the Demons took him to bolster their midfield. Very quick and is a well-balanced player who should step straight

into senior football. An All-Australian at under-16 and under-18 levels.

## DARREN KOWAL
Had a season he'd prefer to forget last year struggling with injuries and form. Played half the season in the reserves, which was not an encouraging sign at a club lacking in experience and racked by injuries. Played the last game of the year against Fremantle as though his life depended on it and that performance may have helped him win a reprieve for 1998. Best suited in defence.
**Player honors:** AFL Norwich Rising Star nominee 1993.

## HAYDEN LAMARO
Played nine games in the reserves in 1997, but missed the middle part of the season with a broken wrist. Returned in the latter part of '97 and played mainly on a half-back flank. Still only 19 and as he develops physically, should be capable of playing senior football.

## ANDREW LEONCELLI
The former Old Xaverians and Carlton reserves utility played only 12 games struggling with a stress fracture in the second half of the season. Broke a leg the previous season and if he can get himself fully fit, should fulfil the potential he has shown in glimpses. Despite his setback in 1997, still finished third in Melbourne's best and fairest.
**Player honors:** 3rd best and fairest 1997.

## TROY LONGMUIR
Rangy half-back flanker who attacks the ball hard. Played for Western Australia at last year's AFL National Under-18 Championships and will be given plenty of time to develop.

## BRETT LOVETT
The fourth longest-serving player in Melbourne's long and proud history and a wonderful contributor since his debut in 1986. Not the quickest player in the League, but one of the smartest and his ability to read the play, combined with his excellent disposal, has taken him well over the 200-game mark. One of the survivors of Melbourne's revival in the mid and late '80s, Lovett has given the Demons great service after failing to make the grade with Hawthorn reserves in 1984 and '85.
**Player honors:** 2nd best and fairest 1988, 1990.

## GLENN LOVETT
Smooth and crisp ball-handler who should be up around the 200-game mark, but has struggled with persistent injuries over the years. Relies heavily on his running, but has had continual problems with muscle tears and could manage only 14 games last year. Despite that, finished fourth in the club's best and fairest. Fully fit, he is a damaging and creative midfielder and has always shown excellent leadership qualities. Not related to Brett Lovett.
**Player honors:** best and fairest 1992; 2nd best and fairest 1993.

## GARRY LYON
A chronic back problem has restricted the Demons skipper to just 20 games in the past two seasons and many of those were played under considerable duress. Hobbled through the first four games in 1997, came back to be part of Melbourne's memorable win over Richmond in round 10 just after Neil Balme was sacked, but then had to call it quits for the season. Has had back surgery and has taken every precaution possible to make a comeback.
**Player honors:** best and fairest 1990, 1994; 2nd best and fairest 1986; 3rd best and fairest 1989; All-Australian 1993, 1994, 1995; leading goalkicker 1994, 1995; night series premiership sides 1987, 1989; captain since 1991.

## ANTHONY McDONALD
After three previous attempts at AFL level, McDonald finally grabbed his chance with the Demons last year, playing 19 of a possible 22 games. Previously had tried his luck with Carlton reserves (nine games in 1991 and '92) and Hawthorn (11 games in 1992 and '93) and was on Melbourne's supplementary list in 1996, playing all 22 reserves games. Also had stints with Coburg (VFL) and Old Xaverians (VAFA) after starting his career with Ballarat YCW. Persistence rewarded in 1997 and he was a consistent performer in Melbourne's midfield. Older brother Alex plays with Collingwood and another brother, James, is on Melbourne's list.

## JAMES McDONALD
The third of the McDonald brothers to play AFL football, James was promoted from Melbourne's rookie list late in the season and showed considerable promise in four senior appearances. Goes hard at the ball and is a player to watch given more opportunities in 1998.

## DAVID NEITZ
Suffered a terrible injury in round seven last year when he broke his jaw against Fremantle, but recovered well and missed only fives games. Was Melbourne's shining light before being injured and kicked 13 goals in rounds four and five. Used mainly in defence when he returned but finished the season as the Demons' equal leading goalkicker. Rated in the top bracket of AFL players and at 23, should be relishing the best years of his career. Has signed a three-year deal, which will keep him in Demons colors until the end of 2000.
**Player honors:** 2nd best and fairest 1995; All-Australian 1995; AFL Norwich Rising Star nominee 1993; leading goalkicker 1996, 1997 (equal).

## CRAIG NETTELBECK
Played the first 13 games of 1997 for the Demons, but then injury saw him sidelined for several weeks before playing out the season in the reserves. It was Nettelbeck's collision with Wayne Carey in round one that saw the North Melbourne star sidelined for much of the season with a serious shoulder injury. Has done the rounds at Sydney and Fremantle (where he didn't play a game after being a pre-draft selection when the Dockers entered the AFL in 1995), but has settled in well at Melbourne. Can play either end and has the chance to consolidate his career.
**Previous AFL club:** Sydney (1990-94: 45 games, 27 goals).

## LEIGH NEWTON

Proved to be the best of the unknown players in the 1997 Pre-Season Draft when Melbourne took him as the No. 3 selection. Will be all the better for his first season in the AFL and did enough in 13 senior appearances to suggest he has a bright future. Played as a back-up to Jim Stynes, but could also hold down centre half-forward using his height and mobility to advantage. Played for Albury in the Ovens and Murray League and hails from the small township of Whitfield (population 150) south of Wangaratta.

## ALISTAIR NICHOLSON

One of Melbourne's development players, Nicholson managed one senior appearance in round six last year. A late starter in the game, he showed promise as a young player with Claremont in WA before the Demons took him with their second selection and 22nd overall in the 1996 National Draft. He is a tall, athletic type who can play centre half-forward, centre half-back or assist in the ruck.

## LUKE OTTENS

The older brother of the sought-after Brad Ottens, who was taken as the No. 2 selection by Richmond at the 1997 National Draft. Can play in the ruck or in defence, although the Demons are keen to develop him in a key defensive role. Was on Port Adelaide's rookie list in 1997.

## GUY RIGONI

Spent two seasons at Hawthorn before moving to Victorian country side Myrtleford and caught the eye with some impressive performances. Came down to play in the final reserves game for Melbourne in 1997 and won 33 possessions. The last player to go from Hawthorn to Myrtleford and then back to the AFL was a handy player called Gary Ablett.

## RUSSELL ROBERTSON

Had a traumatic introduction to League football when selected by the Demons in the 1996 National Draft and delisted a few months later before being placed on Melbourne's rookie list. Late in the season, he was promoted to the senior list and played the last three games and kicked five goals. A lively forward from Burnie, Tasmania, and could be a player to watch.

## DAVID SCHWARZ

In what was a tough year on and off the field for the Demons, Schwarz's comeback was definitely one of the highlights. Some doubts he would ever play again, let alone in '97, but worked his way back quietly before making a mid-season return. Played his first game in two years in round 11 against Adelaide at the MCG and while understandably a little tentative at first, he was soon throwing himself into the thick of things. Given that his pace and agility have been reduced, it is likely he will spend most of his time at full-forward, where his bulk and marking strength will present headaches for opposition defenders. After three knee reconstructions, every game now is a bonus.
**Player honors:** 3rd best and fairest 1992, 1994.

## MARCUS SEECAMP

After a slow start to the '97 season when he played the first four games in the reserves, Seecamp fought his way back to play some good football for the Demons. A suspension late in the season saw him lose his spot, but generally he was a sound defender, showing some of the dash he displayed at Fitzroy. Finished seventh in Melbourne's best and fairest and has now played 51 games for each of Fitzroy and the Demons.
**Previous AFL club:** Fitzroy (1992-94: 51 games, 10 goals).

## JAMIE SHANAHAN

Ever-reliable full-back who has been the mainstay of St Kilda's defence for a number of seasons. Had another consistent year in 1997, but his season ended on a sour note when he and the Saints could not agree to new pay terms. Asked to be traded to Collingwood, but was knocked back and after several weeks of uncertainty was snapped up by the Demons as the No. 1 pick in the Pre-Season Draft. Had a nightmare finish to the Grand Final when he was matched up with Darren Jarman in the final term, but will bolster Melbourne's defence and fill one of the side's major problem spots.
**Player honors:** night series premiership side 1996.
**Previous AFL club:** St Kilda (1992-97: 125 games, 0 goals).

## SHAUN SMITH

High flying but injury-prone forward who certainly does not lack any courage when launching his body into the air. Made a successful return to League ranks in 1995 after a two-year stint with Werribee in the VFL and will long be remembered for his mark against the Brisbane Bears in 1996. Has been used in defence in the past two seasons with great success, but a broken arm, suffered late in 1996, has been a constant worry and last year he was restricted to just 12 games.
**Previous AFL club:** North Melbourne (1987-93: 47 games, 38 goals).

## CRAIG SMOKER

Former West Coast Eagles rover who was drafted by the Eagles in 1995, but did not play a League game in his two years on the list. Melbourne gave up its third round draft pick, believing Smoker can bolster its small man department. Has played mainly in the forward pocket, but will add some badly needed pace to the midfield.

## JIM STYNES

The endurance man of the AFL continues to defy the odds and keeps passing records as though he is on some sort of football marathon. Has not missed a game since round 16, 1987, and has already claimed the League record of 204 consecutive games held for more than 50 years by Richmond's Jack 'Skinny' Titus. Last year, Stynes celebrated a decade without missing a game and at that rate — he had played 244 — he should pass Robert Flower's games record for Melbourne (272) in 1999. Once again, he carried the Demons' ruck department and by the season's end had collected his fourth best and fairest award — equalling the club record.
**Player honors:** Brownlow Medal 1991; best and fairest 1991, 1995, 1996, 1997; 3rd best and fairest 1990; All-Australian 1991, 1993; AFLPA 1991; night series premiership sides 1987, 1989.

### STEPHEN TINGAY
On his day, Tingay is one of the best wingmen in the League, but has faced a continual battle with injuries over the past two seasons. In 1996, had a slow start due to a pelvic complaint and last season managed only three games because of a severe hip/buttock problem. The Demons need him fit and firing if they are to lift themselves from the bottom of the ladder. Hopefully he will have lost none of his dash and drive because he is a most exciting player to watch.
**Player honors:** 2nd best and fairest 1994, 3rd best and fairest 1993; All-Australian 1994; night series premiership side 1989.

### TODD VINEY
A great contributor for more than a decade, Viney is renowned for his fearless approach at the ball and his aggression and leadership qualities. Once again, he was Melbourne's most damaging midfielder in what was a very lean season for the Demons in 1997 and was rewarded with another high placing in the best and fairest. Turned 32 at the start of 1998, but keeps himself in superb condition and sets a fine example to his younger players. Thoroughly deserves his approaching 200-game milestone.
**Player honors:** best and fairest 1993; 2nd best and fairest 1991, 1997.

### JEFF WHITE
The biggest and most expensive deal of the 1997 end-of-season trading period saw White emerge as a Melbourne player last October. The former Victorian and No. 1 pick in the 1994 National Draft had indicated to Fremantle he wanted to return to his home state and the rush was on to sign him. In the end, he chose Melbourne and was able to negotiate a hefty pay packet — one that has taken him into the top bracket of players. There will be added pressure on him, but he showed enough in 32 games with Fremantle to suggest he is an outstanding prospect and one of the finest in the country for his age. The Demons believe they have secured a ruckman/forward who will lead them well into the next millennium.
**Previous AFL club:** Fremantle (1995-97: 32 games, 18 goals).

### BRENT WILLIAMS
Talented youngster who played in Adelaide's first seven games last year, but his form tapered off and he did not regain his spot. Had an impressive record at under-age level in Victoria and like former teammate Matthew Collins will be happier in more familiar surroundings. Has a good build and the Demons believe it was worth giving up one player — Nathan Bassett — to snare both Williams and Collins.
**Previous AFL club:** Adelaide (1997: 7 games, 4 goals).

### SHANE WOEWODIN
One of only four Melbourne players to appear in all 22 games last year and had an excellent debut season. Won an AFL Norwich Rising Star nomination — a fitting reward for his work ethic and commitment to break into the AFL. Showed versatility and maturity beyond his years playing in a variety of positions and did a fine job shadowing some of the game's biggest names, including Nathan Buckley.
**Player honors:** AFL Norwich Rising Star nominee 1997.

### ADEM YZE
Young player blessed with heaps of talent. Played nine games in 1995, 19 in 1996 and another 19 in 1997, indicating he is finding his feet in the AFL. Natural left-footer with great skills, he should be starting to put his stamp on the game as he approaches his fourth season at senior level. Took on extra responsibility in a young side last year and finished seventh in Melbourne's best and fairest.
**Player honors:** AFL Norwich Rising Star nominee 1996.

## ROOKIE LIST

### BEN BEAMS
Lightly built but highly skilled youngster from Glenorchy in Tasmania. Played for the Tassie Mariners before moving into senior ranks last year with Glenorchy and was leading the club best and fairest until he injured a knee. Was recommended by Chris Fagan (ex-Mariners coach) who is now on Melbourne's coaching staff.

### MATTHEW BISHOP
Tall key position player who was close to making Melbourne's senior list after being on the rookie list in 1997. A strong mark and a long, accurate kick, Bishop played well in the Demons' practice matches.

### JAMIE CANN
Another product of Assumption College, one of the most successful school football programs in the country. Has played in the TAC Cup for the Calder Cannons and is a speedy rover.

### PETER WALSH
Just 20 years old but something of a journeyman. Went to school at St Patrick's, Ballarat, and played school football alongside Melbourne's James McDonald. Spent two years in the army based in Queensland and playing little football before making his way to Adelaide where he joined West Adelaide. Hard-working midfielder.

### DANIEL WARD
Spent 1997 on Melbourne's rookie list and was close to making the senior list this year. Half-back flanker with good disposal.

### LUKE WILLIAMS
Quick forward/winger who played a handful of games with the Oakleigh Chargers in the TAC Cup competition last year. Had a major commitment with St Kevin's College where he was coached by former Fitzroy and Adelaide coach Robert Shaw. Was the No. 1 pick in the rookie draft.

# MELBOURNE

| Name (# = rookie) | No. | Born | Height | Weight | Recruited from |
|---|---|---|---|---|---|
| Matthew Blake | 49 | 4/10/79 | 186 | 76 | SANDHURST/BENDIGO U18 |
| Mark Bradly | 40 | 24/1/77 | 197 | 95 | EAST FREMANTLE (WA) |
| Nathan D. Brown | 52 | 14/8/76 | 180 | 74 | WEST ADELAIDE (SA) |
| David Cockatoo-Collins | 30 | 1/4/78 | 180 | 71 | PORT ADELAIDE (SA) |
| Donald Cockatoo-Collins | 31 | 1/4/78 | 181 | 77 | PORT ADELAIDE (SA) |
| Matthew Collins | 38 | 2/2/77 | 184 | 93 | MACLEOD/NORTHERN U18/ADELAIDE |
| Jeff Farmer | 33 | 24/6/77 | 178 | 80 | TAMBELLUP (WA) |
| Matthew Febey | 20 | 19/8/69 | 183 | 83 | DEVONPORT(TAS)/MELB RESERVES/ROCHESTER |
| Steven Febey | 21 | 19/8/69 | 183 | 83 | DEVONPORT (TAS) |
| Damien Gaspar | 32 | 28/3/75 | 193 | 94 | SOUTH FREMANTLE (WA) |
| Brent Grgic | 48 | 8/10/79 | 192 | 86 | BELL POST HILL/GEELONG U18 |
| Paul Hopgood | 15 | 21/7/73 | 179 | 80 | CHELSEA |
| Anthony Ingerson | 27 | 13/10/69 | 193 | 95 | CENTRAL DISTRICT (SA)/ADELAIDE |
| Travis Johnstone | 41 | 17/7/80 | 186 | 78 | CHELSEA/DANDENONG U18 |
| Darren Kowal | 7 | 18/6/72 | 173 | 75 | CLAREMONT (WA) |
| Hayden Lamaro | 46 | 3/10/78 | 185 | 76 | EUROA/MURRAY U18 |
| Andrew Leoncelli | 36 | 17/7/74 | 186 | 85 | OLD XAVERIANS/CARLTON RES |
| Troy Longmuir | 56 | 27/5/79 | 184 | 78 | WEST PERTH (WA) |
| Brett Lovett | 17 | 20/5/66 | 180 | 92 | INVERLOCH-KONGWAK/HAWTHORN RESERVES |
| Glenn Lovett | 6 | 23/7/69 | 180 | 82 | MHSOB |
| Garry Lyon | 3 | 13/9/67 | 193 | 96 | KYABRAM |
| Anthony McDonald | 35 | 13/6/72 | 183 | 80 | YCWCYC/CA RES/COBURG/HAWTH RES/OLD XAVS |
| James McDonald | 54 | 5/10/76 | 180 | 73 | BALLARAT YCW/B'RAT U18/OLD XAVERIANS |
| David Neitz | 9 | 22/1/75 | 193 | 98 | PARKMORE |
| Craig Nettelbeck | 18 | 26/5/72 | 193 | 96 | LEETON (NSW)/SYDNEY/FREMANTLE LIST |
| Leigh Newton | 14 | 25/3/76 | 198 | 100 | MURRAY U18/ALBURY (NSW) |
| Alistair Nicholson | 44 | 4/3/78 | 197 | 98 | CLAREMONT (WA) |
| Luke Ottens | 50 | 22/5/76 | 195 | 95 | GLENELG (SA) |
| Guy Rigoni | 53 | 27/7/74 | 180 | 83 | MYRTLEFORD/HAWTH RES/MYRTLEFORD |
| Russell Robertson | 42 | 24/11/78 | 184 | 88 | BURNIE/TAS U18 |
| David Schwarz | 5 | 24/7/72 | 195 | 105 | SUNBURY |
| Marcus Seecamp | 10 | 27/7/72 | 188 | 92 | EAST PERTH (WA)/FITZROY |
| Jamie Shanahan | 1 | 6/12/67 | 194 | 106 | HOBART (TAS)/FITZROY RESERVES/ST. KILDA |
| Shaun Smith | 29 | 22/6/69 | 184 | 90 | AINSLIE (ACT)/NORTH MELB/WERRIBEE |
| Craig Smoker | 39 | 4/4/78 | 173 | 76 | WEST PERTH (WA)/WEST COAST LIST |
| Jim Stynes | 11 | 23/4/66 | 199 | 99 | IRELAND |
| Stephen Tingay | 2 | 13/8/70 | 181 | 86 | SHEPPARTON |
| Todd Viney | 12 | 30/3/66 | 183 | 92 | STURT (SA) |
| Jeff White | 34 | 19/2/77 | 194 | 92 | FRANKSTON YCW/SOUTHERN U18/FREMANTLE |
| Brent Williams | 37 | 13/2/78 | 190 | 96 | PARKMORE/PRAHRAN U18/ADELAIDE |
| Shane Woewodin | 22 | 12/7/76 | 185 | 85 | EAST FREMANTLE (WA) |
| Adem Yze | 13 | 21/9/77 | 185 | 85 | SHEPPARTON UNITED/MURRAY U18 |
| Ben Beams # | 51 | 17/8/77 | 183 | 76 | GLENORCHY/TAS U18 |
| Matthew Bishop # | 48 | 11/7/75 | 196 | 96 | BOX HILL |
| Jamie Cann # | 50 | 23/8/79 | 176 | 72 | CRAIGIEBURN/CALDER U18 |
| Peter Walsh # | 52 | 24/7/76 | 182 | 87 | WEST ADELAIDE (SA) |
| Daniel Ward # | 49 | 9/7/77 | 183 | 85 | HOPPERS CROSSING/WESTERN U18/FITZROY RES |
| Luke Williams # | 47 | 29/12/79 | 183 | 79 | ST KEVINS/OAKLEIGH U18 |
| Total/(Average)  *On 26/2/98 | | (23.6 yrs)* | (186) | (87) | |

# PLAYERS 1998

| Debut | HOME & AWAY Gms | Gls | 1997 Gms | Gls | FINALS Gms | Gls | GRAND FINALS Gms | Gls | Won | NIGHT SERIES Gms | Gls | STATE OF ORIGIN Gms | Gls |
|---|---|---|---|---|---|---|---|---|---|---|---|---|---|
| | 0 | 0 | 0 | 0 | | | | | | 0 | 0 | 0 | 0 |
| | 0 | 0 | 0 | 0 | | | | | | 0 | 0 | 0 | 0 |
| | 0 | 0 | 0 | 0 | | | | | | 0 | 0 | 0 | 0 |
| 1996 | 2 | 0 | 1 | 0 | | | | | | 0 | 0 | 0 | 0 |
| 1996 | 6 | 1 | 4 | 1 | | | | | | 0 | 0 | 0 | 0 |
| 1996 | 14 | 2 | 6 | 0 | | | | | | 2 | 0 | 0 | 0 |
| 1995 | 43 | 71 | 17 | 30 | | | | | | 3 | 5 | 0 | 0 |
| 1992 | 103 | 27 | 11 | 0 | 3 | 0 | | | | 7 | 3 | 3 | 1 |
| 1988 | 180 | 24 | 20 | 2 | 11 | 0 | 1 | 0 | 0 | 7 | 3 | 4 | 0 |
| 1995 | 28 | 0 | 12 | 0 | | | | | | 2 | 0 | 0 | 0 |
| 1997 | 9 | 5 | 9 | 5 | | | | | | 0 | 0 | 0 | 0 |
| 1993 | 81 | 8 | 20 | 2 | 3 | 1 | | | | 4 | 2 | 0 | 0 |
| 1992 | 77 | 39 | 22 | 4 | | | | | | 6 | 2 | 0 | 0 |
| | 0 | 0 | 0 | 0 | | | | | | 0 | 0 | 0 | 0 |
| 1992 | 80 | 31 | 6 | 1 | | | | | | 5 | 0 | 0 | 0 |
| | 0 | 0 | 0 | 0 | | | | | | 0 | 0 | 0 | 0 |
| 1996 | 19 | 4 | 12 | 1 | | | | | | 1 | 0 | 0 | 0 |
| | 0 | 0 | 0 | 0 | | | | | | 0 | 0 | 0 | 0 |
| 1986 | 235 | 48 | 18 | 4 | 16 | 4 | 1 | 0 | 0 | 15 | 1 | 6 | 0 |
| 1987 | 125 | 73 | 14 | 3 | 5 | 4 | | | | 6 | 2 | 2 | 0 |
| 1986 | 203 | 383 | 5 | 7 | 10 | 23 | 1 | 2 | 0 | 14 | 22 | 9 | 5 |
| 1997 | 19 | 7 | 19 | 7 | | | | | | 1 | 1 | 0 | 0 |
| 1997 | 4 | 3 | 4 | 3 | | | | | | | | | |
| 1993 | 105 | 138 | 17 | 30 | 3 | 0 | | | | 6 | 4 | 2 | 0 |
| 1990 | 78 | 42 | 13 | 5 | | | | | | 6 | 3 | 1 | 0 |
| 1997 | 13 | 6 | 13 | 6 | | | | | | 0 | 0 | 0 | 0 |
| 1997 | 1 | 0 | 1 | 0 | | | | | | 0 | 0 | 0 | 0 |
| | 0 | 0 | 0 | 0 | | | | | | | | | |
| | 0 | 0 | 0 | 0 | | | | | | | | | |
| 1997 | 3 | 5 | 3 | 5 | | | | | | 0 | 0 | 0 | 0 |
| 1991 | 74 | 113 | 10 | 18 | 3 | 6 | | | | 6 | 3 | 0 | 0 |
| 1992 | 102 | 15 | 15 | 0 | | | | | | 11 | 3 | 3 | 1 |
| 1992 | 125 | 0 | 25 | 0 | 5 | 0 | 1 | 0 | | 12 | 1 | 6 | 0 |
| 1987 | 98 | 119 | 12 | 9 | 1 | 1 | | | | 5 | 4 | 2 | 2 |
| | 0 | 0 | 0 | 0 | | | | | | 0 | 0 | 0 | 0 |
| 1987 | 244 | 128 | 22 | 3 | 16 | 9 | 1 | 0 | 0 | 18 | 3 | 10 | 6 |
| 1989 | 138 | 68 | 3 | 0 | 7 | 2 | | | | 6 | 6 | 1 | 0 |
| 1987 | 194 | 69 | 22 | 7 | 14 | 7 | 1 | 0 | 0 | 7 | 2 | 4 | 0 |
| 1995 | 32 | 18 | 13 | 2 | | | | | | 3 | 0 | 0 | 0 |
| 1997 | 7 | 4 | 7 | 4 | | | | | | 0 | 0 | 0 | 0 |
| 1997 | 22 | 4 | 22 | 4 | | | | | | 1 | 0 | 0 | 0 |
| 1995 | 47 | 21 | 19 | 9 | | | | | | 2 | 0 | 0 | 0 |
| | 0 | 0 | 0 | 0 | | | | | | 0 | 0 | | |
| | 0 | 0 | 0 | 0 | | | | | | 0 | 0 | | |
| | 0 | 0 | 0 | 0 | | | | | | 0 | 0 | | |
| | 0 | 0 | 0 | 0 | | | | | | 0 | 0 | | |
| | 0 | 0 | 0 | 0 | | | | | | 0 | 0 | | |
| | 0 | 0 | 0 | 0 | | | | | | 0 | 0 | | |
| | (60) | (35) | 417 | 172 | 97 | 57 | 6 | 2 | 0 | 156 | 70 | 53 | 15 |

## Kangaroos at a glance

**ADDRESS:** Fogarty Street, North Melbourne 3051
**POSTAL ADDRESS:** PO Box 158, North Melbourne 3051
**TELEPHONE:** (03) 9326 8666
**FACSIMILE:** (03) 9329 7114
**MARKETING OFFICE ADDRESS:** Level 3, Great Southern Stand, MCG
**MARKETING OFFICE TELEPHONE:** 9654 1744;
**FACSIMILE:** 9654 2892
**CHAIRMAN:** Ron Casey
**CHIEF EXECUTIVE:** Greg Miller
**FOOTBALL MANAGER:** Geoff Walsh
**MARKETING MANAGER:** Francis Trainor
**COMMUNICATIONS MANAGER:** Bryce Lewis
**RECRUITING MANAGER:** Neville Stibbard
**FOOTBALL DEVELOPMENT MANAGER:** Tony Elshaug.
**COACHING STAFF:** Denis Pagan (senior), Norm Dare (assistant), Tony Elshaug (reserves), Tim Harrington (skills)
**SELECTION COMMITTEE:** Mark Dawson (chairman), Denis Pagan, Norm Dare, Tony Elshaug, Tim Harrington, Geoff Walsh
**CLUB DOCTOR:** Harry Unglik
**CLUB PHYSIOTHERAPIST:** Gordon McDonald, Roger Moore
**FOUNDED:** 1869
**JOINED AFL:** 1925
**HOME GROUND:** MCG, Yarra Park, Jolimont
**GROUND DIMENSIONS:** 161m by 140m.
**TRAINING VENUE:** Arden St Oval, North Melbourne
**OFFICIAL COLORS:** Guernsey: Royal blue and white vertical stripes. Socks: Royal blue. Shorts: Royal blue
**PREMIERSHIPS:** 1975, 1977, 1996
**BROWNLOW MEDALLISTS:** N. Teasdale (1965 tied), K. Greig (1973-74), M. Blight (1978), R. Glendinning (1983)
**RECORD HOME ATTENDANCE** (MCG): 72,216 — May 21, 1994 v Collingwood

# NORTH MELBOURNE
## 'Big two' to lift Roos near the top again

The hard part for North Melbourne in 1997 was defending its premiership title. It failed, but went close enough to suggest it will be near the top again in '98.

There was the injured Carey factor in 1997; the part-injured McKernan factor and, in the end, the suspension and absence of experienced campaigners Schwass and Archer from crucial finals encounters.

North was never higher on the ladder than fifth in the home and away series and, for eight weeks, was outside the top eight. In 1996, it occupied top spot eight times and was second on seven occasions.

Many believe the season was undone in the opening round when skipper Wayne Carey dislocated his shoulder. Certainly the first-round shock defeat against wooden spoon favorite Melbourne was a setback and Carey's injury had a lasting effect.

Corey McKernan, the club's second best player, got through the season, missing only three games and despite club reports that he was near enough to 100 per cent right, I feel it was shielding its champion.

He did not finish in the top 10 in North's 1997 best and fairest voting and after the season had medical attention to shoulder and knee injuries.

Carey, too, had further surgery to his shoulder. He and McKernan are the 'Big Two' and while there is solid back-up, the show depends on how they perform.

Wayne Schwass is now in Sydney. He has been an excellent player, but needs a change of scenery to recharge him. Shannon Grant's arrival from Sydney will add bite, but he is an enthusiastic worker rather than a key operator.

Mark Stevens and Stuart Anderson have gone and I feel North has done best in the deals by getting Fremantle's Winston Abraham, a dangerous but moody forward, and Adelaide's Jason McCartney, a centre half-back option.

A batch of North players are getting up in years and cannot be expected to get any better. The over-30s are Craig Sholl, John Blakey, Darren Crocker, Dean Laidley and Mark Roberts. Mick Martyn, Robert Scott and Anthony Rock are getting on and John Longmire had a major knee operation in 1996 and isn't the goalkicker he was.

So it comes back largely to players such as Carey, McKernan, Glen Archer, Peter Bell (a most improved rover), David King, Anthony Stevens, Martin Pike and a group of youngsters headed by Brent Harvey and Danny Stevens. **— Greg Hobbs**

## THE YEAR AHEAD

| Rd | Date | Opponent | Venue | Home/Away | Time (local) |
|----|------|----------|-------|-----------|--------------|
| 1 | March 27 (N) | West Coast | MCG | H | 7.40pm |
| 2 | April 4 | Melbourne | MCG | A | 3.30pm |
| 3 | April 11 (N) | Port Adelaide | FP | A | 8.10pm |
| 4 | April 19 | Brisbane Lions | MCG | H | 2.10pm |
| 5 | April 25 (N) | Fremantle | W | A | 6.40pm |
| 6 | May 3 | Adelaide | MCG | H | 2.10pm |
| 7 | May 10 | Western Bulldogs | OO | A | 2.10pm |
| 8 | May 16 | Sydney | MCG | H | 2.10pm |
| 9 | May 23 | Carlton | OO | A | 2.10pm |
| 10 | May 31 | Geelong | MCG | H | 2.10pm |
| 11 | June 8 | Collingwood | MCG | H | 2.10pm |
| 12 | June 14 | Richmond | MCG | A | 2.10pm |
| 13 | June 20 | Hawthorn | P | A | 2.10pm |
| 14 | June 26 (N) | Essendon | MCG | H | 7.40pm |
| 15 | July 4 | St Kilda | P | A | 2.10pm |
| 16 | July 19 | West Coast | S | A | 1.20pm |
| 17 | July 25 | Melbourne | MCG | H | 2.10pm |
| 18 | August 1 | Port Adelaide | MCG | H | 2.10pm |
| 19 | August 7 (N) | Brisbane Lions | G | A | 7.40pm |
| 20 | August 14 (N) | Fremantle | MCG | H | 7.40pm |
| 21 | August 22 (N) | Adelaide | FP | A | 8.10pm |
| 22 | August 28 (N) | Western Bulldogs | MCG | H | 7.40pm |

## 1997 AT A GLANCE

**L:** R1: North Melbourne 7.13 (55) v Melbourne 10.10 (70) (MCG)

**W:** R2: North Melbourne 12.14 (86) v Carlton 8.12 (60) (MCG)

**L:** R3: Essendon 18.14 (122) v North Melbourne 12.8 (80) (MCG)

**L:** R4: Brisbane Lions 15.19 (109) v North Melbourne 12.11 (83) (G)

**W:** R5: North Melbourne 21.15 (141) v Richmond 7.4 (46) (MCG)

**W:** R6: Hawthorn 14.9 (93) v North Melbourne 16.7 (103) (P)

**L:** R7: North Melbourne 9.14 (68) v Collingwood 17.9 (111) (MCG)

**W:** R8: North Melbourne 19.14 (128) v Port Adelaide 15.10 (100) (OO)

**L:** R9: Western Bulldogs 16.7 (103) v North Melbourne 10.11 (71) (MCG)

**W:** R10: North Melbourne 15.13 (103) v West Coast 9.4 (58) (OO)

### SNAPSHOT

**Games:** 25
**Won:** 14 **Lost:** 11
**Ladder finish:** 7th
**Players used:** 33

**W:** R11: North Melbourne 15.15 (105) v Fremantle 12.7 (79) (MCG)

**W:** R12: Adelaide 12.11 (83) v North Melbourne 16.9 (105) (FP)

**L:** R13: Sydney 8.17 (65) v North Melbourne 7.13 (55) (SCG)

**L:** R14: St Kilda 20.13 (133) v North Melbourne 11.13 (79) (P)

**L:** R15: North Melbourne 14.8 (92) v Geelong 15.12 (102) (MCG)

**W:** R16: Melbourne 7.16 (58) v North Melbourne 17.12 (114) (MCG)

**W:** R17: Carlton 7.16 (58) v North Melbourne 14.12 (96) (OO)

**W:** R18: North Melbourne 11.17 (83) v Essendon 8.16 (64) (MCG)

**W:** R19: North Melbourne 17.14 (116) v Brisbane Lions 9.5 (59) (MCG)

**L:** R20: Richmond 14.13 (97) v North Melbourne 14.12 (96) (MCG)

**W:** R21: North Melbourne 10.21 (81) v Hawthorn 6.7 (43) (MCG)

**L:** R22: Collingwood 18.14 (122) v North Melbourne 15.21 (111) (MCG)

## The Coach

### Denis Pagan

**Born:** 24/9/47

Even a coach with the premiership touch of Denis Pagan could not beat the 'next season' jinx of the 1990s.

Not one premiership team in the '90s has reached the Grand Final the next year. In 1996, North Melbourne won the title under Pagan's coaching; in 1997, North departed after the second preliminary final.

Pagan, the player, had 120 games, mainly in the back pocket, for North Melbourne, from 1967 to '74. He later played 23 games with South Melbourne from 1975 to '76.

He gained his premiership reputation with North Melbourne's under-19s, coaching them from 1982 to '91 for five premierships from nine grand finals.

In 1992, he coached Essendon reserves and immediately won another premiership.

Then, on the eve of season 1993, he received the call from North Melbourne, which had decided to replace senior coach Wayne Schimmelbusch. At that point, North had not played in the finals since 1987.

Pagan had North into the finals in 1995, into the preliminary finals in 1994-95, all the way in 1996 (the club's first flag since 1977) and into another preliminary final in 1997 — a most imposing record.

### AT A GLANCE

**COACHING RECORD**
**North Melbourne**

| Season | P | W | L | D | Pos |
|--------|-----|----|----|---|-----|
| 1993 | 21 | 13 | 8 | — | 5 |
| 1994 | 24 | 14 | 10 | — | 3 |
| 1995 | 25 | 16 | 9 | — | 3 |
| 1996 | 25 | 19 | 6 | — | 1 |
| 1997 | 25 | 14 | 11 | — | 7 |
| **Total** | **120** | **76** | **44** | **—** | |

## WIN/LOSS RECORD

| Against | P | W (N) | L (N) | D (N) |
|---|---|---|---|---|
| Adelaide | 10 | 6 (3) | 4 (2) | 0 |
| Brisbane Bears | 17 | 12 (3) | 5 (3) | 0 |
| Brisbane Lions | 2 | 1 (1) | 1 | 0 |
| Carlton | 128 | 39 (3) | 89 (4) | 0 |
| Collingwood | 131 | 39 (3) | 90 (2) | 2 |
| Essendon | 128 | 41 (5) | 86 | 1 |
| Fitzroy | 128 | 65 (3) | 62 (2) | 1 |
| Fremantle | 3 | 3 (1) | 0 | 0 |
| Geelong | 128 | 48 (3) | 79 (3) | 1 |
| Hawthorn | 141 | 61 (3) | 78 (4) | 2 |
| Melbourne | 128 | 53 (2) | 74 (4) | 1 |
| Port Adel | 1 | 1 | 0 | 0 |
| Richmond | 131 | 54 (6) | 76 (2) | 1 |
| St Kilda | 127 | 60 (5) | 65 (2) | 2 |
| Sydney | 129 | 64 (5) | 65 (2) | 0 |
| West Coast | 19 | 10 (5) | 9 (4) | 0 |
| W Bulldogs | 128 | 62 (3) | 63 | 3 |
| **TOTALS** | **1479** | **619 (54)** | **846 (34)** | **14 (0)** |

*(N) Premiership matches played at night*

## WINNING RUNS

16 v Melbourne (1976–1984)
10 v Western Bulldogs (1973–1978)
10 v Hawthorn (1950–1955)
9 v St Kilda (1974–1978)
8 v Geelong (1976–1979)
8 v SM/Sydney (1990–1994)
7 v Brisbane Bears (1990–1993)
7 v Collingwood (1977–1979)
7 v Fitzroy (1975–1978)
7 v Richmond (1990–1993)
4 v Essendon (1957–1959)
3 v Carlton (1973–1974); (1975–1976); (1996– )
3 v Adelaide (1996–)
2 v West Coast (1987–1988); (1989–1990); (1995); (1997– )
2 v Fremantle (1995– )
1 v Port Adelaide (1997– )
1 v Brisbane Lions (1997– )

## 1997 BEST AND FAIREST

Four members of the match committee award up to 10 votes to as many players as warrant votes.

1 Anthony Stevens (494)
2 David King (397)
3 Peter Bell (387)
4 Michael Martyn (341)
5 Craig Sholl (308)
6 Mark Roberts (297)
7 John Blakey (294)
8 Martin Pike (261)
9 John Longmire (259)
10 Glen Archer (252)
   Robert Scott (252)

## GAMES RECORDS

306 Wayne Schimmelbusch (1973–87)
294 Keith Greig (1971–85)
275 David Dench (1969–84)
248 John Dugdale (1955–70)
226 Stephen McCann (1977–88)
224 Ross Smith (1984–96)
220 Allen Aylett (1952–64)
219 John Law (1978–89)
217 Ian Fairley (1983–96)
201 Laurie Dwyer (1956–58; 1960–64; 1966–70)
201 Michael Martyn (1988– )

## GOALS RECORDS

504 John Longmire (1988–95; 1997– )
475 Jock Spencer (1948–57)
444 Malcolm Blight (1974–82)
411 Sel Murray (1937–44; 1948)
411 Wayne Carey (1989– )
358 John Dugdale (1955–70)
354 Wayne Schimmelbusch (1973–87)
352 Bill Findlay (1935–45)
321 Sid Dyer (1937–47)
311 Allen Aylett (1952–64)

## HIGHS AND LOWS

| Against | Highest | Lowest | G. W. Margin | G. L. Margin |
|---|---|---|---|---|
| Adelaide | 23.14.152 (1996) | 7.12.54 (1995) | 80 (1994) | 73 (1991) |
| Brisbane Bears | 24.22.166 (1993) | 8.11.59 (1996) | 94 (1989) | 83 (1989) |
| Brisbane Lions | 17.14.116 (1997) | 12.11.83 (1997) | 57 (1997) | 26 (1997) |
| Carlton | 29.19.193 (1983) | 3.5.23 (1971) | 111 (1983) | 137 (1984) |
| Collingwood | 25.15.165 (1974) | 2.8.20 (1934) | 91 (1974) | 113 (1937) |
| Essendon | 22.20.152 (1985) | 3.10.28 (1961) | 59 (1985) | 104 (1985) |
| Fitzroy | 30.24.204 (1995) | 5.9.39 (1958) | 105 (1996) | 150 (1983) |
| Fremantle | 22.11.143 (1995) | 9.20.74 (1996) | 71 (1995) | — |
| Geelong | 24.10.154 (1986) | 2.7.19 (1930) | 68 (1982) | 114 (1981) |
| Hawthorn | 25.23.173 (1994) | 3.6.24 (1931) | 127 (1994) | 95 (1988) |
| Melbourne | 31.14.200 (1990) | 3.9.27 (1927) | 129 (1981) | 122 (1937) |
| Port Adel | 19.14.128 (1997) | 19.14.128 (1997) | 28 (1997) | — |
| Richmond | 32.17.209 (1990) | 2.9.21 (1928) | 141 (1990) | 168 (1931) |
| St Kilda | 27.17.179 (1990) | 4.8.32 (1963) | 104 (1982) | 86 (1969) |
| Sydney | 35.19.229 (1993) | 4.11.35 (1932) | 140 (1983) | 92 (1934) |
| West Coast | 18.21.129 (1995) | 5.13.43 (1995) | 62 (1995) | 74 (1987) |
| W Bulldogs | 29.15.189 (1983) | 3.7.25 (1953) | 131 (1996) | 92 (1971) |

## THE LEADERSHIP AT NORTH MELBOURNE

| Year | Pos | Coach | Captain | Best & Fairest | Leading Goalkicker | |
|---|---|---|---|---|---|---|
| 1931 | 12 | N. Clark/J. Pemberton | J. Lewis | | J. Lewis | 25 |
| 1932 | 8 | D. Taylor | D. Taylor | | T. Fitzmaurice | 62 |
| 1933 | 8 | D. Taylor | D. Taylor | | T. Fitzmaurice | 60 |
| 1934 | 12 | D. Taylor | D. Taylor | | T. Fitzmaurice | 63 |
| | | T. Fitzmaurice | T. Fitzmaurice | | | |
| 1935 | 12 | P. Scanlan | G. Lewellen | | J. Lewis | 23 |
| 1936 | 11 | P. Scanlan | C. Gaudion | | D. Cassidy | 48 |
| 1937 | 12 | P. Scanlan | J. Adamson | W. Carter | S. Anderson | 18 |
| 1938 | 9 | K. Forbes | K. Forbes | J. Cordner | S. Murray | 56 |
| 1939 | 9 | K. Forbes | K. Forbes | S. Dyer | S. Murray | 78 |
| 1940 | 12 | L. Thomas | L. Thomas | J. Adamson | S. Murray | 58 |
| | | J. Adamson | J. Adamson | | | |
| | | W. Carter | | | | |
| 1941 | 9 | R. McCaskill | B. Findlay | G. Kennedy | S. Murray | 88 |
| 1942 | 9 | R. McCaskill | B. Findlay | J. Allister | S. Murray | 42 |
| | | B. Findlay | | | | |
| 1943 | 9 | B. Findlay | B. Findlay | D. Kemp | B. Findlay | 43 |
| 1944 | 6 | R. McCaskill | H. O'Brien | A. Crawford | B. Findlay | 56 |
| 1945 | 4 | R. McCaskill | H. O'Brien | L. Foote | B. Findlay | 49 |
| 1946 | 9 | R. McCaskill | F. Fairweather | D. Condon | S. Dyer | 55 |
| 1947 | 10 | R. McCaskill | K. Dynon | K. McKenzie | S. Dyer | 47 |
| 1948 | 8 | W. Carter | L. Foote | H. O'Brien | D. Condon | 38 |
| 1949 | 3 | W. Carter | L. Foote | L. Foote | J. Spencer | 65 |
| 1950 | 2 | W. Carter | L. Foote | L. Foote | J. Spencer | 86 |
| 1951 | 9 | W. Carter | L. Foote | J. Spencer | J. Spencer | 57 |
| 1952 | 7 | W. Carter | K. Dynon | J. McCorkell | J. Spencer | 51 |
| 1953 | 7 | W. Carter | K. Dynon | J. O'Halloran | G. Marchesi | 49 |
| 1954 | 4 | J. McCorkell | G. Marchesi | J. Brady | J. Spencer | 38 |
| 1955 | 11 | J. McCorkell | V. Lawrence | R. Brooker | J. Spencer | 68 |
| 1956 | 12 | C. Gaudion | R. Brooker | J. Edwards | J. Spencer | 40 |
| 1957 | 8 | C. Gaudion | J. Brady | B. Martyn | J. Dugdale | 37 |
| 1958 | 3 | W. Carter | J. Brady | A. Aylett | J. Dugdale | 57 |
| 1959 | 6 | W. Carter | J. Brady | A. Aylett | P. Schofield | 47 |
| 1960 | 11 | W. Carter | A. Mantello | A. Aylett | J. Dugdale | 38 |
| 1961 | 12 | W. Carter | A. Aylett | L. Dwyer | J. Dugdale | 47 |
| 1962 | 11 | W. Carter | A. Aylett | W. Serong | J. Dugdale | 44 |
| 1963 | 7 | A. Killigrew | A. Aylett | N. Teasdale | J. Dugdale | 30 |
| 1964 | 8 | A. Killigrew/N. Teasdale | A. Aylett | N. Teasdale | J. Dugdale | 46 |
| 1965 | 9 | A. Killigrew | N. Teasdale | N. Teasdale | F. Goode | 38 |
| 1966 | 7 | A. Killigrew | N. Teasdale | N. Teasdale | F. Goode | 49 |
| 1967 | 8 | K. McKenzie | N. Teasdale | L. Dwyer | G. Farrant | 26 |
| 1968 | 12 | K. McKenzie | J. Dugdale | J. Dugdale | D. Farrant | 35 |
| 1969 | 8 | K. McKenzie | J. Dugdale | S. Kekovich | S. Kekovich | 56 |
| 1970 | 12 | K. McKenzie | J. Dugdale | B. Cable | G. Farrant | 32 |
| 1971 | 9 | B. Dixon | B. Goodingham | D. Dench | S. Kekovich | 35 |
| 1972 | 12 | B. Dixon | D. Dench | K. Montgomery | S. Kekovich/V. Doolan | 19 |
| 1973 | 6 | R. Barassi | B. Davis | B. Davis | D. Wade | 73 |
| 1974 | 2 | R. Barassi | B. Davis | J. Rantall | D. Wade | 103 |
| 1975 | 1 | R. Barassi | B. Davis | B. Davis | D. Wade | 47 |
| 1976 | 2 | R. Barassi | K. Greig | D. Dench | W. Schimmelbusch | 43 |
| 1977 | 1 | R. Barassi | K. Greig | D. Dench | B. Crosswell | 42 |
| 1978 | 2 | R. Barassi | K. Greig | M. Blight | M. Blight | 77 |
| 1979 | 3 | R. Barassi | W. Schimmelbusch | G. Dempsey | M. Blight | 60 |
| 1980 | 5 | R. Barassi | W. Schimmelbusch | K. Greig | A. Briedis | 53 |
| 1981 | 8 | M. Blight/B. Cable | W. Schimmelbusch | D. Dench | M. Blight | 70 |
| 1982 | 4 | B. Cable | W. Schimmelbusch | R. Glendinning | M. Blight | 103 |
| 1983 | 3 | B. Cable | W. Schimmelbusch | R. Glendinning | J. Krakouer,P. Krakouer | 44 |
| 1984 | 11 | B. Cable | W. Schimmelbusch | K. Hodgeman | D. McDonald | 38 |
| 1985 | 4 | J. Kennedy | W. Schimmelbusch | M. Larkin | P. Krakouer | 35 |
| 1986 | 7 | J. Kennedy | W. Schimmelbusch | J. Krakouer | J. Krakouer | 32 |
| 1987 | 5 | J. Kennedy | W. Schimmelbusch | M. Larkin | P. Krakouer | 43 |
| 1988 | 11 | J. Kennedy | J. Law | M. Larkin | J. Krakouer | 35 |
| 1989 | 9 | J. Kennedy | J. Law | M. Martyn | I. Fairley | 28 |
| 1990 | 6 | W. Schimmelbusch | M. Larkin | J. Longmire | J. Longmire | 98 |
| 1991 | 7 | W. Schimmelbusch | M. Larkin | C. Sholl/M. Martyn | J. Longmire | 91 |
| 1992 | 12 | W. Schimmelbusch | M. Larkin | W. Carey | J. Longmire | 64 |
| 1993 | 5 | D. Pagan | W. Carey | W. Carey | J. Longmire | 75 |
| 1994 | 3 | D. Pagan | W. Carey | W. Schwass | J. Longmire | 78 |
| 1995 | 3 | D. Pagan | W. Carey | W. Schwass | W. Carey | 65 |
| 1996 | 1 | D. Pagan | W. Carey | W. Carey | W. Carey | 82 |
| 1997 | 4 | D. Pagan | W. Carey | A. Stevens | B. Allison | 43 |

# PLAYER PROFILES

## WINSTON ABRAHAM

Was bordering on sensational when he started with the Dockers, but has not been able to maintain the magic. It is still in him. Aged 23 and is a destructive forward when the ball is running sweetly. Will quickly realise he will be more accountable under coach Denis Pagan, who will demand more than just fancy footwork.

**Previous AFL club:** Fremantle (1995-97: 38 games, 55 goals).

## BRETT ALLISON

Smart performer across half-forward who loves to drift in and kick goals. Has rammed through 255, mainly left-footers, at vital stages in a senior career that started in 1987. Was the subject of big discussions with Sydney after last season, particularly when his wife's job took her to the Harbour City. It seemed Allison would be part of the Shannon Grant swap, but Wayne Schwass filled that bill. Allison needs one game for his 200. Has had a hernia operation since last year and hindered by back injury in lead up to '98 season.

**Player honors:** premiership side 1996; night series premiership side 1995; 3rd best and fairest 1990.

## BRADY ANDERSON

The second of North's two selections at the 1998 pre-season draft. Anderson won the 1997 Sandover Medal in WA in controversial circumstances after being heavily favored by football punters. Played with East Perth, the club which provided the Roos with 1983 Brownlow Medallist, Ross Glendinning, in 1978. A centreline player and hard-running type who was first drafted by Geelong as its sixth pick (68th overall) at the 1995 National Draft. Played 23 reserves games with the Cats in 1996 and returned to East Perth in 1997.

## GLEN ARCHER

Aggressive all-rounder who will be looking to regain top rating. Brilliant in the premiership season of 1996, when he captured the Norm Smith Medal, but not as prominent in 1997, when he slipped to equal 10th in best and fairest voting. Two Tribunal suspensions, which included two finals, also cut into his season. Only 25, has strength and plays well at either end.

**Player honors:** AFL Norwich Rising Star nominee 1993; All-Australian 1996; premiership side 1996; Norm Smith Medal 1996.

## PETER BELL

Hard working rover and one of the most improved players in the AFL in 1997. Has had two very good seasons with North after an ill-fated start to his AFL career with Fremantle in 1995, when he could manage only two games. Despite some claims that he was too small for the 1996 pre-season draft. He played in the 1996 premiership side and last year finished third in the best and fairest voting.

**Player honors:** AFL Norwich Rising Star nominee 1996; premiership side 1996; 3rd best and fairest 1997.

**Previous AFL club:** Fremantle (1995: 2 games, 2 goals).

## JOHN BLAKEY

He will be 32 in July, but football is not wearying this honest utility who is equally at home in defence as he is ruck-roving or tagging. Not a high-profile Roo, but is always on hand to lend support. At the start of 1998, needed one game for 250.

**Player honors:** premiership side 1996; night series premiership side 1995.

**Previous AFL club:** Fitzroy (1985-92: 135 games, 38 goals).

## MATTHEW CAPUANO

Will be very anxious to pick up the threads of his career after missing all games in 1997 due to knee surgery. Damaged the anterior cruciate ligament in his left knee in an Ansett Australia Cup match in late February 1997 and had to undergo his second knee reconstruction in two years. Promising ruckman who desperately needs a change of luck.

**Player honors:** AFL Norwich Rising Star nominee 1995; premiership side 1996; night series premiership side 1995.

## WAYNE CAREY

Acknowledged as the best centre half-forward in the game, but 1997 wasn't his year. The North skipper suffered a dislocated shoulder in the first game against Melbourne and did not reappear in the side until round 13. He took time to wind up and at the season's end, after North was eliminated in the second preliminary final, he had further surgery to his shoulder and also to a knee.

**Player honors:** best and fairest 1992, 1993, 1996; 2nd best and fairest 1990, 1995; All-Australian 1993-96; All-Australian captain 1996; captain since 1993; AFLPA award 1995; leading goalkicker 1995, 1996; premiership side 1996; night series premiership side 1995.

## BRETT CHANDLER

Has proved to be one of the success stories from the 1996 Fitzroy side following the merge with the Brisbane Bears. Given a second chance by North when selected at the 1997 pre-season draft. Leading up to that, Chandler had trained with Collingwood. The smallish utility did not let North down and jumped from Fitzroy's 1996 wooden spoon side into the reigning premiership side with style, missing only one match due to an ankle injury.

**Previous AFL club:** Fitzroy (1995-96: 28 games, 2 goals).

## STUART COCHRANE

Tall, running wing/utility player who is expected to break into the seniors in 1998 after 47 games and two seasons in the reserves. Is strong and has excellent endurance capacity. All-Australian junior at under-17 level and played in North's 1996 reserves' premiership side.

## DARREN CROCKER

Only a youngster when thrown club dual Brownlow Medallist Keith Greig's famous No. 27 guernsey, but time has marched on and he starts the 1998 season as a 31-year-old. Had another interrupted season in '97, missed several games with groin trouble and his form took a dive. However, this talented, well-built forward was recalled for the three finals and in the losing second preliminary final, kicked four goals. Suffered a further knee injury blow in the 1998 Ansett Australia Cup game against Carlton in Hobart and was sidelined for several weeks.

**Player honors:** 2nd best and fairest 1992; premiership side 1996.

### GLENN FREEBORN

Made his football name when he kicked three of North's five second-quarter goals in the 1996 Grand Final. Played the first 11 games of 1997, lost his place, regained it and then spent further time in the reserves before returning for the three finals. North selectors had obviously not forgotten his '96 Grand Final goals, but this time he kicked a total of two. Needs a strong 1998.

**Player honors:** premiership side 1996.

### SHANNON GRANT

Young Sydney player who was swapped with veteran Wayne Schwass in the pre-national draft trading. A middle-sized player who was in Sydney's losing 1996 Grand Final side, he can run off half-back or play closer to goal. Made it clear he wanted to return to Melbourne and if North had not done a deal, Melbourne Football Club, which also courted him, would have nabbed him.

**Player honors:** AFL Norwich Rising Star nominee 1996.

**Previous AFL club:** Sydney (1995-97: 58 games, 38 goals)

### CHRIS GROOM

Still a virtual stranger to North supporters after playing just two senior games in the past two seasons. Broke down with knee trouble at training in March 1996, had surgery but broke down again the following August and had more surgery. Finally made his senior debut with the Roos in round 20, 1997. A big man with ruck/centre half-forward flair.

**Previous AFL clubs:** Adelaide (1993-94: 12 games, 8 goals); Fremantle (1995: 7 games, 18 goals).

### BRENT HARVEY

Forward pocket/rover who played one game in 1996 and 17 last year, including the lead-up matches to the finals. However, he lost his place for the September action and was one of North's best in the reserve-grade second elimination final win. Not 20 until May, has ability and his turn will come. Troubled by a shoulder complaint in the pre-season.

### ADAM HAY

Selected as North's sixth choice (70th overall) at the 1996 National Draft and starts 1998 still without a senior game. Turns 20 in July and is a ruckman with promise, but needs to put on more weight.

### EVAN HEWITT

Promising WA state junior basketballer and keen tennis player who turned to football later than most but quickly made headway as a ruckman with Subiaco, WA. Selected first (23rd overall) at the National Draft in 1996, when he was WA's best player in the under-18 championships. Turns 20 in July and starts 1998 having played just one senior game — in round 13 last year against Sydney.

### DAMIAN HOULIHAN

North's first choice at the 1998 pre-season draft, the Roos decided to give Houlihan a second chance after he appeared lost to League football. Played senior football with Corowa/Rutherglen as a teenager and was drafted by Collingwood late in 1992 as a prospective goalkicker, but played several of his 11 games in defence. Played a total of 31 reserves games for the Pies. Delisted at end of 1995 and played 1996-97 with Tatura in country Victoria. Trained at North over the summer.

**Previous AFL club:** Collingwood (1994: 11 games, 6 goals).

### DAVID KING

Attacking defender who late last year was involved in the pinch report that saw West Coast Eagles forward Chris Lewis outed for a game. King had his best season, finished second in the club voting and won a back pocket position in the All-Australian side. A late starter in League football at 22, but the former Port boy has made great progress in four seasons.

**Player honors:** premiership side 1996; night series premiership side 1995; All-Australian 1997; 2nd best and fairest 1997.

### KENT KINGSLEY

Full-forward who is waiting in the wings. A fast leader in the Scott Cummings (Port Adelaide) mould and was equal AFL reserves goalkicking champion with 50 in 19 games in 1997. He and twin brother Wade, who is also on North's list, got to North in a deal which saw Paul Geister go to Port Adelaide. Led the SANFL under-19s goalkicking when he played with Woodville-West Torrens.

### JOHN LONGMIRE

After missing all of 1996 — and the premiership glory — he made a successful comeback in 1997 after a knee reconstruction. The club's all-time top goalkicker, but no longer the focal point in attack. Last year he was used in the ruck and at centre half-back and while he didn't set the world on fire, he played in all matches without a setback to the knee and was ninth in best and fairest voting.

**Player honors:** best and fairest 1990; 3rd best and fairest 1991; All-Australian 1990; Coleman Medal 1990; leading goalkicker 1990, 1991, 1992, 1993, 1994; all-time leading goalkicker (504); night series premiership side 1995.

### MICHAEL MARTYN

This strong and mean full-back started 1998 having not missed a game since round 19, 1995. Form in 1997 summed up by his fourth placing in the best and fairest voting. Has tackled all the stars — Ablett, Dunstall, Lockett, Modra and so on — and has held his ground. Reached his 200-game milestone last year.

**Player honors:** best and fairest 1989, 1991 (equal); premiership side 1996; night series premiership side 1995; Michael Tuck Medal 1995.

### JASON McCARTNEY

Former top junior (fourth pick overall at 1990 National Draft) who did not live up to expectations at Collingwood and for the past three seasons has battled for recognition at Adelaide. Not sighted in the Crows side after round six last year. North exchanged Mark Stevens for him in pre-draft trading which, on paper, looked to be a standard swap. He is big, can play at centre half-back and this is make or break.

**Previous AFL clubs:** Collingwood (1991-94: 38 games, 28 goals); Adelaide (1995-97: 37 games, 20 goals).

### LUKE McCORMICK

Quick, stocky, barrel-chested rover who could get his chance in 1998 after 21 games in North's reserves in '97. Does not turn 20 until late in the season and the Roos see him as a senior player. He captained the NSW-ACT Rams before North moved in at the 1996 National Draft and selected him as its third choice (50 overall). Dislocated an elbow in a bike accident in pre-season training.

### COREY McKERNAN

Had medical attention to a shoulder and knee at 1997 season's end and just when he looked ready for a big 1998, suffered a stress fracture to his lower right leg in February, again sidelining him for several weeks. This champion follower/forward, who in 1996 was denied a Brownlow Medal because of Tribunal suspension, missed only three games in 1997 but niggling injuries throughout took the edge off his play. The latest shin injury is a real setback and he will have to be patient. At 24, he still has a long way to go, but he needs a clearer run.

**Player honors:** AFL Norwich Rising Star nominee 1994; 3rd best and fairest 1995, 1996; All-Australian 1996; AFLPA award 1996; premiership side 1996; night series premiership side 1995.

### PAUL McMAHON

Another of North's country contingent from the 1997 National Draft when chosen third (30th overall). Played with the Bendigo Pioneers and is a talented rover adept at kicking goals on the run. Has had some experience with Essendon and Carlton reserves. Is a fine all-round athlete, having competed in the state finals of the high jump, triple jump and 200 metres.

### ANTHONY MELLINGTON

Has shown flair at full-forward and was Fitzroy's final leading goalkicker in 1996. The Roos took him at the 1997 pre-season draft and by the fourth game, he was in the senior side. Kicked five goals in his first game and had 12 after three games, but a broken jaw upset his flow.

**Player honors:** Fitzroy leading goalkicker 1996.

**Previous AFL club:** Fitzroy (1995-96: 24 games, 24 goals).

### DION MILES

The last of North's five selections (62nd overall) at the 1997 National Draft, Miles is a midfielder promoted from North's supplementary list. Won North's reserves' best and fairest award in 1997 and played well in the reserves finals.

### CAMERON MOONEY

Younger brother of Sydney's Jason Mooney, but Cameron was written off as a 'season job' before the start of play in 1997. Had a total knee reconstruction after rupturing an anterior cruciate ligament during an intra-club practice match at Waverley Park in February 1997. Plenty of him and he hopes to get another start with the Roos this year after earlier looking a good prospect with the NSW-ACT Rams. Aged 17 and the youngest player on North's list.

### BYRON PICKETT

Blessed with plenty of football skill, this running half-back/utility should be just about ready to put up his hand in 1998. Has been at North for one year and in 1997 played 21 games in the reserves. Hails from Port Adelaide and was chosen by North at the 1996 National Draft as its fifth selection (67th overall).

### MARTIN PIKE

Settled in nicely in defence at North, his third AFL club, in 1997. Not included on the Brisbane Lions list after the Fitzroy–Brisbane Bears merger in 1996. Proved to be a successful draft choice, finishing eighth in the club voting. Played in all bar one game, courtesy of a one-week suspension following an off-field incident in Adelaide.

**Player honors:** Fitzroy best and fairest 1996.

**Previous AFL clubs:** Melbourne (1993-94: 24 games, 25 goals); Fitzroy (1995-96: 36 games; 15 goals).

### MARK ROBERTS

'The Fridge' — so called because of the condition he carried early in his career — hit back strongly in 1997 with a sixth placing in the club best and fairest voting. In 1996, he was not in the top 10. The big roaming forward, 33 in June, missed only three games due to injury in a most satisfying season. He isn't the key to North's attack, but he complements Carey and McKernan with his height and experience and it takes an opposition player of size to stand him.

**Player honors:** premiership side 1996; night series premiership side 1995.

**Previous AFL clubs:** Sydney (1985-86: 18 games, 5 goals); Brisbane Bears (1987-90: 59 games, 14 goals).

### JOSHUA ROBERTSON

Left-footer who has impressed with the Murray Bushrangers and Wodonga Raiders in Victoria's north-east. Up-and-coming midfielder with pace and a keen football sense. North's fourth selection at the 1997 National Draft (46th overall), Robertson's style has been likened to that of top Roo Anthony Stevens. An eye-catching season in 1997 attracted North's attention. Suffered a broken nose in an incident with Port Adelaide captain Gavin Wanganeen in a 1998 pre-season practice match, which resulted in Wanganeen being suspended for three games.

### ANTHONY ROCK

Gutsy, experienced small man who gives the side plenty of drive out of the centre. Has been part of the senior woodwork at Arden Street since 1988 and his 22 games in 1997 took his aggregate to 159. Best finish in the best and fairest voting is fourth on two occasions and while he didn't appear in the top 10 in 1997, had his share of the play with just on 300 kicks and a sound 115 handballs. Suspended for two matches when found guilty of striking during a 1998 Ansett Australia Cup match against Carlton.

**Player honors:** premiership side 1996; night series premiership side 1995.

### ROBERT SCOTT

Soldiering on in a variety of middle-sized roles. Who would have believed a few years back when he was laboring at Geelong that he would go beyond 200 games. He did just that last season and has missed only one game, with a hamstring injury, in the past three seasons. In his last season at Geelong (1994), he managed a mere nine games.

**Player honors:** premiership side 1996; night series premiership side 1995.

**Previous AFL club:** Geelong (1986-94: 132 games, 164 goals).

### CRAIG SHOLL

Shifted on to the forward line in 1996 and played there again in '97 after making his name in defence and on the wing. Second to only Corey McKernan in the marking division in 1997 (134 to 122) and did much more on the forward line than just kick 40 goals. Shared the best and fairest award with Mick Martyn in 1991 and was fifth last year. A very good hand with 176 games and with an ounce of luck will be close to 200 at this season's end.

**Player honors:** equal best and fairest 1991; premiership side 1996; night series premiership side 1995.

### BRADLEY STEPHENS

North's second selection (27th overall) at the 1997 National Draft. Is from Barooga, on the NSW side of the Murray River, and played for the Murray Bushrangers in 1997. Has played very well at half-back where his disposal has been a strong point

### ADAM SIMPSON

Natural left-footer who has done best on the wing and while he played in 19 games in 1997, needs a special season to consolidate. Was a victim of the selectors' axe a couple of times in '97. At 22 and with 46 games behind him, should be ready to show his best. Was North's first choice at the 1993 National Draft when he was a year 12 student and a member of the Preston Knights' under-18 side. Also played with Eltham.

**Player honors:** AFL Norwich Rising Star nominee 1996.

### ANTHONY STEVENS

North's engine-room player, who not surprisingly won the club best and fairest award. This midfielder/on-baller repeatedly cleared the ball out of the centre and his kicks tally (453) at season's end on second preliminary final day was equal top in the competition with Nathan Buckley, of Collingwood. A real play-maker, who has had recent medical attention to a knee.

**Player honors:** best and fairest 1997; 2nd best and fairest 1993, 1994, 1996; premiership side 1996; night series premiership side 1995.

### DANNY STEVENS

In the past two seasons has had two small tastes of senior football — one game in 1996 and eight in '97. Played in two finals last year, but left out of the second preliminary final side when selectors opted for Jason Daniltchenko. Played in the reserves premiership side in 1996 and the Preston Knights' 1994 title

side. Shapes as a likely wingman/rover and has been blooded with 54 games in North's reserves, one with Fitzroy and two with Sydney.

### SHANNON WATT

From Cavendish, in Victoria's western district, and North's first choice (No. 14) overall at the 1997 National Draft. Taken as a 16-year-old from North Ballarat Rebels and showed his skill at under-16 level where he earned All-Australian selection. Athletic, alert centre half-forward who looks the right material. One of the stars for Victoria Country against Victoria Metro in the AFL National Under-18 Championships in 1997. North will be patient in developing him.

### SCOTT WELSH

Has played 44 games in North's reserves and just two in the seniors — one in 1996 and one in '97. Has been with North since 1996 and that season played in the reserves premiership team. Before that, he was attached to West Adelaide and was North's first selection (17 overall) at the 1995 National Draft. Represented SA in the AFL under-17 championship in Wagga/Albury. Does best on the half-back/half-forward lines.

## ROOKIE LIST

### CRAIG FOLINO

Football-educated with Boronia and the Eastern Ranges. Rover who won 1997 best and fairest award with the Ranges and last year won All-Australian selection as a Victoria Metro player at the AFL National Under-18 Championships. Trained at St Kilda during the 1998 pre-season and will be 19 in August.

### WADE KINGSLEY

Delisted by North in October 1997 before the National Draft, but the Roos decided he was worth another chance and he was listed in February in the rookie draft. Tall youngster from South Australia who played 20 reserves games for North in 1997, but none in the seniors. Plays centre half-back/back pocket and not 20 until late September.

### JULIAN KIRZNER

Delisted by North before the 1997 National Draft, but back on the list in February, courtesy of the rookie draft. Made his senior AFL debut with Essendon in 1994, but has played only three senior games since — with North last year. Has had to contend with a knee operation and has built up 62 reserves games (Essendon/Carlton/North). Kicked four goals against Port Power in 1997.

**Previous AFL club:** Essendon (1994: 1 game, 1 goal).

### DAVID ROUND

Ruckman son of Brownlow Medallist Barry Round who has been given another chance in the AFL following the rookie draft in February. Played 21 games with the Western Bulldogs reserves in 1997, taking his total to 40. Also played two senior games early in 1997. Played with Strathmore and the Calder Canons. Delisted by the Bulldogs before the pre-season draft this year.

**Previous AFL club:** Western Bulldogs (1997: 2 games, 0 goals).

# NORTH MELBOURNE

| Name (# = rookie) | No. | Born | Height | Weight | Recruited from |
|---|---|---|---|---|---|
| Winston Abraham | 15 | 29/9/74 | 175 | 79 | PERTH (WA)/FREMANTLE |
| Brett Allison | 33 | 26/5/68 | 182 | 78 | BELCONNEN (ACT) |
| Brady Anderson | 14 | 12/6/75 | 178 | 79 | EAST PERTH (WA)/GEEL RES/EAST PERTH (WA) |
| Glen Archer | 11 | 24/3/73 | 182 | 94 | NOBLE PARK |
| Peter Bell | 26 | 1/3/76 | 175 | 72 | SOUTH FREMANTLE (WA)/FREMANTLE |
| John Blakey | 12 | 24/7/66 | 187 | 85 | EAST DONCASTER/FITZROY |
| Matthew Capuano | 16 | 2/9/75 | 198 | 97 | CRESWICK/GEELONG U18 |
| Wayne Carey | 18 | 27/5/71 | 192 | 94 | NORTH ADELAIDE (SA) |
| Brett Chandler | 9 | 11/7/75 | 173 | 70 | DONCASTER HEIGHTS/EASTERN U18/FITZROY |
| Stuart Cochrane | 45 | 20/7/78 | 189 | 79 | CENTRAL DISTRICT (SA) |
| Darren Crocker | 27 | 26/3/67 | 189 | 88 | SCORESBY |
| Glenn Freeborn | 17 | 6/2/73 | 180 | 74 | WOODVILLE-WEST TORRENS (SA) |
| Shannon Grant | 6 | 19/4/77 | 178 | 86 | FLEMINGTON/WESTERN U18/SYDNEY |
| Chris Groom | 23 | 28/8/73 | 194 | 95 | SOUTH ADELAIDE (SA)/ADELAIDE/FREMANTLE |
| Brent Harvey | 29 | 14/5/78 | 168 | 68 | PRESTON RSL/NORTHERN U18 |
| Adam Hay | 41 | 27/7/78 | 198 | 90 | EAST PERTH (WA) |
| Evan Hewitt | 21 | 7/7/78 | 194 | 87 | SUBIACO (WA) |
| Damian Houlihan | 1 | 30/7/75 | 188 | 93 | COROWA-RUTHERGLEN/COLL/TATURA |
| David King | 34 | 7/3/72 | 183 | 88 | PORT MELBOURNE |
| Kent Kingsley | 42 | 26/9/78 | 193 | 83 | WOODVILLE-WEST TORRENS (SA) |
| John Longmire | 35 | 31/12/70 | 194 | 102 | COROWA-RUTHERGLEN (NSW) |
| Michael Martyn | 4 | 31/8/68 | 190 | 100 | NEWPORT CENTRAL |
| Jason McCartney | 5 | 14/3/74 | 191 | 95 | NHILL/COLLINGWOOD/ADELAIDE |
| Luke McCormick | 44 | 5/8/78 | 173 | 70 | AINSLIE/NSW-ACT U18 |
| Corey McKernan | 31 | 19/12/73 | 197 | 101 | WESTMEADOWS |
| Paul McMahon | 46 | 5/2/79 | 175 | 66 | LOCKINGTON-BAMAWN/BENDIGO U18 |
| Anthony Mellington | 20 | 27/7/74 | 187 | 84 | SHEPPARTON/FITZROY |
| Dion Miles | 32 | 9/8/78 | 176 | 77 | CHANEL COLLEGE/WESTERN U18 |
| Cameron Mooney | 19 | 26/9/79 | 193 | 90 | TURVEY PARK/NSW-ACT U18 |
| Byron Pickett | 28 | 11/8/77 | 178 | 80 | PORT ADELAIDE (SA) |
| Martin Pike | 13 | 14/11/72 | 190 | 92 | NORWOOD (SA)/MELBOURNE/FITZROY |
| Mark Roberts | 22 | 28/6/65 | 189 | 92 | ST GEORGE(NSW)/SYDNEY/BRISBANE |
| Josh Robertson | 39 | 15/6/79 | 180 | 80 | WODONGA RAIDERS/MURRAY U18 |
| Anthony Rock | 3 | 29/9/70 | 170 | 73 | HADFIELD |
| Robert Scott | 8 | 1/3/69 | 173 | 74 | TORQUAY/GEELONG |
| Craig Sholl | 24 | 30/12/67 | 189 | 87 | HORSHAM |
| Adam Simpson | 37 | 16/2/76 | 185 | 77 | ELTHAM/NORTHERN U18 |
| Brad Stephens | 43 | 11/7/79 | 186 | 79 | BAROOGA (NSW)/MURRAY U18 |
| Anthony Stevens | 10 | 2/7/71 | 178 | 82 | SHEPPARTON |
| Danny Stevens | 38 | 10/11/76 | 180 | 77 | GREENSBOROUGH/NORTHERN U18 |
| Shannon Watt | 36 | 26/11/80 | 192 | 86 | HAMILTON/NORTH BALLARAT U18 |
| Scott Welsh | 30 | 1/12/78 | 190 | 84 | WEST ADELAIDE (SA) |
| Craig Folino # | 52 | 28/8/79 | 176 | 75 | BORONIA/EASTERN U18 |
| Wade Kingsley # | 40 | 26/9/78 | 188 | 90 | WOODVILLE-WEST TORRENS (SA) |
| Julian Kirzner # | 48 | 24/10/76 | 188 | 90 | AJAX/CENTRAL U18/ESSENDON |
| David Round # | 54 | 25/6/78 | 192 | 90 | STRATHMORE/CALDER U18/WSTRN BLDGS |
| Total/(Average) *On 26/2/98 | | (23.5 yrs)* | (185) | (84) | |

# PLAYERS 1998

| Debut | HOME & AWAY | | 1997 | | FINALS | | GRAND FINALS | | | NIGHT SERIES | | STATE OF ORIGIN | |
|---|---|---|---|---|---|---|---|---|---|---|---|---|---|
| | Gms | Gls | Gms | Gls | Gms | Gls | Gms | Gls | Won | Gms | Gls | Gms | Gls |
| 1995 | 38 | 55 | 13 | 16 | | | | | | 3 | 2 | 0 | 0 |
| 1987 | 199 | 255 | 24 | 43 | 12 | 28 | 1 | 2 | 1 | 20 | 27 | 7 | 5 |
| | 0 | 0 | | | | | | | | 0 | 0 | 0 | 0 |
| 1992 | 117 | 82 | 21 | 15 | 10 | 8 | 1 | 0 | 1 | 10 | 2 | 2 | 4 |
| 1995 | 50 | 49 | 25 | 24 | 6 | 2 | 1 | 1 | 1 | 7 | 7 | 1 | 0 |
| 1985 | 249 | 75 | 24 | 6 | 15 | 4 | 1 | 0 | 1 | 28 | 3 | 0 | 0 |
| 1994 | 36 | 12 | 0 | 0 | 3 | 1 | 1 | 0 | 1 | 7 | 1 | 0 | 0 |
| 1989 | 162 | 411 | 14 | 25 | 12 | 34 | 1 | 1 | 1 | 19 | 46 | 3 | 4 |
| 1995 | 52 | 6 | 24 | 4 | 3 | 0 | | | | 2 | 1 | 0 | 0 |
| | 0 | 0 | 0 | 0 | | | | | | 0 | 0 | 0 | 0 |
| 1985 | 158 | 116 | 9 | 10 | 13 | 11 | 1 | 3 | 1 | 11 | 9 | 0 | 0 |
| 1995 | 46 | 22 | 18 | 5 | 9 | 8 | 1 | 3 | 1 | 3 | 0 | 0 | 0 |
| 1995 | 58 | 38 | 23 | 18 | 4 | 1 | 1 | 0 | 0 | 3 | 4 | 0 | 0 |
| 1993 | 21 | 26 | 2 | 0 | | | | | | 6 | 5 | 0 | 0 |
| 1996 | 18 | 10 | 17 | 10 | 2 | 0 | | | | 1 | 0 | 0 | 0 |
| | 0 | 0 | 0 | 0 | | | | | | 0 | 0 | 0 | 0 |
| 1997 | 1 | 0 | 1 | 0 | | | | | | 0 | 0 | 0 | 0 |
| 1994 | 11 | 6 | 0 | 0 | | | | | | 5 | 3 | 0 | 0 |
| 1994 | 89 | 25 | 23 | 8 | 11 | 3 | 1 | 0 | 1 | 10 | 4 | 1 | 0 |
| | 0 | 0 | 0 | 0 | | | | | | 0 | 0 | 0 | 0 |
| 1988 | 180 | 504 | 25 | 10 | 8 | 15 | | | | 19 | 30 | 5 | 17 |
| 1988 | 201 | 14 | 25 | 0 | 12 | 1 | 1 | 0 | 1 | 18 | 2 | 2 | 0 |
| 1991 | 75 | 48 | 6 | 3 | 2 | 1 | | | | 13 | 8 | 0 | 0 |
| | 0 | 0 | 0 | 0 | | | | | | 0 | 0 | 0 | 0 |
| 1993 | 93 | 96 | 22 | 22 | 11 | 11 | 1 | 0 | 1 | 7 | 6 | 1 | 2 |
| | 0 | 0 | 0 | 0 | | | | | | 0 | 0 | 0 | 0 |
| 1995 | 38 | 41 | 14 | 17 | | | | | | 1 | 0 | 0 | 0 |
| | 0 | 0 | 0 | 0 | | | | | | | | | |
| | 0 | 0 | 0 | 0 | | | | | | 0 | 0 | 0 | 0 |
| 1997 | 1 | 0 | 1 | 0 | | | | | | 0 | 0 | 0 | 0 |
| 1993 | 84 | 46 | 24 | 6 | 6 | 4 | | | | 8 | 3 | 0 | 0 |
| 1985 | 186 | 155 | 22 | 17 | 11 | 10 | 1 | 2 | 1 | 19 | 12 | 4 | 2 |
| | 0 | 0 | 0 | 0 | | | | | | 0 | 0 | 0 | 0 |
| 1988 | 159 | 130 | 22 | 14 | 12 | 3 | 1 | 1 | 1 | 18 | 16 | 3 | 3 |
| 1986 | 206 | 208 | 25 | 14 | 16 | 12 | 3 | 0 | 1 | 23 | 24 | 7 | 9 |
| 1987 | 176 | 96 | 25 | 40 | 12 | 12 | 1 | 2 | 1 | 19 | 8 | 6 | 0 |
| 1995 | 46 | 21 | 19 | 5 | 6 | 2 | 1 | 1 | 1 | 5 | 0 | 0 | 0 |
| | 0 | 0 | 0 | 0 | | | | | | 0 | 0 | 0 | 0 |
| 1989 | 156 | 77 | 25 | 10 | 9 | 2 | 1 | 2 | 1 | 18 | 10 | 3 | 0 |
| 1996 | 9 | 5 | 8 | 4 | 2 | 0 | | | | 0 | 0 | 0 | 0 |
| | 0 | 0 | 0 | 0 | | | | | | 0 | 0 | 0 | 0 |
| 1996 | 2 | 0 | 1 | 0 | | | | | | 0 | 0 | 0 | 0 |
| | 0 | 0 | 0 | 0 | | | | | | 0 | 0 | | |
| | 0 | 0 | 0 | 0 | | | | | | 0 | 0 | | |
| 1994 | 4 | 6 | 3 | 5 | | | | | | 1 | 0 | | |
| 1997 | 2 | 0 | 2 | 0 | | | | | | 1 | 0 | | |
| | (69) | (63) | 502 | 346 | 207 | 173 | 20 | 18 | 17 | 303 | 233 | 45 | 46 |

## Port Power at a glance

**ADDRESS:** Queen Street, Alberton, SA 5014

**POSTAL ADDRESS:** PO Box 379, Port Adelaide, SA 5015

**TELEPHONE:** (08) 8447 4044 Football Department (08) 8447 8155

**FACSIMILE:** (08) 8447 8633

**WEB SITE:** www.portpower.com.au

**MELBOURNE OFFICE:** PO Box 285, Hawthorn, Vic 3122

**PRESIDENT:** Greg Boulton

**CHIEF EXECUTIVE OFFICER:** Brian Cunningham

**FOOTBALL OPERATIONS MANAGER:** Rob Snowdon

**VICTORIAN MANAGER:** Chris Pelchen

**COMMUNICATIONS MANAGER:** Matt Cross

**RECRUITING MANAGER:** Alan Stewart

**MARKETING MANAGER:** Mark Brayshaw

**PLAYER WELFARE AND DEVELOPMENT MANAGER:** Bob Clayton

**COACHING STAFF:** John Cahill (senior), Mark Williams (assistant), David Arnfield (training and rehabilitation)

**SELECTION COMMITTEE:** Brian Fairclough (chairman), John Cahill, Mark Williams, Geoff Morris

**TRAINING/REHABILITATION MANAGER:** Stephen Traynor

**CLUB DOCTOR:** Peter Barnes

**CLUB PHYSIOTHERAPIST:** Patrick Custance

**FOUNDED:** 1870

**JOINED AFL:** 1997

**HOME GROUND:** Football Park

**GROUND DIMENSIONS:** 170m by 135m

**TRAINING VENUE:** Alberton Oval

**OFFICIAL COLORS:** Black body with white lightning stripes on left side, teal chest panels, and black lightning panels on left side, black neck and teal trim. Socks: Black. *Alternate strip:* Guernsey: black with white and teal lightning stripes down left side. Shorts: white with silver, white, black and teal trim. Socks: Black.

**RECORD HOME ATTENDANCE** (Football Park): 45,498 — August 10, 1997 v Adelaide

# PORT ADELAIDE

## A powerful start; now to hold ground

Port Adelaide slipped into the AFL with far less frustration than most imagined and in the end, it was the length of the season that cost it a place in the finals in its maiden season.

Few people expected much from Port last year and were surprised. This year, expectations will be higher and if Port can hold its ground — it finished ninth in 1997, out of the finals on percentage only — it will have filled the bill.

Big Brett Chalmers, from Adelaide, and rover Chris Naish, from Richmond, have joined Port in return for Ian Downsborough and John Rombotis and there is probably nothing in those transactions that will sway things one way or the other.

Gavin Wanganeen leads by example and must again be at the coal-face. So must Scott Cummings, the full-forward who kicked 70.50 in 1997. If Cummings can straighten his kicking — and some players never master the art — it could often mean the difference between victory and defeat.

Darren Mead had a successful first season at centre half-back and was club best and fairest, Stephen Paxman slotted nicely into full-back, Matthew Primus is gaining in status as a ruckman, Donald Dickie has style on the wing and Brayden Lyle and David Brown are strong smaller-sized players.

Michael Wilson is a youngster with great talent and was rewarded in 1997 with the Norwich Rising Star, while other youngsters with a future are Nathan Eagleton, Bowen Lockwood, Brendon Lade and Adam Heuskes. Heuskes, 22 in March, last year won a place in the All-Australian side and in 1996 played in Sydney's Grand Final side.

Coach John Cahill has extracted every ounce of that win-at-all-costs SANFL Port background and has engineered an exciting and successful brand of forceful football.

Port should have made the finals in 1997. It had Adelaide's measure in round 19 before going down by seven points and it should never have had to settle for a draw against the Brisbane Lions at the Gabba in round 20.

Port still had a chance to play in the finals in the last match of the season. But, even at Football Park, and when right up with St Kilda at three-quarter time, it could not find the energy to go on and win — and grab a finals spot.

The season was just too long, but it was a great foundation for 1998.

— **Greg Hobbs**

## THE YEAR AHEAD

| Rd | Date | Opponent | Venue | Home/Away | Time (local) |
|----|------|----------|-------|-----------|--------------|
| 1 | March 29 | Sydney | FP | H | 12.10pm |
| 2 | April 4 | Hawthorn | P | A | 2.10pm |
| 3 | April 11 (N) | North Melbourne | FP | H | 8.10pm |
| 4 | April 19 | Adelaide | FP | H | 1.40pm |
| 5 | April 26 | Melbourne | MCG | A | 2.10pm |
| 6 | May 2 (N) | Fremantle | FP | H | 8.10pm |
| 7 | May 9 | Carlton | OO | A | 2.10pm |
| 8 | May 16 | St Kilda | P | A | 7.40pm |
| 9 | May 24 | Collingwood | FP | H | 2.50pm |
| 10 | May 30 | Richmond | MCG | A | 2.10pm |
| 11 | June 6 (N) | West Coast | FP | H | 8.10pm |
| 12 | June 14 | Brisbane Lions | G | A | 2.10pm |
| 13 | June 21 | Western Bulldogs | FP | H | 8.10pm |
| 14 | June 27 (N) | Geelong | FP | H | 8.10pm |
| 15 | July 4 | Essendon | MCG | A | 2.10pm |
| 16 | July 19 | Sydney | SCG | A | 12.40pm |
| 17 | July 25 (N) | Hawthorn | FP | H | 8.10pm |
| 18 | August 1 | North Melbourne | MCG | A | 2.10pm |
| 19 | August 9 | Adelaide | FP | A | 2.50pm |
| 20 | August 16 | Melbourne | FP | H | 12.10pm |
| 21 | August 23 | Fremantle | S | A | 12.10pm |
| 22 | August 30 | Carlton | FP | H | 2.50pm |

## 1997 AT A GLANCE

**L:** R1: Collingwood 26.10 (166) v Port Adelaide 13.9 (87) (MCG)

**L:** R2: Port Adelaide 8.12 (60) v Essendon 14.9 (93) (FP)

**W:** R3: Port Adelaide 18.21 (129) v Geelong 14.6 (90) (FP)

**W:** R4: Adelaide 11.6 (72) v Port Adelaide 11.17 (83) (FP)

**W:** R5: Port Adelaide 10.13 (73) v Brisbane Lions 10.11 (71) (FP)

**W:** R6: Port Adelaide 19.8 (122) v Richmond 8.10 (58) (FP)

**L:** R7: St Kilda 20.6 (126) v Port Adelaide 8.13 (61) (P)

**L:** R8: Nth Melb 19.14 (128) v Port Adelaide 15.10 (100) (OO)

### SNAPSHOT

**Games:** 22
**Won:** 10 **Lost:** 11
**Drew:** 1
**Ladder Finish:** 9th
**Players Used:** 35

**W:** R9: Port Adelaide 10.18 (78) v Melbourne 3.9 (27) (FP)

**W:** R10: Port Adelaide 14.9 (93) v Carlton 7.13 (55) (FP)

**L:** R11: Port Adelaide 4.17 (41) v Sydney 10.16 (76) (FP)

**W:** R12: Western Bulldogs 12.10 (82) v Port Adelaide 14.10 (94) (OO)

**W:** R13: Port Adelaide 10.9 (69) v Fremantle 7.12 (54) (FP)

**L:** R14: Hawthorn 18.16 (124) v Port Adelaide 13.14 (92) (P)

**L:** R15: West Coast 12.13 (85) v Port Adelaide 9.13 (67) (S)

**W:** R16: Port Adelaide 17.9 (111) v Collingwood 8.10 (58) (FP)

**W:** R17: Essendon 10.12 (72) v Port Adelaide 18.14 (122) (MCG)

**L:** R18: Geelong 25.9 (159) v Port Adelaide 11.8 (74) (KP)

**L:** R19: Port Adelaide 9.4 (58) v Adelaide 9.11 (65) (FP)

**D:** R20: Brisbane Lions 13.15 (93) v Port Adelaide 13.15 (93) (G)

**L:** R21: Richmond 22.14 (146) v Port Adelaide 8.13 (61) (MCG)

**L:** R22: Port Adelaide 12.12 (84) v St Kilda 17.15 (117) (FP)

## The Coach

**John Cahill**

**Born:** 27/4/40

Cahill came close to becoming the first coach of the recently admitted clubs to figure in the finals in his first season.

Port Adelaide had a splendid season, however, finishing ninth and out of the top eight by percentage only. As late as the round 17, it was fifth, but registered four losses and a draw in the last five games.

Cahill had Port playing a fast and exciting brand of football, with the best run being four wins from rounds three to six.

He started coaching Port in the SANFL in 1974 and had an unbroken run until 1982. In 1983 and '84, he coached Collingwood and on returning to SA, coached West Adelaide from 1985 to '87. He went back to Port as coach in 1988 and remained until the 11th game of 1996 when he stepped down to start preparing for the AFL Port Adelaide.

Cahill coached Port to 10 SANFL premierships and had West Adelaide and Collingwood in the finals.

He played 267 games with Port from 1958 to '73 and was captain from 1967 to '73.

### AT A GLANCE

**COACHING RECORD**

**Collingwood**

| Season | P | W | L | D | Pos |
|--------|----|----|----|----|-----|
| 1983 | 22 | 12 | 10 | — | 6 |
| 1984 | 25 | 15 | 10 | — | 3 |
| | 47 | 27 | 20 | | |

**Port Adelaide**

| Season | P | W | L | D | Pos |
|--------|----|----|----|----|-----|
| 1997 | 22 | 10 | 11 | — | 9 |
| **Total** | **69** | **37** | **31** | | |

## WIN/LOSS RECORD

| Against | P | W (N) | L (N) | D (N) |
|---|---|---|---|---|
| Adelaide | 2 | 1 | 1 | 0 |
| Brisbane Lions | 2 | 1 | 0 | 1 (1) |
| Carlton | 1 | 1 (1) | 0 | 0 |
| Collingwood | 2 | 1 (1) | 1 | 0 |
| Essendon | 2 | 1 (1) | 1 | 0 |
| Fremantle | 1 | 1 (1) | 0 | 0 |
| Geelong | 2 | 1 (1) | 1 | 0 |
| Hawthorn | 1 | 0 | 1 | 0 |
| Melbourne | 1 | 1 (1) | 0 | 0 |
| North Melb | 1 | 0 | 1 | 0 |
| Richmond | 2 | 1 | 1 | 0 |
| St Kilda | 2 | 0 | 2 (2) | 0 |
| Sydney | 1 | 0 | 1 (1) | 0 |
| West Coast | 1 | 0 | 1 | 0 |
| W Bulldogs | 1 | 1 | 0 | 0 |
| **TOTALS** | **22** | **10 (6)** | **11 (3)** | **1 (1)** |

*(N) Premiership matches played at night*

## WINNING RUNS

1 v Adelaide (1997)
1 v Brisbane Lions (1997)
1 v Carlton (1997– )
1 v Collingwood (1997– )
1 v Essendon (1997– )
1 v Fremantle (1997– )
1 v Geelong (1997)
1 v Melbourne (1997– )
1 v Richmond (1997)
1 v Western Bulldogs (1997– )

## 1997 BEST AND FAIREST

The five-man match committee rates every player in every game on a scale of 0-4. Individual player votes from each match committee member are then averaged out for each game and this figure is awarded to the player.

**1** Darren Mead (22)
**2** Matthew Primus (21)
**3** Stephen Paxman (19)
Michael Wilson (19)
**5** Shane Bond (17)
Brayden Lyle (17)
Adam Heuskes (17)
Gavin Wanganeen (17)
**9** David Brown (13)
Brendon Lade (13)

## GAMES RECORDS

| | |
|---|---|
| **22** | Shane Bond (1997– ) |
| **22** | Donald Dickie (1997– ) |
| **22** | Josh Francou (1997– ) |
| **22** | Adam Heuskes (1997– ) |
| **22** | Brendon Lade (1997– ) |
| **22** | Darren Mead (1997– ) |
| **22** | Stephen Paxman (1997– ) |
| **22** | Matthew Primus (1997– ) |
| **22** | Michael Wilson (1997– ) |

## GOALS RECORDS

| | |
|---|---|
| **70** | Scott Cummings (1997– ) |
| **17** | Shayne Breuer (1997– ) |
| **17** | David Brown (1997– ) |
| **16** | Josh Francou (1997– ) |

## THE LEADERSHIP AT PORT ADELAIDE

| Year | Pos | Coach | Captain | Best & Fairest | Leading Goalkicker | |
|---|---|---|---|---|---|---|
| 1997 | 9 | J. Cahill | G. Wanganeen | D. Mead | S. Cummings | 70 |

## HIGHS AND LOWS

| Against | Highest | Lowest | G. W. Margin | G. L. Margin |
|---|---|---|---|---|
| Adelaide | 11.17.83 (1997) | 9.4.58 (1997) | 11 (1997) | 7 (1997) |
| Brisbane Lions | 13.15.93 (1997) | 10.13.73.(1997) | 2 (1997) | — |
| Carlton | 14.9.93 (1997) | 14.9.93 (1997) | 38 (1997) | — |
| Collingwood | 17.9.111 (1997) | 13.9.87 (1997) | 53 (1997) | 79 (1997) |
| Essendon | 18.14.122 (1997) | 8.12.60 (1997) | 50 (1997) | 33 (1997) |
| Fremantle | 10.9.69 (1997) | 10.9.69 (1997) | 15 (1997) | — |
| Geelong | 18.21.129 (1997) | 11.8.74 (1997) | 39 (1997) | 85 (1997) |
| Hawthorn | 13.14.92 (1997) | 13.14.92 (1997) | — | 32 (1997) |
| Melbourne | 10.18.78 (1997) | 10.18.78 (1997) | 51 (1997) | |
| North Melb | 15.10.100 (1997) | 15.10.100 (1997) | | 28 (1997) |
| Richmond | 19.8.122 (1997) | 8.13.61 (1997) | 64 (1997) | 85 (1997) |
| St Kilda | 12.12.84 (1997) | 8.13.61 (1997) | — | 65 (1997) |
| Sydney | 4.17.41 (1997) | 4.17.41 (1997) | — | 35 (1997) |
| West Coast | 9.13.67 (1997) | 9.13.67 (1997) | — | 18 (1997) |
| W Bulldogs | 14.10.94 (1997) | 14.10.94 (1997) | 12 (1997) | |

# PLAYER PROFILES

**SCOTT BASSETT**
Promising 19-year-old utility. A foundation list player, attached to Norwood, who has yet to get a run in the AFL side. A good mark and had played only one game with Norwood when selected by Port before the 1997 season. Should make his senior debut in '98.

**MATTHEW BODE**
Interesting choice by Port at the 1998 pre-season draft. Bode has yet to play senior football and will probably spend most, possibly all, of 1998 with Glenelg. Did enough in the pre-season training with Port to warrant selection. A teenage rover who represented SA at the 1996 AFL National Under-18 Championships. Spent 1997 playing cricket in England.

**SHANE BOND**
Didn't miss a game in 1997 and Port executed a telling move by switching him into defence a few games into the season. He found his niche and finished equal fifth in club best and fairest voting. Previously played 34 games, including the 1994 premiership, with the West Coast Eagles. Has proved to be a cool customer in the forward pocket, but it seems he is even better suited to the back line. Initially played with Port Adelaide in the SA League and it wasn't surprising that he would find his way back to SA, particularly when his brother, Troy, left Carlton after being left out of its 1995 premiership side and joined the Adelaide Crows in 1996.
**Player honors:** West Coast Eagles 1994 premiership side.
**Previous AFL club:** West Coast Eagles (1994-96: 34 games, 20 goals).

**SHAYNE BREUER**
Is having his second football stint in South Australia. From the Wimmera in Victoria and represented Victoria Country in Teal Cup competition in 1989. Started his senior career with Woodville/West Torrens and was second in the 1993 Magarey Medal. Joined Geelong in '94, played in two losing Grand Final sides, then moved back to SA to Port in 1997. Played a total of eight finals with Geelong. Excellent half-forward and a very capable goalkicker with impressive on-field leadership qualities. Has an excellent strike rate and since making his debut with Geelong in 1994 has missed only four games. Starts 1998 in the shadows of two milestones — he needs eight games for 100 and six goals for his century.
**Previous AFL club:** Geelong (1994-96: 71 games, 77 goals).

**DAVID BROWN**
Left Port Adelaide (SA League) in 1991 to play with the Adelaide Crows, but returned when Port started to assemble its AFL squad. Busy small man who doesn't mind attending to the untidy work in the packs, but was forced to miss a few games last year with hamstring trouble. In the top 10 in club voting last year and had solid kicks and marks statistics. Has played in four Port Adelaide (SANFL) premiership sides and won the Jack Oatey Medal when best on ground in 1996.

**Previous AFL club:** Adelaide (1991-96: 69 games, 55 goals).

**PETER BURGOYNE**
Made his debut with Port Adelaide Magpies (SA league) in 1996 and a handful of games there convinced Port Power he was AFL material. Son of Port Magpie Peter Burgoyne senior and played junior football in Darwin from age of 12. He earned All-Australian junior honors with the Northern Territory in 1995 and joined the under-19 academy at Port. Small, elusive, quick and clever wing/half-forward who played much of the first half of 1997, but then struggled through the second half. Played the last three games, taking his tally to 15, so it was a creditable first season.

**TOM CARR**
All-Australian at under-17 level in 1995 who has had two well-spaced games with the Power. Played in the big one — the first match between Port and the Adelaide Crows at Football Park in round four — and broke ribs. The year before, he broke a collarbone. Shapes as a promising defender who had not played a senior game with the Port Adelaide Magpies when listed for the 1997 season.

**BRETT CHALMERS**
Hopefully will find his football niche back where his football life started — at Port Adelaide. Left the Port Magpies amid controversy when he let it be known before the 1992 National Draft that he wanted to play for Collingwood — and only Collingwood. The Pies drafted him, but he stayed in SA and was traded to the Crows in 1994. A big man who was sidelined with ankle and hamstring injuries in 1997 and missed all finals. Runs hot and cold, but has had minor surgery to a knee and will give it everything in '98.
**Previous AFL club:** Adelaide (1994-97: 50 games, 8 goals).

**CHAD CORNES**
The reputation of his father, former SA star and foundation Adelaide coach Graham Cornes, preceded his arrival on an AFL list. Cornes is now in an 'opposition' camp, but that re-adjustment will have already taken place. Port's No. 1 choice at the 1997 National Draft, strong overhead and a fast-leading forward who kicks accurately. (Graham also played five games with North Melbourne in the VFL).

**JARROD COTTON**
Scored a goal with his first kick in League football against Carlton at Football Park last year and followed with another later in the game, which Port won. Had limited exposure from four games in his first season, but is a smart half-forward with a future. Had experience with North Adelaide and Central District before Port swooped. Should kick on.

**SCOTT CUMMINGS**
Kicked 70 goals to finish fourth on the AFL list in 1997, but also kicked 50 behinds. If he can steady, could kick 100 in a season as he leads sharply and gives the side a focal point. Was allowed to settle at full-forward — unlike his days at Essendon where he played at both ends and struggled to hold his place. Big, a strong mark and in 1997, won the Graham

Moss Medal for being best man afield for WA (kicking eight goals) against The Allies in State of Origin football. Surprisingly did not finish in Port's top 10 in the best and fairest voting, despite his high finish on the goalkicking ladder. Had medical attention to a knee after the 1997 season.

**Player honors:** AFL Norwich Rising Star nominee 1994; Essendon leading goalkicker 1994; Port Adelaide leading goalkicker 1997; Graham Moss Medal 1997.

**Previous AFL club:** Essendon (1994-96: 40 games, 83 goals).

### STEPHEN DANIELS

Talented centre half-back, full-back, back-pocket who has had to contend with a chronic groin injury. Had 10 games in 1997, but significantly they included the last eight. Started with Norwood in 1994 and had played 42 games when Port signed him. Should get more game time in '98.

### STUART DEW

Solidly built wingman who is a quick big-kicking left-footer. Has had only one senior outing, but should become more familiar to fans this year. One of the best 17-year-old players in Australia and an All-Australian at the 1996 National Under-18 Championships. Had played only two games with Central District when Port included him on its original list.

### DONALD DICKIE

Burst into League football with great impact in 1997 on the wing. Has polish, pace and an ability to be in the right place at the right time. His season evened out, but if he can become mentally tougher, will once more be a driving force from the centre line. Troubled for a time with a groin injury but appeared to be in fine fettle in the lead up to 1998. From New Zealand and came to Australia when he was seven. Played with Sturt, SA country football and with Norwood before Port realised he was something special. Did not miss a match in 1997 and gave Port plenty of drive through the midfield.

### NATHAN EAGLETON

Coach John Cahill admits he was a bonus to Port in 1997. The club knew he had talent as a half-forward/rover but, according to Cahill, he "jumped out of the ground". Promoted for his first game in round five and stayed in for the rest of the season. Had almost no senior experience with West Adelaide when Port took him on and will not be 20 until after this season. A good prospect.

**Player honors:** AFL Norwich Rising Star nominee 1997.

### PAUL EVANS

In the SA team at the under-17 national championships, winning All-Australian selection in 1995 but had not played a senior game with Port Adelaide Magpies when Port Power listed him. Yet to make an AFL appearance, but is best suited at full-forward or in the forward pocket. Will have trouble getting the spearhead role ahead of Scott Cummings, but a spot may be found for him. Did not harm his chances when he kicked five goals in Port's opening practice match in 1998.

### NIGEL FIEGERT

Had four games last year, but spent most of the season with the Port Adelaide Magpies, polling strongly in their club voting. A centre half-back/back pocket who first played with Port (SANFL) in 1996. In round 12 last year at Optus Oval, he was the hero of the win when he was moved to centre half-forward and kicked three goals, including the sealer. It was a memorable second game for Fiegert, but he must grasp his chances this year.

### FABIAN FRANCIS

Before 1997, his last AFL game was with the Brisbane Bears in 1994. He played 22 games with the Queensland club and, in 1991, one game with Melbourne. However, he showed there was still League football left in him on returning to SA and was second in the 1996 Magarey Medal voting playing with the Port Adelaide Magpies. Has played with Southern Districts (NT) and in two Magpies premiership sides. In 1997, Port Power got value from him on the wing and in associated areas. Despite being around the AFL fringes for a good while, he will not be 25 until October.

**Previous AFL clubs:** Melbourne (1991: 1 game, 0 goals); Brisbane Bears (1993-94: 22 games, 17 goals).

### JOSH FRANCOU

Plenty to like about him in his first season in the AFL in 1997. The 1996 Magarey Medallist has a touch of class on the half-forward and centre lines. Did not miss a match, kicked 16 goals and generally can be well satisfied with his debut year. Had 56 games with North Adelaide before he pulled on a boot for Port in round one. Wins the ball often and shows all the signs of developing further. Many Magarey Medallists have become top-flight VFL/AFL players — such as Malcolm Blight, John Platten, Tony McGuinness and Andrew Jarman. Francou has a lot to like about him too.

### DARREN FRASER

Port lifted him with its fourth pick at the 1997 National Draft from Essendon's supplementary list where he had played 80 games (1994-97) in the reserves — on top of his 38 (1991-93) with Collingwood reserves. A senior game a long time coming and one of the more surprising draft picks by Port. From the famous Essendon Fraser family — father Ken captained the Dons and brother Mark is a current player. Has done well in the midfield and if he makes the grade, it will be a late start at 25.

### PAUL GEISTER

The AFL career of this dour defender has moved along at snail's pace. In three seasons with North Melbourne, had just three games and a sizeable 70 in the reserves. Surprisingly, two of Geister's senior games at North were in finals, when he played in the 1995 series. Then it was back to 'boiled lollies' again at Arden Street in 1996 before Port put up its hand. The situation didn't improve with Port last year and he got the nod in just one game — the last of the season. Is 26 and unless he can win a regular position this year, will struggle to hold his place on the list.

**Previous AFL club:** North Melbourne (1995: 3 games, 0 goals).

### TOM HARLEY
Unsighted in the senior side in 1997. A member of the 1996 SA national under-18 team and won All-Australian honors. A Norwood youngster who has height for the half-back line and back pocket. Had not played a senior game with Norwood when Port took the punt with him. Turns 20 in July and will be anxious to get his body into the AFL action this year. Had ankle trouble last year, but did play in one Ansett Australia Cup game.

### MARK HARWOOD
The third of four players taken by Port at the 1996 National Draft, a half-forward who is a good mark and is tough. From Tasmania and is still to open his account with Port. Tasmanian under-18 representative at 1996 national titles. Many great players have come out of the Apple Isle — whether Harwood joins them remains to be seen. Has speed and spring and turns 20 just into the 1998 season.

### BRENT HEAVER
Has had plenty of injuries on his winding journey in League football and last year was no exception. Played early in the season, suffered a thigh injury and did not return until the second half. Hit a further hurdle late in the season and was sidelined with a stress fracture in a lower leg. Then, in a 1998 preseason practice game against Melbourne, tore a quad muscle and again out of action for several weeks. Started his AFL career with Melbourne in 1990 (he kicked two goals in his first game), left the AFL briefly and played with Epping (an outer Melbourne suburb) and was recalled by Carlton before Port took him. Has played in four finals — all with Carlton and the last of them in 1996. His best scoring year was with Carlton in 1993 when he kicked 48.26.
**Previous AFL clubs:** Melbourne (1990-91: 12 games, 12 goals); Carlton (1992-96: 64 games, 106 goals).

### ADAM HEUSKES
A surprising choice in the 1997 All-Australian side on a half-back flank and the only Port player in the lineup. Finished equal fifth in Port's best and fairest voting, but won only four Brownlow Medal votes. Despite the disparity, he had a solid season following his move from Sydney and its Grand Final team of 1996. Was Port's second best kick-getter, played in all 22 games and his return to SA, where he previously played with Norwood, was a success. Turned 22 shortly before start of 1998 season.
**Player honors:** All-Australian team 1997.
**Previous AFL club:** Sydney (1994-96: 49 games, 6 goals).

### ROGER JAMES
Wing/half-forward who had a sound, rather than standout season in 1997 when he played in all games except one from round five on. Suffered a setback in practice match in February when he injured a knee, which interrupted his preparation. A talented performer when he gets the ball, but will do himself no harm by getting involved in more of the play. Started with Norwood in 1995 and had played 35 games when Port listed him. Older brother Brett plays for Adelaide after a stint with Collingwood.

### ADAM KINGSLEY
Was with Essendon and Port went with him on the recommendation of assistant coach Mark Williams, who coached Kingsley in the Essendon reserves. Played the first 12 games with Port — and played very well in some of them — on the backline and on the ball, but then suffered a shoulder injury, which required surgery. Was missing from round 13 on but looked to be in good shape approaching 1998. Port secured him as the last of its four choices at the 1996 National Draft. Played 72 Essendon reserves games (1994-96) and two with the Western Bulldogs (1993).

### BRENDON LADE
Ruckman and forward who was prominent last year, finishing equal eighth in the club voting. Was also an AFL Norwich Rising Star nominee and received one vote at the final judging — an accolade as only 10 of the 22 nominees made it on to the final board. The scene looks set for a top career for this big man, who first played in the seniors at South Adelaide in 1994. Equal ninth in 1997 club voting after going through the season without a miss.
**Player honors:** AFL Norwich Rising Star nominee 1997.

### BOWEN LOCKWOOD
Port's second selection (behind the since-departed John Rombotis) at the 1996 National Draft and had a tougher 1998 pre-season than in 1997. Spent considerable time in the gymnasium after the 1997 season and this year he should be able to stand the strain for longer periods. Port realises he has talent and it is a matter of conditioning him for the rigors of ruck play. Much hope is held for him as a forward/follower and he should improve on his 13 games last year, the best of them early. Won an AFL Norwich Rising Star nomination and should be an acquisition when he matures. Is a Victorian and previously played with the Geelong Falcons.
**Player honors:** AFL Norwich Rising Star nominee 1997.

### BRAYDEN LYLE
Busy middle-sized campaigner who is back in home territory with Port Adelaide after two seasons at the West Coast Eagles where he achieved moderate success with 26 games. Previously played 25 games with Port Adelaide Magpies and when Port started assembling an AFL side, he was an obvious target and was handed the vice-captaincy. Had the honor of leading the side in its first AFL game against Collingwood when skipper Gavin Wanganeen was out serving suspension arising from a practice match. Lyle also is in the record books as being the first Port player to win three Brownlow Medal votes in a game — in round two against Essendon. Overall, did not let down the recruiting men. Was equal fifth in the club voting in 1997 and in State of Origin football, he won the Fos Williams Medal for being SA's best against Victoria.
**Player honors:** Fos Williams Medal 1997.
**Previous AFL club:** West Coast Eagles (1995-96: 26 games, 5 goals).

### SCOTT MATTHEWS
One of a batch of youngsters waiting in the wings to play his first AFL game. From the Woodville-West Tor-

rens club and in 1996 represented SA in the AFL National Under-18 Championships and won All-Australian selection. Plays the half-forward line and wing with effect and his game is enhanced by his marking. Was only a rookie in the SANFL when Port claimed him.

## DARREN MEAD

One of the success stories at Port in 1997 and winner of the inaugural club best and fairest award — by one vote over Matthew Primus. A leading centre half-back who played his first AFL season like a veteran after previously playing 118 games with Port Adelaide Magpies, where he played in premiership sides. Was 26 when he made his debut with Port Power, but he made light of those years and the first best and fairest winner on the new honor board is there for keeps. Surprisingly, the umpires gave him only three Brownlow Medal votes — in the game that had all South Australia stirred up when Port beat Adelaide in their first clash in round four. One of SA's best in the State of Origin game against Victoria in 1997. As far back as 1987, Essendon selected him in the National Draft as its 10th pick (107th overall) and the Brisbane Bears nabbed him as their fifth choice (36th overall) at the 1993 Pre-Season Draft. However, he stayed with Port Adelaide and didn't make his debut in the AFL until 1997 with Port Power.
**Player honor:** best and fairest 1997.

## DANNY MORTON

One of only three players with AFL experience taken at the 1997 National Draft. He was Port's third pick and the 41st overall. Played 30 games with Fitzroy (1993-96) and after that club's merge with the Brisbane Bears, played with North Adelaide, his first club. Did well enough in the roving department to earn another chance in the AFL. Turns 25 in July and is an interesting selection. A handful of the Fitzroy players not included on the Brisbane Lions list have done well, such as Brett Chandler and Martin Pike at North Melbourne, so Morton will be eager to follow suit. Will be 25 in July, was busy in the Port practice match sessions and realises this year is make or break for him.
**Previous AFL club:** Fitzroy (1993-96: 30 games, 17 goals).

## CHRIS NAISH

Has arrived at Port this year with vast experience gained over eight seasons and 143 games at Richmond. A smart goalsneak who should give a good account of himself in his new colors and because he has already played eight seasons in the AFL will be expected to take an on-field leadership role. Exchanged for John Rombotis which, on paper, looks a good deal for the Power. Naish played 12 games for the Tigers in his final year at Punt Road and looked to be a classic case of a player needing to recharge his batteries in different surroundings. He is still only 26, has kicked 212 goals and should be an asset helping set up full-forward Scott Cummings or swooping on what he misses. Naish, from country Wangaratta in north-east Victoria, realises this is his big chance to re-ignite his career.
**Previous AFL club:** Richmond (1990-97: 143 games, 212 goals).

## STEPHEN PAXMAN

Was consistently good at full-back and finished equal third in club best and fairest voting. One of the Fitzroy 'leftovers' — with 102 games experience — after the merger between Fitzroy and the Brisbane Bears. Switched to Port, quickly put his experience to work on the backline and did not miss a game. Has been in senior AFL football since 1991 and, with Gavin Wanganeen, was the only player at the club last year with more than 100 League games.
**Player honors:** equal 3rd Port Adelaide best and fairest 1997.
**Previous AFL club:** Fitzroy (1991-96: 102 games, 18 goals).

## DARRYL POOLE

Fierce competitor, is tough, quick with his hands and backs up for the second effort. Turns 26 at start of the season and, if free in movement, will quickly add to his 10 games of last season. In 1997, he suffered a groin injury which has proved to be a nagging complaint. He still hadn't thrown it off when the 1998 practice matches started. Last year, he also earned the displeasure of the Tribunal and received a two-match suspension. Port Power could well do with Poole and his spirited aggression playing in front of full-forward Scott Cummings.

## MATTHEW PRIMUS

Decided when Fitzroy was merging and Port Adelaide was starting that he wanted to be in SA, not with the Brisbane Lions in Queensland. The former Fitzroy ruckman set his sights on being a key component in the big man division with Port and accomplished his mission with flying colors. Finished runner-up in the club best and fairest award, beaten by one vote by Darren Mead. In '96, he was narrowly beaten in Fitzroy's top award. Tremendous responsibility rests with Primus and if he can continue to emerge as a ruckman on the way to stardom, Port Power will prosper. Played a handful of reserves games with Geelong in 1992 and '93 and then 39 games for Norwood before being drafted by Fitzroy.
**Player honors:** AFL Norwich Rising Star nominee 1996; 2nd Fitzroy best and fairest 1996; 2nd Port Adelaide best and fairest 1997.
**Previous AFL club:** Fitzroy (1996: 20 games, 5 goals).

## NATHAN STEINBERNER

One of the fittest players going around and after a very brief taste of the AFL — one game late in the season — should be seen to advantage this year on the wing when over a broken arm suffered in a pre-season practice game against Melbourne. Polled well in Magarey Medal voting in 1997 playing with Central District and looked ready to spring out of the 1998 blocks until his arm mishap. The mere fact that Port threw him into the senior side late in '97 showed he was being groomed for 1998.

## NICK STEVENS

All-Australian at under-16 level and is well suited to half-back and ruck-roving. Played with the Preston Knights and has a very clean delivery. Was marked down as one of the pick of the draft crop in the lead-up to selection day and Port selected him at No. 2

(25th overall). Represented Victoria Metro at the 1997 National Under-18 Championships, kicking four goals against SA. Is a brother of North Melbourne player Danny Stevens.

### WARREN TREDREA

Made his AFL debut in round two last year, was dropped and not sighted again — in part due to a broken arm. Before that, played in Port's only pre-season Ansett Australia Cup match. Became a forgotten player with Port Power and must quickly make up ground. Has good height and can play in the key forward posts. Represented SA at the national under-17s championships in 1995 and reached All-Australian status (as did current teammates Tom Carr and Paul Evans), then in 1996 played in the Port Adelaide Magpies premiership side. Had played only nine Magpies matches before being brought into the AFL.

### GAVIN WANGANEEN

The skipper and inspiration, whether gathering the ball in defence, weaving his way through the forward line or directing traffic around the midfield. Is not tall, but can leap with the best of them and has uncanny ball skills. The 1993 Brownlow Medallist did everything he could to lift the side into the 1998 finals and proved to be an excellent captain after it seemed he wasn't breaking his neck to get the job. Was equal fifth in club voting and his 11 Brownlow Medal votes was the best in the club. He was ineligible in the medal count as he was suspended twice during the season. In fact, he did not lead the club in its first match as he was serving a week's suspension following a striking misdemeanor in a practice match at Port Lincoln, SA, against Richmond. Reported for striking in a pre-season practice match against North Melbourne in 1998 and suspended for three games.

**Player honors:** Brownlow Medal 1993; Essendon premiership side 1993; Essendon night series premiership side 1993, 1994; All-Australian 1992, 1993, 1995; 2nd Essendon best and fairest 1992; 3rd Essendon best and fairest 1993, 1994; Michael Tuck Medal 1993.

**Previous AFL club:** Essendon (1991-96: 127 games, 64 goals).

### MICHAEL WILSON

Voted the 1997 rookie of the year by the AFL Norwich Rising Star judges. When the final votes were cast in a field of 22 nominations, Wilson polled 27 to clinch victory. This gave the brilliant left-footer a clear-cut win as joint runners-up Blake Caracella (Essendon) and Stefan Carey (Sydney) polled 15 votes. Wilson was also equal third in the club voting and gave every impression he will be an on-baller and general utility of the future. It was a dream start to his AFL career and even more pleasing because he is a home-grown Port Adelaide Magpies player, having played in two premiership sides in his 39 games before joining Port Power. Season 1998 will be a testing year now that Wilson's name has made the headlines, but he appears equal to the task of handling the pressure that will accompany his rise in status.

**Player honors:** AFL Norwich Rising Star 1997; equal 3rd Port Adelaide best and fairest 1997.

## ROOKIE LIST

### BARNABY FRENCH

Tall ruckman who played in the Adelaide Hills League with Ironbank in 1997. Expected to play most of his football with Sturt in 1998. Worked well with Port in the 1998 pre-season. Twice represented Australia at the world rowing championships.

### ANTONY SHEEHAN

Has come up through the junior ranks with the Port Adelaide Magpies and is a strongly built midfielder. Has had limited senior experience with the Magpies. Has also played for SA in under-18 representative football for the past two years and will be 19 in October.

# PORT ADELAIDE

| Name (# = rookie) | No. | Born | Height | Weight | Recruited from |
|---|---|---|---|---|---|
| Scott Bassett | 41 | 9/10/78 | 190 | 85 | NORWOOD (SA) |
| Matthew Bode | 25 | 29/6/79 | 178 | 71 | GLENELG (SA) |
| Shane Bond | 5 | 9/7/75 | 182 | 76 | PORT ADELAIDE (SA)/WEST COAST |
| Shayne Breuer | 3 | 10/9/72 | 184 | 84 | KALKEE/WOODVILLE-WEST TORRENS (SA)/GEELONG |
| David Brown | 21 | 29/9/69 | 172 | 75 | PORT ADELAIDE (SA)/ADELAIDE |
| Peter Burgoyne | 26 | 29/1/78 | 180 | 81 | PORT ADELAIDE (SA) |
| Tom Carr | 32 | 16/6/78 | 183 | 80 | PORT ADELAIDE (SA) |
| Brett Chalmers | 7 | 23/4/73 | 195 | 97 | PORT ADELAIDE (SA)/ADELAIDE |
| Chad Cornes | 35 | 12/11/79 | 191 | 82 | GLENELG (SA) |
| Jarrod Cotton | 44 | 3/4/76 | 185 | 80 | CENTRAL DISTRICT (SA) |
| Scott Cummings | 6 | 18/1/74 | 196 | 98 | SWAN DISTRICTS (WA)/ESSENDON |
| Stephen Daniels | 28 | 3/9/76 | 192 | 83 | NORWOOD (SA) |
| Stuart Dew | 37 | 18/8/79 | 183 | 85 | CENTRAL DISTRICT (SA) |
| Donald Dickie | 19 | 8/5/72 | 187 | 82 | NORWOOD (SA) |
| Nathan Eagleton | 11 | 10/11/78 | 176 | 75 | WEST ADELAIDE (SA) |
| Paul Evans | 40 | 29/12/78 | 187 | 89 | PORT ADELAIDE (SA) |
| Nigel Fiegert | 17 | 28/1/76 | 191 | 88 | PORT ADELAIDE (SA) |
| Fabian Francis | 8 | 24/10/73 | 175 | 80 | SOUTHERN DISTRICTS (NT)/MELB/BRIS/PORT AD (SA) |
| Josh Francou | 10 | 7/8/74 | 185 | 80 | NORTH ADELAIDE (SA) |
| Darren Fraser | 24 | 25/2/73 | 180 | 82 | MONTMORENCY/COLL RES/ESS RES |
| Paul Geister | 31 | 29/1/72 | 191 | 95 | CENTRAL DISTRICT (SA)/NORTH MELB |
| Tom Harley | 27 | 18/7/78 | 191 | 84 | NORWOOD (SA) |
| Mark Harwood | 18 | 8/4/78 | 188 | 84 | TRIABUNNA/TAS U18 |
| Brent Heaver | 12 | 15/6/71 | 173 | 77 | EPPING/MELBOURNE/CARLTON |
| Adam Heuskes | 39 | 20/3/76 | 190 | 86 | NORWOOD (SA)/SYDNEY |
| Roger James | 38 | 21/10/75 | 177 | 84 | NORWOOD (SA) |
| Adam Kingsley | 29 | 20/8/75 | 181 | 80 | DONCASTER HEIGHTS/EASTERN U18/ESS RES |
| Brendon Lade | 20 | 10/7/76 | 198 | 98 | SOUTH ADELAIDE (SA) |
| Bowen Lockwood | 22 | 1/7/78 | 194 | 87 | GEELONG COLLEGE/GEELONG U18 |
| Brayden Lyle | 9 | 6/3/73 | 179 | 85 | PORT ADELAIDE (SA)/WEST COAST |
| Scott Mathews | 23 | 4/11/78 | 188 | 78 | WOODVILLE-WEST TORRENS (SA) |
| Darren Mead | 33 | 29/3/71 | 190 | 90 | PORT ADELAIDE (SA) |
| Danny Morton | 13 | 1/7/73 | 175 | 68 | NTH ADELAIDE (SA)/FITZROY/NTH ADELAIDE (SA) |
| Chris Naish | 4 | 27/9/71 | 172 | 71 | WANGARATTA/RICHMOND |
| Stephen Paxman | 14 | 4/12/70 | 188 | 93 | EAST DONCASTER/FITZROY |
| Darryl Poole | 30 | 1/4/72 | 195 | 98 | PORT ADELAIDE (SA) |
| Matthew Primus | 2 | 12/1/75 | 200 | 106 | GROVEDALE/GEEL RES/NORWOOD (SA)/FITZROY |
| Nathan Steinberner | 34 | 11/3/77 | 176 | 86 | CENTRAL DISTRICT (SA) |
| Nick Stevens | 36 | 3/1/80 | 180 | 82 | ST MARYS (VMFL)/PRESTON U18 |
| Warren Tredrea | 16 | 24/12/78 | 192 | 80 | PORT ADELAIDE (SA) |
| Gavin Wanganeen | 1 | 16/6/73 | 181 | 80 | PORT ADELAIDE (SA)/ESSENDON |
| Michael Wilson | 15 | 21/11/76 | 181 | 85 | PORT ADELAIDE (SA) |
| Barnaby French # | 42 | 25/11/75 | 197 | 98 | STURT (SA) |
| Antony Sheehan # | 43 | 13/10/79 | 181 | 83 | PORT ADELAIDE (SANFL) |
| **Total/(Average)**  *On 26/2/98 | | **(22.5 yrs)*** | **(185)** | **(84)** | |

# PLAYERS 1998

| Debut | HOME & AWAY | | 1997 | | FINALS | | GRAND FINALS | | | NIGHT SERIES | | STATE OF ORIGIN | |
|---|---|---|---|---|---|---|---|---|---|---|---|---|---|
| | Gms | Gls | Gms | Gls | Gms | Gls | Gms | Gls | Won | Gms | Gls | Gms | Gls |
| | 0 | 0 | 0 | 0 | | | | | | 0 | 0 | 0 | 0 |
| | 0 | 0 | 0 | 0 | | | | | | 0 | 0 | 0 | 0 |
| 1994 | 56 | 27 | 22 | 7 | 4 | 3 | 1 | 2 | 1 | 4 | 4 | 1 | 0 |
| 1994 | 92 | 94 | 21 | 17 | 8 | 10 | 2 | 1 | 0 | 4 | 1 | 0 | 0 |
| 1991 | 87 | 72 | 18 | 17 | 3 | 2 | | | | 12 | 17 | 0 | 0 |
| 1997 | 15 | 12 | 15 | 12 | | | | | | 1 | 0 | 0 | 0 |
| 1997 | 2 | 0 | 2 | 0 | | | | | | 0 | 0 | 0 | 0 |
| 1994 | 50 | 8 | 8 | 2 | | | | | | 10 | 2 | 0 | 0 |
| | 0 | 0 | 0 | 0 | | | | | | 0 | 0 | 0 | 0 |
| 1997 | 4 | 4 | 4 | 4 | | | | | | 0 | 0 | 0 | 0 |
| 1994 | 61 | 153 | 21 | 70 | | | | | | 2 | 7 | 2 | 13 |
| 1997 | 10 | 1 | 10 | 1 | | | | | | 0 | 0 | 0 | 0 |
| 1997 | 1 | 0 | 1 | 0 | | | | | | 0 | 0 | 0 | 0 |
| 1997 | 22 | 6 | 22 | 6 | | | | | | 1 | 0 | 0 | 0 |
| 1997 | 18 | 10 | 18 | 10 | | | | | | 0 | 0 | 0 | 0 |
| | 0 | 0 | 0 | 0 | | | | | | 0 | 0 | 0 | 0 |
| 1997 | 4 | 3 | 4 | 3 | | | | | | 1 | 0 | 0 | 0 |
| 1991 | 38 | 22 | 15 | 5 | | | | | | 6 | 5 | 1 | 1 |
| 1997 | 22 | 16 | 22 | 16 | | | | | | 1 | 0 | 0 | 0 |
| | 0 | 0 | 0 | 0 | | | | | | 0 | 0 | 0 | 0 |
| 1995 | 4 | 0 | 1 | 0 | 2 | 0 | | | | 2 | 0 | 0 | 0 |
| | 0 | 0 | 0 | 0 | | | | | | 0 | 0 | 0 | 0 |
| | 0 | 0 | 0 | 0 | | | | | | 0 | 0 | 0 | 0 |
| 1990 | 84 | 127 | 8 | 9 | 4 | 7 | 1 | 1 | 0 | 5 | 4 | 0 | 0 |
| 1994 | 71 | 6 | 22 | 0 | 3 | 1 | 1 | 0 | 0 | 5 | 3 | 1 | 0 |
| 1997 | 17 | 5 | 17 | 5 | | | | | | 0 | 0 | 0 | 0 |
| 1997 | 12 | 2 | 12 | 2 | | | | | | 1 | 0 | 0 | 0 |
| 1997 | 22 | 14 | 22 | 14 | | | | | | 0 | 0 | 1 | 0 |
| 1997 | 13 | 8 | 13 | 8 | | | | | | 0 | 0 | 0 | 0 |
| 1995 | 46 | 10 | 20 | 5 | 2 | 0 | | | | 3 | 1 | 1 | 0 |
| | 0 | 0 | 0 | 0 | | | | | | 0 | 0 | 0 | 0 |
| 1997 | 22 | 1 | 22 | 1 | | | | | | 1 | 0 | 1 | 0 |
| 1993 | 30 | 17 | 0 | 0 | | | | | | 3 | 2 | 0 | 0 |
| 1990 | 143 | 212 | 12 | 12 | 3 | 6 | | | | 11 | 13 | 1 | 0 |
| 1991 | 124 | 18 | 22 | 0 | | | | | | 9 | 2 | 0 | 0 |
| 1997 | 10 | 8 | 10 | 8 | | | | | | 1 | 0 | 0 | 0 |
| 1996 | 42 | 11 | 22 | 6 | | | | | | 2 | 0 | 0 | 0 |
| 1997 | 1 | 0 | 1 | 0 | | | | | | 0 | 0 | 0 | 0 |
| | 0 | 0 | 0 | 0 | | | | | | 0 | 0 | 0 | 0 |
| 1997 | 1 | 0 | 1 | 0 | | | | | | 1 | 0 | 0 | 0 |
| 1991 | 147 | 78 | 20 | 14 | 10 | 4 | 1 | 1 | 1 | 8 | 6 | 7 | 1 |
| 1997 | 22 | 13 | 22 | 13 | | | | | | 1 | 0 | 1 | 1 |
| | 0 | 0 | 0 | 0 | | | | | | 0 | 0 | | |
| | 0 | 0 | 0 | 0 | | | | | | 0 | 0 | | |
| | (31) | (23) | 450 | 267 | 39 | 33 | 6 | 5 | 2 | 95 | 67 | 17 | 16 |

## Tigers at a glance

**ADDRESS:** Punt Rd., Richmond 3121

**POSTAL ADDRESS:** PO Box 48, Richmond 3121

**TELEPHONE:** (03) 9429 5333

**FACSIMILE:** (03) 9429 4686

**WEB SITE:** www.richmondfc.com.au

**EMAIL:** nicole@richmondfc.com.au

**PRESIDENT:** Leon Daphne

**GENERAL MANAGER:** Jim Malone

**FOOTBALL MANAGER:** Garry O'Sullivan

**RECRUITING MANAGER:** Greg Beck

**MARKETING MANAGER:** Hague Shier

**COACHING STAFF:** Jeff Gieschen (senior), Ross Lyon (assistant), Brendan McCartney (development/reserves)

**SELECTION COMMITTEE:** Tony Jewell (chairman), Jeff Gieschen, Ross Lyon, Brendan McCartney, Garry O'Sullivan, Matthew Knights

**CLUB DOCTOR:** Chris Bradshaw

**CLUB PHYSIOTHERAPIST:** Paul Coburn

**JOINED AFL:** 1908

**HOME GROUND:** MCG, Yarra Park, Jolimont, 3002

**GROUND DIMENSIONS:** 161m by 140m.

**TRAINING VENUE:** Punt Road Oval

**OFFICIAL COLORS:** Guernsey: Black with yellow sash across. Socks: Black and yellow hoops. Shorts: Black

**PREMIERSHIPS:** 1920-21, 1932, 1934, 1943, 1967, 1969, 1973-74, 1980

**BROWNLOW MEDALLISTS:** S. Judkins (1930 tied), J. W. Morris (1948), G. R. Wright (1952, 1954), I. Stewart (1971)

**RECORD HOME ATTENDANCE** (MCG): 91,936 — April 25, 1977 v Collingwood

# RICHMOND

# Richardson the key in any Tiger revival

Richmond finished with a spurt in 1997, which was enough to keep stand-in coach Jeff Gieschen in the job and, at the same time, give the club's restless supporters hope for '98.

The Tiger fans have had to be patient and when the situation hit near rock bottom during 1997 and Gieschen took over from Robert Walls, it seemed that only a miracle could resurrect a group of hapless, unconfident players.

I don't know about a miracle, but Gieschen brought with him a sharp turnaround in fortunes. He engineered four wins in his five games and while the Tigers finished 13th, they were less than one game out of the finals.

The late form of '97 must be maintained, which means that players such as Matthew Richardson, Brendon Gale, Wayne Campbell, Darren Gaspar, Duncan Kellaway, Matthew Knights and Paul Broderick must perform at an upper level.

Richardson is the key. He is always under enormous pressure to take control on the forward line and in 1997, he started like a house on fire. However, a broken arm interrupted his flow and he didn't finish with the same flourish.

He finished seventh in club voting, compared with his second in 1996, when he kicked 91 goals.

The Tigers used 37 players in 1997. Skipper Knights missed the first half of the season with knee problems; up-and-coming Joel Bowden was sidelined for nine matches with a broken collarbone; Matthew Rogers, Robert Powell and David Bourke had injury worries and there was the drug drama that saw Justin Charles suspended late in the year for 16 matches.

Richmond has lost Chris Naish (to Port Adelaide), Chris Bond (to Fremantle) and Jamie Tape (to Collingwood) and in pre-national draft trading, it picked up Aaron James (Collingwood), Ashley Blurton (West Coast) and John Rombotis (Port Adelaide). Bond will be most missed. James, who played his first game with Collingwood in 1994, has promised much but, for a variety of reasons, has delivered little.

In the draft, the Tigers secured one of the prize recruits in Brad Ottens — a big youngsters with spotless credentials.

Richmond has played in only one finals series — in 1995 — since it reached its last Grand Final in 1982 and its last premiership was in 1980. This is the club that was all-powerful in the 1960s and '70s and at the start of the '80s.

Over to you, Jeff Gieschen. **— Greg Hobbs**

**SUPERMAN:** Essendon's Matthew Lloyd kicked 63 goals in 1997, being, at times, a lone hand on the Bomber forward line. His performances earned him State of Origin representation, a third placing in the club best and fairest and he polled the most Brownlow votes of any individual at Windy Hill. To think he has played only 36 games, and only turns 20 in April.

**UPS:** Richmond's Matthew Richardson is an enigma. His highs are very, very high…

**DOWNS:** But his low moments can leave him with more than just egg on his face.

**A BIT OF G AND D:**
David Neitz (right) showed plenty of courage in 1997, returning late in the season from a broken jaw. He is an important part of the masterplan for success demanded by Melbourne's president Joseph Gutnick. Former Essendon star Neale Daniher (top) was appointed coach in September 1997 after an extensive selection process that saw him replace caretaker coach Greg Hutchison, who has remained with the club as assistant coach.

**SEE THE FUTURE:** Nick Holland's knee injury towards the end of the 1997 season cost the Hawks dearly. He missed the first five games in their eight-game losing streak.

**CATCH OF THE DAY:** Paul Salmon has been at Hawthorn two years and has won two best and fairests.

**COLEMAN MEDALLIST:** Tony Modra won his first Coleman Medal in 1997, kicking 84 goals for the season (including finals). He was the first player since 1990 to win the medal without kicking at least 100 goals. He also won All-Australian selection at full-forward, but missed Adelaide's flag because of a knee injury which required a reconstruction. He is not expected back until after July.

**NUGGET:** Michael Wilson's ethic of hard-working, tough-running football impressed many football watchers and culminated in him winning the 1997 Norwich Rising Star award.

**BROWNLOW:** Robert Harvey was a fantastic winner of the Brownlow Medal in 1997 in a historic result. His effort through the year was topped only by his performance for the Saints in the 1997 Grand Final. It was one man trying to do the work of 10. In the Brownlow Medal, Harvey polled 26 votes to win. The Western Bulldogs' Chris Grant polled 27 votes but was ineligible because of suspension. It was the first time the player who polled the most votes in the Brownlow did not win.

**NORM SMITH MEDAL:** Andrew McLeod became the third player from the Northern Territory to win the Norm Smith Medal since it was first awarded in 1979. Richmond's Maurice Rioli, in 1982, and Essendon's Michael Long, in 1993, were the previous winners from the north.

**THE ALLIES:** The Allies defeated Western Australia in a thriller, earning the right to take on the might of Victoria this year.

**VICTORIA, EUPHORIA:** The Victorians were the pride of their state when they defeated South Australia by eight points at Football Park on a Saturday night in June.

**OLD, NEW AND NEWEST:** Collingwood and Carlton have been at it for years. West Coast and Fremantle have their local derby, but a Fremantle victory is needed to confirm the depth of the rivalry. Adelaide and Port Adelaide began last year, and their first game was a clash to rival those that have taken generations to build. Their tally now stands at one-all.

**WE HAVE POWER:** Port Adelaide's Brent Heaver played only eight games for Port Adelaide last year, but he was there enjoying the early moments of the club's first AFL game, when Collingwood thumped the new arrivals by 79 points. By year's end, Port Adelaide had won 10 games and drawn one in an amazingly successful first season.

**WE HAVE LIFT-OFF:** Geelong's 1997 best and fairest winner, Liam Pickering, played an excellent finals series for the Cats, despite their two losses. Unfortunately the results in those games made September more of a low time than a high one for Pickering.

**BREAKTHROUGH:** Fremantle's Dale Kickett finally played his 100th game of AFL football, with his fifth club, in 1997, and he won the club's best and fairest after being runner-up the previous two seasons.

**TEST OF ANDREW:** No one was expecting the 1997 that Andrew Wills produced. He was both attacking and aggressive. He polled 15 votes in the Brownlow Medal, finishing in the top 10.

**A VINTAGE FOOTBALLER:** Stephen Silvagni was named at full-back in the All-Australian side for the fourth year in succession, despite the fact that many of his most memorable performances came when playing full-forward in the second half of the season. He re-signed with Carlton at the end of last season in a deal that should see the champion finish his career with the Blues.

**HEADS UP:** There was much controversy surrounding Anthony Koutoufides during 1997, but none of it appeared to be caused by him. Unfortunately his form suffered, but he still showed flashes of brilliance during what was a long season for the Blues star.

**A MILLION BUCKS:** Collingwood star Nathan Buckley had another fantastic season for Collingwood where he was named in Collingwood's Team of the Century, the only current player to make the elite group. Playing in his 100th game against Fremantle, he picked up more than 40 possessions.

**SPEEDSTER:** Collingwood had to rely on too few players in 1997. Paul Williams was one of the few who performed well consistently.

**REAL VALUE:** Gavin Wanganeen's captaincy of Port Adelaide in its first year was a case of leadership by example. His tenacity, skill and courage was inspiring and his team responded with some fantastic results.

## THE YEAR AHEAD

| Rd | Date | Opponent | Venue | Home/ Away | Time (local) |
|----|------|----------|-------|------------|--------------|
| 1 | March 29 | Essendon | MCG | H | 2.10pm |
| 2 | April 4 | Geelong | KP | A | 2.10pm |
| 3 | April 11 | Hawthorn | MCG | H | 3.30pm |
| 4 | April 17 (N) | Collingwood | MCG | A | 7.40pm |
| 5 | April 24 (N) | West Coast | MCG | H | 7.40pm |
| 6 | May 1 (N) | Brisbane Lions | G | A | 7.40pm |
| 7 | May 10 | Melbourne | MCG | H | 2.10pm |
| 8 | May 17 | Adelaide | FP | A | 12.10pm |
| 9 | May 23 | Western Bulldogs | P | A | 2.10pm |
| 10 | May 30 | Port Adelaide | MCG | H | 2.10pm |
| 11 | June 8 | St Kilda | P | A | 2.10pm |
| 12 | June 14 | North Melbourne | MCG | H | 2.10pm |
| 13 | June 21 | Sydney | SCG | A | 12.40pm |
| 14 | June 27 | Fremantle | MCG | H | 2.10pm |
| 15 | July 3 (N) | Carlton | MCG | H | 7.40pm |
| 16 | July 19 | Essendon | MCG | A | 2.10pm |
| 17 | July 26 | Geelong | MCG | H | 2.10pm |
| 18 | August 2 | Hawthorn | P | A | 2.10pm |
| 19 | August 9 | Collingwood | MCG | H | 2.10pm |
| 20 | August 16 | West Coast | S | A | 1.20pm |
| 21 | August 22 | Brisbane Lions | MCG | H | 2.10pm |
| 22 | August 30 | Melbourne | MCG | A | 2.10pm |

## 1997 AT A GLANCE

**W:** R1: Richmond 15.14 (104) v Geelong 13.17 (95) (MCG)
**W:** R2: Richmond 19.14 (128) v Adelaide 15.10 (100) (MCG)
**L:** R3: Western Bulldogs 16.9 (105) v Richmond 12.14 (86) (MCG)
**W:** R4: Richmond 10.11 (71) v Fremantle 10.7 (67) (OO)
**L:** R5: North Melbourne 21.15 (141) v Richmond 7.4 (46) (MCG)
**L:** R6: Port Adelaide 19.8 (122) v Richmond 8.10 (58) (FP)

**SNAPSHOT**

**Games:** 22
**Wins:** 10  **Losses:** 12
**Ladder Finish:** 13th
**Players Used:** 37

**L:** R7: Richmond 10.16 (76) v Carlton 14.14 (98) (MCG)
**W:** R8: Richmond 18.11 (119) v West Coast 9.13 (67) (MCG)
**L:** R9: St Kilda 22.9 (141) v Richmond 14.10 (94) (P)
**L:** R10: Richmond 9.13 (67) v Melbourne 14.8 (92) (MCG)
**W:** R11: Collingwood 10.11 (71) v Richmond 11.11 (77) (MCG)
**L:** R12: Sydney 26.8 (164) v Richmond 16.14 (110) (SCG)
**L:** R13: Richmond 4.10 (34) v Essendon 19.13 (127) (MCG)
**L:** R14: Brisbane Lions 7.26 (68) v Richmond 7.8 (50) (G)
**W:** R15: Richmond 22.13 (145) v Hawthorn 10.9 (69) (MCG)
**L:** R16: Geelong 16.14 (110) v Richmond 12.6 (78) (KP)
**L:** R17: Adelaide 29.11 (185) v Richmond 7.6 (48) (FP)
**W:** R18: Richmond 17.13 (115) v Western Bulldogs 15.10 (100) (OO)
**L:** R19: Fremantle 12.13 (85) v Richmond 5.12 (42) (W)
**W:** R20: Richmond 14.13 (97) v North Melbourne 14.12 (96) (MCG)
**W:** R21: Richmond 22.14 (146) v Port Adelaide 8.13 (61) (MCG)
**W:** R22: Carlton 13.11 (89) v Richmond 13.13 (91) (OO)

## The Coach

**Jeff Gieschen**

**Born:** 22/9/56

Gieschen had five games as a senior AFL coach in 1997 before Richmond decided he was the man to continue in the job this year.

From those five games after the dismissal of Robert Walls, he notched four wins and the Tigers finished only half a game (and percentage) out of the top eight.

At the end of 1997, he also completed his coaching assignment with the Richmond reserves with a premiership.

Gieschen's association with League football goes back to 1974 when he was recruited from Maffra, in the Gippsland area of Victoria, to play with Footscray (now the Western Bulldogs). He played 24 senior games and 81 in the reserves.

He returned to Maffra as captain and coach from 1979 to '85 and coached Wodonga, in the Ovens and Murray League, from 1986 to '91. This stint included two premierships.

From 1992 to '94, he coached West Perth, which secured a second and third finish, and in 1995-96, he coached Geelong reserves. In 1997, he started off coaching the Richmond reserves, coached the seniors from rounds 19 to 22 and then took the reserves to the title.

It has been a long coaching apprenticeship.

### AT A GLANCE

**COACHING RECORD**

| Richmond | | | | | |
|----------|---|---|---|---|---|
| Season | P | W | L | D | Pos |
| 1997 | 5 | 4 | 1 | — | 13 |

## WIN/LOSS RECORD

| Against | P | W (N) | L (N) | D (N) |
|---|---|---|---|---|
| Adelaide | 11 | 5 (4) | 6 (2) | 0 |
| Brisbane Bears | 17 | 9 (3) | 8 (3) | 0 |
| Brisbane Lions | 1 | 0 | 1 | 0 |
| Carlton | 184 | 76 (1) | 106 (2) | 2 |
| Collingwood | 177 | 74 (2) | 102 | 1 |
| Essendon | 163 | 73 | 86 | 4 (1) |
| Fitzroy | 166 | 94 (1) | 72 (1) | 0 |
| Fremantle | 5 | 3 | 2 (1) | 0 |
| Geelong | 166 | 81 | 82 | 3 |
| Hawthorn | 129 | 74 (1) | 55 | 0 |
| Melbourne | 157 | 87 | 68 (2) | 2 |
| North Melb | 131 | 76 (2) | 54 (6) | 1 |
| Port Adel | 2 | 1 | 1 | 0 |
| St Kilda | 153 | 98 | 53 | 2 |
| Sydney | 163 | 94 (2) | 68 (3) | 1 |
| West Coast | 17 | 5 (1) | 12 (1) | 0 |
| W Bulldogs | 126 | 69 | 56 | 1 |
| University | 14 | 9 | 5 | 0 |
| **TOTALS** | **1782** | **928 (17)** | **837 (21)** | **17 (1)** |

*(N) Premiership matches played at night*

## WINNING RUNS

21 v Hawthorn (1925–1936)
18 v North Melb (1925–1936)
15 v St Kilda (1940–1949)
12 v Fitzroy (1931–1938)
12 v Fitzroy (1962–1969)
11 v Essendon (1914–1921)
11 v Hawthorn (1947–1953)
11 v SM/Sydney (1970–1975)
10 v Geelong (1939–1947)
10 v SM/Sydney (1964–1969)
9 v Melbourne (1965–1970); (1971–1975)
8 v Western Bulldogs (1927–1931)
6 v Carlton (1965–1968)
6 v Collingwood (1920–1922)
5 v Adelaide (1994–1997)
4 v Brisbane Bears (1990–1993)
3 v West Coast (1987–1989)
2 v Fremantle (1995–1996)
1 v Port Adelaide (1997– )

## 1997 BEST AND FAIREST

Four match committee members each award up to 15 votes per home and away game. No player can receive more than four votes per game from each member.

1 Wayne Campbell (112)
2 Duncan Kellaway (91)
3 Darren Gaspar (76)
4 Michael Gale (66)
5 Brendon Gale (60)
6 Nick Daffy (58)
7 Matthew Richardson (57)
8 Joel Bowden (54)
9 Paul Broderick (47)
10 Chris Bond (43)
  Paul Bulluss (43)

## GAMES RECORDS

403 Kevin Bartlett (1965–83)
312 Jack Dyer (1931–49)
300 Francis Bourke (1967–81)
294 Jack Titus (1926–43)
274 Dale Weightman (1978–93)
263 Vic Thorp (1910–25)
263 Percy Bentley (1925–40)
251 Kevin Sheedy (1967–79)
245 Roger Dean (1957–73)
238 Merv Keane (1972–84)

## GOALS RECORDS

970 Jack Titus (1926–43)
778 Kevin Bartlett (1965–83)
607 Michael Roach (1977–89)
548 Dick Harris (1934–44)
443 Jack Dyer (1931–49)
369 Royce Hart (1967–77)
351 Ray Poulter (1946–56)
344 Dale Weightman (1978–93)
306 Jeff Hogg (1986–93)
275 Percy Bentley (1925–40)

## HIGHS AND LOWS

| Against | Highest | Lowest | G. W. Margin | G. L. Margin |
|---|---|---|---|---|
| Adelaide | 19.14.128 (1997) | 4.8.32 (1993) | 46 (1996) | 139 (1993) |
| Brisbane Bears | 22.21.153 (1990) | 5.15.45 (1989) | 82 (1990) | 77 (1995) |
| Brisbane Lions | 7.8.50 (1997) | 7.8.50 (1997) | — | 18 (1997) |
| Carlton | 25.24.174 (1978) | 2.9.21 (1958) | 77 (1978) | 115 (1984) |
| Collingwood | 25.25.175 (1942) | 1.7.13 (1927) | 138 (1942) | 101 (1986) |
| Essendon | 25.22.172 (1982) | 3.11.29 (1911) | 74 (1983) | 125 (1960) |
| Fitzroy | 29.25.199 (1980) | 3.7.25 (1909) | 151 (1996) | 76 (1915) |
| Fremantle | 12.18.90 (1995) | 5.12.42 (1997) | 7 (1995) | 54 (1996) |
| Geelong | 25.23.173 (1944) | 4.5.29 (1910) | 118 (1969) | 134 (1989) |
| Hawthorn | 29.14.188 (1985) | 2.20.32 (1975) | 114 (1967) | 101 (1986) |
| Melbourne | 30.16.196 (1942) | 1.6.12 (1908) | 93 (1980) | 121 (1993) |
| North Melb | 30.19.199 (1931) | 3.8.26 (1960) | 168 (1931) | 141 (1990) |
| Port Adel | 22.14.146 (1997) | 8.10.58 (1997) | 85 (1997) | 64 (1997) |
| St Kilda | 34.18.222 (1980) | 0.8.8 (1961) | 152 (1980) | 89 (1912) |
| Sydney | 26.11.167 (1975) | 3.8.26 (1909) | 107 (1975) | 93 (1909) |
| West Coast | 18.15.123 (1995) | 5.9.39 (1994) | 60 (1995) | 96 (1994) |
| W Bulldogs | 27.18.180 (1980) | 2.11.23 (1958) | 115 (1980) | 78 (1989) |

## THE LEADERSHIP AT RICHMOND

| Year | Pos | Coach | Captain | Best & Fairest | Leading Goalkicker | |
|------|-----|-------|---------|----------------|--------------------|---|
| 1931 | 2 | F. Hughes | M. Hunter | | D. Strang | 68 |
| 1932 | 1 | F. Hughes | P. Bentley | J. Dyer | D. Strang | 49 |
| 1933 | 2 | B. Schmidt | P. Bentley | M. Hunter | D. Strang | 51 |
| 1934 | 1 | P. Bentley | P. Bentley | R. Martin | J. Titus | 80 |
| 1935 | 3 | P. Bentley | P. Bentley | R. Martin | J. Titus | 83 |
| 1936 | 6 | P. Bentley | P. Bentley | M. Bolger | J. Titus | 83 |
| 1937 | 4 | P. Bentley | P. Bentley | J. Dyer | J. Titus/R. Harris | 65 |
| 1938 | 6 | P. Bentley | P. Bentley | J. Dyer | J. Titus | 72 |
| 1939 | 4 | P. Bentley | P. Bentley | J. Dyer | J. Titus | 48 |
| 1940 | 2 | P. Bentley | P. Bentley | J. Dyer | J. Titus | 100 |
| 1941 | 4 | J. Dyer | J. Dyer | J. Titus | J. Titus | 87 |
| 1942 | 2 | J. Dyer | J. Dyer | L. Merrett | J. Titus | 67 |
| 1943 | 1 | J. Dyer | J. Dyer | R. Durham | R. Harris | 63 |
| 1944 | 2 | J. Dyer | J. Dyer | L. Merrett | R. Harris | 66 |
| 1945 | 7 | J. Dyer | J. Dyer | W. Morris | F. Burge | 55 |
| 1946 | 5 | J. Dyer | J. Dyer | J. Dyer | A. Mooney | 49 |
| 1947 | 4 | J. Dyer | J. Dyer | W. Wilson | J. Dyer | 46 |
| 1948 | 5 | J. Dyer | J. Dyer | W. Morris | J. Dyer | 64 |
| 1949 | 6 | J. Dyer | J. Dyer | G. Spring | R. Poulter | 51 |
| 1950 | 6 | J. Dyer | W. Morris | W. Morris | R. Poulter | 56 |
| 1951 | 6 | J. Dyer | W. Morris | D. Rowe/R. Wright | J. O'Rourke | 58 |
| 1952 | 9 | J. Dyer | D. Rowe | R. Wright | J. O'Rourke | 43 |
| 1953 | 10 | A. Pannam | D. Rowe | H. Rowe | R. Branton | 22 |
| 1954 | 5 | A. Pannam | D. Rowe | R. Wright | R. Branton | 33 |
| 1955 | 6 | A. Pannam | D. Rowe | D. Rowe | R. Poulter | 49 |
| 1956 | 10 | M. Oppy | D. Rowe | L. Sharp | R. Dummett | 32 |
| 1957 | 7 | A. McDonald | D. Rowe | R. Wright | R. Dummett | 41 |
| 1958 | 10 | A. McDonald | R. Wright | D. Cuzens | E. Langridge | 28 |
| 1959 | 11 | A. McDonald | R. Wright | D. Cuzens | R. Dummett | 45 |
| 1960 | 12 | A. McDonald | R. Branton | R. Branton | G. Wilkinson | 21 |
| 1961 | 10 | D. Rowe | R. Branton | R. Branton | E. Langridge | 29 |
| 1962 | 8 | D. Rowe | R. Branton | R. Branton | E. Langridge | 42 |
| 1963 | 10 | D. Rowe | N. Crowe | N. Crowe | I. Hayden | 25 |
| 1964 | 9 | L. Smith | N. Crowe | N. Crowe | R. Dean | 23 |
| 1965 | 5 | L. Smith/J. Titus | N. Crowe | W. Barrot | M. Erwin | 32 |
| 1966 | 5 | T. Hafey | N. Crowe | N. Crowe | P. Guinane | 50 |
| 1967 | 1 | T. Hafey | F. Swift | K. Bartlett | R. Hart | 55 |
| 1968 | 5 | T. Hafey | R. Dean | K. Bartlett | P. Guinane | 41 |
| 1969 | 1 | T. Hafey | R. Dean | R. Hart | R. Hunt | 55 |
| 1970 | 6 | T. Hafey | R. Dean | F. Bourke | E. Moore | 39 |
| 1971 | 3 | T. Hafey | R. Dean | I. Stewart | R. Hart | 59 |
| 1972 | 2 | T. Hafey | R. Hart | R. Hart | R. McLean, N. Balme | 55 |
| 1973 | 1 | T. Hafey | R. Hart | K. Bartlett | N. Balme | 34 |
| 1974 | 1 | T. Hafey | R. Hart | K. Bartlett | K. Bartlett | 47 |
| 1975 | 3 | T. Hafey | R. Hart | K. Morris | K. Bartlett | 42 |
| 1976 | 7 | T. Hafey | F. Bourke | K. Sheedy | R. Lamb | 38 |
| 1977 | 4 | B. Richardson | F. Bourke | K. Bartlett | K. Bartlett | 55 |
| 1978 | 7 | B. Richardson | K. Sheedy | G. Raines | B. Monteath | 55 |
| 1979 | 8 | T. Jewell | K. Bartlett | B. Rowlings | M. Roach | 90 |
| 1980 | 1 | T. Jewell | B. Monteath | G. Raines | M. Roach | 112 |
| 1981 | 7 | T. Jewell | B. Wood | G. Raines | M. Roach | 86 |
| 1982 | 2 | F. Bourke | D. Cloke | M. Rioli | B. Taylor | 71 |
| 1983 | 10 | F. Bourke | B. Rowlings | M. Rioli | K. Bartlett, M. Roach | 37 |
| 1984 | 8 | M. Patterson | B. Rowlings | M. Lee | B. Taylor | 61 |
| 1985 | 8 | P. Sproule | M. Lee | T. Poole | M. Roach | 80 |
| 1986 | 10 | T. Jewell | M. Lee | D. Weightman | M. Roach | 62 |
| 1987 | 14 | T. Jewell | M. Lee | D. Weightman | M. Roach | 43 |
| 1988 | 10 | K. Bartlett | D. Weightman | M. Pickering | J. Hogg | 57 |
| 1989 | 14 | K. Bartlett | D. Weightman | T. Free | J. Hogg | 34 |
| 1990 | 14 | K. Bartlett | D. Weightman | M. Knights | S. Ryan | 28 |
| 1991 | 13 | K. Bartlett | D. Weightman | C. Lambert | J. Hogg | 68 |
| 1992 | 13 | A. Jeans | D. Weightman | M. Knights | J. Hogg | 45 |
| 1993 | 14 | J. Northey | J. Hogg | T. Free | J. Hogg | 57 |
| 1994 | 9 | J. Northey | T. Free | C. Bond | M. Richardson | 56 |
| 1995 | 4 | J. Northey | T. Free | W. Campbell | N. Daffy | 45 |
| 1996 | 9 | R. Walls | T. Free | P. Broderick | M. Richardson | 91 |
| 1997 | 13 | R. Walls | M. Knights | W. Campbell | M. Richardson | 47 |
| | | J. Gieschen | | | | |

# PLAYER PROFILES

## ASHLEY BLURTON

Quick and creative utility with good hands who found the competition at the West Coast Eagles too hot to win regular senior selection. Ten games in the last three seasons (three last year) was his sum total with the Eagles. But he is a better player than those statistics suggest and a new club may bring with it more games. Richmond exchanged him for a third round national draft pick (Todd Holmes, Subiaco). At West Perth, Blurton was coached by current Richmond coach Jeff Gieschen.

**Previous AFL club:** West Coast Eagles (1995-97: 10 games, 2 goals).

## DAVID BOURKE

Dislocated a shoulder in round two last year against Adelaide. Missed four games, but was never really free of the injury and near the end of the season was forced out again and underwent surgery. Showed heaps of promise in his first season. Has ability, is tall and marks brilliantly, but needs a solid and consistent season. Son of former Tiger champion Francis Bourke.

**Player honors:** AFL Norwich Rising Star nominee 1995.

## JOEL BOWDEN

Unquestionably one of the best young talents in the AFL but stricken with bad luck. The latest blow was a fractured shoulder suffered in the Ansett Australia Cup game against Adelaide in February. He was expected to be out for at least six weeks. This is a similar injury to the one that sidelined him for nine matches. Won an AFL Norwich Rising Star nomination in 1997 and in the final voting, polled 10 votes for fourth place. Left-footer who is well suited to the wing/half-forward, but his shoulder is the problem. Son of Richmond 1969 premiership player Michael Bowden.

**Player honors:** AFL Norwich Rising Star nominee 1997.

## NATHAN BOWER

Had a knee operation in 1996, regained his position in round eight last year and did well against the West Coast Eagles. But there was more trouble in store and he tore an Achilles tendon, broke down badly in the finals and required surgery. Is a pacy wingman/flanker whose association with the Tigers goes back to the reserves in 1990 and his first senior game in 1991. Has shown patches of brilliance in a patient 65 games.

## PAUL BRODERICK

One of the side's play-makers, but slipped in the ratings in 1997 when he finished ninth in the club voting. He won in 1996, was third in '95 and second in '94 and at Fitzroy, he was third in '93 and '91. Plays the midfield with aplomb and has considerable use of the ball. Had 242 kicks in 1997 and his 229 handballs was fifth best in AFL in home and away series.

**Player honors:** best and fairest 1996; 2nd best and fairest 1994; 3rd best and fairest 1995; 3rd Fitzroy best and fairest 1991, 1993.

**Previous AFL club:** Fitzroy (1988-93: 93 games, 80 goals).

## PAUL BULLUSS

After an injury-riddled 1996, he came back with 17 games last year, despite having to contend with a shoulder injury early. Is generally stationed at centre half-back — full-back at times — and in 1997, came in equal 10th in the club best and fairest award. Has yet to figure among the award leaders since his debut in 1993, but plays it hard and with spirit in defence with the likes of Darren Gaspar and Duncan Kellaway. Restricted early in 1998 with a groin injury.

## WAYNE CAMPBELL

Best and fairest winner in 1997 — for the second time. Has an uncanny capacity to repeatedly win the ball and in the home and away series in 1997 was the competition's eighth best kick-winner with 350. His disposals grew to 555 with his 205 handballs to make him fifth overall. Plays well from half-back to the goals and in 1997 had much of the captaincy duties when Matthew Knights missed several games with injury. Had a shoulder injury repaired after the 1997 season.

**Player honors:** best and fairest 1995, 1997; 2nd best and fairest 1992, 1993; All-Australian 1995.

## MARK CHAFFEY

Medium-build player who does well on the flanks and played 12 senior games in 1997 — a bonus, as the club had not counted on him making his debut last year. A couple of years ago this former Caulfield Grammar player spent time in the US on a collegiate baseball scholarship, but has put football first and will be keen to establish himself in '98. Lost his senior place near the end of last season and was a member of the Richmond reserves' premiership side.

## JUSTIN CHARLES

Will not be available until late in the season following a 16-match suspension by the Tribunal last September when he pleaded guilty to taking anabolic steroids. It was the first case of its kind in AFL history. Charles said he had taken the drug in an attempt to overcome injuries. It was a tremendous blow to player and club as big Charles, when right, is a key element at Punt Road, in the ruck or at centre half-forward. Plans to play again.

**Player honors:** 3rd best and fairest 1996.

**Previous AFL club:** Footscray (1989-93: 36 games, 24 goals).

## NICK DAFFY

Seemed he might have been looking for another club after 1997, but player and club reached agreement, he signed a two-year contract and will play his seventh season in 1998. The former North Gambier player is noted for his ability to kick goals from the half-forward line. He picked up 26 in '97, which followed 28 in '96. Also had some time in defence/midfield in '97 when Jeff Gieschen took over as coach. Sixth in beat and fairest voting — his best finish since joining the club. Has had attention to a knee injury.

**Player honors:** leading goalkicker 1995.

## DANIEL DONATI

Old Xaverian who made his debut when the 1997 season was in full swing, but lost his place after one game. Totted up 23 reserves matches and played in the premiership side. Selected at the 1996 National Draft because of his prowess in the amateurs and last year kicked 29 goals with the reserves. Is best suited to half-forward/wing/half-back.

### BRETT EVANS
Suffered a depressed fracture of the cheekbone in an Ansett Australia Cup game against Adelaide in February and was sidelined for several weeks. A member of VFL club Springvale's 1995 and '96 premiership sides and Richmond's No. 1 selection (sixth overall) at the 1997 pre-season draft. Has played just two senior games so far and, as he turns 26 in May, this season will either make or break him at Punt Road. Played 17 reserves games last year, including the premiership.

### ROSS FUNCKE
Born at Minyip, in the Victorian Wimmera, and played at Minyip and with the Ballarat Rebels before getting his first senior game in 1996. Leading junior who represented Victoria Country in the national under-17 titles in 1994 and drafted by the Tigers the same year. Now facing his third season and aided by 49 reserves games, must be ready to make his run. Promising half-back and maybe his 11 games in 1997 will be the springboard for a more prod-uctive input in 1998. Shows signs of becoming a regular.

### BRENDON GALE
The side's best hope in the ruck and even more emphasis on his play following teammate Justin Charles' long Tribunal suspension. Has bordered on top-line material for several years at centre half-forward, but the ruck may prove to be his best spot — something akin to Hawthorn's Paul Salmon. Big, strapping player who is strong in the air. If he can play a dominant role in 1998, the Tigers will be well on the way. Fifth in club voting in '97.

### MICHAEL GALE
At 31 is starting his 13th season in the AFL and if he performs to his 1997 standard, will be right up there again. Finished fourth in Richmond's voting last year — his best finish since joining the club in 1994. Plenty of fibre about him on the wing and at half-back. Was with Fitzroy from 1986 to '93 when he moved to Punt Road to be with younger brother Brendon. Needs just 20 for 200 senior games.
**Previous AFL club:** Fitzroy (1986-93: 105 games, 29 goals).

### DARREN GASPAR
Not an easy task fulfilling the expectations of a No. 1 National Draft selection, but after a moderate start to his career is now starting to bloom. Played two seasons with Sydney, but wanted a change and landed at Richmond after a Melbourne bid failed. Has found his niche in the Richmond defence and last season — his fourth and best — finished third in best and fairest voting. Worried by a hamstring injury in 1998 pre-season, but gives every impression of going to greater heights. Topped club Brownlow Medal voting in 1997 with 12.
**Player honors:** 3rd best and fairest 1997.

**Previous AFL club:** Sydney (1994-95: 21 games, 1 goal).

### PAUL GREENHAM
Port Melbourne rover with plenty of toe who does not turn 20 until after the '98 season. Polled fourth best in the VFL Rookie of the Year voting in 1997, winning a senior place midway through the year. Was reputedly the fastest player over the first 20 metres in the VFL. Richmond's third pick (69th overall) at the 1997 National Draft.

### BEN HARRISON
Had his most productive year in 1997, taking giant strides with his 16 games and handy 16 goals. Came from Devonport in Tasmania and started off with Carlton, but could manage only two games with the Blues and was exchanged for Tiger Justin Murphy before the '96 season. He finished 1997 with his best-ever run, playing in all games from round 11 on. Must maintain the pressure.
**Previous AFL club:** Carlton (1995: 2 games, 0 goals).

### BEN HOLLAND
Has been given a chance on the forward line. Turns 21 in May and must start making a bigger impression. Hit a couple of form lapses in 1997, but had 16 senior games and could be ready to show his best. Drafted by Fitzroy, but Richmond won him by exchanging draft selections. A brother of Hawthorn's strong-marking centre half-forward, Nick, but Ben, a tall utility, hasn't had the same impact.

### AARON JAMES
Hasn't made much of his career so far and Collingwood lost patience with him. Has ability but must settle down as a disciplined player now that he has his second chance. Still only 21, so the ball is in his court to quickly build on his 23 games which have mounted slowly since his debut in 1994. A knee reconstruction ruined his 1996 season and he came back last year to play five matches. Centre half-back material.
**Previous AFL club:** Collingwood (1994-95, 1997: 23 games, 6 goals).

### ANDREW KELLAWAY
On Richmond's supplementary list in 1996-97 and a brother of senior Tigers' defender Duncan Kellaway. Earned his promotion with several impressive 1997 performances in defender/tagging roles and, at 22, must make quick headway if he is to succeed. Has played 33 games with Richmond's reserves, was second in reserves' best and fairest voting in 1997 (to Justin Plapp) and was one of the stars of the 1997 premiership side.

### DUNCAN KELLAWAY
One of the club's most honest and consistent players — a defender who is seldom beaten, but rarely in the limelight. Does a job every week with a minimum of fuss and does it well. Second in Richmond's club voting in 1997 — his best finish. Starts 1998 on 99 games and with just one goal to his name, kicked in round 21, 1997. Is one of only two players to have won two AFL Norwich Rising Star nominations.
**Player honors:** 2nd best and fairest 1997; 3rd best

and fairest 1994; AFL Norwich Rising Star nominee 1993, 1994.

## MATTHEW KNIGHTS

Appointed captain in 1997, but knee surgery kept him out of the senior side until round 12. He tore a lateral ligament in a collision with North Melbourne's Glen Archer in an Ansett Australia Cup match in March 1997. In 1996, he was also sidelined for a long period with a broken ankle that needed reconstructive surgery. The utility/on-baller has plenty of competitive spirit and ball-winning skills and will be hoping for a full season so he can re-assert his influence.

**Player honors:** best and fairest 1990, 1992; 2nd best and fairest 1995; 3rd best and fairest 1993; captain 1997–.

## MATTHEW MANFIELD

Needed a big season in 1997, but persistent hamstring injuries hampered him badly and he played only two senior games (plus 11 in the reserves). It has been a battle to win games and he has managed just seven in three seasons, including five with Fitzroy (1995-96). Must make headway this year or this former Woodville-West Torrens wing/half-forward will be up against it to hold his place. In 1994, he played Teal Cup for SA with Tiger teammate Ben Holland.

**Previous AFL club:** Fitzroy (1995-96: 5 games, 0 goals).

## STEVEN McKEE

From Myrtleford, in Victoria's north-east, McKee had his first full season in the reserves in 1997. Not 20 until June, but a ruckman with promise and must start putting up his hand. Won Myrtleford's best and fairest award in the Ovens and Murray League. With big man Justin Charles unavailable for much of this year, chances of senior inclusion have been boosted.

## MARK MERENDA

Fifth in the club best and fairest voting in 1996, but did not have the same impact in 1997. There were reasons: he carried a hernia and torn groin muscle for much of the time and had surgery at the end of the season. Fremantle made unsuccessful moves to win his services after last season. Has talent as a wing/half-forward and will be anxious to get back on the right track. Season 1997 also saw him serve a two-match suspension so it wasn't a memorable year.

## BEN MOORE

Had his longest sequence of games — five — in the latter part of 1997 when recalled at the same time Jeff Gieschen replaced Robert Walls as coach. Gieschen obviously believes Moore, a wing/half-forward with pace, has something to offer. He had 16 games in the reserves, including the grand final win, taking his tally in that grade to 32. In the final analysis, the club decided he would be better value in the future than Chris Naish, who has gone to Port Adelaide.

## TRENT NICHOLS

Goes back a long way at Richmond — to his senior debut in 1988. He then left for the West Coast Eagles, joined North Melbourne and landed back at Punt Road last year. On his return, he played 12 of the first 13 games, was dropped, did not reappear in the seniors, had 12 reserves matches and was one of the best in the grand final win. Will be 29 early this season, is a rover/forward and while his best football is probably behind him, his experience will be an asset in helping the younger Tigers.

**Player honors:** Gardiner Medal 1996; North Melbourne night series premiership side 1995; 2nd Richmond best and fairest 1990.

**Previous AFL clubs:** Richmond (1988-91: 56 games, 46 goals); West Coast Eagles (1992: 4 games, 3 goals); North Melbourne (1994-96: 33 games, 39 goals).

## BRAD OTTENS

Ottens and Travis Johnstone were all the rage before the 1997 National Draft. Melbourne had selection No. 1 and took Johnstone, which allowed the Tigers to snap up Ottens — an All-Australian at under-16 and under-18 — with the second selection. A tall young player with a big leap. Should make quick headway if his junior form is a guide. The son of former SA leading ruckman Dean Ottens.

## JUSTIN PLAPP

Upgraded last year from Richmond's 1997 rookie list and best and fairest in the reserves in '97. Kicked two goals and played strongly in the 1997 reserves premiership side and has worked hard for his promotion. Kicked 99 goals with the Burnie Dockers (Tasmania) before joining Richmond and last year was the equal leading goalkicker in the AFL reserves (50 goals). Is quick and comfortable on the forward line and very capable further up the ground around the midfield.

## ROBERT POWELL

Arrived at Richmond in 1996 via North Heidelberg, the Preston Knights and Collingwood reserves, where he played 12 games but couldn't crack it for a senior berth. Tied for Richmond's best first year player award in 1996 and last year missed several games with a severe back injury suffered in the round two match against Adelaide. Handy goalkicker who won an AFL Norwich Rising Star nomination late in the season when best on ground in the one-point win over North Melbourne.

**Player honors:** AFL Norwich Rising Star nominee 1997.

## ASHLEY PRESCOTT

Utility player who has produced his best football at half-back. Took him a good while to get into the groove, hence his 73 reserves games. Started to pull everything together in 1995, continued to progress in 1996, but suffered a setback with a broken collarbone. Last year played a further 19 matches. Often thrown tagging, defensive roles, but can play his own attacking game.

## LIONEL PROCTOR

Richmond's second pick at the 1997 National Draft (53rd overall) and a likely wingman. Quick, has the skills required in top company and disposal is impressive. Did not do his draft chances any harm with a strong showing in the 1997 finals with the Preston Knights.

## JASON RAMSEY

Has stepped up from the rookie list and is having his second shot in the seniors. Was previously on Fitzroy's list and played two senior games in 1996 after coming from the Port Adelaide Magpies. The Tigers picked him up after the Fitzroy-Brisbane Bears merge and last year in the reserves he was a straight-at-the-ball, tough half-back with ample pace. Has had to pick up the pieces, is 23, and Richmond has been impressed with the way he has handled his situation. Member of the 1997 reserves' premiership side.

**Previous AFL club:** Fitzroy (1996: 2 games, 0 goals).

## MATTHEW RICHARDSON

A 1998 Ansett Australia Cup victim with a severely injured arm. It was feared he had broken his left elbow, but an X-ray and bone scan revealed no structural damage. Expected to be out for at least a month. Richardson broke an arm last year and missed three matches. To a large degree, the forward line relies on the influence of this brilliant young athlete, whose marking ranks with the best in the game. Seventh in 1997 club best and fairest voting.

**Player honors:** 2nd best and fairest 1996; All-Australian 1996; AFL Norwich Rising Star nominee 1993; Alex Jesaulenko Medal 1996; leading goalkicker 1994, 1996.

## MATTHEW ROGERS

Robust South Australian who has given solid service over four seasons in a utility role. Had to contend with thigh injuries in 1997, which sidelined him for several games in the first half. Won an AFL Norwich Rising Star nomination in his first season (1994) and his best finish in club voting was fourth in 1996. An injury-free 1998 will see him land close to his 100th game, as he needs another 22.

**Player honors:** AFL Norwich Rising Star nominee 1994.

## JOHN ROMBOTIS

Didn't miss a game in Fitzroy's last season in the competition in 1996, but found it tougher going with Port Adelaide where last season he played nine games. Handy player used mainly in defence by Port. Swapped for Chris Naish, a good player and handy goalsneak over the years. Rombotis is looked on as insurance around the midfield.

**Previous AFL clubs:** Fitzroy (1995-96: 26 games, 16 goals); Port Adelaide (1997: 9 games, 5 goals).

## DAMIEN RYAN

Youngster facing up to his third season. Tied with Robert Powell for the club's best first year player award in 1996, but found it tough going in '97 and was in and out of the senior side. Played in the reserves premiership side. Half-back/full-back, still only young and will be striving to put it together in 1998. Showed promise early on at Richmond and, before that, in junior football.

## PAT STEINFORT

The subject of plenty of discussion among the recruiting scouts before Richmond selected him as its No. 1 (16th overall) pick at the 1996 National Draft. Won the Larke Medal as the top player at the AFL National Under-18 Championships in 1996, won All-Australian selection and was chosen in the first ruck in the VSFL Team of the Year in 1996. Is a developing ruckman/key position player who has always barracked for Richmond and played 24 games in the reserves last year, which included a premiership.

## JASON TORNEY

Has been at Punt Road since 1995 and has put together 31 games, including the last nine matches in 1997. Hails from South Adelaide and was Richmond's second choice at the 1994 National Draft. Has shown up as a likely half-back/back pocket and must take the next step. The opening is there for players of his type now that Jamie Tape and Chris Bond have left. Has done the groundwork, which includes 39 reserves games.

## SCOTT TURNER

Experienced full-back who has had a series of knee operations in the past few seasons. His last senior appearance was in round 14, 1997, when he lost his place, could not get back and finished the year with a groin injury. Still troubled with knee soreness in the lead-up to 1998 season. The pressure is right on him to win back his old position. The one-time Ararat and Melbourne reserves player has given sound service since his debut in 1991, but he will need to pull out something special to regain a regular berth. Will be remembered as the last man to play on Gary Ablett in a reserves match (round one) last year.

# ROOKIE LIST

### CHRIS BOSSONG

From St Kevin's Old Boys in Melbourne. Had an ankle injury in 1997 which sidelined him for a time. A left-foot wing/half-forward/half-back who did the whole 1998 pre-season with Richmond after missing selection in the 1997 National Draft.

### BEN HOLLANDS

Played with North Albury in the Ovens and Murray League in 1997. Turned 20 in January, plays in the midfield and on the ball, and is having his second shot at League football as he was with Sydney (no senior games) in 1996 before being delisted. Represented New South Wales at the 1995 AFL under-17 championships and reached All-Australian status.

### GREG TIVENDALE

Left-foot midfielder from the Gippsland Power club who impressed sufficiently in the Tigers' training build-up to 1998 to warrant selection. Nice kick, has pace and third in Power's best and fairest voting in 1997.

# RICHMOND

| Name (# = rookie) | No. | Born | Height | Weight | Recruited from |
|---|---|---|---|---|---|
| Ashley Blurton | 24 | 5/3/75 | 177 | 84 | WEST PERTH (WA)/WEST COAST |
| David Bourke | 30 | 9/1/76 | 193 | 80 | ASSUMPTION COLLEGE/CENTRAL U18 |
| Joel Bowden | 11 | 21/6/78 | 188 | 86 | WEST ALICE SPRINGS (NT) |
| Nathan Bower | 22 | 8/6/72 | 185 | 80 | MILDURA |
| Paul Broderick | 17 | 3/1/70 | 178 | 82 | CAMPERDOWN/FITZROY |
| Paul Bulluss | 21 | 23/1/70 | 194 | 95 | WOODVILLE-WEST TORRENS (SA) |
| Wayne Campbell | 9 | 23/9/72 | 187 | 87 | GOLDEN SQUARE |
| Mark Chaffey | 6 | 6/5/77 | 176 | 75 | CAULFIELD GRAMMAR |
| Justin Charles | 15 | 28/9/70 | 196 | 100 | NORTH FOOTSCRAYFOOTSCRAY |
| Nick Daffy | 10 | 11/5/73 | 183 | 85 | NORTH GAMBIER (SA) |
| Daniel Donati | 42 | 29/9/77 | 187 | 83 | OLD XAVERIANS |
| Brett Evans | 19 | 26/5/72 | 186 | 87 | SPRINGVALE |
| Ross Funcke | 27 | 16/11/77 | 182 | 84 | MINYIP/BALLARAT U18 |
| Brendon Gale | 25 | 18/7/68 | 198 | 104 | BURNIE HAWKS (TAS) |
| Michael Gale | 1 | 21/12/66 | 188 | 93 | PENGUIN (TAS)/FITZROY |
| Darren Gaspar | 2 | 20/5/76 | 193 | 87 | SOUTH FREMANTLE (WA)/SYDNEY |
| Paul Greenham | 34 | 9/2/77 | 178 | 76 | PORT MELBOURNE |
| Ben Harrison | 20 | 17/1/75 | 191 | 93 | DEVONPORT (TAS)/CARLTON |
| Ben Holland | 16 | 10/5/77 | 196 | 99 | NORTH ADELAIDE (SA) |
| Aaron James | 23 | 31/10/76 | 194 | 95 | MELTON/WESTERN U18/COLLINGWOOD |
| Andrew Kellaway | 39 | 23/11/75 | 190 | 87 | SANDRINGHAM |
| Duncan Kellaway | 3 | 17/2/73 | 185 | 84 | GLEN WAVERLEY ROVERS |
| Matthew Knights | 33 | 5/10/70 | 178 | 75 | MERBEIN |
| Matthew Manfield | 36 | 14/4/77 | 192 | 88 | WOODVILLE-WEST TORRENS (SA)/FITZROY |
| Steven McKee | 38 | 20/6/78 | 198 | 96 | MYRTLEFORD |
| Mark Merenda | 8 | 29/10/75 | 181 | 83 | WEST PERTH (WA) |
| Ben Moore | 28 | 4/7/77 | 180 | 76 | GLENELG (SA) |
| Trent Nichols | 26 | 7/4/69 | 173 | 77 | SANDY BAY (TAS)/RICH/WEST C/NTH MLB |
| Brad Ottens | 5 | 25/1/80 | 199 | 92 | GLENELG (SA) |
| Justin Plapp | 14 | 22/6/77 | 186 | 84 | BURNIE (TAS) |
| Robert Powell | 13 | 19/3/76 | 180 | 76 | NORTH HEIDELBERG/NORTHERN U18/COLL RES |
| Ashley Prescott | 7 | 11/9/72 | 188 | 87 | MT WAVERLEY |
| Lionel Proctor | 40 | 27/11/79 | 179 | 70 | ALPHINGTON/PRESTON U18 |
| Jason Ramsey | 44 | 24/1/75 | 189 | 88 | PORT ADELAIDE (SA)/FITZROY |
| Matthew Richardson | 12 | 19/3/75 | 195 | 102 | DEVONPORT (TAS) |
| Matthew Rogers | 4 | 25/11/73 | 184 | 86 | SOUTH ADELAIDE (SA) |
| John Rombotis | 35 | 13/10/76 | 181 | 82 | CAULFIELD GRAMMAR/CENTRAL U18/FITZ/PT ADEL |
| Damien Ryan | 37 | 3/8/77 | 188 | 84 | HEATHERDALE/EASTERN U18 |
| Pat Steinfort | 18 | 20/2/79 | 197 | 95 | MAZENOD OC/OAKLEIGH U18 |
| Jason Torney | 29 | 16/6/77 | 185 | 82 | SOUTH ADELAIDE (SA) |
| Scott Turner | 41 | 31/5/70 | 198 | 101 | ARARAT/MELBOURNE RESERVES |
| Chris Bossong # | 31 | 12/7/78 | 188 | 80 | ST KEVINS |
| Ben Hollands # | 43 | 12/1/78 | 177 | 75 | NORTH ALBURY (NSW)/SYDNEY RESERVES |
| Greg Tivendale # | 32 | 19/4/79 | 182 | 77 | R.O.C./GIPPSLAND U18 |
| Total/(Average) *On 26/2/98 | | (23.2 yrs)* | (187) | (87) | |

# PLAYERS 1998

| Debut | HOME & AWAY | | 1997 | | FINALS | | GRAND FINALS | | | NIGHT SERIES | | STATE OF ORIGIN | |
|---|---|---|---|---|---|---|---|---|---|---|---|---|---|
| | Gms | Gls | Gms | Gls | Gms | Gls | Gms | Gls | Won | Gms | Gls | Gms | Gls |
| 1995 | 10 | 2 | 3 | 0 | | | | | | 4 | 0 | 0 | 0 |
| 1995 | 47 | 12 | 13 | 9 | 1 | 0 | | | | 0 | 0 | 0 | 0 |
| 1996 | 18 | 25 | 13 | 21 | | | | | | 1 | 1 | 0 | 0 |
| 1991 | 65 | 21 | 3 | 2 | 3 | 1 | | | | 4 | 2 | 0 | 0 |
| 1988 | 184 | 126 | 22 | 7 | 3 | 0 | | | | 16 | 8 | 0 | 0 |
| 1993 | 79 | 19 | 17 | 6 | 2 | 1 | | | | 7 | 0 | 2 | 0 |
| 1991 | 140 | 80 | 21 | 4 | 3 | 0 | | | | 10 | 6 | 1 | 1 |
| 1997 | 12 | 2 | 12 | 2 | | | | | | 0 | 0 | 0 | 0 |
| 1989 | 88 | 61 | 13 | 14 | 5 | 4 | | | | 7 | 6 | 0 | 0 |
| 1992 | 89 | 115 | 22 | 26 | 3 | 5 | | | | 6 | 3 | 1 | 1 |
| 1997 | 1 | 0 | 1 | 0 | | | | | | 0 | 0 | 0 | 0 |
| 1997 | 2 | 0 | 2 | 0 | | | | | | 1 | 0 | 0 | 0 |
| 1996 | 15 | 0 | 11 | 0 | | | | | | 1 | 0 | 0 | 0 |
| 1990 | 163 | 173 | 19 | 12 | 3 | 3 | | | | 9 | 4 | 4 | 5 |
| 1986 | 180 | 47 | 18 | 3 | 3 | 0 | | | | 14 | 3 | 6 | 1 |
| 1994 | 62 | 2 | 21 | 0 | | | | | | 8 | 0 | 1 | 0 |
| | 0 | 0 | 0 | 0 | | | | | | 0 | 0 | 0 | 0 |
| 1995 | 26 | 16 | 16 | 16 | | | | | | 1 | 0 | 0 | 0 |
| 1996 | 27 | 16 | 16 | 13 | | | | | | 2 | 0 | 0 | 0 |
| 1994 | 23 | 6 | 5 | 0 | | | | | | 3 | 1 | 0 | 0 |
| | 0 | 0 | 0 | 0 | | | | | | | | | |
| 1993 | 99 | 1 | 22 | 1 | 3 | 0 | | | | 6 | 0 | 2 | 0 |
| 1988 | 174 | 103 | 11 | 2 | 3 | 4 | | | | 13 | 5 | 5 | 2 |
| 1995 | 7 | 1 | 2 | 1 | | | | | | 1 | 0 | 0 | 0 |
| | 0 | 0 | 0 | 0 | | | | | | 0 | 0 | 0 | 0 |
| 1994 | 60 | 44 | 16 | 18 | 3 | 0 | | | | 4 | 9 | 2 | 1 |
| 1996 | 12 | 7 | 8 | 5 | | | | | | 0 | 0 | 0 | 0 |
| 1988 | 105 | 104 | 12 | 16 | 3 | 0 | | | | 13 | 10 | 4 | 2 |
| | 0 | 0 | 0 | 0 | | | | | | 0 | 0 | 0 | 0 |
| | 0 | 0 | 0 | 0 | | | | | | 0 | 0 | 0 | 0 |
| 1996 | 21 | 33 | 13 | 18 | | | | | | 3 | 2 | 0 | 0 |
| 1993 | 68 | 10 | 19 | 3 | 3 | 0 | | | | 4 | 0 | 0 | 0 |
| | 0 | 0 | 0 | 0 | | | | | | 0 | 0 | 0 | 0 |
| 1996 | 2 | 0 | 2 | 0 | | | | | | 0 | 0 | 0 | 0 |
| 1993 | 83 | 252 | 19 | 47 | | | | | | 6 | 23 | 3 | 6 |
| 1994 | 78 | 68 | 14 | 10 | 3 | 5 | | | | 5 | 2 | 1 | 1 |
| 1995 | 35 | 21 | 9 | 5 | | | | | | 0 | 0 | 0 | 0 |
| 1996 | 20 | 1 | 9 | 0 | | | | | | 2 | 0 | 0 | 0 |
| | 0 | 0 | 0 | 0 | | | | | | 0 | 0 | 0 | 0 |
| 1995 | 31 | 2 | 12 | 0 | | | | | | 4 | 0 | 0 | 0 |
| 1991 | 117 | 32 | 13 | 0 | 3 | 2 | | | | 11 | 5 | 0 | 0 |
| | 0 | 0 | 0 | 0 | | | | | | 0 | 0 | | |
| | 0 | 0 | 0 | 0 | | | | | | 0 | 0 | | |
| | 0 | 0 | 0 | 0 | | | | | | 0 | 0 | | |
| | (52) | (34) | 429 | 261 | 47 | 25 | 0 | 0 | 0 | 166 | 90 | 32 | 20 |

## Saints at a glance

**ADDRESS:** Linton Street, Moorabbin, Vic 3189

**POSTAL ADDRESS:** PO Box 34, Moorabbin, Vic 3189

**TELEPHONE:** (03) 9555 6688

**FACSIMILE:** (03) 9553 2553

**PRESIDENT:** Andrew Plympton

**CHIEF EXECUTIVE OFFICER:** Don Hanly

**FOOTBALL MANAGER:** Phil Anstey

**RECRUITING MANAGER:** John Beveridge

**DEVELOPMENT MANAGER:** Gary Colling

**COACHING STAFF:** Stan Alves (senior), Peter Banfield (assistant coach), Peter Russo (reserves),

**SELECTION COMMITTEE:** Norm Goss (chairman), Stan Alves, Gary Colling, Peter Russo, Peter Banfield, Phil Anstey

**CLUB DOCTORS:** Rohan White, Peter Edwards, Ian Stone

**CLUB PHYSIOTHERAPISTS:** Peter Thomas, Michael Vadiveloo, Daniel Pilbrow

**JOINED AFL:** 1897

**HOME GROUND:** Waverley Park, Wellington Rd., Mulgrave

**GROUND DIMENSIONS:** 200m by 160m (fence to fence). Playing arena: 165m x 142m

**TRAINING VENUE:** Moorabbin Oval, Linton St, Moorabbin

**OFFICIAL COLORS:** Guernsey: Red yoke with black cross, white and red bodice. Crest on left breast. Black and red back. White neckband and armholes. Socks: Black with red and white stripes on top. Shorts: Black with red and white panel. Away guernsey: Red white and black vertical stripes. Crest on left breast. Black back. White neckband and armholes.

**PREMIERSHIP:** 1966

**BROWNLOW MEDALLISTS:** C. Watson (1925), B. Gleeson (1957), N. Roberts (1958), V. Howell (1959 tied), I. Stewart (1965-66), R. Smith (1967), T. Lockett (1987 tied), R. Harvey (1997)

**RECORD HOME ATTENDANCE** (Waverley Park): 54,699 — April 12, 1997 v Collingwood

# ST KILDA
# Saints hungry to go one better

Even on Grand Final day, some St Kilda supporters were pinching themselves. "This can't be real?" they asked as they lapped up the euphoria of the game's biggest day.

Sadly for the Saints, they discovered that even the biggest day of all can be unrelenting and unforgiving. St Kilda was punished in the second half by the Adelaide Crows and the premiership that promised to materialise from nowhere is still another season away.

But to undermine what the Saints achieved up until about half-time of the last Saturday in September would be doing the club a great disservice.

They fought their way back from a ladder finish of 10th in 1996 to be one of the AFL's most consistent and reliable teams in 1997 — after starting the season with one win from five games.

From that point on, St Kilda lost only four more games, including the Grand Final. Stan Alves was named coach of the year, Robert Harvey won the Brownlow Medal and the Players' Association MVP (and a stack of media awards) and Peter Everitt, Nathan Burke and Austinn Jones joined Harvey in the All-Australian team.

While Harvey, Burke and, to a lesser extent, Stewart Loewe, were all grand performers and leaders in 1997, the Saints had more willing and able help. Justin Peckett and Jamie Shanahan both enjoyed outstanding seasons in defence; Jones, Tony Brown, Barry Hall, Matthew Lappin, Max Hudghton and Joel Smith were the young guns and Everitt had a stellar season. Unfortunately, both Shanahan and Smith are gone.

Perhaps the biggest surprise was spearhead Jason Heatley who stepped up from some cameo appearances with the West Coast Eagles to be a dominant forward for the Saints.

Andrew Thompson was another eyebrow-raiser having spent time in the Victorian amateur competition and on supplementary lists with St Kilda and the Bulldogs.

Unfortunately, St Kilda had no luck at the end with Everitt (shoulder), Smith (knee) and Lazar Vidovic (knee) all missing and Nicky Winmar playing in the Grand Final after learning his father had passed away just 24 hours earlier.

But having lost a Grand Final will only make Alves' men hungrier. Given the fact they have tasted so many highs and lows in recent seasons, surely the Saints will have their sights raised to the limit in 1998.

— **Michael Lovett**

## THE YEAR AHEAD

| Rd | Date | Opponent | Venue | Home/ Away | Time (local) |
|----|------|----------|-------|------------|--------------|
| 1 | March 28 | Geelong | P | H | 2.10pm |
| 2 | April 5 | Essendon | MCG | A | 2.10pm |
| 3 | April 12 | Adelaide | P | H | 2.10pm |
| 4 | April 18 | Hawthorn | P | A | 3.30pm |
| 5 | April 26 | Carlton | P | H | 2.10pm |
| 6 | May 3 | West Coast | S | A | 1.20pm |
| 7 | May 9 | Brisbane Lions | P | H | 2.10pm |
| 8 | May 16 | Port Adelaide | P | H | 7.40pm |
| 9 | May 22 (N) | Fremantle | W | A | 6.40pm |
| 10 | May 30 (N) | Sydney | SCG | A | 7.40pm |
| 11 | June 8 | Richmond | P | H | 2.10pm |
| 12 | June 14 | Collingwood | P | A | 2.10pm |
| 13 | June 21 | Melbourne | MCG | A | 2.10pm |
| 14 | June 27 | Western Bulldogs | P | H | 2.10pm |
| 15 | July 4 | North Melbourne | P | H | 2.10pm |
| 16 | July 18 | Geelong | KP | A | 2.10pm |
| 17 | July 26 | Essendon | P | H | 2.10pm |
| 18 | August 1 (N) | Adelaide | FP | A | 8.10pm |
| 19 | August 8 | Hawthorn | P | H | 2.10pm |
| 20 | August 16 | Carlton | MCG | A | 2.10pm |
| 21 | August 22 | West Coast | P | H | 2.10pm |
| 22 | August 29 | Brisbane Lions | G | A | 7.40pm |

## 1997 AT A GLANCE

**L:** R1: St Kilda 10.11 (71) v Hawthorn 11.11 (77) (P)

**L:** R2: Brisbane Lions 23.16 (154) v St Kilda 7.15 (57) (G)

**W:** R3: St Kilda 19.11 (125) v Collingwood 17.16 (118) (P)

**L:** R4: St Kilda 12.9 (81) v Sydney 18.19 (127) (P)

**L:** R5: Fremantle 16.11 (107) v St Kilda 15.11 (101) (S)

**W:** R6: St Kilda 17.19 (121) v Melbourne 4.11 (35) (P)

**W:** R7: St Kilda 20.6 (126) v Port Adelaide 8.13 (61) (P)

**W:** R8: Essendon 14.16 (100) v St Kilda 18.16 (124) (MCG)

**W:** R9: St Kilda 22.9 (141) v Richmond 14.10 (94) (P)

**L:** R10: Geelong 16.11 (107) v St Kilda 11.13 (79) (KP)

### SNAPSHOT

**Games:** 25
**Won:** 17 **Lost:** 8
**Ladder finish:** 1
**Players used:** 34

**W:** R11: West Coast 11.7 (73) v St Kilda 13.11 (89) (S)

**W:** R12: St Kilda 16.20 (116) v Carlton 12.13 (85) (P)

**L:** R13: St Kilda 11.18 (84) v Western Bulldogs 15.11 (101) (P)

**W:** R14: St Kilda 20.13 (133) v North Melbourne 11.13 (79) (P)

**L:** R15: Adelaide 10.16 (76) v St Kilda 9.12 (66) (FP)

**W:** R16: Hawthorn 9.8 (62) v St Kilda 20.21 (141) (P)

**W:** R17: St Kilda 12.20 (92) v Brisbane Lions 5.14 (44) (P)

**W:** R18: Collingwood 12.17 (89) v St Kilda 15.21 (111) (MCG)

**W:** R19: Sydney 17.17 (119) v St Kilda 18.20 (128) (SCG)

**W:** R20: St Kilda 12.5 (77) v Fremantle 9.10 (64) (P)

**W:** R21: Melbourne 8.14 (62) v St Kilda 17.12 (114) (MCG)

**W:** R22: Port Adelaide 12.12 (84) v St Kilda 17.15 (117) (FP)

# The Coach

**Stan Alves**

**Born:** 27/6/46

As a player with Melbourne and North Melbourne, Stan Alves had poise and balance. As a coach, he has also shown balance, often walking along a knife's edge.

Five weeks into the 1997 season, the drums were beating that quite possibly the loser of the St Kilda-Melbourne match could say goodbye to their coach. Melbourne did, a month later.

Alves and St Kilda not only turned their season around, but took all before them. By the season's end, he was 'King Stan' and his elevation to coach-of-the-year status was thoroughly deserved.

No coach had ridden an emotion roller-coaster in football and in private life like Alves and while the Saints could not pull off the big one, their arrival as a football force was due in no small part to Alves.

As his coaching record indicates, Alves had overseen small improvements each year until last year's rush to the top of the charts. The hardest job will be keeping them there, but the club knows it is in good hands.

## AT A GLANCE

**COACHING RECORD**

St Kilda

| Season | P | W | L | D | Pos |
|--------|----|----|----|----|-----|
| 1994 | 22 | 7 | 14 | 1 | 13 |
| 1995 | 22 | 8 | 14 | — | 14 |
| 1996 | 22 | 10 | 12 | — | 10 |
| 1997 | 25 | 17 | 8 | — | 10 |
| **Total** | **91** | **42** | **48** | **1** | |

## WIN/LOSS RECORD

| Against | P | W (N) | L (N) | D (N) |
|---|---|---|---|---|
| Adelaide | 12 | 4 (1) | 7 (3) | 1 |
| Brisbane Bears | 15 | 9 | 6 (1) | 0 |
| Brisbane Lions | 3 | 2 | 1 | 0 |
| Carlton | 186 | 33 | 151 | 2 |
| Collingwood | 189 | 48 (1) | 140 (1) | 1 |
| Essendon | 186 | 56 | 126 (1) | 4 |
| Fitzroy | 183 | 77 | 105 | 1 |
| Fremantle | 4 | 2 | 2 (1) | 0 |
| Geelong | 181 | 71 | 110 | 0 |
| Hawthorn | 130 | 62 (1) | 67 (1) | 1 |
| Melbourne | 181 | 72 (1) | 108 | 1 |
| North Melb | 127 | 65 (2) | 60 (5) | 2 |
| Port Adel | 2 | 2 (2) | 0 | 0 |
| Richmond | 153 | 53 | 98 | 2 |
| Sydney | 182 | 66 | 114 (1) | 2 |
| West Coast | 16 | 5 | 11 (3) | 0 |
| W Bulldogs | 127 | 62 | 63 | 2 |
| University | 14 | 8 | 6 | 0 |
| **TOTALS** | **1891** | **697 (8)** | **1175 (17)** | **19 (0)** |

*(N) Premiership matches played at night*

## WINNING RUNS

13 v Fitzroy (1962–1969)
11 v Hawthorn (1933–1940)
10 v North Melb (1963–1968)
10 v SM/Sydney (1990–1995)
9 v Western Bulldogs (1965–1969)
7 v Richmond (1958–1962)
6 v Geelong (1970–1973)
6 v Melbourne (1967–1970); (1971–1974)
5 v Brisbane Bears (1990–1993)
5 v Carlton (1963–1966)
5 v Essendon (1966–1968)
4 v Collingwood (1962–1963); (1996– )
3 v Adelaide (1991–1992)
2 v West Coast (1989–1990)
2 v Port Adelaide (1997– )
2 v Brisbane Lions (1997– )
1 v Fremantle (1996); (1997– )

## 1997 BEST AND FAIREST

Four match committee members each have 10 votes to allocate for each match. The maximum awarded to any one player in a game is four votes, but members can use their 10 votes in any combination. They are not obligated to use all 10 votes.

1 Robert Harvey (120)
2 Nathan Burke (108)
3 Justin Peckett (84)
4 Peter Everitt (78)
5 Stewart Loewe (75)
6 Austinn Jones (59)
7 Tony Brown (43)
8 Steven Sziller (35)
9 Andrew Thompson (31)
10 Jason Heatley (30)

## GAMES RECORDS

300 Barry Breen (1965–82)
265 Gary Colling (1968–81)
256 Kevin Neale (1965–77)
240 Danny Frawley (1984–95)
237 Stewart Loewe (1986– )
234 Ross Smith (1961–72; 1975)
230 Trevor Barker (1975–89)
227 Nathan Burke (1987– )
226 Jeff Sarau (1973–83)
224 Geoff Cunningham (1977–89)

## GOALS RECORDS

898 Tony Lockett (1983–94)
735 Bill Mohr (1929–41)
474 Stewart Loewe (1986– )
308 Allan Davis (1966–75)
308 Barry Breen (1965–82)
301 Kevin Neale (1965–77)
284 George Young (1973–78)
274 Bill Young (1956–61)
267 Nicky Winmar (1987– )
258 Peter Bennett (1944; 1947–51; 1953–54)

## HIGHS AND LOWS

| Against | Highest | Lowest | G. W. Margin | G. L. Margin |
|---|---|---|---|---|
| Adelaide | 24.18.162 (1991) | 3.8.26 (1995) | 131 (1991) | 93 (1993) |
| Brisbane Bears | 27.12.174 (1991) | 5.15.45 (1994) | 120 (1991) | 53 (1994) |
| Brisbane Lions | 20.15.135 (1997) | 7.15.57 (1997) | 48 (1997) | 97 (1997) |
| Carlton | 23.17.155 (1991) | 1.1.7 (1915) | 56 (1995) | 140 (1985) |
| Collingwood | 22.16.148 (1982) | 1.0.6 (1898) | 62 (1963) | 178 (1979) |
| Essendon | 24.14.158 (1973) | 0.3.3 (1897) | 68 (1975) | 120 (1911) |
| Fitzroy | 23.23.161 (1970) | 1.8.14 (1906) | 110 (1970) | 99 (1900) |
| Fremantle | 15.11.101 (1997) | 9.6.60 (1995) | 23 (1996) | 71 (1995) |
| Geelong | 27.15.177 (1993) | 0.1.1 (1899) | 94 (1971) | 161 (1899) |
| Hawthorn | 24.12.156 (1965) | 3.9.27 (1956) | 109 (1950) | 129 (1983) |
| Melbourne | 31.18.204 (1978) | 1.5.11 (1957) | 86 (1997) | 105 (1948) |
| North Melb | 22.19.151 (1937) | 4.5.29 (1996) | 86 (1969) | 104 (1982) |
| Port Adel | 20.6.126 (1997) | 17.15.117 (1997) | 65 (1997) | — |
| Richmond | 24.21.165 (1972) | 1.10.16 (1910) | 89 (1912) | 152 (1980) |
| Sydney | 24.14.158 (1991) | 0.2.2 (1897) | 75 (1990) | 171 (1919) |
| West Coast | 18.19.127 (1990) | 3.18.36 (1988) | 66 (1992) | 88 (1987) |
| W Bulldogs | 23.19.157 (1981) | 4.5.29 (1953) | 81 (1967) | 107 (1978) |

## THE LEADERSHIP AT ST KILDA

| Year | Pos | Coach | Captain | Best & Fairest | Leading Goalkicker | |
|------|-----|-------|---------|----------------|--------------------|---|
| 1931 | 9 | C. Hardy | H. Matthews | H. Neill | W. Mohr | 57 |
| 1932 | 11 | C. Hardy | S. King | W. Mohr | W. Mohr | 68 |
| 1933 | 9 | C. Deane | C. Deane/C. Hindson | H. Comte/C. Hindson | W. Mohr | 74 |
| 1934 | 7 | C. Watson | C. Watson | J. Davis | W. Mohr | 66 |
| 1935 | 5 | D. Minogue | C. Hindson | J. Davis | W. Mohr | 83 |
| 1936 | 7 | D. Minogue | J. Perkins | W. Mohr | W. Mohr | 101 |
| 1937 | 6 | D. Minogue | W. Mohr | J. Davis | W. Mohr | 58 |
| 1938 | 8 | A. Clarke | A. Clarke | S. Lloyd | W. Mohr | 34 |
| 1939 | 3 | A. Clarke | A. Clarke | R. Fountain | W. Mohr | 47 |
| 1940 | 11 | A. Clarke | S. Lloyd | A. Killigrew | W. Mohr | 25 |
| 1941 | 11 | J. Knight | J. Knight | R. Garvin | R. Flegg | 47 |
| 1942 | 7 | R. Garvin | R. Garvin | K. Walker | F. Kelly | 21 |
| 1943 | 11 | R. Garvin | R. Garvin | K. Walker | J. Connelly | 27 |
| 1944 | 9 | H. Thomas | J. Kelly/C. Vontom | R. Garvin/C. Vontom | S. Loxton | 52 |
| 1945 | 12 | H. Thomas | C. Vontom | H. Bray | L. Hall/S. Snell | 20 |
| 1946 | 11 | A. Hird | A. Hird | K. Rosewarne | S. Loxton | 40 |
| 1947 | 12 | A. Hird | A. Hird | H. Bray | P. Bennett | 37 |
| 1948 | 12 | F. Froude | H. Bray | R. Hancock | P. Bennett | 32 |
| 1949 | 11 | F. Froude | F. Green | J. Ross | J. McDonald | 33 |
| 1950 | 9 | F. Froude | F. Green | B. Phillips | P. Bennett | 59 |
| 1951 | 10 | F. Green | K. Drinan | J. Ross | P. Bennett | 47 |
| 1952 | 12 | C. Williamson | K. Drinan | J. Ross | J. McDonald | 31 |
| 1953 | 9 | C. Williamson | K. Drinan | K. Drinan | P. Bennett | 36 |
| 1954 | 12 | L. Foote | L. Foote | L. Foote | J. Ross | 34 |
| 1955 | 12 | L. Foote | L. Foote | N. Roberts | J. McDonald | 24 |
| 1956 | 11 | A. Killigrew | K. Drinan | K. Drinan | W. Young | 56 |
| 1957 | 9 | A. Killigrew | K. Drinan | B. Gleeson | W. Young | 56 |
| 1958 | 8 | A. Killigrew | N. Roberts | N. Roberts | W. Young | 56 |
| 1959 | 8 | J. Francis | N. Roberts | V. Howell | W. Young | 45 |
| 1960 | 6 | J. Francis | N. Roberts | L. Oswald | W. Young | 37 |
| 1961 | 4 | A. Jeans | N. Roberts | L. Oswald | I. Rowland | 26 |
| 1962 | 6 | A. Jeans | N. Roberts | D. Baldock | D. Baldock | 33 |
| 1963 | 4 | A. Jeans | D. Baldock | D. Baldock | D. Baldock | 36 |
| 1964 | 6 | A. Jeans | D. Baldock | I. Stewart | D. Baldock | 29 |
| 1965 | 2 | A. Jeans | D. Baldock | D. Baldock | D. Baldock | 44 |
| 1966 | 1 | A. Jeans | D. Baldock | I. Stewart | K. Neale | 55 |
| 1967 | 5 | A. Jeans | D. Baldock | R. Smith | K. Neale | 37 |
| 1968 | 4 | A. Jeans | D. Baldock | C. Ditterich | K. Neale | 32 |
| 1969 | 7 | A. Jeans | I. Stewart | R. Murray | K. Neale | 50 |
| 1970 | 3 | A. Jeans | R. Smith | D. Griffiths | B. Breen | 35 |
| 1971 | 2 | A. Jeans | R. Smith | R. Smith | A. Davis | 70 |
| 1972 | 3 | A. Jeans | R. Smith | S. Trott | J. Stephens | 53 |
| 1973 | 4 | A. Jeans | S. Trott | K. Neale | A. Davis | 49 |
| 1974 | 10 | A. Jeans | B. Lawrence | G. Elliott | B. Duperouzel | 28 |
| 1975 | 6 | A. Jeans | B. Lawrence | J. Sarau | G. Young | 53 |
| 1976 | 9 | A. Jeans | C. Ditterich | T. Barker | G. Young | 52 |
| 1977 | 12 | R. Smith | C. Ditterich | J. Sarau | G. Young | 58 |
| 1978 | 6 | M. Patterson | G. Colling | G. Gellie | G. Young | 70 |
| 1979 | 12 | M. Patterson | B. Breen | J. Dunne | G. Sidebottom | 56 |
| 1980 | 11 | M. Patterson | | | | |
| | | A. Jesaulenko | G. Sidebottom | J. Dunne | M. Scott | 48 |
| 1981 | 10 | A. Jesaulenko | B. Duperouzel | T. Barker | C. Gorozidis | 34 |
| 1982 | 11 | A. Jesaulenko | B. Duperouzel | P. Kiel | M. Scott | 45 |
| 1983 | 12 | T. Jewell | T. Barker | M. Crow | M. Jackson | 41 |
| 1984 | 12 | T. Jewell/G. Gellie | T. Barker | G. Burns | T. Lockett | 77 |
| 1985 | 12 | G. Gellie | T. Barker | P. Morwood | T. Lockett | 79 |
| 1986 | 12 | G. Gellie | T. Barker | G. Burns | T. Lockett | 60 |
| 1987 | 10 | D. Baldock | D. Frawley | T. Lockett | T. Lockett | 117 |
| 1988 | 14 | D. Baldock | D. Frawley | D. Frawley | N. Winmar | 43 |
| 1989 | 12 | D. Baldock | D. Frawley | N. Winmar | T. Lockett | 78 |
| 1990 | 9 | K. Sheldon | D. Frawley | S. Loewe | T. Lockett | 65 |
| 1991 | 5 | K. Sheldon | D. Frawley | T. Lockett | T. Lockett | 127 |
| 1992 | 4 | K. Sheldon | D. Frawley | R. Harvey | T. Lockett | 132 |
| 1993 | 12 | K. Sheldon | D. Frawley | N. Burke | T. Lockett | 53 |
| 1994 | 13 | S. Alves | D. Frawley | R. Harvey | T. Lockett | 56 |
| 1995 | 14 | S. Alves | D. Frawley | N. Winmar | S. Loewe | 76 |
| 1996 | 10 | S. Alves | N. Burke/S. Loewe | N. Burke | S. Loewe | 90 |
| 1997 | 2 | S. Alves | N. Burke/S. Loewe | R. Harvey | J. Heatley | 73 |

# PLAYER PROFILES

### KRISTIAN BARDSLEY
Found the going tough in 1997, playing just three senior games and spending most of the season in the reserves. Best suited playing out of the back pocket, but found his opportunities limited last year because of the excellent form of Justin Peckett. At 25, he faces a testing season.
**Player honors:** night series premiership side 1996.
**Previous AFL club:** North Melbourne (1992-93: 5 games, 4 goals).

### LUKE BEVERIDGE
Has been a handy spare parts player, but can't seem to take his reserve grade form into the seniors on a consistent basis. Certainly boosts St Kilda's midfield depth and is a dangerous player around goals, but at 27, probably has other players in front of him. His experience at both levels (96 games in the seniors and 96 in the reserves at the start of 1998) is in his favor.
**Player honors:** night series premiership side 1996.
**Previous AFL clubs:** Melbourne (1989-92: 42 goals, 41 goals), Western Bulldogs (1993-95: 31 games, 29 goals).

### TONY BROWN
Highly regarded young midfielder who played a leading role in St Kilda's youth-led recovery. Covers plenty of territory and loves to get on to his favored left foot. Has the chance to hold down the centre position for many years and looks to have a long career ahead of him. One of many Saints who looked overwhelmed on Grand Final day, but finished seventh in the best and fairest and should go on to become a 200-game player.
**Player honors:** night series premiership side 1996.

### NATHAN BURKE
There can be no doubt about his lofty standing in the AFL after another outstanding season. He made the All-Australian team for the third time, finished second in his club's best and fairest and was equal fifth in the Brownlow Medal behind Harvey. More importantly, he gave the Saints continued drive and leadership out of the centre and only Harvey had more possessions during the season (finals included). Burke was gallant in the beaten Grand Final side and having tasted the big day in September for the first time, will be keen to get back there again. A thorough professional both on and off the field and sets a great example for his younger teammates.
**Player honors:** 3rd (equal) Brownlow Medal 1996; best and fairest 1993, 1996; 2nd best and fairest 1995, 1997; 3rd best and fairest 1994; All-Australian 1993, 1996, 1997; night series premiership side 1996; co-captain since 1996.

### BRAD CAMPBELL
Played four successive games from rounds six to nine last year and showed some promise in the back pocket. From Corowa-Rutherglen, Campbell arrived at St Kilda via Port Melbourne in the VFL and should get more chances to prove himself at the highest level.

### MATTHEW CARR
Tall utility with excellent disposal and rated a chance to play senior football in 1998. Spent one season with Collingwood in 1996 but found it difficult to settle in Melbourne and found his way back to Western Australia last year where he played East Fremantle. His junior career in WA was highly promising and is best suited on a flank or on the wing. Lightly built but has impressed the Saints with his attitude and was given a second chance at League level via the 1998 Pre-Season Draft.

### GLEN COGHLAN
Key position player who virtually split his time between seniors and reserves last year, but was not part of the Saints' finals campaign. Approaching his fourth season at senior level, he needs to make the most of his opportunities, although his strong marking has always had appeal. Could have a greater role to play in defence this year following the departure of Jamie Shanahan.

### BRETT COOK
Former Fitzroy ruckman who found himself in the right place at the right time last season. With Lazar Vidovic going down in the final home and away game and Peter Everitt injured in the qualifying final against the Brisbane Lions, Cook was suddenly thrust into the No. 1 ruck position. Took on one of the best big men in the game in Adelaide's Shaun Rehn on Grand Final day and for three quarters, performed manfully. Has to consolidate his position, but with Vidovic retiring, will get his chances.
**Previous AFL club:** Fitzroy (1994-96: 25 games, 7 goals).

### BRENT COWELL
Young ruck-rover from Gippsland Power who has excellent skills and is very cool under pressure. Represented Victoria Country at under-16 level. A shoulder injury interrupted his progress in 1997, but is rated highly and will improve further.

### SAM CRANAGE
Left-footer who is the son of former Collingwood utility Paul Cranage, who played 48 games with the Magpies. A neat looking half-forward with a smart football brain, Cranage is the product of a very successful junior program.

### JASON CRIPPS
Improved defender who stepped up in 1997, played 23 games and did well in the finals series. Runs hard and straight at the football and his close-checking style made him a regular in a hardened defence. Had a well-publicised incident with Stan Alves in one game, but coach and player later played it down and Cripps finished among the Saints' most consistent players for the season. Unfortunately, had a pre-season setback when he was diagnosed with glandular fever.

### JAYSON DANIELS
One of the club's unsung heroes. A great worker who has enjoyed a successful return to his original club after a three-year stint with Sydney. Experienced utility who missed half the season with a serious shoulder injury, but returned in time for the finals. Unfortu-

nately, had a down day in the Grand Final. Achieved an important milestone when he played his 100th game for the Saints during the season.

**Player honors:** night series premiership side 1996.
**Previous AFL clubs:** St Kilda (1988-92: 74 games, 19 goals), Sydney (1993-95: 58 games, 4 goals).

### JAMIE ELLIOTT

Journeyman utility who has enjoyed little luck in his bid to re-establish his AFL career after a promising start with Fitzroy back in 1991. Spent two unsuccessful years with Richmond in 1994-95 and has struggled with injuries in his two years at St Kilda. Was delisted by the Saints at the end of 1997, but continued to train and the club was convinced his fitness level was up to the required standard and he was re-drafted in the Pre-Season Draft. Popular club man and will certainly improve the Saints' depth.

**Player honors:** night series premiership side 1996.
**Previous AFL clubs:** Fitzroy (1991-93: 40 games, 7 goals), Richmond (1994-95: 9 games, 1 goal).

### TIM ELLIOTT

Young ruckman who has patiently served a lengthy apprenticeship in the reserves. Has played 65 reserves game in the past three seasons, but is yet to crack it for a senior game. Could push himself forward now following the retirement of Lazar Vidovic.

### PETER EVERITT

Took a major step forward in 1997 when, to the delight of St Kilda fans, he fulfilled his enormous potential. Played a crucial role in the Saints' rapid charge up the ladder and capped off a great season winning All-Australian selection and finishing fourth in the best and fairest. His improved ruckwork and strong marking in front of goal — he booted 44 goals for the season — were a big asset. Sorely missed after breaking his collarbone in the qualifying final against the Brisbane Lions and would have made a big difference to the Saints' chances on Grand Final day.

**Player honors:** All-Australian 1997; AFL Norwich Rising Star nominee 1993; night series premiership side 1996.

### LUCAS FLEMING

Spent 1997 in the reserves, but was given a solid grounding and should be ready to take the next step. Came through the highly successful Preston Knights program and will develop into a running player as he gains more strength. Plays his best football on the wing.

### RYAN GRINTER

Another young ruckman serving a lengthy apprenticeship in the reserves. Has played two full seasons in the reserves without appearing at senior level. Has the talent, now needs the opportunity. Chances had been limited, but both he and Tim Elliott can now push themselves forward.

### BARRY HALL

Big, imposing youngster who stamped his authority in several games last year, not the least being the Grand Final in which he booted three goals in the second quarter. Needs to add more consistency to his game because he faded out of the Grand Final almost as quickly as he came into it. Has raw strength and potential and is certainly not frightened to put his body on the line. A hefty suspension in the reserves last year set him back, but he looks a most likely type in attack. Another three-week suspension incurred from a practice match incident at the start of the 1998 season was a blow. With a couple of 'priors' he will have to make sure his aggression is directed at the ball.

### ROBERT HARVEY

With the exception of a premiership medallion, Harvey took home just about every award that counted in 1997, confirming his status as the AFL's No. 1 midfielder. Won the Brownlow Medal in dramatic circumstances, was voted the AFL Players' Association most valuable player, won a host of media awards and was again outstanding for Victoria in the State of Origin game against South Australia. Led the League in possessions (765 for the year) and gathered 36 possessions in the Grand Final, despite taking a heavy knock. Harvey's disposal was crisp and precise and he was one of the major reasons why the Saints made such a big improvement. Still has years of good football ahead of him.

**Player honors:** Brownlow Medal 1997; best and fairest 1992, 1994, 1997; 3rd best and fairest 1990, 1993, 1996; All-Australian 1992, 1994, 1995, 1996, 1997; EJ Whitten Medal 1992, 1993, 1996; AFLPA Award 1997; night series premiership side 1996.

### DANIEL HEALY

Took a major step forward in 1997, playing 15 games in the seniors after making just one appearance in 1996. Best suited on the wing and half-forward flank and proved a handy player, although started several games on the interchange bench. Lost his place in the senior line-up in the final two rounds of the home and away season and was overlooked for the finals.

### JASON HEATLEY

Overcame a slow start to the season to become one of the competition's bright lights in front of goal. Had tried his luck with other AFL clubs and earned a reputation as a top goalkicker in Melbourne's Diamond Valley competition, however it took a move to WA to kick-start his career. Played some great games with Subiaco, but was given only limited opportunities by the West Coast Eagles and jumped at the chance to return to Victoria last year. Played the first two games in the reserves and had a couple in the seniors before being injured. Returned to play a crucial role in St Kilda's push to the finals. Had one bag of nine against North Melbourne and played an outstanding game against the Roos in the preliminary final, booting seven. Finished with 73 goals for the season and should go on to become a leading full-forward.

**Player honors:** leading goalkicker 1997.
**Previous AFL club:** West Coast Eagles (1995-96: 3 games, 8 goals).

### MAX HUDGHTON

Turned in an excellent debut season, playing 17 games in defence, and proved to be a tough stumbling block for opposition forwards. Won a handsome reputation as a quality defender in the QAFL competition and certainly was not over-awed stepping into AFL company in his first year. Did a reasonable job on Nigel Smart in the Grand Final and looks to have a very exciting future.

### AUSTINN JONES
Developed into a top-class wingman in 1997 after earning a reputation as a goalsneak in 1995 and '96. His blistering pace and clever use of the ball saw him win selection in the All-Australian side, joining three other Saints (Nathan Burke, Robert Harvey and Peter Everitt). His dashing runs, particularly on big grounds such as Waverley Park and the MCG, were a highlight. Kicked one of the goals of the season in the Grand Final and is an engaging and extremely popular character with Saints fans.
**Player honors:** All-Australian 1997; AFL Norwich Rising Star nominee 1995; night series premiership side 1996.

### ROD KEOGH
Tough as nails on-baller who won a late season reprieve when he was recalled to the Saints line-up for the final six games, including three finals. Had a great game against the Brisbane Lions in the qualifying final and a Grand Final appearance was a fine reward for a player who has persevered in his bid to make it to the top. Unfortunately, he was one of many St Kilda players who found the big day too much to handle. One of only three players to win the Gardiner Medal twice, taking out the reserves competition best and fairest in 1990 and 1991 when he was with Melbourne.
**Previous AFL club:** Melbourne (1990-92: 22 games, 8 goals).

### BRETT KNOWLES
Played 18 reserves games in 1997, overcoming a slow start because of injury. But the Saints liked what they saw of this youngster towards the end of the season and as he gains more consistency, could prove a handy utility.

### ANDREW LAMB
Young back pocket who has had to overcome a persistent battle with shin splint problems. Played 18 games in the reserves last season and could be ready to make the next step.

### MATTHEW LAPPIN
Slightly built utility who had his best season at senior level in 1997, playing 20 games, including all three finals. Blessed with good skills and pace, he became a vital player as the season wore on and his confidence will be greatly improved. Nerves seemed to get the better of him in the Grand Final, but he will be a better player for the experience.

### STEWART LOEWE
Approaching his 13th season in the AFL, Loewe still possesses the biggest and safest hands of any player in the competition. Took the most marks (192) in 1997 and with the arrival and impact of Jason Heatley, he was able to move further up the ground. Had a quiet Grand Final and will be keen to atone if the Saints get another opportunity. Will turn 30 this year, but still playing top-class football and should be able to press on to 300 games.
**Player honors:** best and fairest 1990; 2nd best and fairest 1991, 1992, 1993, 1996; 3rd best and fairest 1995; All-Australian 1991, 1992; EJ Whitten Medal 1992; leading goalkicker 1995; night series premiership side 1996; co-captain since 1996.

### JOE McLAREN
Played the first two games in the seniors last year, but his form fell away and he did not regain his spot. After a successful rookie season in 1996, when he played 11 senior games and was a member of the Saints' historic Ansett Australia Cup premiership, McLaren would be disappointed with his '97 season.
**Player honors:** night series premiership side 1996.

### GAVIN MITCHELL
Former Fremantle rover who made a big impression in his debut season in 1996, but did not quite kick on in 1997. Played 21 games in '96 and certainly was given closer attention last year when he played 15 games. Has plenty of pace and could prove a handy pick-up if he settles into his new club.
**Previous AFL club:** Fremantle (1996-97: 36 games, 18 goals).

### JUSTIN PECKETT
Fought his way back from an ordinary season in 1996 to be among the Saints' most consistent and reliable players in '97. Was a key player in a tight defensive unit and capped off a fine season finishing third behind champion players Robert Harvey and Nathan Burke in the club's best and fairest. Had a couple of nervous moments in the Grand Final, but was a grand player who appeared in all 25 games for the Saints.
**Player honors:** 2nd best and fairest 1994; 3rd best and fairest 1997; night series premiership side 1996.

### DAVID SIERAKOWSKI
Missed the first five games of the 1997 premiership season because of suspension and was dropped twice later in the year. Lost his place in the seniors for the last three games of the home and away season, but fought back for the finals and was asked to help out in the ruck in the absence of Peter Everitt and Lazar Vidovic. Has played his best football in defence and will be keen to settle in a set position in 1998.
**Player honors:** night series premiership side 1996.

### STEVEN SZILLER
Tough, robust utility who works extremely hard in the midfield, usually in a negating role. Has been a fine acquisition and gives the Saints a hard edge around the middle of the ground. Tried hard in the beaten Grand Final side and is a highly regarded player when it comes to matching up with opposition on-ballers. Eighth in St Kilda's best and fairest.
**Player honors:** night series premiership side 1996.

### ANDREW THOMPSON
One of the most improved players in the competition, Thompson was finally rewarded after several attempts to make it in the AFL. Before last year, he spent time on the supplementary lists at St Kilda (1994), the Western Bulldogs (1995) and was back at St Kilda in 1996. Was drafted as a mature age player and certainly showed plenty of maturity in 1997 playing 23

games. Can play on the ball, is lively around goals and should be a confident player approaching the 1998 season. Completed a fine season by finishing ninth in the best and fairest.

### BEN THOMPSON

Ready-made senior player from South Australia who has had two fine seasons in 1996 and 1997 with Glenelg. Won Glenelg's best and fairest in his first season and last year represented SA against the ACT. Best suited on a half-back flank or back pocket and is a long kick.

### JASON TRAIANIDIS

Elusive goalkicker who endured an indifferent season in 1997, playing just seven senior games. Missed more than a month in the middle part of the season through injury, but came back for the final two home and away games and the qualifying final against the Brisbane Lions. Lost his spot thereafter and will have to work hard to establish himself as a regular senior player.
**Player honors:** night series premiership side 1996.

### DARRYL WAKELIN

After a slow start to the 1997 season when he played the first five games in the reserves, Wakelin fought his way back in round six and did not lose his spot for the rest of the year. Consolidated his place at centre half-back and performed some big tasks — none bigger than his effort on Wayne Carey in the preliminary final.
**Player honors:** night series premiership side 1996.

### SHANE WAKELIN

Did not enjoy a great year in 1997. Played just five games and apart from a four-goal haul against Collingwood in round 18, there were few highlights. Was dropped after round 21 and did not appear during the finals. His versatility gives the Saints some depth, but needs to push his name forward on a more consistent basis.
**Player honors:** AFL Norwich Rising Star nominee 1994.

### BEN WALTON

Young half-forward from South Australia who was most impressive at last year's AFL National Under-18 Championships. Uses the ball well, is a long kick and an excellent team player. Could be capable of playing senior football in 1998.

### NICKY WINMAR

Endured a difficult year off the field in 1997, finding himself dropped twice for disciplinary reasons and then had a personal tragedy when his father died on the eve of the Grand Final. At 32, he is still a grand player and remains a popular figure with supporters and teammates. Probably best suited running off the half-back flank and despite Sydney's best efforts to secure him before the 1997 National Draft, he will almost certainly see out his playing days with the Saints. Last year, he became the first Aborigine to play 200 AFL games.
**Player honors:** 3rd (equal) Brownlow Medal 1989; best and fairest 1989, 1995; 2nd best and fairest 1987, 1988; All-Australian 1991, 1995; Michael Tuck Medal 1996; night series premiership side 1996; leading goalkicker 1988.

### MATTHEW YOUNG

This talented half-back flanker has been a great pick-up for the Saints. He was a steal in the 1996 Pre-Season Draft at pick No. 20 and has given his new club fine service in the past two seasons. A back injury slowed him down towards the end of 1997. He played in the preliminary final but had to be ruled out for the Grand Final. A very disciplined and purposeful player.
**Previous AFL club:** Hawthorn (1994-95: 21 games, 6 goals).

## ROOKIE LIST

### LACHLAN BROWN

Late developing midfielder who was on St Kilda's supplementary list in 1997 and played half a season in the reserves. Originally hails from Castlemaine in central Victoria and played in the under-18s for the Bendigo Pioneers. Had a minor ankle operation before the start of the 1998 season.

# ST KILDA

| Name (# = rookie) | No. | Born | Height | Weight | Recruited from |
|---|---|---|---|---|---|
| Kristian Bardsley | 14 | 13/9/72 | 172 | 77 | SCORESBY/NORTH MELB |
| Luke Beveridge | 27 | 23/8/70 | 175 | 78 | ST PETERS/MELBOURNE/FOOTSCRAY |
| Tony Brown | 2 | 28/5/77 | 176 | 77 | LEOPOLD/GEELONG U18 |
| Nathan Burke | 3 | 6/2/70 | 180 | 85 | PINES |
| Brad Campbell | 41 | 21/12/75 | 181 | 78 | PORT MELBOURNE |
| Matthew Carr | 16 | 29/12/78 | 190 | 89 | EAST FREMANTLE (WA)/COLL RES/EAST FREM (WA) |
| Glen Coghlan | 30 | 29/7/74 | 193 | 89 | KYABRAM |
| Brett Cook | 42 | 19/4/73 | 195 | 90 | BROKEN HILL (NSW)/NORWOOD (SA)/FITZROY |
| Brent Cowell | 44 | 7/2/80 | 176 | 66 | BAIRNSDALE/GIPPSLAND U18 |
| Sam Cranage | 45 | 27/4/79 | 185 | 70 | MONIVAE COLLEGE/NORTH BALLARAT U18 |
| Jason Cripps | 18 | 14/10/76 | 184 | 85 | DE LA SALLE/CENTRAL U18/ST KILDA RESERVES |
| Jayson Daniels | 34 | 19/2/71 | 183 | 86 | PARKMORE/ST KILDA/SYDNEY |
| Jamie Elliott | 28 | 6/2/73 | 185 | 85 | MARYBOROUGH/FITZROY/RICHMOND |
| Tim Elliott | 38 | 12/9/76 | 197 | 86 | LUCKNOW/GIPPSLAND U18 |
| Peter Everitt | 10 | 3/5/74 | 201 | 100 | HASTINGS |
| Lucas Fleming | 40 | 25/2/79 | 181 | 67 | GREENSBOROUGH/NORTHERN U18 |
| Ryan Grinter | 37 | 2/1/78 | 198 | 85 | OCEAN GROVE/GEELONG U18 |
| Barry Hall | 25 | 8/2/77 | 194 | 92 | BROADFORD/MURRAY U18 |
| Robert Harvey | 35 | 21/8/71 | 180 | 85 | SEAFORD |
| Daniel Healy | 6 | 3/5/74 | 188 | 83 | CENTRAL DISTRICT (SA) |
| Jason Heatley | 24 | 21/2/72 | 187 | 92 | SUBIACO (WA)/WEST COAST |
| Max Hudghton | 8 | 2/9/76 | 193 | 91 | WEST BRISBANE (QLD) |
| Austinn Jones | 5 | 28/9/76 | 176 | 75 | BEACONSFIELD/SOUTHERN U18 |
| Rod Keogh | 17 | 25/3/71 | 180 | 83 | CASTLEMAINE/MELBOURNE |
| Brett Knowles | 36 | 13/5/78 | 185 | 77 | YINNAR/GIPPSLAND U18 |
| Andrew Lamb | 39 | 23/12/78 | 190 | 80 | WODONGA RAIDERS/MURRAY U18 |
| Matthew Lappin | 22 | 17/2/76 | 181 | 73 | CHILTERN |
| Stewart Loewe | 23 | 23/5/68 | 196 | 106 | MT ELIZA |
| Joe McLaren | 26 | 11/12/77 | 187 | 80 | KOROIT/GEELONG U18 |
| Gavin Mitchell | 11 | 28/12/72 | 171 | 73 | CLAREMONT (WA)/FREMANTLE |
| Justin Peckett | 1 | 5/10/72 | 175 | 78 | KARINGAL |
| David Sierakowski | 13 | 29/12/74 | 194 | 98 | SUBIACO (WA) |
| Steven Sziller | 19 | 15/12/72 | 180 | 78 | WOODVILLE-WEST TORRENS (SA) |
| Andrew Thompson | 29 | 21/10/72 | 174 | 76 | OLD MELBURNIANS |
| Ben Thompson | 21 | 4/9/73 | 193 | 92 | GLENELG (SA) |
| Jason Traianidis | 32 | 7/11/74 | 189 | 91 | SHEPPARTON UNITED |
| Darryl Wakelin | 15 | 12/8/74 | 194 | 94 | PORT ADELAIDE (SA) |
| Shane Wakelin | 12 | 12/8/74 | 193 | 94 | PORT ADELAIDE (SA) |
| Ben Walton | 33 | 12/11/79 | 188 | 87 | CENTRAL DISTRICT (SA) |
| Nicky Winmar | 7 | 25/9/65 | 183 | 83 | SOUTH FREMANTLE (WA) |
| Matthew Young | 20 | 17/9/72 | 185 | 86 | ST PATRICKS,LAUNCESTON (TAS)/HAWTHORN |
| Lachlan Brown # | 43 | 1/8/76 | 180 | 87 | CASTLEMAINE |
| **Total/(Average)** *On 26/2/98 | | **(23.4 yrs)*** | **(186)** | **(84)** | |

# PLAYERS 1998

| Debut | HOME & AWAY | | 1997 | | FINALS | | GRAND FINALS | | | NIGHT SERIES | | STATE OF ORIGIN | |
|---|---|---|---|---|---|---|---|---|---|---|---|---|---|
| | Gms | Gls | Gms | Gls | Gms | Gls | Gms | Gls | Won | Gms | Gls | Gms | Gls |
| 1992 | 57 | 22 | 3 | 1 | | | | | | 5 | 7 | 0 | 0 |
| 1989 | 96 | 90 | 7 | 4 | 5 | 5 | | | | 12 | 5 | 0 | 0 |
| 1995 | 57 | 34 | 24 | 16 | 3 | 0 | 1 | 0 | | 7 | 4 | 0 | 0 |
| 1987 | 227 | 83 | 25 | 9 | 6 | 2 | 1 | 1 | | 16 | 6 | 9 | 3 |
| 1997 | 4 | 0 | 4 | 0 | | | | | | 0 | 0 | 0 | 0 |
| | 0 | 0 | | | | | | | | 0 | 0 | 0 | 0 |
| 1995 | 29 | 7 | 9 | 0 | | | | | | 6 | 2 | 0 | 0 |
| 1994 | 33 | 7 | 8 | 0 | 2 | 0 | 1 | 0 | | 4 | 0 | 0 | 0 |
| | 0 | 0 | 0 | 0 | | | | | | 0 | 0 | 0 | 0 |
| | 0 | 0 | 0 | 0 | | | | | | 0 | 0 | 0 | 0 |
| 1996 | 34 | 6 | 23 | 3 | 3 | 0 | 1 | 0 | | 6 | 0 | 0 | 0 |
| 1988 | 166 | 29 | 13 | 1 | 5 | 0 | 1 | 0 | | 13 | 4 | 0 | 0 |
| 1991 | 58 | 9 | 0 | 0 | | | | | | 11 | 1 | 0 | 0 |
| | 0 | 0 | 0 | 0 | | | | | | 0 | 0 | 0 | 0 |
| 1993 | 91 | 146 | 23 | 44 | 1 | 2 | | | | 11 | 15 | 1 | 0 |
| | 0 | 0 | 0 | 0 | | | | | | 0 | 0 | 0 | 0 |
| | 0 | 0 | 0 | 0 | | | | | | 0 | 0 | 0 | 0 |
| 1996 | 19 | 16 | 15 | 14 | 3 | 4 | 1 | 3 | | 2 | 3 | 0 | 0 |
| 1988 | 179 | 108 | 25 | 18 | 6 | 4 | 1 | 1 | | 14 | 6 | 8 | 4 |
| 1996 | 16 | 6 | 15 | 5 | | | | | | 0 | 0 | 0 | 0 |
| 1995 | 23 | 81 | 20 | 73 | 3 | 11 | 1 | 3 | | 3 | 2 | 0 | 0 |
| 1997 | 17 | 0 | 17 | 0 | 3 | 0 | 1 | 0 | | 3 | 0 | 0 | 0 |
| 1995 | 66 | 57 | 25 | 22 | 3 | 2 | 1 | 1 | | 10 | 9 | 1 | 1 |
| 1990 | 76 | 28 | 6 | 5 | 3 | 3 | 1 | 0 | | 9 | 0 | 0 | 0 |
| | 0 | 0 | 0 | 0 | | | | | | 0 | 0 | 0 | 0 |
| | 0 | 0 | 0 | 0 | | | | | | 0 | 0 | 0 | 0 |
| 1994 | 39 | 21 | 20 | 20 | 3 | 1 | 1 | 0 | | 1 | 0 | 0 | 0 |
| 1986 | 237 | 474 | 24 | 54 | 6 | 13 | 1 | 2 | | 18 | 55 | 10 | 18 |
| 1996 | 13 | 2 | 2 | 0 | | | | | | 7 | 2 | 0 | 0 |
| 1996 | 36 | 18 | 15 | 7 | | | | | | 3 | 0 | 1 | 1 |
| 1992 | 96 | 4 | 25 | 2 | 3 | 1 | 1 | 1 | | 9 | 0 | 0 | 0 |
| 1994 | 52 | 5 | 15 | 1 | 3 | 1 | 1 | 0 | | 4 | 1 | 0 | 0 |
| 1995 | 56 | 13 | 23 | 4 | 3 | 0 | 1 | 0 | | 10 | 7 | 0 | 0 |
| 1997 | 23 | 13 | 23 | 13 | 3 | 1 | 1 | 0 | | 1 | 0 | 0 | 0 |
| | 0 | 0 | 0 | 0 | | | | | | 0 | 0 | 0 | 0 |
| 1996 | 20 | 15 | 7 | 6 | 1 | 1 | | | | 7 | 7 | 0 | 0 |
| 1995 | 56 | 6 | 20 | 4 | 3 | 2 | 1 | 0 | | 7 | 0 | 1 | 0 |
| 1994 | 50 | 17 | 5 | 6 | | | | | | 1 | 0 | 0 | 0 |
| | 0 | 0 | 0 | 0 | | | | | | 0 | 0 | 0 | 0 |
| 1987 | 207 | 267 | 21 | 27 | 6 | 6 | 1 | 1 | | 17 | 11 | 8 | 11 |
| 1994 | 58 | 12 | 18 | 1 | 2 | 1 | | | | 6 | 2 | 0 | 0 |
| | 0 | 0 | 0 | 0 | | | | | | 0 | 0 | | |
| | (53) | (39) | 480 | 360 | 79 | 60 | 19 | 13 | 0 | 223 | 149 | 39 | 38 |

SYDNEY SWANS

## Swans at a glance

**ADDRESS:** Sydney Football Stadium, Driver Avenue, Moore Park, NSW 2021.
**POSTAL ADDRESS:** PO Box 173, Paddington, NSW 2021
**TELEPHONE:** (02) 9332 3888
**FACSIMILE:** (02) 9339 9100
**MELBOURNE OFFICE:** PO Box 211, Albert Park, VIC 3206
**TELEPHONE:** (03) 9645 0600
**FACSIMILE:** (03) 9645 0611
**WEB SITE:** sydneyswans.com.au
**CHAIRMAN:** Richard Colless
**CHIEF EXECUTIVE:** Kelvin Templeton
**GENERAL MANAGER FOOTBALL:** Colin Seery
**FOOTBALL OPERATIONS MANAGER:** Steve Laussen
**MEDIA AND PUBLIC RELATIONS MANAGER:** Stephen Brassel
**COACHING STAFF:** Rodney Eade (senior); Damian Drum (reserves), George Stone (development)
**SELECTION COMMITTEE:** Rodney Eade, Dennis Carroll, Damian Drum, Craig Holden, George Stone
**CLUB DOCTORS:** Nathan Gibbs, Tom Cross
**CLUB PHYSIOTHERAPISTS:** Paul Hedger, Mat Cameron
**JOINED AFL:** 1897
**RE-LOCATED TO SYDNEY:** 1982 and changed name to Sydney
**HOME GROUND:** SCG
**GROUND DIMENSIONS:** 151m by 138m. Goals run north to south
**OFFICIAL COLORS:** Guernsey: White with red yoke, red back on guernsey, white numbers, red cuffs and collar. Socks: Red. Shorts: Red
**PREMIERSHIPS:** 1909, 1918, 1933
**BROWNLOW MEDALLISTS:** H. Matthews (1940 tied), R. Clegg (1949 tied), F. W. Goldsmith (1955), R. Skilton (1959 tied, 1963, 1968), P. Bedford (1970), G. Teasdale (1977), B. Round (1981 tied), G. Williams (1986 tied), G. Healy (1988), P. Kelly (1995)
**RECORD HOME ATTENDANCE** (SCG): 46,168 — August 30, 1997 v Geelong

# SYDNEY
# Swans have the goods for a flag

Real estate is all about position, position, position and so is a bid for the flag in the final eight. As Sydney discovered, finishing sixth wasn't good enough.

There were two reasons for this placing. Sydney's year began slowly with four wins — including only one from seven away games — in the first 10 rounds.

By round 19, the Swans had fought their way back to third spot, only to lose four of their last five games, as injuries, suspensions and poor form thwarted their challenge.

Tony Lockett kicked only 37 goals in 12 games — 18 of them in a four-game winning streak before he was suspended for striking Melbourne's Shaun Smith. A groin injury destroyed his output.

Sydney lost to St Kilda and Geelong at the SCG in the last four weeks. Its loss to St Kilda was especially galling as after leading at one stage by 38 points, it lost by nine points, with suspended pair Lockett and Dale Lewis, who had a sensational year, sitting on the sidelines. Adam Heuskes, who crossed to Port Adelaide, left a hole that was never adequately replaced, although Rowan Warfe and Mark Orchard tried hard in their defensive roles. Andrew Dunkley and Troy Luff

were down on their previous year's form and Craig O'Brien kicked 15 goals in the first six rounds, then one more for the season.

Despite this, Sydney can approach 1998 with confidence. Picking up Wayne Schwass in exchange for Shannon Grant, who has returned to Melbourne, is a bonus, but rewards must be reaped early as Schwass is 28. Paul Roos, an essential player, has been convinced to play another year and a more settled year from Lockett, who underwent a groin operation mid-season last year, will be a bonus.

Jason Mooney needs to play a disciplined role at centre half-forward, while the much-improved trio of Matthew Nicks, Simon Arnott and Leo Barry adds depth to the line-up. Sydney still has a great midfield with champion Paul Kelly being matched for consistency by Daryn Cresswell. Wade Chapman and Troy Cook provide toughness around the ball, while Stuart Maxfield and Michael O'Loughlin can cause great damage with their pace. The inclusion of Robert Ahmat also adds bite around the forward line.

Sydney has a team that is good enough to win the flag, but Lockett has only a few years left and Roos is playing his last year, so alarm bells should be sounding.

— **Peter Ryan**

## THE YEAR AHEAD

| Rd | Date | Opponent | Venue | Home/ Away | Time (local) |
|----|------|----------|-------|------------|--------------|
| 1 | March 29 | Port Adelaide | FP | A | 12.10pm |
| 2 | April 4 (N) | Brisbane Lions | SCG | H | 7.40pm |
| 3 | April 12 | Geelong | SCG | H | 12.40pm |
| 4 | April 18 (N) | West Coast | W | A | 6.40pm |
| 5 | April 26 | Western Bulldogs | SCG | H | 12.40pm |
| 6 | May 3 | Melbourne | SCG | H | 12.40pm |
| 7 | May 10 | Collingwood | P | A | 2.10pm |
| 8 | May 16 | North Melbourne | MCG | A | 2.10pm |
| 9 | May 24 | Hawthorn | SCG | H | 12.40pm |
| 10 | May 30 (N) | St Kilda | SCG | H | 7.40pm |
| 11 | June 5 (N) | Essendon | MCG | A | 7.40pm |
| 12 | June 13 | Carlton | OO | A | 2.10pm |
| 13 | June 21 | Richmond | SCG | H | 12.40pm |
| 14 | June 28 | Adelaide | SCG | H | 12.40pm |
| 15 | July 5 | Fremantle | S | A | 1.20pm |
| 16 | July 19 | Port Adelaide | SCG | H | 12.40pm |
| 17 | July 26 | Brisbane Lions | G | A | 2.10pm |
| 18 | August 1 | Geelong | KP | A | 2.10pm |
| 19 | August 9 | West Coast | SCG | H | 12.40pm |
| 20 | August 15 | Western Bulldogs | P | A | 2.10pm |
| 21 | August 24 (N) | Melbourne | MCG | A | 7.40pm |
| 22 | August 30 | Collingwood | SCG | H | 12.40pm |

## 1997 AT A GLANCE

**L:** R1: West Coast 12.6 (78) v Sydney 5.7 (37) (S)

**L:** R2: Western Bulldogs 13.12 (90) v Sydney 12.11 (83) (OO)

**W:** R3: Sydney 15.9 (99) v Melbourne 14.7 (91) (SCG)

**W:** R4: St Kilda 12.9 (81) v Sydney 18.19 (127) (P)

**L:** R5: Hawthorn 15.9 (99) v Sydney 11.8 (74) (P)

**W:** R6: Sydney 21.16 (142) v Carlton 11.17 (83) (SCG)

**L:** R7: Geelong 11.10 (76) v Sydney 6.8 (44) (KP)

**L:** R8: Adelaide 22.12 (144) v Sydney 8.7 (55) (FP)

**W:** R9: Sydney 16.15 (111) v Collingwood 11.8 (74) (SCG)

**L:** R10: Brisbane Lions 13.14 (92) v Sydney 13.11 (89) (G)

**W:** R11: Port Adelaide 4.17 (41) v Sydney 10.16 (76) (FP)

**W:** R12: Sydney 26.8 (164) v Richmond 16.14 (110) (SCG)

### SNAPSHOT

**Games:** 23
**Wins:** 12
**Losses:** 11
**Ladder Finish:** 6th
**Players Used:** 37

**W:** R13: Sydney 8.17 (65) v North Melbourne 7.13 (55) (SCG)

**L:** R14: Fremantle 6.12 (48) v Sydney 3.15 (33) (W)

**W:** R15: Sydney 11.13 (79) v Essendon 11.12 (78) (SCG)

**W:** R16: Sydney 15.22 (112) v West Coast 11.9 (75) (SCG)

**W:** R17: Sydney 22.17 (149) v Western Bulldogs 7.10 (52) (SCG)

**W:** R18: Melbourne 7.11 (53) v Sydney 25.19 (169) (MCG)

**L:** R19: Sydney 17.17 (119) v St Kilda 18.20 (128) (SCG)

**W:** R20: Sydney 20.15 (135) v Hawthorn 11.11 (77) (SCG)

**L:** R21: Carlton 11.10 (76) v Sydney 5.11 (41) (OO)

**L:** R22: Sydney 13.12 (90) v Geelong 15.10 (100) (SCG)

## The Coach

**Rodney Eade**

**Born:**
4/4/58

Rodney Eade is a passionate coach. During the week — and especially after a win — he is full of humor. But on game day, his passion and ambitions take over. No one is spared if a point is to be made and some of his quarter-time addresses in 1997 made great television.

Eade's players respect him greatly and in two years, he has made Sydney one of the best sides in the competition.

Tactically, he is one of the best brains in the business. For much of last year he had to build a forward line and a gameplan without his trump card, a fit Tony Lockett.

He has been credited with the tactic of flooding the backline, but isn't sure it was his idea.

In the end, it was the skill level of his players which failed in the last two games of 1997. When that happens, the best coach in the world can't make an impact on the result.

Eade is one of the best and will be glad if the memories of 1997 can be erased with a more successful finish to '98.

### AT A GLANCE

**COACHING RECORD**

| Season | Sydney P | W | L | D | Pos |
|--------|---|---|---|---|-----|
| 1996 | 25 | 18 | 6 | 1 | 2 |
| 1997 | 23 | 12 | 11 | 0 | 6 |
| **Total** | **48** | **30** | **17** | **1** | |

## WIN/LOSS RECORD

| Against | P | W (N) | L (N) | D (N) |
|---|---|---|---|---|
| Adelaide | 11 | 5 (2) | 6 (4) | 0 |
| Brisbane Bears | 16 | 6 (2) | 10 (2) | 0 |
| Brisbane Lions | 1 | 0 | 1 | 0 |
| Carlton | 197 | 69 (2) | 122 (1) | 6 |
| Collingwood | 196 | 71 (2) | 124 (1) | 1 |
| Essendon | 190 | 72 (3) | 117 (2) | 1 (1) |
| Fitzroy | 185 | 77 (2) | 104 (3) | 4 |
| Fremantle | 5 | 0 | 5 (1) | 0 |
| Geelong | 187 | 85 (1) | 102 (4) | 0 |
| Hawthorn | 127 | 53 (2) | 72 (1) | 2 |
| Melbourne | 177 | 93 (1) | 83 | 1 |
| North Melb | 129 | 65 (2) | 64 (5) | 0 |
| Port Adel | 1 | 1 (1) | 0 | 0 |
| Richmond | 163 | 68 (3) | 94 (2) | 1 |
| St Kilda | 182 | 114 (1) | 66 | 2 |
| West Coast | 17 | 7 (2) | 10 (3) | 0 |
| W Bulldogs | 130 | 63 (1) | 66 (1) | 1 |
| University | 14 | 13 | 1 | 0 |
| **TOTALS** | **1928** | **862 (27)** | **1047 (30)** | **19 (1)** |

*(N) Premiership matches played at night*

## WINNING RUNS

15 v Hawthorn (1929–1937)
14 v North Melb (1929–1937)
14 v St Kilda (1941–1949)
13 v Hawthorn (1944–1951)
13 v St Kilda (1897–1902)
12 v Melbourne (1909–1914)
10 v Western Bulldogs (1933–1938)
10 v St Kilda (1909–1913); (1931–1937);
  (1950–1956)
8 v Collingwood (1941–1945)
8 v Essendon (1915–1920)
8 v Geelong (1906–1909; 1940–1946)
8 v Richmond (1915–1919)
6 v Fitzroy (1910–1912)
5 v Carlton (1917–1919)
4 v West Coast (1987–1988)
3 v Adelaide (1994–1995)
1 v Brisbane Bears (1987); (1988); (1989);
  (1990); (1992); (1996)
1 v Port Adelaide (1997– )

## 1997 BEST AND FAIREST

Members of the match committee allocate up to five votes for any one player, with no limit on how many players can receive votes.

**1** Paul Kelly (218)
**2** Daryn Cresswell (168)
**3** Dale Lewis (160)
**4** Michael O'Loughlin (137)
**5** Paul Roos (128)
**6** Brad Seymour (113)
**7** Stefan Carey (77)
**8** Troy Cook (75)
**9** Mark Orchard (74)
**10** Stuart Maxfield (71)

## GAMES RECORDS

**260** John Rantall (1963–72; 1976–79)
**251** Mark Browning (1975–87)
**246** Steven Wright (1979–92)
**237** Bob Skilton (1956–68; 1970–71)
**236** Mark Bayes (1985– )
**231** Ron Clegg (1945–54; 1956–60)
**229** Tony Morwood (1978–89)
**227** Jack Graham (1935–49)
**226** Vic Belcher (1907–15; 1917–20)
**222** Jim Cleary (1934–48)

## GOALS RECORDS

**681** Bob Pratt (1930–39; 1946)
**412** Bob Skilton (1956–68; 1970–71)
**397** Tony Morwood (1978–89)
**385** Ted Johnson (1923–31)
**325** Peter Bedford (1968–76)
**317** Warwick Capper (1983–87; 1991)
**289** Len Mortimer (1906–15)
**268** Tony Lockett (1995– )
**250** Austin Robertson Senior (1927–37)
**247** Steven Wright (1979–92)

## HIGHS AND LOWS

| Against | Highest | Lowest | G. W. Margin | G. L. Margin |
|---|---|---|---|---|
| Adelaide | 20.24.144 (1995) | 6.4.40 (1996) | 57 (1995) | 90 (1996) |
| Brisbane Bears | 19.23.137 (1987) | 8.9.57 (1993) | 74 (1992) | 162 (1993) |
| Brisbane Lions | 13.11.89 (1997) | 13.11.89 (1997) | — | 3 (1997) |
| Carlton | 23.13.151 (1934) | 0.5.5 (1899) | 77 (1970) | 102 (1982) |
| Collingwood | 25.15.165 (1987) | 1.7.13 (1898) | 91 (1987) | 99 (1991) |
| Essendon | 36.20.236 (1987) | 0.9.9 (1899) | 163 (1987) | 165 (1964) |
| Fitzroy | 27.8.170 (1995) | 1.4.10 (1898) | 126 (1995) | 103 (1961) |
| Fremantle | 19.13.127 (1995) | 3.15.33 (1997) | — | 58 (1995) |
| Geelong | 24.11.155 (1978) | 1.2.8 (1898) | 109 (1933) | 104 (1976) |
| Hawthorn | 28.15.183 (1980) | 4.7.31 (1974) | 123 (1932) | 99 (1987) |
| Melbourne | 29.15.189 (1986) | 2.3.15 (1898) | 124 (1986) | 107 (1939) |
| North Melb | 24.8.152 (1996) | 5.9.39 (1963) | 92 (1934) | 140 (1983) |
| Port Adel | 10.16.76 (1997) | 10.16.76 (1997) | 35 (1997) | — |
| Richmond | 31.12.198 (1987) | 3.10.28 (1984) | 93 (1909) | 107 (1975) |
| St Kilda | 30.19.199 (1982) | 4.2.26 (1908) | 171 (1919) | 75 (1990) |
| West Coast | 30.21.201 (1987) | 5.7.37 (1997) | 130 (1987) | 61 (1990) |
| W Bulldogs | 31.9.195 (1979) | 3.10.28 (1948) | 108 (1987) | 87 (1954) |

# THE LEADERSHIP AT SYDNEY

| Year | Pos | Coach | Captain | Best & Fairest | Leading Goalkicker | |
|------|-----|-------|---------|----------------|--------------------|--|
| 1931 | 7 | P. Scanlan | J. Scanlan | L. Thomas | A. Robertson | 38 |
| 1932 | 4 | J. Leonard | J. Leonard | W. Faul | R. Pratt | 71 |
| 1933 | 1 | J. Bissett | J. Bissett | H. Clarke | R. Pratt | 109 |
| 1934 | 2 | J. Bissett | J. Bissett | T. Brain | R. Pratt | 150 |
| 1935 | 2 | J. Bissett | J. Bissett | R. Hillis | R. Pratt | 103 |
| 1936 | 2 | J. Bissett | J. Bissett | H. Matthews | R. Pratt | 64 |
| 1937 | 9 | R. Cazaly | L. Nash | H. Matthews | L. Nash | 37 |
| 1938 | 12 | R. Cazaly | H. Matthews | L. Thomas | R. Moore | 34 |
| 1939 | 12 | H. Matthews | H. Matthews | H. Matthews | R. Pratt | 72 |
| 1940 | 10 | J. Baggott | H. Matthews | H. Matthews | L. Reiffel | 33 |
| 1941 | 11 | J. Kelly | H. Matthews | R. Ritchie | J. Graham | 33 |
| 1942 | 3 | J. Kelly | H. Matthews | J. Cleary | L. White | 80 |
| 1943 | 8 | J. Kelly | H. Matthews | H. Matthews | C. Culph | 35 |
| 1944 | 7 | J. Kelly | H. Matthews | J. Cleary | R. Hartridge | 31 |
| 1945 | 2 | W. Adams | H. Matthews | J. Graham | L. Nash | 56 |
| 1946 | 7 | W. Adams | J. Graham | W. Williams | H. Mears | 32 |
| 1947 | 8 | W. Adams | J. Graham | W. Williams | W. Williams | 38 |
| 1948 | 10 | W. Adams/J. Hale | J. Graham | R. Clegg | J. Graham | 33 |
| 1949 | 10 | J. Hale | B. Lucas | R. Clegg | R. Jones | 27 |
| 1950 | 11 | G. Lane | G. Lane | W. Williams | G. Lane | 47 |
| 1951 | 8 | G. Lane | G. Lane | R. Clegg | W. Williams | 41 |
| 1952 | 5 | G. Lane | G. Lane | K. Schaefer | G. Lane | 33 |
| 1953 | 8 | L. Nash | R. Clegg | J. Taylor | I. Gillett | 34 |
| 1954 | 10 | H. Matthews | R. Clegg | E. Lane | E. Lane | 28 |
| 1955 | 10 | H. Matthews | W. Gunn | I. Gillett | E. Lane | 36 |
| 1956 | 9 | H. Matthews | I. Gillett | J. Dorgan | W. Gunn | 28 |
| 1957 | 10 | H. Matthews | R. Clegg | J. Taylor | F. Goldsmith | 43 |
| 1958 | 9 | R. Clegg | R. Clegg | R. Skilton | M. Oaten | 34 |
| 1959 | 8 | R. Clegg | R. Clegg | R. Skilton | R. Skilton | 60 |
| 1960 | 8 | W. Faul | R. Clegg | F. Johnson | M. Oaten | 39 |
| 1961 | 11 | W. Faul | R. Skilton | R. Skilton | B. McGowan | 38 |
| 1962 | 12 | N. McMahen | R. Skilton | R. Skilton | R. Skilton | 36 |
| 1963 | 11 | N. McMahen | R. Skilton | R. Skilton | R. Skilton | 36 |
| 1964 | 11 | N. McMahen | R. Skilton | R. Skilton | M. Papley | 25 |
| 1965 | 8 | R. Skilton | R. Skilton | R. Skilton | R. Kingston | 48 |
| 1966 | 8 | R. Skilton | R. Skilton | M. Papley | A. Robertson | 60 |
| 1967 | 9 | A. Miller | R. Skilton | R. Skilton | J. Sudholz | 35 |
| 1968 | 9 | A. Miller | R. Skilton | R. Skilton | J. Sudholz | 36 |
| 1969 | 9 | N. Smith | J. Rantall | P. Bedford | J. Sudholz | 35 |
| 1970 | 4 | N. Smith | R. Skilton | P. Bedford | J. Sudholz | 60 |
| 1971 | 12 | N. Smith | R. Skilton | P. Bedford | P. Bedford | 44 |
| 1972 | 11 | N. Smith | J. Rantall | R. Cook | P. Bedford | 28 |
| 1973 | 12 | G. John | P. Bedford | P. Bedford | P. Bedford | 52 |
| 1974 | 9 | G. John | P. Bedford | N. Goss | N. Goss | 37 |
| 1975 | 12 | G. John | P. Bedford | P. Bedford | G. Teasdale | 38 |
| 1976 | 8 | I. Stewart | P. Bedford | R. Quade | R. Dean | 37 |
| 1977 | 5 | I. Stewart | R. Quade | G. Teasdale | G. Teasdale | 38 |
| 1978 | 8 | D. Tuddenham | R. Quade | J. Murphy | J. Murphy | 31 |
| 1979 | 10 | I. Stewart | R. Quade | B. Round | T. Morwood | 56 |
| 1980 | 6 | I. Stewart | B. Round | D. Ackerly | J. Roberts | 67 |
| 1981 | 9 | I. Stewart | B. Round | B. Round | J. Roberts | 51 |
| 1982 | 7 | R. Quade | B. Round | D. Ackerly | T. Morwood | 45 |
| 1983 | 11 | R. Quade | B. Round | M. Browning | C. Braddy | 48 |
| 1984 | 10 | R. Quade | B. Round | B. Evans | W. Capper | 39 |
| | | R. Hammond | M. Browning | | | |
| 1985 | 10 | J. Northey | M. Browning | S. Wright | W. Capper | 45 |
| 1986 | 4 | T. Hafey | D. Carroll | G. Healy | W. Capper | 92 |
| 1987 | 4 | T. Hafey | D. Carroll | G. Healy | W. Capper | 103 |
| 1988 | 7 | T. Hafey | D. Carroll | G. Healy | B. Mitchell | 35 |
| 1989 | 7 | C. Kinnear | D. Carroll | M. Bayes | B. Toohey | 27 |
| 1990 | 13 | C. Kinnear | D. Carroll | S. Wright | J. West | 34 |
| 1991 | 12 | C. Kinnear | D. Carroll | B. Mitchell | J. Love | 52 |
| 1992 | 15 | G. Buckenara | D. Carroll | P. Kelly | S. Minton-Connell | 60 |
| 1993 | 15 | G. Buckenara/ | P. Kelly | P. Kelly | S. Minton-Connell | 41 |
| | | R. Barassi | | | | |
| 1994 | 15 | R. Barassi | P. Kelly | D. Cresswell | S. Minton-Connell | 68 |
| 1995 | 12 | R. Barassi | P. Kelly | T. Lockett | T. Lockett | 110 |
| 1996 | 2 | R. Eade | P. Kelly | P. Kelly | T. Lockett | 121 |
| 1997 | 7 | R. Eade | P. Kelly | P. Kelly | T. Lockett | 37 |

# PLAYER PROFILES

## ROBBIE AHMAT
Has great pace and is a genuine goalsneak. Form at Collingwood tapered off and by year's end he wasn't the same player he'd looked at the start and chose to leave. Requires a quality defender as an opponent and is capable of chiming in with bags of three and four goals.
**Previous AFL club:** Collingwood (1995-97: 25 games, 22 goals).

## SIMON ARNOTT
'Biscuits' has developed well in his three years at Sydney. In 1997, he played 11 games, mainly in the forward line. Lacks a bit of pace, but is a good mark for his size and can bob up with a couple of goals. His performance against North Melbourne in round 13, when he kicked four goals on a bog track (only 15 were kicked in the game), was match-winning stuff, displaying what this Victorian is capable of.

## LEO BARRY
Left-footer came on in leaps and bounds at the end of last season, marking strongly and providing a target up forward in the absence of Tony Lockett. Made the jump to senior football last year after playing more than 50 reserves games and is a versatile player.

## MARK BAYES
Experienced player who was a little inconsistent last year, managing 15 games before hamstring problems forced him to miss Sydney's final. Turned the game against Essendon in round 15 with a couple of goals in the last quarter, then kicked six against Melbourne in round 18. His left-foot kicking is legendary, but gets less of the ball than he used to. Fifth on the club's all-time games' list and needs only 16 to move into second place. Turns 31 in March so will be keen for a tilt at glory.
**Player honors:** best and fairest 1989, 2nd best and fairest 1994.

## FRED CAMPBELL
Extremely quick Aborigine from Alice Springs who won the Harrison Medal as the best player in the second division of the AFL National Under-18 Championships. Played for the Eastern Ranges in Victoria before returning to play in the Northern Territory in 1997. Can take a spectacular mark and is very tough.

## STEFAN CAREY
Exciting tall youngster who came of age this season. A couple of best on ground performances at centre half-forward and a high placing in the AFL Norwich Rising Star award showed his quality. Only needs to get a bit harder — and that will come with experience — to move close to being the complete package required in a mobile tall. Marks strongly, is a good kick and is deceptively mobile.
**Player honors:** AFL Norwich Rising Star nominee 1997.

## WADE CHAPMAN
On a football field, Chapman goes where angels don't even think about treading, such is his courage. It cost him again in 1997 with two bouts of concussion. On one occasion, Carlton's Matthew Hogg collected him in a sickening collision that had him considering wearing a helmet. Not overly quick, but a great deliverer of the ball by hand and foot and good in close. An Achilles problem ruined the second half of his '97 season. If he puts in a full season, Sydney will reap the benefits.

## ADAM COGHLAN
Originally from Lemnos, Coghlan came to Sandringham in the VFL after time spent with the Murray Bushrangers in the TAC Cup under-18 competition. Played at full-back in Sandringham's 1997 premiership last year becoming respected as one of the best key defenders in the VFL in his two years in the competition. Was selected in the VFL state squad in 1997, but didn't play. Coghlan is strong, has good recovery and is a good mark. He trained with Collingwood over the pre-season before playing in defence for Sydney in two practice matches.

## TROY COOK
Young Aboriginal rover from Western Australia who had a magnificent debut year playing 20 games, plus State of Origin football. His likeness to Derek Kickett and rapid improvement after an impetuous debut to become a reliable midfielder made him something of a cult figure with Sydney crowds. Still has a lot to learn, but provided one of the more exciting debuts in the AFL for a few years. A tough skilful rover, he excels at centre clearances and tackles ferociously. Needs to work on his disposal and goalkicking, but gives the crowds as much enjoyment as he looks to be having.
**Player honors:** AFL Norwich Rising Star nominee 1997.

## DARYN CRESSWELL
Last season went from being a good off-sider to captain Paul Kelly to an equal and was runner-up in the club's best and fairest. Tough (whacked a knee back into place on the ground after it was dislocated against Geelong), skilful and with an incredible ability to get the ball (third most disposals in the AFL in 1997). Played every game last year even though he was battered from week to week before suffering a shoulder injury in Sydney's only final. Underwent surgery on his shoulder and kneecap over summer, but was back running early in December.
**Player honors:** best and fairest 1994, 2nd best and fairest 1997, 3rd best and fairest 1996; All-Australian 1997.

## JARED CROUCH
Selected at No. 8 in the 1995 National Draft, but stress fractures suffered in 1996 slowed his development. Progressed slowly, but was able to put together a full season of reserves football and should make the jump this season. A handy midfield type of player.

## ANDREW DUNKLEY
Coming off a controversial suspension following an incident in the 1996 preliminary final, he struggled to recapture the form of the year before. Known as much for his wonky kicking style as for his great marking and has the ability to beat the best full-forwards in

the game. Remains a very good full-back even when down on form. Keen to bounce back this year to make amends for a disappointing 1997, but will have to wait again because he starts the year with a two-week suspension.
**Player honors:** 2nd best and fairest 1996.

### PETER FILANDIA
Required a second knee reconstruction early last year, but is expected to make a full recovery. Very small, but is a genuine crumbing rover difficult to match up on when forward. Needs only to lift his goalscoring to a regular two or three per game to become settled in the senior line-up.
**Player honors:** Essendon night series premiership sides 1990, 1993.
**Previous AFL club:** Essendon (1991-92: 13 games, 14 goals).

### ADAM GOODES
Showed match-winning capacity at under-18 level, being Victoria Country's best player in the first game of the AFL National Under-18 Championships before breaking a hand. Returned just before the finals and kicked six for North Ballarat in the TAC Cup grand final to be best on ground. Taken as a 17-year-old so has plenty of time to develop, but is an exciting player and needs only to develop more consistency to take the step.

### BRENT GREEN
From the Gold Coast and was at the Brisbane Bears as a 15-year-old — when Rodney Eade was still there — but played only five games in seven years. A tall, athletic youngster who will provide depth in Sydney's big man department. Has been on the scene for a while, but with the opportunity provided by the move, will be looking to force his way into senior football and put pressure on Greg Stafford.
**Previous AFL club:** Brisbane Bears (1995-96: 3 games, 0 goals), Brisbane Lions (1997: 2 games, 0 goals).

### SIMON HAWKING
Former Fitzroy player who has had three years in the football wilderness because of injury and the unsettling impact of the Brisbane Bears-Fitzroy merger. Didn't play a game with the Brisbane Lions and was traded to Sydney. Fantastic left-foot kick and has great versatility but needs to really lift his intensity.
**Player honors:** 3rd best and fairest Fitzroy 1994, AFL Norwich Rising Star nominee 1994.
**Previous AFL club:** Fitzroy (1993-96: 60 games, 30 goals).

### PAUL KELLY
A modern day champion and as good as they get in terms of midfielders. Won the AFL Players' Association's most courageous player for the fourth year in a row last season, finished in the top four in the Brownlow, was named All-Australian captain for the second year in a row and won his fourth club best and fairest. His great talent is his ability to grab the ball and accelerate. Explosive over the first five metres, a good mark for a midfielder and tackles and holds opponents as tightly as a sleeping python. Was involved in three memorable duels with Western Bull-

dogs tagger Tony Liberatore last year that had Sydney people irate about what they considered the use of unfair tactics. At 27 and with 160 games under his belt, Kelly couldn't possibly get any better. Could he?
**Player honors:** Brownlow Medal 1995, 3rd Brownlow Medal 1997; best and fairest 1992, 1993, 1996, 1997; 3rd best and fairest 1991, 1994; All-Australian 1995, 1996, 1997; All-Australian captain 1996, 1997; captain since 1993.

### MARK KINNEAR
Played three games last year after being the No. 4 draft pick in 1996 and is progressing nicely. Runs hard at the football, has good skills, is a strong mark and gives every indication that with time and continued hard work, he will develop into a key forward/defender.

### DALE LEWIS
Delivered the goods in 1997 with his best year of football. Finished third in the best and fairest and was Sydney's best player in its one final. Only blemish was a suspension for charging near the end of the year. Has enormous ability and courage and last year combined those attributes with a desperate work ethic. Whether playing up forward, where he kicked a few bags of four and five, or in the midfield and across half-back, he was tremendous value. Was seventh in marks in the AFL last year — a magnificent effort for a player of his height (188cm) — and managed to get more of the ball than ever before. At 28 and nearing 150 games, he will build on his most consistent year yet, despite a delayed start to the pre-season because of a shoulder reconstruction.
**Player honors:** 3rd best and fairest 1997.

### PAUL LICURIA
About to enter his third year with the Swans, Licuria has played four senior games and 36 reserves games and was recovering from a knee reconstruction before he joined the Swans. Rated very highly, with good pace and strong skills off a left foot. Capable of breaking into a role in the midfield or becoming a running defender.

### TONY LOCKETT
A disappointing and frustrating year because of constant problems with his groin and when hitting top form again late in the season, copped a two-match suspension for charging Melbourne's Shaun Smith. Was eased back into the fray in round four with half games, but had surgery on June 4, just before round 11. Returned in round 15 and Sydney won four in a row with Lockett kicking 18 goals before being suspended. A total of 37 goals was his lowest return from a year of football since 1988, when he kicked 34, but injury and off-field distractions had their impact and his marking deserted him at times. However, Lockett is a champion and the biggest drawcard in the game. For the first time in four years, he has been able to start a pre-season without undergoing an operation. Needs to kick 134 goals to become the greatest goalkicker in the history of the game.
**Player honors:** Brownlow Medal 1987 (equal); St Kilda best and fairest 1987, 1991; St Kilda 2nd best and fairest 1992; St Kilda 3rd best and fairest 1989; Sydney best and fairest 1995; All-Australian 1991,

1992 1995 1996; EJ Whitten Medal 1995; AFLPA MVP 1987; Coleman Medal 1987, 1991, 1996; St Kilda leading goalkicker 1984, 1985, 1986, 1987, 1989, 1990, 1991, 1992, 1993, 1994; Sydney leading goalkicker 1995, 1996, 1997.
**Previous AFL club:** St Kilda (1983-94: 183 games, 898 goals).

### TROY LUFF
The sensational improver of 1996 inexplicably — at least from the outside — struggled again in '97. Too many errors and a lack of confidence saw him dropped after round five. He played four in a row in the middle and returned for the last two games, including the final, but his year could only be described as disheartening. Needs to work hard to prove his 1996 wasn't an aberration. A versatile player who can mark well and cut the opposition apart with his mobility.

### BEN MATTHEWS
Broke through in 1997 with four senior games, after being picked up with one of Sydney's 1995 local priority choices. A high possession-winner who runs hard to make contests and is looking to consolidate a spot in the senior side.

### STUART MAXFIELD
Enjoyed a productive year playing an important role in the Swans' game-plan. The long-kicking speedster is the prime architect in swinging the ball quickly from defence into attack. Is good in this role and a great tackler. His long left-foot bombs on the run have become one of the most exciting sights in the game.
**Previous AFL club:** Richmond (1990-95: 89 games, 65 goals).

### DAVID McEWAN
Drafted by Hawthorn as a highly rated youngster then traded to Sydney at the end of 1996. Injuries have cost him any opportunity to play senior football. Groin problems last year kept him to just 10 reserves games. The tall youngster was able to begin his preseason injury free and, hopefully, could break his duck in 1998.

### DANIEL McPHERSON
Played in the 1996 Grand Final, but went backwards in '97 and was dropped for the finals after only five games. Entering his sixth year with the club, this back pocket must win more contests and believe in his abilities at AFL level. Runs straight but must improve.
**Player honors:** AFL Norwich Rising Star nominee 1996.

### JASON MOONEY
A bulky forward who plays with a passion that sometimes gets him into trouble and he was reported three times in 1997. A great mark and mobile for his size, the left-footer has the ability to turn a game and never takes a backward step. Needs to concentrate on putting together four quarters of controlled aggression.

### MATTHEW NICKS
Played mainly across half-back showing an ability to run with the footy and take solid marks. Doesn't give up easily in a contest and 20 games was just reward for this emerging young South Australian who was picked up at No. 21 in the 1994 National Draft, but missed his first season with a broken leg.

### CRAIG O'BRIEN
His 100th AFL game in 1997 was the highlight in a year he'd probably rather forget. Struggled with a shoulder injury before his form deserted him after a promising start to the season. Returned for the last two games in which he showed some form and grit in an uncustomary role deep in defence. Looked to have the ability to attack from the backline with poise and may have added another string to his bow. A gritty, nuggety forward who marks exceptionally well for his size, has surprising acceleration and is capable of kicking bags of five or six goals.
**Previous AFL clubs:** Essendon (1989-91: 21 games, 16 goals); St Kilda (1993-95: 52 games, 116 goals).

### BRETT O'FARRELL
The big youngster is an excellent mark and had a reasonable first year in 1997, kicking 38 goals in 19 reserves games. Was not considered ready for senior football as his lack of pace would have been exposed. Can play but needs to work hard to improve his running ability so that as a marking forward, it is less easy for defenders to run off him.

### MICHAEL O'LOUGHLIN
Heightened his soaring reputation as a young star making the All-Australian team for the first time, although his selection did surprise some. His explosive pace, startling skills and great finishing had a greater impact on games than more ever before. Played more of a midfield role as the year progressed and looks likely to move into the engine room as he matures.
**Player honors:** All-Australian 1997; AFL Norwich Rising Star nominee 1995.

### MARK ORCHARD
Came from Collingwood as part of the deal involving Anthony Rocca and had his most productive year yet, playing 20 games including his first final. Made some unforced errors in the final, but it was his first game in a month. Playing across half-back or tagging, he displays great pace and evasive skills. Must improve his disposal, but looks to be a valuable acquisition adding depth to the line-up.
**Previous AFL club:** Collingwood (1995-96: 12 games, 4 goals).

### PAUL ROOS
Convinced to play on for one more year, Roos would love to add a premiership chapter to the book he released in 1997. The champion centre half-back was named in the All-Australian side for the seventh time and second year in succession last year. It's an amazing effort from the 34-year-old who is now the most experienced — and oldest — player in the AFL with 335 games at the start of '98. Reads the play magnificently, has incredible poise and is a courageous, strong mark.
**Player honors:** 3rd Brownlow Medal 1985, 1986; Fitzroy best and fairest 1985, 1986, 1991, 1992, 1994; Fitzroy 3rd best and fairest 1987, 1989; All-Australian 1985, 1987, 1988, 1991, 1992, 1996,

1997; All-Australian captain 1991, 1992; EJ Whitten Medal 1985, 1988; AFLPA MVP award 1986; Fitzroy leading goalkicker 1990; Fitzroy captain 1988-1990, 1992-1994.
**Previous AFL club:** Fitzroy (1982-94: 269 games, 270 goals).

### BRETT ROSE
Works very hard at every contest and is never beaten. Named Victoria Metro's best player in the AFL National Under-18 Championships and was an under-18 All-Australian last year. Sydney likes his hard-working attitude and personality. The left-footed ruck rover/defender with a long penetrating kick is likely to begin his career in defence.

### JASON SADDINGTON
Had a great season for Eastern Ranges in 1997. Lightly built at this stage (he grew eight centimetres between the ages of 16 and 17), but is a good mark and capable in a key post either in defence or attack. Has good skills, is very coachable and prepared to commit himself.

### WILL SANGSTER
Finely built big man who arrived at the club fairly raw, but impressed with his work ethic and willingness to learn the art of ruckwork. Still needs to work hard on his skills and Sydney isn't going to rush him. Probably facing another development year.

### WAYNE SCHWASS
A star player for North Melbourne in the 1990s, with two best and fairests and a premiership to his name, Schwass was the trade shock of the October trading period. Exchanged for the homesick Shannon Grant and a second-round draft selection, he is a real gain as the Swans were resigned to losing Grant. Both he and former coach Denis Pagan denied there was any falling out after Schwass was reported and suspended after North Melbourne's first final. At 29, the pacy, aggressive left-footer with brilliant evasive skills should revel in the challenge a new environment provides.
**Player honors:** North Melbourne best and fairest 1994, 1995; North Melbourne premiership side 1996; North Melbourne night series premiership side 1996.
**Previous AFL club:** North Melbourne (1988-97: 184 games, 97 goals).

### BRAD SEYMOUR
Improved in 1997 on his very solid form of '96. A tough disciplined defender who is prepared to back his judgment and is capable of beating the elite. An arm injury kept him out of the last two games, including Sydney's final, and he underwent a shoulder reconstruction in the off season. An underrated back pocket player who will take on even bigger roles in defence in 1998.

### GREG STAFFORD
Registered a consistent performance and played all but one game in 1997, despite being hampered by a broken toe in the pre-season. Is one of the best big men in the AFL with great skills, a good understanding with his midfield and a strong mark. At 23 and with 61 games under his belt, he is still developing and

was beaten early in the Swans' '97 final by Scott Wynd.

### JOHN STEVENS
Speedy left-footer picked up in the 1997 pre-season draft. Gave good value from the wing and in run-with roles, playing in 19 games including the final. Was found out early in the final when pushed to the last line of defence, matching up with Rohan Smith. Didn't look comfortable, but fought on. Has undergone heart surgery to overcome Wolff-Parkinson-White syndrome, played for Collingwood reserves, did pre-seasons at Richmond, Fitzroy and Geelong and played in the Victorian amateurs. Can be explosive and with a year under his belt, looks a great mature pick-up.

### ROWAN WARFE
Recruited from Fitzroy amid great expectations, but injuries held him back. Found a place late in the season only to miss the last two games, including the final. Has pace, courage and good mental application. Was used across half-back in 1997 and will improve on an interrupted year.
**Previous AFL club:** Fitzroy (1994-96: 26 games, 1 goal).

### BEN WILSON
Looked to be travelling well in defence pre-season and played in the first three games. Made a few errors and then lacked confidence. Very conscientious, but sometimes too hard on himself. Capable of playing at either end of the ground, but probably more suited to defence at this stage.
**Previous AFL club:** Collingwood (1996: 2 games, 0 goals).

## ROOKIE LIST

### MARK BROWN
A left-footer from Numurkah, near Shepparton in Victoria, Brown trained with St Kilda over the summer. Played in Canberra in 1996 before joining Numurkah last year. Described as a utility player.

### JAMES BYRNE
Went from Assumption to the Calder Cannons before being put on Sydney's supplementary list last year. A midfielder with good pace who is about to turn 20.

### MARK LIVY
Led the goalkicking in the TAC Cup for much of last season before switching to ruck roving. Kicked 39 goals for the season for the NSW/ACT Rams. The right-footer performed reasonably well for NSW in last year's AFL National Under-18 Championships. Sydney sees him as a goalkicking forward.

### BRAD MCMAHON
A solidly built key defender from Southport who played last year in the QAFL. Has reasonable pace and shows good strength.

### JASON MCPHERSON
From Ganmain Grong Grong-Matong — a name which brought a few laughs at the draft — in the Riverina. A pacy wingman who needs to bulk up a bit, but has been training with Sydney over summer and impressed in practice matches. The brother of Sydney's Daniel McPherson.

# SYDNEY

| Name (# = rookie) | No. | Born | Height | Weight | Recruited from |
|---|---|---|---|---|---|
| Robert Ahmat | 9 | 19/7/77 | 175 | 75 | DARWIN (NT)/COLLINGWOOD |
| Simon Arnott | 42 | 14/2/76 | 184 | 78 | COLLEGIANS |
| Leo Barry | 21 | 19/5/77 | 184 | 85 | DENILIQUIN (NSW) |
| Mark Bayes | 30 | 15/3/67 | 190 | 94 | NOBLE PARK |
| Fred Campbell | 40 | 14/12/79 | 174 | 65 | PIONEERS (NT) |
| Stefan Carey | 31 | 25/1/76 | 197 | 100 | PENNANT HILLS (NSW) |
| Wade Chapman | 27 | 3/1/76 | 178 | 76 | NORTH SHORE/GEELONG U18 |
| Adam Coghlan | 26 | 27/12/75 | 187 | 82 | LEMNOS/MURRAY U18/SANDRINGHAM |
| Troy Cook | 41 | 12/8/76 | 177 | 75 | PERTH (WA) |
| Daryn Cresswell | 8 | 22/5/71 | 181 | 86 | NORTH HOBART (TAS) |
| Jared Crouch | 28 | 5/3/78 | 173 | 77 | NORWOOD (SA) |
| Andrew Dunkley | 6 | 29/6/68 | 187 | 99 | DEVON/ST KILDA RES/NORTH LAUNCESTON (TAS) |
| Peter Filandia | 10 | 14/5/70 | 172 | 75 | DOUTTA STARS/ESSENDON |
| Adam Goodes | 37 | 8/1/80 | 191 | 85 | HORSHAM/NORTH BALLARAT U18 |
| Brent Green | 16 | 29/3/76 | 197 | 94 | SOUTHPORT (QLD)/BRISBANE |
| Simon Hawking | 25 | 5/3/73 | 193 | 86 | BULLEEN-TEMPLESTOWE/FITZROY/BRISBANE LIST |
| Paul Kelly | 14 | 28/7/69 | 178 | 82 | WAGGA TIGERS (NSW) |
| Mark Kinnear | 39 | 21/8/79 | 190 | 86 | KILMORE/CALDER U18 |
| Dale Lewis | 3 | 4/5/69 | 188 | 84 | NORTH BALLARAT |
| Paul Licuria | 38 | 4/1/78 | 180 | 83 | KEON PARK STARS/NORTHERN U18 |
| Tony Lockett | 4 | 9/3/66 | 191 | 110 | NORTH BALLARAT/ST KILDA |
| Troy Luff | 34 | 22/11/69 | 190 | 88 | NELSON BAY (NSW) |
| Ben Mathews | 36 | 29/11/78 | 180 | 83 | COROWA-RUTHERGLEN (NSW)/MURRAY U18 |
| Stuart Maxfield | 11 | 9/4/72 | 178 | 85 | GLEN WAVERLEY ROVERS/RICHMOND |
| David McEwan | 18 | 10/4/78 | 187 | 81 | ST MARYS (VMFL)/NORTHERN U18/HAWTHORN RES |
| Daniel McPherson | 13 | 5/7/75 | 179 | 83 | GANMAIN (NSW) |
| Jason Mooney | 17 | 5/6/73 | 191 | 96 | TURVEY PARK (NSW) |
| Matthew Nicks | 23 | 13/5/75 | 184 | 82 | WEST ADELAIDE (SA) |
| Craig O'Brien | 5 | 3/3/70 | 174 | 88 | RYE/ESSENDON/ST KILDA |
| Brett O'Farrell | 12 | 3/1/78 | 195 | 98 | EAST SANDRINGHAM/PRAHRAN U18 |
| Michael O'Loughlin | 19 | 20/2/77 | 188 | 87 | CENTRAL DISTRICT (SA) |
| Mark Orchard | 24 | 2/4/76 | 172 | 72 | EAST BALLARAT/BALLARAT U18/COLLINGWOOD |
| Paul Roos | 1 | 27/6/63 | 188 | 88 | BEVERLEY HILLS/FITZROY |
| Brett Rose | 35 | 21/1/79 | 178 | 74 | EAST BURWOOD/EASTERN U18 |
| Jason Saddington | 22 | 23/10/79 | 192 | 83 | MITCHAM/EASTERN U18 |
| Will Sangster | 29 | 11/10/78 | 198 | 86 | BAYSIDE/PRAHRAN U18 |
| Wayne Schwass | 2 | 27/11/68 | 180 | 81 | SOUTH WARRNAMBOOL/NORTH MELB |
| Brad Seymour | 7 | 3/5/76 | 186 | 84 | WAGGA TIGERS (NSW) |
| Greg Stafford | 15 | 27/8/74 | 202 | 102 | WESTERN SUBURBS (NSW) |
| John Stevens | 20 | 15/6/71 | 187 | 85 | OLD IVANHOE GRAMMARIANS/COLL RESERVES |
| Rowan Warfe | 33 | 23/6/76 | 188 | 88 | GOLDEN SQUARE/BENDIGO U18/FITZROY |
| Ben Wilson | 32 | 25/2/77 | 191 | 87 | NORWOOD (SA)/COLLINGWOOD |
| Mark Brown # | 43 | 20/7/77 | 180 | 84 | NUMURKAH |
| James Byrne # | 48 | 23/4/78 | 181 | 82 | ASSUMPTION COLLEGE/CALDER U18 |
| Mark Livy # | 44 | 25/7/79 | 187 | 80 | NORTH SHORE (NSW)/NSW-ACT U18 |
| Brad McMahon # | 45 | 13/3/77 | 194 | 87 | SOUTHPORT (QLD) |
| Jason McPherson # | 46 | 7/8/75 | 180 | 80 | GANMAIN-GRONG GRONG-MATONG (NSW) |
| **Total/(Average)** *On 26/2/98 | | **(23.5 yrs)*** | **(185)** | **(85)** | |

# PLAYERS 1998

| Debut | HOME & AWAY | | 1997 | | FINALS | | GRAND FINALS | | | NIGHT SERIES | | STATE OF ORIGIN | |
|---|---|---|---|---|---|---|---|---|---|---|---|---|---|
| | Gms | Gls | Gms | Gls | Gms | Gls | Gms | Gls | Won | Gms | Gls | Gms | Gls |
| 1995 | 25 | 22 | 14 | 16 | | | | | | 2 | 2 | 0 | 0 |
| 1995 | 26 | 14 | 11 | 8 | 2 | 0 | | | | 1 | 0 | 0 | 0 |
| 1995 | 16 | 15 | 10 | 12 | 1 | | | | | 0 | 0 | 0 | 0 |
| 1985 | 236 | 171 | 15 | 21 | 7 | 5 | 1 | 0 | 0 | 19 | 8 | 5 | 1 |
| | 0 | 0 | 0 | 0 | | | | | | 0 | 0 | 0 | 0 |
| 1996 | 24 | 19 | 20 | 18 | 1 | | | | | 1 | 2 | 1 | 1 |
| 1994 | 48 | 18 | 13 | 8 | 2 | 0 | 1 | 0 | 0 | 4 | 0 | 0 | 0 |
| | 0 | 0 | 0 | 0 | | | | | | 0 | 0 | 0 | 0 |
| 1997 | 20 | 7 | 20 | 7 | 1 | | | | | 1 | 0 | 1 | 0 |
| 1992 | 116 | 92 | 23 | 16 | 4 | 5 | 1 | 1 | 0 | 5 | 6 | 1 | 0 |
| | 0 | 0 | 0 | 0 | | | | | | 0 | 0 | 0 | 0 |
| 1992 | 121 | 7 | 21 | 0 | 4 | 0 | 1 | 0 | 0 | 6 | 1 | 0 | 0 |
| 1991 | 51 | 39 | 5 | 3 | | | | | | 11 | 10 | 0 | 0 |
| | 0 | 0 | 0 | 0 | | | | | | 0 | 0 | 0 | 0 |
| 1995 | 5 | 0 | 2 | 0 | | | | | | 3 | 0 | 0 | 0 |
| 1993 | 60 | 30 | 0 | 0 | | | | | | 4 | 2 | 0 | 0 |
| 1990 | 160 | 109 | 23 | 26 | 4 | 4 | 1 | 0 | 0 | 10 | 6 | 3 | 0 |
| 1997 | 3 | 1 | 3 | 1 | | | | | | 0 | 0 | 0 | 0 |
| 1990 | 133 | 148 | 21 | 28 | 4 | 5 | 1 | 0 | 0 | 8 | 4 | 1 | 0 |
| 1997 | 4 | 1 | 4 | 1 | | | | | | 1 | 0 | 0 | 0 |
| 1983 | 236 | 1166 | 12 | 37 | 6 | 28 | 1 | 6 | 0 | 11 | 51 | 5 | 19 |
| 1990 | 76 | 58 | 11 | 5 | 4 | 5 | 1 | 2 | 0 | 3 | 3 | 0 | 0 |
| 1997 | 4 | 1 | 4 | 1 | | | | | | 0 | 0 | 0 | 0 |
| 1990 | 135 | 88 | 22 | 9 | 7 | 1 | 1 | 0 | 0 | 11 | 5 | 0 | 0 |
| | 0 | 0 | 0 | 0 | | | | | | 0 | 0 | 0 | 0 |
| 1994 | 29 | 3 | 5 | 0 | 3 | 0 | 1 | 0 | 0 | 0 | 0 | 0 | 0 |
| 1992 | 76 | 40 | 18 | 14 | 4 | 5 | 1 | 1 | 0 | 5 | 3 | 1 | 0 |
| 1996 | 26 | 8 | 20 | 6 | 1 | | | | | 0 | 0 | 0 | 0 |
| 1989 | 102 | 182 | 11 | 16 | 5 | 5 | 1 | 0 | 0 | 12 | 12 | 0 | 0 |
| | 0 | 0 | 0 | 0 | | | | | | 0 | 0 | 0 | 0 |
| 1995 | 59 | 59 | 23 | 26 | 4 | 3 | 1 | 2 | 0 | 2 | 2 | 1 | 0 |
| 1995 | 32 | 8 | 20 | 4 | 1 | | | | | 3 | 5 | 0 | 0 |
| 1982 | 335 | 287 | 21 | 6 | 10 | 1 | 1 | 0 | 0 | 26 | 26 | 14 | 11 |
| | 0 | 0 | 0 | 0 | | | | | | 0 | 0 | 0 | 0 |
| | 0 | 0 | 0 | 0 | | | | | | 0 | 0 | 0 | 0 |
| | 0 | 0 | 0 | 0 | | | | | | 0 | 0 | 0 | 0 |
| 1988 | 184 | 97 | 20 | 7 | 10 | 5 | 1 | 0 | 1 | 20 | 15 | 3 | 0 |
| 1994 | 61 | 3 | 21 | 2 | 3 | 0 | 1 | 0 | 0 | 7 | 0 | 0 | 0 |
| 1993 | 61 | 12 | 22 | 5 | 4 | 1 | 1 | 0 | 0 | 1 | 0 | 1 | 0 |
| 1997 | 19 | 10 | 19 | 10 | 1 | 1 | | | | 0 | 0 | 0 | 0 |
| 1994 | 38 | 1 | 12 | 0 | | | | | | 2 | 0 | 0 | 0 |
| 1996 | 6 | 0 | 4 | 0 | | | | | | 1 | 0 | 0 | 0 |
| | 0 | 0 | 0 | 0 | | | | | | 0 | 0 | | |
| | 0 | 0 | 0 | 0 | | | | | | 0 | 0 | | |
| | 0 | 0 | 0 | 0 | | | | | | 0 | 0 | | |
| | 0 | 0 | 0 | 0 | | | | | | 0 | 0 | | |
| | 0 | 0 | 0 | 0 | | | | | | 0 | 0 | | |
| | (60) | (65) | 470 | 313 | 93 | 74 | 17 | 12 | 1 | 180 | 163 | 37 | 32 |

**Eagles at a glance**

**WEST COAST EAGLES**

**ADDRESS:** Subiaco Oval, Subiaco Rd, Subiaco, WA 6008
**POSTAL ADDRESS:** PO Box 508, Subiaco, WA 6904
**TELEPHONE:** (08) 9381 1111
**FACSIMILE:** (08) 9388 2541
**WEB SITE:** www.westcoasteagles.com.au
**EMAIL:** westcoasteagles@westcoast eagles.com.au
**MELBOURNE OFFICE:** Level 3, Great Southern Stand, MCG, Jolimont, Vic 3002
**TELEPHONE:** (03) 9650 8016
**FACSIMILE:** (03) 9650 7972
**CHAIRMAN:** Murray McHenry
**CHIEF EXECUTIVE OFFICER:** Brian Cook
**FOOTBALL MANAGER:** Trevor Nisbett
**VICTORIAN MANAGER:** Stephen Nash
**PR COORDINATOR:** Chris Summers
**MARKETING MANAGER:** Ross Nicholas
**NATIONAL RECRUITING MANAGER:** Gary Merrington (based in Victoria)
**RECRUITING OFFICER:** Trevor Woodhouse
**COACHING STAFF:** Michael Malthouse (senior); Robert Wiley (assistant)
**TEAM MANAGER:** Rod Lester-Smith
**SELECTION COMMITTEE:** Ian Miller (chairman); Michael Malthouse, Robert Wiley, Tim Gepp, George Young, Rod Lester-Smith
**CLUB DOCTORS:** Rod Moore, Ken Fitch
**CLUB PHYSIOTHERAPISTS:** Brian Edwards, Chris Barrett
**JOINED AFL:** 1987
**HOME GROUND:** Subiaco Oval
**GROUND DIMENSIONS:** Subiaco Oval — 173m by 129m. WACA — 165m by 129m.
**OFFICIAL COLORS:** Guernsey: Navy with gold chest panels and white border featuring Eagles logo on centre front. Socks: Navy with gold hoop at top. Shorts: Navy
**ALTERNATIVE STRIP:** Guernsey: Royal blue with gold chest panels and white border featuring Eagle logo on the centre front. Socks: Royal blue with gold top. Shorts: White with royal blue trim.
**PREMIERSHIPS:** 1992, 1994
**RECORD HOME ATTENDANCE** (WACA): 32,121 — August 27, 1993 v Geelong.
(Subiaco): 42,209 — June 30, 1991 v St Kilda

# WEST COAST

## Youth, experience key for Eagles

For the fourth successive season since their 1994 premiership success, the West Coast Eagles will have no shortage of admirers when the ball is bounced for the first time in 1998.

Feared on all parts of the continent, the Eagles attract nothing but the utmost respect from opposition teams and an expectation from their own fans that another flag is just round the corner.

But the harsh reality is that the Eagles have been hit harder than most by retirements and injuries. In the past two seasons, knee injuries have claimed some of the club's most senior and respected players in Glen Jakovich, John Worsfold, Chris Mainwaring and Mitchell White.

While Worsfold and Jakovich returned after delayed starts, Mainwaring and White played just six games between them in 1997 and the loss of such experience and talent told dearly as the season wore on.

The Eagles won 13 games during the home and away season, but bowed out of the finals, losing to eventual premier Adelaide (in Adelaide) and North Melbourne (at the MCG). West Coast was gallant in defeat against North, but the fact remains that the Eagles have lost four of their past five finals since the '94 premiership.

The positive side is what the football world has known for some time — the Eagles have traded wisely and professionally to land some of the most exciting young talent in the country.

Sooner, rather than later, that is going to put the club back to the top of the tree. West Coast netted the No. 1 draft pick in Michael Gardiner last year and in just 10 appearances, he served notice of just what a giant of a young player he will be.

Chad Morrison and Fraser Gehrig were both excellent performers in 1997 and if Ben Cousins can return to his 1996 Norwich Rising Star best, the Eagles have an outstanding platform to build on.

Peter Matera, Guy McKenna and Dean Kemp are all within 12 to 14 months of their 30th birthdays and while all three have been champion performers, they will have to be managed carefully in their training and playing programs over the next couple of years.

Apart from All-Australians Matera and Gehrig, the bonus for the Eagles was the return of clever forward Brett Heady and the consistent season of Paul Symmons, one of three West Coast players to appear in all 24 games in 1997.

— **Michael Lovett**

## THE YEAR AHEAD

| Rd | Date | Opponent | Venue | Home/ Away | Time (local) |
|---|---|---|---|---|---|
| 1 | March 27 | North Melbourne (N) | MCG | A | 7.40pm |
| 2 | April 3 | Collingwood (N) | S | H | 6.40pm |
| 3 | April 12 | Fremantle | S | A | 1.20pm |
| 4 | April 18 | Sydney (N) | W | H | 6.40pm |
| 5 | April 24 | Richmond (N) | MCG | A | 7.40pm |
| 6 | May 3 | St Kilda | S | H | 1.20pm |
| 7 | May 10 | Adelaide | FP | A | 1.40pm |
| 8 | May 17 | Carlton | S | H | 1.20pm |
| 9 | May 23 | Geelong | KP | A | 2.10pm |
| 10 | May 29 (N) | Western Bulldogs | W | H | 6.40pm |
| 11 | June 6 (N) | Port Adelaide | FP | A | 8.10pm |
| 12 | June 12 (N) | Hawthorn | W | H | 6.40pm |
| 13 | June 19 (N) | Essendon | MCG | A | 7.40pm |
| 14 | June 28 | Melbourne | S | H | 1.20pm |
| 15 | July 4(N) | Brisbane Lions | G | A | 7.40pm |
| 16 | July 19 | North Melbourne | S | H | 1.20pm |
| 17 | July 25 | Collingwood | P | A | 2.10pm |
| 18 | August 2 | Fremantle | S | H | 12.10pm |
| 19 | August 9 | Sydney | SCG | A | 12.40pm |
| 20 | August 16 | Richmond | S | H | 1.20pm |
| 21 | August 22 | St Kilda | P | A | 2.10pm |
| 22 | August 29(N) | Adelaide | S | H | 6.40pm |

## 1997 AT A GLANCE

**W:** R1: West Coast 12.6 (78) v Sydney 5.7 (37) (S)
**L:** R2: Geelong 11.12 (78) v West Coast 11.6 (72) (KP)
**W:** R3: West Coast 16.15 (111) v Fremantle 9.17 (71) (S)
**W:** R4: West Coast 17.10 (112) v Hawthorn 13.10 (88) (S)
**W:** R5: Melbourne 12.6 (78) v West Coast 19.12 (126) (MCG)
**L:** R6: West Coast 14.15 (99) v Western Bulldogs 17.11 (113) (W)

### SNAPSHOT

**Games:** 24
**Wins:** 13 **Losses:** 11
**Players Used:** 37
**Ladder Finish:** 5th

**W:** R7: Brisbane Lions 8.12 (60) v West Coast 21.13 (139) (G)
**L:** R8: Richmond 18.11 (119) v West Coast 9.13 (67) (MCG)
**W:** R9: West Coast 16.14 (110) v Essendon 13.7 (85) (S)
**L:** R10: North Melbourne 15.13 (103) v West Coast 9.4 (58) (OO)

**L:** R11: West Coast 11.7 (73) v St Kilda 13.11 (89) (S)
**W:** R12: Collingwood 7.13 (55) v West Coast 11.5 (71) (VP)
**L:** R13: West Coast 11.13 (79) v Carlton 12.14 (86) (S)
**L:** R14: Adelaide 16.10 (106) v West Coast 4.7 (31) (FP)
**W:** R15: West Coast 12.13 (85) v Port Adelaide 9.13 (67) (S)
**L:** R16: Sydney 15.22 (112) v West Coast 11.9 (75) (SCG)
**W:** R17: West Coast 20.9 (129) v Geelong 12.10 (82) (S)
**W:** R18: Fremantle 7.7 (49) v West Coast 13.4 (82) (S)
**W:** R19: Hawthorn 10.6 (66) v West Coast 13.9 (87) (P)
**W:** R20: West Coast 15.7 (97) v Melbourne 7.17 (59) (W)
**L:** R21: Western Bulldogs 12.14 (86) v West Coast 10.8 (68) (WO)
**W:** R22: West Coast 18.12 (120) v Brisbane Lions 11.15 (81) (W)

# The Coach

**Michael Malthouse**

**Born:** 17/8/53

Mick Malthouse has completed 14 seasons coaching at the highest level and his remarkable record both with Footscray and the West Coast Eagles is reflected in the table below.

Only once in that 14-year journey has Malthouse been through a 'losing' season — one with a win-loss ratio of less than 50 per cent. That was back in 1989, his final year with the Bulldogs.

In his eight years with West Coast, Malthouse has guided the Eagles into the finals every season, collecting two premierships along the way. He has coached in 331 games and is 14th on the all-time list of coaches at the start of 1998.

His attention to detail is second to none and while he sets high standards and strict guidelines for his players, West Coast's record through the '90s shows what an outstanding coach he is.

## AT A GLANCE

### COACHING RECORD

**Footscray**

| Season | P | W | L | D | Pos |
|---|---|---|---|---|---|
| 1984 | 22 | 11 | 11 | — | 7 |
| 1985 | 25 | 17 | 8 | — | 3 |
| 1986 | 22 | 11 | 11 | — | 8 |
| 1987 | 22 | 11 | 10 | 1 | 7 |
| 1988 | 22 | 11 | 11 | — | 8 |
| 1989 | 22 | 6 | 15 | 1 | 13 |
| | 135 | 67 | 66 | 2 | |

**West Coast Eagles**

| Season | P | W | L | D | Pos |
|---|---|---|---|---|---|
| 1990 | 26 | 17 | 8 | 1 | 3 |
| 1991 | 26 | 21 | 5 | — | 2 |
| 1992 | 25 | 18 | 6 | 1 | 1 |
| 1993 | 22 | 13 | 9 | — | 4 |
| 1994 | 25 | 19 | 6 | — | 1 |
| 1995 | 24 | 14 | 10 | — | 6 |
| 1996 | 24 | 16 | 8 | — | 5 |
| 1997 | 24 | 13 | 11 | — | 5 |
| | 196 | 131 | 63 | 2 | |
| **Total** | **331** | **198** | **129** | **4** | |

## WIN/LOSS RECORD

| Against | P | W (N) | L (N) | D (N) |
|---|---|---|---|---|
| Adelaide | 12 | 7 (2) | 5 (4) | 0 |
| Brisbane Bears | 16 | 13 (3) | 2 (1) | 1 (1) |
| Brisbane Lions | 2 | 2 (1) | 0 | 0 |
| Carlton | 19 | 9 (2) | 10 (1) | 0 |
| Collingwood | 19 | 11 (1) | 7 | 1 |
| Essendon | 22 | 8 (1) | 14 (2) | 0 |
| Fitzroy | 15 | 9 (3) | 6 (3) | 0 |
| Fremantle | 6 | 6 | 0 | 0 |
| Geelong | 23 | 15 (2) | 8 (1) | 0 |
| Hawthorn | 19 | 12 (2) | 7 | 0 |
| Melbourne | 22 | 15 (3) | 7 (2) | 0 |
| North Melb | 19 | 9 (4) | 10 (5) | 0 |
| Port Adel | 1 | 1 | 0 | 0 |
| Richmond | 17 | 12 (1) | 5 (1) | 0 |
| St Kilda | 16 | 11 (3) | 5 | 0 |
| Sydney | 17 | 10 (3) | 7 (2) | 0 |
| W Bulldogs | 18 | 12 (4) | 6 (1) | 0 |
| **TOTALS** | **263** | **162 (35)** | **99 (23)** | **2 (1)** |

*(N) Premiership matches played at night*

## WINNING RUNS

10 v Richmond (1989–1994)
8 v Brisbane Bears (1987–1991)
8 v Western Bulldogs (1988–1992)
8 v Melbourne (1994– )
6 v Geelong (1989–1991)
6 v Fremantle (1995– )
5 v St Kilda (1993–1996)
5 v Sydney (1992–1997)
5 v Collingwood (1994– )
4 v Essendon (1991–1993)
4 v North Melb (1993–1995)
4 v Fitzroy (1994–1996)
4 v Hawthorn (1995– )
2 v Brisbane Lions (1997– )
3 v Adelaide (1991–1992)
3 v Carlton (1989–1990)
1 v Port Adelaide (1997– )

## 1997 BEST AND FAIREST

Each player is awarded one vote per game on selection in the West Coast team. The match committee allocates up to 10 votes per game to be shared among the best players.

| | | | | |
|---|---|---|---|---|
| 1 | Peter Matera (37) | | 6 | Drew Banfield (30) |
| 2 | Dean Kemp (35) | | 7 | Guy McKenna (29) |
| 3 | Chad Morrison (33) | | | Fraser Gehrig (29) |
| | Paul Symmons (33) | | 9 | Ilija Grgic (28) |
| 5 | Brett Heady (31) | | 10 | Ryan Turnbull (27) |

## GAMES RECORDS

**213** Guy McKenna (1988– )
**197** Chris Lewis (1987– )
**193** Chris Mainwaring (1987– )
**192** John Worsfold (1987– )
**184** David Hart (1987–97)
**179** Michael Brennan (1987–95)
**176** Dean Kemp (1990– )
**163** Peter Matera (1990– )
**155** Chris Waterman (1988– )
**151** Dwayne Lamb (1987–94)

## GOALS RECORDS

**514** Peter Sumich (1989–97)
**244** Chris Lewis (1987– )
**216** Brett Heady (1990– )
**157** Peter Matera (1990– )
**111** Ross Glendinning (1987–88)
**107** Karl Langdon (1988–95)

## THE LEADERSHIP AT WEST COAST

| Year | Pos | Coach | Captain | Best & Fairest | Leading Goalkicker | |
|---|---|---|---|---|---|---|
| 1987 | 8 | R. Alexander | R. Glendinning | S. Malaxos | R. Glendinning | 38 |
| 1988 | 5 | J. Todd | R. Glendinning | J. Worsfold | R. Glendinning | 73 |
| 1989 | 11 | J. Todd | M. Rance | G. McKenna | P. Sumich | 45 |
| 1990 | 3 | M. Malthouse | S. Malaxos | C. Lewis | P. Sumich | 90 |
| 1991 | 2 | M. Malthouse | J. Worsfold | C. Turley | P. Sumich | 111 |
| 1992 | 1 | M. Malthouse | J. Worsfold | D. Kemp | P. Sumich | 82 |
| 1993 | 4 | M. Malthouse | J. Worsfold | D. Pyke/G. Jakovich | P. Sumich | 76 |
| 1994 | 1 | M. Malthouse | J. Worsfold | G. Jakovich | P. Sumich | 49 |
| 1995 | 6 | M. Malthouse | J. Worsfold | G. Jakovich | J. Ball | 48 |
| 1996 | 5 | M. Malthouse | J. Worsfold | D. Banfield | M. White | 37 |
| 1997 | 6 | M. Malthouse | J. Worsfold | Peter Matera | P. Sumich | 33 |

## HIGHS AND LOWS

| Against | Highest | Lowest | G. W. Margin | G. L. Margin |
|---|---|---|---|---|
| Adelaide | 26.21.177 (1995) | 4.7.31 (1997) | 135 (1995) | 75 (1997) |
| Brisbane Bears | 29.18.192 (1988) | 11.11.77 (1996) | 131 (1992) | 47 (1996) |
| Brisbane Lions | 21.13.139 (1997) | 18.12.120 (1997) | 79 (1997) | — |
| Carlton | 21.22.148 (1989) | 5.11.41 (1989) | 76 (1989) | 87 (1987) |
| Collingwood | 19.23.137 (1987) | 8.7.55 (1988) | 81 (1991) | 59 (1990) |
| Essendon | 26.19.175 (1988) | 1.12.18 (1989) | 99 (1988) | 142 (1989) |
| Fitzroy | 20.11.131 (1996) | 5.10.40 (1989) | 99 (1991) | 70 (1988) |
| Fremantle | 23.13.151 (1995) | 9.13.67 (1996) | 85 (1995) | — |
| Geelong | 20.23.143 (1994) | 9.10.64 (1995) | 80 (1994) | 95 (1989) |
| Hawthorn | 21.18.144 (1991) | 6.14.50 (1989) | 82 (1991) | 91 (1989) |
| Melbourne | 24.12.156 (1996) | 9.7.61 (1990) | 106 (1996) | 61 (1987) |
| North Melb | 24.18.162 (1987) | 7.2.44 (1995) | 74 (1987) | 62 (1995) |
| Port Adel | 12.13.85 (1997) | 12.13.85 (1997) | 18 (1997) | — |
| Richmond | 22.21.153 (1990) | 9.9.63 (1995) | 96 (1994) | 60 (1995) |
| St Kilda | 26.19.175 (1987) | 3.11.29 (1992) | 88 (1987) | 66 (1992) |
| Sydney | 19.14.128 (1990) | 6.14.50 (1996) | 61 (1990) | 130 (1987) |
| W Bulldogs | 25.15.165 (1991) | 3.5.23 (1992) | 118 (1991) | 42 (1993) |

# PLAYER PROFILES

### DAVID ANTONOWICZ
Key position player who moves well for his size and will certainly improve with more experience. Had an interrupted season in 1997 because of a knee injury and is not expected to be rushed this year. An All-Australian selection at under-16 level, Antonowicz can play centre-half forward, centre-half back or in the ruck. Like many of the West Coast Eagles' younger brigade, he was given a taste of what to expect when he appeared in some practice matches before the Eagles' Ansett Australia Cup campaign. The tall left-footer was the West Coast Eagles' sixth selection, 44th overall in the 1997 National Draft. Takes over the famous No. 4 jumper from Peter Sumich.

### JASON BALL
More than capable big man who has been hampered by injuries over the past two seasons. Played the first nine games of 1997, but managed only another five, including the semi-final against North Melbourne. The previous season he managed only 13 games and his absence has been crucial in that time. Provides an extra option up forward and presents match-up problems because of his height advantage. Has struggled, mainly with ankle injuries, but his form has also taken a dip and needs a big season to re-establish himself as one of the competition's best big men. Will be keen for an injury-free run in '98 in a bid to return to the form he showed in 1994 and '95. Perhaps his best shot now might be at full-forward with Peter Sumich gone.
**Player honors:** premiership side 1994; leading goal-kicker 1995.

### DREW BANFIELD
Hard-working midfielder who is just one game away from 100 games at the start of the 1998 season. Has been an integral part of the Eagles' midfield for the past five seasons and his consistency recently has been rewarded with a club best and fairest in 1996 and sixth placing in '97. A former No. 1 draft pick (in 1992), Banfield is now rated as one of the leading on-ballers in the AFL and can set up play with his attacking handball. Last year, he was the West Coast Eagles' second leading handballer with 176, behind Dean Kemp (192). A very fit, industrious player who can run all day.
**Player honors:** best and fairest 1996; AFL Norwich Rising Star nominee 1994; premiership side 1994.

### MICHAEL BRAUN
Victorian youngster who was given some tagging assignments in his brief stint at senior level in 1997. Played seven senior games from rounds 11 to 17 and despite his inexperience, acquitted himself well and was one of two Eagles to earn AFL Norwich Rising Star nominations. Missed the latter part of the season because of a groin injury which required surgery. Will be looking for more opportunities in '98. Not afraid to put himself in and is the sort of player who will continue to develop under Mick Malthouse's guidance.
**Player honors:** AFL Norwich Rising Star nominee 1997.

### CALLUM CHAMBERS
Lightly built wingman from country Victoria who has excellent poise and is blessed with tons of pace. Will have to build himself up, but played some games for Essendon's reserves in 1997 and looks to have a promising future. Hails from Lucknow in Gippsland and was the West Coast Eagles' second selection, 13th overall, at the 1997 National Draft.

### BEN COUSINS
Faced a difficult year in 1997 being forced to cope with extra attention after his standout season the previous year when he won the AFL Norwich Rising Star award. To complicate matters, he broke a leg and missed six games mid-season. His temperament was also tested and he will have to be careful not to be sucked in by close-checking opponents. In particular, he was subjected to some close attention by wily Western Bulldog Tony Liberatore and lost his way for a while. However, he remains a classy forward with an exciting future.
**Player honors:** AFL Norwich Rising Star 1996.

### JAXON CRABB
Dashing young wingman who made his senior debut for Claremont in 1997 after gaining selection in the All-Australian side at the AFL National Under-18 Championships. Played some senior football for Claremont in 1997. Has been touted as a future replacement for Chris Mainwaring and gained some experience in practice matches in the pre-season. Was the West Coast Eagles' first pick, 12th overall, at the 1997 National Draft.

### TRENT CUMMINGS
Former Fitzroy utility who is having no luck with injuries as he tries to establish himself at his second club. Spent most of the early part of 1997 recovering from a knee injury and eventually forced his way into the senior line-up in rounds nine and 10. Could not establish himself as a permanent player, but worked hard in the pre-season only to be cut down with another knee injury in a practice match against Fremantle. Faces a long haul back, but will be retained on the West Coast Eagles' list.
**Previous AFL club:** Fitzroy (1994-96: 27 games, 18 goals).

### ANDREW DONNELLY
After a fine debut season in 1996, Donnelly struggled with groin injuries and form last season, managing only 10 games. His marking fell away and he did not appear the confident player he was the previous season. Fully fit, he would be a regular in the Eagles' best 21. Must have total confidence in his marking to be an effective player, but certainly has the talent. Will be 25 at the start of the season and faces competition from younger players for a regular spot.

### TONY EVANS
Fell off the pace last year, playing only 14 games after being a regular in the Eagles' midfield for the past few seasons. Struggled to get into the action although he finished the season strongly and, at 28, still has plenty to offer. Was hampered by ankle and back injuries in 1997. Has always put his hand up in big games and his experience will be an asset as the

Eagles develop younger players. Kicked three goals and played a key role in the West Coast Eagles' first premiership back in 1992.
**Player honors:** Graham Moss Medal 1995; premiership sides 1992, 1994.

## BRENDON FEWSTER
Young big man with heaps of potential as evidenced by his performance against North Melbourne in last year's semi-final. Plucked from virtual obscurity for that game, but kicked some handy goals and looked the part. Has been hampered by knee problems, but shapes as an exciting prospect. Will be part of the West Coast Eagles' continued push to develop youth as the club goes through the next phase in its short AFL history.

## MICHAEL GARDINER
Showed why he was such hot property in the 1996 National Draft with an eye-catching debut season. After just a handful of games, he was elevated to the No. 1 ruck position and given a thorough grounding, including a hotly contested game against the Western Bulldogs in round 21. Virtually became a fixture, missing just one game after round 15. Big and still very raw, but looks to have the world at his feet and should be a dominant ruckman over the next decade. Together with Geelong's Steven King, he shapes as one of the new breed of young AFL ruckmen.
**Player honors:** AFL Norwich Rising star nominee 1997.

## FRASER GEHRIG
Versatile and athletic and a fine example of how well the Eagles have used the draft in recent seasons. He can run all day, take a strong mark, kick a team-lifting goal and play big or small and at either end. Capped off a great season by winning selection in the All-Australian team, however, he was reported four times during 1997. Does not give the impression he is a temperamental player, but one or two incidents probably fitted into the needless category. Booted 31 goals for the season, just two behind leading goalkicker Peter Sumich, and could find himself in a forward role as the Eagles try to find a regular goalkicker. Came out of contract at the end of the season and was feted by several Victorian-based clubs before agreeing to new terms with the Eagles. An exciting long-term prospect.
**Player honors:** All-Australian 1997; AFL Norwich Rising Star nominee 1995.

## ILIJA GRGIC
Former Western Bulldogs big man who played 22 of a possible 24 games with his new club. Was able to lead the way in the ruck when required and was a good option up forward. Hampered by a back injury towards the end of the season, but did enough to suggest the Eagles made a good trade. Missed the semi-final against North Melbourne because of his back problem, but led the West Coast Eagles in hitouts for the season, with 161 (15th in the AFL for '97). Unfortunately, had a setback over summer when he required surgery to correct a disc problem in his back and had a delayed start to the season. With the emergence of Michael Gardiner, his playing time could be limited, although the extra man on the bench

and the fact he can be used in attack should have him in the Eagles' best 22.
**Player honors:** AFL Norwich Rising Star nominee 1993.
**Previous AFL club:** Western Bulldogs (1993-96: 62 games, 92 goals).

## BRETT HEADY
Classy performer who mixed his roles between half-forward and half-back last year. Tremendously skilled, has always shown great courage and dished out the best hip and shoulder of the season on Geelong star Leigh Colbert in round 17. Has been injury-prone and just when he looked to be on top of his setbacks, he hurt a knee in the qualifying final against Adelaide. Finished fifth in best and fairest voting last year and is a great mark for his size — he was the West Coast Eagles' second leading mark-taker with 104. Another experienced player who thrives on the pressure of big games, Heady still has plenty to offer the Eagles.
**Player honors:** premiership sides 1992, 1994.

## TODD HOLMES
Young left-footer who played several games for Subiaco last season and showed plenty of potential. Played for WA at the 1996 AFL National Under-18 Championships. Can play in attack or defence and his precise skills suggest he has a real future. Was the West Coast Eagles' fifth selection, 37th overall, in the 1997 National Draft.

## GLEN JAKOVICH
Made his long-awaited return from a knee reconstruction in round six last year and by the end of the season was starting to look in ominous form. Played a great game against North Melbourne champion Wayne Carey in the semi-final and while his pace will never be blistering, his strength, sure hands and straight-at-the-ball approach make him a feared opponent. Loves the challenge of playing at the very top and some of his battle with opposing key forwards, particularly Carey, have taken on epic proportions. Has been a champion defender for the Eagles and only turned 25 at the start of the 1998 season. There have been some calls for the Eagles to play Jakovich in attack this season and it will be interesting to see whether Mick Malthouse uses him back or forward.
**Player honors:** best and fairest 1993 (equal), 1994, 1995; 3rd best and fairest 1992; All-Australian 1994, 1995; premiership sides 1992, 1994.

## ROWAN JONES
Local youngster who has very good evasive skills and reads the play well for one so young. Missed the AFL National Under-18 Championships because of injury and might have been overlooked by other clubs earlier in the 1997 draft. Played for Scotch College in Perth and made the Claremont colts grand final team. Jones, who is studying engineering and commerce, is expected to develop further. Was the West Coast Eagles' third selection, 28th overall, in the 1997 National Draft.

## DEAN KEMP
Outstanding midfielder and the key link man in getting the Eagles moving out of the centre. His tremendous skills and running ability have seen him run opposi-

tion players into the ground and he again excelled in last year's finals. Filled another placing in the Eagles' best and fairest and the bigger the occasion, the better he seems to play. His performance in the 1994 Grand Final was one of the best displays of running football imaginable and opposing teams spent countless hours devising ways of negating him. Led the Eagles in disposals last season — 296 kicks and 192 handballs for a total of 498 disposals — despite missing two games with a knee injury. He was also the West Coast Eagles' leading tackler for 1997 (63 tackles) but finished well back in Brownlow Medal voting, polling seven votes, 14 behind the best Eagle, Peter Matera. Traditionally — and somewhat surprisingly — he has never polled well in the Brownlow.
**Player honors:** best and fairest 1992; 2nd best and fairest 1995 (equal), 1997; Norm Smith Medal 1994; All-Australian 1992; premiership sides 1992, 1994.

### CHRIS LEWIS
Returned to his best form in the early part of 1997, playing with the flair and skill that saw him rocket to stardom in the early '90s. However, his well-documented history of indiscretions was boosted when he received a seven-week suspension for striking. He was injured on his return, but came back to play in the Eagles' two finals, where he incurred another suspension. Despite his record, the umpires still recognise his talent and he was equal second in Brownlow Medal voting for the Eagles (seven votes). On the verge of becoming only the second West Coast Eagle player to reach 200 games and his experience and talent still make him a viable option.
**Player honors:** best and fairest 1990; 3rd best and fairest 1989; premiership sides 1992, 1994.

### ANTHONY LOVELL
Did not quite repeat the success of his first season with the Eagles, but there were mitigating circumstances. The tragic death of his father in Tasmania obviously affected him and he struggled, particularly in the second half of '97. Lively midfielder who goes hard at the ball and should bounce back in 1998. Keeps himself very fit and is another player who adds depth and experience to the Eagles' list.
**Player honors:** Melbourne 2nd best and fairest 1992.
**Previous AFL club:** Melbourne (1988-95: 121 games, 141 goals).

### CHRIS MAINWARING
Champion wingman who seriously injured a knee against Geelong in round two last year and was sidelined for the rest of the season. His absence across the centre was a big blow for the Eagles, who sorely missed his drive, leadership and experience. Prides himself on his fitness and is sure to return keener than ever, even though he is 32. Getting to the latter stages of his career, but has worked hard to get himself back and has the resolve to go out on a successful note. One of three foundation members of the Eagles, together with Chris Lewis and John Worsfold, Mainwaring is on the verge of completing 200 games. Not expected back until the middle of the season and it will be a bonus if he can regain his All-Australian form.
**Player honors:** 2nd best and fairest 1989, 1992,

1996; 3rd best and fairest 1987, 1988; All-Australian 1991, 1996; premiership sides 1992, 1994.

### NEIL MARSHALL
Young defender who has been on the Eagles' list for the past two seasons, but has managed only two senior games, both in 1997. Can be used as an option across half-back, but will need to push up to ensure his future. Neat-looking left-footer who can also play on the wing and has been used in tagging roles.

### PETER MATERA
Brilliant wingman who has been used with great success as a running half-back in recent seasons. Had another outstanding season, finishing high in the Brownlow Medal voting and taking his club's best and fairest award — surprisingly for the first time. Won All-Australian selection for the fifth time and although he managed just five goals for the season, one of them against Sydney in round one was a gem. His dashing runs and long, penetrating kicks are the feature of his game. Last year, he was the West Coast Eagles' leading kick-getter with 336 and finished second to Dean Kemp in total possessions (471 to Kemp's 498). Has signed a new long-term deal after Melbourne made a bold effort to lure him east. The Demons thought they had netted him, but Matera's decision to stay should ensure he sees out his playing days with the Eagles.
**Player honors:** 2nd Brownlow Medal 1994; 3rd (equal) Brownlow Medal 1997; best and fairest 1997; 3rd best and fairest 1991; Norm Smith Medal 1992; All-Australian 1991, 1993, 1994, 1996, 1997; premiership sides 1992, 1994.

### PHILLIP MATERA
Stepped out of the shadow of his older brother and virtually established himself as a permanent member of the Eagles' forward line. Has a ton of pace and is very dangerous near goals. Booted 30 goals for the season, to be the third leading goalkicker behind Peter Sumich (33) and Fraser Gehrig (31). It needs a very disciplined opponent to mind him. Should be approaching 1998 with plenty of confidence, particularly after brother Peter's decision to remain with the Eagles.

### ASHLEY McINTOSH
One of the young veterans of the West Coast Eagles' line-up who has given the club great service in the past couple of seasons. Leg injuries hampered his progress last year, but he played 19 of 24 games and the previous season played every game. Came through the pre-season in good shape and if his knees hold up, looks set for a big year. Used mainly at full-back, but can move forward and give the Eagles another marking option in attack. Still only 25 and if he can get himself fully fit, will play a crucial role.
**Player honors:** premiership sides 1992, 1994.

### GUY McKENNA
Ultra consistent defender whose importance to the Eagles was underlined when he missed last year's semi-final against North Melbourne with an out of character suspension. Has shown amazing consistency and endurance over the years, running off half-

back and delivering the ball with precision to his for-wards. Became the first West Coast Eagle player to reach 200 games last year and still has plenty of top-class football ahead of him. His sure hands, ability to read the play and his will to win have made him one of the best players the Eagles have produced. Is consistently among the West Coast Eagles' leading tacklers and has always shown a willingness to put his body on the line in second and third efforts.

**Player honors:** best and fairest 1989; 2nd best and fairest 1988, 1991; 3rd best and fairest 1993, 1994, 1996; All-Australian 1991, 1993, 1994; pre-miership sides 1992, 1994.

### DANIEL METROPOLIS

Played the first three games last season before being sidelined for the rest of the year with a serious groin injury. Forward-turned-defender who has excellent skills but would need to bounce back quickly to reclaim a permanent place in what is a fairly settled backline. Probably facing a make or break year and was still struggling to return to full fitness in the pre-season. On his day, Metropolis is a more than com-petent player and his skills are neat and tidy.

### CHAD MORRISON

Looks an outstanding prospect and there were cer-tainly no second-year blues for this talented young-ster. Was given more defensive roles in 1997 after making his debut in '96 as a forward. Looked more than accomplished running out of defence and was one of three players to appear in all 24 games. A strong mark, Morrison took 103 marks for the sea-son, a tally bettered only by Fraser Gehrig (115) and Brett Heady (104). Could be tried in the Eagles' mid-field. Coming up for his third season and looks to have the football world at his feet. One of the exciting new breed of players coming through for the Eagles, whose performances in both trading and drafting in recent years have been outstanding.

**Player honors:** 3rd (equal) best and fairest 1997; AFL Norwich Rising Star nominee 1996.

### PHILLIP READ

Another youngster who is expected to bolster the West Coast Eagles' midfield further down the track. Will be given time to develop, but impressed as a rover for Western Australia at last year's AFL National Under-18 Championships. Has plenty of pace and will be well suited to the dry grounds and goes hard at the ball. Was the West Coast Eagles' final selection, 60th overall, at the 1997 National Draft.

### JARRAD SCHOFIELD

Hard-running and long-kicking midfielder who has developed into a vital cog in the midfield. Has made considerable improvement in the past two seasons and should go on to establish himself as a regular player. His season ended on a sour note when it was feared he had broken a leg in the semi-final against North Melbourne. While there was no break, he did damage an ankle but has had plenty of time to recover. At 23, his career should be starting to blossom.

**Player honors:** AFL Norwich Rising Star nominee 1996.

### SHANE SIKORA

Played two games in 1996, but last season was troubled by a groin injury which ultimately required surgery. Young winger who was a high selection in the 1994 National Draft and, providing he is fully fit, should add to his games tally. Quick and has good ball skills.

### NICHOLAS STONE

One of the oldest players to make his AFL debut in 1997, the 25-year-old proved a more than handy acquisition. The former Claremont premiership defender played 14 senior games, including both finals, and was able to hold his place for most of the second half of the season. Slotted nicely into the backline and his close-checking style suited the Eagles.

### PAUL SYMMONS

Had his best year in the AFL in 1997 after an indif-ferent '96. A dashing player with great ball skills, Symmons played in all 24 games and finished equal third in the club's best and fairest. Was the third lead-ing handballer for the Eagles with 168 and his run and drive around the flanks can set up goalscoring opportunities. Has a great chance to move into the top bracket of AFL players if he can continue the form and consistency he showed last year.

**Player honors:** 3rd (equal) best and fairest 1997.

### RYAN TURNBULL

Played every game in 1997 to make amends for a disappointing '96. Just as his career appeared to be waning, Turnbull played with authority, albeit in a slightly different role. With the arrival of Ilija Grgic and the emergence of Michael Gardiner, he was able to do more work around the ground. Played in the 1994 premiership side and but did not kick on as expected, particularly in 1996. On the verge of 100 games and has plenty of football ahead of him.

**Player honors:** premiership side 1994.

### CHRIS WATERMAN

Experienced and sometimes under-rated utility who has been struggling with injuries over the past two seasons. For the second successive year, he was injured in round one and did not return until round 14, but his versatility ensured he did not lose his spot thereafter. Has played more than 150 games for the Eagles and is highly regarded because of his ability to play tight, disciplined football. Gets the job done with-out any fuss or fanfare, but will have to remain injury-free to get past the 200-game mark he so richly deserves.

**Player honors:** premiership sides 1992, 1994.

### MITCHELL WHITE

A knee injury in round five — requiring a 12-month break — was a bitter blow for the Eagles who missed his leadership and direction at both ends of the ground. After making the All-Australian side in 1996, he will be hoping for a change of fortune and a has-sle-free return. Has worked tirelessly to get himself back and will be like a new recruit when the 1998 season starts. He could be the player to help take the Eagles back into Grand Final and, quite possibly, premiership territory. The Eagles hope to use White at

centre half-forward in 1998 with Jason Ball and Fraser Gehrig the other marking options.
**Player honors:** 2nd (equal) best and fairest 1995; All-Australian 1996; leading goalkicker 1996; premiership side 1992.

### ANDREW WILLIAMS
Quick half-forward/wingman who has great skills on both sides of his body. Played for Victoria Metro at last year's AFL National Under-18 Championships and was part of a successful TAC Cup side. Will be given time to develop, but is considered the ideal size for today's football. Was the West Coast Eagles' fourth selection, 34th overall, at the 1997 National Draft.

### DAVID WIRRPUNDA
Exciting young talent who played six games in 1997, following on from five in 1996. Another groin 'victim', Wirrpunda had two operations last year but is now back fully fit. Has not been rushed along by the Eagles who know they have a player of considerable promise. Played six games last year, but only one after round 10. Turned 19 just before the '98 season and will be a player to watch as the year unfolds. Had an excellent pre-season and looks set to live up to the big fanfare that greeted his drafting and junior career.

### JOSH WOODEN
Young defender who played with a poise and maturity beyond his years in his debut season. Appeared in 18 games and the fact he was able to establish a place in such a strong side suggests he has a long career ahead of him. After round eight, he played every game, except the qualifying final for the Eagles. Looked best suited in defence, but can play in the midfield.

### JOHN WORSFOLD
The evergreen and ever-reliable leader has already ensured his name will go into Eagles' history as captain of the club's first two premiership sides. Made a successful return from a knee reconstruction, but struggled for consistency and had frequent spells on the bench. Might be slower but is still as competitive as ever and his on-field presence remains a source of discomfort for opposition players and supporters. Highly disciplined and possesses one of the sharpest football brains of any player in the competition. Has

never given anything less than 100 per cent each time he has taken the field and is set to reach a thoroughly deserved 200-game milestone in 1998.
**Player honors:** best and fairest 1988; 3rd best and fairest 1990; premiership sides 1992, 1994; West Coast Eagles captain since 1991.

# ROOKIE LIST

### LAURIE BELLOTTI
Still raw in terms of his football development but the Eagles have been most impressed with his athletic capabilities. Originally from Port Hedland, he has played senior football with Claremont, but has had only limited exposure to the game.

### CONRAD CHAMBERS
Athletic young forward whose development will be monitored closely by the Eagles over the next 12 months. Has only played junior football in WA and the experience of being part of a successful program will certainly benefit his progress.

### CHAD FLETCHER
Small left-footer with good skills and will improve by being part of an AFL club. Has represented Western Australia twice at the AFL National Under-18 Championships.

### TODD NENER
Played senior football for East Perth in 1997 and is best suited in defence, mainly centre half-back. Was on the Eagles' rookie list in 1997 and hails from Southport in Queensland.

### TRENT SIMPSON
Another Southport product, this smart left-footer caught the eye in a couple of practice matches for the Eagles earlier this year. Midfielder who has played senior football with Subiaco.

### HEATH YOUNIE
Was rated a leading chance to be selected at the 1997 National Draft but was overlooked. A high possession winner from the Murray Bushrangers in the TAC Cup competition, Younie was going to head to WA to play for West Perth before the Eagles selected him in the rookie draft. Very creative, goes hard at the ball and is smart around goals. Sure to develop playing senior football for West Perth and training with the Eagles.

# WEST COAST

| Name (# = rookie) | No. | Born | Height | Weight | Recruited from |
|---|---|---|---|---|---|
| David Antonowicz | 4 | 1/6/80 | 194 | 85 | ST ALBANS (VMFL)/WESTERN U18 |
| Jason Ball | 26 | 21/11/72 | 200 | 102 | SWAN DISTRICTS (WA) |
| Drew Banfield | 6 | 27/2/74 | 183 | 88 | SUBIACO (WA) |
| Michael Braun | 10 | 24/3/78 | 174 | 72 | ECHUCA UNITED/BENDIGO U18 |
| Callum Chambers | 15 | 19/11/79 | 182 | 71 | LUCKNOW/GIPPSLAND U18 |
| Ben Cousins | 9 | 30/6/78 | 178 | 79 | EAST FREMANTLE (WA) |
| Jaxon Crabb | 35 | 7/11/79 | 179 | 81 | CLAREMONT (WA) |
| Trent Cummings | 20 | 28/12/73 | 182 | 84 | CENTRAL DISTRICT (SA)/FITZROY |
| Andrew Donnelly | 29 | 29/3/73 | 190 | 92 | SUBIACO (WA)/SYDNEY RESERVES |
| Tony Evans | 18 | 14/6/69 | 175 | 82 | CLAREMONT (WA) |
| Brendon Fewster | 23 | 4/1/74 | 193 | 97 | WEST PERTH (WA) |
| Michael Gardiner | 19 | 5/7/79 | 198 | 101 | CLAREMONT (WA) |
| Fraser Gehrig | 7 | 3/3/76 | 195 | 101 | WODONGA/MURRAY U18 |
| Ilija Grgic | 14 | 5/3/72 | 203 | 104 | MHSOB/FOOTSCRAY |
| Brett Heady | 1 | 4/1/70 | 183 | 84 | SUBIACO (WA) |
| Todd Holmes | 25 | 14/7/79 | 186 | 86 | SUBIACO (WA) |
| Glen Jakovich | 27 | 24/3/73 | 193 | 104 | SOUTH FREMANTLE (WA) |
| Rowan Jones | 31 | 19/11/79 | 185 | 83 | CLAREMONT (WA) |
| Dean Kemp | 2 | 17/2/69 | 182 | 81 | SUBIACO (WA) |
| Chris Lewis | 28 | 17/3/69 | 183 | 79 | CLAREMONT (WA) |
| Anthony Lovell | 5 | 28/7/70 | 180 | 82 | GLENORCHY (TAS)/MELBOURNE |
| Chris Mainwaring | 3 | 27/12/65 | 177 | 83 | EAST FREMANTLE (WA) |
| Neil Marshall | 43 | 6/7/77 | 185 | 88 | CLAREMONT (WA) |
| Peter Matera | 30 | 3/4/69 | 181 | 89 | SOUTH FREMANTLE (WA) |
| Phillip Matera | 33 | 27/11/75 | 171 | 75 | SOUTH FREMANTLE (WA) |
| Ashley McIntosh | 11 | 20/10/72 | 192 | 96 | CLAREMONT (WA) |
| Guy McKenna | 17 | 11/5/69 | 185 | 91 | CLAREMONT (WA) |
| Daniel Metropolis | 8 | 17/3/72 | 187 | 86 | SUBIACO (WA) |
| Chad Morrison | 42 | 29/3/78 | 183 | 87 | DANDENONG/SOUTHERN U18 |
| Phillip Read | 36 | 20/10/79 | 178 | 77 | EAST FREMANTLE (WA) |
| Jarrad Schofield | 21 | 30/1/75 | 178 | 83 | SUBIACO (WA) |
| Shane Sikora | 34 | 11/3/77 | 179 | 80 | COBRAM/MURRAY U18 |
| Nicholas Stone | 22 | 19/9/72 | 186 | 89 | CLAREMONT (WA) |
| Paul Symmons | 16 | 2/9/73 | 188 | 87 | WEST PERTH (WA) |
| Ryan Turnbull | 50 | 23/9/71 | 195 | 100 | CLAREMONT (WA) |
| Chris Waterman | 39 | 19/9/68 | 180 | 86 | EAST FREMANTLE (WA) |
| Mitchell White | 12 | 28/3/73 | 192 | 94 | SUBIACO (WA) |
| Andrew Williams | 37 | 1/3/79 | 185 | 78 | SOUTH BELGRAVE/DANDENONG U18 |
| David Wirrpunda | 44 | 3/8/79 | 174 | 80 | HEALESVILLE/EASTERN U18 |
| Josh Wooden | 13 | 14/11/78 | 182 | 84 | LOCKHART/NSW-ACT U18 |
| John Worsfold | 24 | 25/9/68 | 180 | 87 | SOUTH FREMANTLE (WA) |
| Laurie Bellotti # | N/A | 28/2/76 | | | CLAREMONT (WA) |
| Conrad Chambers # | N/A | 23/10/79 | | | EAST FREMANTLE (WA) |
| Chad Fletcher # | N/A | 30/8/79 | | | SUBIACO (WA) |
| Todd Nener # | N/A | 6/3/78 | 193 | 95 | SOUTHPORT (QLD)/EAST PERTH (WA) |
| Trent Simpson # | N/A | 18/8/76 | 180 | 72 | SOUTHPORT (QLD)/SUBIACO (WA) |
| Heath Younie # | N/A | 26/6/79 | 177 | 70 | WODONGA/MURRAY U18 |
| Total/(Average)  *On 26/2/98 | | (23.6 yrs)* | (185) | (87) | |

# PLAYERS 1998

| Debut | HOME & AWAY | | 1997 | | FINALS | | GRAND FINALS | | | NIGHT SERIES | | STATE OF ORIGIN | |
|---|---|---|---|---|---|---|---|---|---|---|---|---|---|
| | Gms | Gls | Gms | Gls | Gms | Gls | Gms | Gls | Won | Gms | Gls | Gms | Gls |
| | 0 | 0 | 0 | 0 | | | | | | 0 | 0 | 0 | 0 |
| 1992 | 67 | 89 | 14 | 6 | 7 | 5 | 1 | 2 | 1 | 4 | 0 | 1 | 1 |
| 1993 | 99 | 38 | 21 | 14 | 7 | 4 | 1 | 1 | 1 | 8 | 2 | 2 | 0 |
| 1997 | 7 | 1 | 7 | 1 | | | | | | 0 | 0 | 0 | 0 |
| | 0 | 0 | 0 | 0 | | | | | | 0 | 0 | 0 | 0 |
| 1996 | 38 | 56 | 18 | 22 | 4 | 6 | | | | 3 | 1 | 0 | 0 |
| | 0 | 0 | 0 | 0 | | | | | | 0 | 0 | 0 | 0 |
| 1994 | 29 | 19 | 2 | 1 | | | | | | 3 | 3 | 0 | 0 |
| 1996 | 30 | 34 | 10 | 6 | 3 | 1 | | | | 2 | 4 | 1 | 0 |
| 1991 | 103 | 78 | 14 | 7 | 14 | 16 | 2 | 6 | 2 | 9 | 4 | 1 | 1 |
| 1996 | 6 | 6 | 3 | 6 | 1 | 2 | | | | 3 | 1 | 0 | 0 |
| 1997 | 10 | 9 | 10 | 9 | 1 | 0 | | | | 0 | 0 | 0 | 0 |
| 1995 | 62 | 63 | 22 | 30 | 5 | 9 | | | | 5 | 1 | 0 | 0 |
| 1993 | 84 | 107 | 22 | 15 | 3 | 3 | | | | 7 | 2 | 0 | 0 |
| 1990 | 140 | 216 | 21 | 23 | 20 | 33 | 3 | 6 | 2 | 11 | 11 | 3 | 2 |
| | 0 | 0 | 0 | 0 | | | | | | 0 | 0 | 0 | 0 |
| 1991 | 139 | 25 | 16 | 3 | 16 | 2 | 3 | 0 | 2 | 11 | 3 | 7 | 3 |
| | 0 | 0 | 0 | 0 | | | | | | 0 | 0 | 0 | 0 |
| 1990 | 176 | 99 | 22 | 13 | 22 | 18 | 3 | 2 | 2 | 4 | 2 | 2 | 1 |
| 1987 | 197 | 241 | 15 | 20 | 20 | 22 | 3 | 4 | 2 | 15 | 11 | 5 | 0 |
| 1988 | 160 | 165 | 16 | 6 | 12 | 10 | 1 | 0 | 0 | 13 | 7 | 2 | 2 |
| 1987 | 193 | 83 | 1 | 0 | 18 | 6 | 3 | 0 | 2 | 16 | 2 | 8 | 0 |
| 1997 | 2 | 0 | 2 | 0 | | | | | | 0 | 0 | 0 | 0 |
| 1990 | 163 | 157 | 21 | 7 | 18 | 22 | 3 | 5 | 2 | 13 | 7 | 5 | 4 |
| 1996 | 24 | 37 | 19 | 29 | 2 | 4 | | | | 3 | 5 | 1 | 1 |
| 1991 | 130 | 91 | 19 | 5 | 15 | 1 | 3 | 0 | 2 | 6 | 3 | 3 | 0 |
| 1988 | 213 | 26 | 20 | 1 | 22 | 4 | 3 | 0 | 2 | 16 | 0 | 4 | 1 |
| 1992 | 48 | 28 | 3 | 0 | 3 | 1 | | | | 7 | 1 | 0 | 0 |
| 1996 | 42 | 33 | 24 | 9 | 4 | 2 | | | | 2 | 1 | 0 | 0 |
| | 0 | 0 | 0 | 0 | | | | | | 0 | 0 | 0 | 0 |
| 1993 | 49 | 28 | 20 | 4 | 4 | 0 | | | | 4 | 1 | 1 | 0 |
| 1996 | 2 | 0 | 0 | 0 | | | | | | 2 | 1 | 0 | 0 |
| 1997 | 14 | 4 | 14 | 4 | 2 | 0 | | | | 1 | 0 | 0 | 0 |
| 1994 | 63 | 23 | 24 | 15 | 4 | 1 | | | | 8 | 2 | 1 | 0 |
| 1991 | 96 | 25 | 24 | 6 | 8 | 0 | 1 | 0 | 1 | 8 | 2 | 2 | 0 |
| 1988 | 155 | 70 | 12 | 0 | 21 | 13 | 3 | 2 | 2 | 9 | 4 | 4 | 0 |
| 1991 | 101 | 51 | 5 | 4 | 10 | 3 | 1 | 0 | 1 | 10 | 1 | 1 | 1 |
| | 0 | 0 | 0 | 0 | | | | | | 0 | 0 | 0 | 0 |
| 1996 | 11 | 6 | 6 | 2 | | | | | | 1 | 0 | 0 | 0 |
| 1997 | 18 | 3 | 18 | 3 | 1 | 0 | | | | 0 | 0 | 0 | 0 |
| 1987 | 192 | 35 | 14 | 0 | 21 | 1 | 3 | 0 | 2 | 16 | 8 | 5 | 0 |
| | 0 | 0 | 0 | 0 | | | | | | 0 | 0 | | |
| | 0 | 0 | 0 | 0 | | | | | | 0 | 0 | | |
| | 0 | 0 | 0 | 0 | | | | | | 0 | 0 | | |
| | 0 | 0 | 0 | 0 | | | | | | 0 | 0 | | |
| | 0 | 0 | 0 | 0 | | | | | | 0 | 0 | | |
| | 0 | 0 | 0 | 0 | | | | | | 0 | 0 | | |
| | (70) | (47) | 479 | 271 | 288 | 189 | 37 | 28 | 26 | 220 | 90 | 59 | 17 |

**Bulldogs
at a glance**

**ADDRESS:** 412 Barkly St,
Footscray West, 3012
**POSTAL ADDRESS:** PO Box
4112, Footscray West, 3012
**TELEPHONE:** (03) 9689 3100
**FACSIMILE:** (Admin, Football,
Marketing) (03) 9689 8094;
(Social, Memberships, Finance)
(03) 9687 4486
**EMAIL:** leman@vicnet.net.au
**WEB SITE:**
www.westernbulldogs.com.au
**PRESIDENT:** David Smorgon
**CHIEF EXECUTIVE OFFICER:**
Mark Patterson
**GENERAL MANAGER
FOOTBALL OPERATIONS:**
Paul Armstrong
**RECRUITING MANAGER:**
Mark Kleiman
**MARKETING AND
COMMUNICATIONS MANAGER:**
Leigh Mawby
**COACHING STAFF:** Terry Wallace
(senior), Brian Royal (assistant),
David Noble (development coach)
**SELECTION COMMITTEE:** Phil
Maylin (chairman), Terry
Wallace, Brian Royal, Gordon
Casey, Oberon Pirak, David
Noble
**CLUB DOCTOR:** Jake
Landsberger, Gary Zimmerman
**CLUB PHYSIOTHERAPISTS:**
Simon Macauley, Sue Cautley
**JOINED AFL:** 1925
**HOME GROUND:** E.J. Whitten
Oval, Barkly Street, Footscray
West; Optus Oval, Princes Park,
Royal Parade, North Carlton
**GROUND DIMENSIONS:** E.J.
Whitten Oval — 176m by 123m.
Optus Oval — 160m by 137m
**OFFICIAL COLORS:** Royal blue,
red and white hoop, and
featuring a stylised white
Bulldog logo on chest. Socks:
Royal blue with red and white
band. Shorts: Royal blue
(home), white (away).
**PREMIERSHIPS:** 1954
**BROWNLOW MEDALLISTS:** A.
Hopkins (1930 tied), N. Ware
(1941), P. Box (1956), J. Schultz
(1960), G. Dempsey (1975),
K. Templeton (1980), B. Hardie
(1985), T. Liberatore (1990),
S. Wynd (1992)
**RECORD HOME ATTENDANCE**
(Whitten Oval): 42,354 — July
9, 1955 v Collingwood; (Optus
Oval): 24,897 — June 7, 1997
v Geelong

# WESTERN BULLDOGS

## Dogs made the leap; now to hold the form

In terms of rungs on the ladder, the Western Bulldogs made the biggest jump of all clubs in 1997 — 12 very big steps from 15th to third.

They came ever so close to playing in their first Grand Final since 1961 when they led Adelaide by 31 points at half-time in the first preliminary final, but could manage only 3.7 in the last half to lose by two points. Two days later, star performer Chris Grant polled the most Brownlow Medal votes, but was ineligible to win due to a one-week Tribunal suspension.

As hard as those events were, I see it as all part of the toughening-up process.

In 1998, all clubs start from scratch again. What happened in 1997 doesn't count for anything when the field umpire puts the ball into play in March.

The major intangible ingredient the Bulldogs hopefully have retained from 1997 is self-belief. The players showed they were good enough with 15 wins and the pressure is on to repeat that with, maybe, a better ending.

Grant, Scott West, Brad Johnson, Rohan Smith, Tony Liberatore, Luke Darcy, Scott Wynd and possibly James Cook are the players who must keep a tight hold on things.

There is barely a risk with the above-mentioned players, with the possible exception of full-forward Cook. He had an eye-catching, solid-scoring finish to the season and if he can hold that form, the Dogs' forward division with be outstanding.

Grant, at centre half-forward, is a top aerialist and a winning Grant-Cook combination could be lethal.

Simon Minton-Connell, another specialist full-forward at Whitten Oval, started well last year, but the goals dried up as the season entered the home straight. He was the club's chief goal-kicker in '97 with 43 in 17 games and will again be putting in his claim.

Paul Hudson, another forward, lost his place for a while in '97 and will be under as much strain as ever to win the ball and kick his twos and threes.

The Bulldogs lost Daniel Hargreaves to Fremantle, which will not upset the status quo, and at the National Draft picked up a fine youngster in Mark Alvey, from the Bendigo Pioneers. In exchange for draft selections, they also secured Simon Garlick (Sydney) and Matthew Robbins (Geelong), who could be helpful.

The Bulldogs put themselves back on the map in 1997. We now wait with interest to see if the lift in status continues into 1998.

**— Greg Hobbs**

## THE YEAR AHEAD

| Rd | Date | Opponent | Venue | Home/ Away | Time (local) |
|----|------|----------|-------|------------|--------------|
| 1 | March 28 (N) | Brisbane Lions | G | A | 7.40pm |
| 2 | April 5 | Carlton | OO | H | 2.10pm |
| 3 | April 11 | Collingwood | OO | H | 2.10pm |
| 4 | April 18 | Geelong | KP | A | 2.10pm |
| 5 | April 26 | Sydney | SCG | A | 12.40pm |
| 6 | May 2 | Essendon | OO | H | 2.10pm |
| 7 | May 10 | North Melbourne | OO | H | 2.10pm |
| 8 | May 17 | Hawthorn | P | A | 2.10pm |
| 9 | May 23 | Richmond | P | H | 2.10pm |
| 10 | May 29 (N) | West Coast | W | A | 6.40pm |
| 11 | June 7 | Adelaide | OO | H | 2.10pm |
| 12 | June 14 | Fremantle | OO | H | 2.10pm |
| 13 | June 21 | Port Adelaide | FP | A | 8.10pm |
| 14 | June 27 | St Kilda | P | A | 2.10pm |
| 15 | July 4 | Melbourne | OO | H | 2.10pm |
| 16 | July 18 | Brisbane Lions | OO | H | 2.10pm |
| 17 | July 25 | Carlton | OO | A | 2.10pm |
| 18 | July 31 (N) | Collingwood | MCG | A | 7.40pm |
| 19 | August 8 | Geelong | OO | H | 2.10pm |
| 20 | August 15 | Sydney | P | H | 2.10pm |
| 21 | August 21 (N) | Essendon | MCG | A | 7.40pm |
| 22 | August 28 (N) | North Melbourne | MCG | A | 7.40pm |

## 1997 AT A GLANCE

**L:** R1: Western Bulldogs 11.10 (76) v Fremantle 10.20 (80) (OO)

**W:** R2: Western Bulldogs 13.12 (90) v Sydney 12.11 (83) (OO)

**W:** R3: Western Bulldogs 16.9 (105) v Richmond 12.14 (86) (MCG)

**W:** R4: Melbourne 13.9 (87) v Western Bulldogs 13.11 (89) (MCG)

**L:** R5: Western Bulldogs 9.17 (71) v Adelaide 19.7 (121) (OO)

**W:** R6: West Coast 14.15 (99) v Western Bulldogs 17.11 (113) (W)

### SNAPSHOT

**Games:** 24
**Won:** 15
**Lost:** 9
**Ladder finish:** 3rd
**Players used:** 36

**W:** R7: Western Bulldogs 19.19 (133) v Hawthorn 13.10 (88) (OO)

**L:** R8: Collingwood 19.15 (129) v Western Bulldogs 11.17 (83) (MCG)

**W:** R9: Western Bulldogs 16.7 (103) v Nth Melbourne 10.11 (71) (MCG)

**W:** R10: Essendon 17.12 (114) v Western Bulldogs 20.16 (136) (MCG)

**W:** R11: Western Bulldogs 14.12 (96) v Geelong 11.9 (75) (OO)

**L:** R12: Western Bulldogs 12.10 (82) v Port Adelaide 14.10 (94) (OO)

**W:** R13: St Kilda 11.18 (84) v Western Bulldogs 15.11 (101) (P)

**W:** R14: Carlton 11.8 (74) v Western Bulldogs 16.14 (110) (OO)

**L:** R15: Western Bulldogs 11.7 (73) v Brisbane Lions 21.11 (137) (OO)

**L:** R16: Fremantle 15.7 (97) v Western Bulldogs 13.13 (91) (S)

**L:** R17: Sydney 22.17 (149) v Western Bulldogs 7.10 (52) (SCG)

**L:** R18: Richmond 17.13 (115) v Western Bulldogs 15.10 (100) (OO)

**W:** R19: Western Bulldogs 14.18 (102) v Melbourne 9.10 (64) (OO)

**W:** R20: Adelaide 7.18 (60) v Western Bulldogs 16.7 (103) (FP)

**W:** R21: Western Bulldogs 12.14 (86) v West Coast 10.8 (68) (WO)

**W:** R22: Hawthorn 13.9 (87) v Western Bulldogs 15.15 (105) (P)

## The Coach

### Terry Wallace

**Born:** 13/12/58

Wallace went close to taking the Western Bulldogs from 15th place in 1996 into the Grand Final in his first full season as senior coach. A second-half fade-out in the first preliminary final against Adelaide ended their season.

However, Wallace did a magnificent job and pressed for selection as coach of the AFL's All-Australian side.

He started 1997 with 10 games' experience as a senior coach (in 1996) following the departure of Alan Joyce and amid widespread criticism for starting training in October.

At the end of the home and away series in 1997, the Bulldogs were third (14 wins/eight losses). They won their second qualifying final, but crashed at the next hurdle.

Wallace played League football with three clubs, but it was at Hawthorn that he won acclaim as a three-times premiership player, playing 174 games (1978-86) and winning two best and fairest awards.

He then played with Richmond (11 games, 1987) and with the Bulldogs (69 games, 1988-91).

He coached the Bulldogs' reserves from 1992 to '95, landing a premiership in 1994.

### AT A GLANCE

**COACHING RECORD**
**Footscray**

| Season | P | W | L | D | Pos |
|--------|-----|-----|-----|-----|-----|
| 1996 | 10 | 3 | 7 | — | 15 |
| 1997 | 24 | 15 | 9 | — | 3 |
| **Total** | **34** | **18** | **16** | | |

## WIN/LOSS RECORD

| Against | P | W (N) | L (N) | D (N) |
|---|---|---|---|---|
| Adelaide | 12 | 7 | 5 (3) | 0 |
| Brisbane Bears | 17 | 13 (2) | 4 (1) | 0 |
| Brisbane Lions | 1 | 0 | 1 | 0 |
| Carlton | 120 | 40 | 76 | 4 |
| Collingwood | 123 | 31 | 91 (2) | 1 |
| Essendon | 130 | 50 | 79 (1) | 1 |
| Fitzroy | 126 | 72 | 54 | 0 |
| Fremantle | 5 | 2 | 3 | 0 |
| Geelong | 127 | 45 | 80 (2) | 2 |
| Hawthorn | 132 | 66 | 65 (1) | 1 |
| Melbourne | 132 | 88 (1) | 73 | 1 |
| North Melb | 128 | 63 | 62 (3) | 3 |
| Port Adel | 1 | 0 | 1 | 0 |
| Richmond | 126 | 56 | 69 | 1 |
| St Kilda | 127 | 63 | 62 | 2 |
| Sydney | 130 | 66 (1) | 63 (1) | 1 |
| West Coast | 18 | 6 (1) | 12 (4) | 0 |
| **TOTALS** | **1455** | **638 (5)** | **800 (18)** | **17 (0)** |

*(N) Premiership matches played at night*

## WINNING RUNS

11 v Fitzroy (1990–1996)
10 v Brisbane Bears (1990–1996)
9 v Hawthorn (1944–1948)
9 v SM/Sydney (1961–1966)
8 v Richmond (1960–1964)
7 v Essendon (1952–1955)
6 v Collingwood (1942–1946)
6 v Geelong (1941–1946)
6 v North Melb (1984–1986)
5 v St Kilda (1992–1994)
4 v Melbourne (1931–1933);
4 v (1953–1954)
4 v Carlton (1984–1986)
3 v Adelaide (1991–1992)
2 v West Coast (1997– )
1 v Fremantle (1995); (1996)

## 1997 BEST AND FAIREST

The match committee awards votes on a 4, 3, 2, 1 system, with four votes being awarded only for an outstanding game.

**1** Scott West (35)
**2** Chris Grant (32)
**3** Tony Liberatore (31)
**4** Jose Romero (29)
**5** Brad Johnson (26)
**6** Scott Wynd (25)
**7** Rohan Smith (24)
**8** Craig Ellis (18)
**9** Luke Darcy (16)
**10** Matthew Dent (15)

## GAMES RECORDS

**329** Doug Hawkins (1978–94)
**321** Ted Whitten Senior (1951–70)
**272** Arthur Olliver (1935–50)
**261** Steven Wallis (1983–96)
**224** Albie Morrison (1928–38; 1941–42; 1946)
**207** Gary Dempsey (1967–78)
**205** Wally Donald (1946–58)
**200** Norman Ware (1932–42; 1944–46)
**199** Brian Royal (1983–93)
**197** Tony Liberatore (1986– )

## GOALS RECORDS

**575** Simon Beasley (1982–89)
**494** Kelvin Templeton (1974–82)
**385** Jack Collins (1950–58)
**369** Albie Morrison (1928–38; 1941–42; 1946)
**360** Ted Whitten Senior (1951–70)
**354** Arthur Olliver (1935–50)
**314** Chris Grant (1990– )
**299** Brian Royal (1983–93)
**294** Bill Wood (1944; 1946–51)
**288** George Bisset (1963–72)

## HIGHS AND LOWS

| Against | Highest | Lowest | G. W. Margin | G. L. Margin |
|---|---|---|---|---|
| Adelaide | 22.11.143 (1992) | 6.10.46 (1995) | 87 (1992) | 50 (1997) |
| Brisbane Bears | 22.21.153 (1987) | 3.4.22 (1996) | 82 (1987) | 87 (1996) |
| Brisbane Lions | 11.7.73 (1997) | 11.7.73 (1997) | — | 64 (1997) |
| Carlton | 22.10.142 (1985) | 4.1.25 (1966) | 59 (1989) | 129 (1982) |
| Collingwood | 18.16.124 (1976) | 3.10.28 (1966) | 56 (1955) | 126 (1926) |
| Essendon | 29.15.189 (1977) | 3.5.23 (1989) | 100 (1977) | 146 (1982) |
| Fitzroy | 25.17.167 (1980) | 4.6.30 (1951) | 104 (1994) | 77 (1981) |
| Fremantle | 18.9.117 (1996) | 11.10.76 (1997) | 18 (1996) | 31 (1995) |
| Geelong | 26.14.170 (1985) | 1.8.14 (1965) | 83 (1968) | 88 (1995) |
| Hawthorn | 23.27.165 (1946) | 3.3.21 (1964) | 112 (1946) | 143 (1982) |
| Melbourne | 26.13.169 (1985) | 3.6.24 (1963) | 120 (1985) | 80 (1943) |
| North Melb | 25.14.164 (1984) | 5.7.37 (1996) | 92 (1971) | 131 (1996) |
| Port Adel | 12.10.82 (1997) | 12.10.82 (1997) | — | 12 (1997) |
| Richmond | 25.16.166 (1985) | 3.11.29 (1935) | 78 (1989) | 115 (1980) |
| St Kilda | 33.15.213 (1978) | 3.12.30 (1927) | 107 (1978) | 81 (1967) |
| Sydney | 25.14.164 (1992) | 4.11.35 (1991) | 87 (1954) | 108 (1987) |
| West Coast | 18.13.121 (1987) | 3.11.29 (1988) | 42 (1993) | 118 (1991) |

# THE LEADERSHIP AT THE WESTERN BULLDOGS

| Year | Pos | Coach | Captain | Best & Fairest | Leading Goalkicker | |
|------|-----|-------|---------|----------------|--------------------|---|
| 1931 | 5 | B. Cubbins | B. Cubbins | A. Hopkins | A. Morrison | 36 |
| 1932 | 7 | B. Cubbins | B. Cubbins | I. McAlpine | L. Dayman | 37 |
| 1933 | 7 | B. Cubbins | I. McAlpine | A. Morrison | A. Rait | 59 |
| 1934 | 9 | A. Morrison | A. Morrison | N. Ware | A. Morrison | 46 |
| 1935 | 11 | A. Morrison | A. Morrison | G. Bennett | J. Ryan | 25 |
| 1936 | 10 | S. Coventy | S. Penberthy | A. Morrison | A. Olliver | 37 |
| 1937 | 11 | S. Coventry/ | S. Dockendorf, | N. Ware | A. Olliver | 39 |
|  |  | J. Kelly | A. Morrison |  |  |  |
| 1938 | 4 | J. Kelly | R. Evans | N. Ware | C. Luke | 44 |
| 1939 | 11 | J. Kelly | R. Evans | H. Hickey | C. Page | 31 |
| 1940 | 6 | J. Kelly | N. Ware | N. Ware | C. Page | 52 |
| 1941 | 6 | N. Ware | N. Ware | N. Ware/A. Olliver | A. Collins | 35 |
| 1942 | 4 | N. Ware | N. Ware | E. Ellis | N. Ware | 51 |
| 1943 | 6 | A. Olliver | A. Olliver | A. Collins | A. Collins | 40 |
| 1944 | 4 | A. Olliver | A. Olliver | A. Olliver | W. Wood | 51 |
| 1945 | 5 | A. Olliver | A. Olliver | H. Hickey | J. Ryan | 37 |
| 1946 | 4 | A. Olliver | A. Olliver | J. Ryan | W. Wood | 52 |
| 1947 | 9 | J. Crowe | H. Hickey | J. Ryan | W. Wood | 75 |
| 1948 | 4 | A. Olliver | A. Olliver | H. Hickey | W. Wood | 41 |
| 1949 | 9 | A. Olliver | A. Olliver | W. Donald | A. Olliver | 28 |
| 1950 | 10 | A. Olliver | A. Olliver | C. Sutton | W. Wood | 45 |
| 1951 | 4 | C. Sutton | C. Sutton | J. Collins | C. Sutton/A. Linton | 23 |
| 1952 | 10 | C. Sutton | C. Sutton | J. Collins | R. Duffy | 20 |
| 1953 | 3 | C. Sutton | C. Sutton | H. Stevens | J. Collins | 50 |
| 1954 | 1 | C. Sutton | C. Sutton | E. Whitten | J. Collins | 84 |
| 1955 | 5 | C. Sutton | C. Sutton | P. Box | J. Collins | 60 |
| 1956 | 3 | C. Sutton | C. Sutton/W. Donald | D. Ross | M.Cross | 52 |
| 1957 | 6 | C. Sutton/E. Whitten | H. Stevens/E. Whitten | E. Whitten | J. Collins | 74 |
| 1958 | 11 | E. Whitten | E. Whitten | E. Whitten | J. Collins | 49 |
| 1959 | 12 | E. Whitten | E. Whitten | E. Whitten | R. Baxter | 35 |
| 1960 | 10 | E. Whitten | E. Whitten | J. Schultz | R. Baster | 37 |
| 1961 | 2 | E. Whitten | E. Whitten | E. Whitten | E. Whitten | 42 |
| 1962 | 5 | E. Whitten | E. Whitten | J. Schultz | E. Whitten | 38 |
| 1963 | 9 | E. Whitten | E. Whitten | R. Walker | M. Hobbs/G. Bisset | 16 |
| 1964 | 7 | E. Whitten | E. Whitten | J. Schultz | G. Bisset/E. Whitten | 24 |
| 1965 | 10 | E. Whitten | E. Whitten | J. Schultz | M. Hobbs | 24 |
| 1966 | 10 | E. Whitten | E. Whitten | J. Schultz | K. Jackman | 28 |
| 1967 | 12 | C. Sutton | E. Whitten | J. Jillard | G. Bisset | 27 |
| 1968 | 10 | C. Sutton | E. Whitten | D. Thorpe | E. Whitten | 36 |
| 1969 | 11 | E. Whitten | E. Whitten | G. Bisset | G. Bisset | 45 |
| 1970 | 7 | E. Whitten | E. Whitten/S. Magee | G. Dempsey | G. Bisset | 45 |
| 1971 | 8 | E. Whitten | G. Dempsey | D. Thorpe | B. Quinlan | 48 |
| 1972 | 7 | R. Rose | G. Dempsey | P. Welsh | L. Sandilands | 39 |
| 1973 | 9 | R. Rose | D. Thorpe | G. Dempsey | L. Sandilands | 34 |
| 1974 | 5 | R. Rose | L. Sandilands | G. Dempsey | L. Sandilands | 50 |
| 1975 | 7 | R. Rose | L. Sandilands | G. Dempsey | L. Sandilands | 47 |
| 1976 | 5 | W. Goggin | L. Sandilands | G. Dempsey | K. Templeton | 82 |
| 1977 | 7 | W. Goggin | G. Dempsey | G. Dempsey | K. Templeton | 40 |
| 1978 | 11 | W. Goggin/ | G. Dempsey | K. Templeton | K.Templeton | 118 |
|  |  | D. McKenzie |  |  |  |  |
| 1979 | 9 | D. McKenzie | G. Jennings | I. Dunstan | K. Templeton | 91 |
| 1980 | 10 | R. Hart | G. Jennings | K. Templeton | K. Templeton | 75 |
| 1981 | 11 | R. Hart | G. Jennings | I. Dunstan | J. Edmond/S. Loveless | 25 |
| 1982 | 12 | R. Hart/I. Hampshire | K. Templeton | I. Dunstan | S. Beasley | 82 |
| 1983 | 7 | I. Hampshire | J. Edmond | B. Royal | S. Beasley | 69 |
| 1984 | 7 | M. Malthouse | J. Edmond | A. Purser | S. Beasley | 61 |
| 1985 | 3 | M. Malthouse | J. Edmond | D. Hawkins | S. Beasley | 105 |
| 1986 | 8 | M. Malthouse | R. Kennedy | B. Hardie | S. Bealsey | 88 |
| 1987 | 7 | M. Malthouse | R. Kennedy | A. McGuinness | S. Beasley | 73 |
| 1988 | 8 | M. Malthouse | R. Kennedy | T. Wallace | S. Beasley | 82 |
| 1989 | 13 | M. Malthouse | S. Wallis | T. Wallace | A. Campbell | 21 |
| 1990 | 7 | T. Wheeler | D. Hawkins | P. Foster | C. Grant | 51 |
| 1991 | 10 | T. Wheeler | D. Hawkins | T. Liberatore | D. Hawkins | 38 |
| 1992 | 3 | T. Wheeler | D. Hawkins | S. Wynd | D. Del-Re | 70 |
| 1993 | 9 | T. Wheeler | D. Hawkins | L. Cameron | D. Del-Re | 36 |
| 1994 | 6 | T. Wheeler/A. Joyce | S. Wynd | C. Grant | C. Grant | 71 |
| 1995 | 7 | A. Joyce | S. Wynd | S. West | R. Osborne | 53 |
| 1996 | 15 | A. Joyce/T. Wallace | S. Wynd | C. Grant/J. Romero | J. Watts | 44 |
| 1997 | 3 | T. Wallace | S. Wynd | S. West | S. Minton-Connell | 43 |

# PLAYER PROFILES

### ANTHONY ALOI
Won the Western Jets' best and fairest in 1997 and has had experience with Melton. A member of the Victoria Metro squad in the AFL National Under-18 Championships in '97, but did not make the final list. However, his form was not affected and he showed out as a centreman/half-back who obviously caught the eye of the Bulldogs' recruiting team. The Dogs' third choice (63rd overall) at the 1997 National Draft.

### MARK ALVEY
Brilliant on-baller who moved from Wentworth, NSW, into the Bendigo Pioneers side and had a star-studded 1997 season, winning the club's best and fairest. Was the Bulldogs' first selection (18th overall) at the 1997 National Draft. Recruiting experts had predicted he would be snapped up in the first 20. Has an uncanny ability to kick goals and should quickly make his presence felt with the Dogs.

### NATHAN BROWN
Left-footer who won the club's best first-year player award in 1997. Clever and quick on the wing/half-forward/forward pocket and should quickly add to his 14 games last year. Was the Bulldogs' first selection at the 1996 National Draft after grooming with Victorian country clubs Golden Square and Bendigo Pioneers.
**Player honors:** Morrish Medal 1996.

### LEON CAMERON
A senior player since 1990 and over the distance has had to contend with plenty of injuries. Is regarded as one of the elder statesmen at the club, coming out of the same National Draft batch in 1988 as the side's champion forward, Chris Grant. Cameron was the Bulldogs' first pick (seventh overall) and Grant the ninth and last (105 overall). Cameron is well accustomed to the wing/half-back and it was the old Cameron who starred in the qualifying final win over Sydney at the MCG last year.
**Player honors:** best and fairest 1993; 3rd best and fairest 1995.

### ADAM CONTESSA
Nuggety half-back who spent two seasons on North Melbourne's supplementary list (1995-96), where he played 46 reserves games. Also played reserves games with St Kilda (three) and Sydney (three) in 1994. His 17 reserves games with the Bulldogs in '97 took his total to 71. Played four games in senior ranks in 1997, after being promoted from the rookie list during the season in place of Scott Taylor. Has had surgery to an injured shoulder since last year and was a reserve grade best and fairest winner in 1997.

### JAMES COOK
Snatched the full-forward position from Simon Minton-Connell last season and finished in fine fettle. Many believe Cook is one of the keys to 1998. If he can hold his form from late 1997, when he kicked seven goals in the last home and away game, four in the qualifying final and six in the first preliminary final, the Bulldogs will be ecstatic. Bold forward with strength, who was at the crossroads when he grabbed his chance last year. Won club award for being best player in the 1997 finals.
**Player honors:** AFL Norwich Rising Star nominee 1994.
**Previous AFL club:** Carlton (1994-95: 25 games, 35 goals).

### SIMON COX
Winner of club's 'most promising player' award in 1997 after shining in latter half of season. The tall defender won his way back into the senior line-up in round 18 and stayed until the end after picking up just three senior games earlier in the season. The former Glenelg player had 11 reserves games in 1997.

### MATTHEW CROFT
His name first appeared on the Bulldogs' books when taken as the club's No. 2 selection at the 1989 National Draft. Made his senior debut in 1991 and his career has rolled along without reaching dizzy heights. A competent spare parts player who can hold down full-back, centre half-back or take a place up forward. Had 20 games in 1997 — his best season's haul. Has played 63 games, plus another 43 in the reserves. The pleasing part for him is that none of those reserves games were in 1997.

### TODD CURLEY
Hit his straps late in 1997, was part of the finals make-up and will be anxious to hold down a place on the half-back line or maybe at half-forward. Had to fight hard to win his stripes last year and in with his 10 senior appearances were 11 in the reserves. Journeyed from WA and made his debut with Collingwood in 1994, but after one season and three games, returned to West Perth. Did well and the Bulldogs jumped in at the 1995 National Draft and took him as their second pick.
**Previous AFL club:** Collingwood (1994: 3 games, 1 goal).

### LUKE DARCY
Continues to show the right signs of developing into a top-liner. Strong in the air — took 131 marks in 1997 to be second at the club behind Chris Grant (170) — and is a long left-foot kick. Takes his turn in the ruck and has the height to hold down key forward positions. Missed only one game in 1997 when given a short spell in the reserves to sharpen up. Will continue to work in tandem with captain/ruckman Scott Wynd.
**Player honors:** AFL Norwich Rising Star nominee 1996.

### MATTHEW DENT
Aggressive at half-back and a real bonus for the Bulldogs. One of the players not picked up by Brisbane following the Brisbane Bears-Fitzroy merger. The Bulldogs selected him second at the 1996 National Draft and were repaid with 20 games in 1997. He relished being in a side with depth and playing in his first finals series. Missed two games due to suspension and had one run in the reserves in 1997.
**Previous AFL club:** Fitzroy (1994-96: 47 games, 9 goals).

### PAUL DIGIOVINE
A ruckman with potential. Put in an impressive 1997

with the Oakleigh Chargers, easily winning their best and fairest award and finishing second in the TAC Cup coaches' award. A member of the Victoria Metro side at the 1997 National Under-18 Championships. His credentials are spotless and he will be brought along without haste.

## PAUL DIMATTINA

Season 1997 was vital as a poor year may have spelt the end for him as an AFL player. He had his best year, but unfortunately missed the club's two finals because of a Tribunal suspension. He was also suspended for one game in round eight. Apart from those blemishes, he worked strongly in the midfield with Jose Romero and Tony Liberatore and his 17 games for the season was much better than his two in 1995 and 10 in 1996. Has had ankle surgery since last season.

## PAUL DOOLEY

A 22-year-old ruckman waiting in the wings for his senior chance. Dooley played 13 games with Melbourne reserves in 1995, won the Liston Trophy with Williamstown in '96 and was selected by the Bulldogs at the 1996 National Draft as their sixth selection and 58th overall. Season 1997 was a development year for Dooley when he won the reserve coach's award. Time has arrived when he must start making a noise.
**Player honors:** Liston Trophy 1996.

## CRAIG ELLIS

One of the most improved players in the AFL last year. Ellis was strong at centre half-back, which freed up Chris Grant, the star centre half-back in 1996, to play at centre half-forward. Ellis did not miss a match in 1997 and played in his first finals. He starts 1998 with 46 senior games and 46 in the reserves. Season 1997 was the making of Ellis, following eight games in '94, two in '95 and 12 in '96. A shoulder injury has been attended to since last year.

## SIMON GARLICK

One of the newcomers at Whitten Oval this year after an up-and-down stint of 44 games with Sydney, including only two last year. Had knee trouble and suffered a broken collarbone in 1997, but finished the year in the reserves' finals. Was good enough to play in all Sydney's finals, including the Grand Final, in 1996. Probably does his best on the forward line, but the Bulldogs may have other ideas. Traded for a second-round draft pick (No. 31) and will be trying to resurrect his career.
**Previous AFL club:** Sydney (1994-97: 44 games, 27 goals).

## CHRIS GRANT

Champion centre half-forward in 1997, who was also brilliant at centre half-back the year before. Has grace and poise, was the AFL's second most prolific mark in 1997 with 170 grabs (behind only Stewart Loewe of St Kilda), and polled the most Brownlow Medal votes (27), but was ineligible because of a Tribunal suspension. One of the AFL's champions and a member of the 1997 All-Australian side.
**Player honors:** best and fairest 1994, 1996 (equal); 2nd best and fairest 1997; 3rd Brownlow Medal 1996; All-Australian 1997; leading club goalkicker 1990, 1994.

## PAUL HUDSON

Had his first season with the Bulldogs in 1997 after being drafted for his goalkicking prowess and general nous on the half-forward line. Made his name at Hawthorn, as did his father, Peter, of goalkicking fame, but was in need of a change. Kicked 27 goals last year to take his career total to 291. His father kicked 727 for the Hawks so the father/son grand total reached 1018. Not all plain sailing in 1997 and Hudson had three games in the reserves.
**Player honors:** Hawthorn premiership side 1991; Hawthorn night premiership sides 1991, 1992; Michael Tuck Medal 1992.
**Previous AFL club:** Hawthorn (1990-96: 134 games, 264 goals).

## BRAD JOHNSON

Class act across the centre-line and unlucky not to have won a wing position in the 1997 All-Australian side. Has pace, courage and works in well with his forwards. Won selection in the Victorian State of Origin side in 1997 in a season which saw him top the club's kicks list (375 — seventh best in the competition). Had surgery to a knee after last season and starts 1998 as a 21-year-old with 76 games behind him. His fourth season last year was his best.
**Player honors:** AFL Norwich Rising Star nominee 1995.

## STEVE KOLYNIUK

A long-time servant of the club, his first game was against North Melbourne in round 20, 1987, when Mick Malthouse was coach. Senior (137) and reserves (62) games total 199, so there has been much mileage in this roving, opportunist forward. Hit two suspension hurdles in 1997 — the second hitting him severely as he missed the qualifying final and was not recalled for the preliminary final. Also dropped in the countdown to the finals, so it wasn't a happy finish.

## STEVE KRETIUK

Hard-nosed defender who had thigh troubles and played a few games in the reserves in the first half of last season. In the second half, he missed only one senior game. Started with the Bulldogs' reserves in 1990, made his senior debut in 1992 and has played six finals with the club at senior level. Will press on this year and should be in the shadows of 100 games at season's end. Had surgery on a wrist after the 1997 season.
**Player honors:** 2nd best and fairest 1994.

## TYSON LANE

Has struggled to progress from his opening season in 1995, when he won an AFL Norwich Rising Star nomination. Has an overall games tally of 14 in three seasons. Last season, played a further 21 games in the reserves. Has ability at half-forward and in a couple of memorable games, kicked five goals against Melbourne in 1995 and put in a classy effort against Carlton in the solid win at Optus Oval last year.
**Player honors:** AFL Norwich Rising Star nominee 1995.

### TONY LIBERATORE

Still the pocket dynamo of League football. Thickly set and standing at only 164cm, he bores in at the bottom of packs, tackles fiercely, tags tenaciously and talks incessantly. An old hand at upsetting more polished rivals with his close-checking tactics, a player with immense spirit and an unbending will to win. Needs three games in '98 for his 200 — an innings that reached a high point in 1990 when he won the Brownlow Medal. Has since fought back from a couple of 'lows' and was third in the 1997 best and fairest.
**Player honors:** Brownlow Medal 1990; best and fairest 1991; 2nd best and fairest 1992, 1993, 1995; 3rd best and fairest 1994, 1997; Gardiner Medal 1986, 1988; Morrish Medal 1984.

### MICHAEL MARTIN

Quick and can kick long distances, generally from half-back or the wing. The club's first choice at the 1994 National Draft, he came across from Hobart and made his senior debut in 1995. Has managed only 17 senior games in three seasons and in that time has played 48 in the reserves, including 13 last year. Had six senior games in 1997 at the important end of the season, including two in the finals. That should be the stimulus for 1998.

### SIMON MINTON-CONNELL

Had a bright start with the Bulldogs in 1997 and looked like being the answer at full-forward. Had 39 on the board in the first 11 games, but his next five games produced only four goals. Lost his place to James Cook, who finished the season as the spearhead. A good mark and kick, but seemed to lose his confidence when his goals dried up. Now faces a task to win back his position at his fourth AFL club. A very handy forward to have on stand-by.
**Player honors:** Sydney leading goalkicker 1992, 1993, 1994; Bulldogs leading goalkicker 1997.
**Previous AFL clubs:** Carlton (1989-91: 19 games, 50 goals); Sydney (1992-94: 46 games, 168 goals); Hawthorn (1995-96: 22 games, 34 goals).

### BRETT MONTGOMERY

On the Bulldogs' supplementary list in 1996 and was drafted later that year. Played 22 reserves games in '96 and won club best and fairest in that grade. Played four games with Essendon reserves in 1991, but then played with Springvale. Overcame injuries to play 16 games last year and proved to be a more than useful half-forward/goalkicker. Got his act together at the business end of the season and played in the finals. Came from virtual obscurity to a preliminary final in one year.

### JIM PLUNKETT

Crafty midfielder in the mould of former Bulldog Simon Atkins. Polled fourth in the 1997 Gardiner Medal voting, is waiting for his senior chance and gives the impression he will not look back when the break comes. Well-schooled in football at Montmorency and the Preston Knights. In 1996, he played six games in Collingwood's reserves, was picked in the VSFL team of the year on a forward flank and was selected in the national under-17 All-Australian side. Has spotless credentials.

### STEPHEN POWELL

Left-footer and a tough customer on the wing/half-forward/ruck-roving. Spent two years on the Bulldogs' supplementary list and was runner-up in its best and fairest voting in 1996. A product of St Kevin's College in Melbourne, he has played 59 reserves games — one with Carlton in 1994 and 58 with the Dogs over the past three seasons. Thrown in the deep end last year in his first senior game against the West Coast's Peter Matera and did well. A thigh injury hampered his season.

### PETER QUILL

Wing/centreman who had four senior games in 1997, which was by far his worst effort since his debut in 1993. Played 15 games in the reserves in 1997 and will have to work very hard to win back a regular senior berth and add to his 67 games. In his first four seasons, his lowest total in one season was 13, so four last year is of real concern for this former East Fremantle player who will be 29 in August. Has had a knee injury repaired since last year.

### JACOB RHODES

The youngest player on the Bulldogs' list in 1997, Rhodes turned 19 in January. Came up through South Warrnambool and the Geelong Falcons, where he won a best and fairest award in 1996. Last year, played 22 games in the reserves, including the losing preliminary final, and shows plenty of promise. Broke a leg in a pre-season practice game.

### MATTHEW ROBBINS

Became a Bulldog in the pre-national draft trading last October after seven senior games with Geelong (one in 1996 and six in '97). His last senior appearance was in round six, 1997, so is almost a forgotten player. Was traded for draft picks and the Bulldogs see him as a smallish, quick, solid and improving backline player.
**Previous AFL club:** Geelong (1996-97: 7 games, 0 goals).

### JOSE ROMERO

Works desperately hard in the midfield and his clearances out of this heavy traffic area were up with the best in 1997. Went through the season without missing a match, despite damaging a shoulder in a qualifying final against Sydney. Had intensive treatment, got the all-clear to play in the preliminary final and suffered further injury to the shoulder and has since had more medical attention. Has signed on for another two years with the Bulldogs.
**Player honors:** equal best and fairest 1996.
**Previous AFL club:** North Melbourne (1988-94: 89 games, 98 goals).

### SEDAT SIR

Dour defender who had to contend with a nasty groin injury in 1997. Played eight senior games and 10 in the reserves and missed the senior finals action. His last game was in the losing reserves' preliminary final. A total of 23 games in three seasons is not setting the world on fire and he will be eager to post a double figures quota.

### ROHAN SMITH

Had another excellent season in 1997. Probably best

known at half-back, but won All-Australian selection in '97 as a half-forward. Kicked a couple of damaging goals in the qualifying final against Sydney last year. Has played 99 senior games and 41 in the reserves, but only one in the lower grade in past three seasons. Voted 'best clubman' in 1997.

**Player honors:** 3rd best and fairest 1996; All-Australian 1997.

## DANIEL SOUTHERN

Colorful character who spent his holidays after last season on the Amazon River in South America. Looks a way-out customer, but takes his football seriously and was disappointed to miss the 1997 qualifying final because of a Tribunal suspension. Had a back-related hamstring injury and also missed the preliminary final. It was a sour end after playing in 17 straight games to the eve of the finals. A keen defender with 64 games behind him and at 23, should play many more.

**Player honors:** AFL Norwich Rising Star nominee 1994.

## ROBERT STEVENSON

Picked up by Essendon at the 1993 National Draft as a promising defender from the Western Jets. However, he has managed only 11 senior games — six in 1994 and five last year. One of only three players with previous AFL experience taken at the 1997 National Draft, he was the Bulldogs' second pick and 47th overall. Turns 22 in June, so there is time to make good.

**Previous AFL club:** Essendon (1994-97: 11 games, 0 goals).

## SCOTT TAYLOR

Former Geelong Falcons captain who played his first AFL game with the Dogs in round one, 1996, and has not played a senior game since. In his debut, he broke a bone in a foot. First drafted by the Bulldogs late in 1994 and played '95 in the reserves. Was on the Bulldogs' list at the start of 1997, but delisted mid-season because of back trouble. Won his way back on to the list at the 1998 pre-season draft. Played a total of 42 reserves games — 38 for 55 goals with the Bulldogs, three with Geelong and one with Sydney. Not 22 until October so he has another chance to point his career in the right direction.

## JASON WATTS

Goalkicking forward pocket who was starved for opportunities in 1997, playing just four games after 20 in 1996. Played 19 games in the reserves, taking his total there to 61. Won the Bulldogs' goalkicking in 1996 with 44 goals, which included two bags of six. Needs to produce something special to win regular selection.

**Player honors:** leading goalkicker 1996.

## MARK WEST

Played the game of his life in the first preliminary final last year when the Dogs went down to Adelaide. He was in everything with 19 kicks, five handballs and two goals and if he can reproduce that form this year, the Bulldogs have a real live-wire wingman/rover. Had previously played only five home and away games in '97 and four in '96. Played with Brisbane Bears' reserves in 1991-92, then returned to South Australia.

## SCOTT WEST

Brilliant in the midfield and winner of the club best and fairest award for the second time in 1997. He was free of nagging injuries and was a play-maker with more disposals (367 kicks and 240 handballs for fourth in the AFL) than any of his teammates. Was still going strongly at the finish, winning votes in the qualifying and preliminary finals. Reached 100 games in 1997.

**Player honors:** best and fairest 1995, 1997; AFL Norwich Rising Star nominee 1993.

## BRAD WIRA

One of the unlucky Bulldogs who missed the 1997 senior finals, finishing the season in the reserves' preliminary final. Played the first 11 games, then missed two serving suspension following an incident with Geelong's Garry Hocking that sparked an AFL investigation. Returned for another five matches and was dropped after round 18, which was his last senior appearance.

**Previous AFL club:** Fremantle (1995: 1 game, 0 goals).

## SCOTT WYND

Club captain since 1994 and its chief ruckman in the 1990s. His peak year was 1992 when he won the Brownlow Medal. Has had plenty of knee-related injuries since his medal win and in 1994 was restricted to only nine games. It seemed he would be only the third player to captain the Dogs into a Grand Final (joining Charlie Sutton and Ted Whitten) in 1997, but a second-half fade-out in the first preliminary final put paid to that. Winner of 'most consistent player' award in 1997.

**Player honors:** Brownlow Medal 1992; best and fairest 1992; 2nd best and fairest 1991; third best and fairest 1993; All-Australian 1992; captain since 1994.

# ROOKIE LIST

## LINCOLN REYNOLDS

A grandson of Essendon triple Brownlow Medallist Dick Reynolds. From Port Melbourne and can play in key positions at either end of ground. Bulldogs are looking to him to develop into a defender. Trained with Melbourne and Essendon before being listed by the Bulldogs.

## SHAUN TINSLEY

Trained with Melbourne over the summer and the Bulldogs think he could have a future in the back half. Has height and uses the ball well.

# WESTERN BULLDOGS

| Name (# = rookie) | No. | Born | Height | Weight | Recruited from |
|---|---|---|---|---|---|
| Anthony Aloi | 19 | 25/9/79 | 184 | 79 | MELTON/WESTERN U18 |
| Mark Alvey | 31 | 1/6/80 | 179 | 72 | WENTWORTH (NSW)/BENDIGO U18 |
| Nathan G. Brown | 17 | 10/2/78 | 179 | 72 | GOLDEN SQUARE/BENDIGO U18 |
| Leon Cameron | 18 | 2/9/72 | 185 | 88 | SOUTH WARRNAMBOOL |
| Adam Contessa | 43 | 29/12/76 | 177 | 78 | COBURG/NORTHERN U18/NTH MLB RES |
| James Cook | 12 | 7/1/74 | 190 | 94 | NORTH HOBART (TAS)/CARLTON |
| Simon Cox | 26 | 25/1/77 | 192 | 92 | GLENELG (SA) |
| Matthew Croft | 16 | 26/2/73 | 185 | 88 | MILDURA IMPERIALS |
| Todd Curley | 11 | 14/1/73 | 188 | 80 | WEST PERTH (WA)/COLLINGWOOD |
| Luke Darcy | 14 | 12/7/75 | 195 | 96 | SOUTH ADELAIDE (SA) |
| Matthew Dent | 21 | 17/1/72 | 184 | 77 | STURT (SA)/FITZROY |
| Paul Digiovine | 42 | 2/7/79 | 195 | 87 | BEVERLEY HILLS/OAKLEIGH U18 |
| Paul Dimattina | 28 | 22/11/74 | 180 | 80 | SANDRINGHAM |
| Paul Dooley | 20 | 3/10/75 | 198 | 90 | WILLIAMSTOWN |
| Craig Ellis | 32 | 4/7/75 | 189 | 88 | STAWELL/WESTERN U18 |
| Simon Garlick | 4 | 10/4/75 | 176 | 78 | GLEN WAVERLEY ROVERS/CENTRAL U18/SYDNEY |
| Chris Grant | 3 | 13/12/72 | 192 | 94 | DAYLESFORD |
| Paul Hudson | 9 | 20/7/70 | 185 | 88 | GLENORCHY (TAS)/HAWTHORN |
| Brad Johnson | 6 | 18/7/76 | 182 | 85 | WILLIAMSTOWN/WESTERN U18 |
| Steven Kolyniuk | 2 | 5/7/70 | 176 | 84 | ST ALBANS |
| Steven Kretiuk | 35 | 4/7/72 | 183 | 86 | ST ALBANS |
| Tyson Lane | 27 | 25/8/76 | 179 | 82 | MELTON |
| Tony Liberatore | 39 | 11/2/66 | 164 | 76 | BRUNSWICK CITY/NORTH MELB RESERVES |
| Michael Martin | 23 | 25/2/77 | 179 | 80 | HOBART (TAS) |
| Simon Minton-Connell | 1 | 26/4/69 | 194 | 92 | NORTH HOBART (TAS)/CARLTON/SYDNEY/HAWTHORN |
| Brett Montgomery | 10 | 1/6/73 | 180 | 80 | SOUTH CROYDON/ESS RES/SPRINGVALE |
| Jim Plunkett | 13 | 26/7/78 | 178 | 74 | MONTMORENCY/NORTHERN U18 |
| Stephen Powell | 29 | 7/9/76 | 181 | 78 | ST KEVINS/CENTRAL U18 |
| Peter Quill | 22 | 23/8/69 | 182 | 84 | EAST FREMANTLE (WA) |
| Jacob Rhodes | 40 | 8/1/79 | 175 | 75 | SOUTH WARRNAMBOOL/GEELONG U18 |
| Matthew Robbins | 30 | 8/5/77 | 174 | 76 | ORMOND AMATEURS/CENTRAL U18/GEELONG |
| Jose Romero | 36 | 1/8/71 | 175 | 73 | JACANA/NORTH MELB |
| Sedat Sir | 38 | 6/3/75 | 188 | 85 | WEST COBURG/CENTRAL U18 |
| Rohan Smith | 5 | 31/5/73 | 182 | 80 | KINGSVILLE |
| Daniel Southern | 8 | 1/1/75 | 188 | 88 | CLAREMONT (WA) |
| Robert Stevenson | 37 | 14/6/76 | 188 | 90 | TAYLORS LAKES/WESTERN U18/ESSENDON |
| Scott Taylor | 44 | 22/10/76 | 180 | 76 | GROVEDALE/GEELONG U18 |
| Jason Watts | 25 | 29/7/71 | 185 | 80 | WERRIBEE |
| Mark West | 34 | 3/4/73 | 180 | 85 | SOUTH ADELAIDE (SA) |
| Scott West | 7 | 14/11/74 | 175 | 78 | STRATHMORE/ESSENDON GRAMMAR |
| Brad Wira | 24 | 16/3/72 | 179 | 75 | CLAREMONT (WA)/FREMANTLE |
| Scott Wynd | 15 | 25/1/70 | 201 | 105 | JACANA |
| Lincoln Reynolds # | 41 | 11/9/77 | 190 | 90 | GEELONG U18/PORT MELBOURNE |
| Shaun Tinsley # | 48 | 11/5/77 | 190 | 83 | EAST SANDRINGHAM/PRAHRAN U18/PORT MELB |
| **Total/(Average)** *On 26/2/98* | | **(23.6 yrs)*** | **(183)** | **(83)** | |

# PLAYERS 1998

| Debut | HOME & AWAY | | 1997 | | FINALS | | GRAND FINALS | | | NIGHT SERIES | | STATE OF ORIGIN | |
|---|---|---|---|---|---|---|---|---|---|---|---|---|---|
| | Gms | Gls | Gms | Gls | Gms | Gls | Gms | Gls | Won | Gms | Gls | Gms | Gls |
| | 0 | 0 | 0 | 0 | | | | | | 0 | 0 | 0 | 0 |
| | 0 | 0 | 0 | 0 | | | | | | 0 | 0 | 0 | 0 |
| 1997 | 14 | 10 | 14 | 10 | 2 | 2 | | | | 0 | 0 | 0 | 0 |
| 1990 | 133 | 55 | 17 | 6 | 5 | 2 | | | | 9 | 2 | 1 | 0 |
| 1997 | 4 | 0 | 4 | 0 | | | | | | 0 | 0 | 1 | 0 |
| 1994 | 44 | 76 | 14 | 36 | 4 | 15 | | | | 4 | 9 | 0 | 0 |
| 1995 | 15 | 6 | 10 | 3 | 2 | 1 | | | | 4 | 1 | 0 | 0 |
| 1991 | 63 | 35 | 20 | 17 | 4 | 0 | | | | 5 | 0 | 0 | 0 |
| 1994 | 31 | 25 | 10 | 2 | 2 | 0 | | | | 2 | 0 | 0 | 0 |
| 1994 | 47 | 36 | 23 | 24 | 2 | 0 | | | | 3 | 4 | 1 | 0 |
| 1994 | 67 | 14 | 20 | 5 | 2 | 1 | | | | 3 | 0 | 0 | 0 |
| | 0 | 0 | 0 | 0 | | | | | | 0 | 0 | 0 | 0 |
| 1995 | 29 | 10 | 17 | 8 | | | | | | 3 | 2 | 0 | 0 |
| | 0 | 0 | 0 | 0 | | | | | | 0 | 0 | 0 | 0 |
| 1994 | 46 | 1 | 24 | 1 | 2 | 0 | | | | 1 | 0 | 0 | 0 |
| 1994 | 44 | 27 | 2 | 1 | 3 | 0 | 1 | 0 | 0 | 6 | 3 | 0 | 0 |
| 1990 | 167 | 314 | 23 | 37 | 8 | 17 | | | | 9 | 11 | 4 | 4 |
| 1990 | 154 | 291 | 20 | 27 | 8 | 16 | 1 | 2 | 1 | 13 | 23 | 3 | 7 |
| 1994 | 76 | 47 | 24 | 16 | 5 | 4 | | | | 5 | 2 | 1 | 1 |
| 1987 | 137 | 141 | 17 | 14 | 3 | 1 | | | | 12 | 7 | 1 | 0 |
| 1992 | 76 | 9 | 15 | 0 | 6 | 0 | | | | 5 | 2 | 0 | 0 |
| 1995 | 14 | 9 | 3 | 1 | | | | | | 2 | 2 | 0 | 0 |
| 1986 | 197 | 89 | 24 | 8 | 8 | 1 | | | | 12 | 1 | 2 | 1 |
| 1995 | 17 | 5 | 6 | 1 | 2 | 0 | | | | 4 | 2 | 0 | 0 |
| 1989 | 104 | 295 | 17 | 43 | 1 | 0 | | | | 7 | 17 | 6 | 4 |
| 1997 | 16 | 18 | 16 | 18 | 2 | 2 | | | | 1 | 1 | 0 | 0 |
| | 0 | 0 | 0 | 0 | | | | | | 0 | 0 | 0 | 0 |
| 1997 | 3 | 2 | 3 | 2 | | | | | | 0 | 0 | 0 | 0 |
| 1993 | 67 | 20 | 4 | 1 | 1 | 0 | | | | 6 | 3 | 0 | 0 |
| | 0 | 0 | 0 | 0 | | | | | | 0 | 0 | 0 | 0 |
| 1996 | 7 | 0 | 6 | 0 | | | | | | 5 | 2 | 0 | 0 |
| 1988 | 150 | 130 | 24 | 11 | 3 | 0 | | | | 17 | 15 | 1 | 2 |
| 1995 | 23 | 0 | 8 | 0 | | | | | | 2 | 0 | 0 | 0 |
| 1992 | 99 | 66 | 24 | 26 | 5 | 3 | | | | 5 | 2 | 1 | 0 |
| 1994 | 64 | 10 | 17 | 2 | 2 | 1 | | | | 2 | 0 | 0 | 0 |
| 1994 | 11 | 0 | 5 | 0 | | | | | | 3 | 0 | 0 | 0 |
| 1996 | 1 | 0 | 1 | 0 | | | | | | 0 | 0 | 0 | 0 |
| 1994 | 56 | 51 | 4 | 2 | 2 | 1 | | | | 3 | 1 | 0 | 0 |
| 1996 | 11 | 2 | 7 | 2 | 2 | 2 | | | | 2 | 0 | 0 | 0 |
| 1993 | 102 | 41 | 24 | 5 | 5 | 2 | | | | 8 | 5 | 0 | 0 |
| 1995 | 38 | 2 | 16 | 1 | | | | | | 3 | 0 | 0 | 0 |
| 1988 | 170 | 27 | 23 | 3 | 5 | 0 | | | | 7 | 0 | 3 | 0 |
| | 0 | 0 | 0 | 0 | | | | | | 0 | 0 | | |
| | 0 | 0 | 0 | 0 | | | | | | 0 | 0 | | |
| | (55) | (44) | 506 | 333 | 96 | 71 | 2 | 2 | 1 | 173 | 117 | 25 | 19 |

# BRISBANE BEARS

## FAST FACTS

**Players:** 143

**Joined AFL:** 1987

**Ownership:** Original licence for Brisbane Bears was issued by the then VFL in October 1986, to a group headed by Paul Cronin. That organisation was subsequently backed by the Qintex group of companies led by Christopher Skase. After the Qintex group collapsed in 1989, control of the company went to Natala Investments led by Reuben Pelerman. It took over the running of the club in February 1990.
On November 28, 1991, it was announced that agreement had been reached with Reuben Pelerman to transfer the ownership of the Bears to a traditional membership-based structure.
The Brisbane Bears' membership grew from 5401 members in 1992 to 10,627 in 1996.

**Coaches:** Peter Knights 1987-R15 1989, Paul Feltham R15-R22 1989, Norm Dare 1990, Robert Walls 1991-1995, John Northey 1996.

### THE LAST BRISBANE BEARS TEAM

**1st Preliminary Final, September 21, 1996**
**Brisbane Bears v North Melbourne, MCG**
**B:** Chris Scott, Richard Champion, Danny Dickfos
**HB:** Nathan Chapman, Matthew Kennedy, Andrew Gowers
**C:** Craig McRae, Adrian Fletcher, Nigel Lappin
**HF:** Gilbert McAdam*, Dion Scott, Darryl White
**F:** Justin Leppitsch, Alastair Lynch, Shaun Hart
**R:** Matthew Clarke, Marcus Ashcroft, Craig Lambert
**I/C:** Michael McLean, Roger Merrett, Tristan Lynch
**COACH:** John Northey
*Michael Voss was replaced in the selected side by Gilbert McAdam due to an ankle injury.*

**Captains:** Mark Mickan 1987-1989, Roger Merrett 1990-1996.

**Games (includes finals):** played — 223 (won 72, lost 149, drew 2)

**Premierships:** nil

**Wooden spoons:** 1990, 1991

**Finals:** played — 4 (won 2, lost 2)

**Home grounds:** Carrara 1987-1992, Gabba 1993-1997

**Record attendance:** 21,964 v Essendon, Gabba, 2nd QF, 1996

**Record attendance:** 66,719 v North Melbourne PF, 1996

**Most games:** 164 Roger Merrett

**Most goals:** 169 Roger Merrett

**Most goals in a season:** 60 Roger Merrett 1993

**Most goals in finals:** 13 Alastair Lynch

**Most best and fairests:** 2 — John Gastev 1989, 1992; Michael McLean 1991, 1993; Michael Voss 1995, 1996

**Brownlow Medals:** Michael Voss 1996 (tied)

**Highest score:** 33.21.(219) v Sydney 1993 (Gabba)

**Lowest score:** 2.5.(17) v Haw 1988

**Highest finish:** 3rd 1996

**Most consecutive wins:** 7 — R15 1996-R21 1996

**Most consecutive losses:** 12 — R10 1990-R14 1991.

## WIN/LOSS RECORD

| Against | P | W (N) | L (N) | D (N) |
|---|---|---|---|---|
| Adelaide | 9 | 2(1) | 7(2) | 0 |
| Carlton | 17 | 4(1) | 13(2) | 0 |
| Collingwood | 15 | 2(1) | 13(3) | 0 |
| Essendon | 15 | 4(2) | 11(3) | 0 |
| Fitzroy | 17 | 11 | 6 | 0 |
| Footscray | 17 | 4(1) | 13(2) | 0 |
| Fremantle | 3 | 2(1) | 1 | 0 |
| Geelong | 15 | 4(1) | 10(1) | 1 |
| Hawthorn | 16 | 3(1) | 13(1) | 0 |
| Melbourne | 17 | 5(2) | 12(4) | 0 |
| North Melb | 17 | 5(3) | 12(3) | 0 |
| Richmond | 17 | 8(3) | 9(3) | 0 |
| St Kilda | 15 | 6(1) | 9 | 0 |
| Sydney | 16 | 10(2) | 6(2) | 0 |
| West Coast | 16 | 2(1) | 13(3) | 1(1) |
| **TOTALS** | **222** | **72(21)** | **148(29)** | **2(1)** |

*(N) Premiership matches played at night*

## WINNING RUNS

6 v Sydney (1992–1995)
5 v Fitzroy (1990–1993)
4 v Richmond (1987–1988)
3 v St Kilda (1994–1995)
3 v Essendon (1995–1996)
2 v Adelaide (1995)
2 v Carlton (1989)
2 v Geelong (1987)
2 v Melbourne (1992–1993); (1995– )
2 v St Kilda (1988); (1994– )
2 v Footscray (1996– )
2 v Hawthorn (1995– )
2 v North Melb (1996)
2 v West Coast (1996– )
2 v Fremantle (1996– )
1 v Collingwood (1996)

## GAMES RECORDS

**164** Roger Merrett (1988–96)
**152** Marcus Ashcroft (1989–)
**138** Scott McIvor (1988–)
**119** Richard Champion (1991– )
**113** John Gastev (1989–94)
**113** Matthew Kennedy (1990–)
**107** Martin Leslie (1989–95)
**102** Shaun Hart (1990–)
**101** Brad Hardie (1987–91)
**90** Darryl White (1992–)

## GOALS RECORDS

**285** Roger Merrett (1988–96)
**192** Brad Hardie (1987–91)
**106** Darryl White (1992–)
**89** Alastair Lynch (1994–)
**84** Marcus Ashcroft (1989–)
**81** Shaun Hart (1990–)
**77** Scott McIvor (1988–)
**72** Michael Voss (1992–)
**71** Warwick Capper (1988–90)
**65** Cameron O'Brien (1987–91)

## HIGHS AND LOWS

| Against | Highest | Lowest | G. W. Margin | G. L. Margin |
|---|---|---|---|---|
| Adelaide | 18.18.126 (1995) | 11.8.74 (1992) | 30 (1995) | 66 (1991) |
| Carlton | 26.14.170 (1996) | 5.8.38 (1996) | 97 (1996) | 103 (1987) |
| Collingwood | 17.19.121 (1994) | 6.15.51 (1996) | 44 (1994) | 101 (1991) |
| Essendon | 17.14.116 (1995) | 3.9.27 (1987) | 35 (1996) | 140 (1988) |
| Fitzroy | 29.13.187 (1996) | 5.13.43 (1993) | 109 (1996) | 104 (1993) |
| Footscray | 29.15.141 (1996) | 4.12.36 (1996) | 87 (1996) | 82 (1987) |
| Fremantle | 17.8.110 (1996) | 8.6.54 (1995) | 25 (1996) | 66 (1995) |
| Geelong | 25.13.163 (1990) | 6.14.50 (1989) | 66 (1990) | 164 (1992) |
| Hawthorn | 15.16.106 (1993) | 2.5.17 (1988) | 63 (1996) | 99 (1994) |
| Melbourne | 18.15.123 (1996) | 4.6.30 (1994) | 77 (1996) | 89 (1993) |
| North Melb | 25.17.167 (1989) | 7.12.54 (1990) | 83 (1989) | 94 (1989) |
| Richmond | 26.13.169 (1987) | 3.8.26 (1989) | 77 (1995) | 82 (1990) |
| St Kilda | 22.19.151 (1990 | 7.8.50 (1996) | 53 (1994) | 120 (1991) |
| Sydney | 33.21 219 (1993) | 7.13.55 (1990) | 162 (1993) | 74 (1992) |
| West Coast | 25.13.163 (1996) | 6.10.46 (1993) | 47 (1996) | 131 (1992) |

## THE LEADERSHIP AT THE BRISBANE BEARS

| Year | Pos | Coach | Captain | Best & Fairest | Leading Goalkicker | |
|---|---|---|---|---|---|---|
| 1987 | 13 | P. Knights | M. Mickan | P. Walsh | J. Edmond | 34 |
| 1988 | 13 | P. Knights | M. Mickan | M. Withers | W. Capper | 45 |
| 1989 | 10 | P. Knights/P. Feltham | M. Mickan | J. Gastev | B. Hardie | 54 |
| 1990 | 14 | N. Dare | R. Merrett | D. Bain/M. Leslie | B. Hardie | 37 |
| 1991 | 15 | R. Walls | R. Merrett | M. McLean | L. Schache | 47 |
| 1992 | 14 | R. Walls | R. Merrett | J. Gastev | J. Hutton | 43 |
| 1993 | 13 | R. Walls | R. Merrett | M. McLean | R. Merrett | 60 |
| 1994 | 12 | R. Walls | R. Merrett | C. Lambert | R. Merrett | 41 |
| 1995 | 8 | R. Walls | R. Merrett | M. Voss | R. Merrett | 44 |
| 1996 | 3 | J. Northey | R. Merrett | M. Voss | A. Lynch | 52 |

# FITZROY

## FAST FACTS

**Formed:** 1883 Fitzroy Town Hall

**Joined AFL:** 1897

**Merger History:** On October 3, 1989, the AFL announced that the Fitzroy FC would merge with the Footscray FC and start playing games under the banner of the Fitzroy Bulldogs with a redesigned jumper. On October 24, after a fundraising campaign by members of the Footscray FC, the VFL Commission supported Footscray continuing in the competition in its own right from 1990. The merger was abandoned. On Friday, June 28, 1996, the Nauru Insurance Corporation, a creditor of the Fitzroy FC, appointed Michael Brennan, to administer the affairs of the Fitzroy Football Club in order to ensure a loan of $1.25 million was to be repaid. The AFL guaranteed funds to allow Fitzroy to continue in the competition for the remainder of 1996. On July 4, 1996, the Fitzroy FC merged with the Brisbane Bears, to be based in Brisbane at the Gabba — an arrangement ensuring all creditors were repaid. At least eight Fitzroy players were to be selected by the Brisbane Lions before the

## THE LAST FITZROY TEAM

**September 1, 1996**
**Fitzroy v Fremantle, Subiaco Oval**

**B:** Brett Chandler, Jarrod Molloy, Stephen Paxman
**HB:** Martin Pike, Rowan Warfe, Shane Clayton
**C:** John Barker, Simon Atkins, Nick Carter
**HF:** Brad Boyd, John McCarthy, Chris Johnson
**F:** Marty Warry, Simon Hawking, John Rombotis
**R:** Matthew Primus, Matthew Dent, Scott Bamford
**I/C:** Peter Doyle, Jeffrey Hogg, Danny Morton
**COACH:** Alan McConnell

1996 National Draft and three Fitzroy representatives were to be on the new club's 11-member board.

**Games (includes finals):** played — 1928 (won 869, lost 1034, drew 25)

**Premierships:** 1898, 1899, 1904, 1905, 1913, 1916, 1922, 1944

**Wooden spoons:** 1936, 1963, 1964, 1966, 1980, 1995, 1996

**Finals:** played — 59 (won 34, lost 25)

**Home grounds:** Brunswick Street Oval 1897-1966, Junction Oval 1970-85, Victoria Park 1985-1986, Princes Park 1967-1969, 1987-1993, Whitten Oval 1994-1996

**Record home attendance:** 34,765 v Essendon, Brunswick St Oval, R14, 1923

**Most games:** 333 Kevin Murray

**Most goals:** 626 Jack Moriarty (1924-1933)

**Most goals in a season:** 116 Bernie Quinlan 1983

**Most goals in finals:** 42 Jim Freake

**Leading league goalkickers:** Jim Freake (56 — 1913, 66 — 1915), Jack Moriarty (82 — 1924), Bernie Quinlan (116 — 1983, 105 — 1984)

**Most best and fairests:** 9 — Kevin Murray

**Brownlow Medals:** Haydn Bunton (1931, 1932, 1935), Wilfred 'Chicken' Smallhorn (1933), Dinny Ryan (1936), Allan Ruthven (1950), Kevin Murray (1969), Bernie Quinlan (1981 tied)

**Highest score:** 36.22 (238) v Melbourne 1979

**Lowest score:** 1.0 (6) v Fitzroy 1953

**Most consecutive wins:** 14 — R10, 1898-R4 1899

**Most consecutive losses:** 27 — R11, 1963-R1, 1965

## GAMES RECORDS

| | |
|---|---|
| **333** | Kevin Murray (1955–64; 1967–74) |
| **269** | Paul Roos (1982–94) |
| **268** | Garry Wilson (1971–84) |
| **249** | Frank Curcio (1932–36; 1938–43; 1945–48) |
| **228** | Norm Johnstone (1944–57) |
| **222** | Alan Ruthven (1940–41; 1943–54) |
| **218** | David McMahon (1973–84) |
| **214** | John Murphy (1967–77) |
| **213** | Alan Gale (1948–61) |
| **213** | Warwick Irwin (1970–80; 1983) |

## GOALS RECORDS

| | |
|---|---|
| **626** | Jack Moriarty (1924–33) |
| **576** | Bernie Quinlan (1978–86) |
| **452** | Garry Wilson (1971–84) |
| **442** | Jimmy Freake (1912–24) |
| **442** | Alan Ruthven (1940–41; 1943–54) |
| **411** | Richard Osborne (1982–92) |
| **395** | Michael Conlan (1977–89) |
| **326** | John Murphy (1967–77) |
| **323** | Eddie Hart (1941; 1944; 1946–51) |
| **291** | Bob Beecroft (1976–80) |

## THE LEADERSHIP AT FITZROY

| Year | Pos | Coach | Captain | Best & Fairest | Leading Goalkicker | |
|------|-----|-------|---------|----------------|--------------------|--|
| 1931 | 10 | C. Niven | C. Niven | | J. Moriarty | 53 |
| 1932 | 10 | F. Maher | H. Bunton | | J. Moriarty | 81 |
| 1933 | 5 | F. Maher | J. Sexton | | J. Moriarty | 70 |
| 1934 | 8 | J. Cashman | J. Cashman | | L. Pye | 39 |
| 1935 | 7 | P. Rowe | C. Cameron | | D. Ryan | 46 |
| 1936 | 12 | H. Bunton | H. Bunton | | H. Bunton | 33 |
| 1937 | 7 | G. Rattray | H. Bunton | | H. Bunton | 37 |
| 1938 | 10 | G. Rattray | F. Curcio | | F. Hughson | 62 |
| 1939 | 8 | G. Rattray | F. Curcio | | C. Denning | 37 |
| 1940 | 7 | D. Minogue | F. Curcio | | C. Curtin | 56 |
| 1941 | 7 | D. Minogue | F. Curcio | | C. Curtin | 65 |
| 1942 | 6 | D. Minogue | M. Hearn | | C. Curtin | 61 |
| 1943 | 3 | F. Hughson | F. Hughson | | J. Grant | 42 |
| 1944 | 1 | F. Hughson | F. Hughson | | A. Ruthven | 46 |
| 1945 | 6 | F. Hughson | F. Hughson | | A. Ruthven | 42 |
| 1946 | 8 | F. Hughson | F. Hughson | A. Ruthven | C. Curtin | 56 |
| 1947 | 3 | F. Hughson | F. Hughson | N. Johnstone | E. Hart | 64 |
| 1948 | 7 | C. Cameron | A. Ruthven | A. Ruthven | E. Hart | 61 |
| 1949 | 7 | N. Smith | N. Smith | A. Ruthven | E. Hart | 53 |
| 1950 | 5 | N. Smith | A. Ruthven | W. Stephen | E. Hart | 50 |
| 1951 | 5 | N. Smith | A. Ruthven | V. Chanter | E. Hart | 65 |
| 1952 | 3 | A. Ruthven | A. Ruthven | N. Broderick | A. Ongarello | 50 |
| 1953 | 6 | A. Ruthven | A. Ruthven | D. Furness | J. Hickey | 40 |
| 1954 | 11 | A. Ruthven | A. Ruthven | W. Stephen | A. Ruthven | 31 |
| 1955 | 9 | W. Stephen | W. Stephen | D. Furness | N. Johnstone | 32 |
| 1956 | 8 | W. Stephen | W. Stephen | K. Murray | A. Ongarello | 33 |
| 1957 | 11 | W. Stephen | W. Stephen | G. Campbell | O. Abrahams | 31 |
| 1958 | 4 | L. Smith | A. Gale | K. Murray | A. Ongarello | 53 |
| 1959 | 5 | L. Smith | A. Gale | R. Harvey | K. Wright | 43 |
| 1960 | 3 | L. Smith | A. Gale | K. Murray | K. Wright | 36 |
| 1961 | 5 | L. Smith | A. Gale | K. Murray | O. Abrahams | 32 |
| 1962 | 10 | L. Smith | O. Abrahams | K. Murray | W. Clark | 21 |
| 1963 | 12 | K. Murray | K. Murray | K. Murray | G. Lazarus | 35 |
| 1964 | 12 | K. Murray | K. Murray | K. Murray | R. Rogerson | 27 |
| 1965 | 11 | W. Stephen | R. Rogerson | N. Brown | G. Lazarus | 32 |
| 1966 | 12 | W. Stephen | R. Rogerson/J. Hayes | N. Brown | G. Lazarus | 39 |
| 1967 | 11 | W. Stephen | K. Murray | N. Brown | G. Lazarus | 35 |
| 1968 | 11 | W. Stephen | K. Murray | K. Murray/J. Murphy | D. Searl | 31 |
| 1969 | 10 | W. Stephen | K. Murray | K. Murray | D. Searl | 68 |
| 1970 | 9 | W. Stephen | K. Murray | J. Murphy | A. Ruscuklic | 49 |
| 1971 | 6 | G. Donaldson | K. Murray | J. Murphy | J. Murphy | 47 |
| 1972 | 9 | G. Donaldson | K. Murray | G. Wilson | G. Wilson | 37 |
| 1973 | 8 | G. Donaldson | J. Murphy | J. Murphy | G. Wilson | 43 |
| 1974 | 11 | G. Donaldson, G. Campbell | J. Murphy | H. Merrigan | D. Wall | 35 |
| 1975 | 9 | K. Rose | J. Murphy | W. Irwin | R. Serafini | 34 |
| 1976 | 11 | K. Rose | J. Murphy | G. Wilson | J. Murphy | 35 |
| 1977 | 10 | K. Rose | J. Murphy | J. Murphy | R. Beecroft | 59 |
| 1978 | 9 | G. Campbell | H. Merrigan | G. Wilson | R. Beecroft | 65 |
| 1979 | 4 | W. Stephen | R. Alexander | G. Wilson | R. Beecroft | 87 |
| 1980 | 12 | W. Stephen | R. Alexander | G. Wilson | R. Beecroft | 63 |
| 1981 | 4 | R. Walls | G. Wilson | R. Alexander | B. Quinlan | 73 |
| 1982 | 6 | R. Walls | G. Wilson | M. Rendell | B. Quinlan | 53 |
| 1983 | 4 | R. Walls | G. Wilson | M. Rendell | B. Quinlan | 116 |
| 1984 | 5 | R. Walls | G. Wilson | R. Thornton | B. Quinlan | 105 |
| 1985 | 9 | R. Walls | M. Rendell | P. Roos | B. Quinlan | 84 |
| 1986 | 3 | D. Parkin | M. Rendell | P. Roos | R. Osborne | 62 |
| 1987 | 11 | D. Parkin | M. Rendell | S. McIvor | R. Osborne | 62 |
| 1988 | 12 | D. Parkin | P. Roos | D. Kappler | R. Osborne | 60 |
| 1989 | 6 | R. Austin | P. Roos | G. Pert | R. Osborne | 68 |
| 1990 | 12 | R. Austin | P. Roos | S. Clayton | P. Roos | 49 |
| 1991 | 14 | R. Shaw | R. Osborne | P. Roos | D. Wheildon | 29 |
| 1992 | 10 | R. Shaw | P. Roos | P. Roos | R. Osborne | 58 |
| 1993 | 11 | R. Shaw | P. Roos | A. Lynch | A. Lynch | 68 |
| 1994 | 14 | R. Shaw | P. Roos | P. Roos | D. Wheildon | 26 |
| 1995 | 16 | B. Quinlan A. McConnell | B. Boyd | B. Boyd | C. Johnson | 25 |
| 1996 | 16 | M. Nunan A. McConnell | B. Boyd | M. Pike | A. Mellington | 22 |

## WIN/LOSS RECORD

| Against | P | W (N) | L (N) | D (N) |
|---|---|---|---|---|
| Adelaide | 9 | 3(1) | 6(4) | 0 |
| Brisbane Bears | 17 | 6 | 11 | 0 |
| Carlton | 197 | 72 | 120 | 5 |
| Collingwood | 209 | 75 | 131 | 3 |
| Essendon | 197 | 80 | 112(1) | 5 |
| Footscray | 126 | 54 | 72 | 0 |
| Fremantle | 4 | 1 | 3 | 0 |
| Geelong | 183 | 79 | 103 | 1 |
| Hawthorn | 116 | 52 | 63 | 1 |
| Melbourne | 179 | 88 | 88 | 3 |
| North Melb | 128 | 62(2) | 65(3) | 1 |
| Richmond | 166 | 72(1) | 94(1) | 0 |
| St Kilda | 183 | 105 | 77 | 1 |
| Sydney | 185 | 104(3) | 77(2) | 4 |
| West Coast | 15 | 6(3) | 9(3) | 0 |
| University | 14 | 10 | 3 | 1 |
| **TOTALS** | **1928** | **869(10)** | **1034(14)** | **25(0)** |

*(N) Premiership matches played at night*

## WINNING RUNS

14 v Carlton (1897–1902)
14 v St Kilda (1897–1903)
11 v Richmond (1911–1916)
9 v Melbourne (1903–1906)
9 v SM/Sydney (1898–1901)
8 v Geelong (1902–1904); (1940–1946)
7 v North Melb (1927–1931)
6 v Hawthorn (1944–1948)
5 v Collingwood (1912–1914)
5 v Essendon (1898–1900); (1903–1904)
4 v Footscray (1950–1952); (1959–1961);
   (1966– 1968); (1970–1971); (1978–1980);
   (1981–1982)
3 v West Coast (1988–1989)
2 v Brisbane Bears (1987)
1 v Adelaide (1992); (1993); (1995)
1 v Fremantle (1996)

## HIGHS AND LOWS

| Against | Highest | Lowest | G. W. Margin | G. L. Margin |
|---|---|---|---|---|
| Adelaide | 19.16.130 (1992) | 7.5.47 (1992) | 33 (1995) | 99 (1996) |
| Brisbane Bears | 22.15.147 (1993) | 6.13.49 (1996) | 104 (1993) | 109 (1996) |
| Carlton | 20.22.142 (1980) | 2.9.21 (1909) | 94 (1904) | 97 (1995) |
| Collingwood | 25.10.160 (1985) | 3.1.19 (1905) | 95 (1945) | 101 (1967) |
| Essendon | 25.22.172 (1979) | 2.4.16 (1898) | 96 (1979) | 103 (1985) |
| Footscray | 23.22.160 (1982) | 1.0.6 (1953) | 77 (1981) | 104 (1994) |
| Fremantle | 16.11.107 (1996) | 9.10.64 (1995) | 31 (1996) | 86 (1996) |
| Geelong | 25.29.179 (1944) | 1.6.12 (1900) | 123 (1944) | 127 (1996) |
| Hawthorn | 27.8.170 (1982) | 4.12.36 (1965) | 84 (1925) | 157 (1991) |
| Melbourne | 36.22.238 (1979) | 2.11.23 (1901) | 190 (1979) | 131 (1991) |
| North Melb | 34.16.220 (1983) | 1.8.14 (1989) | 150 (1983) | 105 (1996) |
| Richmond | 24.17.161 (1992) | 2.9.21 (1964) | 76 (1915) | 151 (1996) |
| St Kilda | 24.20.164 (1984) | 2.3.15 (1963) | 99 (1900) | 110 (1970) |
| Sydney | 25.29.179 (1961) | 2.6.18 (1908) | 103 (1961) | 126 (1995) |
| West Coast | 19.20.134 (1988) | 3.8.26 (1994) | 70 (1988) | 99 (1991) |

# UNIVERSITY

Years ago there was another League club — University, but it did not continue after 1914. This is the story:

In 1908 the Victorian Football League introduced two new clubs — Richmond and University — to bring the number of clubs to ten. The success of Richmond since that time is well known, but the performances of University have not had the same airing.

The University team adopted Blue and Black as their colors; a black jersey with a blue "V" collar and cuffs; white shorts and black hose with blue tops. Eligibility to play with the students was the holding of the Matriculation Certificate or higher degree. From 1908 until 1910 the club shared the old East Melbourne ground with Essendon and from 1911 to 1914 the MCG with Melbourne.

The initial season saw eight wins and ten losses for the students to finish sixth. The following season seven wins and two draws gave them seventh place. Sixth position was regained in 1910 with 10 wins, but only two victories came in the last four seasons and the demise of the University Football Club came at the end of the 1914 season.

University's total reward for 126 League games was 27 wins and two draws. All clubs were beaten at least once except Collingwood with which it drew once.

Examinations, school term holidays, a constant chang-

ing eighteen and the entry of Australia into the First World War were all obstacles that the University Club could not overcome and its end in 1914 was not altogether unexpected.

Many famous names appeared for the Club during their seven year stay including Dave Browning, Harry Cordner, Chris Fogarty, Tom Fogarty, Mark Gardner, Albert Hartkopf (the great Public School athlete), Herbert Hurrey (who also played in six of the seven seasons), Edgar Kneen, Tom Ogilvie, Martin Ratz, Leo Seward (a great all-rounder), A. S. M. Timms and Edward Cordner (father of the famous Melbourne quartet) to name just a few.

## UNIVERSITY PERFORMANCES

| Against | Won | Lost | Tied | Pld. |
|---|---|---|---|---|
| Carlton | 1 | 13 | – | 14 |
| Collingwood | – | 13 | 1 | 14 |
| Essendon | 2 | 12 | – | 14 |
| Fitzroy | 3 | 10 | 1 | 14 |
| Geelong | 6 | 8 | – | 14 |
| Melbourne | 3 | 11 | – | 14 |
| Richmond | 5 | 9 | – | 14 |
| South Melbourne | 1 | 13 | – | 14 |
| St Kilda | 6 | 8 | – | 14 |
| | 27 | 97 | 2 | 126 |

# 1997 AFL NATIONAL DRAFT

| Selection | Drafted Player | AFL Club | Club Of Origin | Body |
|---|---|---|---|---|
| 1 | Travis Johnstone | Melbourne | Dandenong U18 | U18 VMFL |
| 2 | Brad Ottens | Richmond | Glenelg | SANFL |
| 3 | Trent Croad | Hawthorn | Dandenong U18 | U18 VMFL |
| 4 | Mark Bolton | Essendon | Eastern U18 | U18 VMFL |
| 5 | Luke Power | Bris Lions | Oakleigh U18 | U18 VMFL |
| 6 | James Walker | Fremantle | North Ballarat U18 | U18 VCFL |
| 7 | Kris Massie | Carlton | Dandenong U18 | U18 VMFL |
| 8 | Chris Tarrant | Collingwood | Bendigo U18 | U18 VCFL |
| 9 | Chad Cornes | Port Adel | Glenelg | SANFL |
| 10 | Shane O'bree | Brisbane Lions | North Ballarat U18 | U18 VCFL |
| 11 | Jason Saddington | Sydney | Eastern U18 | U18 VMFL |
| 12 | Jaxon Crabb | West Coast | Claremont | WAFL |
| 13 | Callum Chambers | West Coast | Gippsland U18 | U18 VCFL |
| 14 | Shannon Watt | North Melb | North Ballarat U18 | U18 VCFL |
| 15 | Joel Mckay | Geelong | Murray U18 | U18 VCFL |
| 16 | Ben Walton | St Kilda | Central District | SANFL |
| 17 | Lance Picioane | Adelaide | Western U18 | U18 VMFL |
| 18 | Mark Alvey | Footscray | Bendigo U18 | U18 VCFL |
| 19 | Chris Obst | Hawthorn | Western U18 | U18 VMFL |
| 20 | Dean Solomon | Essendon | Bendigo U18 | U18 VCFL |
| 21 | Clem Michael | Fremantle | South Fremantle | WAFL |
| 22 | Troy Longmuir | Melbourne | West Perth | WAFL |
| 23 | Adam Chatfield | Carlton | Nsw-act U18 | NSW-ACT U18 |
| 24 | James Wasley | Collingwood | Norwood | SANFL |
| 25 | Nick Stevens | Port Adel | Preston U18 | U18 VMFL |
| 26 | Brodie Holland | Fremantle | Tasmania U18 | U18 TAS |
| 27 | Brad Stephens | North Melb | Murray U18 | U18 VCFL |
| 28 | Rowan Jones | West Coast | Claremont | WAFL |
| 29 | Marc Woolnough | Geelong | Southport | QLD |
| 30 | Paul Mcmahon | North Melb | Bendigo U18 | U18 VCFL |
| 31 | Simon Black | Brisbane Lions | East Fremantle | WAFL |
| 32 | Troy Johnson | Fremantle | South Fremantle | WAFL |
| 33 | James Thiessen | Adelaide | Norwood | SANFL |
| 34 | Andrew Williams | West Coast | Dandenong U18 | U18 VMFL |
| 35 | Marcus Baldwin | Hawthorn | Calder U18 | U18 VMFL |
| 36 | Judd Lalich | Essendon | East Perth | WAFL |
| 37 | Todd Holmes | West Coast | Subiaco | WAFL |
| 38 | James Rahilly | Geelong | Geelong U18 | U18 VCFL |
| 39 | Matthew Blake | Melbourne | Bendigo U18 | U18 VCFL |
| 40 | Fred Campbell | Sydney | Alice Springs Pioneers | NT |
| 41 | Danny Morton | Port Adel | North Adelaide | SANFL |
| 42 | Matthew Dennis | Hawthorn | Old Brighton | VAFA |
| 43 | Adam Goodes | Sydney | North Ballarat U18 | U18 VCFL |
| 44 | Daviid Antonowicz | West Coast | Western U18 | U18 VMFL |
| 45 | Matthew Scarlett | Geelong | Geelong U18 | U18 VCFL |
| 46 | Josh Robertson | North Melb | Murray U18 | U18 VCFL |
| 47 | Robert Stevenson | Footscray | Essendon | AFL |
| 48 | Ben Thompson | St Kilda | Glenelg | SANFL |
| 49 | Ian Perrie | Adelaide | East Perth | WAFL |
| 50 | Luke Ottens | Melbourne | Glenelg | SANFL |
| 51 | Scott Ralph | Brisbane Lions | Morningside | QLD |
| 52 | Jordon Doering | Essendon | Bendigo U18 | U18 VCFL |
| 53 | Lionel Proctor | Richmond | Preston U18 | U18 VMFL |
| 54 | Justin Wood | Geelong | Tasmania U18 | U18 TAS |
| 55 | Craig Black | Carlton | Dandenong U18 | U18 VMFL |
| 56 | Ben Kinnear | Collingwood | Central District | SANFL |
| 57 | Darren Fraser | Port Adel | Essendon Reserves | AFL RES |
| 58 | Marcus Picken | Brisbane Lions | North Ballarat U18 | U18 VCFL |

**183**

| Selection | Drafted Player | AFL Club | Club Of Origin | Body |
|---|---|---|---|---|
| 59 | Brett Rose | Sydney | Eastern U18 | U18 VMFL |
| 60 | Phillip Read | West Coast | East Fremantle | WAFL |
| 61 | Tim Finocchiaro | Geelong | Eastern U18 | U18 VMFL |
| 62 | Dion Miles | North Melb | North Melb Reserves | AFL RES |
| 63 | Anthony Aloi | Footscray | Western U18 | U18 VMFL |
| 64 | Sam Cranage | St Kilda | North Ballarat U18 | U18 VCFL |
| 65 | Linden Stevens | Adelaide | Sturt | SANFL |
| 66 | Nathan Brown | Melbourne | West Adelaide | SANFL |
| 67 | Brad Lloyd | Hawthorn | Hawthorn Reserves | AFL RES |
| 68 | Simon Eastaugh | Essendon | Norwood | SANFL |
| 69 | Paul Greenham | Richmond | Port Melbourne | VFA |
| 70 | Trent Hoppner | Carlton | Preston U18 | U18 VMFL |
| 71 | Andrew Kellaway | Richmond | Richmond Reserves | AFL RES |
| 72 | Not Utilized | Port Adel | | |
| 73 | Beau Mcdonald | Brisbane Lions | Swan Districts | WAFL |
| 74 | Paul Digiovine | Footscray | Oakleigh U18 | U18 VMFL |
| 75 | Brent Cowell | St Kilda | Gippsland U18 | U18 VCFL |
| 76 | Not Utilized | Adelaide | | |
| 77 | Guy Rigoni | Melbourne | Myrtleford | VCFL |
| 78 | Richard Vandenberg | Hawthorn | University Blues | VAFA |
| 79 | Not Utilized | Richmond | | |
| 80 | John Hynes | Carlton | Prahran U18 | U18 VMFL |
| 81 | Troy Kirwen | Collingwood | Preston U18 | U18 VMFL |
| 82 | Nathan Thompson | Hawthorn | Hawthorn Reserves | AFL RES |
| 83 | Ben Thompson | Carlton | Kedron Grange | QLD |
| 84 | Frankie Raso | Collingwood | Preston U18 | U18 VMFL |
| 85 | Hayden Burgiel | Hawthorn | Gippsland U18 | U18 VCFL |
| 86 | Scott Whiston | Collingwood | Central District | SANFL |

# 1998 AFL PRE-SEASON DRAFT

| Selection | Drafted Player | AFL Club | Club Of Origin | Body |
|---|---|---|---|---|
| 1 | Jamie Shanahan | Melbourne | St Kilda | AFL |
| 2 | Joel Smith | Hawthorn | St Kilda | AFL |
| 3 | Matthew Bode | Port Adel | Glenelg | SANFL |
| 4 | Adam Coghlan | Sydney | Sandringham | VFA |
| 5 | Damian Houlihan | North Melb | Tatura | VCFL |
| 6 | Scott Taylor | Footscray | Western Bulldogs | AFL |
| 7 | Matthew Carr | St Kilda | East Fremantle | WAFL |
| 8 | Not Utilized | Adelaide | | |
| 9 | Jason Daniltchenko | Hawthorn | North Melbourne | AFL |
| 10 | Brady Anderson | North Melb | East Perth | WAFL |
| 11 | Jamie Elliott | St Kilda | St Kilda | AFL |
| 12 | Hayden Kilmartin | Hawthorn | East Fremantle | WAFL |
| 13 | Not Utilized | St Kilda | | |
| 14 | Not Utilized | Hawthorn | | |

# THE TRADES 1997

| Player gained | Draft result |
| --- | --- |

**ADELAIDE**
Nathan Bassett — Traded by Melbourne for Matthew Collins/Brent Williams
Ian Downsborough — Traded by Port Adelaide for Brett Chalmers
Mark Stevens — Traded by North Melbourne for Jason McCartney
**BRISBANE LIONS**
Brad Scott — Traded by Hawthorn for John Barker/Nathan Chapman, draft selection 42 (Matthew Dennis)

**CARLTON**
Sean Charles — Traded by Melbourne for draft selection 39 (Matthew Blake)
**COLLINGWOOD**
Shannon Gibson — Traded by Hawthorn for Paul Sharkey
Clinton King — Traded by Sydney for Robert Ahmat, draft selection 40 (Fred Campbell)
Stuart Mangin — Traded by Sydney for Robert Ahmat, draft selection 40 (Fred Campbell)
Brad Smith — Traded by Richmond for Aaron James, draft selection 71 (Andrew Kellaway)
Jamie Tape — Traded by Richmond for Aaron James, draft selection 71 (Andrew Kellaway)
**ESSENDON**
None
**FREMANTLE**
Chris Bond — Traded by Richmond for draft selection 2 (Brad Ottens)
Adrian Fletcher — Traded by Brisbane Lions for draft selection 5 (Luke Power)
Daniel Hargraves — Traded by Footscray for draft selection 18 (Mark Alvey)
Stuart Anderson — Traded by North Melbourne for Winston Abraham
**GEELONG**
Brett Spinks — Traded by West Coast for draft selection 13 (Callum Chambers)
**HAWTHORN**
John Barker — Traded by Brisbane Lions for Brad Scott, draft selection 51 (Scott Ralph)
Nathan Chapman — Traded by Brisbane Lions for Brad Scott, draft selection 51 (Scott Ralph)
Paul Sharkey — Traded by Collingwood for Shannon Gibson
**MELBOURNE**
Jeff White — Traded by Fremantle for draft selections 2 (Brad Ottens) and 18 (Mark Alvey)
Craig Smoker — Traded by West Coast for draft selection 34 (Andrew Williams)
Matthew Collins — Traded by Adelaide for Nathan Bassett
Brent Williams — Traded by Adelaide for Nathan Bassett
**NORTH MELBOURNE**
Winston Abraham — Traded by Fremantle for Stuart Anderson
Shannon Grant — Traded by Sydney for Wayne Schwass
Jason Mccartney — Traded by Adelaide for Mark Stevens
**PORT ADELAIDE**
Brett Chalmers — Traded by Adelaide for Ian Downsborough
Chris Naish — Traded by Richmond for John Rombotis
**RICHMOND**
Ashley Blurton — Traded by Wst Cst for draft selection 37 (Todd Holmes)
Aaron James — Traded by Collingwood for Jamie Tape/Brad Smith
John Rombotis — Traded by Port Adelaide for Chris Naish
**ST KILDA**
Gavin Mitchell — Traded by Fremantle for draft selection 32 (Troy Johnson)
**SYDNEY**
Brent Green — Traded by Brisbane Lions for draft selection 31 (Simon Black)
Simon Hawking — Traded by Brisbane Lions for draft selection 31 (Simon Black)
Ribert Ahmat — Traded by Collingwood for Clinton King/Stuart Mangin
Wayne Schwass — Traded by North Melbourne for Shannon Grant, draft selection 27 (Brad Stephens)
**WEST COAST**
None
**WESTERN BULLDOGS**
Matthew Robbins — Traded by Geelong for draft selections 15 (Joel Mckay) and 38 (James Rahilly)
Simon Garlick — Traded by Sydney for draft selection 31 (Simon Black)

# THE DRAFT: CLUB BY CLUB

| Draft | Selection | Drafted player | Club of origin | Body | Matches with this club |
|---|---|---|---|---|---|

## ADELAIDE

### 1992

| | | | | | |
|---|---|---|---|---|---|
| Mid-Seas | 6 | Jim West | Sydney | AFL | 0 |
| Mid-Seas | 21 | Andrew Geddes | Strathmerton | VCFL | 0 |
| Mid-Seas | 32 | Alan Schwartz | Essendon | AFL | 0 |
| National | 26 | Martin McKinnon | Central District | SANFL | 25 |
| National | 41 | Brooke Fogden | West Adelaide | SANFL | 0 |
| National | 56 | Matthew Powell | South Adelaide | SANFL | 16 |
| National | 86 | Sam Smart | Norwood | SANFL | 0 |
| National | 116 | Michael Godden | West Adelaide | SANFL | 0 |
| National | Trade | Matthew Robran | Hawthorn | AFL | 67 |
| | | *Traded by Hawthorn for draft selection 11 (Jonathon Robran)* | | | |
| National | Trade | Stuart Wigney | Sydney | AFL | 10 |
| | | *Traded by Sydney for draft selection 71 (Matthew Aston)* | | | |

### 1993

| | | | | | |
|---|---|---|---|---|---|
| Pre-Seas | 11 | Darryl Wakelin | Port Adelaide | SANFL | 0 |
| Pre-Seas | 27 | Joshua Mail | North Adelaide | SANFL | 4 |
| Pre-Seas | 41 | Nick Pesch | Woodville-West Torrens | SANFL | 31 |
| Pre-Seas | 55 | Simon Pedler | Port Adelaide | SANFL | 0 |
| Mid-Seas | 8 | Tim Perkins | North Adelaide | SANFL | 0 |
| National | 44 | Eugene Warrior | Port Adelaide | SANFL | 0 |
| | | *Draft choice 44 traded by Collingwood for Brenton Sanderson* | | | |
| National | Trade | Tony Hall | Hawthorn | AFL | 17 |
| | | *Traded by Hawthorn for draft selection 17 (Angelo Lekkas)* | | | |
| National | Trade | Brett Chalmers | Collingwood | AFL | 50 |
| | | *Traded by Collingwood for draft selection 34 (Stephen Patterson)* | | | |

### 1994

| | | | | | |
|---|---|---|---|---|---|
| Pre-Seas | 18 | Shane Tongerie | Central District | SANFL | 4 |
| Pre-Seas | 31 | Matthew Kluzek | Woodville-West Torrens | SANFL | 24 |
| National | 27 | Toby Kennett | Sturt | SANFL | 0 |
| National | 31 | Allen Nash | Western U18 | U18 VMFL | 0 |
| | | *Draft choice 31 traded by Hawthorn for Randall Bone* | | | |
| National | 38 | Matthew Collins | Northern U18 | U18 VMFL | 14 |
| | | *Draft choice 38 traded by Fremantle for Chris Groom* | | | |
| National | 50 | Brett Higgins | Port Adelaide | SANFL | 0 |
| | | *Draft choice 50 traded by Carlton for Peter Turner* | | | |
| National | Trade | Jason McCartney | Collingwood | AFL | 37 |
| | | *Traded by Collingwood for draft selection 9 (Ben Wilson), draft selection 53 (Mark Orchard)* | | | |
| National | Trade | Matthew Connell | West Coast | AFL | 52 |
| | | *Traded by West Coast for draft selection 44 (Jeremy Dyer)* | | | |
| National | Trade | Andrew McLeod | Fremantle | AFL | 60 |
| | | *Traded by Fremantle for Chris Groom* | | | |

### 1995

| | | | | | |
|---|---|---|---|---|---|
| Pre-Seas | 7 | Peter Vardy | Central District | SANFL | 31 |
| Pre-Seas | 21 | Tyson Edwards | West Adelaide | SANFL | 46 |
| National | 18 | Brent Williams | Prahran U18 | U18 VMFL | 7 |
| | | *Draft choice 18 traded by Geelong for Martin McKinnon* | | | |
| National | 27 | Kane Johnson | Eastern U18 | U18 VMFL | 25 |
| | | *Draft choice 27 traded by Melbourne for Anthony Ingerson* | | | |
| National | 45 | Scott Hodges | Port Adelaide | SANFL | 2 |
| | | *Draft choice 45 traded by Essendon for Sean Wellman* | | | |
| National | 53 | Adam Ugrinic | Woodville-West Torrens | SANFL | 0 |
| National | 70 | Ashley Fernee | Calder U18 | U18 VMFL | 2 |
| National | Trade | Kym Koster | Footscray | AFL | 33 |
| | | *Traded by Footscray for draft selection 9 (Allen Jakovich)* | | | |
| National | Trade | Darren Jarman | Hawthorn | AFL | 43 |
| | | *Traded by Hawthorn for draft selection 25 (Daniel Chick)* | | | |

## YOUR GUIDE TO THE DRAFT

| | | | |
|---|---|---|---|
| Addit Sel | Additional selection | Pre-Dr Supp | Pre-draft Supplementary |
| Comp Sel | Compensatory selection | Pre-seas | Pre-season draft |
| Fath-son | Father-son rule | Rook Elev | Rookie list elevation |
| Mid-seas | Mid-season draft | Trade | Trading of players |
| National | National draft | Unctr Pl Sel | Uncontracted player selection |
| Pre-Dr Sel | Pre-draft selection | Zone Sel | Zone selection |

*At the end of the 1996 season Footscray became the Western Bulldogs. All references to this club up until September 1996 remain as Footscray. From the 1996 national draft onwards the club is referred to as the Western Bulldogs.*

| Draft | Selection | Drafted player | Club of origin | Body | Matches with this club |
|---|---|---|---|---|---|
| National | Trade | Troy Bond | Carlton | AFL | 38 |
| | | *Traded by Carlton for draft selection 63 (Jacob Anstey)* | | | |
| National | Trade | Peter Caven | Sydney | AFL | 42 |
| | | *Traded by Sydney for Paul Rouvray* | | | |

**1996**

| | | | | | |
|---|---|---|---|---|---|
| Pre-Seas | 8 | Shane Ellen | Footscray | AFL | 27 |
| Pre-Seas | 18 | Simon Goodwin | South Adelaide | SANFL | 10 |
| Pre-Seas | 21 | Brendon Logan | West Perth | WAFL | 0 |
| National | 13 | Tom Gilligan | Dandenong-Southern U18 | U18 VMFL | 3 |
| National | 60 | Andrew Eccles | Northern U18 | U18 VMFL | 0 |
| National | 69 | Chad Rintoul | East Fremantle | WAFL | 11 |
| National | 76 | Greg Dempsey | West Adelaide | SANFL | 0 |
| National | 86 | Ben Parker | Murray U18 | U18 VCFL | 0 |
| National | Trade | Barry Standfield | Footscray | AFL | 13 |
| | | *Traded by Footscray for draft selection 32 (Jim Plunkett), draft selection 47 (Brett Montgomery)* | | | |
| National | Trade | Trent Ormond-Allen | Melbourne | AFL | 18 |
| | | *Traded by Melbourne for draft selection 83 (Ashley Gehling)* | | | |
| National | Trade | Tim Cook | Central District | SANFL | 4 |
| | | *Traded by Port Adelaide for Scott Hodges* | | | |
| National | Trade | Brett James | Collingwood | AFL | 17 |
| | | *Traded by Collingwood for Jonathon Ross* | | | |
| National | Trade | Aaron Keating | Norwood | SANFL | 3 |
| | | *Traded by Port Adelaide for Scott Hodges* | | | |
| National | Trade | Nick Laidlaw | Sturt | SANFL | 0 |
| | | *Traded by Port Adelaide for David Brown* | | | |
| National | Trade | Clay Sampson | Melbourne | AFL | 10 |
| | | *Traded by Melbourne for Nick Pesch* | | | |

**1997**

| | | | | | |
|---|---|---|---|---|---|
| National | 17 | Lance Picioane | Western U18 | U18 VMFL | 0 |
| National | 33 | James Thiessen | Norwood | SANFL | 0 |
| National | 49 | Ian Perrie | East Perth | WAFL | 0 |
| National | 65 | Linden Stevens | Sturt | SANFL | 0 |
| National | 76 | Not utilised | | | 0 |
| National | Trade | Nathan Bassett | Melbourne | AFL | 0 |
| | | *Traded by Melbourne for Matthew Collins/Brent Williams* | | | |
| National | Trade | Ian Downsborough | Port Adel | AFL | 0 |
| | | *Traded by Port Adelaide for Brett Chalmers* | | | |
| National | Trade | Mark Stevens | North Melb | AFL | 0 |
| | | *Traded by North Melbourne for Jason McCartney* | | | |

**1998**

| | | | | | |
|---|---|---|---|---|---|
| Pre-Seas | 8 | Not utilised | | | 0 |

# BRISBANE BEARS

**1986**

| | | | | | |
|---|---|---|---|---|---|
| National | 1 | Martin Leslie | Port Adelaide | SANFL | 107 |
| National | 14 | Scott Adams | Clarence | TAS | 0 |
| National | 27 | Adam Garton | Glenelg | SANFL | 3 |
| National | 40 | Stephen Williams | Port Adelaide | SANFL | 4 |
| National | 53 | Michael Templeton | Woodville | SANFL | 0 |
| National | Pre-Dr Sel | Matthew Campbell | North Adelaide | SANFL | 79 |
| National | Pre-Dr Sel | Stephen Connelly | Central District | SANFL | 0 |
| National | Pre-Dr Sel | Ben Harris | Port Adelaide | SANFL | 14 |
| National | Pre-Dr Sel | Neil Hein | Norwood | SANFL | 15 |
| National | Pre-Dr Sel | Colin McDonald | Woodville | SANFL | 0 |
| National | Pre-Dr Sel | Mark Mickan | West Adelaide | SANFL | 48 |

**1987**

| | | | | | |
|---|---|---|---|---|---|
| National | 2 | Chris McDermott | Glenelg | SANFL | 0 |
| National | 15 | Andrew Jarman | North Adelaide | SANFL | 0 |
| National | 28 | Andrew Bishop | Ainslie | ACT | 0 |
| National | 41 | Michael Kennedy | Queanbeyan | ACT | 23 |
| National | 54 | Adam Ladbrook | Pakenham | VCFL | 0 |

**1988**

| | | | | | |
|---|---|---|---|---|---|
| National | 16 | David Bain | East Perth | WAFL | 86 |
| National | 30 | Richard Champion | Woodville | SANFL | 140 |
| National | 58 | Lachlan Sim | Moe | VCFL | 21 |
| National | 72 | Chris O'Sullivan | Coralynn | VCFL | 8 |
| National | 100 | David Kupsch | North Adelaide | SANFL | 0 |
| National | Trade | Alex Ishchenko | West Coast | AFL | 42 |
| | | *Traded by West Coast for draft selection 2 (Todd Breman)* | | | |
| National | Trade | Mark Zanotti | West Coast | AFL | 64 |
| | | *Traded by West Coast for draft selection 44 (Scott Williamson)* | | | |
| National | Trade | Craig Somerville | Footscray | AFL | 0 |
| | | *Traded by Footscray for draft selection 86 (Ben Sexton)* | | | |

**1989**

| | | | | | |
|---|---|---|---|---|---|
| Pre-Seas | 2 | John Gastev | West Coast | AFL | 113 |
| Pre-Seas | 16 | David Wittey | St Kilda | AFL | 0 |
| Pre-Seas | 30 | Simon Hose | Sydney | AFL | 5 |
| Pre-Seas | 44 | Glen Reeves | Hawthorn | AFL | 0 |
| National | 5 | Brad Rowe | East Fremantle | WAFL | 14 |
| National | 33 | Shaun Hart | Shepparton United | VCFL | 121 |

| Draft | Selection | Drafted player | Club of origin | Body | Matches with this club |
|-------|-----------|----------------|----------------|------|------------------------|
| National | 43 | Chris Guerts | Warragul | VCFL | 0 |
| National | 44 | Jonathon Solomon | Seymour | VCFL | 2 |
| National | 51 | Joe Wilson | Wangaratta Rovers | VCFL | 0 |
| National | 79 | David Brown | Port Adelaide | SANFL | 0 |
| National | 93 | Tony Paynter | Pakenham | VCFL | 0 |
| National | 107 | Sean Valenta | Morningside | QLD | INELIG |
| National | Addit Sel | Chris Guerts | Warragul | VCFL | 0 |
| National | Pre-Dr Sel | Darren Jarman | North Adelaide | SANFL | 0 |
| National | Pre-Dr Sel | Kevin Caton | West Coast | AFL | 8 |
| National | Pre-Dr Sel | Peter Davidson | West Coast | AFL | 7 |
| National | Pre-Dr Sel | Brian Hinkley | Essendon | AFL | 0 |
| National | Pre-Dr Sel | Andrew Jarman | North Adelaide | SANFL | 0 |
| National | Pre-Dr Sel | Doug Smart | North Adelaide | SANFL | 0 |
| National | Trade | Gavin Keane | Essendon | AFL | 7 |
| | | *Traded by Essendon for draft selection 19 (Ashley Green), draft selection 65 (Alan Schwartz)* | | | |

## 1990

| Draft | Selection | Drafted player | Club of origin | Body | Matches with this club |
|-------|-----------|----------------|----------------|------|------------------------|
| Pre-Seas | 5 | Brad Edwards | Fitzroy | AFL | 10 |
| Pre-Seas | 11 | Richard Umbers | Geelong | AFL | 4 |
| Pre-Seas | 25 | Scott Lawton | Brisbane Bears | AFL | 0 |
| Pre-Seas | 39 | David Wearne | Brisbane Bears | AFL | 18 |
| Mid-Seas | 1 | Laurie Schache | West Torrens | SANFL | 29 |
| Mid-Seas | 15 | David Greenhill | Wodonga | VCFL | 0 |
| Mid-Seas | 28 | Dean Strauch | Golden Square | VCFL | 0 |
| Mid-Seas | 38 | Glen Bartlett | East Perth | WAFL | 0 |
| National | 10 | David Ogg | Swan Districts | WAFL | 9 |
| | | *Draft choice 10 traded by Hawthorn for Darren Jarman* | | | |
| National | 15 | Andrew Harrison | Benalla | VCFL | 0 |
| National | 23 | Ben Thomas | Port Fairy | VCFL | 0 |
| National | 25 | Peter Worsfold | South Fremantle | WAFL | 31 |
| National | 39 | Nigel Palfreyman | Sandy Bay | TAS | 15 |
| National | 47 | Luke Chambers | Lucknow | VCFL | 0 |
| | | *Draft choice 47 traded by North Melbourne for Mark Roberts* | | | |
| National | 68 | Peter Whyte | South Barwon | VCFL | 0 |
| | | *Draft choice 68 traded by Sydney for Warwick Capper* | | | |
| National | Pre-Dr Sel | Paul Mifka | West Coast | AFL | 0 |
| National | Pre-Dr Sel | Danny Noonan | Clarence | TAS | 55 |
| National | Pre-Dr Sel | Shane Strempel | Swan Districts | WAFL | 3 |
| National | Trade | David Cameron | Geelong | AFL | 16 |
| | | *Traded by Geelong for draft selection 1 (Stephen Hooper)* | | | |
| National | Trade | Shane Hamilton | Geelong | AFL | 31 |
| | | *Traded by Geelong for draft selection 1 (Stephen Hooper)* | | | |
| National | Trade | Travis Martin-Beynon | North Melb | AFL | 0 |
| | | *Traded by North Melbourne for draft selection 53 (Stephen Pears)* | | | |
| National | Trade | Craig Potter | Sydney | AFL | 13 |
| | | *Traded by Sydney for draft selection 67 (David Griffin)* | | | |
| National | Trade | Peter Curran | Hawthorn | AFL | 14 |
| | | *Traded by Hawthorn for draft selection 81 (Luan Morley)* | | | |
| National | Trade | Robert Dickson | Hawthorn | AFL | 2 |
| | | *Traded by Hawthorn for draft selection 81 (Luan Morley)* | | | |
| National | Zone Sel | Darryl White | Alice Springs | NT | 109 |
| National | Zone Sel | Roger Smith | Southern District | NT | 0 |

## 1991

| Draft | Selection | Drafted player | Club of origin | Body | Matches with this club |
|-------|-----------|----------------|----------------|------|------------------------|
| Pre-Seas | 1 | Michael McLean | Footscray | AFL | 88 |
| Pre-Seas | 7 | Matthew Ryan | Sydney | AFL | 18 |
| Pre-Seas | 24 | Ian Kidgell | Hawthorn | AFL | 0 |
| Pre-Seas | 38 | Jon Henry | Carlton | AFL | 0 |
| Mid-Seas | 1 | Ashley Byrne | Box Hill | VFA | 0 |
| Mid-Seas | 14 | Simon Kenny | Kedron Grange | QLD | 0 |
| Mid-Seas | 27 | Peter Bennett | North Adelaide | SANFL | 0 |
| Mid-Seas | 36 | David Ryan | Terang | VCFL | 0 |
| National | 1 | John Hutton | Claremont | WAFL | 18 |
| National | 14 | Fabian Francis | Southern District | NT | 22 |
| National | 27 | Terry Board | Fitzroy | AFL | 0 |
| National | 65 | Heath Shephard | Burnie Hawks | TAS | 4 |
| National | 71 | Luke Chambers | Brisbane Bears | AFL | 0 |
| | | *Draft choice 71 traded by Essendon for Shane Strempel* | | | |
| National | 76 | Matthew Rendell | Fitzroy | AFL | 13 |
| National | Trade | Rod Owen | Melbourne | AFL | 9 |
| | | *Traded by Melbourne for draft selection 40 (Nick White)* | | | |
| National | Trade | Russell Jeffrey | St Kilda | AFL | 8 |
| | | *Traded by St Kilda for draft selection 53 (Alistair Gray)* | | | |
| National | Trade | Colin Alexander | Collingwood | AFL | 5 |
| | | *Traded by Collingwood (not utilised)* | | | |
| National | Trade | Brendon Retzlaff | Collingwood | AFL | 15 |
| | | *Traded by Collingwood (not utilised)* | | | |

## 1992

| Draft | Selection | Drafted player | Club of origin | Body | Matches with this club |
|-------|-----------|----------------|----------------|------|------------------------|
| Pre-Seas | 1 | Ashley Green | Essendon | AFL | 23 |
| Pre-Seas | 15 | Jason Jones | Darwin | NT | 0 |
| Pre-Seas | 29 | Darren Bartsch | West Adelaide | SANFL | 0 |
| Pre-Seas | 43 | Matthew Clarke | Richmond | AFL | 90 |
| Pre-Seas | 51 | Campbell Black | Southport | QLD | 0 |
| Mid-Seas | 1 | John Parker | Frankston | VFA | 3 |

| Draft | Selection | Drafted player | Club of origin | Body | Matches with this club |
|---|---|---|---|---|---|
| Mid-Seas | 16 | Brad Pearce | South Launceston | TAS | 2 |
| Mid-Seas | 29 | Brian Stanislaus | North Launceston | TAS | 0 |
| Mid-Seas | 38 | Adam Aherne | North Launceston | TAS | 0 |
| Mid-Seas | 43 | Brett Sherriff | Devonport | TAS | 0 |
| National | 2 | Nathan Chapman | Kangaroo Flat | VCFL | 60 |
| National | 4 | Justin Leppitsch | Southern U18 | U18 VMFL | 66 |
| National | 36 | Tim Sherman | Geelong U18 | U18 VCFL | 0 |
| National | 51 | Adam Williamson | Central U18 | U18 VMFL | 0 |
| National | 66 | Aaron Lord | Central U19 | U18 VMFL | 0 |
| National | 81 | Michael Murphy | Adelaide | AFL | 10 |
| National | 96 | Trent Mills | South Adelaide | SANFL | 0 |
| National | Trade | Paul Spargo | North Melb | AFL | 9 |
| | | *Traded by North Melbourne for draft selection 6 (Robert Pyman)* | | | |
| National | Trade | Paul Peos | West Coast | AFL | 33 |
| | | *Traded by West Coast for draft selection 21 (Shane Bond)* | | | |
| National | Trade | Dion Scott | Sydney | AFL | 56 |
| | | *Traded by Sydney for draft selection 111 (Michael Gaffney)* | | | |

## 1993

| Draft | Selection | Drafted player | Club of origin | Body | Matches with this club |
|---|---|---|---|---|---|
| Pre-Seas | 2 | Brendan McCormack | Fitzroy | AFL | 12 |
| Pre-Seas | 4 | Adrian Fletcher | St Kilda | AFL | 107 |
| Pre-Seas | 6 | Martin Heffernan | Geelong | AFL | 2 |
| Pre-Seas | 22 | Craig Mcrae | Glenelg | SANFL | 57 |
| Pre-Seas | 36 | Darren Meade | Port Adelaide | SANFL | 0 |
| Pre-Seas | 50 | Julian Waite | Port Adelaide | SANFL | 0 |
| Pre-Seas | 62 | John Klug | Adelaide | AFL | 0 |
| Pre-Seas | 71 | Julian Burton | Port Adelaide | SANFL | 0 |
| Pre-Seas | 78 | Danny Craven | St Kilda | AFL | 25 |
| Mid-Seas | 4 | Damian Bourke | Geelong | AFL | 22 |
| Mid-Seas | 18 | Damian Ryan | Port Adelaide | SANFL | 0 |
| National | 2 | Nigel Lappin | Chiltern | VCFL | 82 |
| National | 12 | Chris Scott | Eastern U18 | U18 VMFL | 60 |
| | | *Draft choice 12 traded by Collingwood for Nathan Buckley* | | | |
| National | 21 | Shane Hodges | North Adelaide | SANFL | 4 |
| National | 24 | Cameron Bennett | North Adelaide | SANFL | 0 |
| National | 45 | Trent Bartlett | Deloraine | TAS | 22 |
| | | *Draft choice 45 traded by Geelong for Aaron Lord* | | | |
| National | 64 | Shane Hamilton | Brisbane Bears | AFL | 16 |
| | | *Draft choice 64 traded by Fitzroy for David Bain, Nigel Palfreyman* | | | |
| National | Trade | Alastair Lynch | Fitzroy | AFL | 52 |
| | | *Traded by Fitzroy for draft selection 7 (Chris Johnson)* | | | |
| National | Trade | Troy Lehmann | Collingwood | AFL | 13 |
| | | *Traded by Collingwood for draft selection 39 (Jason Wild)* | | | |
| National | Trade | Craig Starcevich | Collingwood | AFL | 20 |
| | | *Traded by Collingwood for draft selection 39 (Jason Wild)* | | | |
| National | Zone Sel | Steven Lawrence | Southport | QLD | 22 |

## 1994

| Draft | Selection | Drafted player | Club of origin | Body | Matches with this club |
|---|---|---|---|---|---|
| Pre-Seas | 2 | Andrew Bews | Geelong | AFL | 69 |
| Pre-Seas | 8 | Craig Lambert | Richmond | AFL | 65 |
| National | 75 | Gerard Jess | Ballarat U18 | U18 VCFL | 0 |
| National | 85 | Michael Agnello | Southern U18 | U18 VMFL | 0 |
| National | 93 | Michael Murphy | Brisbane Bears | AFL | 0 |
| National | Trade | Andrew Gowers | Hawthorn | AFL | 48 |
| | | *Traded by Hawthorn for draft selection 8 (Daniel Harford), draft selection 60 (Bradley Scott)* | | | |
| National | Trade | Gilbert McAdam | St Kilda | AFL | 58 |
| | | *Traded by St Kilda for draft selection 26 (Tim Elliott), draft selection 43 (Dean Matthews)* | | | |
| National | Zone Sel | Jason Akermanis | Mayne | QLD | 55 |

## 1995

| Draft | Selection | Drafted player | Club of origin | Body | Matches with this club |
|---|---|---|---|---|---|
| Pre-Seas | 6 | Ross Lyon | Fitzroy | AFL | 2 |
| Pre-Seas | 20 | Shannon Corcoran | Footscray | AFL | 5 |
| National | 12 | Andrew Gowling | South Adelaide | SANFL | 0 |
| National | 28 | Nicholas Trask | Eastern U18 | U18 VMFL | 5 |
| National | 42 | Troy Johnson | South Fremantle | WAFL | 2 |
| National | 56 | Daniel Bradshaw | Wodonga | VCFL | 19 |
| National | Trade | Ben Robbins | West Coast | AFL | 17 |
| | | *Traded by West Coast for draft selection 66 (Neil Marshall)* | | | |
| National | Zone Sel | Danny Dickfos | North Brisbane | QLD | 44 |
| National | Zone Sel | Brett Voss | Morningside | QLD | 3 |
| National | Zone Sel | Derek Wirth | Mt Gravatt | QLD | 0 |

## 1996

| Draft | Selection | Drafted player | Club of origin | Body | Matches with this club |
|---|---|---|---|---|---|
| Pre-Seas | 11 | Tristan Lynch | Sale | VCFL | 42 |
| Pre-Seas | 19 | Matthew Waters | North Brisbane | QLD | 0 |

# BRISBANE LIONS

## 1996

| Draft | Selection | Drafted player | Club of origin | Body | Matches with this club |
|---|---|---|---|---|---|
| National | 3 | Rory Hilton | Murray U18 | U18 VCFL | 0 |
| National | 26 | Tim Notting | Ballarat U18 | U18 VCFL | 0 |
| National | Merger Sel | Scott Bamford | Fitzroy | AFL | 11 |
| National | Merger Sel | Brad Boyd | Fitzroy | AFL | 1 |
| National | Merger Sel | Nick Carter | Fitzroy | AFL | 2 |
| National | Merger Sel | Shane Clayton | Fitzroy | AFL | 3 |
| National | Merger Sel | Chris Johnson | Fitzroy | AFL | 19 |

| Draft | Selection | Drafted player | Club of origin | Body | Matches with this club |
|---|---|---|---|---|---|
| National | Merger Sel | Jarrod Molloy | Fitzroy | AFL | 10 |
| National | Merger Sel | John Barker | Fitzroy | AFL | 8 |
| National | Merger Sel | Simon Hawking | Fitzroy | AFL | 0 |

**1997**

| National | 5 | Luke Power | Oakleigh U18 | U18 VMFL | 0 |
|---|---|---|---|---|---|

*Draft choice 5 traded by Fremantle for Adrian Fletcher*

| National | 10 | Shane O'Bree | North Ballarat U18 | U18 VCFL | 0 |
|---|---|---|---|---|---|
| National | 31 | Simon Black | East Fremantle | WAFL | 0 |

*Draft choice 31 traded by Sydney for Simon Hawking/Brent Green*

| National | 51 | Scott Ralph | Morningside | QLD | 0 |
|---|---|---|---|---|---|

*Draft choice 51 traded by Hawthorn for John Barker/Nathan Chapman, draft selection 42 (Matthew Dennis)*

| National | 58 | Marcus Picken | North Ballarat U18 | U18 VCFL | 0 |
|---|---|---|---|---|---|
| National | 73 | Beau McDonald | Swan Districts | WAFL | 0 |
| National | Trade | Brad Scott | Hawthorn | AFL | 0 |

*Traded by Hawthorn for John Barker/Nathan Chapman, draft selection 42 (Matthew Dennis)*

# CARLTON

**1986**

| National | 12 | Dominic Fotia | West Torrens | SANFL | 18 |
|---|---|---|---|---|---|
| National | 25 | Doug Smart | North Adelaide | SANFL | 0 |
| National | 38 | Simon Minton-Connell | North Hobart | TAS | 19 |
| National | 51 | Andrew Herring | Wynyard | TAS | 0 |
| National | 64 | Darren Newlan | Golden Square | VCFL | 0 |

**1987**

| National | 13 | Peter Bubner | Central District | SANFL | 0 |
|---|---|---|---|---|---|
| National | 26 | Stephen Oliver | Castlemaine | VCFL | 13 |
| National | 39 | David Kernahan | Glenelg | SANFL | 53 |
| National | 52 | Stephen Gemmill | Cobram | VCFL | 0 |
| National | 65 | Dean Adams | Shepparton | VCFL | 0 |

**1988**

| National | 40 | Glen Johnston | North Launceston | TAS | 0 |
|---|---|---|---|---|---|
| National | 54 | Michael Sexton | Sandhurst | VCFL | 148 |
| National | 68 | Grant Povey | Claremont | WAFL | 0 |
| National | 82 | Anthony Loone | Deloraine | TAS | 0 |
| National | 96 | Michael James | St Patricks,Ballarat | APS | 12 |
| National | 110 | Chris Mulcair | Marist Brothers,Bendigo | APS | 0 |
| National | Trade | Glenn Hawker | Essendon | AFL | 27 |

*Traded by Essendon for draft selection 12 (Brad Fox), draft selection 26 (David Regan)*

**1989**

| Pre-Seas | 12 | Simon Verbeek | Richmond | AFL | 38 |
|---|---|---|---|---|---|
| Pre-Seas | 26 | Ashley Matthews | Carlton | AFL | 9 |
| Pre-Seas | 40 | Paul Payne | Melbourne | AFL | 5 |
| Pre-Seas | 54 | Tim Taylor | Therry | VAFA | 0 |
| National | 7 | Stephen Edgar | East Fremantle | WAFL | 14 |
| National | 21 | Peter Doyle | Union | VCFL | 0 |
| National | 35 | Chris Bond | North Hobart | TAS | 22 |
| National | 53 | Derek Coghlan | Lemnos | VCFL | 0 |
| National | 67 | Ben Judd | Sturt | SANFL | 0 |
| National | 81 | Sam Gross | Boort | VCFL | 0 |
| National | 95 | Jeremy Smith | Sandy Bay | TAS | 1 |
| National | 109 | Colin Corkery | Ireland | IRELAND | 0 |

**1990**

| Pre-Seas | 13 | Adrian Bassett | Coburg | VFA | 31 |
|---|---|---|---|---|---|
| Pre-Seas | 27 | Tim Rieniets | Coburg | VFA | 24 |
| Pre-Seas | 41 | Craig Hucker | Carlton | AFL | 0 |
| Pre-Seas | 49 | Ben Robertson | Sydney | AFL | 3 |
| Mid-Seas | 6 | Craig Cross | Burnie Hawks | TAS | 0 |
| Mid-Seas | 20 | Darren Read | Dandenong | VFA | 0 |
| National | 2 | James Cook | North Hobart | TAS | 25 |

*Draft choice 2 traded by Sydney for Warren McKenzie*

| National | 7 | Damian Hampson | Subiaco | WAFL | 0 |
|---|---|---|---|---|---|
| National | 31 | Nick Faull | Golden Point | VCFL | 0 |
| National | 59 | Cameron James | Morwell | VCFL | 0 |
| National | 73 | Anthony McDonald | Ballarat Ycw | VCFL | 0 |
| National | 87 | Danny Morgan | Boolarra | VCFL | 0 |
| National | Trade | Mark Arceri | North Melb | AFL | 17 |

*Traded by North Melbourne for draft selection 45 (Craig Jennings)*

**1991**

| Pre-Seas | 13 | Darren Tarczon | North Melb | AFL | 11 |
|---|---|---|---|---|---|
| Pre-Seas | 30 | Ben Robertson | Noble Park | VMFL | 3 |
| Pre-Seas | 44 | Mark Bouw | Carlton | AFL | 0 |
| Pre-Seas | 52 | Paul Williams | St Kilda | AFL | 0 |
| Mid-Seas | 7 | Brendan Parker | Tongala | VCFL | 5 |
| Mid-Seas | 20 | Trevor Robinson | Sturt | SANFL | 0 |
| Mid-Seas | 32 | Not utilised | | | |
| Mid-Seas | 38 | Not utilised | | | |
| National | 18 | Matthew Hogg | Footscray | AFL | 93 |
| National | 28 | Cale O'Keefe | South Launceston | TAS | 0 |

*Draft choice 28 traded by Fitzroy for Ashley Matthews*

| Draft | Selection | Drafted player | Club of origin | Body | Matches with this club |
|-------|-----------|----------------|----------------|------|------------------------|
| National | 44 | Brett Sholl | North Melb | AFL | 35 |
| National | 54 | Leigh Snooks | Derinallum | VCFL | 0 |
| | | *Draft choice 54 traded by Fitzroy for Peter Sartori* | | | |
| National | 57 | Anthony McDonald | Carlton | AFL | 0 |
| National | 78 | Matthew Dickson | Sandhurst | VCFL | 0 |
| | | *Draft choice 78 traded by Sydney for Simon Minton-Connell* | | | |
| National | 79 | Bevan Smillie | Essendon | AFL | 0 |
| National | Trade | Earl Spalding | Melbourne | AFL | 102 |
| | | *Traded by Melbourne for draft selection 5 (Jason Norrish)* | | | |
| National | Trade | Ron De Iulio | North Melb | AFL | 69 |
| | | *Traded by North Melbourne (not utilised)* | | | |
| National | Trade | Greg Williams | Sydney | AFL | 109 |
| | | *Traded by Sydney (not utilised)* | | | |

## 1992

| Draft | Selection | Drafted player | Club of origin | Body | Matches with this club |
|-------|-----------|----------------|----------------|------|------------------------|
| Pre-Seas | 5 | Mark Athorn | Sydney | AFL | 30 |
| Pre-Seas | 19 | Paul McCormack | Dandenong | VFA | 14 |
| Pre-Seas | 33 | Rohan Welsh | Dandenong | VFA | 42 |
| Pre-Seas | 46 | Paul Tuddenham | Collingwood | AFL | 0 |
| Pre-Seas | 54 | Jeremy Smith | Carlton | AFL | 1 |
| Pre-Seas | 56 | Not utilised | | | |
| Mid-Seas | 10 | Brent Heaver | Epping | VMFL | 64 |
| Mid-Seas | 24 | Justin Clarkson | Ormond | VAFA | 0 |
| Mid-Seas | 35 | David Glascott | Carlton | AFL | 0 |
| National | 13 | Andrew McKay | Glenelg | SANFL | 108 |
| National | 43 | Adrian Whitehead | Wodonga | VCFL | 62 |
| National | 58 | Chris Peel | Swan Districts | WAFL | 0 |
| National | 61 | Luke Rayner | Geelong U18 | U18 VCFL | 0 |
| | | *Draft choice 61 traded by St Kilda for Ian Aitken* | | | |
| National | 73 | Tony Plim | Golden Square | VCFL | 0 |
| National | 88 | Troy Bond | Port Adelaide | SANFL | 36 |
| National | 103 | Ben Harrison | Devonport | TAS | 2 |
| National | 118 | Scott Spalding | Perth | WAFL | 0 |
| National | Fath-Son | Darren Walsh | Golden Square | VCFL | 0 |
| National | Trade | Tim Powell | Richmond | AFL | 11 |
| | | *Traded by Richmond for draft selection 28 (Jamie Tape)* | | | |

## 1993

| Draft | Selection | Drafted player | Club of origin | Body | Matches with this club |
|-------|-----------|----------------|----------------|------|------------------------|
| Pre-Seas | 13 | Andrew Leoncelli | Xavier College | APS | 0 |
| Pre-Seas | 29 | Damien Sheehan | Port Adelaide | SANFL | 0 |
| Pre-Seas | 43 | Matthew Penny | Box Hill | VFA | 0 |
| Pre-Seas | 57 | Chris O'Dwyer | Sydney | AFL | 0 |
| Pre-Seas | 67 | Kelvin Holmes | Claremont | WAFL | 0 |
| Pre-Seas | 74 | Christian Davidson | Collegians | VAFA | 0 |
| Mid-Seas | 6 | Tony Lynn | Central District | SANFL | 27 |
| Mid-Seas | 19 | Haami Williams | South Barwon | VCFL | 0 |
| National | 18 | Simon Beaumont | Central U18 | U18 VMFL | 16 |
| National | 48 | Matthew Hopkins | West Adelaide | SANFL | 0 |
| National | Trade | Barry Mitchell | Collingwood | AFL | 28 |
| | | *Traded by Collingwood for draft selection 35 (Aaron James)* | | | |

## 1994

| Draft | Selection | Drafted player | Club of origin | Body | Matches with this club |
|-------|-----------|----------------|----------------|------|------------------------|
| Pre-Seas | 19 | Dean Rice | St Kilda | AFL | 37 |
| Pre-Seas | 32 | Brad Pearce | Brisbane Bears | AFL | 51 |
| Pre-Seas | 35 | Peter Green | Sydney | AFL | 1 |
| National | 15 | Scott Camporeale | Woodville-West Torrens | SANFL | 59 |
| National | 33 | Mark Cullen | Eastern U18 | U18 VMFL | 0 |
| | | *Draft choice 33 traded by Fitzroy for Andrew Cavedon* | | | |
| National | 41 | Adam White | Eastern U18 | U18 VMFL | 10 |
| National | 67 | Tony Bourke | Ballarat U18 | U18 VCFL | 0 |
| National | 79 | Aaron Hamill | Tuggeranong | ACT | 23 |
| National | 89 | David Nicholson | Western U18 | U18 VMFL | 0 |
| National | Pre-Dr Supp | Matthew Blagrove | Carlton | VSFL | 0 |
| National | Trade | Peter Turner | Adelaide | AFL | 2 |
| | | *Traded by Adelaide for draft selection 50 (Brett Higgins)* | | | |

## 1995

| Draft | Selection | Drafted player | Club of origin | Body | Matches with this club |
|-------|-----------|----------------|----------------|------|------------------------|
| Pre-Seas | 13 | Matt Clape | West Coast | AFL | 51 |
| Pre-Seas | 27 | Glenn Manton | Essendon | AFL | 56 |
| Pre-Seas | 36 | Alan Thorpe | Footscray | AFL | 0 |
| National | 62 | Adrian Burdon | Tas U18 | U18 TAS | 0 |
| National | 63 | Jacob Anstey | Tuggeranong | ACT | 9 |
| | | *Draft choice 63 traded by Adelaide for Troy Bond* | | | |
| National | 69 | Daniel Marshall | Dandenong-Southern U18 | U18 VMFL | 0 |
| National | Fath-Son | David Walls | Southport | QLD | 0 |
| National | Trade | Craig Devonport | St Kilda | AFL | 0 |
| | | *Traded by St Kilda for draft selection 19 (Barry Hall)* | | | |
| National | Trade | Adrian Hickmott | Geelong | AFL | 39 |
| | | *Traded by Geelong for draft selection 49 (Ronnie Burns)* | | | |
| National | Trade | Justin Murphy | Richmond | AFL | 37 |
| | | *Traded by Richmond for Ben Harrison, draft selection 35 (Brad Smith)* | | | |
| National | Trade | Ben Sexton | Footscray | AFL | 4 |
| | | *Traded by Footscray for James Cook* | | | |

## 1996

| Draft | Selection | Drafted player | Club of origin | Body | Matches with this club |
|-------|-----------|----------------|----------------|------|------------------------|
| National | 38 | Sam Smart | Norwood | SANFL | 1 |

| Draft | Selection | Drafted player | Club of origin | Body | Matches with this club |
|---|---|---|---|---|---|
| National | 52 | Damien Lock | Bendigo U18 | U18 VCFL | 0 |
| National | 74 | Chris Jackson | Nsw-Act U18 | U18 NSW-ACT | 0 |
| National | 81 | Anthony Franchina | Carlton Reserves | AFL RES | 2 |
| National | Fath-Son | Lance Whitnall | Northern U18 | U18 VMFL | 18 |
| National | Trade | Mick McGuane | Collingwood | AFL | 3 |
| | | *Traded by Collingwood for draft selection 19 (Brent Tuckey), draft selection 65 (Brad Cassidy)* | | | |
| National | Trade | Andrew Balkwill | Central District | SANFL | 1 |
| | | *Traded by Port Adelaide for Brent Heaver* | | | |
| National | Trade | Ben Nelson | Sturt | SANFL | 1 |
| | | *Traded by Port Adelaide for Brent Heaver* | | | |

**1997**

| Draft | Selection | Drafted player | Club of origin | Body | Matches with this club |
|---|---|---|---|---|---|
| Pre-Seas | 8 | Darren Hulme | Dandenong-Southern U18 | U18 VMFL | 8 |
| National | 7 | Kris Massie | Dandenong U18 | U18 VMFL | 0 |
| National | 23 | Adam Chatfield | Nsw-Act U18 | NSW-ACT U18 | 0 |
| National | 55 | Craig Black | Dandenong U18 | U18 VMFL | 0 |
| National | 70 | Trent Hoppner | Preston U18 | U18 VMFL | 0 |
| National | 80 | John Hynes | Prahran U18 | U18 VMFL | 0 |
| National | 83 | Ben Thompson | Kedron Grange | QLD | 0 |
| National | Trade | Sean Charles | Melbourne | AFL | 0 |
| | | *Traded by Melbourne for draft selection 39 (Matthew Blake)* | | | |
| Rookie Elev | Rook Elev | Mark Porter | Coburg | VFA | 4 |

# COLLINGWOOD

**1986**

| Draft | Selection | Drafted player | Club of origin | Body | Matches with this club |
|---|---|---|---|---|---|
| National | 8 | Grant Fielke | West Adelaide | SANFL | 16 |
| National | 21 | David Robertson | North Adelaide | SANFL | 17 |
| National | 34 | Craig Kelly | Norwood | SANFL | 122 |
| National | 47 | Brendan Hogan | Assumption College | APS | 0 |
| National | 60 | Wayne Tanner | Norwood | SANFL | 0 |

**1987**

| National | 3 | Graham Wright | East Devonport | TAS | 182 |
|---|---|---|---|---|---|
| National | 16 | Chris Grumley | Sale | VCFL | 0 |
| National | 29 | Andrew Pascoe | Norwood | SANFL | 0 |
| National | 42 | Tim Wilson | North Launceston | TAS | 0 |
| National | 55 | Brendan Tranter | Maryborough | VCFL | 8 |

**1988**

| National | 11 | Mark Bayliss | South Fremantle | WAFL | 4 |
|---|---|---|---|---|---|
| National | 25 | Colin Alexander | Clarence | TAS | 24 |
| National | 39 | Scott Russell | Sturt | SANFL | 167 |
| National | 53 | Michael Smith | Devonport | TAS | 0 |
| National | 67 | Peter Divenuto | Sandy Bay | TAS | 0 |
| National | 81 | Nick Probert | Burnie Hawks | TAS | 0 |
| National | 95 | Tony Francis | Norwood | SANFL | 132 |
| National | 109 | Heath Shephard | Robinvale | VCFL | 11 |

**1989**

| Pre-Seas | 11 | Murray Wrensted | West Coast | AFL | 10 |
|---|---|---|---|---|---|
| Pre-Seas | 25 | James Pyke | Norwood | SANFL | 0 |
| Pre-Seas | 39 | John McKay | Old Xaverians | VAFA | 0 |
| Pre-Seas | 53 | Nick Foley | Narrandera | NSW | 0 |
| National | 10 | Daryl Groves | Maryborough | VCFL | 0 |
| National | 22 | Matthew Hanrahan | Lake Bolac | VCFL | 0 |
| | | *Draft choice 22 traded by Sydney for Matthew Ryan* | | | |
| National | 24 | Michael Styles | Glenorchy | TAS | 0 |
| National | 38 | Gavin Rose | East Perth | WAFL | 0 |
| National | 56 | Shayne Bennett | North Adelaide | SANFL | 0 |
| National | 70 | Paul Williams | North Hobart | TAS | 70 |
| National | 82 | Troy Lehmann | North Adelaide | SANFL | 31 |
| | | *Draft choice 82 traded by Sydney for Matthew Ryan* | | | |
| National | 84 | Matthew Kelly | Norwood | SANFL | 0 |
| National | 98 | Kym Russell | Sturt | SANFL | 3 |
| National | 106 | Ernie Hug | Sale | VCFL | 0 |

**1990**

| Pre-Seas | 16 | Rod Gladman | East Ballarat | VCFL | 0 |
|---|---|---|---|---|---|
| Pre-Seas | 30 | David Kupsch | North Adelaide | SANFL | 0 |
| Pre-Seas | 44 | Kane O'Brien | Collingwood | AFL | 0 |
| Pre-Seas | 52 | Dallas Normington | Kyabram | VCFL | 0 |
| Mid-Seas | 13 | Andrew Hardiman | South Warrnambool | VCFL | 0 |
| Mid-Seas | 26 | Stephen Anderson | South Warrnambool | VCFL | 0 |
| Mid-Seas | 36 | Jason Morton | Wagga Tigers | NSW | 0 |
| National | 4 | Jason McCartney | Nhill | VCFL | 38 |
| | | *Draft choice 4 traded by Richmond for Terry Keays* | | | |
| National | 14 | Andrew Hamer | Lakes Entrance | VCFL | 0 |
| National | 22 | Paul Sharkey | Catholic College, Bendigo | VCFL | 26 |
| National | 38 | Grant McFarlane | Wodonga | VCFL | 0 |
| National | 52 | Brendon Retzlaff | Swan Districts | WAFL | 0 |
| National | 66 | Bowden Hamilton | Colbinabbin | VCFL | 0 |
| National | 80 | Scott O'Donohue | Bungaree | VCFL | 0 |
| National | 94 | Chris Ryan | St Vincents, Morwell | VCFL | 0 |

| Draft | Selection | Drafted player | Club of origin | Body | Matches with this club |
|---|---|---|---|---|---|
| **1991** | | | | | |
| Pre-Seas | 20 | Derek Percival | Golden Square | VCFL | 0 |
| Pre-Seas | 37 | Stephen Anderson | South Warrnambool | VCFL | 4 |
| Pre-Seas | 51 | Ross Duffy | North Hobart | TAS | 0 |
| Pre-Seas | 59 | Gerard Healy | Sydney | AFL | 0 |
| Mid-Seas | 4 | Fraser Murphy | Carlton | AFL | 0 |
| Mid-Seas | 17 | Dean Strauch | Golden Square | VCFL | 0 |
| Mid-Seas | 30 | Not utilised | | | |
| National | 30 | Kane Purcell | North Shore | VCFL | 0 |
| | | *Draft choice 30 traded by Sydney for Gavin Rose* | | | |
| National | 41 | Todd Curley | West Perth | WAFL | 0 |
| | | *Draft choice 41 traded by Fitzroy for Brad Boyd* | | | |
| National | 46 | Bruno Italiano | South Fremantle | WAFL | 0 |
| National | 59 | Greg Turner | South Fremantle | WAFL | 0 |
| National | 70 | Jon Lister | Sandy Bay | TAS | 0 |
| National | 81 | Brendan Barrows | Claremont | WAFL | 0 |
| | | *Draft choice 81 traded by Brisbane Bears for Colin Alexander* | | | |
| National | Trade | Gary Pert | Fitzroy | AFL | 70 |
| | | *Traded by Fitzroy for draft selection 2 (Marcus Seecamp), draft selection 20 (Brett Cook)* | | | |
| National | Trade | Tony Woods | Fitzroy | AFL | 18 |
| | | *Traded by Fitzroy for draft selection 33 (Paul Morrish)* | | | |
| National | Trade | Brad Hardie | Brisbane Bears | AFL | 2 |
| | | *Traded by Brisbane Bears (not utilised)* | | | |
| National | Trade | Brad Rowe | Brisbane Bears | AFL | 51 |
| | | *Traded by Brisbane Bears (not utilised)* | | | |
| **1992** | | | | | |
| Pre-Seas | 8 | Ross Napoli | Essendon | AFL | 0 |
| Pre-Seas | 22 | Ross Johns | Carlton | AFL | 0 |
| Pre-Seas | 36 | Paul Docherty | Essendon | AFL | 0 |
| Pre-Seas | 48 | Derek Percival | Collingwood | AFL | 0 |
| Mid-Seas | 11 | James McLure | Geelong | AFL | 0 |
| Mid-Seas | 25 | Ian McMullin | Essendon | AFL | 4 |
| Mid-Seas | 36 | Daniel Tramontana | Northern U18 | U18 VMFL | 0 |
| Mid-Seas | 42 | Darren Fraser | Collingwood | AFL | 0 |
| Mid-Seas | 47 | Jon Hassall | Collingwood | AFL | 50 |
| Mid-Seas | 49 | Nick Probert | Prahran | VFA | 0 |
| National | 10 | Brett Chalmers | Port Adelaide | SANFL | 0 |
| | | *Draft choice 10 traded by Fitzroy for James Manson* | | | |
| National | 15 | Damian Houlihan | Corowa-Rutherglen | VCFL | 11 |
| National | 30 | Paul Ridley | Subiaco | WAFL | 0 |
| National | 45 | Scott Thompson | Subiaco | WAFL | 0 |
| National | 60 | Tim Scott-Branagan | Central U18 | U18 VMFL | 0 |
| National | 75 | Chris Batka | Subiaco | WAFL | 0 |
| National | 85 | Tristan Lynch | Sale | VCFL | 0 |
| | | *Draft choice 85 traded by Fitzroy for James Manson* | | | |
| National | 90 | Scott Burns | Norwood | SANFL | 56 |
| National | 105 | Julian Waite | Port Adelaide | SANFL | 0 |
| National | 120 | Troy Olsen | Port Adelaide | SANFL | 0 |
| **1993** | | | | | |
| Pre-Seas | 15 | Barry Mitchell | Sydney | AFL | 13 |
| Pre-Seas | 31 | Brett James | Norwood | SANFL | 42 |
| Pre-Seas | 45 | Kent Butcher | Geelong | AFL | 22 |
| Pre-Seas | 59 | Jason Williams | Williamstown | VFA | 0 |
| Pre-Seas | 68 | Andrew Tranquilli | Marcellin | APS | 12 |
| Pre-Seas | 75 | Terry Board | Brisbane Bears | AFL | 0 |
| Mid-Seas | 12 | Terry Keays | Frankston | VFA | 0 |
| Mid-Seas | 24 | Kane Batzloff | Chelsea | VCFL | 0 |
| National | 34 | Stephen Patterson | Norwood | SANFL | 57 |
| | | *Draft choice 34 traded by Adelaide for Brett Chalmers* | | | |
| National | 35 | Aaron James | Western U18 | U18 VMFL | 23 |
| | | *Draft choice 35 traded by Carlton for Barry Mitchell* | | | |
| National | 39 | Jason Wild | Collingullie | NSW | 47 |
| | | *Draft choice 39 traded by Brisbane Bears for Craig Starcevich, Troy Lehmann* | | | |
| National | 53 | Justin Mallon | Northern U18 | U18 VMFL | 0 |
| | | *Draft choice 53 traded by Melbourne for Paul Ridley* | | | |
| National | 66 | Andrew Schauble | Xavier College | APS | 45 |
| National | Trade | Nathan Buckley | Brisbane Bears | AFL | 87 |
| | | *Traded by Brisbane Bears for draft selection 12 (Chris Scott)* | | | |
| National | Trade | Brad Plain | Essendon | AFL | 9 |
| | | *Traded by Essendon for draft selection 29 (Scott Mollard)* | | | |
| National | Trade | Brenton Sanderson | Adelaide | AFL | 4 |
| | | *Traded by Adelaide for draft selection 44 (Eugene Warrior)* | | | |
| **1994** | | | | | |
| Pre-Seas | 13 | Jon Ballantyne | Footscray | AFL | 9 |
| Pre-Seas | 28 | Trent Hotton | Preston | VFA | 17 |
| Pre-Seas | 34 | Stephen Ryan | Richmond | AFL | 8 |
| Pre-Seas | 37 | Justin Staritski | North Melb | AFL | 1 |
| National | 9 | Ben Wilson | Norwood | SANFL | 2 |
| | | *Draft choice 9 traded by Adelaide for Jason McCartney* | | | |
| National | 30 | Chad Liddell | Southern U18 | U18 VMFL | 20 |

| Draft | Selection | Drafted player | Club of origin | Body | Matches with this club |
|---|---|---|---|---|---|
| National | 47 | Robert Ahmat | Darwin | NT | 25 |
| | | *Draft choice 47 traded by Geelong for Brenton Sanderson* | | | |
| National | 53 | Mark Orchard | Ballarat U18 | U18 VCFL | 12 |
| | | *Draft choice 53 traded by Adelaide for Jason McCartney* | | | |
| National | 61 | Stephen Zavalas | Western U18 | U18 VMFL | 0 |
| National | 64 | Robert Powell | Northern U18 | U18 VMFL | 8 |
| National | Pre-Dr Supp | Chris Curran | Collingwood | VSFL | 31 |
| National | Trade | Lee Walker | West Coast | AFL | 16 |
| | | *Traded by West Coast for draft selection 12 (Shane Sikora)* | | | |

## 1995

| Draft | Selection | Drafted player | Club of origin | Body | Matches with this club |
|---|---|---|---|---|---|
| Pre-Seas | 10 | Dermott Brereton | Sydney | AFL | 15 |
| Pre-Seas | 24 | Nick Hider | Camperdown | VCFL | 2 |
| Pre-Seas | 34 | Ryan Aitken | Southern U18 | U18 VMFL | 0 |
| National | 10 | Simon Prestigiacomo | Northern U18 | U18 VMFL | 18 |
| National | 40 | Luke Godden | Northern U18 | U18 VMFL | 3 |
| National | 64 | Matthew Carr | East Fremantle | WAFL | 0 |
| National | 71 | Jason Bevan | South Adelaide | SANFL | 2 |
| National | 74 | Mark Bradley | Gippsland U18 | U18 VCFL | 0 |
| National | 76 | Ben Kemp | Norwood | SANFL | 0 |
| National | 77 | Steven Pitt | Norwood | SANFL | 13 |
| National | Trade | Robert Pyman | North Melb | AFL | 5 |
| | | *Traded by North Melbourne for draft selection 26 (Chris Groom)* | | | |
| National | Trade | Scott Crow | Hawthorn | AFL | 36 |
| | | *Traded by Hawthorn for draft selection 54 (Adam Ansell)* | | | |
| National | Trade | Alex McDonald | Hawthorn | AFL | 41 |
| | | *Traded by Hawthorn for draft selection 54 (Adam Ansell)* | | | |
| National | Trade | Matthew Francis | Richmond | AFL | 25 |
| | | *Traded by Richmond for Robert Powell* | | | |
| National | Trade | Adrian McAdam | North Melb | AFL | 0 |
| | | *Traded by North Melbourne for Bradley Plain* | | | |

## 1996

| Draft | Selection | Drafted player | Club of origin | Body | Matches with this club |
|---|---|---|---|---|---|
| Pre-Seas | 9 | Mark Pitura | Richmond | AFL | 0 |
| National | 19 | Brent Tuckey | Ballarat U18 | U18 VCFL | 0 |
| | | *Draft choice 19 traded by Carlton for Mick McGuane* | | | |
| National | 48 | Marty Warry | Fitzroy | AFL | 0 |
| National | 65 | Brad Cassidy | Fitzroy | AFL | 2 |
| | | *Draft choice 65 traded by Carlton for Mick McGuane* | | | |
| National | 77 | Marcus Barham | Calder U18 | U18 VMFL | 0 |
| National | 84 | Josh Mahoney | Williamstown | VFA | 8 |
| National | 87 | Brad Fuller | Nsw-Act U18 | U18 NSW-ACT | 1 |
| National | 89 | Dwayne Griffin | Swan Districts | WAFL | 1 |
| National | 90 | Leigh Singline | South Launceston | TAS | 0 |
| National | Trade | Richard Osborne | Footscray | AFL | 15 |
| | | *Traded by Footscray for draft selection 61 (Stephen Powell)* | | | |
| National | Trade | John Barnett | North Melb | AFL | 8 |
| | | *Traded by North Melbourne for draft selection 70 (Adam Hay)* | | | |
| National | Trade | Anthony Rocca | Sydney | AFL | 21 |
| | | *Traded by Sydney for Ben Wilson, Mark Orchard, draft selection 14 (Brett O'Farrell), draft selection 33 (Will Sangster)* | | | |
| National | Trade | Jonathan Ross | Adelaide | AFL | 0 |
| | | *Traded by Adelaide for Brett James* | | | |

## 1997

| Draft | Selection | Drafted player | Club of origin | Body | Matches with this club |
|---|---|---|---|---|---|
| Pre-Seas | 4 | Jason Taylor | Hawthorn | AFL | 4 |
| Pre-Seas | 14 | Robert Schaefer | Central District | SANFL | 0 |
| Pre-Seas | 19 | Michael Gardiner | Subiaco | WAFL | 0 |
| National | 8 | Chris Tarrant | Bendigo U18 | U18 VCFL | 0 |
| National | 24 | James Wasley | Norwood | SANFL | 0 |
| National | 56 | Ben Kinnear | Central District | SANFL | 0 |
| National | 81 | Troy Kirwen | Preston U18 | U18 VMFL | 0 |
| National | 84 | Frank Raso | Preston U18 | U18 VMFL | 0 |
| National | 86 | Scott Whiston | Central District | SANFL | 0 |
| Rookie Elev | Rook Elev | Malcolm Michael | Morningside | QLD | 13 |
| Rookie Elev | Rook Elev | Andrew Pugsley | Scoresby | VMFL | 0 |
| National | Trade | Shannon Gibson | Hawth | AFL | 0 |
| | | *Traded by Hawthorn for Paul Sharkey* | | | |
| National | Trade | Clinton King | Sydney | AFL | 0 |
| | | *Traded by Sydney for Robert Ahmat, draft selection 40 (Fred Campbell)* | | | |
| National | Trade | Stuart Mangin | Sydney | AFL | 0 |
| | | *Traded by Sydney for Robert Ahmat, draft selection 40 (Fred Campbell)* | | | |
| National | Trade | Brad Smith | Richmond | AFL | 0 |
| | | *Traded by Richmond for Aaron James, draft selection 71 (Andrew Kellaway)* | | | |
| National | Trade | Jamie Tape | Richmond | AFL | 0 |
| | | *Traded by Richmond for Aaron James, draft selection 71 (Andrew Kellaway)* | | | |

# ESSENDON

## 1986

| Draft | Selection | Drafted player | Club of origin | Body | Matches with this club |
|---|---|---|---|---|---|
| National | 9 | Andrew Payze | West Torrens | SANFL | 0 |
| National | 22 | Kieran Sporn | West Adelaide | SANFL | 72 |
| National | 35 | Peter Reid | Sturt | SANFL | 0 |
| National | 48 | Stephen Riley | North Adelaide | SANFL | 0 |
| National | 61 | Andrew Underwood | Sturt | SANFL | 12 |

| Draft | Selection | Drafted player | Club of origin | Body | Matches with this club |
|---|---|---|---|---|---|
| **1987** | | | | | |
| National | 6 | Andrew Rogers | Woodville | SANFL | 8 |
| National | 19 | Jamie Cox | Wynyard | TAS | 0 |
| National | 32 | John Cook | Hamilton Imperials | VCFL | 0 |
| National | 45 | David Grenvold | Glenelg | SANFL | 112 |
| National | 58 | Peter Bennett | North Adelaide | SANFL | 0 |
| **1988** | | | | | |
| National | 9 | Michael Werner | West Torrens | SANFL | 40 |
| National | 12 | Brad Fox | Perth | WAFL | 17 |
| | | *Draft choice 12 traded by Carlton for Glenn Hawker* | | | |
| National | 23 | Michael Long | St Marys | NT | 131 |
| National | 26 | David Regan | East Ballarat | VCFL | 0 |
| | | *Draft choice 26 traded by Carlton for Glenn Hawker* | | | |
| National | 37 | Michael Strickland | Glenorchy | TAS | 0 |
| National | 51 | Adrian Burns | Dromana | VCFL | 11 |
| National | 65 | Rod Saunders | Mooroopna | VCFL | 0 |
| National | 79 | Simon Jorgensen | Castlemaine | VCFL | 0 |
| National | 93 | Paul Hills | North Ballarat | VCFL | 63 |
| National | 107 | Darren Mead | Port Adelaide | SANFL | 0 |
| **1989** | | | | | |
| Pre-Seas | 9 | Brian Hinkley | Geelong | AFL | 0 |
| Pre-Seas | 23 | Paul McWilliam | Sturt | SANFL | 0 |
| Pre-Seas | 37 | Rodney Lawson | Kalkee | VCFL | 0 |
| Pre-Seas | 51 | Gary Barrow | Essendon | AFL | 0 |
| National | 11 | Darren Smith | Port Adelaide | SANFL | 0 |
| | | *Draft choice 11 traded by Melbourne for Trevor Spencer* | | | |
| National | 12 | Gavin Wanganeen | Port Adelaide | SANFL | 127 |
| National | 19 | Ashley Green | Warragul | VCFL | 23 |
| | | *Draft choice 19 traded by Brisbane Bears for Gavin Keane* | | | |
| National | 26 | Alister Carr | South Bendigo | VCFL | 0 |
| National | 39 | Peter Cransberg | East Perth | WAFL | 79 |
| | | *Draft choice 39 traded by Melbourne for Steven Clark* | | | |
| National | 40 | Travis St Clair | South Bendigo | VCFL | 0 |
| National | 46 | Shane Radbone | Sturt | SANFL | 0 |
| National | 58 | Jason Dullard | Bairnsdale | VCFL | 0 |
| National | 65 | Alan Schwartz | West Torrens | SANFL | 0 |
| | | *Draft choice 65 traded by Brisbane Bears for Gavin Keane* | | | |
| National | 72 | Glenn Crawford | Barooga | NSW | 0 |
| National | 86 | Gerrard Harrington | Southport | QLD | 0 |
| National | 99 | Nick Tsiotanis | Bulleen-Templestowe | VMFL | 0 |
| | | *Draft choice 99 traded by Melbourne for Trevor Spencer* | | | |
| National | 100 | David Pittman | Norwood | SANFL | 0 |
| National | 114 | Jason Walsgott | West Gambier | SA | 0 |
| **1990** | | | | | |
| Pre-Seas | 18 | Derek Kickett | North Melb | AFL | 67 |
| Pre-Seas | 32 | Ian McMullin | Old Melburnians | VAFA | 23 |
| Pre-Seas | 46 | Neale Daniher | Essendon | AFL | 7 |
| Pre-Seas | 54 | Rohan Welsh | Essendon | AFL | 0 |
| Mid-Seas | 14 | Paul Morrish | Richmond | AFL | 7 |
| Mid-Seas | 27 | David Robertson | Euroa | VCFL | 3 |
| Mid-Seas | 37 | Andrew Mills | North Shore | NSW | 0 |
| Mid-Seas | 43 | Michael Thomson | Richmond | AFL | 0 |
| National | 13 | Todd Ridley | Claremont | WAFL | 25 |
| National | 21 | Richard Ambrose | Shepparton | VCFL | 0 |
| National | 24 | John Fidge | Glenelg | SANFL | 0 |
| National | 37 | Glen Hoffman | Jeparit | VCFL | 0 |
| National | 51 | Jarrod Carter | North Hobart | TAS | 0 |
| National | 65 | Stephen Fry | Clarence | TAS | 0 |
| National | 79 | James Hird | Ainslie | ACT | 95 |
| National | 93 | Adam Houlihan | Kyabram | VCFL | 0 |
| **1991** | | | | | |
| Pre-Seas | 19 | Matthew Medew | Essendon | AFL | 0 |
| Pre-Seas | 36 | Darren Williams | Essendon | AFL | 0 |
| Pre-Seas | 50 | Michael Strickland | Essendon | AFL | 0 |
| Pre-Seas | 58 | Shane Heard | Essendon | AFL | 11 |
| Mid-Seas | 13 | David McMurray | Keilor | VMFL | 0 |
| Mid-Seas | 26 | Rod Saunders | North Adelaide | SANFL | 0 |
| National | 8 | Michael Symons | Subiaco | WAFL | 92 |
| National | 21 | Willie Dick | Perth | WAFL | 7 |
| National | 37 | Ryan O'Connor | Ulverstone | TAS | 49 |
| | | *Draft choice 37 traded by Geelong for John Barnes* | | | |
| National | 47 | Glenn Manton | Essendon | AFL | 21 |
| National | 48 | Kevin Mitchell | Claremont | WAFL | 0 |
| | | *Draft choice 48 traded by St Kilda for Craig O'Brien* | | | |
| National | 60 | James Billington | Subiaco | WAFL | 0 |
| National | 63 | Brendan Bower | Richmond | AFL | 3 |
| | | *Draft choice 63 traded by West Coast for David Regan* | | | |
| National | Trade | Russell Evans | North Melb | AFL | 0 |
| | | *Traded by North Melbourne for draft selection 34 (Tim Leng)* | | | |
| National | Trade | Shane Strempel | Brisbane Bears | AFL | 0 |
| | | *Traded by Brisbane Bears for draft selection 71 (Luke Chambers)* | | | |

| Draft | Selection | Drafted player | Club of origin | Body | Matches with this club |
|---|---|---|---|---|---|
| National | Trade | Sean Denham | Geelong | AFL | 115 |
|  |  | *Traded by Geelong (not utilised)* |  |  |  |

**1992**

| Draft | Selection | Drafted player | Club of origin | Body | Matches with this club |
|---|---|---|---|---|---|
| Pre-Seas | 9 | Alan Schwartz | Essendon | AFL | 0 |
| Pre-Seas | 23 | Paul McMaster | Carlton | AFL | 0 |
| Pre-Seas | 37 | Glenn Kilpatrick | North Melb | AFL | 26 |
| Mid-Seas | 7 | Kane Batzloff | Southern U18 | U18 VMFL | 0 |
| Mid-Seas | 22 | John McNamara | Geelong | AFL | 0 |
| Mid-Seas | 33 | Eric Lissenden | North Melb | AFL | 0 |
| Mid-Seas | 40 | Daniel Winkel | Southern U18 | U18 VMFL | 0 |
| Mid-Seas | 45 | Mark Garthwaite | Essendon | AFL | 0 |
| National | 3 | Michael Prior | East Perth | WAFL | 47 |
|  |  | *Draft choice 3 traded by Sydney for Michael Werner, Ed Considine* |  |  |  |
| National | 12 | Tony Delaney | Claremont | WAFL | 15 |
| National | 20 | Scott Cummings | Swan Districts | WAFL | 40 |
|  |  | *Draft choice 20 traded by Sydney for Richard Ambrose* |  |  |  |
| National | 27 | Kieran Murrihy | Geelong U18 | U18 VCFL | 0 |
| National | 42 | Che Cockatoo-Collins | Port Adelaide | SANFL | 71 |
| National | 57 | Russell Williams | South Fremantle | WAFL | 3 |
| National | 72 | Matthew Wadewitz | South Adelaide | SANFL | 0 |
| National | 87 | Damien Hardwick | Springvale | VFA | 65 |
| National | 102 | Jason Bell | Red Cliffs | VCFL | 0 |
| National | 117 | Vince Cappadona | Geelong U18 | U18 VCFL | 0 |
| National | Fath-Son | Dustin Fletcher | Western U18 | U18 VMFL | 91 |

**1993**

| Draft | Selection | Drafted player | Club of origin | Body | Matches with this club |
|---|---|---|---|---|---|
| Pre-Seas | 12 | Tim Watson | West Coast | AFL | 25 |
| Pre-Seas | 20 | Ben Doolan | Sydney | AFL | 58 |
| Pre-Seas | 28 | Lachlan Ross | West Adelaide | SANFL | 2 |
| Pre-Seas | 42 | Brad Fox | Essendon | AFL | 0 |
| Pre-Seas | 56 | Brendan Duncan | Western U18 | U18 VMFL | 0 |
| Pre-Seas | 66 | Darren Bartsch | West Adelaide | SANFL | 0 |
| Mid-Seas | 11 | Dale Kickett | Claremont | WAFL | 8 |
| Mid-Seas | 23 | Danny Morgan | Preston | VFA | 0 |
| National | 19 | Robert Stevenson | Western U18 | U18 VMFL | 11 |
| National | 29 | Scott Mollard | Central U18 | U18 VMFL | 0 |
|  |  | *Draft choice 29 traded by Collingwood for Brad Plain* |  |  |  |
| National | 36 | Julian Kirzner | Central U18 | U18 VMFL | 1 |

**1994**

| Draft | Selection | Drafted player | Club of origin | Body | Matches with this club |
|---|---|---|---|---|---|
| Pre-Seas | 20 | Barry Young | Richmond | AFL | 53 |
| National | 4 | Scott Lucas | Geelong U18 | U18 VCFL | 36 |
|  |  | *Draft choice 4 traded by Fremantle for Tony Delaney* |  |  |  |
| National | 10 | Blake Caracella | Northern U18 | U18 VMFL | 17 |
| National | 28 | Shawn Lewfatt | Western U18 | U18 VMFL | 3 |
| National | 39 | Stephen Carter | Port Adelaide | SANFL | 0 |
|  |  | *Draft choice 39 traded by Fremantle for Dale Kickett* |  |  |  |
| National | 45 | Gary Moorcroft | Northern U18 | U18 VMFL | 1 |
| National | 62 | Justin Blumfield | Tuggeranong | ACT | 25 |
| National | Pre-Dr Supp | Danny Morgan | Essendon | VSFL | 16 |

**1995**

| Draft | Selection | Drafted player | Club of origin | Body | Matches with this club |
|---|---|---|---|---|---|
| Pre-Seas | 8 | Mark Fraser | Collingwood | AFL | 24 |
| Pre-Seas | 22 | Tim Darcy | Geelong | AFL | 14 |
| Pre-Seas | 33 | Matthew Banks | Eastern U18 | U18 VMFL | 0 |
| Pre-Seas | Comp Sel | Matthew Lloyd | Western U 18 | U18 VMFL | 36 |
|  |  | *Compensatory selection from Fremantle for uncontracted player selection Todd Ridley* |  |  |  |
| National | 15 | Darren Wheildon | West Adelaide | SANFL | 0 |
| National | 31 | Andrew Ukovic | Northern U18 | U18 VMFL | 5 |
| National | 58 | Peter Berbakov | Essendon Supp List | AFL RES | 28 |
| National | Trade | Sean Wellman | Adelaide | AFL | 31 |
|  |  | *Traded by Adelaide for draft selection 45 (Scott Hodges)* |  |  |  |
| National | Trade | Paul Barnard | Hawthorn | AFL | 20 |
|  |  | *Traded by Hawthorn for Paul Salmon* |  |  |  |

**1996**

| Draft | Selection | Drafted player | Club of origin | Body | Matches with this club |
|---|---|---|---|---|---|
| Pre-Seas | 14 | Richard Peck | Claremont | WAFL | 0 |
| National | 2 | Chris Heffernan | Geelong U18 | U18 VCFL | 3 |
| National | 5 | Daniel McAlister | Tas U18 | U18 TAS | 2 |
|  |  | *Draft choice 5 traded by Port Adelaide for draft selection US (Gavin Wanganeen)* |  |  |  |
| National | 21 | Tim Williams | East Perth | WAFL | 0 |
| National | 25 | Andrew Bomford | Sydney Supp List | AFL RES | 3 |
| National | 28 | Jason Johnson | Calder U18 | U18 VMFL | 3 |
|  |  | *Draft choice 28 traded by Port Adelaide for Scott Cummings* |  |  |  |
| National | 40 | Forfeited: Breach Of Salary Cap Rules |  |  |  |
| National | 54 | Matthew Watson | Essendon Supp List | AFL RES | 1 |
| National | 66 | Paul Hills | Essendon | AFL | 0 |

**1997**

| Draft | Selection | Drafted player | Club of origin | Body | Matches with this club |
|---|---|---|---|---|---|
| Pre-Seas | 9 | Matthew Banks | Eastern U18 | U18 VMFL | 2 |
| National | 4 | Mark Bolton | Eastern U18 | U18 VMFL | 0 |
| National | 20 | Dean Solomon | Bendigo U18 | U18 VCFL | 0 |
| National | 36 | Judd Lalich | East Perth | WAFL | 0 |
| National | 52 | Jordon Doering | Bendigo U18 | U18 VCFL | 0 |
| National | 68 | Simon Eastaugh | Norwood | SANFL | 0 |
| Rookie Elev | Rook Elev | Gary Moorcroft | Preston | VFA | 11 |

| Draft | Selection | Drafted player | Club of origin | Body | Matches with this club |
|---|---|---|---|---|---|
| **FITZROY** | | | | | |
| **1986** | | | | | |
| National | 11 | Jason Taylor | New Norfolk | TAS | 7 |
| National | 24 | Matthew Armstrong | Hobart | TAS | 132 |
| National | 37 | Chris Duthy | Glenelg | SANFL | 3 |
| National | 50 | Alastair Lynch | Hobart | TAS | 120 |
| National | 63 | Peter Winter | West Adelaide | SANFL | 0 |
| **1987** | | | | | |
| National | 4 | Andrew Brockhurst | South Adelaide | SANFL | 38 |
| National | 17 | Chris Waterson | Cohuna | VCFL | 13 |
| National | 30 | Ashley Byrne | Boort | VCFL | 0 |
| National | 43 | Darren Wheildon | Newborough | VCFL | 70 |
| National | 56 | Keith Allan | Central District | SANFL | 0 |
| **1988** | | | | | |
| National | 3 | Carl Dilena | Sturt | SANFL | 23 |
| National | 17 | Brad Edwards | Perth | WAFL | 6 |
| National | 31 | Brenton Klaebe | Norwood | SANFL | 5 |
| National | 45 | Damian Simmonds | Wangaratta | VCFL | 0 |
| National | 48 | Scott Jordon | South Launceston | TAS | 0 |
| | | *Draft choice 48 traded by Geelong for Ken Hinkley* | | | |
| National | 59 | Matthew Dundas | Assumption College | APS | 73 |
| National | 73 | Stephen Walker | North Hobart | TAS | 0 |
| National | 87 | Dwaine Kretschmer | North Gambier | SA | 0 |
| National | 101 | Leigh Funcke | Minyip | VCFL | 0 |
| **1989** | | | | | |
| Pre-Seas | 3 | Wally Matera | West Coast | AFL | 32 |
| Pre-Seas | 17 | Kevin Caton | West Coast | AFL | 9 |
| Pre-Seas | 31 | Peter Bourke | Essendon | AFL | 22 |
| Pre-Seas | 45 | Dean Lupson | Essendon | AFL | 6 |
| National | 9 | Dale Kickett | Claremont | WAFL | 15 |
| National | 23 | Roger Delaney | Port Adelaide | SANFL | 1 |
| National | 27 | Joel Saunders | Bairnsdale | VCFL | 0 |
| | | *Draft choice 27 traded by Geelong for Gary Keane* | | | |
| National | 37 | Shayne Stevenson | Sandy Bay | TAS | 11 |
| National | 45 | Sasha Dyson-Holland | Leongatha | VCFL | 0 |
| National | 55 | Grant Coffee | Central District | SANFL | 0 |
| National | 69 | Jamie Elliott | Maryborough | VCFL | 40 |
| National | 83 | Mark Robinson | Glenorchy | TAS | 0 |
| National | 97 | Paul McConville | Golden Square | VCFL | 0 |
| National | 111 | David Noble | North Hobart | TAS | 2 |
| **1990** | | | | | |
| Pre-Seas | 15 | Robert Cummings | Hawthorn | AFL | 1 |
| Pre-Seas | 29 | Andrew Johnston | Essendon | AFL | 9 |
| Pre-Seas | 43 | Nick Beardsley | Hawthorn | AFL | 1 |
| Pre-Seas | 51 | Mark Athorn | Footscray | AFL | 21 |
| Mid-Seas | 3 | Mark Brady | Old Scotch | VAFA | 1 |
| Mid-Seas | 17 | Darron Wilkinson | Camberwell | VFA | 1 |
| Mid-Seas | 30 | Darren Collins | Port Melbourne | VFA | 4 |
| National | 3 | David Donato | Clarence | TAS | 12 |
| National | 27 | Brad Davis | Burnie Hawks | TAS | 5 |
| National | 41 | Mark Jenkinson | Willaura | VCFL | 0 |
| National | 55 | Steven Byers | New Norfolk | TAS | 0 |
| National | 78 | Dean Harding | Wangaratta Rovers | VCFL | 19 |
| | | *Draft choice 78 traded by West Coast for Dale Kickett* | | | |
| National | Trade | David O'Connell | West Coast | AFL | 21 |
| | | *Traded by West Coast for draft selection 69 (Gavin Cooney)* | | | |
| National | Trade | Joe Cormack | West Coast | AFL | 26 |
| | | *Traded by West Coast for draft selection 83 (Mark Williams)* | | | |
| **1991** | | | | | |
| Pre-Seas | 3 | Matthew Bourke | Hawthorn | AFL | 2 |
| Pre-Seas | 9 | Justin McGrath | Hawthorn | AFL | 8 |
| Pre-Seas | 26 | Wayne Peters | Richmond | AFL | 0 |
| Pre-Seas | 40 | Jamie Bond | Hawthorn | AFL | 1 |
| Mid-Seas | 2 | David Giles | Clarence | TAS | 0 |
| Mid-Seas | 15 | David Morrison | Melbourne | AFL | 0 |
| Mid-Seas | 28 | Alan Thorpe | Tatura | VCFL | 0 |
| National | 2 | Marcus Seecamp | East Perth | WAFL | 51 |
| | | *Draft choice 2 traded by Collingwood for Gary Pert* | | | |
| National | 7 | Jeremy Guard | Claremont | WAFL | 68 |
| National | 20 | Brett Cook | Broken Hill | NSW | 25 |
| | | *Draft choice 20 traded by Collingwood for Gary Pert* | | | |
| National | 33 | Paul Morrish | Essendon | AFL | 20 |
| | | *Draft choice 33 traded by Collingwood for Tony Woods* | | | |
| National | 64 | Chris Barrett | Geelong | AFL | 4 |
| | | *Draft choice 64 traded by Hawthorn for Jason Taylor* | | | |
| National | Trade | Paul Abbott | Hawthorn | AFL | 26 |
| | | *Traded by Hawthorn for draft selection 15 (Kieran O'Dwyer)* | | | |
| National | Trade | Dale Fleming | Hawthorn | AFL | 13 |
| | | *Traded by Hawthorn for draft selection 15 (Kieran O'Dwyer)* | | | |

| Draft | Selection | Drafted player | Club of origin | Body | Matches with this club |
|-------|-----------|----------------|----------------|------|------------------------|
| National | Trade | Ashley Matthews | Carlton | AFL | 6 |
| | | *Traded by Carlton for draft selection 28 (Cale O'Keefe)* | | | |
| National | Trade | Brad Boyd | Collingwood | AFL | 70 |
| | | *Traded by Collingwood for draft selection 41 (Todd Curley)* | | | |
| National | Trade | Peter Sartori | Carlton | AFL | 23 |
| | | *Traded by Carlton for draft selection 54 (Leigh Snooks)* | | | |

## 1992

| Draft | Selection | Drafted player | Club of origin | Body | Matches with this club |
|-------|-----------|----------------|----------------|------|------------------------|
| Pre-Seas | 2 | Gavin Exell | Geelong | AFL | 5 |
| Pre-Seas | 16 | Danny Sexton | North Melb | AFL | 0 |
| Pre-Seas | 30 | Simon Taylor | Montmorency | VMFL | 0 |
| Mid-Seas | 9 | David Johnston | Essendon | AFL | 25 |
| National | 25 | John Barker | Northern U18 | U18 VMFL | 47 |
| National | 40 | Michael Dunstan | South Fremantle | WAFL | 38 |
| National | 68 | Travis Miller | Warragul | VCFL | 0 |
| | | *Draft choice 68 traded by North Melbourne for John Blakey* | | | |
| National | 70 | Danny Morton | North Adelaide | SANFL | 30 |
| National | 100 | Troy Davies | Devonport | TAS | 0 |
| National | 115 | Richard Marr | Central District | SANFL | 0 |
| National | Trade | James Manson | Collingwood | AFL | 47 |
| | | *Traded by Collingwood for draft selection 10 (Brett Chalmers), draft selection 85 (Tristan Lynch)* | | | |
| National | Trade | John McCarthy | North Melb | AFL | 72 |
| | | *Traded by North Melbourne for draft selection 55 (Matthew Capuano)* | | | |

## 1993

| Draft | Selection | Drafted player | Club of origin | Body | Matches with this club |
|-------|-----------|----------------|----------------|------|------------------------|
| Pre-Seas | 10 | Mark Zanotti | Brisbane Bears | AFL | 57 |
| Pre-Seas | 26 | Adam Sheridan | St Marys | VCFL | 0 |
| Pre-Seas | 40 | Brett Rowe | North Brisbane | QLD | 0 |
| Pre-Seas | 54 | James Saywell | Central District | SANFL | 0 |
| Pre-Seas | 65 | Nick Mitchell | St Bernards | VMFL | 9 |
| Pre-Seas | 73 | Simon Farrer | Stawell | VCFL | 0 |
| Mid-Seas | 10 | Danny Dickfos | North Brisbane | QLD | 0 |
| Mid-Seas | 22 | Tom Kavanagh | Castlemaine | VCFL | 8 |
| Mid-Seas | 28 | Anthony McGregor | Prahran | VFA | 41 |
| Mid-Seas | 30 | Dallas Normington | Werribee | VFA | 0 |
| National | 6 | Trent Cummings | Central District | SANFL | 27 |
| | | *Draft choice 6 traded by Richmond for Michael Gale, Matthew Dundas, Paul Broderick* | | | |
| National | 7 | Chris Johnson | Northern U18 | U18 VMFL | 59 |
| | | *Draft choice 7 traded by Brisbane Bears for Alastair Lynch* | | | |
| National | 9 | Rowan Warfe | Bendigo U18 | U18 VCFL | 26 |
| National | 41 | Kieran Sporn | Essendon | AFL | 12 |
| National | 52 | Matthew Dent | Sturt | SANFL | 47 |
| National | 58 | Jeff Bruce | Corowa-Rutherglen | VCFL | 7 |
| National | 62 | Graeme Wood | Mildura | VCFL | 0 |
| National | 65 | Paul Mullarvey | Box Hill | VFA | 0 |
| National | Fath-Son | Jarrod Molloy | Box Hill | VFA | 59 |
| National | Trade | Jeff Hogg | Richmond | AFL | 40 |
| | | *Traded by Richmond for draft selection 26 (Stephen Jurica)* | | | |
| National | Trade | David Bain | Brisbane Bears | AFL | 12 |
| | | *Traded by Brisbane Bears for draft selection 64 (Shane Hamilton)* | | | |
| National | Trade | Nigel Palfreyman | Brisbane Bears | AFL | 1 |
| | | *Traded by Brisbane Bears for draft selection 64 (Shane Hamilton)* | | | |

## 1994

| Draft | Selection | Drafted player | Club of origin | Body | Matches with this club |
|-------|-----------|----------------|----------------|------|------------------------|
| Pre-Seas | 5 | Steven Stretch | Melbourne | AFL | 25 |
| Pre-Seas | 10 | Matthew Mansfield | Footscray | AFL | 0 |
| National | 23 | John Rombotis | Central U18 | U18 VMFL | 26 |
| Pre-Seas | 25 | Peter Doyle | Carlton | AFL | 12 |
| National | 6 | Robert McMahon | Gippsland U18 | U18 VCFL | 2 |
| National | 19 | Ben Holland | North Adelaide | SANFL | 0 |
| | | *Draft choice 19 traded by West Coast for Michael Dunstan* | | | |
| National | 24 | Matthew Manfield | Woodville-West Torrens | SANFL | 5 |
| National | 35 | Marty Warry | Central U18 | U18 VMFL | 8 |
| | | *Draft choice 35 traded by North Melbourne for Matthew Armstrong* | | | |
| National | 58 | Peter Bird | Geelong U18 | U18 VCFL | 15 |
| National | 84 | Doug Hawkins | Footscray | AFL | 21 |
| National | Pre-Dr Supp | Brett Chandler | Fitzroy | VSFL | 28 |
| National | Trade | Andrew Cavedon | Carlton | AFL | 5 |
| | | *Traded by Carlton for draft selection 33 (Mark Cullen)* | | | |
| National | Trade | Darren Holmes | Sydney | AFL | 21 |
| | | *Traded by Sydney for draft selection 74 (Troy Luff)* | | | |
| National | Trade | Martin Pike | Melbourne | AFL | 36 |
| | | *Traded by Melbourne for Marcus Seecamp* | | | |
| National | Trade | Grant De Mamiel | North Melb | AFL | 0 |
| | | *Traded by North Melbourne for Matthew Armstrong* | | | |
| National | Trade | Wayne Lamb | Melbourne | AFL | 19 |
| | | *Traded by Melbourne for Marcus Seecamp* | | | |
| National | Trade | Adam McCarthy | North Melb | AFL | 15 |
| | | *Traded by North Melbourne for Matthew Armstrong* | | | |

## 1995

| Draft | Selection | Drafted player | Club of origin | Body | Matches with this club |
|-------|-----------|----------------|----------------|------|------------------------|
| Pre-Seas | 4 | Jason Ramsey | Port Adelaide | SANFL | 2 |
| Pre-Seas | 18 | Anthony Mellington | Shepparton | VCFL | 24 |
| Pre-Seas | 32 | Simon Atkins | Footscray | AFL | 41 |
| National | 2 | Matthew Primus | Norwood | SANFL | 20 |

| Draft | Selection | Drafted player | Club of origin | Body | Matches with this club |
|---|---|---|---|---|---|
| National | 4 | Scott Bamford | North Adelaide | SANFL | 22 |
| National | 16 | Shane Clayton | Northern U18 | U18 VMFL | 13 |
| | | *Draft choice 16 traded by Richmond for Ben Holland* | | | |
| National | 20 | Nick Carter | Bendigo U18 | U18 VCFL | 17 |
| National | 32 | Nigel Credlin | Geelong U18 | U18 VCFL | 0 |
| | | *Draft choice 32 traded by Richmond for Ben Holland* | | | |
| National | 50 | Brad Cassidy | Fremantle | AFL | 14 |
| National | Trade | Mick Dwyer | St Kilda | AFL | 8 |
| | | *Traded by St Kilda for draft selection 36 (Andrew Lamb)* | | | |

**1996**

| | | | | | |
|---|---|---|---|---|---|
| Pre-Seas | 1 | Brian McInnes | Cairns | QLD | 0 |
| Pre-Seas | 4 | Brent Frewen | South Mildura | VCFL | 2 |

# FREMANTLE

**1994**

| | | | | | |
|---|---|---|---|---|---|
| National | 1 | Jeff White | Southern U18 | U18 VMFL | 32 |
| National | 22 | Winston Abraham | Perth | WAFL | 38 |
| National | 42 | Douglas Headland | Perth | WAFL | 0 |
| | | *Draft choice 42 traded by St Kilda for Darryl Wakelin* | | | |
| National | 56 | Ryan Smith | West Perth | WAFL | 0 |
| National | 72 | Dean Grainger | Northern U18 | U18 VMFL | 0 |
| National | 73 | Sam McFarlane | Subiaco | WAFL | 0 |
| National | 82 | Not utilised | | | |
| National | 83 | Not utilised | | | |
| National | 91 | Not utilised | | | |
| National | 92 | Not utilised | | | |
| National | 96 | Not utilised | | | |
| National | 97 | Not utilised | | | |
| National | Pre-Dr Sel | Daniel Bandy | Perth | WAFL | 34 |
| National | Pre-Dr Sel | David Muir | North Melb | AFL | 20 |
| National | Pre-Dr Sel | Shane Parker | Subiaco | WAFL | 45 |
| National | Pre-Dr Sel | Luke Toia | Subiaco | WAFL | 31 |
| National | Pre-Dr Sel | Craig Nettelbeck | Sydney | AFL | 0 |
| National | Pre-Dr Sel | Jay Burton | Subiaco | WAFL | 2 |
| National | Pre-Dr Sel | Brad Cassidy | Ballarat U18 | U18 VCFL | 0 |
| National | Pre-Dr Sel | Anthony Ljubic | Gippsland U18 | U18 VCFL | 0 |
| National | Pre-Dr Sel | Neil Mildenhall | West Perth | WAFL | 7 |
| National | Pre-Dr Sel | Peter Miller | East Perth | WAFL | 16 |
| National | Pre-Dr Sel | Nathan Mourish | Perth | WAFL | 0 |
| National | Trade | Tony Delaney | Essendon | AFL | 25 |
| | | *Traded by Essendon for draft selection 4 (Scott Lucas)* | | | |
| National | Trade | Scott Watters | Sydney | AFL | 26 |
| | | *Traded by Sydney for draft selection 21 (Matthew Nicks)* | | | |
| National | Trade | Dale Kickett | Essendon | AFL | 63 |
| | | *Traded by Essendon for draft selection 39 (Stephen Carter)* | | | |
| National | Trade | Phil Gilbert | Melbourne | AFL | 14 |
| | | *Traded by Melbourne for Jeff Farmer* | | | |
| National | Trade | Chris Groom | Adelaide | AFL | 7 |
| | | *Traded by Adelaide for Matthew Collins, Andrew McLeod* | | | |
| National | Trade | Brendan Krummel | West Coast | AFL | 1 |
| | | *Traded by West Coast for Chad Morrison* | | | |
| National | Trade | Troy Polak | North Melb | AFL | 0 |
| | | *Traded by North Melbourne for Glen Freeborn, draft selection 55 (Mark Belleville)* | | | |
| National | Unctr Pl Sel | Ben Allan | Hawthorn | AFL | 47 |
| | | *Uncontracted player selection from Hawthorn for compensatory selection David McEwan* | | | |
| National | Zone Sel | Travis Edmonds | Swan Districts | WAFL | 1 |
| National | Zone Sel | John Hutton | Palm Beach-Currumbin | QLD | 13 |
| National | Zone Sel | Todd Menegola | Swan Districts | WAFL | 0 |
| National | Zone Sel | Clinton Wolf | Claremont | WAFL | 4 |

**1995**

| | | | | | |
|---|---|---|---|---|---|
| Pre-Seas | 2 | Greg Madigan | Hawthorn | AFL | 26 |
| Pre-Seas | Unctr Pl Sel | Peter Mann | North Melb | AFL | 58 |
| | | *Uncontracted player selection from North Melbourne for compensatory selection Stuart Cochrane* | | | |
| Pre-Seas | Unctr Pl Sel | Jason Norrish | Melbourne | AFL | 42 |
| | | *Uncontracted player selection from Melbourne for compensatory selection David Cockatoo-Collins* | | | |
| Pre-Seas | Unctr Pl Sel | Stephen O'Reilly | Geelong | AFL | 62 |
| | | *Uncontracted player selection from Geelong for compensatory selection Steven King* | | | |
| Pre-Seas | Unctr Pl Sel | Andrew Wills | Geelong | AFL | 51 |
| | | *Uncontracted player selection from Geelong for compensatory selection Adam Houlihan* | | | |
| Pre-Seas | Unctr Pl Sel | Brendan Krummel | West Coast | AFL | 1 |
| | | *Uncontracted player selection from West Coast for compensatory selection Chad Morrison* | | | |
| Pre-Seas | Unctr Pl Sel | Todd Ridley | Essendon | AFL | 21 |
| | | *Uncontracted player selection from for compensatory selection Matthew Lloyd* | | | |
| National | 1 | Clive Waterhouse | Port Adelaide | SANFL | 26 |
| National | 7 | Ben Edwards | Claremont | WAFL | 0 |
| National | 13 | Brad Rowe | Collingwood | AFL | 8 |
| | | *Draft choice 13 traded by Footscray for Brad Wira, Hugh Reimers* | | | |
| National | 23 | Jay Burton | Fremantle | AFL | 2 |
| National | Pre-Dr Sel | Daniel Parker | Subiaco | WAFL | 12 |
| National | Trade | David Hynes | West Coast | AFL | 13 |
| | | *Traded by West Coast for Phillip Matera, draft selection 3 (Brendon Fewster)* | | | |

| Draft | Selection | Drafted player | Club of origin | Body | Matches with this club |
|---|---|---|---|---|---|
| National | Zone Sel | Michael Brown | Swan Districts | WAFL | 14 |
| National | Zone Sel | Trent Carroll | Claremont | WAFL | 6 |
| National | Zone Sel | Michael Clark | Swan Districts | WAFL | 0 |
| National | Zone Sel | James Clement | South Fremantle | WAFL | 33 |
| National | Zone Sel | Brendon Feddema | East Fremantle | WAFL | 0 |
| National | Zone Sel | Greg Harding | Claremont | WAFL | 36 |
| National | Zone Sel | Steven Koops | West Perth | WAFL | 10 |
| National | Zone Sel | Martin Whitelaw | West Perth | WAFL | 1 |
| National | Zone Sel | Gavin Mitchell | West Kimberley | WA | 36 |
| **1996** | | | | | |
| Pre-Seas | Unctr Pl Sel | Tony Godden | West Coast | AFL | 7 |
| | | *Uncontracted player selection from West Coast for compensatory selection David Wirrpunda* | | | |
| National | 12 | Heath Black | Oakleigh U18 | U18 VMFL | 15 |
| National | 31 | Jess Sinclair | Eastern U18 | U18 VMFL | 9 |
| National | 46 | Matthew Clucas | East Fremantle | WAFL | 1 |
| **1997** | | | | | |
| National | 6 | James Walker | North Ballarat U18 | U18 VCFL | 0 |
| National | 21 | Clem Michael | South Fremantle | WAFL | 0 |
| | | *Draft choice 21 traded by Richmond for Jeff White* | | | |
| National | 26 | Brodie Holland | Tasmania U18 | U18 TAS | 0 |
| | | *Draft choice 26 traded by Brisbane Lions for draft selection 5 (Luke Power)* | | | |
| National | 32 | Troy Johnson | South Fremantle | WAFL | 0 |
| | | *Draft choice 32 traded by St Kilda for Gavin Mitchell* | | | |
| National | Trade | Chris Bond | Richmond | AFL | 0 |
| | | *Traded by Richmond for draft selection 2 (Brad Ottens)* | | | |
| National | Trade | Adrian Fletcher | Brisbane Lions | AFL | 0 |
| | | *Traded by Brisbane Lions for draft selection 5 (Luke Power)* | | | |
| National | Trade | Daniel Hargraves | Western Bulldogs | AFL | 0 |
| | | *Traded by Footscray for draft selection 18 (Mark Alvey)* | | | |
| National | Trade | Stuart Anderson | North Melb | AFL | 0 |
| | | *Traded by North Melbourne for Winston Abraham* | | | |

# GEELONG

| Draft | Selection | Drafted player | Club of origin | Body | Matches with this club |
|---|---|---|---|---|---|
| **1986** | | | | | |
| National | 5 | Michael Taylor | Port Fairy | VCFL | 0 |
| National | 18 | Mark O'Keefe | Warrnambool | VCFL | 0 |
| National | 31 | Glen Keast | North Gambier | SA | 0 |
| National | 44 | Tim Britt | Dunnstown | VCFL | 0 |
| National | 57 | Michael Billman | Boort | VCFL | 0 |
| **1987** | | | | | |
| National | 8 | Darren Jones | Moe | VCFL | 0 |
| National | 21 | Shane Korth | Natimuk | VCFL | 0 |
| National | 34 | Stephen Hewitt | Warracknabeal | VCFL | 0 |
| National | 47 | Stephen McQueen | North Hobart | TAS | 0 |
| National | 60 | Pat Gribble | Traralgon | VCFL | 0 |
| **1988** | | | | | |
| National | 6 | Ray Sterrett | East Fremantle | WAFL | 20 |
| National | 20 | Adrian Fletcher | Glenorchy | TAS | 23 |
| National | 34 | Daryn Cresswell | Glenorchy | TAS | 0 |
| National | 62 | David Welsby | Sturt | SANFL | 2 |
| National | 76 | David Preston | Bairnsdale | VCFL | 0 |
| National | 90 | Kym Nicholls | Norwood | SANFL | 0 |
| National | 104 | Andrew Gribble | St Peters | VCFL | 0 |
| National | Trade | Ken Hinkley | Fitzroy | AFL | 121 |
| | | *Traded by Fitzroy for draft selection 48 (Scott Jordan)* | | | |
| **1989** | | | | | |
| Pre-Seas | 6 | Andrew Rogers | Essendon | AFL | 75 |
| Pre-Seas | 20 | Spiro Malakellis | Geelong | AFL | 67 |
| Pre-Seas | 34 | Darren Savickas | Geelong | AFL | 0 |
| Pre-Seas | 48 | Garry Phillips | Old Haileybury | VAFA | 3 |
| National | 59 | Daniel Frawley | Wangaratta | VCFL | 0 |
| National | 73 | Tim Birthisel | Inglewood | VCFL | 0 |
| National | 87 | Ashley Coutts | Kaniva | VCFL | 0 |
| National | 101 | Richard Harrison | South Adelaide | SANFL | 0 |
| National | 113 | Shane Crothers | Grovedale | VCFL | 0 |
| | | *Draft choice 113 traded by Melbourne for Michael Scott* | | | |
| National | 115 | Colum McManamon | Ireland | IRELAND | 0 |
| National | Trade | Trevor Poole | Richmond | AFL | 54 |
| | | *Traded by Richmond for draft selection 13 (Allister Scott), draft selection 41 (Chris Waterworth)* | | | |
| National | Trade | Gary Keane | Fitzroy | AFL | 0 |
| | | *Traded by Fitzroy for draft selection 27 (Joel Saunders)* | | | |
| **1990** | | | | | |
| Pre-Seas | 19 | Lynton Fitzpatrick | Footscray | AFL | 0 |
| Pre-Seas | 33 | Bret Bailey | Melbourne | AFL | 1 |
| Pre-Seas | 47 | Simon Goosey | Mornington | VCFL | 0 |
| Pre-Seas | 55 | Michael Garvey | Carlton | AFL | 0 |
| Mid-Seas | 7 | Darren Bartsch | West Adelaide | SANFL | 0 |
| Mid-Seas | 21 | Luke Hampshire | Tyrendarra | VCFL | 0 |
| Mid-Seas | 31 | Damian Hancock | Leitchville | VCFL | 0 |
| National | 1 | Stephen Hooper | East Perth | WAFL | 21 |
| | | *Draft choice 1 traded by Brisbane Bears for David Cameron, Shane Hamilton* | | | |

| Draft | Selection | Drafted player | Club of origin | Body | Matches with this club |
|---|---|---|---|---|---|
| National | 5 | Stewart Devlin | Horsham | VCFL | 0 |
| National | 17 | Brendan Hehir | Darley | VCFL | 0 |
| National | 29 | Byron Donnellan | Donald | VCFL | 0 |
| National | 43 | Glen Thomlinson | Rochester | VCFL | 0 |
| National | 57 | Chris Barzon | Mooroopna | VCFL | 0 |
| National | 71 | Dennis Ryan | Kyabram | VCFL | 0 |
| National | 85 | Brad Dowling | Mooroopna | VCFL | 0 |
| **1991** | | | | | |
| Pre-Seas | 5 | Sean Simpson | St Kilda | AFL | 100 |
| Pre-Seas | 11 | Jamie Lamb | St Kilda | AFL | 14 |
| Pre-Seas | 21 | Adrian Menara | North Melb | AFL | 0 |
| Pre-Seas | 28 | Russell Merriman | St Josephs | VCFL | 25 |
| Pre-Seas | 42 | Stephen Jankowicz | East Gambier | SA | 0 |
| Mid-Seas | 11 | Trevor Spencer | Melbourne | AFL | 10 |
| Mid-Seas | 24 | Steven Handley | Swan Districts | WAFL | 73 |
| Mid-Seas | 34 | Dean Smith | St Josephs | VCFL | 0 |
| Mid-Seas | 40 | Darren Enever | Werribee | VFA | 0 |
| Mid-Seas | 42 | Tony Lithgow | Casterton | VCFL | 0 |
| Mid-Seas | 43 | Brad Nicholls | Bell Park | VCFL | 0 |
| Mid-Seas | 44 | Rob Gilbert | South Barwon | VCFL | 0 |
| National | 9 | Stephen O'Reilly | Swan Districts | WAFL | 36 |
| National | 11 | Leigh Willison | East Perth | WAFL | 3 |
| | | *Draft choice 11 traded by St Kilda for Adrian Fletcher* | | | |
| National | 35 | Darryl Donald | Wangaratta | VCFL | 0 |
| | | *Draft choice 35 traded by St Kilda for Darren Flanigan* | | | |
| National | 62 | Peter MacLean | Seymour | VCFL | 0 |
| National | 73 | Cameron Burke | Warragul | VCFL | 0 |
| National | 83 | Peter Jacks | Ballarat Ycw | VCFL | 0 |
| National | Trade | Geoff Miles | West Coast | AFL | 20 |
| | | *Traded by West Coast for draft selection 24 (Kane Morphett)* | | | |
| National | Trade | John Barnes | Essendon | AFL | 114 |
| | | *Traded by Essendon for draft selection 37 (Ryan O'Connor)* | | | |
| National | Trade | Colin Gasden | North Melb | AFL | 0 |
| | | *Traded by North Melbourne for draft selection 50 (Bruce Hando)* | | | |
| National | Trade | John McNamara | North Melb | AFL | 0 |
| | | *Traded by North Melbourne for draft selection 50 (Bruce Hando)* | | | |
| **1992** | | | | | |
| Pre-Seas | 12 | Tim McGrath | North Melb | AFL | 128 |
| Pre-Seas | 26 | Garry Phillips | Geelong | AFL | 0 |
| Pre-Seas | 40 | Ben Graham | Geelong | AFL | 73 |
| Mid-Seas | 14 | Andrew Macnish | Subiaco | WAFL | 3 |
| Mid-Seas | 27 | Mark Ballan | Western U18 | U18 VMFL | 0 |
| Mid-Seas | 37 | Darren King | Southern U18 | U18 VMFL | 0 |
| National | 18 | Leigh Colbert | South Bendigo | VCFL | 85 |
| National | 33 | Corey Robertson | Burnie Hawks | TAS | 0 |
| National | 48 | Andrew Osborn | South Adelaide | SANFL | 0 |
| National | 63 | Matthew McMurray | Perth | WAFL | 0 |
| National | 65 | Gerrad Power | Northern U18 | U18 VMFL | 0 |
| | | *Draft choice 65 traded by Sydney for Tony Malakellis* | | | |
| National | 78 | Damian Crowe | De La Salle | APS | 0 |
| National | 93 | Adam Shanahan | South Bendigo | VCFL | 0 |
| National | 108 | Bryan Beinke | Port Adelaide | SANFL | 0 |
| National | Trade | Liam Pickering | North Melb | AFL | 85 |
| | | *Traded by Geelong for draft selection 123 (Marty Christensen)* | | | |
| National | Trade | Darren Steele | North Melb | AFL | 18 |
| | | *Traded by Geelong for draft selection 123 (Marty Christensen)* | | | |
| National | Trade | Leigh Tudor | North Melb | AFL | 60 |
| | | *Traded by Geelong for draft selection 123 (Marty Christensen)* | | | |
| **1993** | | | | | |
| Pre-Seas | 18 | Matthew McCartin | Colac | VCFL | 0 |
| Pre-Seas | 34 | Shane Crothers | Grovedale | VCFL | 4 |
| Pre-Seas | 48 | Mark Ballan | Geelong | AFL | 0 |
| Pre-Seas | 61 | Daniel Fletcher | Geelong U18 | U18 VCFL | 1 |
| Pre-Seas | 70 | Shayne Breuer | Woodville-West Torrens | SANFL | 71 |
| Pre-Seas | 77 | Damon Lukins | Claremont | WAFL | 0 |
| Mid-Seas | 9 | John Cunningham | Port Melbourne | VFA | 2 |
| Mid-Seas | 21 | Cristian O'Brien | Norwood | SANFL | 2 |
| Mid-Seas | 27 | Stephen Cochrane | Richmond | AFL | 0 |
| National | 13 | David Ugrinic | Woodville-West Torrens | SANFL | 0 |
| National | 30 | Paul Lewis | Murray U18 | U18 VCFL | 0 |
| National | 38 | David Innella | Western U18 | U18 VMFL | 0 |
| | | *Draft choice 38 traded by Richmond for Mark Neeld* | | | |
| National | 55 | Grant Tanner | Norwood | SANFL | 69 |
| National | 59 | Craig Biddiscombe | Gippsland U18 | U18 VCFL | 22 |
| National | Trade | Aaron Lord | Brisbane Bears | AFL | 32 |
| | | *Traded by Brisbane Bears for draft selection 45 (Trent Bartlett)* | | | |
| **1994** | | | | | |
| Pre-Seas | 14 | Cain Liddle | Western U18 | U18 VMFL | 4 |
| National | 17 | Carl Steinfort | Central U18 | U18 VMFL | 24 |
| | | *Draft choice 17 traded by North Melbourne for Robert Scott* | | | |
| National | 18 | Robert Di Rosa | Western U18 | U18 VMFL | 3 |

| Draft | Selection | Drafted player | Club of origin | Body | Matches with this club |
|-------|-----------|----------------|----------------|------|------------------------|
| National | 36 | Matthew Robbins | Central U18 | U18 VMFL | 7 |
| National | 69 | Dean Helmers | Western U18 | U18 VMFL | 0 |
| | | *Draft choice 69 traded by North Melbourne for Robert Scott* | | | |
| National | 70 | Adam Benjamin | Assumption College | APS | 0 |
| National | 81 | Tim Allen | Hawthorn | AFL | 1 |
| National | Pre-Dr Supp | James McLure | Geelong | VSFL | 3 |
| National | Trade | Brenton Sanderson | Collingwood | AFL | 55 |
| | | *Traded by Collingwood for draft selection 47 (Robert Ahmat)* | | | |
| National | Trade | Brad Sholl | North Melb | AFL | 71 |
| | | *Traded by North Melbourne for Robert Scott* | | | |

## 1995

| Draft | Selection | Drafted player | Club of origin | Body | Matches with this club |
|-------|-----------|----------------|----------------|------|------------------------|
| Pre-Seas | 16 | Derek Hall | West Perth | WAFL | 51 |
| Pre-Seas | 30 | Dean Talbot | East Perth | WAFL | 0 |
| Pre-Seas | Comp Sel | Adam Houlihan | Murray U18 | U18 VCFL | 14 |
| | | *Compensatory selection from Fremantle for uncontracted player selection Andrew Wills* | | | |
| Pre-Seas | Comp Sel | Steven King | Murray U18 | U18 VCFL | 35 |
| | | *Compensatory selection from Fremantle for uncontracted player selection Stephen O'Reilly* | | | |
| National | 34 | Jason Snell | Eastern U18 | U18 VMFL | 13 |
| National | 39 | Glenn Kilpatrick | West Adelaide | SANFL | 35 |
| National | 48 | Darren Milburn | Calder U18 | U18 VMFL | 10 |
| National | 49 | Ronnie Burns | St Marys | NT | 45 |
| | | *Draft choice 49 traded by Carlton for Adrian Hickmott* | | | |
| National | 61 | Daniel Lowther | Northern U18 | U18 VMFL | 3 |
| National | 68 | Brady Anderson | East Perth | WAFL | 0 |
| National | 73 | Stuart Lamond | Woodville-West Torrens | SANFL | 0 |
| National | 75 | Clint Bizzell | Kedron Grange | QLD | 4 |
| National | Fath-Son | Simon Fletcher | Geelong U18 | U18 VCFL | 0 |
| National | Trade | Martin McKinnon | Adelaide | AFL | 43 |
| | | *Traded by Adelaide for draft selection 18 (Brent Williams)* | | | |

## 1996

| Draft | Selection | Drafted player | Club of origin | Body | Matches with this club |
|-------|-----------|----------------|----------------|------|------------------------|
| National | 8 | Leigh Brockman | Tas U18 | U18 TAS | 0 |
| | | *Draft choice 8 traded by Port Adelaide for draft selection 37 (Adam Kingsley), Shayne Breuer* | | | |
| National | 18 | Gerrard Bennett | Tas U18 | U18 TAS | 0 |
| National | 43 | Paul Corrigan | Melbourne Supp List | AFL RES | 15 |
| | | *Draft choice 43 traded by Port Adelaide for draft selection 37 (Adam Kingsley), Shayne Breuer* | | | |
| National | Trade | Cameron Roberts | North Adelaide | SANFL | 3 |
| | | *Traded by Port Adelaide for draft selection 37 (Adam Kingsley), Shayne Breuer* | | | |
| National | Trade | Hamish Simpson | Woodville-West Torrens | SANFL | 0 |
| | | *Traded by Port Adelaide for draft selection 37 (Adam Kingsley), Shayne Breuer* | | | |
| National | Trade | Tim Hargreaves | Hawthorn | AFL | 11 |
| | | *Traded by Hawthorn for Aaron Lord* | | | |

## 1997

| Draft | Selection | Drafted player | Club of origin | Body | Matches with this club |
|-------|-----------|----------------|----------------|------|------------------------|
| National | 15 | Joel McKay | Murray U18 | U18 VCFL | 0 |
| | | *Draft choice 15 traded by Western Bulldogs for Matthew Robbins* | | | |
| National | 29 | Marc Woolnough | Southport | QLD | 0 |
| | | *Father/son rule* | | | |
| National | 38 | James Rahilly | Geelong U18 | U18 VCFL | 0 |
| | | *Draft choice 38 traded by Western Bulldogs for Matthew Robbins* | | | |
| National | 45 | Matthew Scarlett | Geelong U18 | U18 VCFL | 0 |
| | | *Father/son rule* | | | |
| National | 54 | Justin Wood | Tasmania U18 | U18 TAS | 0 |
| | | *Draft choice 54 traded by Western Bulldogs for Matthew Robbins* | | | |
| National | 61 | Tim Finocchiaro | Eastern U18 | U18 VMFL | 0 |
| National | Trade | Brett Spinks | West Coast | AFL | 0 |
| | | *Traded by West Coast for draft selection 13 (Callum Chambers)* | | | |

# HAWTHORN

## 1986

| Draft | Selection | Drafted player | Club of origin | Body | Matches with this club |
|-------|-----------|----------------|----------------|------|------------------------|
| National | 13 | Clayton Lamb | West Adelaide | SANFL | 0 |
| National | 26 | Darrin Pritchard | Sandy Bay | TAS | 211 |
| National | 39 | Matthew Queen | Glenorchy | TAS | 0 |
| National | 52 | Robin McKinnon | West Adelaide | SANFL | 0 |
| National | 65 | Tony Symonds | Glenelg | SANFL | 3 |

## 1987

| Draft | Selection | Drafted player | Club of origin | Body | Matches with this club |
|-------|-----------|----------------|----------------|------|------------------------|
| National | 12 | Grant Williams | Sandy Bay | TAS | 0 |
| National | 25 | Damien Trezise | Union | VCFL | 0 |
| National | 38 | John Polkinghorne | North Ballarat | VCFL | 0 |
| National | 51 | Anthony Dessent | Maffra | VCFL | 0 |
| National | 64 | Peter Nunn | Koo Wee Rup | VCFL | 0 |

## 1988

| Draft | Selection | Drafted player | Club of origin | Body | Matches with this club |
|-------|-----------|----------------|----------------|------|------------------------|
| National | 1 | Alex McDonald | Ballarat Ycw | VCFL | 46 |
| | | *Draft choice 1 traded by St Kilda for Paul Harding, Peter Russo, Robert Handley* | | | |
| National | 14 | Stephen Byers | New Norfolk | TAS | 0 |
| National | 28 | Chris Martin | Seymour | VCFL | 0 |
| National | 42 | Dion Rhook | Hamilton Imperials | VCFL | 0 |
| National | 56 | Justin McGrath | Ballarat Ycw | VCFL | 0 |
| National | 70 | Russell Wilding | Lexton | VCFL | 0 |
| National | 78 | Jamie Bond | Beaufort | VCFL | 0 |
| | | *Draft choice 78 traded by Sydney for Rudi Mandemacher* | | | |
| National | 84 | Justin Crough | Bungaree | VCFL | 0 |
| National | 98 | Michael Barrett | Morwell Tigers | VCFL | 0 |

| Draft | Selection | Drafted player | Club of origin | Body | Matches with this club |
|---|---|---|---|---|---|
| National | 112 | Troy Reid | Woorinen | VCFL | 0 |
| **1989** | | | | | |
| Pre-Seas | 14 | Matthew Shinners | Hawthorn | AFL | 0 |
| Pre-Seas | 28 | Jon Gahan | Hawthorn | AFL | 0 |
| Pre-Seas | 42 | Brett Sherrif | Hawthorn | AFL | 0 |
| Pre-Seas | 56 | Adam Ladbrook | Brisbane Bears | AFL | 0 |
| National | 14 | Ben Allan | Claremont | WAFL | 98 |
| National | 28 | Jason Gibson | Deloraine | TAS | 0 |
| National | 42 | Matthew Robran | Norwood | SANFL | 7 |
| National | 60 | Chris Sharp | East Ballarat | VCFL | 0 |
| National | 74 | Alistair Burke | Tatura | VCFL | 0 |
| National | 88 | Tim Leng | Mildura | VCFL | 0 |
| National | 102 | Dion Sheehan | Mansfield | VCFL | 0 |
| National | 116 | Brendan Bicknall | Shepparton | VCFL | 0 |
| **1990** | | | | | |
| Pre-Seas | 20 | Greg Whittlesea | Sturt | SANFL | 4 |
| Pre-Seas | 34 | Peter Lodge | Richmond | AFL | 0 |
| Pre-Seas | 48 | Michael Bawden | Coorparoo | QLD | 0 |
| Pre-Seas | 56 | Lachlan McLean | Warrandyte | VCFL | 0 |
| Mid-Seas | 11 | Damian Stoney | Old Xaverians | VAFA | 0 |
| Mid-Seas | 24 | James Weeding | Norwood | SANFL | 0 |
| Mid-Seas | 34 | Stephen Moloney | North Melb Old Boys | VAFA | 0 |
| Mid-Seas | 41 | Martin Cameron | Traralgon | VCFL | 0 |
| Mid-Seas | 45 | Jolyon Keeble | Old Melburnians | VAFA | 0 |
| National | 30 | Matthew Young | St Patricks,Launceston | TAS | 21 |
| | | *Draft choice 30 traded by St Kilda for Russell Morris* | | | |
| National | 34 | Brad Read | East Fremantle | WAFL | 0 |
| National | 44 | Scott Crow | Port Fairy | VCFL | 13 |
| | | *Draft choice 44 traded by St Kilda for Sean Ralphsmith* | | | |
| National | 48 | Willie Rioli | South Fremantle | WAFL | 0 |
| National | 62 | Ben Herrald | Assumption College | APS | 0 |
| National | 76 | Robert Bowden | Robinvale | VCFL | 0 |
| National | 81 | Luan Morley | North Ballarat | VCFL | 0 |
| | | *Draft choice 81 traded by Brisbane Bears for Peter Curran, Robert Dickson* | | | |
| National | 90 | Adam Ahern | Devonport | TAS | 0 |
| National | Trade | Darren Jarman | Brisbane Bears | AFL | 109 |
| | | *Traded by Brisbane Bears for draft selection 10 (David Ogg)* | | | |
| **1991** | | | | | |
| Pre-Seas | 16 | Dale Fleming | Hawthorn | AFL | 0 |
| Pre-Seas | 33 | Anthony Paynter | Brisbane Bears | AFL | 0 |
| Pre-Seas | 47 | Mark McLeod | Richmond | AFL | 0 |
| Pre-Seas | 55 | Craig Young | Hawthorn | AFL | 0 |
| Mid-Seas | 8 | Michael Ryan | St Marys | VCFL | 0 |
| Mid-Seas | 21 | Simon Palmer | Western Suburbs | NSW | 0 |
| Mid-Seas | 33 | Ross Hart | Golden Point | VCFL | 0 |
| Mid-Seas | 39 | Shaun Ballans | Lara | VCFL | 0 |
| National | 13 | Shane Crawford | Finley | VCFL | 93 |
| National | 15 | Kieran O'Dwyer | Barooga | NSW | 0 |
| | | *Draft choice 15 traded by Fitzroy for Paul Abbott, Dale Fleming* | | | |
| National | 22 | Simon Crawshay | Hawthorn | AFL | 19 |
| | | *Draft choice 22 traded by St Kilda for Laurence Bingham* | | | |
| National | 26 | Ben Herrald | Hawthorn | AFL | 0 |
| National | 39 | Richard Taylor | Hawthorn | AFL | 4 |
| National | 52 | Matthew Henderson | Morwell | VCFL | 0 |
| National | 75 | Travis Edmonds | Swan Districts | WAFL | 0 |
| National | 84 | Alistair Burke | Hawthorn | AFL | 0 |
| National | 88 | Aiden Bussell | Whorouly | VCFL | 0 |
| National | Trade | Jason Taylor | Fitzroy | AFL | 80 |
| | | *Traded by Fitzroy for draft selection 64 (Chris Barret)* | | | |
| **1992** | | | | | |
| Pre-Seas | 14 | Ricky Nixon | St Kilda | AFL | 8 |
| Pre-Seas | 28 | Ernie Hug | Prahran | VFA | 0 |
| Pre-Seas | 42 | Austin McCrabb | Geelong | AFL | 9 |
| Mid-Seas | 8 | Greg Lochhead | University Blues | VAFA | 0 |
| Mid-Seas | 23 | Michael Blood | Old Melburnians | VAFA | 0 |
| Mid-Seas | 34 | Kevin O'Donnell | Springvale | VFA | 0 |
| Mid-Seas | 41 | Anthony McDonald | Coburg | VFA | 1 |
| Mid-Seas | 46 | Travis St Clair | Kangaroo Flat | VCFL | 0 |
| National | 11 | Jonathan Robran | Norwood | SANFL | 39 |
| | | *Draft choice 11 traded by Adelaide for Matthew Robran* | | | |
| National | 14 | Nick Holland | North Adelaide | SANFL | 55 |
| National | 44 | Chris Gerreyn | Claremont | WAFL | 0 |
| National | 74 | Tim Hargreaves | Berrigan | NSW | 42 |
| National | 89 | Hamish Stewart | Glenelg | SANFL | 0 |
| National | 104 | Andrew Kemp | West Adelaide | SANFL | 0 |
| National | 121 | Ben Ellinghaus | Melbourne Grammar | APS | 0 |
| | | *Draft choice 121 traded by St Kilda for Dean Anderson, Chris Wittman* | | | |
| National | Trade | Darren Baxter | Footscray | AFL | 27 |
| | | *Traded by Footscray for draft selection 29 (Sam Phillipou), draft selection 59 (Scott Allen)* | | | |
| National | Trade | Tim Allen | St Kilda | AFL | 17 |
| | | *Traded by St Kilda for draft selection 119 (Scott Morrison)* | | | |

| Draft | Selection | Drafted player | Club of origin | Body | Matches with this club |
|---|---|---|---|---|---|
| **1993** | | | | | |
| Pre-Seas | 14 | Robert Walker | Richmond | AFL | 0 |
| Pre-Seas | 30 | Mark Bunn | Fitzroy | AFL | 23 |
| Pre-Seas | 44 | Austin McCrabb | Hawthorn | AFL | 0 |
| Pre-Seas | 58 | Guy Rigoni | Myrtleford | VCFL | 0 |
| Mid-Seas | 14 | Simon Luhrs | Central District | SANFL | 0 |
| National | 15 | Luke McCabe | Central District | SANFL | 28 |
| National | 17 | Angelo Lekkas | Northern U18 | U18 VMFL | 25 |
| | | *Draft choice 17 traded by Adelaide for Tony Hall* | | | |
| National | 23 | Shannon Gibson | Northern U18 | U18 VMFL | 25 |
| | | *Draft choice 23 traded by Richmond for Greg Dear* | | | |
| National | 32 | Paul Barnard | East Perth | WAFL | 11 |
| National | 47 | Chris Palmer | West Adelaide | SANFL | 0 |
| National | 56 | Rayden Tallis | Eastern U18 | U18 VMFL | 53 |
| | | *Draft choice 56 traded by North Melbourne for John Barnett* | | | |
| **1994** | | | | | |
| Pre-Seas | 16 | Simon Lethlean | Camberwell Grammar | APS | 0 |
| Pre-Seas | 30 | Shayne Stevenson | Fitzroy | AFL | 34 |
| National | 8 | Daniel Harford | Northern U18 | U18 VMFL | 55 |
| | | *Draft choice 8 traded by Brisbane Bears for Andrew Gowers* | | | |
| National | 59 | Nathan Saunders | Geelong U18 | U18 VCFL | 0 |
| | | *Draft choice 59 traded by St Kilda for Joshua Kitchen, Glenn Nugent, draft selection 59 (Chris Hemley)* | | | |
| National | 60 | Bradley Scott | Eastern U18 | U18 VMFL | 0 |
| | | *Draft choice 60 traded by Brisbane Bears for Andrew Gowers* | | | |
| National | 65 | Lee Fraser | Western U18 | U18 VMFL | 0 |
| National | 77 | Ben Dixon | Assumption College | APS | 11 |
| National | 94 | Jade Rawlings | Devonport | TAS | 8 |
| National | Pre-Dr Supp | Adam Hilton | Hawthorn | VSFL | 0 |
| National | Trade | Randall Bone | Adelaide | AFL | 15 |
| | | *Traded by Adelaide for draft selection 31 (Allen Nash)* | | | |
| National | Trade | Simon Minton-Connell | Sydney | AFL | 22 |
| | | *Traded by Sydney for draft selection 87 (Simon Arnott)* | | | |
| **1995** | | | | | |
| Pre-Seas | 11 | Richard Taylor | Hawthorn | AFL | 49 |
| Pre-Seas | 25 | Tony Woods | Collingwood | AFL | 62 |
| Pre-Seas | Comp Sel | David McEwan | Northern U18 | U18 VMFL | 0 |
| | | *Compensatory selection from Fremantle for uncontracted player selection Ben Allan* | | | |
| National | 5 | Brendan Krummel | Fremantle | AFL | 32 |
| National | 25 | Daniel Chick | East Fremantle | WAFL | 43 |
| | | *Draft choice 25 traded by Adelaide for Darren Jarman* | | | |
| National | 37 | Scott Grainger | Northern U18 | U18 VMFL | 0 |
| National | 51 | Kane Fraser | Eastern U18 | U18 VMFL | 3 |
| National | 54 | Adam Ansell | West Adelaide | SANFL | 0 |
| | | *Draft choice 54 traded by Collingwood for Scott Crow, Alex McDonald* | | | |
| National | Trade | Darren Kappler | Sydney | AFL | 30 |
| | | *Traded by Sydney for draft selection 21 (Clinton King)* | | | |
| National | Trade | Leon Higgins | Sydney | AFL | 1 |
| | | *Traded by Sydney for draft selection 21 (Clinton King)* | | | |
| National | Trade | Paul Salmon | Essendon | AFL | 39 |
| | | *Traded by Essendon for Paul Barnard* | | | |
| **1996** | | | | | |
| Pre-Seas | 5 | Gordon Fode | St Kilda | AFL | 0 |
| Pre-Seas | 16 | Craig Treleven | East Fremantle | WAFL | 40 |
| National | 29 | Nathan Turvey | South Fremantle | WAFL | 0 |
| | | *Draft choice 29 traded by Footscray for Simon Minton-Connell* | | | |
| National | 36 | Johathan Hay | East Fremantle | WAFL | 4 |
| National | 51 | Robert McMahon | Fitzroy | AFL | 0 |
| National | 64 | Darren Collins | Port Adelaide | SANFL | 0 |
| National | 73 | Brett Howman | Nsw-Act U18 | U18 NSW-ACT | 0 |
| National | 80 | Chris Holcombe | Dandenong-Southern U18 | U18 VMFL | 0 |
| National | 85 | Brad Scott | Hawthorn Supp List | AFL RES | 22 |
| National | 88 | Phillip Smith | West Perth | WAFL | 0 |
| National | Trade | Justin Crawford | Sydney | AFL | 15 |
| | | *Traded by Sydney for David McEwan, draft selection 17 (Rowan Warfe)* | | | |
| National | Trade | Aaron Lord | Geelong | AFL | 22 |
| | | *Traded by Geelong for Tim Hargreaves* | | | |
| **1997** | | | | | |
| Pre-Seas | 7 | Jon Hassall | Collingwood | AFL | 15 |
| Pre-Seas | 16 | Todd Ridley | Fremantle | AFL | 2 |
| Pre-Seas | 20 | Nigel Credlin | Fitzroy | AFL | 0 |
| National | 3 | Trent Croad | Dandenong U18 | U18 VMFL | 0 |
| National | 19 | Chris Obst | Western U18 | U18 VMFL | 0 |
| National | 35 | Marcus Baldwin | Calder U18 | U18 VMFL | 0 |
| National | 42 | Matthew Dennis | Old Brighton | VAFA | 0 |
| | | *Draft choice 42 traded by Brisbane Lions for Brad Scott, draft selection 51 (Scott Ralph)* | | | |
| National | 67 | Brad Lloyd | Hawthorn Reserves | AFL RES | 0 |
| National | 78 | Richard Vandenberg | University Blues | VAFA | 0 |
| National | 82 | Nathan Thompson | Hawthorn Reserves | AFL RES | 0 |
| National | 85 | Hayden Burgiel | Gippsland U18 | U18 VCFL | 0 |

| Draft | Selection | Drafted player | Club of origin | Body | Matches with this club |
|---|---|---|---|---|---|
| National | Trade | John Barker | Brisbane Lions | AFL | 0 |
| | | *Traded by Brisbane Lions for Brad Scott, draft selection 51 (Scott Ralph)* | | | |
| National | Trade | Nathan Chapman | Brisbane Lions | AFL | 0 |
| | | *Traded by Brisbane Lions for Brad Scott, draft selection 51 (Scott Ralph)* | | | |
| National | Trade | Paul Sharkey | Collingwood | AFL | 0 |
| | | *Traded by Collingwood for Shannon Gibson* | | | |

**1998**

| | | | | | |
|---|---|---|---|---|---|
| Pre-Seas | 2 | Joel Smith | St Kilda | AFL | 0 |
| Pre-Seas | 9 | Jason Daniltchenko | North Melbourne | AFL | 0 |
| Pre-Seas | 12 | Hayden Kilmartin | East Fremantle | WAFL | 0 |
| Pre-Seas | 14 | Not utilised | | | 0 |

# MELBOURNE

**1986**

| | | | | | |
|---|---|---|---|---|---|
| National | 3 | Steven Febey | Devonport | TAS | 180 |
| National | 16 | Matthew Febey | Devonport | TAS | 0 |
| National | 29 | Craig Walker | North Hobart | TAS | 0 |
| National | 42 | Anthony Lovell | Glenorchy | TAS | 121 |
| National | 55 | Darren Jarman | North Adelaide | SANFL | 0 |

**1987**

| | | | | | |
|---|---|---|---|---|---|
| National | 11 | Tim McNeil | Norwood | SANFL | 0 |
| National | 24 | Mark Ducker | Norwood | SANFL | 0 |
| National | 37 | Andrew Obst | Port Adelaide | SANFL | 149 |
| National | 50 | Stephen Tingay | Shepparton | VCFL | 138 |
| National | 63 | Jay Viney | Sturt | SANFL | 23 |

**1988**

| | | | | | |
|---|---|---|---|---|---|
| National | 13 | Darren Bennett | East Fremantle | WAFL | 74 |
| National | 27 | Rod Keogh | Castlemaine | VCFL | 22 |
| National | 41 | Michael Hobbes | Eastlake | ACT | 0 |
| National | 55 | Andrew Ford | North Ballarat | VCFL | 8 |
| National | 69 | Matthew Mahoney | Eastlake | ACT | 6 |
| National | 83 | Brian Stynes | Ireland | IRELAND | 2 |
| National | 97 | Tom Grehan | Ireland | IRELAND | 0 |
| National | 111 | Tom Kavanagh | Castlemaine | VCFL | 2 |

**1989**

| | | | | | |
|---|---|---|---|---|---|
| Pre-Seas | 13 | Dannie Seow | Collingwood | AFL | 7 |
| Pre-Seas | 27 | James Tonkins | Melbourne | AFL | 0 |
| Pre-Seas | 41 | Michael Atkins | Footscray | AFL | 0 |
| Pre-Seas | 55 | Matthew Febey | Melbourne | AFL | 0 |
| National | 25 | Paul Rouvray | Glenelg | SANFL | 0 |
| National | 57 | Tim Moreland | Shepparton | VCFL | 0 |
| National | 71 | Glenn Wilkins | North Ballarat | VCFL | 0 |
| National | 85 | Anthony Tohill | Ireland | IRELAND | 0 |
| National | Trade | Trevor Spencer | Essendon | AFL | 3 |
| | | *Traded by Essendon for draft selection 11 (Darren Smith), draft selection 99 (Nick Tsiotanis)* | | | |
| National | Trade | Steven Clark | Essendon | AFL | 21 |
| | | *Traded by Essendon for draft selection 39 (Peter Cransberg)* | | | |
| National | Trade | Michael Scott | Geelong | AFL | 0 |
| | | *Traded by Geelong for draft selection 113 (Shane Crothers)* | | | |

**1990**

| | | | | | |
|---|---|---|---|---|---|
| Pre-Seas | 17 | Stuart Cameron | Fitzroy | AFL | 5 |
| Pre-Seas | 31 | Scott Williamson | Wangaratta Rovers | VCFL | 0 |
| Pre-Seas | 45 | Robert Hickmott | Essendon | AFL | 2 |
| Pre-Seas | 53 | Matthew Sexton | Sandhurst | VCFL | 0 |
| Mid-Seas | 12 | Jamie Duursma | Melbourne | AFL | 0 |
| Mid-Seas | 25 | Peter Van Der Meer | Frankston | VFA | 0 |
| Mid-Seas | 35 | Paul Hogarth | Northern United | VCFL | 0 |
| Mid-Seas | 42 | David Morrison | Devonport | TAS | 0 |
| National | 6 | Allen Jakovich | Woodville | SANFL | 47 |
| | | *Draft choice 6 traded by St Kilda for Stephen Newport* | | | |
| National | 19 | Gary Merritt | Tatura | VCFL | 0 |
| National | 63 | Fabian Francis | Southern District | NT | 1 |
| National | 75 | Robert Panozza | Wodonga Raiders | VCFL | 0 |
| | | *Draft choice 75 traded by North Melbourne for John Ahern* | | | |
| National | 77 | Niall Buckley | County Kildare | IRELAND | 0 |
| National | Trade | Paul Bryce | North Melb | AFL | 26 |
| | | *Traded by Nth Melbourne for draft selection 11 (Danny Sexton), draft selection 35 (Stuart Anderson)* | | | |
| National | Trade | Phil Egan | Richmond | AFL | 1 |
| | | *Traded by Richmond for draft selection 49 (Nick Daffy)* | | | |
| National | Trade | Rod Owen | St Kilda | AFL | 9 |
| | | *Traded by St Kilda for draft selection 91 (Adam Rudd)* | | | |

**1991**

| | | | | | |
|---|---|---|---|---|---|
| Pre-Seas | 17 | Nick Sebo | St Kilda | AFL | 0 |
| Pre-Seas | 23 | Leigh Capsalis | Melbourne | AFL | 0 |
| Pre-Seas | 34 | Kevin Dyson | Oakleigh | VFA | 70 |
| Pre-Seas | 48 | George Gorozidis | St Kilda | AFL | 0 |
| Pre-Seas | 56 | Not utilised | | | |
| Mid-Seas | 9 | Grant Williams | Sandy Bay | TAS | 4 |
| Mid-Seas | 22 | Stephen Wearne | Sandringham | VFA | 3 |
| National | 3 | Darren Kowal | Claremont | WAFL | 80 |
| | | *Draft choice 3 traded by Richmond for Steven O'Dwyer* | | | |

| Draft | Selection | Drafted player | Club of origin | Body | Matches with this club |
|---|---|---|---|---|---|
| National | 5 | Jason Norrish | Claremont | WAFL | 20 |
| | | *Draft choice 5 traded by Carlton for Earl Spalding* | | | |
| National | 10 | Andrew Lamprill | Hobart | TAS | 36 |
| National | 19 | Phil Gilbert | Claremont | WAFL | 25 |
| | | *Draft choice 19 traded by Footscray for Ricky Jackson* | | | |
| National | 23 | Matthew McKay | Hawthorn | AFL | 0 |
| National | 31 | Haydon Kilmartin | North Hobart | TAS | 0 |
| | | *Draft choice 31 traded by Footscray for Tony Campbell* | | | |
| National | 32 | Micah Berry | Melbourne Grammar | APS | 0 |
| National | 36 | Jason Dullard | Essendon | AFL | 0 |
| National | 40 | Nick White | Richmond | AFL | 0 |
| | | *Draft choice 40 traded by Brisbane Bears for Rod Owen* | | | |
| National | Trade | Michael Pickering | Richmond | AFL | 15 |
| | | *Traded by Richmond for draft selection 49 (Todd Hawes)* | | | |

## 1992
| | | | | | |
|---|---|---|---|---|---|
| Pre-Seas | 11 | Wayne Henwood | Sydney | AFL | 1 |
| Pre-Seas | 25 | Andy Goodwin | Richmond | AFL | 17 |
| Pre-Seas | 39 | Ben Judd | Sturt | SANFL | 0 |
| Pre-Seas | 50 | Cristian O'Brien | Melbourne | AFL | 0 |
| Mid-Seas | 2 | Greg Doyle | Dandenong | VFA | 31 |
| Mid-Seas | 17 | Matthew Febey | Rochester | VCFL | 103 |
| National | 9 | Martin Pike | Norwood | SANFL | 24 |
| National | 24 | Brett Jeffrey | Boort | VCFL | 0 |
| National | 39 | Matthew Kluzek | Woodville-West Torrens | SANFL | 0 |
| National | 54 | Daniel Clarke | West Brisbane | QLD | 0 |
| National | 69 | Scott Simister | Springvale | VFA | 3 |
| National | 84 | Damien Gaspar | South Fremantle | WAFL | 28 |
| National | 99 | Jeff Hilton | St Kilda | AFL | 43 |
| National | 122 | Damon Munt | Norwood | SANFL | 0 |
| | | *Draft choice 122 traded by Footscray for Luke Beveridge* | | | |
| National | Fath-Son | Bradley Campbell | Tongala | VCFL | 1 |
| National | Fath-Son | Glenn Molloy | Norwood | SANFL | 20 |
| National | Trade | Adrian Campbell | Footscray | AFL | 2 |
| | | *Traded by Footscray for draft selection 114 (Paul Whelan)* | | | |

## 1993
| | | | | | |
|---|---|---|---|---|---|
| Pre-Seas | 9 | Glenn Freeborn | Woodville-West Torrens | SANFL | 0 |
| Pre-Seas | 25 | Ivan Bartul | South Fremantle | WAFL | 0 |
| Pre-Seas | 39 | Matthew McKay | Melbourne | AFL | 0 |
| Pre-Seas | 53 | Paul Prymke | Woodville-West Torrens | SANFL | 49 |
| Mid-Seas | 5 | Brett Evans | Springvale | VFA | 0 |
| National | 10 | Trent Ormond-Allen | Port Adelaide | SANFL | 8 |
| National | 27 | Brad Hall | Assumption College | APS | 0 |
| National | 42 | Michael Prentice | Southern U18 | U18 VMFL | 0 |
| National | Trade | Paul Ridley | Collingwood | AFL | 0 |
| | | *Traded by Collingwood for draft selection 53 (Justin Mallon)* | | | |

## 1994
| | | | | | |
|---|---|---|---|---|---|
| Pre-Seas | 11 | Dean Irving | West Coast | AFL | 23 |
| Pre-Seas | 26 | John Carroll | St Bedes | VAFA | 0 |
| National | 16 | Adem Yze | Murray U18 | U18 VCFL | 47 |
| National | 34 | Michael Polley | Northern U18 | U18 VMFL | 5 |
| National | 51 | Clay Sampson | South Adelaide | SANFL | 13 |
| National | 68 | Luke Norman | Wangaratta | VCFL | 16 |
| National | 76 | Todd McHardy | Western U18 | U18 VMFL | 5 |
| | | *Draft choice 76 traded by Richmond for Chris Sullivan* | | | |
| National | Trade | Jeff Farmer | Fremantle | AFL | 43 |
| | | *Traded by Fremantle for Phil Gilbert* | | | |
| National | Trade | Marcus Seecamp | Fitzroy | AFL | 51 |
| | | *Traded by Fitzroy for Wayne Lamb, Martin Pike* | | | |

## 1995
| | | | | | |
|---|---|---|---|---|---|
| Pre-Seas | 14 | Shaun Smith | Werribee | VFA | 51 |
| Pre-Seas | 28 | Martin Heppell | St Kilda | AFL | 2 |
| Pre-Seas | Comp Sel | David Cockatoo-Collins | Port Adelaide | SANFL | 2 |
| | | *Compensatory selection from Fremantle for uncontracted player selection Jason Norrish* | | | |
| National | 11 | Donald Cockatoo-Collins | Wesley College | APS | 6 |
| National | 55 | Mark Bradly | East Fremantle | WAFL | 0 |
| National | 60 | Darren O'Brien | West Perth | WAFL | 24 |
| National | 72 | Ashley Gehling | Dandenong-Southern U18 | U18 VMFL | 0 |
| National | Trade | Anthony Ingerson | Adelaide | AFL | 40 |
| | | *Traded by Adelaide for draft selection 27 (Kane Johnson)* | | | |
| National | Trade | David Grant | St Kilda | AFL | 7 |
| | | *Traded by St Kilda for draft selection 41 (Ryan Grinter)* | | | |
| National | Trade | Alastair Clarkson | North Melb | AFL | 41 |
| | | *Traded by North Melbourne for draft selection 65 (Eric Lissenden)* | | | |
| National | Trade | Craig Turley | West Coast | AFL | 16 |
| | | *Traded by West Coast for Anthony Lovell* | | | |

## 1996
| | | | | | |
|---|---|---|---|---|---|
| Pre-Seas | 2 | Craig Nettelbeck | Fremantle | AFL | 33 |
| Pre-Seas | 10 | Andrew Leoncelli | Old Xaverians | VAFA | 19 |
| National | 11 | Brent Grgic | Geelong U18 | U18 VCFL | 9 |
| National | 22 | Alistair Nicholson | Claremont | WAFL | 1 |
| National | 30 | Hayden Lamaro | Murray U18 | U18 VCFL | 0 |

| Draft | Selection | Drafted player | Club of origin | Body | Matches with this club |
|---|---|---|---|---|---|
| National | 45 | Clayton Gardiner | Claremont | WAFL | 0 |
| National | 59 | Anthony McDonald | Melbourne Supp List | AFL RES | 19 |
| National | 68 | Russell Robertson | Tas U18 | U18 TAS | 0 |
| National | 75 | Mark Winterton | Dandenong-Southern U18 | U18 VMFL | 0 |
| National | 82 | Duncan O'Toole | Devonport | TAS | 0 |
| National | 83 | Ashley Gehling | Melbourne | AFL | 0 |

*Draft choice 83 traded by Adelaide for Trent Ormond-Allen*

| National | Trade | Nick Pesch | Adelaide | AFL | 4 |

*Traded by Adelaide for Clay Sampson*

**1997**

| Pre-Seas | 3 | Leigh Newton | Albury | NSW | 13 |
|---|---|---|---|---|---|
| Pre-Seas | 13 | Robert Pyman | Collingwood | AFL | 19 |
| Pre-Seas | 18 | Shane Woewodin | East Fremantle | WAFL | 22 |
| National | 1 | Travis Johnstone | Dandenong U18 | U18 VMFL | 0 |
| National | 22 | Troy Longmuir | West Perth | WAFL | 0 |

*Draft choice 22 traded by Fremantle for draft selection 2 (Brad Ottens), draft selection 18 (Mark Alvey)*

| National | 39 | Matthew Blake | Bendigo U18 | U18 VCFL | 0 |

*Draft choice 39 traded by Carlton for Sean Charles*

| National | 50 | Luke Ottens | Glenelg | SANFL | 0 |
| National | 66 | Nathan Brown | West Adelaide | SANFL | 0 |
| National | 77 | Guy Rigoni | Myrtleford | VCFL | 0 |
| National | Trade | Jeff White | Fremantle | AFL | 0 |

*Traded by Fremantle for draft selection 2 (Brad Ottens), draft selection 18 (Mark Alvey)*

| National | Trade | Craig Smoker | West Coast | AFL | 0 |

*Traded by West Coast for draft selection 34 (Andrew Williams)*

| National | Trade | Matthew Collins | Adelaide | AFL | 0 |

*Traded by Adelaide for Nathan Bassett*

| National | Trade | Brent Williams | Adelaide | AFL | 0 |

*Traded by Adelaide for Nathan Bassett*

| Rook Prom | Rook Elev | Nathan Bassett | Norwood | SANFL | 0 |
| Rook Prom | Rook Elev | James McDonald | Old Xaverians | VAFA | 4 |
| Rook Prom | Rook Elev | Russell Robertson | Tasmania U18 | U18 TAS | 3 |

**1998**

| Pre-Seas | 1 | Jamie Shanahan | St Kilda | AFL | 0 |

# NORTH MELBOURNE

**1986**

| National | 7 | Chris Lindsay | West Torrens | SANFL | 0 |
|---|---|---|---|---|---|
| National | 20 | Brenton Harris | South Adelaide | SANFL | 2 |
| National | 33 | Malcolm Shippen | Moulamein | NSW | 0 |
| National | 46 | Gary Brooker | Casterton | VCFL | 0 |
| National | 59 | Wayne Morrissey | Northern United | VCFL | 0 |

**1987**

| National | 9 | Michael Murphy | Glenelg | SANFL | 3 |
|---|---|---|---|---|---|
| National | 22 | Scott Christie | Strathmerton | VCFL | 0 |
| National | 35 | Craig Patrick | Wangaratta Rovers | VCFL | 0 |
| National | 48 | Liam Pickering | Stawell | VCFL | 22 |
| National | 61 | Darren Read | Leongatha | VCFL | 0 |

**1988**

| National | 4 | John McNamara | Port Fairy | VCFL | 0 |
|---|---|---|---|---|---|
| National | 18 | Anthony Stevens | Shepparton | VCFL | 156 |
| National | 32 | Brad Sholl | Horsham | VCFL | 0 |
| National | 46 | Simon McCarty | Rochester | VCFL | 0 |
| National | 60 | Derek Kickett | Central District | SANFL | 12 |
| National | 74 | Stephen Hamilton | North Adelaide | SANFL | 6 |
| National | 88 | Justin Staritski | Norwood | SANFL | 25 |
| National | 92 | Stephen Vizy | Queanbeyan | ACT | 0 |

*Draft choice 92 traded by Sydney for Mark O'Donoghue*

| National | 102 | Shaun Holloway | Ballarat Ycw | VCFL | 0 |

**1989**

| Pre-Seas | 4 | Travis Martin-Beynon | Western Districts | QLD | 0 |
|---|---|---|---|---|---|
| Pre-Seas | 18 | Leigh Tudor | North Melb | AFL | 5 |
| Pre-Seas | 32 | Chris Lindsay | West Torrens | SANFL | 0 |
| Pre-Seas | 46 | Tony Furey | North Melb | AFL | 0 |
| National | 6 | Mark Brayshaw | Claremont | WAFL | 32 |
| National | 20 | Brett Hawkey | Nathalia | VCFL | 0 |
| National | 34 | Andrew Venner | Ballarat Ycw | VCFL | 0 |
| National | 52 | Rod Jameson | Glenelg | SANFL | 0 |
| National | 66 | Shannon Bergmann | Swan Hill | VCFL | 0 |
| National | 80 | Damian Murray | West Adelaide | SANFL | 2 |
| National | 94 | John Bingham | Old Haileybury | VAFA | 0 |
| National | 108 | Eric Lissenden | Neerim-Neerim South | VCFL | 0 |

**1990**

| Pre-Seas | 6 | Michael Gallagher | Carlton | AFL | 38 |
|---|---|---|---|---|---|
| Pre-Seas | 12 | Gavin Lloyd | Darley | VCFL | 0 |
| Pre-Seas | 26 | Darren Tarczon | North Melb | AFL | 0 |
| Pre-Seas | 40 | Ken Rainsford | Port Melbourne | VFA | 0 |
| Mid-Seas | 5 | Tim Williamson | Casterton | VCFL | 0 |
| Mid-Seas | 19 | Anthony Pavey | Churchill | VCFL | 0 |

| Draft | Selection | Drafted player | Club of origin | Body | Matches with this club |
|---|---|---|---|---|---|
| National | 11 | Danny Sexton | Lemnos | VCFL | 0 |
| | | *Draft choice 11 traded by Melbourne for Paul Bryce* | | | |
| National | 18 | Dan Miller | Morwell | VCFL | 0 |
| National | 33 | Matthew Kelly | Wedderburn | VCFL | 0 |
| National | 35 | Stuart Anderson | Sale | VCFL | 61 |
| | | *Draft choice 35 traded by Melbourne for Paul Bryce* | | | |
| National | 45 | Craig Jennings | Traralgon | VCFL | 0 |
| | | *Draft choice 45 traded by Carlton for Mark Arceri* | | | |
| National | 50 | Craig Ellis | Stawell | VCFL | 0 |
| | | *Draft choice 50 traded by West Coast for Mark Hepburn* | | | |
| National | 53 | Stephen Pears | Perth | WAFL | 0 |
| | | *Draft choice 53 traded by Brisbane Bears for Travers Martin-Beynon* | | | |
| National | 61 | Michael Scoon | Monbulk | VCFL | 0 |
| National | 89 | Simon Wood | St Arnaud | VCFL | 0 |
| National | Trade | Peter Mann | West Coast | AFL | 39 |
| | | *Traded by West Coast for draft selection 9 (Matt Clape)* | | | |
| National | Trade | Mark Roberts | Brisbane Bears | AFL | 109 |
| | | *Traded by Brisbane Bears for draft selection 47 (Luke Chambers)* | | | |
| National | Trade | John Ahern | Melbourne | AFL | 0 |
| | | *Traded by Melbourne for draft selection 75 (Robert Panozza)* | | | |
| **1991** | | | | | |
| Pre-Seas | 15 | Carl Dilena | Fitzroy | AFL | 10 |
| Pre-Seas | 32 | Peter Baldwin | Geelong | AFL | 0 |
| Pre-Seas | 46 | Anthony Palmer | North Melb | AFL | 0 |
| Pre-Seas | 54 | Dean Barwick | North Melb | AFL | 0 |
| Mid-Seas | 10 | Stephen Zamykal | Williamstown | VFA | 0 |
| Mid-Seas | 23 | Not utilised | | | |
| National | 34 | Tim Leng | North Melb | AFL | 0 |
| | | *Draft choice 34 traded by Essendon for Russell Evans* | | | |
| National | 50 | Bruce Hando | St Arnaud | VCFL | 0 |
| | | *Draft choice 50 traded by Geelong for Col Gasden, John McNamara* | | | |
| National | 69 | Brad Sholl | North Melb | AFL | 2 |
| National | Trade | Tim Bourke | Geelong | AFL | 0 |
| | | *Traded by Geelong for* | | | |
| National | Trade | Richard Dennis | Carlton | AFL | 13 |
| | | *Traded by Carlton for* | | | |
| **1992** | | | | | |
| Pre-Seas | 7 | Alex Ishchenko | Brisbane Bears | AFL | 97 |
| Pre-Seas | 21 | Marty Christensen | Geelong | AFL | 2 |
| Pre-Seas | 35 | Leigh Tudor | North Melb | AFL | 3 |
| Pre-Seas | 47 | Glen Page | Sydney | AFL | 5 |
| Pre-Seas | 55 | Michael Scoon | North Melb | AFL | 0 |
| Mid-Seas | 4 | Tim Perkins | North Adelaide | SANFL | 0 |
| Mid-Seas | 19 | Mark Attard | Eastern U18 | U18 VMFL | 3 |
| National | 6 | Robert Pyman | Woodville-West Torrens | SANFL | 16 |
| | | *Draft choice 6 traded by Brisbane Bears for Paul Spargo* | | | |
| National | 23 | Warren Campbell | South Fremantle | WAFL | 19 |
| National | 38 | David Dighton | Westbrook | NSW | 0 |
| National | 53 | Matthew Moon | Central U18 | U18 VMFL | 0 |
| National | 55 | Matthew Capuano | Geelong U18 | U18 VCFL | 36 |
| | | *Draft choice 55 traded by Fitzroy for John McCarthy* | | | |
| National | 83 | Jeremy Silcock | East Perth | WAFL | 0 |
| National | 98 | Adrian McAdam | South Alice Springs | NT | 36 |
| National | 110 | Jeff Chandler | North Melb | AFL | 0 |
| | | *Draft choice 110 traded by Sydney for Dean McRae* | | | |
| National | 113 | Damon Armstrong | Moama | NSW | 0 |
| National | 123 | Marty Christensen | North Melb | AFL | 0 |
| | | *Draft choice 123 traded by Geelong for Liam Pickering, Darren Steele, Leigh Tudor* | | | |
| National | Trade | Dean Laidley | West Coast | AFL | 99 |
| | | *Traded by West Coast for draft selection 8 (Paul Symmons)* | | | |
| National | Trade | John Blakey | Fitzroy | AFL | 114 |
| | | *Traded by Fitzroy for draft selection 68 (Travis Miller)* | | | |
| **1993** | | | | | |
| Pre-Seas | 8 | Greg Eppelstun | Footscray | AFL | 1 |
| Pre-Seas | 24 | Paul Geister | Central District | SANFL | 3 |
| Pre-Seas | 38 | Brendan Bower | Essendon | AFL | 2 |
| Pre-Seas | 52 | Rodney McKay | North Melb | AFL | 0 |
| Pre-Seas | 64 | Darren Tarczon | Carlton | AFL | 0 |
| Mid-Seas | 15 | Andrew Krakouer | Sandringham | VFA | 0 |
| National | 14 | Adam Simpson | Northern U18 | U18 VMFL | 46 |
| National | 31 | Mark Stevens | Gippsland U18 | U18 VCFL | 21 |
| National | 46 | David King | Port Melbourne | VFA | 89 |
| National | 60 | Troy Polak | Perth | WAFL | 0 |
| National | 63 | Gareth John | Sydney | AFL | 1 |
| National | Trade | John Barnett | Hawthorn | AFL | 6 |
| | | *Traded by Hawthorn for draft selection 56 (Rayden Tallis)* | | | |
| **1994** | | | | | |
| Pre-Seas | 15 | Trent Nichols | West Coast | AFL | 33 |
| Pre-Seas | 29 | David Muir | Claremont | WAFL | 0 |
| National | 52 | Danny Stevens | Northern U18 | U18 VMFL | 9 |
| National | 55 | Mark Belleville | Western U18 | U18 VMFL | 0 |
| | | *Draft choice 55 traded by Fremantle for Troy Polak* | | | |

| Draft | Selection | Drafted player | Club of origin | Body | Matches with this club |
|-------|-----------|----------------|----------------|------|------------------------|
| National | 80 | Ben Atkins | Glenorchy | TAS | 0 |
| National | 90 | Matthew Joy | Southern U18 | U18 VMFL | 0 |
| National | 95 | Kym Eyers | Central District | SANFL | 0 |
| National | Trade | Matthew Armstrong | Fitzroy | AFL | 43 |
| | | *Traded by Fitzroy for draft selection 35 (Marty Warry), Grant Demamiel, Adam McCarthy* | | | |
| National | Trade | Glenn Freeborn | Fremantle | AFL | 46 |
| | | *Traded by Fremantle for Troy Polak* | | | |
| National | Trade | Robert Scott | Geelong | AFL | 74 |
| | | *Traded by Geelong for Brad Sholl, draft selection 17 (Carl Steinfort) and selection 69 (Dean Helmers)* | | | |

**1995**

| | | | | | |
|-------|-----------|----------------|----------------|------|------------------------|
| Pre-Seas | 15 | Keenan Reynolds | Footscray | AFL | 12 |
| Pre-Seas | 29 | Glenn Gorman | Sydney | AFL | 2 |
| Pre-Seas | Comp Sel | Stuart Cochrane | Central District | SANFL | 0 |
| | | *Compensatory selection from Fremantle for uncontracted player selection Peter Mann* | | | |
| National | 17 | Scott Welsh | West Adelaide | SANFL | 2 |
| National | 26 | Chris Groom | Fremantle | AFL | 2 |
| | | *Draft choice 26 traded by Collingwood for Robert Pyman* | | | |
| National | 33 | Sam McFarlane | Subiaco | WAFL | 2 |
| National | 47 | Brent Harvey | Northern U18 | U18 VMFL | 18 |
| National | 65 | Eric Lissenden | Warragul Industrials | VCFL | 2 |
| | | *Draft choice 65 traded by Melbourne for Alastair Clarkson* | | | |
| National | Trade | Bradley Plain | Collingwood | AFL | 1 |
| | | *Traded by Collingwood for Adrian McAdam* | | | |

**1996**

| | | | | | |
|-------|-----------|----------------|----------------|------|------------------------|
| Pre-Seas | 15 | Peter Bell | Fremantle | AFL | 48 |
| National | 23 | Evan Hewitt | Subiaco | WAFL | 1 |
| National | 42 | Martin Pike | Fitzroy | AFL | 24 |
| National | 50 | Luke McCormick | Nsw-Act U18 | U18 NSW-ACT | 0 |
| | | *Draft choice 50 traded by Richmond for Trent Nichols* | | | |
| National | 56 | Cameron Mooney | Nsw-Act U18 | U18 NSW-ACT | 0 |
| National | 67 | Byron Pickett | Port Adelaide | SANFL | 1 |
| National | 70 | Adam Hay | East Perth | WAFL | 0 |
| | | *Draft choice 70 traded by Collingwood for John Barnett* | | | |
| National | Trade | Kent Kingsley | Woodville-West Torrens | SANFL | 0 |
| | | *Traded by Port Adelaide for Paul Geister* | | | |
| National | Trade | Wade Kingsley | Woodville-West Torrens | SANFL | 0 |
| | | *Traded by Port Adelaide for Paul Geister* | | | |

**1997**

| | | | | | |
|-------|-----------|----------------|----------------|------|------------------------|
| Pre-Seas | 11 | Brett Chandler | Fitzroy | AFL | 24 |
| Pre-Seas | 17 | Anthony Mellington | Fitzroy | AFL | 14 |
| Pre-Seas | 21 | Not utilised | | | |
| National | 14 | Shannon Watt | North Ballarat U18 | U18 VCFL | 0 |
| National | 27 | Brad Stephens | Murray U18 | U18 VCFL | 0 |
| | | *Draft choice 27 traded by Sydney for Wayne Schwass* | | | |
| National | 30 | Paul McMahon | Bendigo U18 | U18 VCFL | 0 |
| National | 46 | Josh Robertson | Murray U18 | U18 VCFL | 0 |
| National | 62 | Dion Miles | North Melb Reserves | AFL RES | 0 |
| Rookie Elev | Rook Elev | Julian Kirzner | Ajax | VAFA | 3 |
| National | Trade | Winston Abraham | Fremantle | AFL | 0 |
| | | *Traded by Fremantle for Stuart Anderson* | | | |
| National | Trade | Shannon Grant | Sydney | AFL | 0 |
| | | *Traded by Sydney for Wayne Schwass* | | | |
| National | Trade | Jason McCartney | Adelaide | AFL | 0 |
| | | *Traded by Adelaide for Mark Stevens* | | | |
| Rook Prom | Rook Elev | Julian Kirzner | Carlton Reserves | AFL RES | 3 |

**1998**

| | | | | | |
|-------|-----------|----------------|----------------|------|------------------------|
| Pre-Seas | 5 | Damian Houlihan | Tatura | VCFL | 0 |
| Pre-Seas | 10 | Brady Anderson | East Perth | WAFL | 0 |

# PORT ADELAIDE

**1996**

| | | | | | |
|-------|-----------|----------------|----------------|------|------------------------|
| National | 6 | John Rombotis | Fitzroy | AFL | 9 |
| National | 7 | Bowen Lockwood | Geelong U18 | U18 VCFL | 13 |
| National | 9 | Mark Harwood | Tas U18 | U18 TAS | 0 |
| National | 37 | Adam Kingsley | Essendon Supp List | AFL RES | 12 |
| | | *Draft choice 37 traded by Geelong for Cameron Roberts, Hamish Simpson* | | | |
| National | Trade | Scott Cummings | Essendon | AFL | 21 |
| | | *Traded by Essendon for draft selection 2 (Chris Heffernan), draft selection 28 (Jason Johnson)* | | | |
| National | Trade | Shane Bond | West Coast | AFL | 22 |
| | | *Traded by West Coast for draft selection 57 (Trent Cummings)* | | | |
| National | Trade | Brayden Lyle | West Coast | AFL | 20 |
| | | *Traded by West Coast for draft selection 57 (Trent Cummings)* | | | |
| National | Trade | Shayne Breuer | Geelong | AFL | 21 |
| | | *Traded by Geelong for Hamish Simpson, Cameron Roberts, draft selection 8 (Leigh Brockman), draft selection 43 (Paul Corrigan)* | | | |
| National | Trade | David Brown | Adelaide | AFL | 18 |
| | | *Traded by Adelaide for Nick Laidlaw* | | | |
| National | Trade | Paul Geister | North Melb | AFL | 1 |
| | | *Traded by North Melbourne for Kent Kingsley, Wade Kingsley* | | | |
| National | Trade | Brent Heaver | Carlton | AFL | 8 |
| | | *Traded by Carlton for Ben Nelson, Andrew Balkwill* | | | |

| Draft | Selection | Drafted player | Club of origin | Body | Matches with this club |
|---|---|---|---|---|---|
| National | Trade | Scott Hodges | Adelaide | AFL | 0 |
| | | *Traded by Adelaide for Aaron Keating, Tim Cook* | | | |
| National | Unctr Pl Sel | Ian Downsborough | West Coast | AFL | 7 |
| | | *Uncontracted player selection from West Coast for compensatory selection Michael Gardiner* | | | |
| National | Unctr Pl Sel | Matthew Primus | Fitzroy | AFL | 22 |
| | | *Uncontracted player selection from Brisbane Bears for compensatory selection Rory Hilton* | | | |
| National | Unctr Pl Sel | Adam Heuskes | Sydney | AFL | 22 |
| | | *Uncontracted player selection from Sydney for compensatory selection Mark Kinnear* | | | |
| National | Unctr Pl Sel | Gavin Wanganeen | Essendon | AFL | 20 |
| | | *Uncontracted player selection from Essendon for compensatory selection Daniel McAlister* | | | |
| National | Zone Sel | Scott Bassett | Norwood | SANFL | 0 |
| National | Zone Sel | Peter Burgoyne | Port Adelaide | SANFL | 15 |
| National | Zone Sel | Tom Carr | Port Adelaide | SANFL | 2 |
| National | Zone Sel | Jarrod Cotton | Central District | SANFL | 4 |
| National | Zone Sel | Stephen Daniels | Norwood | SANFL | 10 |
| National | Zone Sel | Stuart Dew | Central District | SANFL | 1 |
| National | Zone Sel | Donald Dickie | Norwood | SANFL | 22 |
| National | Zone Sel | Nathan Eagleton | West Adelaide | SANFL | 18 |
| National | Zone Sel | Paul Evans | Port Adelaide | SANFL | 0 |
| National | Zone Sel | Nigel Fiegert | Port Adelaide | SANFL | 4 |
| National | Zone Sel | Fabian Francis | Port Adelaide | SANFL | 15 |
| National | Zone Sel | Josh Francou | North Adelaide | SANFL | 22 |
| National | Zone Sel | Tom Harley | Norwood | SANFL | 0 |
| National | Zone Sel | Roger James | Norwood | SANFL | 17 |
| National | Zone Sel | Brendon Lade | South Adelaide | SANFL | 22 |
| National | Zone Sel | Scott Mathews | Woodville-West Torrens | SANFL | 0 |
| National | Zone Sel | Darren Meade | Port Adelaide | SANFL | 22 |
| National | Zone Sel | Darryl Poole | Port Adelaide | SANFL | 10 |
| National | Zone Sel | Nathan Steinberner | Central District | SANFL | 1 |
| National | Zone Sel | Warren Tredrea | Port Adelaide | SANFL | 1 |
| National | Zone Sel | Michael Wilson | Port Adelaide | SANFL | 22 |
| National | Zone Sel | Rhett Biglands | Woodville-West Torrens | SANFL | 0 |
| National | Zone Sel | Stephen Carter | Port Adelaide | SANFL | 10 |
| National | Zone Sel | Mark Conway | Central District | SANFL | 1 |
| National | Zone Sel | Scott Freeborn | Woodville-West Torrens | SANFL | 0 |
| National | Zone Sel | Jake Lynch | Woodville-West Torrens | SANFL | 0 |
| National | Zone Sel | Andrew Osborn | South Adelaide | SANFL | 0 |
| National | Zone Sel | Damian Squire | North Adelaide | SANFL | 5 |
| National | Zone Sel | Jonathon Yerbury | Norwood | SANFL | 0 |
| **1997** | | | | | |
| Pre-Seas | 1 | Stephen Paxman | Fitzroy | AFL | 22 |
| National | 9 | Chad Cornes | Glenelg | SANFL | 0 |
| National | 25 | Nick Stevens | Preston U18 | U18 VMFL | 0 |
| National | 41 | Danny Morton | North Adelaide | SANFL | 0 |
| National | 57 | Darren Fraser | Essendon Reserves | AFL RES | 0 |
| National | 72 | Not utilised | | | 0 |
| National | Trade | Brett Chalmers | Adelaide | AFL | 0 |
| | | *Traded by Adelaide for Ian Downsborough* | | | |
| National | Trade | Chris Naish | Richmond | AFL | 0 |
| | | *Traded by Richmond for John Rombotis* | | | |
| **1998** | | | | | |
| Pre-Seas | 3 | Matthew Bode | Glenelg | SANFL | 0 |

# RICHMOND

| | | | | | |
|---|---|---|---|---|---|
| **1986** | | | | | |
| National | 4 | Richard Anderson | Norwood | SANFL | 0 |
| National | 17 | Trent Nichols | Sandy Bay | TAS | 56 |
| National | 30 | Matthew Sexton | Sandhurst | VCFL | 0 |
| National | 43 | Andrew Gray | St Patricks,Ballarat | APS | 0 |
| National | 56 | Greg Whittlesea | Sturt | SANFL | 0 |
| **1987** | | | | | |
| National | 1 | Richard Lounder | Central District | SANFL | 4 |
| National | 14 | Wayne Peters | Morwell | VCFL | 5 |
| National | 27 | Brendon Gale | Burnie Hawks | TAS | 163 |
| National | 40 | Bevan Cox | Wodonga | VCFL | 0 |
| National | 53 | Andrew Wisken | Hastings | VCFL | 0 |
| **1988** | | | | | |
| National | 5 | Chris Naish | Wangaratta | VCFL | 143 |
| National | 19 | Matthew Francis | Ballan | VCFL | 19 |
| National | 33 | Bruce Lennon | Sturt | SANFL | 28 |
| National | 47 | Glen Leaf | Mildura Imperials | VCFL | 0 |
| National | 61 | Julian Moloney | Mildura Imperials | VCFL | 0 |
| National | 75 | Ty Esler | Koo Wee Rup | VCFL | 12 |
| National | 89 | Adam Crudden | Nar Nar Goon | VCFL | 0 |
| National | 103 | Sean Bowden | Mildura Imperials | VCFL | 6 |
| **1989** | | | | | |
| Pre-Seas | 5 | Jeremy Crough | West Coast | AFL | 0 |
| Pre-Seas | 19 | Matt Richardson | West Coast | AFL | 0 |
| Pre-Seas | 33 | Stuart Griffiths | Old Melburnians | VAFA | 17 |
| Pre-Seas | 47 | Justin Paul | Richmond | AFL | 0 |
| National | 1 | Anthony Banik | Won Wron Woodside | VCFL | 49 |

**210**

| Draft | Selection | Drafted player | Club of origin | Body | Matches with this club |
|---|---|---|---|---|---|
| National | 13 | Allister Scott | Inverloch-Kongwak | VCFL | 19 |
| | | *Draft choice 13 traded by Geelong for Trevor Poole* | | | |
| National | 15 | Nathan Bower | Mildura | VCFL | 65 |
| National | 18 | Robert Wren | Assumption College | APS | 0 |
| | | *Draft choice 18 traded by West Coast for Peter Wilson* | | | |
| National | 29 | Wayne Campbell | Golden Square | VCFL | 140 |
| National | 32 | Shaun Slater | St Arnaud | VCFL | 0 |
| | | *Draft choice 32 traded by West Coast for Peter Wilson* | | | |
| National | 41 | Chris Waterworth | Sandy Bay | TAS | 0 |
| | | *Draft choice 41 traded by Geelong for Trevor Poole* | | | |
| National | 47 | Ricky Gerke | Woodville | SANFL | 0 |
| National | 61 | Simon Eastaugh | Shepparton | VCFL | 0 |
| National | 75 | Stephen Pearce | Echuca | VCFL | 0 |
| National | 89 | Jason Smith | Lockington | VCFL | 1 |
| National | 103 | Brett Chalmers | Woodville | SANFL | 0 |

### 1990

| Draft | Selection | Drafted player | Club of origin | Body | Matches with this club |
|---|---|---|---|---|---|
| Pre-Seas | 1 | David Cloke | Collingwood | AFL | 43 |
| Pre-Seas | 7 | David Williams | Melbourne | AFL | 0 |
| Pre-Seas | 21 | Chris Martin | Hawthorn | AFL | 0 |
| Pre-Seas | 35 | David Sullivan | Camberwell | VFA | 0 |
| Mid-Seas | 4 | Andrew Payze | West Torrens | SANFL | 0 |
| Mid-Seas | 18 | Scott Turner | Ararat | VCFL | 117 |
| National | 16 | Todd Menegola | Swan Districts | WAFL | 19 |
| National | 28 | Chris Smith | Assumption College | APS | 0 |
| National | 42 | Mark McQueen | North Hobart | TAS | 5 |
| National | 49 | Nick Daffy | North Gambier | SA | 89 |
| | | *Draft choice 49 traded by Melbourne for Phil Egan* | | | |
| National | 56 | Matthew Clarke | West Gambier | SA | 0 |
| National | 70 | Stuart Johnstone | Melbourne | AFL | 0 |
| National | 84 | John Peter-Budge | St Kilda | AFL | 0 |
| National | Trade | Terry Keays | Collingwood | AFL | 25 |
| | | *Traded by Collingwood for draft selection 4 (Jason McCartney)* | | | |

### 1991

| Draft | Selection | Drafted player | Club of origin | Body | Matches with this club |
|---|---|---|---|---|---|
| Pre-Seas | 4 | Mark Trewella | Fitzroy | AFL | 4 |
| Pre-Seas | 10 | Andrew Underwood | Essendon | AFL | 12 |
| Pre-Seas | 27 | John Mrakov | Collingwood | AFL | 8 |
| Pre-Seas | 41 | David Cloke | Richmond | AFL | 22 |
| Mid-Seas | 5 | Athos Hrysoulakis | Prahran | VFA | 0 |
| Mid-Seas | 18 | Shane Fell | Glenorchy | TAS | 0 |
| National | 49 | Todd Hawes | Swan Districts | WAFL | 0 |
| | | *Draft choice 49 traded by Melbourne for Michael Pickering* | | | |
| National | 51 | Shaun Brooker | Sydney | AFL | 0 |
| | | *Draft choice 51 traded by West Coast for Trent Nichols* | | | |
| National | 55 | Glen Hoffman | Essendon | AFL | 0 |
| National | 66 | Nick Roney | North Launceston | TAS | 0 |
| National | 77 | Jay Burton | Subiaco | WAFL | 0 |
| National | 85 | John Kennedy | Hawthorn | AFL | 0 |
| National | 89 | Paul Dimattina | Richmond | AFL | 0 |
| National | Trade | Steven O'Dwyer | Melbourne | AFL | 5 |
| | | *Traded by Melbourne for draft selection 3 (Darren Kowal)* | | | |
| National | Trade | Stevan Jackson | West Coast | AFL | 21 |
| | | *Traded by West Coast for draft selection 16 (Daniel Metropolis)* | | | |
| National | Trade | Todd Breman | West Coast | AFL | 25 |
| | | *Traded by West Coast for draft selection 42 (Peter Freeman)* | | | |

### 1992

| Draft | Selection | Drafted player | Club of origin | Body | Matches with this club |
|---|---|---|---|---|---|
| Pre-Seas | 3 | Mark McQueen | Richmond | AFL | 29 |
| Pre-Seas | 17 | David Honybun | Richmond | AFL | 16 |
| Pre-Seas | 31 | Brad Gwilliam | West Coast | AFL | 4 |
| Pre-Seas | 44 | Simon Dennis | Richmond | AFL | 2 |
| Pre-Seas | 52 | Adam Jones | Xavier College | APS | 0 |
| Mid-Seas | 3 | Ian Herman | Carlton | AFL | 14 |
| Mid-Seas | 18 | Andrew Tarpey | Sandringham | VFA | 0 |
| Mid-Seas | 30 | Tim Livingstone | Box Hill | VFA | 8 |
| National | 7 | Wayne Hernaman | South Fremantle | WAFL | 20 |
| National | 22 | Mark Jones | Norwood | SANFL | 0 |
| National | 28 | Jamie Tape | Woodville-West Torrens | SANFL | 75 |
| | | *Draft choice 28 traded by Carlton for Tim Powell* | | | |
| National | 37 | Matthew Rogers | South Adelaide | SANFL | 78 |
| National | 52 | Paul Bulluss | Woodville-West Torrens | SANFL | 79 |
| National | 67 | Brady Leckie | West Perth | WAFL | 0 |
| National | 82 | Robert Schaefer | Sturt | SANFL | 11 |
| National | 97 | John Howat | Melbourne | AFL | 45 |
| National | 112 | Ben Careless | Glenorchy | TAS | 0 |
| National | Fath-Son | Matthew Richardson | Devonport | TAS | 83 |

### 1993

| Draft | Selection | Drafted player | Club of origin | Body | Matches with this club |
|---|---|---|---|---|---|
| Pre-Seas | 7 | Stuart Steele | Hawthorn | AFL | 2 |
| Pre-Seas | 23 | Chris Bond | Carlton | AFL | 100 |
| Pre-Seas | 37 | Simon Verbeek | Carlton | AFL | 0 |
| Pre-Seas | 51 | Simon Eishold | Melbourne | AFL | 5 |
| Pre-Seas | 63 | Tim Livingstone | Richmond | AFL | 6 |
| Pre-Seas | 72 | Adam Jones | Richmond | AFL | 0 |

| Draft | Selection | Drafted player | Club of origin | Body | Matches with this club |
|---|---|---|---|---|---|
| Mid-Seas | 2 | James Thiessen | Richmond | VFA | 7 |
| Mid-Seas | 17 | Brad Fox | Essendon | AFL | 4 |
| Mid-Seas | 26 | Brad Read | East Fremantle | WAFL | 0 |
| National | 3 | Justin Murphy | Central U18 | U18 VMFL | 12 |
| National | 26 | Stephen Jurica | South Fremantle | WAFL | 18 |
| | | *Draft choice 26 traded by Fitzroy for Jeff Hogg* | | | |
| National | 50 | Mark Merenda | West Perth | WAFL | 60 |
| National | Trade | Paul Broderick | Fitzroy | AFL | 91 |
| | | *Traded by Fitzroy for draft selection 6 (Trent Cummings)* | | | |
| National | Trade | Michael Gale | Fitzroy | AFL | 75 |
| | | *Traded by Fitzroy for draft selection 6 (Trent Cummings)* | | | |
| National | Trade | Matthew Dundas | Fitzroy | AFL | 14 |
| | | *Traded by Fitzroy for draft selection 6 (Trent Cummings)* | | | |
| National | Trade | Greg Dear | Hawthorn | AFL | 53 |
| | | *Traded by Hawthorn for draft selection 23 (Shannon Gibson)* | | | |
| National | Trade | Mark Neeld | Geelong | AFL | 26 |
| | | *Traded by Geelong for draft selection 38 (David Innella)* | | | |

**1994**

| Draft | Selection | Drafted player | Club of origin | Body | Matches with this club |
|---|---|---|---|---|---|
| Pre-Seas | 3 | Jamie Elliott | Fitzroy | AFL | 9 |
| Pre-Seas | 7 | Haydn Robins | Melbourne | AFL | 4 |
| Pre-Seas | 23 | Adam Slater | Richmond | AFL | 3 |
| National | 11 | Damien Ryan | Eastern U18 | U18 VMFL | 20 |
| National | 29 | Jason Torney | South Adelaide | SANFL | 31 |
| National | 46 | Justin Charles | Footscray | AFL | 52 |
| National | 63 | Ross Funcke | Ballarat U18 | U18 VCFL | 15 |
| National | 86 | Shaun Gordon | Murray U18 | U18 VCFL | 0 |
| National | Fath-Son | David Bourke | Central U18 | U18 VMFL | 47 |
| National | Trade | Chris Sullivan | Melbourne | AFL | 8 |
| | | *Traded by Melbourne for draft selection 76 (Todd McHardy)* | | | |

**1995**

| Draft | Selection | Drafted player | Club of origin | Body | Matches with this club |
|---|---|---|---|---|---|
| Pre-Seas | 9 | Stuart Wigney | Adelaide | AFL | 14 |
| Pre-Seas | 23 | Mark McQueen | Woodville-West Torrens | SANFL | 0 |
| National | 35 | Brad Smith | Claremont | WAFL | 0 |
| | | *Draft choice 35 traded by Carlton for Justin Murphy* | | | |
| National | 46 | Ben Moore | Glenelg | SANFL | 12 |
| National | 59 | Ewan Thompson | Northern U18 | U18 VMFL | 4 |
| National | 67 | Michael Raidis | Glenelg | SANFL | 0 |
| National | Fath-Son | Joel Bowden | West Alice Springs | NT | 18 |
| National | Fath-Son | Nicholas Jewell | Prahran U18 | U18 VMFL | 1 |
| National | Trade | Ben Holland | Fitzroy | AFL | 27 |
| | | *Traded by Fitzroy for draft selection 16 (Shane Clayton), draft selection 32 (Nigel Credlin)* | | | |
| National | Trade | Ben Harrison | Carlton | AFL | 24 |
| | | *Traded by Carlton for Justin Murphy* | | | |
| National | Trade | Robert Powell | Collingwood | AFL | 21 |
| | | *Traded by Collingwood for Matthew Francis* | | | |
| National | Trade | Wayne Thornborrow | St Kilda | AFL | 0 |
| | | *Traded by St Kilda for Jamie Elliott* | | | |

**1996**

| Draft | Selection | Drafted player | Club of origin | Body | Matches with this club |
|---|---|---|---|---|---|
| Pre-Seas | 3 | Darren Gaspar | Sydney | AFL | 41 |
| National | 16 | Pat Steinfort | Oakleigh U18 | U18 VMFL | 0 |
| National | 35 | Mark Chaffey | Caulfield Grammar | APS | 12 |
| National | 41 | Matthew Manfield | Fitzroy | AFL | 2 |
| National | 55 | Steven McKee | Myrtleford | VCFL | 0 |
| National | 63 | Jason Baldwin | Fitzroy | AFL | 2 |
| National | 72 | Brent Frewen | Fitzroy | AFL | 0 |
| National | 79 | Daniel Donati | Old Xavierans | VAFA | 1 |
| National | Trade | Trent Nichols | North Melb | AFL | 12 |
| | | *Traded by North Melbourne for draft selection 50 (Luke McCormick)* | | | |

**1997**

| Draft | Selection | Drafted player | Club of origin | Body | Matches with this club |
|---|---|---|---|---|---|
| Pre-Seas | 6 | Brett Evans | Springvale | VFA | 2 |
| National | 2 | Brad Ottens | Glenelg | SANFL | 0 |
| | | *Draft choice 2 traded by Fremantle for Chris Bond, draft selection 21 (Clem Michael)* | | | |
| National | 53 | Lionel Proctor | Preston U18 | U18 VMFL | 0 |
| National | 69 | Paul Greenham | Port Melbourne | VFA | 0 |
| National | 71 | Andrew Kellaway | Richmond Reserves | AFL RES | 0 |
| | | *Draft choice 71 traded by Collingwood for Jamie Tape/Brad Smith* | | | |
| National | 79 | Not utilised | | | 0 |
| Rookie Elev | Rook Elev | Justin Plapp | Burnie | TAS | 0 |
| Rookie Elev | Rook Elev | Jason Ramsey | Fitzroy | AFL | 0 |
| National | Trade | Ashley Blurton | West Coast | AFL | 0 |
| | | *Traded by West Coast for draft selection 37 (Todd Holmes)* | | | |
| National | Trade | Aaron James | Collingwood | AFL | 0 |
| | | *Traded by Collingwood for Jamie Tape/Brad Smith* | | | |
| National | Trade | John Rombotis | Port Adel | AFL | 0 |
| | | *Traded by Port Adelaide for Chris Naish* | | | |

# ST KILDA

**1986**

| Draft | Selection | Drafted player | Club of origin | Body | Matches with this club |
|---|---|---|---|---|---|
| National | 2 | Steven Sims | West Torrens | SANFL | 0 |
| National | 15 | Andrew Wickham | Latrobe | TAS | 0 |
| National | 28 | Darren Mansell | Penola | SA | 0 |

| Draft | Selection | Drafted player | Club of origin | Body | Matches with this club |
|-------|-----------|----------------|----------------|------|------------------------|
| National | 41 | Brett Jaffray | Latrobe | TAS | 0 |
| National | 54 | Paul Page | Kennington | VCFL | 0 |
| **1987** | | | | | |
| National | 5 | Michael Quirk | Myrtleford | VCFL | 0 |
| National | 18 | Patrick Browne | North Albury | NSW | 0 |
| National | 31 | Jamie Keane | Koroit | VCFL | 0 |
| National | 44 | Bob Jones | Devonport | TAS | 20 |
| National | 57 | Damien Kischke | Sturt | SANFL | 29 |
| **1988** | | | | | |
| National | 15 | Danny Craven | Wangaratta | VCFL | 33 |
| National | 29 | Tim Allen | Mornington | VCFL | 22 |
| National | 43 | Daryl Griffiths | North Launceston | TAS | 0 |
| National | 57 | Pat Lambert | Manangatang | VCFL | 0 |
| National | 71 | Graeme Kettle | South Launceston | TAS | 0 |
| National | 85 | Ian Dargie | Subiaco | WAFL | 10 |
| National | 99 | Dermott McNicholl | Ireland | IRELAND | 3 |
| National | Trade | Robert Handley | Hawthorn | AFL | 4 |
| | | *Traded by Hawthorn for draft selection 1 (Alex McDonald)* | | | |
| National | Trade | Paul Harding | Hawthorn | AFL | 62 |
| | | *Traded by Hawthorn for draft selection 1 (Alex McDonald)* | | | |
| National | Trade | Peter Russo | Hawthorn | AFL | 33 |
| | | *Traded by Hawthorn for draft selection 1 (Alex McDonald)* | | | |
| **1989** | | | | | |
| Pre-Seas | 1 | Brian Winton | Essendon | AFL | 5 |
| Pre-Seas | 15 | Brendan Lowther | Carlton | AFL | 0 |
| Pre-Seas | 29 | Tony Elshaug | Collingwood | AFL | 0 |
| Pre-Seas | 43 | Lazar Vidovic | Castlemaine | VCFL | 80 |
| National | 3 | Jody Arnol | North Hobart | TAS | 13 |
| National | 17 | Gilbert McAdam | Central District | SANFL | 53 |
| National | 31 | Darrel Hart | North Adelaide | SANFL | 0 |
| National | 49 | Greg Jones | Swan Districts | WAFL | 2 |
| National | 63 | Wayne Thornborrow | Glenelg | SANFL | 13 |
| National | 77 | Christian Lister | Golden Square | VCFL | 1 |
| National | 91 | Grant Lawrie | Box Hill | VFA | 17 |
| National | 105 | Stuart Annand | Redan | VCFL | 0 |
| **1990** | | | | | |
| Pre-Seas | 3 | Jim Krakouer | North Melb | AFL | 13 |
| Pre-Seas | 9 | Tim Pekin | Fitzroy | AFL | 112 |
| Pre-Seas | 23 | Russell Jeffrey | Jerilderie | NSW | 27 |
| Pre-Seas | 37 | Glen Kendall | Dromana | VCFL | 0 |
| Mid-Seas | 9 | Steven Cummings | Sandringham | VFA | 14 |
| Mid-Seas | 23 | Damian Sexton | Yarrawonga | VCFL | 4 |
| Mid-Seas | 33 | Bernie Harris | Terang | VCFL | 5 |
| Mid-Seas | 40 | Chris Melican | Glenelg | SANFL | 0 |
| National | 72 | Brian Wilson | Melbourne | AFL | 7 |
| National | 86 | Sam Jones | Sandy Bay | TAS | 3 |
| National | 91 | Adam Rudd | Numurkah | VCFL | 0 |
| | | *Draft choice 91 traded by Melbourne for Rod Owen* | | | |
| National | 92 | Jamie Shanahan | Sandy Bay | TAS | 125 |
| | | *Draft choice 92 traded by West Coast for Ian Dargie* | | | |
| National | Trade | Stephen Newport | Melbourne | AFL | 39 |
| | | *Traded by Melbourne for draft selection 6 (Allen Jakovich)* | | | |
| National | Trade | Russell Morris | Hawthorn | AFL | 66 |
| | | *Traded by Hawthorn for draft selection 30 (Matthew Young)* | | | |
| National | Trade | Sean Ralphsmith | Hawthorn | AFL | 30 |
| | | *Traded by Hawthorn for draft selection 44 (Scott Crow)* | | | |
| National | Trade | Rohan Smith | Sydney | AFL | 3 |
| | | *Traded by Sydney for draft selection 58 (Adrian Goldup)* | | | |
| **1991** | | | | | |
| Pre-Seas | 6 | Tony Antrobus | Essendon | AFL | 6 |
| Pre-Seas | 12 | Darren Davies | Footscray | AFL | 2 |
| Pre-Seas | 29 | Damien Pearce | St Kilda | AFL | 0 |
| Pre-Seas | 43 | Dean Greig | Camberwell | VFA | 33 |
| Mid-Seas | 12 | Jason Briggs | Robinvale | VCFL | 0 |
| Mid-Seas | 25 | Justin Pascoe | Whorouly | VCFL | 0 |
| Mid-Seas | 35 | Not utilised | | | |
| Mid-Seas | 41 | Not utilised | | | |
| National | 12 | Rob Malone | Claremont | WAFL | 0 |
| | | *Draft choice 12 traded by West Coast for Paul Harding* | | | |
| National | 53 | Alistair Gray | Carey Grammar | APS | 0 |
| | | *Draft choice 53 traded by Brisbane Bears for Russell Jeffrey* | | | |
| National | 61 | Michael Addison | Carey Grammar | APS | 0 |
| National | 72 | Michael Shields | St Kilda | AFL | 0 |
| National | 82 | Scott Morrison | North Melb | AFL | 0 |
| National | 87 | Sam Jones | Sandy Bay | TAS | 3 |
| National | Trade | Adrian Fletcher | Geelong | AFL | 22 |
| | | *Traded by Geelong for draft selection 11 (Leigh Willison)* | | | |
| National | Trade | Lawrence Bingham | Hawthorn | AFL | 22 |
| | | *Traded by Hawthorn for draft selection 22 (Simon Crawshay)* | | | |
| National | Trade | Darren Flanigan | Geelong | AFL | 8 |
| | | *Traded by Geelong for draft selection 35 (Darryl Donald)* | | | |

| Draft | Selection | Drafted player | Club of origin | Body | Matches with this club |
|---|---|---|---|---|---|
| National | Trade | Craig O'Brien | Essendon | AFL | 52 |
| | | *Traded by Essendon for draft selection 48 (Kevin Mitchell)* | | | |

## 1992

| Draft | Selection | Drafted player | Club of origin | Body | Matches with this club |
|---|---|---|---|---|---|
| Pre-Seas | 10 | Michael Ford | Footscray | AFL | 2 |
| Pre-Seas | 24 | Steven Clark | Melbourne | AFL | 6 |
| Pre-Seas | 38 | Dale Kickett | West Coast | AFL | 21 |
| Pre-Seas | 49 | Justin Peckett | St Kilda | AFL | 96 |
| Mid-Seas | 12 | Garry Merritt | Tatura | VCFL | 0 |
| Mid-Seas | 26 | Stephen Edgar | Carlton | AFL | 0 |
| National | 16 | Brodie Atkinson | North Adelaide | SANFL | 2 |
| National | 31 | Shane Wakelin | Port Adelaide | SANFL | 50 |
| National | 46 | Matthew Jackson | Brighton Grammar | APS | 0 |
| National | 76 | Hugh Reimers | Central District | SANFL | 0 |
| National | 80 | Stephen Newport | Melbourne | AFL | 1 |
| | | *Draft choice 80 traded by Sydney for Jayson Daniels* | | | |
| National | 91 | Jeremy McVay | Central U18 | U18 VMFL | 0 |
| National | 106 | Craig Treleven | East Fremantle | WAFL | 0 |
| National | 119 | Scott Morrison | St Kilda | AFL | 0 |
| | | *Draft choice 119 traded by Hawthorn for Tim Allen* | | | |
| National | Fath-Son | David Sierakowski | Subiaco | WAFL | 52 |
| National | Trade | Ian Aitken | Carlton | AFL | 5 |
| | | *Traded by Carlton for draft selection 61 (Luke Rayner)* | | | |
| National | Trade | Dean Anderson | Hawthorn | AFL | 67 |
| | | *Traded by Hawthorn for draft selection 121 (Ben Ellinghaus)* | | | |
| National | Trade | Chris Wittman | Hawthorn | AFL | 9 |
| | | *Traded by Hawthorn for draft selection 121 (Ben Ellinghaus)* | | | |

## 1993

| Draft | Selection | Drafted player | Club of origin | Body | Matches with this club |
|---|---|---|---|---|---|
| Pre-Seas | 16 | Mark Arceri | Carlton | AFL | 5 |
| Pre-Seas | 32 | Martin Heppell | Carey Grammar | APS | 5 |
| Pre-Seas | 46 | Chris Hollow | Dandenong | VFA | 24 |
| Pre-Seas | 60 | Darren Bourke | Dandenong | VFA | 32 |
| Pre-Seas | 69 | Leigh Capsalis | Keysborough | VMFL | 1 |
| Pre-Seas | 76 | Nick Hanson | Sandringham | VFA | 1 |
| Pre-Seas | 79 | Greg Wootton | South Fremantle | WAFL | 0 |
| Pre-Seas | 80 | David Nienann | Woodville-West Torrens | SANFL | 0 |
| Pre-Seas | 81 | Jason Mifsud | Mortlake | VCFL | 0 |
| Mid-Seas | 3 | Anthony Harvey | Frankston | VFA | 4 |
| National | 8 | Michael Frost | Footscray | AFL | 11 |
| National | 25 | Clinton Shaw | Southern U18 | U18 VMFL | 6 |
| National | 40 | Matthew Lappin | Chiltern | VCFL | 39 |
| National | 51 | Kristian Pascoe | Northern U18 | U18 VMFL | 0 |

## 1994

| Draft | Selection | Drafted player | Club of origin | Body | Matches with this club |
|---|---|---|---|---|---|
| Pre-Seas | 4 | David Strooper | Sydney | AFL | 6 |
| Pre-Seas | 9 | Rod Keogh | Melbourne | AFL | 54 |
| Pre-Seas | 24 | Adrian Burns | Essendon | AFL | 4 |
| Pre-Seas | 33 | Doug Bailey | Old Xaverians | VAFA | 11 |
| Pre-Seas | 36 | Kristian Bardsley | North Melb | AFL | 52 |
| Pre-Seas | 38 | Daniel McCarthy | Frankston | VFA | 0 |
| Pre-Seas | 39 | Alister Carr | Essendon | AFL | 4 |
| National | 5 | Joel Smith | Murray U18 | U18 VCFL | 58 |
| | | *Draft choice 5 traded by Sydney for Tony Lockett* | | | |
| National | 7 | Tony Brown | Geelong U18 | U18 VCFL | 57 |
| National | 13 | Chris Hemley | Geelong U18 | U18 VCFL | 1 |
| | | *Draft choice 13 traded by Hawthorn for draft selection 59 (Nathan Saunders)* | | | |
| National | 25 | Steven Sziller | Woodville-West Torrens | SANFL | 56 |
| National | 26 | Tim Elliott | Gippsland U18 | U18 VCFL | 0 |
| | | *Draft choice 26 traded by Brisbane Bears for Gilbert McAdam* | | | |
| National | 43 | Dean Matthews | Bulleen-Templestowe | VMFL | 1 |
| | | *Draft choice 43 traded by Brisbane Bears for Gilbert McAdam* | | | |
| National | 48 | Austinn Jones | Southern U18 | U18 VMFL | 66 |
| National | Pre-Dr Supp | Matthew Jackson | St Kilda | VMFL | 4 |
| National | Trade | Darryl Wakelin | Fremantle | AFL | 56 |
| | | *Traded by Fremantle for draft selection 42 (Douglas Headland)* | | | |
| National | Trade | Joshua Kitchen | Hawthorn | AFL | 3 |
| | | *Traded by Hawthorn for draft selection 59 (Nathan Saunders)* | | | |
| National | Trade | Glenn Nugent | Hawthorn | AFL | 11 |
| | | *Traded by Hawthorn for draft selection 59 (Nathan Saunders)* | | | |
| National | Trade | Robert Neill | Sydney | AFL | 23 |
| | | *Traded by Sydney for Tony Lockett* | | | |

## 1995

| Draft | Selection | Drafted player | Club of origin | Body | Matches with this club |
|---|---|---|---|---|---|
| Pre-Seas | 5 | Glen Coghlan | Kyabram | VCFL | 29 |
| Pre-Seas | 19 | Mark Kennedy | Woodville-West Torrens | SANFL | 8 |
| National | 6 | Daniel Healy | Central District | SANFL | 16 |
| National | 19 | Barry Hall | Murray U18 | U18 VCFL | 19 |
| | | *Draft choice 19 traded by Carlton for Craig Devonport* | | | |
| National | 22 | Joe McLaren | Geelong U18 | U18 VCFL | 13 |
| National | 36 | Andrew Lamb | Murray U18 | U18 VCFL | 0 |
| | | *Draft choice 36 traded by Fitzroy for Mick Dwyer* | | | |
| National | 38 | Jason Cripps | St Kilda Supp List | AFL RES | 34 |
| National | 41 | Ryan Grinter | Geelong U18 | U18 VCFL | 0 |
| | | *Draft choice 41 traded by Melbourne for David Grant* | | | |

| Draft | Selection | Drafted player | Club of origin | Body | Matches with this club |
|---|---|---|---|---|---|
| National | Trade | Luke Beveridge | Footscray | AFL | 23 |
| | | *Traded by Footscray for draft selection 52 (Tony Campbell)* | | | |
| National | Trade | Jayson Daniels | Sydney | AFL | 34 |
| | | *Traded by Sydney for Craig O'Brien* | | | |
| National | Trade | Jamie Elliott | Richmond | AFL | 9 |
| | | *Traded by Richmond for Wayne Thornborrow* | | | |

**1996**

| Draft | Selection | Drafted player | Club of origin | Body | Matches with this club |
|---|---|---|---|---|---|
| Pre-Seas | 6 | Andrew McLean | North Launceston | TAS | 6 |
| Pre-Seas | 17 | Jason Traianidis | Shepparton United | VCFL | 20 |
| Pre-Seas | 20 | Matthew Young | Hawthorn | AFL | 37 |
| Pre-Seas | 22 | Anthony Darcy | Port Adelaide | SANFL | 3 |
| National | 15 | Max Hudghton | West Brisbane | QLD | 17 |
| National | 49 | Jason Heatley | West Coast | AFL | 20 |
| National | 62 | Andrew Thompson | St Kilda Supp List | AFL RES | 23 |
| National | 71 | Brett Knowles | Gippsland U18 | U18 VCFL | 0 |
| National | 78 | Lucas Fleming | Northern U18 | U18 VMFL | 0 |
| National | Trade | Troy Gray | Sydney | AFL | 9 |
| | | *Traded by Sydney for draft selection 34 (Shannon Corcoran)* | | | |

**1997**

| Draft | Selection | Drafted player | Club of origin | Body | Matches with this club |
|---|---|---|---|---|---|
| Pre-Seas | 5 | Brett Cook | Fitzroy | AFL | 8 |
| Pre-Seas | 15 | Brad Campbell | Port Melbourne | VFA | 4 |
| National | 16 | Ben Walton | Central District | SANFL | 0 |
| National | 48 | Ben Thompson | Glenelg | SANFL | 0 |
| National | 64 | Sam Cranage | North Ballarat U18 | U18 VCFL | 0 |
| National | 75 | Brent Cowell | Gippsland U18 | U18 VCFL | 0 |
| National | Trade | Gavin Mitchell | Fremantle | AFL | 0 |
| | | *Traded by Fremantle for draft selection 32 (Troy Johnson)* | | | |

**1998**

| Draft | Selection | Drafted player | Club of origin | Body | Matches with this club |
|---|---|---|---|---|---|
| Pre-Seas | 7 | Matthew Carr | East Fremantle | WAFL | 0 |
| Pre-Seas | 11 | Jamie Elliott | St Kilda | AFL | 0 |
| Pre-Seas | 13 | Not utilised | | | 0 |

# SYDNEY

**1986**

| Draft | Selection | Drafted player | Club of origin | Body | Matches with this club |
|---|---|---|---|---|---|
| National | 10 | John Brinkkotter | Barooga | NSW | 5 |
| National | 23 | Lyndon Dakin | Longford | TAS | 0 |
| National | 36 | Donald Thompson | Albury | NSW | 0 |
| National | 49 | Craig Elias | Eastlake | ACT | 0 |
| National | 62 | Laurie Menhenut | Tocumwal | NSW | 0 |

**1987**

| Draft | Selection | Drafted player | Club of origin | Body | Matches with this club |
|---|---|---|---|---|---|
| National | 10 | Michael Parsons | North Adelaide | SANFL | 25 |
| National | 23 | Scott Salisbury | Glenelg | SANFL | 0 |
| National | 36 | Tony Virgona | Jerilderie | NSW | 0 |
| National | 49 | Jim Silvestro | Traralgon | VCFL | 8 |
| National | 62 | David Querzoli | West Torrens | SANFL | 0 |

**1988**

| Draft | Selection | Drafted player | Club of origin | Body | Matches with this club |
|---|---|---|---|---|---|
| National | 8 | Dion Scott | Devonport | TAS | 6 |
| National | 22 | Paul Holdsworth | Clarence | TAS | 6 |
| National | 36 | Nick Chigwidden | Glenelg | SANFL | 0 |
| National | 50 | Jim West | Glenelg | SANFL | 37 |
| National | 64 | Andrew Bishop | Ainslie | ACT | 0 |
| National | 106 | Gareth John | Gisborne | VCFL | 21 |
| National | Trade | Rudi Mandemacher | Hawthorn | AFL | 0 |
| | | *Traded by Hawthorn for draft selection 78 (Jamie Bond)* | | | |
| National | Trade | Mark O'Donoghue | North Melb | AFL | 0 |
| | | *Traded by North Melbourne for draft selection 92 (Stephen Vizy)* | | | |

**1989**

| Draft | Selection | Drafted player | Club of origin | Body | Matches with this club |
|---|---|---|---|---|---|
| Pre-Seas | 8 | Robert Teal | Hawthorn | AFL | 18 |
| Pre-Seas | 22 | Darren Ogier | North Melb | AFL | 8 |
| Pre-Seas | 36 | Brett Scott | Sydney | AFL | 7 |
| Pre-Seas | 50 | Michael Phyland | Sydney | AFL | 13 |
| National | 8 | Brad Tunbridge | East Fremantle | WAFL | 50 |
| National | 36 | Rohan Smith | Port Adelaide | SANFL | 0 |
| National | 54 | Steven Bozicevic | Myrtleford | VCFL | 0 |
| National | 68 | Scott Tomlinson | Shepparton United | VCFL | 0 |
| National | 96 | Gary Stevens | Waaia | VCFL | 5 |
| National | 110 | Craig Budarick | Glenelg | SANFL | 0 |
| National | Pre-Dr Sel | Darren Denneman | Geelong | AFL | 3 |
| National | Pre-Dr Sel | Shane Fell | Geelong | AFL | 15 |
| National | Pre-Dr Sel | John Fidge | Brisbane Bears | AFL | 0 |
| National | Pre-Dr Sel | Paul Starbuck | Carlton | AFL | 0 |
| National | Trade | Matthew Ryan | Collingwood | AFL | 10 |
| | | *Traded by Collingwood for draft selection 22 (Matthew Hanrahan), draft selection 82 (Troy Lehmann)* | | | |

**1990**

| Draft | Selection | Drafted player | Club of origin | Body | Matches with this club |
|---|---|---|---|---|---|
| Pre-Seas | 14 | Michael Kennedy | Carlton | AFL | 15 |
| Pre-Seas | 28 | David Wittey | Brisbane Bears | AFL | 1 |
| Pre-Seas | 42 | Robbie Kerr | Brunswick | VFA | 10 |
| Pre-Seas | 50 | Damian Tresize | Golden Square | VCFL | 0 |
| Mid-Seas | 2 | Dale Lewis | North Ballarat | VCFL | 133 |
| Mid-Seas | 16 | Paul Smit | Springvale | VFA | 0 |

| Draft | Selection | Drafted player | Club of origin | Body | Matches with this club |
|---|---|---|---|---|---|
| Mid-Seas | 29 | Tim Symes | Benalla | VCFL | 0 |
| National | 26 | Dale Hall | Hobart | TAS | 0 |
| National | 40 | Mark Collins | South Fremantle | WAFL | 0 |
| National | 54 | Brian Stanislaus | St Marys | NT | 1 |
| National | 58 | Adrian Goldup | Redcliffs | VCFL | 0 |
| | | *Draft choice 58 traded by St Kilda for Rohan Smith* | | | |
| National | 67 | David Griffin | South Bendigo | VCFL | 0 |
| | | *Draft choice 67 traded by Brisbane Bears for Craig Potter* | | | |
| National | 82 | Leigh Campbell | Campbelltown | NSW | 0 |
| National | Pre-Dr Sel | Justin Clarkson | Melbourne | AFL | 3 |
| National | Pre-Dr Sel | Jason Love | North Melb | AFL | 23 |
| National | Pre-Dr Sel | Darren Morgan | Geelong | AFL | 0 |
| National | Pre-Dr Sel | Brad Sparks | Melbourne | AFL | 0 |
| National | Trade | Warren McKenzie | Carlton | AFL | 21 |
| | | *Traded by Carlton for draft selection 2 (James Cook)* | | | |
| National | Trade | Warwick Capper | Brisbane Bears | AFL | 13 |
| | | *Traded by Brisbane Bears for draft selection 68 (Peter Whyte)* | | | |
| National | Zone Sel | Ben Aulich | Belconnen | ACT | 0 |
| National | Zone Sel | Robert Neill | Eastlake | ACT | 21 |

## 1991

| Draft | Selection | Drafted player | Club of origin | Body | Matches with this club |
|---|---|---|---|---|---|
| Pre-Seas | 2 | Paul Hawke | Collingwood | AFL | 1 |
| Pre-Seas | 8 | Mark Athorn | Fitzroy | AFL | 15 |
| Pre-Seas | 25 | Andrew Peck | Melbourne | AFL | 0 |
| Pre-Seas | 39 | Darren McAsey | Sydney | AFL | 3 |
| Mid-Seas | 3 | Ernie Hug | Prahran | VFA | 0 |
| Mid-Seas | 16 | Mark Stockdale | Traralgon | VCFL | 0 |
| Mid-Seas | 29 | Damian Hogan | Sale | VCFL | 0 |
| National | 4 | Andrew McGovern | Claremont | WAFL | 29 |
| National | 6 | Paul Burton | Claremont | WAFL | 0 |
| | | *Draft choice 6 traded by Footscray for Bernard Toohey* | | | |
| National | 17 | Anthony Cole | North Hobart | TAS | 0 |
| National | 43 | David Strooper | Fitzroy | AFL | 32 |
| National | 56 | Andrew Dunkley | North Launceston | TAS | 121 |
| National | 68 | Matthew Bell | Sydney | AFL | 0 |
| | | *Draft choice 68 traded by Footscray for Darren Morgan* | | | |
| National | Trade | Gavin Rose | Collingwood | AFL | 55 |
| | | *Traded by Collingwood for draft selection 30 (Kane Purcell)* | | | |
| National | Trade | Stuart Wigney | Footscray | AFL | 1 |
| | | *Traded by Footscray for draft selection 67 (Shane Ellen)* | | | |
| National | Trade | Simon Minton-Connell | Carlton | AFL | 46 |
| | | *Traded by Carlton for draft selection 78 (Matt Dickson)* | | | |
| National | Trade | Darren Kappler | Fitzroy | AFL | 59 |
| | | *Traded by Fitzroy (not utilised)* | | | |

## 1992

| Draft | Selection | Drafted player | Club of origin | Body | Matches with this club |
|---|---|---|---|---|---|
| Pre-Seas | 4 | Damien Mellow | Adelaide | AFL | 0 |
| Pre-Seas | 18 | Alan Thorpe | Fitzroy | AFL | 3 |
| Pre-Seas | 32 | Allan McKellar | Footscray | AFL | 2 |
| Pre-Seas | 45 | Andrew Peck | Sydney | AFL | 0 |
| Pre-Seas | 53 | Phil Krakouer | Footscray | AFL | 0 |
| Mid-Seas | 5 | Dwaine Kretschmer | Glenelg | SANFL | 0 |
| Mid-Seas | 20 | Peter Baldwin | North Hobart | TAS | 0 |
| Mid-Seas | 31 | Paul McMaster | Essendon | AFL | 0 |
| Mid-Seas | 39 | Daryn Cresswell | North Hobart | TAS | 116 |
| Mid-Seas | 44 | Paul Atkins | Burnie Hawks | TAS | 2 |
| Mid-Seas | 48 | Stephen Pears | Perth | WAFL | 0 |
| National | 5 | Jason Spinks | South Fremantle | WAFL | 0 |
| National | 35 | Scott Robinson | Norwood | SANFL | 0 |
| National | 50 | Andrew Donnelly | Subiaco | WAFL | 0 |
| National | 71 | Matthew Aston | Geelong U18 | U18 VCFL | 0 |
| | | *Draft choice 71 traded by Adelaide for Stuart Wigney* | | | |
| National | 95 | Scott Direen | New Norfolk | TAS | 52 |
| National | 101 | Troy Hull | Port Adelaide | SANFL | 0 |
| | | *Draft choice 101 traded by Adelaide for Stuart Wigney* | | | |
| National | 111 | Michael Gaffney | Port Adelaide | SANFL | 0 |
| | | *Draft choice 111 traded by Brisbane Bears for Dion Scott* | | | |
| National | Trade | Tony Begovich | West Coast | AFL | 5 |
| | | *Traded by West Coast for draft selection 1 (Drew Banfield)* | | | |
| National | Trade | Scott Watters | West Coast | AFL | 37 |
| | | *Traded by West Coast for draft selection 1 (Drew Banfield)* | | | |
| National | Trade | Ed Considine | Essendon | AFL | 55 |
| | | *Traded by Essendon for draft selection 3 (Michael Prior)* | | | |
| National | Trade | Michael Werner | Essendon | AFL | 20 |
| | | *Traded by Essendon for draft selection 3 (Michael Prior)* | | | |
| National | Trade | Richard Ambrose | Essendon | AFL | 3 |
| | | *Traded by Essendon for draft selection 20 (Scott Cummings)* | | | |
| National | Trade | Tony Malakellis | Geelong | AFL | 5 |
| | | *Traded by Geelong for draft selection 65 (Gerrad Power)* | | | |
| National | Trade | Jayson Daniels | St Kilda | AFL | 58 |
| | | *Traded by St Kilda for draft selection 80 (Stephen Newport)* | | | |
| National | Trade | Dean McRae | North Melb | AFL | 60 |
| | | *Traded by North Melbourne for draft selection 110 (Jeff Chandler)* | | | |

| Draft | Selection | Drafted player | Club of origin | Body | Matches with this club |
|-------|-----------|----------------|----------------|------|-----------|
| **1993** | | | | | |
| Pre-Seas | 1 | Richard Osborne | Fitzroy | AFL | 16 |
| Pre-Seas | 3 | Paul Bryce | Melbourne | AFL | 17 |
| Pre-Seas | 5 | John Hutton | Brisbane Bears | AFL | 5 |
| Pre-Seas | 21 | Ryan Humphreys | Subiaco | WAFL | 0 |
| Mid-Seas | 1 | Matthew Ahmat | Norwood | SANFL | 2 |
| Mid-Seas | 16 | Aldo Dipetta | Ainslie | ACT | 2 |
| Mid-Seas | 25 | James Little | Sydney | AFL | 0 |
| Mid-Seas | 29 | Jamie Grant | Daylesford | VCFL | 0 |
| Mid-Seas | 31 | Phillip Rowston | Sydney | AFL | 0 |
| Mid-Seas | 32 | Brad Hardie | South Fremantle | WAFL | 0 |
| National | 1 | Darren Gaspar | South Fremantle | WAFL | 21 |
| National | 4 | Glenn Gorman | Geelong U18 | U18 VCFL | 0 |
| National | 5 | Adam Heuskes | Norwood | SANFL | 49 |
| National | 20 | Wade Chapman | Geelong U18 | U18 VCFL | 48 |
| National | 22 | Dion Myles | Baulkham Hills | NSW | 8 |
| National | 28 | Daryl Griffin | Western U18 | U18 VMFL | 0 |
| | | *Draft choice 28 traded by Footscray for Richard Osborne* | | | |
| National | 37 | Ashley Thompson | Nyah-Nyah West United | VCFL | 0 |
| National | 49 | Simon Garlick | Central U18 | U18 VMFL | 44 |
| National | 57 | Mark Hepburn | West Coast | AFL | 7 |
| National | 61 | Shayne Smith | Southern U18 | U18 VMFL | 4 |
| National | Zone Sel | Stefan Carey | Pennant Hills | NSW | 24 |
| National | Zone Sel | Brad Seymour | Wagga Tigers | NSW | 61 |
| National | Zone Sel | Damian Lang | Leeton | NSW | 5 |
| **1994** | | | | | |
| Pre-Seas | 1 | Dermott Brereton | Hawthorn | AFL | 7 |
| Pre-Seas | 6 | Peter Filandia | Essendon | AFL | 38 |
| Pre-Seas | 21 | Derek Kickett | Essendon | AFL | 63 |
| Pre-Seas | 22 | Andrew Bomford | North Shore | NSW | 0 |
| National | 2 | Anthony Rocca | Northern U18 | U18 VMFL | 22 |
| National | 3 | Shannon Grant | Western U18 | U18 VMFL | 58 |
| National | 20 | Stuart Mangin | Northern U18 | U18 VMFL | 0 |
| National | 21 | Matthew Nicks | West Adelaide | SANFL | 26 |
| | | *Draft choice 21 traded by Fremantle for Scott Watters* | | | |
| National | 40 | Michael O'Loughlin | Central District | SANFL | 59 |
| National | 57 | Emil Parthenides | Eastern U18 | U18 VMFL | 0 |
| National | 74 | Troy Luff | Sydney | AFL | 44 |
| | | *Draft choice 74 traded by Fitzroy for Darren Holmes* | | | |
| National | 87 | Simon Arnott | Collegians | VAFA | 26 |
| | | *Draft choice 87 traded by Hawthorn for Simon Minton-Connell* | | | |
| National | Trade | Tony Lockett | St Kilda | AFL | 53 |
| | | *Traded by St Kilda for Robert Neill, draft selection 5 (Joel Smith)* | | | |
| National | Unctr Pl Sel | Peter Caven | Fitzroy | AFL | 18 |
| | | *Uncontracted player selection from Fitzroy for compensatory selection John Rombotis* | | | |
| National | Zone Sel | Justin Crawford | Tocumwal | NSW | 17 |
| National | Zone Sel | Leo Barry | Deniliquin | NSW | 16 |
| National | Zone Sel | Tim Scott | Albury | NSW | 1 |
| **1995** | | | | | |
| Pre-Seas | 1 | Paul Roos | Fitzroy | AFL | 66 |
| Pre-Seas | 3 | Not utilised | | | |
| National | 8 | Jared Crouch | Norwood | SANFL | 0 |
| National | 21 | Clinton King | Eastern U18 | U18 VMFL | 9 |
| | | *Draft choice 21 traded by Hawthorn for Darren Kappler, Leon Higgins* | | | |
| National | 24 | Paul Licuria | Northern U18 | U18 VMFL | 4 |
| National | Trade | Craig O'Brien | St Kilda | AFL | 29 |
| | | *Traded by St Kilda for Jayson Daniels* | | | |
| National | Trade | Paul Rouvray | Adelaide | AFL | 0 |
| | | *Traded by Adelaide for Peter Caven* | | | |
| National | Zone Sel | Ben Mathews | Murray U18 | U18 VCFL | 4 |
| National | Zone Sel | Ben Hollands | North Albury | NSW | 0 |
| National | Zone Sel | Leigh Marshall | Murray U18 | U18 VCFL | 0 |
| **1996** | | | | | |
| Pre-Seas | 7 | Kent Butcher | Collingwood | AFL | 0 |
| Pre-Seas | Unctr Pl Sel | Stuart Maxfield | Richmond | AFL | 46 |
| | | *Uncontracted player selection from Richmond for compensatory selection Darren Gaspar* | | | |
| Pre-Seas | Unctr Pl Sel | Kevin Dyson | Melbourne | AFL | 35 |
| | | *Uncontracted player selection from Melbourne for compensatory selection Craig Nettlebeck* | | | |
| National | 4 | Mark Kinnear | Calder U18 | U18 VMFL | 3 |
| National | 14 | Brett O'Farrell | Prahran U18 | U18 VMFL | 0 |
| | | *Draft choice 14 traded by Collingwood for Anthony Rocca* | | | |
| National | 17 | Rowan Warfe | Fitzroy | AFL | 12 |
| | | *Draft choice 17 traded by Hawthorn for Justin Crawford* | | | |
| National | 27 | Troy Cook | Perth | WAFL | 20 |
| National | 33 | Will Sangster | Prahran U18 | U18 VMFL | 0 |
| | | *Draft choice 33 traded by Collingwood for Anthony Rocca* | | | |
| National | 34 | Shannon Corcoran | Brisbane Bears | AFL | 2 |
| | | *Draft choice 34 traded by St Kilda for Troy Gray* | | | |
| National | Trade | David McEwan | Hawthorn | AFL | 0 |
| | | *Traded by Hawthorn for Justin Crawford* | | | |
| National | Trade | Mark Orchard | Collingwood | AFL | 20 |
| | | *Traded by Collingwood for Anthony Rocca* | | | |

| Draft | Selection | Drafted player | Club of origin | Body | Matches with this club |
|---|---|---|---|---|---|
| National | Trade | Ben Wilson | Collingwood | AFL | 4 |
| | | *Traded by Collingwood for Anthony Rocca* | | | |

**1997**

| Draft | Selection | Drafted player | Club of origin | Body | Matches with this club |
|---|---|---|---|---|---|
| Pre-Seas | 10 | John Stevens | Old Ivanhoe Grammarians | APS | 19 |
| National | 11 | Jason Saddington | Eastern U18 | U18 VMFL | 0 |
| National | 40 | Fred Campbell | Alice Springs Pioneers | NT | 0 |
| | | *Draft choice 40 traded by Collingwood for Clinton King/Stuart Mangin* | | | |
| National | 43 | Adam Goodes | North Ballarat U18 | U18 VCFL | 0 |
| National | 59 | Brett Rose | Eastern U18 | U18 VMFL | 0 |
| National | Trade | Brent Green | Brisbane Lions | AFL | 3 |
| | | *Traded by Brisbane Lions for draft selection 31 (Simon Black)* | | | |
| National | Trade | Simon Hawking | Brisbane Lions | AFL | 4 |
| | | *Traded by Brisbane Lions for draft selection 31 (Simon Black)* | | | |
| National | Trade | Robert Ahmat | Collingwood | AFL | 0 |
| | | *Traded by Collingwood for Clinton King/Stuart Mangin* | | | |
| National | Trade | Wayne Schwass | North Melb | AFL | 4 |
| | | *Traded by North Melbourne for Shannon Grant, draft selection 27 (Brad Stephens)* | | | |

**1998**

| Draft | Selection | Drafted player | Club of origin | Body | Matches with this club |
|---|---|---|---|---|---|
| Pre-Seas | 4 | Adam Coghlan | Sandringham | VFA | 0 |

# WEST COAST

**1988**

| Draft | Selection | Drafted player | Club of origin | Body | Matches with this club |
|---|---|---|---|---|---|
| National | 2 | Todd Breman | Subiaco | WAFL | 23 |
| | | *Draft choice 2 traded by Brisbane Bears for Alex Ishchenko* | | | |
| National | 10 | Peter Higgins | Claremont | WAFL | 4 |
| National | 24 | David Hynes | Port Adelaide | SANFL | 73 |
| National | 38 | Jeremy Crough | South Bendigo | VCFL | 0 |
| National | 44 | Scott Williamson | Wangaratta Rovers | VCFL | 0 |
| | | *Draft choice 44 traded by Brisbane Bears for Mark Zanotti* | | | |
| National | 52 | Darren Bartsch | West Adelaide | SANFL | 0 |
| National | 66 | Matt Richardson | Warracknabeal | VCFL | 0 |
| National | 80 | Damian Berto | St Marys | NT | 0 |
| National | 94 | Andrew Geddes | Katunga | VCFL | 0 |
| National | 108 | Peter Melesso | Claremont | WAFL | 6 |
| National | Pre-Dr Sel | Craig Turley | West Perth | WAFL | 115 |
| National | Pre-Dr Sel | Stevan Jackson | South Fremantle | WAFL | 38 |
| National | Pre-Dr Sel | Don Pyke | Claremont | WAFL | 132 |
| National | Pre-Dr Sel | Peter Sumich | South Fremantle | WAFL | 150 |
| National | Pre-Dr Sel | Scott Watters | South Fremantle | WAFL | 46 |

**1989**

| Draft | Selection | Drafted player | Club of origin | Body | Matches with this club |
|---|---|---|---|---|---|
| Pre-Seas | 10 | Shane Cable | Perth | WAFL | 1 |
| Pre-Seas | 24 | Clinton Browning | East Fremantle | WAFL | 4 |
| Pre-Seas | 38 | Shane Ellis | East Fremantle | WAFL | 10 |
| Pre-Seas | 52 | Richard Geary | South Fremantle | WAFL | 2 |
| National | 4 | Peter Matera | South Fremantle | WAFL | 163 |
| National | 50 | Dean Irving | South Fremantle | WAFL | 41 |
| National | 64 | Tony Evans | Claremont | WAFL | 103 |
| National | 78 | Steven Schwerdt | Central District | SANFL | 0 |
| National | 92 | Brett Heady | Subiaco | WAFL | 140 |
| National | 112 | Ashley McIntosh | Claremont | WAFL | 130 |
| National | Addit Sel | Dean Kemp | Subiaco | WAFL | 176 |
| National | Addit Sel | Anthony Begovich | Claremont | WAFL | 9 |
| National | Addit Sel | Brad Gwilliam | West Perth | WAFL | 4 |
| National | Pre-Dr Sel | Peter Mann | Claremont | WAFL | 0 |
| National | Pre-Dr Sel | Ryan Turnbull | Claremont | WAFL | 96 |
| National | Trade | Peter Wilson | Richmond | AFL | 117 |
| | | *Traded by Richmond for draft selection 18 (Robert Wren), draft selection 32 (Shaun Slater)* | | | |

**1990**

| Draft | Selection | Drafted player | Club of origin | Body | Matches with this club |
|---|---|---|---|---|---|
| Pre-Seas | 4 | Craig McGrath | Fitzroy | AFL | 15 |
| Pre-Seas | 10 | Phil Narkle | West Coast | AFL | 9 |
| Pre-Seas | 24 | Warren Dean | Melbourne | AFL | 0 |
| Pre-Seas | 38 | Bret Hutchinson | Subiaco | WAFL | 0 |
| Mid-Seas | 10 | Craig McNaughton | Sandhurst | VCFL | 0 |
| National | 9 | Matt Clape | East Perth | WAFL | 29 |
| | | *Draft choice 9 traded by North Melbourne for Peter Mann* | | | |
| National | 12 | Shane Porter | North Launceston | TAS | 0 |
| National | 20 | Robert West | Wodonga | VCFL | 13 |
| National | 36 | Matthew Burton | Subiaco | WAFL | 0 |
| National | 64 | Derek Hall | West Perth | WAFL | 2 |
| National | 69 | Gavin Cooney | Clarence | TAS | 0 |
| | | *Draft choice 69 traded by Fitzroy for David O'Connell* | | | |
| National | 83 | Mark Williams | Sandhurst | VCFL | 0 |
| | | *Draft choice 83 traded by Fitzroy for Joe Cormack* | | | |
| National | Trade | Mark Hepburn | North Melb | AFL | 13 |
| | | *Traded by North Melbourne for draft selection 50 (Craig Ellis)* | | | |
| National | Trade | Dale Kickett | Fitzroy | AFL | 2 |
| | | *Traded by Fitzroy for draft selection 78 (Dean Harding)* | | | |
| National | Trade | Ian Dargie | St Kilda | AFL | 1 |
| | | *Traded by St Kilda for draft selection 92 (Jamie Shanahan)* | | | |
| National | Zone Sel | Glen Jakovich | South Fremantle | WAFL | 139 |
| National | Zone Sel | Mitchell White | Subiaco | WAFL | 101 |

| Draft | Selection | Drafted player | Club of origin | Body | Matches with this club |
|---|---|---|---|---|---|
| **1991** | | | | | |
| Pre-Seas | 18 | Corey Young | Richmond | AFL | 1 |
| Pre-Seas | 35 | Craig McNaughton | West Coast | AFL | 0 |
| Pre-Seas | 49 | Brad Edwards | Brisbane Bears | AFL | 0 |
| Pre-Seas | 57 | Peter Higgins | West Coast | AFL | 0 |
| National | 16 | Daniel Metropolis | Subiaco | WAFL | 48 |
| | | *Draft choice 16 traded by Richmond for Stevan Jackson* | | | |
| National | 24 | Kane Morphett | East Fremantle | WAFL | 0 |
| | | *Draft choice 24 traded by Geelong for Geoff Miles* | | | |
| National | 25 | Steven Davies | Subiaco | WAFL | 0 |
| National | 29 | Matthew Connell | Subiaco | WAFL | 3 |
| National | 42 | Peter Freeman | St Kilda | AFL | 0 |
| | | *Draft choice 42 traded by Richmond for Todd Breman* | | | |
| National | 74 | Brendan Krummel | East Fremantle | WAFL | 9 |
| National | Trade | Paul Harding | St Kilda | AFL | 43 |
| | | *Traded by St Kilda for draft selection 12 (Rob Malone)* | | | |
| National | Trade | Paul Gow | Footscray | AFL | 0 |
| | | *Traded by Footscray for draft selection 38 (Jamie Rundle)* | | | |
| National | Trade | Trent Nichols | Richmond | AFL | 4 |
| | | *Traded by Richmond for draft selection 51 (Shaun Brooker)* | | | |
| National | Trade | David Regan | Essendon | AFL | 0 |
| | | *Traded by Essendon for draft selection 63 (Brendan Bower)* | | | |
| National | Zone Sel | Jason Ball | Swan Districts | WAFL | 67 |
| **1992** | | | | | |
| Pre-Seas | 13 | Tim Watson | Essendon | AFL | 0 |
| Pre-Seas | 27 | David Ogg | Brisbane Bears | AFL | 0 |
| Pre-Seas | 41 | Jason Disney | Richmond | AFL | 0 |
| Mid-Seas | 13 | Damian Hampson | Carlton | AFL | 4 |
| National | 1 | Drew Banfield | Subiaco | WAFL | 99 |
| | | *Draft choice 1 traded by Sydney for Scott Watters, Tony Begovich* | | | |
| National | 8 | Paul Symmons | West Perth | WAFL | 63 |
| | | *Draft choice 8 traded by North Melbourne for Dean Laidley* | | | |
| National | 19 | Lee Walker | East Perth | WAFL | 0 |
| National | 21 | Shane Bond | Port Adelaide | SANFL | 34 |
| | | *Draft choice 21 traded by Brisbane Bears for Paul Peos* | | | |
| National | 34 | Travis Burton | Subiaco | WAFL | 0 |
| National | 49 | Jarrad Schofield | Subiaco | WAFL | 49 |
| National | 64 | Tony Godden | Subiaco | WAFL | 13 |
| National | 79 | Brett Spinks | South Fremantle | WAFL | 21 |
| National | 94 | Rhys Croxford | Claremont | WAFL | 0 |
| National | 109 | David Muir | Claremont | WAFL | 0 |
| National | 124 | Brayden Lyle | Port Adelaide | SANFL | 26 |
| **1993** | | | | | |
| Pre-Seas | 19 | Brendon Retzlaff | Brisbane Bears | AFL | 3 |
| Pre-Seas | 35 | Travis Edmonds | Hawthorn | AFL | 0 |
| Pre-Seas | 49 | Brendan Green | Claremont | WAFL | 0 |
| Mid-Seas | 13 | Not utilised | | | |
| National | 16 | Fraser Gehrig | Murray U18 | U18 VCFL | 62 |
| National | 33 | Ben Robbins | Gippsland U18 | U18 VCFL | 0 |
| National | 43 | Jason Heatley | Subiaco | WAFL | 3 |
| | | *Draft choice 43 traded by Footscray for Robert West* | | | |
| **1994** | | | | | |
| Pre-Seas | 17 | Scott Thomson | Subiaco | WAFL | 0 |
| National | 12 | Shane Sikora | Murray U18 | U18 VCFL | 2 |
| | | *Draft choice 12 traded by Collingwood for Lee Walker* | | | |
| National | 37 | Ashley Blurton | West Perth | WAFL | 10 |
| National | 44 | Jeremy Dyer | Geelong U18 | U18 VCFL | 0 |
| | | *Draft choice 44 traded by Adelaide for Matthew Connell* | | | |
| National | 54 | Ian Downsborough | West Perth | WAFL | 20 |
| National | 71 | Jason Spinks | Sydney | AFL | 0 |
| National | Trade | Michael Dunstan | Fitzroy | AFL | 5 |
| | | *Traded by Fitzroy for draft selection 19 (Ben Holland)* | | | |
| **1995** | | | | | |
| Pre-Seas | 17 | Paul Peos | Brisbane Bears | AFL | 4 |
| Pre-Seas | 31 | Jason Spinks | Sydney | AFL | 0 |
| Pre-Seas | Comp Sel | Chad Morrison | Southern U18 | U18 VMFL | 42 |
| | | *Compensatory selection from Fremantle for uncontracted player selection Brendan Krummel* | | | |
| National | 3 | Brendon Fewster | West Perth | WAFL | 6 |
| | | *Draft choice 3 traded by Fremantle for David Hynes* | | | |
| National | 14 | Luke Trew | Murray U18 | U18 VCFL | 0 |
| National | 30 | Craig Smoker | West Perth | WAFL | 0 |
| National | 44 | Jonson Clifton | Swan Districts | WAFL | 0 |
| National | 57 | Paul Whitelaw | West Perth | WAFL | 0 |
| National | 66 | Neil Marshall | Claremont | WAFL | 2 |
| | | *Draft choice 66 traded by Brisbane Bears for Ben Robbins* | | | |
| National | Fath-Son | Ben Cousins | East Fremantle | WAFL | 38 |
| National | Trade | Anthony Lovell | Melbourne | AFL | 39 |
| | | *Traded by Melbourne for Craig Turley* | | | |
| National | Trade | Phillip Matera | South Fremantle | WAFL | 24 |
| | | *Traded by Fremantle for David Hynes* | | | |

| Draft | Selection | Drafted player | Club of origin | Body | Matches with this club |
|---|---|---|---|---|---|
| **1996** | | | | | |
| Pre-Seas | 13 | Andrew Donnelly | Subiaco | WAFL | 30 |
| Pre-Seas | Comp Sel | David Wirrpunda | Eastern U18 | U18 VMFL | 11 |
| | | *Compensatory selection from Fremantle for uncontracted player selection Tony Godden* | | | |
| National | 1 | Michael Gardiner | Claremont | WAFL | 10 |
| National | 24 | Josh Wooden | Nsw-Act U18 | U18 NSW-ACT | 18 |
| National | 39 | Nicholas Stone | Claremont | WAFL | 14 |
| National | 53 | Michael Braun | Bendigo U18 | U18 VCFL | 7 |
| National | 57 | Trent Cummings | Fitzroy | AFL | 2 |
| | | *Draft choice 57 traded by Port Adelaide for Brayden Lyle, Shane Bond* | | | |
| National | Trade | Ilija Grgic | Footscray | AFL | 22 |
| | | *Traded by Footscray for Luke Trew, draft selection 20 (Matthew Dent)* | | | |
| **1997** | | | | | |
| National | 12 | Jaxon Crabb | Claremont | WAFL | 13 |
| National | 13 | Callum Chambers | Gippsland U18 | U18 VCFL | 11 |
| | | *Draft choice 13 traded by Geelong for Brett Spinks* | | | |
| National | 28 | Rowan Jones | Claremont | WAFL | 0 |
| National | 34 | Andrew Williams | Dandenong U18 | U18 VMFL | 4 |
| | | *Draft choice 34 traded by Melbourne for Craig Smoker* | | | |
| National | 37 | Todd Holmes | Subiaco | WAFL | 0 |
| | | *Draft choice 37 traded by Richmond for Ashley Blurton* | | | |
| National | 44 | Daviid Antonowicz | Western U18 | U18 VMFL | 0 |
| National | 60 | Phillip Read | East Fremantle | WAFL | 3 |

# WESTERN BULLDOGS
## (Footscray until 1996 National Draft)

| Draft | Selection | Drafted player | Club of origin | Body | Matches with this club |
|---|---|---|---|---|---|
| **1986** | | | | | |
| National | 6 | Richard Cousins | Central District | SANFL | 60 |
| National | 19 | Matthew Mansfield | Glenorchy | TAS | 32 |
| National | 32 | Wayne Mahoney | Port Adelaide | SANFL | 0 |
| National | 45 | James Pyke | Norwood | SANFL | 0 |
| National | 58 | Perry Meka | Lemnos | VCFL | 0 |
| **1987** | | | | | |
| National | 7 | Darren Davies | North Hobart | TAS | 37 |
| National | 20 | Stuart Wigney | Leongatha | VCFL | 47 |
| National | 33 | Rod Gunn | Hamilton | VCFL | 0 |
| National | 46 | Gary Gunn | Hamilton | VCFL | 1 |
| National | 59 | Simon Tregenza | Port Adelaide | SANFL | 0 |
| **1988** | | | | | |
| National | 7 | Leon Cameron | South Warrnambool | VCFL | 133 |
| National | 21 | Anthony Reynolds | Wodonga | VCFL | 0 |
| National | 35 | John Georgiades | Subiaco | WAFL | 15 |
| National | 49 | Shannon Corcoran | Glenelg | SANFL | 23 |
| National | 63 | Scott Davies | North Launceston | TAS | 0 |
| National | 77 | Robert Bloom | Ulverstone | TAS | 0 |
| National | 86 | Ben Sexton | Sandhurst | VCFL | 39 |
| | | *Draft choice 86 traded by Brisbane Bears for Craig Somerville* | | | |
| National | 91 | Matthew Queen | Glenorchy | TAS | 0 |
| National | 105 | Chris Grant | Daylesford | VCFL | 167 |
| **1989** | | | | | |
| Pre-Seas | 7 | Mark Williams | Carlton | AFL | 14 |
| Pre-Seas | 21 | Tim Harrington | Collingwood | AFL | 18 |
| Pre-Seas | 35 | Anthony Evans | St Kilda | AFL | 3 |
| Pre-Seas | 49 | Jolyon Keeble | Hawthorn | AFL | 0 |
| National | 2 | Matthew Croft | Mildura Imperials | VCFL | 63 |
| National | 16 | Jason Shields | Moe | VCFL | 0 |
| National | 30 | Glenn Coleman | Sydney | AFL | 69 |
| National | 48 | Dennis Rapacholi | West Perth | WAFL | 0 |
| National | 62 | John Brunner | Yarrawonga | VCFL | 0 |
| National | 76 | Shayne Ward | Darley | VCFL | 0 |
| National | 90 | Ben Cross | East Warrnambool | VCFL | 0 |
| National | 104 | Tony Trigg | Bungaree | VCFL | 0 |
| **1990** | | | | | |
| Pre-Seas | 2 | Keenan Reynolds | Essendon | AFL | 74 |
| Pre-Seas | 8 | Danny Del-Re | Williamstown | AFL | 62 |
| Pre-Seas | 22 | Anthony Alessio | Parkside | VMFL | 0 |
| Pre-Seas | 36 | Ian Rickman | Williamstown | VFA | 0 |
| Mid-Seas | 8 | Phil Krakouer | North Melb | AFL | 0 |
| Mid-Seas | 22 | Jamie Grant | Daylesford | VCFL | 5 |
| Mid-Seas | 32 | Michael Frost | Swan Hill | VCFL | 13 |
| Mid-Seas | 39 | Nick Tsiotinas | Essendon | AFL | 0 |
| Mid-Seas | 44 | Barry Spierings | Werribee | VFA | 0 |
| National | 8 | Paul Gow | Swan Districts | WAFL | 7 |
| National | 32 | Matthew Moylan | Shepparton | VCFL | 0 |
| National | 46 | Brian McInnes | Wickliffe-Lake Bolac | VCFL | 0 |
| National | 60 | Rodney Harvey | Trinity,Ararat | VCFL | 0 |
| National | 74 | Paul Campbell | Cobram | VCFL | 0 |
| National | 88 | Peter Jacks | Ballarat Ycw | VCFL | 0 |

| Draft | Selection | Drafted player | Club of origin | Body | Matches with this club |
|---|---|---|---|---|---|
| **1991** | | | | | |
| Pre-Seas | 14 | Allan McKellar | Richmond | AFL | 0 |
| Pre-Seas | 22 | Saade Ghazi | Central District | SANFL | 0 |
| Pre-Seas | 31 | Scott McDonald | Bell Post Hill | VCFL | 0 |
| Pre-Seas | 45 | David Ross | Darwin | NT | 0 |
| Pre-Seas | 53 | Phil Krakouer | Footscray | AFL | 7 |
| Mid-Seas | 6 | Mark Naley | South Adelaide | SANFL | 0 |
| Mid-Seas | 19 | Paul Brown | Dandenong | VFA | 0 |
| Mid-Seas | 31 | David Preston | Grovedale | VCFL | 0 |
| Mid-Seas | 37 | Daryl Argus | Kyabram | VCFL | 0 |
| National | 38 | Jamie Rundle | Dandenong | VFA | 0 |
| | | *Draft choice 38 traded by West Coast for Paul Gow* | | | |
| National | 45 | Gary Barrow | Essendon | AFL | 6 |
| National | 58 | Justin Pickering | Richmond | AFL | 0 |
| National | 67 | Shane Ellen | Footscray | AFL | 11 |
| | | *Draft choice 67 traded by Sydney for Stuart Wigney* | | | |
| National | 80 | Damian Ryan | Coburg | VFA | 0 |
| National | 86 | Jamie Madigan | Footscray | AFL | 0 |
| National | Trade | Bernard Toohey | Sydney | AFL | 40 |
| | | *Traded by Sydney for draft selection 6 (Paul Burton)* | | | |
| National | Trade | Ricky Jackson | Melbourne | AFL | 0 |
| | | *Traded by Melbourne for draft selection 19 (Phil Gilbert)* | | | |
| National | Trade | Tony Campbell | Melbourne | AFL | 35 |
| | | *Traded by Melbourne for draft selection 31 (Haydon Kilmartin)* | | | |
| National | Trade | Darren Morgan | Sydney | AFL | 0 |
| | | *Traded by Sydney for draft selection 68 (Matthew Bell)* | | | |
| **1992** | | | | | |
| Pre-Seas | 6 | Greg Jones | St Kilda | AFL | 0 |
| Pre-Seas | 20 | Mark Majerczak | Carlton | AFL | 0 |
| Pre-Seas | 34 | Paul Satterley | Footscray | AFL | 0 |
| Mid-Seas | 15 | Julian Shanks | Williamstown | VFA | 0 |
| Mid-Seas | 28 | Brian McInnes | Williamstown | VFA | 0 |
| National | 17 | Kym Koster | South Adelaide | SANFL | 38 |
| National | 29 | Sam Phillipou | Woodville-West Torrens | SANFL | 3 |
| | | *Draft choice 29 traded by Hawthorn for Darren Baxter* | | | |
| National | 32 | Peter Quill | East Fremantle | WAFL | 67 |
| National | 47 | Dylan Flavell | South Bendigo | VCFL | 0 |
| National | 59 | Scott Allen | Portarlington | VCFL | 15 |
| | | *Draft choice 59 traded by Hawthorn for Darren Baxter* | | | |
| National | 62 | Damian Ryan | Footscray | AFL | 0 |
| National | 77 | Brad Copeland | Western U18 | U18 VMFL | 0 |
| National | 92 | Daniel Southern | Claremont | WAFL | 64 |
| National | 107 | Gary Barrow | Footscray | AFL | 6 |
| National | 114 | Paul Whelan | Ainslie | ACT | 0 |
| | | *Draft choice 114 traded by Melbourne for Adrian Campbell* | | | |
| National | Fath-Son | Luke Darcy | South Adelaide | SANFL | 47 |
| National | Trade | Luke Beveridge | Melbourne | AFL | 31 |
| | | *Traded by Melbourne for draft selection 122 (Damon Munt)* | | | |
| **1993** | | | | | |
| Pre-Seas | 17 | Anthony Darcy | Geelong | AFL | 14 |
| Pre-Seas | 33 | Brad Nicholson | Eastern U18 | U18 VMFL | 34 |
| Pre-Seas | 47 | Craig Ellis | Western U18 | U18 VMFL | 46 |
| Mid-Seas | 7 | Alan Thorpe | Oakleigh | VFA | 12 |
| Mid-Seas | 20 | Russell Evans | Coburg | VFA | 0 |
| National | 11 | Brad Johnson | Western U18 | U18 VMFL | 76 |
| National | 54 | Sedat Sir | Central U18 | U18 VMFL | 23 |
| National | Trade | Richard Osborne | Sydney | AFL | 51 |
| | | *Traded by Sydney for draft selection 28 (Daryl Griffin)* | | | |
| National | Trade | Robert West | West Coast | AFL | 6 |
| | | *Traded by West Coast for draft selection 43 (Jason Heatley)* | | | |
| **1994** | | | | | |
| Pre-Seas | 12 | Jason Watts | Werribee | VFA | 56 |
| Pre-Seas | 27 | Daniel Hargraves | Eastern U18 | U18 VMFL | 38 |
| National | 14 | Michael Martin | Hobart | TAS | 17 |
| National | 32 | Simon Cox | Glenelg | SANFL | 15 |
| National | 49 | Shaun Baxter | Geelong U18 | U18 VCFL | 0 |
| National | 66 | Scott Taylor | Geelong U18 | U18 VCFL | 1 |
| National | 78 | Daryl Griffin | Sydney | AFL | 18 |
| National | 88 | Nathon Irvin | Norwood | SANFL | 0 |
| National | Pre-Dr Supp | Trent Churchill | Footscray | VSFL | 0 |
| **1995** | | | | | |
| Pre-Seas | 12 | Jose Romero | North Melb | AFL | 61 |
| Pre-Seas | 26 | Paul Dimattina | Sandringham | VFA | 29 |
| Pre-Seas | 35 | Michael Johnston | Hawthorn | AFL | 2 |
| Pre-Seas | 37 | Andrew Nichol | Box Hill | VFA | 3 |
| National | 9 | Allen Jakovich | Melbourne | AFL | 7 |
| | | *Draft choice 9 traded by Adelaide for Kym Koster* | | | |
| National | 29 | Todd Curley | West Perth | WAFL | 28 |
| National | 43 | Mark West | South Adelaide | SANFL | 11 |
| National | 52 | Tony Campbell | Perth | WAFL | 8 |
| | | *Draft choice 52 traded by St Kilda for Luke Beveridge* | | | |

**221**

| Draft | Selection | Drafted player | Club of origin | Body | Matches with this club |
|-------|-----------|----------------|----------------|------|------------------------|
| National | Fath-Son | David Round | Calder U18 | U18 VMFL | 2 |
| National | Trade | Brad Wira | Fremantle | AFL | 37 |
| | | *Traded by Fremantle for draft selection 13 (Brad Rowe)* | | | |
| National | Trade | Hugh Reimers | Central District | SANFL | 0 |
| | | *Traded by Fremantle for draft selection 13 (Brad Rowe)* | | | |
| National | Trade | James Cook | Carlton | AFL | 19 |
| | | *Traded by Carlton for Ben Sexton* | | | |
| **1996** | | | | | |
| Pre-Seas | 12 | Jason Lappin | Wodonga Raiders | VCFL | 0 |
| National | 10 | Nathan Brown | Bendigo U18 | U18 VCFL | 14 |
| National | 20 | Matthew Dent | Fitzroy | AFL | 20 |
| | | *Draft choice 20 traded by West Coast for Ilija Grgic* | | | |
| National | 32 | Jim Plunkett | Northern U18 | U18 VMFL | 0 |
| | | *Draft choice 32 traded by Adelaide for Barry Standfield* | | | |
| National | 44 | Jacob Rhodes | Geelong U18 | U18 VCFL | 0 |
| National | 47 | Brett Montgomery | Footscray Supp List | AFL RES | 16 |
| | | *Draft choice 47 traded by Adelaide for Barry Standfield* | | | |
| National | 58 | Paul Dooley | Williamstown | VFA | 0 |
| National | 61 | Stephen Powell | Footscray Supp List | AFL RES | 3 |
| | | *Draft choice 61 traded by Collingwood for Richard Osborne* | | | |
| National | Trade | Simon Minton-Connell | Hawthorn | AFL | 17 |
| | | *Traded by Hawthorn for draft selection 29 (Nathan Turvey)* | | | |
| National | Trade | Luke Trew | West Coast | AFL | 0 |
| | | *Traded by West Coast for Ilija Grgic* | | | |
| **1997** | | | | | |
| Pre-Seas | 2 | Paul Hudson | Hawthorn | AFL | 20 |
| Pre-Seas | 12 | Steven Pitt | Collingwood | AFL | 0 |
| National | 18 | Mark Alvey | Bendigo U18 | U18 VCFL | 0 |
| | | *Draft choice 18 traded by Fremantle for Daniel Hargraves* | | | |
| National | 47 | Robert Stevenson | Essendon | AFL | 0 |
| National | 63 | Anthony Aloi | Western U18 | U18 VMFL | 0 |
| National | 74 | Paul Digiovine | Oakleigh U18 | U18 VMFL | 0 |
| National | Trade | Matthew Robbins | Geelong | AFL | 0 |
| | | *Traded by Geelong for draft selection 15 (Joel McKay), draft selection 38 (James Rahilly)* | | | |
| National | Trade | Simon Garlick | Sydney | AFL | 0 |
| | | *Traded by Sydney for draft selection 31 (Simon Black)* | | | |
| Rookie Elev | Rook Elev | Adam Contessa | North Melb Reserves | AFL RES | 4 |
| **1998** | | | | | |
| Pre-Seas | 6 | Scott Taylor | Western Bulldogs | AFL | 0 |

---

## AFL ROOKIE DRAFT SELECTIONS 1998

Rookies may be promoted to the AFL list during the season. A listed AFL player must be deleted for this to occur. De-listed players are able to play in the Reserves and can be reinstated to an AFL list through the Draft process.

**Adelaide:** Sudjai Cook, Norwood (SANFL); Tim Davis, North Adelaide (SANFL); Steven Hall, Woodville-West Torrens (SA) (SANFL); Ben Marsh, West Adelaide (SANFL)

**Brisbane:** Tate Day, Gold Coast (QLD)

**Carlton:** Cameron Blight, Devonport/Tas U18 (U18 TAS); Clint Evans, Berwick/Dandenong U18 (U18 VMFL); Simon Fletcher, Grovedale/Geelong U18/Geelong Reserves (U18 VCFL); Shane Flynn, Basin/Eastern U18 (U18 VMFL); Scott Freeborn, Woodville-West Torrens/Port Adel List (SANFL); Damian Lang, Leeton (NSW)

**Collingwood:** George Bakoulas, Tullamarine/Calder U18 (U18 VMFL); Marcus Barham, Gisborne/Calder U18 (U18 VMFL); Adam Collings, Croydon/Eastern U18 (U18 VMFL); Frank Dimattina, Bulleen-Templestowe/Oakleigh U18 (U18 VMFL); Tarkyn Lockyer, East Fremantle (WAFL); Mark Matthews, Box Hill (VFA)

**Essendon:** Robert DiRosa, Werribee/Western U18/Geelong/Foots Res (U18 VMFL); Winis Imbi, Portland/Ballarat U18 (U18 VCFL); Mark Johnson, Sunbury/Calder U18 (U18 VMFL); Lachlan Oakley, Sandringham (VFA); Dean Rioli, South Fremantle (WAFL)

**Fremantle:** Brad Dodd, East Fremantle (WAFL); Cameron Jackson, No Club: Basketballer (VIC); Paul Maher, Perth (WAFL); John Neesham, East Fremantle (WAFL)

**Geelong:** Shaun Baxter, Bannockburn/Geelong U18/Foots Res (U18 VCFL); Chris Hemley, Bell Post Hill/Geelong U18/St Kilda (U18 VCFL); Paul Lindsay, East Fremantle (WAFL)

**Hawthorn:** Glen Bowyer, Murray U18 (U18 VCFL); Stephen Jurica, South Fremantle (WAFL)

**Melbourne:** Ben Beams, Glenorchy/Tas U18 (U18 TAS); Matthew Bishop, Box Hill (VFA); Jamie Cann, Calder U18 (U18 VMFL); Peter Walsh, West Adelaide (SANFL); Daniel Ward, Hoppers Crossing/Western U18/Fitzroy Res (U18 VMFL); Luke Williams, St Kevins/Oakleigh U18 (U18 VMFL)

**North Melbourne:** Craig Folino, Eastern U18 (U18 VMFL); Wade Kingsley, Woodville-West Torrens (SANFL); Julian Kirzner, Ajax/Central U18/Essendon (U18 VMFL); David Round, Strathmore/Calder U18/Wstrn Bldgs (U18 VMFL);

**Port Adelaide:** Barnaby French, Sturt (SANFL); Antony Sheehan, Port Adelaide (SANFL)

**Richmond:** Chris Bossong, St Kevins (VAFA); Ben Hollands, North Albury/Sydney Reserves (NSW); Greg Tivendale, ROC./Gippsland U18 (U18 VCFL)

**St Kilda:** Lachlan Brown, Castlemaine (VCFL)

**Sydney:** Mark Brown, Numurkah (VCFL); James Byrne, Assumption College/Calder U18 (U18 VMFL); Mark Livy, North Shore/NSW-ACT U18 (U18 NSW-ACT); Brad McMahon, Southport (QLD); Jason McPherson, Ganmain-Grong Grong-Matong (NSW)

**West Coast:** Laurie Bellotti, Claremont (WAFL); Conrad Chambers, East Fremantle (WAFL); Chad Fletcher, Subiaco (WAFL); Todd Nener, Southport/East Perth (WAFL); Trent Simpson, Southport/Subiaco (WAFL); Heath Younie, Wodonga/Murray U18 (U18 VCFL)

**Western Bulldogs:** Lincoln Reynolds, Geelong U18/Port Melbourne (U18 VCFL); Shaun Tinsley, East Sandringham/Prahran U18/Port Melb (U18 VMFL)

# PLAYER BY PLAYER INDEX

| Player | Club, drafted |
|---|---|
| Capsalis, Leigh | St K 1993 |
| Capuano, Matthew | NM 1992 |
| Caracella, Blake | Ess 1994 |
| Careless, Ben | Rich 1992 |
| Carey, Stefan | Syd 1993 |
| Carr, Alister | Ess 1989 |
| Carr, Alister | St K 1994 |
| Carr, Matthew | Coll 1995 |
| Carr, Matthew | St K 1998 |
| Carr, Tom | Pt Ad 1996 |
| Carroll, John | Melb 1994 |
| Carroll, Trent | Fre 1995 |
| Carter, Jarrod | Ess 1990 |
| Carter, Nick | Fitz 1995 |
| Carter, Nick | B Lions 1996 |
| Carter, Stephen | Ess 1994 |
| Carter, Stephen | Pt Ad 1996 |
| Cassidy, Brad | Fre 1994 |
| Cassidy, Brad | Fitz 1995 |
| Cassidy, Brad | Coll 1996 |
| Caton, Kevin | Fitz 1989 |
| Caton, Kevin | B Bears 1989 |
| Cavedon, Andrew | Fitz 1994 |
| Caven, Peter | Syd 1994 |
| Caven, Peter | Adel 1995 |
| Chaffey, Mark | Rich 1996 |
| Chalmers, Brett | Rich 1989 |
| Chalmers, Brett | Coll 1992 |
| Chalmers, Brett | Adel 1993 |
| Chalmers, Brett | Pt Ad 1997 |
| Chambers, Callum | WC 1997 |
| Chambers, Luke | B Bears 1990 |
| Chambers, Luke | B Bears 1991 |
| Champion, Richard | B Bears 1988 |
| Chandler, Brett | Fitz 1994 |
| Chandler, Brett | NM 1997 |
| Chandler, Jeff | NM 1992 |
| Chapman, Nathan | B Bears 1992 |
| Chapman, Nathan | Haw 1997 |
| Chapman, Wade | Syd 1993 |
| Charles, Justin | Rich 1994 |
| Charles, Sean | Carl 1997 |
| Chatfield, Adam | Carl 1997 |
| Chick, Daniel | Haw 1995 |
| Chigwidden, Nick | Syd 1988 |
| Christensen, Marty | NM 1992 |
| Christensen, Marty | NM 1992 |
| Christie, Scott | NM 1987 |
| Churchill, Trent | Foots 1994 |
| Clape, Matt | WC 1992 |
| Clape, Matt | Carl 1995 |
| Clark, Michael | Fre 1995 |
| Clark, Steven | Melb 1989 |
| Clark, Steven | St K 1992 |
| Clarke, Daniel | Melb 1992 |
| Clarke, Matthew | Rich 1990 |
| Clarke, Matthew | B Bears 1992 |
| Clarkson, Alastair | Melb 1995 |
| Clarkson, Justin | Syd 1990 |
| Clarkson, Justin | Carl 1992 |
| Clayton, Shane | Fitz 1995 |
| Clayton, Shane | B Lions 1996 |
| Clement, James | Fre 1995 |
| Clifton, Jonson | WC 1995 |
| Cloke, David | Rich 1990 |
| Cloke, David | Rich 1991 |
| Clucas, Matthew | Fre 1996 |
| Cochrane, Stephen | Gee 1993 |
| Cochrane, Stuart | NM 1995 |
| Cockatoo-Collins, Che | Ess 1992 |
| Cockatoo-Collins, David | Mel 1995 |
| Cockatoo-Collins, Donald | Mel 1995 |
| Coffee, Grant | Fitz 1989 |
| Coghlan, Adam | Syd 1998 |
| Coghlan, Derek | Carl 1989 |
| Coghlan, Glen | St K 1995 |
| Colbert, Leigh | Gee 1992 |
| Cole, Anthony | Syd 1991 |
| Coleman, Glenn | Foots 1989 |
| Collins, Darren | Fitz 1990 |
| Collins, Darren | Haw 1996 |
| Collins, Mark | Syd 1990 |
| Collins, Matthew | Adel 1994 |
| Collins, Matthew | Melb 1997 |

| Player | Club, drafted |
|---|---|
| Connell, Matthew | WC 1991 |
| Connell, Matthew | Adel 1994 |
| Connelly, Stephen | B Bears 1986 |
| Considine, Ed | Syd 1992 |
| Contessa, Adam | W Bull 1997 |
| Conway, Mark | Pt Ad 1996 |
| Cook, Brett | Fitz 1991 |
| Cook, Brett | St K 1997 |
| Cook, James | Carl 1990 |
| Cook, James | Foots 1995 |
| Cook, John | Ess 1987 |
| Cook, Tim | Adel 1996 |
| Cook, Troy | Syd 1996 |
| Cooney, Gavin | WC 1990 |
| Copeland, Brad | Foots 1992 |
| Corcoran, Shannon | Foots 1988 |
| Corcoran, Shannon | B Bears 1995 |
| Corcoran, Shannon | Syd 1996 |
| Corkery, Colin | Carl 1989 |
| Cormack, Joe | Fitz 1990 |
| Cornes, Chad | Pt Ad 1997 |
| Corrigan, Paul | Gee 1996 |
| Cotton, Jarrod | Pt Ad 1996 |
| Cousins, Ben | WC 1995 |
| Cousins, Richard | Foots 1986 |
| Coutts, Ashley | Gee 1989 |
| Cowell, Brent | St K 1997 |
| Cox, Bevan | Rich 1987 |
| Cox, Jamie | Ess 1987 |
| Cox, Simon | Foots 1994 |
| Crabb, Jaxon | WC 1997 |
| Cranage, Sam | St K 1997 |
| Cransberg, Peter | Ess 1989 |
| Craven, Danny | St K 1988 |
| Craven, Danny | B Bears 1993 |
| Crawford, Glenn | Ess 1989 |
| Crawford, Justin | Syd 1994 |
| Crawford, Justin | Haw 1996 |
| Crawford, Shane | Haw 1991 |
| Crawshay, Simon | Haw 1991 |
| Credlin, Nigel | Fitz 1995 |
| Credlin, Nigel | Haw 1997 |
| Cresswell, Daryn | Gee 1988 |
| Cresswell, Daryn | Syd 1992 |
| Cripps, Jason | St K 1995 |
| Croad, Trent | Haw 1997 |
| Croft, Matthew | Foots 1989 |
| Cross, Ben | Foots 1989 |
| Cross, Craig | Carl 1990 |
| Crothers, Shane | Gee 1989 |
| Crothers, Shane | Gee 1993 |
| Crouch, Jared | Syd 1995 |
| Crough, Jeremy | WC 1988 |
| Crough, Jeremy | Rich 1989 |
| Crough, Justin | Haw 1988 |
| Crow, Scott | Haw 1990 |
| Crow, Scott | Coll 1995 |
| Crowe, Damian | Gee 1992 |
| Croxford, Rhys | WC 1992 |
| Crudden, Adam | Rich 1988 |
| Cullen, Mark | Carl 1994 |
| Cummings, Robert | Fitz 1990 |
| Cummings, Scott | Ess 1992 |
| Cummings, Scott | Pt Ad 1996 |
| Cummings, Steven | St K 1990 |
| Cummings, Trent | Fitz 1993 |
| Cummings, Trent | WC 1996 |
| Cunningham, John | Gee 1993 |
| Curley, Todd | Coll 1991 |
| Curley, Todd | Foots 1995 |
| Curran, Chris | Coll 1994 |
| Curran, Peter | B Bears 1990 |
| Daffy, Nick | Rich 1990 |
| Dakin, Lyndon | Syd 1986 |
| Daniels, Jayson | Syd 1992 |
| Daniels, Jayson | St K 1995 |
| Daniels, Stephen | Pt Ad 1996 |
| Daniher, Neale | Ess 1990 |
| Daniltchenko, Jason | Haw 1998 |
| Darcy, Anthony | Foots 1993 |
| Darcy, Anthony | St K 1996 |
| Darcy, Luke | Foots 1992 |
| Darcy, Tim | Ess 1995 |
| Dargie, Ian | St K 1988 |

| Player | Club, drafted |
|---|---|
| Dargie, Ian | WC 1990 |
| Davidson, Christian | Carl 1993 |
| Davidson, Peter | B Bears 1989 |
| Davies, Darren | Foots 1987 |
| Davies, Darren | St K 1991 |
| Davies, Scott | Foots 1988 |
| Davies, Steven | WC 1991 |
| Davies, Troy | Fitz 1992 |
| Davis, Brad | Fitz 1990 |
| De Iulio, Ron | Carl 1991 |
| De Mamiel, Grant | Fitz 1994 |
| Dean, Warren | WC 1990 |
| Dear, Greg | Rich 1993 |
| Del-Re, Danny | Foots 1990 |
| Delaney, Roger | Fitz 1989 |
| Delaney, Tony | Ess 1992 |
| Delaney, Tony | Fre 1994 |
| Dempsey, Greg | Adel 1996 |
| Denham, Sean | Ess 1991 |
| Denneman, Darren | Syd 1989 |
| Dennis, Matthew | Haw 1997 |
| Dennis, Richard | NM 1991 |
| Dennis, Simon | Rich 1992 |
| Dent, Matthew | Fitz 1993 |
| Dent, Matthew | W Bull 1996 |
| Dessent, Anthony | Haw 1987 |
| Devlin, Stewart | Gee 1990 |
| Devonport, Craig | Carl 1995 |
| Dew, Stuart | Pt Ad 1996 |
| Di Rosa, Robert | Gee 1994 |
| Dick, Willie | Ess 1991 |
| Dickfos, Danny | Fitz 1993 |
| Dickfos, Danny | B Bears 1995 |
| Dickie, Donald | Pt Ad 1996 |
| Dickson, Matthew | Carl 1991 |
| Dickson, Robert | B Bears 1990 |
| Dighton, David | NM 1992 |
| Digiovine, Paul | W Bull 1997 |
| Dilena, Carl | Fitz 1988 |
| Dilena, Carl | NM 1991 |
| Dimattina, Paul | Rich 1991 |
| Dimattina, Paul | Foots 1995 |
| Dipetta, Aldo | Syd 1993 |
| Direen, Scott | Syd 1992 |
| Disney, Jason | WC 1992 |
| Divenuto, Peter | Coll 1988 |
| Dixon, Ben | Haw 1994 |
| Docherty, Paul | Coll 1992 |
| Doering, Jordon | Ess 1997 |
| Donald, Darryl | Gee 1991 |
| Donati, Daniel | Rich 1996 |
| Donato, David | Fitz 1990 |
| Donnellan, Byron | Gee 1990 |
| Donnelly, Andrew | Syd 1992 |
| Donnelly, Andrew | WC 1996 |
| Doolan, Ben | Ess 1993 |
| Dooley, Paul | W Bull 1996 |

| Player | Club, drafted |
|---|---|
| Dowling, Brad | Gee 1990 |
| Downsborough, Ian | WC 1990 |
| Downsborough, Ian | WC 1994 |
| Downsborough, Ian | Pt Ad 1996 |
| Downsborough, Ian | Adel 1997 |
| Doyle, Greg | Melb 1992 |
| Doyle, Peter | Carl 1989 |
| Doyle, Peter | Fitz 1994 |
| Ducker, Mark | Melb 1987 |
| Duffy, Ross | Coll 1991 |
| Dullard, Jason | Ess 1989 |
| Dullard, Jason | Melb 1991 |
| Duncan, Brendan | Ess 1993 |
| Dundas, Matthew | Fitz 1988 |
| Dundas, Matthew | Rich 1993 |
| Dunkley, Andrew | Syd 1991 |
| Dunstan, Michael | Fitz 1992 |
| Dunstan, Michael | WC 1994 |
| Duthy, Chris | Fitz 1986 |
| Duursma, Jamie | Melb 1990 |
| Dwyer, Mick | Fitz 1995 |
| Dyer, Jeremy | WC 1994 |
| Dyson, Kevin | Melb 1991 |
| Dyson, Kevin | Syd 1996 |
| Dyson-Holland, Sasha | Fitz 1989 |
| Eagleton, Nathan | Pt Ad 1996 |
| Eastaugh, Simon | Rich 1989 |
| Eastaugh, Simon | Ess 1997 |
| Eccles, Andrew | Adel 1996 |
| Edgar, Stephen | Carl 1989 |
| Edgar, Stephen | St K 1992 |
| Edmonds, Travis | Haw 1991 |
| Edmonds, Travis | WC 1993 |
| Edmonds, Travis | Fre 1994 |
| Edwards, Ben | Fre 1995 |
| Edwards, Brad | Fitz 1988 |
| Edwards, Brad | B Bears 1990 |
| Edwards, Brad | WC 1991 |
| Edwards, Tyson | Adel 1995 |
| Egan, Phil | Melb 1990 |
| Eishold, Simon | Rich 1993 |
| Elias, Craig | Syd 1986 |
| Ellen, Shane | Foots 1991 |
| Ellen, Shane | Adel 1996 |
| Ellinghaus, Ben | Haw 1992 |
| Elliott, Jamie | Fitz 1989 |
| Elliott, Jamie | Rich 1994 |
| Elliott, Jamie | St K 1995 |
| Elliott, Jamie | St K 1998 |
| Elliott, Tim | St K 1994 |
| Ellis, Craig | NM 1990 |
| Ellis, Craig | Foots 1993 |
| Ellis, Shane | WC 1989 |
| Elshaug, Tony | St K 1989 |
| Enever, Darren | Gee 1991 |
| Eppelstun, Greg | NM 1993 |
| Esler, Ty | Rich 1988 |
| Evans, Anthony | Foots 1989 |
| Evans, Brett | Melb 1993 |
| Evans, Brett | Rich 1997 |
| Evans, Paul | Pt Ad 1996 |
| Evans, Russell | Ess 1991 |
| Evans, Russell | Foots 1993 |
| Evans, Tony | WC 1989 |
| Exell, Gavin | Fitz 1992 |
| Eyers, Kym | NM 1994 |
| Farmer, Jeff | Melb 1994 |
| Farrer, Simon | Fitz 1993 |
| Faull, Nick | Carl 1990 |
| Febey, Matthew | Melb 1986 |
| Febey, Matthew | Melb 1989 |
| Febey, Matthew | Melb 1992 |
| Febey, Steven | Melb 1986 |
| Feddema, Brendan | Fre 1995 |
| Fell, Shane | Syd 1989 |
| Fell, Shane | Rich 1991 |
| Fernee, Ashley | Adel 1995 |
| Fewster, Brendon | WC 1995 |
| Fidge, John | Syd 1989 |
| Fidge, John | Ess 1990 |
| Fiegert, Nigel | Pt Ad 1996 |
| Fielke, Grant | Coll 1986 |
| Filandia, Peter | Syd 1994 |
| Finocchiaro, Tim | Gee 1997 |
| Fitzpatrick, Lynton | Gee 1990 |

| Player | Club, drafted |
|---|---|
| McCartin, Matthew | Gee 1993 |
| McCartney, Jason | Coll 1990 |
| McCartney, Jason | Adel 1994 |
| McCartney, Jason | NM 1997 |
| McCarty, Simon | NM 1988 |
| McConville, Paul | Fitz 1989 |
| McCormack, Brendan | B Bears 1993 |
| McCormack, Paul | Carl 1992 |
| McCormick, Luke | NM 1996 |
| McCrabb, Austin | Haw 1992 |
| McCrabb, Austin | Haw 1993 |
| McDermott, Chris | B Bears 1987 |
| McDonald, Alex | Haw 1988 |
| McDonald, Alex | Coll 1995 |
| McDonald, Anthony | Carl 1990 |
| McDonald, Anthony | Carl 1991 |
| McDonald, Anthony | Haw 1992 |
| McDonald, Anthony | Melb 1996 |
| McDonald, Beau | B Lions 1997 |
| McDonald, Colin | B Bears 1996 |
| McDonald, James | Melb 1997 |
| McDonald, Scott | Foots 1991 |
| McEwan, David | Haw 1995 |
| McEwan, David | Syd 1996 |
| McFarlane, Grant | Coll 1990 |
| McFarlane, Sam | Fre 1994 |
| McFarlane, Sam | NM 1995 |
| McGovern, Andrew | Syd 1991 |
| McGrath, Craig | WC 1990 |
| McGrath, Justin | Haw 1988 |
| McGrath, Justin | Fitz 1991 |
| McGrath, Tim | Gee 1992 |
| McGregor, Anthony | Fitz 1993 |
| McGuane, Mick | Carl 1996 |
| McHardy, Todd | Melb 1994 |
| McInnes, Brian | Foots 1990 |
| McInnes, Brian | Foots 1992 |
| McInnes, Brian | Fitz 1996 |
| McIntosh, Ashley | WC 1989 |
| McKay, Andrew | Carl 1992 |
| McKay, Joel | Gee 1997 |
| McKay, John | Coll 1989 |
| McKay, Matthew | Melb 1991 |
| McKay, Matthew | Melb 1993 |
| McKay, Rodney | NM 1993 |
| McKee, Steven | Rich 1996 |
| McKellar, Allan | Foots 1991 |
| McKellar, Allan | Syd 1992 |
| McKenzie, Warren | Syd 1990 |
| McKinnon, Martin | Adel 1992 |
| McKinnon, Martin | Gee 1995 |
| McKinnon, Robin | Haw 1986 |
| McLaren, Joe | St K 1995 |
| McLean, Andrew | St K 1996 |
| McLean, Lachlan | Haw 1990 |
| McLean, Michael | B Bears 1991 |
| McLeod, Andrew | Adel 1994 |
| McLeod, Mark | Haw 1991 |
| McLure, James | Coll 1992 |
| McLure, James | Gee 1994 |
| McMahon, Paul | NM 1997 |
| McMahon, Robert | Fitz 1994 |
| McMahon, Robert | Haw 1996 |
| McManamon, Colum | Gee 1989 |
| McMaster, Paul | Ess 1992 |
| McMaster, Paul | Syd 1992 |
| McMullin, Ian | Ess 1990 |
| McMullin, Ian | Coll 1992 |
| McMurray, David | Ess 1991 |
| McMurray, Matthew | Gee 1992 |
| McNamara, John | NM 1988 |
| McNamara, John | Gee 1991 |
| McNamara, John | Ess 1992 |
| McNaughton, Craig | WC 1990 |
| McNaughton, Craig | WC 1991 |
| McNeil, Tim | Melb 1987 |
| McNicholl, Dermott | St K 1988 |
| McQueen, Mark | Rich 1990 |
| McQueen, Mark | Rich 1992 |
| McQueen, Mark | Rich 1995 |
| McQueen, Stephen | Gee 1992 |
| McRae, Craig | B Bears 1993 |
| McRae, Dean | Syd 1992 |
| McVay, Jeremy | St K 1992 |
| McWilliam, Paul | Ess 1989 |
| Mead, Fraser | Ess 1988 |
| Meade, Darren | B Bears 1993 |
| Meade, Darren | Pt Ad 1996 |
| Medew, Matthew | Ess 1991 |
| Meka, Perry | Foots 1986 |
| Melesso, Peter | WC 1988 |
| Melican, Chris | St K 1990 |
| Mellington, Anthony | Fitz 1995 |
| Mellington, Anthony | NM 1997 |
| Mellow, Damien | Syd 1992 |
| Menara, Adrian | Gee 1991 |
| Menegola, Todd | Rich 1990 |
| Menegola, Todd | Fre 1994 |
| Menhenut, Laurie | Syd 1986 |
| Merenda, Mark | Rich 1993 |
| Merriman, Russell | Gee 1991 |
| Merritt, Garry | St K 1992 |
| Merritt, Gary | Melb 1990 |
| Metropolis, Daniel | WC 1991 |
| Michael, Clem | Fre 1997 |
| Michael, Malcolm | Coll 1997 |
| Mickan, Mark | B Bears 1986 |
| Mifka, Paul | B Bears 1990 |
| Mifsud, Jason | St K 1993 |
| Milburn, Darren | Gee 1995 |
| Mildenhall, Neil | Fre 1994 |
| Miles, Dion | NM 1997 |
| Miles, Geoff | Gee 1991 |
| Miller, Dan | NM 1990 |
| Miller, Peter | Fre 1994 |
| Miller, Travis | Fitz 1992 |
| Mills, Andrew | Ess 1990 |
| Mills, Trent | B Bears 1992 |
| Minton-Connell, Simon | Carl 1986 |
| Minton-Connell, Simon | Syd 1991 |
| Minton-Connell, Simon | Haw 1994 |
| Minton-Connell, Simon | W Bull 1996 |
| Mitchell, Barry | Coll 1993 |
| Mitchell, Barry | Carl 1993 |
| Mitchell, Gavin | Fre 1995 |
| Mitchell, Gavin | St K 1997 |
| Mitchell, Kevin | Ess 1991 |
| Mitchell, Nick | Fitz 1993 |
| Mollard, Scott | Ess 1993 |
| Molloy, Glenn | Melb 1992 |
| Molloy, Jarrod | Fitz 1993 |
| Molloy, Jarrod | B Lions 1996 |
| Moloney, Julian | Rich 1988 |
| Moloney, Stephen | Haw 1990 |
| Montgomery, Brett | W Bull 1996 |
| Moon, Matthew | NM 1992 |
| Mooney, Cameron | NM 1996 |
| Moorcroft, Gary | Ess 1994 |
| Moorcroft, Gary | Ess 1997 |
| Moore, Ben | Rich 1995 |
| Moreland, Tim | Melb 1989 |
| Morgan, Danny | Carl 1990 |
| Morgan, Danny | Ess 1993 |
| Morgan, Danny | Ess 1994 |
| Morgan, Darren | Syd 1990 |
| Morgan, Darren | Foots 1991 |
| Morley, Luan | Haw 1990 |
| Morphett, Kane | WC 1991 |
| Morris, Russell | St K 1990 |
| Morrish, Paul | Ess 1990 |
| Morrish, Paul | Fitz 1991 |
| Morrison, Chad | WC 1995 |
| Morrison, David | Melb 1990 |
| Morrison, David | Fitz 1991 |
| Morrison, Scott | St K 1991 |
| Morrison, Scott | St K 1992 |
| Morrissey, Wayne | NM 1986 |
| Morton, Danny | Fitz 1992 |
| Morton, Danny | Pt Ad 1997 |
| Morton, Jason | Coll 1990 |
| Mourish, Nathan | Fre 1994 |
| Moylan, Matthew | Foots 1990 |
| Mrakov, John | Rich 1991 |
| Muir, David | WC 1992 |
| Muir, David | Fre 1994 |
| Muir, David | NM 1994 |
| Mulcair, Chris | Carl 1988 |
| Mullarvey, Paul | Fitz 1993 |
| Munt, Damon | Melb 1992 |
| Murphy, Fraser | Coll 1991 |
| Murphy, Justin | Rich 1993 |
| Murphy, Justin | Carl 1995 |
| Murphy, Michael | NM 1987 |
| Murphy, Michael | B Bears 1992 |
| Murphy, Michael | B Bears 1994 |
| Murray, Damian | NM 1989 |
| Murrihy, Kieran | Ess 1992 |
| Myles, Dion | Syd 1993 |
| Naish, Chris | Rich 1988 |
| Naish, Chris | Pt Ad 1997 |
| Naley, Mark | Foots 1991 |
| Napoli, Ross | Coll 1992 |
| Narkle, Phil | WC 1990 |
| Nash, Allen | Adel 1994 |
| Neeld, Mark | Rich 1993 |
| Neill, Robert | Syd 1990 |
| Neill, Robert | St K 1994 |
| Nelson, Ben | Carl 1996 |
| Nettelbeck, Craig | Fre 1994 |
| Nettelbeck, Craig | Melb 1996 |
| Newlan, Darren | Carl 1986 |
| Newport, Stephen | St K 1990 |
| Newport, Stephen | St K 1992 |
| Newton, Leigh | Melb 1997 |
| Nichol, Andrew | Foots 1995 |
| Nicholls, Brad | Gee 1991 |
| Nicholls, Kym | Gee 1988 |
| Nichols, Trent | Rich 1986 |
| Nichols, Trent | WC 1991 |
| Nichols, Trent | NM 1994 |
| Nichols, Trent | Rich 1996 |
| Nicholson, Alistair | Melb 1996 |
| Nicholson, Brad | Foots 1993 |
| Nicholson, David | Carl 1994 |
| Nicks, Matthew | Syd 1994 |
| Nienann, David | St K 1993 |
| Nixon, Ricky | Haw 1992 |
| Noble, David | Fitz 1989 |
| Noonan, Danny | B Bears 1990 |
| Norman, Luke | Melb 1994 |
| Normington, Dallas | Coll 1990 |
| Normington, Dallas | Fitz 1993 |
| Norrish, Jason | Melb 1991 |
| Norrish, Jason | Fre 1995 |
| Notting, Tim | B Lions 1996 |
| Nugent, Glenn | St K 1994 |
| Nunn, Peter | Haw 1987 |
| O'Bree, Shane | B Lions 1997 |
| O'Brien, Craig | St K 1991 |
| O'Brien, Craig | Syd 1995 |
| O'Brien, Cristian | Melb 1992 |
| O'Brien, Cristian | Gee 1993 |
| O'Brien, Darren | Melb 1995 |
| O'Brien, Kane | Coll 1990 |
| O'Connell, David | Fitz 1990 |
| O'Connor, Ryan | Ess 1991 |
| O'Donnell, Kevin | Haw 1992 |
| O'Donoghue, Mark | Syd 1988 |
| O'Donohue, Scott | Coll 1990 |
| O'Dwyer, Chris | Carl 1993 |
| O'Dwyer, Kieran | Haw 1991 |
| O'Dwyer, Steven | Rich 1991 |
| O'Farrell, Brett | Syd 1996 |
| O'Keefe, Cale | Carl 1991 |
| O'Keefe, Mark | Gee 1986 |
| O'Loughlin, Michael | Syd 1994 |
| O'Reilly, Stephen | Gee 1991 |
| O'Reilly, Stephen | Fre 1995 |
| O'Sullivan, Chris | B Bears 1988 |
| O'Toole, Duncan | Melb 1996 |
| Obst, Andrew | Melb 1987 |
| Obst, Chris | Haw 1997 |
| Ogg, David | B Bears 1990 |
| Ogg, David | WC 1992 |
| Ogier, Darren | Syd 1989 |
| Oliver, Stephen | Carl 1987 |
| Olsen, Troy | Coll 1992 |
| Orchard, Mark | Coll 1994 |
| Orchard, Mark | Syd 1996 |
| Ormond-Allen, Trent | Melb 1993 |
| Ormond-Allen, Trent | Adel 1996 |
| Osborn, Andrew | Gee 1992 |
| Osborn, Andrew | Pt Ad 1996 |
| Osborne, Richard | Syd 1993 |
| Osborne, Richard | Foots 1993 |
| Osborne, Richard | Coll 1996 |
| Ottens, Brad | Rich 1997 |
| Ottens, Luke | Melb 1997 |
| Owen, Rod | Melb 1990 |
| Owen, Rod | B Bears 1991 |
| Page, Glen | NM 1992 |
| Page, Paul | St K 1986 |
| Palfreyman, Nigel | B Bears 1990 |
| Palfreyman, Nigel | Fitz 1993 |
| Palmer, Anthony | NM 1991 |
| Palmer, Chris | Haw 1993 |
| Palmer, Simon | Haw 1991 |
| Panozza, Robert | Melb 1990 |
| Parker, Ben | Adel 1996 |
| Parker, Brendan | Carl 1991 |
| Parker, Daniel | Fre 1995 |
| Parker, John | B Bears 1992 |
| Parker, Shane | Fre 1994 |
| Parsons, Michael | Syd 1987 |
| Parthenides, Emil | Syd 1994 |
| Pascoe, Andrew | Coll 1987 |
| Pascoe, Justin | St K 1991 |
| Pascoe, Kristian | St K 1993 |
| Patrick, Craig | NM 1987 |
| Patterson, Stephen | Coll 1993 |
| Paul, Justin | Rich 1990 |
| Pavey, Anthony | NM 1990 |
| Paxman, Stephen | Pt Ad 1997 |
| Payne, Paul | Carl 1989 |
| Paynter, Anthony | Haw 1991 |
| Paynter, Tony | B Bears 1989 |
| Payze, Andrew | Ess 1986 |
| Payze, Andrew | Rich 1990 |
| Pearce, Brad | B Bears 1992 |
| Pearce, Brad | Carl 1994 |
| Pearce, Damien | St K 1991 |
| Pearce, Stephen | Rich 1989 |
| Pears, Stephen | NM 1990 |
| Pears, Stephen | Syd 1992 |
| Peck, Andrew | Syd 1991 |
| Peck, Andrew | Syd 1992 |
| Peck, Richard | Ess 1996 |
| Peckett, Justin | St K 1992 |
| Pedler, Simon | Adel 1993 |
| Peel, Chris | Carl 1992 |
| Pekin, Tim | St K 1990 |
| Penny, Matthew | Carl 1993 |
| Peos, Paul | B Bears 1992 |
| Peos, Paul | WC 1995 |
| Percival, Derek | Coll 1991 |
| Percival, Derek | Coll 1993 |
| Perkins, Tim | NM 1992 |
| Perkins, Tim | Adel 1993 |
| Perrie, Ian | Adel 1997 |

## THE DRAFT

### Club by club

| Player | Club, drafted |
|---|---|
| Pert, Gary | Coll 1991 |
| Pesch, Nick | Adel 1993 |
| Pesch, Nick | Melb 1996 |
| Peter-Budge, John | Rich 1990 |
| Peters, Wayne | Rich 1987 |
| Peters, Wayne | Fitz 1991 |
| Phillipou, Sam | Foots 1992 |
| Phillips, Garry | Gee 1989 |
| Phillips, Garry | Gee 1992 |
| Phyland, Michael | Syd 1989 |
| Picioane, Lance | Adel 1997 |
| Picken, Marcus | B Lions 1997 |
| Pickering, Justin | Foots 1991 |
| Pickering, Liam | NM 1987 |
| Pickering, Liam | Gee 1992 |
| Pickering, Michael | Melb 1991 |
| Pickett, Byron | NM 1996 |
| Pike, Martin | Melb 1992 |
| Pike, Martin | Fitz 1994 |
| Pike, Martin | NM 1996 |
| Pitt, Steven | Coll 1995 |
| Pitt, Steven | W Bull 1997 |
| Pittman, David | Ess 1989 |
| Pitura, Mark | Coll 1996 |
| Plain, Brad | Coll 1993 |
| Plain, Bradley | NM 1995 |
| Plapp, Justin | Rich 1997 |
| Plim, Tony | Carl 1992 |
| Plunkett, Jim | W Bull 1996 |
| Polak, Troy | NM 1993 |
| Polak, Troy | Fre 1994 |
| Polkinghorne, John | Haw 1987 |
| Polley, Michael | Melb 1994 |
| Poole, Darryl | Pt Ad 1996 |
| Poole, Trevor | Gee 1989 |
| Porter, Mark | Carl 1997 |
| Porter, Shane | WC 1990 |
| Potter, Craig | B Bears 1990 |
| Povey, Grant | Carl 1988 |
| Powell, Matthew | Adel 1992 |
| Powell, Robert | Coll 1994 |
| Powell, Robert | Rich 1995 |
| Powell, Stephen | W Bull 1996 |
| Powell, Tim | Carl 1992 |
| Power, Gerrad | Gee 1992 |
| Power, Luke | B Lions 1997 |
| Prentice, Michael | Melb 1993 |
| Prestigiacomo, Simon | Coll 1995 |
| Preston, David | Gee 1988 |
| Preston, David | Foots 1991 |
| Primus, Matthew | Fitz 1995 |
| Primus, Matthew | Pt Ad 1996 |
| Prior, Michael | Ess 1992 |
| Pritchard, Darrin | Haw 1986 |
| Probert, Nick | Coll 1988 |
| Probert, Nick | Coll 1992 |
| Proctor, Lionel | Rich 1997 |
| Prymke, Paul | Melb 1993 |
| Pugsley, Andrew | Coll 1997 |
| Purcell, Kane | Coll 1991 |
| Pyke, Don | WC 1988 |
| Pyke, James | Foots 1986 |
| Pyke, James | Coll 1988 |
| Pyman, Robert | NM 1992 |
| Pyman, Robert | Coll 1995 |
| Pyman, Robert | Melb 1997 |
| Queen, Matthew | Haw 1986 |
| Queen, Matthew | Foots 1988 |
| Querzoli, David | Syd 1987 |
| Quill, Peter | Foots 1992 |
| Quirk, Michael | St K 1987 |
| Radbone, Shane | Ess 1989 |
| Rahilly, James | Gee 1997 |
| Raidis, Michael | Rich 1995 |
| Rainsford, Ken | NM 1990 |
| Ralph, Scott | B Lions 1997 |
| Ralphsmith, Sean | St K 1990 |
| Ramsey, Jason | Fitz 1995 |
| Ramsey, Jason | Rich 1997 |
| Rapacholi, Dennis | Foots 1989 |
| Raso, Frank | Coll 1997 |
| Rawlings, Jade | Haw 1994 |
| Rayner, Luke | Carl 1992 |
| Read, Brad | Haw 1990 |

| Player | Club, drafted |
|---|---|
| Read, Brad | Rich 1993 |
| Read, Darren | NM 1987 |
| Read, Darren | Carl 1990 |
| Read, Phillip | WC 1997 |
| Reeves, Glen | B Bears 1989 |
| Regan, David | Ess 1988 |
| Regan, David | WC 1991 |
| Reid, Peter | Ess 1986 |
| Reid, Troy | Haw 1988 |
| Reimers, Hugh | St K 1992 |
| Reimers, Hugh | Foots 1995 |
| Rendell, Matthew | B Bears 1991 |
| Retzlaff, Brendon | Coll 1990 |
| Retzlaff, Brendon | B Bears 1991 |
| Retzlaff, Brendon | WC 1993 |
| Reynolds, Anthony | Foots 1988 |
| Reynolds, Keenan | Foots 1990 |
| Reynolds, Keenan | NM 1995 |
| Rhodes, Jacob | W Bull 1996 |
| Rhook, Dion | Haw 1988 |
| Rice, Dean | Carl 1994 |
| Richardson, Matt | WC 1988 |
| Richardson, Matt | Rich 1989 |
| Richardson, Matthew | Rich 1992 |
| Rickman, Ian | Foots 1990 |
| Ridley, Paul | Coll 1992 |
| Ridley, Paul | Melb 1993 |
| Ridley, Todd | Ess 1990 |
| Ridley, Todd | Fre 1995 |
| Ridley, Todd | Haw 1997 |
| Rieniets, Tim | Carl 1990 |
| Rigoni, Guy | Haw 1993 |
| Rigoni, Guy | Melb 1997 |
| Riley, Stephen | Ess 1986 |
| Rintoul, Chad | Adel 1996 |
| Rioli, Willie | Haw 1990 |
| Robbins, Ben | WC 1993 |
| Robbins, Ben | B Bears 1995 |
| Robbins, Matthew | Gee 1994 |
| Robbins, Matthew | W Bull 1997 |
| Roberts, Cameron | Gee 1996 |
| Roberts, Mark | NM 1990 |
| Robertson, Ben | Carl 1990 |
| Robertson, Ben | Carl 1991 |
| Robertson, Corey | Gee 1992 |
| Robertson, David | Coll 1986 |
| Robertson, David | Ess 1990 |
| Robertson, Josh | NM 1997 |
| Robertson, Russell | Melb 1996 |
| Robertson, Russell | Melb 1997 |
| Robins, Haydn | Rich 1994 |
| Robinson, Mark | Fitz 1989 |
| Robinson, Scott | Syd 1992 |
| Robinson, Trevor | Carl 1991 |
| Robran, Jonathan | Haw 1992 |
| Robran, Matthew | Haw 1989 |
| Robran, Matthew | Adel 1992 |
| Rocca, Anthony | Coll 1996 |
| Rocca, Anthony | Syd 1994 |
| Rogers, Andrew | Ess 1987 |
| Rogers, Andrew | Gee 1989 |
| Rogers, Matthew | Rich 1992 |
| Rombotis, John | Fitz 1994 |
| Rombotis, John | Pt Ad 1996 |
| Rombotis, John | Rich 1997 |
| Romero, Jose | Foots 1995 |
| Roney, Nick | Rich 1991 |
| Roos, Paul | Syd 1995 |
| Rose, Brett | Syd 1997 |
| Rose, Gavin | Coll 1989 |
| Rose, Gavin | Syd 1991 |
| Ross, David | Foots 1991 |
| Ross, Jonathan | Coll 1996 |
| Ross, Lachlan | Ess 1993 |
| Round, David | Foots 1995 |
| Rouvray, Paul | Melb 1989 |
| Rouvray, Paul | Syd 1995 |
| Rowe, Brad | B Bears 1989 |
| Rowe, Brad | Coll 1991 |
| Rowe, Brad | Fre 1995 |
| Rowe, Brett | Fitz 1993 |
| Rowston, Phillip | Syd 1993 |
| Rudd, Adam | St K 1990 |
| Rundle, Jamie | Foots 1991 |

| Player | Club, drafted |
|---|---|
| Russell, Kym | Coll 1989 |
| Russell, Scott | Coll 1988 |
| Russo, Peter | St K 1988 |
| Ryan, Chris | Coll 1990 |
| Ryan, Damian | Foots 1991 |
| Ryan, Damian | Foots 1992 |
| Ryan, Damian | B Bears 1993 |
| Ryan, Damien | Rich 1994 |
| Ryan, David | B Bears 1991 |
| Ryan, Dennis | Gee 1990 |
| Ryan, Matthew | Syd 1989 |
| Ryan, Matthew | B Bears 1991 |
| Ryan, Michael | Haw 1991 |
| Ryan, Stephen | Coll 1994 |
| Saddington, Jason | Syd 1997 |
| Salisbury, Scott | Syd 1987 |
| Salmon, Paul | Haw 1995 |
| Sampson, Clay | Melb 1994 |
| Sampson, Clay | Adel 1996 |
| Sanderson, Brenton | Coll 1993 |
| Sanderson, Brenton | Gee 1994 |
| Sangster, Will | Syd 1996 |
| Sartori, Peter | Fitz 1991 |
| Satterley, Paul | Foots 1992 |
| Saunders, Joel | Fitz 1989 |
| Saunders, Nathan | Haw 1994 |
| Saunders, Rod | Ess 1988 |
| Saunders, Rod | Ess 1991 |
| Savickas, Darren | Gee 1989 |
| Saywell, James | Fitz 1993 |
| Scarlett, Matthew | Gee 1997 |
| Schache, Laurie | B Bears 1990 |
| Schaefer, Robert | Rich 1992 |
| Schaefer, Robert | Coll 1997 |
| Schauble, Andrew | Coll 1993 |
| Schofield, Jarrad | WC 1992 |
| Schwartz, Alan | Ess 1989 |
| Schwartz, Alan | Ess 1992 |
| Schwartz, Alan | Adel 1992 |
| Schwass, Wayne | Syd 1997 |
| Schwerdt, Steven | WC 1989 |
| Scoon, Michael | NM 1990 |
| Scoon, Michael | NM 1992 |
| Scott, Allister | Rich 1989 |
| Scott, Brad | Haw 1996 |
| Scott, Brad | B Lions 1997 |
| Scott, Bradley | Haw 1994 |
| Scott, Brett | Syd 1989 |
| Scott, Chris | B Bears 1993 |
| Scott, Dion | Syd 1988 |
| Scott, Dion | B Bears 1992 |
| Scott, Michael | Melb 1989 |
| Scott, Robert | NM 1994 |
| Scott, Tim | Syd 1994 |
| Scott-Branagan, Tim | Coll 1992 |
| Sebo, Nick | Melb 1991 |
| Seecamp, Marcus | Fitz 1991 |

| Player | Club, drafted |
|---|---|
| Seecamp, Marcus | Melb 1994 |
| Seow, Dannie | Melb 1989 |
| Sexton, Ben | Foots 1988 |
| Sexton, Ben | Carl 1995 |
| Sexton, Damian | St K 1990 |
| Sexton, Danny | NM 1990 |
| Sexton, Danny | Fitz 1992 |
| Sexton, Matthew | Rich 1986 |
| Sexton, Matthew | Melb 1990 |
| Sexton, Michael | Carl 1988 |
| Seymour, Brad | Syd 1993 |
| Shanahan, Adam | Gee 1992 |
| Shanahan, Jamie | St K 1990 |
| Shanahan, Jamie | Melb 1998 |
| Shanks, Julian | Foots 1992 |
| Sharkey, Paul | Coll 1990 |
| Sharkey, Paul | Haw 1997 |
| Sharp, Chris | Haw 1989 |
| Shaw, Clinton | St K 1993 |
| Sheehan, Damien | Carl 1993 |
| Sheehan, Dion | Haw 1989 |
| Shephard, Heath | Coll 1988 |
| Shephard, Heath | B Bears 1991 |
| Sheridan, Adam | Fitz 1993 |
| Sherman, Tim | B Bears 1992 |
| Sherrif, Brett | Haw 1989 |
| Sherriff, Brett | B Bears 1992 |
| Shields, Jason | Foots 1989 |
| Shields, Michael | St K 1991 |
| Shinners, Matthew | Haw 1989 |
| Shippen, Malcolm | NM 1986 |
| Sholl, Brad | NM 1988 |
| Sholl, Brad | NM 1991 |
| Sholl, Brad | Gee 1994 |
| Sholl, Brett | Carl 1991 |
| Sierakowski, David | St K 1992 |
| Sikora, Shane | WC 1994 |
| Silcock, Jeremy | NM 1992 |
| Silvestro, Jim | Syd 1987 |
| Sim, Lachlan | B Bears 1988 |
| Simister, Scott | Melb 1992 |
| Simmonds, Damian | Fitz 1988 |
| Simpson, Adam | NM 1993 |
| Simpson, Hamish | Gee 1996 |
| Simpson, Sean | Gee 1991 |
| Sims, Steven | St K 1986 |
| Sinclair, Jess | Fre 1996 |
| Singline, Leigh | Coll 1996 |
| Sir, Sedat | Foots 1993 |
| Slater, Adam | Rich 1994 |
| Slater, Shaun | Rich 1989 |
| Smart, Doug | Carl 1986 |
| Smart, Doug | B Bears 1989 |
| Smart, Sam | Adel 1992 |
| Smart, Sam | Carl 1996 |
| Smillie, Bevan | Carl 1991 |
| Smit, Paul | Syd 1990 |
| Smith, Brad | Rich 1995 |
| Smith, Brad | Coll 1997 |
| Smith, Chris | Rich 1990 |
| Smith, Darren | Ess 1989 |
| Smith, Dean | Gee 1991 |
| Smith, Jason | Rich 1989 |
| Smith, Jeremy | Carl 1989 |
| Smith, Jeremy | Carl 1992 |
| Smith, Joel | St K 1994 |
| Smith, Joel | Haw 1998 |
| Smith, Michael | Coll 1988 |
| Smith, Phillip | Haw 1996 |
| Smith, Roger | B Bears 1990 |
| Smith, Rohan | Syd 1989 |
| Smith, Rohan | St K 1990 |
| Smith, Ryan | Fre 1994 |
| Smith, Shaun | Melb 1995 |
| Smith, Shayne | Syd 1993 |
| Smoker, Craig | WC 1995 |
| Smoker, Craig | Melb 1997 |
| Snell, Jason | Gee 1995 |
| Snooks, Leigh | Carl 1991 |
| Solomon, Dean | Ess 1997 |
| Solomon, Jonathon | B Bears 1989 |
| Somerville, Craig | B Bears 1988 |
| Southern, Daniel | Foots 1992 |
| Spalding, Earl | Carl 1991 |

| Player | Club, drafted |
|---|---|
| Spalding, Scott | Carl 1992 |
| Spargo, Paul | B Bears 1992 |
| Sparks, Brad | Syd 1990 |
| Spencer, Trevor | Melb 1989 |
| Spencer, Trevor | Gee 1991 |
| Spierings, Barry | Foots 1990 |
| Spinks, Brett | WC 1992 |
| Spinks, Brett | Gee 1997 |
| Spinks, Jason | Syd 1992 |
| Spinks, Jason | WC 1994 |
| Spinks, Jason | WC 1995 |
| Sporn, Kieran | Ess 1986 |
| Sporn, Kieran | Fitz 1993 |
| Squire, Damian | Pt Ad 1996 |
| St Clair, Travis | Ess 1989 |
| St Clair, Travis | Haw 1992 |
| Standfield, Barry | Adel 1996 |
| Stanislaus, Brian | Syd 1990 |
| Stanislaus, Brian | B Bears 1992 |
| Starbuck, Paul | Syd 1989 |
| Starcevich, Craig | B Bears 1993 |
| Staritski, Justin | NM 1988 |
| Staritski, Justin | Coll 1994 |
| Steele, Darren | Gee 1992 |
| Steele, Stuart | Rich 1993 |
| Steinberner, Nathan | Pt Ad 1996 |
| Steinfort, Carl | Gee 1994 |
| Steinfort, Pat | Rich 1996 |
| Stephens, Brad | NM 1997 |
| Sterrett, Ray | Gee 1988 |
| Stevens, Anthony | NM 1988 |
| Stevens, Danny | NM 1994 |
| Stevens, Gary | Syd 1989 |
| Stevens, John | Syd 1997 |
| Stevens, Linden | Adel 1997 |
| Stevens, Mark | NM 1993 |
| Stevens, Mark | Adel 1997 |
| Stevens, Nick | Pt Ad 1997 |
| Stevenson, Robert | Ess 1993 |
| Stevenson, Robert | W Bull 1997 |
| Stevenson, Shayne | Fitz 1989 |
| Stevenson, Shayne | Haw 1992 |
| Stewart, Hamish | Haw 1992 |
| Stockdale, Mark | Syd 1991 |
| Stone, Nicholas | WC 1996 |
| Stoney, Damian | Haw 1990 |
| Strauch, Dean | B Bears 1990 |
| Strauch, Dean | Coll 1991 |
| Strempel, Shane | B Bears 1990 |
| Strempel, Shane | Ess 1991 |
| Stretch, Steven | Fitz 1994 |
| Strickland, Michael | Ess 1988 |
| Strickland, Michael | Ess 1991 |
| Strooper, David | Syd 1991 |
| Strooper, David | St K 1994 |
| Styles, Michael | Coll 1989 |
| Stynes, Brian | Melb 1988 |
| Sullivan, Chris | Rich 1994 |
| Sullivan, David | Rich 1990 |
| Sumich, Peter | WC 1988 |
| Symes, Tim | Syd 1990 |
| Symmons, Paul | WC 1992 |
| Symonds, Tony | Haw 1986 |
| Symons, Michael | Ess 1991 |
| Sziller, Steven | St K 1994 |
| Talbot, Dean | Gee 1995 |
| Tallis, Rayden | Haw 1993 |
| Tanner, Grant | Gee 1993 |
| Tanner, Wayne | Coll 1986 |
| Tape, Jamie | Rich 1992 |
| Tape, Jamie | Coll 1997 |
| Tarczon, Darren | NM 1990 |
| Tarczon, Darren | Carl 1991 |
| Tarczon, Darren | NM 1993 |
| Tarpey, Andrew | Rich 1992 |
| Tarrant, Chris | Coll 1997 |
| Taylor, Jason | Fitz 1986 |
| Taylor, Jason | Haw 1991 |
| Taylor, Jason | Coll 1997 |
| Taylor, Michael | Gee 1986 |
| Taylor, Richard | Haw 1991 |
| Taylor, Richard | Haw 1995 |
| Taylor, Scott | Foots 1994 |
| Taylor, Scott | W Bull 1998 |

| Player | Club, drafted |
|---|---|
| Taylor, Simon | Fitz 1992 |
| Taylor, Tim | Carl 1989 |
| Teal, Robert | Syd 1989 |
| Templeton, Michael | B Bears 1986 |
| Thiessen, James | Rich 1993 |
| Thiessen, James | Adel 1997 |
| Thomas, Ben | B Bears 1990 |
| Thomlinson, Glen | Gee 1990 |
| Thompson, Andrew | St K 1996 |
| Thompson, Ashley | Syd 1993 |
| Thompson, Ben | Carl 1997 |
| Thompson, Ben | St K 1997 |
| Thompson, Donald | Syd 1986 |
| Thompson, Ewan | Rich 1995 |
| Thompson, Nathan | Haw 1997 |
| Thompson, Scott | Coll 1992 |
| Thomson, Michael | Ess 1990 |
| Thomson, Scott | WC 1994 |
| Thornborrow, Wayne | St K 1993 |
| Thornborrow, Wayne | Rich 1995 |
| Thorpe, Alan | Fitz 1991 |
| Thorpe, Alan | Syd 1992 |
| Thorpe, Alan | Foots 1993 |
| Thorpe, Alan | Carl 1995 |
| Tingay, Stephen | Melb 1987 |
| Tohill, Anthony | Melb 1989 |
| Toia, Luke | Fre 1994 |
| Tomlinson, Scott | Syd 1989 |
| Tongerie, Shane | Adel 1994 |
| Tonkins, James | Melb 1989 |
| Toohey, Bernard | Foots 1991 |
| Torney, Jason | Rich 1994 |
| Traianidis, Jason | St K 1996 |
| Tramontana, Daniel | Coll 1990 |
| Tranquilli, Andrew | Coll 1993 |
| Tranter, Brendan | Coll 1987 |
| Trask, Nicholas | B Bears 1995 |
| Tredrea, Warren | Pt Ad 1996 |
| Tregenza, Simon | Foots 1987 |
| Treleven, Craig | St K 1992 |
| Treleven, Craig | Haw 1996 |
| Tresize, Damian | Syd 1990 |
| Trew, Luke | WC 1995 |
| Trew, Luke | W Bull 1996 |
| Trewella, Mark | Rich 1991 |
| Trezise, Damien | Haw 1987 |
| Trigg, Tony | Foots 1989 |
| Tsiotanis, Nick | Ess 1989 |
| Tsiotinas, Nick | Foots 1990 |
| Tuckey, Brent | Coll 1996 |
| Tuddenham, Paul | Carl 1992 |
| Tudor, Leigh | NM 1989 |
| Tudor, Leigh | NM 1992 |
| Tudor, Leigh | Gee 1992 |
| Tunbridge, Brad | Syd 1989 |
| Turley, Craig | WC 1988 |
| Turley, Craig | Melb 1995 |
| Turnbull, Ryan | WC 1989 |
| Turner, Greg | Coll 1991 |
| Turner, Peter | Carl 1994 |
| Turner, Scott | Rich 1990 |
| Turvey, Nathan | Haw 1996 |
| Ugrinic, Adam | Adel 1995 |
| Ugrinic, David | Gee 1993 |
| Ukovic, Andrew | Ess 1989 |
| Umbers, Richard | B Bears 1990 |
| Underwood, Andrew | Ess 1986 |
| Underwood, Andrew | Rich 1991 |
| Valenta, Sean | B Bears 1989 |
| Van Der Meer, Peter | Melb 1990 |
| Vandenberg, Richard | Haw 1997 |
| Vardy, Peter | Adel 1995 |
| Venner, Andrew | NM 1989 |
| Verbeek, Simon | Carl 1989 |
| Verbeek, Simon | Rich 1993 |
| Vidovic, Lazar | St K 1989 |
| Viney, Jay | Melb 1987 |
| Virgona, Tony | Syd 1987 |
| Vizy, Stephen | NM 1988 |
| Voss, Brett | B Bears 1995 |
| Wadewitz, Matthew | Ess 1992 |
| Waite, Julian | Coll 1992 |
| Waite, Julian | B Bears 1993 |
| Wakelin, Darryl | Adel 1993 |

| Player | Club, drafted |
|---|---|
| Wakelin, Darryl | St K 1994 |
| Wakelin, Shane | St K 1992 |
| Walker, Craig | Melb 1986 |
| Walker, James | Fre 1997 |
| Walker, Lee | WC 1992 |
| Walker, Lee | Coll 1994 |
| Walker, Robert | Haw 1993 |
| Walker, Stephen | Fitz 1988 |
| Walls, David | Carl 1995 |
| Walsgott, Jason | Ess 1989 |
| Walsh, Darren | Carl 1992 |
| Walton, Ben | St K 1997 |
| Wanganeen, Gavin | Ess 1989 |
| Wanganeen, Gavin | Pt Ad 1996 |
| Ward, Shayne | Foots 1989 |
| Warfe, Rowan | Fitz 1993 |
| Warfe, Rowan | Syd 1996 |
| Warrior, Eugene | Adel 1993 |
| Warry, Marty | Fitz 1994 |
| Warry, Marty | Coll 1996 |
| Wasley, James | Coll 1997 |
| Waterhouse, Clive | Fre 1995 |
| Waters, Matthew | B Lions 1996 |
| Waterson, Chris | Fitz 1987 |
| Waterworth, Chris | Rich 1989 |
| Watson, Matthew | Ess 1996 |
| Watson, Tim | WC 1992 |
| Watson, Tim | Ess 1993 |
| Watt, Shannon | NM 1997 |
| Watters, Scott | WC 1988 |
| Watters, Scott | Syd 1992 |
| Watters, Scott | Fre 1994 |
| Watts, Jason | Foots 1994 |
| Wearne, David | B Bears 1990 |
| Wearne, Stephen | Melb 1991 |
| Weeding, James | Haw 1990 |
| Wellman, Sean | Ess 1995 |
| Welsby, David | Gee 1988 |
| Welsh, Rohan | Ess 1990 |
| Welsh, Rohan | Carl 1992 |
| Welsh, Scott | NM 1995 |
| Werner, Michael | Ess 1988 |
| Werner, Michael | Syd 1992 |
| West, Jim | Syd 1988 |
| West, Jim | Adel 1992 |
| West, Mark | Foots 1995 |
| West, Robert | WC 1990 |
| West, Robert | Foots 1993 |
| Wheildon, Darren | Fitz 1987 |
| Wheildon, Darren | Ess 1995 |
| Whelan, Paul | Foots 1992 |
| Whiston, Scott | Coll 1997 |
| White, Adam | Carl 1994 |
| White, Darryl | B Bears 1990 |
| White, Jeff | Fre 1994 |
| White, Jeff | Melb 1997 |
| White, Mitchell | WC 1990 |

**THE DRAFT**

**Club by club**

| Player | Club, drafted |
|---|---|
| White, Nick | Melb 1991 |
| Whitehead, Adrian | Carl 1992 |
| Whitelaw, Martin | Fre 1995 |
| Whitelaw, Paul | WC 1995 |
| Whitnall, Lance | Carl 1996 |
| Whittlesea, Greg | Rich 1986 |
| Whittlesea, Greg | Haw 1990 |
| Whyte, Peter | B Bears 1990 |
| Wickham, Andrew | St K 1986 |
| Wigney, Stuart | Foots 1987 |
| Wigney, Stuart | Syd 1991 |
| Wigney, Stuart | Adel 1992 |
| Wigney, Stuart | Rich 1995 |
| Wild, Jason | Coll 1993 |
| Wilding, Russell | Haw 1988 |
| Wilkins, Glenn | Melb 1989 |
| Wilkinson, Darron | Fitz 1990 |
| Williams, Andrew | WC 1997 |
| Williams, Brent | Adel 1995 |
| Williams, Brent | Melb 1997 |
| Williams, Darren | Ess 1991 |
| Williams, David | Rich 1990 |
| Williams, Grant | Haw 1987 |
| Williams, Grant | Melb 1991 |
| Williams, Greg | Carl 1991 |
| Williams, Haami | Carl 1993 |
| Williams, Jason | Coll 1993 |
| Williams, Mark | Foots 1989 |
| Williams, Mark | WC 1990 |
| Williams, Paul | Coll 1989 |
| Williams, Paul | Carl 1991 |
| Williams, Russell | Ess 1992 |
| Williams, Stephen | B Bears 1986 |
| Williams, Tim | Ess 1996 |
| Williamson, Adam | B Bears 1992 |
| Williamson, Scott | WC 1988 |
| Williamson, Scott | Melb 1990 |
| Williamson, Tim | NM 1990 |
| Willison, Leigh | Gee 1991 |
| Wills, Andrew | Fre 1995 |
| Wilson, Ben | Coll 1994 |
| Wilson, Ben | Syd 1990 |
| Wilson, Brian | St K 1990 |
| Wilson, Joe | B Bears 1989 |
| Wilson, Michael | Pt Ad 1996 |
| Wilson, Peter | WC 1989 |
| Wilson, Tim | Coll 1987 |
| Winkel, Daniel | Ess 1992 |
| Winter, Peter | Fitz 1986 |
| Winterton, Mark | Melb 1996 |
| Winton, Brian | St K 1989 |
| Wira, Brad | Foots 1995 |
| Wirrpunda, David | WC 1996 |
| Wirth, Derek | B Bears 1995 |
| Wisken, Andrew | Rich 1987 |
| Wittey, David | B Bears 1989 |
| Wittey, David | Syd 1990 |
| Wittman, Chris | St K 1992 |
| Woewodin, Shane | Melb 1997 |
| Wolf, Clinton | Fre 1994 |
| Wood, Graeme | Fitz 1993 |
| Wood, Justin | Gee 1997 |
| Wood, Simon | NM 1990 |
| Wooden, Josh | WC 1996 |
| Woods, Tony | Coll 1991 |
| Woods, Tony | Haw 1995 |
| Woolnough, Marc | Gee 1997 |
| Wootton, Greg | St K 1993 |
| Worsfold, Peter | B Bears 1990 |
| Wren, Robert | Rich 1989 |
| Wrensted, Murray | Coll 1989 |
| Wright, Graham | Coll 1987 |
| Yerbury, Jonathon | Pt Ad 1996 |
| Young, Barry | Ess 1994 |
| Young, Corey | WC 1991 |
| Young, Craig | Haw 1991 |
| Young, Matthew | Haw 1990 |
| Young, Matthew | St K 1996 |
| Yze, Adem | Melb 1994 |
| Zamykal, Stephen | NM 1991 |
| Zanotti, Mark | B Bears 1988 |
| Zanotti, Mark | Fitz 1989 |
| Zavalas, Stephen | Coll 1994 |

# BROWNLOW MEDAL KEY POINTS

● The Charles Brownlow Medal was instituted in 1924 for the fairest and best player in the League's home-and-away competition. It perpetuates the memory of Charles Brownlow, the Geelong administrator who died aged 64 on January 23, 1924.

● The first medal was won by a Geelong player — Edward 'Carji' Greeves.

● From 1924-30, the field umpire awarded just one vote to the fairest and best player, hence the low tally of votes.

● In 1931, the system was changed whereby the umpire would award six votes per game — three to the best player, two to the second best and one to the third best. The only change to that system occurred in 1976 and 1977 when, under the two-umpire system, both umpires awarded a set of votes, resulting in the winners recording a high number of votes.

● A countback system was introduced in 1930 when Stan Judkins (Richmond), Harry Collier (Collingwood) and Allan Hopkins (Footscray) all polled four votes. Judkins was awarded the medal because he played fewer games that season.

● Under the subsequent countback system, the equal winners would be separated with the medal going to the player who polled the most three votes. If the three votes were the same, it would be counted back to the two votes and, if required, further back to the one votes. In 1940, Collingwood's Des Fothergill and South Melbourne's Herb Matthews both polled 32 votes and could not be separated after a countback. Each received a replica

of the medal and the original was held at League headquarters.

● At the end of the 1980 season, the countback system was scrapped and it was decided to award a medal to all players finishing on the same number of votes. The new rule was used the following season when South Melbourne's Barry Round and Fitzroy's Bernie Quinlan tied on 22 votes. Under the old system, Quinlan would have been the sole winner.

● Since the abolition of the countback, there have been dual medallists on four occasions — 1981, 1986, 1987 and 1996.

● In 1989, the League decided to recognise all players previously beaten on a countback and awarded retrospective medals to eight players, including Fothergill and Matthews who could not be separated in 1940. The others were: Harry Collier (Collingwood, 1930), Allan Hopkins (Footscray, 1930), Col Austen (Hawthorn, 1949), Bill Hutchison (Essendon, 1952), Verdun Howell (St Kilda, 1959), Noel Teasdale (North Melbourne, 1965).

● From 1924 until 1988 players who were reported in any match, found guilty and suspended could not win the award in that season. In 1979 it was ruled that a player reported and suspended during a finals match could remain eligible to win the Medal. In 1989 a player remained eligible to win the honor unless he was found guilty of a reportable offence, other than time-wasting, in a match in which Brownlow Medal votes were cast. Since 1996 a player fined or reprimanded after being found guilty of any offence has been deemed to be eligible for the award.

## BROWNLOW WINNERS LIST

| Year | Winner | Club | Votes | Age | No. | Position |
|------|--------|------|-------|-----|-----|----------|
| 1924 | E. 'Carji' Greeves | Geelong | 7 | 20 | 20 | Centre |
| 1925 | Colin Watson | St Kilda | 9 | 24 | 31 | Wing/Centre |
| 1926 | Ivor Warne Smith | Melbourne | 9 | 28 | 14 | Foll/Centre |
| 1927 | Syd Coventry | Collingwood | 7 | 28 | 7 | Foll/Defender |
| 1928 | Ivor Warne Smith | Melbourne | 8 | 30 | 14 | Foll/Centre |
| 1929 | Albert Collier | Collingwood | 6 | 20 | 5 | Centre half-back |
| 1930 | Stan Judkins | Richmond | 4 | 22 | 6 | Winger |
|      | Allan Hopkins | Footscray | 4 | 26 | 1 | Centre |
|      | Harry Collier | Collingwood | 4 | 22 | 7 | Rover |
| 1931 | Haydn Bunton | Fitzroy | 26 | 20 | 7 | Rover |
| 1932 | Haydn Bunton | Fitzroy | 23 | 21 | 7 | Rover |
| 1933 | W. 'Chicken' Smallhorn | Fitzroy | 18 | 22 | 21 | Winger |
| 1934 | Dick Reynolds | Essendon | 19 | 19 | 3 | Rover |
| 1935 | Haydn Bunton | Fitzroy | 24 | 24 | 7 | Rover |
| 1936 | Dinny Ryan | Fitzroy | 26 | 20 | 4 | Centre half-back |
| 1937 | Dick Reynolds | Essendon | 27 | 22 | 3 | Rover |
| 1938 | Dick Reynolds | Essendon | 18 | 23 | 3 | Rover |
| 1939 | Marcus Whelan | Collingwood | 23 | 25 | 28 | Centre |

# BROWNLOW WINNERS LIST

| Year | Winner | Club | Votes | Age | No. | Position |
|------|--------|------|-------|-----|-----|----------|
| 1940 | Des Fothergill | Collingwood | 32 | 20 | 6 | Rover |
| | Herbie Matthews | S. Melbourne | 32 | 26 | 1 | Centre |
| 1941 | Norman Ware | Footscray | 23 | 30 | 4 | Follower |

*Award suspended during W.W.2 — 1942-45*

| Year | Winner | Club | Votes | Age | No. | Position |
|------|--------|------|-------|-----|-----|----------|
| 1946 | D.P. (Don) Cordner | Melbourne | 20 | 24 | 21 | Follower |
| 1947 | Bert Deacon | Carlton | 20 | 24 | 23 | Centre half-back |
| 1948 | W. (Bill) Morris | Richmond | 24 | 26 | 5 | Follower |
| 1949 | Ron Clegg | S. Melbourne | 23 | 21 | 23 | Centre half-back |
| | Col Austen | Hawthorn | 23 | 28 | 9 | Half-back flank |
| 1950 | Allan Ruthven | Fitzroy | 21 | 28 | 7 | Rover |
| 1951 | Bernie Smith | Geelong | 23 | 23 | 11 | Back Pocket |
| 1952 | Roy Wright | Richmond | 21 | 23 | 2 | Follower |
| | Bill Hutchison | Essendon | 21 | 29 | 7 | Rover |
| 1953 | Bill Hutchison | Essendon | 26 | 30 | 7 | Rover |
| 1954 | Roy Wright | Richmond | 29 | 25 | 2 | Follower |
| 1955 | Fred Goldsmith | S. Melbourne | 21 | 23 | 2 | Full Back |
| 1956 | Peter Box | Footscray | 22 | 24 | 5 | Centre |
| 1957 | Brian Gleeson | St Kilda | 24 | 22 | 30 | Follower |
| 1958 | Neil Roberts | St Kilda | 20 | 25 | 10 | Centre half-back |
| 1959 | Bob Skilton | S. Melbourne | 20 | 20 | 14 | Rover |
| | Verdun Howell | St Kilda | 20 | 22 | 16 | Full Back |
| 1960 | John Schultz | Footscray | 20 | 21 | 14 | Follower |
| 1961 | John James | Carlton | 21 | 27 | 10 | Half-back flank |
| 1962 | Alistair Lord | Geelong | 28 | 22 | 4 | Centre |
| 1963 | Bob Skilton | S. Melbourne | 20 | 24 | 14 | Rover |
| 1964 | Gordon Collis | Carlton | 27 | 23 | 17 | Centre half-back |
| 1965 | Ian Stewart | St Kilda | 20 | 22 | 5 | Centre |
| | Noel Teasdale | N. Melbourne | 20 | 27 | 2 | Ruckman |
| 1966 | Ian Stewart | St Kilda | 21 | 23 | 5 | Centre |
| 1967 | Ross Smith | St Kilda | 24 | 24 | 3 | Rover |
| 1968 | Bob Skilton | S. Melbourne | 24 | 29 | 14 | Rover |
| 1969 | Kevin Murray | Fitzroy | 19 | 31 | 1 | Ruck-rover |
| 1970 | Peter Bedford | S. Melbourne | 25 | 22 | 11 | Rover/Centre |
| 1971 | Ian Stewart | Richmond | 21 | 28 | 2 | Centre |
| 1972 | Len Thompson | Collingwood | 25 | 25 | 3 | Ruckman |
| 1973 | Keith Greig | N. Melbourne | 27 | 21 | 27 | Winger |
| 1974 | Keith Greig | N. Melbourne | 27 | 22 | 27 | Winger |
| 1975 | Gary Dempsey | Footscray | 20 | 26 | 24 | Ruckman |
| 1976 | Graham Moss | Essendon | 48 | 26 | 25 | Ruckman |
| 1977 | Graham Teasdale | S. Melbourne | 59 | 22 | 20 | Ruckman |
| 1978 | Malcolm Blight | N. Melbourne | 22 | 28 | 15 | Ruck-rover |
| 1979 | Peter Moore | Collingwood | 22 | 22 | 30 | Ruckman |
| 1980 | Kelvin Templeton | Footscray | 23 | 23 | 31 | Centre half-forward |
| 1981 | Bernie Quinlan | Fitzroy | 22 | 30 | 5 | Ruck-rover |
| | Barry Round | S. Melbourne | 22 | 31 | 25 | Ruckman |
| 1982 | Brian Wilson | Melbourne | 23 | 20 | 7 | Centre |
| 1983 | Ross Glendinning | N. Melbourne | 24 | 27 | 4 | Centre half-back |
| 1984 | Peter Moore | Melbourne | 24 | 27 | 30 | Ruckman |
| 1985 | Brad Hardie | Footscray | 22 | 22 | 4 | Back Pocket |
| 1986 | Robert DiPierdomenico | Hawthorn | 17 | 28 | 9 | Winger |
| | Greg Williams | Sydney | 17 | 22 | 2 | Centre |
| 1987 | Tony Lockett | St Kilda | 20 | 21 | 14 | Full Forward |
| | John Platten | Hawthorn | 20 | 24 | 44 | Rover |
| 1988 | Gerard Healy | Sydney | 20 | 27 | 3 | Ruck-rover |
| 1989 | Paul Couch | Geelong | 22 | 25 | 7 | Centre |
| 1990 | Tony Liberatore | Footscray | 18 | 24 | 39 | Rover |
| 1991 | Jim Stynes | Melbourne | 25 | 25 | 11 | Ruckman |
| 1992 | Scott Wynd | Footscray | 20 | 22 | 15 | Ruckman |
| 1993 | Gavin Wanganeen | Essendon | 18 | 20 | 4 | Back Pocket |
| 1994 | Greg Williams | Carlton | 30 | 30 | 2 | Centre |
| 1995 | Paul Kelly | Sydney | 21 | 26 | 14 | Ruck-Rover |
| 1996 | James Hird | Essendon | 21 | 23 | 5 | Centre half-forward |
| | Michael Voss | Brisbane Bears | 21 | 21 | 3 | Ruck-rover |
| 1997 | Robert Harvey | St Kilda | 26 | 26 | 35 | Ruck-rover/Centre |

# TOP BROWNLOW SCORES — 1924–1997

*= not eligible due to suspension*

**Season 1924 voting**
E. Greeves (Geel) . . . . . . 7
A. Chadwick (Melb) . . . . . 6
G. Shorten (Ess) . . . . . . 6
D. Hayes (Rich) . . . . . . 4
A. Pink (Geel) . . . . . . . 3
J. Moriarty (Fitzroy) . . . . 3
P. O'Brien (Carl) . . . . . . 3
M. Tandy (Sth Melb) . . . . 3

**Season 1925 voting**
C. Watson (St K) . . . . . . 9
E. Greeves (Geel) . . . . . . 7
A. Chadwick (Melb) . . . . . 4
F. Maher (Ess) . . . . . . . 4
R. Taylor (Melb) . . . . . . 3
S. Coventry (Coll) . . . . . 3
L. Woodfield (Sth Melb) . . 3
L. Wigraft (Fitzroy) . . . . . 3
C. Splatt (Haw) . . . . . . 3

**Season 1926 voting**
I. Warne-Smith (Melb) . . . 9
E. Greeves (Geel) . . . . . . 5
A. Geddes (Rich) . . . . . . 5
R. Johnson (Melb) . . . . . 5
D. Walsh (N Melb) . . . . . 4
R. Baker (Coll) . . . . . . . 4
K. Millar (Rich) . . . . . . . 4
W. Adams (Fitzroy) . . . . . 4
G. Campbell (Ess) . . . . . 4
A. Duncan (Carl) . . . . . . 3
S. Coventry (Coll) . . . . . 3
L. Dwyer (N Melb) . . . . . 3

**Season 1927 voting**
S. Coventry (Coll) . . . . . 7
R. Taylor (Melb) . . . . . . 6
A. Duncan (Carl) . . . . . . 6
A. Geddes (Rich) . . . . . . 5
E. Greeves (Geel) . . . . . . 5
L. Dwyer (N Melb) . . . . . 3
T. O'Halloran (Rich) . . . . 3
A. Robertson (S Melb) . . . 3
G. Jerram (Geel) . . . . . . 3
E. Utting (Haw) . . . . . . 3
G. Stockdale (Ess) . . . . . 3

**Season 1928 voting**
I. Warne-Smith (Melb) . . . 8
E. Greeves (Geel) . . . . . . 5
C. Chapman (Fitzroy) . . . . 4
J. Baggott (Rich) . . . . . . 4
L. Dwyer (N Melb) . . . . . 4
S. Coventry (Coll) . . . . . 3
A. Hopkins (Foots) . . . . . 3
B. McCormack (Rich) . . . . 3
H. Clarke (Melb) . . . . . . 3
C. Gambetta (St K) . . . . . 3

**Season 1929 voting**
A. Collier (Coll) . . . . . . . 6
A. Batchelor (Fitzroy) . . . . 4
I. Warne-Smith (Melb) . . . 4
A. Hopkins (Foots) . . . . . 4
J. Titus (Rich) . . . . . . . 3
R. Hickey (Geel) . . . . . . 3
E. Utting (Haw) . . . . . . 3
J. Collins (Geel) . . . . . . 3
H. Matthews (St K) . . . . . 3
C. Cameron (N Melb) . . . . 3
H. Vallence (Carl) . . . . . 3
A. Ludlow (St K) . . . . . . 3
R. Makeham (Coll) . . . . . 3

**Season 1930 voting**
S. Judkins (Rich) . . . . . . 4
A. Hopkins (Foots) . . . . . 4
H. Collier (Coll) . . . . . . . 4
B. Foster (Rich) . . . . . . 3
K. Forbes (Ess) . . . . . . 3
A. Collier (Coll) . . . . . . . 3
R. Johnson (Melb) . . . . . 3
G. Todd (Geel) . . . . . . . 3
J. Sharpley (Haw) . . . . . 3
C. Chapman (Fitzroy) . . . . 3
P. Reville (Sth Melb) . . . . 3

**Season 1931 voting**
H. Bunton (Fitzroy) . . . . 26
A. Hopkins (Foots) . . . . 25
R. Hickey (Geel) . . . . . . 19
J. Lewis (N Melb) . . . . . 17
I. McAlpine (Foots) . . . . 15
S. Judkins (Rich) . . . . . 15
P. Beames (Melb) . . . . . 15
F. Phillips (St K) . . . . . . 14
A. Martyn (Carl) . . . . . . 11
H. Okey (Ess) . . . . . . . 11
E. Utting (Haw) . . . . . . 11
H. Matthews (St K) . . . . . 11
H. Rumney (Coll) . . . . . 11
J. Gregory (N Melb) . . . . 10
G. Moloney (Geel) . . . . . 10
H. Comte (St.Kilda) . . . . 10

**Season 1932 voting**
H. Bunton (Fitzroy) . . . . 23
G. Moloney (Geel) . . . . . 16
W. Faul (Sth Melb) . . . . . 16
I. McAlpine (Foots) . . . . 15
P. Beames (Melb) . . . . . 12
S. Judkins (Rich) . . . . . 12
J. Dyer (Rich) . . . . . . . 12
J. Lewis (N Melb) . . . . . 12
W. Smallhorn (Fitzroy) . . 10
F. Phillips (St K) . . . . . . 10
R. Hickey (Geel) . . . . . . 10
G. Strang (Rich) . . . . . . 10

**Season 1933 voting**
W. Smallhorn (Fitzroy) . . 18
W. Lowenthal (Ess) . . . . 17
J. Davis (St K) . . . . . . . 15
A. Hopkins (Foots) . . . . 13
N. Ware (Foots) . . . . . . 13
K. O'Neill (Rich) . . . . . . 13
J. Beveridge (Coll) . . . . . 12
H. Bunton (Fitzroy) . . . . 12
R. Reynolds (Ess) . . . . . 12
R. Martin (Rich) . . . . . . 11

**Season 1934 voting**
R. Reynolds (Ess) . . . . . 19
H. Bunton (Fitzroy) . . . . 18
K. Shea (Carl) . . . . . . . 17
J. Regan (Coll) . . . . . . . 17
R. Martin (Rich) . . . . . . 17
W. Smallhorn (Fitzroy) . . 16
G. Strang (Rich) . . . . . . 14
T. Pratt (Sth Melb) . . . . . 13
N. Ware (Foots) . . . . . . 12

**Season 1935 voting**
H. Bunton (Fitzroy) . . . . 25
H. Forbes (Ess) . . . . . . 17
K. Shea (Carl) . . . . . . . 16
A. La Fontaine (Melb) . . 15
J. Davis (St K) . . . . . . . 13

J. Regan (Coll) . . . . . . . 13
R. Reynolds (Ess) . . . . . 13
G. Bennett (Foots) . . . . . 12
G. Strang (Rich) . . . . . . 11
V. Doherty (Coll) . . . . . . 11
L. Metherell (Geel) . . . . . 11
J. Reid (Sth Melb) . . . . . 11

**Season 1936 voting**
D. Ryan (Fitzroy) . . . . . . 26
R. Hickey (Geel) . . . . . . 21
H. Matthews (S Melb) . . 20
A. La Fontaine (Melb) . . 19
A. Morrison (Foots) . . . . 19
W. Mohr (St K) . . . . . . . 17
J. Regan (Coll) . . . . . . . 17
T. Quinn (Geel) . . . . . . 16
R. Reynolds (Ess) . . . . . 15
N. Ware (Foots) . . . . . . 14
K. Shea (Carl) . . . . . . . 13
V. Randall (Haw) . . . . . . 12

**Season 1937 voting**
R. Reynolds (Ess) . . . . . 27
H. Matthews (S Melb) . . 23
J. Mueller (Melb) . . . . . 17
K. Shea (Carl) . . . . . . . 16
J. Regan (Coll) . . . . . . . 16
N. Ware (Foots) . . . . . . 15
J. Graham (Sth Melb) . . . 14
D. Fothergill (Coll) . . . . . 13
J. Davis (St K) . . . . . . . 12
D. Ryan (Fitzroy) . . . . . . 12
J. Francis (Carl) . . . . . . 12
R. Hickey (Geel) . . . . . . 11
W. Carter (N Melb) . . . . 10

**Season 1938 voting**
R. Reynolds (Ess) . . . . . 18
S. Spinks (Haw) . . . . . . 17
A. Morrison (Foots) . . . . 15
M. Boyall (Coll) . . . . . . 15
W. Smallhorn (Fitzroy) . . 15
J. Cordner (N Melb) . . . . 14
J. Collins (Geel) . . . . . . 13
N. Ware (Foots) . . . . . . 13

**Season 1939 voting**
M. Whelan (Coll) . . . . . . 23
H. Hickey (Foots) . . . . . 20
R. Reynolds (Ess) . . . . . 19
J. Dyer (Rich) . . . . . . . 17
W. Smallhorn (Fitzroy) . . 16
S. Dyer (N Melb) . . . . . 14
J. Cordner (N Melb) . . . . 14
H. Matthews (S Melb) . . 13
S. Spinks (Haw) . . . . . . 12
A. Pannam (Coll) . . . . . 11
H. Torney (Ess) . . . . . . 11
*J. Mueller (Melb) . . . . . 11
J. Cleary (Sth Melb) . . . . 11
G. Kennedy (N Melb) . . . 10
N. Ware (Foots) . . . . . . 10

**Season 1940 voting**
H. Matthews (S Melb) . . 32
D. Fothergill (Coll) . . . . . 32
H. Torney (Ess) . . . . . . 24
N. Ware (Foots) . . . . . . 20
H. Hickey (Foots) . . . . . 15
G. Smeaton (Rich) . . . . 14
J. Dyer (Rich) . . . . . . . 12
S. Spinks (Haw) . . . . . . 12
G. Dougherty (Geel) . . . . 12

R. Baggott (Melb) . . . . . 11
W. Buttsworth (Ess) . . . . 11
J. Graham (Sth Melb) . . . 10
J. Barker (Haw) . . . . . . 10

**Season 1941 voting**
N. Ware (Foots) . . . . . . 23
H. Matthews (S Melb) . . 21
F. Hughson (Fitzroy) . . . 17
*R. Chitty (Carl) . . . . . . 14
R. Garvin (St K) . . . . . . 14
H. Hickey (Foots) . . . . . 13
A. Angwin (Haw) . . . . . 13
G. Kennedy (N Melb) . . . 13
J. Graham (Sth Melb) . . . 13
W. Buttsworth (Ess) . . . . 12
J. Regan (Coll) . . . . . . . 12
J. Cleary (Sth Melb) . . . . 12
A. Olliver (Foots) . . . . . 12

**Brownlow Medal
suspended 1942-45**

**Season 1946 voting**
Don Cordner (Melb) . . . 20
J. Howell (Carl) . . . . . . 19
W. Morris (Rich) . . . . . . 19
B. Deacon (Carl) . . . . . . 17
A. Ruthven (Fitzroy) . . . . 16
F. Flanagan (Geel) . . . . . 15
S. Dyer (N Melb) . . . . . 15
W. Twomey (Coll) . . . . . 14
T. Morrow (Geel) . . . . . 14
W. Pearson (Ess) . . . . . 13
L. Richards (Coll) . . . . . 11
G. Mahon (Geel) . . . . . . 11
H. Mears (Sth Melb) . . . 11
L. Foote (N Melb) . . . . . 10
N. Jarvis (Fitzroy) . . . . . 10
M. Whelan (Coll) . . . . . . 10

**Season 1947 voting**
B. Deacon (Carl) . . . . . . 23
H. Bray (St K) . . . . . . . 21
R. Bywater (Sth Melb) . . 18
W. Culpitt (Haw) . . . . . . 18
F. Flanagan (Geel) . . . . . 17
F. Hughson (Fitzroy) . . . 16
Don Cordner (Melb) . . . 16
W. Morris (Rich) . . . . . . 14
W. Hutchison (Ess) . . . . 13
K. Dynon (N Melb) . . . . 12
W. Williams (Sth Melb) . 12
N. Jarvis (Fitzroy) . . . . . 11
E. Henfry (Carl) . . . . . . 11
L. Richards (Coll) . . . . . 11
J. Howell (Carl) . . . . . . 10
S. McGrath (Melb) . . . . . 10
A. Rodda (Melb) . . . . . . 10
P. Bushby (Ess) . . . . . . 10
K. Rosewarne (St K) . . . 10

**Season 1948 voting**
W. Morris (Rich) . . . . . . 24
O. Grieve (Carl) . . . . . . 21
W. Hutchison (Ess) . . . . 17
R. Clegg (Sth Melb) . . . . 16
W. Twomey (Coll) . . . . . 15
A. Ruthven (Fitzroy) . . . . 13
R. Hancock (St K) . . . . . 13
D. O'Brien (N Melb) . . . . 12
H. Bray (St K) . . . . . . . 12
B. Deacon (Carl) . . . . . . 11
N. Mann (Coll) . . . . . . . 11

B. Morrison (Geel) .... 11
A. Albiston (Haw) ..... 11
A. Rodda (Melb) ..... 11
R. McKenzie (Melb) .... 10
K. Dynon (N Melb) .... 10
W. Wilson (Rich) .... 10

**Season 1949 voting**
R. Clegg (Sth Melb) ... 23
C. Austen (Haw) ...... 23
H. Bray (St K) ...... 20
J. Coleman (Ess) ..... 15
F. Flanagan (Geel).... 14
J. Ross (St K). ...... 14
E. Henfry (Carl) ...... 13
Don Cordner (Melb) ... 12
W. Hutchison (Ess) .... 12
W. Wilson (Rich) ...... 12
L. Foote (N Melb) ..... 11
K. Dynon (N Melb) .... 11
A. Ruthven (Fitzroy) ... 11
B. Morrow (Geel) ..... 11
R. Green (Carl) ...... 10
R. Rose (Coll). ....... 10
C. Sutton (Foots) ..... 10

**Season 1950 voting**
A. Ruthven (Fitzroy) ... 21
F. Flanagan (Geel) .... 18
B. Phillips (St K)...... 17
C. Sutton (Foots) ..... 17
W. Morris (Rich) ...... 17
W. Hutchison (Ess) .... 15
N. McDonald (Ess) .... 12
Denis Cordner (Melb) .. 12
W. Stephen (Fitzroy) ... 12
O. Grieve (Carl)....... 12
H. Bray (St K)........ 11
R. Rose (Coll)........ 11
W. Williams (Sth Melb) . 10
J. Coleman (Ess) ..... 10
J. Hyde (Geel) ....... 10

**Season 1951 voting**
B. Smith (Geel) ...... 23
R. Clegg (Sth Melb) ... 20
W. Hutchison (Ess) .... 16
R. Poulter (Rich)...... 15
H. Bray (St K)........ 14
Denis Cordner (Melb) .. 14
C. Sutton (Foots) ..... 14
R. Rose (Coll)........ 14
J. Clark (Carl) ....... 13
D. Rowe (Rich) ...... 13
J. Kennedy (Haw) ..... 12
B. Phillips (St K)...... 11
A. Ruthven (Fitzroy) ... 11
R. Wearmouth (Foots).. 11
F. Flanagan (Geel) .... 11
L. Foote (N Melb) ..... 10
G. Sibun (Sth Melb) ... 10

**Season 1952 voting**
R. Wright (Rich) ...... 21
W. Hutchison (Ess) .... 21
H. Bray (St K) ....... 19
P. Pianto (Geel) ...... 17
W. Wilson (Rich) ...... 15
T. Merrett (Coll) ...... 12
J. Collins (Foots) ..... 12
Denis Cordner (Melb) .. 11
S. Spencer (Melb) .... 11
J. Kennedy (Haw) ..... 10
W. Gunn (Sth Melb) ... 10
J. Hyde (Geel) ....... 10
J. Ross (St K)........ 10
O. Grieve (Carl)....... 10

**Season 1953 voting**
W. Hutchison (Ess).... 26
R. Rose (Coll)........ 22
N. Mann (Coll) ....... 17
B. Smith (Geel) ...... 16
R. Clegg (Sth Melb) ... 14
D. Rowe (Rich) ...... 13
K. Hands (Carl) ...... 12
T. Merrett (Coll) ...... 12
J. Clarke (Ess) ....... 12
H. Stevens (Foots) .... 12
A. Aylett (N Melb) .... 12
*J. Collins (Foots) .... 10
K. Dynon (N Melb) .... 10
G. Sibun (Sth Melb) ... 10
K. Drinan (St K) ...... 10

**Season 1954 voting**
R. Wright (Rich) ...... 29
N. Mann (Coll) ....... 19
J. Gill (Ess) ......... 14
H. Stevens (Foots) .... 14
E. Lane (Sth Melb) .... 14
L. Crane (Haw) ...... 13
J. Brady (N Melb) .... 13
R. Poulter (Rich) ..... 12
Denis Cordner (Melb) .. 12
J. Ross (St K). ...... 12
J. James (Carl) ...... 12
J. Collins (Foots) ..... 12
P. Pianto (Geel) ...... 12
A. Aylett (N Melb) .... 12
W. Hutchison (Ess) .... 10
B. Phillips (St K)...... 10

**Season 1955 voting**
F. Goldsmith (S Melb) .. 21
W. Hutchison (Ess) ... 20
N. Roberts (St K) ..... 16
J. James (Carl) ...... 15
Denis Cordner (Melb) .. 15
E. Lane (Sth Melb) .... 15
P. Box (Foots) ....... 14
D. Rowe (Rich) ...... 13
L. Sharp (Coll) ...... 12
J. Kerr (Foots) ...... 11
J. Clarke (Ess) ...... 10
T. Merrett (Coll) ...... 10
R. Poulter (Rich) ..... 10

**Season 1956 voting**
P. Box (Foots) ....... 22
P. Pianto (Geel) ...... 16
J. Dorgan (Sth Melb).. 15
J. Beckwith (Melb) .... 13
R. Barassi (Melb) ..... 13
R. Simmonds (Haw) ... 13
N. Roberts (St K) ..... 12
W. Stephen (Fitzroy) .. 11
B. Smith (Geel) ...... 11
Denis Cordner (Melb) .. 11
D. Rowe (Rich) ...... 11
J. O'Mahoney (Haw) ... 11
J. James (Carl) ...... 10
J. Clarke (Ess) ...... 10

**Season 1957 voting**
B. Gleeson (St K) ..... 24
R. Wright (Rich) ...... 20
J. James (Carl) ...... 19
J. Taylor (Sth Melb) ... 16
H. Davies (St K) ..... 14
J. Beckwith (Melb) .... 13
K. Murray (Fitzroy) ... 12
E. Whitten (Foots)..... 12
P. Pianto (Geel) ...... 12
A. Hughes (Haw)..... 12
J. Clarke (Ess) ....... 11
A. Gale (Fitzroy) ...... 11

N. Doolan (N Melb).... 11
A. Woodley (Haw) .... 10

**Season 1958 voting**
N. Roberts (St K) ..... 24
B. Edwards (Haw).... 22
R. Skilton (Sth Melb) .. 19
A. Aylett (N Melb) .... 17
W. Gunn (Sth Melb) .. 16
J. Clarke (Ess) ....... 15
J. Gamble (Ess) ...... 15
J. Birt (Ess) ......... 15
E. Whitten (Foots)..... 14
H. Sullivan (Coll)...... 14
R. Branton (Rich) ..... 13
O. Abrahams (Fitzroy) . 13
*J. Benetti (Carl) ...... 12
R. Gabelich (Coll) ..... 12
P. Falconer (Geel) ..... 11
N. Waller (Coll) ...... 11
J. Beckwith (Melb) .... 11

**Season 1959 voting**
R. Skilton (Sth Melb) .. 20
V. Howell (St K) ...... 20
W. Serong (Coll) ...... 14
R. Gabelich (Coll) ..... 14
H. Mitchell (Ess)...... 14
E. Whitten (Foots) .... 14
T. Merrett (Coll) ...... 12
R. Hovey (Geel) ...... 12
*G. Donaldson (Carl) .. 11
Bob Johnson (Melb) ... 10
B. McGowan (S Melb) . 10

**Season 1960 voting**
J. Schultz (Foots) ..... 20
K. Murray (Fitzroy) ... 19
L. Dwyer (N Melb) .... 18
W. Clark (Fitzroy)..... 17
J. Beckwith (Melb) .... 15
J. James (Carl)....... 12
G. Donaldson (Carl) ... 11
R. Skilton (Sth Melb) .. 11
W. Goggin (Geel) ..... 11
F. Johnson (Sth Melb). 10
L. Oswald (St K) ..... 10
B. Edwards (Haw) .... 10
J. Birt (Ess) ......... 10

**Season 1961 voting**
J. James (Carl) ...... 21
L. Dwyer (N Melb).... 19
I. Law (Haw)......... 17
F. Johnson (Sth Melb). 13
B. Edwards (Haw) .... 12
C. Evans (Foots) ..... 12
E. Whitten (Foots).... 12
J. Taylor (Sth Melb) ... 12
K. Murray (Fitzroy) ... 11
R. Branton (Rich) ..... 11
R. Barassi (Melb) ..... 10
L. Oswald (St K) ..... 10
V. Howell (St K) ...... 10
J. Henderson (Coll) ... 10

**Season 1962 voting**
A. Lord (Geel)........ 28
K. Fraser (Ess) ...... 19
K. Murray (Fitzroy) ... 19
R. Branton (Rich) ..... 19
J. Schultz (Foots) ..... 15
B. Gray (Coll) ....... 13
R. Harvey (Fitzroy) ... 13
V. Howell (St K) ...... 13
R. Skilton (Sth Melb) .. 13
H. Mann (Melb) ...... 11
B. McMaster-Smith (Carl) .10
P. Falconer (Carl) ..... 10
J. Henderson (Coll) .... 10

N. Crompton (Melb) ... 10
W. Serong (N Melb).... 10
D. Baldock (St K) .... 10

**Season 1963 voting**
R. Skilton (Sth Melb) .. 20
G. Farmer (Geel)...... 17
D. Baldock (St K) .... 17
J. Henderson (Coll).... 15
K. Murray (Fitzroy) ... 14
A. Morrow (St K)..... 14
K. Fraser (Ess) ...... 13
I. Law (Haw) ........ 13
J. Wallis (St K) ...... 11
S. Silvagni (Carl)...... 10
C. Youren (Haw) ..... 10
R. Barassi (Melb) ..... 10
B. Dixon (Melb) ...... 10

**Season 1964 voting**
G. Collis (Carl) ....... 27
P. Hay (Haw) ........ 19
K. Fraser (Ess) ...... 19
J. Schultz (Foots) ..... 16
M. Urquhart (Coll)..... 16
I. Stewart (St K) ..... 14
K. Murray (Fitzroy) ... 13
L. Hill (Coll) ......... 11
W. Goggin (Geel) ..... 11
H. Mann (Melb) ...... 11
R. Skilton (Sth Melb) .. 11
J. Wallis (St K) ...... 11
G. Farmer (Geel)...... 10
*R. Barassi (Melb) .... 10
J. Heriot (Sth Melb) ... 10

**Season 1965 voting**
I. Stewart (St K) ..... 20
N. Teasdale (N Melb) .. 20
D. Baldock (St K) .... 18
K. Fraser (Ess) ...... 16
J. Nicholls (Carl)...... 15
R. Skilton (Sth Melb) .. 14
W. Barrot (Rich) ...... 14
J. Jillard (Foots) ...... 13
A. Morrow (St K) ..... 11
G. Farmer (Geel) ..... 11
J. Schultz (Foots) ..... 11
G. John (Sth Melb) ... 10
K. Turner (Coll) ...... 10

**Season 1966 voting**
I. Stewart (St K) ...... 21
J. Nicholls (Carl)...... 17
J. Sharrock (Geel)..... 16
N. Crowe (Rich) ..... 14
D. Baldock (St K) .... 14
D. Marshall (Geel) .... 12
H. Mann (Melb) ...... 12
J. Goold (Carl) ...... 11
I. Bryant (Foots) ...... 10

**Season 1967 voting**
R. Smith (St K) ...... 24
L. Dwyer (N Melb).... 17
A. Jesaulenko (Carl) ... 15
J. Birt (Ess) ........ 13
H. Mann (Melb) ...... 12
R. Clay (Rich) ....... 12
L. Thompson (Coll) .... 11
W. Goggin (Geel) ..... 11
R. Skilton (Sth Melb) .. 11
J. Jillard (Foots) ...... 10

**Season 1968 voting**
R. Skilton (Sth Melb) .. 24
D. Marshall (Geel) .... 21
K. Murray (Fitzroy) ... 18
J. Nicholls (Carl)...... 17
C. Ditterich (St K) .... 17
P. Hudson (Haw)...... 16

P. Steward (N Melb) . . . 14
B. Davis (Ess) . . . . . . . 14
L. Thompson (Coll) . . . . 12
D. Parkin (Haw) . . . . . . 12
I. Stewart (St K) . . . . . 12
J. Schultz (Foots) . . . . . 11
G. Parke (Melb) . . . . . . 11
A. Jesaulenko (Carl) . . . 10
W. Goggin (Geel) . . . . . . 10
D. Meagher (Haw) . . . . . 10
K. Bartlett (Rich) . . . . . 10

**Season 1969 voting**
K. Murray (Fitzroy) . . . . 19
G. Bisset (Foots) . . . . . 18
B. Davis (Ess) . . . . . . . 18
R. Murray (St K) . . . . . 15
K. Bartlett (Rich) . . . . . 14
D. Thorpe (Foots) . . . . . 13
D. Wade (Geel) . . . . . . . 12
S. Kekovich (N Melb) . . . 12
J. Nicholls (Carl) . . . . . 11
L. Thompson (Coll) . . . . 11
M. Green (Rich) . . . . . . 11
K. Sheedy (Rich) . . . . . 11
W. Goggin (Geel) . . . . . 11
T. Waters (Coll) . . . . . . 10

**Season 1970 voting**
P. Bedford (Sth Melb) . . 25
G. Dempsey (Foots) . . . 21
A. Jesaulenko (Carl) . . . 20
B. Cable (N Melb) . . . . . 19
B. Price (Coll) . . . . . . . . 17
J. McIntosh (St K) . . . . . 17
F. Bourke (Rich) . . . . . . 16
P. Hudson (Haw) . . . . . . 14
D. Griffiths (St K) . . . . . 14
N. Zunneberg (Fitzroy) . . 12
P. McKenna (Coll) . . . . . 11
P. Steward (N Melb) . . . 11
B. Quinlan (Foots) . . . . . 10
K. Bartlett (Rich) . . . . . 10
G. Andrews (Geel) . . . . . 10

**Season 1971 voting**
I. Stewart (Rich) . . . . . . 21
B. Davis (Ess) . . . . . . . 18
P. Hudson (Haw) . . . . . . 18
J. McIntosh (St K) . . . . . 18
A. Ruscuklic (Fitzroy) . . 16
G. Dempsey (Foots) . . . 16
R. Smith (St K) . . . . . . . 16
W. Ryan (Geelong) . . . . 16
D. Tuddenham (Coll) . . . 15
J. Murphy (Fitzroy) . . . . 14
B. Price (Coll) . . . . . . . . 13
A. Martello (Haw) . . . . . 13
D. Thorpe (Foots) . . . . . 12
R. Hart (Rich) . . . . . . . . 11
W. Walsh (Sth Melb) . . . 11
J. Bonney (St K) . . . . . . 11
J. Greening (Coll) . . . . . 10
B. Quinlan (Foots) . . . . . 10
G. Wells (Melb) . . . . . . . 10
B. Stevenson (Haw) . . . . 10
L. Matthews (Haw) . . . . 10
S. Alves (Melb) . . . . . . . 10
R. Hunt (Rich) . . . . . . . 10
K. Greig (N Melb) . . . . . 10

**Season 1972 voting**
L. Thompson (Coll) . . . . 25
G. Wells (Melb) . . . . . . . 22
G. Hardeman (Melb) . . . 18
J. Williams (Ess) . . . . . . 18
L. Matthews (Haw) . . . . 16
J. Murphy (Fitzroy) . . . . 15

J. Greening (Coll) . . . . . 14
S. Alves (Melb) . . . . . . . 12
D. Clarke (Geel) . . . . . . 12
G. Dempsey (Foots) . . . 12
A. Jesaulenko (Carl) . . . 11
T. Keogh (Carl) . . . . . . . 11
N. Fields (Ess) . . . . . . . 11
B. Davis (Ess) . . . . . . . 11
K. Greig (N Melb) . . . . . 11
T. Payze (St K) . . . . . . . 11
C. Ditterich (St K) . . . . . 11
R. Cook (Sth Melb) . . . . 10
G. Wilson (Fitzroy) . . . . 10
C. McKellar (Rich) . . . . 10

**Season 1973 voting**
K. Greig (N Melb) . . . . . 27
G. Moss (Ess) . . . . . . . 25
L. Matthews (Haw) . . . . 23
L. Thompson (Coll) . . . . 21
W. Richardson (Coll) . . . 19
D. McKay (Carl) . . . . . . 17
I. Stewart (Rich) . . . . . . 17
G. Wells (Melb) . . . . . . . 16
G. Dempsey (Foots) . . . 15
B. Davis (N Melb) . . . . . 14
G. Wilson (Fitzroy) . . . . 14
D. Clarke (Geel) . . . . . . 13
A. Martello (Haw) . . . . . 11
G. Crane (Carl) . . . . . . . 11
P. Bedford (Sth Melb) . . 11
J. Rantall (N Melb) . . . . 10
N. Fields (Ess) . . . . . . . 10
S. Hoffman (Sth Melb) . . 10
B. Lawrence (St K) . . . . 10
P. Jones (Carl) . . . . . . . 10

**Season 1974 voting**
K. Greig (N Melb) . . . . . 27
G. Hardeman (Melb) . . . 23
K. Bartlett (Rich) . . . . . 22
G. Dempsey (Foots) . . . 19
R. Hunt (Rich/Geel) . . . 15
L. Matthews (Haw) . . . . 15
F. Bourke (Rich) . . . . . . 15
B. Quinlan (Foots) . . . . . 14
J. Hendrie (Haw) . . . . . . 13
G. Moss (Ess) . . . . . . . 12
H. Merrigan (Fitzroy) . . 11
M. Richardson (Coll) . . . 10
G. Elliott (St K) . . . . . . . 10

**Season 1975 voting**
G. Dempsey (Foots) . . . 20
S. Alves (Melb) . . . . . . . 19
G. Moss (Ess) . . . . . . . 18
J. Hendrie (Haw) . . . . . . 18
A. Jesaulenko (Carl) . . . 18
P. Carman (Coll) . . . . . . 17
B. Roberts (Sth Melb) . . 17
K. Greig (N Melb) . . . . . 16
G. Young (St K) . . . . . . . 15
*J. Newman (Geel) . . . . 14
*R. Ashman (Carl) . . . . 11
M. Fitzpatrick (Carl) . . . 11
G. Hardeman (Melb) . . . 11
R. Flower (Melb) . . . . . . 11
C. McKellar (Rich) . . . . 11
W. Irwin (Fitzroy) . . . . . 10
L. Matthews (Haw) . . . . 10
F. Bourke (Rich) . . . . . . 10

**Season 1976 voting**
*(Each field umpire awards votes on 3-2-1 basis)*
G. Moss (Ess) . . . . . . . 48
P. Knights (Haw) . . . . . . 45
F. Bourke (Rich) . . . . . . 36
B. Cable (N Melb) . . . . . 28

G. Dempsey (Foots) . . . 28
G. Wells (Melb) . . . . . . . 28
R. Alexander (Fitzroy) . . 26
B. Nankervis (Geel) . . . . 26
G. Wilson (Fitzroy) . . . . 24
L. Matthews (Haw) . . . . 23
R. Neal (Geel) . . . . . . . 23
J. Hawkins (Geel) . . . . . 22
R. Ashman (Carl) . . . . . 21
T. Barker (St K) . . . . . . 21
K. O'Keeffe (Fitzroy) . . 21
R. Walls (Carl) . . . . . . . 20
S. Alves (Melb) . . . . . . . 19
J. Burns (N Melb) . . . . . 19
A. Jesaulenko (Carl) . . . 19
J. Hendrie (Haw) . . . . . . 19
B. Doull (Carl) . . . ./. . . 18
*R. Andrews (Ess) . . . . 18
G. Osborne (Melb) . . . . 18
K. Sheedy (Rich) . . . . . 18
R. Flower (Melb) . . . . . . 17
R. Huppatz (Foots) . . . . 17
B. Round (Sth Melb) . . . 17
J. Newman (Geel) . . . . . 16
G. Jennings (Foots) . . . . 15
T. Keogh (Carl) . . . . . . . 15
T. Pickett (Carl) . . . . . . 15

**Season 1977 voting**
*(Each field umpire awards votes on 3-2-1 basis)*
G. Teasdale (Sth Melb) . 59
K. Bartlett (Rich) . . . . . 45
W. Picken (Coll) . . . . . . 41
L. Thompson (Coll) . . . . 34
L. Matthews (Haw) . . . . 34
B. Doull (Carl) . . . . . . . 34
*J. Sarau (St K) . . . . . . 30
G. Dempsey (Foots) . . . 27
G. Hardeman (Melb) . . . 27
D. Dench (N Melb) . . . . 26
S. Madden (Ess) . . . . . . 25
S. Icke (N Melb) . . . . . . 23
R. Flower (Melb) . . . . . . 22
G. Wilson (Fitzroy) . . . . 21
M. Tuck (Haw) . . . . . . . 20
G. Wells (Melb) . . . . . . . 20
B. Wood (Rich) . . . . . . . 20
J. Hendrie (Haw) . . . . . . 19
B. Cable (N Melb) . . . . . 18
F. Bourke (Rich) . . . . . . 17

**Season 1978 voting**
M. Blight (N Melb) . . . . 22
P. Knights (Haw) . . . . . . 21
G. Wilson (Fitzroy) . . . . 20
K. Bartlett (Rich) . . . . . 19
G. Dempsey (Foots) . . . 16
G. Teasdale (Sth Melb) . 15
M. Tuck (Haw) . . . . . . . 14
R. Flower (Melb) . . . . . . 14
*R. Shaw (Coll) . . . . . . 14
G. Raines (Rich) . . . . . . 14
R. Alexander (Fitzroy) . . 13
V. Perovic (St K) . . . . . . 13
D. Collins (Carl) . . . . . . 12
R. Barham (Coll) . . . . . . 12
K. Higgins (Geel) . . . . . 12
J. Murphy (Sth Melb) . . . 12
G. Jennings (Foots) . . . . 11
D. McKay (Carl) . . . . . . 10
P. Jones (Carl) . . . . . . . 10
I. Nankervis (Geel) . . . . 10
M. Turner (Geel) . . . . . . 10
*G. Sidebottom (St K) . 10

P. Moore (Coll) . . . . . . . 22
G. Wilson (Fitzroy) . . . . 21
R. Flower (Melb) . . . . . . 19
B. Round (Sth Melb) . . . 17
G. Dempsey (N Melb) . . 16
R. Glendinning (N Melb) . 14
J. Dunne (St K) . . . . . . . 13
*R. Kink (Coll) . . . . . . . 13
T. Daniher (Ess) . . . . . . 13
K. Klomp (Carl) . . . . . . . 13
M. Maclure (Carl) . . . . . 13
W. Harmes (Carl) . . . . . 12
B. Quinlan (Fitzroy) . . . . 12
M. Tuck (Haw) . . . . . . . 12
G. Allan (Fitzroy) . . . . . 11

**Season 1980 voting**
K. Templeton (Foots) . . . 23
M. Neagle (Ess) . . . . . . 20
R. Blake (Geel) . . . . . . . 19
P. Moore (Coll) . . . . . . . 18
T. Watson (Ess) . . . . . . 17
L. Matthews (Haw) . . . . 16
M. Lee (Rich) . . . . . . . . 16
C. Smith (Fitzroy) . . . . . 16
G. Dempsey (N Melb) . . 15
K. Greig (N Melb) . . . . . 15
R. Glendinning (N Melb) . 14
R. Flower (Melb) . . . . . . 14
W. Schimmelbusch (NM) . 13
V. Perovic (Carl) . . . . . . 12
P. Daicos (Coll) . . . . . . . 11
G. Wilson (Fitzroy) . . . . 11
G. Wells (Carl) . . . . . . . 11
B. Duperouzel (St K) . . . 11

**Season 1981 voting**
B. Quinlan (Fitzroy) . . . . 22
B. Round (Sth Melb) . . . 22
R. Ashman (Carl) . . . . . 21
P. Moore (Coll) . . . . . . . 16
T. Barker (St K) . . . . . . 15
J. Mossop (Geel) . . . . . . 15
M. Neagle (Ess) . . . . . . 15
A. Buhagiar (Ess) . . . . . 14
G. Cunningham (St K) . . 13
K. Hunter (Carl) . . . . . . 12
P. Bosustow (Carl) . . . . 11
J. Dunne (St K) . . . . . . . 11
P. Featherby (Geel) . . . . 11
R. Glendinning (N Melb) 11
F. Jackson (Sth Melb) . . 11
L. Matthews (Haw) . . . . 11
V. Perovic (Carl) . . . . . . 11

**Season 1982 voting**
B. Wilson (Melb) . . . . . . 23
R. Glendinning (N Melb) . 18
L. Matthews (Haw) . . . . 17
T. Wallace (Haw) . . . . . 17
G. Dempsey (N Melb) . . 16
*J. Jess (Rich) . . . . . . . 15
B. Round (Syd) . . . . . . . 15
A. Buhagiar (Ess) . . . . . 14
P. Daicos (Coll) . . . . . . . 14
G. Wilson (Fitzroy) . . . . 14
R. Flower (Melb) . . . . . . 13
*V. Perovic (Carl) . . . . . 13
P. Kennan (Melb) . . . . . 12
R. Wiley (Rich) . . . . . . . 12
G. Smith (Syd) . . . . . . . 11

**Season 1983 voting**
R. Glendinning (N Melb) 24
M. Rioli (Rich) . . . . . . . 23
S. Madden (Ess) . . . . . . 22
G. Dempsey (N Melb) . . 17
M. Lee (Rich) . . . . . . . . 16

T. Daniher (Ess) . . . . . . 15
T. Wallace (Haw) . . . . . . 15
V. Perovic (Carl) . . . . . . 14
J. Edmond (Foots) . . . . . 13
S. Icke (Melb) . . . . . . . 13
A. Purser (Foots) . . . . . . 13
M. Neagle (Ess) . . . . . . 12
J. Mossop (Geel) . . . . . . 11
R. Elphinstone (St K) . . 11

**Season 1984 voting**
P. Moore (Melb) . . . . . . 24
D. Cloke (Coll) . . . . . . . 21
R. Flower (Melb) . . . . . . 19
S. Taubert (Syd) . . . . . . 15
M. Byrne (Haw) . . . . . . 14
S. Madden (Ess) . . . . . . 14
D. Hawkins (Foots) . . . . 14
*G. Ayres (Haw) . . . . . . 12
W. Johnston (Carl) . . . . . 12
J. Buckley (Carl) . . . . . . 12
A Sidebottom (St K) . . . 12
R. Merrett (Ess) . . . . . . 12
M. Lee (Rich) . . . . . . . . 12
R. DiPierdomenico (Haw). 12
M. Rioli (Rich) . . . . . . . 12

**Season 1985 voting**
B. Hardie (Foots) . . . . . 22
J. Madden (Carl) . . . . . . 21
P. Roos (Fitzroy) . . . . . . 16
*G. Ablett (Geel) . . . . . . 15
S. Wallis (Foots) . . . . . . 15
M. Larkin (N Melb) . . . . 15
G. Williams (Geel) . . . . . 15
B. Royal (Foots) . . . . . . 15
T. Watson (Ess) . . . . . . 15
*J. Krakouer (N Melb) . . . 14
T. Alvin (Carl) . . . . . . . 14
M. Rioli (Rich) . . . . . . . 14
*P. Van Der Haar (Ess) . 12
J. Ironmonger (Syd) . . . . 12
G. Hawker (Ess) . . . . . . 11
S. Madden (Ess) . . . . . . 11

**Season 1986 voting**
R. DiPierdomenico (Haw) . . 17
G. Williams (Syd) . . . . . . 17
P. Roos (Fitzroy) . . . . . . 16
G. Hawker (Ess) . . . . . . 15
J. Platten (Haw) . . . . . . 14
B. Abernethy (Coll) . . . . 13
*J. Dorotich (Carl) . . . . . 12
W. Harmes (Carl) . . . . . 12
S. Morwood (Coll) . . . . . 12
R. Loveridge (Haw) . . . . 11
D. Carroll (Syd) . . . . . . 10
P. Daicos (Coll) . . . . . . . 10
G. Pert (Fitz) . . . . . . . . 10
M. Dwyer (Fitzroy) . . . . . 10
A. Ezard (Ess) . . . . . . . 10
P. McConville (St K) . . . 10
P. Meldrum (Carl) . . . . . 10

**Season 1987 voting**
T. Lockett (St K) . . . . . . 20
J. Platten (Haw) . . . . . . 20
P. Meldrum (Carl) . . . . . 15
B. Royal (Foots) . . . . . . 15
A. McGuinness (Foots) . 15
C. Bradley (Carl) . . . . . . 14
M. Tuck (Haw) . . . . . . . 14
S. Kernahan (Carl) . . . . 14
*G. Williams (Syd) . . . . . 13
B. Wilson (Melb) . . . . . . 12
M. Naley (Carl) . . . . . . . 12
R. Glendinning (WC) . . . 11
P. Foster (Foots) . . . . . . 11
*G. Raines (B Bears) . . 11

*D. Weightman (Rich) . . 11
M. Larkin (N Melb) . . . . 10
G. Keane (Fitzroy) . . . . . 10
P. Roos (Fitzroy) . . . . . . 10
N. Winmar (St K) . . . . . 10

**Season 1988 voting**
G. Healy (Syd) . . . . . . . 20
S. Madden (Ess) . . . . . . 16
J. Dunstall (Haw) . . . . . 16
T. Hall (Haw) . . . . . . . . 16
D. Millane (Coll) . . . . . . 14
D. Kappler (Fitz) . . . . . . 14
*P. Foster (Foots) . . . . . 14
A. Gleeson (Carl) . . . . . 13
S. Morwood (Coll) . . . . . 13
T. McGuinness (Foots) . 13
C. Mainwaring (WC) . . . 13
W. Johnston (Carl) . . . . 12
*D. Cloke (Coll) . . . . . . . 12
J. Platten (Haw) . . . . . . 12
M. Mitchell (Rich) . . . . . 12
G. Raines (B Bears) . . . 12
T. Watson (Ess) . . . . . . 11
*G. Ayres (Haw) . . . . . . 11
G. Buckenara (Haw) . . . 11
D. Murphy (Syd) . . . . . . 11
P. Couch (Geel) . . . . . . 10
S. O'Dwyer (Melb) . . . . . 10
B. Lovett (Melb) . . . . . . 10
C. Lambert (Rich) . . . . . 10

**Season 1989 voting**
P. Couch (Geel) . . . . . . 22
J. Platten (Haw) . . . . . . 20
T. Watson (Ess) . . . . . . 16
J. Dunstall (Haw) . . . . . 16
N. Winmar (St K) . . . . . 16
*G. Williams (Syd) . . . . . 16
P. Hawke (Coll) . . . . . . 14
R. Merrett (Bris Bears) . 14
G. McKenna (WC) . . . . . 13
P. Daicos (Coll) . . . . . . 12
G. Hocking (Geel) . . . . . 12
J. Madden (Carl) . . . . . . 11
M. Bairstow (Geel) . . . . 11
D. Bain (Bris Bears) . . . 11
G. Dear (Haw) . . . . . . . 11
S. McIvor (Bris Bears) . . 10
S. Newport (Melb) . . . . . 10
J. Stynes (Melb) . . . . . . 10
W. Schwass (N Melb) . . 10
A. McKellar (Rich) . . . . . 10
*T. Lockett (St K) . . . . . 10

**Season 1990 voting**
T. Liberatore (Foots) . . . 18
G. Wright (Coll) . . . . . . 16
S. Silvagni (Carl) . . . . . . 16
D. Bain (Bris Bears) . . . 15
A. Collins (Haw) . . . . . . 15
B. Lovett (Melb) . . . . . . 15
T. McGuinness (Foots) . 14
T. Shaw (Coll) . . . . . . . 13

D. Bewick (Ess) . . . . . . 13
G. Anderson (Ess) . . . . 13
S. Loewe (St K) . . . . . . 12
B. Brownless (Geel) . . . 12
P. Salmon (Ess) . . . . . . 11
J. Platten (Haw) . . . . . . 11
S. Malaxos (WC) . . . . . 11
M. McGuane (Coll) . . . . 10
G. O'Donnell (Ess) . . . . 10
L. Cameron (Foots) . . . . 10
T. Wallace (Foots) . . . . 10
D. Bennett (Melb) . . . . . 10
T. Nichols (Rich) . . . . . . 10

**Season 1991 voting**
J. Stynes (Melb) . . . . . . 25
C. Turley (WC) . . . . . . . 20
G. Hocking (Geel) . . . . . 19
Peter Matera (WC) . . . . 18
M. McLean (Bris Bears) 17
P. Hudson (Haw) . . . . . . 17
M. Knights (Rich) . . . . . 17
D. Bourke (Geel) . . . . . . 16
D. Cloke (Rich) . . . . . . . 16
T. Lockett (St K) . . . . . . 16
M. Bairstow (Geel) . . . . 15
M. Mickan (Adel) . . . . . 14
T. Francis (Coll) . . . . . . 14
P. Foster (Foots) . . . . . . 13
K. Hinkley (Geel) . . . . . 13
J. Platten (Haw) . . . . . . 13
W. Schwass (N Melb) . . 13
S. Wynd (Foots) . . . . . . 12
A. Jarman (Adel) . . . . . 11
P. Dean (Carl) . . . . . . . 11
P. Roos (Fitzroy) . . . . . . 11
P. Couch (Geel) . . . . . . 11
N. Winmar (St K) . . . . . 11
D. Carroll (Syd) . . . . . . 11
A. Jakovich (Melb) . . . . 10
D. Irving (WC) . . . . . . . 10

**Season 1992 voting**
S. Wynd (Foots) . . . . . . 20
J. Dunstall (Haw) . . . . . 18
K. Hinkley (Geel) . . . . . 17
S. Loewe (St K) . . . . . . 16
D. Jarman (Haw) . . . . . . 14
*W. Carey (N Melb) . . . . 14
D. Kickett (Ess) . . . . . . 13
J. Dorotich (Carl) . . . . . 12
R. Harvey (St K) . . . . . . 12
N. Kellett (Foots) . . . . . 12
T. Liberatore (Foots) . . . 12
S. Rehn (Adel) . . . . . . . 12
J. Platten (Haw) . . . . . . 11
*A. Gleeson (Carl) . . . . . 11
G. Wanganeen (Ess) . . . 11
A. Jarman (Adel) . . . . . 11
M. Bairstow (Geel) . . . . 11
S. Russell (Coll) . . . . . . 11
M. McGuane (Coll) . . . . 10
C. Mainwaring (WC) . . . 10

G. Jakovich (WC) . . . . . 10
P. Salmon (Ess) . . . . . . 10
D. Bewick (Ess) . . . . . . 10
P. Roos (Fitzroy) . . . . . . 10
N. Burke (St K) . . . . . . . 10
T. Lockett (St K) . . . . . . 10

**Season 1993 voting**
G. Wanganeen (Ess) . . . 18
G. Williams (Carl) . . . . . 17
*G. Hocking (Geel) . . . . . 17
W. Carey (N Melb) . . . . 16
J. Dunstall (Haw) . . . . . 16
N. Buckley (Bris Bears) . 14
L. Cameron (Foots) . . . . 14
*W. Schwass (N Melb) . 14
M. Knights (Rich) . . . . . 13
*G. Ablett (Geel) . . . . . . 13
R. Harvey (St K) . . . . . . 12
S. Wynd (Foots) . . . . . . 12
*D. Monkhorst (Coll) . . 12
J. Stynes (Melb) . . . . . . 12
T. McGuinness (Adel) . . 11
T. Modra (Adel) . . . . . . 11
S. Rehen (Adel) . . . . . . 11
B. Allan (Haw) . . . . . . . 11
J. Madden (Carl) . . . . . . 11
P. Kelly (Sydney) . . . . . 11
M. Armstrong (Fitzroy) . . 11
S. Tingay (Melb) . . . . . . 10
*Peter Matera (WC) . . . 10
*M. Bairstow (Geel) . . . 10
A. Lynch (Fitzroy) . . . . . 10

**Season 1994 voting**
G. Williams (Carl) . . . . . 30
Peter Matera (WC) . . . . 28
G. Hocking (Geel) . . . . . 20
W. Schwass (N Melb) . . 19
D. Monkhorst (Coll) . . . 17
T. Liberatore (Foots) . . . 16
*W. Carey (N Melb) . . . . 15
C. Grant (Foots) . . . . . . 15
D. Schwarz (Melb) . . . . 15
J. Platten (Haw) . . . . . . 14
L. Cameron (Foots) . . . . 13
S. Rehn (Adel) . . . . . . . 13
J. Dunstall (Haw) . . . . . 12
G. Jakovich (WC) . . . . . 12
J. Madden (Carl) . . . . . . 12
D. Southern (Foots) . . . 12
T. Francis (Coll) . . . . . . 11
*D. Jarman (Haw) . . . . . 11
*P. Kelly (Syd) . . . . . . . 11
C. Langford (Haw) . . . . . 11
M. Mansfield (Geel) . . . 11
A. McIntosh (WC) . . . . . 11
S. Tingay (Melb) . . . . . . 11
P. Broderick (Rich) . . . . 10
G. Lyon (Melb) . . . . . . . 10

**Season 1995 voting**
P. Kelly (Syd) . . . . . . . . 21
*D. Jarman (Haw) . . . . . 18
*G. Hocking (Geel) . . . . . 17
M. Long (Ess) . . . . . . . 16
M. Knights (Rich) . . . . . 16
R. Harvey (St K) . . . . . . 16
P. Couch (Geel) . . . . . . 16
J. Stynes (Melb) . . . . . . 15
W. Carey (N Melb) . . . . 14
T. Liberatore (Foots) . . . 14
*A. Jarman (Adel) . . . . . 13
M. Voss (Bris Bears) . . . 13
S. Chisholm (Fre) . . . . . 13
W. Schwass (N Melb) . . 13
*S. Loewe (St K) . . . . . 13

---

## BROWNLOW MEDAL ELIGIBILTY

A player remains eligible to win the Brownlow Medal unless he is suspended as the result of a charge laid in a match in which votes are cast.

Suspensions resulting from charges laid in practice matches, the Ansett Australia Cup competition or finals matches do not affect a player's chances. A suspension carried over from the previous season does not deem a player ineligible.

**235**

Peter Matera (WC) . . . . 13
G. McAdam (Bris Bears) 12
A. Koutoufides (Carl). . . 12
P. Somerville (Ess) . . . . 12
R. Smith (Foots) . . . . . . 12
**Season 1996 voting**
M. Voss (Bris Bears). . . 21
J. Hird (Ess) . . . . . . . . . 21
*C. McKernan (N Melb) . 21
C. Grant (Foots) . . . . . . 20
N. Burke (St K) . . . . . . . 20
G. Hocking (Geel) . . . . . 19
P. Salmon (Haw) . . . . . . 18
J. Charles (Rich) . . . . . . 17
S. Loewe (St K) . . . . . . 17
R. Harvey (St K) . . . . . . 17
G. McKenna (WC) . . . . . 17
J. Platten (Haw) . . . . . . 15
W. Carey (NM) . . . . . . . 15
M. Merenda (Rich) . . . . 15
A. Fletcher (Bris Bears) . 14
P. Kelly (Syd) . . . . . . . . 14
P. Roos (Syd) . . . . . . 14
T. Lockett (Syd) . . . . . . 14
S. Russell (Coll) . . . . . . 13
M. Richardson (Rich) . . 13
F. Brown (Carl) . . . . . . . 12
A. Koutoufides (Carl). . . 12
C. Mainwaring (WC) . . . 12
**Season 1997 voting**
*C. Grant (WB) . . . . . . . 27
R. Harvey (St K) . . . . . . 26
P. Kelly (Syd) . . . . . . . . 21
Peter Matera (WC) . . . . 21
M. Ricciuto (Adel) . . . . . 18
N. Burke (St K) . . . . . . . 18
B. Sholl (Geel) . . . . . . . 16
C. Bradley (Carl) . . . . . . 15
A. Wills (Fre) . . . . . . . . 15
*D. Jarman (Adel) . . . . . 13
N. Buckley (Coll) . . . . . . 13
P. Salmon (Haw) . . . . . . 13
*D. Lewis (Syd) . . . . . . 13
B. Ratten (Carl) . . . . . . 12
*D. King (N Melb) . . . . . 12
D. Gaspar (Rich). . . . . . 12
S. Loewe (St K) . . . . . . 12
N. Lappin (Bris Lions) . . 11
S. Russell (Coll) . . . . . . 11
*G. Wanganeen (PA). . . 11
G. Brown (Coll) . . . . . . 10
P. Williams (Coll) . . . . . 10
G. Kilpatrick (Geel) . . . . 10
C. McKernan (N Melb) . 10
T. Liberatore (WB) . . . . . 10

## TOP 10 VOTE WINNERS FOR CAREER: 1997 PLAYERS

| Player | Votes |
| --- | --- |
| Greg Williams | 154 |
| John Platten | 143 |
| Paul Roos | 121 |
| Jason Dunstall | 120 |
| Peter Matera | 108 |
| Tony Lockett | 107 |
| Garry Hocking | 106 |
| Stewart Loewe | 103 |
| Jim Stynes | 102 |
| Robert Harvey | 102 |

# TOP BROWNLOW VOTE WINNERS

| Career Votes | Player | Club/s | Brownlow Medallist |
| --- | --- | --- | --- |
| 246 | Gary Dempsey* | FO 1967-78; N 1979-84 | 1975 |
| 202 | Leigh Matthews* | H 1969-85 | |
| 180 | Bob Skilton | SM 1956-68, 1970-71 | 1959, 1963, 1968 |
| 178 | Kevin Murray | Fl 1955-64, 1967-74 | 1969 |
| 172 | Bill Hutchison | E 1942-57 | 1952, 1953 |
| 161 | Garry Wilson* | Fl 1971-84 | |
| 160 | Kevin Bartlett* | R 1965-83 | |
| 154 | Dick Reynolds | E 1933-51 | 1934, 1937, 1938 |
| 154 | Greg Williams | G 1984-85; SY 1986-91; CA 1992-97 | 1986, 1994 |
| 151 | Len Thompson* | CO 1965-78; SM 1979; Fl 1980 | 1972 |
| 151 | Keith Greig* | N 1971-85 | 1973, 1974 |
| 150 | Robert Flower* | M 1973-87 | |
| 143 | John Platten | H 1986-97 | 1987 |
| 139 | Simon Madden* | E 1974-92 | |
| 139 | Francis Bourke | R 1967-81 | |
| 139 | Ian Stewart | SK 1963-70; R 1971-75 | 1965, 1966, 1971 |
| 130 | Norman Ware | FO 1932-42, 1944-46 | 1941 |
| 129 | Bernie Quinlan* | FO 1969-77; Fl 1978-86 | 1981 |
| 129 | Alex Jesaulenko* | CA 1967-79; SK 1980-81 | |
| 129 | Greg Wells* | M 1969-80; CA 1980-82 | |

*The introduction of two umpires in 1976 saw two sets of 3-2-1 votes awarded for each game during seasons 1976 and 1977. This led to the over- all tally being inflated for players who played during these seasons. The votes that players listed in the top 20 polled in 1976-77 were: Gary Dempsey 55 votes (1976-28, 1977-27), Leigh Matthews 57 votes (23, 34) Garry Wilson 45 votes (24, 21) Kevin Bartlett 45 votes (2, 45), Len Thompson 48 votes (14, 34), Keith Greig 14 votes (0, 14) Robert Flower 39 votes ( 17, 22), Simon Madden 28 votes (3, 25), Bernie Quinlan 19 votes (8, 11), Alex Jesaulenko 25 votes (19, 6) and Greg Wells 48 votes (28, 20).*

*Quinlan, Jesaulenko and Wells were the only three players who would not have finished in the top 20 without the extra votes.They omitted Haydn Bunton (122 votes), from an amazing 119 games, David Cloke and Barry Davis (both 121).*

## THE GARY DEMPSEY STORY

Gary Dempsey's name was nailed near the top of the Brownlow Medal leaders board for a decade and a half.

Between the period 1970 and 1983, Dempsey finished in the top 10 in the Brownlow Medal every year bar 1981. A golfer would be happy with that many top 10 finishes.

He polled more than 10 votes in a season 13 out of 14 years between 1970 and 1983 actually winning the medal once — in 1975. In 12 of those seasons his tally for each year was above 15 votes.

Dempsey was an incredibly strong, prolific mark who regularly picked up more than 15 marks per match, as well as being a tap ruckman of the highest order. His mop of black hair and sideburns must have been hard for umpires to miss during the 1970s.

After winning six best and fairests at Footscray, he crossed to North Mel- bourne in 1979 and continued his remarkable record winning the Roos club best and fairest once and continuing his sequence of high Brownlow finishes.

# 1997 ROUND BY ROUND

**ROUND 1**
NM v Melb: 3 S. Smith (M),
2 J. Farmer (M), 1 J. Stynes (M).
Coll v PA: 3 S. Russell (C),
2 G. Brown (C), 1 P. Williams (C).
WB v Frem: 3 A. Wills (F),
2 S. McManus (F), 1 S. West (WB).
St K v Haw: 3 D. Harford (H),
2 R. Harvey (St K), 1 M. Graham (H).
WC v Sydney: 3 Peter Matera (WC),
2 I. Grgic (WC), 1 B. Cousins (WC).
Rich v Geel: 3 W. Campbell (R),
2 G. Kilpatrick (G), 1 M. Richardson (R).
Adel v Bris Lions: 3 B. James (A),
2 M. Ricciuto (A), 1 D. Jarman (A).
Ess v Carlton: 3 D. Fletcher (E),
2 J. Hird (E), 1 D. Rice (C).

**ROUND 2**
Melb v Coll: 3 S. Rocca (C),
2 N. Buckley (C), 1 S. Burns (C).
Rich v Adel: 3 M. Richardson (R),
2 N. Smart (A), 1 P. Broderick (R).
Geel v WC: 3 P. Riccardi (G),
2 B. Graham (G), 1 J. Barnes (G).
WB v Syd: 3 C. Grant (WB),
2 T. Liberatore (WB), 1 B. Johnson (WB).
Bris Lions v St K: 3 S. Hart (BL),
2 A. Fletcher (BL), 1 S. McIvor (BL).
PA v Ess: 3 B. Lyle (PA), 2 M. Long (E), 1 J. Misiti (E).
Frem v Haw: 3 S. McManus (F),
2 D. Harford (H), 1 D. Bandy (F).
NM v Carl: 3 D. King (NM),
2 M. Sexton (C), 1 A. Stevens (NM).

**ROUND 3**
Syd v Melb: 3 R. Pyman (M),
2 B. Seymour (S), 1 P. Kelly (S).
WB v Rich: 3 L. Cameron (WB),
2 R. Smith (WB), 1 M. Richardson (R).
St K v Coll: 3 N. Winmar (StK),
2 S. Russell (C), 1 J. Heatley (StK).
PA v Geel: 3 D. Dickie (PA),
2 M. Primus (PA), 1 S. Paxman (PA).
WC v Frem: 3 L. Grgic (WC),
2 G. McKenna (WC), 1 A. Wills (F).
Ess v NM: 3 M. Symons (E), 2 C. McKernan (NM), 1 J. Blumfield (E).
Carl v Adel: 3 M. Allan (C),
2 C. Bradley (C), 1 J. Murphy (C).
Haw v Bris Lions: 3 C. Treleven (H),
2 A. Lekkas (H), 1 S. Hart (BL).

**ROUND 4**
Melb v WB: 3 C. Grant (WB),
2 L. Darcy (WB), 1 A. Clarkson (M).
Coll v Carl: 3 A. Koutoufides (Carl),
2 C. Bradley (Carl), 1 G. Brown (Coll).
Rich v Frem: 3 D. Kellaway (R),
2 C. Waterhouse (F), 1 W. Campbell (R).
Geel v Ess: 3 J. Barnes (G),
2 D. Hall (G), 1 G. Kilpatrick (G).
St K v Sydney: 3 P. Kelly (S),

2 D. Cresswell (S), 1 J. Mooney (S).
WC v Haw: 3 P. Symmons (WC), 2 D. Banfield (WC), 1 N. Holland (H).
Bris Lions V NM: 3 N. Lappin (BL),
2 D. Dickfos (BL), 1 G. Archer (NM).
Adel v PA: 3 D. Mead (PA),
2 S. Breuer (PA), 1 B. Lade (PA).

**ROUND 5**
Ess v Coll: 3 D. Monkhorst (C),
2 G. Brown (C), 1 M. Lloyd (E).
Frem v St K: 3 A. Wills (F),
2 S. Loewe (F), 1 L. Toia (F).
Melb v WC: 3 P. Symmons (WC),
2 D. Neitz (M), 1 C. Lewis (WC).
WB v Adel: 3 M. Bickley (A),
2 M. Ricciuto (A), 1 T. Modra (A).
Haw v Syd: 3 D. Harford (H),
2 C. Treleven (H), 1 N. Holland (H).
PA v Bris Lions: 3 B. Lade (PA), 2 G. Wanganeen (PA), 1 N. Lappin (BL).
NM v Rich: 3 G. Archer (N),
2 C. McKernan (N), 1 M. Pike (N).
Carl v Geel: 3 L. Colbert (G),
2 G. Kilpatrick (G), 1 B. Sholl (G).

**ROUND 6**
WC v WB: 3 C. Grant (WB),
2 S. Minton-Connell (WB),
1 S. West (WB).
Ess v Bris Lions: 3 S. Lucas (E), 2 R. O'Connor (E), 1 G. O'Donnell (E).
Coll v Adel: 3 N. Buckley (C),
2 N. Smart (A), 1 K. Koster (A).
Geel v Frem: 3 R. Burns (G),
2 L. Pickering (G), 1 A. Wills (F).
Haw v NM: 3 P. Salmon (H),
2 C. McKernan (N) 1 D. Harford (H).
Syd v Carl: 3 P. Kelly (S),
2 D. Lewis (S), 1 G. Stafford (S).
St K v Melb: 3 S. Loewe (StK),
2 R. Harvey (StK), 1 T. Brown (StK).
PA v Rich: 3 S. Bond (PA),
2 G. Wanganeen (PA), 1 B. Lade (PA).

**ROUND 7**
NM v Coll: 3 S. Burns (C),
2 G. Brown (C), 1 A. McDonald (C).
Rich v Carl: 3 C. Bradley (C), 2 A. Koutoufides (C), 1 S. Silvagni (C).
WB v Haw: 3 C. Grant (WB), 2 T. Liberatore (WB), 1 M. Croft (WB).
Geel v Syd: 3 G. Kilpatrick (G),
2 B. Graham (G), 1 T. McGrath (G).
St K v PA: 3 R. Harvey (StK),
2 N. Burke (StK), 1 A. Jones (StK).
Frem v Melb: 3 L. Toia (F),
2 Q. Leach (F), 1 D. Kickett (F).
Bris Lions v WC: 3 C. Lewis (WC),
2 Peter. Matera (WC), 1 F. Gehrig (WC).
Adel v Ess: 3 M. Robran (A),
2 M. Ricciuto (A), 1 D. Jarman (A).

**ROUND 8**
Coll v WB: 3 P. Williams (C),
2 N. Buckley (C), 1 S. Patterson (C).
Melb v Geel: 3 B. Sholl (G),
2 T. McGrath (G), 1 T. Hargraves (G).

NM v PA: 3 M. Pike (NM),
2 A. Stevens (NM), 1 C. Sholl (NM).
Adel v Syd: 3 D. Jarman (A),
2 M. Ricciuto (A), 1 N. Smart (A).
Ess v St K: 3 M. Young (StK),
2 P. Everitt (StK) 1 M. Symons (E).
Carl v Haw: 3 B. Ratten (C),
2 G. Manton (C), 1 A. Lord (H).
Frem v Bris Lions: 3 J. White (F),
2 T. Lynch (BL), 1 C. Callaghan (F).
Rich v WC: 3 P. Broderick (R),
2 M. Gale (R), 1 W. Campbell (R).

**ROUND 9**
PA v Melb: 3 M. Wilson (PA),
2 S. Bond (PA), 1 B. Lade (PA).
Carl v Frem: 3 A. Wills (F),
2 L. O'Sullivan (C), 1 A. Hamill (C).
Haw v Adel: 3 K. Koster (A),
2 M. Ricciuto (A), 1 N. Smart (A).
Syd v Coll: 3 S. Carey (S), 2 P. Kelly (S) 1 D. Lewis (S).
Bris Lions v Geel: 3 N. Lappin (BL),
2 C. McRae (BL), 1 D. Bradshaw (BL).
WB v NM: 3 C. Ellis (WB),
2 P. Dimattina (WB), 1 S. West (WB).
St K v Rich: 3 N. Burke (StK),
2 A. Jones (StK), 1 J. Smith (StK).
WC v Ess: 3 Peter Matera (WC),
2 G. Jakovich (WC), 1 J. Hird (E).

**ROUND 10**
PA v Carl: 3 A. Heuskes (PA),
2 S. Paxman (PA), 1 M. Primus (PA).
NM v WC: 3 A. Stevens (NM),
2 Peter Matera (WC), 1 P. Bell (NM).
Haw v Coll: 3 P. Salmon (H),
2 N. Holland (H), 1 G. Brown (C).
Geel v St K: 3 L. Colbert (G),
2 L. Pickering (G), 1 R. Harvey (StK).
Rich v Melb: 3 J. Stynes (M),
2 D. Gaspar (R), 1 T. Viney (M).
Ess v WB: 3 T. Liberatore (WB),
2 J. Romero (WB), 1 C. Daniher (E).
Bris Lions v Syd: 3 C. Lambert (BL),
2 D. Lewis (S), 1 R. Champion (BL).
Frem v Adel: 3 M. Ricciuto (A),
2 P. Vardy (A), 1 A. Wills (F).

**ROUND 11**
Coll v Rich: 3 M. Richardson (R),
2 G. Brown (C), 1 B. Gale (R).
Ess v Haw: 3 A. Lord (H),
2 N. Holland (H), 1 P. Salmon (H).
WB v Geel: 3 B. Johnson (WB),
2 P. Dimattina (WB), 1 S. West (WB).
PA v Syd: 3 P. Roos (S), 2 T. Cook (S), 1 S. Carey (S).
WC v St K: 3 R. Harvey (StK), 2 N. Burke (StK), 1 G. McKenna (WC).
Melb v Adel: 3 R. Jameson (A),
2 S. Woewodin (M), 1 K. Koster (A).
NM v Frem: 3 C. McKernan (NM),
2 H. Black (F), 1 D. King (NM).
Carl v Bris Lions: 3 G. Williams (C),
A. Hickmott (C), 1 L. O'Sullivan (C).

**ROUND 12**
Syd v Rich: 3 S. Maxfield (S),

2 P. Roos (S), 1 D. Gaspar (R).
WB v PA: 3 B. Lyle (PA), 2 S.
Paxman (PA), 1 D. Southern (WB).
Coll v WC: 3 Peter Matera (WC), 2
P. Williams (C), 1 J. Worsfold (WC).
Geel v Haw: 3 P. Salmon (H),
2 S. Crawford (H), 1 L. Pickering (G).
Frem v Ess: 3 A. Wills (F),
2 C. Callaghan (F), 1 B. Allan (F).
St K v Carl: 3 N. Burke (StK),
2 S. Loewe (StK), 1 P. Everitt (StK).
Adel v NM: 3 D. King (NM), 2 M.
Roberts (NM), 1 J. Longmire (NM).
Melb v Bris Lions: 3 S. Hart (BL),
2 J. Molloy (BL), 1 M. Voss (BL).

## ROUND 13
WC v Carl: 3 Peter Matera (WC),
2 S. Silvagni (C), 1 C Bradley (C).
Rich v Ess: 3 D. Hardwick (E),
2 G. Moorcroft (E), 1 D. Fletcher (E).
St K v WB: 3 C. Grant (WB),
2 S. Wynd (WB), 1 P. Dimattina
(WB).
Geel v Adel: 3 P. Lynch (G),
2 L. Pickering (G), 1 M Mansfield (G).
PA v Frem: 3 M. Wilson (PA),
2 C. Callaghan (F), 1 M Primus (PA).
Haw v Melb: 3 J. Platten (H),
2 J. Robran (H), 1 P. Salmon (H).
Syd v NM: 3 S. Arnott (S), 2 D.
Cresswell (S), 1 A. Stevens (NM).
Bris Lions v Coll: 3 J. Molloy (BL),
2 M. Clarke (BL), 1 N. Buckley (C).

## ROUND 14
Adel v WC: 3 M. Ricciuto (A),
2 D. Jarman (A), 1 A. McLeod (A).
Geel v Coll: 3 B. Sholl (G),
2 P. Lynch (G), 1 P. Williams (C).
Carl v WB: 3 C. Grant (WB), 2 P.
Dimattina (WB), 1 R. Smith (WB).
St K v NM: 3 J. Heatley (StK),
2 J. Smith (StK), 1 T. Brown (StK).
Frem v Syd: 3 Q. Leach (F),
2 L. Toia (F), 1 P. Kelly (S).
Ess v Melb: 3 J. Misiti (E),
2 M. Lloyd (E), 1 M. Mercuri (E).
Haw v PA: 3 A. Lord (H),
2 J. Platten (H), 1 T. Woods (H).
Bris Lions v Rich: 3 N. Lappin (BL), 2
D. Dickfos (BL), 1 M. Richardson (R).

## ROUND 15
NM v Geel: 3 P. Lynch (G),
2 W. Schwass (NM), 1 D. King (NM).
Melb v Carl: 3 W. Viney (M),
2 G. Lovett (M), 1 D Schwarz (M).
WB v Bris Lions: 3 A. Fletcher (BL),
2 M. Clarke (BL), 1 D. Dickfos (BL).
Coll v Frem: 3 N. Buckley (C),
2 S. Crow (C), 1 S. Rocca (C).
Adel v St K: 3 R. Harvey (StK),
2 M. Ricciuto (A), 1 N. Burke (S).
Syd v Ess: 3 D. Lewis (S),
2 P. Roos (S), 1 M. Mercuri (E).
Rich v Haw: 3 D. Gaspar (R),
2 D. Bourke (R), 1 R. Taylor (H).
WC v PA: 3 G. Wanganeen (PA),
2 D. Kemp (WC), 1 M. Gardiner (WC).

## ROUND 16
Bris Lions v Adel: 3. M. Voss (BL), 2
R. Champion (BL), 1 J. Akermanis (BL).
Carl v Ess: 3 B. Ratten (C),

## HOW THE CLUBS POLLED

| Club | Votes | No. of players |
| --- | --- | --- |
| Adelaide | 70 | 14 |
| Brisbane Lions | 73 | 16 |
| Carlton | 60 | 15 |
| Collingwood | 68 | 13 |
| Essendon | 50 | 17 |
| Fremantle | 61 | 14 |
| Geelong | 91 | 15 |
| Hawthorn | 57 | 12 |
| Melbourne | 34 | 11 |
| North Melbourne | 63 | 12 |
| Port Adelaide | 70 | 13 |
| Richmond | 52 | 10 |
| St Kilda | 89 | 12 |
| Sydney | 72 | 13 |
| West Coast | 73 | 15 |
| Western Bulldogs | 83 | 15 |

2 S. Silvagni (C), 1 C. Bradley (C).
Haw v St K: 3 R. Harvey (StK),
2 S. Loewe (StK), 1 P. Everitt (StK).
Geel v Rich: 3 M. Mansfield (G),
2 G. Kilpatrick (G), 1 D. Hall (G).
Syd v WC: 3 P. Kelly (S), 2 D. Lewis
(S), 1 S. Carey (S).
PA v Coll: 3 S. Breuer (PA),
2 M. Primus (PA), 1 P. Williams (C).
Frem v WB: 3 D. Kickett (F),
2 P. Mann (F), 1 C. Grant (WB).
Melb v NM: 3 R. Scott (NM),
2 T. Viney (M), 1 D. King (NM).

## ROUND 17
Ess v PA: 3 M. Primus (PA), 2 S.
Cummings (PA), 1 J. Francou (PA).
Carl v NM: 3 D. King (NM),
2 A. McKay (C), 1 M. Roberts (NM).
Haw v Frem: 3 C. Waterhouse (F),
2 P. Mann (F), 1 P. Salmon (H).
Coll v Melb: 3 S. Russell (C),
2 G. Crosisca (C), 1 T. Francis (C).
Adel v Rich: 3 D. Jarman (A),
2 M. Robran (A), 1 D. Pittman (A).
WC v Geel: 3 C. Lewis (WC),
2 B. Heady (WC), 1 G. Hocking (G).
Syd v WB: 3 T. Cook (S),
2 D. Cresswell (S), 1 T Lockett (S).
St K v Bris Lions: 3 S. Lowe (StK),
2 A. Jones (StK), 1 N. Lappin (BL).

## ROUND 18
NM v Ess: 3 W. Schwass (NM),
2 J. Misiti (E), 1 C. McKernan (NM).
Melb v Syd: 3 P. Kelly (S),
2 M. Bayes (S), 1 T. Cook (S).
Rich v WB: 3 M. Knights (R),
2 N. Brown (WB), 1 W. Campbell (R).
Geel v PA: 3 S. King (G),
2 R. Riccardi (G), 1 B. Sholl (G).
Bris Lions v Haw: 3 A. Fletcher
(BL), 2 D. Bradshaw (BL), 1 S.
Crawford (H).
Adel v Carl: 3 C. Bradley (C),
2 S. Rehn (A), 1 K. Koster (A).
Coll v St K: 3 R. Harvey (StK),
2 N. Buckley (C), 1 P. Everitt (StK).

Frem v WC: 3 Peter Matera (WC), 2
D. Kemp (WC), 1 G. McKenna (WC).

## ROUND 19
NM v Bris Lions: 3 M. Pike (NM),
2 J. Longmire (NM), 1 P. Bell (NM).
Carl v Coll: 3 C. Bradley (Carl),
2 B. Ratten (Carl), 1 A. Koutoufides
(Carl).
WB v Melb: 3. L. Darcy (WB),
2 T. Viney (M), 1 N. Brown (WB).
Haw v WC: 3 F. Gehrig (WC),
2 D. Kemp (WC), 1 B. Heady (WC).
Frem v Rich: 3 G. Dhurrkay (F),
2 J. Sinclair (F), 1 D. Gaspar (R).
Syd v St K: 3 R. Harvey (StK),
2 P. Kelly (S), 1 N. Burke (StK).
Ess v Geel: 3 B. Caracella (E),
2 B. Sholl (G), 1 M. Mansfield (G).
PA v Adel: 3 G. Wanganeen (PA),
2 B. Lade (PA), 1 M. Connell (A).

## ROUND 20
WC v Melb: 3 J. Ball (WC), 2 Peter
Matera (WC), 1 D. Kemp (WC).
Coll v Ess: 3 S. Russell (C),
2 G. Crosisca (C), 1 M. Lloyd (E).
St K v Frem: 3 N. Burke (StK),
2 M. Lappin (StK), 1 J. Peckett (StK).
Geel v Carl: 3 B. Sholl (G),
2 J. Barnes (G), 1 D. Hall (G).
Bris Lions v PA: 3 C. Keating (BL),
2 S. Bond (PA), 1 G. Wanganeen (PA).
Syd v Haw: 3 D. Lewis (S),
2 P. Kelly (S), 1 B. Seymour (S).
Rich v NM: 3 D. Gaspar (R),
2 W. Schwass (NM), 1 R. Powell (R).
Adel v WB: 3 C. Grant (WB),
2 S. Wynd (WB), 1 J. Romero (WB).

## ROUND 21
Melb v St K: 3 N. Burke (StK),
2 J. Heatley (StK), 1 J. Peckett (StK).
NM v Haw: 3 W. Carey (NM), 2 M.
Graham (H), 1 W. Schwass (NM).
Carl v Syd: 3 B. Ratten (C),
2 D. Hulme (C), 1 P. Kelly (S).
WB v WC: 3 C. Grant (WB),
2 L. Darcy (WB), 1 S. West (WB).
Bris Lions v Ess: 3 M. Lloyd (E),
2 C. Daniher (E), 1 D. White (BL).
Frem v Geel: 3 S. King (G),
2 P. Riccardi (G), 1 D. Hall (G).
Rich v PA: 3 P. Broderick (R),
2 M. Knights (R), 1 R. Powell (R).
Adel v Coll: 3 D. Jarman (A),
2 K. Koster (A), 1 M. Connell (A).

## ROUND 22
WC v Bris Lions: 3 J. Schofield (WC),
2 D. Banfield (WC), 1 F. Gehrig (WC).
Melb v Frem: 3 J. Farmer (M),
2 P. Hopgood (M), 1 T. Viney (M).
Carl v Rich: 3 M. Knights (R),
2 D. Gaspar (R), 1 B. Ratten (C).
Haw v WB: 3 T. Liberatore (WB),
2 C. Grant (WB), 1 P. Salmon (H).
Syd v Geel: 3 B. Sholl (G),
2 B. Graham (G), 1 G. Hocking (G).
PA v St K: 3 R. Harvey (StK), 2 J.
Peckett (StK), 1 A. Heuskes (PA).
Coll v NM: 3 S. Patterson (C),
2 P. Williams (C), 1 A. Schauble (C).
Ess v Adel: 3 D. Wallis (E),
2 R. Jameson (A), 1 P. Somerville (E).

## AFL PLAYERS' ASSOCIATION MOST VALUABLE PLAYER AWARD

AFLPA members vote annually for the player among their peers they consider worthy of such an honor.

1982 — Leigh Matthews (Hawthorn)
1983 — Terry Daniher (Essendon)
1984 — Russell Greene (Hawthorn)
1985 — Greg Williams (Geelong)
1986 — Paul Roos (Fitzroy)
1987 — Tony Lockett (St Kilda)
1988 — Gerard Healy (Sydney)
1989 — Tim Watson (Essendon)
1990 — Darren Millane (Collingwood)
1991 — Jim Stynes (Melbourne)
1992 — Jason Dunstall (Hawthorn)
1993 — Gary Ablett (Geelong)
1994 — Greg Williams (Carlton)
1995 — Wayne Carey (North Melb)
1996 — Corey McKernan (North Melb)
1997 — Robert Harvey (St Kilda)

## AFMA MOST VALUABLE PLAYER

Members of the Australian Football Media Association vote annually for the player they consider the most outstanding for that particular season.

1973 — George Bisset (Coll)
1974 — Kevin Sheedy (Rich)
1975 — Alex Jesaulenko (Carl), Brian Roberts (SM)
1976 — Peter Knights (Haw)
1977 — Don Scott (Haw)
1978 — Malcolm Blight (NM)
1979 — Kevin Bartlett (Rich)
1980 — Kelvin Templeton (Foots)
1981 — Peter Moore (Coll)
1982 — Leigh Matthews (Haw)
1983 — Wayne Schimmelbusch (NM)
1984 — Terry Daniher (Ess)
1985 — Simon Beasley (Foots)
1986 — Paul Roos (Fitz)
1987 — John Platten (Haw)
1988 — Gerard Healy (Syd)
1989 — Tim Watson (Ess)
1990 — Peter Daicos (Coll)
1991 — Jim Stynes (Melb)
1992 — Jason Dunstall (Haw)
1993 — Gary Ablett (Geel)
1994 — Greg Williams (Carl)
1995 — Garry Lyon (Melb)
1996 — James Hird (Ess)
1997 — Robert Harvey (St Kilda)

## NORWICH RISING STAR

1993 — Nathan Buckley (Brisbane Bears)
1994 — Chris Scott (Brisbane Bears)
1995 — Nick Holland (Hawthorn)
1996 — Ben Cousins (West Coast)
1997 — Michael Wilson (Port Adelaide)

The Norwich Rising Star Award was instituted in 1993 to recognise and encourage talented young players in the AFL. After each round of home-and-away games, a player is nominated and at the end of the season a panel of experts selects the winner. The winner must be under the age of 21 at January 1 of that year, must not have played more than 10 games to the start of that season and must not have been suspended by the AFL or State League tribunals during the season (as with the Brownlow Medal, players found guilty of certain offences and fined or reprimanded by the Tribunal remain eligible to win the award). The award carries an investment portfolio, plus interest earned, as well as a hand-crafted trophy.

## NORM SMITH MEDAL

1979 — W. Harmes (Carlton)
1980 — K. Bartlett (Richmond)
1981 — B. Doull (Carlton)
1982 — M. Rioli (Richmond)
1983 — C. Robertson (Hawthorn)
1984 — B. Duckworth (Essendon)
1985 — S. Madden (Essendon)
1986 — G. Ayres (Hawthorn)
1987 — D. Rhys-Jones (Carlton)
1988 — G. Ayres (Hawthorn)
1989 — G. Ablett (Geelong)
1990 — A. Shaw (Collingwood)
1991 — P. Dear (Hawthorn)
1992 — P. Matera (West Coast)
1993 — M. Long (Essendon)
1994 — D. Kemp (West Coast)
1995 — G. Williams (Carlton)
1996 — G. Archer (North Melbourne)
1997 — A. McLeod (Adelaide)

Norm Smith was a famous Melbourne Football Club identity who was also associated with Fitzroy and South Melbourne at senior level. Smith played a total of 227 games with Melbourne and Fitzroy and coached in a total of 452 games with Melbourne (310), Fitzroy (55) and South Melbourne (87). During his 310-game tenure coaching Melbourne, he took the club into every Grand Final between 1954 and 1960 and won 6 premierships in the years 1955, 1956, 1957, 1959, 1960, 1964. He played from 1935 to 1950, and coached at senior level every year between 1949 and 1972, except 1968. Smith died in 1973, aged 57. The Norm Smith Medal is presented to the player judged, by an independent panel of football experts, best on ground in the Grand Final.

## JOHN COLEMAN MEDAL

**HOME AND AWAY MATCHES ONLY**

1981 — M. Roach (Richmond) — 86
1982 — M. Blight (Nth. Melb.) — 94
1983 — B. Quinlan (Fitzroy) — 106
1984 — B. Quinlan (Fitzroy) — 102
1985 — S. Beasley (Footscray) — 93
1986 — B. Taylor (Collingwood) — 100
1987 — T. Lockett (St. Kilda) — 117
1988 — J. Dunstall (Hawthorn) — 124
1989 — J. Dunstall (Hawthorn) — 126
1990 — J. Longmire (Nth. Melb.) — 98
1991 — T. Lockett (St. Kilda) — 118
1992 — J. Dunstall (Hawthorn) — 139
1993 — G. Ablett (Geelong) — 124
1994 — G. Ablett (Geelong) — 113
1995 — G. Ablett (Geelong) — 118
1996 — T. Lockett (Sydney) — 114
1997 — T. Modra (Adelaide) — 81

John Coleman was a champion Essendon full-forward. In 1949, with 12 goals on debut, 100 goals in his first season, an Essendon best and fairest, Victorian representation and full-forward in a premiership side, he made a spectacular entry into League ranks. He played 98 games kicking 537 goals before a serious knee injury prematurely ended his playing career. He later coached Essendon to 2 premierships in 1962 and 1965. He died in 1973, aged 44, but left his stamp on Australian Football as one of its greatest ever players. The Coleman Medal is awarded to the League's leading goalkicker at the end of the home-and-away rounds.

## MORRISH MEDALLISTS

The Morrish Medal was first presented the year after the formation of the League Thirds competition and was awarded to the player voted best and fairest in that grade by the field umpires. It perpetuates the memory of long-serving (1922-67) Reserve Grade treasurer Tom Norrish. In 1959 the competition was renamed the VFL 19s. Since 1991 the medal has been presented to the VSFL under-18s player of the season.

| | |
|---|---|
| 1947 | A. Dale (Essendon) |
| 1948 | R. Harvey (Melbourne) |
| 1949 | A. Harbrow (St. Kilda) |
| 1950 | N. Alford (North Melb.) |
| 1951 | F. Williams (Hawthorn) |
| 1952 | P. McPhee (Footscray) |
| 1953 | P. Pratt (Carlton) |
| 1954 | A. Clarke (Carlton) |
| 1955 | M. Job (Carlton) |
| 1956 | G. Rasmussen (Hawthorn) |
| 1957 | P. O'Reilly (South Melb.) |
| 1958 | N. Bowler (North Melb.) |
| 1959 | D. Glassenbury (Fitzroy) |
| 1960 | G. Ryan (Footscray) |
| 1961 | T. Johnston (Melbourne) |
| 1962 | K. Egan (Essendon) |
| 1963 | J. Schram (Geelong) |
| 1964 | P. Gowans (North Melb.) |
| 1965 | R. Petherbridge (St. Kilda) |
| 1966 | B. Wright (Fitzroy) |
| 1967 | M. Gale (Carlton) |
| 1968 | P. Callery (Melbourne) |
| 1969 | K. Gehling (Richmond) |
| 1970 | K. Marks (Fitzroy) |
| 1971 | T. O'Malley (Carlton) |
| 1972 | I. Kilmartin (North Melb.), |
| | V. Catoggio (Carlton)* |
| 1973 | R. Bruerton (South Melb.) |
| 1974 | J. Di-Natale (Foots), |
| | R. Bruerton (Sth Melb.) |
| 1975 | B. Jones (South. Melb) |
| 1976 | C. Jamieson (Richmond) |
| 1977 | D. Williams (Essendon) |
| 1978 | A. McPhie (Fitzroy) |
| | S. Simpson (North Melb.) |
| 1979 | P. Banks (Collingwood) |
| 1980 | P. Lane (Richmond) |
| 1981 | A. Battiston (Melbourne) |
| 1982 | L. Bamblett (Melbourne) |
| 1983 | Greg Healy (Melbourne) |
| 1984 | T. Liberatore (North Melb.) |
| 1985 | F. Zoccali (Essendon) |
| 1986 | D. Ross (North Melb.) |
| 1987 | W. Schwass (North Melb.) |
| 1988 | T. McGrath (North Melb.) |
| 1989 | B. Davies (Essendon) |
| 1990 | B. Roberson (Carlton) |
| | C. Watson (North Melb) |
| 1991 | G. Stevens (Sydney) |
| 1992 | B. Smith (Northern) |
| 1993 | D. Watson (Southern) |
| 1994 | G. Moorcroft (Northern) |
| 1995 | P. Hood (Geelong) |
| 1996 | N. Brown (Bendigo) |
| 1997 | D. Murray (Murray) |

## GARDINER MEDALLISTS

Instituted seven years after the formation of the League Seconds, the Gardiner Medal was named after the late Frank Gardiner, a president of the competition. In 1959 the Seconds was renamed the VFL Reserve Grade. The medal is awarded to the best and fairest player as adjudged by field umpires.

| | |
|---|---|
| 1926 | A. Jacobson (Sth Melb.), R. James (Ess) |
| 1927 | S. Jamieson (Richmond) |
| 1928 | J. Money (Geelong), N. Driver (Melbourne) |
| 1929 | R. Ross (Collingwood) |
| 1930 | M. Kelly (Geelong), S. Baker (Richmond) |
| 1931 | A. Logan (Hawthorn) |
| 1932 | A. Franke (North Melb. ) |
| 1933 | E. Utting (Hawthorn) |
| 1934 | R. Saunders (Richmond) |
| 1935 | J. Kinnear (Melbourne) |
| 1936 | M. Boyall (Collingwood) |
| 1937 | A. Peake (St Kilda) |
| 1938 | B. Calverley (Fitzroy) |
| 1939 | N. Smith (Essendon) |
| 1940 | A. Price (Carlton) |
| 1941 | P. McNamara (South Melb) |
| 1942 | K. Taylor (St Kilda) |
| 1943 | E. Hart (Melbourne) |
| 1944 | R. Wearmouth (Footscray) |
| 1945 | W. Arthur (North Melb. |
| 1946 | J. McLeod (Footscray) |
| 1947 | P. Twomey (Collingwood) |
| 1948 | J. Ryan (Footscray) |
| 1949 | K. Coghlan (Collingwood) |
| 1950 | D. Davies (Geelong) |
| 1951 | N. Doolan (North Melb. ) |
| 1952 | L. O'Halloran (Geelong) |
| 1953 | C. Austen (Richmond) |
| 1954 | N. Pearson (Hawthorn) |
| 1955 | D. Davies (Geelong) |
| 1956 | G. Kerr (Melbourne) |
| 1957 | L. Pridham (Essendon) |
| 1958 | J. Fisher (Hawthorn) |
| 1959 | W. Shelton (Hawthorn) |
| 1960 | N. Trezise (Geelong) |
| 1961 | J. O'Brien (North Melb. ) |
| 1962 | J. Gutterson (Footscray) |
| 1963 | W. Clark (Fitzroy) |
| 1964 | G. Arnold (Richmond) |
| 1965 | K. Jackman (Footscray) |
| 1966 | D. Herrod (Geelong) |
| 1967 | R. Graham (Geelong) |
| 1968 | P. Rhoden (Melbourne) |
| 1969 | K. Emselle (Melbourne) |
| 1970 | M. Redenbach (North Melb) |
| 1971 | B. Brown (Melbourne) |
| 1972 | M. Pokrovsky (Footscray) |
| 1973 | V. Catoggio (Carlton) |
| 1974 | S. Clifford (Collingwood) |
| 1975 | N Chamberlain (Melbourne) |
| 1976 | A. Mangels (Carlton) |
| 1977 | D. Schimmelbusch (North Melb) |
| 1978 | A. Goad (Hawthorn) |
| 1979 | C. Boyd (Essendon) |
| 1980 | W. Valli (Essendon) |
| 1981 | D. Vernon (Richmond) |
| 1982 | R. Merrett (Essendon) |
| 1983 | J. Taylor (Footscray) |

**CONSISTENT:** In a year in which injuries ravaged the Brisbane Lions, Marcus Ashcroft was the only player to play every game. He finished third in the best and fairest.

**MORE PLEASE:** In 1997, Paul Kelly was equal third in the Brownlow, won his fourth club best and fairest, was All-Australian captain for the third year in succession, was named the AFL Players' Association's most courageous player and played his 150th game.

**ROOOOOOS:** It is one of the great sounds in football hearing the crowd collectively say Paul Roos' name as he gathers the ball time after time. Luckily for the punters, and for the Sydney Swans, Roos will be back for his last season in 1998. Last year he was named at centre half-back in the All-Australian team for the second year in a row. At 34, he's the most experienced player in the AFL, having played 335 games, and following the departure of Hawthorn's John Platten, the oldest.

**CONFIDENT:** The West Coast Eagles' Mick Malthouse coached his side into the finals for the eighth time in succession in 1997. He was named a life member of the Eagles in October and believes that everyone should look out for the youngsters that the Eagles are gathering together to attack 1998. All four players (below) played in West Coast's final against North Melbourne in 1997. All were under 20. They are the future of the Eagles.

**MICHAEL GARDINER:** Debut 1997, games 10, born 5/7/1979

**BEN COUSINS:** Debut 1996, games 38, born 30/6/1978

**CHAD MORRISON:** Debut 1996, games 42, born 29/3/1978

**JOSH WOODEN:** Debut 1997, games 18, born 14/11/1978

**NO MARKING TIME:** Geelong's Leigh Colbert is one of the most exciting and consistent youngsters in the game. He finished second in the club best and fairest in 1997, but his season will be remembered for the courageous mark he took — but which was denied by umpire Grant Vernon — in the 1997 second semi final between Geelong and Adelaide.

**HEIR APPARENT:** Teenager Steven King was forced into the number one rucking role for the Cats after John Barnes broke an arm last season.

**BLITZ:** The Western Bulldogs sent Sydney packing with a nine goal to zero opening quarter in the second qualifying final at the MCG. Scott Wynd was brilliant dropping fearlessly into the defensive hole to block off Tony Lockett's leads.

**UP AND AWAY:** It was a fleeting appearance for the Brisbane Lions in the 1997 finals. After leading St Kilda at half-time in the fourth qualifying final, they were overpowered by the Saints in the second half to lose by 46 points.

**CAREY:** In the third qualifying final, Wayne Carey stood between Geelong and a berth in the preliminary final. His match-winning seven goals on a wet night at the MCG was one of the best individual finals performances seen for a long time. It set up a showdown with his arch rival Glen Jakovich, a contest in which he was soundly beaten, but his team won.

**JAKOVICH:** West Coast's Glen Jakovich was back to his best in the 1997 finals series after returning earlier in the year from a knee reconstruction. He thrashed North champion Wayne Carey in the first semi-final, but it wasn't enough to gain victory for his team.

**YOUNGER, YOUNGEST:** Corey McKernan kicked four goals in the first semi-final to be a match-winner for the Roos before injuring a shoulder early in the preliminary final. His opponent on the day, Michael Gardiner, showed enough to be considered a star of the near future.

**CALM BEFORE STORM:** Darren Jarman was the Adelaide Crows' trump card. Against Geelong, he managed 10 kicks in the second quarter to get his team back into the game. Against the Western Bulldogs, he was unleashed up forward in the last quarter of the preliminary final. Against the Saints, he kicked six goals in the second half of the 1997 Grand Final.

**ANGUISH:** Corey McKernan dislocated his shoulder before 10 minutes had gone in the 1997 preliminary final after being tackled by St Kilda's Nathan Burke and Brett Cook. It was the end of his season and that of the Kangaroos.

**PUSHING FOR LUCK:** St Kilda co-captain Stewart Loewe was sensational for the Saints in 1997 and preliminary final night was the club's highpoint as the Saints won their way into their first Grand Final for 26 years, defeating North Melbourne by 31 points.

**HOPE (1):** The Western Bulldogs only needed to kick one goal in the last quarter of the 1997 preliminary final and they would have earned a place in the Grand Final. Tony Liberatore and teammates Brett Montgomery (left) and Paul Hudson (right) thought Libber had just kicked the sealer. He hadn't and the Bulldogs were about to squander a 22-point lead at three-quarter time to lose by two points to the Adelaide Crows in one of the most dramatic games of the season.

**HOPE (2):** Adelaide Crows coach Malcolm Blight moved Darren Jarman to full-forward at three-quarter time of the preliminary final to turn the tide. It worked. He took big marks and kicked winning goals and generally frightened the life out of his Western Bulldogs' opponents.

**FROM OBSCURITY:** Shane Ellen transferred from the Western Bulldogs to the Adelaide Crows in the 1996 pre-season draft and led a relatively obscure life before kicking five goals in the Grand Final. He began the game at full-forward, where he kicked two, and then moved back to half-back, where he kicked a further three. He'd kicked only three goals in his previous 37 games.

**AUSSIE:** The highlight of Grand Final day for St Kilda came late in the first quarter with Austinn Jones' five-bounce run down the Great Southern Stand wing, a run that ended in Jones goaling from just on 50 metres out. It was inspirational.

**LEADERS AND FIGHTERS:** Mark Bickley and Ben Hart (above) endured the hard times with Adelaide as 100 game players. On Grand Final day, they embraced after reaching football's pinnacle — the premiership. David Pittman and Darren Jarman had their knockers. In Pittman's case, even the coach had wondered aloud about his performance after a round two game against Richmond. They answered the critics with unblemished Grand Final performances.

**THE AWFUL TRUTH:** Jayson 'Jack' Daniels is devastated after being part of St Kilda's tilt at the 1997 premiership that ended on Grand Final day in defeat to Adelaide.

**WINMAR:** The death of Nicky Winmar's father, Neal, on the eve of the Grand Final was tragic for the exciting St Kilda playmaker. It was a gutsy effort on Winmar's behalf to take part in the Grand Final.

**SO NEAR, YET SO FAR:** Chris Grant had an awful end to the football season. First, a devastating exit from the finals with a two-point loss and then the result on Brownlow Medal night where despite polling the most votes, he was ineligible to win the award because of a one-match suspension received for striking Hawthorn's Nick Holland. It nearly overshadowed what was a fantastic year.

**ACTION ATTRACTION:** Western Bulldogs coach Terry Wallace promised a new approach from his club and he delivered, giving the public a rare insight into the machinations of a football club. The team didn't let him down on the field, until the last quarter of the preliminary final when they squandered a golden opportunity to play in the club's first Grand Final for 36 years.

**REVITALISED:** Martin Pike really didn't have to prove to himself that he could play football. He knew that. But to the hard noses in the football world there were question marks — some justified, some not — over his capacity to maintain a disciplined approach to football. In 1997, after crossing from Fitzroy to North Melbourne, he silenced the doubters.

**LEAPS AND BOUNDS:** Peter Bell built on the 1996 success at North Melbourne with a fantastic year around the packs for the Kangaroos.

**WIDE EYED:** St Kilda coach Stan Alves was named All-Australian coach in 1997. It was one of the most remarkable performances for many years as speculation abounded that he was facing the sack as the Saints entered round six. The club underwent a form transformation that saw them on top of the ladder after 22 rounds, before making the Grand Final. The big spider — ruckman Peter Everitt — was one of the main causes of the Saints' improved form.

**THE STORY:** St Kilda played as a passionate, unified team last year. They were on a mission, winning nine games straight to enter their first Grand Final in 26 years. They failed at the final hurdle with a loss in the Grand Final, but produced a Brownlow Medallist, Robert Harvey, and had a lot of fun along the way. They were contenders, not pretenders.

**THE VICTORS:** This group of men will be immortalised as the first Adelaide Crows players to win an AFL premiership.

**THE COACH:** Malcolm Blight helped the Adelaide Crows finally fulfil their potential and win the flag in his first season at Football Park. It was a mighty effort from Blight who must have stared down some personal demons entering his fourth Grand Final as coach when the previous three (with Geelong) had ended in defeat.

1984    A. Stephenson (Footscray)
1985    G. Dear (Hawthorn), J. Bennett (Hawthorn)
1986    T. Liberatore (Footscray)
1987    B. Gotch (St. Kilda)
1988    T. Liberatore (Footscray)
1989    M. Kol (Geelong)
1990    R. Keogh (Melbourne)
1991    S. Anderson (Collingwood)
1992    M. Dwyer (St Kilda)
1993    R. Keogh (Melbourne)
1994    D. Bain (Fitzroy)
1995    S. Crawshay (Hawthorn)
1996    T. Nichols (North Melb)
1997    B. Lloyd (Hawthorn)

## MAGAREY MEDALLISTS

Awarded to the best and fairest player in the SANFL as adjudged by field umpires. William Magarey was the first chairman of the South Australian Football League.

1898    A. Green (Norwood)
1899    S. A. Malin (Port Adel)
1900    No Award
1901    P. T. Sandland (North Adel)
1902    T. D. MacKenzie (West Torrens)
1903    H. S. Waye (Sturt)
1904    No Award
1905    T. D. MacKenzie (North Adel)
1906    T. D. MacKenzie (North Adel)
1907    J. Mack (Port Adel)
1908    J. M. Tierney (West Adel)
1909    H. R. Head (West Adel)
1910    S. Hosking (Port Adel)
1911    H. V. Cumberland (Sturt)
1912    D. Low (West Torrens)
1913    T. J. Leahy (North Adel)
1914    W. J. Ashley (Port Adel)
1915    F. M. Barry (South Adel)
1916–18 No Award
1919    D. Moriarty (South Adel)
1920    D. Moriarty (South Adel)
1921    D. Moriarty (South Adel)
1922    R. G. L. Barnes (West Adel)
1923    H. A. Riley (Sturt)
1924    W. Scott (Norwood)
1925    A. . Lill (Norwood)
1926    B. H. McGregor (West Adel)
1927    B. H. McGregor (West Adel)
1928    H. H. Handby (Glenelg)
1929    R. Snell (West Adel)
1930    W. Scott (Norwood)
1931    J. E. G. Sexton (West Adel)
1932    S. M. Pontifex (West Torrens)
1933    W. K. Dunn (Sturt)
1934    G. B. Johnston (Glenelg)
1935    J. Cockburn (South Adel)
1936    W. B. McCallum (Norwood)
1937    H. J. Hawke (North Adel)
1938    R. B. Quinn (Port Adel)
1939    J. H. Pash (North Adel)
1940    P. M. Brock (Glenelg)
1941    M. M. W. Boyall (Glenelg)
1942–44 No Award

1945    R. B. Quinn (Port Adel)
1946    R. W. Hank (West Torrens)
1947    R. W. Hank (West Torrens)
1948    H. R. Phillips (North Adel)
1949    H. R. Phillips (North Adel)
1950    I. L. McKay (North Adel)
1951    J. E. Marriott (Norwood)
1952    L. C. Fitzgerald (Sturt)
1953    J. G. Deane (South Adel)
1954    L. C. Fitzgerald (Sturt)
1955    L. H. Head (West Torrens)
1956    D. E. Boyd (Port Adel)
1957    R. M. Benton (West Adel)
1958    L. H. Head (West Torrens)
1959    L C. Fitzgerald (Sturt)
1960    B. Barbary (North Adel)
1961    J. A. Halbert (Sturt)
1962    K. J Eustice (West Adel)
1963    L. H. Head (West Torrens)
1964    G. P. Motley (Port Adel)
1965    G. C. Window (Central Dist)
1966    R. G. Kneebone (Norwood)
1967    T. D. Obst (Port Adel)
1968    B. C. Robran (North Adel)
1969    D. K. Phillis (Glenelg)
1970    B. C. Robran (North Adel)
1971    R. F. Ebert (Port Adel)
1972    M. J. Blight (Woodville)
1973    B. C. Robran (North Adel)
1974    R. F. Ebert (Port Adel)
1975    P. D. Woite (Port Adel)
1976    R. F. Ebert (Port Adel)
1977    T. F. Grimwood (West Adel)
1978    K. Hodgeman (Glenelg)
1979    A. J. Duckworth (Central Dist)
1980    R. F. Ebert (Port Adel)
1981    M. C. Aish (Norwood)
1982    A. B. McGuinness (Glenelg)
1983    A. J. Antrobus (North Adel)
1984    J. Platten (Central Dist)
1985    G. Fielke (West Adel)
1986    G. Anderson (Port Adel)
1987    A. N. Jarman (North Adel)
1988    G. Whittlesea (Sturt)
1989    Gilbert McAdam (Central Dist)
1990    S. Hodges (Port Adel)
1991    M. Naley (South Adel)
1992    N. Buckley (Port Adel)
1993    B. Phillips (North Adel)
1994    G. McIntosh (Norwood)
1995    G. McIntosh (Norwood)
        G. Kilpatrick (West Adel)
1996    J. Francou (North Adel)
1997    A. Jarman (Norwood)
        B. Atkinson (Sturt)

## SANDOVER MEDALLISTS

Awarded to the best and fairest player in the WAFL as adjudged by field umpires.

In 1921 Perth businessman Alfred Sandover donated a medal for the competition's outstanding player of the season. His descendants have carried on the tradition.

| | |
|---|---|
| 1921 | Tom Outridge (Subiaco) |
| | Tie with Cyril Hoft (Perth) |
| | decided on President's vote |
| 1922 | Harold Boyd (West Perth) |
| 1923 | W. (Digger) Thomas (East Perth) |
| 1924 | Jim Gosnell (West Perth) |
| 1925 | George Owens (East Perth) |
| 1926 | John Leonard (Subiaco) |
| 1927 | Jim Craig (West Perth) |
| 1928 | Jack Rocchi (South Frem) |
| 1929 | W (Billy) Thomas (East Perth) |
| | Tie with John Leonard (Subiaco) |
| | decided on President's vote |
| 1930 | Ted Fleming (West Perth) |
| 1931 | Lin Richards (East Frem) |
| 1932 | Keith Hough (Clarem-Cottesloe) |
| 1933 | Sammy Clarke (Clarem-Cottesloe) |
| 1934 | Sammy Clarke (Clarem-Cottesloe) |
| 1935 | Lou Daily (Subiaco) |
| | George Krepp (Swan Dists) |
| 1936 | George Moloney (Claremont) |
| 1937 | Frank Jenkins (South Frem) |
| 1938 | Haydn Bunton senior (Subiaco) |
| 1939 | Haydn Bunton senior (Subiaco) |
| 1940 | E. (Checker) O'Keefe (West Perth) |
| 1941 | Haydn Bunton senior (Subiaco) |
| 1942 | Laurie Bowen (West Perth) |
| 1943 | Terry Moriarty (Perth) |
| 1944 | Jim Davies (Swan Dists) |
| 1945 | George Bailey (Perth) |
| 1946 | John Loughridge (West Perth) |
| 1947 | Clive Lewington (South Frem) |
| 1948 | Merv McIntosh (Perth) |
| 1949 | George Maffina (Claremont) |
| 1950 | Jim Conway (East Frem) |
| | Won from Frank Allen (East Perth) |
| | on countback of 2nd votes |
| 1951 | Fred Buttsworth (West Perth) |
| 1952 | Steve Marsh (South Frem) |
| 1953 | Merv McIntosh (Perth) |
| 1954 | Merv McIntosh (Perth) |
| 1955 | John Todd (South Frem) |
| 1956 | Graham Farmer (East Perth) |

| | |
|---|---|
| 1957 | Jack Clarke (East Frem) |
| | Won from Graham Farmer (East Perth) |
| | on countback of lst votes |
| 1958 | Ted Kilmurray (East Perth) |
| 1959 | Brian Foley (West Perth) |
| 1960 | Graham Farmer (East Perth) |
| 1961 | Neville Beard (Perth) |
| | Won from Ray Sorrell (East Perth) |
| | on countback of lst votes |
| 1962 | Haydn Bunton junior. (Swan Dists) |
| 1963 | Ray Sorrell (East Frem) |
| 1964 | Barry Cable (Perth) |
| 1965 | Bill Walker (Swan Dists) |
| 1966 | Bill Walker (Swan Dists) |
| 1967 | Bill Walker (Swan Dists) |
| | John Parkinson (Claremont) |
| | Equal first, each presented with a medal |
| 1968 | Barry Cable (Perth) |
| 1969 | Malcolm Brown (East Perth) |
| 1970 | Pat Dalton (Perth) |
| | Won from Bill Walker (Swan Dists) |
| | on countback of lst votes. |
| 1971 | David Hollins (East Frem) |
| 1972 | Ian Miller (Perth) |
| 1973 | Barry Cable (Perth) |
| 1974 | Graham Melrose (East Frem) |
| 1975 | Alan Quartermaine (East Perth) |
| 1976 | Peter Spencer (East Perth) |
| 1977 | Brian Peake (East Frem) |
| 1978 | Phil Kelly (East Perth) |
| 1979 | Phil Kelly (East Perth) |
| 1980 | Stephen Michael (South Frem) |
| 1981 | Stephen Michael (South Frem) |
| 1982 | Phil Narkle (Swan Dists) |
| 1983 | John Ironmonger (East Perth) |
| | Won from Bryan Cousins (Perth) |
| | on countback of 2nd votes |
| 1984 | Peter Spencer (East Perth) |
| | Michael Mitchell (Claremont) |
| | Steve Malaxos (Claremont) |
| 1985 | Murray Wrensted (East Frem) |
| 1986 | Mark Bairstow (South Frem) |
| 1987 | Mark Watson (Perth) |
| 1988 | David Bain (East Perth) |
| 1989 | Craig Edwards (South Frem) |
| 1990 | Mick Grasso (Swan Dists) |
| 1991 | Ian Dargie (Subiaco) |
| 1992 | Robbie West (West Perth) |
| 1993 | Neil Mildenhall (West Perth) |
| 1994 | Ian Dargie (Subiaco) |
| 1995 | Craig Treleven (East Frem) |
| 1996 | Jeremy Wasley (Swan Dists) |
| 1997 | Brady Anderson (East Perth) |

# LEADING GOALKICKERS

## 1897–1997

### TOTALS INCLUDE FINALS MATCHES

1897 — **James, E.** (Geelong) . . . . . . . . . . . . 27
1898 — **Smith, A.** (Collingwood) . . . . . . . . . 31
1899 — **James, E.** (Geelong) . . . . . . . . . . . . 31
1900 — **Thurgood, A.** (Essendon) . . . . . . . . 25
1901 — **Hiskins, F.** (Essendon) . . . . . . . . . . 34
1902 — **Rowell, E.** (Collingwood) . . . . . . . . 33
1903 — **Lockwood, E.** (Collingwood) . . . . . 35
1904 — **Coutie, V.** (Melbourne) . . . . . . . . . . 39
1905 — **Pannam, C.** (Collingwood) . . . . . . . 38
1906 — **Grace, M.** (Carlton) . . . . . . . . . . . . 50
1907 — **Lee, W. H.** (Collingwood) . . . . . . . . 47
1908 — **Lee, W. H.** (Collingwood) . . . . . . . . 54
1909 — **Lee, W. H.** (Collingwood) . . . . . . . . 58
1910 — **Lee, W. H.** (Collingwood) . . . . . . . . 58
1911 — **Gardiner, V.** (Carlton) . . . . . . . . . . 47
1912 — **Brereton, H.** (Melbourne) . . . . . . . . 56
1913 — **Freake, J.** (Fitzroy) . . . . . . . . . . . . 56
1914 — **Lee, W. H.** (Collingwood) . . . . . . . . 57
1915 — **Lee, W. H.** (Collingwood) . . . . . . . . 66
1915 — **Freake, J.** (Fitzroy) . . . . . . . . . . . . 66
1916 — **Lee, W. H.** (Collingwood) . . . . . . . . 48
1917 — **Lee, W. H.** (Collingwood) . . . . . . . . 54
1918 — **Cowley, E.** (Carlton) . . . . . . . . . . . 35
1919 — **Lee, W. H.** (Collingwood) . . . . . . . . 56
1920 — **Bayliss, G.** (Richmond) . . . . . . . . . 63
1921 — **Lee, W. H.** (Collingwood) . . . . . . . . 64
1922 — **Clover, H.** (Carlton) . . . . . . . . . . . . 56
1923 — **Stockdale, G.** (Essendon) . . . . . . . . 68
1924 — **Moriarty, J.** (Fitzroy) . . . . . . . . . . . 82
1925 — **Hagger, L.** (Geelong) . . . . . . . . . . . 78
1926 — **Coventry, G.** (Collingwood) . . . . . . 83
1927 — **Coventry, G.** (Collingwood) . . . . . . 97
1928 — **Coventry, G.** (Collingwood) . . . . . . 89
1929 — **Coventry, G.** (Collingwood) . . . . . 124
1930 — **Coventry, G.** (Collingwood) . . . . . 118
1931 — **Vallence, H.** (Carlton) . . . . . . . . . . 86
1932 — **Moloney, G.** (Geelong) . . . . . . . . . 109
1933 — **Pratt, R.** (South Melbourne) . . . . . 109
1934 — **Pratt, R.** (South Melbourne) . . . . . 150
1935 — **Pratt, R.** (South Melbourne) . . . . . 103
1936 — **Mohr, W.** (St Kilda) . . . . . . . . . . . 101
1937 — **Coventry, G.** (Collingwood) . . . . . . 72
1938 — **Todd, R.** (Collingwood) . . . . . . . . 120
1939 — **Todd, R.** (Collingwood) . . . . . . . . 121
1940 — **Titus, J.** (Richmond) . . . . . . . . . . 100
1941 — **Smith, N.** (Melbourne) . . . . . . . . . . 89
1942 — **White, L.** (South Melbourne) . . . . . 80
1943 — **Harris, R.** (Richmond) . . . . . . . . . . 63
1944 — **Fanning, F.** (Melbourne) . . . . . . . . 87
1945 — **Fanning, F.** (Melbourne) . . . . . . . . 67

1946 — **Brittingham, W.** (Essendon) . . . . . . 66
1947 — **Fanning, F.** (Melbourne) . . . . . . . . . 97
1948 — **White, L.** (Geelong) . . . . . . . . . . . . 86
1949 — **Coleman, J.** (Essendon) . . . . . . . . 100
1950 — **Coleman, J.** (Essendon) . . . . . . . . 120
1951 — **Goninon, G.** (Geelong) . . . . . . . . . . 86
1952 — **Coleman, J.** (Essendon) . . . . . . . . 103
1953 — **Coleman, J.** (Essendon) . . . . . . . . . 97
1954 — **Collins, J.** (Footscray) . . . . . . . . . . 84
1955 — **Rayson, N.** (Geelong) . . . . . . . . . . 80
1956 — **Young, W.** (St Kilda) . . . . . . . . . . . 56
1957 — **Collins, J.** (Footscray) . . . . . . . . . . 74
1958 — **Brewer, I.** (Collingwood) . . . . . . . . 73
1959 — **Evans, R.** (Essendon) . . . . . . . . . . 78
1960 — **Evans, R.** (Essendon) . . . . . . . . . . 67
1961 — **Carroll, T.** (Carlton) . . . . . . . . . . . 54
1962 — **Wade, D.** (Geelong) . . . . . . . . . . . . 68
1963 — **Peck, J.** (Hawthorn) . . . . . . . . . . . 75
1964 — **Peck, J.** (Hawthorn) . . . . . . . . . . . 68
1965 — **Peck, J.** (Hawthorn) . . . . . . . . . . . 56
1966 — **Fordham, E.** (Essendon) . . . . . . . . 76
1967 — **Wade, D.** (Geelong) . . . . . . . . . . . . 96
1968 — **Hudson, P.** (Hawthorn) . . . . . . . . 125
1969 — **Wade, D.** (Geelong) . . . . . . . . . . . 127
1970 — **Hudson, P.** (Hawthorn) . . . . . . . . 146
1971 — **Hudson, P.** (Hawthorn) . . . . . . . . 150
1972 — **McKenna, P.** (Collingwood) . . . . . 130
1973 — **McKenna, P.** (Collingwood) . . . . . . 86
1974 — **Wade, D.** (North Melbourne) . . . . 103
1975 — **Matthews, L.** (Hawthorn) . . . . . . . 68
1976 — **Donohue, L.** (Geelong) . . . . . . . . 105
1977 — **Hudson, P.** (Hawthorn) . . . . . . . . 110
1978 — **Templeton, K.** (Footscray) . . . . . . 118
1979 — **Templeton, K.** (Footscray) . . . . . . . 91
1980 — **Roach, M.** (Richmond) . . . . . . . . 112
1981 — **Roach, M.** (Richmond) . . . . . . . . . 86
1982 — **Blight, M.** (North Melbourne) . . . . 103
1983 — **Quinlan, B.** (Fitzroy) . . . . . . . . . . 116
1984 — **Quinlan, B.** (Fitzroy) . . . . . . . . . . 105
1985 — **Beasley, S.** (Footscray) . . . . . . . . 105
1986 — **Taylor, B.** (Collingwood) . . . . . . . 100
1987 — **Lockett, T.** (St Kilda) . . . . . . . . . 117
1988 — **Dunstall, J.** (Hawthorn) . . . . . . . 132
1989 — **Dunstall, J.** (Hawthorn) . . . . . . . 138
1990 — **Longmire, J.** (North Melbourne) . . . 98
1991 — **Lockett, T.** (St Kilda) . . . . . . . . . 127
1992 — **Dunstall, J.** (Hawthorn) . . . . . . . 145
1993 — **Modra, T.** (Adelaide) . . . . . . . . . 129
1994 — **Ablett, G.** (Geelong) . . . . . . . . . . 129
1995 — **Ablett, G.** (Geelong) . . . . . . . . . . 122
1996 — **Lockett, T.** (Sydney) . . . . . . . . . . 131
1997 — **Modra, T.** (Adelaide) . . . . . . . . . . 84

**243**

# TOP GOALKICKERS

## 1897–1997

The 15 players listed are the most prolific goalkickers in VFL history. Former Collingwood great Gordon Coventry set a magnificent mark of 1299. He retired in 1937 and since then only four players, Doug Wade (Geelong, North Melbourne), Jason Dunstall (Hawthorn), Tony Lockett (St Kilda, Sydney) and Gary Ablett (Hawthorn, Geelong) have managed to reach 1000 career goals.

### GORDON COVENTRY — Collingwood

| | | | | | |
|---|---|---|---|---|---|
| 1920 | 13 | 1926 | 83 | 1932 | 82 |
| 1921 | 19 | 1927 | 97 | 1933 | 108 |
| 1922 | 42 | 1928 | 89 | 1934 | 105 |
| 1923 | 36 | 1929 | 124 | 1935 | 88 |
| 1924 | 28 | 1930 | 118 | 1936 | 60 |
| 1925 | 68 | 1931 | 67 | 1937 | 72 |
| | | | | TOTAL | 1299 |

### JASON DUNSTALL — Hawthorn

| | | | | | |
|---|---|---|---|---|---|
| 1985 | 36 | 1990 | 83 | 1994 | 101 |
| 1986 | 77 | 1991 | 82 | 1995 | 66 |
| 1987 | 94 | 1992 | 145 | 1996 | 102 |
| 1988 | 132 | 1993 | 123 | 1997 | 21 |
| 1989 | 138 | | | TOTAL | 1200 |

### TONY LOCKETT — St Kilda & Sydney

| | | | | | |
|---|---|---|---|---|---|
| 1983 | 19 | 1989 | 78 | 1994 | 56 |
| 1984 | 77 | 1990 | 65 | Trans to Syd | |
| 1985 | 79 | 1991 | 127 | 1995 | 110 |
| 1986 | 60 | 1992 | 132 | 1996 | 121 |
| 1987 | 117 | 1993 | 53 | 1997 | 37 |
| 1988 | 35 | | | TOTAL | 1166 |

### DOUG WADE — Geelong & North Melb.

| | | | | | |
|---|---|---|---|---|---|
| 1961 | 51 | 1967 | 96 | Trans to NM | |
| 1962 | 68 | 1968 | 64 | 1973 | 73 |
| 1963 | 48 | 1969 | 127 | 1974 | 103 |
| 1964 | 41 | 1970 | 74 | 1975 | 47 |
| 1965 | 29 | 1971 | 94 | | |
| 1966 | 52 | 1972 | 90 | TOTAL | 1057 |

### GARY ABLETT — Hawthorn & Geelong

| | | | | | |
|---|---|---|---|---|---|
| 1982 | 9 | 1986 | 65 | 1990 | 75 |
| Trans to Geel | | 1987 | 53 | 1991 | 28 |
| 1984 | 33 | 1988 | 82 | 1992 | 72 |
| 1985 | 82 | 1989 | 87 | 1993 | 124 |
| 1994 | 129 | 1995 | 122 | 1996 | 69 |
| | | | | TOTAL | 1030 |

### JACK TITUS — Richmond

| | | | | | |
|---|---|---|---|---|---|
| 1926 | 1 | 1932 | 41 | 1938 | 72 |
| 1927 | 0 | 1933 | 42 | 1939 | 48 |
| 1928 | 26 | 1934 | 80 | 1940 | 100 |
| 1929 | 54 | 1935 | 83 | 1941 | 87 |
| 1930 | 50 | 1936 | 83 | 1942 | 67 |
| 1931 | 47 | 1937 | 65 | 1943 | 24 |
| | | | | TOTAL | 970 |

### LEIGH MATTHEWS — Hawthorn

| | | | | | |
|---|---|---|---|---|---|
| 1969 | 7 | 1975 | 68 | 1981 | 48 |
| 1970 | 20 | 1976 | 71 | 1982 | 74 |
| 1971 | 43 | 1977 | 91 | 1983 | 79 |
| 1972 | 45 | 1978 | 71 | 1984 | 77 |
| 1973 | 51 | 1979 | 30 | 1985 | 56 |
| 1974 | 52 | 1980 | 32 | TOTAL | 915 |

### PETER McKENNA — Collingwood & Carlton

| | | | | | |
|---|---|---|---|---|---|
| 1965 | 21 | 1970 | 143 | 1975 | 26 |
| 1966 | 20 | 1971 | 134 | 1976 | in Tas |
| 1967 | 47 | 1972 | 130 | Trans to Carl | |
| 1968 | 64 | 1973 | 86 | 1977 | 36 |
| 1969 | 98 | 1974 | 69 | TOTAL | 874 |

### BERNIE QUINLAN — Footscray & Fitzroy

| | | | | | |
|---|---|---|---|---|---|
| 1969 | 18 | 1976 | 34 | 1982 | 53 |
| 1970 | 12 | 1977 | 27 | 1983 | 116 |
| 1971 | 48 | Trans to Fitz | | 1984 | 105 |
| 1972 | 37 | 1978 | 18 | 1985 | 84 |
| 1973 | 20 | 1979 | 48 | 1986 | 52 |
| 1974 | 9 | 1980 | 27 | | |
| 1975 | 36 | 1981 | 73 | TOTAL | 817 |

### KEVIN BARTLETT — Richmond

| | | | | | |
|---|---|---|---|---|---|
| 1965 | 13 | 1972 | 34 | 1979 | 36 |
| 1966 | 19 | 1973 | 31 | 1980 | 84 |
| 1967 | 38 | 1974 | 47 | 1981 | 58 |
| 1968 | 38 | 1975 | 42 | 1982 | 58 |
| 1969 | 30 | 1976 | 27 | 1983 | 37 |
| 1970 | 34 | 1977 | 55 | | |
| 1971 | 53 | 1978 | 44 | TOTAL | 778 |

### STEPHEN KERNAHAN — Carlton

| | | | | | |
|---|---|---|---|---|---|
| 1986 | 62 | 1990 | 69 | 1994 | 82 |
| 1987 | 73 | 1991 | 46 | 1995 | 63 |
| 1988 | 54 | 1992 | 83 | 1996 | 56 |
| 1989 | 59 | 1993 | 68 | 1997 | 23 |
| | | | | TOTAL | 738 |

### BILL MOHR — St Kilda

| | | | | | |
|---|---|---|---|---|---|
| 1929 | 38 | 1934 | 66 | 1939 | 47 |
| 1930 | 83 | 1935 | 83 | 1940 | 25 |
| 1931 | 57 | 1936 | 101 | 1941 | 1 |
| 1932 | 68 | 1937 | 58 | | |
| 1933 | 74 | 1938 | 34 | TOTAL | 735 |

### PETER HUDSON — Hawthorn

| | | | | | |
|---|---|---|---|---|---|
| 1967 | 57 | 1971 | 150 | 1977 | 110 |
| 1968 | 125 | 1972 | 8 | | |
| 1969 | 120 | 1973 | 3 | | |
| 1970 | 146 | 1974 | 3 | TOTAL | 727 |

### HARRY VALLENCE — Carlton

| | | | | | |
|---|---|---|---|---|---|
| 1926 | 19 | 1931 | 86 | 1936 | 86 |
| 1927 | 25 | 1932 | 97 | 1937 | 39 |
| 1928 | 22 | 1933 | 84 | 1938 | 81 |
| 1929 | 64 | 1934 | 35 | | |
| 1930 | 18 | 1935 | 66 | TOTAL | 722 |

### DICK LEE — Collingwood

| | | | | | |
|---|---|---|---|---|---|
| 1906 | 35 | 1912 | 2 | 1918 | 17 |
| 1907 | 47 | 1913 | 8 | 1919 | 56 |
| 1908 | 54 | 1914 | 57 | 1920 | 20 |
| 1909 | 58 | 1915 | 66 | 1921 | 64 |
| 1910 | 58 | 1916 | 48 | 1922 | 38 |
| 1911 | 25 | 1917 | 54 | TOTAL | 707 |

# CAREER GOALS TO 1997

*Club premiership matches only.   * = 1997 player*

| | Total Goals | Total Matches | Game Ave | | Total Goals | Total Matches | Game Ave |
|---|---|---|---|---|---|---|---|
| G. Coventry (Coll) | 1299 | 306 | 4.25 | P. Salmon* (Ess-Haw) | 526 | 248 | 2.12 |
| J. Dunstall* (Haw) | 1200 | 256 | 4.69 | P. Sumich* (West Coast) | 514 | 150 | 3.43 |
| T. Lockett* (St K-Syd) | 1166 | 236 | 4.94 | J. Longmire* (Nth Mel) | 504 | 180 | 2.8 |
| D. Wade (Geel-Nth Melb) | 1057 | 267 | 3.96 | B. Hutchison (Ess) | 496 | 290 | 1.71 |
| G. Ablett (Haw-Geel) | 1030 | 248 | 4.15 | K. Forbes (Ess-Nth Mel-Fitz) | 475 | 187 | 2.54 |
| J. Titus (Rich) | 970 | 294 | 3.3 | J. Peck (Haw) | 475 | 213 | 2.23 |
| L. Matthews (Haw) | 915 | 332 | 2.76 | J. Spencer (Nth Mel) | 475 | 153 | 3.1 |
| P. Mckenna (Coll-Carl) | 874 | 191 | 4.58 | S. Loewe* (St K) | 474 | 237 | 2 |
| B. Quinlan (Foots-Fitz) | 817 | 366 | 2.23 | T. Daniher (Sth Melb-Ess) | 469 | 313 | 1.5 |
| K. Bartlett (Rich) | 778 | 403 | 1.93 | D. Brereton (Haw-Syd-Coll) | 464 | 211 | 2.2 |
| S. Kernahan* (Carl) | 738 | 251 | 2.94 | S. Murray (Nth Mel-Rich) | 461 | 121 | 3.81 |
| B. Mohr (St K) | 735 | 195 | 3.77 | A. Pannam (Coll-Rich) | 459 | 183 | 2.51 |
| P. Hudson (Haw) | 727 | 129 | 5.64 | G. Wilson (Fitz) | 452 | 268 | 1.69 |
| H. Vallence (Carl) | 722 | 204 | 3.54 | M. Blight (Nth Mel) | 444 | 178 | 2.49 |
| D. Lee (Coll) | 707 | 230 | 3.07 | A. Jesaulenko (Carl-St K) | 444 | 279 | 1.59 |
| B. Pratt (Sth Melb) | 681 | 158 | 4.31 | R. Walls (Carl-Fitz) | 444 | 259 | 1.71 |
| J. Moriarty (Ess-Fitz) | 662 | 170 | 3.89 | J. Dyer (Rich) | 443 | 312 | 1.42 |
| M. Moncrieff (Haw) | 629 | 224 | 2.81 | J. Freake (Fitz) | 442 | 174 | 2.54 |
| M. Roach (Rich) | 607 | 200 | 3.04 | D. Reynolds (Ess) | 442 | 320 | 1.38 |
| K. Templeton (Foots-Mel) | 593 | 177 | 3.35 | A. Ruthven (Fitz) | 442 | 222 | 1.99 |
| S. Beasley (Foots) | 575 | 154 | 3.73 | B. Brownless* (Geel) | 441 | 198 | 2.23 |
| S. Madden (Ess) | 575 | 378 | 1.52 | A. Noonan (Ess-Rich) | 434 | 192 | 2.26 |
| N. Smith (Mel-Fitz) | 572 | 227 | 2.52 | R. Merrett (Ess-Bris Bears) | 433 | 313 | 1.38 |
| R. Osborne* (Fitz-Syd-Foots-Coll) | 568 | 269 | 2.11 | L. Richards (Coll) | 423 | 250 | 1.69 |
| P. Daicos (Coll) | 549 | 250 | 2.2 | T. Modra* (Adel) | 421 | 110 | 3.83 |
| D. Harris (Rich) | 548 | 196 | 2.8 | B. Skilton (Sth Melb) | 412 | 237 | 1.74 |
| L. White (Geel-Sth Melb) | 540 | 142 | 3.8 | W. Carey* (Nth Mel) | 411 | 162 | 2.54 |
| J. Coleman (Ess) | 537 | 98 | 5.48 | F. Fanning (Mel) | 411 | 104 | 3.95 |
| B. Taylor (Rich-Coll) | 527 | 140 | 3.76 | C. Rankin (Geel) | 400 | 153 | 2.61 |

## THE GORDON COVENTRY STORY

Gordon Coventry holds the League record for the most career goals kicked. His total of 1299 was scored in an era when freak sporting achievements seemed to be common.

Don Bradman averaged 99.94 in Test cricket, Phar Lap won everything there was to win and Coventry made the walk to Victoria Park an occasion of happiness for Collingwood supporters. 'Nuts' Coventry averaged 4.25 goals a game over 306 games, 72 a season over 18 seasons between 1920 and 1937 and 111 in 31 finals appearances (second highest number of finals appearances behind Michael Tuck).

He kicked 100 goals in a season four times, being the first player, in 1929 (124 goals), to break the century barrier. He led the League's goalkicking six times and Collingwood's 16 times and played in nine Collingwood Grand Finals for five flags. His nine goals in the 1928 Grand Final was unequalled until 1989 (Gary Ablett). Coventry's style was accumulative rather than spectacular, according to those who saw him play. His results are spectacular to those who didn't.

## CENTURIES AGAINST CLUBS

*Players who have kicked 100 or more goals against one club:*

**G. Coventry (Coll)**
114 v Carlton
107 v Essendon
136 v Fitzroy
122 v Geelong
134 v Hawthorn
124 v Melbourne
113 v North Melb.
117 v Richmond
143 v South Melb.
100 v St Kilda

**D. Wade (Geel, NM)**
101 v Footscray
107 v Hawthorn
122 v Richmond

**P. McKenna (Coll, Carlt)**
124 v South Melb.

**W. Lee (Coll)**
112 v Carlton

101 v Richmond

**L. Matthews (Haw)**
113 v North Melb.

**G. Ablett (Haw/Geel)**
117 v Richmond

**T. Lockett (St.K/Syd)**
114 v Fitzroy
102 v North Melb.
112 v Sydney

**J. Dunstall (Haw)**
111 v Richmond
105 v Geelong

103 v Footscray
90 v Melbourne

*Players getting close:*

**J. Dunstall (Haw)**
90 v Collingwood
90 v Melbourne

**T. Lockett (St.K/Syd)**
83 v Essendon
83 v Hawthorn
82 v Western Bulldogs

# BAGS OF SEVEN OR MORE

*The number of times bags of seven or more goals have been kicked by the leading goalkickers.  * = 1997 player*

| | Matches | Goals | Ratio | 18 | 17 | 16 | 15 | 14 | 13 | 12 | 11 | 10 | 9 | 8 | 7 |
|---|---|---|---|---|---|---|---|---|---|---|---|---|---|---|---|
| G. Coventry (1920–37, Coll) | 1299 | 306 | 4.25 | — | 1 | 1 | 1 | 1 | — | — | 5 | 2 | 11 | 16 | 25 |
| J. Dunstall* (1985–97, Haw) | 1200 | 256 | 4.69 | — | 1 | — | — | 1 | — | 4 | 5 | 5 | 13 | 12 | 14 |
| T. Lockett* (1983–97, St K, Syd) | 1166 | 236 | 4.94 | — | — | 1 | 1 | — | 1 | 6 | 4 | 6 | 11 | 15 | 20 |
| D. Wade (1961–75, Geel, Nth Melb) | 1057 | 267 | 3.96 | — | — | — | — | — | 2 | — | 2 | — | 5 | 10 | 21 |
| G. Ablett (1982; 1984–97, Haw, Geel) | 1030 | 248 | 4.15 | — | — | — | — | 3 | — | 2 | 2 | 5 | 6 | 10 | 17 |
| J. Titus (1926–43, Rich) | 970 | 294 | 3.30 | — | — | — | — | — | — | — | — | 3 | 4 | 9 | 3 |
| L. Matthews (1969–85, Haw) | 915 | 332 | 2.76 | — | — | — | — | — | — | — | 2 | — | — | 2 | 10 |
| P. McKenna (1965–75; 1977, Coll, Carl) | 874 | 191 | 4.58 | — | — | 1 | — | — | 1 | 4 | 4 | 3 | 7 | 9 | 16 |
| B. Quinlan (1969–86, Foots, Fitz) | 817 | 366 | 2.23 | — | — | — | — | — | — | — | 1 | 1 | 2 | 3 | 6 |
| K. Bartlett (1965–83, Rich) | 778 | 403 | 1.93 | — | — | — | — | — | — | — | — | — | — | 1 | 3 |
| S. Kernahan* (1986–97, Carl) | 738 | 251 | 2.94 | — | — | — | — | — | — | — | — | 2 | 2 | 1 | 11 |
| B. Mohr (1929–41, St K) | 735 | 195 | 3.77 | — | — | — | — | — | — | — | 2 | 1 | 5 | 9 | 13 |
| P. Hudson (1967–74; 1977, Haw) | 727 | 129 | 5.64 | — | — | 1 | — | — | 2 | 2 | 2 | 5 | 8 | 14 | 10 |
| H. Vallence (1926–38, Carl) | 722 | 204 | 3.54 | — | — | — | — | — | — | — | 4 | — | 3 | 6 | 14 |
| D. Lee (1906–22, Coll) | 707 | 230 | 3.07 | — | — | — | — | — | — | — | 1 | — | 1 | 2 | 8 |
| B. Pratt (1930–39; 1946, Sth Mel) | 681 | 158 | 4.31 | — | — | — | 1 | — | — | 1 | 3 | 3 | 4 | 6 | 14 |
| J. Moriarty (1922; 1924–33, Ess, Fitz) | 662 | 170 | 3.89 | — | — | — | — | — | — | 1 | — | 1 | 3 | 7 | 8 |
| M. Moncrieff (1971–83, Haw) | 629 | 224 | 2.81 | — | — | — | — | — | — | — | — | 3 | 4 | 4 | 7 |
| M. Roach (1977–89, Rich) | 607 | 200 | 3.04 | — | — | — | — | — | — | — | 2 | 3 | 3 | 2 | 15 |
| K. Templeton (1974–85, Foots, Melb) | 593 | 177 | 3.35 | — | — | — | — | 1 | — | — | — | — | 2 | 7 | 6 |
| S. Beasley (1982–89, Foots) | 575 | 154 | 3.73 | — | — | — | — | — | — | 3 | 1 | 1 | 3 | 3 | 8 |
| S. Madden (1974–92, Ess ) | 575 | 378 | 1.52 | — | — | — | — | — | — | — | — | — | — | 2 | 3 |
| N. Smith (1935–50, Melb, Fitz) | 572 | 227 | 2.52 | — | — | — | — | — | — | — | 1 | — | — | 4 | 4 |
| R. Osborne* (1982–97, Fitz, Syd, Foots, Coll) | 568 | 269 | 2.11 | — | — | — | — | — | — | — | 1 | 1 | — | 5 | 4 |
| P. Daicos (1979–93, Coll) | 549 | 250 | 2.20 | — | — | — | — | — | 1 | — | — | — | 1 | 3 | 7 |
| D. Harris (1934–44, Rich) | 548 | 196 | 2.80 | — | — | — | — | — | — | — | — | 1 | — | 1 | 7 |
| L. White (1941–50, Geel, Sth Mel) | 540 | 142 | 3.80 | — | — | — | — | — | — | 1 | 2 | 3 | 4 | 3 | 5 |
| J. Coleman (1949–54, Ess) | 537 | 98 | 5.48 | — | — | — | — | 1 | 2 | 1 | 2 | 6 | 3 | 5 | 10 |
| B. Taylor (1980–90, Rich, Coll) | 527 | 140 | 3.76 | — | — | — | — | — | — | 1 | — | 2 | 3 | 5 | 12 |
| P. Salmon* (1983–97, Ess, Haw) | 526 | 248 | 2.12 | — | — | — | — | — | — | — | 2 | 1 | 2 | 4 | 9 |
| P. Sumich* (1989–97, W Coast) | 514 | 150 | 3.43 | — | — | — | — | — | — | 1 | — | 1 | — | 5 | 3 |
| J. Longmire* (1988–95; 1997, Nth Mel) | 504 | 180 | 2.80 | — | — | — | — | 1 | — | 1 | — | — | 2 | 6 | 8 |
| B. Hutchison (1942–57, Ess) | 496 | 290 | 1.71 | — | — | — | — | — | — | — | — | — | — | — | 2 |
| K. Forbes (1928–40, Ess, Nth Mel, Fitz) | 475 | 187 | 2.54 | — | — | — | — | — | — | — | — | — | 1 | 2 | 1 |
| J. Peck (1954–66, Haw) | 475 | 213 | 2.23 | — | — | — | — | — | — | — | — | — | — | 3 | 5 |
| J. Spencer (1948–57, Nth Mel) | 475 | 153 | 3.10 | — | — | — | — | — | — | — | — | 1 | 1 | 5 | 2 |
| S. Loewe* (1986–97, St K) | 474 | 237 | 2.00 | — | — | — | — | — | — | — | — | — | 2 | 4 | 5 |
| T. Daniher (1976–92, Sth Mel, Ess) | 469 | 313 | 1.50 | — | — | — | — | — | — | — | — | — | — | 1 | 5 |
| D. Brereton (1982–92; 1994–95, Haw, Syd, Coll) | 464 | 211 | 2.20 | — | — | — | — | — | — | — | 1 | — | — | 2 | — |
| S. Murray (1937–46; 1948, Nth Mel, Rich) | 461 | 121 | 3.81 | — | — | — | — | — | — | — | — | 1 | 2 | 4 | 6 |
| A. Pannam (1933–43; 1945; 1947, Coll, Rich) | 459 | 183 | 2.51 | — | — | — | — | — | — | — | — | — | — | — | 4 |
| G. Wilson (1971–84, Fitz ) | 452 | 268 | 1.69 | — | — | — | — | — | — | — | — | — | — | — | 2 |
| M. Blight (1974–82, Nth Melb) | 444 | 178 | 2.49 | — | — | — | — | — | — | — | 1 | — | — | 7 | 9 |

## THE FRED FANNING STORY

Fred Fanning kicked 18 goals against St Kilda at the Junction Oval in the final round of the 1947 season. It was the highest number of goals kicked by one player in a single match in the history of AFL football.

Fanning performed his feat in his last game of football. It took him to 97 goals for the season, still the highest tally of goals kicked in a season by a Melbourne player. Melbourne is the only Victorian-based club not to have a century goalkicker.

Fanning kicked 11 goals in the first half and seven in the second.

In 1995, Sydney's Tony Lockett kicked 16 in one day against Fitzroy and that was after spending 10 minutes on the bench.

Hawthorn spearhead Jason Dunstall kicked 17.5 against Richmond in 1992, and with 11 up until half-time, he had many driving out to Waverley Park in the hope they would witness history. He just failed. Fanning has set a good target.

| | Matches | Goals | Ratio | 18 | 17 | 16 | 15 | 14 | 13 | 12 | 11 | 10 | 9 | 8 | 7 |
|---|---|---|---|---|---|---|---|---|---|---|---|---|---|---|---|
| A. Jesaulenko (1967–81, Carl, St K) | 444 | 279 | 1.59 | — | — | — | — | — | — | — | — | 1 | 2 | 1 | 8 |
| R. Walls (1967–80, Carl, Fitz) | 444 | 259 | 1.71 | — | — | — | — | — | — | — | 1 | — | — | — | — |
| J. Dyer (1931–49, Rich) | 443 | 312 | 1.42 | — | — | — | — | — | — | — | — | — | 1 | 1 | 1 |
| J. Freake (1912–24, Fitz ) | 442 | 174 | 2.54 | — | — | — | — | — | — | — | 1 | 1 | 1 | 1 | 2 |
| A. Ruthven (1940–41; 1943–54, Fitz) | 442 | 222 | 1.99 | — | — | — | — | — | — | — | — | — | 1 | 1 | 1 |
| B. Brownless* (1986–97, Geel) | 441 | 198 | 2.23 | — | — | — | — | — | — | — | 1 | — | 1 | 3 | 4 |
| A. Noonan (1966–77, Ess, Rich) | 434 | 192 | 2.26 | — | — | — | — | — | — | — | — | — | 1 | 5 |
| R. Merrett (1978–96, Ess, Bris Bears) | 433 | 313 | 1.38 | — | — | — | — | — | — | — | — | — | — | 2 | 2 |
| L. Richards (1941–55, Coll) | 423 | 250 | 1.69 | — | — | — | — | — | — | — | — | — | — | — | 1 |
| T. Modra* (1992–97, Adel) | 421 | 110 | 3.83 | — | — | — | — | — | 2 | — | — | 2 | — | 3 | 11 |
| B. Skilton (1956–68; 1970–71, Sth Mel) | 412 | 237 | 1.74 | — | — | — | — | — | — | — | — | 2 | — | 1 | 3 |
| W. Carey* (1989–97, Nth Melb) | 411 | 162 | 2.54 | — | — | — | — | — | — | — | 1 | — | — | — | 6 |
| F. Fanning (1940; 1942–47, Melb ) | 411 | 104 | 3.95 | 1 | — | — | — | — | — | — | 3 | 2 | 3 | 2 | 7 |
| C. Rankin (1915; 1919–28, Geel) | 400 | 153 | 2.61 | — | — | — | — | — | — | — | — | 1 | 1 | 1 | 1 |

## TOP GOALS PER MATCH RATIOS 1897–1997

| Ratio | Player | Club | Matches | Goals |
|---|---|---|---|---|
| 5.636 | Peter Hudson | Hawthorn 1967–74; 1977 | 129 | 727 |
| 5.480 | John Coleman | Essendon 1949–54 | 98 | 537 |
| 4.941 | Tony Lockett | St Kilda 1983–94; Sydney 1995–97 | 236 | 1166 |
| 4.688 | Jason Dunstall | Hawthorn 1985–97 | 256 | 1200 |
| 4.576 | Peter McKenna | Collingwood 1965–75; Carlton 1977 | 191 | 874 |
| 4.310 | Bob Pratt | South Melb 1930–39; 1946 | 158 | 681 |
| 4.303 | Ron Todd | Collingwood 1935–39 | 76 | 327 |
| 4.250 | Jack MacMillan | Footscray 1936 | 4 | 17 |
| 4.245 | Gordon Coventry | Collingwood 1920–37 | 306 | 1299 |
| 4.153 | Gary Ablett | Hawthorn 1982; Geelong 1984–96 | 248 | 1030 |
| 3.959 | Doug Wade | Geelong 1961–72; North Melb 1973–75 | 267 | 1057 |
| 3.952 | Fred Fanning | Melbourne 1940; 1942–47 | 104 | 411 |
| 3.894 | Jack Moriarty | Essendon 1922; Fitzroy 1924–33 | 170 | 662 |
| 3.852 | Allen Jakovich | Melbourne 1991–94; Footscray 1996 | 54 | 208 |
| 3.850 | Dave Lynch | Richmond 1922–23; 1926–27; 1929 | 20 | 77 |
| 3.827 | Tony Modra | Adelaide 1992–97 | 110 | 421 |
| 3.810 | Sel Murray | North Melb 1937–44; 1948; Richmond 1945–46 | 121 | 461 |
| 3.803 | Lindsay White | Geelong 1941; 1944–50; South Melb 1942–43 | 142 | 540 |
| 3.769 | Bill Mohr | St Kilda 1929–41 | 195 | 735 |
| 3.764 | Brian Taylor | Richmond 1980–84; Collingwood 1985–90 | 140 | 527 |
| 3.756 | Mark Jackson | Melbourne 1981–82; St Kilda 1983; Geelong 1984–86 | 82 | 308 |
| 3.734 | Simon Beasley | Footscray 1982–89 | 154 | 575 |
| 3.688 | Noel O'Brien | Carlton 1954–55 | 32 | 118 |
| 3.560 | George Margitich | Melbourne 1930–34 | 75 | 267 |
| 3.539 | Harry Vallence | Carlton 1926–38 | 204 | 722 |
| 3.522 | Jason Heatley | West Coast 1995–96; St Kilda 1997 | 23 | 81 |
| 3.509 | Saverio Rocca | Collingwood 1992–97 | 110 | 386 |
| 3.500 | John Hall | Hawthorn 1938 | 2 | 7 |
| 3.500 | Malcolm Greenslade | Richmond 1971 | 2 | 7 |
| 3.443 | George Moloney | Geelong 1931–35 | 88 | 303 |
| 3.429 | Warren Ralph | Carlton 1984–86 | 21 | 72 |
| 3.427 | Peter Sumich | West Coast 1989–97 | 150 | 514 |
| 3.400 | Jack Metherell | Geelong 1932–37 | 65 | 221 |
| 3.350 | Kelvin Templeton | Footscray 1974–82; Melbourne 1983–85 | 177 | 593 |
| 3.333 | Austin Robertson | South Melb 1966 | 18 | 60 |
| 3.322 | George Goninon | Essendon 1948–50; Geelong 1950–54 | 87 | 289 |
| 3.299 | Jack Titus | Richmond 1926–43 | 294 | 970 |
| 3.296 | Eddie Hart | Fitzroy 1941; 1944; 1946–51 | 98 | 323 |
| 3.281 | Ron Evans | Essendon 1958–62 | 64 | 210 |
| 3.265 | Tom Reynolds | Essendon 1937–44; | 113 | 369 |
| 3.263 | Alan Rait | Footscray 1933–34 | 19 | 62 |
| 3.250 | Bob Galbally | Collingwood 1944 | 8 | 26 |
| 3.250 | Ross Ditchburn | Carlton 1982–83 | 28 | 91 |
| 3.229 | Larry Donohue | Geelong 1973–80 | 105 | 339 |
| 3.207 | Harry Davie | Melbourne 1924–27; Carlton 1928 | 58 | 186 |
| 3.129 | Warwick Capper | Sydney 1983–87; 1991; Brisbane Bears 1988–90 | 124 | 388 |
| 3.105 | Jock Spencer | North Melb 1948–57 | 153 | 475 |

## MOST GOALS BY INDIVIDUALS IN LEAGUE MATCHES: 1897–1997

| G.B. | Player | Result | Season, Round Venue* |
|------|--------|--------|----------------------|
| 18.1 | Fred Fanning | (Melbourne 27.9.171) v St Kilda 10.18.78 | 47-R19-JO |
| 17.5 | Jason Dunstall | (Hawthorn 25.22.172) v Richmond 14.9.93 | 92-R7-WP |
| 17.4 | Gordon Coventry | (Collingwood 25.17.167) v Fitzroy 13.16.94 | 30-R12-VP |
| 16.5 | Gordon Coventry | (Collingwood 22.10.142) v Hawthorn 7.14.56 | 29-R13-VP |
| 16.4 | Peter McKenna | (Collingwood 19.15.129) v South Melbourne 6.22.58 | 69-R19-VP |
| 16.1 | Peter Hudson | (Hawthorn 21.10.136) v Melbourne 14.20.104 | 69-R5-GO |
| 16.0 | Tony Lockett | (Sydney 27.8.170) v Fitzroy 6.8.44 | 95-R19-WO |
| 15.9 | Kelvin Templeton | (Footscray 33.15.213) v St Kilda 16.10.106 | 79-R13-WO |
| 15.5 | Gordon Coventry | (Collingwood 20.19.139) v Essendon 14.14.98 | 33-R11-VP |
| 15.3 | Bob Pratt | (South Melbourne 23.10.142) v Essendon 15.16.106 | 34-R3-LO |
| 15.4 | Tony Lockett | (St Kilda 24.13.157) v Sydney 15.14.104 | 92-R13-M |
| 14.7 | Gary Ablett | (Geelong 19.18.132) v Essendon 23.18.156 | 93-R6-MCG |
| 14.5 | Gordon Coventry | (Collingwood 23.22.160) v Hawthorn 10.13.73 | 34-R14-VP |
| 14.5 | John Coleman | (Essendon 22.13.145) V Fitzroy 7.12.54 | 54-R7-WH |
| 14.5 | Gary Ablett | (Geelong 25.15.165) v Sydney 9.17.71 | 94-R8-SCG |
| 14.3 | Gary Ablett | (Geelong 32.19.211) v Richmond 10.17.77 | 89-R9-MCG |
| 14.2 | John Longmire | (North Melbourne 31.14.200) v Melbourne 10.13.73 | 90-R14-MCG |
| 14.2 | Doug Strang | (Richmond 30.19.199) v North Melbourne 4.7.31 | 31-R2-PR |
| 14.2 | Jason Dunstall | (Hawthorn 20.12.132) v Footscray 10.5.65 | 96-R19-WP |
| 14.1 | Harold Robertson | (South Melbourne 29.19.189) v St Kilda 2.6.18 | 19-R12-LO |

*Venues: Refer to legend, page 239*

## HIGHEST GOALS AT EACH CLUB IN A SEASON

Adelaide — Tony Modra, 129 (1993)
Brisbane Bears — Roger Merrett, 60 (1993)
Brisbane Lions — Justin Leppitsch, 50 (1997)
Carlton — Alex Jesaulenko, 115 (1970)
Collingwood — Peter McKenna, 143 (1970)
Essendon — John Coleman, 120 (1950)
Fitzroy — Bernie Quinlan, 116 (1983)
Footscray — Kelvin Templeton, 118 (1978)
Fremantle — Peter Mann, 33 (1995)
           Kingsley Hunter, 33 (1996)
Geelong — Gary Ablett, 129 (1994)
Hawthorn — Peter Hudson, 150 (1971)
Melbourne — Fred Fanning, 97 (1947)
North Melbourne — Doug Wade, 103 (1974)
           Malcolm Blight, 103 (1982)
Port Adelaide — Scott Cummings, 70 (1997)
Richmond — Michael Roach, 112 (1980)
Sth Melb/Sydney — Bob Pratt, 150 (1934)
St Kilda — Tony Lockett, 132 (1992)
West Coast — Peter Sumich, 111 (1991)

## TOTAL GOALS AT EACH CLUB

Adelaide — Tony Modra, 421 (1992–97)
Brisbane Bears — Roger Merrett, 285 (1988–96)
Brisbane Lions — Justin Leppitsch, 50 (1997– )
Carlton — Stephen Kernahan, 738 (1986–97)
Collingwood — Gordon Coventry, 1299 (1920–37)
Essendon — Simon Madden, 575 (1974–92)
Fitzroy — Jack Moriarty, 626 (1924–33)
Footscray — Simon Beasley, 575 (1982–89)
Fremantle — Peter Man, 79 (1995–97)
Geelong — Gary Ablett, 1021 (1984–96)
Hawthorn — Jason Dunstall, 1200 (1985–97)
Melbourne — Norm Smith, 546 (1935–48)
North Melbourne — John Longmire, 504 (1988–97)
Port Adelaide — Scott Cummings, 70 (1997)
Richmond — Jack Titus, 970 (1926–43)
South Melb/Sydney — Bob Pratt, 681 (1930–46)
St Kilda — Tony Lockett, 898 (1983–94)
West Coast — Peter Sumich, 514 (1989–97)

## MOST CAREER GOALS IN FINALS MATCHES: 1897–1997

| | | Clubs | Finals | Match Ave |
|---|---|-------|--------|-----------|
| 112 | Gordon Coventry | Coll | 31 | 3.61 |
| 78 | Jason Dunstall | Haw | 21 | 3.71 |
| 74 | Jack Titus | Rich | 24 | 3.08 |
| 72 | Leigh Matthews | Hawth | 29 | 2.48 |
| 65 | Stephen Kernahan | Carlt | 18 | 3.61 |
| 64 | Gary Ablett | Geel | 16 | 4.00 |
| 64 | Doug Wade | Geel/NM | 18 | 3.56 |
| 62 | Jack Mueller | Melb | 18 | 3.44 |
| 62 | Dick Lee | Coll | 22 | 2.82 |
| 62 | Kevin Bartlett | Rich | 27 | 2.30 |
| 62 | Peter Sumich | West C | 19 | 3.26 |
| 60 | Billy Brownless | Geel | 17 | 3.53 |
| 55 | Ron Todd | Coll | 11 | 5.00 |
| 53 | Harry Vallence | Carlt | 14 | 3.79 |
| 53 | Dermott Brereton | Hawth | 26 | 2.04 |
| 51 | Dick Reynolds | Ess | 27 | 1.89 |
| 47 | Dick Harris | Rich | 14 | 3.35 |
| 46 | Peter McKenna | Coll | 12 | 3.83 |
| 42 | Jimmy Freake | Fitz | 18 | 2.33 |
| 40 | Alex Jesaulenko | Carlt | 23 | 1.73 |

## NUMBER OF 10 GOALS OR MORE EFFORTS 1897–1997

| | |
|---|---|
| Tony Lockett (St Kilda/Sydney) | 19 |
| Jason Dunstall (Hawthorn) | 16 |
| Peter McKenna (Collingwood/Carlton) | 13 |
| John Coleman (Essendon) | 12 |
| Peter Hudson (Hawthorn) | 12 |
| Gary Ablett (Hawthorn/Geelong) | 12 |
| Gordon Coventry (Collingwood) | 11 |

**248**

## KICKED 100 GOALS IN A SEASON

**150** — R. Pratt (S.M), 1934;
P. Hudson (Haw), 1971
**146** — P. Hudson (Haw), 1970
**145** — J. Dunstall (Haw), 1992
**143** — P. McKenna (Coll), 1970
**138** — J. Dunstall (Haw), 1989
**134** — P. McKenna (Coll), 1971
**132** — J. Dunstall (Haw), 1988;
T. Lockett (St K), 1992
**130** — P. McKenna (Coll), 1972
**129** — T. Modra (Adel), 1993;
G. Ablett (Geel), 1994
**127** — D. Wade (Geel), 1969;
T. Lockett (St K), 1991
**125** — P. Hudson (Haw), 1968
**124** — G. Coventry (Coll), 1929;
G. Ablett (Geel), 1993
**123** — J. Dunstall (Haw), 1993

**122** — G. Ablett (Geel), 1995
**121** — R. Todd (Coll), 1939;
T. Lockett, (Syd) 1996
**120** — R. Todd (Coll), 1938;
J. Coleman (Ess), 1950;
P. Hudson (Haw), 1969
**119** — G. Coventry (Coll), 1930
**118** — K. Templeton (Foot), 1978
**117** — T. Lockett (St K), 1987
**116** — B. Quinlan (Fitz), 1983
**115** — A. Jesaulenko (Carl), 1970
**112** — M. Roach (Rich), 1980
**111** — P. Sumich (W.C.E), 1991
**110** — P. Hudson (Haw), 1977;
T. Lockett (Syd), 1995
**109** — G. Moloney (Geel), 1932;
R. Pratt (SM), 1933
**108** — G. Coventry (Coll), 1933

**107** — G. Blethyn (Ess), 1972
**105** — G. Coventry (Coll), 1934;
L. Donohue (Geel), 1976;
B. Quinland (Fitz), 1984;
S. Beasley (Foots), 1985
**103** — R. Pratt (S.M), 1935;
J. Coleman (Ess), 1952;
D. Wade (NM), 1974;
M. Blight (NM), 1982;
W. Capper (Syd), 1987
**102** — J. Dunstall (Haw), 1996
**101** — W. Mohr (St K), 1936;
J. Dunstall (Haw), 1994
**100** — J. Titus (Rich), 1940;
J. Coleman (Ess), 1949,
B. Taylor (Coll), 1986.

## RECORDS AT VENUES: 1897-1997

| VENUE | MOST IN A MATCH | MOST IN A CAREER |
|---|---|---|
| Football Park: | **Tony Modra** (Adelaide) 13 v Richmond, 1993; **Tony Modra** (Adelaide) 13 v Carlton, 1994 | **Tony Modra** (Adelaide) 184 (1992–96) |
| Gabba: | **Bill Brownless** (Geelong) 11 v Bris Bears, 1991 | **Roger Merrett** (B Bears) 118 (1991–96) |
| Kardinia Park: | **Doug Wade** (Geelong) 13 v North Melb., 1971 | **Doug Wade** (Geel/NM) 413 (1961–75) |
| MCG: | **Gary Ablett** (Geel) 14 v Rich, 1989; v Ess, 1993; **John Longmire** (NM) 14 v Melb, 1990 | **Kevin Bartlett** (Rich) 380 (1965–83) |
| Princes Park: | **Harry Davie** (Melbourne) 13 v Carlton, 1925 | **Harry Vallence** (Carlton) 357 (1926–38) |
| SCG: | **Gary Ablett** (Geelong) 14 v Sydney, 1994 | **Tony Lockett** (St Kilda/Syd) 182 (1983–97) |
| Subiaco Oval: | **Peter Sumich** (W Coast) 8 v Syd, 1990; **Tony Lockett** (St K) 8 v W Coast, 1991; **Darren Bewick** (Ess) 8 v West Coast, 1993 | **Peter Sumich** (West Coast) 176 (1989–97) |
| Victoria Park: | **Gordon Coventry** (Coll) 17 v Fitzroy, 1930 | **Gordon Coventry** (Coll) 675 (1920–37) |
| WACA: | **Peter Sumich** (W Coast) 13 v Foots, 1991 | **Peter Sumich** (W Coast) 101 (1989–97) |
| Waverley Park: | **Jason Dunstall** (Haw) 17 v Rich, 1992 | **Jason Dunstall** (Haw) 532 (1985–97) |
| Whitten Oval: | **Tony Lockett** (Syd) 16 v Fitzroy, 1995 | **Kelvin Templeton** (Foots/Melb) 219 (1974–85); **Simon Beasley** (Footscray) 219 (1982–89) |

## MOST GOALS ROUND BY ROUND

R1: **Tony Modra** (Adelaide) 13 v Carlton, 1994.
R2: **Doug Strang** (Rich) 14 v N Melb., 1931.
R3: **Bob Pratt** (S Melb) 15 v Ess, 1934.
R4: **Tony Lockett** (St Kilda) 12 v Melb, 1987.
R5: **Peter Hudson** (Haw) 16 v Melb, 1969.
R6: **Gary Ablett** (Geel) 14 v Ess, 1993.
R7: **Jason Dunstall** (Haw) 17 v Rich, 1992.
R8: **Gary Ablett** (Geel) 14 v Sydney, 1994.
R9: **Gary Ablett** (Geel) 14 v Rich, 1989.
R10: **Lindsay White** (Geel) 11 v St. Kilda, 1948; **Gary Ablett** (Geel) 11 v Bris Bears, 1988.
R11: **Gordon Coventry** (Coll) 15 v Ess, 1933.
R12: **Gordon Coventry** (Coll) 17 v Fitzroy, 1930.
R13: **Gordon Coventry** (Coll) 16 v Haw, 1929.
R14: **Gordon Coventry** (Coll) 14 v Haw, 1934;

**John Longmire** (N Melb.) 14 v Melb, 1990.
R15: **Bob Pratt** (S Melb) 12 v Foots, 1934;
**Peter Hudson** (Haw) 12 v St. Kilda 1971;
**Simon Beasley** (Foots) 12 v Melb, 1985.
R16: **Tony Modra** (Adel) 13 v Rich, 1993.
R17: **Doug Wade** (Geel) 13 v S Melb, 1967.
R18: **John Coleman** (Ess) 13 v Haw, 1952.
R19: **Fred Fanning** (Melb) 18 v St. Kilda, 1947.
R20: **Doug Wade** (Geel) 13 v N Melb., 1971;
**Peter Daicos** (Coll) 13 v Bris Bears, 1991.
R21: **Tony Lockett** (St Kilda) 13 v Carlton, 1991.
R22: **Peter Hudson** (Haw) 11 v Fitzroy, 1970;
**Jason Dunstall** (Haw) 11 v St Kilda, 1989.
R23: **Scott Hodges** (Adel) 11 v Geel, 1992.
R24: **Tony Lockett** (St Kilda) 11 v Sydney, 1991.

## CLUBS' HIGHEST LOSING SCORES

**Adelaide** — 18.10 (118) v. North Melb 18.12 (120), R9, 1991 (MCG); 16.22 (118) v. Sydney 19.8 (122), R18, 1991 (Football Park)
**Brisbane Bears** — 22.11 (143) v. North Melb 24.22 (166), R1, 1993 (MCG)
**Brisbane Lions** — 15.12 (102) v. Essendon 16.10 (106), R21, 1997 (Gabba)
**Carlton** — 22.13 (145) v. North Melb 22.15 (147), R3, 1985 (Princes Park)
**Collingwood** — 21.16 (142) v. Melbourne 22.21 (153), R16, 1937 (Victoria Park)
**Essendon** — 21.13 (139) v. Collingwood 23.6 (144), R22, 1987 (MCG)
**Fitzroy** — 23.19 (157) v. Melbourne 24.23 (167), R2, 1978 (MCG)
**Footscray** — 19.16 (130) v. St Kilda 20.17 (137), R2, 1978 (Moorabbin)
**Fremantle** — 15.9 (99) v. Footscray 18.9 (117), R15, 1996 (Whitten Oval)
**Geelong** — 25.13 (163) v. Hawthorn 26.15 (171), R6, 1989 (Princes Park)
**Hawthorn** — 21.23 (149) v. Richmond 29.14 (188), R5, 1985 (Princes Park)
**Melbourne** — 22.19 (151) v. Geelong 24.10 (154), R10, 1940 (MCG)
**North Melbourne** — 23.14 (152) v. Fitzroy 25.16 (166), R11, 1984 (Junction Oval)
**Richmond** — 22.18 (150) v. Carlton 28.9 (177), GF, 1972 (MCG)
**St Kilda** — 21.18 (144) v. Collingwood 24.16 (160), R11, 1983 (Moorabbin)
**South Melb/Sydney** — 24.11 (155) v. Geelong 26.11 (167), R20, 1978 (Lake Oval)
**University** — 11.7 (73) v. Fitzroy 13.16 (94), R16, 1908 (Brunsw St Ov)
**West Coast** — 18.10 (118) v. Essendon 21.20 (146), R15, 1987 (WACA)

## CLUBS' LOWEST WINNING SCORES

**Adelaide** — 7.8 (50) d. Fitzroy 7.5 (47), R12, 1991 (Football Park)
**Brisbane Bears** — 4.12 (36) d. Footscray 3.4 (22), R16, 1996 (Whitten Oval)
**Brisbane Lions** — 7.26 (68) d. Richmond 7.8 (50), R14, 1997 (Princes Park)
**Carlton** — 3.6 (24) d. South Melb 0.5 (5), R8, 1899 (Princes Park)
**Collingwood** — 3.3 (21) d. Melbourne 1.7 (13), R9, 1899 (MCG)
**Essendon** — 1.8 (14) d. Melbourne 0.8 (8), Final, 1897 (Lake Oval)
**Fitzroy** — 2.10 (22) d. Collingwood 1.5 (11), SF, 1898 (Brunsw St Ov)
**Footscray** — 4.11 (35) d. Fitzroy 3.16 (34), R21, 1976 (Waverley Park)
**Fremantle** — 12.22 (94) d. Geelong 10.15 (75), R4, 1995 (WACA)
**Geelong** — 1.9 (15) d. Melbourne 0.10 (10), R9, 1897 (Corio Oval)
**Hawthorn** — 5.12 (42) d. North Melb 5.8 (38), R2, 1926 (Arden St Oval)
**Melbourne** — 4.4 (28) d. Fitzroy 3.7 (25), R9, 1908 (MCG)
**North Melbourne** — 5.12 (42) d. Richmond 3.8 (26), R3, 1960 (Arden St Oval)
**Richmond** — 5.4 (34) d. Fitzroy 4.9 (33), R12, 1908 (Brunsw St Ov)
**St Kilda** — 3.8 (26) d. Geelong 2.10 (22), R15, 1909 (Junction Oval)
**South Melb/Sydney** — 2.3 (15) d. Melbourne 1.7 (13), R6, 1898 (MCG)
**University** — 5.9 (39) d. Geelong 4.11 (35), R8, 1908 (Corio Oval)
**West Coast** — 7.11 (53) d. Footscray 3.11 (29), R22, 1988 (Whitten Oval)

## HIGHEST MATCH SCORES

37.17 (239) by Geelong v Bris Bears, R7, 1992 (C)
36.22 (238) by Fitzroy v Melbourne, R17, 1979 (P)
36.20 (236) by Sydney v Essendon, R17, 1987 (SCG)
36.15 (231) by Hawthorn v Fitzroy, R6, 1991 (NH)
35.19 (229) by North Melb v Sydney, R6, 1993 (PP)
35.18 (228) by Geelong v St Kilda, R7, 1989 (KP)
35.15 (225) by Hawthorn v Geelong, R21, 1986 (PP)
34.18 (222) by Richmond v St Kilda, R16, 1980 (SCG)
34.16 (220) by Fitzroy v North Melb, R13, 1983 (JO)
33.21 (219) by Bris Bears v Sydney, R8, 1993 (G)
32.24 (216) by Hawthorn v Essendon, R20, 1992 (MCG)

## LOWEST MATCH SCORES

0.1 (1) by St Kilda v Geelong, R17, 1899 (CO)
0.2 (2) by St Kilda v South Melb, R3, 1897 (LO)
0.2 (2) by St Kilda v Geelong, R14, 1899 (CO)
0.2 (2) by Melbourne v Fitzroy, R16, 1899 (B)
0.3 (3) by St Kilda v South Melb, R10, 1897 (JO)
0.3 (3) by St Kilda v Essendon, R12, 1897 (E)
0.5 (5) by South Melb v Carlton, R8, 1899 (PP)
0.6 (6) by Carlton v Collingwood, R5, 1898 (VP)
1.0 (6) by St Kilda v Collingwood, R13, 1898 (VP)
1.0 (6) by St Kilda v Essendon, R9, 1899 (MCG)
1.0 (6) by Fitzroy v Footscray, R5, 1953 (WO)

## GREATEST WINNING MARGINS

190 — Fitzroy 36.22(238) d Melbourne 6.12 (48), R17, 1979
178 — Collingwood 31.21 (207) d St Kilda 3.11 (29), R4, 1979
171 — South Melb 29.15 (189) d St Kilda 2.6 (18), R12, 1919
168 — Richmond 30.19 (199) d North Melb 4.7 (31), R2, 1931
165 — Essendon 28.16 (184) d South Melb 2.7 (19), R18, 1964
164 — Geelong 37.17 (239) d Bris Bears 11.9 (75), R7, 1992
163 — Sydney 36.20 (236) d Essendon 11.7 (73), R17, 1987
162 — Brisbane Bears 33.21 (219) d Sydney 8.9 (57), R8, 1993
161 — Geelong 23.24 (162) d St Kilda 0.1 (1), R17, 1899
160 — Hawthorn 32.24 (216) d Essendon 8.8 (56), R20, 1992

*MCG — Melbourne Cricket Ground;*
*SCG — Sydney Cricket Ground;*
*P — Waverley Park; PP — Princes Park; KP — Kardinia Park; JO — Junction Oval; VP — Victoria Park; WO — Whitten Oval; C — Carrara; NH — North Hobart; CO — Corio Oval; LO — Lake Oval; B — Brunswick St Oval; E — East Melbourne CG*

# GAMES

## 200 CLUB MEMBERS

At the end of the 1961 season the League formed an exclusive club, bringing together players with 200 or more League matches, including night series and interstate (State of Origin) games.

A further 16 players — Brett Allison, Paul Broderick, Michael Gale, David Hart, Robert Harvey, Craig Lambert, Tony Liberatore, John Longmire, Michael Martyn, Michael McLean, Mark Roberts, Wayne Schwass, Craig Sholl, Barry Stoneham, Todd Viney and John Worsfold — joined 'The Club' in 1997.

The following list shows the '200 Club' members and their total matches for premiership points only. All reached the double century when night series/State of Origin games were added.

*# = Deceased*
*\* = 1997 player*

| | |
|---|---|
| Gary Ablett (Vic: Haw, Geel) 1982; 1984–97 | 248 |
| Geoff Ablett (Vic: Haw, Rich, St K) 1973–85 | 229 |
| David Ackerly (Vic: S Melb, N Melb) 1979–89 | 191 |
| Brett Allison* (ACT: N Melb) 1987–97 | 199 |
| Stan Alves (Vic: Melb, N Melb) 1965–79 | 266 |
| Tom Alvin (Vic: Carl) 1984–94 | 218 |
| Barry Armstrong (Vic: Carl) 1969–81 | 204 |
| Matthew Armstrong (Tas: Fitz, N Melb) 1987–96 | 175 |
| Graham Arthur (Vic: Haw) 1955–68 | 232 |
| Rod Ashman (Vic: Carl) 1973–86 | 236 |
| Rod Austin (Vic: Carl) 1972–85 | 220 |
| Allen Aylett (Vic: N Melb) 1952–64 | 220 |
| Gary Ayres (Vic: Haw) 1978–93 | 269 |
| Ron D. Barassi (Vic: Melb, Carl) 1953–69 | 254 |
| Trevor Barker# (Vic: St K) 1975–89 | 230 |
| Kevin Bartlett (Vic: Rich) 1965–83 | 403 |
| Mark Bayes* (Vic: Syd) 1985–97 | 236 |
| Percy Beames (Vic: Melb) 1931–44 | 213 |
| Peter Bedford (Vic: S Melb, Carl) 1968–78 | 186 |
| Vic Belcher# (Vic: S Melb) 1907–15; 1917–20 | 226 |
| George Bennett# (Vic: Haw, Foots) 1930–40; 1942–44 | 200 |
| Percy Bentley# (Vic: Rich) 1925–40 | 263 |
| Andrew Bews* (Vic: Geel, B Bears, B Lions) 1982–97 | 276 |
| John Birt (Vic: Ess) 1957–67 | 193 |
| George Bisset (Vic: Foots, Coll) 1963–74 | 207 |
| John Blakey* (Vic: Fitz, N Melb) 1985–97 | 249 |
| Malcolm Blight (SA: N Melb) 1974–82 | 178 |
| Mark Bos (Vic: Geel) 1979–89 | 195 |
| Francis Bourke (Vic: Rich) 1967–81 | 300 |
| Craig Bradley* (SA: Carl) 1986–97 | 267 |
| Barry Breen (Vic: St K) 1965–82 | 300 |
| Dermott Brereton (Vic: Haw, Syd, Coll) 1982–92; 1994–95 | 211 |
| Terry Bright (Vic: Geel) 1976–87 | 219 |
| Paul Broderick* (Vic: Fitz, Rich) 1987–97 | 184 |
| Gavin Brown* (Vic: Coll) 1987–97 | 204 |
| Norm Brown (Vic: Fitz) 1975–87 | 181 |
| Mark Browning (Vic: S Melb) 1975–87 | 251 |
| Billy Brownless (NSW: Geel) 1986–97 | 198 |
| Neville Bruns (Vic: Geel) 1978–92 | 223 |
| Nathan Burke* (Vic: St K) 1987–97 | 227 |

| | |
|---|---|
| Ray Byrne (Vic: Carl, Coll, Geel) 1973–84 | 219 |
| Dennis Carroll (NSW: S Melb) 1981–93 | 219 |
| Rod Carter (Vic: Fitz, S Melb) 1974–90 | 293 |
| Roy Cazaly# (Vic: St K, S Melb) 1911–15; 1918–24; 1926–27 | 198 |
| David Clarke (Vic: Geel, Carl) 1971–74; 1976–82 | 211 |
| Jack Clarke (Vic: Ess) 1951–67 | 263 |
| Dick Clay (Vic: Rich) 1966–76 | 213 |
| Jim Cleary# (Vic: S Melb) 1934–48 | 222 |
| Ron Clegg# (Vic: S Melb) 1945–54; 1956–60 | 231 |
| David Cloke (Vic: Rich, Coll) 1974–91 | 333 |
| Glenn Coleman (NSW: Fitz, Syd, Foots) 1980–84; 1986–93 | 194 |
| Albert Collier# (Vic: Coll, Fitz) 1925–30; 1933–39; 1941–42 | 217 |
| Harry Collier# (Vic: Coll) 1926–40 | 253 |
| Gary Colling (Vic: St K) 1968–81 | 265 |
| Andrew Collins (Vic: Haw) 1987–96 | 212 |
| Bruce Comben (Vic: Carl) 1950–61 | 188 |
| Michael Conlan (ACT: Fitz) 1977–89 | 210 |
| Neil Cordy (Vic: Foots, Syd) 1979–93 | 235 |
| Paul Couch (Vic: Geel) 1985–97 | 259 |
| Gordon Coventry# (Vic: Coll) 1920–37 | 306 |
| Syd Coventry# (Vic: Coll) 1922–34 | 227 |
| Gary Cowton (Vic: N Melb, Foots, S Melb) 1971–81; 1983–84 | 199 |
| Gavin Crosisca* (Qld: Coll) 1987–97 | 202 |
| Brent Crosswell (Tas: Carl, N Melb, Melb) 1968–82 | 222 |
| Max Crow (Vic) | 188 |
| Geoff Cunningham (Vic: St K) 1977–89 | 224 |
| Frank Curcio# (Vic: Fitz) 1932–36; 1938–43; 1945–48 | 249 |
| Peter Daicos (Vic: Coll) 1979–93 | 250 |
| Anthony Daniher (NSW: S Melb, Ess) 1981–94 | 233 |
| Terry Daniher (NSW: S Melb, Ess) 1976–92 | 313 |
| Tim Darcy (Vic: Geel, Ess) 1982–83; 1986–95 | 190 |
| Allan Davis (Vic: St K, Melb, Ess, Coll) 1966–80 | 250 |
| Barry Davis (Vic: Ess, N Melb) 1961–75 | 289 |
| Bob Davis (Vic: Geel) 1948–58 | 189 |
| Peter Dean* (Vic: Carl) 1984–97 | 235 |
| Roger Dean (Vic: Rich) 1957–73 | 245 |
| Greg Dear (Vic: Haw, Rich) 1985–96 | 190 |
| Gary Dempsey (Vic: Foots, N Melb) 1967–84 | 329 |
| David Dench (Vic: N Melb) 1969–84 | 275 |
| Charlie Dibbs# (Vic: Coll, Geel) 1924–36 | 223 |
| Robert Dipierdomenico (Vic: Haw) 1975; 1978–91 | 240 |
| Carl Ditterich (Vic: St K, Melb) 1963–80 | 285 |
| Brian Dixon (Vic: Melb) 1954–68 | 252 |
| Wally Donald (Vic: Foots) 1946–58 | 205 |
| Bruce Doull (Vic: Carl) 1969–86 | 356 |
| John Dugdale (Vic: N Melb) 1955–70 | 248 |
| Ross Dunne (Vic: Coll) 1967–78 | 213 |
| Jason Dunstall* (Qld: Haw) 1985–97 | 256 |
| Laurie Dwyer (Vic: N Melb) 1956–58; 1960–64; 1966–70 | 201 |
| Jack Dyer (Vic: Rich) 1931–49 | 312 |
| Rodney Eade (Tas: Haw, Bris Bears) 1976–90 | 259 |
| Bill Eason# (Vic: Geel) 1902–15 | 220 |
| Jim Edmond (Vic: Foots, Syd, Bris Bears) 1977–88 | 188 |
| Wels Eicke# (Vic: St K, N Melb) 1909–15; 1918–26 | 218 |
| Fred Elliott# (Vic: Melb, Carl) 1899–1901; 1903–11 | 209 |

Bernie Evans (Vic: S Melb, Carl) 1978–88   185
Alan Ezard (Vic: Ess) 1983–93   184
Ian Fairley (Vic: N Melb) 1983–96   217
Neville Fields (Vic: Ess, S Melb) 1969–82   200
Tom Fitzmaurice# (Vic: Ess, Geel, N Melb)
1918–20; 1922–28; 1932–35   188
Ken Fletcher (Vic: Ess) 1967–80   264
Robert Flower (Vic: Melb) 1973–87   272
Garry Foulds (Vic: Ess) 1974–89   300
Jim Francis (Vic: Haw, Carl) 1929–43   223
Ken Fraser (Vic: Ess) 1958–68   198
Danny Frawley (Vic: St K) 1984–95   240
Alan Gale# (Vic: Fitz) 1948–61   213
Michael Gale* (Tas: Fitz, Rich) 1986–97   180
Adrian Gallagher (Vic: Carl, Foots, N Melb) 1964–76 220
Peter German (Vic: N Melb) 1984–94   185
Frank Gill# (Vic: Carl) 1929–42   205
Ross Glendinning (WA: N Melb, Wst Cst) 1978–88   230
Bill Goggin (Vic: Geel) 1958–71   248
Norm Goss (Vic: S Melb, Haw) 1972–82   202
Jack Graham# (Vic: S Melb) 1935–49   227
David Grant (Tas: St K, Melb) 1984–96   198
Russell Greene (Vic: St K, Haw) 1974–88   304
Keith Greig (Vic: N Melb) 1971–85   294
Dick Grigg# (Vic: Geel) 1904–14; 1921   194
George Haines (Heinz)# (Vic: Geel, Melb, St K)
1910–14; 1919–25; 1927   194
Ian Hampshire (Vic: Geel, Foots) 1968–82   224
Ken Hands (Vic: Carl) 1945–57   211
Mil Hanna (Vic: Carl) 1986–97   190
Gary Hardeman (Vic: Melb) 1967–77; 1981   219
Dick Harris# (Vic: Rich) 1934–44   196
Leon Harris (Vic: Fitz) 1979–89   186
David Hart (WA: Wst Cst) 1987–97   184
Royce Hart (Tas: Rich) 1967–77   187
Mark Harvey (Vic: Ess) 1984–97   206
Robert Harvey* (Vic: St K) 1988–97   179
Glenn Hawker (Vic: Ess, Carl) 1978–91   227
Doug Hawkins (Vic: Foots, Fitz) 1978–95   350
Gerard Healy (Vic: Melb, Syd) 1979–90   211
Kevin Heath (Vic: Haw, Carl) 1968–80   218
John Hendrie (Vic: Haw) 1972–82   197
Reg Hickey# (Vic: Geel) 1926–40   245
Garry Hocking* (Vic: Geel) 1987–97   207
Steven Hocking (Vic: Geel) 1984–94   199
Les Hughes# (Vic: Coll) 1908–22   225
Rex Hunt (Vic: Rich, Geel, St K) 1968–78   202
Bill Hutchison# (Vic: Ess) 1942–57   290
Steven Icke (Vic: N Melb, Melb) 1975–85   198
Warwick Irwin (Vic: Fitz, Coll) 1970–81; 1983   229
John James (Vic: Carl) 1953–63   195
Ray Jencke (Vic: Haw) 1986–97   194
Alex Jesaulenko (ACT: Carl, St K) 1967–81   279
Jim Jess (Vic: Rich) 1976–88   223
John Jillard (Vic: Foots) 1958–70   189
Robert Johnson (Tas: Melb) 1959–69   202
Wayne Johnston (Vic: Carl) 1979–90   209
Norm Johnstone (Vic: Fitz) 1944–57   228
Peter Jones (Tas: Carl) 1966–79   249
Merv Keane (Vic: Rich) 1972–84   238
Peter Keenan (Vic: Melb, N Melb, Ess) 1970–82   213
John Kennedy (Vic: Haw) 1979–91   241
Trevor Keogh (Vic: Carl) 1970–81   208
Stephen Kernahan (SA: Carl) 1986–97   251
Peter Knights (Vic: Haw) 1969–85   264
Phonse Kyne# (Vic: Coll) 1934–44; 1946–50   245
Craig Lambert* (Vic: Rich, B Bears, B Lions) 1988–97 188

## MOST GAMES

*PREMIERSHIP GAMES ONLY*

| | |
|---|---|
| M. Tuck (Hawthorn) | 426 |
| K. Bartlett (Richmond) | 403 |
| S. Madden (Essendon) | 378 |
| B. Quinlan (Footscray, Fitzroy) | 366 |
| B. Doull (Carlton) | 356 |
| D. Hawkins (Footscray, Fitzroy) | 350 |
| J. Rantall (Sth. Melb., Nth. Melb., Fitzroy) | 336 |
| P. Roos (Fitzroy, Sydney) | 335 |
| D. Cloke (Richmond, Collingwood) | 333 |
| K. Murray (Fitzroy) | 333 |
| L. Matthews (Hawthorn) | 332 |
| J. Madden (Essendon, Carlton) | 332 |
| G. Dempsey (Footscray, Nth. Melb.) | 329 |
| J. Nicholls (Carlton) | 328 |
| B. Round (Footscray, Sydney) | 328 |
| I. Nankervis (Geelong) | 325 |
| E. Whitten (Footscray) | 321 |
| R. Reynolds (Essendon) | 320 |
| T. Daniher (Sth. Melb., Essendon) | 313 |
| T. Shaw (Collingwood) | 313 |
| R. Merrett (Essendon, Brisbane Bears) | 313 |
| J. Dyer (Richmond) | 312 |
| T. Watson (Essendon) | 307 |
| G. Coventry (Collingwood) | 306 |
| W. Schimmelbusch (North Melbourne) | 306 |
| R. Greene (St Kilda, Hawthorn) | 304 |
| C. Langford (Hawthorn) | 303 |
| D. Scott (Hawthorn) | 302 |
| L. Thompson (Collingwood, S. Melb, Fitz) | 301 |
| B. Breen (St Kilda) | 300 |
| J. Newman (Geelong) | 300 |
| F. Bourke (Richmond) | 300 |
| K. Moore (Hawthorn) | 300 |
| G. Foulds (Essendon) | 300 |

## THE MICHAEL TUCK STORY

The wiry frame of Michael Tuck has been off the AFL scene for five seasons, but even in that time no player has looked like getting anywhere near his phenomenal record of 426 League games.

The former Hawthorn captain and ruck-rover appears certain to keep his name as the AFL's games record-holder well into the next century given that the most recent additions to the 300-club — Justin Madden, Paul Roos and Roger Merrett — have either retired or are into the twilight of their careers.

Tuck's durability saw him play senior football from 1972 until his retirement after the 1991 Grand Final, which produced the Hawks' last premiership. He played in seven winning Grand Final sides (a League record) and it is worth noting he played 50 reserves games, the majority before he even managed a senior berth. Tuck and former Richmond champion Kevin Bartlett (403 games) are the only players in VFL/AFL history to pass the 400-game mark.

| | |
|---|---|
| Chris Langford (Vic: Haw) 1983–97 | 303 |
| John Law (Vic: N Melb) 1978–89 | 219 |
| Dick Lee# (Vic: Coll) 1906–22 | 230 |
| Mark Lee (Vic: Rich) 1977–91 | 233 |
| Geoff Leek (Vic: Ess) 1951–62 | 191 |
| Harry Lever# (Vic: St K) 1905–15; 1918–19; 1921–22 | 217 |
| Chris Lewis* (WA: West Coast) 1987–97 | 197 |
| Johnny Lewis* (Vic: N Melb, Melb) 1925–27; 1929–38 | 196 |
| Tony Liberatore* (Vic: Foots) 1986–97 | 197 |
| Tony Lockett* (Vic: St K, Syd) 1983–97 | 236 |
| Stewart Loewe* (Vic: St K) 1986–97 | 237 |
| John Longmire* (NSW: N Melb) 1988–95; 1997 | 180 |
| Brett Lovett* (Vic: Melb) 1986–97 | 235 |
| Garry Lyon* (Vic: Melb) 1986–97 | 203 |
| Mark Maclure (NSW: Carl) 1974–86 | 243 |
| Stephen Macpherson (Tas: Foots) 1982–95 | 188 |
| Justin Madden (Vic: Ess, Carl) 1980–96 | 332 |
| Simon Madden (Vic: Ess) 1974–92 | 378 |
| Stuart Magee (S Melb, Foots) 1962–75 | 216 |
| Chris Mainwaring* (WA: Wst Cst) 1987–97 | 193 |
| Alan Martello (Vic: Haw, Rich) 1970–83 | 255 |
| Mick Martyn* (Vic: N Melb) 1988–97 | 201 |
| Leigh Matthews (Vic: Haw) 1969–85 | 332 |
| Stephen McCann (WA: N Melb) 1977–88 | 226 |
| Peter McConville (Vic: Carl, St K) 1978–89 | 194 |
| Basil McCormack# (Vic: Rich) 1925–36 | 199 |
| Rod McGregor# (Vic: Carl) 1905–12; 1914–20 | 236 |
| Tony McGuinness (SA: Foots, Adel) 1986–96 | 222 |
| Jock McHale# (Vic: Coll) 1903–18; 1920 | 261 |
| Scott McIvor (Qld: Fitz, B Bears, B Lions) 1985–97 | 200 |
| David McKay (Vic: Carl) 1969–81 | 263 |
| Guy McKenna* (WA: Wst Cst) 1988–97 | 213 |
| Peter McKenna (Vic: Coll, Carl) 1965–75; 1977 | 191 |
| Don McKenzie (Vic: Ess) 1960–74 | 266 |
| Michael McLean (NT: Foots, B Bears, B Lions) 1983–89; 1991–97 | 183 |
| David McLeish (Vic: S Melb) 1969–80 | 213 |
| David McMahon (Vic: Fitz) 1973–84 | 218 |
| Des Meagher (Vic: Haw) 1966–76 | 198 |
| Roger Merrett (Vic: Ess, Bris Bears) 1978–96 | 313 |
| Harvey Merrigan (Vic: Fitz) 1969–81 | 197 |
| Chris Mew (Vic: Haw) 1980–92 | 230 |
| Bert Mills# (Vic: Haw) 1930–42 | 196 |
| Barry Mitchell (Vic: Syd, Coll, Carl) 1984–96 | 221 |
| Hugh Mitchell (Vic: Ess) 1953–67 | 224 |
| Bill Mohr# (NSW: St K) 1929–41 | 195 |
| Michael Moncrieff (Vic: Haw) 1971–83 | 224 |
| Ken Montgomery (Vic: N Melb) 1968–81 | 189 |
| Kelvin Moore (Vic: Haw) 1970–84 | 300 |
| Peter Moore (Vic: Coll, Melb) 1974–87 | 249 |
| Albie Morrison# (Vic: Foots) 1928–38; 1941–42; 1946 | 224 |
| Shane Morwood (Vic: Syd, Coll) 1981–93 | 212 |
| Tony Morwood (Vic: Syd) 1978–89 | 229 |
| Jack Mueller (Vic: Melb) 1934–50 | 216 |
| John Murphy (Vic: Fitz, S Melb, N Melb) 1967–80 | 246 |
| Len Murphy# (Vic: Coll, Foots) 1928–37; 1940–41 | 198 |
| Kevin Murray (Vic: Fitz) 1955–64; 1967–74 | 333 |
| Brian Mynott (Vic: St K) 1964–75 | 210 |
| Bruce Nankervis (Vic: Geel) 1970–83 | 253 |
| Ian Nankervis (Vic: Geel) 1967–83 | 325 |
| Merv Neagle (Vic: Ess, Syd) 1977–90 | 203 |
| Robert Neal (Tas: Geel, St K) 1974–88 | 220 |
| Kevin Neale (Vic: St K) 1965–77 | 256 |
| Ken Newland (Vic: Geel, Foots) 1965–78 | 216 |
| John Newman (Vic: Geel) 1964–80 | 300 |

## CONSECUTIVE GAMES

| | |
|---|---|
| J. Stynes (Melbourne) | 240 |
| J. Titus (Richmond) | 204 |
| J. McHale (Collingwood) | 191 |
| A. Collins (Hawthorn) | 189 |
| K. Bartlett (Richmond) | 173 |
| J. Schultz (Footscray) | 169 |
| K. Murray (Fitzroy) | 168 |
| T. Liberatore (W Bulldogs) | 160 |
| J. Murphy (Fitz/SM/NM) | 158 |
| K. Bartlett (Richmond) | 150 |
| A. Ruthven (Fitzroy) | 147 |

## THE JIM STYNES STORY

Of all the tales and folklore involving football at the highest level, surely this is one of the greatest. Big, strapping Irish lad comes to Australia on a flight of fancy to play a game completely foreign to him.

Not only does he adapt quickly to his new code, he excels to the point where he wins the game's highest individual award, the Brownlow Medal (in 1991). And now Jim Stynes' name is in the books for achieving one of the greatest statistical feats the game has seen.

In round nine 1996, the Melbourne ruckman played his 205th consecutive game, breaking the long-standing record of 204 held by former Richmond great Jack Titus. By the end of the 1997 season, Stynes' games sequence had stretched to 240 and he has not missed a game since round 16, 1987. Last year he celebrated the 10th anniversary of his record-breaking achievement.

| | |
|---|---|
| John Nicholls (Vic: Carl) 1957–74 | 328 |
| Alan Noonan (Vic: Ess, Rich) 1966–77 | 192 |
| Gary O'Donnell* (Vic: Ess) 1987–97 | 226 |
| Arthur Olliver# (Vic: Foots) 1935–50 | 272 |
| Kevin O'Neill# (Vic: Rich) 1930–41 | 208 |
| Richard Osborne* (Vic: Fitz, Syd, Foots, Coll) 1982–97 | 269 |
| David Parkin (Vic: Haw) 1961–74 | 211 |
| John Peck# (Vic: Haw) 1954–66 | 213 |
| Tim Pekin (Vic: Fitz, St K) 1984–95 | 219 |
| Gary Pert (Vic: Fitz, Coll) 1982–95 | 233 |
| Bill Picken (Vic: Coll, Syd) 1974–86 | 240 |
| Phillip Pinnell (Vic: Carl, Melb) 1969–81 | 201 |
| John Platten (SA: Haw) 1986–97 | 258 |
| Ted Pool# (WA: Haw) 1926–38 | 200 |
| Darrin Pritchard (Tas: Haw) 1987–97 | 211 |
| Bernie Quinlan (Vic: Foots, Fitz) 1969–86 | 366 |
| Geoff Raines (Vic: Rich, Coll, Ess, B Bears) 1976–89 | 254 |
| John Rantall (Vic: S Melb, N Melb, Fitz) 1963–80 | 336 |
| Jack Regan# (Vic: Coll) 1930–41; 1943; 1946 | 196 |
| Russell Renfrey (Vic: Geel) 1946–56 | 201 |
| Dick Reynolds (Vic: Ess) 1933–51 | 320 |
| David Rhys–Jones (Vic: S Melb, Carl) 1980–92 | 182 |
| Lou Richards (Vic: Coll) 1941–55 | 250 |
| Max Richardson (WA: Coll, Fitz) 1969–80 | 241 |
| Wayne Richardson (Vic: Coll) 1966–78 | 277 |
| Michael Roach (Tas: Rich) 1977–89 | 200 |
| Mark Roberts* (NSW: Syd, B Bears, NM) 1985–97 | 186 |
| Paul Roos* (Vic: Fitz, Syd) 1982–97 | 335 |

| | |
|---|---|
| Barry Round (Vic: Foots, S Melb) 1969–85 | 328 |
| Barry Rowlings (Vic: Haw, Rich) 1975–86 | 234 |
| Brian Royal (Vic: Foots) 1983–93 | 199 |
| Peter Russo (Vic: Haw, St K) 1978–90 | 195 |
| Allan Ruthven (Vic: Fitz) 1940–41; 1943–54 | 222 |
| Paul Salmon* (Vic: Ess, Haw) 1983–97 | 248 |
| Jeff Sarau (Vic: St K) 1973–83 | 226 |
| John Scarlett (Vic: Geel, S Melb) 1967–78 | 212 |
| Wayne Schimmelbusch (Vic: N Melb) 1973–87 | 306 |
| John Schultz (Vic: Foots) 1958–68 | 188 |
| Wayne Schwass* (Vic: N Melb) 1988–97 | 184 |
| Don Scott (Vic: Haw) 1967–81 | 302 |
| Robert Scott* (Vic: Geel, N Melb) 1986–97 | 206 |
| Tony Shaw (Vic: Coll) 1978–94 | 313 |
| Kevin Sheedy (Vic: Rich) 1967–79 | 251 |
| Ken Sheldon (Vic: Carl, St K) 1977–89 | 185 |
| Craig Sholl* (Vic: N Melb) 1987–97 | 176 |
| Sergio Silvagni (Vic: Carl) 1958–71 | 239 |
| Stephen Silvagni* (Vic: Carl) 1985–97 | 230 |
| Roy Simmonds (Vic: Haw) 1950–61 | 192 |
| Bob Skilton (Vic: S Melb) 1956–68; 1970–71 | 237 |
| Norm Smith# (Vic: Melb, Fitz) 1935–50 | 227 |
| Ross G. Smith (Vic: N Melb) 1984–96 | 234 |
| Ross W. Smith (Vic: St K) 1961–72; 1975 | 224 |
| Steven Smith (Vic: Melb) 1974–85 | 203 |
| Geoff Southby (Vic: Carl) 1971–84 | 268 |
| Earl Spalding (WA: Melb, Carl) 1987–97 | 211 |
| Ian Stewart (Tas: St K, Rich) 1963–75 | 205 |
| Allan Stoneham (Vic: Foots, Ess) 1972–83 | 200 |
| Barry Stoneham* (Vic: Geel) 1986–94; 1996–97 | 194 |
| Steven Stretch (SA: Melb, Fitz) 1986–95 | 189 |
| Jim Stynes* (Ire: Melb) 1987–97 | 244 |
| Tony Sullivan (Vic: Melb) 1967–79 | 191 |
| Mark Tandy# (Vic: S Melb) 1911–15; 1917–26 | 207 |
| Dick Taylor# (Vic: Melb, N Melb) 1922–35 | 204 |
| Noel Teasdale (Vic: N Melb) 1956–67 | 178 |
| Bill Thomas# (Vic: S Melb, Rich) 1905–16; 1918–19 | 197 |
| Len Thomas# (Vic: S Melb, Haw, N Melb) 1927–34; 1936–40 | 209 |
| Len Thompson (Vic: Coll, S Melb, Fitz) 1965–80 | 301 |
| Mark Thompson (Vic: Ess) 1983–96 | 202 |
| Vic Thorp# (Vic: Rich) 1910–25 | 263 |
| David Thorpe (Vic: Foots, Rich) 1965–76 | 178 |
| Jack Titus# (Vic: Rich) 1926–43 | 294 |
| George Todd # (Vic: Geel) 1922–34 | 232 |
| Bernard Toohey (NSW: Geel, Syd, Foots) 1981–93 | 263 |
| Stuart Trott (Vic: St K, Haw) 1967–77 | 200 |
| Michael Tuck (Vic: Haw) 1972–91 | 426 |
| Des Tuddenham (Vic: Coll, Ess) 1962–77 | 251 |
| Michael Turner (Vic: Geel) 1974–84; 1986–88 | 245 |
| Harry Vallence# (Vic: Carl) 1926–38 | 204 |
| Paul Van Der Haar (Vic: Ess) 1977–90 | 201 |
| Todd Viney* (SA: Melb) 1987–97 | 194 |
| Doug Wade (Vic: Geel, North Melb) 1961–75 | 267 |
| Terry Wallace (Vic: Haw, Rich, Foots) 1978–91 | 254 |
| Steven Wallis (Vic: Foots) 1983–96 | 261 |
| Robert Walls (Vic: Carl, Fitz) 1967–80 | 259 |
| Norman Ware (Vic: Foots) 1932–42; 1944–46 | 200 |
| Tim Watson (Vic: Ess) 1977–91; 1993–94 | 307 |
| Dale Weightman (Vic: Rich) 1978–93 | 274 |
| Greg Wells (Vic: Melb, Carl) 1969–82 | 267 |
| Ted J. Whitten # (Vic: Foots) 1951–70 | 321 |
| Don Williams# (Vic: Melb) 1953–59; 1964–68 | 205 |
| Greg Williams (Vic: Geel, Syd, Carl) 1984–97 | 250 |
| John Williams (Vic: Ess, Coll) 1965–76 | 196 |
| Mark Williams (SA: Coll, Bris Bears) 1981–90 | 201 |

## MOST MATCHES AS CAPTAIN OF ONE CLUB

| Total | Player | Career Matches |
|---|---|---|
| 226 | Stephen Kernahan (Carl 1986-97) | 251 |
| 224 | Dick Reynolds (Ess 1938-50) | 320 |
| 212 | Ted Whitten (Foots 1951-70) | 321 |
| 187 | John Nicholls (Carl 1957-74) | 328 |
| 177 | Danny Frawley (St K 1984-95) | 240 |
| 168 | Percy Bentley (Rich 1925-40) | 263 |
| 165 | Bob Skilton (SM 1956-68, 70-71) | 237 |
| 160 | Jack Dyer (Rich 1931-49) | 312 |
| 159 | Kevin Murray (Fitz 1955-64, 67-74) | 333 |
| 153 | Syd Coventry (Coll 1922-34) | 227 |
| 153 | Graham Arthur (Haw 1955-68) | 232 |
| 150 | W. Schimmelbusch (NM 1973-87) | 306 |
| 142 | Reg Hickey (Geel 1926-40) | 245 |
| 139 | Michael Tuck (Hawth 1972-91) | 426 |
| 137 | Henry Young (Geel 1897-1910) | 167 |
| 131 | Dennis Carroll (Syd 1981-93) | 219 |
| 127 | Arthur Olliver (Foots 1935-50) | 272 |
| 127 | Robert Flower (Melb 1973-78) | 272 |
| 127 | Terry Daniher (Ess 1978-92) | 313 |
| 125 | Roger Merrett (Bris Bears 1988-96) | 313 |

*Totals include matches as acting captain*

## THE STEPHEN KERNAHAN STORY

Stephen Kernahan was destined for big things long before he joined Carlton in 1986. He had given notice of his pending greatness at state level for South Australia and at club level for Glenelg and the Blues had moved heaven and earth to get him.

After his debut season, Carlton had seen enough in the tall centre half-forward to be convinced he would be leadership material. So at the start of 1987, Kernahan replaced Mark Maclure as captain and kept going ... and going ... and going.

Eleven years later — in the round 18 clash against Adelaide at Football Park in 1997 — Kernahan, a champion leader in every sense, led the Blues for the 225th time. In the process, he set a new mark for a VFL/AFL captain, breaking Dick Reynolds' long-standing record of 224 for Essendon.

No other player in the history of the League has served as club captain longer than Kernahan. He retired at the end of 1997, ending a wonderful career and he has a record that will take some catching.

| | |
|---|---|
| Brian Wilson (Vic: Foots, N Melb, Melb, St K) 1978–91 | 209 |
| Garry Wilson (Vic: Fitz) 1971–84 | 268 |
| Percy Wilson# (Vic: Coll, Melb) 1909–24 | 234 |
| Nicky Winmar* (WA: St K) 1987–97 | 207 |
| Bryan Wood (Vic: Rich, Ess) 1972–86 | 253 |
| John Worsfold* (WA: Wst Cst) 1987–97 | 192 |
| Roy Wright (Vic: Rich) 1946–59 | 195 |
| Steven Wright (Vic: S Melb) 1979–92 | 246 |

## SENIOR MATCHES WITH FOUR OR MORE CLUBS: 1897-1997

**5 clubs**

| | | |
|---|---|---|
| Les Abbott | 39 games | Coll 1904 (1), Carlt 1905 (1), Rich 1910–11 (31), Melb 1912 (3), S Melb 1912 (3) |
| Les Hughson | 73 games | Coll 1927 (1), Hawth 1928 (4), Carlt 1933–34 (12), St K 1934–36 (41), Fitz 1937 (15) |
| Dale Kickett | 109 games | Fitz 1990 (15), W Coast 1991 (2), St K 1992 (21), Ess 1994 (8), Frem 1995–97 (63) |

**4 clubs**

| | | |
|---|---|---|
| Charlie Anderson | 16 games | Carlt 1924 (1), S. Melb 1925-26 (11), Rich 1926 (3), Foots 1927 (1) |
| Mark Athorn | 83 games | Foots 1987–89 (17), Fitz 1990 (21), Syd 1991 (15), Carlt 1992–94 (30) |
| Ted Baker | 142 games | Carlt 1920 (1), Coll 1922–23, 1932 (43), Geel 1927–32 (95), Foots 1934 (3) |
| Phil Carman | 100 games | Coll 1975–78 (66), Melb 1979 (11), Ess 1980–81 (10), N Melb 1982 (13) |
| Richard Chirgwin | 83 games | Rich 1934–39 (64), Foots 1940 (3), S Melb 1940 (1), N Melb 1941–43 (15) |
| Alf Clay | 83 games | Hawth 1937 (3), Foots 1938–39 (8), Fitz 1940–44 (41), N Melb 1944–46 (31) |
| Daryl Cumming | 109 games | Rich 1971–76 (88), Melb 1977 (10), N Melb 1978 (1), S Melb 1979 (10) |
| Allan Davis | 250 games | St K 1966–75 (173), Melb 1976–77 (41), Ess 1978–79 (33), Coll 1980 (3) |
| Craig Davis | 163 games | Carlt 1973–75 (42), N Melb 1977–78 (10), Coll 1979–83 (102), Syd 1988 (9) |
| George Dougherty | 173 games | Carlt 1934–36 (17), Geel 1936–41, 1944–45 (121), Foots 1942–43 (25), S Melb 1945 (10) |
| Peter Francis | 158 games | Carlt 1979–81 (47), Fitz 1981–83 (40), Rich 1984–86 (52), Ess 1987–88 (19) |
| Frank Kelly | 116 games | Coll 1930–31, 1933 (34), Melb 1934–36 (31), Ess 1937–39 (30), St K 1942–44 (21) |
| Norman Le Brun | 50 games | S Melb 1929 (3), Ess 1931–32 (23), Coll 1933–34 (19), Carlt 1935 (5) |
| Simon Minton-Connell | 104 games | Carlt 1989–91 (19), Syd 1992–94 (46), Hawth 1995–96 (22), Western Bulldogs 1997 (17) |
| Vic Nankervis | 46 games | Geel 1941, 1944–45 (33), Foots 1942 (2), St K 1943 (7), S Melb 1946 (4) |
| Richard Osborne | 269 games | Fitz 1982–92 (187), Syd 1993 (16), Foots 1994–96 (51), Coll 1997 (15) |
| Geoff Raines | 254 games | Rich 1976–82 (134), Coll 1983–86 (47), Ess 1986 (14), Bris Bears 1987–89 (59) |
| Lou Sharpe | 34 games | St K 1926–27 (8), Foots 1929–30 (19), Fitz 1932 (6), Ess 1934 (1) |
| Stuart Wigney | 72 games | Foots 1988–91 (47), Syd 1992 (1), Adel 1993–94 (10), Rich 1995–96 (14) |
| Brian Wilson | 209 games | Foots 1978–79 (9), N Melb 1980–81 (39), Melb 1982–90 (154), StK 1991 (7) |

## OLDEST LEAGUE PLAYERS 1897-1997

| Player | Clubs | Last match | Age | Career matches |
|---|---|---|---|---|
| H.V. 'Vic' Cumberland | Melb/StK | 1920 | 43 years 48 days | 176 |
| Sid Barker | Rich/Ess/NM | 1927 | 39 years 239 days | 68 |
| Jim Flynn | Geel/Carl | 1910 | 39 years 180 days | 149 |
| Les 'Flapper' Hughes | Coll | 1922 | 38 years 144 days | 225 |
| Teddy Rankin | Geel | 1910 | 38 years 144 days | 180 |
| Michael Tuck | Hawth | 1991 | 38 years 96 days | 426 |
| Harry Lever | StK | 1922 | 38 years | 217 |
| Charlie Hardy | Ess | 1925 | 38 years | 36 |
| Albie Morrison | Foots | 1946 | 37 years 221 days | 224 |
| Henry 'Tracker' Young | Geel | 1910 | 37 years 77 days | 167 |

## YOUNGEST LEAGUE PLAYERS
## 1897–1997

**15 years 287 days:**
Keith Bromage (Collingwood) on debut 1953, the youngest player to play in senior VFL game.
**15 years 297 days:**
Albert Collier (Collingwood) 1925
**15 years 305 days:**
Tim Watson (Essendon) 1977
**15 years 315 days:**
Wells Eicke (St Kilda) 1909
**15 years 315 days:**
Mick Maguire (Richmond) 1910
**15 years 349 days:**
Len Fitzgerald (Collingwood) 1945

## YOUNGEST PLAYERS, CLUB BY
## CLUB, 1897–1997

| Name | Team | Years | Days |
|------|------|-------|------|
| Ben Hart | Adelaide | 17 | 257 |
| Michael Voss | Brisbane Bears | 17 | 11 |
| Brett Voss | Brisbane Lions | 19 | 65 |
| Jim Buckley | Carlton | 16 | 200 |
| Keith Bromage | Collingwood | 15 | 287 |
| Tim Watson | Essendon | 15 | 305 |
| Andrew Kuka | Fitzroy | 16 | 46 |
| Ron James | Footscray | 16 | 155 |
| Steven Koops | Fremantle | 17 | 277 |
| Ken Newland | Geelong | 16 | 74 |
| John Peck | Hawthorn | 16 | 255 |
| Sid Catlin | Melbourne | 16 | 230 |
| Rob Peterson | North Melbourne | 16 | 45 |
| Stuart Dew | Port Adel | 17 | 329 |
| Mick Maguire | Richmond | 15 | 328 |
| Wells Eicke | St Kilda | 15 | 315 |
| Rob Hay | Sth Melb/Sydney | 16 | 285 |
| David Wirrpunda | West Coast | 16 | 268 |

## PLAYERS WHO MADE THEIR AFL DEBUT IN 1997

| | | | | | |
|---|---|---|---|---|---|
| Tim Cook (Adel) | R2 | Jess Sinclair (Frem) | R10 | Brendon Lade (Port Ad) | R1 |
| Tom Gilligan (Adel) | R3 | Martin Whitelaw (Frem) | R21 | Bowen Lockwood (Port Ad) | R2 |
| Simon Goodwin (Adel) | R1 | Paul Corrigan (Geel) | R1 | Darren Mead (Port Ad) | R1 |
| Aaron Keating (Adel) | R1 | Adam Houlihan (Geel) | R4 | Darryl Poole (Port Ad) | R1 |
| Chad Rintoul (Adel) | R1 | Daniel Lowther (Geel) | R16 | Damian Squire (Port Ad) | R1 |
| Brent Williams (Adel) | R1 | Darren Milburn (Geel) | R1 | Nathan Steinberner | |
| Nick Trask (Bris Lions) | R10 | Cameron Roberts (Geel) | R10 | (Port Ad) | R21 |
| Brett Voss (Bris Lions) | R5 | Ben Dixon (Hawth) | R5 | Warren Tredrea (Port Ad) | R2 |
| Jacob Anstey (Carlt) | R7 | Jonathan Hay (Hawth) | R17 | Michael Wilson (Port Ad) | R1 |
| Andrew Balkwill (Carlt) | R3 | Brad Scott (Hawth) | R1 | Mark Chaffey (Rich) | R4 |
| Anthony Franchina (Carlt) | R20 | Brent Grgic (Melb) | R14 | Daniel Donati (Rich) | R14 |
| Darren Hulme (Carlt) | R10 | Anthony McDonald (Melb) | R4 | Brett Evans (Rich) | R9 |
| Ben Nelson (Carlt) | R3 | James McDonald (Melb) | R17 | Nick Jewell (Rich) | R19 |
| Mark Porter (Carlt) | R16 | Leigh Newton (Melb) | R3 | Ewan Thompson (Rich) | R14 |
| Sam Smart (Carlt) | R21 | Alistair Nicholson (Melb) | R6 | Brad Campbell (St K) | R6 |
| Adam White (Carlt) | R2 | Russell Robertson (Melb) | R20 | Max Hudghton (St K) | R1 |
| Lance Whitnall (Carlt) | R1 | Shane Woewodin (Melb) | R1 | Andrew Thompson (St K) | R1 |
| Brad Fuller (Coll) | R13 | Evan Hewitt (Nth Melb) | R13 | Troy Cook (Syd) | R3 |
| Luke Godden (Coll) | R18 | Byron Pickett (Nth Melb) | R15 | Mark Kinnear (Syd) | R6 |
| Dwayne Griffin (Coll) | R22 | Paul Wynd (Nth Melb) | R11 | Paul Licuria (Syd) | R1 |
| Josh Mahoney (Coll) | R12 | Peter Burgoyne (Port Ad) | R1 | Ben Mathews (Syd) | R16 |
| Mal Michael (Coll) | R7 | Tom Carr (Port Ad) | R4 | John Stevens (Syd) | R3 |
| Matthew Banks (Ess) | R5 | Stephen Carter (Port Ad) | R1 | Michael Braun (West C) | R11 |
| Andrew Bomford (Ess) | R3 | Mark Conway (Port Ad) | R14 | Michael Gardiner (West C) | R4 |
| Blake Caracella (Ess) | R3 | Jarrod Cotton (Port Ad) | R10 | Neil Marshall (West C) | R16 |
| Chris Heffernan (Ess) | R19 | Stephen Daniels (Port Ad) | R4 | Nicholas Stone (West C) | R4 |
| Jason Johnson (Ess) | R18 | Stuart Dew (Port Ad) | R15 | Josh Wooden (West C) | R1 |
| Daniel McAlister (Ess) | R21 | Donald Dickie (Port Ad) | R1 | Nathan Brown (W Bull) | R1 |
| Andrew Ukovic (Ess) | R12 | Nathan Eagleton (Port Ad) | R5 | Adam Contessa (W Bull) | R13 |
| Matthew Watson (Ess) | R21 | Nigel Fiegert (Port Ad) | R2 | Brett Montgomery (W Bull) | R2 |
| Heath Black (Frem) | R4 | Josh Francou (Port Ad) | R1 | Stephen Powell (W Bull) | R6 |
| Trent Carroll (Frem) | R9 | Roger James (Port Ad) | R5 | David Round (W Bull) | R3 |
| Matthew Clucas (Frem) | R6 | Adam Kingsley (Port Ad) | R1 | | |

# STATS '97

## KICKS: THE LEADING 25 PLAYERS

| Player | Club | Total | Games | Average |
|--------|------|-------|-------|---------|
| Nathan Burke | St Kilda | 469 | 25 | 18.76 |
| Robert Harvey | St Kilda | 453 | 25 | 18.12 |
| Anthony Stevens | North Melbourne | 453 | 25 | 18.12 |
| Nathan Buckley | Collingwood | 453 | 22 | 20.59 |
| Craig Bradley | Carlton | 436 | 22 | 19.82 |
| Darren Jarman | Adelaide | 381 | 24 | 15.88 |
| Paul Kelly | Sydney | 376 | 23 | 16.35 |
| Brad Johnson | Western Bulldogs | 375 | 24 | 15.63 |
| Daryn Cresswell | Sydney | 367 | 23 | 15.96 |
| Scott West | Western Bulldogs | 367 | 24 | 15.29 |
| Mark Bickley | Adelaide | 351 | 26 | 13.50 |
| Wayne Campbell | Richmond | 350 | 21 | 16.67 |
| David King | North Melbourne | 348 | 23 | 15.13 |
| Peter Matera | West Coast | 336 | 21 | 16.00 |
| Paul Williams | Collingwood | 332 | 22 | 15.09 |
| Austinn Jones | St Kilda | 323 | 25 | 12.92 |
| Dale Lewis | Sydney | 322 | 21 | 15.33 |
| Liam Pickering | Geelong | 322 | 20 | 16.10 |
| Rohan Smith | Western Bulldogs | 318 | 24 | 13.25 |
| Mark Ricciuto | Adelaide | 316 | 21 | 15.05 |
| Glenn Kilpatrick | Geelong | 316 | 24 | 13.17 |
| Brad Sholl | Geelong | 311 | 24 | 12.96 |
| Craig Callaghan | Fremantle | 302 | 21 | 14.38 |
| Jose Romero | Western Bulldogs | 298 | 24 | 12.42 |
| Anthony Rock | North Melbourne | 297 | 22 | 13.50 |

## MARKS: THE LEADING 25 PLAYERS

| Player | Club | Total | Games | Average |
|--------|------|-------|-------|---------|
| Stewart Loewe | St Kilda | 192 | 24 | 8.00 |
| Chris Grant | Western Bulldogs | 170 | 23 | 7.39 |
| Matthew Richardson | Richmond | 148 | 19 | 7.79 |
| Peter Everitt | St Kilda | 135 | 23 | 5.87 |
| Corey Mc Kernan | North Melbourne | 134 | 22 | 6.09 |
| Luke Darcy | Western Bulldogs | 131 | 23 | 5.70 |
| Dale Lewis | Sydney | 128 | 21 | 6.10 |
| Paul Salmon | Hawthorn | 128 | 21 | 6.10 |
| Nick Holland | Hawthorn | 128 | 17 | 7.53 |
| Jim Stynes | Melbourne | 126 | 22 | 5.73 |
| Matthew Lloyd | Essendon | 125 | 20 | 6.25 |
| Derek Hall | Geelong | 124 | 17 | 7.29 |
| Scott Lucas | Essendon | 123 | 22 | 5.59 |
| Craig Sholl | North Melbourne | 122 | 25 | 4.88 |
| Brad Johnson | Western Bulldogs | 122 | 24 | 5.08 |
| Peter Caven | Adelaide | 116 | 22 | 5.27 |
| Michael Mansfield | Geelong | 116 | 23 | 5.04 |
| Nathan Buckley | Collingwood | 116 | 22 | 5.27 |
| Fraser Gehrig | West Coast | 115 | 22 | 5.23 |
| Leigh Colbert | Geelong | 113 | 20 | 5.65 |
| Matthew Allan | Carlton | 113 | 21 | 5.38 |
| Craig Ellis | Western Bulldogs | 109 | 24 | 4.54 |
| Nigel Lappin | Brisbane Lions | 107 | 21 | 5.10 |
| Justin Murphy | Carlton | 107 | 21 | 5.10 |
| Mark Ricciuto | Adelaide | 106 | 21 | 5.05 |

## GOALS: THE LEADING 25 PLAYERS

| Player | Club | Total | Games | Average |
|---|---|---|---|---|
| Tony Modra | Adelaide | 84 | 25 | 3.36 |
| Saverio Rocca | Collingwood | 76 | 21 | 3.62 |
| Jason Heatley | St Kilda | 73 | 20 | 3.65 |
| Scott Cummings | Port Adelaide | 70 | 21 | 3.33 |
| Matthew Lloyd | Essendon | 63 | 20 | 3.15 |
| Stewart Loewe | St Kilda | 54 | 24 | 2.25 |
| Justin Leppitsch | Brisbane Lions | 50 | 22 | 2.27 |
| Ronnie Burns | Geelong | 50 | 24 | 2.08 |
| Matthew Richardson | Richmond | 47 | 19 | 2.47 |
| Peter Everitt | St Kilda | 44 | 23 | 1.91 |
| Brett Allison | North Melbourne | 43 | 24 | 1.79 |
| Simon Minton-Connell | Western Bulldogs | 43 | 17 | 2.53 |
| Craig Sholl | North Melbourne | 40 | 25 | 1.60 |
| Darren Jarman | Adelaide | 39 | 24 | 1.63 |
| Tony Lockett | Sydney | 37 | 12 | 3.08 |
| Chris Grant | Western Bulldogs | 37 | 23 | 1.61 |
| James Cook | Western Bulldogs | 36 | 14 | 2.57 |
| Daniel Bradshaw | Brisbane Lions | 35 | 16 | 2.19 |
| Anthony Rocca | Collingwood | 34 | 21 | 1.62 |
| Peter Sumich | West Coast | 33 | 13 | 2.54 |
| Kingsley Hunter | Fremantle | 32 | 11 | 2.91 |
| Fraser Gehrig | West Coast | 31 | 22 | 1.41 |
| Phillip Matera | West Coast | 30 | 19 | 1.58 |
| David Neitz | Melbourne | 30 | 17 | 1.76 |
| Jeff Farmer | Melbourne | 30 | 17 | 1.76 |

## HANDBALLS: THE LEADING 25 PLAYERS

| Player | Club | Total | Games | Average |
|---|---|---|---|---|
| Robert Harvey | St Kilda | 303 | 25 | 12.12 |
| Brett Ratten | Carlton | 261 | 21 | 12.43 |
| Daryn Cresswell | Sydney | 244 | 23 | 10.61 |
| Scott West | Western Bulldogs | 240 | 24 | 10.00 |
| Todd Viney | Melbourne | 235 | 22 | 10.68 |
| Craig Lambert | Brisbane Lions | 229 | 16 | 14.31 |
| Paul Broderick | Richmond | 229 | 22 | 10.41 |
| Scott Russell | Collingwood | 209 | 22 | 9.50 |
| Sean Denham | Essendon | 208 | 22 | 9.45 |
| Gavin Brown | Collingwood | 206 | 22 | 9.36 |
| Wayne Campbell | Richmond | 205 | 21 | 9.76 |
| Daniel Harford | Hawthorn | 204 | 22 | 9.27 |
| Joe Misiti | Essendon | 203 | 18 | 11.28 |
| Nathan Burke | St Kilda | 200 | 25 | 8.00 |
| Mark Bickley | Adelaide | 197 | 26 | 7.58 |
| Tony Liberatore | Western Bulldogs | 196 | 24 | 8.17 |
| Scott Wynd | Western Bulldogs | 194 | 23 | 8.43 |
| Mark Ricciuto | Adelaide | 193 | 21 | 9.19 |
| Dean Kemp | West Coast | 192 | 22 | 8.73 |
| Tony Brown | St Kilda | 192 | 24 | 8.00 |
| Garry Hocking | Geelong | 192 | 20 | 9.60 |
| Glenn Kilpatrick | Geelong | 190 | 24 | 7.92 |
| Marcus Ashcroft | Brisbane Lions | 185 | 23 | 8.04 |
| Dale Kickett | Fremantle | 182 | 22 | 8.27 |
| Peter Bell | North Melbourne | 182 | 25 | 7.28 |

## FREES FOR: THE LEADING 25 PLAYERS

| Player | Club | Total | Games | Average |
|---|---|---|---|---|
| Jim Stynes | Melbourne | 48 | 22 | 2.18 |
| Scott West | Western Bulldogs | 48 | 24 | 2.00 |
| Matthew Primus | Port Adelaide | 43 | 22 | 1.95 |
| Nathan Burke | St Kilda | 41 | 25 | 1.64 |
| David Pittman | Adelaide | 40 | 23 | 1.74 |
| Jose Romero | Western Bulldogs | 40 | 24 | 1.67 |
| Peter Everitt | St Kilda | 38 | 23 | 1.65 |
| Gavin Wanganeen | Port Adelaide | 37 | 20 | 1.85 |
| Peter Matera | West Coast | 36 | 21 | 1.71 |
| Stewart Loewe | St Kilda | 36 | 24 | 1.50 |
| Paul Salmon | Hawthorn | 35 | 21 | 1.67 |
| Chris Grant | Western Bulldogs | 35 | 23 | 1.52 |
| Peter Caven | Adelaide | 34 | 22 | 1.55 |
| Corey Mc Kernan | North Melbourne | 34 | 22 | 1.55 |
| Tony Liberatore | Western Bulldogs | 34 | 24 | 1.42 |
| Michael Wilson | Port Adelaide | 33 | 22 | 1.50 |
| Shane Bond | Port Adelaide | 33 | 22 | 1.50 |
| Shaun Rehn | Adelaide | 32 | 22 | 1.45 |
| Ilija Grgic | West Coast | 32 | 22 | 1.45 |
| Dale Lewis | Sydney | 32 | 21 | 1.52 |
| Barry Stoneham | Geelong | 32 | 21 | 1.52 |
| Shane Parker | Fremantle | 31 | 22 | 1.41 |
| Ben Hart | Adelaide | 31 | 26 | 1.19 |
| Brad Sholl | Geelong | 31 | 24 | 1.29 |
| Scott Wynd | Western Bulldogs | 31 | 23 | 1.35 |

## FREES AGAINST: THE LEADING 25 PLAYERS

| Player | Club | Total | Games | Average |
|---|---|---|---|---|
| Darren Jarman | Adelaide | 51 | 24 | 2.13 |
| Jim Stynes | Melbourne | 51 | 22 | 2.32 |
| Corey Mc Kernan | North Melbourne | 48 | 22 | 2.18 |
| Matthew Clarke | Brisbane Lions | 40 | 21 | 1.90 |
| Greg Stafford | Sydney | 40 | 22 | 1.82 |
| Todd Viney | Melbourne | 40 | 22 | 1.82 |
| Stewart Loewe | St Kilda | 37 | 24 | 1.54 |
| John Longmire | North Melbourne | 37 | 25 | 1.48 |
| Craig Callaghan | Fremantle | 36 | 21 | 1.71 |
| Paul Salmon | Hawthorn | 35 | 21 | 1.67 |
| Matthew Primus | Port Adelaide | 35 | 22 | 1.59 |
| Garry Hocking | Geelong | 34 | 20 | 1.70 |
| David Pittman | Adelaide | 33 | 23 | 1.43 |
| Ilija Grgic | West Coast | 33 | 22 | 1.50 |
| Paul Kelly | Sydney | 33 | 23 | 1.43 |
| Chris Grant | Western Bulldogs | 33 | 23 | 1.43 |
| Peter Everitt | St Kilda | 32 | 23 | 1.39 |
| Scott Wynd | Western Bulldogs | 32 | 23 | 1.39 |
| Matthew Allan | Carlton | 32 | 21 | 1.52 |
| Daryn Cresswell | Sydney | 31 | 23 | 1.35 |
| Steven King | Geelong | 31 | 22 | 1.41 |
| Luke Darcy | Western Bulldogs | 31 | 23 | 1.35 |
| Josh Francou | Port Adelaide | 31 | 22 | 1.41 |
| Steven Sziller | St Kilda | 30 | 23 | 1.30 |
| Matthew Richardson | Richmond | 30 | 19 | 1.58 |

## HIT-OUTS: THE LEADING 25 PLAYERS

| Player | Club | Total | Games | Average |
|---|---|---|---|---|
| Paul Salmon | Hawthorn | 352 | 21 | 16.76 |
| Scott Wynd | Western Bulldogs | 350 | 23 | 15.22 |
| Jim Stynes | Melbourne | 320 | 22 | 14.55 |
| David Pittman | Adelaide | 317 | 23 | 13.78 |
| Matthew Clarke | Brisbane Lions | 309 | 21 | 14.71 |
| Peter Everitt | St Kilda | 302 | 23 | 13.13 |
| Greg Stafford | Sydney | 282 | 22 | 12.82 |
| Shaun Rehn | Adelaide | 264 | 22 | 12.00 |
| Matthew Allan | Carlton | 263 | 21 | 12.52 |
| Matthew Primus | Port Adelaide | 255 | 22 | 11.59 |
| Brendon Gale | Richmond | 206 | 19 | 10.84 |
| Steven King | Geelong | 200 | 22 | 9.09 |
| Damian Monkhorst | Collingwood | 178 | 20 | 8.90 |
| Brendon Lade | Port Adelaide | 171 | 22 | 7.77 |
| Ilija Grgic | West Coast | 161 | 22 | 7.32 |
| Corey Mc Kernan | North Melbourne | 143 | 22 | 6.50 |
| Clark Keating | Brisbane Lions | 140 | 20 | 7.00 |
| Peter Somerville | Essendon | 137 | 13 | 10.54 |
| Stewart Loewe | St Kilda | 136 | 24 | 5.67 |
| Luke Darcy | Western Bulldogs | 132 | 23 | 5.74 |
| Jeff White | Fremantle | 131 | 13 | 10.08 |
| Matthew Burton | Fremantle | 131 | 11 | 11.91 |
| Ryan Turnbull | West Coast | 123 | 24 | 5.13 |
| John Barnes | Geelong | 104 | 15 | 6.93 |
| Daniel Bandy | Fremantle | 101 | 18 | 5.61 |

## TACKLES: THE LEADING 25 PLAYERS

| Player | Club | Total | Games | Average |
|---|---|---|---|---|
| Tony Liberatore | Western Bulldogs | 95 | 24 | 3.96 |
| Mark Bickley | Adelaide | 80 | 26 | 3.08 |
| Nathan Burke | St Kilda | 75 | 25 | 3.00 |
| Brett Ratten | Carlton | 68 | 21 | 3.24 |
| Darren Jarman | Adelaide | 67 | 24 | 2.79 |
| Anthony Stevens | North Melbourne | 66 | 25 | 2.64 |
| Dean Kemp | West Coast | 63 | 22 | 2.86 |
| Glenn Kilpatrick | Geelong | 63 | 24 | 2.63 |
| Duncan Kellaway | Richmond | 62 | 22 | 2.82 |
| Craig Callaghan | Fremantle | 61 | 21 | 2.90 |
| Todd Viney | Melbourne | 60 | 22 | 2.73 |
| Adrian Fletcher | Brisbane Lions | 59 | 21 | 2.81 |
| Guy Mc Kenna | West Coast | 58 | 20 | 2.90 |
| Daniel Chick | Hawthorn | 58 | 21 | 2.76 |
| Scott West | Western Bulldogs | 57 | 24 | 2.38 |
| Tristan Lynch | Brisbane Lions | 56 | 21 | 2.67 |
| Danny Dickfos | Brisbane Lions | 54 | 22 | 2.45 |
| Drew Banfield | West Coast | 53 | 21 | 2.52 |
| Marcus Ashcroft | Brisbane Lions | 53 | 23 | 2.30 |
| Andrew Thompson | St Kilda | 52 | 23 | 2.26 |
| Steven Sziller | St Kilda | 52 | 23 | 2.26 |
| Kym Koster | Adelaide | 51 | 24 | 2.13 |
| Andrew Mc Leod | Adelaide | 51 | 26 | 1.96 |
| Garry Hocking | Geelong | 51 | 20 | 2.55 |
| Craig Lambert | Brisbane Lions | 50 | 16 | 3.13 |

*STATISTICS COMPILED BY A.P.B. SPORTS (SPORTS CONSULTANTS), 14 MERRICK CRESCENT, GLEN WAVERLEY, VICTORIA, 3150 PHONE (03)95606509 FAX (03)95618590*

# THE TOP TEN 1981-1997

## KICKS

| Player | Club | Total | Games |
|---|---|---|---|
| Paul Roos | Fitz/Syd | 4410 | 335 |
| Craig Bradley | Carlton | 4318 | 267 |
| Tony Shaw | Collingwood | 4068 | 313 |
| John Platten | Hawthorn | 3850 | 258 |
| Terry Wallace | Haw/Rich/Foots | 3758 | 255 |
| Paul Couch | Geelong | 3750 | 259 |
| Tony McGuinness | Foots/Adel | 3683 | 222 |
| Steven Wallis | Footscray | 3390 | 261 |
| Doug Hawkins | Foots/Fitz | 3390 | 350 |
| Nathan Burke | St Kilda | 3388 | 227 |

## FREES FOR

| Player | Club | Total | Games |
|---|---|---|---|
| Justin Madden | Ess/Carl | 819 | 332 |
| Roger Merrett | Ess/B.Bears | 597 | 313 |
| Bernard Toohey | Geel/Syd/Foots | 579 | 263 |
| Steven Wright | Sydney | 554 | 246 |
| Simon Madden | Essendon | 550 | 379 |
| Jim Stynes | Melbourne | 544 | 244 |
| Matthew Rendell | Fitz/B.Bears | 538 | 176 |
| Dale Weightman | Richmond | 536 | 275 |
| Doug Hawkins | Foots/Fitz | 520 | 350 |
| John Platten | Hawthorn | 516 | 258 |

## MARKS

| Player | Club | Total | Games |
|---|---|---|---|
| Paul Roos | Fitz/Syd | 2067 | 335 |
| Stewart Loewe | St Kilda | 1943 | 237 |
| Stephen Kernahan | Carlton | 1758 | 251 |
| Jason Dunstall | Hawthorn | 1718 | 256 |
| Paul Salmon | Ess/Haw | 1582 | 248 |
| Terry Daniher | Essendon | 1486 | 313 |
| Jim Stynes | Melbourne | 1457 | 244 |
| Tony Lockett | St Kilda/Syd | 1439 | 236 |
| Gary Ablett | Haw/Geel | 1432 | 248 |
| Doug Hawkins | Foots/Fitz | 1389 | 350 |

## FREES AGAINST

| Player | Club | Total | Games |
|---|---|---|---|
| Justin Madden | Ess/Carl | 759 | 332 |
| Roger Merrett | Ess/B.Bears | 752 | 313 |
| Gary Ablett | Haw/Geel | 568 | 248 |
| Mark Lee | Richmond | 544 | 233 |
| Tony Lockett | St Kilda/Syd | 499 | 236 |
| Dermott Brereton | Haw/Syd/Coll | 497 | 211 |
| Garry Hocking | Geelong | 495 | 207 |
| Jim Stynes | Melbourne | 483 | 244 |
| Simon Madden | Essendon | 481 | 379 |
| R. DiPierdomenico | Hawthorn | 477 | 240 |

## GOALS

| Player | Club | Total | Games |
|---|---|---|---|
| Jason Dunstall | Hawthorn | 1200 | 256 |
| Tony Lockett | St Kilda/Syd | 1166 | 236 |
| Gary Ablett | Haw/Geel | 1030 | 248 |
| Leigh Matthews | Hawthorn | 915 | 340 |
| Bernie Quinlan | Foots/Fitz | 817 | 367 |
| Kevin Bartlett | Richmond | 778 | 403 |
| Stephen Kernahan | Carlton | 738 | 251 |
| Michael Moncrieff | Hawthorn | 628 | 225 |
| Michael Roach | Richmond | 607 | 200 |
| Kelvin Templeton | Foots/Melb | 593 | 177 |

## HIT-OUTS

| Player | Club | Total | Games |
|---|---|---|---|
| Justin Madden | Ess/Carl | 5660 | 332 |
| Simon Madden | Essendon | 3860 | 379 |
| Mark Lee | Richmond | 3095 | 233 |
| Jim Stynes | Melbourne | 2857 | 244 |
| John Mossop | Geel/Nth Melb | 2722 | 171 |
| Gary Dempsey | Foots/Nth Melb | 2487 | 337 |
| Matthew Rendell | Fitz/B.Bears | 2439 | 176 |
| Paul Salmon | Hawthorn | 2297 | 248 |
| Scott Wynd | Footscray | 2280 | 170 |
| Greg Dear | Haw/Rich | 2241 | 190 |

## HANDBALLS

| Player | Club | Total | Games |
|---|---|---|---|
| Greg Williams | Geel/Syd/Carl | 3594 | 250 |
| Tony Shaw | Collingwood | 2737 | 313 |
| Craig Lambert | Rch/B.Bears/B.Lions | 2441 | 188 |
| Paul Couch | Geelong | 2304 | 259 |
| Paul Roos | Fitz/Syd | 2246 | 335 |
| Doug Hawkins | Foots/Fitz | 2222 | 350 |
| Dale Weightman | Richmond | 2175 | 275 |
| Barry Mitchell | Syd/Coll/Carl | 2154 | 221 |
| Robert Harvey | St Kilda | 2108 | 179 |
| Garry Hocking | Geelong | 2096 | 207 |

## TACKLES

| Player | Club | Total | Games |
|---|---|---|---|
| Tony Liberatore | Footscray | 888 | 197 |
| Nathan Burke | St Kilda | 595 | 227 |
| Andrew Collins | Hawthorn | 507 | 212 |
| John Platten | Hawthorn | 490 | 258 |
| Dean Kemp | West Coast | 475 | 176 |
| Craig Lambert | Rch/B.Bears/B.Lions | 448 | 188 |
| Garry Hocking | Geelong | 442 | 207 |
| Chris Lewis | West Coast | 436 | 197 |
| Wayne Schwass | North Melbourne | 425 | 184 |
| Paul Kelly | Sydney | 423 | 160 |

# ATTENDANCES

## ATTENDANCES 1944-1997

| Year | Premiership season | Finals | Total | Receipts | Year | Premiership season | Finals | Total | Receipts |
|------|-----------|--------|-------|----------|------|-----------|--------|-------|----------|
| 1944 | 1,409,950 | 137,000 | 1,546,950 | £52,839* | 1972 | 2,934,919 | 591,879 | 3,526,798 | $2,591,619 |
| 1945 | 1,719,500 | 205,375 | 1,924,875 | £70,048 | 1973 | 2,836,694 | 501,956 | 3,338,650 | $2,630,177 |
| 1946 | 2,058,000 | 336,833 | 2,394,833 | £91,562 | 1974 | 2,763,654 | 479,997 | 3,243,651 | $3,379,822 |
| 1947 | 2,047,000 | 299,508 | 2,346,508 | £88,891 | 1975 | 2,755,765 | 450,251 | 3,206,016 | $3,345,377 |
| 1948 | 2,060,000 | 345,293 | 2,405,293 | £92,982 | 1976 | 2,863,112 | 425,358 | 3,288,470 | $5,061,762 |
| 1949 | 1,919,950 | 303,587 | 2,223,537 | £111,498 | 1977 | 2,773,007 | 531,073 | 3,304,080 | $5,607,203 |
| 1950 | 2,102,500 | 296,575 | 2,399,075 | £116,654 | 1978 | 3,024,926 | 453,409 | 3,478,335 | $6,265,200 |
| 1951 | 2,081,200 | 281,487 | 2,362,687 | £137,775 | 1979 | 3,096,945 | 477,341 | 3,574,286 | $7,178,112 |
| 1952 | 2,248,568 | 271,159 | 2,519,727 | £161,697 | 1980 | 3,280,129 | 490,788 | 3,770,917 | $8,336,513 |
| 1953 | 2,065,027 | 286,444 | 2,351,471 | £154,451 | 1981 | 3,354,023 | 476,208 | 3,830,231 | $10,441,540 |
| 1954 | 2,363,716 | 239,734 | 2,603,450 | £171,222 | 1982 | 3,264,284 | 417,272 | 3,681,556 | $11,019,512 |
| 1955 | 2,341,194 | 285,697 | 2,626,891 | £190,463 | 1983 | 3,217,578 | 420,439 | 3,638,017 | $13,444,232 |
| 1956 | 2,371,555 | 380,788 | 2,752,332 | £242,210 | 1984 | 2,951,247 | 443,324 | 3,394,571 | $13,069,124 |
| 1957 | 2,540,236 | 314,101 | 2,854,337 | £301,066 | 1985 | 2,727,217 | 385,956 | 3,113,173 | $13,173,365 |
| 1958 | 2,391,700 | 321,175 | 2,712,875 | £284,681 | 1986 | 2,899,145 | 423,714 | 3,322,859 | $14,409,766 |
| 1959 | 2,351,499 | 103,506 | 2,455,005 | £179,575 | 1987 | 2,924,185 | 429,057 | 3,353,242 | $15,006,785 |
| 1960 | 2,292,556 | 323,763 | 2,616,319 | £333,072 | 1988 | 3,092,679 | 436,199 | 3,528,878 | $16,987,578 |
| 1961 | 2,634,236 | 368,208 | 3,002,444 | £356,864 | 1989 | 3,145,126 | 436,696 | 3,581,822 | $17,753,049 |
| 1962 | 2,720,209 | 463,578 | 3,183,787 | £444,810 | 1990 | 3,587,595 | 475,790 | 4,063,385 | $21,346,308 |
| 1963 | 2,739,372 | 368,140 | 3,107,512 | £427,163 | 1991 | 3,797,177 | 381,707 | 4,178,884 | $20,996,463 |
| 1964 | 2,536,962 | 374,801 | 2,911,763 | £408,238 | 1992 | 4,332,917 | 481,346 | 4,814,263 | $24,895,471 |
| 1965 | 2,550,567 | 388,460 | 2,939,027 | £471,778 | 1993 | 4,185,388 | 471,501 | 4,656,889 | $24,783,921 |
| 1966 | 2,567,643 | 384,487 | 2,952,130 | $932,595 | 1994 | 4,723,023 | 514,375 | 5,237,398 | $32,054,287 |
| 1967 | 2,428,002 | 395,704 | 2,823,706 | $1,025,331 | 1995 | 5,117,774 | 594,919 | 5,712,693 | $36,454,603 |
| 1968 | 2,425,905 | 425,727 | 2,851,632 | $1,292,737 | 1996 | 5,216,148 | 478,773 | 5,694,921 | $38,506,480 |
| 1969 | 2,486,795 | 436,221 | 2,923,016 | $1,405,353 | 1997 | 5,842,591 | 560,406 | 6,402,997 | $41,544,497 |
| 1970 | 2,863,780 | 446,988 | 3,310,768 | $1,754,370 | | | | | |
| 1971 | 2,906,157 | 420,270 | 3,326,427 | $1,753,434 | *1944 receipts are estimated | | | | |

## ROUND BY ROUND ATTENDANCE RECORDS

| | | | | | | | | | |
|---|---|---|---|---|---|---|---|---|---|
| R1 | 329,369 (1997) | R7 | 305,573 (1996) | R13 | 261,336 (1997) | R19 | 276,689 (1997) |
| R2 | 259,424 (1996) | R8 | 276,671 (1996) | R14 | 282,401 (1997) | R20 | 245,514 (1997) |
| R3 | 296,994 (1997) | R9 | 254,764 (1997) | R15 | 267,913 (1997) | R21 | 313,444 (1996) |
| R4 | 316,244 (1997) | R10 | 270,954 (1996) | R16 | 265,949 (1997) | R22 | 283,188 (1996) |
| R5 | 278,707 (1997) | R11 | 296,852 (1997) | R17 | 252,738 (1997) | R23 | 204,780 (1992) |
| R6 | 265,150 (1993) | R12 | 245,334 (1996) | R18 | 275,685 (1997) | R24 | 228,347 (1994) |

## 1997 ATTENDANCES AND RECEIPTS

| | Total | Receipts | Home Games | Highest attendance In 1997 |
|---|-------|----------|-------|----------------------------|
| Adelaide | 724,216 | $2,986,075 | 441,905 | 47,256 v Port Adel, R4 FP |
| Brisbane Lions | 512,728 | $1,606,876 | 215,051 | 37,642 v Essendon, R6 MCG |
| Carlton | 872,375 | $4,549,677 | 369,972 | 82,363 v Essendon, R1 MCG |
| Collingwood | 1,102,961 | $6,765,806 | 535,789 | 83,271 v Essendon, R5 MCG |
| Essendon | 1,033,238 | $5,698,882 | 581,330 | 83,271 v Collingwood, R5 MCG |
| Fremantle | 471,895 | $1,564,718 | 241,801 | 39,711 v West Coast, R18 S |
| Geelong | 700,019 | $3,075,557 | 311,567 | 65,228 v Collingwood, R14 MCG |
| Hawthorn | 710,654 | $2,716,609 | 356,179 | 60,594 v Essendon, R11 MCG |
| Melbourne | 613,713 | $3,039,341 | 304,853 | 61,138 v Collingwood, R2 MCG (N) |
| North Melb | 732,956 | $3,823,272 | 357,725 | 57,978 v Essendon, R3 MCG |
| Port Adel | 695,990 | $1,824,478 | 394,115 | 51,883 v Collingwood, R1 MCG |
| Richmond | 783,517 | $3,976,561 | 379,670 | 70,350 v Collingwood, R11 MCG (N) |
| St Kilda | 794,178 | $3,433,358 | 387,553 | 68,036 v Collingwood, R18 MCG |
| Sydney | 701,141 | $2,594,798 | 393,999 | 46,168 v Geelong, R22 SCG (N) |
| West Coast | 644,697 | $1,956,164 | 358,401 | 39,711 v Fremantle, R18 S |
| W Bulldogs | 590,904 | $2,543,696 | 212,681 | 61,014 v Collingwood, R8 MCG (N) |
| **Totals** | **5,842,591** | **$26,077,934** | | |

## LARGEST ATTENDANCE AT CURRENT LEAGUE VENUES

| Venue | Home And Away Matches | | | Finals | | |
|---|---|---|---|---|---|---|
| MCG | 99,346 | Melb v Coll | R10, 1958 | 121,696 | Coll v Carl | GF, 1970 |
| Waverley Park | 92,935 | Coll v Hawth | R11, 1981 | 75,526 | Geel v Coll | PF, 1980 |
| Kardinia Park | 49,107 | Geel v Carl | R19, 1952 | | | |
| Football Park | 48,522 | Adel v Coll | R22, 1993 | 46,319 | Adel v Geel | SF ,1997 |
| SCG | 46,168 | Syd v Geel | R22, 1997 | 41,731 | Syd v Ess | PF, 1996 |
| Princes Park | 47,514 | Carlt v Geel | R6, 1963 | 62,986 | Sth Melb v Carl | GF, 1945 |
| Victoria Park | 47,224 | Coll v Sth Melb | R2, 1948 | 16,000 | Carlt v Ess | SF, 1904 |
| Whitten Oval | 42,354 | Foots v Coll | R12, 1955 | | | |
| Subiaco | 42,209 | West C v St K | R15, 1991 | 44,142 | West C v Hawth | QF, 1991 |
| WACA | 32,119 | West C v Geel | R22, 1993 | 34,317 | West C v Melb | PF, 1994 |
| Gabba | 21,644 | Bris Bears v Coll | R8, 1996 | 22,003 | Bris Bears v Ess | QF, 1996 |

## LARGEST 1997 ATTENDANCE AT CURRENT LEAGUE VENUES

| | | | | Average | | Total |
|---|---|---|---|---|---|---|
| MCG | 83,271 | Ess v Coll | R5 | 43,488 | | 2,304,865 |
| Waverley Park | 54,699 | St K v Coll | R3 | 33,806 | | 743,732 |
| Football Park | 47,256 | Adel v P Adel | R4 | 38,001 | | 836,020 |
| SCG | 46,168 | Syd v Geel | R22 | 35,818 | | 393,999 |
| Subiaco | 39,711 | Fre v W Coast | R18 | 29,160 | | 466,553 |
| Optus Oval | 34,922 | Carl v Rich | R22 | 20,781 | | 457,182 |
| Whitten Oval | 26,704 | W Bull v W Coast | R21 | 26,704 | | 26,704 |
| Victoria Park | 25,323 | Coll v W Coast | R12 | 24,473 | | 73,419 |
| WACA | 29,838 | W Coast v W Bull | R6 | 22,275 | | 133,649 |
| Kardinia Park | 24,099 | Geel v Rich | R16 | 21,269 | | 191,417 |
| Gabba | 21,348 | Bris Lions v Adel | R16 | 19,550 | | 215,051 |

## LEAGUE MATCH VENUES: 1897–1997

| Venue | All matches | Finals | Clubs/seasons |
|---|---|---|---|
| Football Park | 89 | 2 | Adel 1991–97; Pt Adel 1997 |
| Gabba | 61 | 2 | 1981; B Bears 1991; 1993–96; B Lions 1997 |
| Princes Park | 1200 | 15 | Carl 1897–1997; Sth M 1942–43; Fitz 1967–69; 1987–93; Haw 1974–91; Foots 1997 |
| Victoria Park | 876 | 2 | Coll 1897–1997; Fitz 1985–86 |
| Whitten Oval | 665 | 0 | Foots 1925–41; 1943–97 Fitz 1994–96 |
| Kardinia Park | 506 | 0 | Geel 1941; 1944–97 |
| MCG | 1779 | 348 | Melb 1897–1914; 1919–41; 1946–97; Rich 1965–97; Nth M 1984–97; Ess 1992–97; Coll 1993–97 |
| Waverley Park | 685 | 70 | 1970–97; Haw 1990–97; St K 1993–97 |
| SCG | 189 | 2 | 1903–04; 1952; 1979–81; Syd 1982–97 |
| Subiaco | 106 | 3 | WC 1987–97; Fre 1995–97 |
| Waca | 54 | 2 | WC 1987–97; Fre 1995–97 |
| Carrara | 61 | 0 | Bris Bears 1987–92 |
| East Melb C.G. | 225 | 3 | Ess 1897–1915; 1918–21; Uni 1908–10 |
| Windy Hill | 629 | 1 | Ess 1922–91 |
| Brunswick St Oval | 612 | 4 | Fitz 1897–1966 |
| Junction Oval | 734 | 6 | St K 1897–1915; 1918–41;1944–64; Sth M 1944–46; Fitz 1970–84 |
| Yarraville | 7 | 0 | Foots 1942 |
| Corio Oval | 371 | 1 | Geel 1897–1915; 1917–40 |
| Glenferrie Oval | 443 | 0 | Haw 1925–73 |
| Motordrome | 3 | 0 | Melb 1932 |
| Arden St Oval | 529 | 0 | Nth M 1925–64; 1966–85 |
| Coburg | 9 | 0 | Nth M 1965 |
| Punt Rd Oval | 543 | 0 | Rich 1908–64; Mel 1942–46 |
| Toorak Park | 13 | 0 | St K 1942–43 |
| Moorabbin | 254 | 0 | St K 1965–92 |
| Lake Oval | 704 | 4 | Sth M 1897–1915, 1917–41; 1947–81 |
| Brisbane Exhib Ground | 1 | 0 | 1952 |
| North Hobart | 5 | 0 | 1952; Fitz 1991–92 |
| Albury | 1 | 0 | 1952 |
| Euroa | 1 | 0 | 1952 |
| Yallourn | 1 | 0 | 1952 |
| Bruce Stadium | 1 | 0 | 1995 |
| **Total:** | **11,357** | **465** | |

## PROMOTIONAL ROUND

**Saturday, June 14, 1952**

Collingwood 10.12 (72)
Richmond 5.6 (36)
Umpire: H. Jamieson.
Attendance: 24,174 at the SCG.

South Melbourne 18.10 (118)
North Melbourne 14.12 (96)
Umpire: W. Barbour.
Attendance: 15,000 in Albury.

St Kilda 7.7 (49)
Footscray 5.4 (34)
Umpire: M. Blumfield.
Attendance: 3,500 in Yallourn.

Carlton 17.15 (117)
Hawthorn 11.14 (80)
Umpire: H. Beitzel.
Attendance: 7,500 in Euroa.

Fitzroy 12.10 (82)
Melbourne 10.10 (70)
Umpire: G. Robinson.
Attendance: 18,387 at North Hobart.

**Monday, June 16, 1952 (night)**

Essendon 23.17 (155)
Geelong 12.14 (86)
Umpire: J. McMurray jnr.
Attendance: 40,000 at the Brisbane Exhibition Ground.

## CLUB MEMBERSHIP YEAR BY YEAR

| | 1992 | 1993 | 1994 | 1995 | 1996 | 1997 | % change 1996/97 |
|---|---|---|---|---|---|---|---|
| Adelaide | 38,673 | 40,100 | 40,611 | 41,654 | 42,283 | 41,395 | −2.10 |
| Brisbane Bears | 5,401 | 5,750 | 6,158 | 6,893 | 10,267 | — | |
| Brisbane Lions | — | — | — | — | — | 16,769 | |
| Carlton | 12,354 | 14,445 | 18,308 | 18,032 | 23,278 | 24,984 | +7.33 |
| Collingwood | 18,921 | 21,882 | 20,843 | 22,543 | 20,752 | 22,761 | +9.68 |
| Essendon | 10,034 | 11,546 | 19,720 | 23,833 | 24,324 | 28,063 | +15.37 |
| Fitzroy | 5,177 | 6,853 | 8,164 | 8,806 | 7,628 | — | |
| Fremantle | — | — | — | 18,456 | 19,622 | 19,949 | +1.67 |
| Geelong | 13,535 | 15,500 | 14,312 | 15,922 | 17,346 | 18,858 | +8.72 |
| Hawthorn | 12,338 | 11,388 | 11,245 | 12,728 | 12,484 | 27,005 | +116.32 |
| Melbourne | 8,681 | 10,097 | 10,648 | 9,544 | 12,964 | 15,336 | +18.30 |
| North Melb | 6,083 | 6,851 | 10,296 | 14,027 | 14,438 | 19,368 | +34.15 |
| Port Adel | — | — | — | — | — | 35,809 | |
| Richmond | 8,158 | 9,918 | 8,229 | 14,647 | 20,308 | 24,975 | +22.98 |
| St Kilda | 11,650 | 12,956 | 12,009 | 8,870 | 14,375 | 16,610 | +15.55 |
| Sydney | 3,020 | 3,097 | 3,327 | 6,088 | 9,525 | 22,109 | +132.12 |
| West Coast | 23,902 | 25,779 | 24,265 | 26,821 | 26,663 | 33,286 | +24.84 |
| W Bulldogs | 9,311 | 11,478 | 9,339 | 12,212 | 10,650 | 15,054 | +41.35 |
| **TOTALS:** | **187,238** | **207,640** | **217,474** | **261,076** | **286,907** | **382,331** | **+33.26** |

## 1998 ADMISSION PRICES

The AFL Commission has adopted the following admission and club membership prices for the 1998 Coca-Cola AFL Premiership Season and Ansett Australia Cup:

| Premiership Season: Daily Admission | 1998 | 1997 |
|---|---|---|
| Adult | $13.00 | $12.50 |
| Adult — Visiting Member | $11.00 | $10.50 |
| Daily Concession | $7.00 | $6.50 |
| Family | $26.00 | $25.00 |
| Children Under 15 | $2.00 | $1.70 |
| Children Under 6 | Free | Free |
| **Club Membership (Season Tickets)** | | |
| Adult | $87.00 | $83.00 |
| Vic-based supporters of non-Vic clubs | $67.00 | $63.00 |
| Family | $174.00 | $166.00 |
| Concession 11 Games | $48.00 | $43.00 |
| Concession 22 Games | $72.00 | $67.00 |
| Squadron 11 Games (non-Vic) | $13.00 | $11.00 |
| Squadron 22 Games | $25.00 | $19.00 |
| Country Membership | $51.00 | $48.00 |

| Ansett Australia Cup — Preliminary Rounds | 1998 | 1997 |
|---|---|---|
| Adult | $11.00 | $10.50 |
| Adult Club Member | $7.00 | $6.50 |
| Concession | $6.50 | $6.00 |
| Concession Club Member | $4.00 | $3.80 |
| Family | $22.00 | $21.00 |
| Family Club Member | $14.00 | $13.00 |
| Children Under 15 | $2.00 | $1.70 |
| Children Under 6 | Free | Free |
| **Ansett Australia Cup — Grand Final** | | |
| Adult | $16.00 | $14.00 |
| Concession | $8.00 | $7.00 |
| Family | $32.00 | $28.00 |
| Children Under 15 | $2.00 | $1.70 |
| Children Under 6 | Free | Free |

## ADMISSION PRICES 1949–1997

**1949** Adults 1/3
**1951** Outer 2/1
**1952** Outer 2/6
**1953** Outer 2/1 (grandstand) 3/9
**1955** Outer 2/6 Grandstand 4/6
**1956** Outer 3/- Grandstand 5/-
**1960** Outer 3/6 Grandstand: 6/-
**1961** Outer 4/6 Grandstand 6/6 Children: Stand 2/-, Outer 1/6
**1963** Outer 4/6 Grandstand 6/6 Children: Stand 2/-, Outer 1/6
**1964** Outer 5/-, Grandstand 7/6 Children: Outer 1/6, Stand 2/-
**1966** Outer 50¢, Stand 75¢ Children: Outer 15¢, Stand 20¢
**1967** Outer 60¢, Grandstand 80¢
**1970** Adults: Outer 70¢, Reserve 90¢ Children: Outer 20¢, Res 25¢
**1972** Adults $1, Children 25¢ (Outer areas abandoned)
**1974** Adults $1.50 Children 25¢, Pensioners 50¢
**1976** Adults $2, Pen 50¢, child 25¢
**1978** Adult $2.50 Pen: 60¢, Children (U15) 30¢

**1979** Adults $2.70 Pen 60¢, children U 15 30¢
**1980** Adults $3, pens 60¢, U 15 40¢
**1981** Adults $4; Child and pens 50¢
**1982** Adults $4.50 Child and pen 60¢
**1983** Adults $6, Child and pen $1. Introduction of family admission ticket
**1984** Adults $6; Child and Pen $1
**1985** Adults $7 Child and pen $1; Children U10 (free)
**1987** Adults $7.50 Concession $3
**1988** Adults $8, Adult members' away game concession $6 Concession category $3.20 Children Under 15 $1 Children under 6 (free)
**1989** Adults $8.50 Adult members away game concession $6.50 Concession category $3.50. Children Under 6 (free)
**1990** Adults $9 Adult members' away games $7 Concessions $3.75 Children U15 $1, Children U 6 (free)
**1991** Adults $9.50 Adult members away games concession $7.50 Concession category $4.50

**1992** Adults $10, Adult Members away games $8, Concessions ($4.20 Children U 15 $1.20 Children U 6 Free. Family: Two adults and school aged children $20.
**1993** All same except family up to $21
**1994** H &A $11, visiting adult club member $9, Concession $5, Child U 15 $1.50, Child U 6 (free), Family $22.
**1995** Home and away admission adults $11.50, visiting adult club member $9.50, Concession $5.20, Children U15, $1.60, Children U6 (Free), Family: Two adults and up to four juniors $23.
**1996** Home and away admission adults $12, visiting adult club member $10, Concession $6, Children U15, $1.60, Children U6 (Free), Family: Two adults and up to four juniors $24.
**1997** Home and away admission adults $12.50, visiting adult club member $10.50, Concession $6.50, Children U15, $1.70, Children U6 (Free), Family: Two adults and up to four juniors $25.

# FINALS SYSTEMS

The following is a brief history of the various systems used to determine the premiership team in each season since the VFL was formed in 1896 and the first season played in 1897.

**1897** — eight clubs played each other twice and upon completion of the two rounds, a round-robin series was played among the top four teams with the leader in this series being the premiers.

**1898** — another system was introduced. Again 14 games were played and then teams were split into divisions — the first, third, fifth and seventh teams in "A" Division and the remainder in "B" Division.

The team which finished on top of the ladder and failed to top the list after its "A" Division games was given the right to challenge and this occurred with Essendon having finished second after the additional three games.

Fitzroy topped "A" Division and then beat "B" Division leader Collingwood.

Essendon, however, challenged and the first grand final was played. Essendon lost to Fitzroy.

**1901** — the same system applied but without the right of challenge.

**1902** — the system altered so that the two teams of each section played off with the winners advancing to the grand final.

**1903** — system varied so that first played third and second played fourth with the winners playing for the premiership. The challenge was still in force.

**1904** — the right to challenge was scrapped.

**1924** — the round-robin finals series used 27 years earlier was revived. Despite losing its last finals match, Essendon won the flag.

**1925** — system returned to first playing third and second playing fourth with winners playing off. This system remained in force until 1931.

**1931** — McIntyre Final Four introduced. This system was as follows:

First semi-final — third v fourth.

Winner advanced to preliminary final. Loser eliminated.

Second semi-final — first v second.

Winner advanced to grand final. Loser played in preliminary final.

Preliminary final — loser of second semi v winner of first semi.

Winner advanced to grand final. Loser eliminated.

Grand final — winner of second semi-final v winner of preliminary final.

**1972** — McIntyre Final Five system introduced.

This system was as follows:

Elimination final — fourth v fifth.

Winner advanced to first semi-final. Loser eliminated.

Qualifying final — second v third.

Winner advanced to second semi-final. Loser to first semi-final.

First semi-final — loser of qualifying final v winner of elimination final.

Winner to preliminary final. Loser eliminated.

Second semi-final — first v winner of qualifying final.

Winner to grand final. Loser to preliminary final.

Preliminary final — winner of first semi final v loser

of second semi-final. Winner to grand final. Loser eliminated.

Grand final — Winner of second semi-final v winner of preliminary final.

**1991** — McIntyre Final Six introduced by AFL Commission. Operated as follows:

Week 1: Game A, qualifying final, 1st v 2nd.
Game B, second elimination final, 3rd v 4th.
Game C, first elimination final, 5th v 6th.

Week 2: Game D, second semi-final, winner A v winner B.
Game E, first semi-final, winner C v loser A.

Week 3: Game F, preliminary final, winner E v loser D.

Week 4: Game G, grand final, winner D v winner F.

**1992** — McIntyre Final Six modified by AFL Commission in February 1992, after receiving submissions from AFL clubs.

Of the 15 clubs, 13 favored the final six option of 3rd v 6th and 4th v 5th in first week of finals, instead of 3rd v 4th and 5th v 6th.

**1994** — McIntyre Final Eight adopted by AFL Commission.

# LADDERS, FINALS SCORES 1931-1997

The details on the following pages show the positions in which teams finished after home-and-away matches and finals results since the McIntyre Finals system was introduced in 1931. The McIntyre Final Five did not come in until 1972, while the McIntyre Final Six was introduced in 1991. In 1994, the Final Eight was implemented. On the ladders, numbers in brackets indicate finalists' positions after finals.

## 1931

| | | P | W | L | D | For | Agst | % | Pts |
|---|---|---|---|---|---|---|---|---|---|
| 1 | Geelong (1) | 18 | 15 | 3 | | 1572 | 1038 | 151.4 | 60 |
| 2 | Richmond (2) | 18 | 15 | 3 | | 1627 | 1153 | 141.1 | 60 |
| 3 | Carlton (3) | 18 | 12 | 6 | | 1613 | 1289 | 125.1 | 48 |
| 4 | Collingwood (4) | 18 | 12 | 6 | | 1589 | 1281 | 124.0 | 48 |
| 5 | Footscray | 18 | 12 | 6 | | 1161 | 1054 | 110.2 | 48 |
| 6 | Essendon | 18 | 10 | 8 | | 1416 | 1428 | 99.2 | 40 |
| 7 | South Melb | 18 | 9 | 9 | | 1393 | 1406 | 99.1 | 36 |
| 8 | Melbourne | 18 | 8 | 10 | | 1286 | 1403 | 91.7 | 32 |
| 9 | St Kilda | 18 | 8 | 10 | | 1323 | 1484 | 89.2 | 32 |
| 10 | Fitzroy | 18 | 4 | 14 | | 1380 | 1605 | 86.0 | 16 |
| 11 | Hawthorn | 18 | 3 | 15 | | 1145 | 1395 | 82.1 | 12 |
| 12 | North Melb | 18 | 0 | 18 | | 1000 | 1969 | 50.8 | 0 |

*(18 H & A matches)*

**First Semi Final**
Carlton 20.10 (130) d. Collingwood 5.12 (42)
**Second Semi Final**
Richmond 15.9 (99) d. Geelong 10.6 (66)
**Preliminary Final**
Geelong 11.17 (83) d. Carlton 11.11 (77)

**Grand Final**
Geelong 2.3 5.6 8.11 9.14 (68) d
Richmond 1.2 4.5 5.5 7.6 (48)
Goals — Geelong: Metherell 2, Baker 2, L. Hardiman 2, Troughton, Collins, Moloney. Richmond: D. Strang 3, Titus 2, Ford, Twyford.
Best — Geelong: Hickey, Carney, Lamb, McDonald, H. Hardiman, Williams. Richmond: O'Neill, Foster, Geddes, G. Strang, Zschech, Ford.
Umpire: Scott. Match played at MCG.
Attendance: 60,712
*The first year of operation of the McIntyre Final Four finals system saw a speedy Geelong side end Collingwood's run of domination. Geelong beat Richmond twice during the year, lost to them in the second semi and triumphed in the Grand Final by 20 points.*
GEELONG
B: M. Lamb, G. Todd, H. Hardiman
HB: R. McDonald, R. Hickey, J. Williams
C: J. Carney, E. Greeves, J. Walker
HF: L. Hardiman, J. Collins, R. Troughton
F: J. Evans, G. Moloney, T. Quinn
R: A. Coghlan, L. Metherell, E. Baker (c).
Reserve: F. Mockridge
Coach: C. Clymo
RICHMOND
B: K. O'Neill, A. Murdoch, F. Heifner
HB: M. Bolger, T. Dunne, B. McCormack
C: S. Judkins, E. Zschech, A. Geddes

HF: J. Titus, G. Strang, J. Twyford
F: J. Dyer, D. Strang, F. Ford
R: J. Bissett, H. Foster, H. Hunter (c).
Reserve: T. O'Halloran
Coach: F. Hughes

## 1932

| | | P | W | L | D | For | Agst | % | Pts |
|---|---|---|---|---|---|---|---|---|---|
| 1 | Carlton (2) | 18 | 15 | 3 | | 1803 | 1308 | 137.8 | 60 |
| 2 | Richmond (1) | 18 | 14 | 3 | 1 | 1526 | 1096 | 139.2 | 58 |
| 3 | Collingwood (3) | 18 | 14 | 4 | | 1644 | 1473 | 111.6 | 56 |
| 4 | South Melb (4) | 18 | 13 | 5 | | 1531 | 1297 | 118.0 | 52 |
| 5 | Geelong | 18 | 11 | 6 | 1 | 1825 | 1306 | 139.7 | 46 |
| 6 | Essendon | 18 | 10 | 8 | | 1488 | 1444 | 103.0 | 40 |
| 7 | Footscray | 18 | 9 | 9 | | 1229 | 1188 | 103.5 | 36 |
| 8 | North Melb | 18 | 8 | 10 | | 1535 | 1581 | 97.1 | 32 |
| 9 | Melbourne | 18 | 4 | 14 | | 1281 | 1675 | 76.5 | 16 |
| 10 | Fitzroy | 18 | 3 | 15 | | 1361 | 1786 | 76.2 | 12 |
| 11 | St Kilda | 18 | 3 | 15 | | 1263 | 1753 | 72.0 | 12 |
| 12 | Hawthorn | 18 | 3 | 15 | | 1034 | 1613 | 64.1 | 12 |

*(18 H & A matches)*

**First Semi Final**
Collingwood 17.12 (114) d. South Melbourne 12.16 (88)
**Second Semi Final**
Richmond 18.16 (124) d. Carlton 14.15 (99)
**Preliminary Final**
Carlton 23.19 (157) d. Collingwood 11.16 (82)

**Grand Final**
Richmond 3.3 7.9 8.12 13.14 (92) d
Carlton 2.3 5.6 7.11 12.11 (83)
Goals — Richmond: D. Strang 4, Titus 2, Hunter, Heifner, Martin, G. Strang, Anderson, Bentley, O'Halloran. Carlton: Vallence 5, Shea 2, Clarke 2, Bullen 2, Crisp.
Best — Richmond: G. Strang, McCormack, O'Neill, Baggott, Titus, Bolger. Carlton: C. Martyn, Oprey, Huxtable, Mackie, Crowe, Egan.
Umpire: Scott. Match played at MCG.
Attendance: 69,724
*After finishing runners-up in four of the previous five seasons, Richmond finally cracked it for another flag with a nine-point win over Carlton in a tough, thrilling match that saw Tiger wingman Allan Geddes play the second half with a broken jaw.*
RICHMOND
B: M. Bolger, M. Sheahan, K. O'Neill
HB: J. Baggott, A. Murdoch, B. McCormack
C: S. Judkins, E. Zschech, A. Geddes
HF: W. Benton, G. Strang, J. Titus

F: F. Heifner, D. Strang, M. Hunter
R: P. Bentley (c), T. O'Halloran, R. Martin
Reserve: J. Anderson
Coach: F. Hughes
CARLTON
B: J. Crowe, F. Gill, C. Street
HB: F. Huxtable, G. Mackie, F. Gilby
C: J. Kelly, C. Martyn (c), L. Oprey
HF: K. Shea, J. Green, C. Crisp
F: H. Bullen, H. Vallence, R. Cooper
R: C. Davey, M. Johnson, A. Clarke
Reserve: J. Young
Coach: D. Minogue

# 1933

| | | P | W | L | D | For | Agst | % | Pts |
|---|---|---|---|---|---|---|---|---|---|
| 1 | Richmond (2) | 18 | 15 | 3 | | 1746 | 1237 | 141.1 | 60 |
| 2 | South Melb (1) | 18 | 13 | 5 | | 1764 | 1383 | 127.5 | 52 |
| 3 | Carlton (4) | 18 | 13 | 5 | | 1702 | 1488 | 114.4 | 52 |
| 4 | Geelong (3) | 18 | 12 | 6 | | 1730 | 1327 | 130.4 | 48 |
| 5 | Fitzroy | 18 | 11 | 6 | 1 | 1534 | 1453 | 105.6 | 46 |
| 6 | Collingwood | 18 | 11 | 7 | | 1760 | 1559 | 112.9 | 44 |
| 7 | Footscray | 18 | 11 | 7 | | 1520 | 1555 | 97.7 | 44 |
| 8 | North Melb | 18 | 7 | 10 | 1 | 1463 | 1717 | 85.2 | 30 |
| 9 | St Kilda | 18 | 6 | 12 | | 1380 | 1706 | 80.9 | 24 |
| 10 | Melbourne | 18 | 3 | 15 | | 1511 | 1842 | 82.0 | 12 |
| 11 | Hawthorn | 18 | 3 | 15 | | 1178 | 1607 | 73.3 | 12 |
| 12 | Essendon | 18 | 2 | 16 | | 1392 | 1806 | 77.1 | 8 |

*(18 H & A matches)*

**First Semi Final**
Geelong 12.12 (84) d. Carlton 10.11 (71)
**Second Semi Final**
South Melbourne 14.11 (95) d. Richmond 11.11 (77)
**Preliminary Final**
Richmond 13.5 (83) d. Geelong 10.14 (74)

**Grand Final**
South Melbourne 3.5 6.7 8.12 9.17 (71) d
Richmond 0.2 2.3 3.3 4.5 (29)
Goals — South Melbourne: Pratt 3, Diggins 2, Brain 2, Reville, Thomas. Richmond: Farmer 2, G. Strang, Martin.
Best — South Melbourne: Nash, Diggins, Austin, Clarke, Bowe, Bissett. Richmond: O'Neill, Zschech, Martin, Dyer, Murdoch, McCormack.
Umpire: Scott. Match played at MCG.
Attendance: 75,754
*The year of South Melbourne's famed 'Foreign Legion', in which a side of talent brought from all around Australia by chain-store king Archie Crofts snared what would prove to be South Melbourne's last flag. The side included such legends as Pratt and Nash, and again Richmond was the bridesmaid.*
SOUTH MELBOURNE
B: R. McKenzie, H. McKay, J. Austin
HB: W. Faul, L. Nash, H. McLaughlin
C: H. Clarke, L. Thomas, J. Bowe
HF: J. O'Meara, B. Diggins, H. Reville
F: H. Matthews, R. Pratt, O. Bertram
R: J. Bissett (c), D. Kelleher, T. Brain
Reserve: G. Beard
Coach: J. Bissett

RICHMOND
B: M. Bolger, M. Sheahan, D. O'Neill
HB: J. Stenhouse, A. Murdoch, B. McCormack
C: S. Judkins, E. Zschech, A. Geddes
HF: H. Farmer, T. O'Halloran, J. Baggott
F: J. Dyer, J. Titus, H. Foster
R: P. Bentley (c), G. Strang, R. Martin
Reserve: J. Anderson
Coach: W. Schmidt

# 1934

| | | P | W | L | D | For | Agst | % | Pts |
|---|---|---|---|---|---|---|---|---|---|
| 1 | Richmond (1) | 18 | 15 | 3 | | 1618 | 1334 | 121.3 | 60 |
| 2 | Geelong (3) | 18 | 14 | 3 | 1 | 1834 | 1355 | 135.4 | 58 |
| 3 | South Melb (2) | 18 | 14 | 4 | | 2187 | 1560 | 140.2 | 56 |
| 4 | Collingwood (4) | 18 | 13 | 4 | 1 | 1915 | 1571 | 121.9 | 54 |
| 5 | Carlton | 18 | 12 | 6 | | 1986 | 1707 | 116.3 | 48 |
| 6 | Melbourne | 18 | 9 | 9 | | 1623 | 1670 | 97.2 | 36 |
| 7 | St Kilda | 18 | 9 | 9 | | 1592 | 1661 | 95.8 | 36 |
| 8 | Fitzroy | 18 | 7 | 11 | | 1589 | 1660 | 95.7 | 28 |
| 9 | Footscray | 18 | 6 | 12 | | 1444 | 1699 | 85.0 | 24 |
| 10 | Essendon | 18 | 5 | 13 | | 1635 | 1958 | 83.5 | 20 |
| 11 | Hawthorn | 18 | 3 | 15 | | 1300 | 1917 | 67.8 | 12 |
| 12 | North Melb | 18 | 0 | 18 | | 1245 | 1876 | 66.4 | 0 |

*(18 H & A matches)*

**First Semi Final**
South Melbourne 11.12 (78) d. Collingwood 9.21 (75)
**Second Semi Final**
Richmond 19.20 (134) d. Geelong 7.8 (50)
**Preliminary Final**
South Melbourne 15.18 (108) d. Geelong 7.6 (48)

**Grand Final**
Richmond 4.4 10.8 16.11 19.14 (128)
d South Melbourne 4.3 6.5 6.11 12.17 (89)
Goals — Richmond: Titus 6, O'Halloran 3, Harris 3, Bentley 2, Martin, Baxter, Murdoch, Zschech. South Melbourne: Nash 6, Pratt 2, Brian, Diggins, O'Meara, Bertram.
Best — Richmond: Titus, Bolger, Baggott, McCormack, G. Strang, Martin. South Melbourne: Nash, Austin, Reville, Pratt, McLaughlin, McKay.
Umpire: Scott. Match played at MCG.
Attendance: 65,335
*The Swans and Tigers were there again, but this time it was the yellow and black colors that were flying high. Richmond won easily by 39 points, with Bob Pratt's two goals taking him to 150 for the season. Pratt kicked his record tally in 21 matches — 18 home-and-away and three finals.*
RICHMOND
B: M. Bolger, M. Sheahan, K. O'Neill
HB: J. Baggott, G. Strang, B. McCormack
C: S. Judkins, E. Zschech, A. Geddes
HF: T. O'Halloran, D. Baxter, A. Murdoch
F: H. Foster, J. Titus, R. Harris
R: P. Bentley (c), J. Dyer, R. Martin
Reserve: H. Edmonds
Coach: P. Bentley
SOUTH MELBOURNE
B: H. McKay, J. Austin, R. McKenzie
HB: W. Faul, L. Richards, H. McLaughlin
C: H. Clarke, L. Thomas, H. Matthews

HF: H. Reville, L. Nash, J. O'Meara
F: B. Diggins, R. Pratt, O. Bertram
R: J. Bissett (c), D. Kelleher, T. Brain
Reserve: W. Harris
Coach: J. Bissett

# 1935

| | | P | W | L | D | For | Agst | % | Pts |
|---|---|---|---|---|---|---|---|---|---|
| 1 | South Melb (2) | 18 | 16 | 2 | | 1940 | 1410 | 137.6 | 64 |
| 2 | Collingwood (1) | 18 | 14 | 2 | 2 | 1895 | 1561 | 121.4 | 60 |
| 3 | Carlton (4) | 18 | 14 | 3 | 1 | 1958 | 1383 | 141.6 | 58 |
| 4 | Richmond (3) | 18 | 12 | 6 | | 1572 | 1339 | 117.4 | 48 |
| 5 | St Kilda | 18 | 11 | 7 | | 1708 | 1545 | 110.6 | 44 |
| 6 | Melbourne | 18 | 8 | 9 | 1 | 1601 | 1582 | 101.2 | 34 |
| 7 | Fitzroy | 18 | 8 | 9 | 1 | 1488 | 1649 | 90.2 | 34 |
| 8 | Essendon | 18 | 7 | 11 | | 1526 | 1703 | 89.6 | 28 |
| 9 | Geelong | 18 | 6 | 11 | 1 | 1683 | 1747 | 96.3 | 26 |
| 10 | Hawthorn | 18 | 5 | 13 | | 1460 | 1805 | 80.9 | 20 |
| 11 | Footscray | 18 | 2 | 14 | 2 | 1272 | 1731 | 73.5 | 12 |
| 12 | North Melb | 18 | 1 | 17 | | 1208 | 1856 | 65.1 | 4 |

*(18 H & A matches)*

**First Semi Final**
Richmond 19.11 (125) d. Carlton 14.20 (104)
**Second Semi Final**
South Melbourne 15.14 (104) d. Collingwood 11.17 (83)
**Preliminary Final**
Collingwood 14.10 (94) d. Richmond 9.12 (66)
**Grand Final**
Collingwood 1.3 6.6 8.10 11.12 (78) d
South Melbourne 3.6 4.8 6.10 7.16 (58)
Goals — Collingwood: G. Coventry 4, Kyne 2, Pannam 2, H. Collier, A. Collier, Stackpole. South Melbourne: Davies 2, Moore 2, Nash, Kelleher, McEachen.
Best — Collingwood: H. Collier, Regan, A. Collier, Kyne, Froude, Rumney, Whelan. South Melbourne: Clarke, Hillis, Austin, Diggins, McKenzie, Kelleher.
Umpire: Scott. Match played at MCG.
Attendance: 54,154
Collingwood had been missing from Grand Final action for four years, but returned to take the 1935 flag. Its path to the premiership was smoothed by a Grand Final eve accident to South star Bob Pratt, who was forced out of the game. Pratt was injured when hit by a truck after getting off a tram in Prahran.
COLLINGWOOD
B: J. Ross, C. Dibbs, H. Rumney
HB: B. Woods, J. Regan, F. Froude
C: J. Carmody, M. Whelan, L. Morgan
HF: L. Riley, A. Kyne, V. Doherty
F: K. Fraser, G. Coventry, A. Pannam
R: A. Collier, P. Bowyer, H. Collier (c.)
Reserve:. K. Stackpole
Coach: J. McHale
SOUTH MELBOURNE
B: J. Austin, R. Hillis, R. Humphries
HB: W. Faul, L. Richards, H. McLaughlin
C: H. Clarke, H. Matthews, J. Reid
HF: A. Robertson, L. Nash, J. O'Meara
F: D. Kelleher, R. Moore, F. Davies

R: J. Bissett (c.), B. Diggins, T. Brain
Reserve: R. McEachern
Coach: J. Bissett

# 1936

| | | P | W | L | D | For | Agst | % | Pts |
|---|---|---|---|---|---|---|---|---|---|
| 1 | South Melb (2) | 18 | 16 | 2 | | 1806 | 1524 | 118.5 | 64 |
| 2 | Collingwood (1) | 18 | 15 | 3 | | 1854 | 1367 | 135.6 | 60 |
| 3 | Carlton (4) | 18 | 12 | 6 | | 1877 | 1504 | 124.8 | 48 |
| 4 | Melbourne (3) | 18 | 12 | 6 | | 1755 | 1477 | 118.8 | 48 |
| 5 | Geelong | 18 | 11 | 7 | | 1884 | 1498 | 125.8 | 44 |
| 6 | Richmond | 18 | 10 | 8 | | 1673 | 1550 | 107.9 | 40 |
| 7 | St Kilda | 18 | 9 | 9 | | 1845 | 1919 | 96.1 | 36 |
| 8 | Essendon | 18 | 6 | 12 | | 1565 | 1840 | 85.1 | 24 |
| 9 | Hawthorn | 18 | 6 | 12 | | 1391 | 1720 | 80.9 | 24 |
| 10 | Footscray | 18 | 5 | 13 | | 1462 | 1690 | 86.5 | 20 |
| 11 | North Melb | 18 | 4 | 14 | | 1274 | 1679 | 75.9 | 16 |
| 12 | Fitzroy | 18 | 2 | 16 | | 1367 | 1985 | 68.9 | 8 |

*(18 H & A matches)*

**First Semi Final**
Melbourne 14.13 (97) d. Carlton 11.22 (88)
**Second Semi Final**
Collingwood 12.18 (90) d. South Melbourne 10.17 (77)
**Preliminary Final**
South Melbourne 13.11 (89) d. Melbourne 8.15 (63)
**Grand Final**
Collingwood 3.6 7.16 8.19 11.23 (89) d
South Melbourne 3.4 5.7 8.12 10.18 (78)
Goals — Collingwood: Pannam 5, Todd 4, Knight, Kyne. South Melbourne: Pratt 3, Johnson 2, Moore 2, Nash, Robertson, Evans.
Best — Collingwood: Pannam, Whelan, Kyne, Carmody, Todd, Fraser. South Melbourne: Robertson, Cleary, Hillis, Richards, Nash, Evans.
Umpire: Blackburn. Match played at MCG.
Attendance: 74,091
*Another flag for the Magpies and again it was South that finished second. Collingwood's 11-point victory gave it six premierships in 10 years — a stunning achievement. This one was achieved without star forward Gordon Coventry, controversially suspended for eight weeks late in the season.*
COLLINGWOOD
B: J. Crowe, J. Regan, B. Woods
HB: J. Ross, K. Fraser, F. Froude
C: J. Carmody, M. Whelan, L. Morgan
HF: L. Riley, A. Kyne, V. Doherty
F: J. Knight, R. Todd, A. Pannam
R: A. Collier, P. Bowyer, H. Collier (c.)
Reserve: K. Stackpole
Coach: J. McHale
SOUTH MELBOURNE
B: L. Richards, R. Hillis, J. Austin
HB: W. Faul, J. Graham, J. Cleary
C: H. Matthews, L. Thomas, J. Reid
HF: O. Evans, L. Nash, S. Dineen
F: M. Johnson, R. Pratt, R. Moore
R: J. Bissett (c.), D. Kelleher, A. Robertson
Reserve: C. Pettiona
Coach: J. Bissett

# 1937

| | | P | W | L | D | For | Agst | % | Pts |
|---|---|---|---|---|---|---|---|---|---|
| 1 | Geelong (1) | 18 | 15 | 3 | | 1824 | 1348 | 135.3 | 60 |
| 2 | Melbourne (3) | 18 | 15 | 3 | | 1945 | 1482 | 131.2 | 60 |
| 3 | Collingwood (2) | 18 | 13 | 5 | | 1908 | 1479 | 129.0 | 52 |
| 4 | Richmond (4) | 18 | 11 | 6 | 1 | 1647 | 1525 | 108.0 | 46 |
| 5 | Carlton | 18 | 11 | 7 | | 1624 | 1464 | 110.9 | 44 |
| 6 | St Kilda | 18 | 10 | 8 | | 1600 | 1580 | 101.3 | 40 |
| 7 | Fitzroy | 18 | 7 | 11 | | 1386 | 1488 | 93.1 | 28 |
| 8 | Hawthorn | 18 | 7 | 11 | | 1413 | 1675 | 84.4 | 28 |
| 9 | South Melb | 18 | 6 | 11 | 1 | 1527 | 1698 | 89.9 | 26 |
| 10 | Essendon | 18 | 5 | 13 | | 1530 | 1689 | 90.6 | 20 |
| 11 | Footscray | 18 | 4 | 14 | | 1409 | 1722 | 81.8 | 16 |
| 12 | North Melb | 18 | 3 | 15 | | 1188 | 1851 | 64.2 | 12 |

*(18 H & A matches)*

**First Semi Final**
Collingwood 18.12 (120) d. Richmond 10.9 (69)
**Second Semi Final**
Geelong 19.11 (125) d. Melbourne 16.17 (113)
**Preliminary Final**
Collingwood 16.11 (107) d. Melbourne 7.10 (52)

**Grand Final**
Geelong 3.3 8.5 12.8 18.14 (122) d
Collingwood 6.3 8.10 11.14 12.18 (90)
Goals — Geelong: Evans 6, J. Metherell 4, Coles
4, Abbott 2, Sellwood, Wills. Collingwood: Todd 4,
G. Coventry 3, Pannam 2, Doherty, Kyne,
Fothergill.
Best — Geelong: Muller, Quinn, L. Hardiman, H.
Hardiman, J. Metherell. Collingwood: Regan,
Froude, Ross, Todd, A. Collier, Woods.
Umpire: Batt. Match played at MCG.
Attendance: 88,540
*A record crowd of 88,540 witnessed what is still
regarded as one of the best Grand Finals. Geelong
and Collingwood turned on a display of brilliant,
fast and fair football that eventually saw the Cats
triumph by 32 points.*
GEELONG
B: A. Everett, R. Hickey (c.), B. Hore
HB: J. Grant, J. Sellwood, T. Arklay
C: L. Slack, F. Hawking, A. Muller
HF: J. Wills, G. Abbott, C. Coles
F: G. Dougherty, L. Hardiman, J. Metherell
R: H. Hardiman, J. Evans, T. Quinn
Reserve: G. Mahon
Coach: R. Hickey
COLLINGWOOD
B: H. Rumney, J. Regan, B. Woods
HB: F. Froude, M. Boyall, J. Ross
C: J. Carmody, M. Whelan, R. Dowling
HF: D. Fothergill, R. Todd, V. Doherty
F: A. Kyne, G. Coventry, A. Pannam
R: A. Collier, P. Bowyer, H. Collier (c.)
Reserve: L. Murphy
Coach: J. McHale

# 1938

| | | P | W | L | D | For | Agst | % | Pts |
|---|---|---|---|---|---|---|---|---|---|
| 1 | Carlton (1) | 18 | 14 | 4 | | 1827 | 1574 | 116.1 | 56 |
| 2 | Geelong (3) | 18 | 13 | 5 | | 1897 | 1468 | 129.2 | 52 |
| 3 | Footscray (4) | 18 | 13 | 5 | | 1723 | 1386 | 124.3 | 52 |
| 4 | Collingwood (2) | 18 | 12 | 6 | | 1942 | 1652 | 117.6 | 48 |
| 5 | Melbourne | 18 | 11 | 7 | | 1776 | 1676 | 106.0 | 44 |
| 6 | Richmond | 18 | 10 | 8 | | 1747 | 1563 | 111.8 | 40 |
| 7 | Essendon | 18 | 9 | 9 | | 1801 | 1760 | 102.3 | 36 |
| 8 | St Kilda | 18 | 9 | 9 | | 1474 | 1606 | 91.8 | 36 |
| 9 | North Melb | 18 | 6 | 12 | | 1384 | 1852 | 74.7 | 24 |
| 10 | Fitzroy | 18 | 5 | 13 | | 1543 | 1742 | 88.6 | 20 |
| 11 | Hawthorn | 18 | 4 | 14 | | 1414 | 1717 | 82.4 | 16 |
| 12 | South Melb | 18 | 2 | 16 | | 1353 | 1885 | 71.8 | 8 |

*(18 H & A matches)*

**First Semi Final**
Collingwood 18.9 (117) d. Footscray 10.16 (76)
**Second Semi Final**
Carlton 16.17 (113) d. Geelong 10.21 (81)
**Preliminary Final**
Collingwood 21.9 (135) d. Geelong 14.14 (98)

**Grand Final**
Carlton 3.2 7.6 11.9 15.10 (100) d
Collingwood 3.1 4.4 8.5 13.7 (85)
Goals — Carlton: Wrout 4, Baxter 3, Schmidt 2,
Hale 2, Price, Crisp, Vallence, Green. Collingwood:
Fothergill 4, Todd 3, Pannam 2, Doherty 2, Knight,
Kyne.
Best — Carlton: Hale, Crisp, Wrout, Green,
Diggins, Gill. Collingwood: Whelan, Balfour, Froude,
Fothergill, Williams, Boyall.
Umpire: Blackburn. Match played at MCG.
Attendance: 96,834
*Carlton broke its 23-year premiership drought with
a 15-point victory over Collingwood. There was a
fair bit of feeling in the game, as the Pies went into
it without their captain Harry Collier — suspended
for 14 weeks after a Carlton complaint earlier in
the season.*
CARLTON
B: D. McIntyre, F. Gill, J. Park
HB: F. Anderson, J. Francis, R. Chitty
C: J. Carney, C. Crisp, R. Green
HF: P. Schmidt, J. Wrout, H. Vallence
F: R. McLean, K. Baxter, A. Price
R: B. Diggins (c.), H. Hollingshead, J. Hale
Reserve: C. McInnes
Coach: B. Diggins
COLLINGWOOD
B: D. Balfour, J. Regan, B. Woods
HB: J. Ross, M. Boyall, F. Froude
C: R. Dowling, M. Whelan, L. Morgan
HF: A. Kyne, G. Hocking, V. Doherty
F: J. Knight, R. Todd, A. Pannam
R: A. Collier (c.), A. Williams, K. Fothergill
Reserve: J. Carmody
Coach: J. McHale

# 1939

| | | P | W | L | D | For | Agst | % | Pts |
|---|---|---|---|---|---|---|---|---|---|
| 1 | Melbourne (1) | 18 | 15 | 3 | | 1928 | 1502 | 128.4 | 60 |
| 2 | Collingwood (2) | 18 | 15 | 3 | | 1872 | 1535 | 122.0 | 60 |
| 3 | Richmond (4) | 18 | 13 | 5 | | 1734 | 1469 | 118.0 | 52 |
| 4 | St Kilda (3) | 18 | 13 | 5 | | 1806 | 1550 | 116.5 | 52 |
| 5 | Carlton | 18 | 12 | 6 | | 1796 | 1459 | 123.1 | 48 |
| 6 | Essendon | 18 | 8 | 10 | | 1696 | 1749 | 97.0 | 32 |
| 7 | Geelong | 18 | 7 | 11 | | 1582 | 1713 | 92.4 | 28 |
| 8 | Fitzroy | 18 | 6 | 11 | 1 | 1482 | 1661 | 89.2 | 26 |
| 9 | North Melb | 18 | 6 | 12 | | 1561 | 1709 | 91.3 | 24 |
| 10 | Hawthorn | 18 | 5 | 12 | 1 | 1427 | 1657 | 86.1 | 22 |
| 11 | Footscray | 18 | 4 | 14 | | 1494 | 1809 | 82.6 | 16 |
| 12 | South Melb | 18 | 3 | 15 | | 1367 | 1932 | 70.8 | 12 |

*(18 H & A matches)*

**First Semi Final**
St Kilda 10.12 (72) d. Richmond 6.6 (42)
**Second Semi Final**
Melbourne 15.14 (104) d. Collingwood 12.18 (90)
**Preliminary Final**
Collingwood 20.14 (134) d. St Kilda 15.15 (105)

**Grand Final**
Melbourne 3.5 10.10 15.14 21.22 (148) d
Collingwood 6.5 10.6 13.9 14.11 (95)
Goals — Melbourne: Beames 4, Rodda 4, L. Jones
3, Ball 2, Mueller 2, Truscott 2, Smith, Wartman,
LaFontaine, Baggott. Collingwood: Todd 6,
Fothergill 3, Knight 2, Balfour, McRae, Doherty.
Best — Melbourne: Beames, Roberts, Anderson,
Rodda, Wartman, Truscott. Collingwood: Regan,
Todd, Knight, H. Collier, Kyne, Ross.
Umpires: Coward, Blackburn. Match played at
MCG. Attendance: 78,110
*The Magpies fronted up for their fifth Grand Final in
a row, but left with their third successive runners-up
placing, this time at the hands of a powerful
Melbourne team that handed out a 53-point
thumping.*
MELBOURNE
B: R. Emselle, J. Mueller, R. Fischer
HB: R. Hingston, G. Jones, F. Roberts
C: R. Wartman, A. La Fontaine (c.), S. Anderson
HF: K. Truscott, R. Baggott, L. Jones
F: H. Ball, N. Smith, A. Rodda
R: R. Kimberley, J. Furniss, P. Beames
Reserve: J. O'Keefe
Coach: F. Hughes
COLLINGWOOD
B: G. Hocking, J. Regan, J. Murphy
HB: J. Ross, A. Williams, D. Balfour
C: F. Fricker, M. Whelan, N. Campbell
HF: C. McRae, A. Kyne, V. Doherty
F: J. Knight, R. Todd, D. Fothergill
R: A. Collier, B. Woods, H. Collier (c.)
Reserve: J. Green
Coach: J. McHale

# 1940

| | | P | W | L | D | For | Agst | % | Pts |
|---|---|---|---|---|---|---|---|---|---|
| 1 | Melbourne (1) | 18 | 14 | 4 | | 2110 | 1677 | 125.8 | 56 |
| 2 | Richmond (2) | 18 | 12 | 6 | | 1787 | 1489 | 120.0 | 48 |
| 3 | Essendon (3) | 18 | 12 | 6 | | 1611 | 1489 | 108.2 | 48 |
| 4 | Geelong (4) | 18 | 11 | 7 | | 1645 | 1599 | 102.9 | 44 |
| 5 | Carlton | 18 | 10 | 8 | | 1730 | 1555 | 111.3 | 40 |
| 6 | Footscray | 18 | 9 | 9 | | 1696 | 1558 | 108.9 | 36 |
| 7 | Fitzroy | 18 | 9 | 9 | | 1443 | 1563 | 92.3 | 36 |
| 8 | Collingwood | 18 | 8 | 10 | | 1621 | 1611 | 100.6 | 32 |
| 9 | Hawthorn | 18 | 7 | 11 | | 1549 | 1760 | 88.0 | 28 |
| 10 | South Melb | 18 | 7 | 11 | | 1480 | 1696 | 87.3 | 28 |
| 11 | St Kilda | 18 | 5 | 13 | | 1418 | 1634 | 86.8 | 20 |
| 12 | North Melb | 18 | 4 | 14 | | 1381 | 1840 | 75.1 | 16 |

*(18 H & A matches)*

**First Semi Final**
Essendon 13.14 (92) d. Geelong 10.14 (74)
**Second Semi Final**
Richmond 16.11 (107) d. Melbourne 14.17 (101)
**Preliminary Final**
Melbourne 12.18 (90) d. Essendon 12.13 (85)

**Grand Final**
Melbourne 4.8 10.11 13.15 15.17 (107) d
Richmond 3.0 4.2 5.4 10.8 (68)
Goals — Melbourne: Smith 7, Baggott 2, Beames
2, O'Keefe (2), Truscott, Fanning. Richmond: Harris
5, Titus 3, Crane, Bawden.
Best — Melbourne: Beames, Smith, Baggott,
LaFontaine, Mueller, Ball. Richmond: Harris, Titus,
McDonald, Dyer, Edwards, Cotter.
Umpire: Coward. Match played at MCG.
Attendance: 69,061
*Another resounding Demon win, this time by 39
points and at the expense of Richmond. Tiger star
Jack Dyer was tagged out of the game as
Melbourne coach 'Checker' Hughes triumphed
against the team he had coached to a flag in
1932.*
MELBOURNE
B: R. Emselle, F. Roberts, H. Ball
HB: C. McLean, G. Jones, R. Hingston
C: R. Wartman, A. La Fontaine (c.), S. Anderson
HF: M. Gibb, R. Baggott, K. Truscott
F: F. Fanning, N. Smith, A. Rodda
R: J. Mueller, J. O'Keefe, P. Beames
Reserve: R. Barassi
Coach: F. Hughes
RICHMOND
B: K. O'Neill, G. Smeaton, J. Symons
HB: R. Steele, I. Hull, J. Cotter
C: A. McDonad, B. Waldron, B. Edwards
HF: R. Martin, J. Crane, L. Smith
F: R. Bawden, J. Titus, R. Harris
R: P. Bentley (c.), J. Dyer, J. Quinn
Reserve: L. Merrett
Coach: P. Bentley

# 1941

| | | P | W | L | D | For | Agst | % | Pts |
|---|---|---|---|---|---|---|---|---|---|
| 1 | Carlton (3) | 18 | 14 | 4 | | 1948 | 1619 | 120.3 | 56 |
| 2 | Melbourne (1) | 18 | 14 | 4 | | 1993 | 1701 | 117.2 | 56 |
| 3 | Richmond (4) | 18 | 14 | 4 | | 1714 | 1469 | 116.7 | 56 |
| 4 | Essendon (2) | 18 | 13 | 5 | | 1864 | 1431 | 130.3 | 52 |
| 5 | Collingwood | 18 | 12 | 6 | | 1743 | 1571 | 110.9 | 48 |
| 6 | Footscray | 18 | 10 | 8 | | 1676 | 1517 | 110.5 | 40 |
| 7 | Fitzroy | 18 | 8 | 10 | | 1695 | 1760 | 96.3 | 32 |
| 8 | South Melb | 18 | 8 | 10 | | 1397 | 1552 | 90.0 | 32 |
| 9 | North Melb | 18 | 6 | 12 | | 1759 | 1893 | 92.9 | 24 |
| 10 | Geelong | 18 | 3 | 15 | | 1561 | 1880 | 83.0 | 12 |
| 11 | St Kilda | 18 | 3 | 15 | | 1454 | 1775 | 81.9 | 12 |
| 12 | Hawthorn | 18 | 3 | 15 | | 1367 | 2003 | 68.2 | 12 |

*(18 H & A matches)*

**First Semi Final**
Essendon 21.9 (135) d. Richmond 11.15 (81)
**Second Semi Final**
Melbourne 16.13 (109) d. Carlton 11.16 (82)
**Preliminary Final**
Essendon 13.15 (93) d. Carlton 9.14 (68)

**Grand Final**
Melbourne 6.6 11.9 14.11 19.13 (127) d
Essendon 1.1 2.6 6.12 13.20 (98)
Goals — Melbourne: Beames 6, Smith 3, Mueller 3, Wartman 2, Daly, Dullard, O'Keefe, Anderson, Gibb. Essendon: T. Reynolds 3, R. Reynolds 2, Bryce 2, Abbott, Lane, Regan, Cassin, Exelby, Torney.
Best — Melbourne: Beames, Lock, Heal, Mueller, Dullard, LaFontaine. Essendon: Coward, Buttsworth, R. Reynolds, H. Lambert, Abbott.
Umpire: Hawkins. Match played at MCG.
Attendance: 79,687
*The Demons became the third club to complete a hat-trick of flags with their 29-point victory over Essendon. The win was even more impressive than it seemed, as 12 of Melbourne's senior list were unavailable either through injury or because of war duties.*
MELBOURNE
B: R. Emselle, J. McGrath, D. Cordner
HB: C. McLean, E. Cordner, W. Lock
C: S. Anderson, A. La Fontaine (c.), S. Heal
HF: M. Gibb, R. Baggott, R. Wartman
F: J. O'Keefe, N. Smith, G. Daly
R: J. Mueller, A. Dullard, P. Beames
Reserve: W. Lewis
Coach: F. Hughes
ESSENDON
B: E. Plummer, C. Ruddell, F. Green
HB: R. Flanigan, W. Buttsworth, A. Hird
C: E. Coward, H. Lambert, J. Caesar
HF: G. Lane, L. Griggs, M. Exelby
F: J. Cassin, T. Reynolds, E. Bryce
R: H. Torney, G. Abbott, R. Reynolds (c.)
Reserve: G. Regan
Coach: R. Reynolds

# 1942

| | | P | W | L | D | For | Agst | % | Pts |
|---|---|---|---|---|---|---|---|---|---|
| 1 | Essendon (1) | 15 | 12 | 3 | | 1426 | 1122 | 127.1 | 52 |
| 2 | Richmond (2) | 15 | 11 | 4 | | 1778 | 1322 | 134.5 | 48 |
| 3 | South Melb (3) | 15 | 11 | 4 | | 1513 | 1173 | 129.0 | 48 |
| 4 | Footscray (4) | 14 | 10 | 4 | | 1460 | 1159 | 126.0 | 48 |
| 5 | Carlton | 14 | 10 | 4 | | 1361 | 1132 | 120.2 | 48 |
| 6 | Fitzroy | 15 | 8 | 7 | | 1405 | 1340 | 104.9 | 36 |
| 7 | St Kilda | 14 | 6 | 8 | | 1076 | 1314 | 81.9 | 32 |
| 8 | Melbourne | 15 | 5 | 10 | | 1384 | 1624 | 85.2 | 24 |
| 9 | North Melb | 14 | 4 | 10 | | 1105 | 1413 | 78.2 | 24 |
| 10 | Collingwood | 14 | 2 | 12 | | 1120 | 1474 | 76.0 | 16 |
| 11 | Hawthorn | 15 | 1 | 14 | | 1058 | 1613 | 65.6 | 8 |

*(18 H & A matches) Four match points awarded for a bye. Geelong did not compete.*

**First Semi Final**
South Melbourne 13.13 (91) d. Footscray 7.22 (64)
**Second Semi Final**
Richmond 11.12 (78) d. Essendon 8.8 (56)
**Preliminary Final**
Essendon 19.10 (124) d. South Melbourne 14.12 (96)

**Grand Final**
Essendon 2.6 8.14 14.16 19.18 (132) d
Richmond 2.4 4.4 5.10 11.13 (79)
Goals — Essendon: Lane 6, R. Reynolds 4, Cassin 3, Exelby 2, Dearle 2, Abbott, T. Reynolds. Richmond: Harris 3, Dyer 2, Titus 2, Merrett, D. Martin, Randall, Hay.
Best — Essendon: R. Reynolds, Dearle, Abbott, Coward, Buttsworth, Flanagan. Richmond: Merrett, Steele, Guinane, Edwards, Morris, Hay.
Umpire: Hawkins. Match played at Princes Park.
Attendance: 49,000
*Essendon ended its years in the wilderness with a hefty 53-point defeat of Richmond at Princes Park (Optus Oval). The MCG had been taken over by the US Air Force and re-named Camp Murphy.*
ESSENDON
B: E. Plummer, C. Ruddell, P. Bushby
HB: R. Flanigan, W. Buttsworth, A. Hird
C: E. Coward, L. Dearle, J. Caesar
HF: G. Abbott, G. Lane, W. Hutchison
F: T. Reynolds, E. Leehane, M. Exelby
R: H. Torney, J. Cassin, R. Reynolds (c.)
Reserve: S. Silk
Coach: R. Reynolds
RICHMOND
B: D. Guinane, G. Smeaton, J. Reilly
HB: J. Scott, J. Sullivan, R. Steele
C: L. Merrett, B. Waldron, B. Edwards
HF: B. Randall, J. Symons, R. Hay
F: R. Bawden, J. Titus, F. Burge
R: J. Dyer (c.), W. Morris, R. Harris
Reserve: D. Martin
Coach: J. Dyer

# 1943

| | | P | W | L | D | For | Agst | % | Pts |
|---|---|---|---|---|---|---|---|---|---|
| 1 | Richmond (1) | 15 | 10 | 5 | | 1435 | 1166 | 123.1 | 44 |
| 2 | Essendon (2) | 15 | 10 | 5 | | 1296 | 1125 | 115.2 | 44 |
| 3 | Fitzroy (3) | 15 | 10 | 5 | | 1345 | 1234 | 109.0 | 44 |
| 4 | Carlton (4) | 15 | 9 | 6 | | 1420 | 1136 | 125.0 | 40 |
| 5 | Hawthorn | 15 | 9 | 6 | | 1259 | 1212 | 103.9 | 40 |
| 6 | Footscray | 15 | 7 | 8 | | 1164 | 1244 | 93.6 | 32 |
| 7 | Melbourne | 15 | 7 | 8 | | 1364 | 1537 | 88.7 | 32 |
| 8 | South Melb | 15 | 6 | 9 | | 1346 | 1272 | 105.8 | 28 |
| 9 | North Melb | 15 | 5 | 9 | 1 | 1019 | 1323 | 77.0 | 26 |
| 10 | Collingwood | 15 | 5 | 10 | | 1217 | 1358 | 89.6 | 24 |
| 11 | St Kilda | 10 | 1 | 8 | 1 | 731 | 989 | 73.9 | 10 |

*(16 H & A matches) Four match points awarded for a bye. Geelong did not compete. After Round 11, the bottom club (St Kilda) was eliminated.*

**First Semi Final**
Fitzroy 13.16 (94) d. Carlton 5.13 (43)
**Second Semi Final**
Essendon 13.16 (94) d. Richmond 9.17 (71)
**Preliminary Final**
Richmond 12.14 (86) d. Fitzroy 8.13 (61)

**Grand Final**
Richmond 4.2 6.5 8.8 12.14 (86) d
Essendon 2.4 4.9 8.13 11.15 (81)
Goals — Richmond: Harris 7, Dyer 3, Bawden, Broadstock. Essendon: T. Reynolds 7, Torney 2, Lane, Rawle.
Best — Richmond: Harris, Dyer, Perkins, Merrett, Bawden, Oppy. Essendon: T. Reynolds, Lane, Ruddell, Cassin, R. Reynolds, Buttsworth.
Umpire: Hawkins. Match played at Princes Park.
Attendance: 42,100
*Richmond reversed the 1942 result with a five-point win over Essendon again at Princes Park (Optus Oval). It was the smallest Grand Final margin in 22 years. In a thrilling match, the last quarter was highlighted by two Jack Dyer goals, a nail-biting struggle and a last-ditch effort by the Dons that fell just metres short.*
RICHMOND
B: R. Steele, R. Durham, J. Scott
HB: R. Hunt, L. Maguire, W. Perkins
C: L. Merrett, J. Broadstock, B. Edwards
HF: R. Quinn, B. Randall, B. Waldron
F: M. Oppy, R. Bawden, R. Harris
R: J. Dyer (c.), A. Kemp, L. Cahill
Reserve: L. Ablett
Coach: J. Dyer
ESSENDON
B: E. Plummer, C. Ruddell, P. Bushby
HB: J. Cockburn, W. Buttsworth, A. Hird
C: W. Hutchison, L. Gardiner, E. Coward
HF: L. Dearle, G. Lane, G. Abbott
F: T. Reynolds, J. Cassin, K. Rawle
R: H. Torney, N. Betson, R. Reynolds (c.)
Reserve: G. Langley
Coach: R. Reynolds

# 1944

| | | P | W | L | D | For | Agst | % | Pts |
|---|---|---|---|---|---|---|---|---|---|
| 1 | Richmond (2) | 18 | 13 | 4 | 1 | 1886 | 1438 | 131.2 | 54 |
| 2 | Fitzroy (1) | 18 | 13 | 4 | 1 | 1678 | 1280 | 131.1 | 54 |
| 3 | Essendon (3) | 18 | 12 | 4 | 2 | 1887 | 1408 | 134.0 | 52 |
| 4 | Footscray (4) | 18 | 12 | 5 | 1 | 1529 | 1430 | 106.9 | 50 |
| 5 | Carlton | 18 | 12 | 6 | | 1656 | 1259 | 131.5 | 48 |
| 6 | North Melb | 18 | 10 | 8 | | 1619 | 1614 | 100.3 | 40 |
| 7 | South Melb | 18 | 9 | 9 | | 1358 | 1402 | 96.9 | 36 |
| 8 | Melbourne | 18 | 7 | 11 | | 1521 | 1481 | 102.7 | 28 |
| 9 | St Kilda | 18 | 6 | 10 | 2 | 1358 | 1502 | 90.4 | 28 |
| 10 | Collingwood | 18 | 7 | 11 | | 1452 | 1629 | 89.1 | 28 |
| 11 | Hawthorn | 18 | 2 | 15 | 1 | 1268 | 1914 | 66.2 | 10 |
| 12 | Geelong | 18 | 1 | 17 | | 1210 | 2065 | 58.6 | 4 |

*(18 H & A matches)*

**First Semi Final**
Essendon 14.17 (101) d. Footscray 8.4 (52)
**Second Semi Final**
Fitzroy 11.15 (81) d. Richmond 10.10 (70)
**Preliminary Final**
Richmond 16.12 (108) d. Essendon 12.15 (87)

**Grand Final**
Fitzroy 1.2 4.8 6.10 9.12 (63) d
Richmond 2.2 3.2 5.5 7.9 (51)
Goals — Fitzroy: Sier 3, Stackpole 2, Calverley, Symons, Wright, Ruthven. Richmond: Wilson 3, Randall 2, Burge, Dyer.
Best — Fitzroy: Calverley, Hillard, Price, Hughson, Hearn, B. Clay. Richmond: Smeaton, Oppy, Perkins, Maguire, Edwards, Wilson.
Umpire: Hawkins. Match played at Junction Oval Football Ground.
Attendance: 43,000
*Fitzroy's last moment of premiership triumph in the VFL came on September 30, 1944, in stifling conditions before a packed Junction Oval crowd of 43,000. Richmond had the stars but Fitzroy had the spirit and prevailed by 15 points.*
FITZROY
B: C. Denning, F. Hughson (c.), A. Fields
HB: L. Bickerton, N. Hillard, A. O'Bryan
C: B. Calverley, G. Hoskins, N. Jarvis
HF: S. Dawson, S. Wright, N. Price
F: M. Hearn, K. Sier, K. Stackpole
R: B. Clay, J. Symons, A. Ruthven
Reserve: D. Murray
Coach: F. Hughson
RICHMOND
B: M. Oppy, G. Smeaton, C. Priestley
HB: B. Waldron, L. Maguire, W. Perkins
C: L. Merrett, F. Cook, B. Edwards
HF: A. Mooney, B. Randall, L. Jones
F: R. Rawden, J. Scott, F. Burge
R: J. Dyer (c.), W. Morris, W. Wilson
Reserve: K. Cook
Coach: J. Dyer

# 1945

| | | P | W | L | D | For | Agst | % | Pts |
|---|---|---|---|---|---|---|---|---|---|
| 1 | South Melb (2) | 20 | 16 | 4 | | 1840 | 1396 | 131.8 | 64 |
| 2 | Collingwood (3) | 20 | 15 | 5 | | 1902 | 1477 | 128.8 | 60 |
| 3 | North Melb (4) | 20 | 13 | 7 | | 1696 | 1526 | 111.1 | 52 |
| 4 | Carlton (1) | 20 | 13 | 7 | | 1718 | 1607 | 106.9 | 52 |
| 5 | Footscray | 20 | 12 | 8 | | 1717 | 1576 | 108.9 | 48 |
| 6 | Fitzroy | 20 | 11 | 8 | 1 | 1730 | 1452 | 119.1 | 46 |
| 7 | Richmond | 20 | 11 | 9 | | 1802 | 1742 | 103.4 | 44 |
| 8 | Essendon | 20 | 10 | 9 | 1 | 1837 | 1614 | 113.8 | 42 |
| 9 | Melbourne | 20 | 8 | 12 | | 1683 | 1699 | 99.1 | 32 |
| 10 | Hawthorn | 20 | 6 | 14 | | 1665 | 1944 | 85.6 | 24 |
| 11 | Geelong | 20 | 2 | 18 | | 1415 | 2180 | 64.9 | 8 |
| 12 | St Kilda | 20 | 2 | 18 | | 1305 | 2097 | 62.2 | 8 |

*(20 H & A matches)*

**First Semi Final**
Carlton 14.10 (94) d. North Melbourne 8.20 (68)
**Second Semi Final**
South Melbourne 13.10 (88) d.
Collingwood 11.11 (77)
**Preliminary Final**
Carlton 13.12 (90) d. Collingwood 12.8 (80)

**Grand Final**
Carlton 2.4 7.5 12.9 15.13 (103) d
South Melbourne 0.5 6.9 8.12 10.15 (75)
Goals — Carlton: Hands 3, Price 3, Mooring 2, K.
Baxter 2, Bennett, Chitty, Wines, McLean, Savage.
South Melbourne: Castles 3, Nash 2, Smith 2,
Linden 2, Richards.
Best — Carlton: Brown, Sanger, K. Baxter, Chitty,
Wines, McLean.
Umpire: Spokes. Match played at Princes Park.
Attendance: 62,986
*The infamous 'Bloodbath' between Carlton and
South Melbourne at Princes Park (Optus Oval). The
Blues became the first team to win from fourth
under the McIntyre system, but that was all but
forgotten in a wild match that saw nine players
reported on 15 charges.*
CARLTON
B: A. Sanger, V. Brown, J. Baird
HB: R. Chitty (c.), B. Deacon, J. Clark
C: D. Williams, C. Wines, H. Turner
HF: A. Way, K. Hands, L. Collins
F: R. McLean, K. Baxter, J. Mooring
R: R. Savage, J. Bennett, A. Price
Reserve: C. McInnes
Coach: P. Bentley
SOUTH MELBOURNE
B: B. Kelly, J. Cleary, D. Grossman
HB: R. Matlock, J. Williams, J. Danckert
C: E. Whitfield, H. Matthews (c.), W. King
HF: V. Castles, R. Clegg, K. Smith
F: A. Linden, L. Nash, W. Williams
R: J. Graham, J. Dempsey, R. Richards
Reserve: R. Hartridge
Coach: W. Adams

# 1946

| | | P | W | L | D | For | Agst | % | Pts |
|---|---|---|---|---|---|---|---|---|---|
| 1 | Essendon (1) | 19 | 15 | 4 | | 1980 | 1407 | 140.7 | 60 |
| 2 | Collingwood (3) | 19 | 13 | 6 | | 1849 | 1477 | 125.2 | 52 |
| 3 | Footscray (4) | 19 | 13 | 6 | | 1917 | 1628 | 117.8 | 52 |
| 4 | Melbourne (2) | 19 | 13 | 6 | | 1700 | 1622 | 104.8 | 52 |
| 5 | Richmond | 19 | 11 | 8 | | 1921 | 1659 | 115.8 | 44 |
| 6 | Carlton | 19 | 11 | 8 | | 1724 | 1688 | 102.1 | 44 |
| 7 | South Melb | 19 | 10 | 9 | | 1627 | 1528 | 106.5 | 40 |
| 8 | Fitzroy | 19 | 9 | 10 | | 1589 | 1339 | 118.7 | 36 |
| 9 | North Melb | 19 | 8 | 11 | | 1536 | 1685 | 91.2 | 32 |
| 10 | Geelong | 19 | 4 | 15 | | 1505 | 2124 | 70.9 | 16 |
| 11 | St Kilda | 19 | 4 | 15 | | 1332 | 1902 | 70.0 | 16 |
| 12 | Hawthorn | 19 | 3 | 16 | | 1487 | 2108 | 70.5 | 12 |

*(19 H & A matches)*

**First Semi Final**
Melbourne 17.18 (120) d. Footscray 15.12 (102)
**Second Semi Final**
Essendon 14.16 (100) drew with Collingwood
13.22 (100)
**Replay**
Essendon 10.16 (76) d. Collingwood 8.9 (57)
**Preliminary Final**
Melbourne 16.17 (113) d. Collingwood 14.16
(100)

**Grand Final**
Essendon 7.2 9.8 20.15 22.18 (150) d
Melbourne 8.3 10.4 11.5 13.9 (87)
Goals — Essendon: Lane 7, Brittingham 4,
Hutchison 3, R. Reynolds 3, McClure 2, Equid,
Rawle, Cassin. Melbourne: Mueller 6, Dullard 3,
Fanning, O'Rourke, Rodda, Bowman.
Best — Essendon: Lane, Hutchison, Buttsworth,
Ruddell, Bushby, H. Lambert. Melbourne: Mueller,
Rodda, McGrath, Bickford, Mitchell, Dullard.
Umpire: Bride. Match played at MCG.
Attendance: 73,743
*After drawing with, then beating, Collingwood in the
second semi, Essendon was far too good for
Melbourne in the Grand Final, back at the MCG,
winning by 63 points. The win was set up by a
paralysing 11-goal third-quarter burst.*
ESSENDON
B: L. Gardiner, C. Ruddell, P. Bushby
HB: H. Tonkes, W. Buttsworth, H. Lambert
C: G. Hassell, W. Pearson, A. Harper
HF: H. Equid, G. Lane, R. Reynolds (c.)
F: R. McClure, W. Brittingham, K. Rawle
R: G. Abbott, J. Cassin, W. Hutchison
Reserves: J. Jones, C. Lambert
Coach: R. Reynolds
MELBOURNE
B: W. Deans, J. McGrath, D. Cordner
HB: C. McLean, E. Cordner, W. Lock
C: G. Bickford, L. Dockett, R. Stabb
HF: G. Bowman, F. Fanning, J. Mitchell
F: A. Dullard, N. Smith (c.), E. O'Rourke
R: J. Mueller, S. Rule, A. Rodda
Reserves: F. Kennedy, A. Byfield
Coach: F. Hughes

# 1947

| | | P | W | L | D | For | Agst | % | Pts |
|---|---|---|---|---|---|---|---|---|---|
| 1 | Carlton (1) | 19 | 15 | 4 | | 1833 | 1368 | 134.0 | 60 |
| 2 | Essendon (2) | 19 | 14 | 5 | | 1876 | 1528 | 122.8 | 56 |
| 3 | Fitzroy (3) | 19 | 13 | 6 | | 1736 | 1370 | 126.7 | 52 |
| 4 | Richmond (4) | 19 | 12 | 7 | | 1726 | 1582 | 109.1 | 48 |
| 5 | Collingwood | 19 | 11 | 7 | 1 | 1738 | 1546 | 112.4 | 46 |
| 6 | Melbourne | 19 | 11 | 8 | | 1742 | 1488 | 117.1 | 44 |
| 7 | Geelong | 19 | 11 | 8 | | 1761 | 1705 | 103.3 | 44 |
| 8 | South Melb | 19 | 8 | 10 | 1 | 1602 | 1652 | 97.0 | 34 |
| 9 | Footscray | 19 | 8 | 10 | 1 | 1646 | 1713 | 96.1 | 34 |
| 10 | North Melb | 19 | 4 | 15 | | 1390 | 1789 | 77.7 | 16 |
| 11 | Hawthorn | 19 | 4 | 15 | | 1456 | 1907 | 76.4 | 16 |
| 12 | St Kilda | 19 | 1 | 17 | 1 | 1221 | 2079 | 58.7 | 6 |

*(19 H & A matches)*

**First Semi Final**
Fitzroy 16.7 (103) d. Richmond 11.9 (75)
**Second Semi Final**
Carlton 14.15 (99) d. Essendon 11.17 (83)
**Preliminary Final**
Essendon 16.13 (109) d. Fitzroy 14.12 (96)

**Grand Final**
Carlton 4.0 8.0 10.4 13.8 (86) d
Essendon 3.7 8.11 10.15 11.19 (85)
Goals — Carlton: Davies 4, Baird 3, Turner 2, Stafford, Howell, Garby, Henfry. Essendon: Hutchison 4, Brittingham 2, R. Reynolds 2, Goodingham, Rawle, Cassin.
Best — Carlton: Henfry, Davies, Bennett, Clark, Howell, Grieve. Essendon: Buttsworth, McClure, Hutchison, Jones, R. Reynolds, Bradley.
Umpire: Sawyer. Match played at MCG.
Attendance: 85,815
*Essendon led by 12 points with 10 minutes to go. The lead had been reduced to five points with just 44 seconds left, when Carlton's Fred Stafford grabbed the ball after a boundary throw-in and booted the winning goal.*
CARLTON
B: R. Green, O. Grieve, G. Bailey
HB: V. Brown, B. Deacon, J. Clark
C: F. Fitzgibbon, E. Henfrey (c.), D. Williams
HF: F. Stafford, K. Hands, R. Garby
F: F. Davies, J. Baird, H. Turner
R: J. Howell, J. Bennett, J. Conley
Reserves: K. Baxter, A. Greenshields
Coach: P. Bentley
ESSENDON
B: L. Gardiner, C. Ruddell, R. McClure
HB: N. Allanson, W. Buttsworth, N. McDonald
C: R. Bradley, H. Lambert, G. Hassell
HF: R. Reynolds (c.), J. Jones, A. Harper
F: I. Goodingham, W. Brittingham, K. Rawle
R: P. Bushby, J. Cassin, W. Hutchison
Reserves: K. Newton, G. Tate
Coach: R. Reynolds

# 1948

| | | P | W | L | D | For | Agst | % | Pts |
|---|---|---|---|---|---|---|---|---|---|
| 1 | Essendon (2) | 19 | 16 | 2 | 1 | 1838 | 1340 | 137.2 | 66 |
| 2 | Melbourne (1) | 19 | 13 | 6 | | 1682 | 1347 | 124.9 | 52 |
| 3 | Collingwood (3) | 19 | 13 | 6 | | 1775 | 1500 | 118.3 | 52 |
| 4 | Footscray (4) | 19 | 12 | 7 | | 1499 | 1453 | 103.2 | 48 |
| 5 | Richmond | 19 | 11 | 7 | 1 | 1895 | 1509 | 125.6 | 46 |
| 6 | Carlton | 19 | 10 | 9 | | 1768 | 1564 | 113.0 | 40 |
| 7 | Fitzroy | 19 | 9 | 10 | | 1529 | 1355 | 112.8 | 36 |
| 8 | North Melb | 19 | 8 | 11 | | 1328 | 1589 | 83.6 | 32 |
| 9 | Geelong | 19 | 7 | 12 | | 1558 | 1737 | 89.7 | 28 |
| 10 | South Melb | 19 | 7 | 12 | | 1512 | 1826 | 82.8 | 28 |
| 11 | Hawthorn | 19 | 5 | 14 | | 1280 | 1690 | 75.7 | 20 |
| 12 | St Kilda | 19 | 2 | 17 | | 1124 | 1878 | 59.9 | 8 |

*(19 H & A matches)*

**First Semi Final**
Collingwood 17.17 (119) d. Footscray 12.12 (84)
**Second Semi Final**
Essendon 13.16 (94) d. Melbourne 8.10 (58)
**Preliminary Final**
Melbourne 25.16 (166) d. Collingwood 15.11 (101)

**Grand Final**
Essendon 0.6 2.15 6.21 7.27 (69) drew with
Melbourne 3.2 4.5 6.8 10.9 (69)
Goals — Melbourne: Mueller 6, Smith, Craddock, Arnold, Dullard. Essendon: Hutchison 2, Brittingham 2, Rawle, Bigelow, Bradley.
Best — Melbourne: Rodda, Smith, Collins, Mueller, Bickford, McGrath. Essendon: R. Reynolds, McClure, McDonald, H. Lambert, C. Lambert, Leehane.
Umpire: McMurray. Match played at MCG.
Attendance: 85,658
*The first drawn Grand Final saw Essendon's staggering inaccuracy — 7.27 — give Melbourne a second chance which it accepted with relish, winning the replay by 39 points. Jack Mueller, brought out of retirement for the finals, kicked 20 goals in three games.*
ESSENDON
B: C. Lambert, C. Ruddell, P. Bushby
HB: H. Lambert, W. Buttsworth, N. McDonald
C: R. Bradley, A. Harper, G. Hassell
HF: R. Reynolds (c.), E. Leehane, J. Jones
F: R. Syme, W. Brittingham, K. Rawle
R: R. McClure, D. Bigelow, W. Hutchison
Reserves: W. May, V. Fisher
Coach: R. Reynolds
MELBOURNE
B: W. Deans, J. McGrath, S. Rule
HB: C. McLean, Denis Cordner, G. Collins
C: M. Spittle, G. Bickford, L. Dockett
HF: D. Heywood, L. Arnold, N. McMahen
F: J. Mueller, N. Smith, E. Craddock
R: Don Cordner (c.), A. Dullard, A. Rodda
Reserves: G. Bowman, E. Jackson
Coach: F. Hughes
**Replay**
Melbourne 6.2 9.3 11.8 13.11 (89) d
Essendon 0.3 5.5 6.6 7.8 (50)
Goals — Melbourne: Mueller 6, Arnold 2, Rodda 2, Smith, Dullard, McMahen. Essendon: Brittingham 2, Syme 2, R. Reynolds, Hutchison, Jones.

Best — Melbourne: Mueller, Smith, McGrath, Spittle, Bickford, Arnold. Essendon: McDonald, McClure, Bushby, Syme, Hassell, C. Lambert.
Umpire: McMurray. Match played at MCG.
Attendance: 52,226

**MELBOURNE**
B: W. Deans, J. McGrath, S. Rule
HB: C. McLean, Denis Cordner, G. Collins
C: M. Spittle, G. Bickford, L. Dockett
HF: R. McKenzie, L. Arnold, N. McMahen
F: J. Mueller, N. Smith, E. Craddock
R: Don Cordner (c.), A. Dullard, A. Rodda
Reserves: G. Bowman, E. Jackson
Coach:  F. Hughes

**ESSENDON**
B: C. Lambert, C. Ruddell, R. McClure
HB: L. Gardiner, W. May, N. McDonald
C: R. Bradley, A. Harper, G. Hassell
HF: J. Jones, E. Leehane, R. Reynolds (c.)
F: H. Equid, W. Brittingham, K. Rawle
R: P. Bushby, R. Syme, W. Hutchison
Reserves: V. Fisher, R. McEwin
Coach: R. Reynolds

# 1949

| | | P | W | L | D | For | Agst | % | Pts |
|---|---|---|---|---|---|---|---|---|---|
| 1 | North Melb (3) | 19 | 14 | 5 | | 1471 | 1235 | 119.1 | 56 |
| 2 | Carlton (2) | 19 | 13 | 6 | | 1679 | 1328 | 126.4 | 52 |
| 3 | Collingwood (4) | 19 | 13 | 6 | | 1616 | 1308 | 123.5 | 52 |
| 4 | Essendon (1) | 19 | 13 | 6 | | 1649 | 1366 | 120.7 | 52 |
| 5 | Melbourne | 19 | 12 | 7 | | 1516 | 1341 | 113.0 | 48 |
| 6 | Richmond | 19 | 10 | 9 | | 1733 | 1485 | 116.7 | 40 |
| 7 | Fitzroy | 19 | 10 | 9 | | 1488 | 1521 | 97.8 | 40 |
| 8 | Geelong | 19 | 9 | 10 | | 1722 | 1540 | 111.8 | 36 |
| 9 | Footscray | 19 | 7 | 12 | | 1211 | 1444 | 83.9 | 28 |
| 10 | South Melb | 19 | 6 | 13 | | 1343 | 1669 | 80.5 | 24 |
| 11 | St Kilda | 19 | 4 | 15 | | 1272 | 1730 | 73.5 | 16 |
| 12 | Hawthorn | 19 | 3 | 16 | | 1153 | 1886 | 61.1 | 12 |

*(19 H & A matches)*

**First Semi Final**
Essendon 20.16 (136) d. Collingwood 8.6 (54)
**Second Semi Final**
Carlton 15.13 (103) d. North Melbourne 14.7 (91)
**Preliminary Final**
Essendon 11.12 (78) d. North Melbourne 9.7 (61)
**Grand Final**
Essendon 3.3 7.7 12.15 18.17 (125) d
Carlton 2.4 2.10 3.12. 6.16 (52)
Goals — Essendon: Coleman 6, Rawle 3, Hutchison 2, Syme 2, McEwin 2, Jones, Leehane, R. Reynolds. Carlton: Howell, Turner, Garby, B. Baxter, K. Baxter, Hands.
Best — Essendon: McClure, May, Hutchison, Coleman, Brittingham McDonald. Carlton: Deacon, Grieve, Green, Clark, Howell, Henfry.
Umpire: McMurray. Match played at MCG.
Attendance: 90,453
*Essendon handed Carlton a football lesson and a 73-point drubbing. The coup de grace was applied by Bomber sensation John Coleman, who kicked his 100th goal for the season (his first century) late in the last quarter.*

**ESSENDON**
B: A. Thaw, W. Brittingham, W. May
HB: L. Gardiner, R. McConnell, N. McDonald
C: V. Fisher, H. Lambert, R. Bradley
HF: J. Jones, E. Leehane, R. McEwin
F: R. Reynolds (c.), J. Coleman, K. Rawle
R: R. McClure, R. Syme, W. Hutchison
Reserves: G. Lane, G. Hassell
Coach: R. Reynolds

**CARLTON**
B: R. Green, O. Grieve, F. Davies
HB: J. Baird, B. Deacon, J. Clark
C: A. Hodgson, E. Henfrey (c.), D. Williams
HF: J. Conley, J. Howell, R. Garby
F: G. Brokenshire, K. Baxter, H. Turner
R: K. Hands, F. Bateman, J. Mooring
Reserves: B. Baxter, F. Stafford
Coach: P. Bentley

# 1950

| | | P | W | L | D | For | Agst | % | Pts |
|---|---|---|---|---|---|---|---|---|---|
| 1 | Essendon (1) | 18 | 17 | 1 | | 1942 | 1197 | 162.2 | 68 |
| 2 | North Melb (2) | 18 | 13 | 5 | | 1595 | 1293 | 123.4 | 52 |
| 3 | Melbourne (4) | 18 | 12 | 6 | | 1485 | 1205 | 123.2 | 48 |
| 4 | Geelong (3) | 18 | 10 | 8 | | 1562 | 1256 | 124.4 | 40 |
| 5 | Fitzroy | 18 | 10 | 8 | | 1452 | 1314 | 110.5 | 40 |
| 6 | Richmond | 18 | 10 | 8 | | 1506 | 1476 | 102.0 | 40 |
| 7 | Collingwood | 18 | 9 | 9 | | 1586 | 1437 | 110.4 | 36 |
| 8 | Carlton | 18 | 8 | 9 | 1 | 1528 | 16з7 | 93.3 | 34 |
| 9 | St Kilda | 18 | 8 | 9 | 1 | 1341 | 1553 | 86.3 | 34 |
| 10 | Footscray | 18 | 5 | 13 | | 1475 | 1608 | 91.7 | 20 |
| 11 | South Melb | 18 | 5 | 13 | | 1438 | 1904 | 75.5 | 20 |
| 12 | Hawthorn | 18 | 0 | 18 | | 1022 | 2052 | 49.8 | 0 |

*(18 H & A matches)*

**First Semi Final**
Geelong 13.10 (88) d. Melbourne 6.8 (44)
**Second Semi Final**
Essendon 11.14 (80) d. North Melbourne 11.11 (77)
**Preliminary Final**
North Melbourne 14.16 (100) d. Geelong 12.11 (83)
**Grand Final**
Essendon 7.3 7.6 10.11 13.14 (92) d
North Melbourne 4.0 5.5 7.9 7.12 (54)
Goals — Essendon: Coleman 4, R. Reynolds 2, Syme 2, McEwin, Hutchison, Dale, Harper, Snell. North Melbourne: Spencer 3, Robb 2, Dynon, Brooker.
Best — Essendon: McDonald, R. Reynolds, May, McClure, Syme, Gardiner. North Melbourne: Foote, Robb, Dynon, Jarrard, Brooker, McCorkell.
Umpire: McMurray. Match played at MCG.
Attendance: 87,601
*North Melbourne finally made its first appearance in a VFL Grand Final, but it was not to be a happy day for the Shinboners. Essendon cleaned them up by 38 points, despite some typically physical play.*
**ESSENDON**
B: L. Gardiner, W. Brittingham, W. May
HB: H. Lambert, R. McConnell, N. McDonald
C: C. Lambert, A. Dale, J. Collins
HF: J. Jones, W. Snell, A. Harper
F: R. Reynolds (c.), J. Coleman, R. McEwin

R: R. McClure, R. Syme, W. Hutchison
Reserves: E. Leehane, N. Allanson
Coach: R. Reynolds
NORTH MELBOURNE
B: P. Kelly, J. McCorkell, J. Reeves
HB: E. Jarrard, R. Ryan, L. Reeves
C: K. McKenzie, K. Dynon, L. Mogg
HF: G. Marchesi, F. Jeeves, D. Condon
F: R. Brooker, J. Spencer, H. Robb
R: C. Thornton, L. Foote (c.), J. Malone
Reserves: V. Lawrence, J. Hedley
Coach: W. Carter

# 1951

| | | P | W | L | D | For | Agst | % | Pts |
|---|---|---|---|---|---|---|---|---|---|
| 1 | Geelong (1) | 18 | 14 | 4 | | 1485 | 1097 | 135.4 | 56 |
| 2 | Collingwood (3) | 18 | 14 | 4 | | 1499 | 1193 | 125.6 | 56 |
| 3 | Essendon (2) | 18 | 13 | 5 | | 1530 | 1262 | 121.2 | 52 |
| 4 | Footscray (4) | 18 | 12 | 6 | | 1316 | 1165 | 113.0 | 48 |
| 5 | Fitzroy | 18 | 10 | 6 | 2 | 1373 | 1305 | 105.2 | 44 |
| 6 | Richmond | 18 | 10 | 8 | | 1551 | 1327 | 116.9 | 40 |
| 7 | Carlton | 18 | 8 | 9 | 1 | 1341 | 1253 | 107.0 | 34 |
| 8 | South Melb | 18 | 8 | 9 | 1 | 1399 | 1505 | 93.0 | 34 |
| 9 | North Melb | 18 | 7 | 11 | | 1224 | 1433 | 85.4 | 28 |
| 10 | St Kilda | 18 | 5 | 13 | | 1311 | 1595 | 82.2 | 20 |
| 11 | Hawthorn | 18 | 4 | 14 | | 1136 | 1515 | 75.0 | 16 |
| 12 | Melbourne | 18 | 1 | 17 | | 1230 | 1745 | 70.5 | 4 |

*(18 H & A matches)*

**First Semi Final**
Essendon 8.13 (61) d. Footscray 8.5 (53)
**Second Semi Final**
Geelong 22.20 (152) d. Collingwood 10.10 (70)
**Preliminary Final**
Essendon 10.10 (70) d. Collingwood 10.8 (68)
**Grand Final**
Geelong 3.8 4.10 9.13 11.15 (81) d
Essendon 1.0 6.2 6.5 10.10 (70)
Goals — Geelong: Goninon 4, Davis, Pianto,
McMaster, Turner, Flanagan, Morrow, Norman.
Essendon: K. McDonald 2, Syme 2, May,
Hutchison, Snell, Tate, Jones, Payne.
Best — Geelong: Morrison, Smith, McMaster,
Turner, Hyde, Trezise. Essendon: Gardiner, Mann,
N. McDonald, May, Syme, Bigelow.
Umpire: Jamieson. Match played at MCG.
Attendance: 85,795
*The controversial suspension of John Coleman on
the eve of the finals cleared the way for Geelong to
win the 1951 flag. The Cats got up by 11 points,
but even their own players admitted things might
have been different if Coleman had played.*
GEELONG
B: B. Smith, B. Morrison, L. Stewart
HB: A. Worner, J. Hyde, R. Middlemiss
C: S. Tate, L. Turner, T. Fulton
HF: R. Renfrey, F. Flanagan (c.), R. Davis
F: C. McMaster, G. Goninon, P. Pianto
R: T. Morrow, J. Norman, N. Trezise
Reserves: L. Reed, R. Hovey
Coach: R. Hickey
ESSENDON
B: L. Gardiner, W. Brittingham, D. Bigelow

HB: H. Lambert, R. McConnell, N. McDonald
C: C. Lambert, A. Dale, L. Mann
HF: J. Jones, W. Snell, R. McEwin
F: F. Payne, K. McDonald, G. Tate
R: W. May, R. Syme, W. Hutchison (c.)
Reserves: R. Reynolds, J. Clarke
Coach: R. Reynolds

# 1952

| | | P | W | L | D | For | Agst | % | Pts |
|---|---|---|---|---|---|---|---|---|---|
| 1 | Geelong (1) | 19 | 16 | 2 | 1 | 1594 | 1183 | 134.7 | 66 |
| 2 | Collingwood (2) | 19 | 14 | 5 | | 1528 | 1058 | 144.4 | 56 |
| 3 | Fitzroy (3) | 19 | 13 | 6 | | 1233 | 1170 | 105.4 | 52 |
| 4 | Carlton (4) | 19 | 11 | 6 | 2 | 1473 | 1310 | 112.4 | 48 |
| 5 | South Melb | 19 | 11 | 7 | 1 | 1411 | 1337 | 105.5 | 46 |
| 6 | Melbourne | 19 | 9 | 9 | 1 | 1420 | 1379 | 103.0 | 38 |
| 7 | North Melb | 19 | 9 | 10 | | 1352 | 1396 | 96.8 | 36 |
| 8 | Essendon | 19 | 8 | 10 | 1 | 1579 | 1390 | 113.6 | 34 |
| 9 | Richmond | 19 | 8 | 11 | | 1281 | 1384 | 92.6 | 32 |
| 10 | Footscray | 19 | 5 | 14 | | 1052 | 1364 | 77.1 | 20 |
| 11 | Hawthorn | 19 | 5 | 14 | | 1030 | 1480 | 69.6 | 20 |
| 12 | St Kilda | 19 | 2 | 17 | | 1071 | 1573 | 68.1 | 8 |

*(18 H & A matches)*

**First Semi Final**
Fitzroy 10.9 (69) d. Carlton 8.20 (68)
**Second Semi Final**
Geelong 14.16 (100) d. Collingwood 6.10 (46)
**Preliminary Final**
Collingwood 11.15 (81) d. Fitzroy 9.8 (62)
**Grand Final**
Geelong 4.2 5.3 11.6 13.8 (86) d
Collingwood 1.2 3.3 5.4 5.10 (40)
Goals — Geelong: Goninon 5, Trezise 4, Davis,
McMaster, Flanagan, Worner. Collingwood: Parker
3, Merrett 2.
Best — Geelong: Williams, Trezise, Sharp,
Goninon, B. Smith, Morrison. Collingwood: Merrett,
Mann, R. Rose, Parker, Tuck, M. Twomey.
Umpire: Jamieson. Match played at MCG.
Attendance: 87,601
*By finals time in 1952, Geelong was in the middle
of the longest unbeaten streak in VFL history — 26
games without defeat. And Collingwood presented
few problems for the all-conquering Cats in the
Grand Final, going down by 46 points.*
GEELONG
B: B. Smith, B. Morrison, N. Sharp
HB: R. Middlemiss, J. Hyde, G. Williams
C: A. Worner, D. Palmer, T. Fulton
HF: L. Turner, F. Flanagan (c.), R. Davis
F: J. Norman, G. Goninon, P. Pianto
R: C. McMaster, R. Renfrey, N. Trezise
Reserves: S. Smith, R. Hovey
Coach: R. Hickey
COLLINGWOOD
B: G. Hams, K. Batchelor, W. Rose
HB: F. Tuck, J. Finck, L. Smith
C: D. Healey, W. Twomey, T. Merrett
HF: R. Rose, M. Dunstan, J. Hickey
F: N. Mann, H. Stevens, J. Parker
R: M. Twomey, A. Gooch, L. Richards (c.)
Reserves: R. Kingston, K. Aitken
Coach: P. Kyne

# 1953

| | | P | W | L | D | For | Agst | % | Pts |
|---|---|---|---|---|---|---|---|---|---|
| 1 | Geelong (2) | 18 | 15 | 3 | | 1546 | 1079 | 143.3 | 60 |
| 2 | Collingwood (1) | 18 | 14 | 4 | | 1518 | 1229 | 123.5 | 56 |
| 3 | Footscray (3) | 18 | 13 | 5 | | 1309 | 959 | 136.5 | 52 |
| 4 | Essendon (4) | 18 | 13 | 5 | | 1529 | 1177 | 129.9 | 52 |
| 5 | Carlton | 18 | 10 | 8 | | 1409 | 1310 | 107.6 | 40 |
| 6 | Fitzroy | 18 | 10 | 8 | | 1208 | 1421 | 85.0 | 40 |
| 7 | North Melb | 18 | 9 | 9 | | 1388 | 1287 | 107.8 | 36 |
| 8 | South Melb | 18 | 9 | 9 | | 1385 | 1323 | 104.7 | 36 |
| 9 | St Kilda | 18 | 5 | 13 | | 1065 | 1561 | 68.2 | 20 |
| 10 | Richmond | 18 | 3 | 14 | 1 | 1220 | 1501 | 81.3 | 14 |
| 11 | Melbourne | 18 | 3 | 14 | 1 | 1137 | 1420 | 80.1 | 14 |
| 12 | Hawthorn | 18 | 3 | 15 | | 974 | 1421 | 68.5 | 12 |

*(18 H & A matches)*

**First Semi Final**
Footscray 6.13 (49) d. Essendon 5.11 (41)
**Second Semi Final**
Collingwood 13.12 (90) d. Geelong 8.12 (60)
**Preliminary Final**
Geelong 8.15 (63) d. Footscray 5.7 (37)

**Grand Final**
Collingwood 2.4 5.6 10.10 11.11 (77) d
Geelong 2.3 3.9 5.11 8.17 (65)
Goals — Collingwood: Batchelor 4, R. Rose 3,
Healey 2, L. Richards, M. Twomey. Geelong: Davis
3, Rayson 2, Hovey, Trezise, McMaster.
Best — Collingwood: Healey, Mann, R. Richards, L.
Richards, R. Rose, Merrett. Geelong: B. Smith,
Williams, Renfrey, Turner, McMaster.
Umpire: McMurray. Match played at MCG.
Attendance: 89,060
*In 1953, Collingwood finally put an end to
Geelong's record winning streak. It repeated the
dose in the second semi, and again in the Grand
Final two weeks later. Captain Lou Richards
couldn't stop grinning. Still can't.*
COLLINGWOOD
B: L. Sharp, J. Finck, A. Gooch
HB: J. Parker, N. Waller, R. Kingston
C: D. Healey, W. Twomey, R. Richards
HF: P. Twomey, T. Waites, T. Merrett
F: M. Twomey, K. Batchelor, L. Richards (c.)
R: N. Mann, W. Rose, R. Rose
Reserves: M. Weideman, G. Hams
Coach: P. Kyne
GEELONG
B: B. Smith, B. Morrison, H. Herbert
HB: S. Smith, J. Hyde, G. Williams
C: L. Reed, L. Turner, A. Worner
HF: N. Rayson, F. Flanagan (c.), R. Davis
F: G. Swarbrick, R. Renfrey, N. Trezise
R: C. McMaster, N. Sharp, P. Pianto
Reserves: D. Palmer, R. Hovey
Coach: R. Hickey

# 1954

| | | P | W | L | D | For | Agst | % | Pts |
|---|---|---|---|---|---|---|---|---|---|
| 1 | Geelong (3) | 18 | 13 | 5 | | 1630 | 1225 | 133.1 | 52 |
| 2 | Footscray (1) | 18 | 11 | 6 | 1 | 1423 | 1095 | 130.0 | 46 |
| 3 | North Melb (4) | 18 | 11 | 6 | 1 | 1355 | 1361 | 99.6 | 46 |
| 4 | Melbourne (2) | 18 | 11 | 7 | | 1504 | 1239 | 121.4 | 44 |
| 5 | Richmond | 18 | 10 | 8 | | 1503 | 1310 | 114.7 | 40 |
| 6 | Essendon | 18 | 10 | 8 | | 1471 | 1364 | 107.8 | 40 |
| 7 | Collingwood | 18 | 10 | 8 | | 1312 | 1301 | 100.8 | 40 |
| 8 | Carlton | 18 | 8 | 10 | | 1382 | 1391 | 99.4 | 32 |
| 9 | Hawthorn | 18 | 8 | 10 | | 1177 | 1337 | 88.0 | 32 |
| 10 | South Melb | 18 | 6 | 12 | | 1209 | 1482 | 81.6 | 24 |
| 11 | Fitzroy | 18 | 4 | 13 | 1 | 1174 | 1604 | 73.2 | 18 |
| 12 | St Kilda | 18 | 4 | 13 | 1 | 1149 | 1580 | 72.7 | 18 |

*(18 H & A matches)*

**First Semi Final**
Melbourne 16.14 (110) d. North Melbourne 11.14 (80)
**Second Semi Final**
Footscray 11.19 (85) d. Geelong 8.14 (62)
**Preliminary Final**
Melbourne 10.7 (67) d. Geelong 7.8 (50)

**Grand Final**
Footscray 6.3 8.5 12.9 15.12 (102) d
Melbourne 1.4 4.6 6.7 7.9 (51)
Goals — Footscray: Collins 7, Sutton 3, J. Kerr,
Stevens, Duffy, Reynolds, Stockman. Melbourne:
Clarke, Barassi, Spencer, Mithen, McLean, R.
Johnson, Albiston.
Best — Footscray: J. Kerr, Collins, Bryden, Ross,
Whitten, Reynolds. Melbourne: Den. Cordner,
Collins, Barassi, Mithen, McLean, Albiston.
Umpire: McMurray. Match played at MCG.
Attendance: 80,897
*At last! In its 30th season in the VFL, Footscray
finally got to salute its first premiership flag after a
comprehensive demolition job on Melbourne, with
Ted Whitten and Charlie Sutton starring.
Unfortunately, first is also last for the Dogs.*
FOOTSCRAY
B: W. Donald, H. Henderson, D. Bryden
HB: A. Martin, E. Whitten, J. Gallagher
C: R. McCarthy, D. Ross, D. Reynolds
HF: R. Duffy, P. Box, R. Stockman
F: B. Gilmore, J. Collins, C. Sutton (c.)
R: H. Stevens, A. Edwards, J. Kerr
Reserves: J. Nuttall, A. Abbey
Coach: C. Sutton
MELBOURNE
B: J. Beckwith, L. Arnold, K. Christie
HB: G. Collins (c.), N. McMahen, D. Williams
C: R. Lane, K. Melville, I. McLean
HF: L. Mithen, G. McGivern, G. Case
F: R. Johnson, N. Clarke, K. Albiston
R: D. Cordner, R. Barassi, S. Spencer
Reserves: F. Adams, B. Dixon
Coach: N. Smith

# 1955

| | | P | W | L | D | For | Agst | % | Pts |
|---|---|---|---|---|---|---|---|---|---|
| 1 | Melbourne (1) | 18 | 15 | 3 | | 1559 | 1036 | 150.5 | 60 |
| 2 | Collingwood (2) | 18 | 14 | 4 | | 1526 | 1197 | 127.5 | 56 |
| 3 | Geelong (3) | 18 | 14 | 4 | | 1524 | 1241 | 122.8 | 56 |
| 4 | Essendon (4) | 18 | 12 | 6 | | 1435 | 1099 | 130.6 | 48 |
| 5 | Footscray | 18 | 12 | 6 | | 1323 | 1018 | 130.0 | 48 |
| 6 | Richmond | 18 | 9 | 9 | | 1471 | 1387 | 106.1 | 36 |
| 7 | Carlton | 18 | 9 | 9 | | 1384 | 1403 | 98.6 | 36 |
| 8 | Hawthorn | 18 | 8 | 10 | | 1262 | 1342 | 94.0 | 32 |
| 9 | Fitzroy | 18 | 6 | 12 | | 1258 | 1421 | 88.5 | 24 |
| 10 | South Melb | 18 | 5 | 13 | | 1276 | 1454 | 87.8 | 20 |
| 11 | North Melb | 18 | 3 | 15 | | 1233 | 1617 | 76.3 | 12 |
| 12 | St Kilda | 18 | 1 | 17 | | 861 | 1897 | 45.4 | 4 |

*(18 H & A matches)*

**First Semi Final**
Geelong 9.7 (61) d. Essendon 7.11 (53)
**Second Semi Final**
Melbourne 8.8 (56) d. Collingwood 6.9 (45)
**Preliminary Final**
Collingwood 14.12 (96) d. Geelong 13.6 (84)

**Grand Final**
Melbourne 2.3 3.10 4.13 8.16 (64) d
Collingwood 2.2 2.5 4.6 5.6 (36)
Goals — Melbourne: Clarke 3, Ridley 3, McKenzie,
Laidlaw. Collingwood: Weideman 2, R. Rose,
Smale, Jones.
Best — Melbourne: Den. Cordner, Barassi,
Melville, McLean, McMahen, Marquis. Collingwood:
Hamilton, Lucas, Mann, R. Rose, Sharp, Tuck.
Umpire: Beitzel. Match played at MCG.
Attendance: 88,053
*The start of possibly the finest era enjoyed by any*
*club in football history as the Demons outclassed*
*Collingwood by 28 points. The game was*
*highlighted by the infamous Des Healey-Frank*
*Adams clash which saw both players stretchered*
*off and Healey forced into premature retirement.*
MELBOURNE
B: J. Beckwith, P. Marquis, Trevor Johnson
HB: D. Williams, G. McGivern, N. McMahen (c.)
C: I. McLean, K. Melville, G. Case
HF: L. Mithen, C. Laidlaw, R. McKenzie
F: R. Johnson, N. Clarke, I. Ridley
R: D. Cordner, R. Barassi, S. Spencer
Reserves: T. Gleeson, F. Adams
Coach: N. Smith
COLLINGWOOD
B: L. Sharp, J. Hamilton, N. Waller
HB: P. Lucas, F. Tuck, R. Kingston
C: D. Healey, J. Parker, T. Merrett
HF: W. Jones, K. Smale, M. Weideman
F: M. Twomey, K. Batchelor, R. Rose
R: N. Mann (c.), A. Gooch, R. Richards
Reserves: J. Hickey, R. Kupsch
Coach: P. Kyne

# 1956

| | | P | W | L | D | For | Agst | % | Pts |
|---|---|---|---|---|---|---|---|---|---|
| 1 | Melbourne (1) | 18 | 16 | 2 | | 1429 | 979 | 146.0 | 64 |
| 2 | Collingwood (2) | 18 | 13 | 5 | | 1420 | 1128 | 125.9 | 52 |
| 3 | Geelong (4) | 18 | 13 | 5 | | 1427 | 1171 | 121.9 | 52 |
| 4 | Footscray (3) | 18 | 11 | 7 | | 1323 | 1159 | 114.2 | 44 |
| 5 | Carlton | 18 | 10 | 7 | 1 | 1304 | 1147 | 113.7 | 42 |
| 6 | Essendon | 18 | 10 | 8 | | 1308 | 1365 | 95.8 | 40 |
| 7 | Hawthorn | 18 | 7 | 10 | 1 | 1193 | 1342 | 88.9 | 30 |
| 8 | Fitzroy | 18 | 7 | 11 | | 1190 | 1332 | 89.3 | 28 |
| 9 | South Melb | 18 | 6 | 11 | 1 | 1210 | 1374 | 88.1 | 26 |
| 10 | Richmond | 18 | 6 | 12 | | 1277 | 1471 | 86.8 | 24 |
| 11 | St Kilda | 18 | 4 | 13 | 1 | 1170 | 1330 | 88.0 | 18 |
| 12 | North Melb | 18 | 3 | 15 | | 1038 | 1491 | 69.6 | 12 |

*(18 H & A matches)*

**First Semi Final**
Footscray 5.13 (43) d. Geelong 6.5 (41)
**Second Semi Final**
Melbourne 11.14 (80) d. Collingwood 8.16 (64)
**Preliminary Final**
Collingwood 15.6 (96) d. Footscray 7.15 (57)

**Grand Final**
Melbourne 2.4 6.11 10.16 17.19 (121) d
Collingwood 3.3 4.3 5.6 6.12 (48)
Goals — Melbourne: Spencer 5, Webb 5,
R. Johnson 3, Barassi 3, Ridley. Collingwood:
Smale, Serong, Turner, W. Twomey, Jones, Greve.
Best — Melbourne: Spencer, Barassi, Adams, Den.
Cordner, Beckwith, Melville. Collingwood: Tuck,
Serong, Jones, Mann, Weideman, Waller.
Umpire: Nash. Match played at MCG.
Attendance: 115,802
*A remarkable crowd of 115,802 crammed into the*
*MCG for another Melbourne-Collingwood Grand*
*Final, only to witness a disappointing one-sided*
*game in which the Demons belted the Pies by 73*
*points. They seemed invincible.*
MELBOURNE
B: J. Beckwith, P. Marquis, Trevor Johnson
HB: D. Williams, N. McMahen (c.), K. Carroll
C: F. Adams, K. Melville, B. Dixon
HF: J. Sandral, C. Laidlaw, L. Mithen
F: R. Johnson, A. Webb, I. Ridley
R: D. Cordner, R. Barassi, S. Spencer
Reserves: T. Gleeson, R. Lane
Coach: N. Smith
COLLINGWOOD
B: L. Sharp, H. Sullivan, N. Waller
HB: P. Lucas, F. Tuck, R. Kingston
C: K. Hedt, W. Twomey, T. Merrett
HF: K. Turner, M. Weideman, W. Serong
F: N. Mann (c.), K. Smale, R. Greve
R: R. Gabelich, L. Rymer, W. Jones
Reserves: J. Hamilton, R. Kupsch
Coach: P. Kyne

# 1957

| | | P | W | L | D | For | Agst | % | Pts |
|---|---|---|---|---|---|---|---|---|---|
| 1 | Melbourne (1) | 18 | 12 | 5 | 1 | 1567 | 1129 | 138.8 | 50 |
| 2 | Essendon (2) | 18 | 11 | 7 | | 1447 | 1223 | 118.3 | 44 |
| 3 | Hawthorn (3) | 18 | 11 | 7 | | 1321 | 1132 | 116.7 | 44 |
| 4 | Carlton (4) | 18 | 11 | 7 | | 1341 | 1348 | 99.5 | 44 |
| 5 | Collingwood | 18 | 9 | 8 | 1 | 1390 | 1366 | 101.8 | 38 |
| 6 | Footscray | 18 | 9 | 8 | 1 | 1263 | 1275 | 99.1 | 38 |
| 7 | Richmond | 18 | 9 | 9 | | 1506 | 1604 | 93.9 | 36 |
| 8 | North Melb | 18 | 8 | 10 | | 1404 | 1477 | 95.1 | 32 |
| 9 | St Kilda | 18 | 8 | 10 | | 1318 | 1394 | 94.5 | 32 |
| 10 | South Melb | 18 | 7 | 11 | | 1349 | 1519 | 88.8 | 28 |
| 11 | Fitzroy | 18 | 6 | 12 | | 1355 | 1611 | 84.1 | 24 |
| 12 | Geelong | 18 | 5 | 12 | 1 | 1368 | 1551 | 88.2 | 22 |

*(18 H & A matches)*

**First Semi Final**
Hawthorn 10.11 (71) d. Carlton 6.12 (48)
**Second Semi Final**
Essendon 12.11 (83) d. Melbourne 8.19 (67)
**Preliminary Final**
Melbourne 22.12 (144) d. Hawthorn 11.10 (76)

**Grand Final**
Melbourne 6.2 9.9 12.11 17.14 (116) d
Essendon 2.3 4.4 7.8 7.13 (55)
Goals — Melbourne: Barassi 5, Ridley 4, Webb 3,
R. Johnson 2. Tunbridge 2, Case. Essendon:
Gallagher 3, Birt, Gill, Hebbard, Clarke.
Best — Melbourne: Barassi, R. Johnson, Fenton-
Smith, Lord, Williams, Ridley. Essendon: Clarke,
Shearman, Mitchell, Leek, Towner, Birt.
Umpire: Nash. Match played at MCG.
Attendance: 100,324
*The Melbourne machine rolled on, winning its third
flag in a row. This time the victim was different —
Essendon — but the margin was just as
comprehensive 61 points. Ron Barassi starred, but
he had many mates.*
MELBOURNE
B: J. Beckwith (c.), P. Marquis, R. Fenton-Smith
HB: D. Williams, J. Lord, K. Carroll
C: I. McLean, L. Mithen, B. Dixon
HF: G. Tunbridge, Trevor Johnson, G. Case
F: R. Barassi, A. Webb, I. Ridley
R: R. Johnson, C. Wilson, F. Adams
Reserves: I. Thorogood, P. Brenchley
Coach: N. Smith
ESSENDON
B: R. Suter, J. Knowles, M. Pascoe
HB: R. Shearman, J. Gamble, J. Towner
C: R. Burgess, J. Clarke, G. Sewell
HF: C. Hebbard, R. Fox, S. Booth
F: G. Leek, F. Gallagher, J. Birt
R: J. Gill, H. Mitchell, W. Hutchison (c.)
Reserves: L. Moloney, J. Heenan
Coach: R. Reynolds

# 1958

| | | P | W | L | D | For | Agst | % | Pts |
|---|---|---|---|---|---|---|---|---|---|
| 1 | Melbourne (2) | 18 | 15 | 3 | | 1608 | 1300 | 123.7 | 60 |
| 2 | Collingwood (1) | 18 | 12 | 6 | | 1528 | 1235 | 123.7 | 48 |
| 3 | Fitzroy (4) | 18 | 12 | 6 | | 1551 | 1283 | 120.9 | 48 |
| 4 | North Melb (3) | 18 | 11 | 7 | | 1228 | 1324 | 92.7 | 44 |
| 5 | Essendon | 18 | 10 | 8 | | 1519 | 1365 | 111.3 | 40 |
| 6 | Hawthorn | 18 | 9 | 9 | | 1419 | 1298 | 109.3 | 36 |
| 7 | Carlton | 18 | 8 | 10 | | 1158 | 1260 | 91.9 | 32 |
| 8 | St Kilda | 18 | 7 | 11 | | 1340 | 1454 | 92.2 | 28 |
| 9 | South Melb | 18 | 7 | 11 | | 1450 | 1634 | 88.7 | 28 |
| 10 | Richmond | 18 | 7 | 11 | | 1425 | 1611 | 88.5 | 28 |
| 11 | Footscray | 18 | 6 | 12 | | 1401 | 1440 | 97.3 | 24 |
| 12 | Geelong | 18 | 4 | 14 | | 1192 | 1615 | 73.8 | 16 |

*(18 H & A matches)*

**First Semi Final**
Nth. Melbourne 10.10 (70) d. Fitzroy 9.12 (66)
**Second Semi Final**
Melbourne 11.12 (78) d. Collingwood 4.9 (33)
**Preliminary Final**
Collingwood 14.12 (96) d. Nth. Melbourne 10.16 (76)

**Grand Final**
Collingwood 2.2 7.6 12.9 12.10 (82) d
Melbourne 5.1 7.4 7.6 9.10 (64)
Goals — Collingwood: Weideman 2, Brewer 2,
Beers 2, Bennett 2, Merrett 2, M. Twomey,
Fellowes. Melbourne: Barassi 2, Adams 2,
Brenchley, R. Johnson, McLean, Ridley, Crompton.
Best — Collingwood: Merrett, Harrison, Bennett,
Fellowes, Serong, Gabelich. Melbourne: Beckwith,
Williams, R. Johnson, Adams, McLean, Tunbridge.
Umpire: Nash. Match played at MCG.
Attendance: 97,956
*Melbourne finished three games clear on top of the
ladder in 1958 and walloped Collingwood by 45
points in the second semi. It seemed a formality
that it would equal the Pies' four-in-a-row record of
1927-30. But on a miserable, wet day, Magpie
strongmen such as Murray Weideman and 'Hooker'
Harrison made life uncomfortable for the Demons,
who went down by three goals in a boilover. The
League countered an attempt by* The Sun *to thwart*
The Football Record's *exclusive hold on player
numbers.* The Sun *had published the players' usual
numbers on the morning of the game.*
COLLINGWOOD
B: R. Reeves, H. Sullivan, R. Gabelich
HB: K. Rose, M. Delanty, P. Lucas
C: B. Gray, J. Henderson, K. Turner
HF: B. Beers, M. Weideman (c.), W. Serong
F: M. Twomey, I. Brewer, K. Bennett
R: G. Fellowes, B. Harrison, T. Merrett
Reserves: K. Smale, R. Greve
Coach: P. Kyne
MELBOURNE
B: J. Beckwith (c.), P. Marquis, C. Wilson
HB: K. Carroll, D. Williams, I. Thorogood
C: I. McLean, L. Mithen, B. Dixon
HF: G. Tunbridge, T. Johnson, P. Brenchley
F: R. Johnson, A. Webb, F. Adams
R: R. Fenton-Smith, R. Barassi, I. Ridley
Reserves: T. Gleeson, N. Crompton
Coach: N. Smith

# 1959

| | | P | W | L | D | For | Agst | % | Pts |
|---|---|---|---|---|---|---|---|---|---|
| 1 | Melbourne (1) | 18 | 13 | 4 | 1 | 1731 | 1213 | 142.7 | 54 |
| 2 | Carlton (3) | 18 | 13 | 5 | | 1534 | 1404 | 109.3 | 52 |
| 3 | Collingwood (4) | 18 | 12 | 6 | | 1477 | 1215 | 121.6 | 48 |
| 4 | Essendon (2) | 18 | 11 | 7 | | 1598 | 1422 | 112.4 | 44 |
| 5 | Fitzroy | 18 | 10 | 7 | 1 | 1533 | 1351 | 113.5 | 42 |
| 6 | North Melb | 18 | 10 | 8 | | 1331 | 1490 | 89.3 | 40 |
| 7 | Hawthorn | 18 | 9 | 9 | | 1592 | 1412 | 112.7 | 36 |
| 8 | St Kilda | 18 | 9 | 9 | | 1428 | 1515 | 94.3 | 36 |
| 9 | South Melb | 18 | 8 | 10 | | 1515 | 1465 | 103.4 | 32 |
| 10 | Geelong | 18 | 5 | 13 | | 1320 | 1681 | 78.5 | 20 |
| 11 | Richmond | 18 | 4 | 14 | | 1309 | 1771 | 73.9 | 16 |
| 12 | Footscray | 18 | 3 | 15 | | 1178 | 1607 | 73.3 | 12 |

*(18 H & A matches)*

**First Semi Final**
Essendon 14.16 (100) d. Collingwood 8.14 (62)
**Second Semi Final**
Melbourne 11.15 (81) d. Carlton 4.13 (37)
**Preliminary Final**
Essendon 8.9 (57) d. Carlton 7.8 (50)

**Grand Final**
Melbourne 1.4 8.5 11.10 17.13 (115) d
Essendon 3.5 7.8 10.10 11.12 (78)
Goals — Melbourne: Barassi 4, Rowarth 4, Adams 3, R. Johnson 3, H. Mann, Tunbridge, Ridley. Essendon: Sewell 4, Evans 2, Clarke 2, Shaw 2, Fraser.
Best — Melbourne: Barassi, McLean, R. Johnson, Dixon, Jones, Beckwith. Essendon: Shearman, Birt, Epis, Sewell, Shaw, Clarke.
Umpire: Barbour. Match played at MCG.
Attendance: 103,506
*Football's normal order was restored as the Demons again dominated the competition, beating Carlton by 44 points in the second semi and Essendon by 37 in 'The Big One'. This Melbourne team is now regarded as one of the best of all time.*
MELBOURNE
B: J. Beckwith (c.), "Tassie" Johnson, J. Lord
HB: G. Case, D. Jones, I. Thorogood
C: I. McLean, L. Mithen, B. Dixon
HF: G. Tunbridge, C. Laidlaw, H. Mann
F: R. Barassi, A. Rowarth, I. Ridley
R: B. Johnson, R. Fenton-Smith, F. Adams
Reserves: D. Williams, P. Brenchley
Coach: N. Smith
ESSENDON
B: R. Shearman, J. Towner, B. Sampson
HB: A. Epis, I. Shelton, C. Hebbard
C: A. Murdoch, R. Burgess, B. Capuano
HF: K. Peucker, K. Fraser, G. Sewell
F: D. Shaw, R. Evans, J. Birt
R: G. Leek, H. Mitchell, J. Clarke (c.)
Reserves: B. Mackie, G. Leydin
Coach: R. Reynolds

# 1960

| | | P | W | L | D | For | Agst | % | Pts |
|---|---|---|---|---|---|---|---|---|---|
| 1 | Melbourne (1) | 18 | 14 | 4 | | 1455 | 1017 | 143.1 | 56 |
| 2 | Fitzroy (3) | 18 | 14 | 4 | | 1332 | 1184 | 112.5 | 56 |
| 3 | Essendon (4) | 18 | 13 | 5 | | 1506 | 1204 | 125.1 | 52 |
| 4 | Collingwood (2) | 18 | 11 | 7 | | 1314 | 1150 | 114.3 | 44 |
| 5 | Hawthorn | 18 | 11 | 7 | | 1251 | 1192 | 104.9 | 44 |
| 6 | St Kilda | 18 | 9 | 9 | | 1159 | 1140 | 101.7 | 36 |
| 7 | Carlton | 18 | 8 | 9 | 1 | 1300 | 1313 | 99.0 | 34 |
| 8 | South Melb | 18 | 7 | 11 | | 1304 | 1413 | 92.3 | 28 |
| 9 | Geelong | 18 | 6 | 11 | 1 | 1311 | 1373 | 95.5 | 26 |
| 10 | Footscray | 18 | 6 | 12 | | 1065 | 1178 | 90.4 | 24 |
| 11 | North Melb | 18 | 5 | 13 | | 1183 | 1474 | 80.3 | 20 |
| 12 | Richmond | 18 | 2 | 14 | 2 | 1086 | 1628 | 66.7 | 12 |

*(18 H & A matches)*

**First Semi Final**
Collingwood 9.12 (66) d. Essendon 7.15 (57)
**Second Semi Final**
Melbourne 14.18 (102) d. Fitzroy 4.16 (40)
**Preliminary Final**
Collingwood 9.11 (65) d. Fitzroy 8.12 (60)

**Grand Final**
Melbourne 4.3 5.7 7.11 8.14 (62) d
Collingwood 0.0 1.0 2.0 2.2 (14)
Goals — Melbourne: R. Johnson 2, Adams 2, H. Mann 2, Tunbridge, Rowarth. Collingwood: Henderson, Gabelich.
Best — Melbourne: Mithen, Lord, L. Mann, R. Johnson, Tunbridge, Dixon. Collingwood: Burns, K. Rose, M. Twomey, Thripp, Reeves.
Umpire: Irving. Match played at MCG.
Attendance: 97,457
*Melbourne's status as one of the great teams was further enhanced in 1960 with its seventh successive Grand Final appearance — and its fifth flag in that time. Melbourne won by 48 points in the wet and the hapless Magpies were the victims again, this time managing a paltry 2.2 (14), the lowest Grand Final score since 1927.*
MELBOURNE
B: J. Beckwith, "Tassie" Johnson, Trevor Johnson
HB: G. Case, J. Lord, I. Thorogood
C: B. Dixon, L. Mithen, B. Kenneally
HF: G. Tunbridge, C. Laidlaw, H. Mann
F: R. Johnson, A. Rowarth, F. Adams
R: L. Mann, R. Barassi (c.), I. Ridley
Reserves: B. Leahy, R. Nilsson
Coach: N. Smith
COLLINGWOOD
B: R. Reeves, P. Rosenbrock, M. Twomey
HB: K. Rose, W. Thripp, M. Delanty
C: B. Gray, J. Henderson, E. Hutchesson
HF: K. Turner, M. Weideman (c.), B. Beers
F: G. Fellowes, R. Willett, K. Burns
R: R. Gabelich, B. Harrison, R. O'Dwyer
Reserves: I. Brewer, A. Chapman
Coach: P. Kyne

# 1961

| | | P | W | L | D | For | Agst | % | Pts |
|---|---|---|---|---|---|---|---|---|---|
| 1 | Hawthorn (1) | 18 | 14 | 4 | | 1467 | 1173 | 125.1 | 56 |
| 2 | Melbourne (3) | 18 | 12 | 5 | 1 | 1510 | 1151 | 131.2 | 50 |
| 3 | St Kilda (4) | 18 | 11 | 7 | | 1373 | 1173 | 117.1 | 44 |
| 4 | Footscray (2) | 18 | 11 | 7 | | 1334 | 1216 | 109.7 | 44 |
| 5 | Fitzroy | 18 | 10 | 7 | 1 | 1469 | 1258 | 116.8 | 42 |
| 6 | Geelong | 18 | 10 | 7 | 1 | 1367 | 1362 | 100.4 | 42 |
| 7 | Essendon | 18 | 9 | 8 | 1 | 1462 | 1335 | 109.5 | 38 |
| 8 | Carlton | 18 | 9 | 9 | | 1279 | 1325 | 96.5 | 36 |
| 9 | Collingwood | 18 | 5 | 12 | 1 | 1166 | 1375 | 84.8 | 22 |
| 10 | Richmond | 18 | 5 | 13 | | 1126 | 1428 | 78.9 | 20 |
| 11 | South Melb | 18 | 5 | 13 | | 1187 | 1644 | 72.2 | 20 |
| 12 | North Melb | 18 | 4 | 13 | 1 | 1133 | 1433 | 79.1 | 18 |

*(18 H & A matches)*

**First Semi Final**
Footscray 9.15 (69) d. St Kilda 8.12 (60)
**Second Semi Final**
Hawthorn 12.8 (80) d. Melbourne 11.7 (73)
**Preliminary Final**
Footscray 13.7 (85) d. Melbourne 8.10 (58)

**Grand Final**
Hawthorn 2.4 3.9 9.15 13.16 (94) d
Footscray 4.2 5.5 6.6 7.9 (51)
Goals — Hawthorn: Browne 3, Mort 2, Law 2,
Nalder, Peck, Hill, Cunningham, Arthur, Edwards.
Footscray: Whitten 3, Quarrell 2, McKellar, Hobbs.
Best — Hawthorn: Edwards, Law, Winneke, Fisher,
Mort, Hill. Footscray: Schultz, Evans, Whitten,
Hoiles, Quarrell, Ware.
Umpire: Schwab. Match played at MCG.
Attendance: 107,935
*Hawthorn became the second of the three teams*
*admitted in 1925 to snare a flag when it easily ac-*
*counted for Footscray. The Doggies, with Ted*
*Whitten as captain-coach, led at half-time, but*
*Kennedy's Commandos, captained by Graham*
*Arthur, stormed home with a 10 goal to two*
*second half. Hawks by 43 points.*
HAWTHORN
B: R. Poole, L. Kaine, G. Cooper
HB: S. Hay, J. McArthur, C. McPherson
C: C. Youren, B. Edwards, J. Fisher
HF: I. Mort, G. Young, M. Browne
F: M. Hill, J. Peck, J. Cunningham
R: J. Winneke, G. Arthur (c.), I. Law
Reserves: P. Hay, R. Nalder
Coach: J. Kennedy
FOOTSCRAY
B: C. Evans, B. Lee, R. Ware
HB: J. Jillard, J. Hoiles, B. Ion
C: A. Gardiner, Robt. Spargo, I. Bryant
HF: J. Quarrell, G. Ion, B. McKellar
F: E. Whitten (c.), J. Slattery, K. Beamish
R: J. Schultz, C. McDonald, M. Hobbs
Reserves: K. Duff, C. Stewart
Coach: E. Whitten

# 1962

| | | P | W | L | D | For | Agst | % | Pts |
|---|---|---|---|---|---|---|---|---|---|
| 1 | Essendon (1) | 18 | 16 | 2 | | 1574 | 1207 | 130.4 | 64 |
| 2 | Geelong (3) | 18 | 14 | 4 | | 1690 | 1213 | 139.3 | 56 |
| 3 | Melbourne (4) | 18 | 14 | 4 | | 1374 | 1092 | 125.8 | 56 |
| 4 | Carlton (2) | 18 | 13 | 5 | | 1361 | 1205 | 112.9 | 52 |
| 5 | Footscray | 18 | 11 | 7 | | 1390 | 1281 | 108.5 | 44 |
| 6 | St Kilda | 18 | 9 | 9 | | 1379 | 1267 | 108.8 | 36 |
| 7 | Collingwood | 18 | 9 | 9 | | 1365 | 1386 | 98.5 | 36 |
| 8 | Richmond | 18 | 5 | 13 | | 1308 | 1446 | 90.5 | 20 |
| 9 | Hawthorn | 18 | 5 | 13 | | 1307 | 1510 | 86.6 | 20 |
| 10 | Fitzroy | 18 | 5 | 13 | | 1222 | 1529 | 79.9 | 20 |
| 11 | North Melb | 18 | 4 | 14 | | 1152 | 1575 | 73.1 | 16 |
| 12 | South Melb | 18 | 3 | 15 | | 1193 | 1604 | 74.4 | 12 |

*(18 H & A matches)*

**First Semi Final**
Carlton 11.12 (78) d. Melbourne 11.10 (76)
**Second Semi Final**
Essendon 14.21 (105) d. Geelong 7.17 (59)
**Preliminary Final**
Carlton 12.13 (85) drew with Geelong 13.7 (85)
**Replay**
Carlton 10.18 (78) d Geelong 10.13 (73)

**Grand Final**
Essendon 6.5 7.7 10.10 13.12 (90) d
Carlton 1.1 5.6 7.8 8.10 (58)
Goals — Essendon: Birt 4, Clarke 2, Mitchell 2, C.
Payne 2, Leek, Johnston, Timms. Carlton: Williams
3, J. Nicholls 2, Cross, Greenwood, Donaldson.
Best — Essendon: Clarke, Mitchell, Birt, Leek,
Epis, Beissel. Carlton: Silvagni, Williams, James,
Cox, Donaldson, Sankey.
Umpire: Irving. Match played at MCG.
Attendance: 98,385
*Essendon coasted to a 32-point victory in a Grand*
*Final of contrasting preparations. The Bombers had*
*played only one game in a month, while Carlton*
*had to play three, courtesy of its drawn preliminary*
*final with Geelong — the replay of which was*
*famous for the last-minute free kick paid against*
*Cats' full-forward Doug Wade.*
ESSENDON
B: D. Shaw, P. Doran, D. McKenzie
HB: A. Epis, I. Shelton, B. Davis
C: R. Blew, G. Beissel, B. Capuano
HF: G. Johnston, K. Fraser, J. Somerville
F: K. Timms, C. Payne, J. Birt
R: G. Leek, H. Mitchell, J. Clarke (c.)
Reserves: B. Sampson, G. Gosper
Coach: J. Coleman
CARLTON
B: J. Benetti, P. Barry, M. Sankey
HB: G. Anderson, W. Lofts, R. Crowe
C: I. Collins, B. Cox, M. Kick
HF: G. Donaldson (c.), J. James, J. Gill
F: K. Greenwood, T. Carroll, P. Falconer
R: J. Nicholls, S. Silvagni, B. Williams
Reserves: V. Varlamos, M. Cross
Coach: K. Hands

# 1963

| | | P | W | L | D | For | Agst | % | Pts |
|---|---|---|---|---|---|---|---|---|---|
| 1 | Hawthorn (2) | 18 | 13 | 4 | 1 | 1485 | 1137 | 130.6 | 54 |
| 2 | Geelong (1) | 18 | 13 | 4 | 1 | 1354 | 1056 | 128.2 | 54 |
| 3 | Melbourne (3) | 18 | 13 | 5 | | 1680 | 1136 | 147.9 | 52 |
| 4 | St Kilda (4) | 18 | 13 | 5 | | 1501 | 1071 | 140.1 | 52 |
| 5 | Essendon | 18 | 13 | 5 | | 1470 | 1069 | 137.5 | 52 |
| 6 | Carlton | 18 | 10 | 8 | | 1275 | 1234 | 103.3 | 40 |
| 7 | North Melb | 18 | 8 | 10 | | 1059 | 1244 | 85.1 | 32 |
| 8 | Collingwood | 18 | 7 | 11 | | 1365 | 1427 | 95.7 | 28 |
| 9 | Footscray | 18 | 7 | 11 | | 1126 | 1283 | 87.8 | 28 |
| 10 | Richmond | 18 | 5 | 13 | | 1279 | 1687 | 75.8 | 20 |
| 11 | South Melb | 18 | 4 | 14 | | 1202 | 1722 | 69.8 | 16 |
| 12 | Fitzroy | 18 | 1 | 17 | | 986 | 1716 | 57.5 | 4 |

*(18 H & A matches)*

**First Semi Final**
Melbourne 9.17 (71) d. St Kilda 8.16 (64)
**Second Semi Final**
Geelong 14.17 (101) d. Hawthorn 11.16 (82)
**Preliminary Final**
Hawthorn 11.11 (77) d. Melbourne 10.8 (68)
**Grand Final**
Geelong 3.3 7.10 9.13 15.19 (109) d
Hawthorn 3.6 5.6 8.9 8.12 (60)
Goals — Geelong: Wooller 3, Hynes 3, Yeates 2,
W. Goggin 2, Rice 2, A. Lord 2, Wade. Hawthorn:
Peck 3, Woodley, Law, Coverdale, Mort, Fisher.
Best — Geelong: Farmer, Devine, Scott, W. Goggin,
Walker, Wooller. Hawthorn: Arthur, Nalder,
Coverdale, Mort, Young, Youren.
Umpire: Crouch. Match played at MCG.
Attendance: 101,209
*The great 'Polly' Farmer directed Geelong's charge
to the flag with a magnificent season and a superb
performance on Grand Final day to see the Cats
home by 49 points. The highlight for many was TV
personality Happy Hammond running out with the
Geelong team. Bob Davis, as coach, remains
Geelong's only living premiership coach.*
GEELONG
B: I. Scott, R. West, J. Watts
HB: J. Devine, P. Walker, S. Lord
C: H. Routley, A. Lord, J. Brown
HF: G. Hynes, F. Wooller (c.), J. Sharrock
F: J. Yeates, D. Wade, C. Rice
R: G. Farmer, P. Vinar, W. Goggin
Reserves: K. Goodland, A. Polinelli
Coach: R. Davis
HAWTHORN
B: D. Parkin, P. Hay, G. Cooper
HB: S. Hay, G. Young, C. McPherson
C: J. Fisher, R. Nalder, C. Youren
HF: G. Arthur (c.), K. Coverdale, I. Mort
F: R. Olsson, J. Peck, D. Albiston
R: K. Beck, A. Woodley, I. Law
Reserves: P. Lyon, K. Connell
Coach: J. Kennedy

# 1964

| | | P | W | L | D | For | Agst | % | Pts |
|---|---|---|---|---|---|---|---|---|---|
| 1 | Melbourne (1) | 18 | 14 | 4 | | 1532 | 1109 | 138.1 | 56 |
| 2 | Collingwood (2) | 18 | 13 | 4 | 1 | 1470 | 1104 | 133.2 | 54 |
| 3 | Essendon (4) | 18 | 13 | 4 | 1 | 1499 | 1151 | 130.2 | 54 |
| 4 | Geelong (3) | 18 | 13 | 4 | 1 | 1328 | 1042 | 127.4 | 54 |
| 5 | Hawthorn | 18 | 13 | 5 | | 1382 | 1142 | 121.0 | 52 |
| 6 | St Kilda | 18 | 10 | 8 | | 1408 | 1189 | 118.4 | 40 |
| 7 | Footscray | 18 | 9 | 9 | | 1146 | 1301 | 88.1 | 36 |
| 8 | North Melb | 18 | 8 | 10 | | 1231 | 1411 | 87.2 | 32 |
| 9 | Richmond | 18 | 6 | 12 | | 1143 | 1346 | 84.9 | 24 |
| 10 | Carlton | 18 | 5 | 12 | 1 | 1190 | 1318 | 90.3 | 22 |
| 11 | South Melb | 18 | 2 | 16 | | 1125 | 1654 | 68.0 | 8 |
| 12 | Fitzroy | 18 | 0 | 18 | | 1019 | 1706 | 59.7 | 0 |

*(18 H & A matches)*

**First Semi Final**
Geelong 12.12 (84) d. Essendon 10.5 (65)
**Second Semi Final**
Melbourne 19.20 (134) d. Collingwood 6.9 (45)
**Preliminary Final**
Collingwood 7.6 (48) d. Geelong 5.14 (44)
**Grand Final**
Melbourne 2.6 5.7 7.10 8.16 (64) d
Collingwood 2.5 5.9 5.11 8.12 (60)
Goals — Melbourne: Townsend 3, Lord 2, H.
Mann, Bourke, Crompton. Collingwood: Waters 2,
Gabelich 2, Bone, Steer, Dalton, Tuddenham.
Best — Melbourne: Adams, Dixon, Tas. Johnson,
Wise, H. Mann, Williams. Collingwood: Hill, Steer,
Bone, Potter, Henderson, Dalton.
Umpire: Brophy. Match played at MCG.
Attendance: 102,469
*Another Melbourne-Collingwood Grand Final and
another Demons' victory — but only just. Giant
Magpie Ray Gabelich put his team ahead late in
the last quarter after a now-legendary 70-metre
run. But Melbourne back pocket player Neil
Crompton followed his man up-field, took the ball
when it spilled from a pack and slotted through his
only goal of the season.*
MELBOURNE
B: N. Crompton, B. Massey, "Tassie" Johnson
HB: A. Anderson, B. Roet, F. Davis
C: B. Dixon, D. Williams, F. Adams
HF: B. Kenneally, G. Jacobs, B. Vagg
F: J. Lord, B. Bourke, J. Townsend
R: G. Wise, R. Barassi (c.), H. Mann
Reserves: P. McLean, K. Emselle
Coach: N. Smith
COLLINGWOOD
B: R. Reeves, E. Potter, T. Steer
HB: L. Hill, J. Mahon, D. Wright
C: R. Watt, J. Henderson, A. Chapman
HF: D. Tuddenham, K. McLean, D. Norman
F: T. Waters, I. Graham, D. Dalton
R: R. Gabelich (c.), K. Rose, M. Bone
Reserves: M. Urquhart, K. Turner
Coach: R. Rose

# 1965

| | | P | W | L | D | For | Agst | % | Pts |
|---|---|---|---|---|---|---|---|---|---|
| 1 | St Kilda (2) | 18 | 14 | 4 | | 1573 | 1154 | 136.3 | 56 |
| 2 | Collingwood (3) | 18 | 13 | 5 | | 1473 | 1131 | 130.2 | 52 |
| 3 | Geelong (4) | 18 | 13 | 5 | | 1319 | 1088 | 121.2 | 52 |
| 4 | Essendon (1) | 18 | 12 | 6 | | 1465 | 1102 | 132.9 | 48 |
| 5 | Richmond | 18 | 10 | 8 | | 1561 | 1249 | 125.0 | 40 |
| 6 | Carlton | 18 | 10 | 8 | | 1317 | 1190 | 110.7 | 40 |
| 7 | Melbourne | 18 | 10 | 8 | | 1265 | 1315 | 96.2 | 40 |
| 8 | South Melb | 18 | 9 | 9 | | 1386 | 1550 | 89.4 | 36 |
| 9 | North Melb | 18 | 5 | 13 | | 1143 | 1415 | 80.8 | 20 |
| 10 | Footscray | 18 | 4 | 14 | | 1010 | 1310 | 77.1 | 16 |
| 11 | Fitzroy | 18 | 4 | 14 | | 1114 | 1580 | 70.5 | 16 |
| 12 | Hawthorn | 18 | 4 | 14 | | 1200 | 1742 | 68.9 | 16 |

*(18 H & A matches)*

**First Semi Final**
Essendon 14.19 (103) d. Geelong 7.9 (51)
**Second Semi Final**
St Kilda 13.24 (102) d. Collingwood 14.17 (101)
**Preliminary Final**
Essendon 14.13 (97) d. Collingwood 6.6 (42)

**Grand Final**
Essendon 2.7 5.10 10.18 14.21 (105) d
St Kilda 1.6 4.8 5.11 9.16 (70)
Goals — Essendon: Fordham 7, Sampson 2,
Gosper 2, Fraser, Birt, Mitchell. St Kilda: Howell 3,
Rowland 2, Baldock 2, Smith, K. Roberts.
Best — Essendon: Sampson, Fordham, Fraser,
Gosper, Davis, Birt. St Kilda: Stewart, Baldock,
Cooper, Kennedy, Read, Neale.
Umpire: Crouch. Match played at MCG.
Attendance: 104,846
*Essendon won the 1965 flag the hard way — from
fourth place. The Bombers beat Geelong in the first
semi, Collingwood in the preliminary (the game of
'the Somerville incident') and then St Kilda by 35
points in the Grand Final.*
ESSENDON
B: D. Gerlach, G. Brown, C. Payne
HB: B. Davis, I. Shelton, G. Pryor
C: A. Epis, J. Clarke, R. Blew
HF: G. Johnston, K. Fraser (c.), G. Gosper
F: B. Sampson, E. Fordham, D. Shaw
R: D. McKenzie, H. Mitchell, J. Birt
Reserves: B. Waite, K. Egan
Coach: J. Coleman
ST. KILDA
B: R. Head, R. Murray, K. Neale
HB: B. Sierakowski, I. Synman, D. Griffiths
C: J. Read, I. Stewart, B. McMaster-Smith
HF: I. Cooper, D. Baldock (c.), R. Cross
F: A. Morrow, V. Howell, R. Smith
R: C. Ditterich, D. Kennedy, I. Rowland
Reserves: R. Morton, K. Roberts
Coach: A. Jeans

# 1966

| | | P | W | L | D | For | Agst | % | Pts |
|---|---|---|---|---|---|---|---|---|---|
| 1 | Collingwood (2) | 18 | 15 | 3 | | 1687 | 1073 | 157.2 | 60 |
| 2 | St Kilda (1) | 18 | 14 | 4 | | 1641 | 1149 | 142.8 | 56 |
| 3 | Geelong (4) | 18 | 14 | 4 | | 1599 | 1162 | 137.6 | 56 |
| 4 | Essendon (3) | 18 | 14 | 4 | | 1457 | 1204 | 121.0 | 56 |
| 5 | Richmond | 18 | 13 | 4 | 1 | 1626 | 1320 | 123.2 | 54 |
| 6 | Carlton | 18 | 10 | 8 | | 1233 | 1143 | 107.9 | 40 |
| 7 | North Melb | 18 | 7 | 10 | 1 | 1294 | 1381 | 93.7 | 30 |
| 8 | South Melb | 18 | 7 | 11 | | 1486 | 1505 | 98.7 | 28 |
| 9 | Hawthorn | 18 | 5 | 13 | | 1224 | 1650 | 74.2 | 20 |
| 10 | Footscray | 18 | 4 | 14 | | 1004 | 1458 | 68.9 | 16 |
| 11 | Melbourne | 18 | 3 | 15 | | 1235 | 1580 | 78.2 | 12 |
| 12 | Fitzroy | 18 | 1 | 17 | | 1004 | 1865 | 53.8 | 4 |

*(18 H & A matches)*

**First Semi Final**
Essendon 15.6 (96) d. Geelong 12.14 (86)
**Second Semi Final**
Collingwood 15.9 (99) d. St Kilda 13.11 (89)
**Preliminary Final**
St Kilda 15.4 (94) d. Essendon 7.10 (52)

**Grand Final**
St Kilda 2.5 5.6 8.9 10.14 (74) d
Collingwood 2.1 5.7 7.11 10.13 (73)
Goals — St Kilda: Neale 5, Baldock 2, Griffiths,
Cooper, Moran. Collingwood: Tuddenham 3,
Gabelich 2, W. Richardson 2, Wallis, Pitt, Graham
Best — St Kilda: Cooper, Griffiths, Stewart, Breen,
Sierakowski, Neale. Collingwood: W. Richardson,
Waters, Thompson, Tuddenham, Gabelich, Pitt.
Umpire: Crouch. Match played at MCG.
Attendance: 101,655.
*The end of the longest premiership drought in VFL
history as St Kilda, led by 'Doc' Baldock and
coached by Allan Jeans, scraped home by a single
point against the luckless Magpies — this time on
the back of a wobbly punt kick by Barry Breen and
a match-saving mark by Bob Murray. One of the
most famous of all Grand Finals, thanks largely to
the super-charged commentary provided by Mike
Williamson, 'Butch' Gale and Teddy Whitten.*
ST. KILDA
B: R. Head, R. Murray, B. Sierakowski
HB: V. Howell, I. Synman, J. Bingley
C: J. Moran, I.Stewart, J. Read
HF: I. Cooper, D. Baldock (c.), B. Breen
F: A. Morrow, K. Neale, A. Davis
R: B. Mynott, D. Griffiths, R. Smith
Reserves: T. Payze, K. Billing
Coach: A. Jeans
COLLINGWOOD
B: I. Montgomery, P. Boyne, T. Waters
HB: L. Hill, E. Potter, L. Adamson
C: P. Patterson, C. Tully, E. Hutchesson
HF: D. Tuddenham (c.), D. Searl, M. Pitt
F: R. Gabelich, I. Graham, G. Wallis
R: L. Thompson, K. Rose, W. Richardson
Reserves: T. Steer, J. Henderson
Coach: R. Rose

# 1967

| | | P | W | L | D | For | Agst | % | Pts |
|---|---|---|---|---|---|---|---|---|---|
| 1 | Richmond (1) | 18 | 15 | 3 | | 1869 | 1281 | 145.9 | 60 |
| 2 | Carlton (3) | 18 | 14 | 3 | 1 | 1425 | 1133 | 125.8 | 58 |
| 3 | Geelong (2) | 18 | 13 | 5 | | 1625 | 1323 | 122.8 | 52 |
| 4 | Collingwood (4) | 18 | 12 | 6 | | 1629 | 1232 | 132.2 | 48 |
| 5 | St Kilda | 18 | 11 | 7 | | 1630 | 1328 | 122.7 | 44 |
| 6 | Essendon | 18 | 8 | 9 | 1 | 1406 | 1327 | 106.0 | 34 |
| 7 | Melbourne | 18 | 8 | 10 | | 1258 | 1417 | 88.8 | 32 |
| 8 | North Melb | 18 | 7 | 10 | 1 | 1234 | 1310 | 94.2 | 30 |
| 9 | South Melb | 18 | 5 | 12 | 1 | 1446 | 1763 | 82.0 | 22 |
| 10 | Hawthorn | 18 | 5 | 13 | | 1241 | 1766 | 70.3 | 20 |
| 11 | Fitzroy | 18 | 4 | 14 | | 1193 | 1655 | 72.1 | 16 |
| 12 | Footscray | 18 | 4 | 14 | | 1060 | 1481 | 71.6 | 16 |

*(18 H & A matches)*

**First Semi Final**
Geelong 16.12 (108) d. Collingwood 11.12 (78)
**Second Semi Final**
Richmond 20.21 (141) d. Carlton 14.17 (101)
**Preliminary Final**
Geelong 17.6 (108) d. Carlton 11.13 (79)

**Grand Final**
Richmond 4.3 9.10 12.15 16.18 (114) d
Geelong 3.3 7.6 13.7 15.15 (105)
Goals — Richmond: Ronaldson 3, Hart 3, Brown 3,
Bartlett 3, Barrot, A. Richardson, B. Richardson,
Guinane. Geelong: Sharrock 4, Wade 4, Goggin 3,
Andrews, Eales, Ryan, Hynes.
Best — Richmond: Barrot, Hart, Brown, A.
Richardson, Dean, Bartlett. Geelong: Goggin,
Sharrock, Farmer, West, Polinelli, Newland.
Umpire: Sheales. Match played at MCG.
Attendance: 109,396
*A fast, brilliant game provided a memorable end to
the season. Highlighted by memorable marks from
Royce Hart and Ken Newland, it was a high
standard game from start to finish. The Tigers
grabbed a nine-point lead late in the game and
held on to win their first flag in 24 years.*
RICHMOND
B: Roger Dean, F. Swift (c.), A. Jewell
HB: G. Burgin, M. Perry, G. Strang
C: R. Clay, W. Barrot, F. Bourke
HF: J. Northey, P. Guinane, B. Richardson
F: J. Ronaldson, R. Hart, W. Brown
R: M. Patterson, A. Richardson, K. Bartlett
Reserves: M. Green, J. Perry
Coach: T. Hafey
GEELONG
B: G. Ainsworth, R. West, G. Rosenow
HB: T. Farman, P. Walker, D. Marshall
C: K. Newland, W. Closter, A. Polinelli
HF: J. Sharrock, G. Andrews, G. Eales
F: C. Mitchell, D. Wade, G. Hynes
R: G. Farmer (c.), W. Ryan, W. Goggin
Reserves: R.Graham, J. Scarlett
Coach: P. Pianto

# 1968

| | | P | W | L | D | For | Agst | % | Pts |
|---|---|---|---|---|---|---|---|---|---|
| 1 | Essendon (2) | 20 | 16 | 3 | 1 | 1860 | 1428 | 130.3 | 66 |
| 2 | Carlton (1) | 20 | 15 | 5 | | 1751 | 1343 | 130.4 | 60 |
| 3 | Geelong (3) | 20 | 15 | 5 | | 1528 | 1431 | 106.8 | 60 |
| 4 | St Kilda (4) | 20 | 14 | 5 | 1 | 1718 | 1263 | 136.0 | 58 |
| 5 | Richmond | 20 | 14 | 6 | | 1889 | 1536 | 123.0 | 56 |
| 6 | Hawthorn | 20 | 9 | 10 | 1 | 1934 | 1869 | 103.5 | 38 |
| 7 | Collingwood | 20 | 9 | 11 | | 1623 | 1717 | 94.5 | 36 |
| 8 | Melbourne | 20 | 8 | 12 | | 1434 | 1709 | 83.9 | 32 |
| 9 | South Melb | 20 | 6 | 13 | 1 | 1639 | 1954 | 83.9 | 26 |
| 10 | Footscray | 20 | 5 | 15 | | 1413 | 1710 | 82.6 | 20 |
| 11 | Fitzroy | 20 | 4 | 16 | | 1643 | 2035 | 80.7 | 16 |
| 12 | North Melb | 20 | 3 | 17 | | 1266 | 1703 | 74.3 | 12 |

*(20 H & A matches)*

**First Semi Final**
Geelong 19.13 (127) d. St Kilda 11.17 (83)
**Second Semi Final**
Carlton 13.17 (95) d. Essendon 8.11 (59)
**Preliminary Final**
Essendon 11.25 (91) d. Geelong 9.13 (67)

**Grand Final**
Carlton 2.2 6.8 7.9 7.14 (56) d
Essendon 2.1 5.1 6.4 8.5 (53)
Goals — Carlton: B. Kekovich 4, Crane, Crosswell,
Quirk. Essendon: Blethyn 4, Close, B. Lake,
Noonan, Sproule.
Best — Carlton: Nicholls, Robertson, Crane,
Jesaulkeno, Silvagni, Gallagher. Essendon:
Gerlach, Close, Epis, Williams, Gosper, Pryor.
Umpire: Crouch. Match played at MCG.
Attendance: 116,828
*Ron Barassi's first premiership as coach, though
he was technically a non-playing captain-coach (a
not inappropriate term as well for club president
George Harris). Carlton, flagless since 1947,
kicked a goal less than Essendon, but still
managed to win the game by three points, its
profligacy in front of goal (7.14), nearly proving
costly.*
CARLTON
B: I. Collins, W. Lofts, R. Walls
HB: B. Gill, J. Goold, K. Hall
C: I. Robertson, B. Crosswell, G. Crane
HF: A. Jesaulkeno, W.Bennett, B. Quirk
F: P. Jones, B. Kekovich, D. Munari
R: J. Nicholls (c.), S. Silvagni, A. Gallagher
Reserves: P. McLean, N. Chandler
Coach: R. Barassi
ESSENDON
B: D. Gerlach, G. Pryor, N. Evans
HB: A. Epis, J. Williams, B. Davis
C: K. Fletcher, J. Ellis, R. Blew
HF: R. Close, A. Noonan, D. Shaw
F: E. Fordham, G. Blethyn, P. Sproule
R: D. McKenzie (c.), C. Payne, G. Gosper
Reserves: B. Lake, D. Cross
Coach: J. Clarke

# 1969

| | | P | W | L | D | For | Agst | % | Pts |
|---|---|---|---|---|---|---|---|---|---|
| 1 | Collingwood (3) | 20 | 15 | 5 | | 2129 | 1651 | 129.0 | 60 |
| 2 | Carlton (2) | 20 | 15 | 5 | | 2260 | 1875 | 120.5 | 60 |
| 3 | Geelong (4) | 20 | 13 | 6 | 1 | 2092 | 1745 | 119.9 | 54 |
| 4 | Richmond (1) | 20 | 13 | 7 | | 2060 | 1653 | 124.6 | 52 |
| 5 | Hawthorn | 20 | 13 | 7 | | 2025 | 2050 | 98.8 | 52 |
| 6 | Essendon | 20 | 10 | 9 | 1 | 1941 | 1893 | 102.5 | 42 |
| 7 | St Kilda | 20 | 9 | 11 | | 1803 | 1747 | 103.2 | 36 |
| 8 | North Melb | 20 | 8 | 12 | | 1859 | 2125 | 87.5 | 32 |
| 9 | South Melb | 20 | 7 | 13 | | 1803 | 2186 | 82.5 | 28 |
| 10 | Fitzroy | 20 | 7 | 13 | | 1745 | 2118 | 82.4 | 28 |
| 11 | Footscray | 20 | 6 | 14 | | 1778 | 2079 | 85.5 | 24 |
| 12 | Melbourne | 20 | 3 | 17 | | 1838 | 2211 | 83.1 | 12 |

*(20 H & A matches)*

**First Semi Final**
Richmond 25.17 (167) d. Geelong 7.7 (49)
**Second Semi Final**
Carlton 16.11 (107) d. Collingwood 10.11 (71)
**Preliminary Final**
Richmond 15.17 (107) d. Collingwood 12.9 (81)

**Grand Final**
Richmond 2.2 6.5 8.6 12.13 (85) d
Carlton 1.4 2.7 8.10 8.12 (60)
Goals — Richmond: Barrot 3, Moore 2, Northey 2, Bartlett, Bond, Dean, Hart, Ronaldson. Carlton: Jackson 2, Nicholls 2, Crosswell, Jesaulenko, Gallagher, Walls.
Best — Richmond: Green, Bartlett, Clay, Barrot, Northey, Dean. Carlton: Quirk, Crane, Silvagni, Lofts, Walls, Goold.
Umpire: Crouch. Match played at MCG.
Attendance: 119,165
*Two in three years for the resurgent Tigers. The Tommy Hafey-led combination came from fourth to defeat the more fancied Carlton by 25 points.*
RICHMOND
B: K. Sheedy, B. Richardson, C. Beard
HB: G. Strang, G. Burgin, I. Owen
C: R. Clay, W. Barrot, F. Bourke
HF: J. Northey, R. Hart, Roger Dean (c.)
F: J. Ronaldson, E. Moore, W. Brown
R: M. Green, M. Bowden, K. Bartlett
Reserves: R. Hunt, G. Bond
Coach: T. Hafey
CARLTON
B: B. Gill, W. Lofts, V. Waite
HB: P. Pinnell, J. Goold, K. Hall
C: G. Crane, I. Robertson, B. Quirk
HF: S. Jackson, R. Walls, B. Crosswell
F: P. Jones, A. Jesaulenko, I. Nicoll
R: J. Nicholls (c.), S. Silvagni, A. Gallagher
Reserves: I. Collins, E. Hopkins
Coach: R. Barassi

# 1970

| | | P | W | L | D | For | Agst | % | Pts |
|---|---|---|---|---|---|---|---|---|---|
| 1 | Collingwood (2) | 22 | 18 | 4 | | 2333 | 1709 | 136.5 | 72 |
| 2 | Carlton (1) | 22 | 16 | 6 | | 2146 | 1911 | 112.3 | 64 |
| 3 | St Kilda (3) | 22 | 14 | 8 | | 1926 | 1532 | 125.7 | 56 |
| 4 | South Melb (4) | 22 | 14 | 8 | | 1914 | 1828 | 104.7 | 56 |
| 5 | Geelong | 22 | 12 | 10 | | 1949 | 1903 | 102.4 | 48 |
| 6 | Richmond | 22 | 12 | 10 | | 2029 | 1998 | 101.6 | 48 |
| 7 | Footscray | 22 | 11 | 11 | | 1728 | 1894 | 91.2 | 44 |
| 8 | Hawthorn | 22 | 10 | 12 | | 2264 | 1986 | 114.0 | 40 |
| 9 | Fitzroy | 22 | 9 | 13 | | 1774 | 2155 | 82.3 | 36 |
| 10 | Melbourne | 22 | 6 | 16 | | 1705 | 2043 | 83.5 | 24 |
| 11 | Essendon | 22 | 6 | 16 | | 1734 | 2128 | 81.5 | 24 |
| 12 | North Melb | 22 | 4 | 18 | | 1574 | 1989 | 79.1 | 16 |

*(22 H & A matches)*

**First Semi Final**
St Kilda 22.11 (143) d. South Melbourne 13.12 (90)
**Second Semi Final**
Collingwood 17.16 (118) d. Carlton 17.6 (108)
**Preliminary Final**
Carlton 17.21 (123) d. St Kilda 7.19 (61)

**Grand Final**
Carlton 0.3 4.5 12.5 17.9 (111) d
Collingwood 4.8 10.13 13.16 14.17 (101)
Goals — Carlton: Hopkins 4, Jesaulenko 3, Crosswell 2, Gallagher 2, Nicholls 2, Walls 2, Jackson, Silvagni. Collingwood: McKenna 6, Dunne 2, Thompson 2, Tuddenham 2, Britt, W. Richardson.
Best — Carlton: Jesaulenko, Crosswell, McKay, Silvagni, Robertson, Hopkins. Collingwood: Dunne, Price, Tuddenham, McKenna, W. Richardson, Greening.
Umpire: Jolley. Match played at MCG.
Attendance: 121,696
*Was this the greatest Grand Final of them all? A record crowd (121,696). The greatest Grand Final comeback of all time (Carlton down by 44 points at half-time). Jezza's mark. Teddy Hopkins' moment in the sun. Collingwood's third heart-breaking Grand Final defeat in seven years. The birth of the Colliwobbles and maybe of the modern game. Possibly the most influential game of the era. Handball was here to stay. The Magpies took years to recover.*
CARLTON
B: B. Gill, K. Hall, V. Waite
HB: J. Goold, D. McKay, B. Mulcair
C: G. Crane, I. Robertson, P. Pinnell
HF: B. Crosswell, R. Walls, S. Jackson
F: P. Jones, A. Jesaulenko, B. Thornley
R: J. Nicholls (c.), S. Silvagni, A. Gallagher
Reserves: N. Chandler, E. Hopkins
Coach: R. Barassi
COLLINGWOOD
B: C. Tully, J. Clifton, P. Eakins
HB: D. O'Callaghan, E. Potter, L. Adamson
C: R. Dean, B. Price, J. Greening
HF: M. Richardson, L. Thompson, C. Britt
F: R. Dunne, P. McKenna, W. Richardson
R: G. Jenkin, T. Waters (c.), D. Tuddenham
Reserves: R. Heard, R. Watt
Coach: R. Rose

# 1971

| | | P | W | L | D | For | Agst | % | Pts |
|---|---|---|---|---|---|---|---|---|---|
| 1 | Hawthorn (1) | 22 | 19 | 3 | | 2460 | 1601 | 153.7 | 76 |
| 2 | St Kilda (2) | 22 | 16 | 6 | | 2176 | 1554 | 140.0 | 64 |
| 3 | Richmond (3) | 22 | 16 | 6 | | 2318 | 1890 | 122.6 | 64 |
| 4 | Collingwood (4) | 22 | 14 | 7 | 1 | 2331 | 1840 | 126.7 | 58 |
| 5 | Carlton | 22 | 14 | 8 | | 2103 | 2014 | 104.4 | 56 |
| 6 | Fitzroy | 22 | 12 | 10 | | 2047 | 1915 | 106.9 | 48 |
| 7 | Melbourne | 22 | 11 | 10 | 1 | 1962 | 1791 | 109.5 | 46 |
| 8 | Footscray | 22 | 11 | 11 | | 1966 | 2217 | 88.7 | 44 |
| 9 | North Melb | 22 | 5 | 16 | 1 | 1705 | 2551 | 66.8 | 22 |
| 10 | Geelong | 22 | 5 | 17 | | 2072 | 2523 | 82.1 | 20 |
| 11 | Essendon | 22 | 4 | 17 | 1 | 1705 | 2252 | 75.7 | 18 |
| 12 | South Melb | 22 | 3 | 19 | | 1618 | 2315 | 69.9 | 12 |

*(22 H & A matches)*

**First Semi Final**
Richmond 18.13 (121) d. Collingwood 11.11 (77)
**Second Semi Final**
Hawthorn 12.18 (90) d. St Kilda 12.16 (88)
**Preliminary Final**
St Kilda 16.12 (108) d. Richmond 12.6 (78)

**Grand Final**
Hawthorn 2.2 4.4 5.7 12.10 (82) d
St Kilda 2.1 4.6 8.9 11.9 (75)
Goals — Hawthorn: Keddie 4, Hudson 3, Crimmins
2, L. Matthews, Rice, Scott. St Kilda: Breen 4,
Bonney 2, Davis, Manzie, Smith, Theodore, Trott.
Best — Hawthorn: Scott, Moore, Crimmins, Parkin,
Keddie, Rice. St Kilda: Lawrence, Trott, Smith,
Neale, Besanko, Breen.
Umpire: Sheales. Match played at MCG.
Attendance: 118,192
*A tough, uncompromising game in which Hawthorn
emerged victorious by seven points. St Kilda could
not defend the 20-point lead it enjoyed at three-
quarter time and Peter Hudson could not get the
extra goal he needed to break Bob Pratt's record of
150 goals in a season. He had two easy chances
but missed both — maybe still dazed after being
belted early by 'Cowboy' Neale. Ironically, Bob
Keddie, at full-forward in the last quarter, was the
Hawks' match-winner, not Hudson.*
HAWTHORN
B: D. Parkin (c.), K. Moore, L. Hawken
HB: R. Day, N. Bussell, I. Bremner
C: L. Rice, G. Angus, D. Meagher
HF: R. Keddie, A. Martello, M. Porter
F: K. Heath, P. Hudson, L. Matthews
R: D. Scott, B. Stevenson, P. Crimmins
Reserves: K. Beck, R. Wilson
J. Kennedy
ST. KILDA
B: W. Judson, R. Murray, K. Neale
HB: G. Colling, B. Lawrence, N. Besanko
C: J. Manzie, G. Elliott, S. Trott
HF: J. Moran, B. Breen, S. Theodore
F: C. Ditterich, A. Davis, J. Bonney
R: B. Mynott, T. Payze, R. Smith (c.)
Reserves: R. Galt, S. Rae
Coach: A. Jeans

# 1972

| | | P | W | L | D | For | Agst | % | Pts |
|---|---|---|---|---|---|---|---|---|---|
| 1 | Carlton (1) | 22 | 18 | 3 | 1 | 2237 | 1666 | 134.3 | 74 |
| 2 | Richmond (2) | 22 | 18 | 4 | | 2469 | 2098 | 117.7 | 72 |
| 3 | Collingwood (4) | 22 | 14 | 7 | 1 | 2338 | 1747 | 133.8 | 58 |
| 4 | St Kilda (3) | 22 | 14 | 8 | | 1989 | 1721 | 115.6 | 56 |
| 5 | Essendon (5) | 22 | 14 | 8 | | 2317 | 2140 | 108.3 | 56 |
| 6 | Hawthorn | 22 | 13 | 9 | | 2277 | 2050 | 111.1 | 52 |
| 7 | Footscray | 22 | 11 | 11 | | 1930 | 2038 | 94.7 | 44 |
| 8 | Melbourne | 22 | 10 | 12 | | 2043 | 1929 | 105.9 | 40 |
| 9 | Fitzroy | 22 | 9 | 13 | | 1997 | 2062 | 96.8 | 36 |
| 10 | Geelong | 22 | 7 | 15 | | 1994 | 2369 | 84.2 | 28 |
| 11 | South Melb | 22 | 2 | 20 | | 1513 | 2323 | 65.1 | 8 |
| 12 | North Melb | 22 | 1 | 21 | | 1628 | 2589 | 62.9 | 4 |

*(22 H & A matches)*

**Elimination Final**
St Kilda 18.16 (124) d. Essendon 10.11 (71)
**Qualifying Final**
Richmond 25.14 (164) d. Collingwood 18.12 (120)
**First Semi Final**
St Kilda 11.17 (83) d. Collingwood 8.17 (65)
**Second Semi Final**
Carlton 8.13 (61) drew with Richmond 8.13 (61)
**Second Semi Final Replay**
Richmond 15.20 (110) d. Carlton 9.15 (69)
**Preliminary Final**
Carlton 16.13 (109) d. St Kilda 13.15 (93)

**Grand Final**
Carlton 8.4 18.6 25.9 28.9 (177) d
Richmond 5.4 10.9 15.15 22.18 (150)
Goals — Carlton: Jesaulenko 7, Nicholls 6, Walls
6, Keogh 3, Jackson 2, Hall, Gallagher, Chandler,
Dickson. Richmond: Balme 5, B. Richardson 3,
Sheedy 3, Hart 2, Cumming 2, McMillan 2,
McLean, Hunt, Morris, Sproule, Stewart.
Best — Carlton: Walls, Nicholls, Jones,
Jesaulenko, Armstrong, Doull. Richmond: Bartlett,
Morris, Sproule, Bourke, Sheedy, Balme.
Umpire: Deller. Match played at MCG.
Attendance: 112,393
*The highest scoring Grand Final on record.
Richmond's 22.18 (150) would have been enough
to win any other Grand Final, but Carlton this day
outdid them by 27 points. Jezza kicked seven,
Nicholls and Walls six each.*
CARLTON
B: J. O'Connell, G. Southby, D. McKay
HB: V. Waite, B. Doull, P. Hurst
C: I. Robertson, B. Armstrong, D. Dickson
HF: N. Chandler, R. Walls, S. Jackson
F: J. Nicholls (c.), A. Jesaulenko, T. Keogh
R: P. Jones, K. Hall, A. Gallagher
Reserves: A. Lukas, G. Crane
Coach: J. Nicholls
RICHMOND
B: K. Sheedy, R. Clay, R. Boyanich
HB: W. Walsh, R. Hunt, S. Hywood
C: F. Bourke, P. Sproule, G. Bond
HF: B. Richardson, R. Hart (c.), M. McMillan
F: N. Balme, R. McLean, D. Cumming
R: C. McKellar, K. Morris, K. Bartlett
Reserves: B. Roberts, I. Stewart
Coach: T. Hafey

# 1973

| | | P | W | L | D | For | Agst | % | Pts |
|---|---|---|---|---|---|---|---|---|---|
| 1 | Collingwood (3) | 22 | 19 | 3 | | 2356 | 1878 | 125.5 | 76 |
| 2 | Richmond (1) | 22 | 17 | 5 | | 2301 | 1957 | 117.6 | 68 |
| 3 | Carlton (2) | 22 | 15 | 7 | | 2342 | 1850 | 126.6 | 60 |
| 4 | Essendon (5) | 22 | 13 | 9 | | 2443 | 2341 | 104.4 | 52 |
| 5 | St Kilda (4) | 22 | 12 | 10 | | 2024 | 1922 | 105.3 | 48 |
| 6 | North Melb | 22 | 11 | 10 | 1 | 1938 | 1986 | 97.6 | 46 |
| 7 | Hawthorn | 22 | 11 | 11 | | 2194 | 2002 | 109.6 | 44 |
| 8 | Fitzroy | 22 | 9 | 13 | | 1990 | 2194 | 90.7 | 36 |
| 9 | Footscray | 22 | 7 | 14 | 1 | 1860 | 2109 | 88.2 | 30 |
| 10 | Melbourne | 22 | 7 | 15 | | 1938 | 2111 | 91.8 | 28 |
| 11 | Geelong | 22 | 6 | 16 | | 1903 | 2426 | 78.4 | 24 |
| 12 | South Melb | 22 | 4 | 18 | | 1932 | 2445 | 79.0 | 16 |

*(22 H & A matches)*

**Elimination Final**
St Kilda 24.14 (158) d. Essendon 13.13 (91)
**Qualifying Final**
Carlton 13.13 (91) d. Richmond 10.11 (71)
**First Semi Final**
Richmond 15.18 (108) d. St Kilda 9.14 (68)
**Second Semi Final**
Carlton 15.17 (107) d. Collingwood 12.15 (87)
**Preliminary Final**
Richmond 15.15 (105) d. Collingwood 14.14 (98)

**Grand Final**
Richmond 3.5 11.8 15.11 16.20 (116) d
Carlton 2.2 7.6 9.9 12.14 (86)
Goals — Richmond: Hart 3, Sheedy 3, Stewart 3,
Balme 2, Sproule 2, Bartlett, Carter, Green.
Carlton: Crane 2, Dickson 2, Hall 2, McKay 2,
Walls 2, Chandler, Nicholls.
Best — Richmond: Bartlett, Sheedy, Green,
Stewart, Hart, Sproule. Carlton: Crane, Walls,
McKay, Hall, Pinnell, Jesaulenko.
Umpire: Robinson. Match played at MCG.
Attendance: 116,956
*Richmond exacted its full measure of revenge for*
*1972 with a five-goal win. But that revenge wasn't*
*just limited to the scoreboard. Laurie Fowler laid*
*out John Nicholls with one of footy's most famous*
*shirtfronts, while Neil Balme 'went the knuckle' to*
*knock out Geoff Southby and took on most of the*
*rest of the Blues' defence as well.*
RICHMOND
B: L. Fowler, R. Clay, R. Hunt
HB: M. Keane, F. Bourke, R. McGhie
C: B. Wood, I. Stewart, W. Walsh
HF: K. Sheedy, R. Hart (c.), S. Rae
F: M. Green, N. Balme, N. Carter
R: B. Roberts, P. Sproule, K. Bartlett
Reserves: C. McKellar, K. Morris
Coach: T. Hafey
CARLTON
B: R. Byrne, G. Southby, V. Waite
HB: K. Hall, B. Doull, P. Pinnell
C: D. Dickson, J. O'Connell, G. Crane
HF: D. McKay, R. Walls, A. Jesaulenko
F: J. Nicholls (c.), C. Davis, V. Cattoggio
R: P. Jones, B. Crosswell, B. Welsh
Reserves: N. Chandler, B. Quirk
Coach: J. Nicholls

# 1974

| | | P | W | L | D | For | Agst | % | Pts |
|---|---|---|---|---|---|---|---|---|---|
| 1 | Richmond (1) | 22 | 17 | 5 | | 2558 | 1979 | 129.3 | 68 |
| 2 | North Melb (2) | 22 | 16 | 6 | | 2398 | 1728 | 138.8 | 64 |
| 3 | Hawthorn (3) | 22 | 15 | 7 | | 2168 | 1729 | 125.4 | 60 |
| 4 | Collingwood (4) | 22 | 15 | 7 | | 2131 | 2037 | 104.6 | 60 |
| 5 | Footscray (5) | 22 | 13 | 8 | 1 | 1899 | 1746 | 108.8 | 54 |
| 6 | Geelong | 22 | 11 | 11 | | 1858 | 1989 | 93.4 | 44 |
| 7 | Carlton | 22 | 10 | 11 | 1 | 2053 | 1941 | 105.8 | 42 |
| 8 | Essendon | 22 | 10 | 12 | | 2110 | 2162 | 97.6 | 40 |
| 9 | South Melb | 22 | 9 | 12 | 1 | 1947 | 2327 | 83.7 | 38 |
| 10 | St Kilda | 22 | 7 | 15 | | 1790 | 2018 | 88.7 | 28 |
| 11 | Fitzroy | 22 | 4 | 17 | 1 | 1770 | 2481 | 71.3 | 18 |
| 12 | Melbourne | 22 | 3 | 19 | | 1840 | 2385 | 77.1 | 12 |

*(22 H & A matches)*

**Elimination Final**
Collingwood 19.10 (124) d. Footscray 6.19 (55)
**Qualifying Final**
Nth. Melb. 15.13 (103) d. Hawthorn 8.17 (65)
**First Semi Final**
Hawthorn 21.12 (138) d. Collingwood 13.10 (88)
**Second Semi Final**
Richmond 10.13 (73) d. Nth. Melb. 6.16 (52)
**Preliminary Final**
Nth. Melb. 8.8 (56) d. Hawthorn 7.9 (51)

**Grand Final**
Richmond 3.8 10.11 12.17 18.20 (128) d
North Melbourne 3.2 8.3 11.4 13.9 (87)
Goals — Richmond: B. Richardson 5, Hart 3,
Balme 2, Green 2, Sheedy 2, Cloke, Cumming,
Thorpe, Walsh. North Melbourne: Wade 4, Cable 2,
Kekovich 2, Briedis, Burns, Davis, Greig, Peterson.
Best — Richmond: Sheedy, Hart, Sproule, Green,
Balme, Walsh. North Melbourne: Greig, Cable,
Schimmelbusch, Rantall, Smith, Burns.
Umpire: Robinson. Match played at MCG.
Attendance: 113,839
*North was back in a Grand Final for the first time*
*since 1950, but was no match for the all-*
*conquering Richmond, which cruised to a 41-point*
*win. The highlight for North was Doug Wade's*
*100th goal for the year.*
RICHMOND
B: M. Keane, R. Clay, G. Andrews
HB: F. Bourke, R. McGhie, K. Morris
C: W. Walsh, D. Thorpe, B. Wood
HF: D. Cloke, R. Hart (c.), P. Sproule
F: N. Balme, B. Richardson, D. Cumming
R: M. Green, K. Sheedy, K. Bartlett
Reserves: B. Roberts, C. Clayton
Coach: T. Hafey
NORTH MELBOURNE
B: D. Pagan, D. Dench, B. Smith
HB: J. Rantall, G. Farrant, K. Montgomery
C: K. Greig, J. Burns, W. Schimmelbusch
HF: S. Kekovich, P. Baker, P. Feltham
F: P. Ryan, D. Wade, R. Peterson
R: B. Goodingham, B. Davis (c.), B. Cable
Reserves: G. Cowton, A. Briedis
Coach: R. Barassi

# 1975

| | | P | W | L | D | For | Agst | % | Pts |
|---|---|---|---|---|---|---|---|---|---|
| 1 | Hawthorn (2) | 22 | 17 | 5 | | 2383 | 1735 | 137.3 | 68 |
| 2 | Carlton (4) | 22 | 16 | 6 | | 2360 | 1827 | 129.2 | 64 |
| 3 | North Melb (1) | 22 | 14 | 8 | | 2096 | 1821 | 115.1 | 56 |
| 4 | Richmond (3) | 22 | 13 | 9 | | 2269 | 1999 | 113.5 | 52 |
| 5 | Collingwood (5) | 22 | 13 | 9 | | 1983 | 2112 | 93.9 | 52 |
| 6 | St Kilda | 22 | 11 | 11 | | 1982 | 1954 | 101.4 | 44 |
| 7 | Footscray | 22 | 11 | 11 | | 1968 | 2076 | 94.8 | 44 |
| 8 | Essendon | 22 | 10 | 12 | | 2222 | 2451 | 90.7 | 40 |
| 9 | Fitzroy | 22 | 9 | 13 | | 2079 | 2142 | 97.1 | 36 |
| 10 | Melbourne | 22 | 9 | 13 | | 2092 | 2234 | 93.6 | 36 |
| 11 | Geelong | 22 | 7 | 15 | | 1735 | 2218 | 78.2 | 28 |
| 12 | South Melb | 22 | 2 | 20 | | 1798 | 2398 | 75.0 | 8 |

*(22 H & A matches)*

**Elimination Final**
Richmond 11.11 (77) d. Collingwood 10.13 (73)
**Qualifying Final**
Nth. Melb. 14.12 (96) d. Carlton 12.4 (76)
**First Semi Final**
Richmond 9.17 (71) d. Carlton 9.8 (62)
**Second Semi Final**
Hawthorn 12.10 (82) d. Nth. Melb. 10.11 (71)
**Preliminary Final**
Nth. Melb. 10.16 (76) d. Richmond 8.11 (59)

**Grand Final**
North Melbourne 4.2 9.2 12.6 19.8 (122) d
Hawthorn 2.2 5.6 7.7 9.13 (67)
Goals — North Melbourne: Briedis 5, Wade 4,
Burns 4, Schimmelbusch 2, Blight, Kekovich,
Crosswell, Feltham. Hawthorn: Martello 2,
Moncrieff 2, Rowlings, K. Matthews, Trott,
Meagher, Scott.
Best — North Melbourne: Crosswell, Rantall,
Greig, Burns, Dench, Nolan. Hawthorn: Knights,
Martello, Jaworskyj, Bremner, Moore, Rowlings.
Umpire: Smith. Match played at MCG.
Attendance: 110,551
*North Melbourne, with a second chance at Grand
Final glory, made no mistake this time with a
thumping 55-point win over Hawthorn — giving the
Roos their first ever VFL flag. Supercoach Ron
Barassi masterminded the win, with former
Bomber Barry Davis captain. The club had
completed a remarkable turnaround from its last-
place finish just three years earlier.*
NORTH MELBOURNE
B: R. Henshaw, D. Dench, F. Gumbleton
HB: B. Crosswell, M. Blight, J. Rantall
C: K. Greig, J. Burns, P. Chisnall
HF: W. Schimmelbusch, A. Briedis, S. Kekovich
F: G. Farrant, D. Wade, P. Feltham
R: M. Nolan, B. Davis (c.), B. Cable
Reserves: B. Goodingham, G. Cowton
Coach: R. Barassi
HAWTHORN
B: P. Welsh, K. Moore, M. Moncrieff
HB: B. Jaworskyj, P. Knights, I. Bremner
C: S. Trott, K. Matthews, G. Ablett
HF: S. Murphy, A. Martello, J. Hendrie
F: B. Jones, M. Cooke, B. Rowlings
R: D. Scott (c.), M. Tuck, L. Matthews
Reserves: L. Rice, D. Meagher
Coach: J. Kennedy

# 1976

| | | P | W | L | D | For | Agst | % | Pts |
|---|---|---|---|---|---|---|---|---|---|
| 1 | Carlton (3) | 22 | 16 | 5 | 1 | 2245 | 1690 | 132.8 | 66 |
| 2 | Hawthorn (1) | 22 | 16 | 6 | | 2323 | 2035 | 114.2 | 64 |
| 3 | North Melb (2) | 22 | 15 | 7 | | 2041 | 1748 | 116.8 | 60 |
| 4 | Geelong (4) | 22 | 12 | 10 | | 2251 | 2166 | 103.9 | 48 |
| 5 | Footscray (5) | 22 | 11 | 10 | 1 | 1958 | 2023 | 96.8 | 46 |
| 6 | Melbourne | 22 | 11 | 11 | | 2319 | 2333 | 99.4 | 44 |
| 7 | Richmond | 22 | 10 | 12 | | 2192 | 2224 | 98.6 | 40 |
| 8 | South Melb | 22 | 9 | 13 | | 2223 | 2364 | 94.0 | 36 |
| 9 | St Kilda | 22 | 9 | 13 | | 2056 | 2282 | 90.1 | 36 |
| 10 | Essendon | 22 | 9 | 13 | | 1987 | 2253 | 88.2 | 36 |
| 11 | Fitzroy | 22 | 7 | 15 | | 2005 | 2161 | 92.8 | 28 |
| 12 | Collingwood | 22 | 6 | 16 | | 2033 | 2354 | 86.4 | 24 |

*(22 H & A matches)*

**Elimination Final**
Geelong 14.18 (102) d. Footscray 14.11 (95)
**Qualifying Final**
Hawthorn 14.19 (103) d. Nth. Melb. 12.11 (83)
**First Semi Final**
Nth. Melb. 14.9 (93) d. Geelong 8.12 (60)
**Second Semi Final**
Hawthorn 12.15 (87) d. Carlton 9.16 (70)
**Preliminary Final**
Nth. Melb. 10.7 (67) d. Carlton 9.12 (66)

**Grand Final**
Hawthorn 5.6 9.12 10.18 13.22 (100) d
North Melbourne 4.2 7.5 10.8 10.10 (70)
Goals — Hawthorn: Moncrieff 3, Goad 2, Hendrie
2, K. Matthews 2, L. Matthews, Martello,
Rowlings, Scott. North Melbourne: Burns 2, Cable
2, Icke 2, Byrne, Cowton, Melrose, Moore.
Best — Hawthorn: Hendrie, Knights, Ablett, Douge,
Rowlings, Moore. North Melbourne: Dench, Greig,
Cable, Blight, Icke, Sutton.
Umpires: Deller, Smith. Match played at MCG.
Attendance: 110,143
*This was Crimmo's Cup, the game Hawthorn won
for its champion rover and captain Peter Crimmins,
in hospital with cancer on Grand Final day. The
Hawks won by five goals and that night took the
cup to Crimmo's bedside. 'The little fella' died
three days later.*
HAWTHORN
B: B. Douge, K. Moore, B. Jones
HB: I. Bremner, P. Knights, D. O'Halloran
C: G. Ablett, B. Rowlings, R. Eade
HF: D. Polkinghome, A. Martello, K. Matthews
F: M. Moncrieff, J. Hendrie, A. Goad
R: D. Scott (c.), M. Tuck, L. Matthews
Reserves: L. Rice, P. Murnane
Coach: J. Kennedy
NORTH MELBOURNE
B: J. Byrne, D. Dench, F. Gumbleton
HB: S. Icke, G. Cowton, D. Sutton
C: P. Feltham, J. Burns, K. Greig (c.)
HF: W. Schimmelbusch, T. Moore, M. Blight
F: P. Keenan, B. Crosswell, G. Melrose
R: M. Nolan, M. Dawson, B. Cable
Reserves: R. Henshaw, P. Chisnall
Coach: R. Barassi

# 1977

| | | P | W | L | D | For | Agst | % | Pts |
|---|---|---|---|---|---|---|---|---|---|
| 1 | Collingwood (2) | 22 | 18 | 4 | | 2560 | 1959 | 130.7 | 72 |
| 2 | Hawthorn (3) | 22 | 17 | 5 | | 2618 | 1959 | 133.6 | 68 |
| 3 | North Melb (1) | 22 | 15 | 7 | | 2124 | 1803 | 117.8 | 60 |
| 4 | Richmond (4) | 22 | 14 | 7 | 1 | 2370 | 2085 | 113.7 | 58 |
| 5 | South Melb (5) | 22 | 13 | 8 | 1 | 2148 | 1942 | 110.6 | 54 |
| 6 | Carlton | 22 | 13 | 9 | | 2081 | 1859 | 111.9 | 52 |
| 7 | Footscray | 22 | 10 | 11 | 1 | 2170 | 2141 | 101.4 | 42 |
| 8 | Geelong | 22 | 8 | 14 | | 1930 | 2333 | 82.7 | 32 |
| 9 | Essendon | 22 | 7 | 14 | 1 | 2085 | 2518 | 82.8 | 30 |
| 10 | Fitzroy | 22 | 6 | 16 | | 2072 | 2474 | 83.8 | 24 |
| 11 | Melbourne | 22 | 5 | 17 | | 2117 | 2492 | 85.0 | 20 |
| 12 | St Kilda | 22 | 3 | 17 | 2 | 1966 | 2676 | 73.5 | 16 |

*(22 H & A matches)*

**Elimination Final**
Richmond 13.10 (88) d. Sth. Melb. 7.12 (54)
**Qualifying Final**
Hawthorn 19.11 (125) d. Nth. Melb. 12.15 (87)
**First Semi Final**
Nth. Melb. 16.14 (110) d. Richmond 9.9 (63)
**Second Semi Final**
Collingwood 17.10 (112) d. Hawthorn 16.14 (110)
**Preliminary Final**
Nth. Melb. 16.16 (112) d. Hawthorn 5.15 (45)

**Grand Final**
Collingwood 1.5 4.8 9.12 10.16 (76)
drew North Melbourne 4.4 4.10 4.15 9.22 (76)
Goals — North Melbourne: Baker 6, Dench 2,
Sutton. Collingwood: Moore 4, Kink, 2, Dunne,
Anderson, Shaw, Barham. Best — North
Melbourne: Schimmbusch, Baker, Alves, Dench,
Keenan, Montgomery. Collingwood: Thompson,
Magro, Ireland, Wearmouth, Picken, Moore.
Umpires: Robinson, Sutcliffe. Match played at MCG.
Attendance: 108,224
*Not one but two classic Grand Finals. The first was
drawn, with North edging its way to the front after
overcoming a 27-point deficit at the last change.
Then 'Twiggy' Dunne marked and levelled the
scores with a minute to play. North was never going
to lose the replay, but Phil Manassa provided the
highlight with a running goal from half-back flank
that will never be forgotten.*
COLLINGWOOD
B: R. Hyde, K. Worthington, D. Gott
HB: A. Ireland, W. Picken, P. Manassa
C: R. Barham, S. Magro, W. Gordon
HF: W. Richardson, R. Dunne, G. Anderson
F: P. Moore, R. Kink, R. Shaw
R: L. Thompson, M. Richardson (c.), R. Wearmouth
Reserves: G. Betts, S. Bond
Coach: T. Hafey
NORTH MELBOURNE
B: R. Henshaw, D. Dench (c.), F. Gumbleton
HB: G. Cowton, D. Sutton, K. Montgomery
C: S. Alves, X. Tanner, W. Schimmelbusch
HF: S. Icke, M. Blight, A. Briedis
F: B. Crosswell, P. Baker, J. Cassin
R: P. Keenan, J. Byrne, B. Cable
Reserves: S. McCann, W. Nettlefold
Coach: R. Barassi

**Grand Final Replay**
North Melbourne 5.5 9.12 15.19 21.25 (151) d
Collingwood 3.4 8.7 12.7 19.10 (124)
Goals — North Melbourne: Briedis 5, Baker 3,
Crosswell 2, Cable 2, Blight 2, Schimmelbusch 2,
Bryne 2, Icke, Tanner, Cassin. Collingwood: Moore
5, Manassa 3, Barham 2, Dunne 2, Gordon 2,
Kink, Wearmouth, W. Richardson, Anderson, Ireland.
Best — North Melbourne: Briedis, Tanner, Blight,
Montgomery, Byrne, Cable. Collingwood: Moore,
Manassa, Thompson, Hyde, Wearmouth, Ireland.
Umpires: Robinson, Sutcliffe. Match played at MCG.
Attendance: 98,366
NORTH MELBOURNE
B: R. Henshaw, D. Dench (c), F. Gumbleton
HB: G. Cowton, D. Sutton, K. Montgomery
C: S. Alves, X. Tanner, W. Schimmelbusch
HF: S. Icke, M. Blight, A. Briedis
F: B. Crosswell, P. Baker, J. Cassin
R: P. Keenan, J. Byrne, B. Cable
Reserves: S. McCann, W. Nettlefold
Coach: R. Barassi
COLLINGWOOD
B: R. Hyde, K. Worthington, C. Perry
HB: A. Ireland, W. Picken, P. Manassa
C: R. Barham, S. Magro, W. Gordon
HF: W. Richardson, R. Dunne, G. Anderson
F: P. Moore, R. Kink, R. Shaw
R: L. Thompson, M. Richardson (c.), R. Wearmouth
Reserves: G. Betts, S. Bond
Coach: T. Hafey

# 1978

| | | P | W | L | D | For | Agst | % | Pts |
|---|---|---|---|---|---|---|---|---|---|
| 1 | North Melb (2) | 22 | 16 | 6 | | 2407 | 1991 | 120.9 | 64 |
| 2 | Hawthorn (1) | 22 | 16 | 6 | | 2496 | 2120 | 117.7 | 64 |
| 3 | Collingwood (3) | 22 | 15 | 7 | | 2347 | 2072 | 113.3 | 60 |
| 4 | Carlton (4) | 22 | 14 | 8 | | 2329 | 1994 | 116.8 | 56 |
| 5 | Geelong (5) | 22 | 12 | 10 | | 2153 | 2104 | 102.3 | 48 |
| 6 | St Kilda | 22 | 11 | 10 | 1 | 2330 | 2503 | 93.1 | 46 |
| 7 | Richmond | 22 | 10 | 11 | 1 | 2459 | 2389 | 102.9 | 42 |
| 8 | South Melb | 22 | 9 | 13 | | 2390 | 2383 | 100.3 | 36 |
| 9 | Fitzroy | 22 | 8 | 14 | | 2258 | 2339 | 96.5 | 32 |
| 10 | Essendon | 22 | 8 | 14 | | 2203 | 2337 | 94.3 | 32 |
| 11 | Footscray | 22 | 7 | 15 | | 2272 | 2508 | 90.6 | 28 |
| 12 | Melbourne | 22 | 5 | 17 | | 2025 | 2929 | 69.1 | 20 |

*(22 H & A matches)*

**Elimination Final**
Carlton 15.15 (105) d. Geelong 9.18 (72)
**Qualifying Final**
Hawthorn 23.16 (154) d. Collingwood 14.14 (98)
**First Semi Final**
Collingwood 15.18 (108) d. Carlton 13.15 (93)
**Second Semi Final**
Hawthorn 12.15 (87) d. Nth. Melb. 10.13 (73)
**Preliminary Final**
Nth. Melb. 14.12 (96) d. Collingwood 12.12 (84)
**Grand Final**
Hawthorn 5.3 7.4 14.10 18.13 (121) d
North Melbourne 2.2 7.8 10.12 15.13 (103)
Goals — Hawthorn: Moncrieff 4, L. Matthews 4,
Scott 3, Knights 2, Ablett, Martello, Hendrie, Eade,
Murnane. North Melbourne: Baker 6, Briedis 2,

Huppatz 2, Boyse 2, Smith 2, Melrose.
Best — Hawthorn: DiPierdomenico, L. Matthews,
Eade, Scott, Wallace, Knights. North Melbourne:
Baker, Schimmelbusch, Huppatz, Sutton, Henshaw,
Glendinning.
Umpires: Deller, Robinson. Match played at MCG.
Attendance: 101,701
*A second Hawthorn victory in three years, but a
Grand Final remembered more for the Hawks'
grinding determination than for brilliant football.
That was left to North's Phil Baker, who took a
couple of first class 'screamers'.*
HAWTHORN
B: A. de Wolde, K. Moore, I. Paton
HB: D. Polkinghorne, P. Knights,
R. DiPierdomenico
C: G. Ablett, T. Wallace, R. Eade
HF: P. Murnane, A. Martello, J. Hendrie
F: R. Walter, M. Moncrieff, P. Russo
R: D. Scott (c.), M. Tuck, L. Matthews
Interchange: M. McCarthy, N. Goss
Coach: D. Parkin
NORTH MELBOURNE
B: R. Henshaw, R. Glendinning, G. Cowton
HB: K. Montgomery, D. Sutton, K. Greig (c.)
C: S. Alves, X. Tanner, W. Schimmelbusch
HF: A. Briedis, S. McCann, M. Boyse
F: M. Blight, P. Baker, R. Huppatz
R: M. Nolan, J. Byrne, G. Melrose
Interchange: D. Smith, J. Cassin
Coach: R. Barassi

# 1979

| | | P | W | L | D | For | Agst | % | Pts |
|---|---|---|---|---|---|---|---|---|---|
| 1 | Carlton (1) | 22 | 19 | 3 | | 2772 | 1986 | 139.6 | 76 |
| 2 | North Melb (3) | 22 | 17 | 5 | | 2574 | 2083 | 123.6 | 68 |
| 3 | Collingwood (2) | 22 | 15 | 7 | | 2501 | 1974 | 126.7 | 60 |
| 4 | Fitzroy (4) | 22 | 15 | 7 | | 2699 | 2198 | 122.8 | 60 |
| 5 | Essendon (5) | 22 | 12 | 9 | 1 | 2236 | 2127 | 105.1 | 50 |
| 6 | Geelong | 22 | 12 | 10 | | 2149 | 2140 | 100.4 | 48 |
| 7 | Hawthorn | 22 | 10 | 12 | | 2332 | 2336 | 99.8 | 40 |
| 8 | Richmond | 22 | 9 | 13 | | 2451 | 2512 | 97.6 | 36 |
| 9 | Footscray | 22 | 7 | 14 | 1 | 2015 | 2463 | 81.8 | 30 |
| 10 | South Melb | 22 | 6 | 16 | | 2424 | 2666 | 90.9 | 24 |
| 11 | Melbourne | 22 | 6 | 16 | | 2093 | 2759 | 75.9 | 24 |
| 12 | St Kilda | 22 | 3 | 19 | | 1857 | 2859 | 65.0 | 12 |

*(22 H & A matches)*

**Elimination Final**
Fitzroy 17.22 (124) d. Essendon 5.13 (43)
**Qualifying Final**
Nth. Melb. 18.13 (121) d. Collingwood 9.28 (82)
**First Semi Final**
Collingwood 16.20 (116) d. Fitzroy 12.22 (94)
**Second Semi Final**
Carlton 15.21 (111) d. Nth. Melbourne 11.7 (73)
**Preliminary Final**
Collingwood 18.14 (122) d. Nth. Melb. 13.17 (95)

**Grand Final**
Carlton 0.5 5.7 10.12 11.16 (82) d
Collingwood 2.2 5.6 7.9 11.11 (77)
Goals — Carlton: Sheldon 3, Buckley 2, Maclure 2,
Young, P. Jones, Harmes, Francis. Collingwood:

Davis 4, Wearmouth, Edwards, Brewer, Carlson,
Ohlsen, Kink, Ireland.
Best — Carlton: Harmes, Francis, Johnston,
Buckley, Klomp, Armstrong. Collingwood: Picken,
Morris, Byrne, Davis, Barham, Ohlsen.
Umpires: Deller, Smith. Match played at MCG.
Attendance: 112,845
*Another triumph for Carlton; another heartbreak for
Collingwood. This time the Maggies went down by
five points on a muddy MCG, thanks to Wayne
Harmes' desperate chase and knock-back of his
own kick that had been heading out of bounds.
Sheldon goaled from the knock-back and the gap
was just enough. Harmes won the inaugural Norm
Smith Medal.*
CARLTON
B: W. Harmes, G. Southby, D. McKay
HB: R. Klomp, B. Doull, P. McConville
C: P. Francis, A. Jesaulenko (c.), M. Young
HF: W. Johnston, M. Maclure, T. Keogh
F: M. Fitzpatrick, P. Brown, K. Sheldon
R: P. Jones, B. Armstrong, J. Buckley
Interchange: R. Austin, A. Marcou
Coach: A. Jesaulenko
COLLINGWOOD
B: S. Magro, P. McCormack, K. Worthington
HB: R. Byrne, W. Picken, I. Ireland
C: R. Barham, K. Morris, G. Anderson
HF: R. Kink, A. Edwards, R. Brewer
F: D. Shaw, D. Davis, R. Shaw (c.)
R: P. Moore, R. Ohlsen, R. Wearmouth
Interchange: D. Banks, L. Carlson
Coach: T. Hafey

# 1980

| | | P | W | L | D | For | Agst | % | Pts |
|---|---|---|---|---|---|---|---|---|---|
| 1 | Geelong (3) | 22 | 17 | 5 | | 2362 | 1888 | 125.1 | 68 |
| 2 | Carlton (4) | 22 | 17 | 5 | | 2576 | 2128 | 121.1 | 68 |
| 3 | Richmond (1) | 22 | 16 | 5 | 1 | 2754 | 1990 | 138.4 | 66 |
| 4 | North Melb (5) | 22 | 14 | 7 | 1 | 2345 | 1894 | 123.8 | 58 |
| 5 | Collingwood (2) | 22 | 14 | 7 | 1 | 2491 | 2178 | 114.4 | 58 |
| 6 | South Melb | 22 | 13 | 9 | | 2211 | 2174 | 101.7 | 52 |
| 7 | Essendon | 22 | 10 | 12 | | 2268 | 2151 | 105.4 | 40 |
| 8 | Hawthorn | 22 | 10 | 12 | | 2249 | 2381 | 94.5 | 40 |
| 9 | Melbourne | 22 | 5 | 17 | | 2140 | 2709 | 79.0 | 20 |
| 10 | Footscray | 22 | 5 | 17 | | 2056 | 2737 | 75.1 | 20 |
| 11 | St Kilda | 22 | 4 | 16 | 2 | 1872 | 2704 | 69.2 | 20 |
| 12 | Fitzroy | 22 | 4 | 17 | 1 | 2398 | 2788 | 86.0 | 18 |

*(22 H & A matches)*

**Elimination Final**
Collingwood 14.20 (104) d. Nth. Melb. 14.12 (96)
**Qualifying Final**
Richmond 18.8 (116) d. Carlton 10.14 (74)
**First Semi Final**
Collingwood 22.20 (152) d. Carlton 15.12 (102)
**Second Semi Final**
Richmond 14.11 (95) d. Geelong 11.5 (71)
**Preliminary Final**
Collingwood 13.15 (93) d. Geelong 13.11 (89)

**Grand Final**
Richmond 6.5 11.11 15.17 23.21 (159) d
Collingwood 2.6 4.10 5.18 9.24 (78)

Goals — Richmond: Bartlett 7, Cloke 6, Wiley 3, Roach 2, Keane 2, Weightman, Jess, Rowlings. Collingwood: Picken 3, Davis 2, Wearmouth, R. Shaw, Moore, Ohlsen.

Best — Richmond: Bartlett, Raines, Lee, Welsh, Bourke, Raines. Collingwood: Woolnough, R. Shaw, Picken, Ohlsen, Davis, Magro.

Umpires: Deller, Robinson. Match played at MCG.

Attendance: 113,461

*This was the most one-sided Grand Final that had been seen to that stage in history, with Collingwood only able to get within 81 points of a Richmond side that was a class or two above. Kevin Bartlett kicked seven goals, giving him a record-equalling 21 for the finals series.*

RICHMOND
B: M. Malthouse, E. Dunne, G. Strachan
HB: T. Smith, J. Jess, P. Welsh
C: S. Mount, G. Raines, B. Wood
HF: M. Keane, D. Cloke, K. Bartlett
F: F. Bourke, M. Roach, R. Wiley
R: M. Lee, B. Rowlings, D. Weightman
Interchange: B. Monteath (c.), D. Freame
Coach: T. Jewell

COLLINGWOOD
B: S. Magro, P. McCormack, A. Ireland
HB: K. Morris, W. Picken, R. Byrne
C: R. Barham, P. Daicos, L. Carlson
HF: R. Kink, C. Stewart, I. Low
F: D. Young, C. Davis, R. Shaw (c.)
R: P. Moore, R. Ohlsen, R. Wearmouth
Interchange: A. Shaw, M. Woolnough
Coach: T. Hafey

Goals — Carlton: Ashman 3, Maclure 2, McKay 2, Sheldon 2, Johnston, Harmes, Buckley. Collingwood: Williams 2, Barham 2, A. Shaw, R. Shaw, Stewart, Taylor, Moore, Daicos.

Best — Carlton: Doull, Fitzpatrick, Hunter, Marcou, Glascott, McConville. Collingwood: Picken, Williams, D. Twomey, McCormack, Taylor, Stewart.

Umpires: Robinson, Dye. Match played at MCG.

Attendance: 112,964

*The Magpies' sixth Grand Final in five years — and still they couldn't win one. This time the margin was 20 points, but again the victor was Carlton. Many were convinced that the Collingwood finals' jinx would never be beaten.*

CARLTON
B: D. English, S. Howell, V. Perovic
HB: K. Hunter, B. Doull, W. Harmes
C: P. Maylin, G. Wells, D. Glascott
HF: P. Bosustow, M. Maclure, W. Johnston
F: D. McKay, P. McConville, J. Buckley
R: M. Fitzpatrick (c.), K. Sheldon, R. Ashman
Interchange: A. Marcou, M. Bortolotto
Coach: D. Parkin

COLLINGWOOD
B: I. Cooper, P. McCormack, R. Byrne
HB: D. Twomey, W. Picken, G. Allan
C: R. Barham, M. Williams, W. Irwin
HF: P. Daicos, C. Davis, R. Kink
F: R. Shaw, R. Brewer, C. Stewart
R: P. Moore (c.), M. Taylor, A. Shaw
Interchange: S. Atkin, N. Lovell
Coach: T. Hafey

# 1981

| | | P | W | L | D | For | Agst | % | Pts |
|---|---|---|---|---|---|---|---|---|---|
| 1 | Carlton (1) | 22 | 17 | 5 | | 2303 | 1768 | 130.3 | 68 |
| 2 | Collingwood (2) | 22 | 17 | 5 | | 2399 | 1957 | 122.6 | 68 |
| 3 | Geelong (3) | 22 | 16 | 6 | | 2224 | 1714 | 129.8 | 64 |
| 4 | Essendon (5) | 22 | 16 | 6 | | 2323 | 1821 | 127.6 | 64 |
| 5 | Fitzroy (4) | 22 | 14 | 8 | | 2413 | 2152 | 112.1 | 56 |
| 6 | Hawthorn | 22 | 13 | 9 | | 2313 | 2114 | 109.4 | 52 |
| 7 | Richmond | 22 | 13 | 9 | | 2323 | 2207 | 105.3 | 52 |
| 8 | North Melb | 22 | 10 | 12 | | 2386 | 2293 | 104.1 | 40 |
| 9 | South Melb | 22 | 8 | 14 | | 2165 | 2522 | 85.8 | 32 |
| 10 | St Kilda | 22 | 5 | 17 | | 1930 | 2266 | 85.2 | 20 |
| 11 | Footscray | 22 | 2 | 20 | | 1764 | 2680 | 65.8 | 8 |
| 12 | Melbourne | 22 | 1 | 21 | | 1824 | 2873 | 63.5 | 4 |

*(22 H & A matches)*

**Elimination Final**
Fitzroy 16.13 (109) d. Essendon 13.16 (94)
**Qualifying Final**
Geelong 16.16 (112) d. Collingwood 13.20 (98)
**First Semi Final**
Collingwood 19.19 (133) d. Fitzroy 19.18 (132)
**Second Semi Final**
Carlton 16.17 (113) d. Geelong 11.7 (73)
**Preliminary Final**
Collingwood 12.10 (82) d. Geelong 11.9 (75)

**Grand Final**
Carlton 2.4 5.8 8.13 12.20 (92) d
Collingwood 2.6 5.7 10.10 10.12 (72)

# 1982

| | | P | W | L | D | For | Agst | % | Pts |
|---|---|---|---|---|---|---|---|---|---|
| 1 | Richmond (2) | 22 | 18 | 4 | | 2682 | 2125 | 126.2 | 72 |
| 2 | Hawthorn (3) | 22 | 17 | 5 | | 2828 | 2149 | 131.6 | 68 |
| 3 | Carlton (1) | 22 | 16 | 5 | 1 | 2561 | 2008 | 127.5 | 66 |
| 4 | Essendon (5) | 22 | 16 | 6 | | 2576 | 2057 | 125.2 | 64 |
| 5 | North Melb (4) | 22 | 14 | 8 | | 2693 | 2458 | 109.6 | 56 |
| 6 | Fitzroy | 22 | 12 | 9 | 1 | 2614 | 2550 | 102.5 | 50 |
| 7 | Sydney | 22 | 12 | 10 | | 2621 | 2537 | 103.3 | 48 |
| 8 | Melbourne | 22 | 8 | 14 | | 2488 | 2752 | 90.4 | 32 |
| 9 | Geelong | 22 | 7 | 15 | | 2073 | 2293 | 90.4 | 28 |
| 10 | Collingwood | 22 | 4 | 18 | | 2201 | 2575 | 85.5 | 16 |
| 11 | St Kilda | 22 | 4 | 18 | | 2188 | 3052 | 71.7 | 16 |
| 12 | Footscray | 22 | 3 | 19 | | 2066 | 3035 | 68.1 | 12 |

*(22 H & A matches)*

**Elimination Final**
Nth. Melb. 19.14 (128) d. Essendon 16.19 (115)
**Qualifying Final**
Carlton 25.13 (163) d. Hawthorn 16.9 (105)
**First Semi Final**
Hawthorn 24.22 (166) d. Nth. Melb. 18.6 (114)
**Second Semi Final**
Richmond 16.17 (113) d. Carlton 13.12 (90)
**Preliminary Final**
Carlton 13.16 (94) d. Hawthorn 8.15 (63)

**Grand Final**
Carlton 4.7 6.11 11.15 14.19 (103) d
Richmond 4.3 9.4 9.10 12.13 (85)
Goals — Carlton: Johnston 2, McConville 2,

Ashman 2, Fitzpatrick 2, Harmes, Hunter, Bosustow, Marcou, Maclure, Maylin. Richmond: Bartlett 3, Cloke 3, Rioli 3, Raines, Jess, Weightman.

Best — Carlton: Johnston, Fitzpatrick, Hunter, Perovic, Marcou, Doull. Richmond: Rioli, Weightman, Strachan, Raines, Keane, Wiley.

Umpires: Sawers, James. Match played at MCG.

Attendance: 107,536

*The Blues got home by three goals from Richmond in a spectacular contest dominated by Wayne Johnston and highlighted by the appearance of the first ever Grand Final streaker, Helen D'Amico. Her 'tussle' with Bruce Doull was worth the entrance money alone.*

CARLTON

B: D. English, B. Doull, V. Perovic
HB: M. Bortolotto, K. Hunter, K. Sheldon
C: D. Glascott, J. Buckley, W. Harmes
HF: P. Bosustow, M. Maclure, W. Johnston
F: P. McConville, R. Ditchburn, A. Marcou
R: M. Fitzpatrick (c.), P. Maylin, R. Ashman
Reserves: W. Jones, R. Klomp
Coach: D. Parkin

RICHMOND

B: G. Landy, A. Martello, E. Dunne
HB: M. Keane, J. Jess, G. Strachan
C: S. Williams, G. Raines, B. Wood
HF: K. Bartlett, D. Cloke (c.), M. Rioli
F: M. Roach, I. Sartori, D. Weightman
R: M. Lee, R. Wiley, B. Rowlings
Interchange: B. Tempany, P. Welsh
Coach: F. Bourke

Goals — Hawthorn: L. Matthews 6, Byrne 3, Loveridge 2, Greene 2, Judge 2, Tuck, Knights, Kennedy, Wallace, O'Halloran. Essendon: T. Daniher 2, Kink, Ezard, Walsh, Copping, S. Madden, Wood.

Best — Hawthorn: Tuck, Knights, L. Matthews, Robertson, Kennedy, Greene. Essendon: T. Daniher, Foulds, S. Madden, Heard, Williams, Buhagiar.

Umpires: Nash, Smith. Match played at MCG.

Attendance: 110,332

*Hawthorn set a new record-winning margin for a Grand Final with its 83-point annihilation of Essendon. Even Collingwood fans cheered. The Magpies' reign as biggest Grand Final losers had lasted just three years.*

HAWTHORN

B: G. Ayres, C. Mew, D. O'Halloran
HB: R. Greene, M. McCarthy, J. Kennedy
C: P. Schwab, T. Wallace, R. Eade
HF: G. Buckenara, D. Brereton, P. Knights
F: L. Matthews (c.), M. Byrne, R. Loveridge
R: I. Paton, M. Tuck, C. Robertson
Interchange: R. DiPierdomenico, K. Judge
Coach: A. Jeans

ESSENDON

B: S. Heard, P. Weston, S. Carey
HB: G. Foulds, K. Walsh, P. Bradbury
C: G. Hawker, M. Neagle, B. Wood
HF: R. Kink, R. Merrett, A. Ezard
F: D. Williams, T. Daniher (c.), P. Van Der Haar
R: S. Madden, T. Watson, T. Buhagiar
Interchange: S. Copping, C. Clayton
Coach: K. Sheedy

# 1983

| | | P | W | L | D | For | Agst | % | Pts |
|---|---|---|---|---|---|---|---|---|---|
| 1 | North Melb (3) | 22 | 16 | 6 | | 2789 | 2183 | 127.8 | 64 |
| 2 | Hawthorn (1) | 22 | 15 | 7 | | 2675 | 2078 | 128.7 | 60 |
| 3 | Fitzroy (4) | 22 | 15 | 7 | | 2608 | 2059 | 126.7 | 60 |
| 4 | Essendon (2) | 22 | 15 | 7 | | 2664 | 2215 | 120.3 | 60 |
| 5 | Carlton (5) | 22 | 13 | 9 | | 2360 | 2244 | 105.2 | 52 |
| 6 | Collingwood | 22 | 12 | 10 | | 2315 | 2247 | 103.0 | 48 |
| 7 | Footscray | 22 | 10 | 12 | | 2102 | 2428 | 86.6 | 40 |
| 8 | Melbourne | 22 | 9 | 13 | | 2220 | 2557 | 86.8 | 36 |
| 9 | Geelong | 22 | 8 | 14 | | 1932 | 2197 | 87.9 | 32 |
| 10 | Richmond | 22 | 7 | 15 | | 2124 | 2392 | 88.8 | 28 |
| 11 | Sydney | 22 | 7 | 15 | | 2068 | 2670 | 77.5 | 28 |
| 12 | St Kilda | 22 | 5 | 17 | | 2150 | 2737 | 78.6 | 20 |

*(22 H & A matches)*

**Elimination Final**
Essendon 17.12 (114) d. Carlton 12.9 (81)
**Qualifying Final**
Hawthorn 19.13 (127) d. Fitzroy 19.9 (123)
**First Semi Final**
Essendon 16.13 (109) d. Fitzroy 12.14 (86)
**Second Semi Final**
Hawthorn 13.10 (88) d. Nth. Melb. 6.12 (48)
**Preliminary Final**
Essendon 25.14 (164) d. Nth. Melb. 12.6 (78)

**Grand Final**
Hawthorn 5.6 12.10 16.18 20.20 (140) d
Essendon 3.0 4.1 4.3 8.9 (57)

# 1984

| | | P | W | L | D | For | Agst | % | Pts |
|---|---|---|---|---|---|---|---|---|---|
| 1 | Essendon (1) | 22 | 18 | 4 | | 2556 | 1994 | 128.2 | 72 |
| 2 | Hawthorn (2) | 22 | 17 | 5 | | 2724 | 2069 | 131.7 | 68 |
| 3 | Carlton (4) | 22 | 13 | 9 | | 2332 | 2014 | 115.8 | 52 |
| 4 | Collingwood (3) | 22 | 13 | 9 | | 2260 | 2072 | 109.1 | 52 |
| 5 | Fitzroy (5) | 22 | 11 | 11 | | 2405 | 2345 | 102.6 | 44 |
| 6 | Geelong | 22 | 11 | 11 | | 2112 | 2239 | 94.3 | 44 |
| 7 | Footscray | 22 | 11 | 11 | | 1992 | 2123 | 93.8 | 44 |
| 8 | Richmond | 22 | 10 | 12 | | 2157 | 2373 | 90.9 | 40 |
| 9 | Melbourne | 22 | 9 | 13 | | 2328 | 2233 | 104.3 | 36 |
| 10 | Sydney | 22 | 9 | 13 | | 2223 | 2522 | 88.1 | 36 |
| 11 | North Melb | 22 | 5 | 17 | | 2174 | 2661 | 81.7 | 20 |
| 12 | St Kilda | 22 | 5 | 17 | | 1904 | 2522 | 75.5 | 20 |

*(22 H & A matches)*

**Elimination Final**
Collingwood 23.15 (153) d. Fitzroy 15.17 (107)
**Qualifying Final**
Hawthorn 18.14 (122) d. Carlton 13.14 (92)
**First Semi Final**
Collingwood 17.16 (118) d. Carlton 14.9 (93)
**Second Semi Final**
Hawthorn 16.17 (113) d. Essendon 15.15 (105)
**Preliminary Final**
Essendon 28.6 (174) d. Collingwood 5.11 (41)

**Grand Final**
Essendon 2.4 3.11 5.15 14.21 (105) d
Hawthorn 6.1 8.6 10.8 12.9 (81)

Goals — Essendon: Baker 4, Duckworth 2, Watson 2, T. Daniher, Bradbury, Thompson, Merrett, Weston, Neagle. Hawthorn: L. Matthews 4, Brereton 2, Robertson 2, Loveridge, Tuck, Judge, Curran.
Best — Essendon: Duckworth, Watson, Harvey, Hawker, Heard, Baker. Hawthorn: Wallace, Loveridge, Schwab, Greene, Matthews, Ayres.
Umpires: James, Sawers, Match played at MCG.
Attendance: 92,685
*Spurred on by the debacle of '83, Essendon stormed home with a nine-goal final term to take a famous 24-point victory over Hawthorn. For the first time since 1966, a team other than Richmond, Carlton, Hawthorn or North had won the flag.*
ESSENDON
B: G. Foulds, W. Duckworth, P. Weston
HB: P. Bradbury, K. Walsh, G. Hawker
C: M. Neagle, L. Baker, S. Heard
HF: T. Watson, T. Daniher (c.), P. Van Der Haar
F: A. Ezard, S. Madden, F. Dunell
R: R. Merrett, N. Clarke, D. Williams
Interchange: M. Harvey, M. Thompson
Coach: K. Sheedy
HAWTHORN
B: G. Ayres, D. O'Halloran, C. Robertson
HB: R. Lester-Smith, C. Mew, P. Schwab
C: R. DiPierdomenico, T. Wallace, P. Russo
HF: K. Judge, D. Brereton, P. Curran
F: M. McCarthy, L. Matthews (c.), R. Loveridge
R: M. Byrne, M. Tuck, R. Greene
Interchange: I. Paton, R. Eade
Coach: A. Jeans

# 1985

| | | P | W | L | D | For | Agst | % | Pts |
|---|---|---|---|---|---|---|---|---|---|
| 1 | Essendon (1) | 22 | 19 | 3 | | 2755 | 1991 | 138.4 | 76 |
| 2 | Footscray (3) | 22 | 16 | 6 | | 2417 | 2000 | 120.9 | 64 |
| 3 | Hawthorn (2) | 22 | 15 | 6 | 1 | 2647 | 2024 | 130.8 | 62 |
| 4 | Carlton (5) | 22 | 15 | 7 | | 2430 | 2104 | 115.5 | 60 |
| 5 | North Melb (4) | 22 | 13 | 8 | 1 | 2379 | 2431 | 97.9 | 54 |
| 6 | Geelong | 22 | 12 | 10 | | 2277 | 2263 | 100.6 | 48 |
| 7 | Collingwood | 22 | 10 | 12 | | 2197 | 2180 | 100.8 | 40 |
| 8 | Richmond | 22 | 9 | 13 | | 2362 | 2590 | 91.2 | 36 |
| 9 | Fitzroy | 22 | 7 | 15 | | 2301 | 2452 | 93.8 | 28 |
| 10 | Sydney | 22 | 6 | 16 | | 2219 | 2349 | 94.5 | 24 |
| 11 | Melbourne | 22 | 6 | 16 | | 1965 | 2527 | 77.8 | 24 |
| 12 | St Kilda | 22 | 3 | 19 | | 1899 | 2937 | 64.7 | 12 |

*(22 H & A matches)*

**Elimination Final**
Nth. Melb. 20.6 (126) d. Carlton 16.11 (107)
**Qualifying Final**
Hawthorn 22.23 (155) d. Footscray 8.14 (62)
**First Semi Final**
Footscray 19.23 (137) d. Nth. Melb. 16.11 (107)
**Second Semi Final**
Essendon 14.18 (102) d. Hawthorn 9.8 (62)
**Preliminary Final**
Hawthorn 16.13 (109) d. Footscray 15.9 (99)

**Grand Final**
Essendon 6.4 11.9 15.11 26.14 (170) d
Hawthorn 5.1 9.3 11.5 14.8 (92)

Goals — Essendon: Salmon 6, Merrett 5, Harvey 4, Watson 3, Baker 2, Ezard 2, Williams 2, Thompson, Duckworth. Hawthorn: Brereton 8, L. Matthews, Loveridge, McCarthy, Judge, Lester-Smith, DiPierdomenico.
Best — Essendon: S. Madden, Merrett, Salmon, Watson, Baker, Thompson. Hawthorn: Brereton, Lester-Smith, Kennedy, Morris, O'Halloran, Loveridge.
Umpires: Cameron, Robinson. Match played at MCG.
Attendance: 100,042
*The Bombers were hailed as one of the best teams in AFL history after their 78-point demolition job on Hawthorn in the teams' third successive Grand Final meeting. There were highlights aplenty — a wild brawl to kick off proceedings, Dermott Brereton kicking a record eight goals for the losers and Leigh Matthews being chaired from the ground in tears after his final game.*
ESSENDON
B: M. Thompson, P. Weston, W. Duckworth
HB: G. Foulds, K. Walsh, G. Hawker
C: B. Wood, T. Watson, N. Clarke
HF: T. Daniher (c.), R. Merrett, M. Harvey
F: L. Baker, P. Salmon, P. Van Der Haar
R: S. Madden, D. Williams, T. Elshaug
Interchange: S. Carey, A. Ezard
Coach: K. Sheedy
HAWTHORN
B: G. Ayres, C. Mew, P. Schwab
HB: R. Morris, R. Lester-Smith, R. Greene
C: R. DiPierdomenico, T. Wallace, P. Russo
HF: J. Kennedy, D. Brereton, K. Judge
F: M. McCarthy, J. Dunstall, L. Matthews (c.)
R: C. Langford, R. Handley, R. Loveridge
Interchange: M. Tuck, D. O'Halloran
Coach: A. Jeans

# 1986

| | | P | W | L | D | For | Agst | % | Pts |
|---|---|---|---|---|---|---|---|---|---|
| 1 | Hawthorn (1) | 22 | 18 | 4 | | 2698 | 1906 | 141.6 | 72 |
| 2 | Sydney (4) | 22 | 16 | 6 | | 2470 | 2087 | 118.4 | 64 |
| 3 | Carlton (2) | 22 | 15 | 7 | | 2566 | 1809 | 141.9 | 60 |
| 4 | Fitzroy (3) | 22 | 13 | 9 | | 2068 | 2063 | 100.2 | 52 |
| 5 | Essendon (5) | 22 | 12 | 10 | | 2379 | 1978 | 120.3 | 48 |
| 6 | Collingwood | 22 | 12 | 10 | | 2261 | 2070 | 109.2 | 48 |
| 7 | North Melb | 22 | 12 | 10 | | 2324 | 2356 | 98.6 | 48 |
| 8 | Footscray | 22 | 11 | 11 | | 1963 | 2010 | 97.7 | 44 |
| 9 | Geelong | 22 | 7 | 15 | | 2133 | 2599 | 82.1 | 28 |
| 10 | Richmond | 22 | 7 | 15 | | 2151 | 2745 | 78.4 | 28 |
| 11 | Melbourne | 22 | 7 | 15 | | 2003 | 2673 | 74.9 | 28 |
| 12 | St Kilda | 22 | 2 | 20 | | 1846 | 2566 | 71.9 | 8 |

*(22 H & A matches)*

**Elimination Final**
Fitzroy 8.10 (58) d. Essendon 8.9 (57)
**Qualifying Final**
Carlton 18.12 (120) d. Sydney 15.14 (104)
**First Semi Final**
Fitzroy 13.16 (94) d. Sydney 13.11 (89)
**Second Semi Final**
Carlton 16.16 (112) d. Hawthorn 13.6 (84)
**Preliminary Final**
Hawthorn 16.14 (110) d. Fitzroy 7.12 (54)

**Grand Final**

Hawthorn 5.6 8.8 15.9 16.14 (110) d
Carlton 1.5 4.11 6.13 9.14 (68)
Goals — Hawthorn: Dunstall 6, Buckenara 4,
Brereton 3, Curran, Russo, Ayres. Carlton:
Meldrum 3, Kernahan 2, Glascott, McKenzie, Rhys-
Jones, Evans.
Best — Hawthorn: Ayres, Eade, Dunstall,
Buckenara, Wallace, Langford. Carlton: Alvin,
Meldrum, Glascott, Madden, English, Motley.
Umpires: Cameron, Russo. Match played at MCG.
Attendance: 101,861
*Hawthorn showed its spirit had not been broken by*
*the crushing losses of '84 and '85 with a*
*comprehensive 42-point win. It was Bruce Doull's*
*last game, but he lowered his colors to young*
*Hawk spearhead Jason Dunstall.*
HAWTHORN
B: G. Ayres, C. Langford, R. Greene
HB: R. Morris, C. Mew, P. Schwab
C: R. DiPierdomenico, T. Wallace, R. Eade
HF: G. Buckenara, D. Brereton, J. Kennedy
F: P. Curran, J. Dunstall, J. Platten
R: G. Dear, M. Tuck (c.), R. Loveridge
Interchange: P. Abbott, P. Russo
Coach: A. Jeans
CARLTON
B: W. Harmes, B. Doull, P. Dean
HB: D. English, J. Dorotich, P. Motley
C: D. Rhys-Jones, C. Bradley, W. Blackwell
HF: W. Johnston, S. Kernahan, P. Meldrum
F: B. Evans, K. Hunter, M. Maclure (c.)
R: J. Madden, T. Alvin, D. Glascott
Interchange: W. McKenzie, S. Robertson
Coach: R. Walls

# 1987

| | | P | W | L | D | For | Agst | % | Pts |
|---|---|---|---|---|---|---|---|---|---|
| 1 | Carlton (1) | 22 | 18 | 4 | | 2599 | 1883 | 138.0 | 72 |
| 2 | Hawthorn (2) | 22 | 17 | 5 | | 2781 | 1891 | 147.1 | 64 |
| 3 | Sydney (4) | 22 | 15 | 7 | | 2846 | 2197 | 129.5 | 60 |
| 4 | North Melb (5) | 22 | 13 | 8 | 1 | 2402 | 2417 | 99.4 | 54 |
| 5 | Melbourne (3) | 22 | 12 | 10 | | 2189 | 2026 | 108.0 | 48 |
| 6 | Geelong | 22 | 11 | 10 | 1 | 2355 | 2348 | 100.3 | 46 |
| 7 | Footscray | 22 | 11 | 10 | 1 | 1959 | 2046 | 95.7 | 46 |
| 8 | West Coast | 22 | 11 | 11 | | 2386 | 2438 | 97.9 | 44 |
| 9 | Essendon | 22 | 9 | 12 | 1 | 2075 | 2318 | 89.5 | 38 |
| 10 | St Kilda | 22 | 9 | 13 | | 2150 | 2369 | 90.8 | 36 |
| 11 | Fitzroy | 22 | 8 | 14 | | 2328 | 2544 | 91.5 | 32 |
| 12 | Collingwood | 22 | 7 | 15 | | 1853 | 2425 | 76.4 | 28 |
| 13 | Brisbane Bears | 22 | 6 | 16 | | 2113 | 2666 | 79.3 | 24 |
| 14 | Richmond | 22 | 5 | 17 | | 2199 | 2667 | 82.5 | 20 |

*(22 H & A matches)*

**Elimination Final**
Melbourne 22.26 (158) d. Nth. Melb. 5.10 (40)
**Qualifying Final**
Hawthorn 23.18 (156) d. Sydney 8.9 (57)
**First Semi Final**
Melbourne 21.23 (149) d. Sydney 10.13 (73)
**Second Semi Final**
Carlton 11.14 (80) d. Hawthorn 10.5 (65)
**Preliminary Final**
Hawthorn 11.14 (80) d. Melbourne 10.18 (78)

**294**

**Grand Final**

Carlton 3.5 6.8 10.11 15.14 (104) d
Hawthorn 4.2 4.9 7.13 9.17 (71)
Goals — Carlton: Kernahan 3, Bradley 3, Johnston
2, Dorotich, Gleeson, Murphy, Hunter, Naley,
McKenzie, Meldrum. Hawthorn: Kennedy 3, Curran,
Collins, Pritchard, Platten, DiPierdomenico, G.
Dear.
Best — Carlton: Rhys-Jones, Johnston, Glascott,
Aitken, Madden, Alvin. Hawthorn: Langford,
DiPierdomenico, Tuck, Collins, Ayres, Greene.
Umpires: Robinson, Sawers. Match played at MCG.
Attendance: 92,754
*An outstanding performance by David Rhys-Jones*
*set up Carlton for a 33-point win on a day when the*
*temperature soared into the 30s. The Hawks*
*looked drained after their post-siren win in the*
*preliminary final against Melbourne the previous*
*week.*
CARLTON
B: T. Alvin, S. Silvagni, D. Glascott
HB: I. Aitken, D. Rhys-Jones, P. Dean
C: M. Kennedy, C. Bradley, S. Robertson
HF: R. Dennis, S. Kernahan (c.), K. Hunter
F: P. Meldrum, J. Dorotich, M. Naley
R: J. Madden, W. Johnston, F. Murphy
Interchange: A. Gleeson, W. McKenzie
Coach: R. Walls
HAWTHORN
B: G. Ayres, C. Mew, A. Collins
HB: R. Jencke, C. Langford, J. Kennedy
C: R. Greene, M. Tuck (c.), R. DiPierdomenico
HF: P. Curran, D. Brereton, R. Morris
F: G. Buckenara, P. Dear, P. Russo
R: G. Dear, P. Schwab, J. Platten
Interchange: P. Abbott, D. Pritchard
Coach: A. Jeans

# 1988

| | | P | W | L | D | For | Agst | % | Pts |
|---|---|---|---|---|---|---|---|---|---|
| 1 | Hawthorn (1) | 22 | 19 | 3 | | 2791 | 1962 | 142.3 | 76 |
| 2 | Collingwood (4) | 22 | 15 | 6 | 1 | 1948 | 1728 | 112.7 | 62 |
| 3 | Carlton (3) | 22 | 15 | 7 | | 2342 | 1961 | 119.4 | 60 |
| 4 | West Coast (5) | 22 | 13 | 9 | | 2199 | 1966 | 111.9 | 52 |
| 5 | Melbourne (2) | 22 | 13 | 9 | | 2003 | 1961 | 102.1 | 52 |
| 6 | Essendon | 22 | 12 | 10 | | 2186 | 2017 | 108.4 | 48 |
| 7 | Sydney | 22 | 12 | 10 | | 2169 | 2176 | 99.7 | 48 |
| 8 | Footscray | 22 | 11 | 11 | | 1880 | 1803 | 104.3 | 44 |
| 9 | Geelong | 22 | 10 | 12 | | 2356 | 2246 | 104.9 | 40 |
| 10 | Richmond | 22 | 8 | 14 | | 2161 | 2540 | 85.1 | 32 |
| 11 | North Melb | 22 | 7 | 14 | 1 | 2361 | 2638 | 89.5 | 30 |
| 12 | Fitzroy | 22 | 7 | 15 | | 2128 | 2538 | 83.8 | 28 |
| 13 | Brisbane Bears | 22 | 7 | 15 | | 1806 | 2421 | 74.6 | 28 |
| 14 | St Kilda | 22 | 4 | 18 | | 1708 | 2081 | 82.1 | 16 |

*(22 H & A matches)*

**Elimination Final**
Melbourne 11.7 (73) d. West Coast 10.11 (71)
**Qualifying Final**
Carlton 22.13 (145) d. Collingwood 16.11 (107)
**First Semi Final**
Melbourne 13.17 (95) d. Collingwood 12.10 (82)
**Second Semi Final**
Hawthorn 9.12 (66) d. Carlton 6.9 (45)

**Preliminary Final**
Melbourne 19.6 (120) d. Carlton 14.14 (98)

**Grand Final**
Hawthorn 4.4 10.9 14.16 22.20 (152) d
Melbourne 1.5 2.8 5.14 6.20 (56)
Goals — Hawthorn: Dunstall 7, Abbott 6, Brereton
5, Schwab, Kennedy, Morrissy, DiPierdomenico.
Melbourne: Lyon 2, Williams 2, Greg Healy,
Johnson.
Best — Hawthorn: Ayres, Abbott, Platten, Schwab,
Dunstall, Brereton. Melbourne: B. Lovett, Stynes,
Greg Healy, Grinter, Lovell, Johnson.
Umpires: Cameron, Sheehan. Match played at MCG.
Attendance: 93,754
*Melbourne made its first appearance in a Grand
Final since 1964 — and probably wished it hadn't.
The Hawks crushed the Demons by 96 points, the
biggest Grand Final thumping in history. The
hapless Demons could manage only 6.20 (56).
Gary Ayres won his second Norm Smith Medal, the
only player to have won it twice.*
HAWTHORN
B: A. Collins, C. Langford, G. Ayres
HB: S. Maginness, C. Mew, M. Tuck (c.)
C: R. DiPierdomenico, P. Schwab, T. Hall
HF: C. Wittman, D. Brereton, J. Kennedy
F: P. Abbott, J. Dunstall, J. Morrissey
R: G. Dear, G. Buckenara, J. Platten
Interchange: R. Greene, D. Pritchard
Coach: A. Joyce
MELBOURNE
B: A. Johnson, S. Stretch, R. Grinter
HB: S. Newport, J. Duursma, B. Lovett
C: T. Viney, B. Wilson, G. Yeats
HF: G. Lyon, E. Spalding, D. Williams
F: J. Stynes, S. Wight, R. Jackson
R: D. Hughes, A. Lovell, G. Healy (c.)
Interchange: D. Flintoff, S. Febey
Coach: J. Northey

# 1989

| | | P | W | L | D | For | Agst | % | Pts |
|---|---|---|---|---|---|---|---|---|---|
| 1 | Hawthorn (1) | 22 | 19 | 3 | | 2678 | 1748 | 153.2 | 76 |
| 2 | Essendon (3) | 22 | 17 | 5 | | 2240 | 1705 | 131.4 | 68 |
| 3 | Geelong (2) | 22 | 16 | 6 | | 2916 | 1987 | 146.8 | 64 |
| 4 | Melbourne (4) | 22 | 14 | 8 | | 1876 | 1944 | 96.5 | 56 |
| 5 | Collingwood (5) | 22 | 13 | 9 | | 2216 | 1964 | 112.8 | 52 |
| 6 | Fitzroy | 22 | 12 | 10 | | 2069 | 2125 | 97.4 | 48 |
| 7 | Sydney | 22 | 11 | 11 | | 1959 | 1958 | 100.1 | 44 |
| 8 | Carlton | 22 | 9 | 12 | 1 | 1921 | 2079 | 92.4 | 38 |
| 9 | North Melb | 22 | 9 | 13 | | 2061 | 2301 | 89.6 | 36 |
| 10 | Brisbane Bears | 22 | 8 | 14 | | 1792 | 2274 | 78.8 | 32 |
| 11 | West Coast | 22 | 7 | 15 | | 1948 | 2247 | 86.7 | 28 |
| 12 | St Kilda | 22 | 7 | 15 | | 2108 | 2502 | 84.3 | 28 |
| 13 | Footscray | 22 | 6 | 15 | 1 | 1614 | 1855 | 87.0 | 26 |
| 14 | Richmond | 22 | 5 | 17 | | 1725 | 2434 | 70.9 | 20 |

*(22 H & A matches)*

**Elimination Final**
Melbourne 17.9 (111) d. Collingwood 13.10 (88)
**Qualifying Final**
Essendon 24.13 (157) d. Geelong 11.15 (81)
**First Semi Final**
Geelong 22.21 (153) d. Melbourne 12.18 (90)
**Second Semi Final**
Hawthorn 16.16 (112) d. Essendon 11.10 (76)
**Preliminary Final**
Geelong 24.20 (164) d. Essendon 10.10 (70)

**Grand Final**
Hawthorn 8.4 12.9 18.13 21.18 (144) d
Geelong 2.0 7.2 13.7 21.12 (138)
Goals — Hawthorn: Dunstall 4, Anderson 4,
Buckenara 4, Brereton 3, Curran 3,
DiPierdomenico, Wittman, Morrissey. Geelong:
Ablett 9, Brownless 2, Stoneham 2, Hamilton 2,
Cameron 2, Bews, Bairstow, Bruns, Flanigan.
Best — Hawthorn: Pritchard, Anderson,
DiPierdomenico, Buckenara, Dunstall, Curran.
Geelong: Ablett, Lindner, Flanigan, Hamilton, Bews,
Couch.
Umpires: Carey, Sheehan. Match played at MCG.
Attendance: 94,796
*Unquestionably the finest Grand Final of the modern
era. A game that had everything, right from
Dermott Brereton being 'crunched' by Mark Yeates
at the opening bounce, then getting up to mark and
goal. Platten was concussed, 'Dipper' had a
punctured lung, Ayres, Tuck, Pritchard and Curran
were all injured. But the Hawks held on desperately
to win by a goal — despite heroics from Gary
Ablett that produced nine goals.*
HAWTHORN
B: A. Collins, C. Langford, G. Ayres
HB: S. Maginness, C. Mew, J. Kennedy
C: D. Pritchard, A. Condon, R. DiPierdomenico
HF: D. Anderson, D. Brereton, G. Buckenara
F: P. Curran, J. Dunstall, C. Wittman
R: G. Dear, M. Tuck (c.), J. Platten
Interchange: J. Morrissey, G. Madigan
Coach: A. Jeans
GEELONG
B: S. Malakellis, T. Darcy, S. Hocking
HB: M. Bos, M. Schulze, B. Lindner
C: N. Bruns, P. Couch, M. Yeates
HF: G. Hocking, B. Stoneham, G. Ablett
F: D. Cameron, B. Brownless, R. Scott
R: D. Bourke (c.), M. Bairstow, A. Bews
Interchange: D. Flanigan, S. Hamilton
Coach: M. Blight

# 1990

| | | P | W | L | D | For | Agst | % | Pts |
|---|---|---|---|---|---|---|---|---|---|
| 1 | Essendon (2) | 22 | 17 | 5 | | 2526 | 1815 | 139.2 | 68 |
| 2 | Collingwood (1) | 22 | 16 | 6 | | 2376 | 1825 | 130.2 | 64 |
| 3 | West Coast (3) | 22 | 16 | 6 | | 2274 | 1920 | 118.4 | 64 |
| 4 | Melbourne (4) | 22 | 16 | 6 | | 2339 | 2066 | 113.2 | 64 |
| 5 | Hawthorn (5) | 22 | 14 | 8 | | 2414 | 2002 | 120.6 | 56 |
| 6 | North Melb | 22 | 12 | 10 | | 2519 | 2210 | 114.0 | 48 |
| 7 | Footscray | 22 | 12 | 10 | | 2016 | 2031 | 99.3 | 48 |
| 8 | Carlton | 22 | 11 | 11 | | 2277 | 2187 | 104.1 | 44 |
| 9 | St Kilda | 22 | 9 | 13 | | 2328 | 2313 | 100.6 | 36 |
| 10 | Geelong | 22 | 8 | 14 | | 2248 | 2398 | 93.7 | 32 |
| 11 | Richmond | 22 | 7 | 15 | | 1988 | 2530 | 78.6 | 28 |
| 12 | Fitzroy | 22 | 7 | 15 | | 1874 | 2389 | 78.4 | 28 |
| 13 | Sydney | 22 | 5 | 17 | | 1904 | 2704 | 70.4 | 20 |
| 14 | Brisbane Bears | 22 | 4 | 18 | | 1733 | 2426 | 71.4 | 16 |

*(22 H & A matches)*

**Elimination Final**
Melbourne 10.13 (73) d. Hawthorn 8.16 (64)
**Qualifying Final**
Collingwood 13.12 (90) drew with West Coast 13.12 (90)
**Qualifying Final Replay**
Collingwood 19.12 (126) d. West Coast 9.13 (67)
**First Semi Final**
West Coast 19.16 (130) d. Melbourne 15.10 (100)
**Second Semi Final**
Collingwood 17.15 (117) d. Essendon 7.12 (54)
**Preliminary Final**
Essendon 18.13 (121) d. West Coast 8.10 (58)

**Grand Final**
Collingwood 2.5 8.9 11.10 13.11 (89) d
Essendon 2.2 3.5 5.6 5.11 (41)
Goals — Collingwood: Brown 2, Barwick 2, Crosisca, Russell 2, Daicos 2, Monkhorst, Starcevich, McGuane. Essendon: Salmon 2, Derek Kickett, Somerville, Grenvold.
Best — Collingwood: A. Shaw, Russell, Monkhorst, Millane, Francis, Kerrison. Essendon; Watson, Sporn, T. Daniher, Derek Kickett, Ezard, O'Donnell.
Umpires: Sawers, Rich. Match played at MCG.
Attendance: 98,944
*The first ever AFL flag and the first time Hawthorn has missed a Grand Final since 1982. This was the one the Magpie Army had waited 32 years for. Inspired by Tony Shaw, Darren Millane and Peter Daicos, the Pies ground their way to a premiership in what was otherwise a fairly forgettable spectacle of football. But try telling that to the black and white hordes.*
COLLINGWOOD
B: S. Kerrison, M. Christian, M. Gayfer
HB: S. Morwood, C. Kelly, G. Crosisca
C: D. Millane, T. Shaw (c.), G. Wright
HF: D. Banks, J. Manson, D. Barwick
F: S. Russell, G. Brown, P. Daicos
R: D. Monkhorst, M. McGuane, T. Francis
Interchange: J. Turner, C. Starcevich
Coach: L. Matthews
ESSENDON
B: M. Thompson, A. Daniher, P. Hamilton
HB: D. Grenvold, T. Daniher, G. O'Donnell
C: G. Anderson, D. Kickett, M. Long
HF: M. Harvey, P. Van Der Haar, P. Cransberg
F: A. Ezard, P. Salmon, K. Sporn
R: S. Madden, T. Watson (c.), D. Bewick
Interchange: C. Daniher, P. Somerville
Coach: K. Sheedy

# 1991

| | | P | W | L | D | For | Agst | % | Pts |
|---|---|---|---|---|---|---|---|---|---|
| 1 | West Coast (2) | 22 | 19 | 3 | | 2485 | 1532 | 162.2 | 76 |
| 2 | Hawthorn (1) | 22 | 16 | 6 | | 2793 | 2055 | 135.9 | 64 |
| 3 | Geelong (3) | 22 | 16 | 6 | | 2660 | 2021 | 131.6 | 64 |
| 4 | St Kilda (5) | 22 | 14 | 7 | 1 | 2512 | 2087 | 120.4 | 58 |
| 5 | Melbourne (4) | 22 | 13 | 9 | | 2355 | 2123 | 110.9 | 52 |
| 6 | Essendon (6) | 22 | 13 | 9 | | 2203 | 2017 | 109.2 | 52 |
| 7 | Collingwood | 22 | 12 | 9 | 1 | 2349 | 2033 | 115.5 | 50 |
| 8 | North Melb | 22 | 12 | 10 | | 2456 | 2693 | 91.2 | 48 |
| 9 | Adelaide | 22 | 10 | 12 | | 2041 | 2282 | 89.4 | 40 |
| 10 | Footscray | 22 | 9 | 12 | 1 | 1815 | 2064 | 87.9 | 38 |
| 11 | Carlton | 22 | 8 | 14 | | 1878 | 2113 | 88.9 | 32 |
| 12 | Sydney | 22 | 7 | 14 | 1 | 2360 | 2778 | 85.0 | 30 |
| 13 | Richmond | 22 | 7 | 15 | | 2141 | 2450 | 87.4 | 28 |
| 14 | Fitzroy | 22 | 4 | 18 | | 1837 | 2771 | 66.3 | 16 |
| 15 | Brisbane Bears | 22 | 3 | 19 | | 1976 | 2842 | 69.5 | 12 |

*(22 H & A matches)*

**First Elimination Final**
Melbourne 17.11 (113) d. Essendon 11.9 (75)
**Second Elimination Final**
Geelong 15.14 (104) d. St Kilda 14.13 (97)
**Qualifying Final**
Hawthorn 18.16 (124) d. West Coast 15.11 (101)
**First Semi Final**
West Coast 17.15 (117) d. Melbourne 12.7 (79)
**Second Semi Final**
Hawthorn 13.17 (95) d. Geelong 13.15 (93)
**Preliminary Final**
West Coast 11.13 (79) d. Geelong 8.16 (64)

**Grand Final**
Hawthorn 3.4 7.12 12.15 20.19 (139) d
West Coast 5.1 7.2 12.5 13.8 (86)
Goals — Hawthorn: Dunstall 6, Brereton 4, P. Dear 2, Pritchard 2, Hudson 2, Hall, Condon, Anderson, Morrissey. West Coast: Sumich 5, Heady 4, Lewis 2, Wilson, Pyke.
Best — Hawthorn: P. Dear, Lawrence, Morrissey, Platten, Brereton, Condon. West Coast: McKenna, Pyke, Heady, P. Matera, Mainwaring, Sumich.
Umpires: Russo, Sheehan. Match played at VFL Park.
Attendance: 75,230
*The first, and only, Grand Final to be played at Waverley, due to reconstruction work at the MCG. Different venue maybe, but the same old Hawks, who comfortably accounted for new chum West Coast by 53 points.*
HAWTHORN
B: A. Collins, C. Langford, G. Ayres
HB: M. Tuck (c.), C. Mew, R. Jencke
C: D. Pritchard, B. Allan, A. Gowers
HF: P. Hudson, D. Brereton, T. Hall
F: D. Jarman, J. Dunstall, P. Dear
R: S. Lawrence, A. Condon, J. Platten
Interchange: D. Anderson, J. Morrissey
Coach: A. Joyce

WEST COAST
B: J. Worsfold (c.), M. Brennan, G. McKenna
HB: C. Turley, A. Lockyer, C. Waterman
C: D. Kemp, S. Watters, P. Matera
HF: B. Heady, A. McIntosh, C. Lewis
F: G. Jakovich, P. Sumich, D. Hart
R: D. Irving, D. Lamb, D. Pyke
Interchange: C. Mainwaring, P. Wilson
Coach: M. Malthouse

# 1992

| | | P | W | L | D | For | Agst | % | Pts |
|---|---|---|---|---|---|---|---|---|---|
| 1 | Geelong (2) | 22 | 16 | 6 | | 3057 | 2099 | 145.6 | 64 |
| 2 | Footscray (3) | 22 | 16 | 6 | | 2384 | 1836 | 129.8 | 64 |
| 3 | Collingwood (5) | 22 | 16 | 6 | | 2195 | 1911 | 114.9 | 64 |
| 4 | West Coast (1) | 22 | 15 | 6 | 1 | 2206 | 1752 | 125.9 | 62 |
| 5 | Hawthorn (6) | 22 | 14 | 8 | | 2579 | 2098 | 122.9 | 56 |
| 6 | St Kilda (4) | 22 | 14 | 8 | | 2415 | 2009 | 120.2 | 56 |
| 7 | Carlton | 22 | 14 | 8 | | 2362 | 2103 | 112.3 | 56 |
| 8 | Essendon | 22 | 12 | 10 | | 2241 | 2414 | 92.8 | 48 |
| 9 | Adelaide | 22 | 11 | 11 | | 2317 | 2286 | 101.4 | 44 |
| 10 | Fitzroy | 22 | 9 | 13 | | 2166 | 2398 | 90.3 | 36 |
| 11 | Melbourne | 22 | 7 | 14 | 1 | 2083 | 2386 | 87.3 | 30 |
| 12 | North Melb | 22 | 7 | 15 | | 2269 | 2535 | 89.5 | 28 |
| 13 | Richmond | 22 | 5 | 17 | | 2160 | 2938 | 73.5 | 20 |
| 14 | Brisbane Bears | 22 | 4 | 17 | 1 | 1770 | 2742 | 64.6 | 18 |
| 15 | Sydney | 22 | 3 | 18 | 1 | 1997 | 2694 | 74.1 | 14 |

*(22 H & A matches)*

**First Elimination Final**
West Coast 14.16 (100) d. Hawthorn 12.15 (87)
**Second Elimination Final**
St Kilda 13.13 (91) d. Collingwood 12.11 (83)
**Qualifying Final**
Geelong 26.16 (172) d. Footscray 17.9 (111)
**First Semi Final**
Footscray 19.5 (119) d. St Kilda 14.6 (90)
**Second Semi Final**
West Coast 20.13 (133) d. Geelong 14.11 (95)
**Preliminary Final**
Geelong 22.17 (149) d. Footscray 12.13 (85)

**Grand Final**
West Coast 2.6 6.8 11.15 16.17 (113) d
Geelong 5.5 8.8 9.10 12.13 (85)
Goals — West Coast: Sumich 6, P. Matera 5,
Evans 3, Wilson 2. Geelong: Brownless 3, Ablett 3,
Bruns, Couch, Hinkley, Poole, Riccardi, Stoneham.
Best — West Coast: P. Matera, McIntosh, Kemp,
Heady, Evans, Worsfold. Geelong: Hinkley,
McGrath, Bairstow, Stoneham, Couch, G. Hocking.
Umpires: Carey, Rich. Match played at MCG.
Attendance: 95,007
*The day Victorian footy fans had dreaded, as the
cherished premiership cup headed west, safe in
the hands of Eagles coach Mick Malthouse,
skipper John Worsfold, Norm Smith Medallist Peter
Matera and their West Coast teammates. Geelong
was the villain of the piece, going down by 28
points, after leading by two goals at half-time.*
WEST COAST
B: G. McKenna, M. Brennan, D. Pyke
HB: J. Worsfold (c.), G. Jakovich, M. White
C: P. Matera, D. Kemp, C. Waterman

HF: C. Mainwaring, K. Langdon, C. Lewis
F: A. McIntosh, P. Sumich, D. Lamb
R: P. Harding, C. Turley, T. Evans
Interchange: P. Wilson, B. Heady
Coach: M. Malthouse
GEELONG
B: S. Simpson, T. Darcy, A. Rogers
HB: K. Hinkley, T. McGrath, T. Poole
C: P. Riccardi, P. Couch, R. Scott
HF: G. Ablett, B. Stoneham, R. Merriman
F: G. Miles, B. Brownless, M. Mansfield
R: J. Barnes, M. Bairstow (c.), G. Hocking
Interchange: A. Wills, N. Bruns
Coach: M. Blight

# 1993

| | | P | W | L | D | For | Agst | % | Pts |
|---|---|---|---|---|---|---|---|---|---|
| 1 | Essendon (1) | 20 | 13 | 6 | 1 | 2333 | 1959 | 119.1 | 54 |
| 2 | Carlton (2) | 20 | 13 | 6 | 1 | 2315 | 1968 | 117.6 | 54 |
| 3 | North Melb (5) | 20 | 13 | 7 | | 2597 | 2150 | 120.8 | 52 |
| 4 | Hawthorn (6) | 20 | 13 | 7 | | 2166 | 1858 | 116.6 | 52 |
| 5 | Adelaide (3) | 20 | 12 | 8 | | 2168 | 1840 | 117.8 | 48 |
| 6 | West Coast (4) | 20 | 12 | 8 | | 1912 | 1651 | 115.8 | 48 |
| 7 | Geelong | 20 | 12 | 8 | | 2354 | 2109 | 111.6 | 48 |
| 8 | Collingwood | 20 | 11 | 9 | | 2086 | 2060 | 101.3 | 44 |
| 9 | Footscray | 20 | 11 | 9 | | 1978 | 1997 | 99.0 | 44 |
| 10 | Melbourne | 20 | 10 | 10 | | 2101 | 1873 | 112.2 | 40 |
| 11 | Fitzroy | 20 | 10 | 10 | | 2001 | 2011 | 99.5 | 40 |
| 12 | St Kilda | 20 | 10 | 10 | | 2040 | 2166 | 94.2 | 40 |
| 13 | Brisbane Bears | 20 | 4 | 16 | | 1886 | 2504 | 75.3 | 16 |
| 14 | Richmond | 20 | 4 | 16 | | 1753 | 2480 | 70.7 | 16 |
| 15 | Sydney | 20 | 1 | 19 | | 1837 | 2901 | 63.3 | 4 |

*(20 H & A matches)*

**First Elimination Final**
Adelaide 16.14 (110) d. Hawthorn 13.17 (95)
**Second Elimination Final**
West Coast 17.18 (120) d. North Melb. 11.3 (69)
**Qualifying Final**
Carlton 15.10 (100) d. Essendon 14.14 (98)
**First Semi Final**
Essendon 16.12 (108) d. West Coast 11.10 (76)
**Second Semi Final**
Carlton 13.8 (86) d. Adelaide 8.20 (68)
**Preliminary Final**
Essendon 17.9 (111) d. Adelaide 14.16 (100)

**Grand Final**
Essendon 5.8 10.9 16.11 20.13 (133) d
Carlton 1.2 5.2 10.9 13.11 (89)
Goals — Essendon: Salmon 5, Mercuri 3, Hird 2,
Long 2, Harvey, Wanganeen, C. Daniher, Bewick,
Wallis, Misiti, Denham, Calthorpe. Carlton:
Kernahan 7, Welsh 2, Williams, Heaver, Bradley,
Alvin.
Best — Essendon: Long, Mercuri, O'Donnell,
Salmon, Thompson, Harvey. Carlton: Kernahan,
Hogg, Bradley, Williams, Madden, McKay.
Umpires: Goldspink, Carey. Match played at MCG.
Attendance: 96,862
*Kevin Sheedy's second generation of 'Baby Bomb-
ers' came from nowhere to pinch a flag that had
seemed out of reach at half-time of the preliminary
final, when they trailed Adelaide by 42 points. But*

*the Bombers charged home in the second half of that game, then carried the form into 'The Big One' against the Blues, with the individual brilliance of Michael Long the most memorable feature.*

ESSENDON
B: G. Wanganeen, D. Fletcher, D. Wallis
HB: D. Grenvold, M. Harvey, M. Thompson (c.)
C: R. Olarenshaw, S. Denham, P. Hills
HF: M. Mercuri, J. Hird, J. Misiti
F: T. Watson, P. Salmon, M. Long
R: P. Somerville, G. O'Donnell, D. Bewick
Interchange: C. Daniher, D. Calthorpe
Coach: K. Sheedy

CARLTON
B: B. Ratten, S. Silvagni, A. McKay
HB: A. Christou, M. Sexton, M. Hanna
C: B. Sholl, G. Williams, F. Brown
HF: T. Alvin, E. Spalding, T. Powell
F: R. Welsh, S. Kernahan (c.), B. Heaver
R: J. Madden, C. Bradley, A. Gleeson
Interchange: M. Athorn, M. Hogg
Coach: D. Parkin

# 1994

| | | P | W | L | D | For | Agst | % | Pts |
|---|---|---|---|---|---|---|---|---|---|
| 1 | West Coast (1) | 22 | 16 | 6 | | 2078 | 1572 | 132.2 | 64 |
| 2 | Carlton (5) | 22 | 15 | 7 | | 2351 | 1774 | 132.5 | 60 |
| 3 | North Melb (3) | 22 | 13 | 9 | | 2383 | 1848 | 129.0 | 52 |
| 4 | Geelong (2) | 22 | 13 | 9 | | 2403 | 2104 | 114.2 | 52 |
| 5 | Footscray (6) | 22 | 13 | 9 | | 2106 | 1905 | 110.6 | 52 |
| 6 | Hawthorn (7) | 22 | 13 | 9 | | 2188 | 2005 | 109.1 | 52 |
| 7 | Melbourne (4) | 22 | 12 | 10 | | 2190 | 1879 | 116.6 | 48 |
| 8 | Collingwood (8) | 22 | 12 | 10 | | 2017 | 2019 | 99.9 | 48 |
| 9 | Richmond | 22 | 12 | 10 | | 2033 | 2167 | 93.8 | 48 |
| 10 | Essendon | 22 | 11 | 11 | | 2075 | 2119 | 97.9 | 44 |
| 11 | Adelaide | 22 | 9 | 12 | 1 | 1876 | 2159 | 86.9 | 38 |
| 12 | Brisbane Bears | 22 | 9 | 13 | | 1940 | 2195 | 88.4 | 36 |
| 13 | St Kilda | 22 | 7 | 14 | 1 | 1809 | 2415 | 74.9 | 30 |
| 14 | Fitzroy | 22 | 5 | 17 | | 1726 | 2456 | 70.3 | 20 |
| 15 | Sydney | 22 | 4 | 18 | | 1987 | 2545 | 78.1 | 16 |

*(22 H & A matches)*

**First Qualifying Final**
Geelong 15.16 (106) d. Footscray 15.11 (101)
**Second Qualifying Final**
North Melb. 15.24 (114) d. Hawthorn 13.13 (91)
**Third Qualifying Final**
Melbourne 18.15 (123) d. Carlton 14.12 (96)
**Fourth Qualifying Final**
West Coast 11.16 (82) d. Collingwood 12.8 (80)
**First Semi Final**
Melbourne 21.18 (144) d. Footscray 9.11 (65)
**Second Semi Final**
Geelong 15.15 (105) d. Carlton 10.12 (72)
**First Preliminary Final**
Geelong 16.13 (109) d. Nth. Melb. 14.19 (103)
**Second Preliminary Final**
West Coast 16.21 (117) d. Melbourne 8.4 (52)

**Grand Final**
West Coast 4.4 8.12 12.18 20.23 (143) d
Geelong 4.3 5.7 7.12 8.15 (63)
Goals — West Coast: Evans 3, Heady 2, Kemp 2,
Sumich 2, Wilson 2, Bond 2, Ball 2, Lewis 2,

Waterman 2, Banfield. Geelong: Brownless 4, Wills, Ablett, Couch, Riccardi.
Best — West Coast: Kemp, Jakovich, Pyke, McKenna, Brennan, Evans. Geelong: Mansfield, O'Reilly, Brownless, Riccardi, Couch, Handley.
Umpires: Rich, Sheahan, Howlett.
Match played at MCG.
Attendance: 93,860

*A repeat of 1992, except that this time West Coast gave Geelong an embarrassingly hefty 80-point shellacking. Not a great quality game, certainly not if you were a Geelong fan. Cats coach Malcolm Blight called it a day. Three Grand Final losses were too much to bear.*

WEST COAST
B: D. Hart, M. Brennan, A. McIntosh
HB: G. McKenna, G. Jakovich, J. Worsfold (c.)
C: P. Matera, D. Pyke, C. Mainwaring
HF: P. Wilson, J. Ball, B. Heady
F: C. Lewis, P. Sumich, S. Bond
R: D. Hynes, D. Kemp, T. Evans
Interchange: R. Turnbull, D. Banfield, C. Waterman
Coach: M. Malthouse

GEELONG
B: S. Hocking, S. O'Reilly, S. Handley
HB: M. Mansfield, T. McGrath, K. Hinkley
C: S. Breuer, P. Couch, P. Riccardi
HF: D. Mensch, B. Brownless, A. Hickmott
F: L. Pickering, G. Ablett, L. Tudor,
R: J. Barnes, M. Bairstow (c.), G. Hocking
Interchange: A. Wills, P. Brown, L. Colbert
Coach: M. Blight

# 1995

| | | P | W | L | D | For | Agst | % | Pts |
|---|---|---|---|---|---|---|---|---|---|
| 1 | Carlton (1) | 22 | 20 | 2 | | 2357 | 1711 | 137.8 | 80 |
| 2 | Geelong (2) | 22 | 16 | 6 | | 2558 | 1939 | 131.9 | 64 |
| 3 | Richmond (4) | 22 | 15 | 6 | 1 | 2096 | 1943 | 107.9 | 62 |
| 4 | Essendon (5) | 22 | 14 | 6 | 2 | 2464 | 1931 | 127.6 | 60 |
| 5 | West Coast (6) | 22 | 14 | 8 | | 2079 | 1692 | 122.9 | 56 |
| 6 | North Melb (3) | 22 | 14 | 8 | | 2311 | 2013 | 114.8 | 56 |
| 7 | Footscray (7) | 22 | 11 | 10 | 1 | 1879 | 2054 | 91.5 | 46 |
| 8 | Bris Bears (8) | 22 | 10 | 12 | | 2104 | 2207 | 95.3 | 40 |
| 9 | Melbourne | 22 | 9 | 13 | | 1938 | 1925 | 100.7 | 36 |
| 10 | Collingwood | 22 | 8 | 12 | 2 | 2043 | 2111 | 96.8 | 36 |
| 11 | Adelaide | 22 | 9 | 13 | | 1749 | 2184 | 80.1 | 36 |
| 12 | Sydney | 22 | 8 | 14 | | 2314 | 2299 | 100.7 | 32 |
| 13 | Fremantle | 22 | 8 | 14 | | 2051 | 2209 | 92.8 | 32 |
| 14 | St Kilda | 22 | 8 | 14 | | 1814 | 2258 | 80.3 | 32 |
| 15 | Hawthorn | 22 | 7 | 15 | | 1857 | 1975 | 94.0 | 28 |
| 16 | Fitzroy | 22 | 2 | 20 | | 1617 | 2780 | 58.2 | 8 |

*(22 H & A matches)*

**First Qualifying Final**
Essendon 11.8 (74) d. West Coast 8.7 (55)
**Second Qualifying Final**
North Melb. 17.12 (114) d. Richmond 12.12 (84)
**Third Qualifying Final**
Geelong 24.11 (155) d. Footscray 10.13 (73)
**Fourth Qualifying Final**
Carlton 13.12 (90) d. Brisbane Bears 12.5 (77)
**First Semi Final**
North Melb. 18.21 (129) d. West Coast 10.11 (71)

**Second Semi Final**
Richmond 12.14 (86) d. Essendon 11.7 (73)
**First Preliminary Final**
Geelong 20.9 (129) d. Richmond 6.4 (40)
**Second Preliminary Final**
Carlton 18.10 (118) d. North Melb. 8.8 (56)

**Grand Final**
Carlton 4.5 10.8 16.11 21.15 (141) d
Geelong 2.4 3.10 6.12 11.14 (80)
Goals — Carlton: Williams 5, Kernahan 5, Pearce
4, Bradley 2, Spalding, Camporeale, Rice, Madden,
Whitehead. Geelong: Handley 3, Brownless 3,
Couch, Breuer, Pickering, Riccardi, Mensch.
Best — Carlton: Williams, Silvagni, Christou,
Koutoufides, Dean, Ratten. Geelong: Mansfield,
Pickering, Riccardi, Hickmott, Graham, Barnes.
Umpires: Carey, Goldspink, Kennedy.
Match played at MCG.
Attendance: 93,670
*Statistically, Carlton became the most successful
team in 99 years of the VFL/AFL when it took
Geelong on Grand Final day. That win was its 16th
on the trot, for its 16th premiership, in a season in
which the team lost only twice. For Geelong, four
unsuccessful Grand Final appearances in seven
years was a bitter pill to swallow.*
CARLTON
B: M. Sexton, S. Silvagni, A. Christou
HB: M. Hogg, P. Dean, A. McKay
C: M. Hanna, B. Ratten, A. Koutoufides
HF: D. Rice, E. Spalding, M. Clape
F: G. Williams, S. Kernahan (c.), B. Pearce
R: J. Madden, C. Bradley, F. Brown
Interchange: S. Camporeale, A. Whitehead, G.
Manton
Coach: D. Parkin
GEELONG
B: T. McGrath, B. Graham, M. Mansfield
HB: B. Sholl, S. Handley, P. Brown
C: A. Lord, P. Couch, L. Colbert
HF: L. Tudor, D. Mensch, S. Breuer
F: B. Brownless, G. Ablett (c.), P. Riccardi,
R: J. Barnes, L. Pickering, G. Hocking
Interchange: G. Tanner, K. Hinkley, A. Hickmott
Coach: G. Ayres

# 1996

| | | P | W | L | D | For | Agst | % | Pts |
|---|---|---|---|---|---|---|---|---|---|
| 1 | Sydney (2) | 22 | 16 | 5 | 1 | 2152 | 1737 | 123.9 | 66 |
| 2 | North Melb (1) | 22 | 16 | 6 | | 2526 | 1982 | 127.4 | 64 |
| 3 | Bris Bears (3) | 22 | 15 | 6 | 1 | 2174 | 1731 | 125.6 | 62 |
| 4 | West Coast (5) | 22 | 15 | 7 | | 2201 | 1758 | 125.2 | 60 |
| 5 | Carlton (6) | 22 | 15 | 7 | | 2116 | 1909 | 110.8 | 60 |
| 6 | Essendon (4) | 22 | 14 | 7 | 1 | 2209 | 2023 | 109.2 | 58 |
| 7 | Geelong (7) | 22 | 13 | 8 | 1 | 2353 | 2047 | 114.9 | 54 |
| 8 | Hawthorn (8) | 22 | 11 | 10 | 1 | 1893 | 1921 | 98.5 | 46 |
| 9 | Richmond | 22 | 11 | 11 | | 2282 | 1944 | 117.4 | 44 |
| 10 | St Kilda | 22 | 10 | 12 | | 2053 | 2033 | 101.0 | 40 |
| 11 | Collingwood | 22 | 9 | 13 | | 2203 | 2142 | 102.8 | 36 |
| 12 | Adelaide | 22 | 8 | 14 | | 2233 | 2327 | 96.0 | 32 |
| 13 | Fremantle | 22 | 7 | 15 | | 1830 | 1983 | 92.3 | 28 |
| 14 | Melbourne | 22 | 7 | 15 | | 1743 | 2463 | 70.8 | 28 |
| 15 | Footscray | 22 | 5 | 16 | 1 | 1654 | 2139 | 77.3 | 22 |
| 16 | Fitzroy | 22 | 1 | 21 | | 1452 | 2935 | 49.5 | 4 |

*(22 H & A matches)*

**First Qualifying Final**
West Coast 18.17 (125) d. Carlton 10.10 (70)
**Second Qualifying Final**
Bris Bears 15.11 (101) d. Essendon 15.10 (100)
**Third Qualifying Final**
North Melbourne 19.17 (131) d. Geelong 9.17 (71)
**Fourth Qualifying Final**
Sydney 13.12 (90) d. Hawthorn 12.12 (84)
**First Semi Final**
Essendon 22.12 (144) d. West Coast 8.19 (67)
**Second Semi Final**
Brisbane Bears 26.14 (170) d. Carlton 10.13 (73)
**First Preliminary Final**
North Melbourne 17.12 (114) d. Brisbane Bears
11.10 (76)
**Second Preliminary Final**
Sydney 10.10 (70) d. Essendon 10.9 (69)

**Grand Final**
North Melbourne 3.2 8.7 12.14 19.17 (131) d
Sydney 6.2 8.5 9.7 13.10 (88)
Goals — North Melbourne: Freeborn 3, Crocker 3,
A. Stevens 2, Roberts 2, C. Sholl 2, Allison 2, Rock,
Fairley, Carey, Bell, Simpson. Sydney: Lockett 6,
Luff 2, O'Loughlin 2, Cresswell, Mooney, Kickett.
Best — North Melbourne: Archer, McKernan,
Carey, A. Stevens, Schwass, Rock. Sydney: Roos,
Cresswell, Stafford, Lewis, Luff, Heuskes.
Umpires: Dore, Sheehan, Nash.
Match played at MCG.
Attendance: 93,102
*The AFL's Centenary Year was crowned by North
Melbourne which made amends for the
disappointment of three successive failed finals
campaigns. The Roos won their third flag despite a
slow start against a side which was playing in its
first Grand Final since 1945. The Sydney Swans
might have been South Melbourne back then, but
they added a new dimension and although
overwhelmed in the finish, performed admirably.
Led by the bullocking Glen Archer and superstars
Corey McKernan and Wayne Carey, the Roos were
hell-bent in their premiership quest.*

NORTH MELBOURNE
B: R. Scott, M. Martyn, G. Archer
HB: W. Schwass, I. Fairley, J. Blakey
C: D. King, A. Simpson, D. Laidley
HF: G. Freeborn, W. Carey (c), B. Allison
F: C. Sholl, C. McKernan, D Crocker
R: M. Capuano, A. Rock, A. Stevens
Interchange: S. Anderson, M. Roberts, P. Bell
Coach: D. Pagan
SYDNEY
B: B. Seymour, A. Dunkley, M. Bayes
HB: A. Heuskes, P. Roos, M. O'Loughlin
C: W. Chapman, D. Cresswell, S. Grant

HF: T. Luff, J. Mooney, D. Lewis
F: C. O'Brien, T. Lockett, S. Maxfield,
R: G. Stafford, K. Dyson, P. Kelly (c.)
Interchange: D. Kickett, D. McPherson, S. Garlick
Coach: R. Eade

# 1997

| | | P | W | L | D | For | Agst | % | Pts |
|---|---|---|---|---|---|---|---|---|---|
| 1 | St Kilda (2) | 22 | 15 | 7 | | 2294 | 1918 | 119.6 | 60 |
| 2 | Geelong (5) | 22 | 15 | 7 | | 2111 | 1791 | 117.9 | 60 |
| 3 | W Bulldogs (3) | 20 | 14 | 8 | | 2100 | 2062 | 101.8 | 56 |
| 4 | Adelaide (1) | 22 | 13 | 9 | | 2151 | 1769 | 121.6 | 52 |
| 5 | West Coast (6) | 22 | 13 | 9 | | 1969 | 1770 | 111.2 | 52 |
| 6 | Sydney (7) | 22 | 12 | 10 | | 2093 | 1801 | 116.2 | 48 |
| 7 | North Melb (4) | 22 | 12 | 10 | | 2051 | 1835 | 111.8 | 48 |
| 8 | Bris Lions (8) | 22 | 10 | 11 | 1 | 2076 | 1973 | 105.2 | 42 |
| 9 | Port Adel | 22 | 10 | 11 | 1 | 1852 | 2017 | 91.8 | 42 |
| 10 | Collingwood | 22 | 10 | 12 | | 2138 | 1919 | 111.4 | 40 |
| 11 | Carlton | 22 | 10 | 12 | | 1978 | 2045 | 96.7 | 40 |
| 12 | Fremantle | 22 | 10 | 12 | | 1748 | 1902 | 91.9 | 40 |
| 13 | Richmond | 22 | 10 | 12 | | 1883 | 2253 | 83.6 | 40 |
| 14 | Essendon | 22 | 9 | 13 | | 2004 | 2170 | 92.4 | 36 |
| 15 | Hawthorn | 22 | 8 | 14 | | 1873 | 2144 | 87.4 | 32 |
| 16 | Melbourne | 22 | 4 | 18 | | 1477 | 2429 | 60.8 | 16 |

*(22 H & A matches)*

**1st Qualifying Final**
Adelaide 14.15 (99) d. West Coast 9.12 (66)
**2nd Qualifying Final**
Western Bulldogs 18.11 (119) d. Sydney 12.12 (84)
**3rd Qualifying Final**
North Melbourne 11.13 (79) d. Geelong 9.7 (61)
**4th Qualifying Final**
St Kilda 20.15 (135) d. Brisbane Lions 13.11 (89)
**1st Semi-Final**
North Melbourne 15.8 (98) d. West Coast 12.13 (85)
**2nd Semi-Final**
Adelaide 11.10 (76) d. Geelong 9.14 (68)
**1st Preliminary Final**
Adelaide 12.21 (93) d. Western Bulldogs 13.13 (91)
**2nd Preliminary Final**
St Kilda 15.14 (104) d. North Melbourne 11.7 (73)

**Grand Final**
Scores: Adelaide 3.8 5.10 11.11 19.11 (125) d
St Kilda 3.6 7.11 9.13 13.16 (94)
Goals — Adelaide: Jarman 6, Ellen 5, Bond 4,
Smart, Goodwin, Rintoul, Caven. St Kilda: Hall,
Heatley 3, Loewe 2, Peckett, Burke, Jones,
Winmar, Harvey.
Best — Adelaide: McLeod, Jarman, Ellen, Bond,
Pittman, Rehn, Hart. St Kilda: Jones, Burke Harvey,
D. Wakelin, Hall, Keogh.
Umpires: Kennedy, Sheehan, Nash.
Match played at MCG.
Attendance: 98,828
*A record-breaking finals series capped by two firsts
— Adelaide won its first premiership and in the
process became the first side to win four finals and
take the flag. Malcolm Blight, after suffering the
disappointment of three losing Grand Finals with
Geelong, landed his first premiership as a coach,
guiding his inspired Crows to a 31-point victory.
The Saints were making their first Grand Final*

## FINALS APPEARANCES OF ALL CLUBS 1897–1997

| | Premiers | Second | Third | Fourth | Fifth | Sixth | Seventh | Eighth | Total |
|---|---|---|---|---|---|---|---|---|---|
| Collingwood | 14 | 23 | 17 | 14 | 3 | — | — | 1 | 72 |
| Carlton | 16 | 12 | 14 | 15 | 3 | 1 | — | — | 61 |
| Essendon | 15 | 13 | 7 | 11 | 7 | 1 | — | — | 54 |
| Geelong | 6 | 8 | 15 | 13 | 2 | — | 1 | — | 45 |
| Richmond | 10 | 12 | 3 | 8 | — | — | — | — | 33 |
| Melbourne | 12 | 4 | 7 | 9 | — | — | — | — | 32 |
| Fitzroy | 8 | 5 | 9 | 6 | 1 | — | — | — | 29 |
| Sth Mlb/Syd | 3 | 9 | 6 | 6 | 1 | — | 1 | — | 26 |
| Hawthorn | 9 | 5 | 4 | — | 1 | 2 | 1 | 1 | 23 |
| North Melb | 3 | 4 | 6 | 5 | 3 | — | — | — | 21 |
| St Kilda | 1 | 4 | 5 | 7 | 1 | — | — | — | 18 |
| Wstrn Bldgs | 1 | 1 | 5 | 6 | 2 | 1 | 1 | — | 17 |
| West Coast | 2 | 1 | 1 | 1 | 2 | 2 | — | — | 9 |
| Bris Bears | — | — | 1 | — | — | — | — | 1 | 2 |
| Adelaide | 1 | — | 1 | — | — | — | — | — | 2 |
| Bris Lions | — | — | — | — | — | — | — | 1 | 1 |
| Fremantle | — | — | — | — | — | — | — | — | 0 |
| Port Adel | — | — | — | — | — | — | — | — | 0 |
| University | — | — | — | — | — | — | — | — | 0 |

## FINALS MATCHES: 1897–1997

| Club | Wins | Losses | Ties | Total |
|---|---|---|---|---|
| Adelaide | 5 | 2 | — | 7 |
| Bris Bears | 2 | 2 | — | 4 |
| Bris Lions | — | 1 | — | 1 |
| Carlton | 59 | 62 | 2 | 123 |
| Collingwood | 63 | 85 | 4 | 152 |
| Essendon | 60 | 49 | 2 | 111 |
| Fitzroy | 34 | 25 | — | 59 |
| Fremantle | — | — | — | 0 |
| Geelong | 35 | 50 | 1 | 86 |
| Hawthorn | 34 | 21 | — | 55 |
| Melbourne | 43 | 27 | 2 | 72 |
| North Melb | 24 | 27 | 1 | 52 |
| Port Adelaide | — | — | — | 0 |
| Richmond | 45 | 29 | 1 | 75 |
| St Kilda | 14 | 19 | — | 33 |
| Sth Mlb/Sydney | 20 | 29 | — | 49 |
| University | — | — | — | 0 |
| West Coast | 11 | 11 | 1 | 23 |
| Western Bulldogs | 9 | 19 | — | 28 |
| **Total:** | | | | **465** |

*appearance since 1971. Andrew McLeod gathered 31 disposals and took 11 marks to win the Norm Smith Medal. In the absence of the injured Tony Modra, Darren Jarman booted six goals, including five in the final term. The Saints led by 13 points at half-time, but were no match in the second half.*

ADELAIDE
B: P. Caven, R. Jameson, B. Hart
HB: A, McLeod, D. Pittman, S. Goodwin
C: M. Connell, D. Jarman, K. Koster
HF: C. Sampson, M. Robran, N. Smart
F: C. Rintoul, S. Ellen, T. Bond
R: S. Rehn, K. Johnson, M. Bickley (c.)
Interchange: T. Edwards, B. James, A. Keating
Coach: M. Blight
ST KILDA
B: S. Sziller, J. Shanahan, J. Peckett
HB: J. Cripps, D. Wakelin, M. Hudghton
C: J. Daniels, A. Thompson, A. Jones
HF: M. Lappin, S. Loewe, R. Keogh
F: B. Hall, J. Heatley, N. Winmar
R: B. Cook, R. Harvey, N. Burke (c.)
Interchange: T. Brown, D. Sierakowski, R. Neill
Coach: S. Alves

## VFL/AFL PREMIERSHIPS 1897-1997

**16** Carlton (1906, 1907, 1908, 1914, 1915, 1938, 1945, 1947, 1968, 1970, 1972, 1979, 1981, 1982, 1987, 1995)

**15** Essendon (1897, 1901, 1911, 1912, 1923, 1924, 1942, 1946, 1949, 1950, 1962, 1965, 1984, 1985, 1993)

**14** Collingwood (1902, 1903, 1910, 1917, 1919, 1927, 1928, 1929, 1930, 1935, 1936, 1953, 1958, 1990)

**12** Melbourne (1900, 1926, 1939, 1940, 1941, 1948, 1955, 1956, 1957, 1959, 1960, 1964)

**10** Richmond (1920, 1921, 1932, 1934, 1943, 1967, 1969, 1973, 1974, 1980)

**9** Hawthorn (1961, 1971, 1976, 1978, 1983, 1986, 1988, 1989, 1991)

**8** Fitzroy (1898, 1899, 1904, 1905, 1913, 1916, 1922, 1944)

**6** Geelong (1925, 1931, 1937, 1951, 1952, 1963)

**3** South Melbourne (Sydney) (1909, 1918, 1933)

**3** North Melbourne (1975, 1977, 1996)

**2** West Coast (1992, 1994)

**1** Footscray (1954)

**1** St Kilda (1966)

**1** Adelaide (1997)

**0** Brisbane Bears, Brisbane Lions, Fremantle, Port Adelaide, University

# LADDER POSITIONS

No team has won the Premiership from fifth place, although Collingwood created history in 1980 by becoming the first Elimination Final team to win through to the Grand Final.

The following clubs have won the Premiership from FIRST place on the League ladder:

| | | | |
|---|---|---|---|
| 1931 | Geelong | 1961 | Hawthorn |
| 1934 | Richmond | 1962 | Essendon |
| 1937 | Geelong | 1964 | Melbourne |
| 1938 | Carlton | 1967 | Richmond |
| 1939 | Melbourne | 1971 | Hawthorn |
| 1940 | Melbourne | 1972 | Carlton |
| 1942 | Essendon | 1974 | Richmond |
| 1943 | Richmond | 1979 | Carlton |
| 1946 | Essendon | 1981 | Carlton |
| 1947 | Carlton | 1984 | Essendon |
| 1950 | Essendon | 1985 | Essendon |
| 1951 | Geelong | 1986 | Hawthorn |
| 1952 | Geelong | 1987 | Carlton |
| 1955 | Melbourne | 1988 | Hawthorn |
| 1956 | Melbourne | 1989 | Hawthorn |
| 1957 | Melbourne | 1993 | Essendon |
| 1959 | Melbourne | 1994 | West Coast |
| 1960 | Melbourne | 1995 | Carlton |

The following clubs have won the Premiership from SECOND place on the ladder:

| | | | |
|---|---|---|---|
| 1932 | Richmond | 1966 | St Kilda |
| 1933 | Sth Melbourne | 1968 | Carlton |
| 1935 | Collingwood | 1970 | Carlton |
| 1936 | Collingwood | 1973 | Richmond |
| 1941 | Melbourne | 1976 | Hawthorn |
| 1944 | Fitzroy | 1978 | Hawthorn |
| 1948 | Melbourne | 1983 | Hawthorn |
| 1953 | Collingwood | 1990 | Collingwood |
| 1954 | Footscray | 1991 | Hawthorn |
| 1958 | Collingwood | 1996 | Nth Melbourne |
| 1963 | Geelong | | |

The following clubs have won the Premiership from THIRD place on the League ladder:

| | | | |
|---|---|---|---|
| 1975 | Nth Melbourne | 1980 | Richmond |
| 1977 | Nth Melbourne | 1982 | Carlton |

The following clubs have won the Premiership from FOURTH place on the ladder:

| | | | |
|---|---|---|---|
| 1945 | Carlton | 1969 | Richmond |
| 1949 | Essendon | 1992 | West Coast |
| 1965 | Essendon | 1997 | Adelaide |

# FINALS PERFORMANCES — 1897-1997

| Team | Round Robin 1897; 1924 | | | | Elimination Finals 1972-93 | | | | Qualifying Finals 1972-96 | | | | Semi Finals 1901-23; 1925-96 | | | | Preliminary Finals 1898-1923; 1925-96 | | | | Grand Finals 1898-1923; 1925-96 | | | | TOTAL | | | | Highest | | GWM | | GLM | |
|---|---|---|---|---|---|---|---|---|---|---|---|---|---|---|---|---|---|---|---|---|---|---|---|---|---|---|---|---|---|---|---|---|---|---|
| | P | W | L | T | P | W | L | T | P | W | L | T | P | W | L | T | P | W | L | T | P | W | L | T | P | W | L | T | Score | Year | | Year | | Year |
| Adelaide | | | | | 1 | 1 | 0 | 0 | 1 | 1 | 0 | 0 | 2 | 1 | 1 | 0 | 2 | 1 | 1 | 0 | 1 | 1 | 0 | 0 | 7 | 5 | 2 | 0 | 19.11 (125) | 1997 | 33 | 1997 | 18 | 1993 |
| Brisbane Bears | | | | | | | | | 2 | 1 | 1 | 0 | 1 | 1 | 0 | 0 | 1 | 0 | 1 | 0 | | | | | 4 | 2 | 2 | 0 | 26.14 (170) | 1996 | 97 | 1996 | 38 | 1996 |
| Brisbane Lions | | | | | | | | | 1 | 0 | 1 | 0 | | | | | | | | | | | | | 1 | 0 | 1 | 0 | | | | | 46 | 1997 |
| Carlton | 3 | 1 | 2 | 0 | 3 | 1 | 2 | 0 | 11 | 6 | 5 | 0 | 55 | 26 | 28 | 1 | 23 | 9 | 13 | 1 | 28 | 16 | 12 | 0 | 123 | 59 | 62 | 2 | 28.9 (177) | 1972 | 88 | 1931 | 97 | 1996 |
| Collingwood | 6 | 5 | 1 | 0 | 6 | 3 | 3 | 0 | 8 | 1 | 6 | 1 | 64 | 24 | 38 | 2 | 30 | 16 | 14 | 0 | 38 | 14 | 23 | 1 | 152 | 63 | 85 | 4 | 23.15 (153) | 1984 | 69 | 1974 | 133 | 1984 |
| Essendon | 3 | 1 | 2 | 0 | 8 | 1 | 7 | 0 | 4 | 2 | 2 | 0 | 47 | 29 | 17 | 1 | 22 | 14 | 8 | 0 | 27 | 13 | 13 | 1 | 111 | 60 | 49 | 2 | 28.6 (174) | 1984 | 133 | 1984 | 94 | 1989 |
| Fitzroy | 3 | 1 | 2 | 0 | 4 | 3 | 1 | 0 | 1 | 0 | 1 | 0 | 24 | 16 | 8 | 0 | 14 | 6 | 8 | 0 | 13 | 8 | 5 | 0 | 59 | 34 | 25 | 0 | 19.18 (132) | 1981 | 81 | 1979 | 62 | 1960 |
| Fremantle | | | | | | | | | | | | | | | | | | | | | | | | | 0 | 0 | 0 | 0 | | | | | | |
| Geelong | 3 | 2 | 1 | 0 | 3 | 2 | 1 | 0 | 7 | 4 | 3 | 0 | 40 | 13 | 26 | 1 | 21 | 8 | 12 | 1 | 13 | 6 | 7 | 0 | 87 | 35 | 50 | 2 | 26.16 (172) | 1992 | 94 | 1989 | 118 | 1969 |
| Hawthorn | | | | | 3 | 0 | 3 | 0 | 12 | 8 | 4 | 0 | 18 | 13 | 5 | 0 | 8 | 4 | 4 | 0 | 14 | 9 | 5 | 0 | 55 | 34 | 21 | 0 | 24.22 (166) | 1982 | 99 | 1987 | 78 | 1985 |
| Melbourne | 3 | 0 | 3 | 0 | 5 | 5 | 0 | 0 | | | | | 32 | 18 | 13 | 1 | 15 | 8 | 7 | 0 | 17 | 12 | 4 | 1 | 72 | 43 | 27 | 2 | 25.16 (166) | 1948 | 118 | 1987 | 96 | 1988 |
| North Melb | | | | | 5 | 2 | 3 | 0 | 9 | 7 | 2 | 0 | 16 | 5 | 11 | 0 | 14 | 7 | 7 | 0 | 8 | 3 | 4 | 1 | 52 | 24 | 27 | 1 | 21.25 (151) | 1977 | 69 | 1977 | 118 | 1987 |
| Port Adel | | | | | | | | | | | | | | | | | | | | | | | | | 0 | 0 | 0 | 0 | | | | | | |
| Richmond | 3 | 2 | 1 | 0 | 2 | 2 | 0 | 0 | 4 | 2 | 2 | 0 | 32 | 21 | 11 | 0 | 12 | 8 | 4 | 0 | 21 | 10 | 11 | 0 | 74 | 45 | 29 | 0 | 25.17 (167) | 1969 | 118 | 1969 | 89 | 1995 |
| St Kilda | | | | | 4 | 3 | 1 | 0 | 1 | 1 | 0 | 0 | 16 | 5 | 11 | 0 | 7 | 4 | 3 | 0 | 5 | 1 | 4 | 0 | 33 | 14 | 19 | 0 | 24.14 (158) | 1973 | 67 | 1973 | 62 | 1970 |
| Sth Mlb/syd | 3 | 1 | 2 | 0 | 1 | 0 | 1 | 0 | 4 | 1 | 3 | 0 | 21 | 11 | 10 | 0 | 8 | 4 | 4 | 0 | 12 | 3 | 9 | 0 | 49 | 20 | 29 | 0 | 15.18 (108) | 1934 | 60 | 1934 | 99 | 1987 |
| University | | | | | | | | | | | | | | | | | | | | | | | | | 0 | 0 | 0 | 0 | | | | | | |
| West Coast | | | | | 3 | 2 | 1 | 0 | 7 | 2 | 4 | 1 | 7 | 3 | 4 | 0 | 3 | 2 | 1 | 0 | 3 | 2 | 1 | 0 | 23 | 11 | 11 | 1 | 20.23 (143) | 1994 | 80 | 1994 | 77 | 1996 |
| Wstrn Bldgs | | | | | 2 | 0 | 2 | 0 | 5 | 1 | 4 | 0 | 13 | 6 | 7 | 0 | 6 | 1 | 5 | 0 | 2 | 1 | 1 | 0 | 28 | 9 | 19 | 0 | 19.23 (137) | 1985 | 51 | 1954 | 93 | 1985 |
| Totals | 24 | 12 | 12 | 0 | 50 | 25 | 25 | 0 | 39 | 38 | 38 | 1 | 195 | 192 | 192 | 3 | 93 | 92 | 92 | 1 | 101 | 99 | 99 | 2 | 465 | 458 | 458 | 7 | | | | | | |

*Preliminary Final: a match between Semi Finals and Grand Final.*

# HOW CLUBS HAVE FINISHED 1897–1997

| | 1948 | 1947 | 1946 | 1945 | 1944 | 1943 | 1942 | 1941 | 1940 | 1939 | 1938 | 1937 | 1936 | 1935 | 1934 | 1933 | 1932 | 1931 | 1930 | 1929 | 1928 | 1927 | 1926 | 1925 | 1924 | 1923 | 1922 | 1921 | 1920 | 1919 | 1918 | 1917 | 1916 | 1915 | 1914 | 1913 | 1912 | 1911 | 1910 | 1909 | 1908 | 1907 | 1906 | 1905 | 1904 | 1903 | 1902 | 1901 | 1900 | 1899 | 1898 | 1897 |
|---|---|---|---|---|---|---|---|---|---|---|---|---|---|---|---|---|---|---|---|---|---|---|---|---|---|---|---|---|---|---|---|---|---|---|---|---|---|---|---|---|---|---|---|---|---|---|---|---|---|---|---|---|
| CARLTON | 6 | 6 | 1 | 1 | 5 | 5 | 3 | 5 | 5 | 5 | 1 | 4 | 4 | 4 | 5 | 4 | 3 | 3 | 3 | 3 | 4 | 4 | 6 | 9 | 7 | 4 | 4 | 3 | 4 | 4 | 3 | 3 | 2 | 1 | 1 | 6 | 3 | 4 | 2 | 1 | 2 | 1 | 1 | 3 | 2 | 3 | 6 | 7 | 7 | 7 | 1 | 7 |
| COLLINGWOOD | 3 | 3 | 4 | 3 | 6 | 2 | 1 | 3 | 1 | 1 | 2 | 2 | 3 | 2 | 4 | 5 | 2 | 4 | 1 | 1 | 4 | 2 | 2 | 2 | 6 | 7 | 7 | 2 | 3 | 4 | 1 | 1 | 1 | 1 | 5 | 1 | 1 | 1 | 1 | 2 | 3 | 1 | 3 | 1 | 2 | 1 | 1 | 4 | 4 | 3 | 2 | 3 |
| ESSENDON | 1 | 1 | 1 | 9 | 1 | 1 | 5 | 2 | 2 | 2 | 2 | 2 | 8 | 10 | 2 | 3 | 6 | 6 | 6 | 6 | 5 | 5 | 8 | 3 | 2 | 5 | 1 | 3 | 2 | 6 | 8 | 5 | 2 | 8 | 2 | 4 | 7 | 2 | 4 | 3 | 6 | 4 | 4 | 4 | 3 | 1 | 2 | 2 | 3 | 3 | 5 | 6 |
| FITZROY | 9 | 5 | 8 | 6 | 10 | 10 | 2 | 1 | 8 | 6 | 7 | 10 | 7 | 9 | 10 | 5 | 12 | 11 | 10 | 8 | 12 | 12 | 3 | 5 | 3 | 1 | 2 | 4 | 5 | 5 | — | 5 | 3 | 3 | 6 | 8 | 4 | 2 | 4 | 3 | 6 | 7 | 7 | 2 | 1 | 4 | 7 | 1 | 4 | 1 | 1 | 6 |
| FOOTSCRAY | 4 | 6 | 3 | 5 | 4 | 2 | 6 | 6 | 7 | 8 | 7 | 11 | 12 | 5 | 5 | 11 | 11 | 5 | 9 | 11 | 7 | 9 | 5 | 11 | — | — | — | — | — | — | — | — | — | — | — | — | — | — | — | — | — | — | — | — | — | — | — | — | — | — | — | — |
| GEELONG | 4 | 3 | 8 | 8 | — | — | — | — | 4 | 7 | 1 | 3 | 9 | 11 | 3 | 3 | 7 | 7 | 2 | 9 | 1 | 3 | 4 | 1 | 5 | 6 | 9 | 9 | 7 | 7 | 5 | 7 | 6 | 9 | 4 | 5 | 5 | 9 | 5 | 9 | 6 | 6 | 6 | 6 | 7 | 4 | 3 | 3 | 5 | 5 | 3 | 2 |
| HAWTHORN | — | — | 9 | — | — | — | — | 10 | 9 | 8 | 11 | 9 | 5 | 8 | 8 | 8 | 8 | 9 | 12 | 7 | 9 | 7 | 12 | 12 | — | — | — | — | — | — | — | — | — | — | — | — | — | — | — | — | — | — | — | — | — | — | — | — | — | — | — | — |
| MELBOURNE | 5 | 7 | 12 | 4 | — | — | 4 | 4 | 9 | 9 | 8 | 1 | 1 | 1 | 8 | 9 | 10 | 10 | 5 | 2 | 2 | 2 | 2 | 10 | 4 | 9 | 6 | 6 | 6 | 2 | 4 | 2 | 4 | 7 | 9 | 2 | 9 | 6 | 7 | 9 | 9 | 5 | 8 | 7 | 4 | 6 | 4 | 8 | 8 | 8 | 8 | 5 |
| NTH. MELB. | 11 | 11 | 11 | 7 | 12 | 1 | — | — | 11 | 12 | 1 | 8 | 3 | 3 | 2 | 8 | 9 | 11 | 12 | 12 | 11 | 11 | 11 | 6 | — | — | — | — | — | — | — | — | — | — | — | — | — | — | — | — | — | — | — | — | — | — | — | — | — | — | — | — |
| RICHMOND | 8 | 9 | 2 | 10 | 7 | 7 | 2 | 11 | 3 | 3 | 4 | 6 | 4 | 6 | 1 | 2 | 1 | 2 | 4 | 4 | 8 | 6 | 6 | 7 | 1 | 7 | 5 | 2 | 1 | 6 | 2 | 4 | 4 | — | — | 9 | 8 | 9 | 8 | 9 | 9 | 9 | 7 | 5 | 8 | 8 | 5 | 8 | 5 | 6 | 6 | — |
| ST KILDA | 7 | 10 | 10 | 11 | 12 | 12 | — | 9 | 11 | 12 | 12 | 12 | 11 | 7 | 11 | 10 | 9 | 12 | 8 | 10 | 6 | 10 | 9 | 8 | 7 | 9 | 8 | 11 | 9 | 7 | 4 | 1 | 4 | 7 | 7 | 10 | 7 | 5 | 10 | 5 | 7 | 6 | 5 | 5 | 8 | 8 | 8 | 8 | 6 | 6 | 2 | 5 |
| STH. MELB. | 2 | 2 | 5 | 12 | 3 | 4 | 7 | 7 | 10 | 2 | 6 | 5 | 6 | 6 | 6 | 2 | 4 | 9 | 11 | 5 | 4 | 5 | 10 | 10 | 8 | 3 | 3 | 5 | 8 | 9 | 7 | 4 | 1 | 4 | 2 | 10 | 6 | 3 | 3 | 1 | 5 | 8 | 8 | 8 | 5 | 8 | 5 | 6 | 8 | 4 | 5 | 1 |
| UNIVERSITY | — | — | — | — | — | — | — | — | — | — | — | — | — | — | — | — | — | — | — | — | — | — | — | — | — | — | — | — | — | — | — | — | — | — | 8 | 10 | 10 | 7 | 6 | 7 | 4 | 2 | 2 | — | — | — | — | — | — | — | — | — |

| | 1997 | 1996 | 1995 | 1994 | 1993 | 1992 | 1991 | 1990 | 1989 | 1988 | 1987 | 1986 | 1985 | 1984 | 1983 | 1982 | 1981 | 1980 | 1979 | 1978 | 1977 | 1976 | 1975 | 1974 | 1973 | 1972 | 1971 | 1970 | 1969 | 1968 | 1967 | 1966 | 1965 | 1964 | 1963 | 1962 | 1961 | 1960 | 1959 | 1958 | 1957 | 1956 | 1955 | 1954 | 1953 | 1952 | 1951 | 1950 | 1949 |
|---|---|---|---|---|---|---|---|---|---|---|---|---|---|---|---|---|---|---|---|---|---|---|---|---|---|---|---|---|---|---|---|---|---|---|---|---|---|---|---|---|---|---|---|---|---|---|---|---|---|
| ADELAIDE | 1 | 8 | 11 | 11 | 9 | 9 | — | — | — | — | — | — | — | — | — | — | — | — | — | — | — | — | — | — | — | — | — | — | — | — | — | — | — | — | — | — | — | — | — | — | — | — | — | — | — | — | — | — | — |
| BRISBANE BEARS | — | 3 | 12 | 13 | 9 | 14 | 13 | 13 | 13 | 8 | 13 | — | — | — | — | — | — | — | — | — | — | — | — | — | — | — | — | — | — | — | — | — | — | — | — | — | — | — | — | — | — | — | — | — | — | — | — | — | — |
| BRISBANE LIONS | — | — | — | — | 11 | 15 | 14 | 14 | 13 | 11 | 11 | 2 | 3 | 5 | 5 | 5 | 4 | 4 | 4 | 5 | 6 | 4 | 7 | 2 | 5 | 5 | 8 | 6 | 3 | 7 | 3 | 6 | 6 | 6 | 6 | 8 | 5 | 8 | 3 | 3 | 4 | 8 | 9 | 8 | 5 | 4 | 2 | 2 | 8 |
| CARLTON | 10 | 3 | 1 | 1 | 2 | 7 | 8 | 1 | 6 | 6 | 4 | 2 | 1 | 6 | 5 | 2 | 2 | 1 | 4 | 9 | 9 | 12 | 10 | 7 | 4 | 8 | 9 | 11 | 3 | 6 | 3 | 3 | 3 | 4 | 12 | 7 | 8 | 2 | 1 | 3 | 4 | 7 | 3 | 2 | 1 | 5 | 6 | 12 | 9 |
| COLLINGWOOD | 11 | 10 | 8 | 12 | 12 | 14 | 2 | 1 | 6 | 3 | 5 | 12 | 2 | 9 | 3 | 10 | 5 | 4 | 1 | 11 | 1 | 11 | 4 | 8 | 10 | 6 | 1 | 6 | 2 | 8 | 6 | 6 | 12 | 2 | 6 | 9 | 7 | 3 | 3 | 1 | 5 | 7 | 9 | 7 | 4 | 7 | 4 | 4 | 12 |
| ESSENDON | 11 | 11 | 8 | 5 | 1 | 4 | 1 | 4 | 2 | 3 | 6 | 1 | 6 | 1 | 4 | 5 | 7 | 4 | 12 | 10 | 12 | 8 | 5 | 8 | 11 | 11 | 10 | 2 | 9 | 10 | 2 | 4 | 2 | 2 | 6 | 5 | 7 | 7 | 3 | 6 | 5 | 5 | 2 | 4 | 2 | 7 | 4 | 1 | 2 |
| FITZROY | 12 | 8 | 10 | 10 | 7 | 10 | 6 | 2 | 6 | 11 | 12 | 11 | 9 | 3 | 7 | 6 | 11 | 9 | 12 | 7 | 11 | 5 | 11 | 9 | 7 | 3 | 11 | 1 | 7 | 11 | 12 | 12 | 12 | 1 | 12 | 7 | 11 | 3 | 11 | 6 | 6 | 10 | 11 | 7 | 5 | 2 | 12 | 8 | 8 |
| FOOTSCRAY | 2 | 4 | 4 | 16 | 7 | 11 | 12 | 12 | 3 | 7 | 8 | 8 | 11 | 4 | 9 | 2 | 5 | 10 | 10 | 5 | 7 | 5 | 7 | 5 | 9 | 8 | 8 | 12 | 10 | 12 | 11 | 10 | 7 | 3 | 10 | 2 | 5 | 5 | 6 | 11 | 8 | 6 | 3 | 6 | 1 | 3 | 5 | 8 | 10 |
| FREMANTLE | 3 | 14 | 16 | — | — | — | — | — | — | — | — | — | — | — | — | — | — | — | — | — | — | — | — | — | — | — | — | — | — | — | — | — | — | — | — | — | — | — | — | — | — | — | — | — | — | — | — | — | — |
| GEELONG | 12 | 16 | 3 | 3 | 3 | 3 | 10 | 3 | 2 | 13 | 7 | 7 | 4 | 6 | 6 | 9 | 6 | 7 | 5 | 4 | 4 | 4 | 8 | 6 | 9 | 10 | 5 | 10 | 2 | 3 | 10 | 10 | 4 | 5 | 3 | 6 | 10 | 4 | 2 | 7 | 10 | 5 | 12 | 12 | 3 | 9 | 5 | 10 | 6 |
| HAWTHORN | 9 | 13 | 13 | 11 | 5 | 1 | 1 | 5 | 1 | 1 | 1 | 8 | 9 | 1 | 1 | 1 | 2 | 6 | 6 | 1 | 5 | 6 | 2 | 1 | 1 | 5 | 6 | 6 | 5 | 6 | 11 | 1 | 11 | 9 | 8 | 8 | 5 | 11 | 7 | 3 | 7 | 9 | 12 | 11 | 11 | 12 | 9 | 10 | 11 |
| MELBOURNE | 5 | 4 | 4 | 4 | 5 | 4 | 4 | 5 | 4 | 4 | 3 | 11 | 12 | 12 | 11 | 12 | 8 | 11 | 11 | 11 | 10 | 10 | 12 | 10 | 10 | 10 | 9 | 8 | 9 | 4 | 6 | 2 | 6 | 11 | 6 | 6 | 11 | 12 | 12 | 4 | 3 | 6 | 6 | 9 | 6 | 4 | 4 | 5 | 5 |
| NTH. MELB. | 2 | 1 | 3 | 4 | 10 | 10 | 5 | 9 | 9 | 9 | 5 | 4 | 7 | 7 | 8 | 4 | 3 | 5 | 11 | 3 | 2 | 11 | 3 | 1 | 7 | 11 | 12 | 10 | 11 | 11 | 8 | 7 | 8 | 7 | 7 | 11 | 7 | 11 | 9 | 8 | 11 | 12 | 7 | 2 | 7 | 12 | 3 | 8 | 3 |
| PORT ADELAIDE | 14 | 10 | 14 | 13 | 13 | 3 | 2 | 10 | 12 | 11 | 12 | 12 | — | — | — | — | — | — | — | — | — | — | — | — | — | — | — | — | — | — | — | — | — | — | — | — | — | — | — | — | — | — | — | — | — | — | — | — | — |
| RICHMOND | 4 | 10 | 16 | 12 | 13 | 4 | 11 | 4 | 12 | 2 | 10 | 12 | 12 | 12 | 8 | 12 | 1 | 2 | 9 | 4 | 8 | 9 | 8 | 12 | 3 | 4 | 3 | 10 | 8 | 1 | 2 | 9 | 8 | 6 | 8 | 10 | 4 | 6 | 4 | 6 | 10 | 4 | 8 | 6 | 4 | 6 | 6 | 6 | 6 |
| ST KILDA | 1 | 3 | 5 | 12 | 10 | 2 | 10 | 2 | 5 | 7 | 13 | 12 | 9 | 4 | 9 | 6 | 9 | 7 | 9 | 12 | 10 | 8 | 11 | 11 | 13 | 12 | 12 | 9 | 4 | 9 | 9 | 9 | 8 | 1 | 11 | 11 | 8 | 6 | 10 | 9 | 7 | 11 | 9 | 12 | 12 | 11 | 8 | 5 | 5 |
| S. MELB/SYDNEY | 8 | 11 | 12 | 15 | 15 | 15 | 13 | 12 | 12 | 6 | 11 | 9 | 6 | 11 | 4 | 5 | 10 | 9 | 8 | 8 | 9 | 2 | 9 | 9 | 10 | 11 | 9 | 12 | 9 | 10 | 9 | 11 | 2 | 3 | 14 | 10 | 2 | 6 | 11 | 5 | 4 | 12 | 11 | 10 | 2 | 1 | 6 | 5 | 10 |
| WEST COAST | 6 | 9 | 6 | 1 | 12 | 2 | 3 | 8 | 8 | 16 | 9 | — | — | — | — | — | — | — | — | — | — | — | — | — | — | — | — | — | — | — | — | — | — | — | — | — | — | — | — | — | — | — | — | — | — | — | — | — | — |

303

# McCLELLAND TROPHY

From 1951–1990 inclusive, the "Dr Wm. C. McClelland Trophy" was awarded to the club accumulating the highest number of points by its senior, reserve grade and under 19 grade teams. With the move to a one team national competition, the AFL Commission decided that as from 1991, the trophy would be awarded to the team finishing on top of the ladder at the end of the AFL premiership season. The trophy was instituted to recognise the service of Dr Wm. C. McClelland as a player, club delegate for Melbourne, official and VFL President from 1926–1955.

| | First | Second | Third | | First | Second | Third |
|---|---|---|---|---|---|---|---|
| 1951 | Essendon | Geelong | Collingwood | 1975 | Richmond | Hawthorn | Carlton |
| 1952 | Geelong | Collingwood | Carlton | 1976 | North Melb. | Hawthorn | Carlton |
| 1953 | Essendon | Collingwood | Geelong | 1977 | Richmond | Collingwood | North Melb. |
| 1954 | Geelong | Melbourne | North Melb. | 1978 | North Melb. | Hawthorn | Geelong |
| 1955 | Melbourne | Collingwood | Footscray | 1979 | Carlton | North Melb. | Collingwood |
| 1956 | Melbourne | Collingwood | Geelong | 1980 | Geelong | Richmond | Carlton |
| 1957 | Essendon | Melbourne | Hawthorn | 1981 | Geelong | Essendon | Carlton |
| 1958 | Melbourne | Collingwood | Essendon | 1982 | Richmond | Hawthorn | Carlton |
| 1959 | Collingwood | Melbourne | Hawthorn | 1983 | North Melb. | Fitzroy | Collingwood |
| 1960 | Collingwood | Essendon | Melbourne | 1984 | Hawthorn | Essendon | Carlton |
| 1961 | Hawthorn | Melbourne | Footscray | 1985 | Hawthorn Carlton | — | Essendon |
| 1962 | Geelong | Essendon | Melbourne | 1986 | Hawthorn | Carlton | North Melb. |
| 1963 | Geelong | Essendon | (Hawthorn) (St Kilda) | 1987 | Carlton | Hawthorn | North Melb. |
| 1964 | Collingwood | Melbourne | Geelong | 1988 | Hawthorn | Carlton | Collingwood |
| 1965 | Collingwood | St Kilda | Geelong | 1989 | Essendon | Geelong | Hawthorn |
| 1966 | Collingwood | St Kilda | Richmond | 1990 | Melbourne | Essendon | Collingwood |
| 1967 | Richmond | Collingwood | Geelong | 1991 | West Coast | Geelong | Hawthorn |
| 1968 | Essendon | Richmond | St Kilda | 1992 | Geelong | Footscray | Collingwood |
| 1969 | Carlton | Richmond | Collingwood | 1993 | Essendon | Carlton | North Melb. |
| 1970 | Collingwood | Richmond | Hawthorn | 1994 | West Coast | Carlton | North Melb. |
| 1971 | Hawthorn | Richmond | Collingwood | 1995 | Carlton | Geelong | Richmond |
| 1972 | Richmond | Carlton | Hawthorn | 1996 | Sydney | North Melb. | Bris Bears |
| 1973 | Richmond | Collingwood | Essendon | 1997 | St Kilda | Geelong | W Bulldogs |
| 1974 | Richmond | Footscray | Hawthorn | | | | |

# WOODEN SPOON

Adelaide, Carlton, Fremantle, Port Adelaide and West Coast are the only teams to have never finished at the bottom of the ladder, while St Kilda has finished last 25 times.

In 1976 Collingwood finished last for the first time in the club's history, but it won six games which is more than any previous bottom side.

**Below are the occasions on which clubs were wooden spooners with their winning games of that season shown in brackets.**

ADELAIDE — Nil.

BRISBANE BEARS — 1990 (4), 1991 (3).

CARLTON — Nil.

COLLINGWOOD — 1976 (6).

ESSENDON — 1907 (5), 1918 (3), 1921 (3), 1933 (2).

FITZROY — 1916 (2). Only four clubs competed and Fitzroy finally won Premiership and Collingwood won only one match in the "Second Round" when all teams against played each other. 1936 (2), 1963 (1), 1964 (0), 1966 (1), 1980 (4), 1995 (2), 1996 (1).

FOOTSCRAY — 1959 (3), 1967 (4), 1982 (3).

FREMANTLE — Nil.

GEELONG — 1908 (2), 1915 (3), 1944 (1), 1957 (5 1/2 ), 1958 (4).

HAWTHORN — 1925 (3), 1927 (1), 1928 (0), 1932 (3), 1941 (3), 1942 (1), 1946 (3), 1949 (3), 1950 (0), 1953 (3), 1965 (4).

MELBOURNE — 1905 (3), 1906 (1), 1919 (0), 1923 (3), 1951 (1), 1969 (3), 1974 (3), 1978 (5), 1981 (1), 1997 (4).

NORTH MELBOURNE — 1926 (0), 1929 (1), 1930 (1), 1931 (0), 1934 (0), 1935 (1), 1937 (3), 1940 (4), 1956 (3), 1961 (4 1/2 ), 1968 (3), 1970 (4), 1972 (1), 1997 (4).

RICHMOND — 1917 (3), 1960 (3), 1987 (5), 1989 (5).

SOUTH MELB/SYDNEY — 1903 (2), 1922 (4), 1938 (2), 1939 (3), 1962 (3), 1971 (3), 1973 (4), 1975 (2), 1992 (3), 1993 (1), 1994 (4).

ST KILDA — 1897 (0), 1898 (0), 1899 (0), 1900 (1), 1901 (1), 1902 (0), 1904 (3), 1909 (2), 1910 (1), 1920 (2), 1924 (4), 1943 (2), 1945 (2), 1947 (1), 1948 (2), 1952 (2), 1954 (4), 1955 (1), 1977 (3), 1979 (3), 1983 (5), 1984 (5), 1985 (3), 1986 (2), 1988 (4).

UNIVERSITY — 1911 (1), 1912 (1), 1913 (0), 1914 (0).

WEST COAST — Nil.

# GRAND FINALS: 1897-1930

## 1897

Collingwood 7.9 (51) d. Melbourne 7.5 (47)
Essendon 5.5 (35) d. Geelong 3.11 (29)
Essendon 9.16 (70) d. Collingwood 4.6 (30)
Geelong 5.16 (46) d. Melbourne 5.7 (37)
Essendon 1.8 (14) d. Melbourne 0.8 (8)
Geelong 8.4 (52) d. Collingwood 6.12 (48)
Unfortunately, there was no grand final as such. All eight teams in the competition played each twice during the home-and-away season, and the top four sides — Geelong, Essendon, Melbourne and Collingwood — met each other in a round robin series. Each side played three 'finals' and there was no grand final as we know it today. Essendon was the only side to win all three round robin games and was declared the premier team. The grand final system was introduced the following season and has remained since, although in 1924, the League again reverted to a best-of-three finals system for just one season.

## 1898

Fitzroy 5.8 (38) d. Essendon 3.5 (23)
**Captains:** Alec Sloan (Fitz), George Stuckey (Ess)
Attendance: 16,538
Fitzroy opened its VFL flag account with a 15-point victory at the Junction Oval against minor premier Essendon. The Grace brothers, Mick and Jim, played key roles in the Maroons' barnstorming finish which saw them win all five of their finals matches after finishing third on the ladder.

## 1899

Fitzroy 3.9 (27) d. South Melb 3.8 (26)
**Captains:** Alec Sloan (Fitz), Dave Adamson (SM)
Attendance: 4,823
The Roys became the first team to win back-to-back flags in the VFL with a thrilling one-point win over South Melbourne. Fitzroy had finished the home-and-away season on top of the ladder, and had the two players of the year in Pat Hickey and Mick Grace.

## 1900

Melbourne 4.10 (34) d. Fitzroy 3.12 (30)
**Captains:** Dick Wardill (Melb), Alec Sloan (Fitz)
Attendance: 20,181
Fitzroy was favored to make it three in a row after finishing two games clear on top of the ladder, but Melbourne showed up the farcical nature of the finals system to come from sixth to snatch the flag by four points.

## 1901

Essendon 6.7 (43) d. Collingwood 2.4 (16)
**Captains:** George Stuckey (Ess), Bill Proudfoot (Coll)
Attendance: 30,000
Essendon comfortably beat Collingwood by 27 points at Albert Park to take its second flag, on the back of

an outstanding season — and an even better finals campaign — from Albert 'The Great' Thurgood, ranked as the greatest player of his day.

## 1902

Collingwood 9.6 (60) d. Essendon 3.9 (27)
**Captains:** Lardie Tulloch (Coll), Hugh Gavin (Ess)
Attendance: 35,202
The first Grand Final played at the MCG, and Collingwood reversed the previous year's result to win by 23 points, thanks to a six-goals-to-one second half. This was the first Grand Final played under the Argus system.

## 1903

Collingwood 4.7 (31) d. Fitzroy 3.11 (29)
**Captains:** Lardie Tulloch (Coll), Gerald Brosnan (Fitz)
Attendance: 32,363
For the first time in VFL history, the result of the Grand Final rested with the final kick of the day. Fitzroy captain Gerald Brosnan missed his set shot and Collingwood got home by two points.

## 1904

Fitzroy 9.7 (61) d. Carlton 5.7 (37)
**Captains:** Gerald Brosnan (Fitz), Joe McShane (Carl)
**Coaches:** — (Fitz), Jack Worrall (Carl)
Attendance: 32,688
After a decade in the doldrums, Carlton returned as a power and made its first VFL Grand Final appearance. But it was no match for Fitzroy and its great champion Percy Trotter. Fitzroy won by four goals.

## 1905

Fitzroy 4.6 (30) d. Collingwood 2.5 (17)
**Captains:** Gerald Brosnan (Fitz), Charlie Pannam senior (Coll)
**Coaches:** — (Fitz), Dick Condon (Coll)
Attendance: 30,000
Fitzroy avenged its nail-biting loss to Collingwood in 1903 with a 13-point victory in heavy conditions. The Pies had finished the season well clear on top of the ladder, but the Maroons' finals campaign was superb.

## 1906

Carlton 15.4 (94) d. Fitzroy 6.9 (45)
**Captains:** Jim Flynn (Carl), Ern Jenkins (Fitz)
**Coaches:** Jack Worrall (Carl) — (Fitz)
Attendance: 44,437
Carlton's return to power was completed with its first flag in any competition since 1887. Fitzroy, appearing in its fourth successive Grand Final, proved no match for the Blues and was overpowered by 49 points.

## 1907

Carlton 6.14 (50) d. South Melb 6.9 (45)
**Captains:** Jim Flynn (Carl), Bill Dolphin (SM)
**Coaches:** Jack Worrall (Carl), — (SM)
Attendance: 40,485

The Blues went back-to-back with a hard-fought five point win over South Melbourne. The MCG was watered before this game, after the semi-finals had been plagued by a rock hard surface and clouds of dust.

# 1908

Carlton 5.5 (35) d. Essendon 3.8 (26)
**Captains:** Fred Elliott (Carl), William Griffith (Ess)
**Coaches:** Jack Worrall (Carl), Dave Smith (Ess)
Attendance: 50,261
Carlton became the first VFL team to win three flags in a row, firmly establishing coach Jack Worrall as a master of his craft. The Blues lost only one match for the year, and outlasted Essendon by nine points in the Grand Final.

# 1909

South Melb 4.14 (38) d. Carlton 4.12 (36)
**Captains:** Charlie Ricketts (SM), Fred Elliott (Carl)
**Coaches:** Charlie Ricketts (SM), Jack Worrall (Carl)
Attendance: 36,700
Jack Worrall resigned amid player dissatisfaction at Carlton, but the Blues still finished equal with South Melbourne on top. South spoiled the Blues' winning run, however, with a two-point win in the Grand Final.

# 1910

Collingwood 9.7 (61) d. Carlton 6.11 (47)
**Captains:** George Angus (Coll), Fred Elliott (Carl)
**Coaches:** George Angus (Coll), Fred Elliott (Carl)
Attendance: 42,577
The first Grand Final meeting between Carlton and Collingwood was packed with sensations. Two Carlton players were suspended during the finals for having 'played dead', and players from both clubs suffered lengthy suspensions following a series of wild brawls in a Grand Final that some dubbed a 'blood bath'. The Magpies concentrated on the footy long enough to win by 14 points.

# 1911

Essendon 5.11 (41) d. Collingwood 4.11 (35)
**Captains:** Dave Smith (Ess), Dick Lee (Coll)
**Coaches:** Jack Worrall (Ess), George Angus (Coll)
Attendance: 43,905
The Pies were back on Grand Final day again, this time opposed to Essendon, now under the generalship of Jack Worrall. The Same Olds won by a goal, after the Pies' Tom Baxter twice kicked into the man on the mark during the last quarter.

# 1912

Essendon 5.17 (47) d. South Melb 4.9 (33)
**Captains:** Allan Belcher (Ess), Charlie Ricketts (SM)
**Coaches:** Jack Worrall (Ess), Charlie Ricketts (SM)
Attendance: 54,463
Essendon toppled favorite South Melbourne to join Fitzroy, Collingwood and Carlton as teams to have won back-to-back flags. The crowd of 54,463 was the largest to have witnessed a sporting event in Australia.

# 1913

Fitzroy 7.14 (56) d. St Kilda 5.13 (43)
**Captains:** Bill Walker (Fitz), Harry Lever (St K)
**Coaches:** Percy Parratt (Fitz), George Sparrow (St K)
Attendance: 59,479

Fitzroy denied St Kilda its first premiership when it defeated the gallant Saints by 13 points. The 'Roys were the best team all year and were strong enough to hold out the Saints when they got to within a point during the final quarter.

# 1914

Carlton 6.9 (45) d. South Melb 4.15 (39)
**Captains:** Billy Dick (Carl), Vic Belcher (SM)
**Coaches:** Norman Clark (Carl), Vic Belcher (SM)
Attendance: 30,427
Carlton returned to the top of the tree, heading the ladder and defeating South Melbourne by a goal in the Grand Final, to mark the 50th anniversary of its birth as a club in the best way possible.

# 1915

Carlton 11.12 (78) d. Collingwood 6.9 (45)
**Captains:** Alf Baud (Carl), Dan Minogue (Coll)
**Coaches:** Norman Clark (Carl), Jock McHale (Coll)
Attendance: 39,211
The Blues and Magpies met in another classic Grand Final, following two memorable home-and-away matches which produced margins of two points and one point. The Grand Final was also tight, but Carlton broke away late in the game to win by more than five goals.

# 1916

Fitzroy 12.13 (85) d. Carlton 8.8 (56)
**Captains:** Wal Johnson (Fitz), Billy Dick (Carl)
**Coaches:** George Holden (Fitz), Norman Clark (Carl)
Attendance: 20,953
A slightly farcical season in which four teams met each other four times, owing to Melbourne, South, Essendon, Geelong and St Kilda having abandoned the VFL because of the war. Fitzroy finished last on the ladder, but beat Carlton by 29 points in the Grand Final.

# 1917

Collingwood 9.20 (74) d. Fitzroy 5.9 (39)
**Captains:** Percy Wilson (Coll), George Holden (Fitz)
**Coaches:** Jock McHale (Coll), George Holden (Fitz)
Attendance: 28,385
Geelong and South Melbourne re-joined the competition, but it was old rivals Collingwood and Fitzroy who contested the premiership match. Despite shocking inaccuracy (they kicked 9.20), the Magpies were too strong and won by 35 points.

# 1918

South Melb 9.8 (62) d. Collingwood 7.15 (57)
**Captains:** Jim Caldwell (SM), Percy Wilson (Coll)
**Coaches:** Herb Howson/Henry Elms (SM), Jock McHale (Coll)
Attendance: 39,168
South Melbourne lost only one game for the season, but was still lucky to beat Collingwood in the Grand Final with a kick off the ground in the last minute that secured a win by five points.

# 1919

Collingwood 11.12 (78) d. Richmond 7.11 (53)
**Captains:** Con McCarthy (Coll), Percy Maybury (Rich)
**Coaches:** Jock McHale (Coll), Norman Clark (Rich)
Attendance: 45,413
Collingwood and South Melbourne remained the two

strongest teams in the competition, but Richmond fought its way from fourth to contest the Grand Final against the Magpies. They weren't quite up to it, however, and went down by 25 points.

# 1920

Richmond 7.10 (52) d. Collingwood 5.5 (35)
**Captains:** Dan Minogue (Rich), Ern Lumsden (Coll)
**Coaches:** Dan Minogue (Rich), Jock McHale (Coll)
Attendance: 53,908
The Tigers avenged the 1919 result with a 17-point victory over the Pies to give the Punt Road boys their first flag. The architect of the Tigers' win was former Collingwood skipper Dan Minogue, recently returned from the war.

# 1921

Richmond 5.6 (36) d. Carlton 4.8 (32)
**Captains:** Dan Minogue (Rich), Gordon Green (Carl)
**Coaches:** Dan Minogue (Rich), Norman Clark (Carl)
Attendance: 43,122
Carlton lost only one game during the home-and-away season, but it was Richmond which lifted when it counted to win its second flag in succession, this one by four points. The final was marked by a fierce hailstorm, while the Grand Final was played in almost constant drizzle.

# 1922

Fitzroy 11.13 (79) d. Collingwood 9.14 (68)
**Captains:** Chris Lethbridge (Fitz), Tom Drummond (Coll)
**Coaches:** Vic Belcher (Fitz), Jock McHale (Coll)
Attendance: 50,054
Fitzroy again, giving them seven flags — clearly the best record of any club in the VFL's first 26 seasons. The Roys beat Collingwood by 11 points, in what proved to be the last match for two champions — Magpie forward Dick Lee and central umpire Jack Elder.

# 1923

Essendon 8.15 (63) d. Fitzroy 6.10 (46)
**Captains:** Sid Barker (Ess), Gordon Rattray (Fitz)
**Coaches:** Sid Barker (Ess), Vic Belcher (Fitz)
Attendance: 46,566
Essendon's famed 'Mosquito Fleet' — with more than half a dozen players under 5'8" — ran away from Fitzroy to take the flag by 17 points. The game was played on October 20 after being postponed the week before due to bad weather. The Grand Final had to compete with the Caulfield Cup!

# 1924

Essendon 8.10 (58) d. Fitzroy 2.6 (18)
Richmond 13.7 (85) d. South Melb 9.3 (57)
Essendon 10.12 (72) d. South Melb 4.15 (39)
Fitzroy 11.10 (76) d. Richmond 8.8 (56)
Richmond 9.13 (67) d. Essendon 6.11 (47)
South Melb 13.8 (86) d. Fitzroy 10.13 (73)
**Captains:** Sid Barker (Ess), Dan Minogue (Rich)
**Coaches:** Sid Barker (Ess), Dan Minogue (Rich)
The 'Mosquito Fleet' took out successive flags, but under a bizarre twist of the finals system then in place, did so despite losing the last game to Richmond. That anti-climax was overshadowed by the

Dons' subsequent loss to VFA champions Footscray, and allegations that Essendon players had been bribed to 'play dead' in both matches.

# 1925

Geelong 10.19 (79) d. Collingwood 9.15 (69)
**Captains:** Cliff Rankin (Geel), Charlie Tyson (Coll)
**Coaches:** Cliff Rankin (Geel), Jock McHale (Coll)
Attendance: 64,288
A then record crowd of 64,288 saw Geelong hold off a fast finishing Collingwood to secure the Pivotonians' first VFL Premiership by 10 points. It was Geelong's first title in the VFA since 1886.

# 1926

Melbourne 17.17 (119) d. Collingwood 9.8 (62)
**Captains:** Bert Chadwick (Melb), Charlie Tyson (Coll)
**Coaches:** Bert Chadwick (Melb), Jock McHale (Coll)
Attendance: 59,362
The Melbourne Fuchsias thumped Collingwood by 57 points, thus ending a 26-year drought. The father of Australian football, Henry Harrison, then 96 years old, was among those at the triumph.

# 1927

Collingwood 2.13 (25) d. Richmond 1.7 (13)
**Captains:** Syd Coventry (Coll), Alan Geddes (Rich)
**Coaches:** Jock McHale (Coll), 'Checker' Hughes (Rich)
Attendance: 34,551
After being runners-up for the past two seasons, Collingwood took the extra step in 1927 to take its sixth flag. It did so in torrential rain and freezing cold winds, conditions reflected in the final scores.

# 1928

Collingwood 13.18 (96) d. Richmond 9.9 (63)
**Captains:** Syd Coventry (Coll), Donald Don (Rich)
**Coaches:** Jock McHale (Coll), 'Checker' Hughes (Rich)
Attendance: 50,026
The Magpies again triumphed with a stunning display of football that produced a then record finals' score of 13.18 (96), and a record haul of goals — nine — to Gordon Coventry. Richmond did well to get within 32 points.

# 1929

Collingwood 11.13 (79) d. Richmond 7.8 (50)
**Captains:** Syd Coventry (Coll), 'Dooley' Lilburne (Rich)
**Coaches:** Jock McHale (Coll), 'Checker' Hughes (Rich)
Attendance: 63,336
Collingwood became the first team to go through the home-and-away season undefeated, only to lose the second semi-final. There was no repeat upset in the Grand Final, however, with the Magpies eclipsing the Tigers by 29 points.

# 1930

Collingwood 14.16 (100) d. Geelong 9.16 (70)
**Captains:** Syd Coventry (Coll), Arthur Coghlan (Geel)
**Coaches:** Jock McHale (Coll), Arthur Coghlan (Geel)
Attendance: 45,022
The mighty Magpie machine, led by Syd Coventry and inspired by Jock McHale, established one of football's most enduring records in 1930 by capturing its fourth flag in a row — a feat not equalled. They did so with a five-goal win over Geelong.

# GRAND FINAL TEAM CAPTAINS AND COACHES

| Year | Team | Captain | Coach | Team | Captain | Coach |
|------|------|---------|-------|------|---------|-------|
| 1897 | Collingwood | G. Stuckey * | — | Melbourne | J. Conway * | — |
| 1898 | Fitzroy | A. Sloan | — | Essendon | G. Stuckey | — |
| 1899 | Fitzroy | A. Sloan | — | South Melb | D. Adamson | — |
| 1900 | Melbourne | R. Wardill | — | Fitzroy | A. Sloan | — |
| 1901 | Essendon | G. Stuckey | — | Collingwood | W.I Proudfoot | — |
| 1902 | Collingwood | L. Tulloch | — | Essendon | H. Gavin | — |
| 1903 | Collingwood | L. Tulloch | — | Fitzroy | G. Brosnan | — |
| 1904 | Fitzroy | G. Brosnan | — | Carlton | J. McShane | J. Worrall |
| 1905 | Fitzroy | G. Brosnan | — | Collingwood | C. Pannam sen. | W. Condon |
| 1906 | Carlton | J. Flynn | J. Worrall | Fitzroy | E. Jenkins | — |
| 1907 | Carlton | J. Flynn | J. Worrall | South Melb | W. Dolphin | — |
| 1908 | Carlton | F. Elliott | J. Worrall | Essendon | W. Griffith | D. Smith |
| 1909 | South Melb | C. Ricketts | C. Ricketts | Carlton | F. Elliott | J. Worrall |
| 1910 | Collingwood | G. Angus | G. Angus | Carlton | F. Elliott | F. Elliott |
| 1911 | Essendon | D. Smith | J. Worrall | Collingwood | D. Lee | G. Angus |
| 1912 | Essendon | A. Belcher | J. Worrall | South Melb | C. Ricketts | C. Ricketts |
| 1913 | Fitzroy | W. Walker | P. Parratt | St Kilda | H. Lever | G. Sparrow |
| 1914 | Carlton | W. Dick | N. Clark | South Melb | V. Belcher | V. Belcher |
| 1915 | Carlton | A. Baud | N. Clark | Collingwood | D. Minogue | J. McHale |
| 1916 | Fitzroy | W. Johnson | G. Holden | Carlton | W. Dick | N. Clark |
| 1917 | Collingwood | P. Wilson | J. McHale | Fitzroy | G. Holden | G. Holden |
| 1918 | South Melb | J. Caldwell | H. Howson/H. Elms | Collingwood | P. Wilson | J. McHale |
| 1919 | Collingwood | C. McCarthy | J. McHale | Richmond | P. Maybury | N. Clark |
| 1920 | Richmond | D. Minogue | D. Minogue | Collingwood | E. Lumsden | J. McHale |
| 1921 | Richmond | D. Minogue | D. Minogue | Carlton | G. Green | N. Clark |
| 1922 | Fitzroy | C. Lethbridge | V. Belcher | Collingwood | T. Drummond | J. McHale |
| 1923 | Essendon | S. Barker | S. Barker | Fitzroy | G. Rattray | V. Belcher |
| 1924 | South Melb | S. Barker* | S. Barker* | Fitzroy | D. Minogue* | D. Minogue * |
| 1925 | Geelong | C. Rankin | C. Rankin | Collingwood | C. Tyson | J. McHale |
| 1926 | Melbourne | A. Chadwick | B. Chadwick | Collingwood | C. Tyson | J. McHale |
| 1927 | Collingwood | S. Coventry | J. McHale | Richmond | A. Geddes | F. Hughes |
| 1928 | Collingwood | S. Coventry | J. McHale | Richmond | D. Don | F. Hughes |
| 1929 | Collingwood | S. Coventry | J. McHale | Richmond | C. Lilburne | F. Hughes |
| 1930 | Collingwood | S. Coventry | J. McHale | Geelong | A. Coghlan | A. Coghlan |
| 1931 | Geelong | E. Baker | C. Clymo | Richmond | M. Hunter | F. Hughes |
| 1932 | Richmond | P. Bentley | F. Hughes | Carlton | C. Martyn | D. Minogue |
| 1933 | South Melbourne | J. Bissett | J. Bissett | Richmond | P. Bentley | W. Schmidt |
| 1934 | Richmond | P. Bentley | P. Bentley | South Melbourne | J. Bissett | J. Bissett |
| 1935 | Collingwood | H. Collier | J. McHale | South Melbourne | J. Bissett | J. Bissett |
| 1936 | Collingwood | H. Collier | J. McHale | South Melbourne | J. Bissett | J. Bissett |
| 1937 | Geelong | R. Hickey | R. Hickey | Collingwood | H. Collier | J. McHale |
| 1938 | Carlton | B. Diggins | B. Diggins | Collingwood | A. Collier | J. McHale |
| 1939 | Melbourne | A. LaFontaine | F. Hughes | Collingwood | H. Collier | J. McHale |
| 1940 | Melbourne | A. LaFontaine | F. Hughes | Richmond | J. Dyer | P. Bentley |
| 1941 | Melbourne | A. LaFontaine | F. Hughes | Essendon | R. Reynolds | R. Reynolds |
| 1942 | Essendon | R. Reynolds | R. Reynolds | Richmond | J. Dyer | J. Dyer |
| 1943 | Richmond | J. Dyer | J. Dyer | Essendon | R. Reynolds | R. Reynolds |
| 1944 | Fitzroy | F. Hughson | F. Hughson | Richmond | J. Dyer | J. Dyer |
| 1945 | Carlton | R. Chitty | P. Bentley | South Melbourne | H. Matthews | W. Adams |
| 1946 | Essendon | R. Reynolds | R. Reynolds | Melbourne | N. Smith | F. Hughes |
| 1947 | Carlton | E. Henfry | P. Bentley | Essendon | R. Reynolds | R. Reynolds |
| 1948 | Melbourne | Don Cordner | F. Hughes | Essendon | R. Reynolds | R. Reynolds |
| 1949 | Essendon | R. Reynolds | R. Reynolds | Carlton | E. Henfry | P. Bentley |
| 1950 | Essendon | R. Reynolds | R. Reynolds | North Melbourne | L. Foote | W. Carter |
| 1951 | Geelong | F. Flanagan | R. Hickey | Essendon | W. Hutchison | R. Reynolds |
| 1952 | Geelong | F. Flanagan | R. Hickey | Collingwood | L. Richards | P. Kyne |
| 1953 | Collingwood | L. Richards | P. Kyne | Geelong | F. Flanagan | R. Hickey |
| 1954 | Footscray | C. Sutton | C. Sutton | Melbourne | G. Collins | N. Smith |
| 1955 | Melbourne | N. McMahen | N. Smith | Collingwood | N. Mann | P. Kyne |
| 1956 | Melbourne | N. McMahen | N. Smith | Collingwood | N. Mann | P. Kyne |
| 1957 | Melbourne | J. Beckwith | N. Smith | Essendon | W. Hutchison | R. Reynolds |
| 1958 | Collingwood | M. Weideman | P. Kyne | Melbourne | J. Beckwith | N. Smith |
| 1959 | Melbourne | J. Beckwith | N. Smith | Essendon | J. Clarke | R. Reynolds |
| 1960 | Melbourne | R. Barassi | N. Smith | Collingwood | M. Weideman | P. Kyne |
| 1961 | Hawthorn | G. Arthur | J. Kennedy | Footscray | E. Whitten | E. Whitten |
| 1962 | Essendon | J. Clarke | J. Coleman | Carlton | G. Donaldson | K. Hands |

308

# GRAND FINAL TEAM CAPTAINS AND COACHES

| | | | | | | |
|---|---|---|---|---|---|---|
| 1963 | Geelong | F. Wooller | B. Davis | Hawthorn | G. Arthur | J. Kennedy |
| 1964 | Melbourne | R. Barassi | N. Smith | Collingwood | R. Gabelich | B. Rose |
| 1965 | Essendon | K. Fraser | J. Coleman | St. Kilda | D. Baldock | A. Jeans |
| 1966 | St. Kilda | D. Baldock | A. Jeans | Collingwood | D. Tuddenham | B. Rose |
| 1967 | Richmond | F. Swift | T. Hafey | Geelong | G. Farmer | P. Pianto |
| 1968 | Carlton | J. Nicholls | R. Barassi | Essendon | D. McKenzie | J. Clarke |
| 1969 | Richmond | R. Dean | T. Hafey | Carlton | J. Nicholls | R. Barassi |
| 1970 | Carlton | J. Nicholls | R. Barassi | Collingwood | T. Waters | B. Rose |
| 1971 | Hawthorn | D. Parkin | J. Kennedy | St. Kilda | R. Smith | A. Jeans |
| 1972 | Carlton | J. Nicholls | J. Nicholls | Richmond | R. Hart | T. Hafey |
| 1973 | Richmond | R. Hart | T. Hafey | Carlton | J. Nicholls | J. Nicholls |
| 1974 | Richmond | R. Hart | T. Hafey | North Melbourne | B. Davis | R. Barassi |
| 1975 | North Melbourne | B. Davis | R. Barassi | Hawthorn | D. Scott | J. Kennedy |
| 1976 | Hawthorn | D. Scott | J. Kennedy | North Melbourne | K. Greig | R. Barassi |
| 1977 | North Melbourne | D. Dench | R. Barassi | Collingwood | M. Richardson | T. Hafey |
| 1978 | Hawthorn | D. Scott | D. Parkin | North Melbourne | K. Greig | R. Barassi |
| 1979 | Carlton | A. Jesaulenko | A. Jesaulenko | Collingwood | R. Shaw | T. Hafey |
| 1980 | Richmond | B. Monteath | T. Jewell | Collingwood | R. Shaw | T. Hafey |
| 1981 | Carlton | M. Fitzpatrick | D. Parkin | Collingwood | P. Moore | T. Hafey |
| 1982 | Carlton | M. Fitzpatrick | D. Parkin | Richmond | D. Cloke | F. Bourke |
| 1983 | Hawthorn | L. Matthews | A. Jeans | Essendon | T. Daniher | K. Sheedy |
| 1984 | Essendon | T. Daniher | K. Sheedy | Hawthorn | L. Matthews | A. Jeans |
| 1985 | Essendon | T. Daniher | K. Sheedy | Hawthorn | L. Matthews | A. Jeans |
| 1986 | Hawthorn | M. Tuck | A. Jeans | Carlton | M. Maclure | R. Walls |
| 1987 | Carlton | S. Kernahan | R. Walls | Hawthorn | M. Tuck | A. Jeans |
| 1988 | Hawthorn | M. Tuck | A. Joyce | Melbourne | G. Healy | J. Northey |
| 1989 | Hawthorn | M. Tuck | A. Jeans | Geelong | D. Bourke | M. Blight |
| 1990 | Collingwood | A. Shaw | L. Matthews | Essendon | T. Watson | K. Sheedy |
| 1991 | Hawthorn | M. Tuck | A. Joyce | West Coast | J. Worsfold | M. Malthouse |
| 1992 | West Coast | J. Worsfold | M. Malthouse | Geelong | M. Bairstow | M. Blight |
| 1993 | Essendon | M. Thompson | K. Sheedy | Carlton | S. Kernahan | D. Parkin |
| 1994 | West Coast | J. Worsfold | M. Malthouse | Geelong | M. Bairstow | M. Blight |
| 1995 | Carlton | S. Kernahan | D. Parkin | Geelong | G. Ablett | G. Ayres |
| 1996 | North Melb | W. Carey | D. Pagan | Sydney | P. Kelly | R. Eade |
| 1997 | Adelaide | M. Bickley | M. Blight | St Kilda | N. Burke | S. Alves |

*= Round robin finals series*

## COACHED MOST GRAND FINALS 1897–1997

The following coaches have coached in the most Grand Finals. (Premierships shown in brackets)

| | |
|---|---|
| 17 (8) | Jock McHale (Collingwood) |
| 12 (4) | Dick Reynolds (Essendon) |
| 11 (5) | 'Checker' Hughes (Richmond, Melbourne) |
| 10 (4) | Tom Hafey (Richmond, Collingwood) |
| 9 (4) | Allan Jeans (St Kilda, Hawthorn) |
| 9 (4) | Ron Barassi (Carlton, North Melbourne) |
| 8 (6) | Norm Smith (Melbourne) |
| 7 (5) | Jack Worrall (Carlton, Essendon) |
| 6 (2) | Phonse Kyne (Collingwood) |
| 5 (2) | Norm Clark (Carlton, Richmond) |
| 5 (3) | Percy Bentley (Richmond, Carlton) |
| 5 (3) | John Kennedy (Hawthorn) |
| 5 (4) | David Parkin (Hawthorn, Carlton) |
| 5 (3) | Kevin Sheedy (Essendon) |

# FINAL BY FINAL STATS

## ELIMINATION FINALS

**1972–1993**

**Highest Score:** St Kilda 24.14 (158) v. Essendon 13.13 (91), 1973.
Melbourne 22.16 158) v. North Melbourne 5.10 (40), 1987.

**Lowest Score:** North Melb. 5.10 (40) v. Melbourne 22.16 (158), 1987.

**Highest winning margin:** 118 points — Melbourne 22.16 (158) v. North Melb. 5.10 (40), 1987.

**Lowest winning margin:** 1 point — Fitzroy 8.10 (58) v. Essendon 8.9 (57), 1986.

**Highest Aggregate:** 260 points — Collingwood 23.15 (153) v. Fitzroy 15.17 (107).

**Highest scoring quarters**

First — 9.4 by Fitzroy v. Essendon, 1979
Second — 7.4 by Carlton v North Melb, 1985
Third — 9.2 by Melbourne v. Collingwood, 1989
Fourth — 10.7 by Collingwood v. Fitzroy, 1984

**Highest Attendance:** 82,952 — Nth. Melb. v. Collingwood (1980).

**Lowest Attendance:** 29,147 — North Melb. v. West Coast (1993).

**Best Goalscorers:** 9 — T. Lockett (St Kilda), 1991; 8 — B. Brownless (Geelong), 1991.

## QUALIFYING FINALS

**1972–1997**

**Highest Score:** Geelong 26.16 (172) v. Footscray 17.9 (111), 1992.

**Lowest Score:** West Coast 8.7 (55) v. Essendon 11.8 (74), 1995.

**Lowest winning margin:** 1 point — Brisbane Bears 15.11 (101) v. Essendon 15.10 (100), 1996.

**Highest winning margin:** 99 points — Hawthorn 23.18 (156) v. Swans 8.9 (57), 1987.

**Highest Aggregate:** 284 points. Richmond 25.14 (164) v. Collingwood 18.12 (120), 1972.

**Highest scoring quarters**

First — 10.2 by Geelong v. Footscray, 1995
Second — 8.4 by Collingwood v. Carlton, 1988
Third — 11.4 by Carlton v. Hawthorn, 1982
Fourth — 8.7 by Geelong v. Footscray, 1992

**Highest Attendance:** 91,900 — Richmond v. Collingwood, 1972.

**Lowest Attendance:** 22,003 — Brisbane Bears v. Essendon (1996).

**Drawn Game:** Collingwood 13.12 drew with West Coast Eagles 13.12 in 1990. Collingwood won the play-off 19.12 to 9.13.

North Melbourne 15.24 114 d Hawthorn 13.13 91 This 1994 final was decided in extra time after the scores were tied (North Melbourne 12.19 91 Hawthorn 13.13 91) when the siren went at the end of the last quarter. Under a rule introduced in 1991,

all finals, except for the Grand Final, which are tied at the end of normal time are decided by playing extra time consisting of two five minute halves plus time on.

**Best Goalscorers:** 9 — B. Brownless (Geelong), 1992. 8 — W. Ralph (Carlton), 1984. M. Moncrieff (Hawthorn), 1978. B. Quinlan (Fitzroy), 1983.

## SEMI-FINALS

**1931–1997**

**Highest Score:** Richmond 25.17 (167) v. Geelong 7.7 (49), 1969.

**Lowest Score:** Collingwood 4.9 (33) v. Melbourne 11.12 (78), 1958.

**Highest winning margin:** 118 points — Richmond 25.17 (167) v. Geelong 7.7 (49), 1969.

**Lowest winning margin:** 1 point — St.Kilda 13.24 (102) v. Collingwood 14.17 (101, 1965.

1 point — Collingwood 19.19 (133) v. Fitzroy 19.18 (132), 1981.

**Highest Aggregate:** 280 points — Hawthorn 24.22 (166) v North Melbourne 18.6 (114), 1982.

**Highest scoring quarters**

First — 10.2 by Geelong v. Footscray, 1995
Second — 9.3 by Essendon v. Melbourne, 1957
Third — 10.4 by Melbourne v. Footscray, 1994
Fourth — 10.10 by Geelong v. Melbourne, 1989

**Highest Attendance:** 112,838 — Collingwood v. Carlton, 1970.

**Lowest Attendance:** 21,767 — Brisbane Bears v. Carlton, 1996.

**Drawn Games:** Essendon 14.16 drew with Collingwood 13.22. Essendon won play-off in 1946. Carlton 8.13 drew with Richmond (VFL Park) 1972. Richmond won replay.

**Postponements:** August 24, 1918, because of rain. Following week, 35,855 saw South Melbourne 8.10 defeat Carlton 7.11.

**Best Goalscorers:** 11 — H. Vallence (Carlton), 1931; G. Goninon (Geelong), 1951. 9 — P. McKenna (Collingwood), 1970). 8 — L. Collins (Carlton), 1945; W. Twomey (Collingwood), 1948. D. Wade (Geelong), 1967.

## PRELIMINARY FINALS

**1931–1997**

**Highest Score:** Essendon 28.6 (174) v. Collingwood 5.11 (41), 1984.

**Lowest Score:** Footscray 5.7 (37) v. Geelong 8.15 (63), 1953.

**Highest winning margin:** 133 points — Essendon 28.6 (174) v. Collingwood 5.11 (41), 1984.

**Lowest winning margin:** 1 point — North Melbourne 10.7 (67) v. Carlton 9.12 (66), 1976. Sydney 10.10 (70) v Essendon 10.9 (69), 1996.

**Highest scoring quarters**
First — 8.3 by North Melb v. Brisbane Bears, 1996
Second — 9.5 by Essendon v. Collingwood, 1984
Third — 10.7 by Carlton v. Collingwood, 1932
Fourth — 8.4 by Essendon v. North Melb., 1983
**Highest Aggregate:** 267 points — Melbourne
25.16 (166) v Collingwood 15.11 (101), 1948.
**Highest Attendance:** 108,215 — Carlton v. St
Kilda, 1970.
**Lowest Attendance:** 26,000 — Essendon v. South
Melbourne, 1942.
**Drawn games:** Carlton 12.13 drew with Geelong
13.7 in 1962. Carlton won the play-off but lost
Grand Final to Essendon.
**Best Goalscorers:** 11 — H. Vallence (Carlton),
1932. 11 — R. Todd (Collingwood), 1938 and
1939. 9 — L. White (South Melbourne), 1942; J.
Dyer (Richmond), 1944.

# GRAND FINALS

**1931-1997**
**Highest Score:** Carlton 28.9 (177), v. Richmond,
1972.
**Lowest Score:** Collingwood 2.2 (14) v. Melbourne,
1960.
**Highest Aggregate:** 327 points. Carlton 28.9
(177), Richmond 22.18 (150), 1972.
**Greatest winning margin:** 96 points — Hawthorn
22.20 (152) v. Melbourne 6.20 (56), 1988.
**Lowest winning margin:** 1 point — Carlton 13.8
(86) v. Essendon 11.19 (85), 1947; St Kilda
10.14 (74) v. Collingwood 10.13 (73), 1966.
**Drawn games:** Essendon 7.27 v. Melbourne 10.9,
1948; Collingwood 10.16 v. North Melbourne
9.22, 1977.
**Highest scoring quarters**
First — 8.4 by Carlton v. Richmond, 1972
First — 8.4 by Hawthorn v. Geelong, 1989
Second — 10.2 by Carlton v. Richmond, 1972
Third — 11.8 by Essendon v. Melbourne, 1946
Fourth — 11.3 by Essendon v. Hawthorn, 1985
**Highest Attendance:** 121,696 — Carlton v.
Collingwood, 1970.
**Lowest Attendance:** 42,100 — Richmond v.
Essendon, 1943.

Postponements — The 1923 match was postponed
one week because the MCG was waterlogged.
Essendon 8.15 (63) defeated Fitzroy 6.10 (46).
**Best Goalscorers:** 9 to G. Ablett (Geelong), 1989;
8 to D. Brereton (Hawthorn), 1985; 7 each to
N. Smith (Melbourne), 1940; R. Harris (Richmond),
1943; T. Reynolds (Essendon), 1943; G. Lane
(Essendon), 1946; J. Collins (Footscray), 1954;
E. Fordham (Essendon). 1965; A. Jesaulenko
(Carlton), 1972; K. Bartlett (Richmond), 1980,
S. Kernahan (Carlton), 1993.

## MOST FINALS MATCHES 1897-1997

The following players have appeared in the most
finals matches.

| | |
|---|---|
| 39 | M. Tuck (Hawthorn) |
| 31 | G. Coventry (Collingwood) |
| 29 | W. Schimmelbusch (North Melb.) |
| 29 | L. Matthews (Hawthorn) |
| 29 | B. Doull (Carlton) |
| 29 | C. Mew (Hawthorn) |
| 28 | W. Hutchison (Essendon) |
| 28 | G. Ayres (Hawthorn) |
| 27 | H. Collier (Collingwood) |
| 27 | R. Reynolds (Essendon) |
| 27 | K. Bartlett (Richmond) |

## MOST GRAND FINALS 1897-1997

The following players have appeared in the most
Grand Finals.

| | |
|---|---|
| 11 | M. Tuck (Hawthorn). |
| 10 | G. Coventry (Collingwood). |
| 10 | A. Collier (Collingwood). |
| 10 | W. Hutchison (Essendon). |
| 10 | R. Reynolds (Essendon). |

## MOST PREMIERSHIPS 1897-1997

The following players have played in the most premiership winning teams.

| | |
|---|---|
| 7 | M. Tuck (Hawthorn). |
| 6 | A. Collier (Collingwood). |
| 6 | H. Collier (Collingwood). |
| 6 | F. Adams (Melbourne). |
| 6 | R. Barassi (Melbourne). |

## PREMIERSHIPS IN ALL GRADES

| Club | Sen. | Res | U19 | Tot. | Night | Tot. |
|---|---|---|---|---|---|---|
| Melbourne | 12 | 12 | 6 | 30 | 3 | 33 |
| Richmond | 10 | 8 | 11 | 29 | 1 | 30 |
| Carlton | 16 | 8 | 6 | 30 | 2 | 32 |
| Essendon | 15 | 7 | 5 | 27 | 5 | 32 |
| Collingwood | 14 | 7 | 4 | 25 | 1 | 26 |
| Geelong | 6 | 13 | 1 | 20 | 1 | 21 |
| Hawthorn | 9 | 4 | 1 | 14 | 8 | 22 |
| North Melbourne | 3 | 7 | 7 | 17 | 4 | 21 |
| Fitzroy | 8 | 3 | 2 | 13 | 2 | 15 |
| Footscray | 1 | 5 | 1 | 7 | 4 | 11 |
| Sth Melb/Sydney | 3 | 0 | 1 | 4 | 4 | 8 |
| St Kilda | 1 | 3 | 1 | 5 | 2 | 7 |
| West Coast | 2 | 0 | 0 | 2 | 0 | 2 |
| Brisbane Bears | 0 | 1 | 0 | 1 | 0 | 1 |
| Adelaide | 1 | 0 | 0 | 0 | 0 | 0 |
| Fremantle | 0 | 0 | 0 | 0 | 0 | 0 |
| Brisbane Lions | 0 | 0 | 0 | 0 | 0 | 0 |
| Port Adelaide | 0 | 0 | 0 | 0 | 0 | 0 |
| **Total** | **100** | **78** | **46** | **224** | **37** | **261** |

## WINNING STREAKS

| 23 | Geelong | (R12, 1952–R13, 1953) |
|----|---------|-----------------------|
| 20 | Collingwood | (SFR, 1928–R18, 1929) |
| 19 | Melbourne | (R15, 1955–R13, 1956) |
| 18 | Carlton | (R10, 1995–R2, 1996) |
| 17 | Collingwood | (R5, 1903–R2, 1904) |
| 16 | Essendon | (R12, 1949–R5, 1950) |
| 16 | Essendon | (R7, 1950–R2, 1951) |
| 15 | Carlton | (R16, 1907–R11, 1908) |
| 15 | Essendon | (R7, 1981–R21, 1981) |

## LOSING STREAKS

| 51 | University | (R4, 1912–R18, 1914) |
|----|------------|----------------------|
| 48 | St Kilda | (R1, 1897–R17, 1899) |
| 35 | North Melb | (R17, 1933–R14, 1935) |
| 33 | North Melb | (R6, 1930–R2, 1932) |
| 29 | South Melb | (R7, 1972–R13, 1973) |
| 27 | St Kilda | (R2, 1900–R11, 1901) |
| 27 | Hawthorn | (R16, 1927–R6, 1929) |
| 27 | Fitzroy | (R11, 1963–R1, 1965) |
| 26 | Sydney | (R9, 1992–R12, 1993) |
| 23 | St Kilda | (R13, 1901–R1, 1903) |

## EXTRA TIME IN FINALS

1n 1991, the AFL Commission introduced a procedure to prevent any final, apart from the Grand Final being tied.

The procedure is as follows:

If a Grand Final is tied at the end of regular time, the game will be replayed. In all other finals, if the game is tied at the end of regular time, extra time consisting of two five-minute halves plus time-on will be played.

Teams will maintain the same ends as at the completion of play for the first five-minute period of extra time and will then change ends.

If the scores remain tied after extra time, additional periods of extra time will be played until a result is achieved. Each additional period will also consist of two five-minute halves plus time-on.

## LAST TIME CLUBS DREW WITH EACH OTHER

| | Adel | B Brs | B Lns | Carlt | Coll | Ess | Fitz | Frem | Geel | Haw | Melb | North | Pt Ad | Rich | St K | Syd | WC | WB |
|---|---|---|---|---|---|---|---|---|---|---|---|---|---|---|---|---|---|---|
| Adelaide | — | — | — | — | — | — | — | — | — | — | — | — | — | — | 1994 | — | — | — |
| Bris Bears | — | — | — | — | — | — | — | — | 1996 | — | — | — | — | — | — | — | 1992 | — |
| Bris Lions | — | — | — | — | — | — | — | — | — | — | — | — | 1997 | — | — | — | — | — |
| Carlton | — | — | — | — | 1972 | 1993 | 1982 | — | 1962 | — | 1952 | — | — | 1972 | 1956 | 1967 | — | 1989 |
| Collingwood | — | — | — | 1972 | — | 1995 | 1980 | — | 1934 | — | 1957 | 1988 | — | 1917 | 1991 | 1947 | 1990 | 1995 |
| Essendon | — | — | — | 1993 | 1995 | — | 1945 | — | 1987 | — | 1948* | — | — | 1995 | 1966 | 1996 | — | 1979 |
| Fitzroy | — | — | — | 1982 | 1980 | 1945 | — | — | 1919 | 1939 | 1961 | 1933 | — | — | 1954 | 1974 | — | — |
| Fremantle | — | — | — | — | — | — | — | — | — | — | — | — | — | — | — | — | — | — |
| Geelong | — | 1996 | — | 1962 | 1934 | 1987 | 1919 | — | — | 1963 | 1911 | 1961 | — | 1960 | — | — | — | 1957 |
| Hawthorn | — | — | — | — | — | — | 1939 | — | 1963 | — | — | 1985 | — | 1944 | 1968 | — | — | 1997 |
| Melbourne | — | — | — | 1952 | 1957 | 1948* | 1961 | — | 1911 | — | — | 1971 | — | 1953 | 1921 | 1992 | — | 1929 |
| Nth Melb | — | — | — | — | 1988 | 1967 | 1933 | — | 1961 | 1985 | 1971 | — | — | 1966 | 1980 | — | — | 1987 |
| Port Ad | — | — | 1997 | — | — | — | — | — | — | — | — | — | — | — | — | — | — | — |
| Richmond | — | — | — | 1972 | 1917 | 1995 | — | — | 1960 | 1944 | 1953 | 1966 | — | — | 1980 | 1937 | — | 1944 |
| St Kilda | 1994 | — | — | 1956 | 1991 | 1966 | 1954 | — | — | 1968 | 1921 | 1980 | — | 1980 | — | 1977 | — | 1977 |
| Sydney | — | — | — | 1967 | 1947 | 1996 | 1974 | — | — | — | 1992 | — | — | 1937 | 1977 | — | — | 1991 |
| West Coast | — | 1992 | — | — | 1990 | — | — | — | — | — | — | — | — | — | — | — | — | — |
| W Bulldogs | — | — | — | 1989 | 1995 | 1979 | — | — | 1957 | 1997 | 1929 | 1987 | — | 1944 | 1977 | 1991 | — | — |

*Grand Final

# TEAMS OF THE YEAR

At the conclusion of the 1950 Australian Football Carnival held in Brisbane a team was selected from the best performed players. The practice continued after each such series until the 1988 Bicentenary Carnival in Adelaide. In 1987, the first AFL team of the year was chosen by the Victorian selectors. With the development of the national competition, the concept was changed slightly and in 1991, the first AFL All-Australian Team was selected. In 1997, the selection panel for the Coca-Cola AFL All-Australian team included Rod Austin, Kevin Bartlett, Ian Collins, Ross Glendinning, Gerard Healy, Neil Kerley and Leigh Matthews, with Wayne Jackson as non-voting chairman.

## ALL-AUSTRALIAN TEAMS

**1950**
SA — B. Hank, J. Marriot, D. Olds, D. Russell, F. Williams.
VFA — J. Whelan.
Vic — B. Brittingham, J. Coleman, B. Davis, L. Dockett, F. Flanagan, D. Fraser, G. Hocking, A. Hodgson, W. Hutchison, B. Morris, C. Sutton.
WA — M. McIntosh.
**1953**
SA — N. Davies, L. Fitzgerald, B. Hank, J. Lynch, J. Marriott, C. Thompson.
Tas — J. Leedham.
VFA — T. Henrys, F. Johnson.
Vic — J.E. Clarke, J. Coleman, D. Healey, J. Howell, W. Hutchison, B. Rose, B. Smith.
WA — J.K. Clarke, S. Marsh, M. McIntosh, F. Sparrow.
**1956**
SA — J. Abley, H. Bunton junior, S. Costello, L. Head.
Tas — G. Long, B. Strange.
VFA — F. Johnson (Capt.).
Vic — R. Barassi, J. Chick, J.E. Clarke, W. Hutchison, P. Pianto, D. Rowe, E. Whitten, R. Wright.
WA — J.K. Clarke, G. Farmer, J. Gerovich, K. Harper, C. Hillier.
**1958**
SA — J. Abley.
Tas — D. Gale, J. Ross, S. Spencer.
VFA — B. Metcalfe.
Vic — O. Abrahams, A. Aylett, R. Barassi, R. Burgess, J.E. Clarke, R. Davis (Capt.), J. Dugdale, K. Murray, N. Roberts, E. Whitten.

WA — J.K. Clarke, G. Farmer, A. Preen, N. Rogers, R. Sorrell.
**1961**
SA — J. Abley, J. Halbert, N. Kerley, G. Kingston, D. Lindner, D. Roach, R. Shearman, W. Wedding.
Tas — D. Baldock, R. Withers.
Vic — A. Aylett, R. Barassi (Capt.), B. Dixon, J. Schultz, E. Whitten.
WA — J.K. Clarke, G. Farmer, R. Gabelich, R. Sorrell, J. Todd.
**1966**
SA — B. Adcock, R. Day, R. Schoff.
Tas — P. Hudson, G. Lee.
Vic — D. Baldock (Capt.), I. Bryant, N. Crowe, J. Goold, G. John, H. Mann, D. Marshall, J. Nicholls, I. Stewart, N. Teasdale.
WA — B. Cable, K. Doncon, J. McIntosh, K. Murray, B. Sarre.
**1969**
SA — J. Cahill, B. Colbey, P. Darley, G. Molloy, R. Schoff.
Vic — N. Crowe, R. Hart, P. Hudson, A. Jesaulenko, R. Keddie, R. Murray, J. Newman, J. Nicholls (Capt.), N. Teasdale.
WA — G. Brehaut, B. Cable, P. Eakins, J. McIntosh, W. Walker.
**1972**
SA — M. Blight, A. Burgan.
Tas — J. Leitch.
Vic — D. Clarke, G. Dempsey, G. Hardeman, A. Jesaulenko, L. Matthews, P. McKenna, T. Payze, L. Thompson, D. Thorpe, J. Williams.
WA — R. Beecroft, M. Brown (Capt.), B. Ciccotosto, K. McAullay, I. Miller, A. Watling, G. Young.
**1979**
SA — P. Carey, G. Cornes, K. Hodgeman, P. Jonas, G. Morris.
Tas — D. James, M. Roach, D. Sutton.
Vic — D. Cloke, B. Doull, P. Moore, K. Moore, M. Tuck, M. Turner, G. Wilson.
WA — A. Buhagiar, K. Hunter, G. Malarkey, B. Monteath, B. Peake (Capt.), B. Cable (Non-Playing Coach).
**1980**
SA — P. Carey, G. Cornes, R. Davies (Capt.), R. Klomp, K. Kuhlmann, G. Phillips, J. Roberts, M. Williams.
Tas — R. Stubbs, D. Sutton.
Vic — R. Flower, J. Jess, M. Lee, I. Nankervis, G. Raines, G. Southby, G. Wilson.
WA — B. Duperouzel, K. Hunter, B. Peake.
Vic — T. Hafey (Non-Playing Coach).

**1983**
SA — M. Aish, C. Bradley, S. Curtis, A. Giles, P. Motley, M. Rendell, C. Williams.
Vic — T. Daniher, R. Flower, K. Greig, M. Lee, S. Madden, S. McCann, M. Tuck.
WA — G. Buckenara, R. Glendinning, S. Michael (Capt.), Michael Richardson, M. Rioli, K. Taylor, J. Todd (Non-Playing Coach).
**1985**
SA — M. Blight, C. Bradley, S. Kernahan, P. Motley, J. Platten.
Vic — D. Brereton, T. Daniher (Capt.), G. Foulds, R. Greene, M. Harvey, M. Lee, R. Merrett, G. Pert, G. Raines, P. Roos, D. Weightman.
WA — L. Baker, G. Buckenara, R. Lester-Smith, M. Mitchell.
Vic — K. Sheedy (Non-Playing Coach).
**1986**
SA — M. Aish, C. Bradley, A. Jarman, S. Kernahan, C. McDermott, M. Naley, J. Platten.
Vic — Gerard Healy, B. Royal, K. Walsh, D. Weightman, G. Williams.
WA — G. Buckenara, S. Hardie, L. Keene, A. MacNish, S. Malaxos, M. Mitchell, B. Peake (Capt.), M. Rioli, R. Wiley, P. Wilson, R. Alexander (Non-Playing Coach).
**1987**
SA — G. Anderson, M. Campbell, A. Jarman, B. Lindner, C. McDermott (Capt.), M. Naley, J. Platten, M. Rendell, A. Rogers, S. Salisbury.
Vic — A. Bews, Gerard Healy, C. Langford, S. Madden, R. Morris, P. Roos, P. Salmon, B. Toohey, G. Williams.
WA — M. Bairstow, C. Holden, P. Narkle.
SA — G. Cornes (Non-Playing Coach).
**1988**
NSW — T. Daniher, D. Murphy.
NT — M. Long, M. McLean, M. Rioli.
SA — A. Hall, D. Hughes, S. Kernahan (Capt.), M. Leslie, B. Lindner, A. McGuinness, M. Mickan, J. Platten, G. Whittlesea.
VFA — T. Wallace.
Vic — D. Frawley, Gerard Healy, S. Madden, P. Roos, P. Salmon, D. Weightman.
WA — S. Malaxos.
SA — G. Cornes (Non-Playing Coach).

**313**

# AFL TEAMS OF THE YEAR

**1982**
B: D. Ackerly, K. Moore, D. O'Halloran.
HB: K. Hunter, R. Glendinning, S. Icke.
C: J. Buckley, B. Wilson, R. Flower.
HF: P. Daicos, P. Van Der Haar,
Gerard Healy.
F: G. Dempsey, M. Blight, L. Matthews.
Foll: M. Fitzpatrick, B. Rowlings.
Rover: R. Ashman.
Inter: T. Wallace, G. Smith.
Coach: D. Parkin.
**1983**
B: D. English, G. Malarkey, G. Ayres.
HB: K. Hunter, R. Glendinning,
R. Greene.
C: R. Flower, T. Wallace,
G. Cunningham.
HF: T. Watson, T. Daniher, M. Rioli.
F: S. Madden, B. Quinlan, L. Matthews.
Foll: M. Lee, M. Tuck.
Rover: B. Royal.
Inter: W. Picken, M. Browning.
Coach: A. Jeans.
**1984**
B: D. Ackerly, C. Mew, P. Moore.
HB: B. Doull, R. Glendinning,
R. Thornton.
C: R. DiPierdomenico, L. Baker,
R. Flower.
HF: Gary Ablett, T. Daniher (Capt.),
Gerard Healy.
F: M. Lee, B. Quinlan, A. Shaw.
Foll: S. Madden, R. Greene.
Rover: K. Hodgeman.
Inter: R. Ashman, D. Banks, A. Purser,
D. Hawkins, G. Burns, B. Evans.
Coach: K. Sheedy.
**1986**
B: M. Thompson, G. Pert, G. Ayres.
HB: G. Hawker, P. Roos, D. Carroll.
C: D. Hawkins, G. Williams,
R. DiPierdomenico.
HF: Gary Ablett, T. Daniher (Capt.),
G. Buckenara.
F: W. Blackwell, B. Taylor, J. Krakouer.
Foll: G. Dear, Gerard Healy.
Rover: D. Weightman.
Inter: C. Bradley, J. Madden,
J. Platten, D. Brereton.
Coach: A. Jeans.
**1987**
B: A. Bews, C. Langford, D. Rhys-
Jones.
HB: S. Wight, P. Roos, M. Bos.
C: R. DiPierdomenico, G. Williams,
S. Stretch.
HF: W. Johnston, S. Kernahan,
A. McGuinness.
F: M. Bairstow, A. Lockett,
D. Weightman.
Foll: J. Madden, Gerard Healy.
Rover: J. Platten.

Inter: S. Madden, R. Morris, J. Krakouer.
Inter: R. Glendinning.
**1988**
B: G. Ayres, C. Langford, D. Frawley.
HB: J. Worsfold, S. Silvagni, B. Lovett.
C: D. Kappler, G. Williams, C. Bradley.
HF: G. Buckenara, S. Kernahan,
P. Daicos.
F: D. Weightman, J. Dunstall,
S. O'Dwyer.
Foll: S. Madden, Gerard Healy.
Rover: J. Platten.
Inter: S. Morwood, D. Brereton,
M. Larkin, B. Mitchell.
**1989**
B: A. Johnson, C. Langford, G. Pert.
HB: B. Lovett, G. Lyon, G. McKenna.
C: D. Pritchard, P. Couch, G. Brown.
HF: N. Winmar, S. Kernahan,
Gary Ablett.
F: B. Stoneham, J. Dunstall, A. Bews.
Foll: S. Madden, M. Bairstow.
Rover: J. Platten.
Inter: T. Daniher, T. Watson,
M. Bayes, G. Williams.
**1990**
B: A. Collins, S. Silvagni, J. Worsfold.
HB: B. Lovett, G. Lyon, G. O'Donnell.
C: D. Millane, A. Shaw (Capt.),
G. Wright.
HF: P. Daicos, S. Loewe, Gary Ablett.
F: S. Kernahan, J. Longmire, S. Russell.
Foll: S. Madden, C. Lewis.
Rover: A. McGuinness.
Inter: M. McGuane, M. Thompson,
A. Liberatore, M. Tuck.
Coach: L. Matthews.
**1991**
B: G. McKenna, A. Daniher, N. Smart.
HB: D. Grant, P. Roos (Capt.), K. Hinkley.
C: C. Mainwaring, P. Couch,
Peter Matera.
HF: G. Brown, S. Loewe, N. Winmar.
F: A. Francis, A. Lockett, G. Hocking.
Foll: J. Stynes, M. Bairstow.
Rover: B. Mitchell.
Inter: B. Brownless, C. Turley.
Coach: M. Malthouse.
Umpire: B. Sheehan.
**1992**
B: B. Hart, P. Roos (Capt.),
G. Wanganeen.
HB: K. Hinkley, B. Stoneham,
M. Hanna.
C: D. Kemp, D. Jarman, M. McGuane.
HF: R. Harvey, S. Loewe, Gary Ablett.
F: A. McGuinness, J. Dunstall,
A. Lockett.
Foll: S. Wynd, C. McDermott.
Rover: J. Platten.
Inter: S. Kernahan, M. Bairstow.
Coach: T. Wheeler.
Umpire: P. Carey.
**1993**
B: B. Hart, A. Lynch, G. Wanganeen.

HB: G. McKenna, M. Harvey, A. McKay.
C: G. Anderson, G. Williams,
Peter Matera.
HF: C. Bradley, W. Carey (Capt.),
G. Lyon.
F: G. Hocking, Gary Ablett, A. Modra.
Foll: J. Stynes, B. Allan.
Rover: A. McGuinness.
Inter: N. Smart, N. Burke.
Coach: K. Sheedy.
Umpire: D. Goldspink.
**1994**
B: D. Hart, S. Silvagni, C. Langford.
HB: G. McKenna, G. Jakovich,
M. Mansfield.
C: S. Tingay, G. Williams (Capt.),
Peter Matera.
HF: G. Brown, W. Carey, G. Lyon.
F: J. Dunstall, Gary Ablett, B. Allan.
Foll: S. Rehn, R. Harvey.
Rover: G. Hocking.
Inter: M. Ricciuto, C. Bradley,
S. Kernahan.
Coach: N. Balme.
Umpire: D. Howlett.
**1995**
B: G. Wanganeen, S. Silvagni,
A. Christou.
HB: M. Mansfield, G. Jakovich,
W. Campbell.
C: N. Winmar, P. Couch, M. Long.
HF: G. Lyon, W. Carey, J. Hird.
F: D. Jarman, Gary Ablett (Capt.),
A. Lockett.
Foll: J. Madden, R. Harvey.
Rover: C. Bradley.
Inter: A. Koutoufides, D. Neitz, P. Kelly.
Coach: D. Parkin.
Umpire: D. Goldspink.
**1996**
B: N. Burke, S. Silvagni, M. Sexton.
HB: N. Buckley, P. Roos, Peter Matera.
C: C. Mainwaring, P. Kelly (Capt.),
S. Crawford.
HF: J. Hird, W. Carey, M. White.
F: M. Voss, A. Lockett, D. Jarman.
Foll: C. McKernan, R. Harvey.
Rover: C. Lambert.
Inter: G. Hocking, G. Archer,
Matthew Richardson.
Coach: R. Eade.
Umpire: M. Nash.
**1997**
B: D. King, S. Silvagni, P. Roos.
HB: Peter Matera, M. Sexton,
A. Heuskes.
C: A. Jones, C. Bradley, N. Buckley.
HF: R. Smith, C. Grant, M. O'Loughlin.
F: F. Gehrig, A. Modra, P. Kelly.
Foll: P. Salmon, R. Harvey.
Rover: N. Burke.
Inter: M. Ricciuto, P. Everitt,
D. Cresswell.
Coach: S. Alves.
Umpire: H. Kennedy.

**314**

# HALL OF FAME

## AUSTRALIAN FOOTBALL HALL OF FAME 1858-1997

### LEGENDS:

Barassi jnr, Ron
Bunton snr, Haydn*
Cazaly, Roy*
Coleman, John*
Dyer, Jack "Captain Blood"
Farmer, Graham "Polly"
Matthews, Leigh
Nicholls, John
Pratt, Bob
Reynolds Dick
Skilton, Bob
Stewart, Ian
Whitten snr, Ted*

### MEMBERS:

#### PLAYERS:

**Era 1858-1900**
Burns, Peter*
Christy, David "Dolly"*
Coulthard, George*
Cumberland, Vic*
Daly, John*
Pannam snr, Charlie*
Reedman, John*
Thurgood, Albert "The Great"*
Worrall, John "Jack"*
Young, Henry "Tracker"*

**Era 1901-1930**
Belcher, Vic*
Bentley, Percy*
Cazaly, Roy*
Chadwick, Bert*
Clover, Horrie*
Collier, Albert "Leeter"*
Collier, Harry*
Coventry, Gordon "Nuts"*
Coventry, Syd*
Eicke, Wels*
Fitzmaurice, Tom*
Greeves jnr, Edward "Carji"*
Hickey, Reg*
Hopkins, Allan
Lee, Dick*
Lewis, Johnny*
Mackenzie, Tom*
McGregor, Rod*
McNamara, Dave*
Minogue, Dan*
Moriarty, Dan*
Scott, Walter*
Tandy, Mark*
Thorp, Vic*

Titus, Jack "Skinny"*
Todd, George "Jocka"*
Truscott, William "Nipper"*
Vallence, Harry "Soapy"*
Warne-Smith, Ivor*
Watson, Colin*

**Era 1931-1960**
Aylett, Allen
Barassi Jnr, Ron
Beames, Percy
Bunton Snr, Haydn*
Clarke, Jack
Clegg, Ron "Smokey"*
Coleman, John*
Davis, Bob "Woofa"
Dyer, Jack "Captain Blood"
Fitzgerald, Len
Foote, Les
Head, Lindsay
Hutchison, Bill*
Kerley, Neil
Kyne, Phonse*
La Fontaine, Allan
Matthews, Herbie snr
McIntosh, Merv
Mohr, Bill*
Moloney, George*
Mueller, Jack
Nash, Laurie*
Pratt, Bob
Quinn, Bob
Regan, Jack*
Reynolds, Dick
Richards, Lou
Rose, Bob
Smith, Bernie*
Sutton, Charlie
Whitten snr, Ted*
Wright, Roy

**Era 1961-1995**
Arthur, Graham
Baldock, Darrel
Bartlett, Kevin
Blight, Malcolm
Bourke, Francis
Cable, Barry
Davis, Barry
Dempsey, Gary
Doull, Bruce
Ebert, Russell
Farmer, Graham "Polly"
Flower, Robert
Greig, Keith
Hart, Royce
Hudson, Peter
Jesaulenko, Alex
Knights, Peter
Madden, Simon

Matthews, Leigh
Moss, Graham
Murray, Kevin "Bulldog"
Nicholls, John
Quinlan, Bernie
Rantall, John "Mopsy"
Robran, Barrie
Schimmelbusch, Wayne
Schultz, John
Skilton, Bob
Stewart, Ian
Tuck, Michael
Wade, Doug
Walker, Bill

#### COACHES:

**Era 1901-1930**
Hughes, Frank "Checker"*
McHale, Jim "Jock"*

**Era 1931-1960**
Leonard, Johnny*
Smith, Norm*
Williams, Fos

**Era 1961-1995**
Bunton jnr, Haydn
Hafey, Tom
Jeans, Allan "Yabbie"
Kennedy snr, John "Kanga"
Oatey, Jack*

#### UMPIRES:

**Era 1901-1930**
Crapp, Ivo*
Elder, Jack*
McMurray, snr Jack*
Scott, Bob*

**Era 1931-1960**
Aplin, Ken
McMurray jnr, Jack

**Era 1961-1995**
Crouch, Jeff*
Deller, Bill
Robinson, Ian
Scott, Ray

#### MEDIA:

**Era 1901-1930**
Wilmott, R.W.E. "Old Boy"*

**Era 1931-1960**
Banks, Norman*
Buggy, Hugh*
DeLacy, Hec*

**Era 1961-1995**
Brown, Alf
Casey, Ron

#### ADMINISTRATORS:

**Era 1858-1900**
Brownlow, Charles*
Harrison, Henry*
Wills, Tom*

**Era 1931-1960**
Andrew, Bruce*
Hill, Thomas*
McBrien, Like*
McClelland, William*

**Era 1961-1995**
Hamilton, Jack*
Luke, Sir Kenneth*
McCutchan, Eric*
Rodriguez, Pat*

*= Deceased

---

### TEAM OF THE CENTURY

**B:** Bernie Smith, (Geelong) , Stephen Silvagni, (Carlton), John Nicholls, (Carlton).
**HB:** Bruce Doull, (Carlton), Ted Whitten, (Footscray), Kevin Murray, (Fitzroy).
**C:** Keith Greig, (North Melbourne), Ian Stewart, (St Kilda, Richmond), Francis Bourke, (Richmond).
**HF:** Alex Jesaulenko, (Carlton, St Kilda), Royce Hart, (Richmond), Dick Reynolds, (Essendon).
**F:** Leigh Matthews, (Hawthorn), John Coleman, (Essendon), Haydn Bunton, (Fitzroy).
**Followers:** Graham Farmer (Geelong), Ron Barassi (Melbourne, Carlton), Rover: Bob Skilton (South Melbourne),
**Interchange:** Gary Ablett (Hawthorn, Geelong), Jack Dyer (Richmond), Greg Williams (Geelong, Sydney, Carlton)

# TRIBUNAL 1997

| Name | Club | Charge category | Rd | Mtchs out | Fine $ | Victim | Club | Video |
|------|------|-----------------|-----|-----------|--------|--------|------|-------|
| Tim Hargreaves | Geelong | Striking | PM | 3 | 0 | A. Parkin | Carlton | No |
| Damien Hardwick | Essendon | Charging | PM | 2 | 0 | M. Graham | Hawthorn | No |
| Joel Bowden | Richmond | Wrestling | PM | 0 | 52 | M. Wilson | Pt Adelaide | No |
| Gavin Wanganeen | Pt Adelaide | Striking | PM | 1 | 0 | A. Prescott | Richmond | No |
| Michael Wilson | Pt Adelaide | Wrestling | PM | 0 | 52 | J. Bowden | Richmond | No |
| Don. Cockatoo-Collins | Melbourne | Striking | PM | 1 | 0 | E. Thompson | Richmond | No |
| Brett Evans | Richmond | Striking | PM | 1 | 0 | T. Weller | Melbourne | No |
| Michael Prior | Essendon | Attempted tripping | NS | 0 | 52 | C. McRae | Bris Lions | Yes |
| Simon Beaumont | Carlton | Wrestling | NS | 0 | 52 | T. Delaney | Fremantle | Yes |
| Garry Hocking | Geelong | Striking | NS | 2 | 0 | M. Hogg | Carlton | Yes |
| Daniel Hargraves | Footscray | Striking | 1 | 0 | 0 | A. Wills | Fremantle | Yes |
| Craig O'Brien | Sydney | Striking | 1 | 0 | 0 | D. Metropolis | West Coast | Yes |
| Ricky Olarenshaw | Essendon | Striking | 1 | 4 | 0 | S. Camporeale | Carlton | Yes |
| Greg Williams | Carlton | Unduly interfering with umpire | 1 | 9 | 0 | A. Coates | Umpire | Yes |
| Darren Jarman | Adelaide | Striking | 2 | 2 | 0 | M. Rogers | Richmond | No |
| Ashley McIntosh | West Coast | Charging | 2 | 0 | 0 | B. Sanderson | Geelong | No |
| Justin Crawford | Hawthorn | Striking | 2 | 2 | 0 | J. Norrish | Fremantle | No |
| Shannon Gibson | Hawthorn | Wrestling | 2 | 0 | 52 | Dale Kickett | Fremantle | Yes |
| Dale Kickett | Fremantle | Wrestling | 2 | 0 | 52 | B. Krummel | Hawthorn | Yes |
| Brendan Krummel | Hawthorn | Wrestling | 2 | 0 | 52 | Dale Kickett | Fremantle | Yes |
| Greg Williams | Carlton | Kneeing | 2 | 3 | 0 | D. Laidley | North Melb | Yes |
| Scott Burns | Collingwood | Striking | 3 | 2 | 0 | S. Loewe | St Kilda | Yes |
| Justin Charles | Richmond | Wrestling | 3 | 0 | 52 | J. Romero | Footscray | Yes |
| Nick Daffy | Richmond | Striking | 3 | 0 | 0 | R. Smith | Footscray | Yes |
| Nick Daffy | Richmond | Wrestling | 3 | 0 | 52 | J. Romero | Footscray | Yes |
| Craig Ellis | Footscray | Wrestling | 3 | 0 | 52 | N. Daffy, J. Charles | Richmond | Yes |
| Mark Merenda | Richmond | Striking | 3 | 2 | 0 | S. West | Footscray | Yes |
| Darryl Poole | Pt Adelaide | Striking | 3 | 2 | 0 | L. Colbert | Geelong | No |
| Jose Romero | Footscray | Wrestling | 3 | 0 | 52 | N. Daffy, J. Charles | Richmond | Yes |
| Steven Sziller | St Kilda | Striking | 3 | 2 | 0 | S. Russell | Collingwood | Yes |
| Darrin Pritchard | Hawthorn | Tripping | 3 | 1 | 0 | C. Johnson | Bris Lions | Yes |
| Jeff Farmer | Melbourne | Striking | 4 | 2 | 0 | B. Wira | Footscray | Yes |
| Andrew Obst | Melbourne | Striking | 4 | 1 | 0 | M. Croft | Footscray | Yes |
| Tony Francis | Collingwood | Striking | 4 | 1 | 0 | B. Ratten | Carlton | Yes |
| Steven Alessio | Essendon | Kneeing | 4 | 3 | 0 | J. Barnes | Geelong | Yes |
| Glen Archer | North Melb | Striking | 4 | 0 | 0 | R. Champion | Bris Lions | No |
| Garry Hocking | Geelong | Striking | 4 | 0 | 0 | M. Lloyd | Essendon | Yes |
| Rod Jameson | Adelaide | Attempted striking | 4 | 3 | 0 | S. Cummings | Pt Adelaide | No |
| Matthew Banks | Essendon | Kneeing | 5 | 0 | 0 | A. Rocca | Collingwood | Yes |
| Michael Prior | Essendon | Racial vilification | 5 | 0 | 0 | R. Ahmat | Collingwood | Yes |
| Jason Mooney | Sydney | Headbutting | 5 | 4 | 0 | B. Krummel | Hawthorn | No |
| Jason Mooney | Sydney | Eye poking | 5 | 0 | 0 | B. Krummel | Hawthorn | No |
| Ashley Prescott | Richmond | Striking | 5 | 1 | 0 | W. Schwass | North Melb | Yes |
| Brett Montgomery | Footscray | Striking | 6 | 2 | 0 | J. Schofield | West Coast | Yes |
| Damien Hardwick | Essendon | Striking | 6 | 2 | 0 | M. Ashcroft | Bris Lions | Yes |
| Justin Leppitsch | Bris Lions | Face gouging | 6 | 0 | 0 | D. Hardwick | Essendon | No |
| Fraser Brown | Carlton | Striking | 6 | 2 | 0 | D. Lewis | Sydney | Yes |
| Robert Harvey | St Kilda | Wrestling | 6 | 0 | 0 | T. Viney | Melbourne | No |
| David Neitz | Melbourne | Wrestling | 6 | 0 | 52 | D. Sierakowski | St Kilda | No |
| Andrew Obst | Melbourne | Striking | 6 | 0 | 0 | M. Young | St Kilda | Yes |

| Name | Club | Charge category | Rd | Mtchs out | Fine $ | Victim | Club | Video |
|------|------|-----------------|----|-----------|--------|--------|------|-------|
| Jamie Shanahan | St Kilda | Wrestling | 6 | 0 | 52 | T. Viney | Melbourne | No |
| David Sierakowski | St Kilda | Wrestling | 6 | 0 | 52 | D. Neitz | Melbourne | No |
| Todd Viney | Melbourne | Wrestling | 6 | 0 | 52 | J. Shanahan | St Kilda | No |
| Matthew Young | St Kilda | Wrestling | 6 | 0 | 0 | D. Neitz | Melbourne | No |
| Matthew Allan | Carlton | Striking | 7 | 0 | 0 | M. Chaffey | Richmond | No |
| Paul Dimattina | Footscray | Striking | 7 | 1 | 0 | D. Harford | Hawthorn | Yes |
| Chris Grant | Footscray | Striking | 7 | 1 | 0 | N. Holland | Hawthorn | Yes |
| Fraser Gehrig | West Coast | Charging | 8 | 0 | 0 | P. Bulluss | Richmond | No |
| Don. Cockatoo-Collins | Melbourne | Headbutting | 9 | 2 | 0 | N. Eagleton | Pt Adelaide | Yes |
| Damien Gaspar | Melbourne | Charging | 9 | 0 | 0 | D. Brown | Pt Adelaide | No |
| Trent Carroll | Fremantle | Charging | 9 | 1 | 0 | L. Whitnall | Carlton | Yes |
| Tony Lockett | Sydney | Striking | 9 | 0 | 0 | S. Burns | Collingwood | No |
| Chris Lewis | West Coast | Striking | 9 | 7 | 0 | D. Morgan | Essendon | Yes |
| Chris Lewis | West Coast | Striking | 9 | 0 | 0 | B. Young | Essendon | No |
| Anthony Stevens | North Melb | Striking | 9 | 0 | 0 | J. Romero | Footscray | Yes |
| Stephen Kernahan | Carlton | Striking | 10 | 0 | 0 | M. Primus | Pt Adelaide | No |
| Justin Charles | Richmond | Headbutting | 10 | 1 | 0 | A. Clarkson | Melbourne | No |
| Sedat Sir | Footscray | Charging | 10 | 1 | 0 | B. Young | Essendon | Yes |
| Garry Hocking | Geelong | Striking | 11 | 1 | 0 | B. Wira | Footscray | No |
| Peter Mann | Fremantle | Charging | 11 | 1 | 0 | D. King | North Melb | No |
| Tim McGrath | Geelong | Striking | 11 | 0 | 0 | T. Liberatore | Footscray | No |
| Brad Wira | Footscray | Testicle squeezing | 11 | 2 | 0 | G. Hocking | Geelong | Yes |
| Darren Mead | Pt Adelaide | Attempted tripping | 12 | 0 | 0 | N. Kellett | Footscray | No |
| Shane Watson | Collingwood | Striking | 12 | 1 | 0 | Peter Matera | West Coast | No |
| Alastair Clarkson | Melbourne | Face gouging | 12 | 0 | 0 | C. Lambert | Bris Lions | Yes |
| Alastair Clarkson | Melbourne | Wrestling | 12 | 0 | 52 | C. Lambert | Bris Lions | Yes |
| Mark Harvey | Essendon | Striking | 12 | 0 | 0 | Dale Kickett | Fremantle | Yes |
| Craig Lambert | Bris Lions | Wrestling | 12 | 0 | 52 | A. Clarkson | Melbourne | Yes |
| Fraser Gehrig | West Coast | Charging | 13 | 1 | 0 | M. Hogg | Carlton | Yes |
| Steven Kolyniuk | Footscray | Striking | 13 | 1 | 0 | J. Peckett | St Kilda | Yes |
| Michael Prior | Essendon | Striking | 13 | 0 | 0 | A. Prescott | Richmond | No |
| Marcus Seecamp | Melbourne | Striking | 13 | 1 | 0 | A. Lord | Hawthorn | No |
| Glen Archer | North Melb | Attempted striking | 14 | 1 | 0 | J. Heatley | St Kilda | No |
| Chris Bond | Richmond | Kneeing | 14 | 0 | 0 | J. Akermanis | Bris Lions | Yes |
| Chris Johnson | Bris Lions | Unduly interfering with umpire | 14 | 3 | 0 | | | No |
| Brad Scott | Hawthorn | Striking | 14 | 0 | 0 | N. Eagleton | Pt Adelaide | Yes |
| Matthew Allan | Carlton | Charging | 15 | 1 | 0 | L. Newton | Melbourne | No |
| Aaron Hamill | Carlton | Charging | 15 | 0 | 0 | D. Neitz | Melbourne | Yes |
| Jason Ball | West Coast | Wrestling | 16 | 0 | 52 | J. Mooney | Sydney | No |
| Ashley Blurton | West Coast | Wrestling | 16 | 0 | 52 | S. Grant | Sydney | Yes |
| Ron De Iulio | Carlton | Kicking | 16 | 4 | 0 | D. Bewick | Essendon | Yes |
| Fraser Gehrig | West Coast | Wrestling | 16 | 0 | 52 | T. Lockett | Sydney | No |
| Shannon Grant | Sydney | Wrestling | 16 | 0 | 52 | A. Blurton | West Coast | Yes |
| Tony Lockett | Sydney | Wrestling | 16 | 0 | 52 | F. Gehrig | West Coast | No |
| Jason Mooney | Sydney | Wrestling | 16 | 0 | 52 | J. Ball | West Coast | No |
| Matthew Dent | Footscray | Striking | 16 | 2 | 0 | L. Toia | Fremantle | Yes |
| Luke Toia | Fremantle | Tripping | 16 | 0 | 0 | M. Croft | Footscray | No |
| Gavin Wanganeen | Pt Adelaide | Charging | 17 | 1 | 0 | B. Doolan | Essendon | No |
| Scott Camporeale | Carlton | Striking | 17 | 2 | 0 | D. King | North Melb | No |
| David King | North Melb | Tripping | 17 | 2 | 0 | S. Silvagni | Carlton | Yes |
| Tony Woods | Hawthorn | Wrestling | 17 | 0 | 52 | M. Brown | Fremantle | Yes |
| Matthew Francis | Collingwood | Striking | 17 | 1 | 0 | J. Stynes | Melbourne | No |
| Kingsley Hunter | Fremantle | Striking | 17 | 0 | 0 | M. Graham | Hawthorn | Yes |
| Jamie Shanahan | St Kilda | Striking | 17 | 0 | 0 | J. Molloy | Bris Lions | No |
| Adem Yze | Melbourne | Wrestling | 17 | 0 | 52 | S. Crow | Collingwood | No |

| Name | Club | Charge category | Rd | Mtchs out | Fine $ | Victim | Club | Video |
|------|------|-----------------|----|-----------|--------|--------|------|-------|
| Scott Chisholm | Fremantle | Charging | 17 | 0 | 0 | S. Crawford | Hawthorn | No |
| Michael Brown | Fremantle | Striking | 17 | 2 | 0 | S. Crawford | Hawthorn | Yes |
| Wayne Campbell | Richmond | Tripping | 18 | 1 | 0 | M. Croft | Footscray | No |
| Justin Charles | Richmond | Striking | 18 | 0 | 0 | J. Romero | Footscray | Yes |
| Dale Lewis | Sydney | Charging | 18 | 1 | 0 | G. Lovett | Melbourne | No |
| Tony Lockett | Sydney | Charging | 18 | 2 | 0 | S. Smith | Melbourne | Yes |
| Darryl White | Bris Lions | Charging | 18 | 0 | 0 | D. Chick | Hawthorn | No |
| Luke O'Sullivan | Carlton | Striking | 18 | 4 | 0 | T. Ormond-Allen | Adelaide | Yes |
| Luke Toia | Fremantle | Striking | 18 | 2 | 0 | P. Symmons | West Coast | No |
| Wayne Carey | North Melb | Tripping | 19 | 0 | 0 | C. McRae | Bris Lions | Yes |
| Tony Evans | West Coast | Striking | 19 | 2 | 0 | B. Krummel | Hawthorn | Yes |
| Brendon Gale | Richmond | Charging | 19 | 1 | 0 | J. Merillo | Fremantle | No |
| Marcus Seecamp | Melbourne | Kneeing | 19 | 2 | 0 | J. Cook | Footscray | No |
| Barry Stoneham | Geelong | Striking | 19 | 3 | 0 | M. Symons | Essendon | Yes |
| Andrew Obst | Melbourne | Striking | 20 | 2 | 0 | P. Sumich | West Coast | No |
| Nathan Buckley | Collingwood | Kneeing | 20 | 0 | 0 | B. Young | Essendon | No |
| Damian Monkhorst | Collingwood | Striking | 20 | 3 | 0 | G. Moorcroft | Essendon | No |
| Damian Monkhorst | Collingwood | Wrestling | 20 | 0 | 52 | R. O'Connor | Essendon | No |
| Ryan O'Connor | Essendon | Wrestling | 20 | 0 | 0 | D. Monkhorst | Collingwood | No |
| Brenton Sanderson | Geelong | Striking | 20 | 2 | 0 | B. Ratten | Carlton | Yes |
| Shane Crawford | Hawthorn | Tripping | 20 | 0 | 0 | S. Grant | Sydney | No |
| Mark West | Footscray | Striking | 20 | 2 | 0 | B. Hart | Adelaide | No |
| Jason Ball | West Coast | Striking | 21 | 2 | 0 | P. Dimattina | Footscray | No |
| Craig Ellis | Footscray | Threatening behaviour | 21 | 0 | 2x52 | M. Gardiner | West Coast | Yes |
| Steven Kolyniuk | Footscray | Striking | 21 | 2 | 0 | Peter Matera | West Coast | Yes |
| Steven Kretuik | Footscray | Threatening behaviour | 21 | 0 | 2x52 | M. Gardiner | West Coast | Yes |
| Daniel Southern | Footscray | Threatening behaviour | 21 | 0 | 2x52 | M. Gardiner | West Coast | Yes |
| Alex McDonald | Collingwood | Striking | 21 | 2 | 0 | S. Rehn | Adelaide | Yes |
| Justin Charles | Richmond | Drug Code violation | 22 | 16 | 0 |  |  | No |
| Paul Dimattina | Footscray | Striking | 22 | 2 | 0 | R. Tallis | Hawthorn | No |
| Gavin Mitchell | Fremantle | Striking | 22 | 1 | 0 | T. Viney | Melbourne | Yes |
| Daniel Southern | Footscray | Wrestling | 22 | 1 | 0 | R. Taylor | Hawthorn | Yes |
| Rayden Tallis | Hawthorn | Striking | 22 | 1 | 0 | J. Cook | Footscray | Yes |
| Richard Taylor | Hawthorn | Wrestling | 22 | 0 | 52 | S. West | Footscray | Yes |
| Scott West | Footscray | Wrestling | 22 | 0 | 0 | R. Taylor | Hawthorn | Yes |
| Scott West | Footscray | Wrestling | 22 | 0 | 52 | R.Taylor, D.Harford | Hawthorn | Yes |
| Stewart Loewe | St Kilda | Attempted tripping | 22 | 0 | 0 | S. Bond | Pt Adelaide | Yes |
| Gary Moorcroft | Essendon | Charging | 22 | 0 | 0 | P. Vardy | Adelaide | Yes |
| Andrew Dunkley | Sydney | Striking | QF | 2 | 0 | J. Cook | Footscray | Yes |
| Jason Mooney | Sydney | Striking | QF | 0 | 0 | J. Romero | Footscray | Yes |
| Glen Archer | North Melb | Tripping | QF | 2 | 0 | G. Hocking | Geelong | No |
| Fraser Gehrig | West Coast | Striking | QF | 2 | 0 | K. Johnson | Adelaide | Yes |
| Guy McKenna | West Coast | Striking | QF | 1 | 0 | T. Bond | Adelaide | Yes |
| Wayne Schwass | North Melb | Stomping on | QF | 4 | 0 | C. Steinfort | Geelong | Yes |
| Simon Beaumont | Carlton | Kicking | NS | 3 | 0 | A. Jones | St Kilda | No |
| David Sierakowski | St Kilda | Striking | NS | 4 | 0 | A. Koutoufides | Carlton | No |
| Chris Lewis | West Coast | Pinching | SF | 1 | 0 | D. King | North Melb | Yes |
| Phillip Matera | West Coast | Tripping | SF | 0 | 0 | P. Bell | North Melb | No |
| David Pittman | Adelaide | Striking | SF | 1 | 0 | P. Riccardi | Geelong | Yes |
| James Cook | Footscray | Striking | PF | 2 | 0 | D. Jarman | Adelaide | No |
| Rohan Smith | Footscray | Attempted kicking | PF | 0 | 0 | A. McLeod | Adelaide | Yes |

NOTE: Under the heading 'Fine' the number 52 indicates a player was fined ½₂ of his base salary, plus one match payment. Where it is indicated '2 x 52', the player was fined ½₂ of his base salary, plus two match payments.

## MOST TRIBUNAL CHARGES

| Number of Charges | Times Guilty | Total Matches Suspended | Player | Club/s |
|---|---|---|---|---|
| 25 | 11 | 22 | David Rhys-Jones | Sth Melb 1980-84; Carl 1985-92 |
| 19 | 11 | 30 | Carl Ditterich | StK 1963-72, 1976-78; Melb 1973-75, 1979-80 |
| 19 | 12 | 34 | Greg Williams | Geel 1984-85; Syd 1986-91; Carl 1992-97 |
| 17 | 9 | 39 | Dermott Brereton | Haw 1982-92; Syd 1994; Coll 1995 |
| 16 | 9 | 25 | Jim Krakouer | Nth Melb 1982-89; StK 1990-91 |
| 16 | 8 | 19 | Dale Weightman | Rich 1978-93 |
| 15 | 7 | 14 | Michael Conlan | Fitz 1977-89 |
| 14 | 10 | 20 | Gary Ablett | Haw 1982; Geel 1984-96 |
| 14 | 10 | 23 | Chris Lewis | WC 1987-97 |
| 13 | 6 | 19 | Mark Lee | Rich 1977-91 |
| 13 | 8 | 23 | Tony Lockett | StK 1983-94; Syd 1995-97 |
| 13 | 9 | 22 | Robert Muir | StK 1974-78, 1980, 1984 |
| 12 | 6 | 13 | Roger Merrett | Ess 1978-87; Bris Bears 1988-96 |
| 11 | 6 | 14 | Greg Burns | StK 1978-89 |
| 11 | 8 | 15 | Mark Jackson | Melb 1981-82; StK 1983; Geel 1984-86 |
| 11 | 6 | 11 | Don Scott | Haw 1967-81 |
| 10 | 7 | 31 | Rod Grinter | Melb 1985-94 |
| 10 | 4 | 13 | Craig Kelly | Coll 1989-96 |
| 10 | 4 | 10 | Stephen Macpherson | Foots 1982-95 |

## LONGEST TRIBUNAL SUSPENSIONS IN A CAREER

| Total Matches | Times Suspended | Player | Club/s |
|---|---|---|---|
| 99 | 1 | Doug Fraser | Carl 1910 |
| 99 | 1 | Alex Lang | Carl 1906-10, 1916-17 |
| 89 | 1 | Fred Rutley | Nth Melb 1925, 1930 |
| 60 | 4 | Tommy Downs | Carl 1927-29, 1931, 1933 |
| 46 | 1 | Bill Burns | Geel 1904; Rich 1908-09, 1912-13, 1916 |
| 40 | 2 | Bert Franks | Sth Melb 1906-10,1912-13 |
| 39 | 9 | Dermott Brereton | Haw 1982-92; Syd 1994; Coll 1995 |
| 35 | 1 | George Topping | Carl 1902-10, 1912, 1914,1916 |
| 34 | 12 | Greg Williams | Geel 1984-85; Syd 1986-91; Carl 1992-97 |
| 31 | 7 | Rod Grinter | Melb 1985-94 |
| 30 | 7 | Ken Boyd | Sth Melb 1957-61 |
| 30 | 12 | Carl Ditterich | St K 1963-72, 1976-78; Melb 1973-75, 1979-80 |
| 29 | 3 | Arthur Coghlan | Geel 1922-25, 1927-32 |
| 29 | 3 | Stan Thomas | Geel 1915, 1917-25 |
| 28 | 1 | Percy Sheehan | Fitz 1904-09; Carl 1910; Rich 1912 |
| 28 | 1 | Jack Shorten | Coll 1909-10, 1912-13 |
| 28 | 2 | Jack Bacquie | Melb 1907-08, 1914-20; Carl 1909-10, 1912-13 |
| 28 | 4 | Rod Mclean | Carl 1935-42, 1944-46 |
| 27 | 3 | Billy Gent | Sth Melb 1903-04, 1906-08 |
| 27 | 5 | Ted Whitfield | Sth Melb 1939-41, 1944-45 |
| 26 | 6 | Peter Reville | Sth Melb 1925-34; Fitz 1938-39 |
| 25 | 9 | Jim Krakouer | Nth Melb 1982-89; St K 1990-91 |

## MOST SEVERE SENTENCES

| Sentence (matches) | Player | Club/s |
|---|---|---|
| 99 | Doug Fraser | Carl 1910 |
| 99 | Alex Lang | Carl 1906-10, 1916-17 |
| 89 | Fred Rutley | Nth Melb 1925, 1930 |
| 46 | Bill Burns | Geel 1904; Rich 1908-09, 1912-13, 1916 |
| 35 | George Topping | Carl 1902-10, 1912, 1914,1916 |
| 33 | Bert Franks | Sth Melb 1906-10,1912-13 |
| 29 | Tommy Downs | Carl 1927-29, 1931, 1933 |
| 28 | Percy Sheehan | Fitz 1904-09; Carl 1910; Rich 1912 |
| 28 | Jack Shorten | Coll 1909-10, 1912-13 |
| 26 | Arthur Coghlan | Geel 1922-25, 1927-32 |
| 26 | Stan Thomas | Geel 1915, 1917-25 |

# COACHES

| Coach | Club | Career span | ALL MATCHES | | | | | | FINALS | | | | | | |
|---|---|---|---|---|---|---|---|---|---|---|---|---|---|---|---|
| | | | Mtchs | Win | Loss | Tie | Win rate | Seasons | Seas | Win | Loss | Tie | Tot | GF | Prem |
| Jock McHale | Collingwood | 1912–49 | 714 | 467 | 237 | 10 | 66% | 38 | 27 | 27 | 30 | 2 | 59 | 17 | 8 |
| Allan Jeans | St Kilda | 1961–76 | 332 | 193 | 138 | 1 | 58% | 16 | 9 | 8 | 10 | 0 | 18 | 3 | 1 |
| | Hawthorn | 1981–87; 1989–90 | 221 | 159 | 61 | 1 | 72% | 9 | 8 | 14 | 9 | 0 | 23 | 6 | 3 |
| | Richmond | 1992 | 22 | 5 | 17 | 0 | 23% | 1 | 0 | 0 | 0 | 0 | 0 | 0 | 0 |
| | Total: | | 575 | 357 | 216 | 2 | 62% | 26 | 17 | 22 | 19 | 0 | 41 | 9 | 4 |
| Tom Hafey | Richmond | 1966–76 | 248 | 173 | 73 | 2 | 70% | 11 | 7 | 15 | 4 | 1 | 20 | 5 | 4 |
| | Collingwood | 1977–82 | 138 | 89 | 47 | 2 | 65% | 6 | 5 | 9 | 8 | 1 | 18 | 5 | 0 |
| | Geelong | 1983–85 | 66 | 31 | 35 | 0 | 47% | 3 | 0 | 0 | 0 | 0 | 0 | 0 | 0 |
| | Sydney | 1986–88 | 70 | 43 | 27 | 0 | 61% | 3 | 2 | 0 | 4 | 0 | 4 | 0 | 0 |
| | Total: | | 522 | 336 | 182 | 4 | 65% | 23 | 14 | 24 | 16 | 2 | 42 | 10 | 4 |
| Ron Barassi | Carlton | 1965–71 | 147 | 99 | 47 | 1 | 68% | 7 | 4 | 5 | 4 | 0 | 9 | 3 | 2 |
| | Nth Mlb | 1973–80 | 198 | 129 | 66 | 3 | 66% | 8 | 7 | 12 | 11 | 1 | 24 | 6 | 2 |
| | Melbourne | (1964); 1981–85 | 111 | 34 | 77 | 0 | 31% | 5 | 0 | 0 | 0 | 0 | 0 | 0 | 0 |
| | Sydney | 1993–95 | 59 | 13 | 46 | 0 | 22% | 3 | 0 | 0 | 0 | 0 | 0 | 0 | 0 |
| | Total: | | 515 | 275 | 236 | 4 | 54% | 23 | 11 | 17 | 15 | 1 | 33 | 9 | 4 |
| Norm Smith | Fitzroy | 1949–51 | 55 | 30 | 23 | 2 | 56% | 3 | 0 | 0 | 0 | 0 | 0 | 0 | 0 |
| | Melbourne | 1952–67 | 310 | 197 | 108 | 5 | 64% | 16 | 11 | 17 | 6 | 0 | 23 | 8 | 6 |
| | Sth Mlb | 1969–72 | 87 | 26 | 61 | 0 | 30% | 4 | 1 | 0 | 1 | 0 | 1 | 0 | 0 |
| | Total: | | 452 | 253 | 192 | 7 | 57% | 23 | 12 | 17 | 7 | 0 | 24 | 8 | 6 |
| David Parkin | Hawthorn | 1977–80 | 94 | 57 | 37 | 0 | 61% | 4 | 2 | 4 | 2 | 0 | 6 | 1 | 1 |
| | Carlton | 1981–85; 1991–97 | 282 | 179 | 101 | 2 | 64% | 12 | 9 | 10 | 10 | 0 | 20 | 4 | 3 |
| | Fitzroy | 1986–88 | 69 | 30 | 39 | 0 | 43% | 3 | 1 | 2 | 3 | 0 | 5 | 0 | 0 |
| | Total: | | 445 | 266 | 177 | 2 | 60% | 19 | 12 | 16 | 15 | 0 | 31 | 5 | 4 |
| Dick Reynolds | Essendon | 1939–60 | 415 | 275 | 134 | 6 | 67% | 22 | 16 | 21 | 14 | 2 | 37 | 12 | 4 |
| Percy Bentley | Richmond | 1934–40 | 133 | 86 | 46 | 1 | 65% | 7 | 5 | 4 | 4 | 0 | 8 | 2 | 1 |
| | Carlton | 1941–55 | 281 | 167 | 110 | 4 | 60% | 15 | 6 | 6 | 5 | 0 | 11 | 3 | 2 |
| | Total: | | 414 | 253 | 156 | 5 | 62% | 22 | 11 | 10 | 9 | 0 | 19 | 5 | 3 |
| John Kennedy | Hawthorn | 1960–63; 1967–76 | 298 | 181 | 115 | 2 | 61% | 14 | 6 | 10 | 5 | 0 | 15 | 5 | 3 |
| | Nth Mlb | 1985–89 | 113 | 55 | 55 | 3 | 50% | 5 | 2 | 1 | 2 | 0 | 3 | 0 | 0 |
| | Total: | | 411 | 236 | 170 | 5 | 58% | 19 | 8 | 11 | 7 | 0 | 18 | 5 | 3 |
| Kevin Sheedy | Essendon | 1981–97 | 400 | 251 | 144 | 5 | 63% | 17 | 12 | 14 | 14 | 0 | 28 | 5 | 3 |
| 'Checker' Hughes | Richmond | 1927–32 | 120 | 87 | 31 | 2 | 73% | 6 | 6 | 7 | 5 | 0 | 12 | 5 | 1 |
| | Melbourne | 1933–41; 1945–48; | | | | | | | | | | | | | |
| | | (1965) | 258 | 157 | 99 | 2 | 61% | 14 | 7 | 11 | 6 | 1 | 18 | 6 | 4 |
| | Total: | | 378 | 244 | 130 | 4 | 65% | 20 | 13 | 18 | 11 | 1 | 30 | 11 | 5 |
| Dan Minogue | Richmond | 1920–25 | 105 | 59 | 45 | 1 | 57% | 6 | 3 | 6 | 2 | 0 | 8 | 3 | 2 |
| | Hawthorn | 1926–27 | 36 | 4 | 31 | 1 | 13% | 2 | 0 | 0 | 0 | 0 | 0 | 0 | 0 |
| | Carlton | 1929–34 | 117 | 85 | 32 | 0 | 73% | 6 | 5 | 3 | 6 | 0 | 9 | 1 | 0 |
| | St Kilda | 1935–37 | 54 | 30 | 24 | 0 | 56% | 3 | 0 | 0 | 0 | 0 | 0 | 0 | 0 |
| | Fitzroy | 1940–42 | 51 | 25 | 26 | 0 | 49% | 3 | 0 | 0 | 0 | 0 | 0 | 0 | 0 |
| | Total: | | 363 | 203 | 158 | 2 | 56% | 20 | 8 | 9 | 8 | 0 | 17 | 4 | 2 |
| Robert Walls | Fitzroy | 1981–85 | 115 | 60 | 54 | 1 | 53% | 5 | 3 | 1 | 4 | 0 | 5 | 0 | 0 |
| | Carlton | 1986–89 | 84 | 56 | 28 | 0 | 67% | 4 | 3 | 5 | 3 | 0 | 8 | 2 | 1 |
| | Bris Bears | 1991–95 | 109 | 30 | 78 | 1 | 28% | 5 | 1 | 0 | 1 | 0 | 1 | 0 | 0 |
| | Richmond | 1996–97 | 39 | 17 | 22 | 0 | 44% | 2 | 0 | 0 | 0 | 0 | 0 | 0 | 0 |
| | Total: | | 347 | 163 | 182 | 2 | 47% | 16 | 7 | 6 | 8 | 0 | 14 | 2 | 1 |
| Michael Malthouse | Footscray | 1984–89 | 135 | 67 | 66 | 2 | 50% | 6 | 1 | 1 | 2 | 0 | 3 | 0 | 0 |
| | West Coast | 1990–97 | 196 | 131 | 63 | 2 | 67% | 8 | 8 | 11 | 10 | 1 | 22 | 3 | 2 |
| | Total: | | 331 | 198 | 129 | 4 | 60% | 14 | 9 | 12 | 12 | 1 | 25 | 3 | 2 |
| Reg Hickey | Geelong | 1932; 1936–40; 1949–59 | 304 | 184 | 117 | 3 | 61% | 18 | 9 | 8 | 10 | 0 | 18 | 4 | 3 |
| John Northey | Sydney | 1985 | 22 | 6 | 16 | 0 | 27% | 1 | 0 | 0 | 0 | 0 | 0 | 0 | 0 |
| | Melbourne | 1986–92 | 167 | 90 | 76 | 1 | 54% | 7 | 5 | 8 | 5 | 0 | 13 | 1 | 0 |
| | Richmond | 1993–95 | 67 | 32 | 34 | 1 | 49% | 3 | 1 | 1 | 2 | 0 | 3 | 0 | 0 |
| | Bris Bears | 1996 | 25 | 17 | 7 | 1 | 70% | 1 | 1 | 2 | 1 | 0 | 3 | 0 | 0 |
| | Bris Lions | 1997 | 23 | 10 | 12 | 0 | 43% | 1 | 1 | 0 | 1 | 0 | 1 | 0 | 0 |
| | Total: | | 304 | 155 | 145 | 4 | 52% | 13 | 8 | 11 | 9 | 0 | 20 | 1 | 0 |

# PRE-SEASON/NIGHT SERIES

## PREMIERSHIPS

| Year | Winner | Runner-up | GF Attend. |
|------|--------|-----------|------------|
| | *At the Lake Oval* | | |
| 1956 | Sth Melb | Carlton | 32,450 |
| 1957 | Sth Melb | Geelong | 25,000 |
| 1958 | St. Kilda | Carlton | 26,400 |
| 1959 | Fitzroy | Hawthorn | 9,200 |
| 1960 | Sth Melb | Hawthorn | 20,000 |
| 1961 | Geelong | Nth Melb | 30,365 |
| 1962 | Richmond | Hawthorn | 24,550 |
| 1963 | Footscray | Richmond | 25,270 |
| 1964 | Footscray | St.Kilda | 36,300 |
| 1965 | Nth Melb | Carlton | 37,750 |
| 1966 | Nth Melb | Hawthorn | 22,800 |
| 1967 | Footscray | Sth Melb | 26,731 |
| 1968 | Hawthorn | Nth Melb | 15,650 |
| 1969 | Hawthorn | Melbourne | 21,067 |
| 1970 | Footscray | Melbourne | 23,882 |
| 1971 | Melbourne | Fitzroy | 21,169 |
| | No matches played 1972–1976 | | |
| | *At Waverley Park* | | |
| 1977 | Hawthorn | Carlton | 27,407 |
| 1978 | Fitzroy | Nth Melb | 26,420 |
| 1979 | Collingwood | Hawthorn | 37,753 |
| 1980 | Nth Melb | Collingwood | 50,478 |
| 1981 | Essendon | Carlton | 24,269 |
| 1982 | Sydney | Nth Melb | 20,028 |
| 1983 | Carlton | Richmond | 32,927 |
| 1984 | Essendon | Sydney | 30,824 |
| 1985 | Hawthorn | Essendon | 24,812 |
| 1986 | Hawthorn | Carlton | 19,627 |
| 1987 | Melbourne | Essendon | 26,860 |
| 1988* | Hawthorn | Geelong | 35,803 |
| 1989 | Melbourne | Geelong | 48,720 |
| 1990 | Essendon | Nth Melb | 48,559 |
| 1991 | Hawthorn | Nth Melb | 46,629 |
| 1992 | Hawthorn | Fitzroy | 49,453 |
| 1993 | Essendon | Richmond | 75,533 |
| 1994 | Essendon | Adelaide | 43,925 |
| 1995 | Nth Melb | Adelaide | 39,393 |
| 1996 | St Kilda | Carlton | 66,888 |
| | *At the MCG* | | |
| 1997 | Carlton | Geelong | 74,786 |

*From 1988 onwards, the pre-season competition has begun in February and been decided before the premiership season begins. The Grand Final is still played at night, but some matches during the preliminary rounds are played during the day.*

## FIRST NIGHT MATCH

The first night football match ever played in Australia took place between Collingwood Artillery and East Melbourne teams on the Melbourne Cricket Ground on Wednesday, August 6, 1879, under a special electric system installed and controlled by a Professor Pepper.

Electric lighting was only in its infancy and the lamps were the large clear glass type, suspended from poles erected around the arena.

As only to be expected at this time, many dark shadows appeared around the playing space, and most of the lamps swayed about in the wind.

The football used was painted white so it could be easily seen by players and spectators. It had to be cleaned every time it became muddy.

Despite the cold and damp night a crowd of 12,000 was present.

The game was drawn, both teams scoring three goals.

On Wednesday evening August 13, Carlton and Melbourne also met under the lights, Carlton winning by three goals to one, with Blues champ George Coulthard, scoring all three goals.

Seven thousand watched this game.

In other matches Richmond and South Melbourne met at Olympic Park in 1935.

## MOST PRE-SEASON/NIGHT SERIES MATCHES

32 — C. Langford* (Hawthorn)
31 — T. Watson (Essendon)
30 — T. Daniher (Sth Melb/Ess)
G. Ayres (Hawthorn)
29 — J. Dunstall* (Hawthorn)
M. Tuck (Hawthorn)
J. Madden* (Ess/Carl)
28 — A. Daniher (Syd/Ess)
J. Blakey* (Fitz/Nth Melb)
27 — R. Dipierdomenico (Hawthorn)
R. Merrett (Ess/Bris Bears)
26 — R. Glendinning (Nth Melb/Wst C)
J. Kennedy Junior (Hawthorn)
P. Schwab (Hawthorn)
T. Wallace (Haw/Foot)
P. Roos* (Fitz/Syd)
M. Armstrong* (Fitz/Nth Melb)
G. Foulds (Essendon)
S. Madden (Essendon)

W. Johnston (Carlton)
25 — J. Platten* (Hawthorn)
P. Abbott (Haw/Fitz)
T. McGuinness (Foot/Adel)
24 — S. McCann (Nth Melb)
G. Dear (Haw/Rich)
23 — B. Evans (Syd/Carl)
R. Greene (St K/Haw)
J. Dugdale (Nth Melb)
G. Arthur (Hawthorn)
D. Brereton (Hawthorn)
C. Mew (Hawthorn)
R. Eade (Haw/Bris Bears)
A. Ezard (Essendon)
P. Couch* (Geelong)
R. Scott* (Geel/Nth Melb)

* = 1997 player

## PRE-SEASON/NIGHT SERIES MATCHES 1956–1997

|  | Played | Won | Lost |
|---|---|---|---|
| Adelaide | 20 | 13 | 7 |
| Brisbane Bears | 12 | 3 | 9 |
| Brisbane Lions | 2 | 1 | 1 |
| Carlton | 73 | 44 | 29 |
| Collingwood | 46 | 20 | 26 |
| Essendon | 61 | 36 | 25 |
| Fitzroy | 62 | 29 | 33 |
| Fremantle | 4 | 1 | 3 |
| Geelong | 52 | 24 | 28 |
| Hawthorn | 82 | 56 | 26 |
| Melbourne | 50 | 24 | 26 |
| North Melb | 77 | 44 | 33 |
| Port Adelaide | 1 | 0 | 1 |
| Richmond | 64 | 31 | 33 |
| St Kilda | 52 | 23 | 29 |
| Sth Melb/Sydney | 68 | 35 | 33 |
| West Coast | 23 | 11 | 12 |
| Western Bulldogs | 64 | 32 | 32 |
| **Total matches played:** | **813** | | |

## MOST PRE-SEASON/NIGHT SERIES GOALS 1956–1997

116 — J. Dunstall* (Hawthorn)
60 — Peter Hudson (Hawthorn)
55 — S. Loewe* (St Kilda)
54 — D. Brereton (Hawthorn)
       T. Modra* (Adelaide)
51 — T. Lockett* (St K/Syd)
49 — J. Dugdale (Nth Melb)
       L. Matthews (Hawthorn)
46 — W. Carey* (Nth Melb)
44 — J. Peck (Hawthorn)
43 — R. Osborne* (Fitz/Syd/Foot/Coll)
39 — S. Kernahan* (Carlton)
36 — B. Quinlan (Foot/Fitz)
35 — B. Brownless* (Geelong)
34 — G. Bisset (Foot/Coll)
       R. Merrett (Ess/Bris Bears)
32 — M. Roach (Richmond)
       A. Ezard (Essendon)
31 — W. Johnston (Carlton)
30 — J. Longmire* (Nth Melb)
29 — G. Arthur (Hawthorn)
       M. Dowdle (Nth Melb)
       F. Goldsmith (Sth Melb)
       B. Skilton (Sth Melb)
28 — M. Conlan (Fitzroy)
       P. Salmon* (Ess/Hawth)
       J. Hogg (Rich/Fitz)

*= 1997 player*

## 1997 RESULTS

**First Round:**
Adelaide 17.14 (116) d Collingwood 9.8 (62)
Football Park
Geelong 9.10 (64) d West Coast 5.4 (34)
Waverley Park
Richmond 11.12 (78) d Hawthorn 9.12 (66)
Waverley Park
North Melbourne 13.9 (87) d Western Bulldogs
11.8 (74) Waverley Park
Carlton 13.9 (87) d Melbourne 9.10 (64)
Waverley Park
Fremantle 11.9 (75) d Port Adelaide 4.15 (39)
Football Park
St Kilda 9.14 (68) d Sydney 10.7 (67)
Bruce Stadium, Canberra
Brisbane Lions 15.13 (103) d Essendon 8.7 (55)
Gabba
**Quarter Finals:**
Geelong 11.14 (80) d Adelaide 7.10 (52)
Football Park
Nth Melb 22.10 (142) d Richmond 9.9 (63)
Waverley Park
Carlton 15.13 (103) d Fremantle 9.11 (65)
Waverley Park
St Kilda 11.10 (76) d Brisbane Lions 11.7 (73)
Waverley Park
**Semi-Finals:**
Geelong 14.13 (97) d North Melbourne 14.12 (96)
Waverley Park
Carlton 12.11 (83) d St Kilda 10.13 (73)
Waverley Park
**Grand Final:**
Carlton 14.13 (97) d Geelong 5. 10 (40) MCG

## MICHAEL TUCK MEDAL

Awarded to the Best and Fairest Player in the Summer Competition Grand Final

| | | |
|---|---|---|
| 1992 | Paul Hudson | Hawthorn |
| 1993 | Gavin Wanganeen | Essendon |
| 1994 | Garry O'Donnell | Essendon |
| 1995 | Mick Martyn | Nth Melb |
| 1996 | Nicky Winmar | St Kilda |
| 1997 | Craig Bradley | Carlton |

# LIGHTNING PREMIERSHIP

## RESULTS

### 1940: Saturday, August 3
*MCG. Attendance: 30,407*
*12 teams competed.*
**ROUND ONE (2x 10-min halves)**
N.Melb. 2.6 (18) d S.Melb. 1.2 (8)
St K. 3.2 (20) d Haw. 2.2 (14)
Rich. 5.5 (35) d Melb. 0.1 (1)
Foots. 4.2 (26) d Coll. 2.4 (16)
Fitz. 4.2 (26) d Ess. 3.1 (19)
Carl. 2.3 (15) d Geel. 0.4 (4)
**QUARTER FINALS (2x 10-min halves)**
N. Melb. & St K. — byes
Rich. 1.2 (8) d Foots 1.0 (6)
Carl. 3.3 (21) d Fitz. 1.2 (8)
**SEMI-FINALS (2x 10-min halves)**
Rich. 5.0 (30) d N.Melb. 2.2 (14)
St K. 1.4 (10) d Carl 1.2 (8)
**GRAND FINAL (2x 10-min halves)**
St K. 4.2 (26) d Rich. 0.2 (2)

### 1941: Saturday, May 24
*MCG. Attendance: 19,572*
*12 teams competed.*
**ROUND 1 (2x 10-min halves)**
Fitz. 4.0 (24) d Haw. 3.1 (19)
St K. 3.5 (23) d N. Melb. 1.2 (8)
Ess. 3.4 (22) d S. Melb. 1.3 (9)
Melb. 2.6 (18) d Carl 2.1 (13)
Coll. 4.1 (25) d Rich. 1.1 (7)
Geel. 2.4 (16) d Foots. 2.2 (14)
**QUARTER FINALS (2x 10-min halves)**
Fitz. & St K. — byes
Melb. 4.3 (27) d Ess. 3.2 (20)
Coll. 2.7 (19) d Geel. 0.0 (0)
**SEMI-FINALS (2x 10-min halves)**
Melb. 2.5 (17) d Fitz. 2.2 (14)
Coll. 2.1 (13) d St K. 2.0 (12)
**GRAND FINAL (2x 15-min halves)**
Coll. 3.2 (20) d Melb. 3.1 (19)

### 1943: Saturday, July 24
*Princes Park. Attendance: 11,000*
*Top four teams competed.*
**SEMI-FINALS (2x 20-min halves)**
Fitz. 5.4 (34) d. Haw. 3.6 (24)
Ess. 2.6 (18) d Rich. 1.2 (8)
**GRAND FINAL (2x 25-min halves)**
Ess. 4.5 (29) d Fitz. 3.3 (21)

### 1951: Wednesday, May 9
*MCG. Attendance: 25,882*
*12 teams competed.*
**ROUND ONE (2x 10-min halves)**
Foots. 3.2 (20) d Carl. 2.2 (14)
Melb. 0.4 (4) d Haw. 0.1 (1)
Ess. 1.5 (11) d. Fitz. 0.2 (2)
Geel. 3.3 (21) d St K. 2.2 (14)
Rich. 4.2 (26) d S.Melb. 2.3 (15)
Coll. 2.1 (13) d N. Melb. 0.3 (3)
**QUARTER FINALS (2x 10-min halves)**
Rich. and Coll. — byes
Melb. 1.2 (8) d Foots. 0.0 (0)
Ess. 4.3 (27) d Geel. 2.1 (13)
**SEMI-FINALS (2x 10-min halves)**
Melb. 3.2 (20) d Rich. 2.2 (14)
Coll. 2.2 (14) d Ess. 2.1 (13)
**GRAND FINAL (2x 10-min halves)**
Coll. 2.0 (12) d Melb. 1.0 (6)

### 1952: Saturday, May 24
*MCG. Attendance: 33,791*
*12 teams competed.*
**ROUND ONE (2x 10-min halves)**
Coll. 4.3 (27) d Haw. 0.4 (4)
Fitz. 2.0 (12) d Carl. 1.1 (7)
Melb. 2.2 (14) d Ess. 1.2 (8)
Geel. 1.4 (10) d Rich. 1.1 (7)
S.Melb. 4.5 (29) d St K. 0.0 (0)
N.Melb. 4.6 (30) d Foots. 1.0 (6)
**QUARTER FINALS (2x 10-min halves)**
S. Melb. & N. Melb. — byes
Coll. 1.2 (8) d Fitz. 0.0 (0)
Melb. 4.1 (25) d Geel. 1.2 (8)
**SEMI-FINALS (2x 10-min halves)**
S.Melb. 3.5 (23) d Coll. 2.1 (13)
Melb. 2.5 (17) d N.Melb. 2.1 (13)
**GRAND FINAL (2x 10-min halves)**
Melb. 1.2 (8) d S. Melb. 0.1 (1)

### 1953: Tuesday, June 2
*MCG. Attendance: 36,715*
*12 teams competed.*
**ROUND ONE (2x 10-min halves)**
S. Melb. 1.2 (8) d Melb. 1.1 (7)
St K. 2.1 (13) d Carl. 0.1 (1)
Foots. 3.2 (20) d Coll. 0.2 (2)
Rich. 4.2 (26) d Fitz. 2.0 (12)
Ess. 2.2 (14) d. Geel. 1.3 (9)
Haw. 3.5 d N.Melb 2.2 (14)
**QUARTER FINALS (2x 10-min halves)**
Ess. and Haw. — byes
St K. 3.3 (21) d S.Melb. 2.2 (14)
Rich. 1.2 (8) d Foots. 0.3 (3)

**SEMI-FINALS (2x 10-min halves)**
St K. 2.5 (17) d Ess. 2.1 (13)
Rich. 1.1 (7) d Haw. 1.0 (6)
**GRAND FINAL (2x 15-min halves)**
Rich. 3.5 (23) d St K. 1.3 (9)

### 1996: Fri/Sat/Sun, February 9/10/11
*Waverley Park. Attendance: 24,276*
*16 teams competed.*
*Experimental rules used.*
**ROUND ONE (2x 17.5-min halves)**
N.Melb. 3.5 (23) d Melb. 3.4 (22)
Coll. 6.4 (40) d Fitz. 2.5 (17)
St K. 7.8 (50) d Haw. 3.2 (20)
B Bears 6.4 (40) d Carl. 3.8 (26)
Rich. 6.1 (37) d W.Cst. 4.8 (32)
Frem. 8.7 (55) d Adel. 6.6 (42)
Ess. 10.7 (67) d Geel. 6.7 (43)
Syd. 6.6 (42) d Foots. 6.4 (40)
**QUARTER FINALS (2x 17.5-min halves)**
Coll. 6.7 (43) d N.Melb. 5.6 (36)
B Bears 6.7 (43) d St K 3.3 (21)
Frem. 8.13 (61) d Rich. 5.1 (31)
Ess. 7.13 (55) d Syd. 3.10 (28)
**SEMI-FINALS (2x 17.5-min halves)**
B Bears 7.13 (55) d Coll. 4.2 (26)
Ess. 6.11 (47) d Frem. 5.8 (38)
**GRAND FINAL (2x 17.5-min halves)**
Ess. 6.2 (38) d B Bears 2.9 (21)

## OVERALL SUMMARY

|  | P | W | L | Prem |
|---|---|---|---|---|
| Adelaide | 1 | 0 | 1 | — |
| Bris Bears | 4 | 3 | 1 | — |
| Carlton | 8 | 2 | 6 | — |
| Collingwood | 15 | 11 | 4 | 2 |
| Essendon | 15 | 10 | 5 | 2 |
| Fitzroy | 11 | 4 | 7 | — |
| Footscray | 9 | 3 | 6 | — |
| Fremantle | 3 | 2 | 1 | — |
| Geelong | 9 | 3 | 6 | — |
| Hawthorn | 8 | 1 | 7 | — |
| Melbourne | 15 | 10 | 5 | 1 |
| North Melb | 9 | 3 | 6 | — |
| Richmond | 15 | 9 | 6 | 1 |
| St Kilda | 13 | 8 | 5 | 1 |
| S Melb/Syd | 10 | 4 | 6 | — |
| West Coast | 1 | 0 | 1 | — |

*Statistics compiled by Stephen Rodgers*

**323**

# STATE OF ORIGIN

## Victoria v Western Australia

### 1977
**Western Australia 23.13.151 d Victoria 8.9.57**
**Western Australia:**
Best: B. Cable, M. Richardson, B. Monteath,
G. Moss, S. Magro, P. Featherby, R. Alexander.
Goals: M. Richardson 6, R. Alexander 3, B. Monteath
2, G. Sidebottom 2, S. Magro 2, G. Moss 2, B. Cable
3, J. Sewell 2, P. Featherby, A. Reid.
Victoria:
Best: R. Flower, I. Nankervis, T. Barker, G. Dempsey,
P. Knights, B. Rowlings, J. Byrne.
Goals: P. Moore 4, J. Hendrie 2, W. Picken,
W. Schimmelbusch.

### 1978
**Victoria 25.13.163 d Western Australia 8.15.63
(June)**
Victoria:
Best: R. Flower, M. Browning, B. Doull, P. Knights,
M. Tuck, G. Teasdale, I. Nankervis, G. Dempsey,
L. Matthews.
Goals: L. Matthews 5, K. Templeton 4, G. Teasdale 4,
M. Browning 3, R. Flower 3, T. Barker 2, M. Tuck 2,
D. McKay, G. Wilson.
Western Australia:
Best: B. Peake, G. Sidebottom, M. Richardson,
P. Featherby, K. Melville.
Goals: R. Beecroft 3, R. Wiley, G. Melrose, R. Day,
B. Monteath, G. Moss.
**Victoria 17.13.115 d Western Australia 14.17.101
(October)**
Victoria:
Best: B. Nankervis, D. Scott, P. Knights, K. Bartlett,
G. Raines, M. Tuck, K. Templeton.
Goals: K. Templeton 6, D. McKay 3, K. Bartlett 2,
W. Irwin 2, G. Wilson 2, M. Browning, W.
Schimmelbusch.
Western Australia:
Best: W. Valli, I. Miller, T. Buhagiar, R. Glendinning,
G. Moss, A. Johnson.
Goals: T. Buhagiar 4, G. Sidebottom 3, G. Moss 2,
P. Bosustow 2, W. Valli, L. Richards, R. Glendinning.

### 1979
**Western Australia 17.21.123 d Victoria 16.12.108**
Western Australia:
Best: B. Peake, B. Monteath, S. Magro, P. Spencer,
T. Buhagiar, J. Sewell.
Goals: P. Spencer 4, S. Michael 4, G. Melrose 3,
P. Bosustow 2, J. Sewell, P. Featherby, B. Monteath,
T. Buhagiar.
Victoria:
Best: B. Doull, K. Moore, M. Tuck, M. Turner,
G. Wilson, K. Bartlett.
Goals: G. Wilson 5, D. Cloke 2, K. Bartlett 2, K.
Templeton, P. Moore, R. Flower, W. Irwin, M. Turner,
G. Raines, G. Allan.

### 1980
**Victoria 18.15.123 d Western Australia 15.12.102
(July)**
Victoria:
Best: R. Flower, J. Dunne, G. Raines, K. Moore,

G. Wilson, T. Watson, L. Matthews.
Goals: K. Templeton 3, L. Matthews 3, T. Watson 2,
D. Clarke 2, K. Bartlett 2, R. Flower, G. Wilson,
K. Grieg, G. Raines, D. Cloke, A. Briedis.
Western Australia:
Best: R. Glendinning, P. Krakouer, M. Rioli, K. Hunter,
B. Monteath, L. Fong.
Goals: G. Moss 4, P. Krakouer 3, P. Bosustow 2,
B. Monteath 2, L. Fong, M. Rioli, J. Hayes, S. Michael.
**Victoria 14.20.104 d Western Australia 9.15.69
(October)**
Victoria:
Best: G. Wilson, K. Sheldon, P. Moore, D. Weightman,
K. Templeton, I. Nankervis, J. Jess.
Goals: G. Wilson 4, K. Templeton 3, K. Sheldon 3,
R. Flower, G. Raines, D. Weightman, K. Bartlett.
Western Australia:
Best: B. Peake, K. Hunter, B. Duperouzel, R. Wiley,
S. Green, R. Prunster.
Goals: P. Spencer 2, B. Duperouzel 2, B. Peake,
M. Rioli, R. Wiley, J. Krakouer, M. Fitzpatrick.

### 1981
**Western Australia 16.23.119 d Victoria 13.12.90**
Western Australia:
Best: S. Beasley, G. Buckenara, G. Moss, R. Lester-
Smith, N. Carter, J. Sewell.
Goals: S. Beasley 6, R. Wiley 3, N. Carter 2,
G. Buckenara 2, B. Peake, M. Fitzpatrick, S. Michael.
Victoria:
Best: G. Dempsey, M. Tuck, R. Ashman, D. Cloke,
K. Moore, P. Moore.
Goals: M. Roach 4, R. Ashman 4, M. Conlan,
T. Daniher, G. Smith, D. Weightman, M. Neagle,
M. Williams.

### 1982
**Victoria 19.10.124 d Western Australia 15.11.101**
Victoria:
Best: R. Flower, G. Smith, S. McCann, B. Rowlings,
A. Marcou, M. Browning.
Goals: A. Marcou 4, G. Healy 3, R. Flower 2, G. Smith
2, D. Cloke 2, B. Rowlings 2, J. Buckley, M. Turner,
G. Wilson, B. Wilson.
Western Australia:
Best: G. Shaw, G. Buckenara, R. Glendinning,
R. Barrett, B. Peake, W. Ralph.
Goals: W. Ralph 5, B. Monteath 3, G. Shaw 2,
K. Taylor, K. Judge, G. Buckenara, B. Vigona, G. Moss.

### 1983
**Western Australia 16.22.118 d Victoria 16.19.115**
Western Australia:
Best: G. Buckenara, M. Rioli, S. Michael, R.
Glendinning, K. Taylor, G. Sidebottom.
Goals: G. Buckenara 7, K. Taylor 2, W. Ralph 2, A.
Johnson, M. Richardson, W. Blackwell, S. Michael, G.
Sidebottom.
Victoria:
Best: T. Wallace, T. Daniher, M. Tuck, D. English, M.
Lee.
Goals: T. Wallace 3, M. Lee 3, P. Knights 2,
S. Madden 2, R. Flower, T. Daniher, W. Johnston,
T. Watson, B. Royal, D. Weightman.

**1984**
**Western Australia 21.16.142 d Victoria 21.12.138**
Western Australia:
Best: R. Glendinning, R. Wiley, B. Hardie, M. Rioli,
N. Carter, P. Harding, S. Malaxos.
Goals: G. Sidebottom 6, R. Wiley 4, S. Malaxos 3,
R. Glendinning 3, A. Daniels 2, K. Taylor, M.
Richardson, P. Bosustow.
Victoria:
Best: G. Ablett, G. Healy, T. Daniher, S. Madden,
C. Mew, R. Greene.
Goals: G. Ablett 8, G. Healy 5, C. Mew 2, J. Buckley,
G. Williams, R. Greene, W. Johnston, B. Evans,
S. Madden.

**1985**
**Victoria 19.16.130 d Western Australia 9.11.65**
Victoria:
Best: P. Roos, R. Merrett, D. Weightman, G. Raines,
G. Pert, T. Alvin, K. Walsh, M. Harvey.
Goals: D. Weightman 4, R. Merrett 2, D. Brereton 2,
S. Wallis 2, S. Madden 2, M. Harvey 2, A. Bews,
T. Lockett, R. Osborne, B. Royal, R. Barham.
Western Australia:
Best: R. Lester-Smith, L. Baker, G. Buckenara,
A. Sidebottom, R. Glendinning, R. Barrett.
Goals: G. Buckenara 2, M. Mitchell 2, S. Beasley,
J. Krakouer, L. Baker, J. Sewell, R. Glendinning.

**1986**
**Western Australia 21.11.137 d Victoria 20.14.134**
Western Australia:
Best: M. Rioli, G. Buckenara, M. Mitchell, P. Narkle,
A. MacNish, L. Baker, B. Peake, L. Keene, B. Hardie.
Goals: B. Peake 7, G. Buckenara 5, A. MacNish 3,
M. Mitchell 2, M. Rioli 2, L. Baker, P. Wilson.
Victoria:
Best: D. Weightman, B. Royal, G. Healy, B. Taylor,
W. Harmes, T. Daniher.
Goals: D. Weightman 5, B. Royal 5, B. Taylor 4,
D. Brereton 3, T. Alvin, A. Bews, G. Healy.

**1987**
**Victoria 16.20.116 d Western Australia 13.14.92**
Victoria:
Best: G. Williams, S. Madden, G. Healy, P. Roos,
A. Bews, R. Jencke, B. Royal, P. Salmon.
Goals: P. Salmon 5, B. Royal 3, D. Rhys-Jones 3,
G. Williams, R. Morris, P. Foster, D. Murphy, W.
Johnston.
Western Australia:
Best: P. Narkle, M. Mitchell, C. Mainwaring, R. Lester-
Smith, M. Bairstow, C. Holden.
Goals: M. Bairstow 3, A. Ishchenko 2, J. Krakouer
2, M. Mitchell, J. Dorotich, D. Hart, P. Narkle,
M. Rance, M. Rioli.

**1988**
**Victoria 20.13.133 d Western Australia 10.13.73**
(March).
Victoria:
Best: D. Weightman, P. Salmon, G. Williams,
G. Healy, S. Madden, A. Bews.
Goals: P. Salmon 7, P. Roos 4, R. Osborne 2,
P. Daicos, G. Healy, L. Harris, R. Smith, G. Williams,
A. Bews, T. Watson.
Western Australia:
Best: R. Dennis, E. Spalding, D. Lamb, S. Malaxos,
D. Laidley.
Goals: A. Lockyer 4, R. Glendinning, G. Buckenara,
J. Annear, E. Spalding, R. Dennis, D. Laidley.

**Victoria 21.23.149 d Western Australia 15.9.99**
**(July)**
Victoria:
Best: G. Healy, B. Mitchell, D. Weightman,
G. Williams, B. Lovett, D. Murphy, S. Morwood.
Goals: G. Healy 5, B. Mitchell 3, D. Weightman 3,
B. Wilson 2, S. Madden 2, D. Murphy, J. Stynes,
D. Millane, G. Williams, T. Daniher, J. Dunstall.
Western Australia:
Best: C. Mainwaring, P. Wilson, J. Worsfold,
A. Lockyer, M. Christian, G. Buckenara, J. Krakouer.
Goals: G. Buckenara 4, M. Bairstow 2, J. Dorotich 2,
C. Starcevich, A Ishchenko, M. Mitchell, J. Krakouer,
M. Christian, D. Pyke, P. Wilson.

**1989**
**Victoria 19.12.126 d Western Australia 10.12.72**
Victoria:
Best: J. Dunstall, D. Weightman, S. Madden,
G. Williams, G. Brown, G. Lyons, B. Lovett, A. Bews,
T. Daniher.
Goals: J. Dunstall 9, R. Scott 2, G. Ablett 2,
T. Daniher 2, G. Williams, A. Bews, A. Collins,
C. Lambert.
Western Australia:
Best: P. Wilson, C. Mainwaring, N. Winmar,
G. Buckenara, S. Jackson, M. Bairstow.
Goals: S. Jackson 3, N. Winmar 2, M. Bairstow,
D. Lamb, E. Spalding, P. Wilson, M. Rance.

**1990**
**Victoria 14.13.97 d Western Australia 8.12.60**
Victoria:
Best: M. McGuane, S. Madden, A. Collins,
B. Stoneham, S. Silvagni, N. Bruns, G. Ablett.
Goals: G. Ablett 6, P. Salmon 4, D. Rice, N. Bruns,
D. Brereton, S. Loewe.
Western Australia:
Best: M. Mitchell, N. Winmar, S. Malaxos, J. Gastev.
Goals: P. Sumich 2, N. Winmar 2, D. Bennett,
D. Bewick, M. Mitchell, B. Heady.

**1991**
**Western Australia 19.13.127 d Victoria 7.9.51**
Western Australia:
Best: M. Bairstow, P. Harding, E. Spalding, P. Sumich,
C. Turley, D. Bewick, G. McKenna.
Goals: P. Sumich 6, M. Bairstow 4, P. Matera 2,
N. Winmar 2, D. Lamb, C. Turley, C. Starcevich,
A. Jakovich, D. Kemp.
Victoria:
Best: B. Mitchell, D. Weightman, A. Collins, P. Roos.
Goals: G. Ablett 2, B. Mitchell 2, D. Weightman,
A. Ezard, G. Hocking.

**1992**
**Victoria 23.19.157 d Western Australia 13.12.90**
Victoria:
Best: Hanna, Brown, Wynd, R. Harvey, Ablett, Loewe,
McGuane.
Goals: Lockett 5, Loewe 4, Ablett 3, Scott 3,
McGuane 3, Mitchell, Brown, Osborne, Bayes,
Stoneham.
Western Australia:
Best: Allan, Kickett, Winmar, Langdon, McIntosh.
Goals: Langdon 2, Winmar 2, Matera 2, Kickett 2,
Wilson 2, Bewick, Watters, Starcevich.

# Victoria v South Australia

## 1979
**Victoria 25.30.180 d South Australia 20.15.135**
Victoria:
Best: G. Wilson, K. Bartlett, W. Picken, D. Cloke,
M. Tuck, W. Irwin.
Goals: K. Bartlett 4, K.Templeton 4, W. Irwin 3, P. Moore
3, G. Wilson 2, W. Schimmelbusch 2, G. Dempsey 2,
M. Tuck, M. Turner, B. Nankervis, D. Cloke, R. Flower.
South Australia:
Best: G. Cornes, M. Blight, P. Carey, P. Jonas,
R. Ebert, K. Hodgeman, B. Lindsay.
Goals: M. Blight 4, A. Bennett 4, M. Graham 3,
P. Jonas 2, B. Lindsay, G. Phillips, R. Ebert, E. Fry,
G. Cornes, G. Morris, R. Davies.

## 1980
**Victoria 15.12.102 d South Australia 12.13.85**
Victoria:
Best: G. Southby, R. Flower, M. Lee, I. Nankervis,
G. Raines, M. Turner.
Goals: K. Templeton 3, K. Bartlett 3, J. Jess 2,
M. Moncrieff 2, R. Flower 2, K. Sheldon, G. Raines,
M. Turner.
South Australia:
Best: G. Cornes, R. Davies, G. Phillips, K. McSporran,
K. Kuhlmann, M. Williams.
Goals: J. Roberts 4, K. McSporran 2, G. Cornes,
P. Heinrich, R. Davies, M. Taylor, G. Phillips, M. James.

## 1982
**Victoria 21.13.139 d South Australia 18.19.127**
Victoria:
Best: P. Moore, B. Rowlings, G. Wilson, T. Buhagiar,
M. Turner, K. Templeton, G. Healy, G. Cunningham.
Goals: K. Templeton 7, G. Healy 5, D. Cloke 2,
R. Wiley 2, G. Wilson 2, G. Hawker, T. Buhagiar,
M. Turner.
South Australia:
Best: M. Naley, G. Phillips, S. Copping, B. Abernethy,
K. Hodgeman, D. Jenkins.
Goals: S. Copping 5, M. Naley 3, B. Abernethy 2,
R. Johnston 2, K. Hodgeman 2, M. Rendell 2, J.
Platten, N. Craig.

## 1983
**South Australia 26.16.172 d Victoria 17.14.116**
South Australia:
Best: M. Aish, P. Motley, N. Craig, A. Giles,
K. Thomas, C. Bradley, B. Lindner.
Goals: B. Lindner 5, P. Motley 3, S. Kernahan 3,
C. Bradley 3, M. Naley 2, M. Aish 2, J. Platten 2,
J. Schneebichler 2, K. Thomas, S. Copping,
G. McAdam, G. McIntosh.
Victoria:
Best: R. Flower, T. Daniher, L. Serafini, B. Wilson,
B. Rowlings, S. Madden.
Goals: R. Flower 4, T. Daniher 3, B. Wilson 3,
S. Madden 2, G. Smith, A. Marcou, G. Cunningham,
R. Ashman, G. Hawker.

## 1984
**Victoria 16.12.108 d South Australia 16.8.104**
Victoria:
Best: S. Madden, P. Salmon, D. Ackerly, W. Johnston,
J. Buckley, D. Hawkins.
Goals: P. Salmon 5, P. Daicos 3, J. Buckley 2,
W. Johnston, G. Wilson, D. Carroll, P. Moore,
D. Hawkins, B. Evans.
South Australia:

Best: S. Kernahan, G. McIntosh, M. Naley, J. Platten,
R. White, N. Craig.
Goals: S. Kernahan 10, N. Roberts 4, P. Motley,
J. Schneebichler.

## 1985
**Victoria 20.13.133 d South Australia 11.10.76**
Victoria:
Best: M. Harvey, D. Weightman, D. Brereton, P. Van
Der Haar, R. Merrett, G. Ablett.
Goals: D. Weightman 6, R. Merrett 4, G. Ablett 4,
P. Van Der Haar 3, M. Harvey, G. Healy, D. Brereton.
South Australia:
Best: R. Johnston, P. Motley, G. Anderson,
G. McIntosh, J. Platten, M. Leslie.
Goals: N. Roberts 3, S. Kernahan 3, M. Redden 2,
J. Platten, K. Thomas, T. Antrobus.

## 1986
**South Australia 18.17.125 d Victoria 17.13.115**
South Australia:
Best: M. Naley, J. Platten, C. McDermott, S.
Kernahan, M. Aish, C. Bradley, D. Bolton.
Goals: S. Kernahan 4, G. Dietrich 4, J. Platten 2,
M. Naley 2, C. McDermott, G. Fielke, M. Aish,
M. Williams, A. McGuinness, K. Thomas.
Victoria:
Best: S. Clark, T. Poole, P. Salmon, D. Brereton,
K. Walsh, T. Alvin.
Goals: P. Salmon 4, D. Brereton 3, S. Clark 3,
T. Poole 3, M. Harvey 2, D. Weightman, G. Williams.

## 1987
**South Australia 12.13.85 d Victoria 11.15.81**
South Australia:
Best: M. Naley, C. McDermott, M. Rendell, A. Robers,
C. Bradley, B. Lindsay, J. Platten.
Goals: B. Lindner 4, M. Naley 4, R. Mandemaker,
C. McDermott, A. McGuinness, S. Stretch.
Victoria:
Best: C. Langford, P. Roos, D. Murphy, B. Royal,
R. Osborne.
Goals: D. Brereton 2, P. Meldrum, R. Osborne,
B. Royal, G. Ablett, D. Barwick, P. Roos, T. Lockett,
A. Bews, M. Larkin.

## 1988
**South Australia 15.12.102 d Victoria 6.6.42**
South Australia:
Best: G. McIntosh, M. Leslie, J. Platten, S. Kernahan,
T. Hall, M. Aish.
Goals: S. Kernahan 6, J. Platten 3, T. Hall 3,
B. Lindner 2, C. McDermott.
Victoria:
Best: G. Healy, P. Roos, S. Silvagni, S. Madden,
D. Frawley.
Goals: R. Morris 2, B. Royal, R. Osborne, P. Salmon,
D. Weightman.

## 1989
**Victoria 22.17.149 d South Australia 9.9.63**
Victoria:
Best: T. Daniher, G. Brown, J. Dunstall, D. Pritchard,
G. Lyon, S. Madden, A. Collins, T. Lockett.
Goals: T. Lockett 5, J. Dunstall 4, D. Brereton 3,
N. Bruns 2, T. Daniher 2, D. Weightman, D. Murphy,
R. Scott, A. Bews, T. Watson, D. Pritchard.
South Australia:
Best: A. Jarman, S. Kernahan, C. Bradley.
Goals: S. Kernahan 4, A. Jarman 2, D. Smith 2,
B. Lindner.

**1991**
**Victoria 12.14.86 d South Australia 11.4.70**
Victoria:
Best: P. Couch, T. Watson, D. Weightman, A. Ezard,
G. Brown, S. Madden.
Goals: S. Madden 4, P. Couch 2, R. Harvey 2,
D. Weightman, G. Lyon, S. Loewe, D. Bourke.
South Australia:
Best: R. Maynard, B. Abernethy, G. Anderson,
M. Leslie, C. Bradley.
Goals: R. Maynard 4, S. Kernahan 3, D. Jarman 3,
A. McGuinness.

**1992**
**South Australia 19.19.133 d Victoria 18.12.120**
South Australia:
Best: S. Kernahan, Francis, Russell, D. Jarman,
Bickley, Wanganeen, Carey.
Goals: S. Kernahan 6, Russell 2, Hall 2, Carey 2,
Francis 2, Obst, D. Jarman, Maynard, McDermott,
Saliba.
Victoria:
Best: McGuane, R. Harvey, Roos, Salmon, Hinkley,
Shaw.
Goals: Salmon 5, Scott 3, Roos 3, Couch 2,
McGuane 2, Stynes, Lambert, R. Harvey.

**1993**
**South Australia 16.13.109 d Victoria 14.13.97**
South Australia:
Best: D. Jarman, Russell, Bradley, Bickley,
Wanganeen, McDermott.
Goals: D. Jarman 6, S. Kernahan 2, Obst 2, Hall 2,
Modra, M. Robran, Bradley, Russell.
Victoria:
Best: R. Harvey, Stynes, Frawley, Williams, Roos,
Langford.
Goals: Ablett 5, G. Lyon 3, Loewe 2, Williams 2,
Roos, McGuane.

**1994**
**South Australia 11.9.75 d Victoria 10.13.73**
South Australia:
Best: Wanganeen, McKay, Kappler, Modra,
D. Jarman, Rehn.
Goals: Modra 6, Kappler, Hynes, Russell, Platten,
D. Jarman.
Victoria:
Best: Calthorpe, Hocking, Stynes, Hanna, Tingay,
Brown.
Goals: Ablett 4, Hocking 2, Brown, Mercuri, Hanna,
Stynes.

**1995**
**Victoria 18.12.120 d South Australia 8.9.57**
Victoria:
Best: Lockett, Mansfield, Couch, Silvagni, Christou,
R. Harvey.
Goals: Lockett 7, Ablett 4, Couch 3, Lyon, Campbell,
Boyd, Monkhorst.
South Australia:
Best: Bulluss, A. Jarman, Wanganeen, Tregenza,
Platten, Bradley.
Goals: Ricciuto 2, Champion, Daffy, D. Jarman,
Wanganeen, Hynes, A. Jarman.

**1997**
**Victoria 13.15.93 d South Australia 12.13.85**
Victoria:
Best: P. Salmon, R. Harvey, G. Brown, S. Loewe,
A. Stevens, B. Johnson, D. King.

Goals: S. Loewe 4, M. Lloyd 3, C. Grant 2,
B. Johnson, A. Jones, G. Archer, N. Burke.
South Australia:
Best: M. Ricciuto, B. Lyle, N. Holland, T. Modra,
M. Wilson, A. McKay
Goals: T. Modra 4, N. Holland 3, S. Russell 2,
D. Jarman, M. Wilson, D. Pittman

## Victoria v Tasmania

**1989**
**Victoria 25.13.163 d Tasmania 15.17.107**
Victoria:
Best: D. Millane, G. Ayres, G. Dear, M. Dwyer,
P. Salmon, P. Roos.
Goals: P. Salmon 7, G. Ayres 4, M. Hanna 3, Greg
Healy 3, G. Hocking 3, P. Roos 2, S. Kerrison,
S. Loewe, S. Newport.
Tasmania:
Best: J. McCarthy, S. MacPherson, S. Atkins,
A. Fletcher, A. Lynch, B. Plain.
Goals: J. McCarthy 3, S. Fell 3, A. Fletcher 2, B. Plain
2, S. Byers, S. Minton-Connell, D. Barwick, S. Atkins,
C. Alexander.

**1990**
**Tasmania 20.14.134 d Victoria 14.17.101**
Tasmania:
Best: J. Manson, D. Pritchard, A. Lynch, G. Wright,
C. Alexander, P. Hudson.
Goals: C. Alexander 4, S. Fell 3, J. McCarthy 3,
P. Hudson 3, D. Barwick 2, B. Gale, G. Wright,
T. Nichols, M. Gale, J. Manson.
Victoria:
Best: B. Toohey, S. Kerrison, G. Ayres, C. Langford,
T. Liberatore.
Goals: R. Lyon 4, B. toohey 3, J. Romero 2,
S. Kerrison, T. Liberatore, P. Foster, J. Longmire,
D. Monkhorst.

**1991**
**Victoria 17.14.116 d Tasmania 14.20.104**
Victoria:
Best: N. Burke, K. Hinkley, M. Knights, M. Larkin,
J. Stynes, S. Wallis.
Goals: K. Hinkley 4, M. Hanna 3, I. McMullin 3,
R. Morris 2, M. Larkin, P. German, T. Alvin,
P. Somerville, J. Stynes.
Tasmania:
Best: A. Lovell, D. Grant, A. Lynch, P. Hudson,
S. MacPherson.
Goals: C. Alexander 4, P. Hudson 3, B. Gale,
P. Williams, D. Barwick, S. Atkins, J. McCarthy,
G. Williams, A. Lovell.

## Victoria v New South Wales

**1990**
**New South Wales 13.8.86 d Victoria 10.16.76**
New South Wales:
Best: J. Longmire, T. Powell, J. Ironmonger, B. Allison,
B. Mitchell, S. Wright.
Goals: J. Longmire 8, T. Daniher, N. Daniher,
B. Toohey, W. Carey, M. Roberts.
Victoria:
Best: D. Weightman, D. Brereton, B. Lovett,
A. Gleeson, S. Silvagni, S. Morwood.
Goals: D. Brereton 3, D. Weightman 2, G. Wright,
P. Salmon, G. Crosisca, S. Silvagni, B. Stoneham.

**1993**
**Victoria 19.16.130 d NSW/ACT 8.17.65**
Victoria:
Best: Roos, Stynes, Hanna, Langford, Knights,
C. Sholl.
Goals: Salmon 6, Ablett 4, Knights 2, Loewe 2,
Silvangi 2, Rock, Lambert, Burke.
NSW/ACT:
Best: Crawford, Hird, Murphy, Kelly, Pyke.
Goals: Hird 3, Barich 3, Crawford, Carey.

## Victoria v Queensland

**1991**
**Queensland 23.14.152 d Victoria 15.18.108**
Queensland:
Best: S. Lawrence, M. Ashcroft, R. Merrett, C. Potter,
S. Luhrs, D. Wearne.
Goals: C. O'Brien 5, R. Merrett 4, C. Bell 2,
M. Ashcroft 2, C. Potter 2, S. Kenny, S. McIvor,
M. Gibson, R. Lester-Smith, A. Taylor, A. Toppenberg,
G. Crosisca, J. Cotter.
Victoria:
Best: A. Phillips, B. Lovett, P. Dean, C. Sholl,
A. Condon, J. Stynes.
Goals: J. Hogg 4, R. Morris 3, J. Stynes 2, A. Rock 2,
A. Phillips, J. Wynd, B. Royal, P. German.

## Victoria v The Allies

**1996**
**Victoria 20.17.137 d The Allies 11.18.84**
Victoria:
Best: R. Harvey, Hocking, Riccardi, Barnes,
McKernan, Burke.
Goals: Mercuri 4, Loewe 3, Archer 3, Grant 2,
McKernan 2, Burke, Riccardi, Colbert, Hocking,
R. Harvey, Williams.
Allies:
Best: Richardson, Buckley, Akermanis, Roberts,
Crawford.
Goals: Richardson 3, Buckley 2, Burns 2, Chisholm,
Roberts, White, Crawford.

## South Australia v Western Aust

**1993**
**South Australia 19.13.127 d Western Australia
14.7.91**
South Australia:
Best: McGuinness, Hart, Platten, Francis, Hall,
Modra.
Goals: Modra 5, Bradley 3, Platten 2, M. Robran,
Russell 2, D. Jarman, McGuinness, Hall, Francis,
A. Jarman.
Western Australia:
Best: Heady, Allan, Winmar, Derek Kickett,
G. Jakovich, A. Jakovich.
Goals: A. Jakovich 3, Bewick 2, Derek Kickett 2,
Rowe 2, Heady, G. Jakovich, Gastev, Allan, Bairstow.

**1996**
**South Australia 20.6.126 d Western Australia
13.13.91**
South Australia:
Best: Modra, Russell, Hart, Champion, Holland,
A. Jarman.
Goals: Modra 8, Kernahan 4, Jarman 2, Francis,
Robran, Rogers, Liptak, Russell, Platten.
Western Australia:

Best: Derek Kickett, Jakovich, Mitchell, Cummings, Ball.
Goals: Cummings 5, Ball, Mitchell, Merenda, Connell,
White, Dale Kickett, Derek Kickett, Bandy.

## Tasmania v South Australia

**1979**
**South Australia 22.20.152 d Tasmania 17.11.113**
South Australia:
Best: K. Hodgeman, M. Taylor, G. Cornes, P. Jonas,
G. Morris, P. Meuret, P. Carey.
Goals: R. Davies 3, P. Meuret 3, P. Jonas 3,
B. Lindsay 3, G. Morris 2, K. Hodgeman 2, G. Hewitt
2, M. Graham, P. Carey, R. Klomp, M. Nunan.
Tasmania:
Best: D. Sutton, C. Robertson, M. Hunnibell,
K. Good, C. Davis, M. Roach.
Goals: M. Roach 6, K. Good 3, C. Davis 2, N. Carter
2, M. Hunnibell 2, T. Pickett, S. Mount.

**1980**
**South Australia 22.18.150 d Tasmania 8.13.61**
South Australia:
Best: G. Cornes, P. Carey, M. Williams, D. Cahill,
J. Lihou, K. McSporran.
Goals: J. Roberts 5, M. Williams 4, T. Hill 3, D. Cahill
2, P. Jonas 2, K. McSporran 2, B. Abernethy,
G. Cornes, D. Kennedy, A. Bennett.
Tasmania:
Best: D. James, G. Linton, R. Eade, N. Carter,
S. Williams.
Goals: C. Reynolds 2, S. Williams, M. Roach,
G. Linton, C. Davis, R. Eade, S. Wade.

## Tasmania v Western Australia

**1979**
**Western Australia 23.33.161 d Tasmania 9.10.64**
Western Australia:
Best: B. Monteath, S. Magro, B. Peake, G. Malarkey,
K. Hunter, G. Moss.
Goals: T. Buhagiar 6, P. Spencer 3, B. Monteath 2, R.
Beecroft 2, G. Moss 2, G. Sidebottom 2, P. Featherby
2, M. Fitzpatrick, G. Melrose, P. Kelly, S. Michael.
Tasmania:
Best: D. Sutton, K. Good, D. James, I. Marsh,
C. Davis, S. Mount.
Goals: I. Marsh, M. Roach, S. Goulding, C. Davis, G.
Towns, N. Carter, S. Williams, T. Martyn, P. Hamilton.

**1980**
**Western Australia 17.23.125 d Tasmania 12.18.90**
Western Australia:
Best: B. Duperouzel, M. Rioli, P. Spencer, L. Fong,
P. Featherby, K. Hunter.
Goals: K. Judge 5, G. Sidebottom 5, P. Arnold 3,
B. Smith 2, L. Fong, R. Alexander.
Tasmania:
Best: D. Scanlon, D. James, D. Sutton, P. Manassa,
R. Eade, C. Davis.
Goals: M. Roach 3, K. Good 2, D. McLeod 2,
D. Sutton, N. Carter, S. Wade, P. Manassa, C. Davis.

## New South Wales v Western Aust

**1988**
**New South Wales 10.8.68 d Western Australia
9.12.66**
New South Wales:
Best: T. Daniher, M. O'Donaghue, N. Cordy, S. Wright,
A. Daniher, D. Murphy, P. Hawke.

Goals: T. Thripp 2, B. Scott 2, B. Brownless,
M. O'Donaghue, P. Bradmore, T. Daniher,
T. Morwood, P. Hawke.
Western Australia:
Best: D. Lamb, C. Mainwaring, P. Mifka,
G. Buckenara, R. Glendinning, S. Malaxos.
Goals: G. Buckenara 2, P. Mifka, P. Scott,
M. Richardson, A. Lockyer, M. Wrensted, W. Dean,
M. Bairstow.

## New South Wales v South Aust

**1988**
**South Australia 12.8.80 d New South Wales 8.11.59**
South Australia:
Best: S. Kernahan, S. Stretch, B. Abernethy,
A. McGuinness, C. Bradley, D. Hughes.
Goals: B. Lindner 4, A. McGuinness 2, S. Kernahan
2, J. Platten 2, A. Payze, T. Hall.
New South Wales:
Best: T. Daniher, S. Morphett, B. Toohey, S. Wright,
D. Murphy.
Goals: T. Daniher 2, B. Brownless 2, T. Morwood 2,
P. Bradmore, P. Hawke.

## New South Wales v Queensland

**1992**
**New South Wales 22.9.141 d Queensland 6.12.48**
New South Wales:
Best: J. Lawson, J. Longmire, B. Brownless,
A. Daniher, M. Gayfer.
Goals: J. Longmire 6, B. Brownless 4, T. Daniher 2,
M. Werner 2, A. Thomson, N. Bruntin, T. Gray,
R. Neill, T. Powell, A. Barich.
Queensland:
Best: R. Willetts, G. Crosisca, S. Handley.
Goals: C. Bell, J. Cotter, J. Grimley, R. Willetts,
B. Stewart, R. Jones.

## Queensland v Tasmania

**1979**
**Tasmania 17.20.122 d Queensland 13.12.90**
Tasmania:
Best: T. Sutton, I. Marsh, D. James, P. Hudson,
R. Neal, K. Good.
Goals: P. Hudson 7, C. Davis 3, N. Carter 3,
M. Roach 2, M. Young, T. Pickett.
Queensland:
Best: B. Clarke, J. Pretty, J. Stackpoole,
R. Rushbrook, F. Dunell, R. Murrie.
Goals: R. Rushbrook 4, F. Dunell 2, B. Clarke 2,
J. Stackpoole, Z. Taylor, O. Backwell, P. Ives, S. Guilford.
**1988**
**Tasmania 11.16.82 d Queensland 10.10.70**
Tasmania:
Best: M. Armstrong, D. Pritchard, S. Nichols,
S. Goulding, R. Eade, D. Barwick.
Goals: S. Nichols 3, M. Armstrong 2, M. Parsons 2,
D. Pearce, S. Goulding, R. Noye, D. Barwick.
Queensland:
Best: S. McIvor, Z. Taylor, R. Mace, P. Riewoldt,
D. Carlson, C. Crowley, M. Gibson.
Goals: J. Dunstall 2, C. Crowley 2, M. Maclure 2,
F. Dunell 2, M. Gibson, R. Willett.

**1993**
**Queensland/NT 16.14.110 d Tasmania 10.15.76**
Queensland/NT:
Best: G. McAdam, Dunstall, Lawrence, Ashcroft,
Lynn, Frigo.

Goals: Dunstall 8, Windsor 2, Ashcroft 2, Francis,
S. Luhrs, White, G. McAdam.
Tasmania:
Best: Williams, Hudson, M. Febey, B. Gale, Manson,
Lovell.
Goals: B. Gale 2, Williams, Lynch, Lovell, Hudgson,
Richardson, M. Febey, McCarthy, Manson.

## Queensland v ACT

**1979**
**Queensland 23.13.151 d ACT 18.12.120**
Queensland:
Best: B. Clarke, R. Rushbrook, B. Karklis, W.
Banfield, M. Gillespie, W. Jones.
Goals: B. Clarke 5, R. Rushbrook 4, W. Banfield 4,
J. Stackpoole 2, W. Jones 2, J. Pretty 2, P. Ives 2,
B. Karklis, H. Thompson.
ACT:
Best: M. Conlan, K. Miller, P. Kenny, S. Widera,
R. Smith, J. Rafferty.
Goals: K. Neale 4, M. Conlan 3, R. Smith 3,
S. Widera 3, M. Manson 3, J. Rafferty 2.

## Northern Territory v Tasmania

**1988**
**Northern Territory 19.20.134 d Tasmania 10.8.68**
Northern Territory:
Best: M. McLean, M. Long, W. Roe, M. Rioli,
N. Briston.
Goals: D. Dunn 5, T. Vigona 4, M. Long 3, A. Mosheni
2, W. Roe 2, J. Ahmat, M. Rioli, N. Briston.
Tasmania:
Best: D. Pritchard, S. Nichols, B. Plain, R. Eade.
Goals: S. Nichols 6, B. Plain 2, M. Armstrong,
S. Goulding.

## The Allies v Western Australia

**1995**
**Allies 13.14.92 d Western Australia 8.13.61**
Allies:
Best: Buckley, O'Connor, McAdam, Pyke, Brownless,
Kelly.
Goals: Brownless 5, Pyke 2, Minton-Connell 2, White,
Buckley, Williams, Allison.
Western Australia:
Best: Evans, Burrows, Allan, Winmar, Zanotti, Laidley.
Goals: Mann 2, Jakovich 2, Winmar, Seecamp,
Evans, Burrows.

**1997**
**Allies 18.8.116 d Western Australia 16.12.108**
Allies:
Best: N. Buckley, P. Williams, D. Cresswell,
A. McLeod, B. Gale, R. Burns.
Goals: N. Buckley 5, P. Williams 4, M. Richardson 2,
S. Minton-Connell, M. Ashcroft, R. Burns, S. Carey,
B. Gale, C. Bond, T. Nichols.
Western Australia:
Best: N. Winmar, S. Cummings, T. Cook, C. Treleven,
Darren Gaspar, C. Callaghan.
Goals: S. Cummings 8, N. Winmar 2, C. Treleven 2,
G. McKenna, J. Clement, Phil Matera, C. Callaghan.

# CAPTAINS, COACHES

## VICTORIA v WESTERN AUSTRALIA

| Year | Venue | Victoria Captain | Coach | Western Australia Captain | Coach |
|------|-------|------------------|-------|---------------------------|-------|
| 1977 | Subiaco | F. Bourke | R. Barassi | G. Moss | G. Farmer |
| 1978 | Waverley Park | K. Greig | R. Barassi | G. Moss | K. Armstrong |
| 1978 | Subiaco | D. Scott | R. Barassi | G. Moss | K. Armstrong |
| 1979 | Subiaco | W. Schimmelbusch | D. Parkin | B. Peake | B. Cable |
| 1980 | Waverley Park | L. Matthews | T. Hafey | B. Peake | B. Smith |
| 1980 | Football Park | K. Bartlett | T. Hafey | B. Peake | B. Smith |
| 1981 | Subiaco | W. Schimmelbusch | T. Jewell | N. Carter | M. Brown |
| 1982 | Subiaco | R. Flower | D. Parkin | G. Moss | M. Brown |
| 1983 | Subiaco | R. Flower | D. Parkin | S. Michael | J. Todd |
| 1984 | Subiaco | M. Tuck | A. Jeans | S. Malaxos | J. Todd |
| 1985 | Subiaco | R. Greene | K. Sheedy | R. Glendinning | J. Todd |
| 1986 | Subiaco | T. Daniher | K. Sheedy | B. Peake | R. Alexander |
| 1987 | Subiaco | D. Weightman | W. Goggin | M. Rioli | J. Todd |
| 1988 | Football Park | D. Weightman | W. Goggin | R. Glendinning | J. Todd |
| 1988 | Subiaco | D. Weightman | W. Goggin | G. Buckenara | M. Brown |
| 1989 | WACA | G. Williams | W. Goggin | G. Buckenara | R. Alexander |
| 1990 | WACA | S. Madden | W. Goggin | S. Malaxos | R. Alexander |
| 1991 | WACA | S. Madden | W. Goggin | C. Mainwaring | M. Malthouse |
| 1992 | MCG | P. Roos | W. Goggin | J. Worsfold | M. Malthouse |

## VICTORIA v SOUTH AUSTRALIA

| Year | Venue | Victoria Captain | Coach | South Australia Captain | Coach |
|------|-------|------------------|-------|--------------------------|-------|
| 1979 | Subiaco | W. Schimmelbusch | D. Parkin | R. Davies | N. Kerley |
| 1980 | Football Park | K. Bartlett | T. Hafey | R. Davies | N. Kerley |
| 1982 | Football Park | M. Fitzpatrick | D. Parkin | P. Weston | J. Cahill |
| 1983 | Football Park | R. Flower | D. Parkin | R. Ebert | R. Hammond |
| 1984 | Football Park | G. Wilson | A. Jeans | N. Craig | N. Kerley |
| 1985 | Football Park | T. Daniher | K. Sheedy | N. Roberts | N. Balme |
| 1986 | Football Park | R. Merrett | K. Sheedy | M. Aish | G. Cornes |
| 1987 | Football Park | W. Schimmelbusch | W. Goggin | B. Lindsay | G. Cornes |
| 1988 | Football Park | D. Weightman | W. Goggin | C. McDermott | G. Cornes |
| 1989 | MCG | S. Madden | W. Goggin | M. Aish | J. Cahill |
| 1991 | Football Park | S. Madden | W. Goggin | C. McDermott | J. Cahill |
| 1992 | Football Park | P. Roos | W. Goggin | C. McDermott | G. Cornes |
| 1993 | MCG | P. Roos | W. Goggin | C. McDermott | G. Cornes |
| 1994 | Football Park | G. Lyon | R. Austin | C. McDermott | G. Cornes |
| 1995 | MCG | G. Ablett | R. Austin | C. McDermott | G. Cornes |
| 1997 | Football Park | G. Brown | L. Matthews | C. Bradley | R. Ebert |

## VICTORIA v TASMANIA

| Year | Venue | Victoria Captain | Coach | Tasmania Captain | Coach |
|------|-------|------------------|-------|------------------|-------|
| 1989 | Nth. Hobart | G. Ayres | D. Parkin | S. Wade | R. Crosby |
| 1990 | Nth. Hobart | G. Ayres | D. Parkin | D. Pritchard | R. Shaw |
| 1991 | Nth. Hobart | J. Madden | R. Austin | D. Pritchard | R. Shaw |

## VICTORIA v NEW SOUTH WALES

| Year | Venue | Victoria Captain | Coach | New South Wales Captain | Coach |
|------|-------|------------------|-------|--------------------------|-------|
| 1990 | SCG | D. Weightman | W. Goggin | T. Daniher | C. Kinnear |
| 1993* | MCG | P. Roos | W. Goggin | W. Carey | T. Daniher |

*NSW/ACT

## VICTORIA v QUEENSLAND

| Year | Venue | Victoria Captain | Coach | Queensland Captain | Coach |
|------|-------|------------------|-------|--------------------|-------|
| 1991 | Gabba | B. Stephens | R. Austin | R. Merrett | N. Dare |

## SOUTH AUST. v WESTERN AUST.

| Year | Venue | South Australia Captain | Coach | Western Australia Captain | Coach |
|------|-------|-------------------------|-------|---------------------------|-------|
| 1993 | Football Park | C. McDermott | G. Cornes | J. Worsfold | M. Malthouse |
| 1996 | Football Park | S. Kernahan | R. Ebert | G. McKenna | R. Glendinning |

## TASMANIA v SOUTH AUSTRALIA

| Year | Venue | Tasmania Captain | Coach | South Australia Captain | Coach |
|------|-------|------------------|-------|-------------------------|-------|
| 1979 | Subiaco | D. Sutton | B. Lawrence | R. Davies | N. Kerley |
| 1980 | Football Park | D. Sutton | P. Daniel | R. Davies | N. Kerley |

## TASMANIA v WESTERN AUSTRALIA

| Year | Venue | Tasmania Captain | Coach | Western Australia Captain | Coach |
|------|-------|------------------|-------|---------------------------|-------|
| 1979 | Subiaco | P. Hudson | B. Lawrence | B. Peake | B. Cable |
| 1980 | Football Park | D. Sutton | P. Daniel | B. Peake | B. Cable |

## NEW SOUTH WALES v WEST. AUST.

| Year | Venue | New South Wales Captain | Coach | Western Australia Captain | Coach |
|------|-------|-------------------------|-------|---------------------------|-------|
| 1988 | Football Park | T. Daniher | T. Hafey | R. Glendinning | J. Todd |

## NEW SOUTH WALES v SOUTH AUST.

| Year | Venue | New South Wales Captain | Coach | South Australia Captain | Coach |
|------|-------|-------------------------|-------|-------------------------|-------|
| 1988 | Football Park | T. Daniher | T. Hafey | C. McDermott | G. Cornes |

## NEW SOUTH WALES v QUEENSLAND

| Year | Venue | New South Wales Captain | Coach | Queensland Captain | Coach |
|------|-------|-------------------------|-------|--------------------|-------|
| 1992 | SGC | T. Daniher | G. Buckenara | G. Crosisca | N. Dare |

## QUEENSLAND v TASMANIA

| Year | Venue | Queensland Captain | Coach | Tasmania Captain | Coach |
|------|-------|--------------------|-------|------------------|-------|
| 1979 | Perth Oval | B. Clarke | W. Roper | P. Hudson | B. Lawrence |
| 1988 | Norwood Oval | Z. Taylor | P. Knights | R. Eade | R. Shaw |
| 1993* | Bellerive | J. Dunstall | N. Dare | D. Pritchard | R. Shaw |

*Qld/N.T.

## QUEENSLAND v ACT

| Year | Venue | Queensland Captain | Coach | ACT Captain | Coach |
|------|-------|--------------------|-------|-------------|-------|
| 1979 | Leederville Oval | B. Clarke | W. Roper | K. Neale | K. Delmenico |

## NORTHERN TERRITORY v TASMANIA

| Year | Venue | Northern Territory Captain | Coach | Tasmania Captain | Coach |
|------|-------|----------------------------|-------|------------------|-------|
| 1988 | Football Park | M. Rioli | J. Taylor | R. Eade | R. Shaw |

## THE ALLIES v WESTERN AUSTRALIA

| Year | Venue | Allies Captain | Coach | Western Australia Captain | Coach |
|------|-------|----------------|-------|---------------------------|-------|
| 1995 | Subiaco | P. Kelly | R. Eade | B. Allan | G. Buckenara |
| 1997 | Subiaco | N. Buckley | N. Daniher | G. McKenna | R. Glendinning |

## THE ALLIES v VICTORIA

| Year | Venue | Allies Captain | Coach | Victoria Captain | Coach |
|------|-------|----------------|-------|------------------|-------|
| 1996 | MCG | J. Dunstall | N. Daniher | S. Silvagni | R. Austin |

# 1997 TEAMS

## The Allies

**Backs:** A. McLeod, J. Shanahan, S. Carey
**Half-backs:** M. Ashcroft, D. Dickfos, D. White
**Centres:** P. Williams, D. Cresswell, M. Gale
**Half-forwards:** J. Akermanis, B. Gale, R. Burns
**Forwards:** G. Dhurrkay, M. Richardson, B. Allison
**Followers:** C. Keating, N. Buckley, C. Bond
**Interchange:** S. Minton-Connell, T. Nichols, J. Mooney
**Captain:** N. Buckley
**Coach:** N. Daniher

## Victoria

**Backs:** D. King, S. Silvagni, G. Archer
**Half-backs:** L. Colbert, M. Sexton, R. Smith
**Centres:** B. Johnson, A. Stevens, G. Brown
**Half-forwards:** N. Lappin, C. Grant, D. Harford
**Forwards:** N. Burke, S. Loewe, M. Lloyd
**Followers:** P. Salmon, B. Ratten, R. Harvey
**Interchange:** M. Mansfield, D. Lewis, P. Everitt, A. Jones
**Captain:** G. Brown
**Coach:** L. Matthews

## Western Australia

**Backs:** B. Krummel, G. Jakovich, M. Prior
**Half-backs:** G. McKenna, Darren Gaspar, T. Cook
**Centres:** Peter Matera, P. Symmons, N. Winmar
**Half-forwards:** C. Treleven, P. Mann, P. Bell
**Forwards:** D. Chick, S. Cummings, Phil Matera
**Followers:** R. Turnbull, L. Toia, C. Callaghan
**Interchange:** M. Merenda, M. Burton, J. Clement, D. Bandy
**Captain:** G. McKenna
**Coach:** R. Glendinning

## South Australia

**Backs:** G. Wanganeen, S. Wellman, B. Lade
**Half-backs:** A. McKay, D. Mead, M. Wilson
**Centres:** M. Ricciuto, M. Bickley, A. Heuskes
**Half-forwards:** D. Jarman, N. Holland, S. Bond
**Forwards:** J. Platten, T. Modra, M. O'Loughlin
**Followers:** M. Clarke, B Lyle, C. Bradley
**Interchange:** T. Viney, D. Pittman, S Russell, B. Hart
**Captain:** C. Bradley
**Coach:** R. Ebert

## STATE OF ORIGIN ELIGIBILITY RULE

The eligibility rule for State of Origin football adopted by the AFL Commission in 1993 provides for a player to be tied to the State or Territory in which he resided for the majority of time between the ages of 10 and 17.

# WIN-LOSS RECORDS 1977-1997

**Victoria**

|  | WON | LOST |
|---|---|---|
| Western Australia | 12 | 7 |
| South Australia | 9 | 7 |
| Tasmania | 2 | 1 |
| New South Wales | 1 | 1 |
| Queensland | 0 | 1 |
| Allies | 1 | 0 |
| TOTALS | 25 | 17 |

**Western Australia**

|  | WON | LOST |
|---|---|---|
| Victoria | 7 | 12 |
| Tasmania | 2 | 0 |
| New South Wales | 0 | 1 |
| South Australia | 0 | 2 |
| Allies | 0 | 2 |
| TOTALS | 9 | 17 |

**South Australia**

|  | WON | LOST |
|---|---|---|
| Victoria | 7 | 9 |
| Tasmania | 2 | 0 |
| New South Wales | 1 | 0 |
| Western Australia | 2 | 0 |
| TOTALS | 12 | 9 |

**Tasmania**

|  | WON | LOST |
|---|---|---|
| Victoria | 1 | 2 |
| Western Australia | 0 | 2 |
| South Australia | 0 | 2 |
| Queensland | 2 | 1 |
| Northern Territory | 0 | 1 |
| TOTALS | 3 | 8 |

**Queensland**

|  | WON | LOST |
|---|---|---|
| Victoria | 1 | 0 |
| Tasmania | 1 | 1 |
| New South Wales | 0 | 2 |
| ACT | 1 | 0 |
| TOTALS | 3 | 3 |

**New South Wales**

|  | WON | LOST |
|---|---|---|
| Western Australia | 1 | 0 |
| South Australia | 0 | 1 |
| Victoria | 1 | 1 |
| Queensland | 1 | 0 |
| TOTALS | 3 | 2 |

**Northern Territory**

|  | WON | LOST |
|---|---|---|
| Tasmania | 1 | 0 |
| Aust. Amateurs | 1 | 0 |
| TOTALS | 2 | 0 |

**ACT**

|  | WON | LOST |
|---|---|---|
| Queensland | 0 | 1 |
| Aust. Amateurs | 0 | 1 |
| TOTALS | 0 | 2 |

**Allies**

|  | WON | LOST |
|---|---|---|
| Western Australia | 2 | 0 |
| Victoria | 0 | 1 |
| TOTALS | 2 | 1 |

# STATE OF ORIGIN MATCHES VICTORIA 1977-1997

| 18 | Dale Weightman | 1980–1991 |
|---|---|---|
| 15 | Chris Lanford | 1987–1994 |
| 14 | Simon Madden | 1983–1991 |
| 14 | Paul Roos | 1985–1993 |
| 14 | Paul Salmon | 1984–1997 |
| 12 | Gerard Healy | 1982–1988 |
| 12 | Andrew Bews | 1985–1992 |
| 11 | Robert Flower | 1977–1983 |
| 11 | Danny Frawley | 1988–1994 |
| 11 | Andrew Collins | 1989–1994 |
| 11 | Gary Ablett | 1984–1995 |
| 11 | Jim Stynes | 1988–1996 |
| 11 | Gavin Brown | 1987–1997 |
| 10 | Garry Wilson | 1978–1984 |
| 10 | Geoff Raines | 1978–1986 |
| 10 | Terry Daniher | 1981–1989 |
| 10 | Tim Watson | 1980–1991 |

# STATE OF ORIGIN GOALS VICTORIA 1977-1997

| 45 | Paul Salmon | 1984–1997 |
|---|---|---|
| 43 | Gary Ablett | 1984–1995 |
| 31 | Kelvin Templeton | 1978–1982 |
| 28 | Dale Weightman | 1980–1991 |
| 21 | Gerard Healy | 1982–1988 |
| 19 | Garry Wilson | 1978–1984 |
| 19 | Tony Lockett | 1985–1995 |
| 18 | Dermott Brereton | 1985–1990 |
| 18 | Stewart Loewe | 1989–1997 |
| 16 | Robert Flower | 1977–1983 |
| 14 | Kevin Bartlett | 1978–1980 |
| 13 | Simon Madden | 1983–1991 |
| 13 | Brian Royal | 1983–1991 |
| 11 | Paul Roos | 1985–1993 |
| 10 | Terry Daniher | 1981–1989 |

# STATE OF ORIGIN MATCHES SOUTH AUSTRALIA 1977-1997

| 15 | John Platten | 1982–1997 |
|---|---|---|
| 14 | Craig Bradley | 1983–1997 |
| 13 | Stephen Kernahan | 1983–1996 |
| 11 | Greg Phillips | 1979–1989 |
| 11 | Chris McDermott | 1985–1995 |
| 9 | Greg Anderson | 1984–1994 |
| 9 | Mark Naley | 1982–1992 |
| 9 | Andrew Jarman | 1987–1996 |
| 9 | Martin Leslie | 1984–1992 |
| 8 | Tony McGuinness | 1986–1993 |

# STATE OF ORIGIN GOALS SOUTH AUSTRALIA 1977-1997

| 47 | Stephen Kernahan | 1983–1996 |
|---|---|---|
| 20 | Tony Modra | 1992–1996 |
| 16 | Bruce Lindner | 1983–1989 |
| 16 | Darren Jarman | 1989–1997 |
| 15 | John Platten | 1982–1996 |
| 11 | Mark Naley | 1989–1992 |

## STATE OF ORIGIN MATCHES
## WESTERN AUSTRALIA 1977-1997

| | | |
|---|---|---|
| 13 | Ross Glendinning | 1977–1988 |
| 11 | Brian Peake | 1978–1986 |
| 10 | Graham Moss | 1977–1982 |
| 10 | Garry Sidebottom | 1977–1985 |
| 10 | Maurice Rioli | 1979–1987 |
| 9 | Gary Buckenara | 1981–1989 |
| 8 | Peter Featherby | 1977–1980 |
| 8 | Ron Alexander | 1977–1980 |
| 8 | Chris Mainwaring | 1987–1992 |
| 8 | Mark Bairstow | 1986–1993 |
| 8 | Paul Harding | 1983–1995 |

## STATE OF ORIGIN GOALS
## WESTERN AUSTRALIA 1977-1997

| | | |
|---|---|---|
| 24 | Gary Buckenara | 1981–1989 |
| 19 | Garry Sidebottom | 1977–1985 |
| 12 | Graham Moss | 1977–1982 |
| 11 | Bruce Monteath | 1977–1982 |
| 11 | Tony Buhagiar | 1978–1983 |
| 11 | Mark Bairstow | 1986–1991 |
| 9 | Robert Wiley | 1978–1985 |
| 9 | Brian Peake | 1978–1986 |
| 9 | Peter Spencer | 1979–1980 |
| 9 | Nicky Winmar | 1988–1995 |

## FOS WILLIAMS MEDAL

Awarded by the South Australian National Football League to the best player for South Australia in State of Origin matches.

| | | |
|---|---|---|
| 1982 | Stephen Copping (Ess) | v Victoria |
| 1983 | Michael Aish (SANFL) | v Victoria |
| 1984 | Stephen Kernahan (SANFL) | v Victoria |
| 1985 | Peter Motley (SANFL) | v Victoria |
| 1986 | Craig Bradley (Carl) | v Victoria |
| 1987 | Chris McDermott (SANFL) | v Victoria |
| 1988 | Mark Mickan (Bris Bears) | v NSW |
| 1988 | Stephen Kernahan (Carl) | v Victoria |
| 1989 | Andrew Jarman (SANFL) | v Victoria |
| 1991 | Craig Bradley (Carl) | v Victoria |
| 1992 | David Hynes (W Coast) | v Victoria |
| 1993 | Greg Anderson (Adel) | v WA |
| 1993 | Craig Bradley (Carl) | v Victoria |
| 1994 | Andrew Jarman (Adel) | v Victoria |
| 1995 | Simon Tregenza (Adel) | v Victoria |
| 1996 | Tony Modra (Adel) | v WA |
| 1997 | Brayden Lyle (Port Adel) | v Victoria |

## THE E. J. WHITTEN MEDAL

Awarded to the best Victorian player in State of Origin matches.

| | | |
|---|---|---|
| 1985 v WA | Paul Roos | (Fitzroy) |
| 1986 v WA | Dale Weightman | (Richmond) |
| 1986 v SA | Kevin Walsh | (Essendon) |
| 1987 v WA | Greg Williams | (Sydney) |
| 1987 v SA | Chris Langford | (Hawthorn) |
| 1988 NFL Champ'ships — Paul Roos (Fitz.) | | |
| 1988 v WA | Gerard Healy | (Sydney) |
| 1989 v SA | Gavin Brown | (Collingwood) |
| 1989 v WA | Jason Dunstall | (Hawthorn) |
| 1990 v WA | Simon Madden | (Essendon) |
| 1990 v NSW | Dale Weightman | (Richmond) |
| 1991 v WA | Barry Mitchell | (Sydney) |
| 1991 v SA | Alan Ezard | (Essendon) |
| 1992 v WA | Stewart Loewe | (St Kilda) |
| 1992 v SA | Robert Harvey | (St Kilda) |
| 1993 v *** | Chris Langford | (Hawthorn) |
| 1993 v SA | Robert Harvey | (St Kilda) |
| 1994 v SA | David Calthorpe | (Essendon) |
| 1995 v SA | Tony Lockett | (Sydney) |
| 1996 v Allies | Robert Harvey | (St Kilda) |
| 1997 v SA | Gavin Brown | (Collingwood) |

***NSW/ACT combined side

## SIMPSON MEDAL

Awarded to the best player in a match involving WA in Perth, and in Australian Championship matches.

| | | |
|---|---|---|
| 1978 | Peter Knights | Victoria |
| 1981 | Simon Beasley | West Australia |
| 1982 | Mark Browning | Victoria |
| 1983 | Maurice Rioli | West Australia |
| 1984 | Brad Hardie | West Australia |
| 1985 | Dale Weightman | Victoria |
| 1986 | Brad Hardie | West Australia |
| 1987 | Andrew Bews | Victoria |
| 1988 | Dwayne Lamb | West Aust (Aus Ch) |
| 1988 | Gerard Healy | Victoria |
| 1989 | Jason Dunstall | Victoria |
| 1990 | Simon Madden | Victoria |
| 1991 | Paul Harding | West Australia |

## GRAHAM MOSS MEDAL

Awarded to the best Western Australian player in State of Origin matches.

| | | |
|---|---|---|
| 1995 | Tony Evans (W Coast) | v Allies |
| 1996 | Derek Kickett (Syd) | v SA |
| 1997 | Scott Cummings (Port Adel) | v Allies |

## ALEX JESAULENKO MEDAL

Awarded to the best Allies player in State of Origin matches.

| | | |
|---|---|---|
| 1995 | Ryan O'Connor (Ess) | v WA |
| 1996 | Matthew Richardson (Rich) | v Victoria |
| 1997 | Nathan Buckley (Coll) | v WA |

# TAC CUP

**TAC** (logo)

The TAC Cup under-18 competition has been a phenomenal success story given it has only been in existence since 1992.

In its short history, it has achieved exactly what administrators at the time had hoped — to provide a well structured, professionally organised competition which covered both country and metropolitan Victoria. In recent years, the competition has expanded to include teams from NSW/ACT (the Rams) and Tasmania (the Tassie Mariners).

At the 1997 National Draft, 45 players were picked from a possible 83 selections and, for the first time, all TAC Cup clubs had players drafted.

The 1997 premiership was won by the North Ballarat Rebels, who became the first country team to win the flag.

## MORRISH MEDAL — 1997

Umpires 3-2-1 votes cast after each game. The Morrish Medal was previously awarded to the fairest and best player in the VFL under-19s.

| | |
|---|---|
| Derek Murray (Murray Bushrangers) | 20 |
| Winnis Imbi (North Ballarat Rebels) | 15 |
| Trent Croad (Dandenong Stingrays) | 13 |
| Ben Lovett (Dandenong Stingrays) | 12 |
| Matthew Bernes (Tassie Mariners) | 12 |
| James Dalton (Geelong Falcons) | 11 |
| Nick Preston (North Ballarat Rebels) | 11 |

## TAC COACHES AWARD — 1997

Each coach votes 5-4-3-2-1 after their game.

| | |
|---|---|
| Matthew Bernes (Tassie Mariners) | 40 |
| Trent Croad (Dandenong Stingrays) | 35 |
| Paul Di Giovine (Oakleigh Chargers) | 29 |
| Matthew Hyde (Murray Bushrangers) | 28 |
| Mark Alvey (Bendigo Pioneers) | 28 |

## TAC CUP WINNERS

| | |
|---|---|
| 1992 | Geelong Falcons |
| 1993 | Preston Knights |
| 1994 | Preston Knights |
| 1995 | Preston Knights |
| 1996 | Preston Knights |
| 1997 | North Ballarat Rebels |

## LEADING GOALKICKERS — 1997

| | |
|---|---|
| Stephen Milne (Dandenong) | 49 |
| Heath Younie (Murray) | 40 |
| Andrew Hewitt (Bendigo) | 39 |
| Brant Chambers (Eastern) | 39 |
| Mark Livy (NSW/ACT) | 39 |
| Adam Skrobalak (Western) | 36 |
| George De Crespigny (Dandenong) | 33 |
| Cameron Ling (Geelong) | 33 |
| Stevie Partsanis (Prahran) | 33 |

## MORRISH MEDAL WINNERS

| | |
|---|---|
| 1992 | Brad Smith (Preston Knights) |
| 1993 | Dean Watson (Dandenong Stingrays) |
| 1994 | Gary Moorcroft (Preston Knights) |
| 1995 | Paul Hood (Geelong Falcons) |
| 1996 | Nathan Brown (Bendigo Pioneers) |
| 1997 | Derek Murray (Murray Bushrangers) |

## GRAND FINALLISTS/BEST ON GROUND (TAC MEDALLIST)

| | |
|---|---|
| 1992 | Geelong Falcons d Western Jets: Daniel Fletcher (Falcons) |
| 1993 | Preston Knights d Western Jets: Shannon Gibson (Knights) |
| 1994 | Preston Knights d Geelong Falcons: Anthony Rocca (Knights) |
| 1995 | Preston Knights d Eastern Ranges: Brent Harvey (Knights) |
| 1996 | Preston Knights d NSW/ACT Rams: David Harrison (Rams) |
| 1997 | North Ballarat Rebels d Dandenong Stingrays: Adam Goodes (Rebels) |

## 1997 TAC CUP TEAM OF THE YEAR

**B:** Brett Rose (Eastern), Matthew Scarlett (Geelong), Mark Bolton (Eastern)
**HB:** Nick Stevens (Preston), Kris Massie (Dandenong), Hayden Burgiel (Gippsland)
**C:** Travis Johnstone (Dandenong), Matthew Bernes (Tassie), James Walker (North Ballarat)
**HF:** Adam Quinn (Prahran), Trent Croad (Dandenong) Heath Younie (Murray)
**F:** Derek Murray (Murray), Mark Livy (NSW/ACT), Mark Alvey (Bendigo) Ballarat)
**R:** Paul Di Giovine (Oakleigh), Matthew Hyde (Murray), Craig Folino (Eastern)
**I/C:** Lance Picioane (Western), Shane Sheppard (Calder), Winnis Imbi (North Ballarat), Dean Solomon (Bendigo)

## 1997 LADDER (HOME & AWAY SEASON)

| | | W | L | D | Pts |
|---|---|---|---|---|---|
| 1 | D'nong Stingrays | 16 | 2 | 0 | 64 |
| 2 | Murray B'Rangers | 14 | 4 | 0 | 56 |
| 3 | N. Ballarat Rebels | 13 | 5 | 0 | 52 |
| 4 | Bendigo Pioneers | 12 | 6 | 0 | 48 |
| 5 | Eastern Ranges | 11 | 7 | 0 | 44 |
| 6 | Preston Knights | 10 | 8 | 0 | 40 |
| 7 | Tassie Mariners | 9 | 9 | 0 | 36 |
| 8 | Prahran Dragons | 7 | 11 | 0 | 28 |
| 9 | Oakleigh Chargers | 6 | 12 | 0 | 24 |
| 10 | Calder Cannons | 6 | 12 | 0 | 24 |
| 11 | Gippsland Power | 6 | 12 | 0 | 24 |
| 12 | NSW/ACT Rams | 6 | 12 | 0 | 24 |
| 13 | Geelong Falcons | 5 | 13 | 0 | 20 |
| 14 | Western Jets | 5 | 13 | 0 | 20 |

# VFL PREMIERS AND RUNNERS-UP

*Before 1903 the team at the top of the ladder was declared Premiership winner. No finals matches were played. In 1896 a play-off match was necessary — the top teams could not be separated by match points or percentage. North Melb was awarded the 1904 Premiership after Richmond objected to the umpire chosen for the match and refused to play. Before 1897 behinds were not registered as scores.*

| Year | Premier | Runner-up |
|---|---|---|
| 1877 | Carlton | Melbourne |
| 1878 | Geelong | Melbourne |
| 1879 | Geelong | Carlton |
| 1880 | Geelong | South Melbourne |
| 1881 | South Melbourne | Geelong |
| 1882 | Geelong | Essendon |
| 1883 | Geelong | South Melbourne |
| 1884 | Geelong | Essendon |
| 1885 | South Melbourne | Essendon |
| 1886 | Geelong | South Melbourne |
| 1887 | Carlton | Geelong |
| 1888 | South Melbourne | Geelong |
| 1889 | South Melbourne | Carlton |
| 1890 | South Melbourne | Carlton |
| 1891 | Essendon | Carlton |
| 1892 | Essendon | Fitzroy |
| 1893 | Essendon | Melbourne |
| 1894 | Essendon | Melbourne |
| 1895 | Fitzroy | Geelong |
| 1896 | Collingwood 6.9.45 | South Melbourne 5.10.40 |
| 1897 | Port Melbourne | North Melbourne |
| 1898 | Footscray | North Melbourne |
| 1899 | Footscray | North Melbourne |
| 1900 | Footscray | Williamstown |
| 1901 | Port Melbourne | Richmond |
| 1902 | Richmond | Port Melbourne |
| 1903 | North Melbourne 7.6.48 | Richmond 3.9.27 |
| 1904 | North Melbourne | Richmond |
| 1905 | Richmond 9.7.61 | North Melbourne 5.6.36 |
| 1906 | West Melbourne 7.8.50 | Footscray 5.9.39 |
| 1907 | Williamstown 7.10.52 | West Melbourne 3.16.34 |
| 1908 | Footscray 9.10.64 | Brunswick 6.4.40 |
| 1909 | Brunswick 10.11.71 | Prahran 8.7.55 |
| 1910 | North Melbourne 9.14.68 | Brunswick 5.9.39 |
| 1911 | Essendon 4.10.34 | Brunswick 3.8.26 |
| 1912 | Essendon 9.8.62 | Footscray 5.11.41 |
| 1913 | Footscray 10.14.74 | North Melbourne 11.7.73 |
| 1914 | North Melbourne 12.14.86 | Footscray 7.9.51 |
| 1915 | North Melbourne 11.10.76 | Brunswick 3.10.28 |
| 1918 | North Melbourne 18.13.121 | Prahran 3.10.28 |
| 1919 | Footscray 8.17.65 | North Melbourne 6.7.43 |
| 1920 | Footscray 10.9.69 | Brunswick 8.18.66 |
| 1921 | Williamstown 8.9.57 | Footscray 5.9.39 |
| 1922 | Port Melbourne 9.6.60 | Footscray 8.10.58 |
| 1923 | Footscray 7.10.52 | Port Melbourne 5.8.38 |
| 1924 | Footscray 11.11.77 | Williamstown 3.4.22 |
| 1925 | Brunswick 10.9.69 | Port Melbourne 7.11.53 |
| 1926 | Coburg 12.9.81 | Brighton 9.11.65 |
| 1927 | Coburg 19.10.124 | Brighton 13.12.90 |
| 1928 | Coburg 17.12.114 | Port Melbourne 16.11.107 |
| 1929 | Northcote 15.21.111 | Port Melbourne 10.9.69 |
| 1930 | Oakleigh 9.6.60 | Northcote 7.9.51 |
| 1931 | Oakleigh 10.14.74 | Northcote 11.5.71 |
| 1932 | Northcote 13.11.89 | Coburg 8.15.63 |
| 1933 | Northcote 11.20.86 | Coburg 9.16.70 |
| 1934 | Northcote 19.16.130 | Coburg 10.9.69 |
| 1935 | Yarraville 10.10.70 | Camberwell 8.13.61 |
| 1936 | Northcote 19.6.120 | Prahran 15.15.105 |
| 1937 | Prahran 12.13.85 | Brunswick 11.17.83 |
| 1938 | Brunswick 19.17.131 | Brighton 14.14.98 |
| 1939 | Williamstown 14.20.104 | Brunswick 14.11.95 |
| 1940 | Port Melbourne 23.22.160 | Prahran 17.11.113 |
| 1941 | Port Melbourne 15.18.108 | Coburg 11.23.89 |
| 1945 | Williamstown 16.21.117 | Port Melbourne 10.20.80 |
| 1946 | Sandringham 14.15.99 | Camberwell 13.14.92 |
| 1947 | Port Melbourne 15.15.105 | Sandringham 8.8.74 |
| 1948 | Brighton 13.16.94 | Williamstown 13.7.85 |
| 1949 | Williamstown 10.5.65 | Oakleigh 8.14.62 |
| 1950 | Oakleigh 13.9.87 | Port Melbourne 9.14.68 |
| 1951 | Prahran 11.13.79 | Port Melbourne 10.10.70 |
| 1952 | Oakleigh 11.18.84 | Port Melbourne 8.15.63 |
| 1953 | Port Melbourne 21.15.141 | Yarraville 12.9.81 |
| 1954 | Williamstown 11.20.86 | Port Melbourne 7.12.54 |
| 1955 | Williamstown 13.19.97 | Port Melbourne 13.10.88 |
| 1956 | Williamstown 14.18.102 | Port Melbourne 10.18.78 |
| 1957 | Moorabbin 15.12.102 | Port Melbourne 7.20.62 |
| 1958 | Williamstown 13.18.96 | Moorabbin 8.16.64 |
| 1959 | Williamstown 15.21.111 | Coburg 11.10.76 |
| 1960 | Oakleigh 18.14.122 | Sandringham 8.14.62 |
| 1961 | Yarraville 22.7.139 | Williamstown 11.10.76 |
| 1961* | Northcote 12.15.87 | Dandenong 9.18.72 |
| 1962 | Sandringham 14.10.94 | Moorabbin 13.15.93 |
| 1962* | Dandenong 16.24.120 | Prahran 8.12.60 |
| 1963 | Moorabbin 19.16.130 | Sandringham 9.12.66 |
| 1963* | Preston 11.14.80 | Waverley 9.15.69 |
| 1964 | Port Melbourne 14.17.101 | Williamstown 10.5.65 |
| 1964* | Geelong West 14.14.98 | Sunshine 11.11.77 |
| 1965 | Waverley 14.13.97 | Port Melbourne 10.25.85 |
| 1965* | Preston 15.12.102 | Mordialloc 9.10.64 |
| 1966 | Port Melbourne 13.12.90 | Waverley 6.11.47 |
| 1966* | Prahran 17.12.114 | Geelong West 5.15.45 |
| 1967 | Dandenong 16.13.109 | Port Melbourne 12.12.84 |
| 1967* | Oakleigh 12.14.86 | Geelong West 11.7.73 |
| 1968 | Preston 15.8.98 | Prahran 12.12.84 |
| 1968* | Geelong West 20.15.135 | Williamstown 18.15.123 |
| 1969 | Preston 12.11.83 | Dandenong 10.11.71 |
| 1969* | Williamstown 15.14.104 | Sunshine 12.12.84 |
| 1970 | Prahran 17.18.120 | Williamstown 10.10.70 |
| 1970* | Coburg 20.17.137 | Box Hill 16.11.107 |
| 1971 | Dandenong 14.14.98 | Preston 13.14.92 |
| 1971* | Sunshine 22.26.158 | Brunswick 16.8.104 |
| 1972 | Oakleigh 25.17.167 | Dandenong 18.15.123 |
| 1972* | Geelong West 14.16.100 | Caulfield 14.10.94 |
| 1973 | Prahran 15.23.113 | Oakleigh 10.18.78 |
| 1973* | Caulfield 18.20.128 | Brunswick 14.22.106 |
| 1974 | Port Melbourne 22.20.152 | Oakleigh 11.17.83 |
| 1974* | Coburg 18.17.125 | Brunswick 9.15.69 |
| 1975 | Geelong West 18.13.121 | Dandenong 14.9.93 |
| 1975* | Brunswick 18.22.130 | Camberwell 12.11.83 |
| 1976 | Port Melbourne 19.18.132 | Dandenong 10.15.75 |
| 1976* | Williamstown 19.13.127 | Mordialloc 9.16.70 |
| 1977 | Port Melbourne 23.19.157 | Sandringham 7.15.57 |
| 1977* | Mordialloc 19.19.133 | Yarraville 14.11.95 |
| 1978 | Prahran 21.15.141 | Preston 17.17.119 |
| 1978* | Frankston 15.13.103 | Camberwell 13.11.89 |
| 1979 | Coburg 16.15.111 | Geelong West 14.19.103 |
| 1979* | Camberwell 18.14.122 | Oakleigh 12.11.83 |
| 1980 | Port Melbourne 11.15.81 | Coburg 10.10.70 |
| 1980* | Brunswick 20.27.147 | Yarraville 14.14.98 |
| 1981 | Port Melbourne 32.19.211 | Preston 15.8.98 |
| 1981* | Camberwell 15.16.106 | Waverley 11.8.74 |
| 1982 | Port Melbourne 21.15.141 | Preston 20.14.134 |
| 1982* | Northcote 12.15.87 | Caulfield 11.16.82 |
| 1983 | Preston 14.10.94 | Geelong West 12.15.87 |
| 1983* | Springvale 17.9.111 | Brunswick 13.16.94 |
| 1984 | Preston 19.21.135 | Frankston 12.9.81 |
| 1984* | Box Hill 32.23.215 | Oakleigh 11.14.80 |
| 1985 | Sandringham 14.16.100 | Williamstown 13.16.94 |
| 1985* | Brunswick 25.18.168 | Oakleigh 22.12.144 |
| 1986 | Williamstown 17.9.111 | Coburg 14.14.98 |
| 1986* | Box Hill 14.14.98 | Sunshine 11.14.80 |
| 1987 | Springvale 14.16.100 | Port Melbourne 7.20.62 |
| 1987* | Prahran 18.9.117 | Waverley 14.14.98 |
| 1988 | Coburg 16.18.114 | Williamstown 12.15.87 |
| 1988* | Oakleigh 29.19.169 | Sunshine 15.9.99 |
| 1989 | Coburg 10.13.73 | Williamstown 7.11.53 |
| 1990 | Williamstown 16.11.107 | Springvale 15.15.105 |
| 1991 | Dandenong 15.15.105 | Werribee 14.12.96 |
| 1992 | Sandringham 19.16.130 | Williamstown 13.8.86 |
| 1993 | Werribee 10.10.70 | Port Melbourne 4.4.28 |
| 1994 | Sandringham 11.12.78 | Box Hill 10.9.69 |
| 1995 | Springvale 14.10.94 | Sandringham 6.15.51 |
| 1996 | Springvale 11.7.73 | Frankston 10.10.70 |
| 1997 | Sandringham 10.13.73 | Frankston 5.14.44 |

*1916–17, competition suspended during World War I.   1942–44, competition suspended during World War II.   * Second division*

# SANFL PREMIERS AND RUNNERS-UP

*Before 1898 the team at the top of the ladder was declared Premiership winner. No finals matches were played. In both 1889 and 1894 a play-off match was necessary — the top teams could not be separated by match points or percentage. Before 1897 behinds were not registered as scores.*

| Year | Premier | Runner-up |
|---|---|---|
| 1877 | South Adelaide | Victorian |
| 1878 | Norwood | South Adelaide |
| 1879 | Norwood | Port Adelaide |
| 1880 | Norwood | Victorian |
| 1881 | Norwood | South Adelaide |
| 1882 | Norwood | South Adelaide |
| 1883 | Norwood | Port Adelaide |
| 1884 | Port Adelaide | Norwood |
| 1885 | South Adelaide | Norwood |
| 1886 | Adelaide | South Adelaide |
| 1887 | Norwood | Port Adelaide |
| 1888 | Norwood | Port Adelaide |
| 1889 | Norwood 7.4. | Port Adelaide 5.9. |
| 1890 | Port Adelaide | Norwood |
| 1891 | Norwood | Port Adelaide |
| 1892 | South Adelaide | Port Adelaide |
| 1893 | South Adelaide | Norwood |
| 1894 | Norwood 4.7. | South Adelaide 3.5. |
| 1895 | South Adelaide | Norwood |
| 1896 | South Adelaide | Norwood |
| 1897 | Port Adelaide | South Adelaide |
| 1898 | South Adelaide 8.8.56 | Port Adelaide 4.8.32 |
| 1899 | South Adelaide 5.12.42 | Norwood 2.2.14 |
| 1900 | North Adelaide 4.3.27 | South Adelaide 1.8.14 |
| 1901 | Norwood 4.9.33 | Port Adelaide 4.5.29 |
| 1902 | North Adelaide 9.14.68 | South Adelaide 4.7.31 |
| 1903 | Port Adelaide 6.6.42 | South Adelaide 5.5.35 |
| 1904 | Norwood 9.8.62 | Port Adelaide 8.10.58 |
| 1905 | North Adelaide 6.8.44 | Port Adelaide 1.6.12 |
| 1906 | Port Adelaide 8.12.60 | North Adelaide 5.9.39 |
| 1907 | Norwood 8.7.55 | Port Adelaide 3.9.27 |
| 1908 | West Adelaide 7.10.52 | Norwood 6.13.49 |
| 1909 | West Adelaide 7.17.59 | Port Adelaide 6.5.41 |
| 1910 | Port Adelaide 8.12.60 | Sturt 5.11.41 |
| 1911 | West Adelaide 7.9.51 | Port Adelaide 6.10.46 |
| 1912 | West Adelaide 6.10.46 | Port Adelaide 5.2.32 |
| 1913 | Port Adelaide 7.12.54 | North Adelaide 5.10.40 |
| 1914 | Port Adelaide 13.15.93 | North Adelaide 1.8.14 |
| 1915 | Sturt 6.10.46 | Port Adelaide 4.10.34 |
| 1919 | Sturt 3.5.23 | North Adelaide 2.6.18 |
| 1920 | North Adelaide 9.15.69 | Norwood 3.3.21 |
| 1921 | Port Adelaide 4.8.32 | Norwood 3.6.24 |
| 1922 | Norwood 9.7.61 | West Adelaide 2.16.28 |
| 1923 | Norwood 9.12.66 | North Adelaide 6.4.40 |
| 1924 | West Torrens 9.12.66 | Sturt 8.10.58 |
| 1925 | Norwood 8.4.52 | West Torrens 7.9.51 |
| 1926 | Sturt 9.10.64 | North Adelaide 7.9.51 |
| 1927 | West Adelaide 10.11.71 | North Adelaide 8.10.58 |
| 1928 | Port Adelaide 15.14.104 | Norwood 7.14.56 |
| 1929 | Norwood 16.14.110 | Port Adelaide 10.9.69 |
| 1930 | North Adelaide 9.13.67 | Port Adelaide 9.9.63 |
| 1931 | North Adelaide 17.13.115 | Sturt 11.11.77 |
| 1932 | Sturt 16.14.110 | North Adelaide 10.9.69 |
| 1933 | West Torrens 13.10.88 | Norwood 9.11.65 |
| 1934 | Glenelg 18.15.123 | Port Adelaide 16.18.114 |
| 1935 | South Adelaide 15.9.99 | Port Adelaide 13.13.91 |
| 1936 | Port Adelaide 13.19.97 | Sturt 14.10.94 |
| 1937 | Port Adelaide 13.16.94 | South Adelaide 9.16.70 |
| 1938 | South Adelaide 23.14.152 | Port Adelaide 15.16.106 |
| 1939 | Port Adelaide 16.28.124 | West Torrens 11.11.77 |
| 1940 | Sturt 14.16.100 | South Adelaide 11.13.79 |
| 1941 | Norwood 14.16.100 | Sturt 10.11.71 |
| 1945 | West Torrens 15.25.115 | Port Adelaide 15.12.102 |
| 1946 | Norwood 13.14.92 | Port Adelaide 9.10.64 |
| 1947 | West Adelaide 10.15.75 | Norwood 5.15.45 |
| 1948 | Norwood 15.16.106 | West Torrens 6.13.49 |
| 1949 | North Adelaide 23.17.155 | West Torrens 9.8.62 |
| 1950 | Norwood 15.16.106 | Glenelg 8.11.59 |
| 1951 | Port Adelaide 10.12.72 | North Adelaide 8.13.61 |
| 1952 | North Adelaide 23.15.153 | Norwood 6.9.45 |
| 1953 | West Torrens 9.13.67 | Port Adelaide 8.12.60 |
| 1954 | Port Adelaide 11.13.79 | West Adelaide 10.16.76 |
| 1955 | Port Adelaide 15.11.101 | Norwood 5.8.38 |
| 1956 | Port Adelaide 12.9.81 | West Adelaide 9.11.65 |
| 1957 | Port Adelaide 15.15.105 | Norwood 13.16.94 |
| 1958 | Port Adelaide 14.10.94 | West Adelaide 14.8.92 |
| 1959 | Port Adelaide 13.9.87 | West Adelaide 11.11.77 |
| 1960 | North Adelaide 14.11.95 | Norwood 13.12.90 |
| 1961 | West Adelaide 16.13.109 | Norwood 11.7.73 |
| 1962 | Port Adelaide 8.10.58 | West Adelaide 7.13.55 |
| 1963 | Port Adelaide 11.14.80 | North Adelaide 7.13.55 |
| 1964 | South Adelaide 9.15.69 | Port Adelaide 5.12.42 |
| 1965 | Port Adelaide 12.8.80 | Sturt 12.5.77 |
| 1966 | Sturt 16.16.112 | Port Adelaide 8.8.56 |
| 1967 | Sturt 13.10.88 | Port Adelaide 10.17.77 |
| 1968 | Sturt 12.18.90 | Port Adelaide 9.9.63 |
| 1969 | Sturt 24.15.159 | Glenelg 13.16.94 |
| 1970 | Sturt 12.13.85 | Glenelg 9.10.64 |
| 1971 | North Adelaide 10.19.79 | Port Adelaide 9.5.59 |
| 1972 | North Adelaide 19.14.128 | Port Adelaide 10.12.72 |
| 1973 | Glenelg 21.11.137 | North Adelaide 19.16.130 |
| 1974 | Sturt 9.16.70 | Glenelg 8.7.55 |
| 1975 | Norwood 9.10.64 | Glenelg 7.10.52 |
| 1976 | Sturt 17.14.116 | Port Adelaide 10.15.75 |
| 1977 | Port Adelaide 17.11.113 | Glenelg 16.9.105 |
| 1978 | Norwood 16.15.111 | Sturt 14.26.110 |
| 1979 | Port Adelaide 9.9.63 | South Adelaide 3.14.32 |
| 1980 | Port Adelaide 11.15.81 | Norwood 9.9.63 |
| 1981 | Port Adelaide 14.11.95 | Glenelg 6.8.44 |
| 1982 | Norwood 20.13.133 | Glenelg 9.17.71 |
| 1983 | West Adelaide 21.16.142 | Sturt 16.12.108 |
| 1984 | Norwood 15.10.100 | Port Adelaide 13.13.91 |
| 1985 | Glenelg 21.15.141 | North Adelaide 12.12.84 |
| 1986 | Glenelg 21.9.135 | North Adelaide 12.15.87 |
| 1987 | North Adelaide 23.7.145 | Glenelg 9.9.63 |
| 1988 | Port Adelaide 12.12.84 | Glenelg 8.7.55 |
| 1989 | Port Adelaide 15.18.108 | North Adelaide 1.8.14 |
| 1990 | Port Adelaide 16.12.108 | Glenelg 13.15.93 |
| 1991 | North Adelaide 21.22.148 | West Adelaide 11.7.73 |
| 1992 | Port Adelaide 17.3.105 | Glenelg 7.7.49 |
| 1993 | W'ville-W Torrens 17.20.122 | Norwood 7.7.49 |
| 1994 | Port Adelaide 15.16.106 | W'ville-W Torrens 10.9.69 |
| 1995 | Port Adelaide 13.16.94 | Central District 6.10.46 |
| 1996 | Port Adelaide 11.14.80 | Central District 6.8.44 |
| 1997 | Norwood 19.12.126 | Port Adelaide 7.11.53 |

*1916–17, competition suspended during World War I. 1942–44, competition suspended during World War II.*

# WAFL PREMIERS AND RUNNERS-UP

*Before 1904 the team at the top of the ladder was declared Premiership winner. No finals matches were played. In 1907 the final scoreboard had East Fremantle as 6.11.47. Perth successfully protested that a goal was wrongly allowed.*

| Year | Premier | Runner-up |
|------|---------|-----------|
| 1885 | Rovers | Victorians |
| 1886 | Fremantle | Victorians |
| 1887 | Unions | Victorians |
| 1888 | Unions | Rovers |
| 1889 | Unions | Rovers |
| 1890 | Fremantle | Metropolitan |
| 1891 | Rovers | West Perth |
| 1892 | Fremantle | West Perth |
| 1893 | Fremantle | West Perth |
| 1894 | Fremantle | West Perth |
| 1895 | Fremantle | Rovers |
| 1896 | Fremantle | Imperials |
| 1897 | West Perth | Fremantle |
| 1898 | Fremantle | West Perth |
| 1899 | West Perth | East Fremantle |
| 1900 | East Fremantle | South Fremantle |
| 1901 | West Perth | East Fremantle |
| 1902 | East Fremantle | North Fremantle |
| 1903 | East Fremantle | West Perth |
| 1904 | East Fremantle 12.11.83 | Perth 3.7.25 |
| 1905 | West Perth 4.7.31 | East Fremantle 3.9.27 |
| 1906 | East Fremantle 12.3.75 | West Perth 5.6.36 |
| 1907 | Perth 6.6.42 | East Fremantle 5.11.41 |
| 1908 | East Fremantle 5.7.37 | Perth 0.8.8 |
| 1909 | East Fremantle 8.8.56 | Perth 4.6.30 |
| 1910 | East Fremantle 5.5.35 | East Perth 2.10.22 |
| 1911 | East Fremantle 14.12.96 | West Perth 7.3.45 |
| 1912 | Subiaco 5.8.38 | East Fremantle 4.3.27 |
| 1913 | Subiaco 6.7.43 | Perth 4.7.31 |
| 1914 | East Fremantle 5.13.43 | South Fremantle 3.6.24 |
| 1915 | Subiaco 3.3.21 | Perth 2.7.19 |
| 1916 | South Fremantle 7.12.54 | East Fremantle 5.5.35 |
| 1917 | South Fremantle 6.5.41 | East Fremantle 3.8.26 |
| 1918 | East Fremantle 11.8.74 | East Perth 8.5.53 |
| 1919 | East Perth 10.8.68 | East Fremantle 7.4.46 |
| 1920 | East Perth 6.16.52 | East Fremantle 4.6.30 |
| 1921 | East Perth 5.9.39 | East Fremantle 4.8.32 |
| 1922 | East Perth 7.13.55 | West Perth 5.9.39 |
| 1923 | East Perth 9.9.63 | East Fremantle 7.4.46 |
| 1924 | Subiaco 7.9.51 | East Fremantle 3.6.24 |
| 1925 | East Fremantle 10.10.70 | Subiaco 6.7.43 |
| 1926 | East Perth 11.19.85 | Subiaco 5.5.35 |
| 1927 | East Perth 10.12.72 | South Fremantle 7.9.51 |
| 1928 | East Fremantle 10.13.73 | East Perth 8.8.56 |
| 1929 | East Fremantle 8.22.70 | South Fremantle 5.9.39 |
| 1930 | East Fremantle 12.15.87 | South Fremantle 9.11.65 |
| 1931 | East Fremantle 9.13.67 | Subiaco 7.7.49 |
| 1932 | West Perth 18.9.117 | East Perth 11.8.74 |
| 1933 | East Fremantle 10.13.73 | Subiaco 7.7.49 |
| 1934 | West Perth 11.7.73 | East Fremantle 5.9.39 |
| 1935 | West Perth 11.8.74 | Subiaco 7.9.51 |
| 1936 | East Perth 11.5.71 | Claremont 9.6.60 |
| 1937 | East Fremantle 14.13.97 | Claremont 13.9.87 |
| 1938 | Claremont 14.17.101 | East Fremantle 11.13.79 |
| 1939 | Claremont 14.11.95 | East Fremantle 11.10.76 |
| 1940 | Claremont 13.13.91 | South Fremantle 9.20.74 |
| 1941 | West Perth 14.14.98 | East Fremantle 10.17.77 |
| 1942 | West Perth 19.16.130 | Claremont 11.13.79 |
| 1943 | East Fremantle 17.15.117 | Swan Districts 11.11.77 |
| 1944 | East Perth 14.13.97 | East Fremantle 4.17.41 |
| 1945 | East Fremantle 12.15.87 | South Fremantle 7.9.51 |
| 1946 | East Fremantle 11.13.79 | West Perth 10.13.73 |
| 1947 | South Fremantle 13.8.86 | West Perth 9.17.71 |
| 1948 | South Fremantle 13.9.87 | West Perth 8.15.63 |
| 1949 | West Perth 16.13.109 | Perth 12.7.79 |
| 1950 | South Fremantle 12.23.95 | Perth 13.11.89 |
| 1951 | West Perth 13.10.88 | South Fremantle 12.13.85 |
| 1952 | South Fremantle 12.19.91 | West Perth 10.10.70 |
| 1953 | South Fremantle 18.12.120 | West Perth 8.13.61 |
| 1954 | South Fremantle 21.14.140 | East Fremantle 9.8.62 |
| 1955 | Perth 11.11.77 | East Fremantle 11.9.75 |
| 1956 | East Perth 10.17.77 | South Fremantle 9.10.64 |
| 1957 | East Fremantle 10.18.78 | East Perth 9.8.62 |
| 1958 | East Perth 8.17.65 | East Fremantle 8.15.63 |
| 1959 | East Perth 12.19.91 | Subiaco 9.14.68 |
| 1960 | West Perth 17.13.115 | East Perth 12.11.83 |
| 1961 | Swan Districts 17.9.111 | East Perth 12.15.87 |
| 1962 | Swan Districts 14.10.94 | East Fremantle 10.16.76 |
| 1963 | Swan Districts 17.10.112 | East Fremantle 13.12.90 |
| 1964 | Claremont 14.18.102 | East Fremantle 15.8.98 |
| 1965 | East Fremantle 18.18.126 | Swan Districts 16.6.102 |
| 1966 | Perth 11.25.91 | East Perth 10.15.75 |
| 1967 | Perth 18.12.120 | East Perth 15.12.102 |
| 1968 | Perth 16.14.110 | East Perth 13.8.86 |
| 1969 | West Perth 21.21.147 | East Perth 10.14.74 |
| 1970 | South Fremantle 15.7.97 | Perth 6.18.54 |
| 1971 | West Perth 14.17.101 | East Perth 9.15.69 |
| 1972 | East Perth 9.17.71 | Claremont 8.8.56 |
| 1973 | Subiaco 10.12.72 | West Perth 6.4.40 |
| 1974 | East Fremantle 17.20.122 | Perth 15.10.100 |
| 1975 | West Perth 23.17.155 | South Fremantle 7.9.51 |
| 1976 | Perth 13.14.92 | East Perth 11.3.69 |
| 1977 | Perth 26.13.169 | East Fremantle 14.12.96 |
| 1978 | East Perth 11.15.81 | Perth 12.7.79 |
| 1979 | East Fremantle 21.19.145 | South Fremantle 16.16.112 |
| 1980 | South Fremantle 23.18.156 | Swan Districts 15.8.98 |
| 1981 | Claremont 16.15.111 | South Fremantle 12.24.96 |
| 1982 | Swan Districts 18.19.127 | Claremont 11.12.78 |
| 1983 | Swan Districts 15.14.104 | Claremont 12.11.83 |
| 1984 | Swan Districts 20.18.138 | East Fremantle 15.12.102 |
| 1985 | East Fremantle 15.12.102 | Subiaco 14.13.97 |
| 1986 | Subiaco 19.16.130 | East Fremantle 8.13.61 |
| 1987 | Claremont 20.20.140 | Subiaco 10.9.69 |
| 1988 | Subiaco 19.8.122 | Claremont 8.12.60 |
| 1989 | Claremont 15.16.106 | South Fremantle 5.9.39 |
| 1990 | Swan Districts 16.7.103 | Claremont 10.17.77 |
| 1991 | Claremont 19.18.132 | Subiaco 8.7.55 |
| 1992 | East Fremantle 12.19.91 | South Fremantle 9.13.67 |
| 1993 | Claremont 13.14.92 | West Perth 8.14.62 |
| 1994 | East Fremantle 13.13.91 | Claremont 10.10.70 |
| 1995 | West Perth 21.11.137 | Subiaco 12.9.81 |
| 1996 | Claremont 13.8.86 | East Perth 12.12.84 |
| 1997 | South Fremantle 13.7.85 | East Fremantle 11.13.79 |

# UMPIRES

## Peter Schwab
## AFL Director of Umpiring

- 171 VFL/AFL matches with Hawthorn, including 20 finals and six Grand Finals. Played in three premiership sides and four night premiership sides
- Started at Hawthorn in 1997
- First game in 1980 v South Melbourne
- Retired in 1991
- Assistant coach at Richmond 1992-94
- Marketing manager Hawthorn 1995
- Assistant coach Hawthorn 1996-97
- Awarded life membership of Hawthorn Football Club
- Wife: Jenny. Children: Emily (dec.), William

## Rowan Sawers
## AFL Umpires' Coach

- Played under-age football with Frankston Rovers before umpiring in 1971 with the Southern Umpires Association and FDJFL. Recruited to VFL senior panel in 1973
- VFL umpiring debut 1977, completing 410 VFL/AFL senior games, including 31 finals and four Grand Finals. Eight State of Origin games and two Irish tours
- Victorian state director of umpiring in 1992 (while injured)
- Junior football coach with Dingley Football Club since 1995
- Appointed AFL Umpires Coach at end of 1997 season
- Wife: Carmel. Children: Travis, Ryan, Aaron.

## 1998 AFL FIELD UMPIRES

**David ACKLAND (VIC)**
**Born:** 17/10/72
**Height:** 176cm **Weight:** 70kg **Number:** 17
**Career background:** recruited from Goulbourn Valley Football League in 1993, invited to join AFL senior squad in 1995. AFL senior debut in 1996.
**AFL games to end of '97:** 14
**Occupation:** credit officer

**Brett ALLEN (VIC)**
**Born:** 14/4/66
**Height:** 178cm **Weight:** 72kg **Number:** 10
**Career background:** recruited from Geelong Umpires and has been on the AFL squad for nine years. Made AFL debut in 1992, officiating in 16 games in first season at senior level. Five AFL finals games. One State of Origin game.
**AFL games to end of '97:** 110
**Occupation:** gardener

**Troy BURTON (SA)**
**Born:** 30/4/71
**Height:** 180cm **Weight:** 70kg **Number:** 33
**Career background:** umpired with Southern Football League before joining South Australian National Football League panel in 1990. Umpired in 1994 Commonwealth Bank Cup. Invited to join AFL senior squad in 1995. Umpired AFL reserves grand final in 1997.
**AFL games to end of '97:** 6
**Occupation:** clerk

**Peter CAREY (VIC)**
**Born:** 16/6/57
**Height:** 178cm **Weight:** 67kg **Number:** 8
**Career background:** promoted to senior list in 1983 from reserve grade squad. Umpired reserve grade grand final 1985. Senior umpiring debut in 1985. 21 VFL/AFL finals including four Grand Finals. Four State of Origin games. All-Australian umpire 1992.
**AFL games to end of '97:** 263
**Occupation:** purchasing officer

**Andrew COATES (VIC)**
**Born:** 6/6/66
**Height:** 175cm **Weight:** 62kg **Number:** 6
**Career background:** umpired with Essendon District League before joining state League panel in 1983. Promoted to senior list in 1986, made umpiring debut in 1989, officiating in two games. Has umpired 10 finals. Four State of Origin games.
**AFL games to end of '97:** 136
**Occupation:** accountant

**Gavin DELLER (VIC)**
**Born:** 28/8/69
**Height:** 175cm **Weight:** 70kg **Number:** 5
**Career background:** recruited from Essendon District League. Joined VSFL in 1994 and invited to join AFL senior squad in 1997. Umpired VSFL under-18 grand final 1994. AFL reserves grand final 1997.
**AFL games to end of '97:** 14
**Occupation:** police officer

**Gavin DORE (VIC)**
**Born:** 25/4/61
**Height:** 177cm **Weight:** 68kg **Number:** 19
**Career background:** joined West Gippsland Umpires Association in 1979. Moved to VFL reserve grade in 1982. Made senior list in 1984 and umpired first senior game in 1986. 10 AFL finals, including 1996 Grand Final. Two State of Origin games.
**AFL games to end of '97:** 175
**Occupation:** teacher

**Craig DURHAM (QLD)**
**Born:** 7/2/69
**Height:** 184cm **Weight:** 72kg **Number:** 15
**Career background:** umpired with QAFL since
1991. Invited to join AFL senior squad 1994.
Umpired QAFL grand final in 1994 and Teal Cup
grand final in 1992
**AFL games to end of '97:** 18
**Occupation:** solicitor

**Martin ELLIS (VIC)**
**Born:** 9/5/69
**Height:** 179cm **Weight:** 63kg **Number:** 23
**Career background:** recruited from Preston District
Junior Football League in 1990, invited to join AFL
senior squad in 1995. VSFL grand final in 1994.
Made AFL senior debut in 1996.
**AFL games to end of '97:** 23
**Occupation:** self-employed

**Darren GOLDSPINK (VIC)**
**Born:** 12/9/64
**Height:** 178cm **Weight:** 76kg **Number:** 32
**Career background:** umpired Preston Districts
Junior Football Association 1981-83. Joined VFL
cadet squad in 1984 and promoted to senior list
in 1986. First senior game in 1989. Played
football with North Reservoir juniors 1979-1980.
12 AFL finals including 1993 and 1995 Grand
Finals. Four State of Origin games. All-Australian
umpire 1993 and 1995.
**AFL games to end of '97:** 154
**Occupation:** accountant

**Steven HANLEY (VIC)**
**Born:** 8/1/71
**Height:** 178cm **Weight:** 66kg **Number:** 18
**Career background:** umpired with Preston District
Junior Football Association before joining Victorian
State Football League panel in 1995. Umpired
1995 Commonwealth Bank Cup grand final and
1995 VFA grand final. Made AFL senior debut in
1996.
**AFL games to end of '97:** 16
**Occupation:** sales manager

**John HARVEY (VIC)**
**Born:** 14/2/64
**Height:** 183cm **Weight:** 72kg **Number:** 25
**Career background:** began umpiring with
Essendon District Football League in 1983. Joined
VFA in 1987 and VFL senior list in 1989. Senior
umpiring debut in 1990. Two AFL finals in 1996.
**AFL games to end of '97:** 80
**Occupation:** bank clerk

**David HOWLETT (VIC)**
**Born:** 2/10/60
**Height:** 175cm **Weight:** 72kg **Number:** 1
**Career background:** umpired with Essendon
District Football League for five years. Joined VFL
in 1982 and umpired two games. 11 AFL finals,
including one Grand Final in 1994. Three State of
Origin games.
**AFL games to end of '97:** 227
**Occupation:** sales manager

**Derek HUMPHERY-SMITH (QLD)**
**Born:** 3/11/69
**Height:** 183cm **Weight:** 81kg **Number:** 27
**Career background:** umpired with Queensland
Australian Football Club before joining Queensland
Australian Football League panel in 1993. Umpired
1994 Commonwealth Bank Cup. Made AFL senior
debut in 1996.
**AFL games to end of '97:** 12
**Occupation:** lawyer

**Hayden KENNEDY (VIC)**
**Born:** 16/10/65
**Height:** 166cm **Weight:** 65kg **Number:** 7
**Career background:** started with Essendon District
Football League in 1983. Recruited to VFL cadet
squad in 1984 and promoted to senior grade list in
1987. Made VFL umpiring debut in 1988. 13 AFL
finals including 1995 and '97 Grand Finals. Two
State of Origin games. All-Australian umpire 1997.
**AFL games to end of '97:** 186
**Occupation:** teacher

**Jamie LOVE (VIC)**
**Born:** 4/6/69
**Height:** 174cm **Weight:** 70kg **Number:** 28
**Career background:** recruited from Ballarat
Umpires in 1993, invited to join AFL senior squad
in 1995. Made AFL senior debut in 1996.
**AFL games to end of '97:** 25
**Occupation:** green-keeper

**Stephen McBURNEY (VIC)**
**Born:** 14/11/67
**Height:** 178cm **Weight:** 68kg **Number:** 29
**Career background:** began umpiring in 1983 with
SESFL joining VFL state panel in 1989. Invited to
join AFL senior squad in 1995. Made AFL senior
debut in 1995.
**AFL games to end of '97:** 42
**Occupation:** solicitor

**Darren McCAULEY (VIC)**
**Born:** 26/12/69
**Height:** 180cm **Weight:** 64kg **Number:** 31
**Career background:** recruited from Essendon
District Football League to VFL cadet squad in
1989. Invited to join AFL squad in 1993 and made
debut in same year.
**AFL games to end of '97:** 29
**Occupation:** carpenter

**Shane McINERNEY (VIC)**
**Born:** 19/10/70
**Height:** 178cm **Weight:** 64kg **Number:** 30
**Career background:** recruited from Ballarat
Umpires, joining Victorian state league panel in
1992. Promoted to AFL squad in 1993 and made
AFL senior debut in 1994.
**AFL games to end of '97:** 46
**Occupation:** research industrial chemist

**Mark McKENZIE (VIC)**
**Born:** 7/5/70
**Height:** 80cm **Weight:** 64kg **Number:** 24
**Career background:** recruited from Doncaster and
District Football League in 1989. Invited to join AFL

squad in 1994 and made debut in 1995. One AFL final in 1995.
**AFL games to end of '97:** 47
**Occupation:** fashion company director

## Scott McLAREN (VIC)
**Born:** 11/4/68
**Height:** 188cm **Weight:** 82kg **Number:** 11
**Career background:** recruited from Eastern District Football League. Joined state league panel in 1993. Invited to join AFL squad in 1994 and made debut in same year.
**AFL games to end of '97:** 55
**Occupation:** pharmacist

## Andrew MALCOLM (VIC)
**Born:** 26/9/71
**Height:** 178cm **Weight:** 70kg **Number:** 20
**Career background:** recruited from ACTAFL and joined AFL in 1994. Made AFL senior umpiring debut in 1997. AFL reserves grand final in 1995 and '97, VFL grand final in 1996.
**AFL games to end of '97:** 11
**Occupation:** customer service representative

## Chris MITCHELL (VIC)
**Born:** 14/4/61
**Height:** 177cm **Weight:** 67kg **Number:** 4
**Career background:** recruited from Footscray District League and joined VFL cadet squad in 1979. Made VFL senior umpiring debut in 1985. Nine AFL finals games and five State of Origin games.
**AFL games to end of '97:** 232
**Occupation:** teacher

## Mark NASH (VIC)
**Born:** 24/6/70
**Height:** 166cm **Weight:** 60kg **Number:** 14
**Career background:** joined state league panel from Waverley Juniors Umpires in 1990. Promoted to AFL squad in 1993. Two State of Origin games. Seven AFL finals including 1996 and '97 Grand Finals. All-Australian umpire 1996.
**AFL games to end of '97:** 90
**Occupation:** planner for pharmaceuticals manufacturer

## Matthew NORDEN (VIC)
**Born:** 2/10/68
**Height:** 170cm **Weight:** 67kg **Number:** 16
**Career background:** started umpiring in 1984 with DDJFL. Invited to join AFL senior squad in 1995 and made debut in same year. Toured Ireland in 1991.
**AFL games to end of '97:** 30
**Occupation:** accountant

## Greg SCROOP (WA)
**Born:** 6/10/66
**Height:** 178cm **Weight:** 76kg **Number:** 21
**Career background:** started with WAFL in 1987 and umpired 70 WAFL games including three finals, plus 1992 WAFL grand final. Joined AFL squad list in 1990 and made AFL senior debut in 1990. Six AFL finals.
**AFL games to end of '97:** 94
**Occupation:** self-employed

## Vince SERCIA (VIC)
**Born:** 26/7/67
**Height:** 173cm **Weight:** 67kg **Number:** 26
**Career background:** umpired with Southern Umpires before joining Victorian State Football League panel in 1989. Umpired in 1995 VFA grand final and 1995 representative game VFA v NSW. Made AFL senior debut in 1996.
**AFL games to end of '97:** 14
**Occupation:** bank officer

## Tim SHEARER (VIC)
**Born:** 25/10/67
**Height:** 178cm **Weight**: 79kg **Number:** 12
**Career background:** umpired with VAFA before joining Victorian State Football League panel in 1994. Umpired 1996 VFL grand Final. Invited to join AFL senior squad in 1997.
**AFL games to end of '97:** 9
**Occupation:** national account manager

## Bryan SHEEHAN (VIC)
**Born:** 3/4/59
**Height:** 167cm **Weight:** 62kg **Number:** 9
**Career background:** recruited from Dandenong and District Junior Football League and joined VFL cadet squad in 1984. Made VFL senior umpiring debut in 1986. 28 AFL finals including six Grand Finals. Four State of Origin games. All-Australian umpire 1991.
**AFL games to end of '97:** 238
**Occupation:** planning manager (printing industry)

## Grant VERNON (WA)
**Born:** 12/11/64
**Height:** 172cm **Weight:** 63kg **Number:** 2
**Career background:** member of first development squad at East Fremantle Junior Council. Umpired 80 games with WAFL, including three grand finals and four State of Origin games. Made VFL senior grade squad in 1987 and umpired seven games in same year. 10 finals matches.
**AFL games to end of '97:** 189
**Occupation:** national manager — investment group

## Stuart WENN (VIC)
**Born:** 30/6/69
**Height:** 179cm **Weight**: 67kg **Number:** 22
**Career background:** began umpiring in 1988 with ESCFA. Invited to join AFL senior squad in 1995 and made debut in same year. Three VSFL finals in 1994.
**AFL games to end of '97:** 25
**Occupation:** banker

## Richard WILLIAMS (SA)
**Born:** 18/4/67
**Height:** 185cm **Weight**: 80kg **Number:** 34
**Career background:** recruited from SANFL. Invited to join AFL senior squad in 1995 and made debut in same year. Two SANFL grand finals 1993 and '94.
**AFL games to end of '97:** 6
**Occupation:** clerk

# GRAND FINAL FIELD UMPIRES 1898–1996

H. Beitzel 1955
W. Blackburn 1936, 1938
G. Batt 1937
W. Barbour 1959
R. Brophy 1964
T. Bride 1946
P. Cameron 1985, 1986 1988
P. Carey 1989, 1992, 1993, 1995
A. Coward 1939, 1940
I. Crapp 1898, 1899, 1901, 1902, 1904, 1905
J. Crouch 1963, 1965, 1966, 1968, 1969
W. Deller OAM 1972, 1976, 1978, 1979, 1980
G. Dore 1996
J. Elder 1908, 1909, 1910, 1911, 1912, 1913, 1918, 1919, 1920, 1922
M. Dye 1981
R. Gibson 1903
D. Goldspink 1993, 1995
E. Hawkins 1941, 1942, 1943, 1944
D. Howlett 1994
J. Irving OAM 1960, 1962
D. Jolley 1970
G. James OAM 1982, 1984
H. Jamieson 1951, 1952
H. Kennedy 1995, 1997
L. Mutch 1923
J. McMurray (Snr) 1921, 1924, 1925, 1926, 1927, 1928
J. McMurray (Jnr) 1948 (2), 1949, 1950, 1953, 1954
A. Nash 1956, 1957, 1958
M. Nash 1996, 1997
N. Nash 1983
A. Norden 1915, 1916, 1917
I. Robinson 1973, 1974, 1977 (2), 1978, 1980, 1981, 1985, 1987
H. Rawle 1914
D. Rich 1990, 1992, 1994
J. Russo 1986, 1991
R. Sawers 1982, 1984, 1987, 1990
R. Scott 1929, 1930, 1931, 1932, 1933, 1934, 1935
R. Sawyer 1947
F. Schwab 1961
P. Sheales 1967, 1971
B. Sheehan 1988, 1989, 1991, 1994, 1996, 1997
K. Smith 1975, 1976, 1979, 1983
F. Spokes 1945
J. Sutcliffe 1977 (2)
L. Tulloch 1907
H. Wregg 1906

## FIELD UMPIRE SYSTEM

Prior to 1976, one field umpire umpired each game. Two field umpires were introduced in 1976. In 1994, a three field umpire system was introduced.

# 200 CLUB UMPIRES

| | |
|---|---|
| P. Cameron | 306 |
| P. Carey | 263 |
| W. Deller OAM | 251 |
| J. Elder | 295 |
| D. Howlett | 227 |
| J. McMurray Jnr | 216 |
| J. McMurray Snr | 303 |
| C. Mitchell | 232 |
| N. Nash | 217 |
| D. Rich | 251 |
| I. Robinson | 353 |
| J. Russo | 222 |
| R. Sawers | 410 |
| B. Sheehan | 238 |
| K. Smith | 303 |
| J. Sutcliffe | 214 |

*Day games only indicated. Night and Interstate games also qualify umpires for 200 Club membership.*

# 1997 HIGHLIGHTS AND HONORS

**Ansett Australia Cup Grand Final**
Field: Gavin Dore, Mark Nash, Bryan Sheehan
Boundary: Matthew Bellizia, Matthew Vitiritti, Scott Hutton
Goal: Anthony Black, Mark Powell
**State of Origin – Allies vs Western Australia**
Field: Andrew Coates, Denis Rich, Rowan Sawers
Boundary: Daniel Gooch, Ian Green, Dean Maxwell
Goal: David Flegg, Mark Powell
**State of Origin — South Australia vs Victoria**
Field: Darren Goldspink, Mark Nash, Greg Scroop
Boundary: Allan Cook, Shane Jansen, Chris MacDonald
Goal: Rodney Davies, Leo Corrieri
**All-Australian Umpire**
Hayden Kennedy
**AFL Grand Final**
Field: Hayden Kennedy, Mark Nash, Bryan Sheehan
Boundary: Allan Cook, Daniel Gooch, Andrew Wheeler
Goal: Rodney Davies, Mark Powell

# MILESTONES ACHIEVED IN 1997

**100 Matches**
Field: Brett Allen
Boundary: Greg Harding, Malcolm Owen
**400 Matches**
Field: Rowan Sawers

# 1997 UMPIRES AND GAMES

| | 1997 Games | Total | First Game | Recruited From |
|---|---|---|---|---|
| David Ackland | 6 | 14 | 1996 | Goulburn Vall. |
| Brett Allen | 22 | 110 | 1992 | VSFL |
| Michael Avon | 5 | 5 | 1997 | SANFL |
| Troy Burton | 6 | 6 | 1997 | SANFL |
| Keith Callaghan | 8 | 56 | 1992 | VSFL |
| Peter Carey | 11 | 263 | 1985 | VFL Reserves |
| Andrew Coates | 24 | 136 | 1989 | Essendon Dist. |
| Gavin Deller | 14 | 14 | 1997 | Essendon Dist. |
| Gavin Dore | 19 | 175 | 1986 | West Gippsland |
| Craig Durham | 3 | 18 | 1995 | QAFL |
| Martin Ellis | 11 | 23 | 1996 | Preston Dist. |
| Michael Forbes | 3 | 3 | 1997 | NSWAFL |
| Darren Goldspink | 23 | 154 | 1989 | Preston Dist. |
| Steven Hanley | 9 | 16 | 1996 | Preston Dist. |
| John Harvey | 13 | 80 | 1990 | VFA |
| David Howlett | 22 | 227 | 1982 | Essendon Dist. |
| Derek Hamper-Smith | 9 | 12 | 1996 | QAFL |
| Hayden Kennedy | 25 | 186 | 1988 | Essendon Dist. |
| Sam Kronja | 6 | 9 | 1996 | WAFL |
| Anton Lewis | 4 | 7 | 1996 | NSWAFL |
| Jamie Love | 14 | 25 | 1996 | Ballarat |
| Stephen McBurney | 13 | 42 | 1995 | South East Sub. |
| Darren McCauley | 10 | 29 | 1993 | Essendon Dist. |
| Shane McInerney | 11 | 46 | 1994 | Ballarat |
| Mark McKenzie | 14 | 47 | 1994 | Doncaster Dist. |
| Scott McLaren | 16 | 55 | 1994 | Eastern Dist. |
| Andrew Malcolm | 11 | 11 | 1997 | ACTAFL |
| Chris. Mitchell | 15 | 232 | 1984 | Footscray Dist. |
| Mark Nash | 26 | 90 | 1994 | Waverley Jnrs. |
| Kieron Nicholls | 4 | 12 | 1996 | Riddell Dist. |
| Matthew Norden | 6 | 30 | 1995 | Doncaster Dist. |
| Tim Pfeiffer | 4 | 44 | 1994 | SANFL |
| Mark Prince | 12 | 59 | 1993 | VSFL |
| Denis Rich | 23 | 251 | 1983 | Western Sub. |
| Rowan Sawers | 23 | 410 | 1977 | Southern Ump. |
| Justin Schmitt | 3 | 3 | 1997 | SANFL |
| Greg. Scroop | 21 | 94 | 1990 | WAFL |
| Vince Sercia | 11 | 14 | 1996 | Southern Ump. |
| Michael Sexton | 6 | 6 | 1997 | Footscray Dist. |
| Tim Shearer | 9 | 9 | 1997 | VAFA |
| Bryan Sheehan | 17 | 238 | 1986 | Dandenong Dist. |
| Grant Vernon | 21 | 189 | 1987 | WAFL |
| Stuart Wenn | 16 | 25 | 1995 | Eastern Sub. |
| Richard Williams | 6 | 30 | 1995 | SANFL |

# 1997 FINALS UMPIRES AND GAMES

| | Elim. | Qual. | 1st | 2nd | Prel. | G.F. | Total |
|---|---|---|---|---|---|---|---|
| Rowan Sawers | 5 | 7 | 6 | 6 | 7 | 4 | 35 |
| Bryan Sheehan | 4 | 5 | 5 | 2 | 6 | 6 | 28 |
| Peter Carey | 3 | 5 | 1 | 4 | 4 | 4 | 21 |
| Denis Rich | 1 | 6 | 3 | 1 | 3 | 3 | 17 |
| Hayden Kennedy | — | 5 | 1 | 2 | 3 | 2 | 13 |
| Darren Goldspink | — | 5 | 1 | — | 4 | 2 | 12 |
| David Howlett | 1 | 3 | 1 | 3 | 2 | 1 | 11 |
| Gavin Dore | 1 | 4 | — | 2 | 2 | 1 | 10 |
| Andrew Coates | — | 4 | 2 | 1 | 3 | — | 10 |
| Grant Vernon | 1 | 4 | 5 | — | — | — | 10 |
| Chris Mitchell | 2 | 4 | 2 | — | 1 | — | 9 |
| Mark Nash | — | 3 | 1 | 1 | 1 | 2 | 8 |
| Greg. Scroop | — | 3 | — | 1 | 2 | — | 6 |
| Brett Allen | — | 2 | — | 1 | 2 | — | 5 |
| John Harvey | — | 2 | — | — | — | — | 2 |
| Mark McKenzie | — | 1 | — | — | — | — | 1 |

## FINALS UMPIRES — 1931-1997

| Year | Grand Final | Preliminary | Second Semi | First Semi |
|------|-------------|-------------|-------------|------------|
| 1931 | R. Scott | R. Scott | R. Scott | P. Ellingsen |
| 1932 | R. Scott | J. McMurray | R. Scott | R. Scott |
| 1933 | R. Scott | A. Blackburn | J. McMurray | P. Ellingsen |
| 1934 | R. Scott | R. Scott | R. Scott | J. McMurray |
| 1935 | R. Scott | W. Blackburn | J. McMurray | W. Blackburn |
| 1936 | W. Blackburn | W. Blackburn | W. Blackburn | W. Blackburn |
| 1937 | G. Batt | G. Batt | G. Batt | W. Blackburn |
| 1938 | W. Blackburn A. Coward | W. Blackburn | W. Blackburn | W. Blackburn |
| 1939 | W. Blackburn | W. Blackburn | A. Coward | A. Coward |
| 1940 | A. Coward | A. Coward | A. Coward | E. Hawkins |
| 1941 | E. Hawkins | T. Bride | A. Coward | E. Hawkins |
| 1942 | E. Hawkins | E. Hawkins | E. Hawkins | E. Hawkins |
| 1943 | E. Hawkins | E. Hawkins | E. Hawkins | E. Hawkins |
| 1944 | E. Hawkins | E. Hawkins | E. Hawkins | E. Hawkins |
| 1945 | F. Spokes | A. Sawyer | A. Sawyer | F. Spokes |
| 1946 | T. Bride | T. Bride | T. Bride (2) | F. Spokes |
| 1947 | A. Sawyer | F. Spokes | F. Spokes | A. Sawyer |
| 1948 | J. McMurray (2) | J. McMurray | A. Sawyer | F. Spokes |
| 1949 | J. McMurray | J. McMurray | A. Sawyer | J. McMurray, Jnr |
| 1950 | J. McMurray | J. McMurray | H. Jamieson | J. McMurray |
| 1951 | H. Jamieson | J. McMurray | H. Jamieson | J. McMurray |
| 1952 | H. Jamieson | G. Robinson | J. McMurray | H. Jamieson |
| 1953 | J. McMurray | H. Jamieson | W. Barbour | J. McMurray |
| 1954 | J. McMurray | H. Jamieson | G. Robinson | W. Barbour |
| 1955 | H. Beitzel | H. Beitzel | J. McMurray | H. Beitzel |
| 1956 | A. Nash | A. Nash | H. Beitzel | A. Nash |
| 1957 | A. Nash | A. Nash | A. Nash | A. Nash |
| 1958 | A. Nash | A. Barbour | A. Nash | W. Barbour |
| 1959 | W. Barbour | W. Barbour | A. Nash | W. Barbour |
| 1960 | J. Irving | J. Irving | F. Schwab | J. Irving |
| 1961 | F. Schwab | F. Schwab | J. Irving | F. Schwab |
| 1962 | J. Irving | F. Schwab/J. Irving | R. Nunn | F. Schwab |
| 1963 | J. Crouch | R. Brophy | J. Crouch | R. Brophy |
| 1964 | R. Brophy | R. Brophy | J. Crouch | R. Brophy |
| 1965 | J. Crouch | R. Brophy | S. Fisher | J. Crouch |
| 1966 | J. Crouch | J. Crouch | L. Perkins | J. Crouch |
| 1967 | P. Sheales | P. Sheales | P. Sheales | J. Crouch |
| 1968 | J. Crouch | J. Crouch | R. Sleeth | J. Crouch |
| 1969 | J. Crouch | D. Jolley | R. Sleeth | J. Crouch |
| 1970 | D. Jolley | D. Jolley | J. Crouch | R. Sleeth |
| 1971 | P. Sheales | I. Coates | W. Deller | P. Sheales |

| Year | Grand Final | Preliminary | Second Semi | First Semi | Qualifying | Elimination |
|------|-------------|-------------|-------------|------------|------------|-------------|
| 1972 | W. Deller | I. Coates | I. Coates Replay W. Deller | R. Sleeth | P. Sheales | W. Deller |
| 1973 | I. Robinson | W. Deller | I. Robinson | I. Coates | I. Robinson | W. Deller |
| 1974 | I. Robinson | K. Smith | I. Robinson | J. Chapman | K. Smith | I. Robinson |
| 1975 | K. Smith | K. Smith | I. Robinson | J. Sutcliffe | M. Henry | K. Smith |
| 1976 | K. Smith W. Deller | I. Robinson K. Smith | M. Henry M. Dye | K. Smith W. Deller | I. Robinson K. Smith | W. Deller J. Sutcliffe |
| 1977 | I. Robinson(2) J. Sutcliffe(2) | K. Smith J. Sutcliffe | W. Deller N. Nash | M. Dye I. Robinson | J. Sutcliffe *I. Robinson | W. Deller K. Smith |
| | (*Robinson inj. replaced by G. Polites (2nd qtr.) | | | | | |
| 1978 | W. Deller I. Robinson | I. Robinson N. Nash | J. Chapman W. Deller | I. Robinson K. Smith | I. Robinson K. Smith | W. Deller N. Nash |
| 1979 | W. Deller K. Smith | W. Deller I. Robinson | J. Chapman N. Nash | K. Smith R. Sawers | K. Smith W. Deller | R. Sawers I. Robinson |
| 1980 | W. Deller I. Robinson | W. Deller K. Smith | R. Sawers J. Sutcliffe | N. Nash K. Smith | W. Deller G. James | P. Cameron I. Robinson |
| 1981 | I. Robinson M. Dye | M. Dye P. Cameron | I. Robinson R. Sawers | P. Cameron M. Dye | I. Robinson R. Sawers | K. Smith N. Nash |
| 1982 | G. James | N. Nash | G. James | R. Sawers | N. Nash | R. Sawers |

## FINALS UMPIRES — 1931-1997

| Year | Grand Final | Preliminary | Second Semi | First Semi | Qualifying | Elimination |
|------|-------------|-------------|-------------|------------|------------|-------------|
|      | R. Sawers | P. Cameron | P. Cameron | K. Smith | I. Robinson | G. James |
| 1983 | K. Smith | N. Nash | G. James | R. Sawers | N. Nash | I. Robinson |
|      | N. Nash | I. Robinson | T. Bryant | K. Smith | G. James | K. Smith |
| 1984 | G. James | R. Sawers | J. Russo | K. Smith | G. James | N. Nash |
|      | R. Sawers | P. Cameron | I. Robinson | R. Sawers | J. Russo | P. Cameron |
| 1985 | P. Cameron | G. James | P. Cameron | G. James | R. Sawers | P. Cameron |
|      | I. Robinson | R. Sawers | T. Bryant | I. Robinson | D. Howlett | I. Robinson |
| 1986 | P. Cameron | R. Sawers | R. Sawers | R. Castle | I. Clayton | P. Cameron |
|      | J. Russo | R. Castle | J. Russo | P. Cameron | I. Robinson | J. Russo |
| 1987 | I. Robinson | I. Robinson | R. Sawers | P. Cameron | R. Sawers | I. Robinson |
|      | R. Sawers | D. Howlett | I. Clayton | D. Howlett | G. Dore | I. Clayton |
| 1988 | B. Sheehan | R. Castle | D. Rich | P. Carey | P. Carey | P. Cameron |
|      | P. Cameron | R. Sawers | P. Cameron | B. Sheehan | J. Russo | B. Sheehan |
| 1989 | P. Carey | D. Rich | I. Clayton | J. Russo | D. Rich | B. Sheehan |
|      | B. Sheehan | P. Carey | P. Cameron | B. Sheehan | C. Mitchell | P. Carey |
| 1990 | R. Sawers | B. Sheehan | P. Carey | R. Sawers | D. Rich | R. Sawers |
|      | D. Rich | P. Carey | B. Sheehan | D. Rich | M. Ball | P. Carey |
|      |           |           |           | Replay |           |           |
|      |           |           |           | B. Sheehan |           |           |
|      |           |           |           | C. Mitchell |           |           |

| Year | Grand Final | Preliminary | 2nd Semi | 1st Semi | Qualifying | 2nd Elim. | 1st Elim. |
|------|-------------|-------------|----------|----------|------------|-----------|-----------|
| 1991 | B. Sheehan | G. Dore | G. Dore | B. Sheehan | D. Goldspink | P. Cameron | B. Sheehan |
|      | J. Russo | R. Sawers | J. Russo | C. Mitchell | J. Russo | R. Sawers | G. Vernon |
| 1992 | P. Carey | D. Goldspink | P. Carey | G. Vernon | D. Goldspink | P. Carey | C. Mitchell |
|      | D. Rich | B. Sheehan | D. Howlett | D. Rich | H. Kennedy | B. Sheehan | D. Rich |
| 1993 | P. Carey | D. Goldspink | P. Carey | A. Coates | P. Carey | C. Mitchell | G. Dore |
|      | D. Goldspink | B. Sheehan | H. Kennedy | B. Sheehan | A. Coates | R. Sawers | D. Howlett |

| Year | 1994 | | | 1995 | | |
|------|------|------|------|------|------|------|
| Grand Final | D. Rich | B. Sheehan | D. Howlett | P. Carey | D. Goldspink | H. Kennedy |
| 2nd Prelim. | R. Sawers | H. Kennedy | D. Rich | A. Coates | D. Goldspink | B. Sheehan |
| 1st Prelim. | P. Carey | B. Allen | C. Mitchell | P. Carey | H. Kennedy | R. Sawers |
| 2nd Semi | D. Howlett | G. Dore | A. Coates | R. Sawers | G. Scroop | B. Sheehan |
| 1st Semi | B. Sheehan | C. Mitchell | G. Vernon | H. Kennedy | D. Rich | G. Vernon |
| 4th Qualif. | P. Carey | C. Mitchell | G. Vernon | A. Coates | G. Dore | M. Nash |
| 3rd Qualif. | D. Howlett | B. Sheehan | B. Allen | P. Carey | M. McKenzie | B. Sheehan |
| 2nd Qualif. | H. Kennedy | R. Sawers | G. Dore | D. Goldspink | G. Scroop | G. Vernon |
| 1st Qualif. | D. Rich | A. Coates | J. Russo | H. Kennedy | D. Rich | R. Sawers |

| Year | 1996 | | | 1997 | | |
|------|------|------|------|------|------|------|
| Grand Final | G. Dore | M. Nash | B. Sheehan | H. Kennedy | M. Nash | B. Sheehan |
| 2nd Prelim. | G. Dore | D. Goldspink | B. Sheehan | B. Allen | G. Scroop | B. Sheehan |
| 1st Prelim. | A. Coates | H. Kennedy | G. Scroop | A. Coates | M. Nash | D. Howlett |
| 2nd Semi | B. Allen | P. Carey | M. Nash | D. Goldspink | G. Vernon | M. Nash |
| 1st Semi | A. Coates | R. Sawers | G. Vernon | H. Kennedy | R. Sawers | D. Howlett |
| 4th Qualif. | P. Carey | J. Harvey | M. Nash | A. Coates | D. Howlett | M. Nash |
| 3rd Qualif. | H. Kennedy | R. Sawers | G. Vernon | H. Kennedy | J. Harvey | G. Scroop |
| 2nd Qualif. | G. Dore | D. Rich | B. Sheehan | R. Sawers | D. Rich | B. Allen |
| 1st Qualif. | D. Goldspink | C. Mitchell | G. Scroop | D. Goldspink | G. Vernon | B. Sheehan |

# AFL COMMISSION

On December 4, 1985, the then VFL Board of Directors resolved to appoint a Commission with specific powers to administer the competition.

Almost a year earlier, the board resolved on December 12, 1984, to appoint a commission for a 12-month period.

At the December 4, 1985, Board of Directors' meeting, it was resolved that the League entrust to and confer upon the commission all of the responsibilities and powers exercisable by it with the restriction that the commission may not, unless otherwise expressly authorised by the League, exercise any of the powers of the League:

(a) To admit any club to or expel or suspend any club for the competition;

(b) to amalgamate or join in any other League;

(c) to take over the administration of any additional football club;

(d) to approve the move of any clubs out of Victoria;

(e) to provide financial assistance to any club (other than by payment of advances of final dividends) or to guarantee the obligations of any club;

(f) except expressly authorised in any budget approved by the Board of Directors, to purchase or dispose of any capital asset with a cost of more than $100,000;

(g) except as expressly authorised in any budget approved by the Board of Directors, to borrow any money otherwise than for the ordinary purposes of the League or to give any security for any such borrowing;

(h) to undertake any major capital works (including major works in relation to existing assets of the league) involving a total expenditure of more than $100,000;

(i) to exercise any of the powers of the League in owning or operating any television or radio station; or

(j) to appoint the representatives of the League on the National Football Championships Pty Limited;

(k) to amend any of the laws of the game.

## CRAWFORD REPORT

On August 11, 1992, the AFL Board of Directors adopted a recommendation from the AFL Commission to conduct an independent review of the AFL administrative structure examining specifically:

(i) the respective role and responsibilities of the Commission, Board of Directors and management of the AFL;

(ii) the structure of the Commission, Board of Directors and management of the AFL;

(iii) the relationship between the Commission, the Board of Directors, management of the AFL and the clubs.

Mr David Crawford, a senior partner in the firm of KPMG Peat Marwick, was subsequently appointed to conduct the review.

On March 1, 1993, Mr Crawford presented his report to the Board of Directors and AFL Commission.

On July 19, 1993, the Board of Directors approved new Memorandum and Articles of Association for the AFL which reflected the recommendations of the Crawford Report.

In effect, this was the last meeting of the Board of Directors, consisting of one representative from each club.

Key recommendations of the Crawford Report included:

● Commissioners — up to eight commissioners to be appointed.

● Chairman — to be appointed by the Commission but who should not be the Chief Executive Officer.

The primary role of the Chairman to include:

— Chairing meetings of the Commission.

— Chairing meetings between the Commission and the clubs.

— Acting as a sounding board for the Chief Executive Officer.

● Chief Executive Officer — appointed by the Commission, to be a Commissioner as a matter of right while retaining his position as Chief Executive Officer. To be a voting member of the Commission.

The role would include:

— being responsible for the operating performance of the AFL.

— being responsible for implementation of policy decided by the Commission.

— being the public face of the Commission.

● Admission, re-location or merger of clubs — the AFL Commission has the power to admit, re-locate or merge clubs.

Any such decision by the Commission can be reversed by the clubs at a duly constituted meeting of clubs called within 14 days of receiving formal notice of a Commission decision to admit or re-locate a club or approve the merger of clubs.

A two thirds majority of clubs is required to reverse any such decision of the Commission.

Three clubs may requisition a meeting of clubs to reverse a Commission decision to admit or re-locate a club or approve the merger of clubs.

Clubs cannot be merged unless the clubs who are party to the merger first agree.

● Expulsion of a club — any decision of the AFL Commission to suspend or expel a club must be ratified at a general meeting of clubs on a vote by a simple majority of all clubs who are members of the league on the date of such meeting.

● Other powers — all other powers to run the AFL competition were transferred to the AFL Commission and the AFL Board of Directors as it was constituted was abolished.

# AFL COMMISSION MEMBERS

## RON EVANS — CHAIRMAN
President of Essendon Football Club 1988-1992.
Played 61 games and kicked 209 goals as a full-forward for Essendon from 1958-1962.
Leading VFL Goalkicker in 1959 and 1960.
Managing Director of Spotless Services Limited.
Bachelor of Science (Melbourne University).
Master of Business Administration (Monash University).
Appointed to AFL Commission 1993.

## WAYNE JACKSON — Chief Executive Officer
Former member of the South Australian National Football League Commission, 1990-1995.
Life member of Woodville West Torrens Football Club.
Played 160 games at senior and seconds level with West Torrens.
Also coached the club at senior and reserves level.
Chairman of West Torrens, 1975-1979.
Managing Director of The South Australian Brewing Company, 1993-1996.
General Manager, Thomas Hardy & Sons 1977-1981.
Managing Director Thomas Hardy & Sons 1981-1992. At that time, Thomas Hardy & Sons merged with Berri Renmano Ltd. to become BRL Hardy Limited and the company was publicly floated.
Appointed Business Development Director of BRL Hardy and to the main board in 1992.
Bachelor of Economics (Adelaide University).
Fellow of Australian Society of Certified Practicing Accountants.
Appointed to AFL Commission 1995.
Appointed Chief Executive Officer, October 1996.

## COLIN CARTER
Director of the Boston Consulting Group and played a key role in the development of the report adopted by the original VFL Commission in 1985 "Establishing the Basis of Future Success".
Director of Geelong Football Club 1987-1993.
Bachelor of Commerce (Melbourne University).
Master of Business Administration (Harvard University).
Appointed to AFL Commission 1993.

## BILL KELTY
Graduated as a Bachelor of Economics from La Trobe University, 1969.
Appointed as an industrial officer, Federated Storeman & Packers Union, 1970.
Appointed research officer for Workers' Education Association, Adelaide, 1974.
Requested by ACTU to prepare and present minimum wage case on behalf of the Port Moresby Council of Trade Unions 1974.
Appointed research officer/advocate for ACTU, 1974.
Elected assistant secretary of the ACTU, 1983.
Appointed to the Reserve Bank Board, 1987.
Appointed Chairman of the Commonwealth Government Regional Development Taskforce, 1993.
Other appointments — member of National Labour

Consultative Council since 1977; Committee for Melbourne since 1980 and member of Netforce since 1994.
Appointed to AFL Commission 1998.

## CRAIG KIMBERLEY
Former president of the South Melbourne Football Club, 1976-1977.
Former South Melbourne VFL director, 1975-1991.
Sydney AFL director 1988-1991, 1993.
Chairman of Just Jeans Holdings Limited and has worked in the clothing and textile industry for more than 30 years.
Just Jeans Holdings Limited consists of three operating groups — Just Jeans, which has 303 stores in Australia and New Zealand; Jays Jays which has 59 stores and the Jacqui E chain which has 62 stores.
Recently appointed Chairman of the Woolmark Melbourne Fashion Festival.
Appointed to AFL Commission 1997.

## TERRY O'CONNOR
Chairman of the West Coast Eagles 1990-1993.
Played 300 games of amateur football in Western Australia.
Bachelor of Laws (University of Western Australia).
Appointed Queen's Counsel 1987.
Chairman Ausdrill Limited and Environmental Solutions Limited.
Chancellor University of Notre Dame, Australia.
Chairman Interim West Australian Football Commission.
Appointed to AFL Commission 1993.

## GRAEME SAMUEL
Left a career in law to become executive director of the Macquarie Bank and is now principal of Grant Samuel and Associates, corporate advisers.
Trustee, MCG Trust.
Chairman, Melbourne and Olympic Parks Trust.
Chairman of Opera Australia.
President of the Australian Chamber of Commerce and Industry.
Chairman of the Inner and Eastern Health Care Network.
Councillor of the National Competition Council.
Bachelor of Laws (Melbourne University).
Master of Laws (Monash University).
Appointed to original VFL Commission in 1984.

## DAVID SHAW
Former President of the Essendon Football Club.
Played 177 games and kicked 55 goals for Essendon between 1959-1968.
Member of 1962 and 1965 Essendon premiership teams.
Essendon board member 1971-1974, 1984-1986.
Essendon vice-president 1987-1992
Appointed president of Essendon in 1993, a position he held until his election to the AFL Commission.
Essendon AFL director 1988-1994.
Partner in Melbourne legal practice, Campbell and Shaw, since 1966.
Bachelor of Laws (Melbourne University).
Appointed to AFL Commission 1997.

# AFL ADMINISTRATION

**Ian Collins — General Manager, Football Operations**
Played 163 games and kicked 52 goals for Carlton from 1961–1971 after being recruited from Sale in country Victoria.
Was a member of Carlton's 1968 premiership team and after finishing his career at Carlton, became captain-coach of Port Melbourne in the VFA.
Executive Director of Carlton from 1981–1993.
Life Member of the Carlton Football Club.
Joined the AFL in November, 1993.

**Finance Manager** — Kevin Lehmann
**Communications Manager** — Tony Peek
**Football Administration Manager** — Rod Austin
**Manager–Ground Operations** — Jill Lindsay
**Marketing Manager** — Grant Burgess
**Special Events Manager** — Dean Moore
**Director of Umpire Coaching** — Peter Schwab
**AFL Umpires Coach** — Rowan Sawers
**AFL Membership Manager** — Jennie Loughnan
**Publications Editor** — Michael Lovett
**Senior Writer, Football Record** — Greg Hobbs
**Licensing Manager** — Andrew McKenzie
**Corporate Sales Manager** — Maris O'Sullivan
**Waverley Park Manager** — Graeme Finn
**Player Payments Commissioner** — Ralph Lane
**Special Investigator** — Michael Easy
**Statistician** — Colin Hutchinson

## MEDIA DEPARTMENT CONTACTS
**Communications Manager** — Tony Peek
**Media Co-Ordinator** — Jenny Cooke
**Media Assistant** — Peta Edebone

## AFL TRIBUNAL
Brian Collis, QC (chairman), Michael Green, Brian Le Brocq, Shane Maguire (deputy chairman), Assoc. Prof. David Shilbury, Elaine Canty, Emmett Dunne.

## AFL LAWS COMMITTEE
Wayne Jackson (chairman), Robert Flower, Bob Skilton, Tim Watson, Ian Collins, Kevin Bartlett, Rod Austin, Peter Schwab, Paul Salmon, Dean Moore (secretary).

## UMPIRING SELECTION COMMITTEE
Peter Schwab, Rowan Sawers, Ian Robinson.

## APPEAL BOARD
Peter O'Callaghan, QC (chairman), Brian Bourke, Graham Sherry, John Shultz, Gavin Francis, Tony Nolan. (Others to be appointed during 1998.)

## PRESIDENTS
1897–1915: Alex McCracken, JP
1915–1917: O. Morrice Williams
1918–1919: Charles Brownlow
1919–1925: Sir Baldwin Spencer
1926–1955: Dr. W. M. C. McClelland, CBE, JP
1956–1971: Sir Kenneth Luke, CM., JP
1971–1976: Sir Maurice Nathan, KBE
1977–1984: Dr Allen Aylett, OBE

## LEGAL ADVISER
Jeff Browne

## MEDICAL COMMISSIONER
Prof. Ken Hardy, Dr. Peter Harcourt (deputy).

## COMMISSIONER
1984–1986: J.C. Hamilton, AM

## CHAIRMAN — COMMISSION
1986–1993: R.G. Oakley
1993–97: J. Kennedy
1998–: R. Evans

## EXECUTIVE COMMISSIONER
1986–1993: A. Schwab

## COMMISSIONERS
1985–1991: The Hon. P. Nixon
1985: G.J. Samuel
1985–1993: P. D. Scanlon
1985–1988: R. J. Seddon
1988–1993: A. Mantello
1986–1996: R. G. Oakley
1991–1993: M. Carlile
1993: C. B. Carter
1993: R. B. Evans
1993: T. E. O'Connor, QC
1993–1995: J. S. Winneke, QC
1995: W. R. Jackson
1997: C. Kimberley
1997: D. H. Shaw
1998: W. Kelty

## SECRETARIES/GENERAL MANGERS
1897–1929: E. L. Wilson
1929–1956: L. H. McBrien, OBE
1956–1976: E. O. McCutchan, OBE
1977–1984: J. C. Hamilton, AM
1985–1986: A. Schwab

## AUSTRALIAN FOOTBALL LEAGUE
Australian Football League
Great Southern Stand, MCG
Brunton Ave., Melbourne, 3002.
Telephone: (03) 9643 1999
Fax: (03) 9654 1143
Postal Address: P.O. Box 1449N, Melbourne, 3001.

# SALARY CAP

The salary cap is one of the most important areas relating to the finances of the AFL and its 16 club — but how does the League arrive at the figure clubs are allowed to spend on players?
The simple answer is the salary cap is determined by AFL and club income streams.

## THE SALARY CAP IN PROFILE

Total player payments are made up of the following elements:
- Salary Cap — consists of a percentage of up to 60 per cent of club membership and gate receipts from the premiership season, controlled by AFL clubs and enhanced by AFL strategies, plus broadcast rights and corporate sponsorship controlled by the AFL.
- For 1997, the salary cap was based on:
— club membership and gate
receipts                                    $46.895 million
— gross finals revenue and
broadcast rights                        $31.685 million

- The salary cap for 1997 was $2.9 million per club or 58.9 per cent of the preceding income streams.
   That, however, is only part of the player payments picture, injury payments, Ansett Australia Cup payments and finals' payments are all additional to the salary cap level and in 1997, total player payments per club ranged between $3 million and $3.9 million.

| The year by year growth in total player payments from 1990–97, excluding any CPI allowance is: | |
| --- | --- |
| **Year** | **Million** |
| 1990 | $22.527 |
| 1991 | $26.110 |
| 1992 | $26.588 |
| 1993 | $28.277 |
| 1994 | $32.061 |
| 1995 | $39.830 |
| 1996 | $47.961 |
| 1997 | $55.674 |

## SALARY CAP HISTORY

| | 1985 | 1986 | 1987 | 1988 | 1989 | 1990 | 1991 |
| --- | --- | --- | --- | --- | --- | --- | --- |
| SALARY CAP TOTAL (millions) | 12.65 | 13.1 | 15.2 | 16.9 | 18.2 | 19.6 | 22.5 |
| PERCENTAGE OF INCOME STREAM | 65 | 62 | 59 | 64 | 64 | 59 | 61 |
| NUMBER OF CLUBS | 12 | 12 | 14 | 14 | 14 | 14 | 15 |
| SALARY CAP PER CLUB (millions) | Variable | Variable | Variable | Variable | 1.3 | 1.4 | 1.5 |

| | 1992 | 1993 | 1994 | 1995 | 1996 | 1997 | 1998 |
| --- | --- | --- | --- | --- | --- | --- | --- |
| SALARY CAP TOTAL (millions) | 24 | 26.25 | 27.75 | 36.8 | 40.8 | 47.25 | 51.17 |
| PERCENTAGE OF INCOME STREAM | 56 | 54 | 47 | 53 | 56 | 59 | 60 |
| NUMBER OF CLUBS | 15 | 15 | 15 | 16 | 16 | 16 | 16 |
| SALARY CAP PER CLUB (millions) | 1.6 | 1.75 | *1.85 | *2.3 | *2.55 | 2.9 | 3.2 |

*Excludes special grants to certain clubs

## SUMMARY OF AFL TOTAL PLAYER PAYMENTS 1990-1997

| Year | Under $20,000 | $20,000– $29,000 | $30,000– $39,000 | $40,000– $59,000 | $60,000– $79,000 | $80,000– $99,000 | $100,000– $149,999 | $150,000– $199,000 | $200,000– $249,999 | $250,000– $299,999 | $300,000– $349,000 | $350,000– $399,000 |
| --- | --- | --- | --- | --- | --- | --- | --- | --- | --- | --- | --- | --- |
| 1990 | 153 | 96 | 82 | 111 | 72 | 16 | 8 | — | — | — | — | — |
| 1991 | 148 | 92 | 80 | 128 | 77 | 23 | 14 | 3 | — | — | — | — |
| 1992 | 132 | 69 | 91 | 117 | 93 | 32 | 18 | 1 | 1 | — | — | — |
| 1993 | 103 | 85 | 67 | 118 | 81 | 45 | 29 | 4 | 1 | — | — | — |
| 1994 | 57 | 84 | 80 | 116 | 89 | 58 | 36 | 9 | 1 | — | — | — |
| 1995 | 49 | 63 | 70 | 125 | 93 | 69 | 73 | 18 | 5 | 4 | — | — |
| 1996 | 6 | 64 | 59 | 131 | 102 | 71 | 96 | 30 | 11 | 1 | 2 | — |
| 1997 | — | 27 | 51 | 100 | 118 | 99 | 119 | 40 | 14 | 3 | 1 | 4 |

# PLAYER AGENTS

|  |  | Business phone |
|---|---|---|
| **NEW SOUTH WALES** | | |
| Greg Keenan | Athlete Mgt International, PO Box 232, Randwick, NSW 2031 | (0411) 310531 |
| Rodney Paech | Event Mgt & Marketing P/L, PO Box 316, North Sydney, NSW 2060 | (02) 9954 6227 |
| Darryl Mather | Proserv/ISM, North Sydney, NSW 2065 | (02) 9957 5014 |
| **QUEENSLAND** | | |
| Richard May | C/- KPMG, GPO Box 223, Brisbane, QLD 4001 | (07) 3233 3204 |
| Stuart Rees | C/- Broadley Rees Lawyers, GPO Box 635, Brisbane, QLD 4000 | (07) 3221 1600 |
| Mark Schampers | Sportmode Mgt Aust, 50 Sterculia Ave, Holland Park, QLD 4121 | (07) 3349 9793 |
| Ian Scott | Dunhill, Madden & Butler, GPO Box 2477, Brisbane, QLD 4001 | (07) 3307 8802 |
| **SOUTH AUSTRALIA** | | |
| Michael Ardlie | Wallmans Solicitors, GPO Box 1018, Adelaide, SA 5001 | (08) 8235 3000 |
| Paul Brown | Ford McCarthy & Associates, 142 Grange Road, Flinders Park, SA 5025 | (08) 8346 9591 |
| Robert Coleman | 3 Dessasenay Cres, Modbury Heights, SA 5092 | (0411) 733 834 |
| John Crouch | Pro Edge, PO Box 196, Prospect, SA 5082 | (08) 8269 1455 |
| Ian Gray | Sportslife Consulting, 312A Unley Road, Hyde Park, SA 5061 | (08) 8373 2055 |
| Gregory Griffin | Griffins, 14th Fl, 26 Flinders St, Adelaide, SA 5000 | (08) 410 2020 |
| Rick Harley | Pro Edge, C/- Ward and Partners, GPO Box 439, Adelaide, SA 5000 | (08) 8414 3373 |
| Brenton Hart | Australian Player Mgt, 68 Beatrice Street, Prospect, SA 5082 | (08) 8344 9018 |
| Peter Krieg | Krieg Sports Management, 13 Campbell Road, Parkside, SA 5063 | (0412) 822 144 |
| David McKay | Sports Power Management, 15 Stuart Road, Dulwich, SA 5065 | (08) 8332 2733 |
| Adrian O'Dea | C/- Arthur Anderson, 12 Pirie Street, Adelaide, SA 5000 | (08) 8217 2975 |
| Kym Richardson | Aussie Sports Action, 18 Blinkbrae Ave., Happy Valley, SA 5159 | (015) 976 240 |
| Max Stevens | Flying Start, PO Box 101, Henley Beach, SA 5022 | (08) 8356 1150 |
| Nigel Thompson | Concept Endeavours, PO Box 284, Belair, SA 5052 | (08) 8363 5224 |
| Craig Vozzo | Bonnins Commercial Lawyers, 14, 100 King William St, Adelaide, SA 5000 | (08) 8231 0360 |
| Timothy White | Tindal, Gask, Bensley, 76 Light Square, Adelaide, SA 5000 | (08) 8212 1077 |
| **VICTORIA** | | |
| Robert Aivatoglou | Advantage International, Suite 16, 663 Victoria St, Abbotsford, VIC 3067 | (03) 9427 9655 |
| Harvey Allatt | Harvey Allatt & Co Pty Ltd, PO Box 71, Hawksburn, VIC 3142 | (03) 9521 2055 |
| John Andrews | Elite Sports Properties, Level 1, 177 Bridge Rd, Richmond, VIC 3121 | (03) 9374 2222 |
| Michael Baker | Baker Smith All Sports Mgt, PO Box 14082, Melbourne, VIC 8001 | (03) 9696 7150 |
| Dominic Barba | Barba & Barba Pty Ltd, PO Box 660, Sunshine, VIC 3020 | (03) 9311 3699 |
| Enrico Belli | E.P.B. Associates Pty Ltd, PO Box 1500, Carlton, VIC 3053 | (03) 9650 0011 |
| Stephen Carr | SGC Management Services, 2 Railway Parade, Murrumbeena, VIC 3163 | (03) 9565 1672 |
| Shane Casley | Elite Sports Properties, Level 1, 177 Bridge Rd, Richmond, VIC 3121 | (03) 9629 1600 |
| Scott Christiansen | Christiansen Sports Mgt., Unit 1, 10 Chippewa Ave, Mitcham, VIC 3132 | (03) 9872 3888 |
| Paul Connors | Flying Start (Aust.) P/L, Level 2, 25–31 Rokeby St, Collingwood, VIC 3066 | (03) 9419 9300 |
| Len Cox | Cox Hanley & Walker, Level 2, 40 Burwood Rd, Hawthorn, VIC 3122 | (03) 9819 1744 |
| Richard Custerson | A Positive Move Pty Ltd, PO Box 4008, Langwarrin, VIC 3910 | (03) 9775 7665 |
| Peter Fitzgerald | PDO Consulting Service, 17th Fl., 500 Collins St, Melbourne, VIC 3000 | (03) 9614 3771 |
| Tony Free | Advantage International Pty Ltd, Abbotsford, VIC 3067 | (03) 9427 9655 |
| Robert Hession | C/- Hardy's Solicitors, PO Box 321, Dandenong, VIC 3175 | (03) 9791 7222 |
| Alan Hickling | Heidelberg Corporate Group , PO Box 448, Heidelberg, VIC 3084 | (03) 9457 1700 |
| Dean Humphries | 21 Miniata Walk, Vermont South, VIC 3133 | (014) 014 442 |
| Manuel Imbardelli | C/- Somerville and Co, PO Box 139, Balwyn, VIC 3103 | (03) 9888 5644 |
| Peter Jess | PO Box 215, Essendon, VIC 3040 | (03) 9375 4225 |
| Bruce Kaider | Priority 1 Sports, 504 Elizabeth Drive, Sunbury, VIC 3429 | (03) 9744 2658 |
| Genc Kalaja | Kalaja Clifton Solicitors, Level 1, 434 St. Kilda Rd, Melbourne, VIC 3004 | (03) 9281 3871 |
| Michael Kearney | Wilson Kearney Sports Mgt, PO Box 624, Ballarat, VIC 3353 | (03) 5331 1599 |
| Robert Krause | Elite Player Services, 212 Bellbridge Drive, Hoppers Crossing, VIC 3029 | (03) 9748 7126 |

**Business phone**

| | | |
|---|---|---|
| Kieran Liston | Kieran Liston & C, 444 Waverly Road, East Malvern, VIC 3145 | (03) 9572 3366 |
| Chris McLeod | Freehill, Hollingdale & Page, Level 47, 101 Collins St, Melbourne, VIC 3000 | (03) 9288 1490 |
| Perry Meka | Sportiff Management, 9 Polworth Place, Shepparton, VIC 3630 | (03) 5831 7676 |
| Peter Niblett | Obbin Management, 35 Arden Avenue, Leopold, VIC 3224 | (0412) 118544 |
| Ricky Nixon | Flying Start (Aust) Pty Ltd, Level 2, 25–31 Rokeby St, Collingwood, VIC 3066 | (03) 9419 9300 |
| Robert Petrie | R.J. Business Development, PO Box 538, Richmond, VIC 3121 | (03) 9844 1663 |
| John Phillips | C.W. Stirling & Co., 5th Fl, 499 St. Kilda Rd, Melbourne, VIC 3004 | (03) 9867 4011 |
| Craig Richards | Madgwicks Solicitors, Fl. 19,535 Bourke Street, Melbourne, VIC 3000 | (03) 9242 4774 |
| Paul Robinson | Sportshow Australia, PO Box 300, Toorak, VIC 3142 | (03) 9826 0099 |
| John Robson | PO Box 441, Mitcham, VIC 3132 | (03) 9874 7744 |
| John Ryan | The Management Works, PO Box 1184, North Fitzroy, VIC 3068 | (03) 9486 7061 |
| Don Smarrelli | Newbury Bell Solicitors, 11/455 Bourke Street, Melbourne, VIC 3000 | (03) 9670 8561 |
| Damien Smith | 160 Whitehorse Road, Balwyn, VIC 3103 | (03) 9618 4252 |
| Geoffrey Turner | G.A. Turner & Associates, PO Box 275, Ivanhoe, VIC 3079 | (03) 9499 7677 |
| Marvin Weinberg | Cohen, Woolf & Weinberg, 3/608 St. Kilda Rd, Melbourne, VIC 3004 | (03) 9521 2244 |
| Peter Wilson | Nevett Ford Lawyers, PO Box 564, Ballarat, VIC 3350 | (03) 5331 4444 |
| Gavan Woodruff | UAS Accountants, PO Box 441, Balwyn, VIC 3103 | (03) 9830 2388 |

**WESTERN AUSTRALIA**

| | | |
|---|---|---|
| Glen Bartlett | Barker Gosling, PO Box 7222, Cloisters Square, WA 6850 | (08) 9321 1211 |
| Colin Emmott | Mann Judd, PO Box 263, West Perth, WA 6872 | (09) 481 0977 |
| Reg Gillard | Specialist Sports Mgt, Grd Floor, 30 Ledgar Rd, Balcutta, WA 6021 | (08) 9240 2836 |
| Nick Greenwood | Nick Greenwood Pty Ltd, 2 Fell Place, Wembley Downs, WA 6019 | (08) 9245 3147 |
| Gavin Jahn | Curtin University, PO Box U1987, Perth, WA 6001 | (0419) 916 201 |
| Phil Lamb | White Line Management, PO Box 1737, West Perth, WA 6872 | (09) 481 0166 |
| Jamie Lockyer | Auspeak Management, 35 Walter Street, East Fremantle, WA 6158 | (08) 9339 5155 |
| Stephen McComish | Wesport Management, Level 11, 15 William St, Perth, WA 6000 | (09) 483 0123 |
| Colin Minson | C.M. Promotions, 138 Seacrest Drive, Sorrento, WA 6020 | (08) 8447 8355 |
| Arthur Papas | Tandem Sports Mgt Group, 11 Stanley Street, Dianella, WA 6059 | (0411) 742 346 |
| Adam Sierakowski | Wesport Management, PO Box H584, Perth, WA 6001 | (08) 9221 9199 |
| Trevor Sprigg | Sprint Consultants, 12 Dowell Place, Bibra Lake, WA 6163 | (09) 417 1971 |
| Jim Tsagalis | Boss Sports Management, PO Box 7117, Cloisters Square, WA 6850 | (0418) 927 462 |

# MAJOR LAWS OF THE GAME

*Some laws, which are not related to the operation of the game during play, have been deleted for space reasons*

## 1.0 PLAYING GROUND, OVAL, GOAL AND BEHIND POSTS

1.1 The playing ground shall be oval in shape, between 135-185 metres in length, and between 110-155 metres in width.

1.1.2 A circle three metres in diameter shall be marked in the centre of the ground and divided with a white line into two semi-circles laterally, such line to extend a maximum two metres on each side of the diameter. A square of 45 metres shall also be marked in white in the centre of the ground. In circumstances where centre areas are deemed to be impractical for bouncing a football, Controlling Bodies may approve relocation of the square.

1.1.3 Two two-metre lines across the boundary line, 15 metres apart, shall mark the interchange area.

1.1.4 The ideal playing area is 165 metres in length and 135 metres in width.

1.2 Two goal posts 6.4 metres apart and not less than six metres in height shall be placed at each end of the playing ground.

1.3 Two behind posts shall be placed at a distance of 6.4 metres from each goal post and in a straight line with them. The minimum height of the posts should be three metres.

1.5 Two lines shall be drawn at right angles to the goal line for a distance of nine metres from each post. The outer end of these lines shall be connected by a straight line. These lines shall be marked in white and known as the kick off lines.

## 2.0 THE BALL

2.1 Dimensions: Footballs shall conform to a standard size of 720-730 millimetres by 545-555 millimetres and to the shape and standard specification approved by the Australian Football League.

2.2 Weight: The dry weight of the inflated ball shall be between 450 and 500 grams.

2.3 Provision of footballs: In the absence of other arrangements, the home team shall provide the ball for the match, giving the visiting team the choice of two new balls which have been approved by the umpires. Unless the captains agree to a change, the same ball shall be used throughout the match.

## 3.0 TEAMS

3.1 The team shall consist of fourteen to eighteen players, on the field of play at any one time and up to four interchange players.

3.1.1 The controlling body shall determine the number of players.

3.1.2 Prior to the commencement of play an official of each team shall hand to the field umpire a list of names and numbers of the players comprising the team and indicating the captain and interchange players who will not take part in the match at its commencement.

3.1.3 At any time during the course of the match, one of the players not then taking part in the match may be interchanged with one of the participating players.

3.1.4 Should circumstances require a player's number to be changed the team runner should advise a field umpire during the next interval, or at the first available opportunity if the change occurs during the final quarter.

3.1.5 The official runner and other team officials approved by the Controlling Body must wear the uniform determined by the Controlling Body and be easily identifiable by the Umpire (by way of arm band or otherwise) and name/s shall appear on the team sheet of the team concerned.

It shall be the responsibility of the Controlling Body to document circumstances in which such officials may enter the playing area and to produce guidelines covering the specific duties when on the arena. Umpires shall report any breach of such guidelines to the controlling body.

3.2 The procedures for the interchange of players shall be as follows:

3.2.1 If there is in attendance a steward appointed by the controlling body to supervise the operation of this law, the captain, the official runner or one other nominated club official, shall request permission from the steward, to make the replacement of one named player by another named player.

3.2.2 The steward shall be stationed throughout the match in a prominent position as close to the boundary line as the controlling body shall approve.

3.2.3 Players shall leave and enter the playing ground through the interchange area during the match unless the player is taken from the playing ground on a stretcher, in which case he may be taken from the playing ground at any point. His replacement shall enter the playing ground through the interchange area. The replaced player may return to the playing ground by way of normal interchange.

3.2.4 The steward, on being satisfied that the proposed replacement is permitted under the provision of this law, shall give his permission which shall hold good for a period of three minutes from it being given, but shall then lapse if not acted upon.

3.2.5 When it is necessary for a player to be taken from the playing ground on a stretcher, the field umpire shall stop play at the first appropriate opportunity after he is advised that a stretcher is on the playing ground and play will not recommence until the stretcher has left the playing ground and is outside the boundary fence or located in an area approved by the controlling body.

3.2.6 When a player has been, or appears to have been, so seriously injured as to prevent his being removed immediately from the playing ground, the steward may approve his replacement prior to leaving the ground.

3.2.7 If a steward is not in attendance, the field umpire shall perform these duties. A request to make a replacement shall only be made during a period when time is being added to the playing time.

3.3 The field umpire shall at the request of either captain, stop the match and call the players of the opposing team into line for the purpose of a team count. Such players shall line up in the centre square and remain until dismissed by the field umpire. The field umpire shall report to the controlling body upon every such request and result.

3.3.1 If a team has been counted and found to have more than the permitted number of players on the field, taking into account players ordered from the field where a replacement of such players is not permitted, a Controlling Body shall impose a penalty by way of reverse of match result, annulment of score or part thereof, fine or censure as it shall consider proper.

3.4 Subject to the approval of the Australian Football League, the controlling body in each State may reduce or increase the number of players who shall take part in any match. A State controlling body may similarly grant this authority to an affiliated league or association.

## 4.0 PLAYERS' BOOTS JEWELLERY AND PROTECTIVE EQUIPMENT

4.1 No player shall be permitted to play in a match with apparel or protective equipment which may cause injury to himself or his opponents. This shall include:

4.1.1 Bootstuds or plates considered dangerous.

4.1.2 A finger ring or other jewellery.

4.1.3 Surgical appliances or guards.

4.2 A field umpire may inspect players boots, hands and guards prior to the commencement of play or at any time prior to the conclusion of the match. The Field Umpire shall have the sole prerogative to determine whether apparel or protective equipment has the potential to cause injury.

## 5.0 STARTING THE MATCH

5.3 Prior to starting the match, the umpire shall consult the captains as to the readiness of their teams.

5.4 Unless a free kick has been awarded, to commence play at the start of each quarter the field umpire shall hold the ball aloft, sound his whistle and bounce the ball in the circle. Match timing shall commence on the sound of the whistle or when the ball is brought into play in the event of a free kick.

5.4.2 The field umpire shall take up a position on the white line either side of the centre circle prior to bouncing the ball.

5.4.3 The above procedure is followed except when a free kick has been given after a goal has been registered and before the ball is bounced in the circle.

5.4.4 The field umpire has the authority to throw the ball in the air in the event of the ground surface being considered unsuitable for bouncing. In such event the umpire shall indicate to players that he intends to throw the ball up.

5.5 A maximum of four players of each team is permitted in the square for the centre bounce. No officials are permitted in the square for the centre bounce. No player or official is permitted to enter the square or centre circle from the time the field umpire commences his approach to the centre circle until the ball touches the ground in the act of bouncing or leaves the umpires hand in the act of being thrown up.

The centre bounce or throw up shall be contested only by one player of each team who shall take up a position outside the centre circle in his team's defensive half. Neither of these players shall enter his team's attacking half until the ball touches the ground in the act of bouncing or leaves the umpire's hand in the act of being thrown up.

Where the umpire determines that a poor bounce has occurred he shall call "play on" and the ball may then be contested by any player.

5.5.1 In the event of a breach of this Law by a player or official, the field umpire shall award a free kick to a player of the opposing side nearest the centre circle.

5.5.2 If an injured player is receiving attention from medical or training staff in the centre square at a time when the centre bounce is to occur, the field umpire will not commence play until the player is removed from the square.

In the event that the field umpire's direction to remove the player is not immediately complied with a free kick shall be awarded to a player of the opposing side nearest the centre circle; unless the field umpire has given permission for the player to leave the ground on a stretcher under Law 3.2.5.

5.6 The field umpire shall report to the controlling body any club which is not ready to start at the appointed time.

## 6.0 GOALS AND BEHINDS

6.1 A goal shall register six points and a behind one point.

6.2 When a ball crosses a goal or behind line or hits a goal post, the field umpire shall give the goal umpire an "All Clear" signal if there have not been any incidents in play which the field umpire intends to penalise.

6.3 A score cannot be registered unless the field umpire calls or indicates "All Clear", or "Touched, All Clear" to the goal umpire.

6.4 Subject to the "All Clear" signal, a goal shall be scored when the ball is kicked over the goal line by a player of the attacking team without touching a player or a goal post. A behind shall be scored in any other case when the ball passes over the goal line, or touches or passes over a goal post or passes over a behind line without touching or passing over a behind post.

6.4.1 If a defending player kicks or takes the ball over the goal or behind line, a behind shall be scored.

6.4.2 If the ball touches or passes over a behind post, it shall be out of bounds.

6.4.3 The fact that the ball has struck or touched an umpire (or any other authorised official or replaced player) shall not prevent the scoring of a goal or a behind.

6.4.4 While the ball is on the ground and a player has his hands on it, and if another player kicks the ball, it shall be deemed to have been touched in transit. If the ball goes over the goal or behind lines, the field umpire shall call "Touched, All Clear" and a behind shall be registered.

6.4.5 In the event that the ball crosses a goal or behind line, or hits a goal post, and the goal umpire does not receive an all clear from the field umpire and play continues, the goal umpire shall run after the field umpire and notify him at once.

On receipt of such advice, the field umpire shall stop play and give the all clear.

The goal umpire shall signal and record the score and play shall recommence in accordance with these laws.

In the event that a free kick has been awarded after the ball crosses the line and before the all clear has been given, the field umpire shall give the all clear and the goal umpires shall signal and record the score. The free kick shall then be taken where the infringement occurred or where the ball is at the time, whichever is the greater penalty against the offending team.

6.4.6 In the event that, after the all clear has been given for a goal, an infringement occurs to a player of the defending team prior to the ball being bounced in the centre circle, the resultant free kick shall be taken at the spot where the infringement occurred, or at the centre circle, whichever is the greater penalty against the offending team.

6.4.7 In the event that, after the all clear has been given for a behind, an infringement occurs to a player of the defending team prior to the ball being kicked off after the behind, the resultant free kick shall be taken at the spot where the infringement occurred, or at the back line of the centre square, whichever is the greater penalty against the offending team.

6.5 The goal umpires shall be the final judges of goals and behinds, but may be assisted by other umpires as required. The goal umpires' decisions are final, except when the ball has become dead by a decision of the field umpire.

6.5.1 Upon receiving "All Clear", the goal umpire shall intitially indicate a goal by raising both index fingers, and a behind by raising one index finger.

6.5.2 The goal umpire shall then signal a goal by waving two flags, and a behind by waving one flag. A score cannot be annulled unless the goal umpire immediately rectifies a mistake by notifying the field umpire before the ball is bounced in the centre if he has wrongly signalled a goal or before the ball is kicked off in the case of a behind except when the ball has been signalled out of bounds and the signal has not been seen by the field umpire.

6.5.3 When a score has been annulled, the goal umpire shall immediately stand on the centre of the goal line and hold both flags above his head in crossed position.

6.5.4 Controlling bodies may provide for field umpires to over-rule decisions of goal umpires not formally appointed by the controlling body concerned.

6.6 At the first sound of the siren, the ball shall be dead, but a player who has, prior to the first sound of the siren, taken a mark or been awarded a free kick shall be allowed to kick or handball the ball. A goal or behind obtained therefrom or from a ball which is in transit prior to the first sound of the siren shall be counted.

In the event that the siren sounds whilst the ball is in transit, or whilst the player taking a kick after the siren is preparing to kick the ball, or after he has kicked the ball, an infringement occurs to a player of the attacking team before the all clear has been given, the field umpire shall blow his whistle and consult with the goal umpire as to whether a goal or behind has been kicked.

If a goal has been kicked the field umpire shall give

the all clear and the goal shall be registered. In the event that a behind has been kicked, the player offended against shall be given the option of taking the free kick at the spot the infringement occurred, or allowing the behind to be registered.

Should the siren sound whilst the ball is in transit, or whilst the player taking a kick after the siren is preparing to kick the ball, or after he has kicked the ball, an infringement occurs to a player of the defending team before the all clear has been given, the field umpire shall award a free kick to the player offended against at the spot where the infringement occurred.

6.6.1 In the event that two or more field umpires are officiating, the ball shall be deemed dead when one of the field umpires hears the first sound of the siren. That field umpire shall be the sole judge of whether the ball has been kicked or handled or whether a free kick has been awarded prior to the first sound of the siren.

6.6.2 If the ball is touched in transit the field umpire must be satisfied that the score was not assisted by a teammate.

6.7 Controlling bodies shall authorise such officials as they deem appropriate to record scores, separate from the goal umpires. In the event of the goal umpires disagreeing on the final scores, the controlling body may take the separately recorded scores into consideration in determining the result of the match.

## 7.0 KICKING OFF FROM BEHIND

7.1 When a behind has been scored, unless a subsequent free kick has been given, any player of the defending team shall kick the ball into the field of play from within the kick off lines, the ball contact being made before the ball completely crosses the line. When the ball is being kicked off, no player shall be allowed within five metres of the kick off lines.

7.2 The player kicking off may regain possession provided the ball has been kicked into the field of play beyond the kick off lines.

7.3 If the ball is not brought into play correctly, the field umpire shall bounce the ball on the centre of the kick off line.

7.4 The ball shall not be kicked off until the goal umpire has finished waving the flag.

7.5 If an opposing player attempts to delay play by moving to or standing within five metres of the kick off line or prevents the player from kicking off, the field umpire shall penalise the offending team by advancing the mark from the kick off line to the back line of the centre square — the kick to be taken at the centre of the line by the nearest player of the team offended against.

In the event of a further offence against this Law, the mark to be advanced to the forward line of the centre square — the kick to be taken at the centre of the line by the nearest player of the team offended against.

7.6 If after the goal umpire has finished waving the flag a player will not kick off (time being added) when directed to do so by the field umpire, or kicks the ball over the goal or behind line, the field umpire shall bounce the ball on the centre of the kick off line.

## 8.0 MARKING THE BALL

8.1 A mark is catching the ball directly from the kick of another player, not less than 10 metres distant, the ball being held a reasonable time and not having been touched in transit from kick to catch.

8.1.1 A mark shall be awarded to a player who crosses the boundary line from the playing ground but controls the ball before it has passed completely over the boundary line. If the field umpire is in doubt he should consult the boundary umpire.

8.1.2 A mark shall be allowed when the ball is caught and controlled on the goal, behind or boundary lines.

8.1.3 A mark will be awarded where a ball in flight strikes an umpire, or any other authorised official or replaced player.

8.2 When a player takes a mark or is given a free kick, an opponent is permitted to stand on the mark or spot where this occurrence took place.

8.2.1 Only one opponent may stand on a player's mark.

8.2.2 No other player is allowed within a corridor which extends from five metres either side of the mark to five metres either side of, and a five metre radius behind, the player with the ball. This corridor is to be known as the ten metre protected area.

8.2.3 In the event of an opponent encroaching over the mark when a player is kicking for goal and a goal is kicked, the field umpire shall give the "All Clear" and the goal shall be registered. If a goal has not been kicked, the player shall be given the option of another kick, and the mark shall be advanced 50 metres.

## 9.0 BALL DISPOSAL

The ball may be kicked or handballed.

9.1 A player shall handball the ball by holding the ball in one hand and hitting it with the clenched fist of the other hand. If the ball is not handballed correctly, a free kick shall be given to the nearest opponent.

9.2 A player may kick the ball by making contact with the ball below the knee.

9.2.1 A player who takes a mark or is awarded a free kick shall play the ball from directly behind the spot where the mark or free kick was awarded. The ten metre protected area shall apply. If the player attempts to play the ball other than in a direct line over the mark, the field umpire shall call "Play On" and the ball shall immediately be in play.

9.2.2 When it is necessary for a defending player, from a free kick or mark, to play the ball from beyond the goal or behind line, or adjacent boundary line, the player on the mark shall not be permitted to come within five metres of the goal or behind lines or adjacent boundary line. In such cases, the ball must be played directly over the mark.

If there is no player on the mark, the ball may be played in any direction provided it is brought into play over the goal, behind or boundary line originally crossed.

9.2.3 When a player is kicking for goal from a mark or a free kick, the kick shall be taken along a direct line through the mark to the centre of the goal line.

9.2.4 The ball shall be deemed to be brought into play when any portion of it is on or above the boundary line.

9.2.5 If a player taking his kick from outside the boundary line after having been awarded a mark or a free kick, fails to take the ball into play, or attempts to

play on outside the boundary line, the ball shall be deemed to be out of bounds. The ball will then be thrown into play by the boundary umpire from the spot where the original mark or free kick took place.

9.2.6 If a player on the defending team, from a free kick or mark, kicks from behind the goal or behind lines and the ball hits either a goal or behind post, the field umpire shall direct the time keepers to add time on and give the player another kick to put the ball into play.

## 10.0 BALL POSSESSION

10.1 A player may hold the ball for any length of time provided he is not held by an opponent.

10.2 If he runs with the ball he must bounce it or touch it on the ground at least once within every 15 metres from the commencement of his run, whether running in a straight line or turning and dodging.

10.3 If a player with the ball bounces it, he is deemed to be in possession of the ball.

10.4 If he runs with the ball and handballs it over an opponent's head and catches it, he must, within 15 metres of commencing his run or striking the ball on the ground, bounce it or touch the ground with it or dispose of the ball.

10.5 A player who lies on or over the ball is deemed to be in possession of the ball.

## 11.0 HOW A PLAYER MAY BE CHECKED OR TACKLED

11.1 A player may be fairly met or checked by an opponent by the use of the hip, shoulder, chest, arms or open hand provided the ball is not more than five metres away.

11.2 A player may be pushed in the chest or side or shepherded by an opponent provided the ball is not more than five metres away.

11.3 A player in possession of the ball may fend off a prospective tackler by pushing him with an open hand in the chest, shoulder or side.

11.4 A player in possession of the ball may be tackled and grasped in the area below the top of the shoulders and on or above the knees. The tackle may be from front, side or behind provided that the tackle from behind does not thrust forward the player with the ball.

11.5 Procedures for administering this law are as follows:

11.5.1 A player in possession of the ball who has had a reasonable time (prior opportunity) to dispose of the ball must, when legally held by an opponent firmly enough to retard his progress, dispose of the ball by a kick or handball within a reasonable time of being held, otherwise a free kick shall be awarded against the player for failing to dispose of the ball in a legal manner.

11.5.2 The field umpire shall bounce the ball when the player with the ball has the ball held to his body by an opponent, unless the player has had a reasonable time to dispose of the ball prior to being tackled in which case a free kick shall be awarded for holding the ball.

11.5.3 A player who elects to dive on the ball and/or drag the ball under him when he is on the ground, will be penalised for holding the ball if he does not immediately hit the ball clear when held legally.

11.5.4 A player not in possession of the ball when held by an opponent, shall be awarded a free kick.

11.5.5 When a player claims a mark, the ball having been touched in transit, and retains possession when held by an opponent, the field umpire shall not award a free kick but bounce the ball if he is satisfied that the player did not hear his call of "Play On". But if the ball has been taken away from the player by another player, the field umpire's call "Play On" shall hold good.

11.5.6 The field umpire shall allow play to continue if a player in the act of kicking or handball, is swung off balance and his foot or hand does not connect with the ball.

11.5.7 The field umpire shall allow play to continue if a player is bumped and the ball falls from his hands.

11.5.8 The field umpire shall allow play to continue when a player's arm is knocked, causing him to drop the ball.

11.5.9 The field umpire shall allow play to continue if a player has his arms pinned to his sides causing him to drop the ball.

11.5.10 The field umpire shall allow play to continue if a player is pulled by one arm or swung causing the ball to fall from his hand.

## 12.0 FREE KICKS

12.1 The spirit of the laws relating to awarding free kicks is:

12.1.1 The player who makes the ball his sole objective shall be given every opportunity to gain possession of the ball.

12.1.2 The player who has possession of the ball and is held by an opponent shall be given a reasonable time to kick or handball the ball.

12.1.3 The ball shall be kept in motion. The field umpire shall call "Play On" even though a free kick should have been awarded but by so doing would penalise the team offended against.

12.2 All breaches of the laws shall be penalised whether the ball is dead or in play. The field umpire shall sound his whistle for the awarding of a free kick. Unless otherwise specified, the player nearest to the opponent who commits a breach of the Laws shall receive the free kick.

12.2.1 If the field umpire has sounded his whistle for a free kick, he may cancel such a free kick by calling "Play On" if the side offended against will be penalised by enforcing the free kick.

Should the field umpire cancel a free kick he may reverse the decision if it is obvious that it is not to the advantage of the team concerned.

12.2.2 A player awarded a free kick must go back to the spot where the breach occurred before being allowed to kick or play the ball. If such player kicks or plays the ball without complying with this law, the field umpire shall stop play and enforce compliance.

12.2.3 A free kick shall be awarded against a player who throws or hands the ball to another player, or to the advantage of play, while the ball is in play.

12.2.4 When a player who has taken a mark or been awarded a free kick is, in the opinion of the field umpire, unable to dispose of the ball through accident or the deliberate action of an opponent, the field umpire shall award a free kick to the nearest player of the same team at the time the incident occurred.

The kick shall be taken at the spot nearest to where the incident occurred.

12.2.5 If a player has been awarded a free kick or a mark, and before the kick is taken a further breach of the laws is made by a player on the same side as the first offender, the field umpire shall sound his whistle and direct the free kick to be taken by a teammate at the spot where the subsequent breach took place, if doing so will penalise the offending team. Where a subsequent breach is committed by a teammate of the player taking the kick, a free kick shall be given to the nearest opponent at the spot of the original free kick, if doing so will penalise the offending team.

12.2.6 If a breach of the laws is committed, regardless of the position on the field, the free kick is to be taken at the spot where the infringement occurred, or where the ball is, or is deemed to be at the time, whichever would be the greater penalty for the offending team.

12.2.7 A free kick shall be given if a player infringes any of the laws between the time the field umpire sounds his whistle and bounces the ball.

12.3 Free kicks for infringements concerning the field umpire bouncing the ball will be awarded against the player who:

12.3.1 Enters the centre circle when the field umpire is in the act of bouncing the ball at the start of the match, the start of each quarter, and after a goal has been scored.

12.3.2 Interferes with an opponent from the time the ball has been bounced in the centre circle until the ball subsequently makes contact with a player or the ground.

12.3.3 Unduly interferes with the bouncing of the ball by the field umpire or deliberately interferes with an umpire during the progress of the match.

12.4 A free kick will be awarded against a player who interferes with an opponent in the following manner:

12.4.1 Interferes with an opponent from the time the ball goes out of bounds, until the ball, after being thrown in by the boundary umpire, makes contact with a player or the ground.

12.4.2 When a goal is kicked by a player, and while the ball is being kicked or is in transit a breach of the laws is made by an opponent, the field umpire shall give the "All Clear" signal and the goal shall be registered; but in the event of a behind being scored the ball not having touched the ground or player, the player shall be given the option of another kick.

12.4.3 After the ball has been kicked and an infringement occurs, and the ball crosses the behind line on the full or hits the goal post on the full, the option of another kick shall be given to the player who originally kicked the ball at the spot from where the kick originated. If the breach of the laws occurred before or during the act of kicking or handball, a free kick shall be taken by the player offended against, at the spot where the breach occurred, provided that the team offended against will not be penalised by the taking of such a free kick.

12.4.4 If a breach of the Laws is made by a player of the attacking side, the field umpire shall not signal "All Clear" but must award a free kick, to the nearest player of the defending team.

12.4.5 If a player is fouled immediately after scoring a goal or behind and after the field umpire has given the "All Clear", the field umpire shall award such player a free kick at the spot where the offence took place. Another score may then be registered without the ball having been bounced in the centre circle or kicked off.

12.4.6 If a breach of the laws is committed against a player who has disposed of the ball, or who is shepherding for a teammate with the ball, and this occurs after the ball has been kicked or handballed, a penalty free kick shall be awarded to a player of the team offended against at the spot where the ball first touched the ground, a player, was marked or went out of bounds. If the awarding of such a free kick will penalise the team offended against, the free kick shall be given to the player who originally kicked the ball.

12.4.7 Trips or kicks, attempts to trip or kick or slings an opponent, or when not in possession of the ball, kicks in a manner likely to cause injury to an opponent, or strikes or attempts to strike an opponent with either hand or arm or deliberately with the knee.

12.5 A free kick shall be awarded against a player who kicks the ball out of bounds in the following manner:

12.5.1 Kicks the ball out of bounds on the full. The free kick shall be taken at the spot where the ball went out of bounds.

12.5.2 When kicking off after a behind has been registered, the ball is kicked out of bounds without it having been touched by any player, a free kick shall be given at the spot where the ball went out of bounds.

12.5.3 Wilfully kicks or forces the ball out of bounds without it being touched by another player.

12.6 A free kick shall be awarded against the player who checks or tackles an opponent in the following manner:

12.6.1 Catches hold of an opponent below the knee or by the neck or head, which includes the top of the shoulder.

12.6.2 Charges an opponent.

12.6.3 Pushes an opponent from behind in any way, except when legitimately going for a mark, a player may interfere with an opponent from behind.

12.6.4 Pushes, bumps or shepherds an opponent in the face, head, neck or in the shoulder.

12.6.5 Pushes, bumps or shepherds an opponent who is in the air for a mark.

12.6.6 Shepherds an opponent when the ball is more than five metres away or is out of play.

12.6.7 Deliberately holds back or throws an opponent after that opponent has kicked or handballed the ball. No free kick shall be given if the player, unable to release his hold at once, throws the opponent down.

12.7 A free kick shall be awarded against a player who interferes with play as follows:

12.7.1 If the ball is in transit towards goal from a free kick, mark or field kick and an opponent shakes the goal post, the field umpire shall give the player the option of a free kick, if in the umpires's opinion, the opponent's action could have affected the result. The free kick is to be taken at the centre of the goal line.

12.7.2 If a teammate shakes the goal post, the field umpire shall award a free kick to the nearest opponent at the spot from where the ball was kicked.

12.8 A free kick shall be awarded against a player who wilfully wastes time by not allowing the ball to be brought into play prior to, or when directed to do so, by the field umpire.

12.9 A free kick shall be awarded against the team as follows:

12.9.1 Any official runner, trainer, medical officer, other approved team official or replaced player who interferes with the ball, the play or a player of the opposing team during the course of the game shall cause the field umpire to award a free kick to the nearest player of the team offended against at the spot of the infringement, or where the ball is at the time, whichever would be a greater penalty to the offending team.

When a player is awarded a set kick at goal and an opposition player climbs on the shoulders of a teammate before the kick is taken, the mark shall be advanced to the centre of the goal line and the player with the kick shall be permitted to kick from directly in front of goal.

12.9.2 A free kick shall be awarded against a player who carries the ball across the boundary line, and after a boundary umpire signals out of bounds, does not give the ball immediately to the boundary umpire or drop it directly to the ground.

12.9.3 A free kick shall be awarded against a player who touches the ball after it has passed outside the boundary line and been signalled out of bounds by the boundary umpire, except for a player of the team to receive the free kick when the ball has been kicked out on the full, kicked out directly from a kick off from a behind, or wilfully kicked or forced out without being touched by another player.

12.9.4 A free kick shall be awarded against a player who uses abusive, insulting or obscene language to an umpire or behaves in an abusive, insulting or obscene manner towards an umpire.

12.10 Controlling bodies may authorise umpires to award a free kick where a breach of the laws has occurred on the field of play prior to the commencement of a quarter. The free kick to be taken where the infringement occurred or at the centre circle, whichever is the greater penalty to the offending team.

## 13.0 50 METRE PENALTY

13.1 A 50 metre penalty will be applied in instances where the actions of a player encroach over the mark, waste time and/or delay the play or where a player uses abusive, insulting or obscene language to an umpire or behaves in an abusive, insulting or obscene language towards an umpire when an opposition player has been awarded a mark or free kick.

13.2 When the umpire applies a 50 metre penalty, he shall signal "time on". The player receiving the penalty shall not be permitted to play on. The mark shall then be advanced 50 metres in a direct line with the centre of the goal. The player receiving the penalty shall be given free access to take up a position behind the advanced mark. When the umpire is satisfied the player has taken up a correct position, he will instruct the time keepers to stop adding time, irrespective of whether an opponent is standing on the mark.

13.3 A 50 metre penalty shall have the same implication as a free kick.

13.4 If a free kick or mark has been awarded and a player of the opposing team runs through the 10 metre protected area, unless accompanying or following an opponent within five metres, a 50 metre penalty shall be awarded.

13.5 Where a 50 metre penalty advances the mark to the centre of the goal line, the kick shall be taken from directly in front of the advanced mark.

13.6 Where a player has been awarded a mark or free kick and another player of the same team is infringed behind the spot of the mark or free kick, a 50 metre penalty shall be awarded to the player originally awarded the mark or free kick.

13.7 Where a free kick is awarded for intentionally tripping, a 50 metre penalty shall automatically apply.

13.8 To suit local requirements controlling bodies may reduce the distance of the penalty to 25 metres.

## 14.0 PLAY ON

The field umpire shall call and indicate "Play On" and the ball shall immediately remain in play in any of the following circumstances:

14.1 When an umpire, or any other authorised official or player is struck by the ball while it is in play.

14.2 When the ball, having been kicked, is touched while still in transit.

14.3 When the ball is caught directly from a kick of another player less than 10 metres distant.

14.4 When the field umpire cancels a free kick.

14.5 When a player who has taken a mark or been awarded a free kick, attempts to run, handball or kick otherwise than over his mark.

## 15.0 BOUNCING THE BALL

15.1 The field umpire shall bounce the ball in the following circumstances:

15.1.1 At the start of the match, at the start of each quarter and after each goal has been kicked, except when a breach of the laws has been penalised by the awarding of a free kick.

15.1.2 When in doubt as to which player has taken a mark.

15.1.3 When a player, in kicking off after a behind has been registered, fails to correctly bring the ball into play, the ball to be bounced on the centre of the kick off line.

15.1.4 In a scrimmage where players are struggling in undue confusion for possession of the ball.

15.1.5 When the field umpire has bounced the ball and it goes over the goal, behind or boundary line without having been touched by any player.

15.1.6 When a player claims a mark, the ball having been touched, and retains possession of the ball when held by an opponent, the field umpire will bounce the ball if he is satisfied that the player did not hear his call of "Play On".

15.1.7 When a goal umpire is unable to see whether the ball goes over the goal or behind lines, and cannot give a decision, the ball shall be bounced on the centre of the kick off line in front of goal.

15.1.8 When there is simultaneous encroachment of players from opposing teams, into the centre square prior to the ball being bounced.

## 16.0 UMPIRES: DUTIES AND INSTRUCTIONS

## 16.1 APPOINTMENT OF UMPIRES

16.1.1 The controlling body shall appoint for each match a field umpire, two boundary umpires, and two goal umpires. The field umpire shall have full control of play and shall award penalties in accordance with the laws.

16.1.2 The controlling body may appoint additional field and boundary umpires to officiate throughout the period of the match. All additional umpires shall have the powers conferred under these laws.

## 16.2 REPLACEMENT OF UMPIRES

16.2.1 When any umpire, before or during the progress of the game, becomes incapable through sickness, injury or accident in performing his duties, a substitute shall be chosen according to arrangements made by the controlling body.

16.2.2 In matches played without boundary umpires, the duties assigned to them by the laws shall be determined by the field umpire.

## 16.3 UMPIRES' ROOMS

16.3.1 No person other than the umpires officiating in the match and their trainers shall enter the umpires' dressing room while the umpires are there. Each umpire is individually responsible for seeing that this law is observed and must report to the controlling body any person who breaches this law.

## 16.5 FIELD UMPIRES

Field umpires shall indicate to the time keepers when "Time On" is to be added due to a delay in play, and shall indicate that "Time On" has ended when satisfied that play is ready to recommence.

## 16.6 BOUNDARY UMPIRES

16.6.1 The boundary umpire shall, subject to being directed by the goal umpire, in relation to a score or when the ball hits or goes directly over the behind post, be the final judge of when the ball is out of bounds or out of bounds on the full. The boundary umpires may seek the advice of field and goal umpires before deciding whether the ball is out of bounds.

16.6.2 To be out of bounds, the ball must be completely outside the boundary line or have hit the behind post after first having touched the ground or having been touched by a player. If any portion of it is on or above the boundary line, the ball is still in play.

16.6.3 When the ball has completely crossed the boundary line, or hit the behind post after first touching the ground, or been touched by a player, the boundary umpire shall immediately signal to the field umpire and bring the ball back to the spot where it crossed the line or hit the post.

16.6.4 Boundary umpires may use a whistle when indicating that the ball is "out of bounds", but the whistle must be used in conjunction with the raising of one arm.

16.6.5 When the ball has been kicked out of bounds on the full, the boundary umpire shall sound his whistle and shall indicate, by raising his arms sideways to shoulder level, that the ball has fully crossed the line without having been touched in transit by a player. The boundary umpire shall indicate to the field umpire the spot on the boundary line where the ball crossed the line and from which a free kick to the nearest opponent shall be awarded.

16.6.6 When the boundary umpire signals that the ball is out of bounds, the field umpire shall immediately sound his whistle to indicate that the ball is out of play. When directed by the field umpire, the boundary umpire shall throw the ball over his head towards the centre of the field to a distance of between 10 and 15 metres and reaching a height not less than 3 metres.

16.6.7 When a goal umpire signals a "behind" and a boundary umpires signals "out of bounds", the decision of the goal umpire shall prevail.

16.6.8 In the event that the boundary umpire signals the ball out of bounds and the signal is not acknowledged by the field umpire and play continues, the boundary umpire shall run after the field umpire and notify him that the ball is out of bounds.

On receipt of such advice the field umpire shall stop play and order the ball to be taken back to the spot where it crossed the boundary line to be thrown in, or kicked in if it has been kicked out on the full.

Where the field umpire has awarded a free kick, or applied a 50 metre penalty, after the ball has crossed the boundary line and prior to the boundary umpire notifying him, out of bounds lapses.

In the event that a score is registered after the ball has crossed the boundary line and prior to the boundary umpire notifying the field umpire, he shall order the score to be annulled and the ball taken back to where it crossed the boundary line to be brought into play in accordance with these laws.

16.6.9 When a goal is scored the boundary umpires shall bring the ball back to the centre as quickly as possible without waiting for the ball to be kicked or handed to them and shall give it to the field umpire.

16.6.10 At centre bounces, players may enter the centre square until the field umpire commences his approach to bounce the ball.

16.6.11 Controlling bodies may provide for field umpires to over-rule decisions of boundary umpires not formally appointed by the controlling body concerned.

Boundary umpires shall penalise only players who step over the white line after the field umpire commences his approach, and until the ball touches the ground in the act of bouncing or is thrown up by the field umpire.

## 16.7 GOAL UMPIRES

16.7.1 Goal umpires shall keep a record of all goals and behinds scored in a match and furnish a report within the time specified by the controlling body.

16.7.2 In the event of a goal umpire observing the field umpire line a team up for the purpose of counting the players, he shall make a record of the scores at that time.

16.7.3 Goal umpires shall signal and record a goal or behind, as the case may be, upon receiving the "all clear" or "touched, all clear" from the field umpire. They shall not concern themselves with the question as to whether the siren has or has not sounded at any period of the match.

16.7.4 The goal umpire must watch the play closely, but if he is unable to decide who kicked the ball over the goal or behind line, he may consult the field umpire before making a decision.

## 16.8 REPORTING PLAYERS AND OFFICIALS

16.8.1 Umpires shall report to the controlling body any player or official who commits a reportable offence during the progress of a match or on the day of the match and within the immediate proximity of venue where the match is conducted. Without limiting their ordinary meaning the words "within the immediate proximity of the venue" shall include any area within 500 metres of the venue where the match is conducted.

16.8.2 Umpires shall report the offending player or official without taking into consideration whether the offending player or official received provocation or not.

16.8.3 Umpires may caution a player or official but

must not at any time threaten a player or official.

16.8.4 For the purposes of these laws, an "official" shall include but is not limited to an officer, coach, assistant coach, trainer, runner, employee or any person performing any duties (paid or unpaid) for or on behalf of the club.

## 16.9 REPORTABLE OFFENCES

The following acts are reportable offences:

16.9.1 Intentionally, recklessly, carelessly or negligently interfering with or assaulting or using threatening language to or behaving in a threatening manner towards or disputing the decision of an umpire.

16.9.2 Assaulting another person.

16.9.3 Intentionally, recklessly, carelessly or negligently kicking or attempting to kick another person.

16.9.4 Any act of misconduct.

16.9.5 Using abusive, insulting or obscene language to an umpire or behaving in an abusive, insulting or obscene manner towards an umpire.

16.9.6 Intentionally, recklessly, carelessly or negligently wasting time; interfering with a player while that player is kicking for goal; shaking a goal post when another player is preparing to kick or is kicking for goal after the player has kicked for goal and the ball is in transit; throwing another player while that player has taken a mark or after the ball is otherwise out of play; tripping or attempting to trip an opponent by foot or leg; striking or attempting to strike a person; engaging in rough play by breaching the Laws of Australian Football against an opponent; or pushes in a violent or threatening manner a player after the player has disposed of the ball; or wrestling with another person; or engaging in a melee.

16.9.7. Using abusive, insulting, obscene or threatening language towards another person.

16.9.8 Remaining on the playing ground in an incorrect uniform after being warned by the umpire.

16.9.9 Wearing boots, jewellery and equipment prohibited under Law 4 of the Laws of Australian Football.

## 16.10 REPORTING PLAYERS

16.10.1 When an umpire intends to make a charge or charges against a player, he shall notify the player concerned as soon as reasonably possible after the incident. If such a charge or charges relate to incidents arising in the first three quarters the umpire shall notify the player, or players, not later than the commencement of the next quarter.

Where a charge is laid in the final quarter, if the umpire is unable to notify the player during the course of the match, notification on the official report sheet handed to team officials at the conclusion of the match will suffice.

16.10.2 Umpires shall make themselves thoroughly familiar with the offences which must be reported and report all offending players.

16.10.3 Umpires may not enter the competing clubs' dressing rooms to notify players of charges laid. In the case of a player charged in the second quarter and who does not return to the field for the third quarter, or who leaves the field injured or interchanged before being notified by the umpire of the charge, advice to the captain or acting captain not later than the commencement of the next quarter shall meet the requirements of this law.

16.10.4 After reporting a player or players, umpires

must not at anytime enter into any conversation with delegates, club officials or players relating to any incident of the match or any charges made against a player.

## 16.11 REPORTING PROCEDURES

16.11.1 Umpires shall be provided by the controlling body with report sheets on which they shall enter particulars of any charge or charges they make against players or officials. This shall be completed at or before the termination of a match.

## 16.12 PLAYER DISQUALIFICATION

16.12.1 A controlling body may disqualify for any term, players of officials who have been reported for and found guilty of breaches of the laws.

16.12.2 Any player disqualified for committing an offence against the Laws of the Game shall not be permitted to play in any match under the control of the AFL, AFL Affiliated Bodies or Bodies Affiliated to AFL Affiliated Bodies.

16.12.3 A disqualified player may seek permission from the Body which imposed the penalty to play in a competition that is conducted between 1 October and 31 March.

16.12.5 A player suspended in a competition conducted between 1 October and 31 March may seek permission from such Body to play in a competition conducted between 31 March and 1 October.

16.12.6 A player or official suspended by a Controlling Body and subsequently transferring to or interchanging with a club of another Controlling Body, shall complete the term of his suspension with his new club, provided that the competition is normally conducted between 31 March and 1 October. The Controlling Body which imposed the suspension may require the player to fulfil any part of the suspension in that competition, should the player subsequently return within 12 months of the completion of the suspension.

## 16.13 STEWARDS

The Controlling Body may appoint a Steward or Stewards who shall have the same power and duty of reporting players as that conferred on umpires under the laws.

## 16.14 ORDER OFF

Applicable in all competitions other than AFL first grade matches.

## 17.0 MATCH — TIME, DUTIES & RESPONSIBILITIES OF UMPIRES & TIME KEEPERS

## 17.1 DURATION OF THE GAME, QUARTERS & INTERVALS

17.1.1 All matches shall be of four quarters each of 20 minutes playing time as determined by the controlling body.

17.1.2 The time allowed between the end of the first quarter and the start of the second quarter shall be sufficient to permit teams to change ends, but shall not exceed three minutes. At half time the players may leave the playing ground for not more than 15 minutes, the match must recommence not later than 20 minutes after the conclusion of the second quarter. At the conclusion of the 20 minute period, the time keepers shall notify the field umpire by sounding the siren. Between the end of the third quarter and the start of the last quarter, there shall be an interval of not more than five minutes.

17.1.3 The time keepers shall indicate the end of each quarter by sounding the siren and the ball shall be deemed dead and play shall cease when any one of the field umpires hears the first sound of the siren. The field umpire shall signify that the siren has been heard by blowing his whistle and holding up both hands provided no breach of the laws has occurred and except when the ball is in transit or when a player has been awarded a mark or free kick prior to the first sound of a siren, the player is permitted to take his kick.

17.1.4 In the event of an encroachment of the area of play by unauthorised persons, or that play is prevented by any other means, the field umpire shall seek the assistance of his fellow umpires and/or other constituted authority to clear the playing arena so that the match may be resumed. If the field umpire is unable to do this within a reasonable time, he shall terminate play at that time and report all circumstances to the controlling body. This body may award the result or declare the match abandoned or call a replay at its discretion.

## 17.2 TIME KEEPERS

The Controlling Body shall appoint two or more independent time keepers, or in the absence of such arrangements, each team shall appoint a time keeper, whose duties shall be:

17.2.1 To keep the time of each quarter on time cards and forward the completed cards in accordance with the procedures of the controlling body.

17.2.2 To sound a siren at the start and finish of each quarter, and to keep sounding it until the field umpire notifies them that he has heard it.

17.2.3 To add time on to the playing time of the quarter whenever directed to do so by the field umpire, or when a goal or behind has been scored or when the ball is signalled out of bounds.

## 17.3 TIME ON

Time keepers shall add "time on" as follows:

17.3.1 When directed to do so by the field umpire when there is any undue delay in play.

17.3.2 When the goal umpire signals that a goal has been scored.

17.3.3 When the goal umpire signals that a behind has been scored.

17.3.4 When a boundary umpire signals that the ball is out of bounds.

## 17.4 TIME ON WHEN CEASED

Time keepers shall stop adding time on when instructed by the field umpire, when the ball is bounced in the centre after a goal, kicked in after a behind has been scored, thrown in by the boundary umpire, returned to play by a player or when the ball is obviously in play.

## 17.5 DOMESTIC PROVISIONS

Controlling bodies may vary the provisions of this law to suit local requirements.

## 17.6 TIME ON INDICATED

The field umpire shall adopt the following procedure for indicating "Time On" to the time keepers.

17.6.1 To indicate the commencement of the time added period, the field umpire shall blow his whistle and raise one arm above his head.

17.6.2 To indicate that the time added period has elapsed, the field umpire shall again blow his whistle and raise one arm above his head.

## 17.7 FORFEIT

Where a team fails to appear or where a team forfeits during the progress of a match, full premiership points should be awarded to the team receiving the forfeit. At the conclusion of the minor round, it should also be credited and debited with the average number of points scored against and by the forfeiting team. Similarly, the forfeiting team should be credited and debited with the average points against and for the team receiving the forfeit.

In the event an affected team considers itself disadvantaged, it may appeal to its Controlling Body for a variation of points credited and debited.

## 18.0 CONTROLLING BODY

18.1 These Laws shall apply to all Bodies Affiliated to the Australian Football League and to Bodies Affiliated to AFL Affiliates.

18.2 The Term Controlling Body contained in these Laws shall refer to the League, Association or Body responsible for a competition's Match Arrangements.

18.3 Affiliated Bodies may seek approval from the AFL to vary the Laws for an indefinite or specified period.

18.4 Other Controlling Bodies may seek approval from the AFL through AFL Affiliated Bodies to vary the laws for an indefinite or specified period.

## 19.0 DOPING POLICY

The Doping Policy of the AFL, shall apply to all matches played under these laws, except where a controlling body has its own specific policy approved by the Australian Sports Drug Agency.

## 20.0 INFECTIOUS DISEASES

The policies of the Australian Sports Medicine Federation shall apply in all matches played under these laws, except where a controlling body has adopted its own specific policy.

### The Game of the People for the People

"This booklet containing the Laws of Australian Football issued by the Australian Football League and it will be an infringement of such copyright if matter from it be reproduced in any publication without written permission, and all rights are reserved"

## METHOD OF TIMEKEEPING

The following method of keeping time was used for the first time during the 1994 AFL premiership season.

The timekeeping procedure is as follows:

20 minute quarters.

Time-on added:

• at the instruction of the field umpire when play is unduly delayed;

• when a goal is scored, the time between the signal of the goal umpire that a goal has been scored and the bouncing of the ball in the centre;

• when a behind is scored, the time between the signal of the goal umpire that a behind has been scored and the kick-off;

• the time between the signal of the boundary umpire that the ball is out of bounds and the ball being brought back into play.

## BLOWING THE WHISTLE — RULE CHANGES

**1897** Present scoring introduced — six points for a goal and one point for a behind.

**1904** Boundary umpires punched the ball back into play.

**1910** Boundary umpires obliged to throw the ball in over their head

**1913** The VFL independent tribunal introduced.

**1925** Boundary umpire required to bounce ball 5 metres in from the boundary.

**1930** Use of a replacement (19th man) permitted for the first time. Once replaced a player could not return to the field.

**1933** System of determining percentage altered. Points for were divided by points against and multiplied by 100. Previously points against were divided by points for and multiplied by 100.

**1939** Re-introduction of general boundary throw in.

**1946** Two reserves (19th and 20th men) permitted for the first time. Once replaced, a player could not return to the field.

**1950** Sirens replaced bells at all grounds

**1955** Introduction of 15 metre penalty for time wasting.

**1964** Coaches were permitted to address players on field at quarter time for the first time. Coaches runners were permitted to speak to team captains and vice-captains only on the field during matches.

**1965** Coaches runners were again free to speak to all team members

"Flick pass" outlawed (June 2)

**1969** Introduction of the free against player kicking ball out of bounds on the full

**1973** Centre Diamond (sides 45m long) introduced. Four players only from each team permitted in the area at centre bounces. Ten year rule introduced.

**1975** Centre diamond amended to become centre square. Video tapes of incidents became admissable evidence at VFL tribunal hearings.

**1978** Interchange player system introduced.

**1980** Field umpires required to carry notebooks to record details of reportable incidents.

**1981** Fifteen metres instead of ten metres allowed for running with ball without it making contact with the ground.

**1986** Video investigations for on-field misconduct introduced.

**1988** Player awarded free obliged to kick the ball. Replacement of 15 metre penalty with 50 metre penalty.

**1990** Player awarded free again given option of kick or handpass.

**1994** Introduction of third interchange player. Introduction of third boundary umpire using rotational interchange system in pairs.

**1995** Tripping by hand no longer reportable. Penalty: Free and 50 metres

**1996** Clarification in the interpretation of the holding the ball law. If a player has had reasonable prior opportunity to dispose, he must kick or handball immediately once tackled.

# 1997 RESULTS

## ROUND 1 (EASTER)

*Thursday, March 27*
NM 7.13 (55) v **Melb 10.10 (70)** MCG
*Saturday, March 29*
**Coll 26.10 (166)** v Port 13.9 (87) MCG
WB 11.10 (76) v **Fre 10.20 (80)** OO
St K 10.11 (71) v **Haw 11.11 (77)** P
**WC 12.6 (78)** v Syd 5.7 (37) S
*Sunday, March 30*
**Rich 15.14 (104)** v Geel 13.17 (95) MCG
**Adel 20.12 (132)** v Bris Lions 14.12 (96) FP
*Monday, March 31*
Ess 16.10 (106) v Carl 15.9 (99) MCG

## ROUND 2

*Friday, April 4*
Melb 7.14 (56) v **Coll 24.19 (163)** MCG (N)
*Saturday, April 5*
**Rich 19.14 (128)** v Adel. 15.10 (100) MCG
**Geel 11.12 (78)** v WC 11.6 (72) KP
**WB 13.12 (90)** v Syd 12.11 (83) OO
*Sunday, April 6*
**Bris Lions 23.16 (154)** v St K 7.15 (57) G
Port 8.12 (60) v **Ess 14.9 (93)** FP
**Fre 13.9 (87)** v Haw 10.13 (73) S
*Monday, April 7*
**NM 12.14 (86)** v Carl 8.12 (60) MCG (N)

## ROUND 3

*Friday, April 11*
Syd 15.9 (99) v **Melb 14.7 (91)** SCG (N)
*Saturday, April 12*
**WB 16.9 (105)** v Rich. 12.14 (86) MCG
**St K 19.11 (125)** v Coll 17.16 (118) P
**Port 18.21 (129)** v Geel 14.6 (90) FP (N)
*Sunday, April 13*
**WC 16.15 (111)** v Fre 9.17 (71) S
**Ess 18.14 (122)** v NM 12.8 (80) MCG
**Carl 15.18 (108)** v Adel 12.8 (80) OO
**Haw 12.15 (87)** v Bris Lions 11.9 (75) P

## ROUND 4

*Friday, April 18*
Melb 13.9 (87) v **WB 13.11 (89)** MCG (N)
*Saturday, April 19*
Coll 12.12 (84) v **Carl 15.11 (101)** MCG
**Rich 10.12 (72)** v Fre 10.7 (67) OO
St K 12.9 (81) v **Syd 18.19 (127)** P
**WC 17.10 (112)** v Haw 13.10 (88) S (N)
*Sunday, April 20*
**Bris Lions 15.19 (109)** v NM 12.11 (83) G
Adel 11.6 (72) v **Port 11.17 (83)** FP
**Geel 11.19 (85)** v Ess 11.12 (78) MCG

## ROUND 5 (ANZAC)

*Friday, April 25*
Ess 10.10 (70) v **Coll 14.15 (99)** MCG
**Frem 16.11 (107)** v St K 15.11 (101) S (N)
*Saturday, April 26*
Melb 12.6 (78) v **WC 19.12 (126)** MCG
WB 9.17 (71) v **Adel 19.7 (121)** OO
**Haw 15.9 (99)** v Syd 11.8 (74) P (N)
*Sunday, April 27*
**Port 10.13 (73)** v Bris Lions 10.11 (71) FP
**NM 21.15 (141)** v Rich 7.4 (46) MCG
Carl 12.14 (86) v **Geel 13.16 (94)** OO

## ROUND 6

*Friday, May 2*
WC 14.15 (99) v **WB 17.11 (113)** W (N)
*Saturday, May 3*
**Ess 15.12 (102)** v Bris Lions 9.17 (71) MCG
**Coll 13.6 (84)** v Adel 11.17 (83) VP
**Geel 14.13 (97)** v Fre 6.7 (43) KP
Haw 14.9 (93) v **NM 16.7 (103)** P (N)
*Sunday, May 4*
**Syd 21.16 (142)** v Carl 11.17 (83) SCG
**St K 17.19 (121)** v Melb 4.11 (35) P
**Port 19.8 (122)** v Rich 8.10 (58) FP

## ROUND 7

*Friday, May 9*
NM 9.14 (68) v **Coll 17.9 (111)** MCG (N)
*Saturday, May 10*
Rich 10.16 (76) v **Carl 14.14 (98)** MCG
**WB 19.19 (133)** v Haw 13.10 (88) OO
**Geel 11.10 (76)** v Syd 6.8 (44) KP
**St K 20.6 (126)** v Port 8.13 (61) P (N)
**Fre 17.22 (124)** v Melb 10.9 (69) W (N)
*Sunday, May 11*
Bris Lions 8.12 (60) v **WC 21.13 (139)** G
**Adel 18.18 (126)** v Ess 11.7 (73) FP

## ROUND 8

*Friday, May 16*
**Coll 19.15 (129)** v WB 11.17 (83) MCG (N)
*Saturday, May 17*
Melb 7.7 (49) v **Geel 19.14 (128)** MCG
**NM 19.14 (128)** v Port 15.10 (100) OO
**Adel 22.12 (144)** v Syd 8.7 (55) FP (N)
*Sunday, May 18*
Ess 14.16 (100) v **St K 18.16 (124)** MCG
**Carl 15.16 (106)** v Haw 12.9 (81) OO
**Frem 14.14 (98)** v Bris Lions 15.3 (93) S
*Monday, May 19*
**Rich 18.11 (119)** v WC 9.13 (67) MCG (N)

## ROUND 9

*Friday, May 23*
Port 10.18 (78) v Melb 3.9 (27) FP (N)

*Saturday, May 24*
**Carl 16.9 (105)** v Fre 14.4 (88) OO
Haw 13.10 (88) v **Adel 14.18 (102)**P
**Syd 16.15 (111)** v Coll 11.8 (74) SCG (N)
*Sunday, May 25*
**Bris Lions 19.12 (126)** v Geel 15.8 (98) G
**WB 16.7 (103)** v NM 10.11 (71) MCG
**St K 22.9 (141)** v Rich 14.10 (94) P
**WC 16.14 (110)** v Ess 13.7 (85) S

## ROUND 10

*Friday, May 30*
**Port 14.9 (93)** v Carl 7.13 (55) FP (N)
*Saturday, May 31*
**NM 15.13 (103)** v WC 9.4 (58) OO
**Haw 16.12 (108)** v Coll 8.7 (55) P
**Geel 16.11 (107)** v St K 11.13 (79) KP
Rich 9.13 (67) v **Melb 14.8 (92)** MCG (N)
*Sunday, June 1*
Ess 17.12 (114) v **WB 20.16 (136)** MCG
**Bris Lions 13.14 (92)** v Syd 13.11 (89) G
*Monday, June 2*
Fre 10.12 (72) v **Adel 16.9 (105)** S (N)

## ROUND 11
## (QUEEN'S BIRTHDAY)

*Friday, June 6*
Coll. 10.11 (71) v **Rich 11.11 (77)** MCG (N)
*Saturday, June 7*
Ess 13.13 (91) v **Haw 17.22 (124)** MCG
**WB 14.12 (96)** v Geel 11.9 (75) OO
Port 4.17 (41) v **Syd 10.16 (76)** FP (N)
*Sunday, June 8*
WC 11.7 (73) v **St K 13.11 (89)** S
Melb 5.15 (45) v **Adel 14.13 (97)** MCG
*Monday, June 9*
**NM 15.15 (105)** v Fre. 12.7 (79) MCG
**Carl 12.12 (84)** v Bris Lions 9.9 (63) OO

## ROUND 12

*Friday, June 13*
**Syd 26.8 (164)** v Rich 16.14 (110) (SCG) N
*Saturday, June 14*
WB 12.10 (82) v **Port 14.10 (94)** OO
Coll 7.13 (55) v **WC 11.5 (71)** VP
Geel 12.10 (82) v **Haw 13.10 (88)** KP
*Sunday, June 15*
**Fre 24.13 (157)** v Ess 9.6 (60) S
**St K 16.20 (116)** v Carl 12.13 (85) P
Adel 12.11 (83) v **NM 16.9 (105)** FP
Melb 7.8 (50) v **Bris Lions 21.9 (135)** MCG

STATE OF ORIGIN
*Friday, June 20*
WA 16.12 (108) v **Allies 18.8 (116)** S (N)
*Saturday, June 21*
SA 12.13 (85) v **Victoria 13.15 (93)** FP (N)

## ROUND 13

*Friday, June 27*
WC 11.13 (79) v **Carl 12.14 (86)** S (N)
*Saturday, June 28*
Rich 4.10 (34) v **Ess 19.13 (127)** MCG
St K 11.18 (84) v **WB 15.11 (101)** P
**Geel 17.8 (110)** v Adel 7.12 (54) KP
**Port 10.9 (69)** v Fre 7.12 (54) FP (N)
**Bris Lions 11.22 (88)** v Coll 11.7 (73) G (N)
*Sunday, June 29*
**Haw 17.16 (118)** v Melb 7.13 (55) P
**Syd 8.17 (65)** v NM 7.13 (55) SCG

## ROUND 14

*Friday, July 4*
**Adel 16.10 (106)** v WC 4.7 (31) FP (N)
*Saturday, July 5*
**Geel. 9.26 (80)** v Coll. 10.12 (72) MCG
Carl 11.8 (74) v **WB 16.14 (110)** OO
**St K 20.13 (133)** v NM 11.13 (79) P
**Frem 6.12 (48)** v Syd 3.15 (33) W (N)
*Sunday, July 6*
**Ess 18.12 (120)** v Melb 8.9 (57) MCG
**Haw 18.16 (124)** v Port 13.14 (92) P
**Bris Lions 7.26 (68)** v Rich 7.8 (50) G

## ROUND 15

*Friday, July 11*
NM 14.8 (92) v **Geel 15.12 (102)** MCG
*Saturday, July 12*
**Melb 18.11 (119)** v Carl.15.10 (100) MCG
WB 11.7 (73) v **Bris Lions 21.11 (137)** OO
**Coll 25.10 (160)** v Fre 9.6 (60) VP
**Adel.10.16 (76)** v St K 9.12 (66) FP
*Sunday, July 13*
**Syd 11.13 (79)** v Ess 11.12 (78) SCG
**Rich 22.13 (145)** v Haw 10.9 (69) MCG
**WC 12.13 (85)** v Port 9.13 (67) S

## ROUND 16

*Friday, July 18*
**Bris Lions 17.16 (118)** v Adel 13.9 (87) G (N)
*Saturday, July 19*
**Carl 25.15 (165)** v Ess 13.9 (87) MCG
Haw 9.8 (62) v **St K 20.21 (141)** P
**Geel 16.14 (110)** v Rich 12.6 (78) KP
**Syd 15.22 (112)** v WC 11.9 (75) SCG (N)
**Port 17.9 (111)** v Coll 8.10 (58) FP (N)
*Sunday, July 20*
**Frem 15.7 (97)** v WB 13.13 (91) S
Melb 7.16 (58) v **NM 17.12 (114)** MCG

## ROUND 17

*Friday, July 25*
Ess 10.12 (72) v **Port 18.14 (122)** MCG (N)

*Saturday, July 26*
Carl.7.16 (58) v **NM 14.12 (96)** OO
Haw 9.8 (62) v **Fre 10.11 (71)** P
**Syd 22.17 (149)** v WB 7.10 (52) SCG
**Adel 29.11 (185)** v Rich 7.6 (48) FP (N)
*Sunday, July 27*
**WC 20.9 (129)** v Geel 12.10 (82) S
**St K 12.20 (92)** d Bris Lions 5.14 (44) P
**Coll 20.14 (134)** v Melb 12.10 (82) MCG

## ROUND 18

*Friday, August 1*
**NM 11.17 (83)** v Ess 8.16 (64) MCG (N)
*Saturday, August 2*
Melb 7.11 (53) v **Syd 25.19 (169)** MCG
**Rich 17.13 (115)** v WB 15.10 (100) OO
**Geel 25.9 (159)** v Port 11.8 (74) KP
**Bris Lions 21.15 (141)** v Haw 11.5 (71) G (N)
*Sunday, August 3*
**Adel 18.19 (127)** v Carl 13.8 (86) FP
Coll 12.17 (89) v **St K 15.21 (111)** MCG
Fre 7.7 (49) v **WC 13.4 (82)** S

## ROUND 19

*Friday, August 8*
**NM 17.14 (116)** v Bris Lions 9.5 (59) MCG (N)
*Saturday, August 9*
**Carl 14.23 (107)** v Coll 13.13 (91) MCG
**WB 14.18 (102)** v Melb 9.10 (64) OO
Haw 10.6 (66) v **WC 13.9 (87)** P
**Fre 12.13 (85)** v Rich 5.12 (42) W (N)
*Sunday, August 10*
Syd 17.17 (119) v **St K 18.20 (128)** SCG
**Ess 11.7 (73)** v Geel 9.14 (68) MCG
Port 9.4 (58) v **Adel 9.11 (65)** FP

## ROUND 20

*Friday, August 15*
**WC 15.7 (97)** v Melb 7.17 (59) W (N)
*Saturday, August 16*
**Coll 13.13 (91)** v Ess 12.9 (81) MCG
**St K 12.5 (77)** v Fre 9.10 (64) P
**Geel 13.17 (95)** v Carl 9.13 (67) KP
Bris Lions 13.15 (93) v Port 13.15 (93) G (N)
*Sunday, August 17*
**Syd 20.15 (135)** v Haw 11.11 (77) SCG
**Rich 14.13 (97)** v NM 14.12 (96) MCG
Adel 7.18 (60) v **WB 16.7 (103)** FP

## ROUND 21

*Friday, August 22*
Melb 8.14 (62) v **St K 17.12 (114)** MCG (N)

*Saturday, August 23*
**NM 10.21 (81)** v Haw 6.7 (43) MCG
**Carl 11.10 (76)** v Syd 5.11 (41) OO
**WB 12.14 (86)** v WC 10.8 (68) WO
Bris Lions. 15.12 (102) v **Ess 16.10 (106)** G (N)
*Sunday, August 24*
Fre 9.14 (68) v **Geel 14.16 (100)** S
**Rich 22.14 (146)** v Port 8.13 (61) MCG
*Monday, August 25*
Adel 6.12 (48) v **Coll 5.9 (39)** FP (N)

## ROUND 22

*Friday, August 29*
**WC 18.12 (120)** v Bris Lions 11.15 (81) (W) N
*Saturday, August 30*
**Melb 18.11 (119)** v Fre 11.13 (79) (MCG)
Carl 13.11 (89) v **Rich 13.13 (91)** (OO)
Haw 13.9 (87) v **WB 15.15 (105)** (P)
Syd 13.12 (90) v **Geel 15.10 (100)** (SCG) N
*Sunday, August 30*
Port 12.12 (84) v **St K 17.15 (117)** (FP)
**Coll 18.14 (122)** v NM 15.21 (111) (MCG)
**Ess 16.6 (102)** v Adel 14.14 (98) (OO)

## FINALS

*Saturday, September 6*
**2nd Qualifying Final**
**WB 18.11 (119)** v Syd. 12.12 (84) MCG
*Sunday, September 7*
**1st Qualifying Final**
**Adel 14.15 (99)** v WC 9.12 (66) FP
**4th Qualifying Final**
**St K 20.15 (135)** v Bris Lions. 13.11 (89) WP
**3rd Qualifying Final**
Geel 9.7 (61) v **NM 11.13 (79)** MCG (N)
*Saturday, September 13*
**1st Semi-Final**
**NM 15.8 (98)** v WC 12.13 (85) MCG
**2nd Semi-Final**
**Adel 11.10 (76)** v Geel 9.14 (68) FP (N)
*Friday, September 19*
**2nd Preliminary Final**
**St K 15.14 (104)** v NM 11.7 (73) MCG (N)
*Saturday, September 20*
**1st Preliminary Final**
WB 13.13 (91) v **Adel 12.21 (93)** MCG
*September 27*
**Grand Final**
**Adel 19.11 (125)** v St K 13.16 (94) MCG

# 1998 COCA-COLA AFL PREMIERSHIP SEASON

*Matches to be played on grounds of first-named clubs except where otherwise determined by the League. N—Night game; (FP)—Football Park, Adelaide; (G)—Gabba; (KP)—Kardinia Park, Geelong; (MO)—Manuka Oval, Canberra; (OO)—Optus Oval; (P)—Waverley; (S)—Subiaco Oval; (SCG)—Sydney; (VP)—Victoria Park, Collingwood; (W)—WACA.*

## ROUND 1
**Friday, March 27**
North Melbourne v West Coast (MCG) N
**Saturday, March 28**
Carlton v Adelaide (OO)
Collingwood v Hawthorn (MCG)
St Kilda v Geelong (P)
Brisbane Lions v Western Bulldogs (G) N
**Sunday, March 29**
Port Adelaide v Sydney (FP)
Richmond v Essendon (MCG)
Fremantle v Melbourne (S)

## ROUND 2
**Friday, April 3**
West Coast v Collingwood (S) N
**Saturday, April 4**
Geelong v Richmond (KP)
Hawthorn v Port Adelaide (P)
Melbourne v North Melbourne (MCG)
Sydney v Brisbane Lions (SCG) N
**Sunday, April 5**
Adelaide v Fremantle (FP)
Essendon v St Kilda (MCG)
Western Bulldogs v Carlton (OO)

## ROUND 3 (EASTER)
**Saturday, April 11 (Easter Saturday)**
Richmond v Hawthorn (MCG)
Western Bulldogs v Collingwood (OO)
Port Adelaide v North Melbourne (FP) N
**Sunday, April 12 (Easter Sunday)**
St Kilda v Adelaide (P)
Sydney v Geelong (SCG)
Fremantle v West Coast (S)
**Monday, April 13 (Easter Monday)**
Brisbane Lions v Melbourne (G)
Carlton v Essendon (MCG)

## ROUND 4
**Friday, April 17**
Collingwood v Richmond (MCG) N
**Saturday, April 18**
Geelong v Western Bulldogs (KP)
Hawthorn v St Kilda (P)
West Coast v Sydney (W) N
**Sunday, April 19**
Port Adelaide v Adelaide (FP)
Carlton v Melbourne (OO)
Essendon v Fremantle (P)
North Melbourne v Brisbane Lions (MCG)

## ROUND 5 (ANZAC)
**Friday, April 24**
Richmond v West Coast (MCG) N
**Saturday, April 25 (Anzac Day)**
Collingwood v Essendon (MCG)
Hawthorn v Brisbane Lions (P)
Fremantle v North Melbourne (W) N

## Sunday, April 26
Melbourne v Port Adelaide (MCG)
St Kilda v Carlton (P)
Sydney v Western Bulldogs (SCG)
Adelaide v Geelong (FP)

## ROUND 6
**Friday, May 1**
Brisbane Lions v Richmond (G) N
**Saturday, May 2**
Carlton v Collingwood (MCG)
Geelong v Hawthorn (KP)
Western Bulldogs v Essendon (OO)
Port Adelaide v Fremantle (FP) N
**Sunday, May 3**
North Melbourne v Adelaide (MCG)
Sydney v Melbourne (SCG)
West Coast v St Kilda (S)

## ROUND 7
**Friday, May 8**
Fremantle v Hawthorn (W) N
**Saturday, May 9**
Carlton v Port Adelaide (OO)
St Kilda v Brisbane Lions (P)
Essendon v Geelong (MCG) N
**Sunday, May 10**
Adelaide v West Coast (FP)
Collingwood v Sydney (P)
Richmond v Melbourne (MCG)
Western Bulldogs v North Melbourne (OO)

## ROUND 8
**Friday, May 15**
Essendon v Brisbane Lions (MCG) N
**Saturday, May 16**
Geelong v Fremantle (KP)
North Melbourne v Sydney (MCG)
St Kilda v Port Adelaide (P)
**Sunday, May 17**
West Coast v Carlton (S)
Hawthorn v Western Bulldogs (P)
Melbourne v Collingwood (MCG)
Adelaide v Richmond (FP)

## ROUND 9
**Friday, May 22**
Fremantle v St Kilda (W) N
**Saturday, May 23**
Carlton v North Melbourne (OO)
Geelong v West Coast (KP)
Melbourne v Essendon (MCG)
Western Bulldogs v Richmond (P)
Brisbane Lions v Adelaide (G) N
**Sunday, May 24**
Sydney v Hawthorn (SCG)
Port Adelaide v Collingwood (FP)

## ROUND 10
**Friday, May 29**
West Coast v Western Bulldogs (W) N

## Saturday, May 30
Carlton v Brisbane Lions (OO)
Hawthorn v Essendon (P)
Richmond v Port Adelaide (MCG)
Sydney v St Kilda (SCG) N
**Sunday, May 31**
Adelaide v Melbourne (FP)
Collingwood v Fremantle (VP)
North Melbourne v Geelong (MCG)

## ROUND 11 (QUEEN'S BIRTHDAY)
**Friday, June 5**
Essendon v Sydney (MCG) N
**Saturday, June 6**
Geelong v Carlton (MCG)
Hawthorn v Melbourne (P)
Port Adelaide v West Coast (FP) N
**Sunday, June 7**
Fremantle v Brisbane Lions (S)
Western Bulldogs v Adelaide (OO)
**Monday, June 8 (Queen's Birthday)**
North Melbourne v Collingwood (MCG)
St Kilda v Richmond (P)

## ROUND 12
**Friday, June 12**
West Coast v Hawthorn (W) N
**Saturday, June 13**
Carlton v Sydney (OO)
Melbourne v Geelong (MCG)
Adelaide v Essendon (FP) N
**Sunday, June 14**
Brisbane Lions v Port Adelaide (G)
Collingwood v St Kilda (P)
Richmond v North Melbourne (MCG)
Western Bulldogs v Fremantle (OO)

## ROUND 13
**Friday, June 19**
Essendon v West Coast (MCG) N
**Saturday, June 20**
Collingwood v Adelaide (MCG)
Geelong v Brisbane Lions (KP)
Hawthorn v North Melbourne (P)
Port Adelaide v Western Bulldogs (FP) N
**Sunday, June 21**
Melbourne v St Kilda (MCG)
Sydney v Richmond (SCG)
Fremantle v Carlton (S)

## ROUND 14
**Friday, June 26**
North Melbourne v Essendon (MCG) N
**Saturday, June 27**
Carlton v Hawthorn (OO)
Richmond v Fremantle (MCG)
St Kilda v Western Bulldogs (P)
Port Adelaide v Geelong (FP) N
**Sunday, June 28**
Brisbane Lions v Collingwood (G)

Sydney v Adelaide (SCG)
West Coast v Melbourne (S)

## ROUND 15
*Friday, July 3*
Richmond v Carlton (MCG) N
*Saturday, July 4*
Essendon v Port Adelaide (MCG)
St Kilda v North Melbourne (P)
Western Bulldogs v Melbourne (OO)
Brisbane Lions v West Coast (G) N
*Sunday, July 5*
Adelaide v Hawthorn (FP)
Collingwood v Geelong (MCG)
Fremantle v Sydney (S)

## STATE OF ORIGIN
*Friday, July 10*
Allies v Victoria (G) N
*Saturday, July 11*
South Australia v Western Australia (FP) N

## ROUND 16
*Friday, July 17*
Adelaide v Carlton (FP) N
*Saturday, July 18*
Geelong v St Kilda (KP)
Hawthorn v Collingwood (P)
Melbourne v Fremantle (MCG)
Western Bulldogs v Brisbane Lions (OO)
*Sunday, July 19*
Essendon v Richmond (MCG)
Sydney v Port Adelaide (SCG)
West Coast v North Melbourne (S)

## ROUND 17
*Friday, July 24*
Fremantle v Adelaide (S) N
*Saturday, July 25*
Carlton v Western Bulldogs (OO)
Collingwood v West Coast (P)
North Melbourne v Melbourne (MCG)
Port Adelaide v Hawthorn (FP) N

*Sunday, July 26*
Brisbane Lions v Sydney (G)
Richmond v Geelong (MCG)
St Kilda v Essendon (P)

## ROUND 18
*Friday, July 31*
Collingwood v Western Bulldogs (MCG) N
*Saturday, August 1*
Geelong v Sydney (KP)
Melbourne v Brisbane Lions (P)
North Melbourne v Port Adelaide (MO)
Adelaide v St Kilda (FP) N
*Sunday, August 2*
Essendon v Carlton (MCG)
Hawthorn v Richmond (P)
West Coast v Fremantle (S)

## ROUND 19
*Friday, August 7*
Brisbane Lions v North Melbourne (G) N
*Saturday, August 8*
Melbourne v Carlton (MCG)
St Kilda v Hawthorn (P)
Western Bulldogs v Geelong (OO)
Fremantle v Essendon (S) N
*Sunday, August 9*
Richmond v Collingwood (MCG)
Sydney v West Coast (SCG)
Adelaide v Port Adelaide (FP)

## ROUND 20
*Friday, August 14*
North Melbourne v Fremantle (MCG) N
*Saturday, August 15*
Essendon v Collingwood (MCG)
Geelong v Adelaide (KP)
Western Bulldogs v Sydney (P)
Brisbane Lions v Hawthorn (G) N
*Sunday, August 16*
Port Adelaide v Melbourne (FP)
Carlton v St Kilda (MCG)
West Coast v Richmond (S)

## ROUND 21
*Friday, August 21*
Essendon v Western Bulldogs (MCG) N
*Saturday, August 22*
Richmond v Brisbane Lions (MCG)
St Kilda v West Coast (P)
Adelaide v North Melbourne (FP) N
*Sunday, August 23*
Fremantle v Port Adelaide (S)
Collingwood v Carlton (MCG)
Hawthorn v Geelong (P)
*Monday, August 24*
Melbourne v Sydney (MCG) N

## ROUND 22
*Friday, August 28*
North Melbourne v Western Bulldogs
(MCG) N
*Saturday, August 29*
Geelong v Essendon (MCG)
Hawthorn v Fremantle (P)
West Coast v Adelaide (S) N
Brisbane Lions v St Kilda (G) N
*Sunday, August 30*
Melbourne v Richmond (MCG)
Sydney v Collingwood (SCG)
Port Adelaide v Carlton (FP)

## FINALS
*Played under the McIntyre
Final Eight System*
*September 5*
Round 1 — Qualifying Finals
Four matches
*September 12*
Round 2 — Semi Finals
Two Matches
*September 19*
Round 3 — Preliminary Finals
Two Matches
*September 26*
Round 4 — Grand Final

# ANSETT AUSTRALIA CUP COMPETITION FIXTURE

*The program of matches for the 1998 Ansett Australia Cup Competition is as follows:*

| MATCH | | DATE | VENUE | DAY/ NIGHT | LOCAL TIME | AEST |
|---|---|---|---|---|---|---|
| **FIRST ROUND** | | | | | | |
| 1 | Carlton v North Melbourne | Sat, Feb 21 | North Hobart Oval | Day | 2.10 pm Tas | 2.10 pm |
| 2 | Brisbane Lions v Fremantle | Sun, Feb 22 | Newlands, Cape Town, South Africa | Day | 2.00 pm SAF | 11.00 pm |
| 3 | Adelaide v Richmond | Mon, Feb 23 | Football Park | Night | 8.10 pm SA | 8.40 pm |
| 4 | West Coast v Collingwood | Wed, Feb 25 | Subiaco | Night | 5.40 pm WA | 8.40 pm |
| 5 | Port Adelaide v St. Kilda | Fri, Feb 27 | Football Park | Night | 8.10 pm SA | 8.40 pm |
| 6 | Hawthorn v Essendon | Sat, Feb 28 | Waverley Park | Night | 8.40 pm Vic | 8.40 pm |
| 7 | Sydney v Melbourne | Sun, Mar 1 | The Basin Reserve, Wellington, NZ | Day | 2.10 pm NZ | 12.10 pm |
| 8 | Geelong v Western Bulldogs | Mon, Mar 2 | Waverley Park | Night | 8.40 pm Vic | 8.40 pm |
| **QUARTER FINALS** | | | | | | |
| 9 | Winner 2 v Winner 3 | Fri, Mar 6 | Waverley/FP | Night | 8.40 pm Vic | 8.40 pm |
| 10 | Winner 1 v Winner 6 | Sat, Mar 7 | MCG | Night | 8.40 pm Vic | 8.40 pm |
| 11 | Winner 4 v Winner 5 | Sun, Mar 8 | Waverley/FP | Night | 8.40 pm Vic | 8.40 pm |
| 12 | Winner 7 v Winner 8 | Mon, Mar 9 | Waverley | Night | 8.40 pm Vic | 8.40 pm |
| **SEMI FINALS** | | | | | | |
| 13 | Winner 9 v Winner 10 | Friday, Mar 13 | Waverley/FP | Night | 8.40 pm Vic | 8.40 pm |
| 14 | Winner 11 v Winner 12 | Saturday, Mar 14 | Waverley/FP | Night | 8.40 pm Vic | 8.40 pm |
| **GRAND FINAL** | | | | | | |
| 15 | Winner 13 v Winner 14 | Saturday, March 21 | Waverley Park/FP | Night | 8.45 pm Vic | 8.45 pm |

*Second mentioned clubs to wear white shorts in accordance with AFL Rules unless otherwise designated.*
*AEST = Australian Eastern Summer Time. Venues for Quarter Finals, Semi-Finals and Grand Final to be decided.*

# INDEX